CALIFORNIA

NATIONAL GEOGRAPHIC | U.S. HISTORY | 1877 to the Present

AMERICA
THROUGH THE LENS

THROUGH THE LENS ON THE COVER

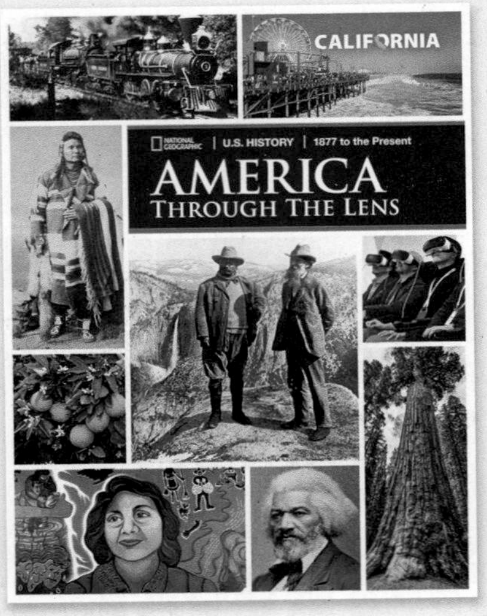

Clockwise from center:

- President Theodore Roosevelt stands with conservationist John Muir in Yellowstone National Park, California.
- Attendees participate in a virtual reality experience at a consumer technology trade show in Nevada.
- The General Sherman Tree, the world's largest living tree, is located in Sequoia National Park, California.
- Born a slave, Frederick Douglass was a famous abolitionist, orator, writer, and social reformer.
- This mural by artist Yreina Cervantes depicts Dolores Huerta, co-founder of the United Farm Workers (UFW).
- Over two-thirds of the fruits and nuts Americans consume each year are grown in California.
- In 1877, Chief Joseph, leader of the Nez Perce tribe in Oregon, led a group of followers across several states to avoid relocation to a reservation.
- Transcontinental train lines began connecting the American East Coast with the West Coast in the mid-1800s.
- Built in 1909, the Santa Monica Pier in California was the first concrete pier on the West Coast. Today it remains a popular fishing spot, and also features an amusement park and aquarium.

NATIONAL GEOGRAPHIC LEARNING | CENGAGE

Acknowledgments

Grateful acknowledgment is given to the authors, artists, photographers, museums, publishers, and agents for permission to reprint copyrighted material. Every effort has been made to secure the appropriate permission. If any omissions have been made or if corrections are required, please contact the Publisher.

Credits

Front Cover: (tr) ©Eduardo Frederiksen/500px. (tl) Underwood Photo Archives/Underwood Photo Archives/Superstock. (cr) David Becker/Getty Images. (cl) nsf/Alamy Stock Photo. (crb) ©Design Pics Inc/National Geographic Creative. (br) ©Design Pics Inc/National Geographic Creative. (bc) The Art Archive/ Superstock. (bl) ©Yreina Cervantez/SPARC.

Back Cover: ©Evgeny Tchebotarev/500px.

Acknowledgments and credits continue on page R115.

Printed in the United States of America.

Print Number: 04
Print Year: 2018

For product information and technology assistance, contact us at Customer & Sales Support, 888-915-3276

For permission to use material from this text or product, submit all requests online at **www.cengage.com/permissions**

Further permissions questions can be emailed to **permissionrequest@cengage.com**

National Geographic Learning | Cengage
1 N. State Street, Suite 900
Chicago, IL 60602

Cengage is a leading provider of customized learning solutions with office locations around the globe, including Singapore, the United Kingdom, Australia, Mexico, Brazil, and Japan. Locate your local office at **www.cengage.com/global.**

Visit National Geographic Learning online at **NGL.Cengage.com/school**

Visit our corporate website at **www.cengage.com**

ISBN: 978-133-711-194-2

87090131

SENIOR CONSULTANTS

FREDRIK HIEBERT

Fred Hiebert is National Geographic's Archaeologist-in-Residence. He has led archaeological expeditions at ancient Silk Roads sites across Asia. Hiebert was curator of National Geographic's exhibition "Afghanistan: Hidden Treasures from the National Museum, Kabul," and its more recent exhibition, "The Greeks: Agamemnon to Alexander the Great."

PEGGY ALTOFF

Peggy Altoff's career includes teaching middle school and high school students, supervising teachers, and serving as adjunct university faculty. Altoff served as a state social studies specialist in Maryland and as a K–12 coordinator in Colorado Springs. She is a past president of the National Council for the Social Studies (NCSS) and served on the task force for the 2012 NCSS National Curriculum Standards.

FRITZ FISCHER

Fritz Fischer is a professor and Director of History Education at the University of Northern Colorado, where he teaches U.S. History and Social Studies Education courses. Fischer is also Chair Emeritus of the Board of Trustees of the National Council for History Education (NCHE), the largest national membership organization focusing on history education at the K–12 level.

NATIONAL GEOGRAPHIC

PROGRAM CONSULTANTS

KATHRYN KEANE
Vice President, National Geographic Exhibitions

ROBERT REID
Travel Writer

National Geographic Digital Nomad

WILLIAM PARKINSON
Associate Curator of Anthropology, Field Museum of Natural History

National Geographic Explorer

ANDRÉS RUZO
Geothermal Scientist

National Geographic Explorer

NATIONAL GEOGRAPHIC TEACHER REVIEWERS

National Geographic works with teachers at all grade levels from across the country. The following teachers reviewed chapters in *U.S. History: America Through the Lens.*

CRYSTAL CULP
McCracken Regional School
Paducah, KY

KAREN DAVIS
St. Joseph School
Conway, AR

NICOLE ESHELMAN
Manheim Township High School
Lancaster, PA

KIMBERLY HENDRICKS
Park Hill South High School
Kansas City, MO

MARY JANZEN
Duncan High School
Fresno, CA

SYLVIA MCBRIDE
Castle Park High School
Chula Vista, CA

NATALIE WOJINSKI
West Contra Costa USD
Richmond, CA

NATIONAL GEOGRAPHIC SOCIETY

The National Geographic Society contributed significantly to *U.S. History: America Through the Lens*. Our collaboration with each of the following has been a pleasure and a privilege: National Geographic Maps, National Geographic Education and Children's Media, and National Geographic Missions programs. We thank the Society for its guidance and support.

NATIONAL GEOGRAPHIC

NATIONAL GEOGRAPHIC EXPLORATION

National Geographic supports the work of a host of anthropologists, archaeologists, adventurers, biologists, educators, writers, and photographers across the world. The individuals below each contributed substantially to *U.S. History: America Through the Lens*.

ROBERT BALLARD
National Geographic Explorer-in-Residence

ARI BESER
Fulbright–National Geographic Fellow

LESLIE DEWAN
National Geographic Explorer

KEVIN HAND
National Geographic Explorer

SANDRA POSTEL
National Geographic Freshwater Fellow (2009-2015)

TRISTRAM STUART
National Geographic Explorer

THROUGH THE LENS PHOTOGRAPHERS

The work of the National Geographic photographers below helps tell the story of America in striking, image-focused lessons.

LYNSEY ADDARIO

JIMMY CHIN

JEFFREY GUSKY

DAVID GUTTENFELDER

PAUL NICKLEN

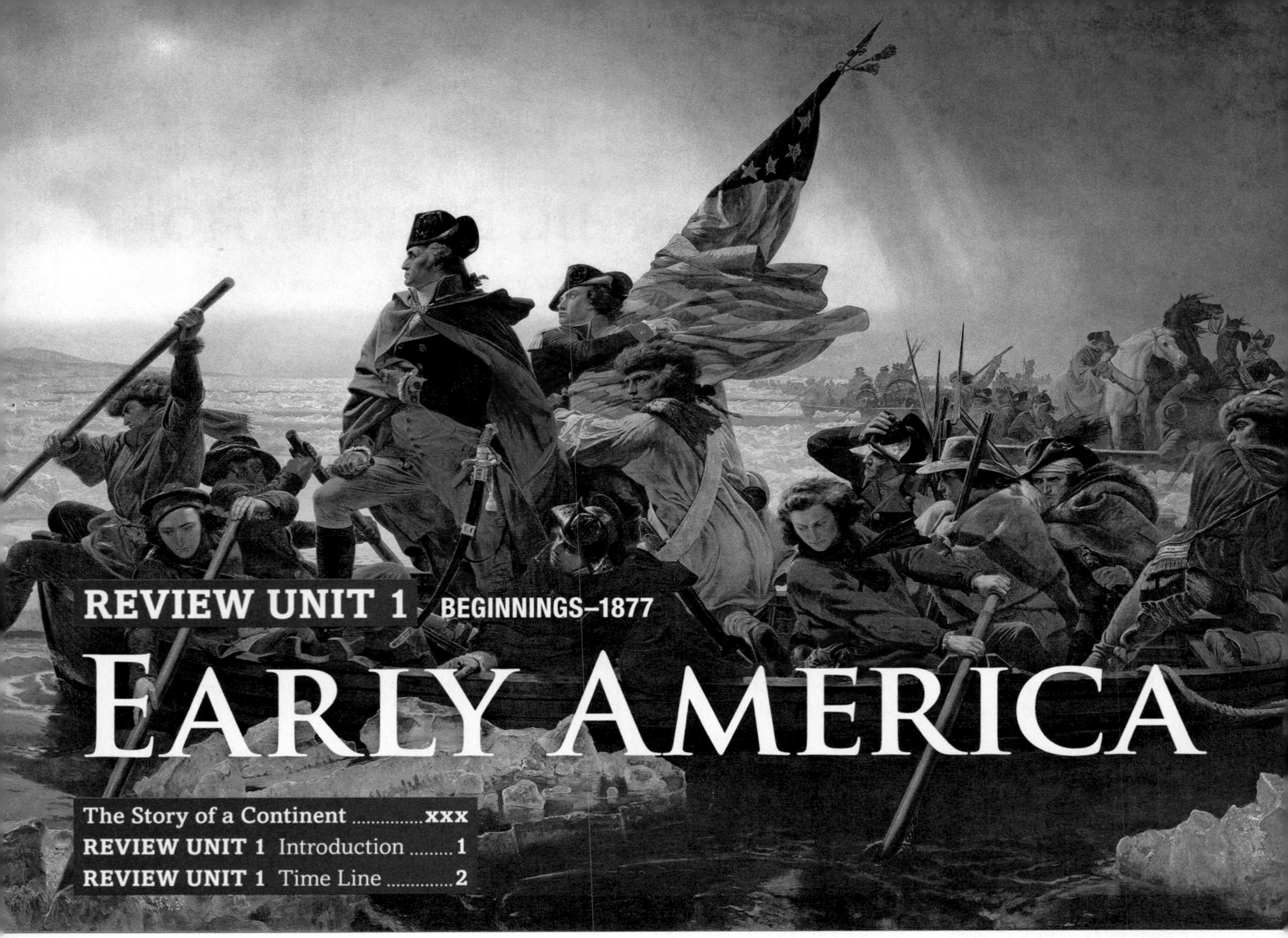

REVIEW UNIT 1 BEGINNINGS–1877

EARLY AMERICA

REVIEW CHAPTER 1 EXPLORATION AND SETTLEMENT 4
Beginnings–1765

AMERICAN STORIES ONLINE
Cahokia
Jamestown

AMERICAN GALLERY ONLINE
Southern Plantations

REVIEW CHAPTER 2 REVOLUTION AND A NEW REPUBLIC 22
1765–1814

AMERICAN STORIES ONLINE
Daily Life During the Revolution
The Northwest Ordinances

AMERICAN GALLERY ONLINE
Valley Forge

REVIEW CHAPTER 3

EXPANSION AND REFORM

1803–1853

AMERICAN STORIES ONLINE

American Inventions

The Cherokee

AMERICAN GALLERY ONLINE

On the Trail with Lewis and Clark

REVIEW CHAPTER 4

CIVIL WAR AND RECONSTRUCTION

1850–1877

AMERICAN STORIES ONLINE

Civil War Naval Battles

The Post–Civil War North

AMERICAN GALLERY ONLINE

The Battle of Vicksburg

UNIT 2 1877–1920

GROWTH AND REFORM

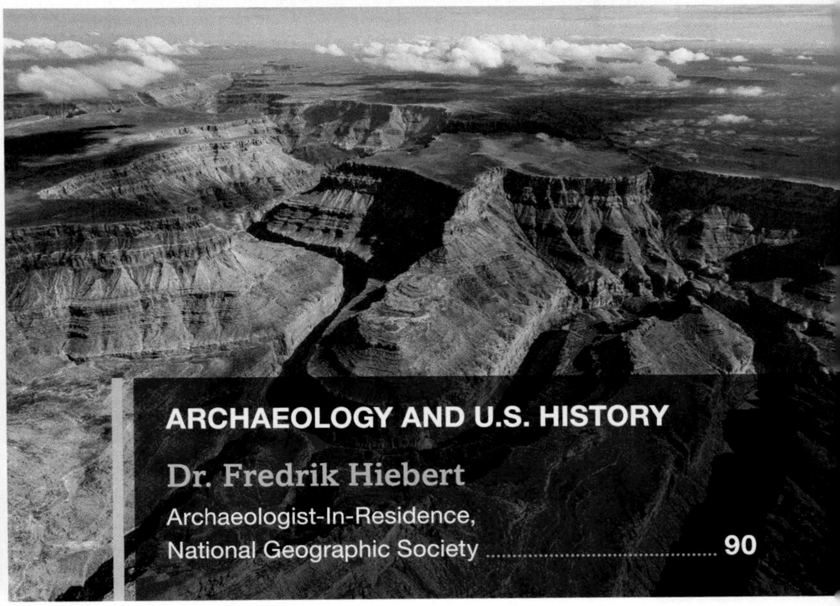

UNIT 3 1914–1940

FROM THE GREAT WAR TO THE NEW DEAL

Franz Kline, *Lower East Side Market Scene* (detail), c. 1938

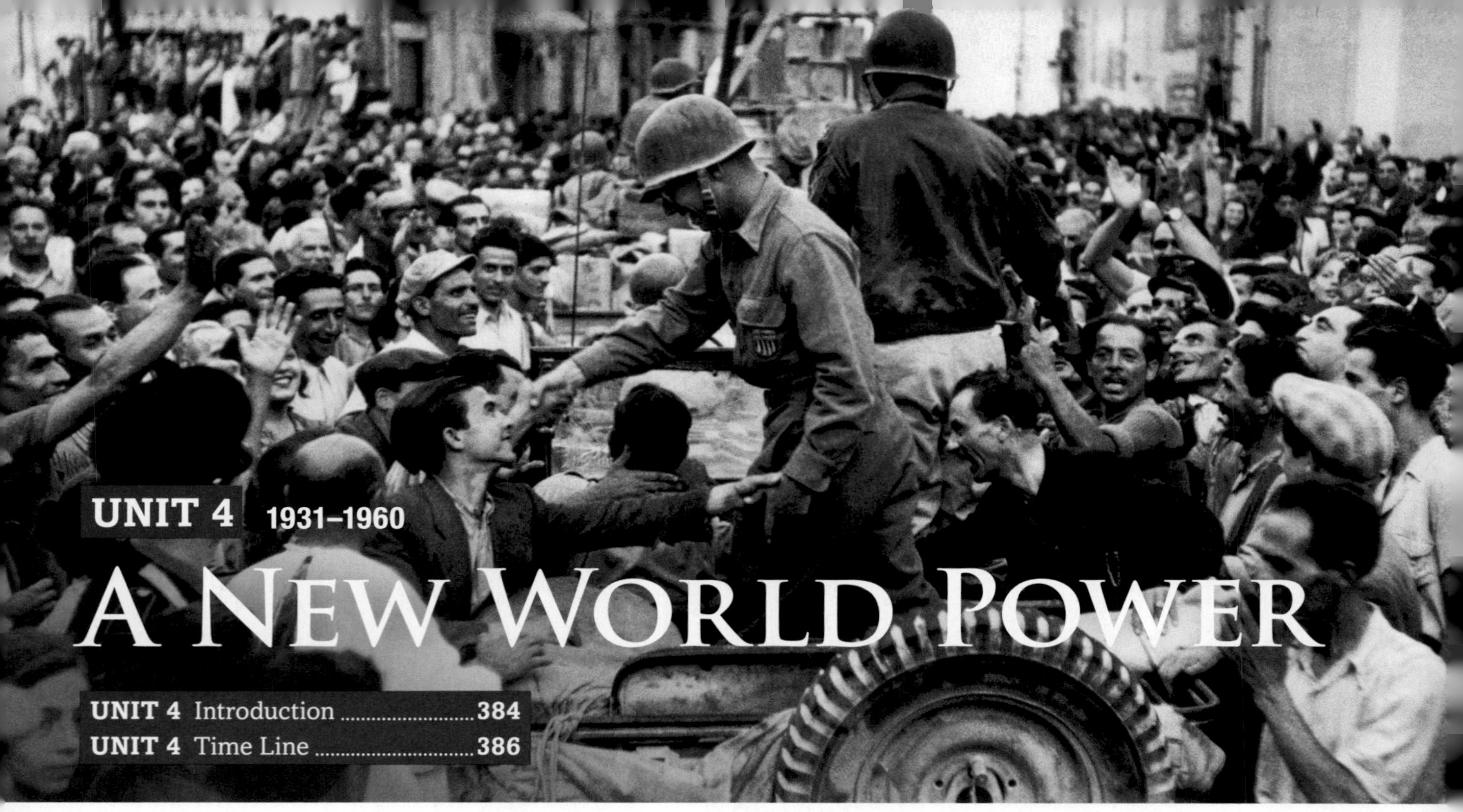

UNIT 4 1931–1960

A NEW WORLD POWER

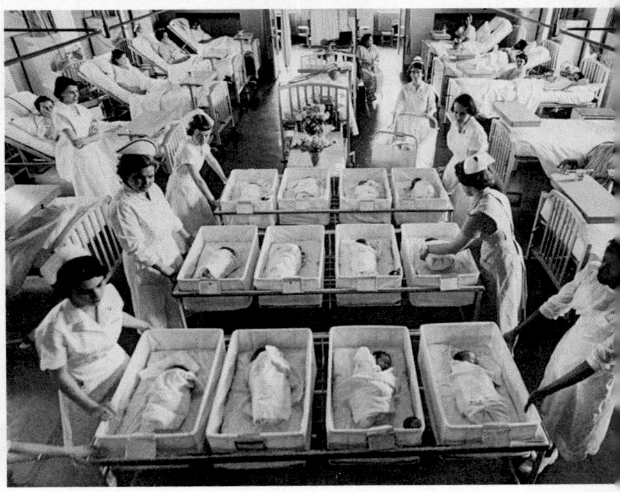

CHAPTER 14

THE COLD WAR AND KOREA

CHAPTER 15

POSTWAR PROSPERITY

UNIT 5 1954–1975

YEARS OF TURBULENCE

CUBA

UNIT 6 1968–PRESENT

CHALLENGES OF A NEW CENTURY

CHAPTER 20 PRESIDENTIAL SUCCESSES AND FAILURES 674

1968–1980

CHAPTER 21 THE CONSERVATIVE REVOLUTION 702

1980–1992

CHAPTER 22

AMERICA IN A GLOBAL SOCIETY

NATIONAL GEOGRAPHIC FEATURES

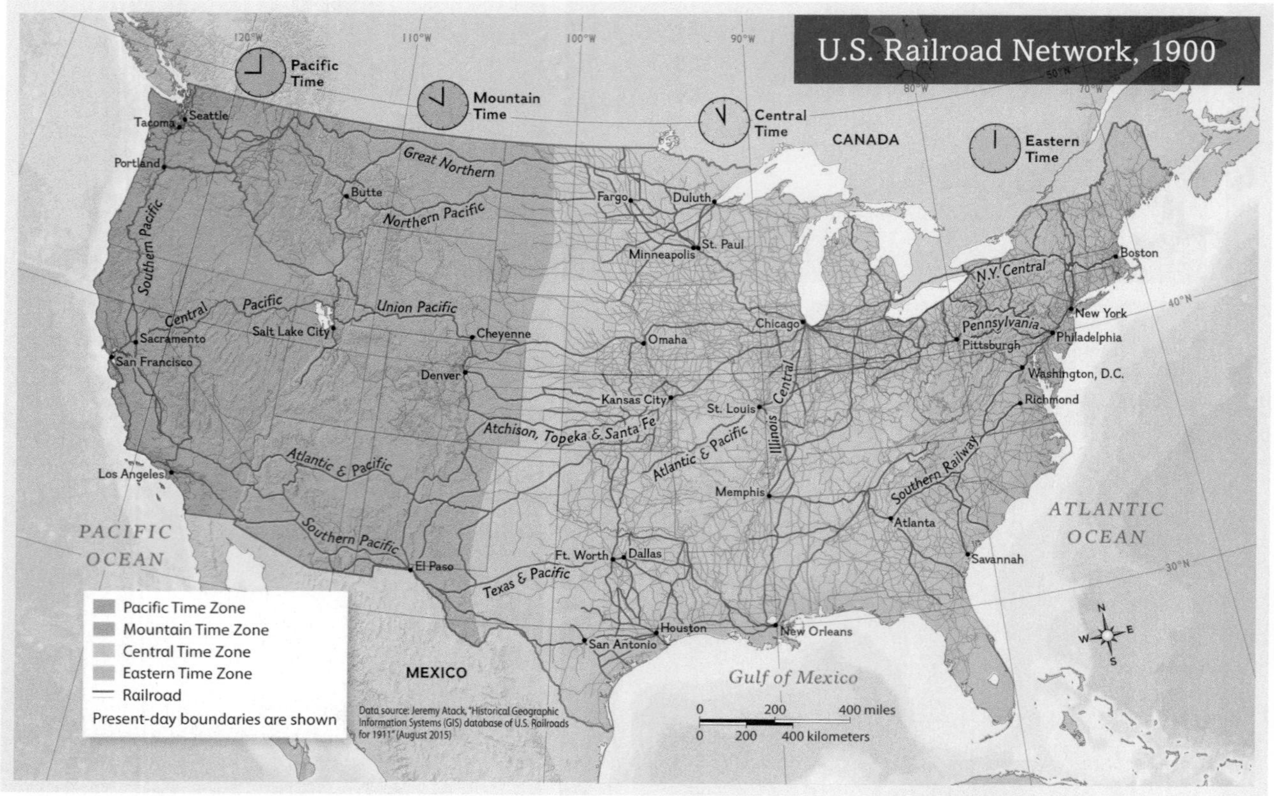

Maps

National Geographic Contributors

Curating History

Document-Based Questions

NATIONAL GEOGRAPHIC EXPLORER TRISTRAM STUART

GREENSBORO SIT-IN, 1960

THE WHITE HOUSE, 2015

American Stories

American Stories Online

American Galleries Online

FRANKLIN ROOSEVELT'S
FIRESIDE CHAT MICROPHONE

Student Handbooks

Geology in History

American Voices Biographies

BARACK AND MICHELLE OBAMA

1959 CADILLAC EL DORADO

KUWAIT, 1991

Through The Lens Features

Featured Themes

Featured Photographers

Featured American Places

History–Social Science Content Standards and Analysis Skills

GRADES 7 AND 8 CONTENT STANDARDS	
STANDARD	**STUDENT EDITION**
7.11 Students analyze political and economic change in the sixteenth, seventeenth, and eighteenth centuries (the Age of Exploration, the Enlightenment, and the Age of Reason).	21
7.11.2 Discuss the exchanges of plants, animals, technology, culture, and ideas among Europe, Africa, Asia, and the Americas in the fifteenth and sixteenth centuries and the major economic and social effects on each continent.	10-11, 20
7.11.3 Examine the origins of modern capitalism; the influence of mercantilism and cottage industry; the elements and importance of a market economy in seventeenth-century Europe; the changing international trading and marketing patterns, including their locations on a world map; and the influence of explorers and map makers.	20
8.1 Students understand the major events preceding the founding of the nation and relate their significance to the development of American constitutional democracy.	16–17, 18–19, 20–21
8.2.1 Discuss the significance of the Magna Carta, the English Bill of Rights, and the Mayflower Compact.	6–7, 20–21
8.3.4 Understand how the conflicts between Thomas Jefferson and Alexander Hamilton resulted in the emergence of two political parties (e.g., view of foreign policy, Alien and Sedition Acts, economic policy, National Bank, funding and assumption of the revolutionary debt).	34–35
8.5.1 Understand the political and economic causes and consequences of the War of 1812 and know the major battles, leaders, and events that led to a final peace.	36–37
8.5.2 Know the changing boundaries of the United States and describe the relationships the country had with its neighbors (current Mexico and Canada) and Europe, including the influence of the Monroe Doctrine, and how those relationships influenced westward expansion and the Mexican-American War.	60–61, 64
8.6.1 Discuss the influence of industrialization and technological developments on the region, including human modification of the landscape and how physical geography shaped human actions (e.g., growth of cities, deforestation, farming, mineral extraction).	44–45, 46–47, 64
8.6.2 Outline the physical obstacles to and the economic and political factors involved in building a network of roads, canals, and railroads (e.g., Henry Clay's American System).	46–47, 64
8.6.4 Study the lives of black Americans who gained freedom in the North and founded schools and churches to advance their rights and communities.	72–73
8.7.1 Describe the development of the agrarian economy in the South, identify the locations of the cotton-producing states, and discuss the significance of cotton and the cotton gin.	44–45, 64
8.7.2 Trace the origins and development of slavery; its effects on black Americans and on the region's political, social, religious, economic, and cultural development; and identify the strategies that were tried to both overturn and preserve it (e.g., through the writings and historical documents on Nat Turner, Denmark Vesey).	44–45, 50–51, 72–73
8.7.4 Compare the lives of and opportunities for free blacks in the North with those of free blacks in the South.	68–69
8.8.1 Discuss the election of Andrew Jackson as president in 1828, the importance of Jacksonian democracy, and his actions as president (e.g., the spoils system, veto of the National Bank, policy of Indian removal, opposition to the Supreme Court).	48–49, 64

STANDARD	STUDENT EDITION
8.8.2 Describe the purpose, challenges, and economic incentives associated with westward expansion, including the concept of Manifest Destiny (e.g., the Lewis and Clark expedition, accounts of the removal of Indians, the Cherokees' "Trail of Tears," settlement of the Great Plains) and the territorial acquisitions that spanned numerous decades.	42–43, 56–57, 64–65
8.8.3 Describe the role of pioneer women and the new status that western women achieved (e.g., Laura Ingalls Wilder, Annie Bidwell; slave women gaining freedom in the West; Wyoming granting suffrage to women in 1869).	62–63
8.8.5 Discuss Mexican settlements and their locations, cultural traditions, attitudes toward slavery, land-grant system, and economies.	58–59
8.8.6 Describe the Texas War for Independence and the Mexican-American War, including territorial settlements, the aftermath of the wars, and the effects the wars had on the lives of Americans, including Mexican Americans today.	58–59, 60–61, 65
8.9.1 Describe the leaders of the movement (e.g., John Quincy Adams and his proposed constitutional amendment, John Brown and the armed resistance, Harriet Tubman and the Underground Railroad, Benjamin Franklin, Theodore Weld, William Lloyd Garrison, Frederick Douglass).	50–51, 64, 70–71, 72–73, 88
8.9.2 Discuss the abolition of slavery in early state constitutions.	70–71
8.9.4 Discuss the importance of the slavery issue as raised by the annexation of Texas and California's admission to the union as a free state under the Compromise of 1850.	68–69, 88
8.9.5 Analyze the significance of the States' Rights Doctrine, the Missouri Compromise (1820), the Wilmot Proviso (1846), the Compromise of 1850, Henry Clay's role in the Missouri Compromise and the Compromise of 1850, the Kansas-Nebraska Act (1854), the *Dred Scott* v. *Sandford* decision (1857), and the Lincoln-Douglas debates (1858).	46–47, 48–49, 70–71, 88
8.10.2 Trace the boundaries constituting the North and the South, the geographical differences between the two regions, and the differences between agrarians and industrialists.	76–77
8.10.4 Discuss Abraham Lincoln's presidency and his significant writings and speeches and their relationship to the Declaration of Independence, such as his "House Divided" speech (1858), Gettysburg Address (1863), Emancipation Proclamation (1863), and inaugural addresses (1861 and 1865).	74–75, 80–81, 82–83, 88
8.10.5 Study the views and lives of leaders (e.g., Ulysses S. Grant, Jefferson Davis, Robert E. Lee) and soldiers on both sides of the war, including those of black soldiers and regiments.	78–79, 80–81, 84–85, 88
8.10.6 Describe critical developments and events in the war, including the major battles, geographical advantages and obstacles, technological advances, and General Lee's surrender at Appomattox.	76–77, 78–79, 80–81, 82–83, 84–85, 88–89
8.10.7 Explain how the war affected combatants, civilians, the physical environment, and future warfare.	78–79, 88
8.11.3 Understand the effects of the Freedmen's Bureau and the restrictions placed on the rights and opportunities of freedmen, including racial segregation and "Jim Crow" laws.	86–87
8.11.4 Trace the rise of the Ku Klux Klan and describe the Klan's effects.	89
8.11.5 Understand the Thirteenth, Fourteenth, and Fifteenth Amendments to the Constitution and analyze their connection to Reconstruction.	84–85, 86–87, 89
8.12.6 Discuss child labor, working conditions, and laissez-faire policies toward big business and examine the labor movement, including its leaders (e.g., Samuel Gompers), its demand for collective bargaining, and its strikes and protests over labor conditions.	52–53
8.12.7 Identify the new sources of large-scale immigration and the contributions of immigrants to the building of cities and the economy; explain the ways in which new social and economic patterns encouraged assimilation of newcomers into the mainstream amidst growing cultural diversity; and discuss the new wave of nativism.	62–63, 65

GRADE 11 CONTENT STANDARDS	
STANDARD	**STUDENT EDITION**
11.1 Students analyze the significant events in the founding of the nation and its attempts to realize the philosophy of government described in the Declaration of Independence.	24–25, 28–29, 30–31, 82–83, R4
11.1.1 Describe the Enlightenment and the rise of democratic ideas as the context in which the nation was founded.	6–7, 12–13, 14–15, 24–27, 38, R2–R3
11.1.2 Analyze the ideological origins of the American Revolution, the Founding Fathers' philosophy of divinely bestowed unalienable natural rights, the debates on the drafting and ratification of the Constitution, and the addition of the Bill of Rights.	24–25, 26–27, 28–29, 30–31, 32–33, 38, R2–R3, R8, R21
11.1.3 Understand the history of the Constitution after 1787 with emphasis on federal versus state authority and growing democratization.	34–35, 39, R10, R20–R21, R27
11.1.4 Examine the effects of the Civil War and Reconstruction and of the industrial revolution, including demographic shifts and the emergence in the late nineteenth century of the United States as a world power.	84–87, 89, 106–109, 112–115, 118–121, 138–141, 144–147, 166–167, 170–173, 208–209
11.2 Students analyze the relationship among the rise of industrialization, large-scale rural-to-urban migration, and massive immigration from Southern and Eastern Europe.	160–163, 176
11.2.1 Know the effects of industrialization on living and working conditions, including the portrayal of working conditions and food safety in Upton Sinclair's *The Jungle*.	144–151, 166–168, 176–177, 180–187, 199–201, 204–206, R40
11.2.2 Describe the changing landscape, including the growth of cities linked by industry and trade, and the development of cities divided according to race, ethnicity, and class.	148–149, 154–157, 160–163, 166–167, 176–177
11.2.3 Trace the effect of the Americanization movement.	154, 160–163, 176, 204
11.2.4 Analyze the effect of urban political machines and responses to them by immigrants and middle-class reformers.	168–169, 185–186, 196–197
11.2.5 Discuss corporate mergers that produced trusts and cartels and the economic and political policies of industrial leaders.	141, 176, 199–201
11.2.6 Trace the economic development of the United States and its emergence as a major industrial power, including its gains from trade and the advantages of its physical geography.	138–141, 144–147, 176, 208–211, 216–217, R40
11.2.7 Analyze the similarities and differences between the ideologies of Social Darwinism and Social Gospel (e.g., using biographies of William Graham Sumner, Billy Sunday, Dwight L. Moody).	139–140, 148–149, 188–189, R41
11.2.8 Examine the effect of political programs and activities of Populists.	114–115, 128, 780–781
11.2.9 Understand the effect of political programs and activities of the Progressives (e.g., federal regulation of railroad transport, Children's Bureau, the Sixteenth Amendment, Theodore Roosevelt, Hiram Johnson).	164–165, 169, 176–177, 190–193, 196–197, 204–207, 220–221, R26
11.3 Students analyze the role religion played in the founding of America, its lasting moral, social, and political impacts, and issues regarding religious liberty.	12–13, 14–15
11.3.1 Describe the contributions of various religious groups to American civic principles and social reform movements (e.g., civil and human rights, individual responsibility and the work ethic, antimonarchy and self-rule, worker protection, family-centered communities).	52–53, 188–189, 190–193, 255, R41
11.3.2 Analyze the great religious revivals and the leaders involved in them, including the First Great Awakening, the Second Great Awakening, the Civil War revivals, the Social Gospel Movement, the rise of Christian liberal theology in the nineteenth century, the impact of the Second Vatican Council, and the rise of Christian fundamentalism in current times.	24–25, 52–53, 64, 189, 283, 574, 658–659, 704–705, R41

STANDARD	STUDENT EDITION
11.3.3 Cite incidences of religious intolerance in the United States (e.g., persecution of Mormons, anti-Catholic sentiment, anti-Semitism).	56–57, 122–123, 152–153, 160–163, 176, 320–321, R46
11.3.4 Discuss the expanding religious pluralism in the United States and California that resulted from large-scale immigration in the twentieth century.	154–157, 160–163
11.3.5 Describe the principles of religious liberty found in the Establishment and Free Exercise clauses of the First Amendment, including the debate on the issue of separation of church and state.	32–33, 704–705, R22
11.4 Students trace the rise of the United States to its role as a world power in the twentieth century.	208–209, 218–219, 220, 266
11.4.1 List the purpose and the effects of the Open Door policy.	210–211, 220–221
11.4.2 Describe the Spanish-American War and U.S. expansion in the South Pacific.	208–209, 212–215, 216–217, 220–221
11.4.3 Discuss America's role in the Panama Revolution and the building of the Panama Canal.	218–219
11.4.4 Explain Theodore Roosevelt's Big Stick diplomacy, William Taft's Dollar Diplomacy, and Woodrow Wilson's Moral Diplomacy, drawing on relevant speeches.	218–219, 220–221, 240–241, 266
11.4.5 Analyze the political, economic, and social ramifications of World War I on the home front.	230–235, 242–243, 244–247, 251, 254–257, 262–265, 266–267, R43
11.4.6 Trace the declining role of Great Britain and the expanding role of the United States in world affairs after World War II.	324–325, 463–464
11.5 Students analyze the major political, social, economic, technological, and cultural developments of the 1920s.	289, 295, 308, R43
11.5.1 Discuss the policies of Presidents Warren Harding, Calvin Coolidge, and Herbert Hoover.	265, 278–279, 289, 308, 320–321, 334–335, 338
11.5.2 Analyze the international and domestic events, interests, and philosophies that prompted attacks on civil liberties, including the Palmer Raids, Marcus Garvey's "back-to-Africa" movement, the Ku Klux Klan, and immigration quotas and the responses of organizations such as the American Civil Liberties Union, the National Association for the Advancement of Colored People, and the Anti-Defamation League to those attacks.	170–176, 255, 278–283, 300–301, 305, 308–309, 327, 562, R55
11.5.3 Examine the passage of the Eighteenth Amendment to the Constitution and the Volstead Act (Prohibition).	282–283, 284, 308, R27
11.5.4 Analyze the passage of the Nineteenth Amendment and the changing role of women in society.	180–187, 256, 275, 296–299, 308–309, R28
11.5.5 Describe the Harlem Renaissance and new trends in literature, music, and art, with special attention to the work of writers (e.g., Zora Neale Hurston, Langston Hughes).	271–273, 302–305, 306–307, 308
11.5.6 Trace the growth and effects of radio and movies and their role in the worldwide diffusion of popular culture.	100–105, 272–277, 287, 290–293, 308, 332–333, 343–344, 352–353, 488
11.5.7 Discuss the rise of mass production techniques, the growth of cities, the impact of new technologies (e.g., the automobile, electricity), and the resulting prosperity and effect on the American landscape.	132–137, 144–147, 176, 184–185, 287–289, 292–293, 308, R44–R45
11.6 Students analyze the different explanations for the Great Depression and how the New Deal fundamentally changed the role of the federal government.	338, 380
11.6.1 Describe the monetary issues of the late nineteenth and early twentieth centuries that gave rise to the establishment of the Federal Reserve and the weaknesses in key sectors of the economy in the late 1920s.	207, 220, 320–321, 322–323, 324–327, 338

History–Social Science

Content Standards, continued

STANDARD	STUDENT EDITION
11.6.2 Understand the explanations of the principal causes of the Great Depression and the steps taken by the Federal Reserve, Congress, and Presidents Herbert Hoover and Franklin Delano Roosevelt to combat the economic crisis.	320–321, 322–323, 324–327, 334–339, 352–353, 358–361, 366–367, 378–381
11.6.3 Discuss the human toll of the Depression, natural disasters, and unwise agricultural practices and their effects on the depopulation of rural regions and on political movements of the left and right, with particular attention to the Dust Bowl refugees and their social and economic impacts in California.	312–319, 324–327, 330–338, 343, 372–375
11.6.4 Analyze the effects of and the controversies arising from New Deal economic policies and the expanded role of the federal government in society and the economy since the 1930s (e.g., Works Progress Administration, Social Security, National Labor Relations Board, farm programs, regional development policies, and energy development projects such as the Tennessee Valley Authority, California Central Valley Project, and Bonneville Dam).	314, 353–355, 356–357, 358–363, 366–367, 374–379, 380–381, R46
11.6.5 Trace the advances and retreats of organized labor, from the creation of the American Federation of Labor and the Congress of Industrial Organizations to current issues of a postindustrial, multinational economy, including the United Farm Workers in California.	132–137, 265, 355, 364–367, 368–369, 518–519, 646–649, 666, R53
11.7 Students analyze America's participation in World War II.	408, 420–421
11.7.1 Examine the origins of American involvement in the war, with an emphasis on the events that precipitated the attack on Pearl Harbor.	394–395, 396–398, 400–403, 404–405, 406–407, 408, 418–421, 457
11.7.2 Explain U.S. and Allied wartime strategy, including the major battles of Midway, Normandy, Iwo Jima, Okinawa, and the Battle of the Bulge.	412–417, 434–437, 438–439, 440–443, 444–447, 456–457
11.7.3 Identify the roles and sacrifices of individual American soldiers, as well as the unique contributions of the special fighting forces (e.g., the Tuskegee Airmen, the 442nd Regimental Combat team, the Navajo Code Talkers).	412–417, 422–423, 456
11.7.4 Analyze Roosevelt's foreign policy during World War II (e.g., Four Freedoms speech).	394–395, 404–405, 406–407, 418–421, 456
11.7.5 Discuss the constitutional issues and impact of events on the U.S. home front, including the internment of Japanese Americans (e.g., *Fred Korematsu* v. *United States of America*) and the restrictions on German and Italian resident aliens; the response of the administration to Hitler's atrocities against Jews and other groups; the roles of women in military production; and the roles and growing political demands of African Americans.	393, 394–395, 424–427, 428–433, 454–455, 456–457, R23
11.7.6 Describe major developments in aviation, weaponry, communication, and medicine and the war's impact on the location of American industry and use of resources.	402–403, 404–405, 416–417, 422, 424, 428–429, 435, 440, 446, 456, 580–581
11.7.7 Discuss the decision to drop atomic bombs and the consequences of the decision (Hiroshima and Nagasaki).	446–447, 448–449, 456
11.7.8 Analyze the effect of massive aid given to Western Europe under the Marshall Plan to rebuild itself after the war and the importance of a rebuilt Europe to the U.S. economy.	460–461, R47
11.8 Students analyze the economic boom and social transformation of post-World War II America.	468–469, 520, 600
11.8.1 Trace the growth of service sector, white collar, and professional sector jobs in business and government.	468–469, 482, 494–495, 498, 774
11.8.2 Describe the significance of Mexican immigration and its relationship to the agricultural economy, especially in California.	373–374, 518–519, 520, 642–643, 666, R53, R54
11.8.3 Examine Truman's labor policy and congressional reaction to it.	469, R48
11.8.4 Analyze new federal government spending on defense, welfare, interest on the national debt, and federal and state spending on education, including the California Master Plan.	468–469, 470, 496–497, 500–501, 502, 588–591, 601

STANDARD	STUDENT EDITION
11.8.5 Describe the increased powers of the presidency in response to the Great Depression, World War II, and the Cold War.	352–355, 358–361, 422, 496–497, 565–566, 568–569
11.8.6 Discuss the diverse environmental regions of North America, their relationship to local economies, and the origins and prospects of environmental problems in those regions.	110–111, 494–495, 514–515, 516–517, 682–684, 733, 736–741
11.8.7 Describe the effects on society and the economy of technological developments since 1945, including the computer revolution, changes in communication, advances in medicine, and improvements in agricultural technology.	494–495, 500–501, 504–505, 508–509, 520, 570–571, 636–641, 662–667, 716–717, 719, 750–751
11.8.8 Discuss forms of popular culture, with emphasis on their origins and geographic diffusion (e.g., jazz and other forms of popular music, professional sports, architectural and artistic styles).	270–277, 290–295, 343–349, 472, 488–493, 510–513, 520–521, 540–541, R45, R50
11.9 Students analyze U.S. foreign policy since World War II.	460–461, 482–483
11.9.1 Discuss the establishment of the United Nations and International Declaration of Human Rights, International Monetary Fund, World Bank, and General Agreement on Tariffs and Trade (GATT) and their importance in shaping modern Europe and maintaining peace and international order.	460–461, 482
11.9.2 Understand the role of military alliances, including NATO and SEATO, in deterring communist aggression and maintaining security during the Cold War.	471, 474–475, 604–605, R49
11.9.3 Trace the origins and geopolitical consequences (foreign and domestic) of the Cold War and containment policy, including the following: • The era of McCarthyism, instances of domestic Communism (e.g., Alger Hiss) and blacklisting • The Truman Doctrine • The Berlin Blockade • The Korean War • The Bay of Pigs invasion and the Cuban Missile Crisis • Atomic testing in the American West, the “mutual assured destruction” doctrine, and disarmament policies • The Vietnam War • Latin American policy	460–467, 473–475, 478–481, 482–483, 496–497, 520–521, 564–570, 572–575, 605–621, 624–631, 642–643, 692–693, 714–715, 732–733, R49, R53
11.9.4 List the effects of foreign policy on domestic policies and vice versa (e.g., protests during the war in Vietnam, the “nuclear freeze” movement).	478–479, 572–574, 616–617, 620–627, 630–631, 632–633, 730–731, 756–757
11.9.5 Analyze the role of the Reagan administration and other factors in the victory of the West in the Cold War.	714–715, 720–723, 726–727, 732–733
11.9.6 Describe U.S. Middle East policy and its strategic, political, and economic interests, including those related to the Gulf War.	680–681, 696–699, 700, 728–729, 732, 756–759, 778–779, 782
11.9.7 Examine relations between the United States and Mexico in the twentieth century, including key economic, political, immigration, and environmental issues.	373–375, 518–519, 746–749, 770–771, 782
11.10 Students analyze the development of federal civil rights and voting rights.	542–543, 562, 585–587, 592–593, 666–667
11.10.1 Explain how demands of African Americans helped produce a stimulus for civil rights, including President Roosevelt’s ban on racial discrimination in defense industries in 1941, and how African Americans’ service in World War II produced a stimulus for President Truman’s decision to end segregation in the armed forces in 1948.	425, 531–533, 538–539, 550–554, 556–557, 562, 586–587, 594–597
11.10.2 Examine and analyze the key events, policies, and court cases in the evolution of civil rights, including *Dred Scott* v. *Sandford, Plessy* v. *Ferguson, Brown* v. *Board of Education, Regents of the University of California* v. *Bakke,* and California Proposition 209.	70–71, 171–173, 532–535, 542–545, 554–555, 558–561, 596–597, 600, 642–643, 660–661, 678–679, 694, 748–749
11.10.3 Describe the collaboration on legal strategy between African American and white civil rights lawyers to end racial segregation in higher education.	532–533, 543, 563

History–Social Science
Content Standards, continued

STANDARD	STUDENT EDITION
11.10.4 Examine the roles of civil rights advocates (e.g., A. Philip Randolph, Martin Luther King, Jr., Malcolm X, Thurgood Marshall, James Farmer, Rosa Parks), including the significance of Martin Luther King, Jr. 's "Letter from Birmingham Jail" and "I Have a Dream" speech.	531–543, 544–545, 548–562, 592–597, 600, 616–617, 660–661, R52
11.10.5 Discuss the diffusion of the civil rights movement of African Americans from the churches of the rural South and the urban North, including the resistance to racial desegregation in Little Rock and Birmingham, and how the advances influenced the agendas, strategies, and effectiveness of the quests of American Indians, Asian Americans, and Hispanic Americans for civil rights and equal opportunities.	516–519, 538–539, 542–543, 549–551, 553–557, 562–563, 596–597, 642–643, 646–655, R56
11.10.6 Analyze the passage and effects of civil rights and voting rights legislation (e.g., 1964 Civil Rights Act, Voting Rights Act of 1965) and the Twenty-Fourth Amendment, with an emphasis on equality of access to education and to the political process.	585–593, 597, 600, 652–653, 666, 678–679, 768–771, 782, R30, R32
11.10.7 Analyze the women's rights movement from the era of Elizabeth Stanton and Susan Anthony and the passage of the Nineteenth Amendment to the movement launched in the 1960s, including differing perspectives on the roles of women.	54–55, 64–65, 190–195, 220, 296–297, 299, 498–499, 656–659, 666, R28
11.11 Students analyze the major social problems and domestic policy issues in contemporary American society.	220–221, 600, 700–701, 732–733, 776–777, 782–783, R59
11.11.1 Discuss the reasons for the nation's changing immigration policy, with emphasis on how the Immigration Act of 1965 and successor acts have transformed American society.	591, 600–601, 642–643, 655, 661, 748–749, 770–771, 780–781, 782–783, R55
11.11.2 Discuss the significant domestic policy speeches of Truman, Eisenhower, Kennedy, Johnson, Nixon, Carter, Reagan, Bush, and Clinton (e.g., with regard to education, civil rights, economic policy, environmental policy).	469, 588, 557, 638, 676, 678, 696, 700, 708–709, 731–733, 747, R50, R52, R60
11.11.3 Describe the changing roles of women in society as reflected in the entry of more women into the labor force and the changing family structure.	370–371, 498–499, 520, 656–659, 666, 712–713, 717–719, 768–769
11.11.4 Explain the constitutional crisis originating from the Watergate scandal.	688–691, 700, R57
11.11.5 Trace the impact of, need for, and controversies associated with environmental conservation, expansion of the national park system, and the development of environmental protection laws, with particular attention to the interaction between environmental protection advocates and property rights advocates.	202–203, 682–685, 694–695, 700–701, 710–713, 731, 738–741, 772–775, 780–781, R61, R72
11.11.6 Analyze the persistence of poverty and how different analyses of this issue influence welfare reform, health insurance reform, and other social policies.	358–361, 514–515, 520, 590, 710–711, 713, 745, 762–765, 782
11.11.7 Explain how the federal, state, and local governments have responded to demographic and social changes such as population shifts to the suburbs, racial concentrations in the cities, Frostbelt-to-Sunbelt migration, international migration, decline of family farms, increases in out-of-wedlock births, and drug abuse.	502–503, 514–519, 623, 705–707, 711, 719, 732, 743–745, 748–749, 760–761, 768–771, 783, R58

HISTORICAL AND SOCIAL SCIENCES ANALYSIS SKILLS (Grades 9–12)

STANDARD	STUDENT EDITION
Chronological and Spatial Thinking	
CST 1 Students compare the present with the past, evaluating the consequences of past events and decisions and determining the lessons that were learned.	65, 129, 180–187, 221, 261, 267, 317, 392–395, 520, 562, 601, 633, 667, 669, R60
CST 2 Students analyze how change happens at different rates at different times; understand that some aspects can change while others remain the same; and understand that change is complicated and affects not only technology and politics but also values and beliefs.	144–147, 168–173, 404–405, 539, 563, 633, 639, 733, 771, 785, R42, R51
CST 3 Students use a variety of maps and documents to interpret human movement, including major patterns of domestic and international migration, changing environmental preferences and settlement patterns, the frictions that develop between population groups, and the diffusion of ideas, technological innovations, and goods.	xxxiv–xxxvii, 119–121, 221, 236–237, 300–301, 396–398, 400–403, 406–407, 420–421, 475–477, 590–591, R44
CST 4 Students relate current events to the physical and human characteristics of places and regions.	110–111, 339, 623, 738–739, 760–761, 777, 780–781
Historical Research, Evidence, and Point of View	
HREP 1 Students distinguish valid arguments from fallacious arguments in historical interpretations.	129, 221, 409, 640, 691, 766–767, R41, R50, R60, R61
HREP 2 Students identify bias and prejudice in historical interpretations.	100–105, 124–125, 213–215, 246–247, 267, 282–283, 381, 609, 640, 691, R40, R42–R43
HREP 3 Students evaluate major debates among historians concerning alternative interpretations of the past, including an analysis of authors' use of evidence and the distinctions between sound generalizations and misleading oversimplifications.	xxxii–xxxiii, 92, 523, 575, 640, R46, R61
HREP 4 Students construct and test hypotheses; collect, evaluate, and employ information from multiple primary and secondary sources; and apply it in oral and written presentations.	175, 223, 257, 356–357, 467, 559, 563, 785
Historical Interpretation	
HI 1 Students show the connections, causal and otherwise, between particular historical events and larger social, economic, and political trends and developments.	148–149, 154–157, 239, 336–337, 338–339, 501, 555, 707, 756–757, 767, 778–779, R53
HI 2 Students recognize the complexity of historical causes and effects, including the limitations on determining cause and effect.	10–11, 58–59, 234, 339, 390–393, 676–677, 681, 701, 745, R44
HI 3 Students interpret past events and issues within the context in which an event unfolded rather than solely in terms of present-day norms and values.	129, 223, 383, 392–393, 482–483, 570, 657, 661, R49
HI 4 Students understand the meaning, implication, and impact of historical events and recognize that events could have taken other directions.	12–13, 114–115, 118–121, 152–153, 181, 390–393, 416–417, 551, 587, 598–599, 753, 780–781, 784, R46
HI 5 Students analyze human modifications of landscapes and examine the resulting environmental policy issues.	108–109, 144–147, 330–331, 504–505, 682–685, 712–713, 740–741, 775, 783, R72
HI 6 Students conduct cost-benefit analyses and apply basic economic indicators to analyze the aggregate economic behavior of the U.S. economy.	323, 324–327, 376–377, 591, 600, 693

THE STORY OF A CONTINENT

BY DR. WILLIAM PARKINSON
National Geographic Explorer
Associate Curator of Anthropology
Field Museum of Natural History

CRITICAL VIEWING This artist's rendering shows the Laurentide Ice Sheet, which, at times, covered large parts of North America during the Pleistocene epoch. Present-day glaciers, particularly in Canada, are remnants of this ice sheet. What does the image reveal about this glacial period?

EARTH'S TIME LINE — 100 Million Years

Earth Forms
4.5 Billion Years Ago

First Life Appears on Earth
3.8 Billion Years Ago

Close your eyes for a minute and try to imagine the United States without any of the familiar trappings of 21st-century life—no smartphones, hoverboards, or tablets. No iTunes, YouTube, or video games.

Imagine traveling from place to place without paved roads to follow—in fact, with no roads at all, and no wheeled vehicles or even horses to carry you. Instead of strip malls, fast-food chains, and electric streetlights, there are lush, dark forests, pristine rivers and streams, and abundant plant and animal life as far as your eye can see.

Take a deep breath while we travel back to the earliest history of North America, from the beginnings of civilization and even further back to a time when mammoths and mastodons, saber-toothed cats, and giant ground sloths roamed the lands of North America. It was a time when your own species, *Homo sapiens*, evolved and spread throughout the world.

This is the moment in a play just before the main curtain rises on North America—a continent with a story much longer than you may think.

GEOLOGY AND LANDSCAPE

North America is geologically dramatic, featuring towering mountains, vast deserts, sandy beaches, and rolling hills. But the landscape that Europeans like Christopher Columbus encountered when they arrived in the "New World" just a few hundred years ago was profoundly different from the world that the earliest humans experienced when they first came to North America.

Let's go way back in time to when the first modern humans arrived in North America. It was at the end of a more than 2-million-year period that geologists refer to as the **Pleistocene epoch** (PLEIS-to-seen EH-puhk). During this period, the climate and ecology of North America was completely different from the climate and ecology of today and included supersized animals and plants that no longer exist. During the Pleistocene epoch, modern humans across the world honed their skills in hunting, created early artwork, developed fire, and began to use language.

Many people think the climate during the Pleistocene was always cold when, in fact, there were dramatic fluctuations in temperature over relatively short periods of time. At some points, the climate during the Pleistocene was about the same as it is today. During **glacial periods**, or **ice ages**, when glaciers expanded across Earth's surface, the global average annual temperature was significantly colder.

During the Pleistocene epoch, there were more than 20 cycles of glacial periods in which the movement of ice and water changed the landscape and shorelines of the continents drastically, especially around the edges of the Arctic Circle and in present-day North America, Europe, and Asia.

In North America, ice sheets extended as far south as the Missouri and Ohio rivers and covered nearly all of Canada and much of the northern Great Plains, the Midwest, and the northeastern United States. Some recognizable bodies of water and landforms created by glacial movement include the Great Lakes, Cape Cod in Massachusetts, Long Island in New York, and Glacier National Park in Montana. When the glaciers retreated about 10,000 years ago, the North American landscape looked much like it does today.

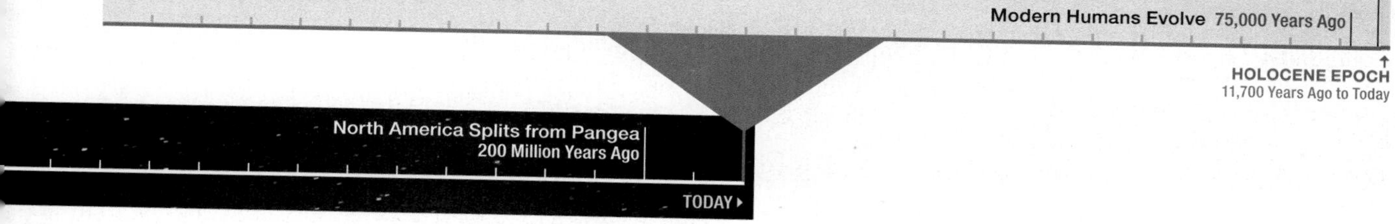

BRIDGING THE CONTINENTS

In Europe, Asia, and Africa, modern humans evolved between 75,000 and 35,000 years ago—long before they arrived in North America. By the end of the Pleistocene, about 12,000 years ago, the only surviving hominid species was modern humans.

Scientists love debates, and one of the biggest debates in archaeology centers around the arrival of the earliest modern humans in North America. We know that when the Pleistocene ended, there were modern human societies living throughout the continent. The debate revolves around pinpointing when during the Pleistocene the first people migrated to the Americas and whether they came by boat or walked. Yes, it was possible for people to have *walked* from Europe and Asia to the Americas! Yes! But the continents are separated by oceans!

Today, the continents are separated by oceans, but during the Pleistocene, there were glacial periods when ice sheets covered the continents. In addition, the oceans contained less water, and the coastlines of the continents were much larger. After the last major glacial period, about 20,000 years ago, the two ice sheets that covered northern North America began to melt, leaving North America temporarily connected to Asia by a large stretch of land between modern-day Alaska and Siberia that scientists call the **Bering Land Bridge**. About 11,000 to 12,000 years ago, the land bridge disappeared as the ice melted, the oceans filled with the water, and the coastlines receded.

A team of paleontologists from the University of Michigan recovered this mastodon skull and more than 60 percent of the animal's skeleton in October 2016. Mastodons are extinct relatives of the elephant.

ENORMOUS ANIMALS

About 12,000 years ago, we entered the Holocene (HO-luh-seen) epoch, which we are still in today. Many animals that lived during the Pleistocene went extinct around the beginning of the Holocene, including many species of large animals, or **megafauna**, such as mammoths, mastodons, and saber-toothed cats. Along with other oversize animals, like giant sloths, giant beavers, and American lions, horses also lived in North America until the end of the Pleistocene but were reintroduced by Europeans a few hundred years ago. They became a critical aspect of Native American culture, especially on the Great Plains. This was the incredible environment the earliest humans encountered when they first arrived in North America at the end of the Pleistocene.

HREP 3 Students evaluate major debates among historians concerning alternative interpretations of the past, including an analysis of authors' use of evidence and the distinctions between sound generalizations and misleading oversimplifications.

THE GREAT DEBATE

Until recently, scientists believed that the earliest people to arrive in the Americas just before the land bridge disappeared were **hunter-gatherers** who specialized in hunting large herd animals that migrated back and forth across the continent. Archaeologists call them the Clovis Culture, based on a kind of stone tool—a Clovis point—that people made at that time.

But there is growing evidence that other groups may have reached the Americas before the Clovis Culture. Sites in Chile and Pennsylvania suggest that there was a pre-Clovis occupation of North America, and some scientists even speculate that people may have arrived by boats earlier in the Pleistocene, perhaps from Europe rather than Asia.

By the end of the Pleistocene, the climate began to stabilize, and modern humans spread throughout the Americas. They were specialized, mobile hunters and gatherers like their contemporaries elsewhere in the world, and they used the same technology—Clovis points—to hunt. These points have been found throughout North America, and similar ones have appeared as far south as Venezuela. People began to settle in different regions of the North American continent that can be distinguished according to the specialized stone tools that were made and used in the Holocene.

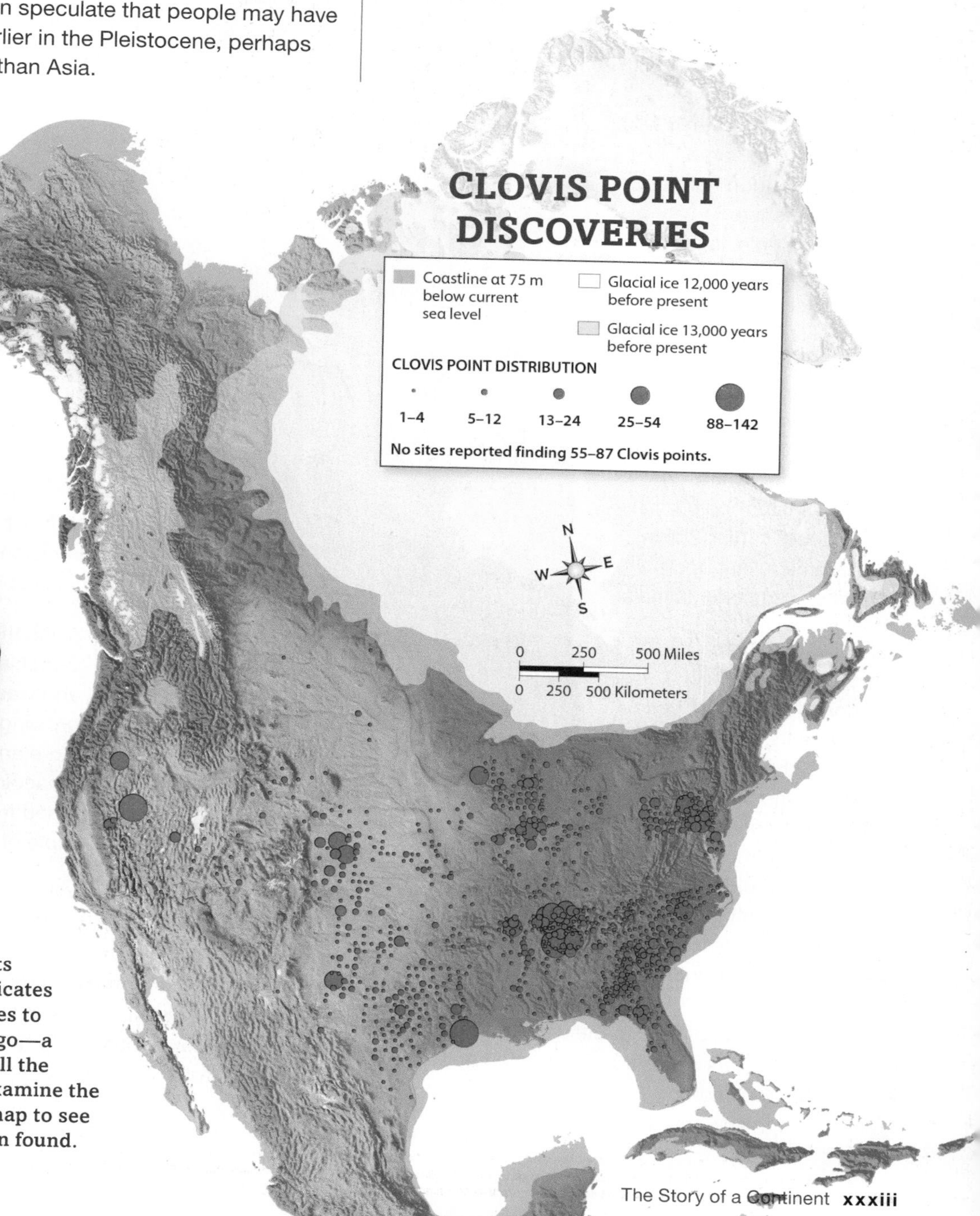

Clovis Point

Carbon dating of points like the one above indicates the Clovis Culture dates to around 11,500 years ago—a time archaeologists call the Paleoindian period. Examine the proportional symbol map to see where points have been found.

THE AGRICULTURAL REVOLUTION

For several thousand years during the Holocene, people continued to live in small groups and move frequently throughout the year, but everything changed when some groups of mobile hunters and gatherers started to experiment with planting their own crops. This transition from relying on gathering wild plants and hunting animals to planting crops and raising animals is called the **Agricultural Revolution**.

The practice of bringing plants and animals under human control is called **domestication**. Almost all the foods we eat today are domesticated instead of wild, which means they have been modified from their wild forms and are to some extent reliant upon humans for their existence. Corn, for example, is the domesticated form of a plant called *teosinte* (TAY-oh-SIN-tay), and cows are the domestic form of a wild herd animal called an *aurochs* (OR-auks). Domestication had a dramatic impact on society and actually transformed human life as people settled down and became reliant upon domestic plants and animals.

Out of all the plants domesticated in North America thousands of years ago, the real game changer was corn. The hunters and gatherers who began experimenting with the domestication of corn had no idea of the impact their little experiment would have on the world in the years to come. Corn is now grown almost everywhere in the world and tied to almost everything Americans eat and many things Americans produce, such as toothpaste and gasoline. But the biggest impact corn had in North America was its unparalleled ability to feed large populations.

This copper plate, discovered in 1906 near Malden, Missouri, provides evidence of Mississippian cultures outside of Cahokia.

SETTLING DOWN

It took a while for corn to be adopted and widely used in North America. In eastern North America, for example, it wasn't a major part of the human diet until about 1,000 years ago. Growing crops like corn and remaining in one location allowed social groups to grow larger and develop more complex political systems. In some places, these groups built massive cities and had extensive trade networks that moved goods across the continent.

One of these cities was located in present-day Illinois along the Mississippi River near the city of St. Louis, Missouri. Founded around A.D. 800, Cahokia would come to be the capital of a large community called a **chiefdom**. By A.D. 1250, Cahokia was a thriving community that controlled a massive geographic area at the confluence of three rivers (the Missouri, Illinois, and Mississippi), and at its height may have had a population of about 15,000 people. It is considered the most sophisticated prehistoric native civilization north of Mexico.

Since the fertile soil of Cahokia was easy to farm and was well suited to growing corn, people farmed more and hunted less. And archaeological evidence unearthed from the site indicates the people of Cahokia ate well.

Although Cahokia and other similar sites in the southeastern United States were heavily dependent upon domestic crops like corn, communities in other parts of North America were not. They continued to hunt and gather wild resources as a major part of their diet.

CST 3 Students use a variety of maps and documents to interpret human movement, including major patterns of domestic and international migration, changing environmental preferences and settlement patterns, the frictions that develop between population groups, and the diffusion of ideas, technological innovations, and goods.

CORN EVOLVES

Corn's wild ancestor, a grass called *teosinte*, doesn't look much like corn but has a very similar genetic makeup. After corn was introduced to North America 6,000 to 10,000 years ago, it spread from Mexico into the American Southwest and across the continent. Early farmers learned to grow types of corn with preferred qualities such as resistance to pests and the ability to grow in different types of soil, which led to a great diversity of species.

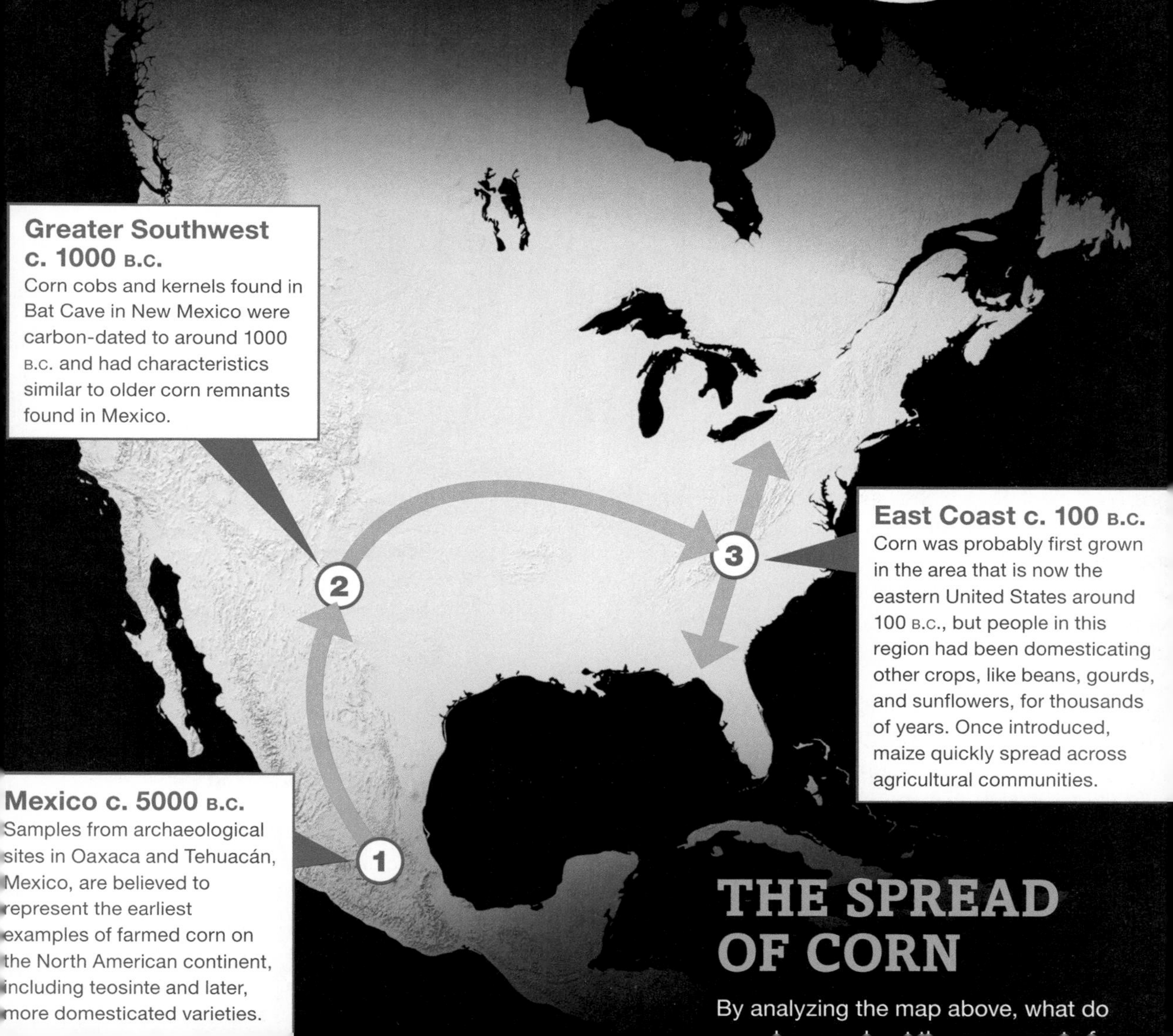

THE SPREAD OF CORN

By analyzing the map above, what do

A CULTURAL MOSAIC

Before the 1500s, the Americas, Europe, and Africa had been isolated from one another, but as Europeans began looking beyond their shores for riches and resources, Africa's mighty empires wanted to show their strength. Both continents were on a collision course with the Americas, but the Europeans got there first.

When the Europeans arrived in the "New World," they experienced a mosaic of diverse cultures and landscapes. From the hierarchical chiefdoms of Florida to the more mobile, less hierarchical groups of the Great Basin, the cultures of North America made up a patchwork quilt of societies with distinct languages, economic practices, political systems, and traditions as varied as the landscape.

These petroglyphs in California's Chidago Canyon are thought to be the visions of ancient Paiute shamans.

Everyone has a personal American story to tell, and those stories often reflect the diversity of our cultural mosaic. It's not always easy to build consensus or get everyone "on the same page," but that diversity is one of the best things about life in the United States. With so many options and perspectives and our persistent American drive, we have the potential to develop amazingly creative solutions to 21st-century issues.

So raise the curtain on this incredibly rich and varied landscape, well equipped to sustain and nurture the promise of a unique new country and a vibrant people. The action and the drama are just about to begin.

THINK ABOUT IT

What does the fact that these diverse cultures all expressed themselves through art suggest about early humans?

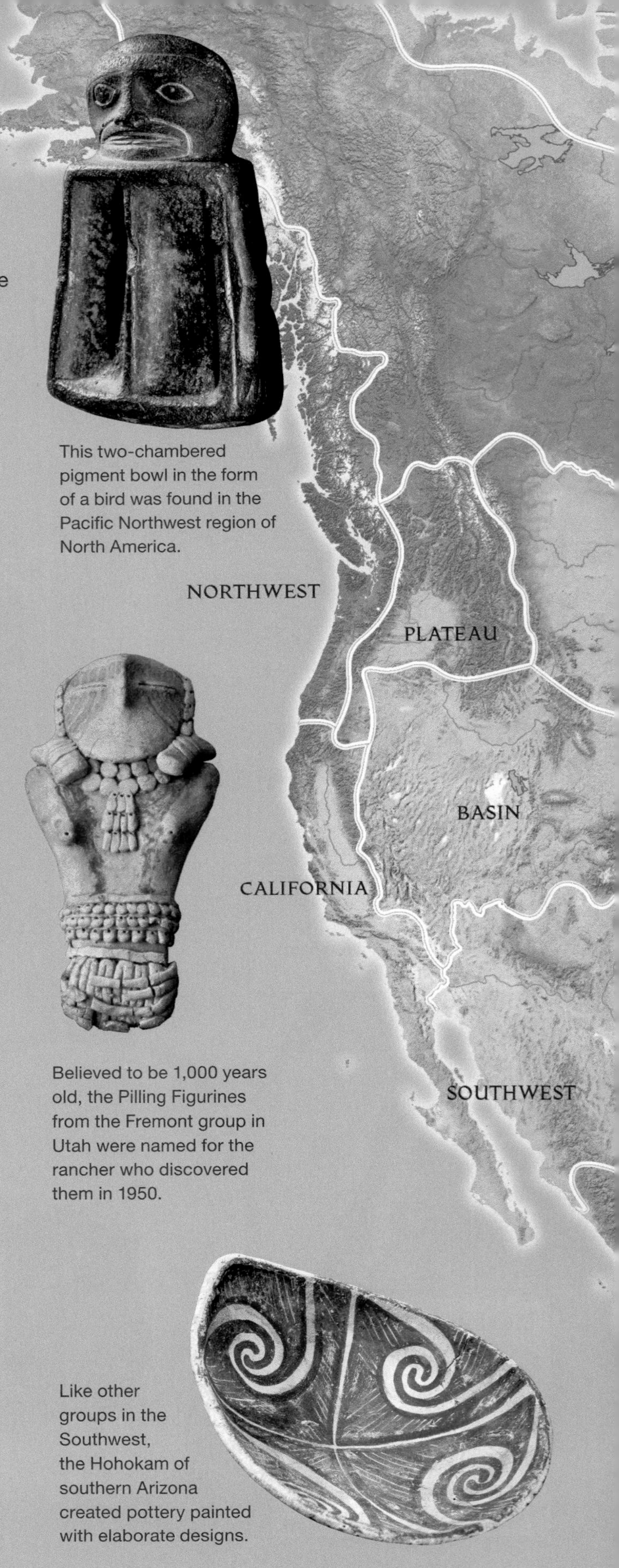

This two-chambered pigment bowl in the form of a bird was found in the Pacific Northwest region of North America.

Believed to be 1,000 years old, the Pilling Figurines from the Fremont group in Utah were named for the rancher who discovered them in 1950.

Like other groups in the Southwest, the Hohokam of southern Arizona created pottery painted with elaborate designs.

CST 3 Students use a variety of maps and documents to interpret human movement, including major patterns of domestic and international migration, changing environmental preferences and settlement patterns, the frictions that develop between population groups, and the diffusion of ideas, technological innovations, and goods.

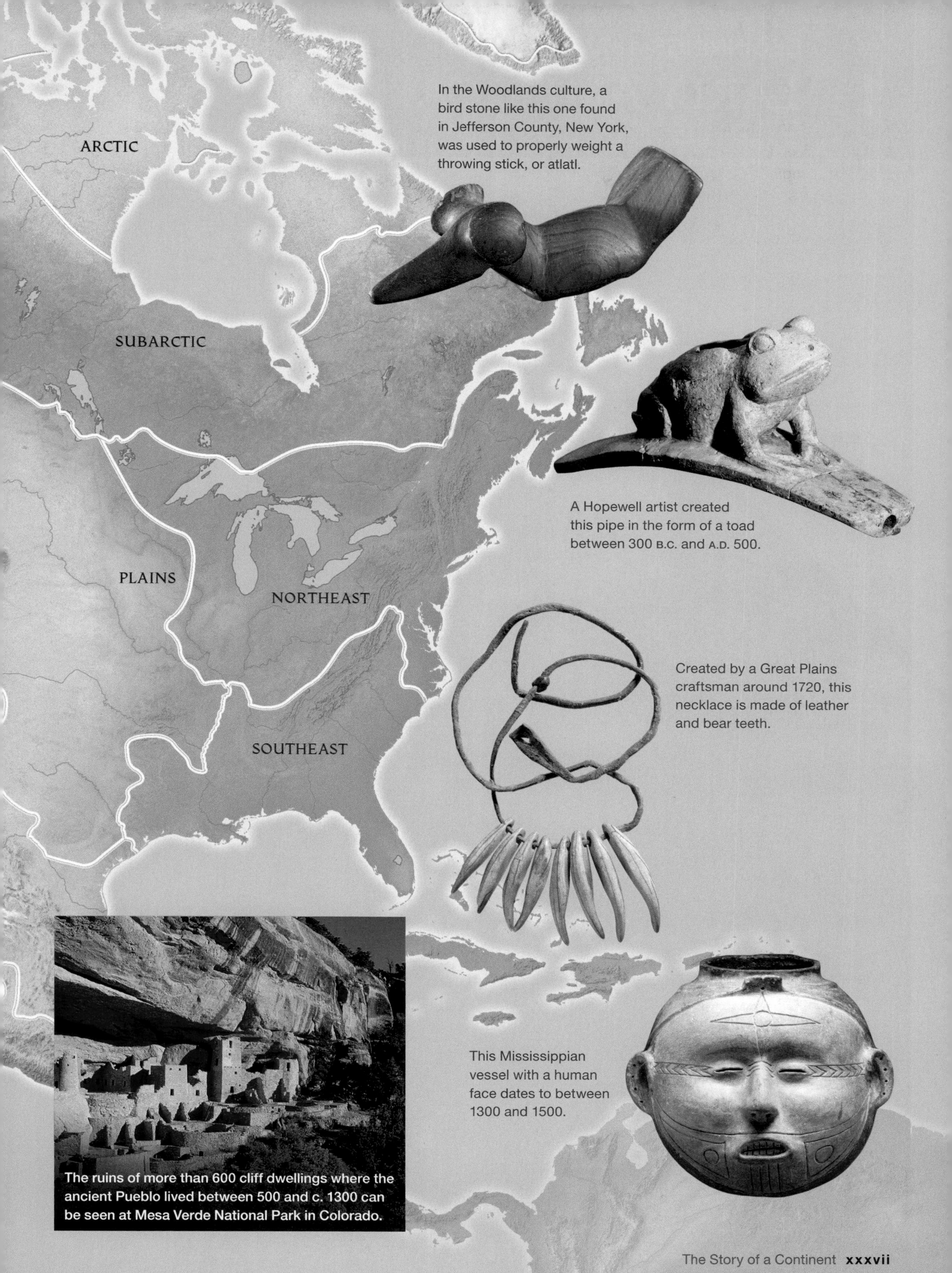

In the Woodlands culture, a bird stone like this one found in Jefferson County, New York, was used to properly weight a throwing stick, or atlatl.

A Hopewell artist created this pipe in the form of a toad between 300 B.C. and A.D. 500.

Created by a Great Plains craftsman around 1720, this necklace is made of leather and bear teeth.

The ruins of more than 600 cliff dwellings where the ancient Pueblo lived between 500 and c. 1300 can be seen at Mesa Verde National Park in Colorado.

This Mississippian vessel with a human face dates to between 1300 and 1500.

REVIEW UNIT 1

BEGINNINGS–1877

EARLY AMERICA

CRITICAL VIEWING Artist Emanuel Leutze's 1851 oil painting, called *Washington Crossing the Delaware*, depicts General Washington's attack on the Hessians in Trenton, New Jersey, on December 25, 1776. This is a large work of art, measuring 149 inches high by 255 inches wide. According to Leutze, what challenges did the soldiers face during the attack on Trenton?

REVIEW UNIT 1 EARLY AMERICA

THE AMERICAS

A.D. 250
The Maya Classic Period begins.
(Maya temple in Tikal, Guatemala)

1000 B.C.
The ancient Pueblo begin to farm in the southwestern region of North America.

1325
The Aztec found Tenochtitlán and build a great civilization.

1450
The Inca build Machu Picchu in the Andes Mountains in South America.

1492
Christopher Columbus makes the first of several voyages to the Americas.

1607
English settlers found Jamestown in Virginia. *(sealing wax stamp owned by Jamestown resident)*

1620
Pilgrims sign the Mayflower Compact, establishing a self-governing colony at Plymouth in New England.

1000 B.C.

A.D. 1

1600

THE WORLD

476 EUROPE
The Western Roman Empire falls, and the period known as the Middle Ages soon begins in Western Europe.

1200 AFRICA
The Mali Empire, built on trade and gold, arises in West Africa.

1300 EUROPE
The Renaissance begins in Europe.
(Renaissance artist Leonardo da Vinci's painting, the Mona Lisa*)*

1368 ASIA
The Ming dynasty begins a 276-year rule in China.

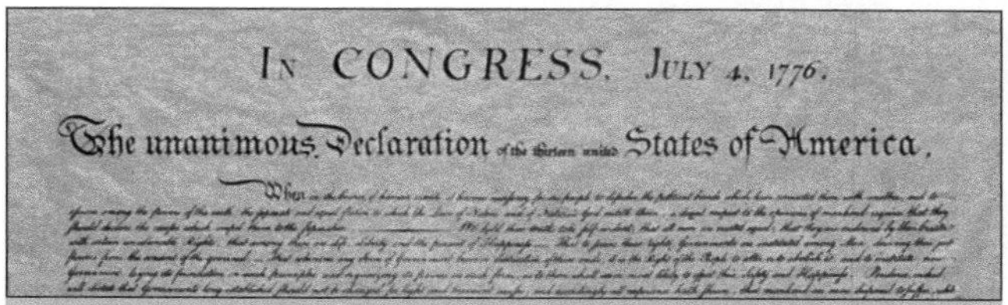
IN CONGRESS, JULY 4, 1776.

The unanimous Declaration of the thirteen united States of America,

1776
The Declaration of Independence, which announces the formation of the United States of America and its independence from Britain, is adopted on July 4.

HISTORICAL THINKING

DETERMINE CHRONOLOGY Which event first indicated that American colonists would favor a democratic form of government?

1789
George Washington becomes the first president of the United States.

1861
The Civil War begins between the Confederate states in the South and the Union North.
(Union soldier cap)

1877
Reconstruction comes to an end but does not fully achieve its goal of granting equal rights to African Americans.

1860
Abraham Lincoln is elected president. Soon after, South Carolina secedes from the Union.

1775
The American Revolution begins with the battles of Lexington and Concord in Massachusetts.

1700

1800

1880

c. 1750 EUROPE
The Industrial Revolution begins in Great Britain.
(spinning jenny, which helped industrialize Britain's textile production)

1876 AFRICA
The European scramble for African territory begins.

1857 ASIA
Indian soldiers revolt against British rule in India.

HI 1 Students show the connections, causal and otherwise, between particular historical events and larger social, economic, and political trends and developments.

REVIEW CHAPTER 1

EXPLORATION AND SETTLEMENT

Beginnings–1765

HISTORICAL THINKING Why did the New England, Middle, and Southern colonies develop differently?

AMERICAN STORIES ONLINE **Cahokia**

AMERICAN STORIES ONLINE **Jamestown**

AMERICAN GALLERY ONLINE **Southern Plantations**

CRITICAL VIEWING Founded in 1947, Plimoth Plantation, a living history museum in Plymouth, Massachusetts, re-creates the community life of the Pilgrims in the 1600s. From details in the photo, what materials can you identify that the Pilgrims used to build houses and everyday objects?

"As a **city upon a hill,**
the eyes of all people are upon us."

—John Winthrop

REVIEW LESSON 1.1 THE ATLANTIC WORLD

When historians refer to the Atlantic World, they mean more than the continents bordering the Atlantic Ocean. They are referring to the exchange of people, goods, ideas, and cultural elements that began to flow across the Atlantic Ocean in the late 1400s as exploration, trade, and colonization connected Europe, Africa, and the Americas. One outcome of this exchange was the meeting of European, African, and Native American cultures in the Americas.

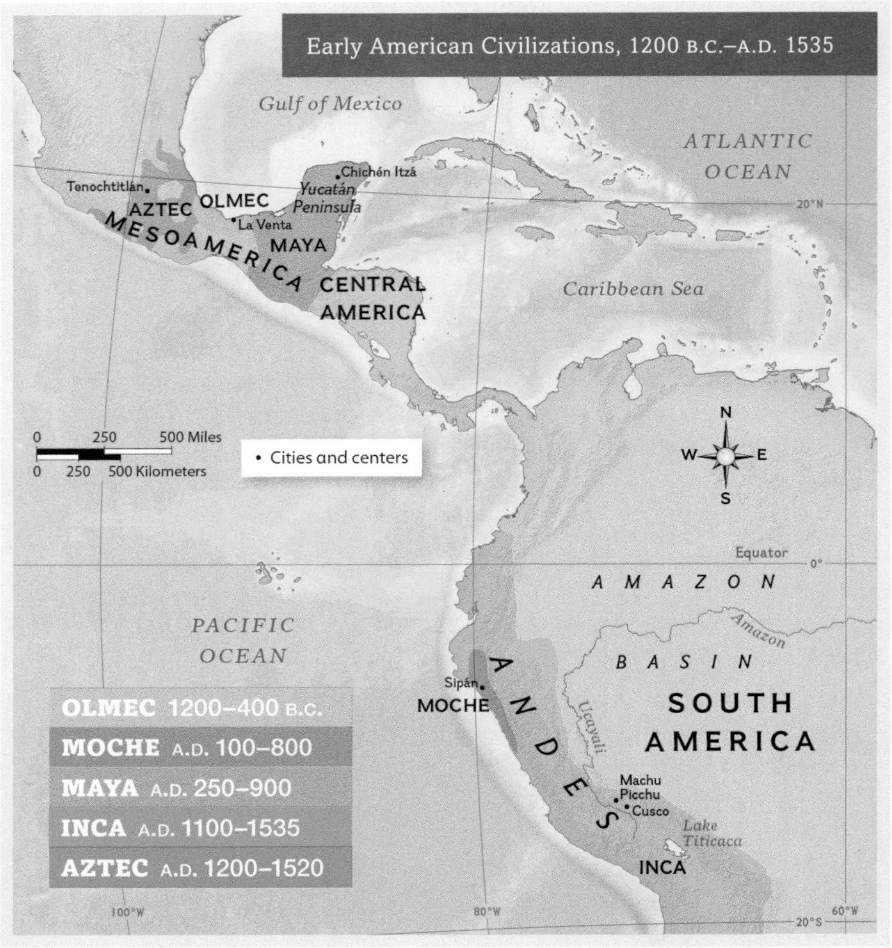

A LAND OF PLENTY The Americas are geographically diverse. North America has towering mountain ranges, grassy plains, rocky coasts, deserts, and broad valleys. **Mesoamerica**, the area from present-day southern Mexico into parts of Central America, is divided into highlands and lowlands. South America contains coastal mountains and plains, dry forests and deserts, and vast river basins covered by rain forests and grasslands. Some scientists believe that during the last ice age, which ended about 10,000 B.C., Asians migrated into the Americas across the Bering land bridge and along the Pacific Coast, creating distinct cultures in every part of the Western Hemisphere. But other theories as to how and when people arrived in North America exist as well. Over thousands of years, American civilizations rose and fell as various empires built pyramids and temple mounds, developed cities and cultures, and competed for territory and trade.

EUROPE AND AFRICA The seeds of the Atlantic World were planted in the Middle Ages, which extended from about A.D. 500 to 1450. The Crusades, religious wars fought by Christians to win the Holy Land from Muslims, had the unintended consequence of increasing trade between northern and western Europe and the eastern Mediterranean region. The feudal society in Europe, headed by kings, began to give way to more democratic systems as barons set limits on the power of monarchs, especially in England. During the **Renaissance**, which began in the 1300s, Europeans developed new ideas in many fields and encouraged more freedom of thought. These changes contributed to the **Reformation**, which split the Roman Catholic Church and gave rise to Protestantism in the 1500s. In West Africa during this period, mighty empires based on trade and conquest rose and fell.

A MEETING OF CULTURES In the 1400s, the desire for trade with Asia spurred Europeans to explore new sea routes after the Ottoman Turks took control of overland routes and made travel difficult. Portuguese navigators successfully sailed around the tip of Africa and on to India and back. Portuguese sailors also explored the western coast of Africa and brought back trade goods. Other explorers traveled westward across the Atlantic in search of a route to Asia. These explorations led to the intermixing of European, African, and Native American cultures that characterizes the Atlantic World.

CST 3 Students use a variety of maps and documents to interpret human movement, including major patterns of domestic and international migration, changing environmental preferences and settlement patterns, the frictions that develop between population groups, and the diffusion of ideas, technological innovations, and goods.

KEY TAKEAWAYS

THE AMERICAS

- Descendants of the people who migrated from Asia during the last ice age settled in Central America and South America as early as 14,000 years ago.
- Mesoamerican civilizations in present-day Mexico, Guatemala, and Belize included the Olmec, Maya, and Aztec, who thrived at different times from around 1200 B.C. to about A.D. 1520.
- South American civilizations included the Moche, who lived on the northern coast of what is now Peru between about A.D. 100 and 800, and the Inca, whose empire arose in Peru in the 1100s.

EUROPE

- The **Magna Carta**, signed by King John and his barons in 1215, launched democratic reforms in England by requiring the monarch to abide by rules laid out by the nobles and by helping give rise to Parliament. Later, Parliament passed the English Bill of Rights of 1689 to formally protect the rights of English citizens and Parliament.
- The Renaissance, which was rooted in the writings and philosophies of ancient Greece and Rome, and the Reformation, which was led by a German monk named **Martin Luther**, brought changes in art, architecture, literature, philosophy, and religion in Europe.
- Political and social changes continued with the **Enlightenment**, an intellectual movement that encouraged people to use reason to question things rather than simply accept the dictates of religious and political leaders.

AFRICA

- The trading empires of West Africa arose in the Sahel, a flat grassland region south of the Sahara.
- First Ghana, then Mali, and then Songhai became rich and powerful kingdoms by controlling the gold and salt trade in West Africa.
- Until the Portuguese introduced chattel slavery—in which people are bought and sold as property—in the mid-1400s, most enslaved people in West Africa were war captives, criminals, political opponents, victims of famine or debt, or foreigners, and their condition of servitude was not passed to their children.

OPENING UP THE OCEAN WORLD

- The desire to avoid the high prices that Turkish merchants charged for Asian goods spurred European sea exploration in the 1400s.
- Technological innovations—such as the magnetic compass for determining direction, the astrolabe for identifying location at sea based on the positions of the stars, and the caravel for sailing into the wind—furthered exploration.
- Prince Henry the Navigator's maritime school in Sagres, Portugal, Bartholomeu Dias's discovery of a route around the southern tip of Africa, and Vasco da Gama's successful round trip to India helped advance sea exploration in the 1400s.

NATIONAL GEOGRAPHIC EXPLORER

Pardis Sabeti

Harvard research scientist Pardis Sabeti uses computer science and mathematical tools to research infectious diseases, which spread from person to person. She studies current outbreaks to learn how they alter over time and influence changes in human biology. Using the knowledge gained, she reveals how diseases have affected history, such as the decimation of Native Americans after they came in contact with the diseases of European settlers.

HISTORICAL THINKING

1. **SUMMARIZE** According to some scientists, how and when did Asians first migrate to the Americas?
2. **MAKE GENERALIZATIONS** How did democratic ideas develop in Europe?
3. **INTERPRET MAPS** Which early civilization developed the largest empire in the Americas?

8.2.1 Discuss the significance of the Magna Carta, the English Bill of Rights, and the Mayflower Compact; 11.1.1 Describe the Enlightenment and the rise of democratic ideas as the context in which the nation was founded.

REVIEW LESSON 1.2

THE CULTURES OF NORTH AMERICA

Built by early Native Americans, Serpent Mound in Adams County, Ohio, resembles a writhing snake. The mound stretches more than 1,300 feet. It is estimated to be between 1,000 and 2,000 years old.

As Native Americans spread from the frozen tundra of the Arctic and subarctic regions across North America, they formed distinct cultures in the various geographic areas in which they settled. These cultures developed in response to the specific climate, landscape, soil, and plant and animal life the people encountered. Resources and challenges differed for the various groups, depending on whether they settled in coastal, arid, or rainy lands.

COASTAL CULTURES The coastal people of the Pacific Northwest and California did not need to farm to survive. The lush evergreen forests of the Pacific Northwest provided a wide variety of plants and animals to eat. The rivers that flowed into the ocean were stocked with fish, including salmon swimming to and from the Pacific Ocean. The ocean provided clams, mussels, oysters, and other shellfish, as well as halibut, herring, and other marine fish.

In some areas, Native Americans hunted whales. Native Americans living along the California coast also ate shellfish and marine fish. In addition, they collected acorns and hunted game. Those who lived farther inland fished in local waters. They hunted deer, elk, rabbit, waterfowl, and other game, and they gathered acorns, plants, and berries.

DESERT CULTURES Native Americans living in the Southwest and on the Great Plains had to adapt to arid conditions. In the deserts, mesas, and canyons of what is now the American Southwest, the ancient Pueblo and Hohokam grew enough squash, beans, and maize to support large populations. The pre-contact tribes of the Great Plains lived on the grasslands that stretched from the Rocky Mountains eastward to the Mississippi River. Such groups as the Mandan settled in river valleys and farmed. But the Blackfeet and other tribes who lived on the dry western grasslands were nomadic. They moved from place to place, hunting bison and other game.

WETLAND CULTURES The Native American cultures of the Mississippi River Valley, Southeast, and Northeast benefited from generous rain in those regions. The Adena and Hopewell, two early cultures known as Mound Builders because of the earthen mounds they constructed, were primarily hunter-gatherers. The later Mississippian culture also created mounds, but the people were primarily farmers. Agriculture was also a mainstay in the Southeast, where the Choctaw, Chickasaw, and other woodland societies lived, and in the heavily wooded forests of the Northeast, where the Eastern Woodlands people lived.

HI 1 Students show the connections, causal and otherwise, between particular historical events and larger social, economic, and political trends and developments.

KEY TAKEAWAYS

PACIFIC NORTHWEST AND CALIFORNIA CULTURES

- Native Americans of the Pacific Northwest lived in the region that is now the states of Washington and Oregon and the Canadian province of British Columbia.
- The influence of the environment on culture can be seen in the importance Native Americans in the Pacific Northwest placed on woodworking, including the carving of totem poles, and on such celebrations as the First Salmon Ceremony.
- California cultures living on or near the coast included the Shasta, Yurok, and Hupa in what is now northwestern California. The Pomo, Ohlone, Patwin, Miwok, and Maidu lived in what is now the San Francisco Bay area and valleys farther inland, such as the Sacramento and San Joaquin valleys.

SOUTHWEST AND GREAT PLAINS CULTURES

- The ancient Pueblo and Hohokam adopted farming practices from Mesoamerican groups of the Southwest with whom they traded.
- By digging canals to carry river water to their fields, the Hohokam were able to farm the desert. The ancient Pueblo built dams, reservoirs, and terraces to control water.
- Bison were important to the Great Plains Native Americans because they could eat the animal's meat, make clothing and tepees from its hide and fur, and make tools from its bones and tendons.

MOUND BUILDERS OF THE MISSISSIPPI VALLEY

- The Adena and Hopewell lived primarily in present-day southern Ohio but also settled in what is now Indiana, Kentucky, West Virginia, Michigan, Wisconsin, and Pennsylvania. The Mississippians spread across North America from present-day Georgia to Minnesota.
- The Mound Builders' earthen mounds served a variety of purposes, from entombing the dead to providing a base for grand temples. Some of the mounds in the Mississippians' capital city of Cahokia in Illinois served as residences for chiefs.
- The Mississippians were able to support a large population, numbering as many as 15,000 people at Cahokia, because of their strong agricultural production of corns, beans, and squash.

SOUTHEAST AND NORTHEAST CULTURES

- A mild climate, fertile soil, and plentiful rainfall made the Southeast a perfect place for Native Americans to grow such crops as maize, beans, pumpkins, and squash.
- The Eastern Woodlands farmers in the heavily forested Northeast practiced slash-and-burn agriculture, which involved cutting down and burning trees to clear land for planting.
- Two language groups were dominant in the Eastern Woodlands—the Algonquian, who lived along the Atlantic coast, and the Iroquois, who lived primarily in the central part of present-day New York State and the southern part of the Canadian province of Ontario.

Ceremonial mask

CURATING HISTORY

National Museum of the American Indian

This western red cedar mask from the museum in Washington, D.C., represents the chief of the undersea, who was believed to live in the ocean in a copper home guarded by sea monsters. Ceremonial masks such as this one usually depict ancestors or supernatural beings. A master carver from a tribe in western Canada carved this mask in the late 1800s or early 1900s.

HISTORICAL THINKING

1. **ANALYZE ENVIRONMENTAL CONCEPTS** How did Native Americans both depend on and change their natural environments?
2. **MAKE CONNECTIONS** How was the social and economic development of the Mound Builders influenced by where they settled?
3. **CATEGORIZE** What were the main ways in which Native Americans obtained food?

REVIEW LESSON 1.3

EUROPEANS IN NORTH AMERICA

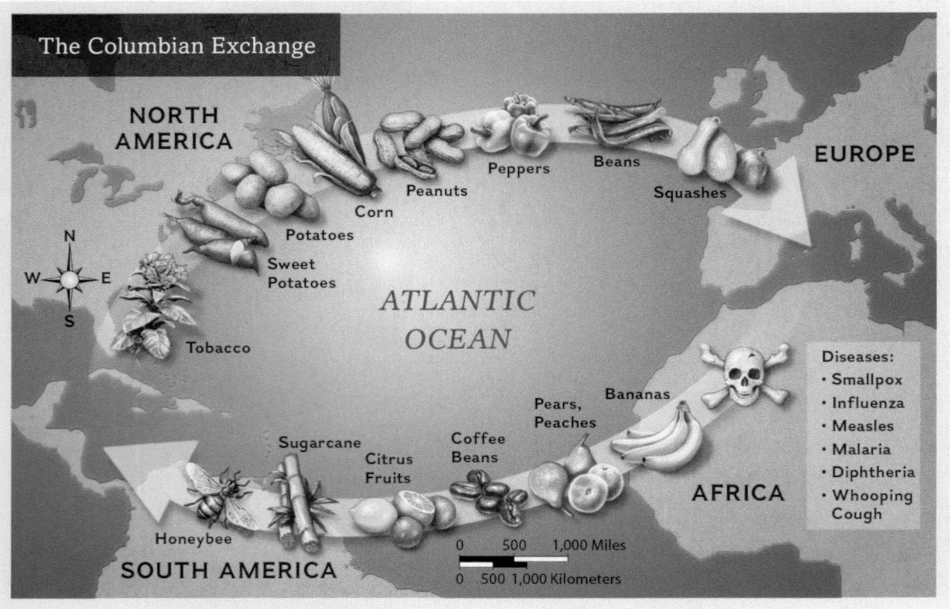

Colonization led to the Columbian Exchange—a biological and cultural exchange among the Americas, Europe, Africa, and Asia following Columbus's voyage to the Americas in 1492.

Portugal's success in establishing trade in West Africa made other countries eager to participate. However, in 1455, Pope Nicholas V gave the Portuguese sole rights to trading in lands they discovered along the African and West Indian coasts. This action spurred Spain, France, the Netherlands, and England to begin their own sea explorations. These European countries wanted to increase trade and colonization, search for gold, and spread Christianity. Trade and colonization were especially important because European economies were based on mercantilism, an economic system in which countries had the sole right to trade with their colonies. More colonies meant more wealth and power. This drive for wealth and power led to fierce competition for colonies in North America.

SPAIN'S QUESTS Despite the pope's decree, King Ferdinand and Queen Isabella of Spain were determined to expand their trade routes. Toward that end, they financed a voyage in 1492 for Italian explorer **Christopher Columbus** to find a westward route to Asia. Columbus, of course, never reached Asia, landing instead in the Caribbean islands. Ferdinand and Isabella petitioned the new pope to allow Spain to colonize the lands Columbus claimed. With permission granted, Spain launched its quest to find gold and convert the inhabitants of the new lands to Christianity. Spain eventually colonized Mexico, Central America, much of South America, and parts of southern North America.

FRENCH AND DUTCH IN NORTH AMERICA

The French and Dutch explored North America in hopes of finding the Northwest Passage, a northwestern water route to Asia. While this effort was unsuccessful, French explorer **Samuel de Champlain** established a fur-trading base along the St. Lawrence River in 1608. It became the first permanent settlement in the French colony of New France. In 1614, after English explorer **Henry Hudson** sailed up the river that now bears his name, the Dutch set up a fur-trading post near what is now Albany, New York, and named their new colony New Netherland. They added the community of New Amsterdam (now New York) in 1626.

ENGLISH VOYAGES AND SETTLEMENT Like the French and the Dutch, the English also searched for a northwestern route to Asia and claimed land in the process. Eager for the wealth, power, and fame that colonies might bring, Queen Elizabeth granted English nobleman **Walter Raleigh** permission to set up a colony in North America in the late 1500s. Raleigh tried but failed to establish a colony on Roanoke Island, part of the island chain now known as the Outer Banks of North Carolina. England tried again to establish a colony in the early 1600s and founded **Jamestown, Virginia**, in 1607.

7.11.2 Discuss the exchanges of plants, animals, technology, culture, and ideas among Europe, Africa, Asia, and the Americas in the fifteenth and sixteenth centuries and the major economic and social effects on each continent.

KEY TAKEAWAYS

SPANISH COLONIZATION

- Spain sponsored a number of voyages of exploration. Columbus made four round-trips to the Americas between 1492 and 1504. Italian navigator Amerigo Vespucci explored the east coast of South America in 1499. Portuguese explorer **Ferdinand Magellan** began a circumnavigation of the globe in 1522. Portuguese navigator Juan Rodríguez Cabrillo explored the California coast in 1542.
- Spanish conquistadors led by **Hernán Cortés** defeated the Aztec Empire in Mexico by laying siege to its capital, Tenochtitlán, in 1521. The forces of Spanish conquistador **Francisco Pizarro** conquered the Inca Empire in South America between 1532 and 1537 by killing their emperor, **Atahualpa**, and crushing the opposition.
- To rule the people they conquered in the Americas, the Spanish set up viceroyalties, territories governed by colonial leaders called viceroys, who were appointed by the king.

FRENCH AND DUTCH COLONIZATION

- Italian navigator Giovanni da Verrazzano explored most of the Atlantic coast for France. French mariner **Jacques Cartier** named the St. Lawrence River and claimed the land he saw for France. Henry Hudson explored the northern Atlantic coast for the Dutch while attempting to find a northwestern water route to Asia.
- The French colony of New France grew slowly, in part because Catholic France refused to allow Protestants to settle there. French peasants saw little chance for advancement in the colony since wealthy settlers controlled large manors.
- After the Dutch established New Amsterdam on the island of Manhattan, they discovered that the Native Americans who sold them the land believed they would share it, which led to war by 1640.

ENGLISH COLONIZATION

- Italian navigator John Cabot discovered Newfoundland in search of a northwestern water route and claimed land for England there.
- Walter Raleigh made two attempts to establish a colony at Roanoke. The first group of colonists returned home after less than a year. The second group vanished.
- With the help of Native Americans, the English colony of Jamestown, Virginia, eventually succeeded, exporting tobacco and establishing the first representative assembly in the American colonies.

IMPACT OF EUROPEAN COLONIZATION

- The **Columbian Exchange** increased agricultural options and enriched diets on the continents of Europe, Africa, and the Americas.
- Colonization and the Columbian Exchange were disastrous for Native Americans. Many groups were forced off their land, and large populations were wiped out by European diseases.
- Colonization introduced chattel slavery to the Americas.

NATIONAL GEOGRAPHIC EXPLORER

William Kelso

American archaeologist William Kelso has spent years investigating, excavating, and reconstructing Fort James, the original fort built by the Jamestown colonists in Virginia. With few clues to go on, Kelso identified evidence of all but one corner of the fort's structure as well as thousands of artifacts. He and his team then began reconstructing the fort, using the kinds of materials and tools available to the Jamestown settlers.

HISTORICAL THINKING

1. **SUMMARIZE** Why did European countries launch competing voyages of exploration?
2. **INTERPRET MAPS** How did the Columbian Exchange negatively affect the health of Native Americans?
3. **ANALYZE CAUSE AND EFFECT** What complex effects did European colonization have on Native Americans?

HI 2 Students recognize the complexity of historical causes and effects, including the limitations on determining cause and effect.

REVIEW LESSON 1.4

NEW ENGLAND COLONIES

European settlers continued to immigrate to the American colonies during the early 1600s. Among the new arrivals to New England were religious dissenters, people who disagreed with the teachings of their church. Coming from the Church of England, these dissenters sought religious freedom. Some dissenters, such as the Pilgrims, were separatists. They wished to create their own congregations outside the Church of England. Others, such as the Puritans, hoped to reform the church from within.

After it was built in 1956, this full-scale replica of the *Mayflower* sailed from England to New England.

SETTLEMENT OF NEW ENGLAND After landing on Cape Cod in 1620, the Pilgrims settled around what is now Plymouth, Massachusetts, surviving with the help of a group of Native Americans called the Pawtuxet. The Puritans first began their Great Migration from England to Massachusetts in 1630. They established the **Massachusetts Bay Colony**, with the church serving as the center of the community and the congregation as the governing authority in the colony. Not all colonists welcomed this arrangement. In 1636, English clergyman **Thomas Hooker** and his followers left to found a colony in Connecticut. In the same year, **Roger Williams**, also an English clergyman, founded Rhode Island after being banished from Massachusetts for dissent. English religious leader **Anne Hutchinson**, another banished dissenter, founded a settlement near present-day Portsmouth, Rhode Island.

COLONIAL TRADE While most New Englanders were farmers, it was fishing, whaling, shipbuilding, and trading that fueled the New England economy. New England quickly became the trading center of eastern North America. New England merchants exchanged goods with other colonies, from Newfoundland to Georgia, and with countries in Europe. The merchants conducted business through a trading network called the triangular trade, which connected the Americas with Europe and Africa.

CULTURE Over time, the Puritans' hold on New England society weakened as their church membership declined. Other Protestant religious groups, such as the Quakers and Baptists, flourished. In 1691, a new plan for the colony further weakened Puritanism by guaranteeing religious freedom and extending the vote to any man who owned property, regardless of his religion. The belief that people needed to be able to read so they could learn about God helped spur the establishment of elementary schools, secondary schools, and universities. The rising rate of literacy led to a greater demand for books and newspapers. As an alternative to pursuing higher education, many colonial boys learned trades by becoming apprentices to master craftsmen. The legal terms of the apprenticeships varied, but an apprentice received room and board instead of wages.

11.1.1 Describe the Enlightenment and the rise of democratic ideas as the context in which the nation was founded; 11.3 Students analyze the role religion played in the founding of America, its lasting moral, social, and political impacts, and issues regarding religious liberty.

KEY TAKEAWAYS

PLYMOUTH AND MASSACHUSETTS BAY COLONIES

- Dissenters and separatists fled England because the Church of England threatened to imprison people who disagreed.
- When their ship, the *Mayflower*, landed on Cape Cod rather than in northern Virginia, the Pilgrims established and signed the **Mayflower Compact**, which laid out a plan of government for the new colony.
- The Puritans' system of self-governance, called the New England Way, gave the congregation the authority to punish members who disagreed with church doctrine, take away the property of those who left the church, and limit voting to males who were church members.

CONNECTICUT AND RHODE ISLAND

- Thomas Hooker, who left Massachusetts over the New England Way's insistence that only church members could vote and hold office, helped formulate the Fundamental Orders of Connecticut. This law established a General Assembly in Connecticut and removed church membership as a requirement for voting and holding office.
- Roger Williams was banished for attacking laws that established tax support for the church and required church attendance. He based the government of his new colony of Rhode Island on the idea that church and state affairs should be kept separate.
- Anne Hutchinson, who established a settlement within Rhode Island, believed ministers were unnecessary and taught that people had to answer directly to God for their actions, not to the church.

WAR AND WITCH TRIALS

- Native Americans helped the colonists adapt to their new environment and were partners in trade. However, the continued takeover of Native American lands by colonists led to increasing conflict.
- King Philip's War, which erupted in the 1670s after Plymouth colonists hanged three Wampanoag for murder, resulted in the deaths of about 600 colonists and thousands of Native Americans.
- Charges of witchcraft rocked New England society in 1692. Nearly 200 women and men in Salem, Massachusetts, were brought to trial as witches, and 20 of the accused were put to death.

ECONOMIC DEVELOPMENT

- Fishing and whaling led to the growth of a thriving shipbuilding industry that took advantage of New England's plentiful forests. The industries kept sawmills, rope makers, and iron foundries busy and made New England a center of colonial trade.
- In the triangular trade, traders from Europe brought goods to West Africa to exchange for captured and enslaved Africans. The African slaves were sold or traded for rum and other goods in the Americas, and ships loaded with products from the Americas returned to Europe.
- Enslaved Africans made up only about 2 to 3 percent of New England's population, but their work was essential in fueling the region's economy.

AMERICAN VOICES
Squanto

Squanto was one of the Pawtuxet who helped the Pilgrims survive in North America. According to some sources, Squanto was kidnapped from his Massachusetts home in 1605 and taken to England, where he learned English. When he eventually returned home, he discovered that most of his people had been wiped out by disease. After being introduced to the Pilgrims, Squanto acted as an interpreter for the colony and helped them plant local crops.

HISTORICAL THINKING

1. **ANALYZE CAUSE AND EFFECT** What complex historical causes led to the migration of the Puritans and Pilgrims to New England?
2. **MAKE GENERALIZATIONS** What role did religion play in the rise of democratic ideas in the New England settlements?
3. **FORM AND SUPPORT OPINIONS** How might the conflict between the New England colonists and Native Americans have been avoided? Support your opinion with evidence from the text.

HI 2 Students recognize the complexity of historical causes and effects, including the limitations on determining cause and effect; HI 4 Students understand the meaning, implication, and impact of historical events and recognize that events could have taken other directions.

REVIEW LESSON 1.5

MIDDLE COLONIES

This relief from the U.S. Capitol Rotunda shows William Penn (center), founder of the colony of Pennsylvania, meeting with leaders of the Lenni Lenape in 1682 in what is now Philadelphia.

Situated in the mid-Atlantic region of North America, the Middle Colonies included New York, New Jersey, Pennsylvania, and Delaware. Settlers from such European countries as England, France, the Netherlands, Germany, Sweden, and Portugal immigrated to the Middle Colonies for various reasons. Some were fleeing religious wars in their home countries. Others were looking for good farmland or pursuing trade opportunities.

NEW NETHERLAND TO NEW YORK Dutch settlers formed peaceful relations with their Native American neighbors in the early years after New Netherland's founding. By 1664, however, the colonists and Native Americans were embroiled in wars over land use. King Charles II of England gave his brother James, the Duke of York, permission to force the Dutch out. The overwhelming English presence in the area made doing so easy and ensured the English complete control of eastern North America. The duke renamed the colony New York, and the English made peace with Native Americans living there. After assuming control of New York, the duke granted land between the Delaware and Hudson rivers to two English noblemen, Lord Berkeley and Sir George Carteret, who named the area New Jersey.

PENN'S WOODS In 1681, King Charles II granted a charter, a written contract giving permission to establish a colony, to **William Penn**, an English Quaker who wanted to create a safe home for his fellow Quakers. The Quakers were members of the Religious Society of Friends, a Christian movement devoted to peace and equality. Because others perceived Quakers as anti-authority and even dangerous, thousands of Quakers were persecuted in England and in the American colonies. Penn named his colony Sylvania, which means "woods." King Charles II renamed it Pennsylvania.

PROSPEROUS AND PRODUCTIVE The Middle Colonies' rich farmland and climate made the region ideal for growing such grains as wheat, corn, rye, and barley. Wheat was the most popular grain in colonial America because it made a fine flour that produced soft bread. Since grinding grain by hand was slow, many colonists built gristmills near rivers to harness the power of water for grinding. As the settlers grew wealthier, they sold more of their harvest and raised livestock for sale and export.

11.1.1 Describe the Enlightenment and the rise of democratic ideas as the context in which the nation was founded; 11.3 Students analyze the role religion played in the founding of America, its lasting moral, social, and political impacts, and issues regarding religious liberty; HI 1 Students show the connections, causal and otherwise, between particular historical events and larger social, economic, and political trends and developments.

KEY TAKEAWAYS

NEW YORK AND NEW JERSEY

- Dutch trader Cornelius Jacobsen May, working on behalf of the Dutch West India Company, founded New Netherland in 1624 to provide a base for trade in the Hudson River region.
- When the English acquired New Netherland and renamed it New York, the colony was already home to a diverse group of settlers: Dutch, Swedes, Finns, Norwegians, and French, as well as free and enslaved Africans who made up about 20 percent of the population.
- Lord Berkeley eventually sold his stake in New Jersey, leading to the colony being divided into East Jersey and West Jersey. Dissatisfaction with this arrangement caused the English government to reunite East and West Jersey into one royal colony in 1702.

PENNSYLVANIA AND DELAWARE

- William Penn set out to create a colony based on the Quaker doctrine that all people are equal in the eyes of God.
- Penn made Pennsylvania into an extremely diverse society by encouraging religious minorities to settle there, keeping peace with Native Americans, and selling land to a variety of buyers from other colonies, Europe, and the West Indies.
- European settlers who lived in the "Lower Counties," located in southern Pennsylvania, did not like living under Penn's government. In 1704, Penn allowed these counties to form their own assembly, and they later established the colony of Delaware.

ALGONQUIANS AND IROQUOIS

- Native Americans in the Middle Colonies were organized into two major language groups: the Algonquian, who were primarily hunter-gatherers living along the Atlantic coast, and the Iroquois, who were farmers in what is now central New York.
- Competition in the fur trade intensified hostilities between the Algonquian tribes, the Iroquois tribes, and European traders.
- In the 1600s, the Mohawk, Onondaga, Oneida, Cayuga, and Seneca banded together as the Iroquois Confederacy, which later became the Six Nations when the Tuscarora joined the alliance.

ECONOMIC AND POLITICAL DEVELOPMENT

- German immigrants brought advanced farming techniques from Europe, contributing to the region's high agricultural production.
- The region's plentiful rivers provided the water power to operate gristmills, where millers ground grain into flour for making bread. For this reason, the Middle Colonies became known as the "breadbasket."
- The Middle Colonies' ethnic diversity and a 1712 slave revolt increased racial tensions and led to restrictive laws in New York City.
- Colonial newspaper publisher **John Peter Zenger** was tried for libel in 1735 for criticizing the colonial governor of New York. However, he was found not guilty on the grounds that his allegations were true, thus paving the way for freedom of the press.

AMERICAN PLACES
Philadelphia Row Houses

Row houses are just what they sound like—individual houses attached in a row along a street. The first row houses in the United States were built in Philadelphia and date to around 1690. At that time, such buildings were built near ports and housed the growing number of people working in jobs on the busy docks where goods were traded. The row houses' unique design made them easier and less expensive to build than separate houses. An urban renewal program in the 1950s led to the restoration of many of the buildings in Philadelphia.

HISTORICAL THINKING

1. **SUMMARIZE** How did New Netherland become New York?
2. **EVALUATE** What role did Penn's religious beliefs play in the founding of Pennsylvania and in the rise of democratic ideas in the colonies?
3. **MAKE GENERALIZATIONS** What factors drove economic development in the Middle Colonies?

REVIEW LESSON 1.6

SOUTHERN COLONIES

Only 9 of the 27 slave houses that once stood at Boone Hall Plantation near Charleston, South Carolina, still remain. The houses together make up what was called a "slave street."

As you have read, the Virginia colony of Jamestown, founded in 1607, was the first successful English colony in North America. Over time, Europeans established settlements in many parts of the South, resulting in five Southern Colonies: Maryland, Virginia, North Carolina, South Carolina, and Georgia.

CHESAPEAKE BAY Virginia continued to grow in the 1600s—slowly at first, hampered in large part by the heavy death toll caused by malaria and other diseases that thrived in the swampy conditions of the **Chesapeake Bay** region. But the introduction of tobacco as a cash crop spurred immigration and increased the demand for land. Farmers tried to produce enough tobacco to supply the growing market for the crop in the colonies and overseas.

In 1632, King Charles I of England authorized carving the new colony of Maryland out of the northern part of Virginia. Most of the settlers there were either owners of small parcels of land or renters. Maryland's location on the Chesapeake Bay provided easy access to trade, and the region's fertile soil was ideal for growing tobacco. Wealthy plantation owners and merchants built docks on such tributaries of Chesapeake Bay as the Potomac and Anacostia rivers. From these docks, they could easily load ships with tobacco to export and receive ships from around the world loaded with goods.

SETTLING THE SOUTHERN COLONIES

The colonies of North Carolina and South Carolina began as the single colony of Carolina. But by 1691, Carolina had split into two colonies: North Carolina, settled by small planters from Virginia, and South Carolina, where many settlers came from Barbados in the West Indies. By 1729, both Carolinas had become royal colonies, each with a governor and council appointed by the king. Settlers were attracted by the fertile soil and mild climate, well suited to growing cash crops. Georgia differed from most of the other American colonies because it was founded by reformers who wanted to start a colony that gave a new start to the very poor, not as a way to make money or escape religious oppression.

PLANTATIONS AND SLAVERY The Chesapeake Bay region and South Carolina became home to many plantations, or large farms, devoted to growing such cash crops as tobacco, rice, and indigo. Running a plantation required a lot of labor. Planters originally hired white indentured servants, who worked for a specified period of time in exchange for payment of their travel expenses to a colony. But in 1698, England gave all English merchants permission to participate in the African slave trade. Many planters turned to chattel slavery—a form of permanent bondage in which people are classified as property and have virtually no human rights.

KEY TAKEAWAYS

VIRGINIA AND MARYLAND

- In 1619, the Virginia Company, which funded the founding of Virginia, tried to build the colony's labor force by offering land to English immigrants who paid their own travel expenses. The company paid transportation costs for indentured servants.
- King Charles I awarded the charter for Maryland to English politician George Calvert, a Catholic. Calvert's son Cecil took over the colony after his father's untimely death, establishing it as a safe haven for Roman Catholics.
- Tobacco became the main cash crop in Virginia after English settler John Rolfe introduced a variety that gained wide popularity in England because it was less bitter than the previous variety.

THE CAROLINAS

- King Charles II chartered Carolina to a group of property owners who created a plan for a feudal society with lords and nobles, which the ordinary settlers in the colony refused to accept.
- Carolina's proprietors found it difficult to govern the northern part of the colony because the area was a haven for pirates and its other settlers were poor formerly indentured servants. The proprietors created North Carolina by appointing a separate governor in 1691.
- South Carolina's settlers established large plantations where they grew tobacco, rice, cotton, sugarcane, and other crops.

GEORGIA: A GRAND EXPERIMENT FAILS

- British general **James Oglethorpe** and Irish viscount John Percival were the reformers behind the plan to found Georgia. While King George II did not share their interest in helping the poor, he understood the value of a military buffer between Spanish Florida and South Carolina, so in 1732 he granted a charter placing control of the colony in the hands of a group of trustees that included Oglethorpe.
- As governor of Georgia, Oglethorpe required all colonists to follow three rules: no slaves, no liquor, and limited land ownership.
- The other trustees recognized that immigration to Georgia would not thrive under Oglethorpe's strict rules, so the laws were changed and Great Britain resumed control of the colony in 1752.

PLANTATIONS AND CHATTEL SLAVERY

- Southern plantations developed in order to support the large-scale production of such cash crops as tobacco, rice, and indigo, which all required large amounts of land and much labor to be profitable.
- Dependence on slave labor increased in the Southern Colonies over time. As a result, Africans living in North America—almost all of whom were enslaved—accounted for more than 40 percent of Virginia's population and more than half of South Carolina's population by 1750.
- Scots-Irish immigrants settled the backcountry along the Appalachian Mountains and developed a culture based on small farms that did not rely on slave labor.

AMERICAN PLACES
The Chesapeake Bay

The Chesapeake Bay is the largest estuary in North America. An estuary is a body of water that forms where one or more rivers flow into the sea. In an estuary, freshwater mixes with salt water. The Chesapeake Bay extends through Virginia, Delaware, and Maryland. It forms a rich ecosystem with more than 150 rivers and streams flowing into it. The area around the bay provided plenty of fertile soil to colonists who established farms and plantations there. Today, the bay is best known for its seafood.

HISTORICAL THINKING

1. **SUMMARIZE** How was Maryland founded?
2. **MAKE INFERENCES** How did Georgia reflect the democratic idea that all are equal before the law?
3. **DRAW CONCLUSIONS** Why did plantation owners rely on enslaved labor during colonial times, and how did the norms and values of the time shape that dependency?

8.1 Students understand the major events preceding the founding of the nation and relate their significance to the development of American constitutional democracy; HI 3 Students interpret past events and issues within the context in which an event unfolded rather than solely in terms of present-day norms and values.

REVIEW LESSON 1.7

EXPANSION OF SLAVERY

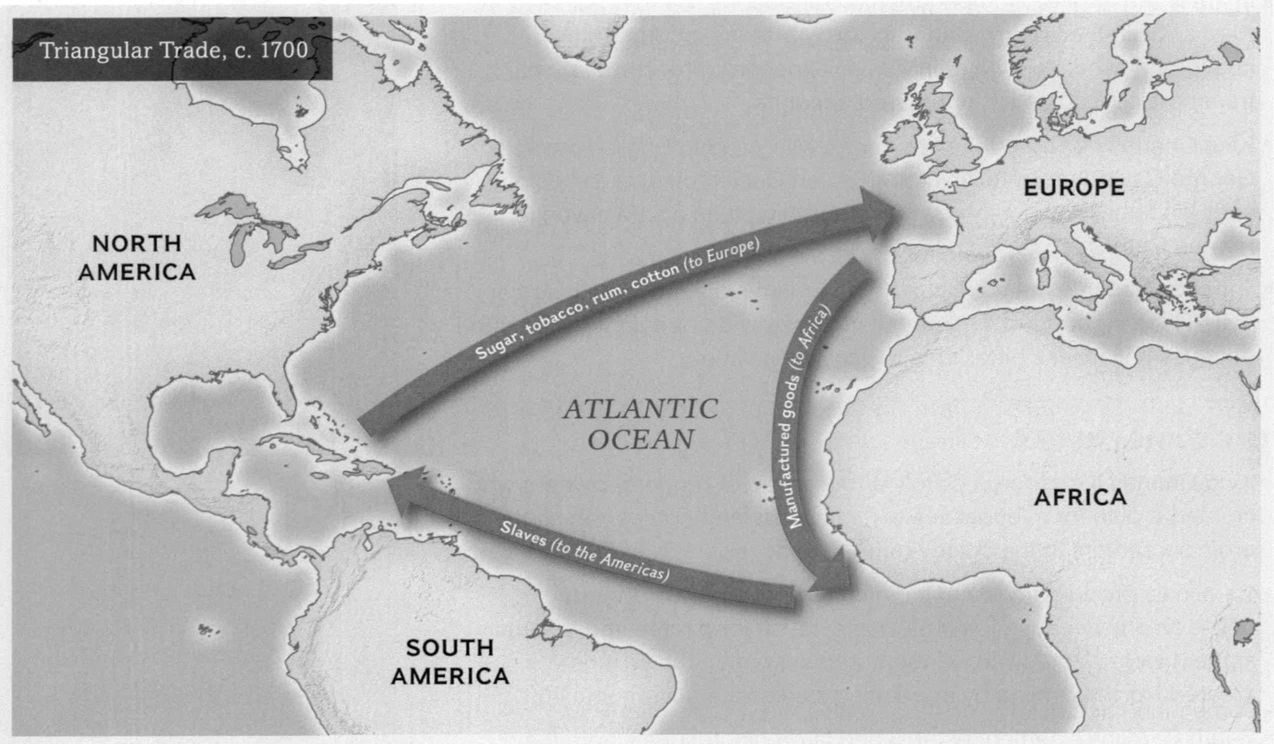

The economies of the colonies and most European countries depended on ships transporting trade goods and slaves between Europe, Africa, and North America.

Chattel slavery originated in the mid-1400s when the Portuguese started to trade with West Africans to obtain slaves to work on sugar plantations. Spain also turned to Africa as a source of captive labor. By the end of the 1500s, 75,000 enslaved Africans worked on Spanish plantations in the Caribbean. The North American slave trade expanded from there. The slave trade between Africa and the Americas started around 1502 and lasted until the 1860s. During that time, traders shipped between 7 and 10 million people to the Western Hemisphere.

ORIGINS OF SLAVERY The Spanish hacienda system, which granted colonists tracts of land to farm, and the encomienda system, which allowed them to enslave Native Americans, encouraged the growth of sugar plantations in the West Indies and set the stage for the expansion of slavery in North America. These plantations required a considerable workforce in order to grow and process enough sugarcane to make a profit. When the Spanish first replaced Native American laborers, they bought Africans who had been enslaved on Portuguese plantations. Soon, however, they began buying enslaved Africans directly from West Africa.

TRIANGULAR TRADE AND THE MIDDLE PASSAGE The enslaved Africans who came to the Americas were part of the triangular trade, a three-part trading network that connected Europe, Africa, and the Americas. On the first leg of the route, European traders traveled to West Africa, where they exchanged various goods for captured and enslaved Africans. On the second leg—the infamous **Middle Passage**—the traders transported the Africans to the Americas on ships where they were confined under inhumane conditions. On the third leg, ships loaded with American products returned to Europe to repeat the cycle. This triangular trade lasted until the slave trade was abolished in the 1800s.

THE USE OF CHATTEL SLAVERY In North America, the use of chattel slavery greatly expanded on the tobacco plantations of Maryland and Virginia and the tobacco and rice plantations of the Carolinas and Georgia. For instance, in 1660, only 900 Africans resided in the Chesapeake Bay area, some of whom had arrived as servants and lived free. By 1770, Africans made up from one-third to one-half of the population in the region, and most of the African population was enslaved.

8.1 Students understand the major events preceding the founding of the nation and relate their significance to the development of American constitutional democracy; HI 2 Students recognize the complexity of historical causes and effects, including the limitations on determining cause and effect.

KEY TAKEAWAYS

SLAVERY IN THE EARLY COLONIES

- In the mid-17th century, enslaved Africans accounted for only 2 to 3 percent of New England's population. The number of enslaved and free Africans rose to about 20 percent of the population in 1664 when the English acquired the land that became the Middle Colonies from New Netherland.
- Faced with a high demand for labor and a dwindling supply of indentured servants, planters in the South viewed the use of enslaved African labor as a good economic decision.
- About 10 to 15 percent of the captives on slave ships died of disease or despair during the 5,000-mile Middle Passage to the Americas.
- After 1698, when England opened the slave trade to any English merchant who wanted to participate, the supply of enslaved Africans in the English colonies soared and slave prices declined, enabling colonists to invest in even more enslaved labor.

VIRGINIA AND MARYLAND

- The shift from indentured labor to enslaved labor increased on Chesapeake tobacco plantations after the decrease in slave prices made owning slaves a more affordable alternative for planters.
- Some plantation owners mistreated their slaves, and the heavy workload took its toll on all the laborers, causing high death rates among enslaved people.
- In the Chesapeake Bay area, most field hands worked for 12 to 14 hours a day and had little free time to attend to family needs.

THE CAROLINAS AND GEORGIA

- Unfamiliar with rice cultivation, planters in the Carolinas depended on enslaved Africans from rice-growing regions in West Africa to tend the rice fields and ensure successful yields.
- Supervisors called overseers sometimes used whips and other harsh instruments and measures to force enslaved people to work harder or more productively.
- Some owners recruited enslaved people to work as drivers, who pushed the enslaved people to increase the pace.

THE REALITIES OF SLAVERY

- Men and women who worked in a planter's household cooked and performed other household chores. Women also cared for their owners' children, and some served as nurses or weavers. Some men became artisans who crafted furniture, tools, or other items.
- Enslaved people married, had children, and gained a network of friends and relatives, but they knew that owners could destroy these relationships by selling them or their loved ones away.
- Many enslaved people actively rebelled against their servitude by staging slowdowns, faking illnesses, secretly destroying crops and tools, or running away. Some even became violent, killing slave owners or setting fire to fields and homes.

Gentleman with Attendant

CURATING HISTORY

New Britain Museum of American Art

In this portrait, which hangs in the museum in Connecticut, American painter Ralph Earl included an African-American free servant or enslaved person with his New England landowner. Such paintings were rare in the 1780s, the time in which it was finished. In the North, enslaved people tended to work in the homes of their owners. In the South, enslaved people worked in the fields. Though New England's economy did not depend on slavery, some merchants there earned huge fortunes from the slave trade.

HISTORICAL THINKING

1. **MAKE INFERENCES** How did slavery take root in the Americas, and what role might it have played in the development of American constitutional democracy?
2. **IDENTIFY MAIN IDEAS AND DETAILS** Why did southern planters adopt chattel slavery?
3. **ANALYZE CAUSE AND EFFECT** What factors might limit our understanding of the impact slavery had on enslaved people in the South?

REVIEW CHAPTER 1

EXPLORATION AND SETTLEMENT

ASSESSMENT

MAIN IDEAS

Choose the best answer for each question from the choices available.

1. What was the significance of the Magna Carta? HSS 8.2.1
   - A It formally protected the rights of English citizens.
   - B It required monarchs to abide by rules and paved the way for a government run by Parliament.
   - C It formally protected the rights of Parliament.
   - D It launched reforms to strengthen the monarchy.

2. What action spurred Spain, France, the Netherlands, and England to begin their own sea explorations? HSS 7.11.2
   - A Portugal financed Christopher Columbus's voyages.
   - B The Portuguese set up the triangular trade.
   - C The Portuguese established trade relations with the African kingdom of Ghana.
   - D Pope Nicholas V gave Portugal sole rights to trading in lands it discovered.

3. What shows the influence that environment had on the culture of Native Americans in the Pacific Northwest? HSS HI 1
   - A their celebration of salmon
   - B their dependence on farming
   - C their hunting of bison
   - D their reliance on trade

4. How did the Hohokam and ancient Pueblo survive in their environment? HSS HI 2
   - A by building canals and dams to control water supplies
   - B by hunting bison
   - C by gathering acorns, plants, and berries
   - D by collecting mussels, oysters, and other shellfish

5. What happened as a result of Europeans' attempts to find a water route to Asia? HSS 7.11.3
   - A Christopher Columbus claimed land in Asia for Spain.
   - B John Cabot claimed land for England in present-day Canada.
   - C Ferdinand Magellan and Sebastian del Cano were able to circumnavigate the globe.
   - D Portugal introduced chattel slavery to West Africa.

6. What was the main purpose of the English Bill of Rights of 1689? HSS 8.2.1
   - A to require monarchs to abide by rules
   - B to bring about changes in architecture, literature, philosophy, and religion in Europe
   - C to encourage people to question religious and political dictates
   - D to protect the rights of English citizens and Parliament

7. Why did Thomas Hooker leave Massachusetts to found his own colony? HSS 8.1
   - A He violated a term in the Mayflower Compact.
   - B The Puritans banished him for believing ministers were unnecessary.
   - C He disagreed with the Puritans' system of government, which gave all power to the church.
   - D He was banished for attacking laws that gave taxes to churches.

8. What was a characteristic of the New England colonial economy? HSS 7.11.3
   - A It was dependent on growing cash crops.
   - B It participated in the triangular trade.
   - C It relied heavily on enslaved labor.
   - D It lacked diversity.

9. Which colonial founder contributed to the rise of democratic ideas by the way he recruited colonists and bought and sold land? HSS 11.1.1
   - A Lord Berkeley
   - B William Penn
   - C James Oglethorpe
   - D Sir George Carteret

10. What was a result of the John Peter Zenger trial? HSS 11.1.1

A It put limits on the slave trade.
B It strengthened libel laws.
C It limited the authority of colonial governors.
D It paved the way for freedom of the press.

11. Which area of the South did not rely on slave labor? HSS 7.11

A the Chesapeake Bay region
B the backcountry
C South Carolina
D Maryland

12. Why did the Georgia colony's grand experiment fail? HSS 8.1

A The trustees believed that Oglethorpe's strict rules would stall immigration to the colony.
B Settlers refused to accept a feudal society.
C The trustees were unable to provide a safe haven for Roman Catholics.
D Parts of the colony were poor, difficult to govern, and a haven for pirates.

13. How did England's 1698 decision to open the slave trade to all English merchants affect plantation labor in the South? HSS 7.11

A It decreased the pool of indentured servants.
B It increased the pool of indentured servants.
C It caused slave prices to drop, enabling colonists to buy more slaves.
D It decreased the supply of slaves.

14. What was the Middle Passage? HSS 7.11

A the voyage of ships carrying slaves from Africa to the Americas
B the voyage of ships carrying trade goods from Europe to Africa
C the voyage of ships carrying trade goods from the Americas to Europe
D the name given to the trading network that connected Europe, Africa, and Asia

15. How many years did the Atlantic slave trade last? HSS 7.11

A about 40 years
B about 100 years
C about 250 years
D about 400 years

ANALYZE SOURCES

The Magna Carta, or "Great Charter," was signed in 1215 and served as a peace treaty between King John of England and his barons, who had rebelled against the heavy taxes the king levied on them. Read the passage and answer the questions that follow.

> No free man shall be seized or imprisoned, or stripped of his rights or possessions, or outlawed or exiled, or deprived of his standing in any other way, nor will we [the king's government] proceed with force against him, or send others to do so, except by the lawful judgment of his equals or by the law of the land.

16. According to the excerpt, what should the king's government not be able to do? HSS 8.2.1

17. Based on the excerpt, how was the Magna Carta a step toward democracy? HSS 8.2.1

WRITE ABOUT HISTORY

18. **EXPLANATORY** European settlers came to the Atlantic colonies seeking economic opportunity and freedom. Over time, they developed distinct economies in the three regions they settled. Think about the economies in the three regions and answer the following question: How and why did the economies of the New England Colonies, Middle Colonies, and Southern Colonies differ? HSS 7.11

TIPS

- Review what you have learned about the economies of the three colonial regions.
- Introduce the topic with a clear main idea statement.
- Develop the topic with relevant facts and concrete details.
- Provide a concluding statement that follows from the information you have presented.

REVIEW CHAPTER 2

REVOLUTION AND A NEW REPUBLIC

1765–1814

HISTORICAL THINKING How did declaring independence and forming a new government help shape the American identity?

AMERICAN STORIES ONLINE **Daily Life During the Revolution**

AMERICAN STORIES ONLINE **The Northwest Ordinances**

AMERICAN GALLERY ONLINE **Valley Forge**

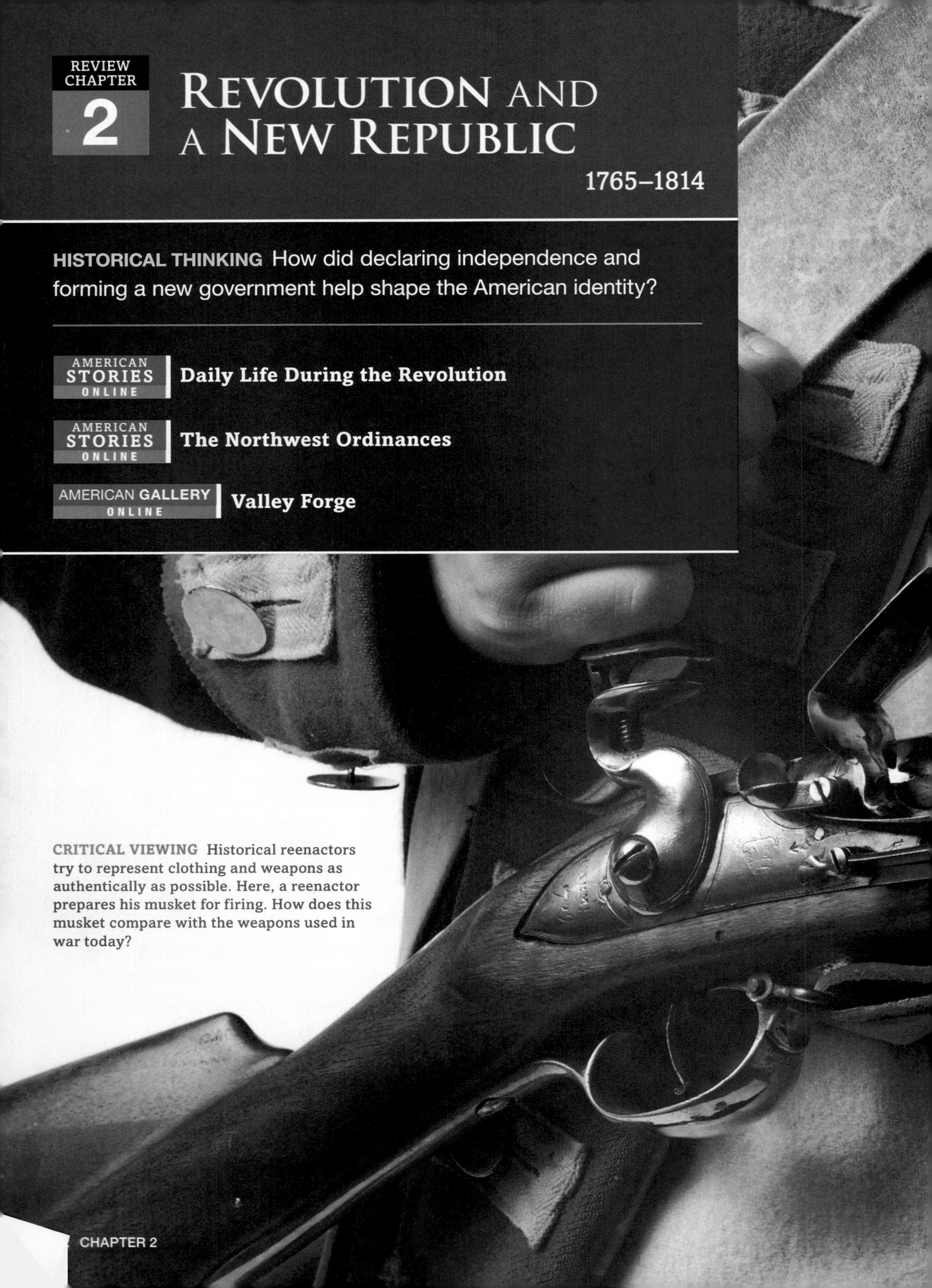

CRITICAL VIEWING Historical reenactors try to represent clothing and weapons as authentically as possible. Here, a reenactor prepares his musket for firing. How does this musket compare with the weapons used in war today?

"It is a common observation here that **our cause is the cause of all mankind.**"
—Benjamin Franklin

REVIEW LESSON 2.1

DECLARING INDEPENDENCE

This painting by John Trumbull, titled *Declaration of Independence*, depicts the presentation of the document to the Continental Congress in 1776.

During the first half of the 1700s, the colonists grew happily accustomed to living in relative isolation from British authority and largely governing themselves. The American colonies modeled their governments after Britain's Parliament by forming elected assemblies similar to the House of Commons. Unlike the British legislators, however, elected officials in the assemblies lived in the area they represented. The colonists believed that representatives who lived among the people who elected them would better understand local interests and needs. The colonists had no representatives in Parliament and resented what they felt was unfair treatment by Britain.

GROWING RESENTMENT The colonists' resentment grew after they fought alongside the British in the **French and Indian War**. After Britain won the war against the French in 1763, the colonists assumed they could expand their settlements westward. But the British government issued a proclamation that colonists could not settle west of the Appalachian Mountains. To make matters worse, King George III of Great Britain, insisting that the role of a colony was to support the mother country, levied a series of taxes against the colonists to help pay for the war.

PROTESTS AND CONFLICT Crying "No taxation without representation," the colonists protested against the British legislation. Then, in 1775, feelings on both sides reached the boiling point. After British troops learned that the colonists had gathered weapons in Concord, Massachusetts, the troops marched to the town. Colonial militiamen rushed to face down the British soldiers in nearby Lexington. Shots rang out at what would later be called the first battles of the American Revolution.

DEMOCRATIC IDEAS In 1776, colonial delegates debated the cause of independence from Britain. Many delegates wanted to ground the American Revolution and their new nation in the democratic political tradition. Thomas Jefferson, who championed the democratizing Enlightenment movement that spread from Britain to the colonies in the 1700s, became the principal author of the Declaration of Independence. Inspired by the movement's philosophy of divinely bestowed natural rights, Jefferson called for "life, liberty, and the pursuit of happiness" in the Declaration. These unalienable rights, he insisted, could not be taken away. Colonists agreed and fought the Revolution to secure them.

11.1 Students analyze the significant events in the founding of the nation and its attempts to realize the philosophy of government described in the Declaration of Independence; 11.1.1 Describe the Enlightenment and the rise of democratic ideas as the context in which the nation was founded; 11.1.2 Analyze the ideological origins of the American Revolution, the Founding Fathers' philosophy of divinely bestowed unalienable natural rights, the debates on the drafting and ratification of the Constitution, and the addition of the Bill of Rights.

KEY TAKEAWAYS

BRITISH AUTHORITY

- At the conclusion of the French and Indian War (1754–1763), Britain angered the colonists by issuing the Proclamation of 1763, which prevented them from settling west of a line drawn along the crest of the Appalachian Mountains from Maine to Georgia.
- To force colonists to help pay for the war, King George III and the British Parliament passed legislation, including the Stamp Act in 1765, which placed a tax on the colonists' printed materials, and the Tea Act in 1773, which gave Britain the right to set the price of tea sold in the colonies.
- To quell rebellion in Boston and force the colonies into obedience, Britain passed what colonists called the Intolerable Acts in 1774, preventing Massachusetts from governing itself.

COLONIAL PROTESTS

- Following the passage of the Stamp Act, colonists calling themselves the Sons of Liberty organized boycotts of British goods.
- As tensions rose in the colonies, violence ensued in 1770 with the Boston Massacre, resulting in the death of five colonists at the hands of British soldiers.
- In response to the Tea Act, colonists staged the **Boston Tea Party** by boarding British ships and throwing more than 300 crates of tea overboard.

SEEDS OF WAR

- In 1774, delegates met at the First Continental Congress to discuss ways to have the Intolerable Acts repealed.
- Militia units across the colonies stepped up their training and stockpiled supplies, and specially trained militia members called minutemen were also assembled.
- The clashes between colonial militiamen and British soldiers at Lexington and Concord, Massachusetts, in 1775 resulted in 73 deaths on the British side and 49 on the American side and marked the beginning of the American Revolution.

BREAK WITH BRITAIN

- When the Continental Congress convened again in 1776, some delegates called for the colonies to separate completely from Britain.
- A committee—which included Thomas Jefferson, John Adams, and Benjamin Franklin, three of America's Founding Fathers—was formed to write an official document to declare independence.
- Democratic ideas in the colonies had been fueled by the **Great Awakening**, a religious revival of the early 1700s that encouraged Americans to challenge authority and consider themselves equal to those in power.
- Jefferson was further influenced by Enlightenment thinkers, such as John Locke, who asserted that humans were born free and equal and that a leader could rule only with the consent of the people.

AMERICAN VOICES
Thomas Jefferson

Thomas Jefferson was chosen to be the main author of the Declaration of Independence when he was only 33. In the Declaration, Jefferson described the democratic ideas upon which the nation would be founded and captured the voice and identity of a new America. In addition to drafting the Declaration, Jefferson served his country for more than 50 years as a historian, diplomat, public official, president, and the founder of the University of Virginia.

HISTORICAL THINKING

1. **SUMMARIZE** What roles did the Enlightenment and the Great Awakening play in the founding of the nation?
2. **DRAW CONCLUSIONS** What steps taken by the colonists suggest they were preparing for war with Britain?
3. **EVALUATE** What are the ideological origins of the American Revolution?

11.3.2 Analyze the great religious revivals and the leaders involved in them, including the First Great Awakening, the Second Great Awakening, the Civil War revivals, the Social Gospel Movement, the rise of Christian liberal theology in the nineteenth century, the impact of the Second Vatican Council, and the rise of Christian fundamentalism in current times.

REVIEW LESSON 2.2

THE AMERICAN REVOLUTION

Artist William T. Trego painted this scene, called *The March to Valley Forge, December 16, 1777,* of a young soldier (center right) saluting George Washington (center left).

When the opening shots of the American Revolution rang out in April 1775, neither side imagined the long road ahead. Fighting continued until 1781, when the British surrendered at Yorktown, Virginia. The war would not officially end until 1783, when the United States and Great Britain signed the Treaty of Paris. The Enlightenment and the rise of democratic ideas shaped the spirit of the American Revolution. Inspiring the rebels were Enlightenment ideas of political freedom and the Founding Fathers' philosophy of divinely bestowed unalienable natural rights, including liberty, equality, and individual pursuit of happiness.

THE EARLY YEARS The Americans, fighting as the **Continental Army**, suffered many defeats at the beginning of the war. Colonial victories at Fort Ticonderoga in May 1775 and at the Battle of Trenton in December 1776 were overshadowed by defeats at Bunker Hill in 1775 and Brooklyn Heights, Fort Washington, and Quebec in 1776. However, the Continental Army began to turn the tide in the fall of 1777 when it defeated the British at Saratoga. The victory boosted American morale and earned the Americans an alliance with France.

THE MIDDLE YEARS In the wake of the victory at Saratoga, France's ally Spain also agreed to help the Americans. Combat moved to the Southern Colonies, where guerrilla fighters, such as those led by Francis Marion, the "Swamp Fox," harassed the British and kept the Americans competitive. Meanwhile, the Continental Army clashed with the British at Monmouth Court House in Pennsylvania, but the fighting ended with no clear winner. The Americans fared better on the western frontier, where they achieved several victories.

PATH TO VICTORY The colonists' fortunes improved after **Nathanael Greene** took over as commander of the Continental Army's southern troops. Greene's troops defeated the British at the Battle of Kings Mountain, helping to turn the war in the Americans' favor. The British hope of victory in the South soon faded. The final blow came at Yorktown, Virginia, where American and French troops surrounded British general **Lord Cornwallis** and his army, who were camped on a peninsula overlooking the York River. Facing certain defeat, the British surrendered.

11.1.1 Describe the Enlightenment and the rise of democratic ideas as the context in which the nation was founded; 11.1.2 Analyze the ideological origins of the American Revolution, the Founding Fathers' philosophy of divinely bestowed unalienable natural rights, the debates on the drafting and ratification of the Constitution, and the addition of the Bill of Rights; HI 4 Students understand the meaning, implication, and impact of historical events and recognize that events could have taken other directions.

KEY TAKEAWAYS

AMERICANS AT WAR

- The British had an experienced, professional army that was well trained and well supplied, while the American forces were disorganized, ill prepared, undisciplined, and cobbled together from local militias.
- The Americans had one big advantage: they were fighting on their own soil to protect their homes and way of life.
- The early British strategy was to end the war quickly by dividing New England from the rest of the colonies. General Washington led the Continental Army in a defensive war, concentrating on trying to wear down the British in a prolonged conflict.
- The Americans won the Battle of Saratoga by surrounding British troops and forcing a surrender. The Americans then made camp at **Valley Forge**, where they struggled through a bitter winter.

THE WAR EXPANDS

- France and Spain played pivotal roles in the war by drawing Britain's military and naval attentions in different directions and supplying the Americans with money for the war.
- Women contributed to the war effort by filling jobs at home traditionally performed by men and working on the front lines as nurses and spies. Some even disguised themselves as men to participate in battle.
- The two sides engaged in naval warfare as well, with the small Continental Navy facing tough odds against the British Royal Navy. However, John Paul Jones's defeat of the British ship *Serapis* proved a critical victory for the Americans.

VICTORY FOR THE AMERICANS

- In addition to the Battle of Kings Mountain, the Americans were victorious at nearby Cowpens in South Carolina and at Guilford Court House in North Carolina.
- Attempting to fight in both the North and the South spread the British forces thin. As a result, the British relied on Loyalists to help fight many battles in the South.
- Cornwallis's defeat and surrender at Yorktown, Virginia, marked the last major battle in the American Revolution.

LEGACY OF THE REVOLUTION

- In 1782, the British Parliament voted to end the war, and in 1783, the United States and Great Britain signed the Treaty of Paris, which officially recognized U.S. independence and set the boundaries for the new nation.
- Now truly independent, Americans set about developing a new national identity based on liberty and equality.
- The United States also began the difficult task of establishing a constitutional republic that stressed civic republicanism and supported the classical liberal principles of private property and individual and religious freedoms embodied in the Enlightenment.

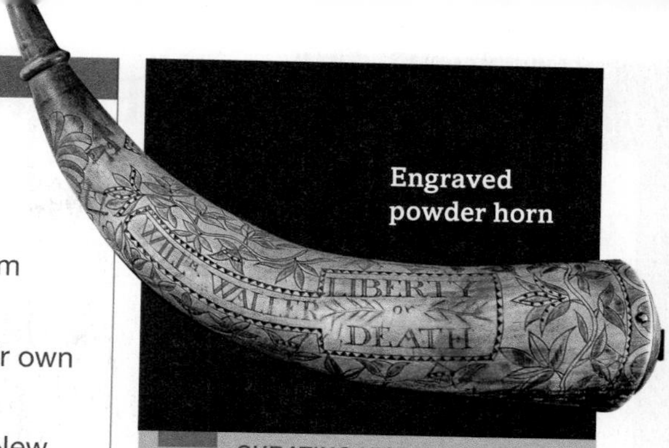

Engraved powder horn

CURATING HISTORY

Museum of the American Revolution

Rifleman William Waller from Virginia used this ornate powder horn as he fought British and Hessian soldiers during a battle at Fort Washington, New York, on November 16, 1776. Powder horns were vital pieces of equipment for soldiers. Riflemen carried a cow, ox, or buffalo horn to store their gunpowder and protect it from moisture. A few popular slogans from the time have been scrimshawed, or carved, into this horn, including "Liberty or Death" and "Kill or be Kill[e]d." The horn is part of a collection at the museum in Philadelphia.

HISTORICAL THINKING

1. **COMPARE AND CONTRAST** How did the American and British armies compare in terms of advantages and disadvantages?
2. **DRAW CONCLUSIONS** How might the outcome of the American Revolution have been different if the Americans hadn't won the Battle of Saratoga?
3. **ANALYZE CAUSE AND EFFECT** What factors helped the Americans win the war?
4. **ANALYZE VISUALS** What mood does the artist convey in the painting?

REVIEW LESSON 2.3

The Articles of Confederation

The Continental Congress was at a disadvantage in the early years of the war because it lacked the authority to provide funding for arms, supplies, and pay for soldiers. Thus, even as the war raged on, Congress moved to create a central government by drafting and adopting the **Articles of Confederation**. The Articles gave Congress the ability to make decisions about the military and the authority to call on the states to help fund the war. The document also outlined a national plan of self-governing states. For eight years, the Articles of Confederation served as the first constitution of the United States.

A protester in Springfield, Massachusetts, attacks an official during Shays's Rebellion in an attempt to disrupt court proceedings on debt repayment.

NATIONAL AND STATE GOVERNMENTS While it helped create greater unity among states, the Articles of Confederation established a weak central government that had little power of its own and no president or court system. Power rested primarily with the states, including the ability to levy taxes. This meant the federal government had to ask the states for funds. Meanwhile, many states decided to organize their governments with a governor and a two-house legislature elected by the people. Organizing a legislature into two parts ensured that lawmakers shared power and further limited each governor's authority. Some states, such as Pennsylvania, opted for no governor at all.

ORDINANCES OF 1785 AND 1787 The Treaty of Paris in 1783 granted the United States most of the territory from the Atlantic Ocean to the Mississippi River. This land extended north to the St. Lawrence River and the Great Lakes and south to the border with the Spanish colony of Florida. Operating under the Articles of Confederation, Congress passed the **Land Ordinance of 1785** and the **Northwest Ordinance of 1787** to organize new settlements and establish a strong government presence in the West. Passage of these settlement laws was the most important accomplishment of the Confederation era.

ISSUES WITH THE ARTICLES The Articles of Confederation provided a much-needed governing structure during the American Revolution, but the document quickly proved inadequate for the requirements of the new nation. The Articles gave the federal government some key powers but not others. The government could not impose taxes or regulate trade, which left it unable to adequately manage the nation's growing financial issues.

11.1 Students analyze the significant events in the founding of the nation and its attempts to realize the philosophy of government described in the Declaration of Independence; 11.1.2 Analyze the ideological origins of the American Revolution, the Founding Fathers' philosophy of divinely bestowed unalienable natural rights, the debates on the drafting and ratification of the Constitution, and the addition of the Bill of Rights.

KEY TAKEAWAYS

THE ARTICLES OF CONFEDERATION

- The Continental Congress drafted and adopted the Articles of Confederation in 1777, but the 13 states took until March 1781 to finally ratify the Articles.
- The Articles provided key powers to the federal government but weakened its authority by limiting its ability to levy taxes and failing to appoint a leader.
- The 13 states mostly governed themselves as small republics, with the federal government serving as an administrator to help the states agree on various matters.

LAND ORDINANCE OF 1785

- The Land Ordinance of 1785 divided the nation's new western territory into a small number of self-governing districts, which helped establish an orderly system for transferring federally owned land into private holdings, townships, and states.
- The ordinance called for surveying and organizing districts into townships that could be further divided into lots, which the government sold at a minimum of $1 per acre, thereby allowing for an equitable distribution of land.
- The 1785 ordinance also stipulated that each township had to set aside land for a school.

NORTHWEST ORDINANCE OF 1787

- The Northwest Ordinance of 1787 renamed much of the country's newly acquired western land the "Northwest Territory."
- The ordinance provided for ownership of land by individuals and a process for creating 3 to 5 new states out of the Northwest Territory, with each state qualified to enter the Union when its population reached 60,000.
- The ordinance prohibited slavery in the Northwest Territory.

DEBT AND OTHER ISSUES

- During the Revolution, the federal government raised funds for the military by asking successful American merchants and European governments to lend money to the cause, so after the war, the federal government owed around $50 million to those who contributed.
- State governments imposed heavy taxes on their own citizens, but because they refused to contribute money for the national government to pay off its debt, the national debt went unpaid.
- At the same time, British merchants demanded that American farmers repay past credit with cash rather than crops and livestock, thus pushing some farmers into financial ruin.
- Opposition to taxation and the debt collection process led to rebellion in some states. The most prominent uprising was **Shays's Rebellion** in Massachusetts, which the state put down by force when Congress could not raise money to send troops.

AMERICAN PLACES
Cumberland Gap

Many Americans who settled in the Northwest Territory traveled through the Cumberland Gap. The Cumberland Gap is located where the states of Virginia, Kentucky, and Tennessee meet. At the time, it was the only reliable travel route through the Appalachian Mountains into Kentucky.

Historians estimate that nearly 300,000 people traveled through the gap between 1760 and 1850. After passing through the valley, the path forked. One trail was called the Wilderness Road and ended near Louisville, Kentucky. The other trail led south and west through Tennessee.

HISTORICAL THINKING

1. **SUMMARIZE** What were the provisions of the Articles of Confederation?
2. **ANALYZE CAUSE AND EFFECT** How did the Northwest Ordinance of 1787 contribute to orderly westward expansion?
3. **EVALUATE** What was the major weakness of the Articles of Confederation?

REVIEW LESSON 2.4

DEBATES ON GOVERNMENT

One of two large-scale scenes painted by Barry Faulkner in 1936, this mural hangs in the National Archives in Washington, D.C. It depicts the leaders of the Constitutional Convention.

By 1787, it was clear the Articles of Confederation were not working. The United States was expanding geographically and economically, and the Articles proved unable to address the complications that arose from such expansion. Political leaders such as Robert Morris of Pennsylvania and Alexander Hamilton of New York believed the country needed a stronger central government to deal with the growing challenges. The nation's leaders convened the **Constitutional Convention** in Philadelphia on May 25, 1787, to discuss reforming the Articles. In the end, the attendees—known as delegates—drafted a new constitution to form "a more perfect union."

PRINCIPLES OF GOVERNMENT The delegates at the Constitutional Convention agreed on the main principles of government. The Framers, as they were called, wanted to create a central government that was neither too strong, like the British monarchy, nor too weak, as the American government was under the Articles of Confederation. In addition, they wanted a government that promoted the principles of federalism, majority rule, separation of powers, checks and balances, and dual sovereignty, which refers to giving state governments certain powers that the national government cannot overrule.

MATTERS OF DEBATE Most delegates favored creating three branches of government—a legislative branch to make the laws, an executive branch to enforce the laws, and a judicial branch to interpret the laws. However, the delegates disagreed on how the legislative branch should work. Delegates Edmund Randolph and William Paterson proposed two different plans: the Virginia Plan, which favored larger states, and the New Jersey Plan, which favored smaller states. Fellow delegate Roger Sherman of Connecticut combined the best ideas from both plans to craft the **Great Compromise** (see opposite page), which resulted in the legislative structure we have today.

DEBATES OVER SLAVERY The institution of slavery was also a major topic of debate, especially in terms of how it affected state representation in Congress. Southern delegates wanted all enslaved people counted as members of a state's population. Doing so would increase the number of delegates representing southern states in the House of Representatives and increase the region's electoral votes. Northerners argued that enslaved people should not be counted because they were legally defined as property.

11.1 Students analyze the significant events in the founding of the nation and its attempts to realize the philosophy of government described in the Declaration of Independence.

KEY TAKEAWAYS

GOALS AND CHALLENGES OF THE CONSTITUTION

- In a republican form of government, citizens elect officials to represent them, and these officials must act and govern according to the law.
- Federalism is a political system in which national, state, and local governments share governing power.
- Majority rule requires that decisions are made with at least one more than one-half of all votes, even when more than two choices exist.
- Separation of powers refers to the principle that each branch of government should have equal but unique authority.
- Checks and balances refers to the idea that each political branch acts as an overseer, monitoring the power of the other two branches.

LARGE STATES VERSUS SMALL STATES

- **The Virginia Plan** called for two houses, an upper house and a lower house, with the number of representatives in each house being proportionate to a state's population.
- **The New Jersey Plan** called for a single house, with each state having an equal number of representatives, regardless of population.
- The Great Compromise called for a House of Representatives, with the number of representatives from each state being proportionate to the state's population, and a Senate, with each state having an equal number of representatives, regardless of population.

POWER OF THE EXECUTIVE BRANCH

- The power of the executive branch concerned people living in a world dominated by kings and princes, so delegates wanted to ensure that the government remained a republic and did not become a monarchy.
- The delegates debated whether to elect the president through direct vote or through the legislature. As a compromise, they adopted the electoral college, with state electoral delegates casting votes for president based on the preferences of voters.
- Though voting rights would eventually expand over time, voting in the new nation was initially limited to white males who owned property.

ROLE OF SLAVERY

- As part of the Great Compromise, delegates agreed that five enslaved African Americans would count as three free persons. This allowed southern states to count some slaves as part of their population—thus giving these states greater political representation. Northern states were satisfied that the South would not be able to count all of its slaves. This agreement was inserted in Article 1 of the Constitution as the **three-fifths clause**.
- The three-fifths clause increased the power of white voters in the South at the expense of enslaved African Americans.
- The delegates included a clause in Article 1 stating that Congress could not ban the importation of slaves for 20 years.

AMERICAN PLACES
Maryland State House

The Maryland State House in Annapolis is the only state capitol building that has also served as the nation's capital. Between November 1783 and August 1784, the Continental Congress met at the Maryland State House. In its Senate Chamber, the Congress accepted Washington's resignation as commander in chief of the Continental Army and ratified the Treaty of Paris, signaling the end of the American Revolution.

HISTORICAL THINKING

1. **IDENTIFY MAIN IDEAS AND DETAILS** What were the main principles of government that guided delegates when drafting the Constitution?
2. **COMPARE AND CONTRAST** How did the large states and small states differ in their views concerning the legislative branch?
3. **DRAW CONCLUSIONS** What impact did the debate and compromise over slavery have on representative government?

11.1.2 Analyze the ideological origins of the American Revolution, the Founding Fathers' philosophy of divinely bestowed unalienable natural rights, the debates on the drafting and ratification of the Constitution, and the addition of the Bill of Rights.

REVIEW LESSON 2.5

The Constitution and Bill of Rights

Through a series of compromises, the delegates at the Constitutional Convention gradually settled the debate over how to divide state and federal power, how much authority to grant the three branches of the federal government, how to elect the president, and how to structure the legislative branch. These compromises resulted in the **U.S. Constitution**.

THREE BRANCHES OF GOVERNMENT

As you have read, the Constitutional Convention established three branches of government: the legislative, the executive, and the judicial. The delegates gave the legislative branch the power to create and pass laws. They assigned the executive branch the power to lead the nation and enforce the laws Congress passed. They gave the judicial branch the job of interpreting the laws. The delegates separated the powers of the three branches and provided checks and balances to keep any one branch from gaining more power than the others. For example, the delegates gave the president the power to veto laws passed by Congress, but they also gave Congress the power to override a presidential veto.

RATIFICATION After the Constitution was drafted, it had to be approved by the state representatives. Those who supported the Constitution as it was written were called **federalists** because they favored a strong federal government. Those who opposed any part of the Constitution were called **antifederalists**. Antifederalists believed the Constitution provided too few barriers against the potential abuse of power by the federal government, and they favored giving the states greater authority.

BILL OF RIGHTS Antifederalists demanded a series of amendments that guaranteed specific freedoms as a condition of ratifying the Constitution. Ten amendments were added to the Constitution, and they became known collectively as the **Bill of Rights**. The Bill of Rights protects such fundamental rights as freedom of religion, speech, press, peaceful assembly, and the right to a fair trial. A controversial amendment states that government and religion should be separate, but does not explicitly state how to achieve that separation. In addition, the Bill of Rights protects rights not specifically mentioned in the Constitution, granting to states and citizens powers not given to the federal government.

The statue *Guardianship* stands in front of the National Archives building in Washington, D.C., where the foundational documents of the United States are housed. The inscription at the base of the statue reads, "Eternal vigilance is the price of liberty."

KEY TAKEAWAYS

LEGISLATIVE BRANCH

- Under the Constitution, only the House of Representatives can initiate spending bills, bring impeachment charges against government officials, and elect the president if an electoral college tie occurs.
- The Senate has the sole power to confirm presidential appointments, try impeachment cases, and ratify treaties.
- Today, U.S. representatives are elected directly by voters every two years. Senators are elected directly by voters every six years.
- When a bill is introduced to Congress, it goes through committees for review. If approved, it is sent to the full House or Senate for debate and a vote. A bill must pass both houses before moving to its final step: consideration by the president.

EXECUTIVE BRANCH

- In addition to being the head of the government and commander in chief, the president is responsible for enforcing the laws passed by Congress. To carry out this duty, the president appoints a Cabinet and the heads of federal agencies.
- The Cabinet and federal agencies are responsible for the day-to-day activities required to carry out federal laws.
- The president makes the final decisions on bills created and passed by Congress—either signing the bill and making it a law or vetoing it.

JUDICIAL BRANCH

- The Constitution establishes the judicial branch but leaves its structure up to Congress, including the number of **Supreme Court** justices. Since 1869, the Court has consisted of eight associate justices and the Chief Justice of the United States.
- Congress also has the responsibility of creating lower courts, which consist of district courts to try federal cases and appellate courts to hear appeals of district court cases.
- The Constitution guarantees a speedy trial by an impartial jury.

LEGACY OF THE BILL OF RIGHTS

- The amendments contained in the Bill of Rights were intended to protect the freedoms of life, liberty, and the pursuit of happiness—all ideals that were put forth in the Declaration of Independence.
- The rights and freedoms that Americans enjoy are the result of a defined set of political principles that are not always basic to citizens of other countries.
- The rights guaranteed under the U.S. Constitution depend on an educated citizenry for their preservation and protection.
- The **Establishment clause** bans the government from declaring a national religion. The **Free Exercise clause** allows Americans to practice their religion in whatever way they choose. The two clauses often conflict each other.

AMERICAN PLACES

The Supreme Court

Surprisingly, the Supreme Court was not provided with its own building until 1935. Chief Justice William Howard Taft, who had also served as president, persuaded Congress to construct a permanent home for the Court. The architect built it in the style of an ancient Roman temple. The result was as Taft wished: "a building of dignity and importance suitable for use as the home of the Supreme Court of the United States."

HISTORICAL THINKING

1. **SUMMARIZE** What are the functions of each branch of government?
2. **ANALYZE CAUSE AND EFFECT** How does the Bill of Rights, specifically the Establishment and Free Exercise clauses, reflect the principles on which the country was founded?
3. **COMPARE AND CONTRAST** How might the conflict between the federalists and antifederalists provide a basis for understanding current constitutional issues?

11.1.2 Analyze the ideological origins of the American Revolution, the Founding Fathers' philosophy of divinely bestowed unalienable natural rights, the debates on the drafting and ratification of the Constitution, and the addition of the Bill of Rights; 11.3.5 Describe the principles of religious liberty found in the Establishment and Free Exercise clauses of the First Amendment, including the debate on the issue of separation of church and state; CST 1 Students compare the present with the past, evaluating the consequences of past events and decisions and determining the lessons that were learned.

REVIEW LESSON 2.6

THE EARLY PRESIDENCIES

When you are the first to do something, you set examples for others to follow. This concept was certainly true of **George Washington** as the first president of the United States. Everything Washington did set a standard for future presidents, since he was inventing the role of president as he went along. The succeeding presidents **John Adams** and **Thomas Jefferson** had the benefit of serving in Washington's administration, but they too faced new challenges in their own presidential administrations. Their leadership also set precedents for future presidents to follow.

Artist Gilbert Stuart painted 104 portraits of George Washington, including the one shown here, which he finished between 1796 and 1803.

WASHINGTON'S ESSENTIAL LEADERSHIP Washington set many precedents during his two terms as president, from establishing that he should be referred to as simply "Mr. President" and giving inaugural addresses to peacefully turning over the reins of government when his second term ended. In his 1796 farewell address, Washington warned against the formation of political parties, arguing that they could pit one group of people against another, thereby harming national unity. Nevertheless, two early political parties did form—the **Federalists** and the **Democratic-Republicans**—setting the country on the two-party path it follows to this day.

ADAMS VERSUS JEFFERSON The Federalists and Democratic-Republicans waged a bitter presidential campaign in 1796. John Adams ran as a Federalist. Thomas Jefferson represented the Democratic-Republicans. After attacks from both sides, Adams emerged victorious. Due to early electoral voting rules, which have long since changed, Jefferson became vice president. The Adams presidency was marked by a number of key events, including the XYZ Affair, the emergence of the issue of states' rights, and the Alien and Sedition Acts, which attempted to expel new immigrants and made speaking out against the government a crime.

JEFFERSON'S VISION FOR AMERICA Thomas Jefferson won the presidential election of 1800 after the House of Representatives broke a tie in electoral votes between Jefferson and Aaron Burr. As president, Jefferson refused to seat judges Adams had appointed as he left office, sparking the historic Supreme Court case *Marbury* v. *Madison*. Jefferson also lowered taxes, reduced the size of the federal judiciary, supported the power of the states, and championed less government spending. His crowning achievement was the **Louisiana Purchase**, which doubled the size of the nation. Jefferson easily won re-election in 1804.

8.3.4 Understand how the conflicts between Thomas Jefferson and Alexander Hamilton resulted in the emergence of two political parties (e.g., view of foreign policy, Alien and Sedition Acts, economic policy, National Bank, funding and assumption of the revolutionary debt); 11.1.3 Understand the history of the Constitution after 1787 with emphasis on federal versus state authority and growing democratization.

KEY TAKEAWAYS

SETTING UP THE GOVERNMENT

- As the Constitution directed, the electoral college determined who would be president. Washington won with all 69 electoral votes. John Adams, the runner-up in the popular vote, became the vice president.
- In his first term, Washington set powerful precedents for future presidents. He bypassed Congress to take control of treaty negotiations after warring countries tried to involve the United States. He insisted it was within the president's power to do so.
- Washington's presidency faced "an ocean of difficulties," from the national debt to wars across the Atlantic.

WASHINGTON'S PRESIDENCY

- Washington picked for his Cabinet men from across the country with differing political views, including Thomas Jefferson as Secretary of State and Alexander Hamilton as Secretary of the Treasury.
- Jefferson favored an agricultural nation and opposed a strong central government and a powerful banking structure. Hamilton envisioned an industrial nation and advocated a strong central government and the creation of a national bank.
- The Federal Judiciary Act of 1789 established a Supreme Court with the Chief Justice and five associate justices and a dual lower court system that split responsibilities between state and federal courts.

ADAMS'S PRESIDENCY

- Adams won the 1796 presidential election with 71 electoral votes to Jefferson's 68 electoral votes.
- When France began seizing U.S. ships in an effort to prevent U.S. trade with Britain, Adams sent an envoy to France to negotiate. But French agents, known to Americans only as X, Y, and Z, demanded a bribe, sparking the so-called XYZ Affair and the threat of war.
- The Democratic-Republicans charged that the Alien and Sedition Acts violated the First Amendment and gave the president too much power.

JEFFERSON'S PRESIDENCY

- Jefferson's preference for an agrarian nation and his fears that a national bank would give the government unlimited power reflected his Democratic-Republican beliefs.
- In *Marbury* v. *Madison*, Chief Justice John Marshall established judicial review—the power of the Supreme Court to invalidate laws it deems unconstitutional.
- The British practice of impressment—forcing captured sailors to serve the British Navy—led to the Embargo Act of 1807, which blocked foreign imports from arriving in American ports.
- Jefferson's biggest accomplishment was the Louisiana Purchase, in which the nation bought France's territory in North America. The transaction doubled the size of the United States.

AMERICAN PLACES
U.S. Treasury Building

In the early years of the nation, the Department of the Treasury was housed in Philadelphia. When the capital moved to Washington, D.C., in 1801, so did the Treasury. After two Treasury buildings burned down, construction on a third structure began in 1836—and this time its architects made it fireproof. A statue of Alexander Hamilton stands before the south entrance of the building, shown here.

HISTORICAL THINKING

1. **FORM AND SUPPORT OPINIONS** What do you think President Washington's most important achievements were?
2. **COMPARE AND CONTRAST** How did Jefferson's vision for the nation differ from Hamilton's?
3. **DRAW CONCLUSIONS** Why might people have questioned the constitutionality of the Alien and Sedition Acts?

REVIEW LESSON 2.7

THE WAR OF 1812

Tom Freeman's painting, called *Burning of the White House, 1814*, shows the structure in flames after British soldiers set it on fire during the War of 1812. Before their arrival, President Madison's wife, Dolley, had a full-length portrait of George Washington removed from the building, saving it from the flames.

American expansion into the Northwest Territory increased conflict with Native Americans in the early 1800s. Rumors swirled that British forces in Canada were encouraging Native Americans to attack U.S. settlers and troops. Some Americans even believed that the British had formed an official alliance with Native Americans against the United States. As a result, the War Hawks, Americans who favored conflict with Britain, issued a call to arms in Washington, D.C.

CAUSES OF THE WAR The United States and Great Britain went to battle in what became known as the **War of 1812**. The conflict had its roots in a larger war between France and Britain that began in 1803. At first, American merchants profited from U.S. neutrality as they sold provisions and weapons to both countries. But soon the British and French navies tried to block U.S. ships from supplying the other side. The British began capturing U.S. ships and forcing sailors into the British Navy, an action called impressment. President Jefferson responded by urging Congress to pass the widely unpopular Embargo Act of 1807, which blocked foreign imports from entering U.S. ports. Tensions continued to mount with Britain until the United States declared war in 1812.

KEY BATTLES The war began badly for the United States when American troops were forced to retreat after attempting to take a British fort near Detroit, Michigan. Things went better for Oliver Hazard Perry and his fleet on Lake Erie. But by the summer of 1814, Britain's war against the French in Europe was drawing to a close, so Britain sent more troops to North America. The British attacked both Washington, D.C., and Baltimore, Maryland, but only succeeded in capturing Washington, D.C.

END OF THE WAR By the end of 1814, the war had become a stalemate with neither side near victory. Delegates from both countries met in Ghent, a city in present-day Belgium, where they signed the **Treaty of Ghent** and formally ended the war. However, news of the treaty did not come soon enough to stop one last British naval and ground attack on New Orleans. The battle resulted in a resounding U.S. victory. Although the Treaty of Ghent did not declare a winner, many Americans felt they'd scored a diplomatic victory in the war.

8.5.1 Understand the political and economic causes and consequences of the War of 1812 and know the major battles, leaders, and events that led to a final peace.

KEY TAKEAWAYS

NATIVE AMERICANS UNITE

- Democratic-Republican **James Madison** won a landslide victory against the Federalist Party in the presidential election of 1808.
- Around 1808, Shawnee chief **Tecumseh** founded Prophetstown on the Tippecanoe River in Indiana Territory, which served as his base from which to recruit Native American allies for a confederacy against the United States. Tecumseh hoped to end the continued U.S. conquest of Native American land.
- In 1811, Tecumseh's brother Tenskwatawa, "the Prophet," clashed with troops led by William Henry Harrison, the governor of Indiana Territory, in what came to be known as the Battle of Tippecanoe. Prophetstown was burned to the ground.
- In June 1812, the War Hawks got their wish when Congress declared war against Britain, accusing the British of encouraging Native American attacks.

LAKE ERIE BATTLES

- As the War of 1812 began, American forces attacked a British fort near Detroit, Michigan, but the British repelled the attack and forced the U.S. militia to surrender Detroit.
- In September 1813, American troops won their first victory when Oliver Hazard Perry and his fleet of ships defeated British forces on Lake Erie.
- Soon after, William Henry Harrison's forces retook Detroit and defeated British troops at the Battle of the Thames, in which Shawnee chief Tecumseh died fighting for the British.

WASHINGTON AND BALTIMORE

- In 1814, British forces captured Washington, D.C., and burned down the Capitol and the White House.
- The British also attacked Baltimore, Maryland, and a fort near the city but failed to take either.
- The American flag flying amid the rockets and bombs during the Battle of Fort McHenry inspired Francis Scott Key to memorialize the scene in his poem "**The Star-Spangled Banner.**" The poem was later set to music and became the national anthem of the United States.

PEACE AND THE BATTLE OF NEW ORLEANS

- The terms of the Treaty of Ghent restored conditions to what they were before the war: all British and American territories captured during the fighting were returned, and all prisoners of war were freed.
- **Andrew Jackson**, a military leader from Tennessee, led a resounding U.S. victory at the Battle of New Orleans, killing, capturing, or wounding more than 2,000 British soldiers, while losing only 13 of his own men.
- The war confirmed U.S. sovereignty, boosted Americans' self-confidence, united the country through patriotism, and encouraged more expansion and economic prosperity.

Andrew Jackson's coat

CURATING HISTORY

Louisiana State Museum

In 1815, wearing this uniform coat, Jackson led the American victory at the Battle of New Orleans. The coat is on display in the Cabildo, a building in New Orleans constructed between 1796 and 1799 during Spanish rule. The building housed the government of New Orleans and the headquarters of the state supreme court before it became the Louisiana State Museum in 1908.

HISTORICAL THINKING

1. **ANALYZE CAUSE AND EFFECT** Why did the War Hawks press for war against Britain?
2. **DRAW CONCLUSIONS** Why did Britain choose not to send its entire army to fight in America before 1814?
3. **MAKE PREDICTIONS** What impact do you think the Battle of New Orleans had on Andrew Jackson's career?

REVIEW CHAPTER 2

REVOLUTION AND A NEW REPUBLIC

ASSESSMENT

MAIN IDEAS

Choose the best answer for each question from the choices available.

1. What policy did the British government adopt toward the colonies in the early 1700s? HSS 11.1.1
   - A The government strictly enforced its authority.
   - B The government largely allowed the colonists to govern themselves.
   - C The government included elected representatives from the colonies in Parliament.
   - D The government allowed the colonies complete freedom.

2. How did colonists react to taxes levied against them to pay for the French and Indian War? HSS 11.1.1
   - A They cried, "No taxation without representation!"
   - B They boycotted British goods.
   - C They staged protests.
   - D all of the above

3. How did the Enlightenment influence the Founding Fathers? HSS 11.1.2
   - A It encouraged the violent overthrow of government.
   - B It awakened religious fervor in the Founding Fathers.
   - C It called for the granting of natural rights, liberty, and equality.
   - D It provided a strategy for reconciling with King George III.

4. What role(s) did women play in the American Revolution? HSS 11.1
   - A They took over the jobs at home traditionally done by men.
   - B They worked as spies.
   - C They worked as nurses on the battlefield.
   - D all of the above

5. What was a key legacy of the American Revolution? HSS 11.1.2
   - A It freed enslaved people.
   - B It established a constitutional republic in the United States.
   - C It inspired other nations to write constitutions.
   - D It established the United States as a major world power.

6. Why did the federal government struggle to pay its debts after the American Revolution? HSS 11.1
   - A because the Articles of Confederation didn't allow the Continental Congress to levy taxes
   - B because the Articles of Confederation didn't allow states to levy taxes
   - C because the Articles of Confederation declared that debts had to be repaid with goods
   - D because the Articles of Confederation declared that debts could be paid on credit

7. Which debate did the development of the electoral college resolve? HSS 11.1.2
   - A the debate over whether representatives should be elected
   - B the debate over how to select the president
   - C the debate over slavery
   - D the debate over voting rights

8. How did Constitutional Convention delegates determine an enslaved African American would be counted within a state's population? HSS 11.1.2
   - A as three-fifths of a person
   - B as one full person
   - C as three people
   - D An enslaved African American would not be counted at all.

9. Why was the Bill of Rights added to the Constitution? HSS 11.1.2
   - A to override laws detailed in state constitutions
   - B to please the federalists
   - C to protect such rights as liberty, equality, and individual pursuit of happiness
   - D to emphasize the difference between the newly formed United States and Britain

10. What powers not enumerated in the Constitution did George Washington assume? HSS 11.1.3

A He created a Cabinet.

B He took control of treaty negotiations.

C He established a Supreme Court.

D He ensured that laws passed by Congress were carried out.

11. Why did Thomas Jefferson oppose Alexander Hamilton's plan for a national bank? HSS 11.1.3

A because he believed it would give the federal government unlimited powers

B because he believed it would give state governments unlimited powers

C because the Constitution expressly forbade the creation of a national bank

D because the Constitution only allowed for the creation of state banks

12. Why did Democratic-Republicans oppose the Alien and Sedition Acts passed under President John Adams? HSS 11.1.3

A They claimed the acts violated citizens' freedom of speech.

B They claimed the acts violated freedom of the press.

C They claimed the acts gave the president too much power.

D all of the above

13. How did the War Hawks affect the War of 1812? HSS 11.1

A They rescued sailors impressed by French and British ship captains.

B They recaptured Detroit from the British.

C They pressured Congress to declare war on Britain.

D They saved a portrait of George Washington from being burned in a fire.

14. What historical event put an end to the War of 1812? HSS 11.1

A Britain defeated the United States.

B The United States defeated Britain.

C The United States won the Battle of New Orleans.

D The Treaty of Ghent was signed.

ANALYZE SOURCES

Thomas Jefferson wrote the Declaration of Independence in 1776 to tell the world why the colonies were breaking away from Britain. The following lines are from the first part of the Declaration. Read the passage and answer the questions that follow.

> We hold these truths to be self-evident, that all men are created equal, that they are endowed by their Creator with certain unalienable Rights, that among these are Life, Liberty and the pursuit of Happiness. That to secure these rights, Governments are instituted among Men, deriving their just powers from the consent of the governed, That whenever any Form of Government becomes destructive of these ends, it is the Right of the People to alter or to abolish it, and to institute new Government.

15. According to the excerpt, when are people justified in overthrowing their government? HSS 11.1

16. Based on the excerpt, what are the key ideas of American democracy? HSS 11.1

WRITE ABOUT HISTORY

17. **EXPLANATORY** From 1763 to 1774, British Parliament passed several laws that limited colonial trade. Think about what you have learned about the Proclamation of 1763, the Tea Act, the Stamp Act, and the Intolerable Acts in the context of the time period and then answer the following question: Which British law most burdened the colonists? HSS HI 3

TIPS

- Introduce the topic with a clear main idea statement.
- Develop the topic with relevant facts and concrete details.
- Infer Britain's motivations for instituting these strict laws.
- Provide a concluding statement that follows from the information you have presented.

REVIEW CHAPTER 3

EXPANSION AND REFORM

1803–1853

HISTORICAL THINKING How did expansion impact the United States politically, economically, and socially?

AMERICAN STORIES ONLINE | **American Inventions**

AMERICAN STORIES ONLINE | **The Cherokee**

AMERICAN GALLERY ONLINE | **On the Trail with Lewis and Clark**

In 1827, a group of enterprising businessmen founded the Baltimore & Ohio (B&O) Railroad, which became the first railroad to transport goods and people in the United States. By 1850, railroad routes crisscrossed much of the country. Some steam locomotives are still in use, including the one shown here, pulling freight through a rural countryside.

"Railroad iron is a magician's wand,
in its power to evoke the sleeping energies of land and water."

—Ralph Waldo Emerson

REVIEW LESSON 3.1 THE LOUISIANA PURCHASE

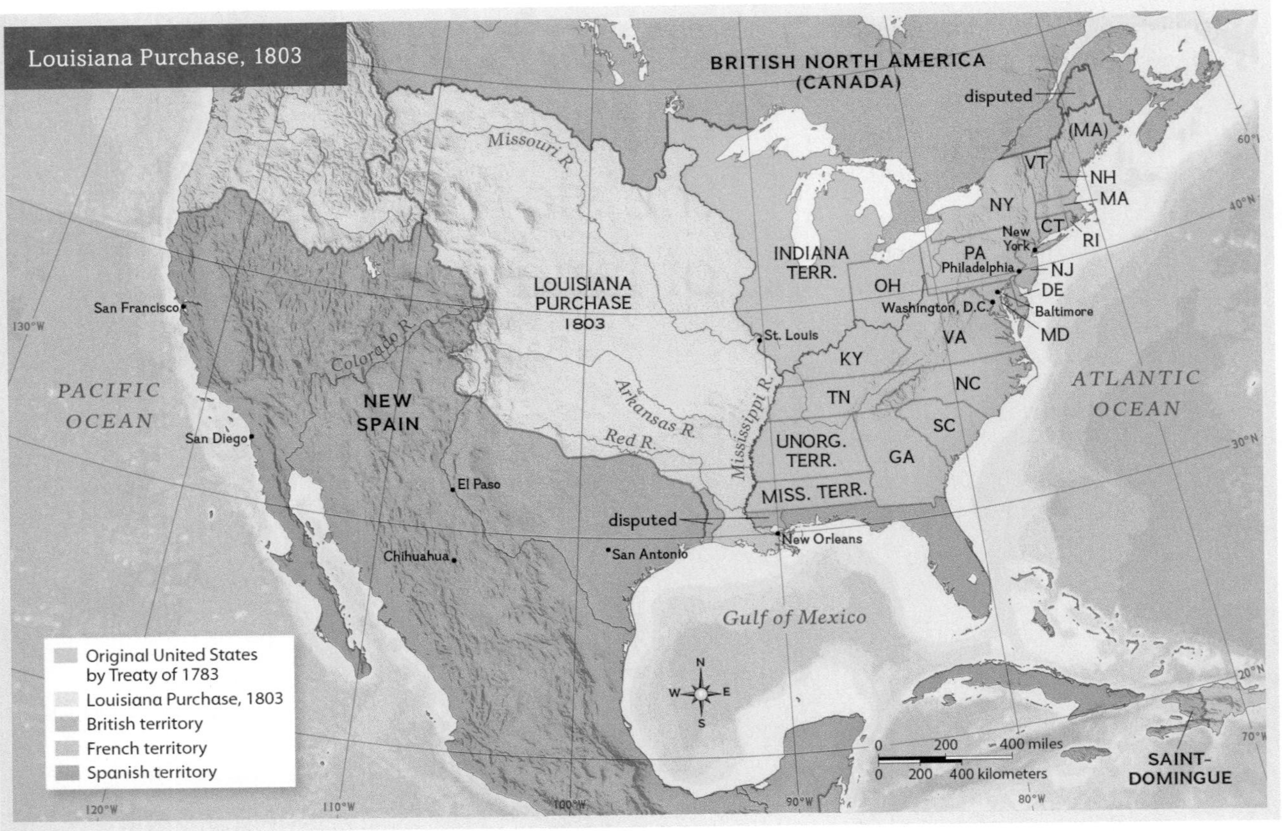

As president, Thomas Jefferson set his sights on expanding the nation to provide land for the agricultural society he envisioned. The population in the region between the Appalachian Mountains and the Mississippi River had grown steadily. Farmers were settling the area and shipping their crops down the tributaries of the Mississippi to the French-held city of New Orleans, where ships carried cargo to ports all over the world. Jefferson wanted to acquire New Orleans to gain control of shipping on the Mississippi River, and only France stood in his way.

NAPOLEON BONAPARTE French general Napoleon Bonaparte overthrew the revolutionary government in France in 1799 and seized power. The next year, he signed a secret treaty requiring Spain to return the area of land called Louisiana—and the Port of New Orleans—to France. In 1803, Jefferson sent James Monroe to France to help negotiate the purchase of territory at the mouth of the Mississippi, including New Orleans. Negotiations between Napoleon and the United States stalled, however, as Napoleon tried to win back the Caribbean colony of Saint-Domingue, now known as Haiti, on the island of Hispaniola. France had lost the colony to revolution in the 1790s.

LOUISIANA TERRITORY After Napoleon surrendered to Haitian independence, he felt that Louisiana had little value without Saint-Domingue. The French leader decided to give up all his territory in continental North America. Instead of selling only New Orleans to the United States, Napoleon suggested selling the entire Louisiana Territory. As a result, in October 1803, the U.S. Senate ratified the treaty that established the Louisiana Purchase.

LEWIS AND CLARK Jefferson funded an expedition to take a good look at the land and natural resources the country had bought. In 1803, he sent **Meriwether Lewis** and **William Clark** to explore the uncharted West and find a water route to the Pacific. Lewis and Clark's Corps of Discovery, initially consisting of 59 men and a dog, traveled almost 8,000 miles from St. Louis, Missouri, to the Pacific Ocean and then back to St. Louis. Few accurate maps of the West existed at that time, and there were many geographic unknowns about the region. Lewis and Clark didn't find the water route, but their recorded observations changed Americans' understanding of the physical landscapes of the West. Their journey resulted in the discovery of plants and animals never seen before by European Americans.

KEY TAKEAWAYS

PORT OF NEW ORLEANS

- Napoleon made a deal with Spain to obtain Louisiana because the Spanish government had decided that, with only 50,000 settlers in all of Louisiana, the area was too expensive to maintain and produced too little profit.
- Jefferson feared that France would interfere with American merchants trying to ship goods out of the Port of New Orleans, which was part of the Louisiana Territory.
- Fortunately for Jefferson, France felt as burdened with Louisiana as Spain had and was very willing to sell the territory to another nation.

NAPOLEON'S OFFER

- Negotiations between the United States and France were slowed but ultimately helped by Napoleon's all-out war to take back control of Saint-Domingue from **Toussaint L'Ouverture**, who had led a successful revolution to free slaves in 1791.
- When Napoleon failed to regain control of Saint-Domingue, the victorious rebels established Haiti as an independent nation in 1804.
- After the U.S. Senate ratified the treaty that finalized the Louisiana Purchase, France officially transferred the land to the United States, doubling the size of the nation.

THE TERRITORY

- The United States paid France $15 million for the 828,000 square miles of land included in the Louisiana Purchase.
- Jefferson had some misgivings about the constitutionality of the Louisiana Purchase, since the U.S. Constitution did not give the federal government the power to acquire new territories. He proceeded anyway.
- After he signed the treaty with France, Jefferson funded an expedition to explore the land. Meriwether Lewis, an amateur scientist, and William Clark, an army officer, headed the expedition.

THE EXPEDITION

- Lewis and Clark's Corps of Discovery traveled westward along the Missouri River, over the Rocky Mountains, and along the Columbia River to the Pacific Ocean. On their return trip, they split into two groups for a time to explore more territory.
- **Sacagawea**, a young Shoshone woman, traveled with the Corps of Discovery, acting as an interpreter for the group as it moved through the territories of many Native American tribes. Some tribes had never seen white men before.
- Lewis and Clark recorded more than 120 new animal species, including mule deer and coyote, and described 178 new species of plants, such as the big leaf maple, the Oregon crab apple, and the ponderosa pine.

Lewis and Clark's journals

CURATING HISTORY
Missouri Historical Society

Among the treasures to emerge from the Corps of Discovery were Lewis and Clark's personal journals, housed today in this museum in St. Louis. In their journals, the men often drew the geography, people, plants, and animals they encountered. This bird from the journals is a type of grouse—a bird that is slightly smaller than a turkey—which they found in March 1806.

HISTORICAL THINKING

1. **SUMMARIZE** Why was Jefferson interested in the Louisiana Territory?
2. **ANALYZE CAUSE AND EFFECT** Explain the complex ways in which the Louisiana Purchase affected the United States and its people.
3. **MAKE PREDICTIONS** What impact do you think the Louisiana Purchase had on Native Americans over time?

8.8.2 Describe the purpose, challenges, and economic incentives associated with westward expansion, including the concept of Manifest Destiny (e.g., the Lewis and Clark expedition, accounts of the removal of Indians, the Cherokees' "Trail of Tears," settlement of the Great Plains) and the territorial acquisitions that spanned numerous decades; HI 2 Students recognize the complexity of historical causes and effects, including the limitations on determining cause and effect.

REVIEW LESSON 3.2 ECONOMIC GROWTH

In the early 1800s, different regions of the United States became more interdependent and connected as the country shifted from an agricultural nation to a market-oriented, industrial one. This economic transition was prompted in part by the **Industrial Revolution**, or the widespread use of machinery to produce goods, which began in Europe in the mid-1700s. The industrial transformation of the new nation is often dated to 1793, when Samuel Slater opened his first cloth factory in Rhode Island. Industrialization in New England transformed social structures and had important consequences for the nation's economy and international position.

THE FACTORY SYSTEM

New machines produced goods more rapidly and efficiently than people could make by hand, one at a time. These machines led to the introduction of factories, places where large crews of people use machines to produce goods. Under the factory system, mechanized production replaced skilled craftspeople. The United States entered the Industrial Revolution and developed the factory system through the rise in New England of the textile industry, which produced cloth and clothing from cotton and other raw materials.

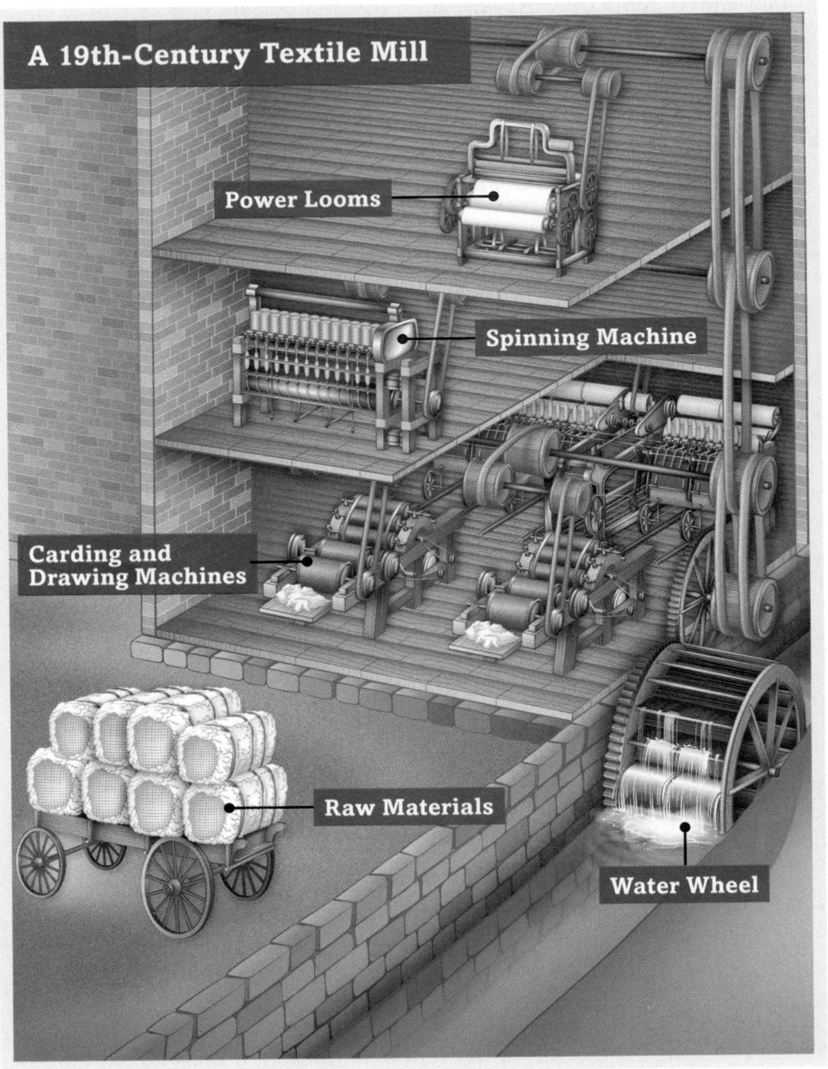

Textile mills in the 19th century relied on water to power the different machines needed to transform raw materials into textiles. Machines inside the mill performed a variety of tasks, including preparing the cotton and fibers for spinning, spinning fibers into threads, and weaving threads into cloth.

NEW INVENTIONS As Americans moved west, new technologies, such as the steel plow and mechanical reaper, were developed to tackle the challenges settlers faced on the new land. Farmers had used cast iron plows to turn up soil before planting seeds, but the plows couldn't handle the hard prairie soil. The shape and material of the new steel plow solved the problem. The mechanical reaper freed farmers from harvesting their crops by hand. Both inventions made farming easier for western settlers and greatly increased productivity.

SOUTHERN ECONOMY While the North industrialized, the South relied largely on an agrarian economy, producing primarily cotton. Both the North and the South relied on cotton. Slave labor in the South produced the cotton and raw materials that workers in the North processed in mills. This system allowed northern textile companies, financial groups, and other businesses to thrive. However, the high demand for cotton resulted in the expansion of slavery, and regional tensions began to grow between slave and free states.

8.6.1 Discuss the influence of industrialization and technological developments on the region, including human modification of the landscape and how physical geography shaped human actions (e.g., growth of cities, deforestation, farming, mineral extraction); 8.7.1 Describe the development of the agrarian economy in the South, identify the locations of the cotton-producing states, and discuss the significance of cotton and the cotton gin.

KEY TAKEAWAYS

AMERICA'S FIRST INDUSTRIAL REVOLUTION

- Blacksmith John Deere developed a plow made of hard, polished steel that didn't allow the prairie soil to clump or stick to the blade.
- Cyrus Hall McCormick developed a horse-drawn mechanical reaper that quickly reaped, or cut, stalks of wheat from the field and gathered them up for processing.
- In the 1790s, **Eli Whitney** designed the cotton gin, a machine that made picking cotton faster and less labor-intensive.
- Samuel F. B. Morse invented a telegraph that sent messages over electrical wires using a series of long and short pulses that became known as Morse code.

NEW ENGLAND TEXTILE MILLS

- Francis Cabot Lowell increased speed and efficiency at his textile mill in Massachusetts by developing a single-operator power loom.
- Carding machines and drawing frames prepared cotton and fibers for spinning, powerful spinning machines combined thread into yarn, and power looms wove yarn into cloth.
- Mill owners hired girls and young women for their factories because they could pay them less than men. The young women lived in boarding houses and worked in the mills instead of attending school.

THE COTTON INDUSTRY

- The cotton gin was fitted with teeth that grabbed the cotton seeds and separated them from cotton tufts.
- The cotton gin increased the productivity of enslaved laborers, helping make cotton the main cash crop on many southern farms that had previously grown tobacco.
- With better production methods, cotton quickly became a central part of the U.S. economy.

EXPANSION OF SLAVERY

- Southern plantation owners tried to maximize profits by increasing their numbers of slaves.
- Slave owners urged enslaved women to have more children, and they then sold the children at auctions to make a profit or trade them for specially skilled slaves.
- A law banning the importation of slaves from outside the United States, which took effect in 1808, caused the interstate slave trade, or the slave trade within the United States, to increase.
- Some enslaved people resisted slavery through passive resistance. Others, such as Nat Turner, chose open rebellion. Turner led a group of fellow slaves in a violent rebellion in 1831 and killed more than 50 people in one night.

Cotton gin

CURATING HISTORY
Henry Ford Museum

Eli Whitney's cotton gin, on exhibit at this museum in Dearborn, Michigan, revolutionized the process of cleaning seeds out of cotton. Whitney had heard about farmers struggling to efficiently process their cotton crops. He solved the problem with a device that pulled cotton through a set of wire teeth. Cotton fibers fit through the teeth, but the seeds could not.

HISTORICAL THINKING

1. **IDENTIFY MAIN IDEAS AND DETAILS** How did work in both the North and the South change in the early 1800s?
2. **DRAW CONCLUSIONS** How did the factory system affect people's social and economic lives?
3. **EVALUATE** How did slavery shape the economic development of both the South and the North?
4. **INTERPRET VISUALS** Why were 19th-century textile mills often located beside rivers?

8.7.2 Trace the origins and development of slavery; its effects on black Americans and on the region's political, social, religious, economic, and cultural development; and identify the strategies that were tried to both overturn and preserve it (e.g., through the writings and historical documents on Nat Turner, Denmark Vesey); HI 1 Students show the connections, causal and otherwise, between particular historical events and larger social, economic, and political trends and developments.

NATIONAL GROWTH

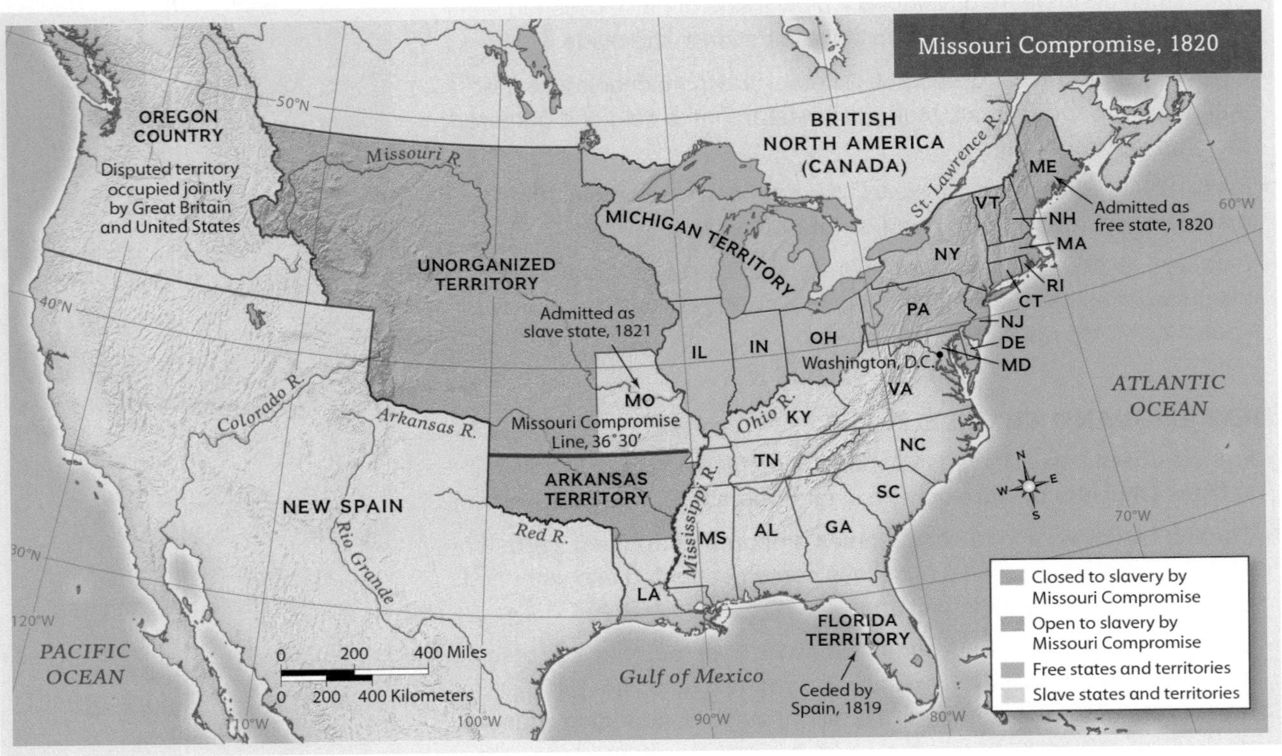

As industry grew in the early 1800s and settlers moved west and south, Americans soon realized they needed more efficient ways to move people and goods across the country. But they faced several geographic challenges, including connecting the nation, traveling over great distances, and crossing the Appalachian Mountains. Americans overcame these geographic challenges by coming up with new solutions and building an enormous transportation network that produced major economic benefits.

INNOVATIONS IN TRANSPORTATION Steamboats, railroads, canals, and improved roads helped move people and goods between the East and the Northwest Territory, and modified the American landscape. The National Road made travel over great distances smoother and more comfortable, while the success of the B&O Railroad encouraged other companies to build more railroads. The Erie Canal made it possible to ship crops and manufactured goods from New York City to New Orleans on a water route. Congressmen **Henry Clay** and **John C. Calhoun** supported many of these improvements as part of the American System, designed to get the federal government involved in financing the nation's infrastructure.

GROWING NATIONALIST SPIRIT The market revolution—the transition from a pre-industrial economy to a market-oriented, capitalist economy—changed how people worked, traveled, and did business. Eventually, the revolution also encouraged a new philosophy of nationalism, the concept of loyalty and devotion to one's nation. Americans developed a strong national identity during the administrations of presidents James Madison and James Monroe.

WESTWARD EXPANSION At the same time, the nation continued to grow in size. In 1819, the United States received Florida from Spain. But territorial growth was accompanied by sectionalism, the identification with and loyalty to a particular part of the country, such as the North or the South. The rise of sectionalism was rooted in economic differences between the North and the South and in the practice of slavery. The issue of slavery came to the forefront when the federal government wanted to admit Missouri to the Union as the 23rd state. The trick was how to do so without upsetting the balance of 11 slave states and 11 free states. Americans worried that admitting Missouri would create an imbalance in power between slave and free states.

8.6.1 Discuss the influence of industrialization and technological developments on the region, including human modification of the landscape and how physical geography shaped human actions (e.g., growth of cities, deforestation, farming, mineral extraction).

KEY TAKEAWAYS

NEW FORMS OF TRANSPORTATION

- Robert Fulton's steamboats, or boats powered by steam boiler engines, revolutionized river travel and made shipping faster.
- The steam-operated Baltimore & Ohio (B&O) Railroad connected Baltimore to the growing cities of the interior, such as Cincinnati, Ohio, and St. Louis, Missouri.
- The National Road, also known as the Cumberland Road, stretched west from Cumberland, Maryland, to Vandalia, Illinois.
- Under the American System, improvements in road systems, trains, and waterways united the country geographically and culturally, and strengthened the nation's market economy.

NATIONALISM AND FOREIGN POLICY

- A sense of national pride and confidence encouraged expansion and a new economic prosperity.
- The presidency of **James Monroe**, who served from 1817 to 1825, marked a period called the Era of Good Feelings for its years of relative peace and economic growth.
- In 1823, Monroe introduced a new approach to foreign policy, declaring the United States would not fight in any European wars. He also warned European nations against interfering in the Western Hemisphere, a statement that became known as the Monroe Doctrine.

EXPANSION

- Under the terms of the Transcontinental Treaty of 1819, the United States formally received Florida from Spain and gave sovereignty over Texas to Spain.
- The federal government wanted to admit the Missouri Territory as the 23rd state but worried that this would increase sectional tensions.
- The lands acquired in the Louisiana Purchase were considered unorganized territory, or lands governed by the federal government but not belonging to any state.

TENSIONS OVER SLAVERY

- As the United States expanded its territory and power, it negotiated how each new state would deal with the issue of slavery.
- The Missouri Territory was located on the same latitude as much of Illinois, Indiana, and Ohio, which seemed to violate the assumption held by many northerners that slavery would expand only in the South.
- Under the terms of the Missouri Compromise of 1820, Missouri was admitted to the Union as a slave state at the same time Maine was admitted as a free state. Any states formed from the unorganized territory north of the 36° 30' N latitude line would be free states.

AMERICAN PLACES
The Mississippi River

The mighty Mississippi is the largest river in North America and one of the largest in the world. It lies entirely within the United States and flows south from Minnesota, collecting water from the Ohio and Missouri rivers and spilling from Louisiana into the Gulf of Mexico. As one of the world's busiest commercial waterways, the river is the lifeblood of a highly industrialized country and moves most of our agricultural products for export.

HISTORICAL THINKING

1. **ANALYZE CAUSE AND EFFECT** What factors caused the development of new modes of transportation?
2. **SYNTHESIZE** How did new methods of transportation improve national unity?
3. **DRAW CONCLUSIONS** Why did expansion increase sectional tensions and divisions?

8.6.2 Outline the physical obstacles to and the economic and political factors involved in building a network of roads, canals, and railroads (e.g., Henry Clay's American System); 8.9.5 Analyze the significance of the States' Rights Doctrine, the Missouri Compromise (1820), the Wilmot Proviso (1846), the Compromise of 1850, Henry Clay's role in the Missouri Compromise of 1850, the Kansas-Nebraska Act (1854), the *Dred Scott* v. *Sandford* decision (1857), and the Lincoln-Douglas debates (1858).

REVIEW LESSON 3.4

JACKSON AND NATIVE AMERICANS

Sculptor Clark Mills created this statue of Andrew Jackson, which stands in a square across the street from the White House in Washington, D.C. The bronze statue—the first one made in the United States—celebrates Jackson's 1815 victory against the British at the Battle of New Orleans during the War of 1812.

Despite a hard childhood in North Carolina, Andrew Jackson achieved great success. He moved to the Tennessee frontier and became a lawyer in 1787. He later made a successful run for Congress and became a plantation owner. After crushing the British at the Battle of New Orleans in the War of 1812, Jackson became a national hero. His success was crowned by his election as president of the United States in 1828, running on the claim that he championed the "common man."

JACKSONIAN DEMOCRACY By 1828, most white men in the United States could vote whether they owned property or not. As a result, about 782,000 more "common men" participated in the 1828 election than in the previous one. The political movement that celebrated the common man—farmers, laborers, and middle-class businessmen—and defended the will of the people was called Jacksonian democracy. Once Jackson took office, he replaced many of John Quincy Adams's government officials with his own supporters, a practice called the spoils system. In Jackson's second term, he sought to destroy the **Second National Bank**, which he believed gave the government too much control over the nation's economy.

STRUGGLES OVER SECESSION Congress passed a bill in 1828 that greatly increased tariffs, or taxes on imported goods. The bill also included a clause that taxed U.S. raw materials, such as cotton and tobacco, sold abroad. Southerners labeled the bill the Tariff of Abominations. South Carolina went so far as to threaten to secede, or leave the Union, if the tariff was enforced, but Jackson made it clear that he considered secession an act of treason. To prevent the country from breaking apart, South Carolina senator John C. Calhoun applied the doctrine of nullification, also called the states' rights doctrine. According to this doctrine, a state could nullify, or reject, a federal law it considered unconstitutional.

TRAIL OF TEARS In 1830, Jackson approved the Indian Removal Act, which forced Native Americans to move to what became known as **Indian Territory**, an area of land in present-day Oklahoma, Kansas, and Nebraska. Many Native Americans gave in and left their homes, but the Seminole took up arms against the U.S. government, and the Cherokee fought removal by taking their case to the Supreme Court. In the end, however, the Cherokee were forced to move in a brutal journey that became known as the **Trail of Tears**.

KEY TAKEAWAYS

JACKSON'S EARLY LIFE

- Jackson's father died three weeks before he was born. Jackson and his brothers were raised in poverty by his mother.
- The young Jackson carried messages for the Continental Army during the American Revolution until he was taken prisoner by the British.
- In the War of 1812, Jackson became a national hero after he and his troops stopped a British naval and ground attack on New Orleans.

JACKSON'S REFORMS

- Critics claimed that Jackson's spoils system was corrupt, but Jackson argued that completely removing officials from time to time would prevent any one party from dominating the government.
- Henry Clay, Jackson's opponent in the 1832 presidential election, sponsored a bill to renew the Second National Bank's charter early. Jackson vetoed it and eventually drove the bank out of business.
- Jackson introduced a new political movement that championed the "common man" and came to be called Jacksonian democracy.

STATES' RIGHTS

- The Tariff of 1828 helped protect industries in the Northeast and enraged southerners. Political leaders in South Carolina hated the tariff so much they began to discuss withdrawing from the Union.
- To prevent the country from dividing, Calhoun applied the doctrine of nullification, which led to the Webster-Hayne debate in 1830.
- Massachusetts senator **Daniel Webster** argued against nullification, claiming that it threatened the Union and freedom, while South Carolina senator **Robert Y. Hayne** made the case for nullification, claiming a state had the right to nullify a federal law.
- When South Carolina's representatives still threatened secession after Jackson reduced the tariff in 1832, Congress authorized the president to use force to collect tariffs.

POLICIES TOWARD NATIVE AMERICANS

- The discovery of gold on Cherokee land in Georgia in 1828 fueled the desire to remove Native Americans from their lands in the Southeast.
- Although the Indian Removal Act of 1830 clearly stated that the government was required to negotiate treaties with Native Americans and not force them off their land, the U.S. government and Jackson ignored this requirement.
- The Sauk and the Fox were forced to surrender their land and move to Indian Territory in 1832. The Florida Seminole resisted removal in 1835 by retreating into the Everglades.
- About 4,000 Cherokee died from cold, illness, and starvation on the Trail of Tears between 1838 and 1839.

Cherokee coat

CURATING HISTORY
National Museum of the American Indian

While the Cherokee assimilated European clothing styles, they also held onto their own culture, as the traditional Cherokee coat from this museum in Washington, D.C., demonstrates. The man's coat dating from the 1820s is made from the hide of deer, which the Cherokee hunted. The fringe channeled rain off the wearer, helping to keep him dry. Cherokee men may have worn a coat like this one on the Trail of Tears.

HISTORICAL THINKING

1. **SYNTHESIZE** How did expanding democratization contribute to Andrew Jackson's rise in politics?
2. **DRAW CONCLUSIONS** Why was the crisis over the doctrine of nullification an important political development?
3. **ANALYZE CAUSE AND EFFECT** What impact did the Trail of Tears have on the Cherokee?
4. **MAKE INFERENCES** Why did southerners call the tariff bill passed in 1828 the Tariff of Abominations?

8.8.1 Discuss the election of Andrew Jackson as president in 1828, the importance of Jacksonian democracy, and his actions as president (e.g., the spoils system, veto of the National Bank, policy of Indian removal, opposition to the Supreme Court); 8.9.5 Analyze the significance of the States' Rights Doctrine, the Missouri Compromise (1820), the Wilmot Proviso (1846), the Compromise of 1850, Henry Clay's role in the Missouri Compromise and the Compromise of 1850, the Kansas-Nebraska Act (1854), the *Dred Scott* v. *Sandford* decision (1857), and the Lincoln-Douglas debates (1858).

REVIEW LESSON 3.5 SLAVERY AND ABOLITION

The white and black men and women in this photo from 1850 gathered for a convention of the American Anti-Slavery Society. The man seated at the left end of the table is Frederick Douglass.

As you know, slavery expanded in the South when the cotton industry boomed. Slaves were considered chattel, or the property of their owners, and were denied rights, freedom, and sometimes even their lives. In the 1830s, abolitionists—people who wanted to end slavery—began speaking out against the treatment of enslaved people.

LIFE UNDER SLAVERY Most plantation slaves—both men and women—spent long hours planting, weeding, watering, and harvesting crops. Many slave owners used harsh treatment to punish enslaved people or force them to work harder. Slave owners sometimes even used chains and other restraints to prevent African Americans from escaping. Perhaps worst of all, enslaved family members were sometimes separated forever when an owner sold a child or parent to another owner.

SPEAKING OUT AGAINST SLAVERY Around the 1830s, abolitionists began speaking out about the injustice of slavery in an attempt to end the institution in the United States. These reformers founded antislavery societies and used pamphlets, newspapers, and other literature to spread their ideas. Former president John Quincy Adams also expressed abolitionist views, arguing that the ideals of the Declaration of Independence applied to all people. Many Americans, however, did not agree with those who opposed slavery. White southerners protested that abolitionist literature invited slaves to revolt. Some northerners were opposed to abolition as well. In some places, mobs rose up and violently attacked abolitionists.

STANDING UP FOR FREEDOM The American Anti-Slavery Society, which **William Lloyd Garrison** helped found, was one of the abolitionist groups that emerged in the early 1830s. By the end of the 1830s, the society claimed more than a quarter million members, including such prominent white abolitionists as **Wendell Phillips**, **Sarah Grimké**, **Angelina Grimké**, and **Theodore Weld.** Both free and enslaved African Americans actively challenged the existence of slavery, too. In the mid-1840s, **Frederick Douglass** and **Sojourner Truth** spoke at society meetings. **David Walker** and **Harriet Jacobs** were also active in the abolition movement.

8.7.2. Trace the origins and development of slavery; its effects on black Americans and on the region's political, social, religious, economic, and cultural development; and identify the strategies that were tried to both overturn and preserve it (e.g., through the writings and historical documents on Nat Turner, Denmark Vesey).

KEY TAKEAWAYS

LIFE FOR ENSLAVED AFRICAN AMERICANS

- Owners sometimes whipped enslaved people or recruited drivers, enslaved people tasked with pushing other slaves to work harder.
- When a child or parent in an enslaved family was sold to another owner, the rest of the family often did not see the relative again.
- Some slave owners used shackles to chain enslaved people. Others restrained slaves using an iron collar, which had prongs that made it impossible to lie down to rest or sleep.

THE ABOLITION MOVEMENT

- Many reformers who protested social issues were also abolitionists.
- Southerners and northerners alike considered abolitionists and their ideas radical, dangerous, un-Christian, and even unpatriotic.
- In 1839, former president John Quincy Adams called for a constitutional amendment to free every child born in the United States after July 4, 1842, and proposed that no new state be admitted to the Union if it allowed slavery, but neither idea became law.

WHITE ABOLITIONISTS

- In 1831, William Lloyd Garrison published the antislavery newspaper *The Liberator*, which called for the immediate emancipation of all enslaved people. Wealthy attorney Wendell Phillips wrote for Garrison's newspaper and contributed financially to the movement.
- Sisters Sarah Grimké and Angelina Grimké became abolitionists after witnessing the cruelty of slavery firsthand while growing up on their parents' plantation in South Carolina. They joined the Quakers and traveled the country giving speeches in support of abolition.
- Theodore Weld, who eventually married Angelina Grimké, served as a trainer and recruiter for the American Anti-Slavery Society.

AFRICAN-AMERICAN ABOLITIONISTS

- Frederick Douglass, an escaped slave who taught himself to read and write, became one of the most powerful and outspoken opponents of slavery. He was also an avid supporter of women's rights.
- David Walker, a free African-American clothing store owner and writer, printed and sewed antislavery pamphlets into the pockets of clothing he sold to sailors, hoping the pamphlets would reach people in southern ports and elsewhere. When his pamphlet "An Appeal to the Coloured Citizens of the World" reached the South, southern states reacted by prohibiting the circulation of abolitionist literature.
- Sojourner Truth, who was born into slavery, was a powerful abolitionist voice. She captivated people with her simple, clear message that all people deserved the same rights as white men.
- Harriet Jacobs, born into slavery, escaped to New York in 1842. She published one of the most extensive slave narratives written by a woman called *Incidents in the Life of a Slave Girl*.

Slave shackles

CURATING HISTORY
Chicago History Museum

The system of slavery relied on preventing escapes. Slave owners placed shackles like these on enslaved people's wrists or ankles. The cuffs were made of heavy wrought iron and held closed by a screw. Abolitionist speakers displayed shackles during their speeches to highlight the cruelty of the system and evoke a strong reaction from the crowd.

HISTORICAL THINKING

1. **SUMMARIZE** Under what conditions did enslaved African Americans live?
2. **MAKE INFERENCES** What ideals in the Declaration of Independence supported John Quincy Adams's call for his constitutional amendment?
3. **DRAW CONCLUSIONS** Why did most Americans consider abolitionists' ideas radical?
4. **SYNTHESIZE** How did abolition leaders spread their message across the country?

8.9.1 Describe the leaders of the movement (e.g., John Quincy Adams and his proposed constitutional amendment, John Brown and the armed resistance, Harriet Tubman and the Underground Railroad, Benjamin Franklin, Theodore Weld, William Lloyd Garrison, Frederick Douglass).

REVIEW LESSON 3.6

RELIGION AND EDUCATIONAL REFORM

In 1839, J. Maze Burbank captured the fervor of a revival in this painting, *Religious Camp Meeting*. Revival meetings, where Christian believers gathered to hear fiery sermons from traveling preachers, were also known as "camp meetings." Most were located on the frontier where settlers had not yet built churches.

In the early 1800s, many Americans began to return to the church due to the influence of a new religious movement. At the same time, reform movements arose to address social problems in American society. As reformers advocated for solutions to these problems, writers in the 19th century set out to shape the American identity.

A RETURN TO THE CHURCH In the 1790s, some Christians re-examined their religious practices. Many believed they should have a direct and emotional relationship with God and returned to the church in a movement called the **Second Great Awakening**. You may remember that a similar movement, called the Great Awakening, occurred in the early 1700s. The Second Great Awakening gained momentum around the 1830s. To reawaken religious enthusiasm, many churches organized revival meetings, informal religious events held outdoors or in tents. The revivals became very popular, especially among the Baptists and Methodists.

REFORMING SOCIAL PROBLEMS **Charles Grandison Finney**, a former lawyer and religious skeptic turned Christian preacher, was one of the most prominent figures of the Second Great Awakening. He was as passionate about social reform as he was about his faith. He believed a just society had the responsibility to improve the lives of all its members. Many other revivalist preachers shared Finney's views. As a result, religious groups actively promoted social reform causes. For example, the temperance movement, which crusaded against the overuse of alcohol, was part of this social reform. Reformers also advocated for such causes as free education for females, African Americans, and immigrants and better treatment for the mentally ill.

FIGHTING FOR BETTER PAY American workers also banded together and demanded better, safer labor conditions. Most factory workers toiled 10 to 14 hours per day, 6 days per week. They operated large and dangerous machines without safety gear. As a result, many machine operators were maimed or killed on the job. In the 1820s, workers began to organize labor unions, or groups that advocate for workers' rights and protections. Craftsmen, such as carpenters and shoemakers, also formed organizations called craft unions.

KEY TAKEAWAYS

SECOND GREAT AWAKENING

- During the Second Great Awakening, preachers evangelized, or spread the Christian gospel, by delivering dramatic sermons and sharing personal experiences.
- Revival meetings drew people out of church buildings and into nature. Some preachers attracted thousands of spectators.
- People felt a sense of freedom in worshiping with their friends and neighbors outside the formal organization of the church.

REFORM MOVEMENTS

- Charles Grandison Finney delivered lively sermons calling for the abolition of slavery, the improvement of education for all citizens, and the passage of women's rights.
- Members of the temperance movement called for moderation in drinking alcohol to preserve the social order. They also sought to protect women and children from mistreatment resulting from their husbands' and fathers' abuse of alcohol.
- Education reformer **Horace Mann** helped to establish a free public education system in Massachusetts for students of all social classes, genders, races, ethnicities, and faiths.
- Reformers such as **Dorothea Dix** and Louis Dwight worked to remove people with mental illnesses from prisons, jails, and poorhouses and place them in hospitals called asylums.

LABOR UNIONS

- Unionized workers had a much more powerful voice in demanding better pay and safer work environments than did individual workers.
- Workers wanted better wages, and they also wanted their employers to be held responsible for accidents on the job.
- **Sarah Bagley**, a millworker in Lowell, Massachusetts, led the way for women's labor unions by helping establish the Lowell Female Labor Reform Association (LFLRA), which advocated for shorter workdays.

CREATIVE EXPRESSION

- Writers and artists in the 19th century used events in U.S. history to help define what it meant to be American.
- An 1820 story by **Washington Irving** called "Rip Van Winkle" commented on the effects of the American Revolution on society, while a novel by **James Fenimore Cooper** called *The Pioneers* described life on the frontier in the late 1700s.
- Visual artists, such as Thomas Cole and Asher B. Durand, shaped American identity through landscape paintings that celebrated America's beauty.

CURATING HISTORY

Crystal Bridges Museum of American Art

In 1848, Asher B. Durand completed the painting above called *Kindred Spirits*, curated at this museum in Bentonville, Arkansas. Durand created it as a tribute to the friendship between painter Thomas Cole and poet William Cullen Bryant. In the painting, the two artists admire Fawns Leap and the Kaaterskill Falls—two sites in the Catskill Mountains of New York that cannot be viewed at the same time.

HISTORICAL THINKING

1. **MAKE INFERENCES** What might have drawn Americans to the Second Great Awakening?
2. **MAKE CONNECTIONS** What was the connection between religion and reform in the 19th century?
3. **IDENTIFY PROBLEMS AND SOLUTIONS** How did reformers attempt to solve the problems of alcohol abuse, education, mental illness, and labor?

8.12.6 Discuss child labor, working conditions, and laissez-faire policies toward big business and examine the labor movement, including its leaders (e.g., Samuel Gompers), its demand for collective bargaining, and its strikes and protests over labor conditions; 11.3.1. Describe the contributions of various religious groups to American civic principles and social reform movements (e.g., civil and human rights, individual responsibility and the work ethic, antimonarchy and self-rule, worker protection, family-centered communities); 11.3.2 Analyze the great religious revivals and the leaders involved in them, including the First Great Awakening, the Second Great Awakening, the Civil War revivals, the Social Gospel Movement, the rise of Christian liberal theology in the nineteenth century, the impact of the Second Vatican Council, and the rise of Christian fundamentalism in current times.

REVIEW LESSON 3.7 WOMEN'S RIGHTS

Throughout the early 1800s, women played active roles in social reform movements and in the abolition movement. An organized movement for women's rights in the United States began in 1840 when women attending the World's Anti-Slavery Convention in London, England, were consigned to seats in a separate area from the men. Delegate **Elizabeth Cady Stanton** felt "humiliated and chagrined" by the experience, but she discovered an important ally at the London meeting: **Lucretia Mott**, a Quaker and feminist. The two women vowed to champion women's rights in the United States, including the right to vote.

In this photo, women's rights leader Susan B. Anthony shows a document to fellow activist Elizabeth Cady Stanton, seated, in 1900. In 1902, Anthony wrote to Stanton: "It is fifty-one years since we first met, and we have been busy through every one of them, stirring up the world to recognize the rights of women."

UNEQUAL TREATMENT

The refusal to grant women's suffrage, or the right to vote, was not the only inequality women faced in the United States. Women lacked full equality with men in many aspects of life, including in property rights, education, employment and wages, and legal matters such as divorce. Furthermore, because educational and career opportunities were so limited for women, marriage was often the only possible path to a financially stable life.

LEADERS FOR WOMEN'S RIGHTS Stanton and Mott emerged as the leaders of the movement for women's rights. Stanton, who was raised in a wealthy family and educated at New York's Troy Female Seminary, married abolitionist Henry Brewster Stanton. Mott was from Massachusetts and housed African Americans who were trying to escape slavery in the South. In 1848, Mott and Stanton organized the **Seneca Falls Convention** in central New York—the first gathering of women's rights advocates in the United States. There, they issued the "Declaration of Sentiments and Resolutions," outlining the injustices women faced in American society and advocating for immediate change, especially in regard to voting rights.

CONTINUING THE WORK The campaign for women's rights began in the early 1800s, but the struggle continued throughout the 19th century. In 1851, Sojourner Truth, who had attended the Seneca Falls Convention, delivered a powerful speech at the Women's Rights Convention in Ohio. That same year, Elizabeth Cady Stanton met **Susan B. Anthony**, and the two women began a friendship and political partnership that lasted more than 50 years. In 1869, Anthony and Stanton founded the National Woman Suffrage Association (NWSA), the first national women's rights organization. The NWSA made securing women's voting rights its top priority but also proposed reforms on issues such as divorce.

KEY TAKEAWAYS

ORIGINS OF THE WOMEN'S MOVEMENT

- The fight for women's rights had its roots in the abolition movement, where female abolitionists gained public speaking and organizational experience. Some began to ask why women were not granted the same rights as men.
- When women earned wages outside of the home, their pay was much lower than the wages men received for doing the same job. In addition, married women could not own or purchase property or enter into financial contracts.
- Single women had all the property rights a man had but were taxed on that property by a government in which they had no voice.

SENECA FALLS CONVENTION

- In their Declaration of Sentiments, Stanton and Mott framed the injustices faced by women in the familiar language of the Declaration of Independence.
- The Declaration of Independence introduced the idea that all men are created equal. Stanton and Mott inserted "and women" into that fundamental idea.
- Even though they knew opponents of women's suffrage would claim the demand was outrageous, Stanton and Mott included women's right to vote as the first grievance in the Declaration of Sentiments.

THE MOVEMENT EXPANDS

- At the Women's Rights Convention in Ohio, Sojourner Truth drew the audience's attention to race in the fight for women's rights by asking in her speech, "Ain't I a woman?"
- Anthony and Stanton traveled together, delivered speeches to lawmakers, planned campaigns, and published *The Revolution*, a newspaper devoted to women's rights.
- Many people who supported equal rights for women also supported the temperance movement because of the impact of alcohol abuse on women and children.

AFTER THE CIVIL WAR

- During the 1850s and 1860s, issues regarding women's rights became less pressing because of the impending Civil War between the North and the South. However, after the war was over, women's rights activists picked up the cause again.
- Anthony believed the best way to bring attention to women's suffrage was to violate the law by voting. When she tried to vote in the 1872 election and was arrested, she refused to pay the fine.
- Mott, Stanton, Truth, Anthony, and many other women's rights activists dedicated their lives to securing political and social equality for women—some working until the day they died.

AMERICAN PLACES
Women's Rights National Historical Park

This park honors the women who produced the Declaration of Sentiments. The statues featured here are the centerpiece of the park's visitors' center lobby. The park is located in Seneca Falls, New York, because the first women's rights conference took place at a church there. The town was also home to three women's suffrage leaders.

HISTORICAL THINKING

1. **SUMMARIZE** Why was the Seneca Falls Convention significant?
2. **MAKE CONNECTIONS** In what ways were the movements for abolition and women's rights entwined?
3. **SYNTHESIZE** How did women's suffrage activists connect women's rights to the Founding Fathers' positions on equality and natural rights?

11.10.7 Analyze the women's rights movement from the era of Elizabeth Stanton and Susan Anthony and the passage of the Nineteenth Amendment to the movement launched in the 1960s, including differing perspectives on the roles of women; HI 1 Students show the connections, causal and otherwise, between particular historical events and larger social, economic, and political trends and developments.

MANIFEST DESTINY

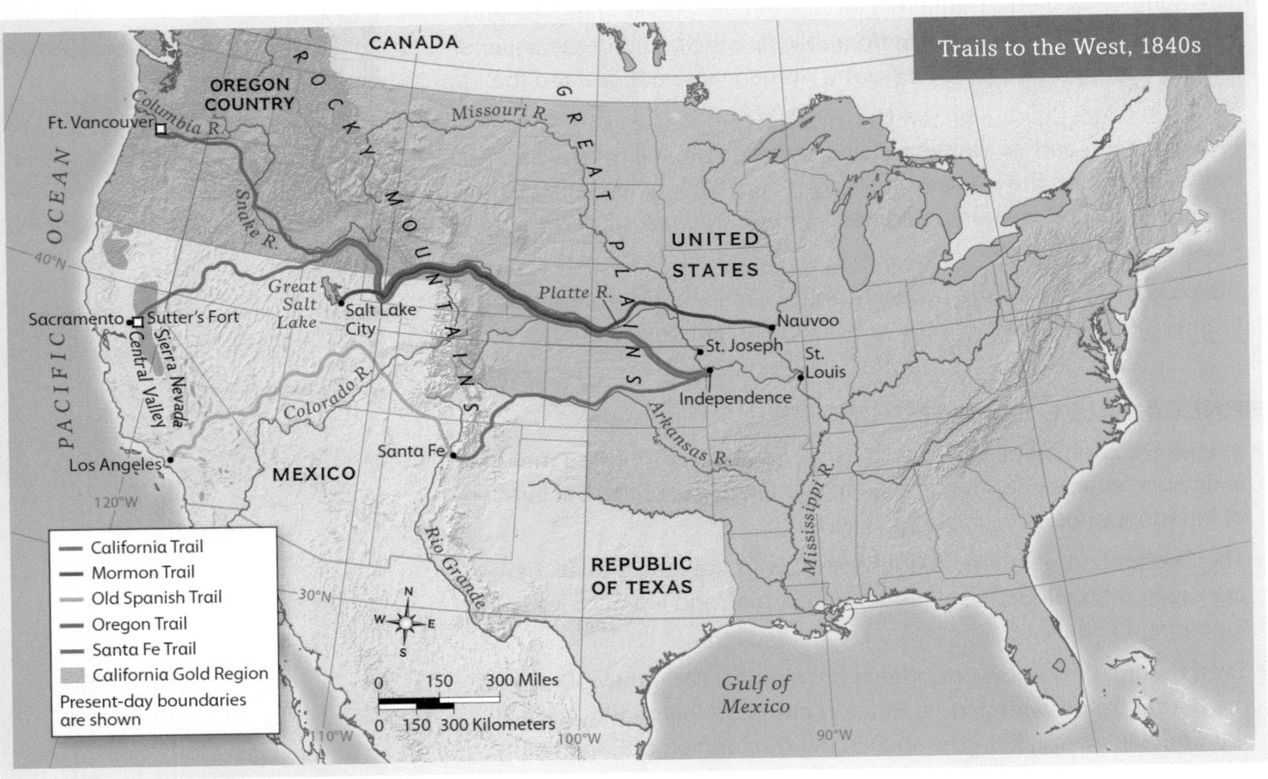

Americans began to explore, move to, and live in the West in the early 1800s. In 1806, Zebulon Pike led an expedition to discover the headwaters of the Arkansas River and was one of the first white men to explore the wilderness of Colorado. Many of the adventurous individuals who first moved to the frontier were fur trappers and explorers called mountain men. The mountain men's explorations opened up trails to the West.

THE PULL OF THE WEST In 1845, magazine editor John O'Sullivan wrote an editorial urging the United States to annex, or add, Texas as a state. He also wrote that Americans had a "manifest destiny to overspread and possess the whole of the continent." For several decades, the federal government pursued the territorial acquisition of western lands. The Oregon Territory, California, and Texas promised fertile farmland and a rich variety of resources. The desire for riches and the belief in manifest destiny inspired settlers and politicians to move westward.

TRAILS TO THE WEST In 1822, William Becknell opened a trade route from Independence, Missouri, to Santa Fe in Mexican territory. The route became known as the **Santa Fe Trail**. From Santa Fe, traders traveled to the Pacific coast along the Old Spanish Trail, which ran through territory controlled by Mexico, to bring goods to California. The Santa Fe Trail represented only one of several important routes to the West. Independence was also the starting point for two other major trails: the **Oregon Trail**, which led settlers to the Oregon Territory in the Northwest, and the **Mormon Trail**, which Mormons followed to present-day Utah in 1846.

DIFFICULT JOURNEYS The people moving to new and unfamiliar lands were called pioneers. They headed west in groups of covered wagons called wagon trains. The journey was grueling and took several months as wagon trains crossed rivers and mountains as well as arid lands where water and vegetation were scarce. The long days demanded difficult chores and wearying travel. In addition, westward trails passed through lands inhabited by various Native American tribes. Most encounters were friendly, and Native Americans and settlers engaged in trade and sometimes helped each other. However, conflicts did arise as new settlers intruded on Native American land.

8.8.2 Describe the purpose, challenges, and economic incentives associated with westward expansion, including the concept of Manifest Destiny (e.g., the Lewis and Clark expedition, accounts of the removal of Indians, the Cherokees' "Trail of Tears," settlement of the Great Plains) and the territorial acquisitions that spanned numerous decades.

KEY TAKEAWAYS

THE WEST OPENS

- The West inspired individualism, or a self-reliant independence, and the rugged life on the western frontier dramatically influenced our national self-image and sense of the American past.
- Several mountain men became legendary. Kit Carson was a successful fur trapper in California. Jedediah Smith explored more of the western territory than any other single person. Former slave Jim Beckwourth discovered a pass through the Sierra Nevada mountains.
- After the economic difficulties of the Panic of 1837, the West started to look attractive to unhappy easterners, new immigrants, independent women, and others who were seeking a new start in life.

MANIFEST DESTINY

- The word *manifest* means "obvious," and *destiny* refers to the unavoidable events of the future. By using the term, O'Sullivan was suggesting that the United States would—indeed, should—one day stretch from the Atlantic Ocean to the Pacific Ocean.
- O'Sullivan's editorial rested on the belief that God intended for white Protestant Americans to take over the continent, an idea that blatantly ignored the fact that people already lived on these lands.
- The belief in manifest destiny led to the territorial acquisition of western lands. The Oregon Territory offered timber, furs, rich fisheries, and ports on the Pacific Ocean. California promised fertile farmland, abundant mineral resources, and ports on the Pacific. Texas held deposits of minerals and metals, such as silver.

WESTWARD TRAILS

- The Santa Fe Trail and the Old Spanish Trail enabled traders to bring Mexican woolen goods to California and trade them for horses.
- Between 1840 and 1860, about 400,000 Americans traveled the Oregon Trail to settle in the present-day states of Oregon, Washington, Idaho, and parts of Montana.
- Mormons, members of the Church of Jesus Christ of Latter-day Saints, forged the Mormon Trail as they sought a new home where they could practice their religion. The Mormons had settled in Illinois but, because of the economic and political power they had achieved there, suffered violence from their non-Mormon neighbors.

PIONEERS AND NATIVE AMERICANS

- Pioneers dealt with severe weather, fought diseases such as cholera and typhoid, and worried constantly about running out of food, water, and supplies between settlements.
- Pioneer women performed tasks such as cooking and cleaning and worked alongside men tending to livestock and repairing wagons.
- Attacks by Native Americans were rare. Of the nearly 400,000 people who traveled the Oregon Trail in the mid-19th century, only about 400 were killed in attacks by Native Americans.

CURATING HISTORY
Autry Museum of the American West

John Gast's 1872 painting *American Progress*, which is displayed in this Los Angeles museum, depicts the "spirit of America" as a goddess-like woman bathed in light and floating westward. She is leading pioneers as they leave their settled communities and lives behind. The woman carries a schoolbook and strings telegraph wire as she moves across the open land. Notice Gast's use of light and dark and how Native Americans and wildlife seem to react to the people headed their way.

HISTORICAL THINKING

1. **SUMMARIZE** How did the concept of manifest destiny encourage Americans to move west?
2. **ANALYZE CAUSE AND EFFECT** What led the Mormons to move west?
3. **IDENTIFY MAIN IDEAS AND DETAILS** What challenges did pioneers face on the journey westward?
4. **ANALYZE VISUALS** What details in the painting above portray a positive view of westward settlement?

11.3.3 Cite incidences of religious intolerance in the United States (e.g., persecution of Mormons, anti-Catholic sentiment, anti-Semitism).

REVIEW LESSON 3.9

TEXAS INDEPENDENCE

A bronze statue of a Tejano sitting astride his horse is part of the striking Tejano Monument, located on the grounds of the Texas state capitol in Austin. The monument honors the contributions of Tejanos and their roles in shaping Tejas—and eventually Texas.

In the early 1800s, some westward-bound Americans ended up in the Spanish territory of **Tejas** (TAY-hahs), what we now know as the state of Texas. Spain was worried about U.S. influence, so it forbade its settlers of Spanish or Mexican descent, called Tejanos, from trading with the Americans. Still, many Tejanos and Americans conducted business illegally. Spain also limited trade between the Native Americans who lived in the territory and the Americans. Resentful of this restriction and distrustful of Spanish missionaries, the Native Americans attacked Spanish settlements.

SETTLEMENT OF TEXAS Relations between the United States and Tejas changed in 1821, when Mexico won its independence from Spain. The new nation of Mexico included the lands that make up present-day Texas, New Mexico, Arizona, California, Nevada, and Utah, as well as parts of Colorado and Wyoming. Few people lived in Tejas, and the Mexican government feared conflicts between Tejanos and Native Americans. Hoping that a larger population would stabilize the territory, Mexico offered land grants to encourage American immigration and settlement and, unlike Spain, welcomed trade between the two cultures.

REBELLION BY TEXANS Though it had invited American settlement, the Mexican government grew concerned as the population of Texas became more American and less Mexican. In response, Mexico placed a ban on further American settlement in Texas, hoping the move would encourage a stronger European presence and lead to the end of slavery in the territory. Texans—Americans and Tejanos alike—disliked these changes and eventually rebelled, triggering the Texas War for Independence. The war started in October 1835 with the Battle of Gonzales, a victory for Texas. More battles followed, including the siege of the **Alamo** and the decisive Texas victory in the Battle of San Jacinto (yah-SIN-toh) against Mexico's president, **Antonio López de Santa Anna**.

INDEPENDENCE AND ANNEXATION With its victory in the war, Texas became the Republic of Texas, an independent nation, in 1836. Texans elected **Sam Houston** as their first president and pushed for annexation by the United States. The United States initially rejected this plan, fearing that annexation might lead to war with Mexico. Also, admitting Texas into the Union would upset the balance between slave and free states.

KEY TAKEAWAYS

LAND GRANTS AND SETTLERS

- The Mexican government gave land grants to American farmers and merchants to persuade them to move to the territory.
- In 1820, when the Tejanos were still under Spanish rule, Moses Austin persuaded the Spanish governor to allow him to bring a few hundred families to settle in Tejas, but Austin died a year later.
- Austin's son, **Stephen F. Austin**, inherited the land grant and moved 300 American families into southeastern Tejas, establishing the territory's first legal American settlement.

GROWING NUMBER OF SETTLERS

- By 1830, about 21,000 Americans lived in Texas, including about 1,000 enslaved African Americans, leading Mexico to ban all further American settlement.
- Texans called for more representation within the Mexican government. They disagreed with Mexico's antislavery position. After staging revolts in 1832 and 1833, Texans declared that they wanted Texas statehood within Mexico.
- When Santa Anna rejected the demand for Texas statehood, Texans launched the Texas War for Independence.

TEXAS WAR FOR INDEPENDENCE

- After the Battle of Gonzales, Santa Anna led an army from Mexico City to put down the rebellion, reaching San Antonio by mid-February 1836, where he encountered roughly 180 Texans guarding the Alamo, a mission building.
- Battling 1,800 Mexican soldiers, the Texans managed to defend the Alamo for 13 days. On March 6, 1836, the Mexican Army breached the Alamo's walls and killed almost everyone inside.
- On April 21, Sam Houston, the Texan Army's commander, attacked the Mexican Army near the San Jacinto River and captured Santa Anna in the Battle of San Jacinto. Santa Anna agreed to withdraw and surrender, giving Texas its independence.

ANNEXATION OF TEXAS

- The newly independent Texas was nicknamed the Lone Star Republic to represent its defiance, pride, and independence.
- Most Texans favored annexation by the United States because Texas lacked an established economy and was vulnerable to further attacks from Mexico.
- Annexation gained support when James K. Polk was elected president in 1844. Polk supported manifest destiny. With Polk as president, Texas was admitted to the Union as the 28th state.

AMERICAN VOICES
Sam Houston

When the Texans won the Battle of San Jacinto, many of Sam Houston's soldiers called for the execution of Santa Anna. After all, the Mexican leader hadn't shown any mercy to the Texans at the Alamo. But Houston wanted independence for Texas, not revenge. He became the first president of the Republic of Texas. After the United States annexed Texas, Houston served as U.S. senator and later as governor of the state. This portrait of Houston by English artist Thomas Flintoff was painted during Houston's term as senator.

HISTORICAL THINKING

1. **DETERMINE CHRONOLOGY** What events led to American settlement of Texas?
2. **ANALYZE CAUSE AND EFFECT** Why did Texans rebel against the Mexican government?
3. **DRAW CONCLUSIONS** Describe the complexity of admitting Texas as a state as it relates to affecting the balance of slave states and free states.

8.8.5 Discuss Mexican settlements and their locations, cultural traditions, attitudes toward slavery, land-grant system, and economies; 8.8.6 Describe the Texas War for Independence and the Mexican-American War, including territorial settlements, the aftermath of the wars, and the effects the wars had on the lives of Americans, including Mexican Americans today; HI 2 Students recognize the complexity of historical causes and effects, including the limitations on determining cause and effect.

REVIEW LESSON 3.10 THE WAR WITH MEXICO

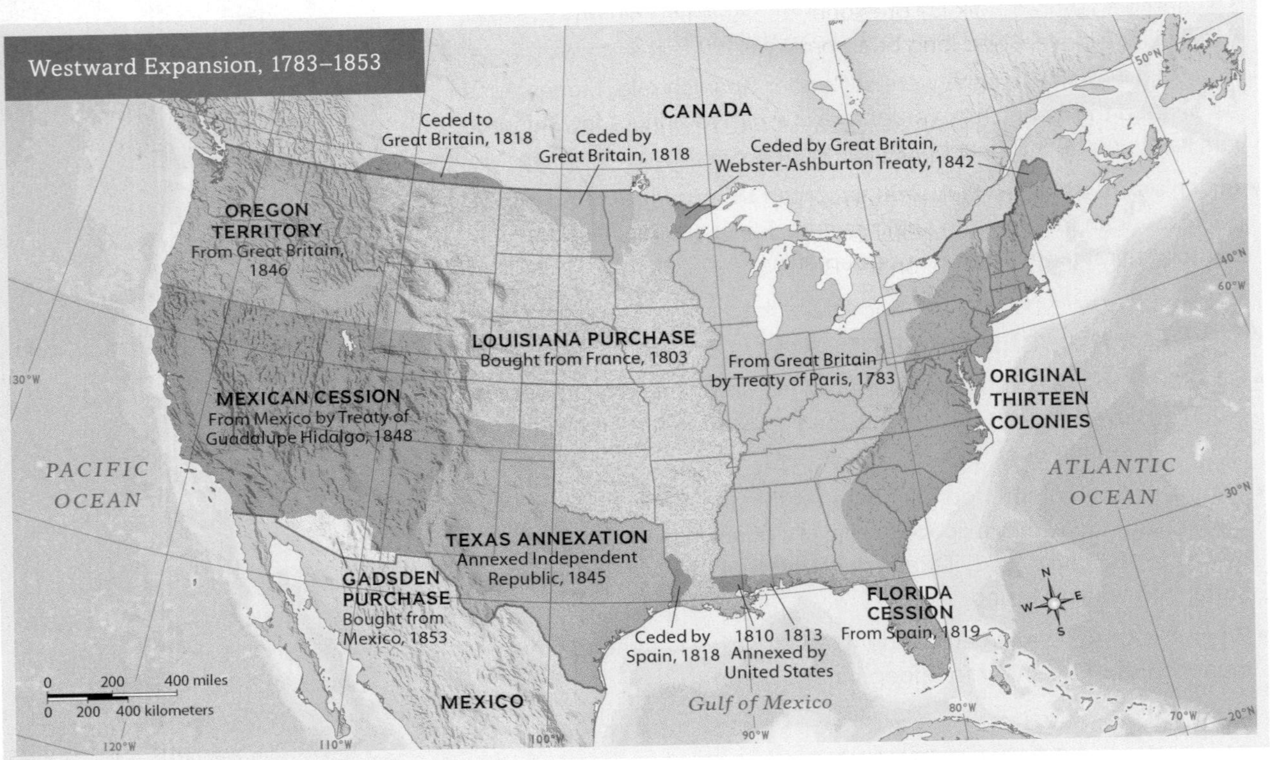

Relations between the United States and Mexico had been tense since the creation of the Republic of Texas. Mexican president Antonio López de Santa Anna had signed the Treaties of Velasco, giving Texas its independence, but the Mexican government never formally acknowledged the treaties as legal. Santa Anna had signed the treaties while he was a prisoner of the Texan Army, it argued, and therefore Texas was still a part of Mexico. Given this history, it's not surprising that Texas's annexation further worsened relations between the United States and Mexico.

EXPANDING THE COUNTRY As a candidate in the 1844 presidential election, James K. Polk had campaigned on a platform arguing not only for the annexation of Texas but also for the acquisition of California and Oregon. He believed the United States should take control of the Oregon Territory, up to the latitude of 54° 40′ N. In fact, one of Polk's campaign slogans was "Fifty-four forty or fight!" As president, Polk turned his political ambitions for expanding the country into policy. Under his leadership, Congress voted to annex Texas as a new slave state in 1845.

CROSSING THE NUECES RIVER When it was annexed, Texas extended only as far south as the Nueces River. Polk insisted that Texas's southern border should be the Rio Grande, much farther south than the Nueces. In July 1845, Polk sent American troops, led by General Zachary Taylor, to secure the area between the Rio Grande and the Nueces River. Polk also sent diplomat John Slidell to Mexico City with an offer to purchase California. However, the Mexican government refused to negotiate. Hearing about the snub, Polk told Taylor to advance on the Rio Grande. After American and Mexican troops clashed near the river, Polk called for war. Congress agreed, and the **Mexican-American War** began on May 13, 1846.

GAINING LAND AND VICTORY The United States had the upper hand from the start of the war. American troops claimed the New Mexico Territory and California for the United States in August 1846. In 1847, Taylor fought Santa Anna at Buena Vista in northern Mexico. Because Taylor was reluctant to mount a large-scale invasion of Mexico, Polk changed the American strategy and ordered General Winfield Scott to take his troops to Mexico by sea. Coming ashore at Veracruz, Scott and his men fought their way to Mexico City, forcing Mexico to surrender. The war officially ended in February 1848, when the United States and Mexico signed the **Treaty of Guadalupe Hidalgo**.

8.5.2. Know the changing boundaries of the United States and describe the relationships the country had with its neighbors (current Mexico and Canada) and Europe, including the influence of the Monroe Doctrine, and how those relationships influenced westward expansion and the Mexican-American War.

KEY TAKEAWAYS

POLK'S MISSION

- Southerners favored Polk for president because of his plans to annex Texas. Since slavery had long been practiced in Texas, it would enter the Union as a slave state.
- When Texas joined the Union as a slave state, northerners were infuriated because slave states then outnumbered free states.
- After Mexico ignored Polk's offer to extend the southern boundary of Texas to the Rio Grande and buy California for $25 million, Polk sent American troops to advance on the Rio Grande.
- A skirmish between American and Mexican troops near the Rio Grande led Polk to urge Congress to declare war on Mexico in 1846.

NEW MEXICO AND CALIFORNIA

- On June 14, 1846, American settlers in California proclaimed their land a republic after taking control of the town of Sonoma. The revolt is known as the Bear Flag Revolt.
- On August 18, 1846, General Stephen Kearny's troops marched into Santa Fe, the capital of the New Mexico Territory, to face the Mexican militia. They found the city unguarded and overtook it without a battle.
- The settlers elected John C. Frémont as leader of the Republic of California, but within days, American forces seized the area and claimed California for the United States in August 1846.

THE MEXICAN-AMERICAN WAR

- Taylor's campaign in northern Mexico seemed to be an even fight until Santa Anna withdrew his troops, leaving Taylor in control of the area.
- Scott and his men captured Veracruz after a three-week siege.
- After a fierce battle, Scott entered the capital, Mexico City, in September 1847 and raised the American flag in victory.

TREATY OF GUADALUPE HIDALGO

- The treaty set the Rio Grande as the border between Texas and Mexico and, in exchange for $15 million, gave the United States Mexico's northernmost territories.
- The addition of so much land worsened regional conflicts over slavery in the United States because the new territories were not part of the Missouri Compromise.
- At the same time, the United States and Britain compromised over the Oregon Territory, setting the northern border of the United States at the 49th parallel, or line of latitude.
- The Gadsden Purchase completed the borders of the contiguous, or connected, United States when Mexico sold land located along the southern edges of present-day Arizona

AMERICAN PLACES
Big Bend National Park

Big Bend National Park is a protected area of canyons and waterfalls at the southernmost bend of the Rio Grande in southwest Texas. The huge bend in the river curves around the largest protected portion of the Chihuahuan Desert, which stretches from central Mexico into the United States. The Rio Grande forms the border between the two countries for about 1,000 miles. At the beginning of the Mexican-American War in 1846, the border, and therefore access to this important river, was disputed.

HISTORICAL THINKING

1. **SEQUENCE EVENTS** What events led to the United State[s] declaring war on Mexico?
2. **DRAW CONCLUSIONS** Why do you think the United States was victorious over M[exico] in the war?
3. **INTERPRET MAPS** Locate present-day state borders. How ... states or parts of states were added to U.S. territory between 1803 and 1853?

8.8.6 D... the Mexican-American War, including territorial ... of the wars, and the effects the wars had on the ... Americans, including Mexican Americans today.

REVIEW LESSON 3.11 SETTLING CALIFORNIA

Long before the United States acquired California, Spanish conquistadors explored and claimed the area in the 16th century. The Spanish were slow to settle in California because the territory was so far from their base in Mexico. In the 1700s, however, British and Russian fur traders expanded westward into the region. Spain responded by establishing communities and founding missions in southern California in 1769. Father **Junípero Serra**, a Catholic priest from Spain, founded the first mission in California at San Diego.

GOLD RUSH! Americans came to settle in California while the territory belonged to Mexico. In the early 1840s, **John Sutter**, a Swiss immigrant, received land grants from the Mexican government to start a colony. By the late 1840s, Sutter's Fort, a huge, high-walled adobe structure in present-day Sacramento, was a thriving farm community that included a sawmill upstream on the American River. On January 24, 1848, workers spotted some gold at the mill. Word soon got out, and a gold rush was on.

In 1858, George W. Northrup posed as a prospector for a photo to send home to his family in Minnesota. He is holding a pickax, a hoe, a pan, and two pistols. Note that he also has a bag labeled "gold" on his lap.

FORTUNE-SEEKERS By the following year, around 80,000 gold-seekers had moved to California. Their arrival in 1849 earned them the nickname forty-niners. California's population increased ...ite rapidly because of the gold rus... Before 1848, about 1,000 non-n... ...e people lived there. By the end of 1849, that num... reached nearly 100,000. The forty-niners came from ...yer ...he United States and the world. Consequently, ...mi...g towns, or boomtowns, that sprang up to ...se ...d feed the forty-niners included diverse mi... ...f na... ...nalities and cultures.

THE MINING FRONT... ... Chile, Mexico, China and many o... crowding into California, ...omtowns in... ...from people who spoke ...ifferent languages, ha... customs, and practiced different religions. Women also came to California. They handled domestic duties for their households and sometimes took on housekeeping tasks for the single men living around them. Among white Americans, prejudices against Native Americans, African Americans, and Chinese immigrants often boiled over into fights. As California's population grew and lawlessness got ...ut of control, many people pushed for California to ...ate. They hoped a strong government ...lence.

KEY TAKEAWAYS

THE SPANISH AND MEXICANS IN CALIFORNIA

- Over time, the Spanish established 21 missions, including those at San Francisco, Santa Clara, and San Luis Obispo.
- The purpose of the missions was to convert Native Americans to Christianity, but some historians believe the Native Americans who lived at the missions were mistreated and enslaved.
- When Mexico gained independence from Spain in 1821, California became one of its northernmost territories. In 1824, Mexico passed an act granting large estates called *ranchos* to settlers.

GOLD IS DISCOVERED

- The California gold rush began when gold was exposed at Sutter's mill after a trickle of water left to run overnight washed away some loose dirt and gravel.
- At first, prospectors found easy access to a wealth of gold deposits, but much of the gold had been depleted by the time most of the fortune-seekers arrived.
- The discovery of gold gave rise to businesses providing goods and services to miners and other new residents of California.

THE FORTY-NINERS

- Most of the fortune-seekers who came to California were single men who hoped to find riches quickly and move on.
- Since slavery was not commonly practiced in California, many free African Americans tried their luck in the gold fields.
- Many *Californios*, or California residents of Spanish or Mexican descent, saw their legal rights ignored and their land seized by newcomers during the gold rush. Native Americans also suffered, dying by the thousands at the hands of gold miners or from the diseases the miners brought.

LIFE IN A MINING CAMP

- Gold rush boomtowns had neither law enforcement nor government of any kind. Thieves often got richer than gold miners.
- Cultural differences in the mining camps sometimes led to misunderstandings or even violence. Bored miners living far from home spent their free time gambling and fighting with each other.
- Many women discovered a liberating independence in California despite being outnumbered by men. Few laws existed to prohibit the women there from owning property or businesses.
- In September 1850, less than two years after gold was found at Sutter's Mill, California became the 31st state.

AMERICAN PLACES
San Francisco's Chinatown

The gold rush attracted thousands of immigrants from China, where they started communities in California towns. Busy, colorful, and thriving, San Francisco's Chinatown is a testament to these immigrants. United through heritage, culture, language, and economics, and living in a new and sometimes unwelcoming country, generations of Chinese immigrants established and still maintain a proud Chinese American community here.

HISTORICAL THINKING

1. **DETERMINE CHRONOLOGY** What events led to the migration of people to California?
2. **SUMMARIZE** What were the contributions and effects of different groups of people migrating to California?
3. **ANALYZE CAUSE AND EFFECT** How did the gold rush lead to statehood for California?

8.8.3. Describe the role of pioneer women and the new status that western women achieved (e.g., Laura Ingalls Wilder, Annie Bidwell; slave women gaining freedom in the West; Wyoming granting suffrage to women in 1869); 8.12.7 Identify the new sources of large-scale immigration and the contributions of immigrants to the building of cities and the economy; explain the ways in which new social and economic patterns encouraged assimilation of newcomers into the mainstream amidst growing cultural diversity; and discuss the new wave of nativism.

REVIEW CHAPTER 3

EXPANSION AND REFORM

ASSESSMENT

MAIN IDEAS

Choose the best answer for each question from the choices available.

1. How did the Lewis and Clark expedition foster westward expansion? HSS 8.8.2
   - A The expedition established the Santa Fe and Oregon trails.
   - B The expedition negotiated treaties with Native Americans in the West.
   - C The expedition helped Americans understand the physical geography of the West.
   - D The expedition guaranteed Americans access to the Mississippi River and the Port of New Orleans.

2. Which of the following technological developments had the greatest impact on the economy and society in the South? HSS 8.7.1
   - A steel plow
   - B cotton gin
   - C mechanical reaper
   - D power loom

3. What was Henry Clay's American System designed to do? HSS 8.6.2
   - A involve the federal government in improving transportation
   - B move the United States from a pre-industrial to a market economy
   - C balance the number of slave and free states
   - D establish and promote the Monroe Doctrine

4. How did the Monroe Doctrine attempt to influence foreign policy? HSS 8.5.2
   - A It promised to defend American allies in Europe in case of war.
   - B It declared U.S. intentions to annex Mexican and Canadian land.
   - C It called for tariff-free trade between North America and Europe.
   - D It warned European nations against interfering in the Western Hemisphere.

5. How did the Erie Canal benefit Americans? HSS 8.6.1
   - A It provided a route between New York City and Philadelphia.
   - B It allowed farmers to ship crops to California.
   - C It allowed farmers to ship their crops from New York to New Orleans.
   - D It improved trade between Americans and Native Americans.

6. How did Andrew Jackson show his opposition to the Second National Bank? HSS 8.8.1
   - A through a veto
   - B through tariffs
   - C through nullification
   - D through the spoils system

7. The "Trail of Tears" refers to what event? HSS 8.8.2
   - A the forced removal of the Cherokee
   - B the Mormons' search for a home in the West
   - C the forging of the Santa Fe Trail
   - D Lewis and Clark's expedition through the Rocky Mountains

8. How did John Quincy Adams show his support for abolition? HSS 8.9.1
   - A by supporting the Missouri Compromise
   - B by calling for the immediate end of slavery
   - C by proposing a constitutional amendment
   - D by founding and editing *The Liberator*

9. Charles Grandison Finney was a prominent figure in which movement? HSS 11.3.2
   - A the Second Great Awakening
   - B free public education
   - C mental health reform
   - D rights for workers

10. Which individuals are most closely associated with the Seneca Falls Convention? HSS 11.10.7
    - A Susan B. Anthony and Sojourner Truth
    - B Elizabeth Cady Stanton and Lucretia Mott
    - C Frederick Douglass and David Walker
    - D Sojourner Truth and Sarah Bagley

11. What document was the Declaration of Sentiments and Resolutions based on? HSS 11.10.7

A the Declaration of Independence
B the U.S. Constitution
C the Bill of Rights
D the Monroe Doctrine

12. What concept did Americans use to justify westward expansion in the mid-1800s? HSS 8.8.2

A Jacksonian democracy
B women's suffrage
C manifest destiny
D individualism

13. The Battle of the Alamo is associated with which conflict? HSS 8.8.6

A Bear Flag Revolt
B Mexican War of Independence
C Mexican American War
D Texas War for Independence

14. The annexation of Texas is associated with which of the following? HSS 8.8.6

A Monroe Doctrine
B Missouri Compromise
C Mexican-American War
D "Fifty-four forty or fight!"

15. What was one of the immediate effects of the Treaty of Guadalupe Hidalgo? HSS 8.8.6

A U.S. acquisition of California
B U.S. acquisition of Oregon
C U.S. acquisition of Texas
D the Gadsden Purchase

16. Which of these had the greatest impact on immigration to California? HSS 8.12.7

A Mexican land grants
B discovery of gold
C the mission system
D western trails

17. Who lived in the boomtowns that formed during the California gold rush? HSS 8.12.7

A people from all over the United States and the world
B mostly single white men
C mostly Chinese immigrants and free African Americans
D only white men and women

ANALYZE SOURCES

Margaret Fuller's *Woman in the Nineteenth Century*, published in 1845, presents an argument for women participating fully in society. Fuller points out that women constitute half of humanity. She goes on to argue that women's development contributes to the growth of men, too. Fuller makes the case that men are better off when women are able to lead fulfilling lives.

> Not a few believe, and men themselves have expressed the opinion that . . . the idea of Man, however imperfectly brought out, has been far more so [expressed] than that of Woman; . . . that she, the other half of the same thought, the other chamber of the heart of life, needs now take her turn in the full pulsation, and that improvement in the daughters will best aid in the reformation of the sons of this age.

18. Why do you think Fuller describes women as "the other half of the same thought"? HSS 11.10.7

19. What do you think Fuller is suggesting when she says, "improvement in the daughters will best aid in the reformation of the sons of this age"? HSS 11.10.7

WRITE ABOUT HISTORY

20. **EXPLANATORY** Think about a 19th-century reform movement and a cause you support today. What common threads can you trace between then and now? Write a paragraph in which you describe how the cause you support can trace its roots to reform movements of the past, including lessons learned. HSS CST 1

TIPS

- Consider the mix of reforms happening at this time, and list the facts and details that best align with the cause you support.
- Explain your reasons for supporting your cause, and connect them with the reasons of early reformers.
- Provide a concluding statement that follows from the information you have presented.

REVIEW CHAPTER 4

CIVIL WAR AND RECONSTRUCTION

1850–1877

HISTORICAL THINKING What led to the Civil War, and what was its aftermath?

AMERICAN STORIES ONLINE **Civil War Naval Battles**

AMERICAN STORIES ONLINE **The Post–Civil War North**

AMERICAN GALLERY ONLINE **The Battle of Vicksburg**

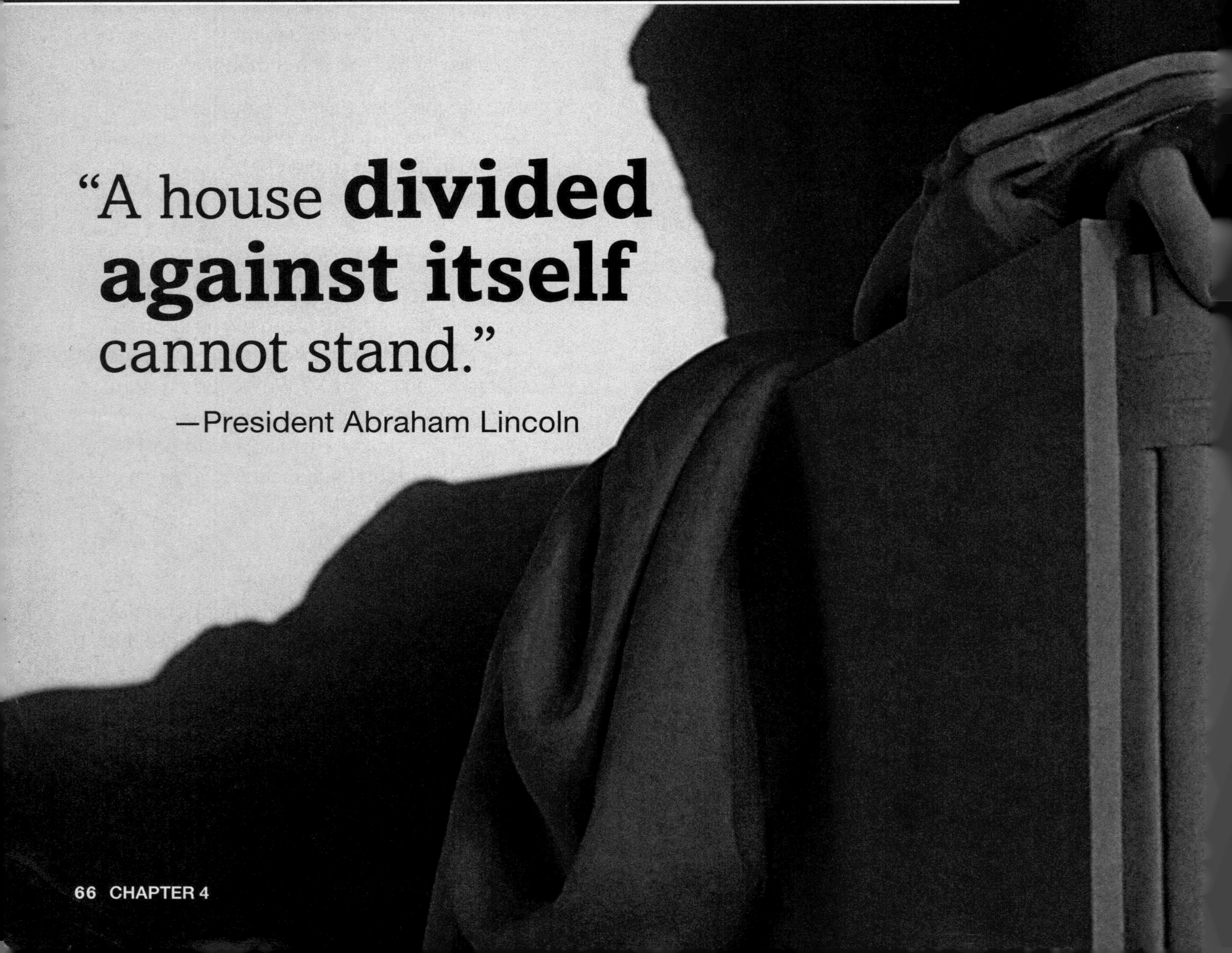

"A house **divided against itself** cannot stand."

—President Abraham Lincoln

CRITICAL VIEWING Completed in 1922, this statue of a seated Abraham Lincoln is situated within the Lincoln Memorial in Washington, D.C. At 19 feet tall and 19 feet wide, it's no wonder it took the sculptor Daniel Chester French 4 years to carve. Why might the sculptor have chosen to make his statue so large?

REVIEW LESSON 4.1 SLAVERY IN THE STATES AND TERRITORIES

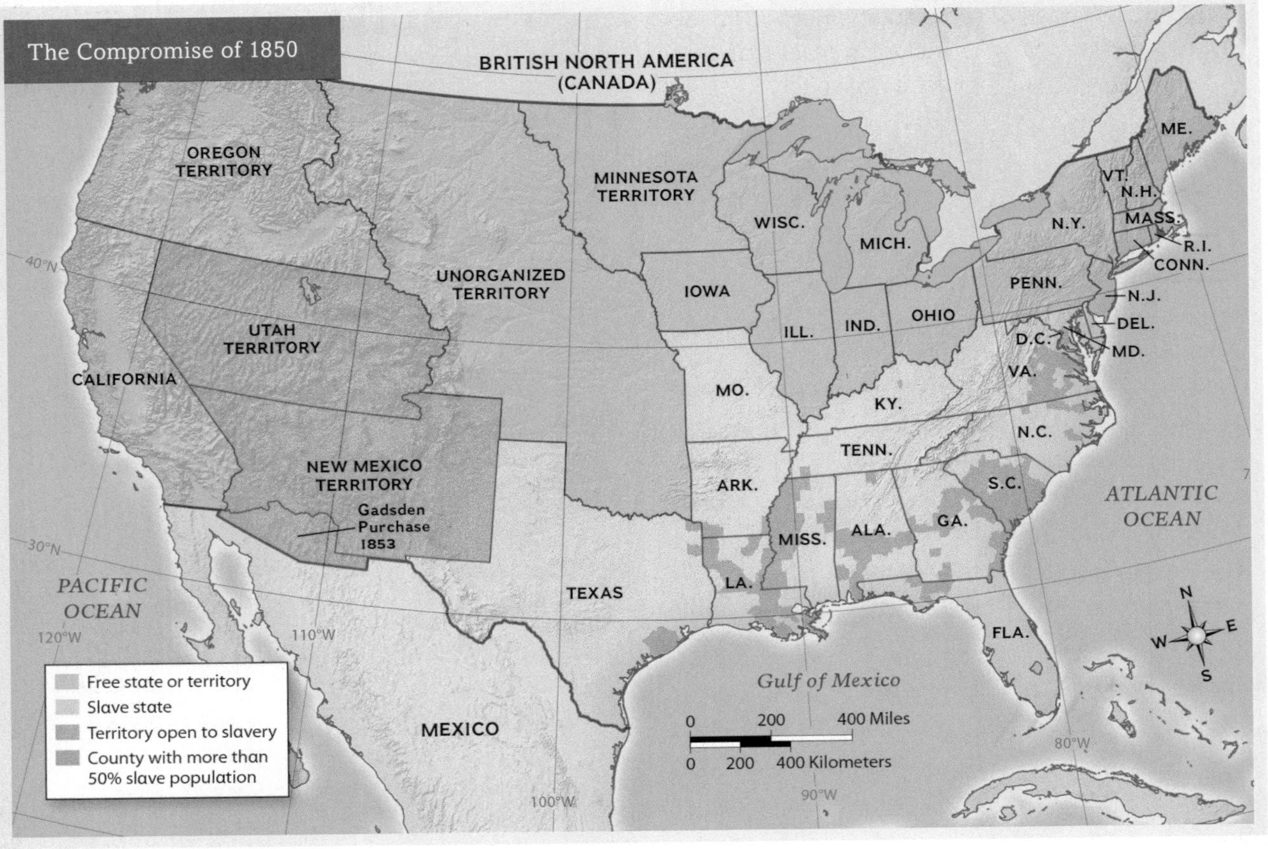

By the mid-1800s, slavery had become so divisive that political leaders could not continue to ignore it. Americans were rapidly populating new territories in the western frontiers, in part due to a gold rush, and those territories were applying for statehood. The main question at hand was whether slavery should be allowed in new territories and states.

CONTROVERSY OVER TERRITORIES The agricultural economy of the South depended on slavery. To protect those interests, southern senators insisted that slaveholding states and the nation's free states maintain equal political power. California's application for admission as a free state in 1849 sent the nation into crisis. If granted, free states would outnumber slaveholding states, and the Missouri Compromise of 1820 would no longer keep the peace between political rivals. As a result, southern states threatened to secede from the Union. Senator **Henry Clay** of Kentucky offered a compromise bill to resolve the free vs. slaveholding argument and settle questions regarding the new territories. After months of debate, the **Compromise of 1850** became law.

SLAVERY AND RACISM By 1860, nearly 4 million enslaved African Americans lived in the South. Most of them led difficult lives marked by fear, overwork, and cruelty due to laws that kept them enslaved. Racist laws also affected the few free African Americans living there. The laws restricted the daily lives of African Americans so much that many tried to escape. However, the situation in the North wasn't much better. Northern states had outlawed slavery and allowed African Americans to meet in groups, but they still endured the same racist attitudes and discrimination as those in the South.

RUNAWAY SLAVES To appease the South, one part of the Compromise of 1850 put more teeth into an earlier law regarding escaped slaves. The new, harsher **Fugitive Slave Act** forced ordinary citizens in both regions to capture runaway slaves and assigned marshals to enforce the law. People who aided escapees faced the possibility of being thrown in jail, and captured fugitives were returned to their owners without a trial. Many northerners were outraged by the act and openly defied it.

8.7.4 Compare the lives of and opportunities for free blacks in the North with those of free blacks in the South; 8.9.4 Discuss the importance of the slavery issue as raised by the annexation of Texas and California's admission to the union as a free state under the Compromise of 1850.

KEY TAKEAWAYS

AFRICAN AMERICANS IN THE SOUTH

- The South's agrarian economy relied on slavery and the slave trade. Without slavery, the plantation system would collapse.
- The racist attitudes of some southerners justified slavery as an institution. Many citizens, including plantation owners, believed that African Americans were inferior to whites.
- Local laws enforced discrimination against free African Americans by preventing people from assembling in large groups, including in churches and schools, and restricting where they could live and work.

AFRICAN AMERICANS IN THE NORTH

- African Americans experienced similar discrimination in the North as in the South. Many northerners did not want to live near, work with, or have their children attend school with African Americans.
- In some states, laws prevented African Americans from voting, owning property, or moving about freely. Laws did not protect free African Americans from being captured and sent into slavery in the South.
- African Americans could freely gather, but segregation prevented African Americans from living, working, or attending schools and churches in white neighborhoods.

THE COMPROMISE OF 1850

- After the Mexican-American War, the United States gained new territory in the West. The short supply of land in the East and the 1848 discovery of gold in California spurred rapid settlement of this region.
- Whigs and antislavery Democrats formed the Free-Soil Party, which was a political group dedicated to preventing slavery in the new states and territories. To relieve the conflict between them and proslavery politicians, Senator Henry Clay drafted the Compromise of 1850.
- Senator John C. Calhoun of South Carolina supported slavery and opposed the compromise, arguing for states' rights and the secession of southern states. He passionately debated Senator Daniel Webster of Massachusetts, who advocated for the compromise.
- The Compromise of 1850 established California as a free state, defined the boundaries of Texas, declared that popular sovereignty would decide the status of slavery in the territories, and enacted a harsher version of the Fugitive Slave Act.

THE FUGITIVE SLAVE ACT

- The new Fugitive Slave Act enforced greater penalties on runaway slaves and compelled citizens to help capture fugitives.
- The act tasked federal marshals with enforcing the new law.
- The northern states responded defiantly. Some states passed laws to protect runaway slaves, while some individuals actively resisted the act by confronting slave catchers and freeing imprisoned fugitives.

Spinning wheel

CURATING HISTORY

The Henry Ford Museum

The museum in Dearborn, Michigan, has dedicated an entire exhibit to agriculture, including artifacts from the cotton industry. Cotton was the primary driver of the South's economy. Before the invention of the cotton gin in 1793 enabled enslaved laborers to harvest more cotton, many households used a spinning wheel to spin cotton fibers into thread for sewing and weaving. With larger cotton crops, more thread and cloth was manufactured in textile mills.

HISTORICAL THINKING

1. **COMPARE AND CONTRAST** How were the lives of free African Americans in the North and those in the South similar, and how were they different?
2. **IDENTIFY PROBLEMS AND SOLUTIONS** What issues did the Compromise of 1850 resolve?
3. **MAKE INFERENCES** In what ways did the Fugitive Slave Act impact slaves in the South?

REVIEW LESSON 4.2 STATES' RIGHTS

This 1918 painting, *Abraham Lincoln and Stephen A. Douglas Debating at Charleston* by Robert Marshall Root, shows one of the many debates between the two men. In the scene, Lincoln addresses the crowd gathered for the outdoor event in Charleston, Illinois. Douglas sits to Lincoln's right, waiting his turn to speak.

After California became a state in 1850, its citizens needed transportation and communication to and from the East Coast. Senator **Stephen A. Douglas** of Illinois proposed building a railroad from Chicago to San Francisco. The tracks would run north of the latitude designated in the Missouri Compromise as the line between free and slave states. Southerners resented that the new railroad would only service the North, and once again the issue of slavery threatened national unity.

"BLEEDING KANSAS" Douglas responded with a new bill called the **Kansas-Nebraska Act** in 1854 that repealed the Missouri Compromise and established that popular sovereignty would determine a new state's slavery status. As a result, both proslavery and antislavery groups in Kansas sought to influence the vote. After the proslavery factions won the election, the antislavery Free-Soilers elected their own government. In 1856, violence erupted between the two governments, and politicians from both sides were convicted of murder. The murders earned the state a grim nickname: "Bleeding Kansas." A militant abolitionist named **John Brown** added to the violence in the state.

DRED SCOTT* V. *SANDFORD The *Dred Scott* v. *Sandford* lawsuit, first filed in 1846, further agitated the national controversy over slavery. Dred Scott, an enslaved African American, sued for his freedom, arguing that his owner had taken him to live in free parts of the country. In 1857, the Supreme Court ruled that Scott's case had no merit because African Americans were not U.S. citizens and had no right to sue. Furthermore, the court determined that since slaves were private property, the federal government could not regulate slavery in the territories.

LINCOLN AND DOUGLAS In the 1858 Illinois senate race, the challenger **Abraham Lincoln,** representing the newly formed Republican Party, and the Democratic incumbent Stephen Douglas held a series of public debates. Although Illinois was a free state, the debates centered on the issue of slavery in the United States. Both men opposed slavery, but they differed on how to resolve the matter. Douglas supported states' rights and believed the issue should be handled impartially. Lincoln, meanwhile, argued that a "house divided against itself cannot stand" and that the country could not continue to exist "half slave and half free."

8.9.1 Describe the leaders of the movement (e.g., John Quincy Adams and his proposed constitutional amendment, John Brown and the armed resistance, Harriet Tubman and the Underground Railroad, Benjamin Franklin, Theodore Weld, William Lloyd Garrison, Frederick Douglass).

KEY TAKEAWAYS

THE KANSAS-NEBRASKA ACT

- Douglas called for the territory west of Minnesota, Iowa, and Missouri to be divided into two states, Kansas and Nebraska.
- To appease the South, Congress repealed the Missouri Compromise, which banned slavery in those territories, in favor of the Kansas-Nebraska Act and states' rights.
- Popular sovereignty would decide policies of slavery in the new states.

VIOLENCE IN KANSAS

- In an effort to swing the vote in Kansas against slavery, members of the Free-Soil Party encouraged abolitionists to settle there.
- Slavery supporters from Missouri called "border ruffians" crossed the state line to vote illegally in Kansas.
- Proslavery forces won control of the Kansas legislature and imposed harsh laws against those who opposed slavery. In response, the Free-Soilers created their own government within the territory and set out to write a new constitution.
- In 1856, a proslavery mob attacked the antislavery town of Lawrence, Kansas. In turn, abolitionist John Brown and his followers murdered five men in the proslavery town of Pottawatomie Creek.

DRED SCOTT AND JOHN BROWN

- The 1857 ruling by Chief Justice Roger Taney in the *Dred Scott* v. *Sandford* case further heightened tensions regarding slavery. Taney declared that African Americans were not U.S. citizens, that slaves were private property, and that the federal government had no constitutional right to regulate slavery.
- The *Dred Scott* decision rendered the Missouri Compromise of 1820, which had banned slavery in northwestern states, unconstitutional.
- John Brown, hoping to trigger a slave revolt, led a raid on Harpers Ferry, in what was then Virginia. His band of 21 men captured a federal arsenal and took dozens of prisoners.
- Although Brown was soon captured and hanged, many northerners sympathized with his actions, which only infuriated southerners more.

LINCOLN-DOUGLAS DEBATES

- Antislavery leaders founded the new Republican Party in 1854 to oppose the expansion of slavery in the territories and new states.
- Lincoln personally opposed slavery on moral grounds, but his main concern was his belief that the Union could not continue as partly free and partly slaveholding.
- Douglas also opposed slavery but believed in a state's right to choose according to the will of its people. He accused Lincoln of favoring racial equality, a tactic aimed at turning voters against Lincoln.

8.9.2 Discuss the abolition of slavery in early state constitutions; 8.9.5 Analyze the significance of the States' Rights Doctrine, the Missouri Compromise (1820), the Wilmot Proviso (1846), the Compromise of 1850, Henry Clay's role in the Missouri Compromise and the Compromise of 1850, the Kansas-Nebraska Act (1854), the *Dred Scott* v. *Sandford* decision (1857), and the Lincoln-Douglas debates (1858); 11.10.2 Examine and analyze the key events, policies, and court cases in the evolution of civil rights, including *Dred Scott* v. *Sandford*, *Plessy* v. *Ferguson*, *Brown* v. *Board of Education*, *Regents of the University of California* v. *Bakke*, and California Proposition 209.

AMERICAN PLACES

Harpers Ferry

Ken Garrett, National Geographic photographer, took this aerial view of the town of Harpers Ferry, West Virginia. At the meeting of the Potomac and Shenandoah rivers, the town is the site of John Brown's 1859 raid on the local armory. Once a part of Virginia, Harpers Ferry is now the easternmost town in West Virginia. Because of its historical significance, as well as its natural beauty, the locale became a national park in 1963. The old firehouse, now called John Brown's Fort, remains today.

HISTORICAL THINKING

1. **SUMMARIZE** Why did the Kansas Territory become known as "Bleeding Kansas"?
2. **DRAW CONCLUSIONS** How did John Brown's raid at Harpers Ferry increase tensions between the North and the South?
3. **SYNTHESIZE** How did the *Dred Scott* case render the Missouri Compromise of 1820 unconstitutional?
4. **ANALYZE CAUSE AND EFFECT** Why did Douglas write the Kansas-Nebraska Act?

THE UNDERGROUND RAILROAD AND HARRIET TUBMAN

African-American artist Jacob Lawrence captured the spirit of the Underground Railroad in his moody, nighttime painting called *Forward Together*. Harriet Tubman is believed to be the figure wearing the red cloak on the right.

The **Underground Railroad** developed as a secret system that helped southern slaves escape to the North. The system functioned for about 50 years, from around 1810 to 1860. Few records exist of how the operation worked, and no one is certain how many people ran it. Some estimates suggest the Underground Railroad helped 100,000 enslaved people achieve freedom.

ESCAPE ROUTES The Underground Railroad consisted of a network of escape routes for slaves to follow. Most fugitives traveled on foot for miles from one way station to the next. They were guided by word of mouth and by "conductors" who escorted them through the railroad's hidden networks. Routes led to northern states and to Canada, where slavery had been banned in the 1830s. However, fugitives had to evade professional bounty hunters, who operated legally in the northern states, throughout the journey. Fugitives also risked the safety of the people who helped them because the conductors were often prosecuted.

UNDERGROUND CONDUCTOR One woman who escaped slavery on the Underground Railroad was **Harriet Tubman**. Tubman had worked for an abusive plantation overseer in Maryland before she escaped to Pennsylvania in 1849. After her escape she frequently endangered herself by returning to slave-holding states as an Underground Railroad conductor. For eight years, she guided other fugitives to freedom. In this capacity, Tubman became a hero of the Underground Railroad, and her achievements are still celebrated today.

LIFE ON THE UNDERGROUND RAILROAD Enslaved men and women were desperate people, and some took dangerous measures to escape from the South. To maintain secrecy, the people operating the Underground Railroad used code words and phrases. Much of this terminology was either biblical in origin or borrowed from railway vocabulary. The terminology made coded conversations seem as ordinary as business transactions, so they attracted less attention in public places.

8.6.4 Study the lives of black Americans who gained freedom in the North and founded schools and churches to advance their rights and communities; 8.7.2 Trace the origins and development of slavery; its effects on black Americans and on the region's political, social, religious, economic, and cultural development; and identify the strategies that were tried to both overturn and preserve it (e.g., through the writings and historical documents on Nat Turner, Denmark Vesey).

KEY TAKEAWAYS

THE UNDERGROUND RAILROAD

- The Underground Railroad involved many safe houses, safe businesses, and people who helped fleeing slaves reach the northern states and Canada.
- Fugitives usually traveled by night and hid during the day.
- Homes and other buildings served as "stations" in which fugitives could rest and eat.

HARRIET TUBMAN'S EARLY LIFE

- Harriet Tubman was born a slave in Maryland around 1822. Her birth name was Araminta Ross.
- Three of Harriet's eight siblings were sold to another owner when she was young. When their owner was about to sell her youngest brother, Harriet's mother successfully protested the transaction.
- Tubman suffered from seizures and severe headaches due to a blow to the head she received from an overseer.
- Following the death of her owner in 1849, Tubman escaped to Pennsylvania in order to avoid being sold to a new owner.

CONDUCTOR AND MILITARY LEADER

- Tubman became a conductor on the Underground Railroad and helped to recruit other conductors.
- Tubman returned to Maryland 19 times to lead more than 300 people from that state to freedom.
- During the Civil War, Tubman worked as an armed scout and spy and led a raid to free slaves in South Carolina. Before the raid, she was sent to the area to gather intelligence on the local land features and the movements of the Confederate Army.
- In 2016, the U.S. Treasury announced that an image of Harriet Tubman would replace Andrew Jackson's image on the $20 bill, beginning in the 2020s.

SURVIVAL ON THE UNDERGROUND RAILROAD

- For both escapees and sympathetic aides, the Underground Railroad was very dangerous. Bounty hunters used harsh and violent methods to capture fugitives.
- The Fugitive Slave Act of 1850 enforced tough penalties against people who helped any fugitive.
- Most of the people who bravely helped escapees were free African Americans, but some were white abolitionists or Quakers.
- The special terminology used on the Underground Railroad included train-related words such as "conductor," "station," and "agent." Other terms, including Tubman's code name "Moses," came from the Bible or other everyday sources.

AMERICAN VOICES
Harriet Tubman

Harriet Tubman is the most recognized hero of the Underground Railroad. She continued helping others after the Civil War. She established a home for elderly and disabled African Americans in Auburn, New York, where she moved and remarried. She raised money to support schools for freed slaves and campaigned for women's suffrage. Today, Tubman is honored as a great American patriot and humanitarian.

HISTORICAL THINKING

1. **IDENTIFY MAIN IDEAS AND DETAILS** Explain how the Underground Railroad worked and what role Harriet Tubman played in its operation.
2. **DESCRIBE** What were some of the qualities Tubman possessed that helped her in her work on the Underground Railroad?
3. **DRAW CONCLUSIONS** Why is Tubman a fitting choice to appear on U.S. currency?

8.9.1 Describe the leaders of the movement (e.g., John Quincy Adams and his proposed constitutional amendment, John Brown and the armed resistance, Harriet Tubman and the Underground Railroad, Benjamin Franklin, Theodore Weld, William Lloyd Garrison, Frederick Douglass).

REVIEW LESSON 4.4

ABRAHAM LINCOLN

As the 1860 election drew near, the United States approached a political crisis. The violence in Kansas, the *Dred Scott* court case decision, and the raid on Harpers Ferry intensified passions and further divided the nation on the question of slavery. Adding to the crisis, arguments among Democrats caused the party to split, and another political group formed to preserve the Union and protect the Constitution.

This 1860 photo by Alexander Hesler reveals Lincoln's lined face and rugged features.

THE NOMINATION OF LINCOLN In 1860, the Republican Party held its national convention in Chicago and nominated Abraham Lincoln, a successful lawyer from a modest background in Illinois. He had served as an Illinois state representative and became famous for his passionate political debates. In addition to Lincoln, three other candidates ran for president that year—Stephen Douglas of the northern Democrats, John Breckinridge of the southern Democrats, and John Bell of the Constitutional Unionists. However, Lincoln became president.

THE CONFEDERACY FORMS Lincoln's victory outraged southerners because the new president had been elected without winning a single southern state. He and the Republicans wanted to prevent the spread of slavery to new states, but southerners suspected he wished to abolish slavery altogether.

In the time between Lincoln's election and his presidency, southern politicians discussed and debated the formation of a separate nation. South Carolina declared its secession from the Union first, and 10 other states followed. These states formed a new nation called the Confederate States of America, or the **Confederacy**. The states also announced a president and adopted a new Constitution that protected slavery and embraced states' rights. Kentucky, Maryland, Delaware, and Missouri held off joining the Confederacy in the hope of a resolution between the two sides. They never seceded from the Union.

LINCOLN'S FIRST YEAR Abraham Lincoln took office in November 1860. To fill his Cabinet, he chose politicians he knew would challenge his opinions. He believed their opposing views would better inform his decisions. He and his administration sprang into action immediately to condemn the seceding states and declare his intentions to protect the Union. Meanwhile, tensions were rising at **Fort Sumter**, a federal property in Charleston, South Carolina, which Confederate forces demanded the U.S. Army evacuate. After President Lincoln approved a shipment to resupply the Union soldiers in the fort, Confederate forces bombarded it. The battle continued for 34 hours.

KEY TAKEAWAYS

ELECTION OF 1860

- Four candidates ran for president in 1860, representing the Republican Party, the two factions of the Democratic Party, and the new Constitutional Unionist Party.
- The Republicans nominated Abraham Lincoln, considered a moderate, as their candidate.
- Lincoln won both the electoral and popular vote, even though he received no electoral votes from the South.

LINCOLN'S LIFE

- Lincoln grew up in a poor family on frontier farms in Kentucky and Indiana. His mother died when he was nine. He had little formal education, but he loved to read.
- When he was 21, he moved to Illinois, taught himself law, and became a lawyer.
- He served four terms in the Illinois state assembly and one term in the U.S. House of Representatives.
- Lincoln gained recognition from his famous "House Divided" speech and his heated 1858 Senate debates with Stephen Douglas.

SOUTHERN SECESSION

- Just over one month after Lincoln won the 1860 presidential election, South Carolina became the first state to secede.
- The Confederate States of America, made up of seceded southern states, formed a new republic in 1861. **Jefferson Davis**, a senator from Mississippi, was named its temporary president.
- Senator **John J. Crittenden** of Kentucky proposed a Union-preserving constitution based on the reinstatement of the 1820 Missouri Compromise line, which would permanently protect slavery in southern states. After much debate, Congress defeated the Crittenden Plan.

PRESIDENT LINCOLN

- Lincoln selected Republicans who held widely opposing views for his Cabinet. Historians, such as Doris Kearns Goodwin, have come to refer to Lincoln's Cabinet as a team of rivals.
- In his first Inaugural Address, Lincoln rejected the southern secession, declaring it illegal. In his view, the Union still existed, and it was his duty as president to protect it.
- Immediately after Lincoln's inauguration, Confederate forces surrounded the island on which Fort Sumter was built. The Union Army inside refused to leave, and on April 12, 1861, the Confederates attacked. After two days, the men stationed in the fort surrendered.
- The attack on Fort Sumter marked the beginning of the Civil War.

8.10.4 Discuss Abraham Lincoln's presidency and his significant writings and speeches and their relationship to the Declaration of Independence, such as his "House Divided" speech (1858), Gettysburg Address (1863), Emancipation Proclamation (1863), and inaugural addresses (1861 and 1865); HI 1 Students show the connections, causal and otherwise, between particular historical events and larger social, economic, and political trends and developments.

AMERICAN PLACES

Fort Sumter

Fort Sumter, built after the War of 1812 with Britain, stands on a small island in Charleston Harbor. The five-sided brick structure was one of a series of forts constructed for coastal defense against outside aggression. Instead, it became the site of the first battle of the Civil War in 1861.

No one was killed during the fort's bombardment, but two Union soldiers accidentally died during a 100-gun salute. Two years later, the fort was destroyed in a second battle. Today the property is part of the Fort Sumter National Monument, operated by the National Park Service and open to visitors.

HISTORICAL THINKING

1. **DETERMINE CHRONOLOGY** What events led to the Republican nomination of Abraham Lincoln for president?
2. **DRAW CONCLUSIONS** How did Lincoln's Cabinet selections reflect the national mood?
3. **SYNTHESIZE** What was the connection between the concept of states' rights and the secession of the southern states?

EW
SON

4.5 STRATEGIC ADVANTAGES AND DISADVANTAGES

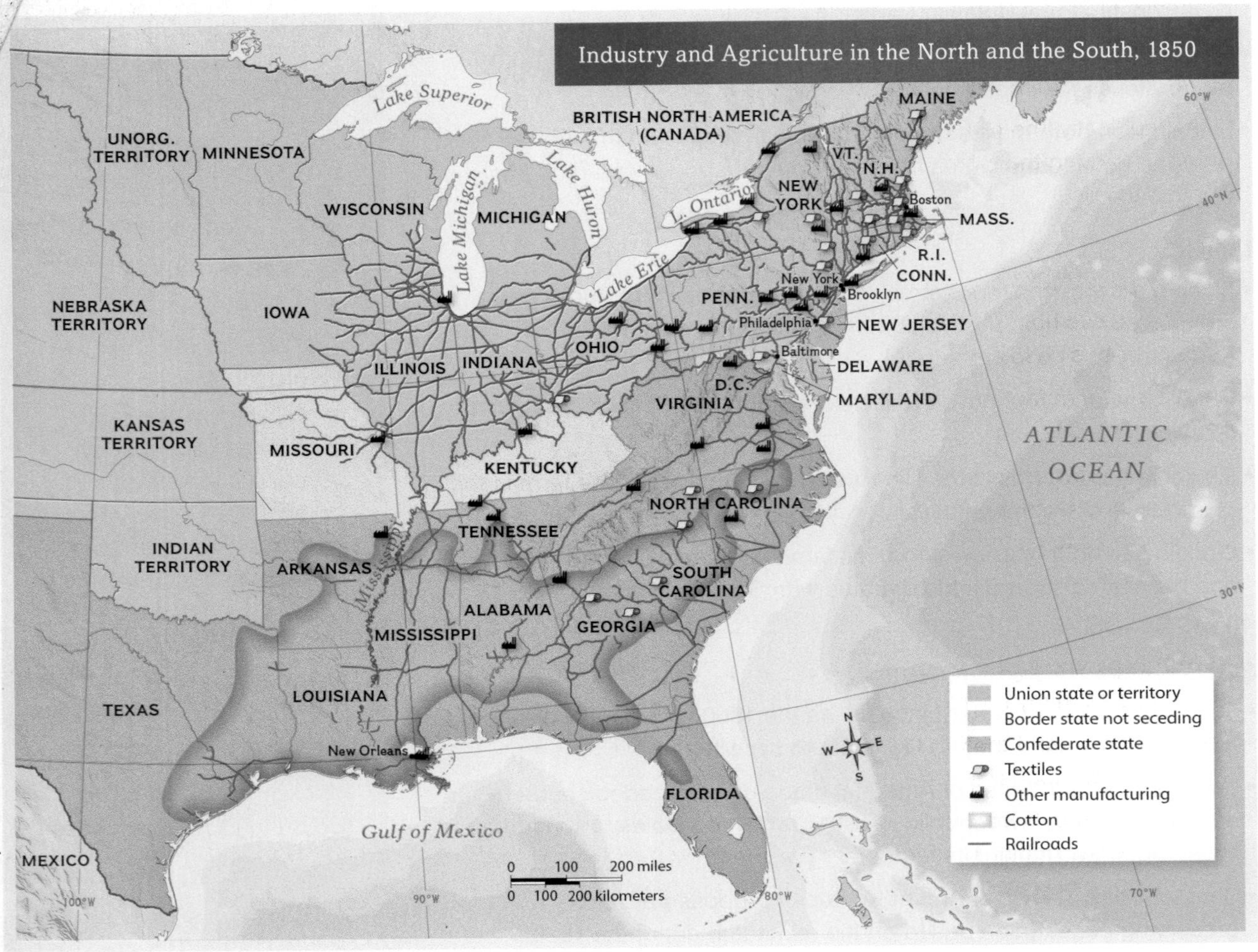

In fighting the Civil War, the Union and the Confederacy each had strategic advantages and disadvantages based on geography, population, economy, railroad routes, and military capabilities. These factors were as critically important to the war's outcome as any military general's strategies or the enthusiasm of the troops for the righteousness of their cause.

PEOPLE AND LAND Throughout the war, the Union had a much larger population than the Confederacy. With more than three times as many free men of military age, the North had the larger army, which made all the difference. However, a higher percentage of southern men joined the Confederate Army, so the Union's military only outnumbered the Confederacy's by about two to one. Most battles were fought in the South where Confederate soldiers knew the terrain.

INDUSTRY AND RAILROADS Industries such as iron and steel manufacturing were critically important during the war. The Union dominated both industries. The North also had more railroads, which was another distinct advantage. On the other hand, the South grew most of the world's cotton. Selling cotton overseas—and even to textile mills in the North—stabilized the Confederacy's economy.

MILITARY READINESS The Union had not only a bigger army but a better organized military than the Confederacy. The Union had more infrastructure, better transportation and communication systems, and better access to the latest advances in weaponry to support its troops. The Union enjoyed a larger and better equipped navy. It also was home to the country's foremost military academy, **West Point**, in New York; however, both northern and southern officers had trained there.

8.10.2 Trace the boundaries constituting the North and the South, the geographical differences between the two regions, and the differences between agrarians and industrialists.

KEY TAKEAWAYS

POPULATION AND GEOGRAPHY

- In 1860, the North had more than 3 times as many free men of fighting age than the South. However, a higher percentage of southern men volunteered to join the Confederate Army.
- The Union's population spread over a wide geographic area, from Maine to California, including the western territories.
- Geographically, the war was fought mostly in the South, which gave an advantage to the Confederates because they were fighting on familiar terrain.

INDUSTRY AND AGRICULTURE

- The North was home to 19 of the nation's largest cities, which were centers of business and industry.
- The Union manufactured more iron and steel and therefore produced more of the rifles, cannons, and other materials its soldiers needed.
- The South grew, harvested, and exported abundant cotton, which helped raise the huge amounts of money necessary for the Confederates to finance the war.

RAILROADS

- Railroads played a critical role in the Civil War. The North had more than twice as many rail lines as the South.
- Both the Union and the Confederacy used railroads to transport equipment, weapons, and troops.
- The Confederacy's leadership did not recognize the importance of railroads at the beginning of the war. They allowed their lines to fall into disrepair, and many railroad workers had left their jobs to fight in the war.
- Civilians owned most of the railroads in the South, and the Confederate government did not believe in overtaking its citizens' sources of income.

MILITARY

- The Union Navy had an advantage over the Confederate Navy. When the war started in 1861, the Union possessed 40 ships. The Confederacy only had 10 ships.
- West Point, located in upstate New York, was the best military academy in the country. The Civil War ripped apart the school as it did the nation. Former classmates and friends found themselves fighting each other on the battlefield.
- Both Union and Confederate generals—including Ulysses S. Grant and Robert E. Lee—trained at West Point.
- Soldiers on both sides carried the latest advancement in weaponry, the Minié bullet. These slim, lead bullets made rifles more accurate and deadly weapons.

Confederate battle flag

CURATING HISTORY

Confederate Memorial Hall

This flag, which can be viewed at the museum in New Orleans, Louisiana, belonged to the Louisiana 22nd Infantry. It was designed from the original Confederate battle flag first flown by a Virginia regiment. By the end of the war, many Confederate regiments used some version of the blue cross with a red background, even though the Confederacy never officially adopted the flag as its own.

HISTORICAL THINKING

1. **COMPARE AND CONTRAST** Compare the population and geographic advantages of the North and the South.
2. **MAKE INFERENCES** In terms of the war, how did having more industries become an advantage for the North?
3. **FORM AND SUPPORT OPINIONS** Of the various strategic advantages and disadvantages that influenced the war, which factor might have been the most important? Support your opinion with evidence from the text.

REVIEW LESSON 4.6

EARLY YEARS OF THE WAR

As this 1862 photograph of the Union Army reveals, soldiers serving in the Civil War used heavy guns and fought from deep trenches. This photograph was taken in Yorktown, Virginia.

When the Civil War began, the Confederate and the Union armies had few professional soldiers and little time to recruit and train more. To ensure a quick victory, both armies made plans to attack the opposition's capitals, Washington, D.C., and Richmond, Virginia. President Lincoln acted first, sending Union troops to seize Richmond. His expectations were dashed after Confederate troops defeated his army. Subsequent losses on both sides made it clear that the war would be bloody and long.

EARLY COURSE OF THE WAR In July 1861, after Union General Irvin McDowell delayed his troops' advance by a week, Union forces battled Confederate troops at Bull Run Creek near Manassas, Virginia. The Confederates proved stronger, more courageous, and better led than the northerners expected and forced the humiliated Union Army to retreat to Washington, D.C.

As the war continued, soldiers on both sides endured great hardships. In addition to facing the enemy's weapons, men lived in harsh conditions and suffered from hunger and disease. Some women traveled to battlefields to nurse wounded soldiers back to health. Others stayed home to make money for their families. Both Confederate and Union soldiers attended religious services called revival meetings to help them make meaning of the war.

The early battles occurred on two fronts. In 1862, the North tried to gain control of western parts of the Confederacy, including New Orleans and ports along the Mississippi—the main suppliers of the Confederate Army. As part of that campaign, the two sides clashed in Shiloh, Tennessee, with many casualties on both sides. In the eastern part of the Confederacy, the Union attempted to take Richmond again. A battle between two ironclad warships, the *Monitor* and the *Merrimack*, ended in a stalemate. In the Seven Days' Battles, the Union's **General George McClellan** marched his troops from the sea toward Richmond, only to be forced back by **General Robert E. Lee**.

THE BATTLES OF 1862 Lee's forces defeated McClellan's troops in the Second Battle of Bull Run and then marched north to Antietam, Maryland. Lee was on the offensive, trying to push his army north into Union states. The Battle of Antietam on September 17 cost the largest number of lives yet, and was later dubbed "America's Bloodiest Day." Union losses finally compelled Lincoln to replace McClellan in the field with General Ambrose Burnside. The new leader set out to capture Richmond, but his troops could advance no further than Fredericksburg, Virginia, where they fought the Confederates for three days before retreating, defeated yet again.

8.10.5 Study the views and lives of leaders (e.g., Ulysses S. Grant, Jefferson Davis, Robert E. Lee) and soldiers on both sides of the war, including those of black soldiers and regiments; 11.3.2 Analyze the great religious revivals and the leaders involved in them, including the First Great Awakening, the Second Great Awakening, the Civil War revivals, the Social Gospel Movement, the rise of Christian liberal theology in the nineteenth century, the impact of the Second Vatican Council, and the rise of Christian fundamentalism in current times.

KEY TAKEAWAYS

BULL RUN

- Lincoln, hoping to end the war quickly, ordered the Union Army to take Richmond. Less than 100 miles outside Richmond, they fought a battle at Bull Run Creek near Manassas, Virginia.
- A Union general's decision to delay his force's departure from Washington, D.C., gave the Confederate Army time to strengthen its numbers and gain reinforcements.
- During the battle, Confederate General Thomas Jackson courageously held back Union attackers "like a stone wall," earning him the nickname "Stonewall" Jackson.
- Confederates won the battle, but troops on both sides suffered staggering casualties.

MEN AND WOMEN IN THE WAR

- Soldiers were often cold and hungry, and disease killed more men than battle.
- New forms of war technology, including advancements in trench warfare and ironclad ships, were developed during the Civil War.
- Women volunteered on the battlefield as much-needed nurses and worked at home as farmers and factory workers, replacing the men who had left to fight.
- Revival meetings, led by ministers, included a sermon and time for soldiers to share their gratitude for survival and struggle with the death they saw on the battlefields.

SHILOH AND THE SEVEN DAYS' BATTLES

- The Battle of Shiloh took place in April 1862 at Shiloh, Tennessee, when Confederate troops ambushed Union troops on their way to capture a major Confederate railroad hub in Mississippi.
- The battle of the ironclad warships, *Monitor* and *Merrimack*, which occurred in the harbor of Hampton Roads, Virginia, heralded a new kind of naval warfare.
- Confederates repelled Union forces outside Richmond during the Seven Days' Battles and succeeded in boosting southern morale.

ANTIETAM AND FREDERICKSBURG

- After a Confederate victory at the second Battle of Bull Run in 1862, Confederate forces under Lee moved north into Maryland.
- Union forces learned Confederate plans before they fought at Antietam Creek, Maryland, in what became "America's Bloodiest Day."
- The Confederate Army defeated Union troops led by General Burnside at Fredericksburg, adding to Lincoln's growing frustration with his military leadership.

NATIONAL GEOGRAPHIC PHOTOGRAPHER

Ken Garrett

National Geographic photographer Ken Garrett uses his craft to document America's Civil War history. His photographs of re-enactments of famous battles help people better understand the past.

Garrett finds photographing the battlefield at Gettysburg, Pennsylvania, to be particularly compelling. "It is a very emotional place, where you really get an understanding of the horror of war," he says. "The thought that those boys walked out into that open field to be killed, sometimes by their own brothers, is shocking."

HISTORICAL THINKING

1. **MAKE INFERENCES** Describe the mood of both the Union and Confederate soldiers after the first battle at Bull Run.
2. **SUMMARIZE** Explain the expanding roles women played during the Civil War.
3. **DETERMINE CHRONOLOGY** Which events precipitated the Battle of Antietam?

8.10.6 Describe critical developments and events in the war, including the major battles, geographical advantages and obstacles, technological advances, and General Lee's surrender at Appomattox; 8.10.7 Explain how the war affected combatants, civilians, the physical environment, and future warfare.

The Emancipation Proclamation

General McClellan and President Lincoln meet in the general's headquarters at Antietam, Maryland, in October 1862.

With the two sides at a standoff, the number of fatalities rising astronomically, and Americans questioning the point of it all, President Lincoln needed to define a moral justification for the war. The dreadful death toll clearly required a higher purpose than preserving the Union. With this idea in mind, Lincoln realized the Union could not defeat the Confederacy without first destroying slavery.

LINCOLN AND THE ISSUE OF SLAVERY

From the beginning of the war, abolitionists had pressured Lincoln to end slavery. Although he personally opposed slavery, he believed banning it outright would be politically disastrous. In his 1858 "House Divided" speech, Lincoln said the Union could not continue with half the country's states being free states and half being slave states. Nevertheless, as president, he thought it best to work toward gradual change. He needed the support of proslavery northern Democrats, who warned against the social, economic, and political consequences of an abrupt end to slavery. He also needed to cut off the South's cotton industry to win the war.

FOREVER FREE As the war dragged on, Lincoln made a dramatic move. In September 1862, he issued the **Emancipation Proclamation**, which declared all slaves in the Confederacy to be "forever free." The decree, to go into effect January 1, 1863, committed the U.S. government to a moral purpose—that of liberating enslaved people in rebel states. It also cleared the way for African Americans to serve in the armed forces, which would help bolster Union troops. The Confederacy, however, refused to acknowledge the legitimacy of the proclamation.

AFRICAN AMERICANS JOIN THE FIGHT After Lincoln's decree, free African-American men began enlisting in the Union Army. They were assigned to the 54th Massachusetts infantry regiment, and their first mission was to storm Fort Wagner, a stronghold near Fort Sumter that also guarded the port of Charleston, South Carolina. Inside the fort, the infantry confronted a much larger force of Confederate soldiers. The resulting battle was brutal. Despite their heroism, the 54th Massachusetts did not succeed in seizing the fort.

8.10.4 Discuss Abraham Lincoln's presidency and his significant writings and speeches and their relationship to the Declaration of Independence, such as his "House Divided" speech (1858), Gettysburg Address (1863), Emancipation Proclamation (1863), and inaugural addresses (1861 and 1865).

KEY TAKEAWAYS

LINCOLN'S PREDICAMENT

- Lincoln personally opposed slavery but wanted to dismantle the institution gradually, easing the impact on the South's economy.
- Lincoln knew that slavery provided an advantage to the Confederacy, keeping the South's economy running while southern white men went to war.
- Lincoln's supporters urged him to allow African-American men to fight for the Union.

THE EMANCIPATION PROCLAMATION

- Lincoln issued the Emancipation Proclamation just five days after the bloody Battle of Antietam.
- The Emancipation Proclamation freed slaves in rebel-held states, but not in the border states of the Union, which Lincoln felt he could not afford to antagonize for fear of secession.
- The Emancipation Proclamation applied the idea in the Declaration of Independence that "all men are created equal" to the issue of slavery.
- Slaveholders in Confederate states refused to acknowledge the proclamation, but many African Americans emancipated themselves by escaping. Other enslaved people, however, did not hear about their emancipation until the end of the war.

AFRICAN AMERICANS IN THE WAR

- The Emancipation Proclamation reversed a 1792 law prohibiting African Americans from serving in the military.
- About 200,000 African-American men served in the U.S. Army and Navy, in segregated units commanded by white officers.
- Many African-American women stayed home and took on the men's tasks in addition to their own work around the house. A few served as nurses, spies, and scouts.
- As a spy and a scout, Harriet Tubman helped free 727 slaves during a raid on the Combahee River in South Carolina in June 1863. The raid was the single largest liberation of slaves in American history.

THE 54TH MASSACHUSETTS REGIMENT

- More than 1,000 African Americans enlisted in the regiment and served under the white commanding officer, **Robert Gould Shaw**.
- In July 1863, Shaw and his men stormed Fort Wagner in the Port of Charleston, South Carolina, where they were met by a group of Confederate soldiers almost 3 times their size.
- Shaw and many of his men died in the fighting, and the regiment lost the battle despite the troop's evident courage.
- For his extraordinary valor, William H. Carney of the 54th Massachusetts became the first African American to receive the Congressional Medal of Honor.

AMERICAN VOICES
Frederick Douglass

Born in Maryland, Frederick Douglass (1818–1895) became a great writer, abolitionist, and civil rights leader. After escaping slavery, Douglass settled in Massachusetts, where he spoke publicly about his former life and called for an end to the institution.

Douglass wrote three autobiographies, founded a newspaper, and became a powerful and eloquent orator. During the Civil War, he advised President Lincoln and recruited African-American soldiers for the Union Army.

HISTORICAL THINKING

1. **SUMMARIZE** How did Lincoln redefine the justification for the war?
2. **MAKE INFERENCES** How did the Emancipation Proclamation extend the premise of the Declaration of Independence?
3. **DRAW CONCLUSIONS** What are some reasons why the 54th Massachusetts Regiment gained respect despite losing the Battle of Fort Wagner?

8.10.5 Study the views and lives of leaders (e.g., Ulysses S. Grant, Jefferson Davis, Robert E. Lee) and soldiers on both sides of the war, including those of black soldiers and regiments; 8.10.6 Describe critical developments and events in the war, including the major battles, geographical advantages and obstacles, technological advances, and General Lee's surrender at Appomattox.

REVIEW LESSON 4.8

THE BATTLES OF VICKSBURG AND GETTYSBURG

In the first months of 1863, the war wasn't going well for the Union. In May, Lincoln's new commander, **General Joseph Hooker**, led Union forces to a crushing defeat against Lee's much smaller army in Chancellorsville, Virginia. Hooker's loss was blamed on miscommunication, confusion, and ultimately, his own indecisiveness. Yet again, one of Lincoln's top generals proved disappointing. Although Lee lost his best commander, "Stonewall" Jackson, and a high percentage of his troops, Chancellorsville was hailed as his greatest victory. But the course of the war would soon change.

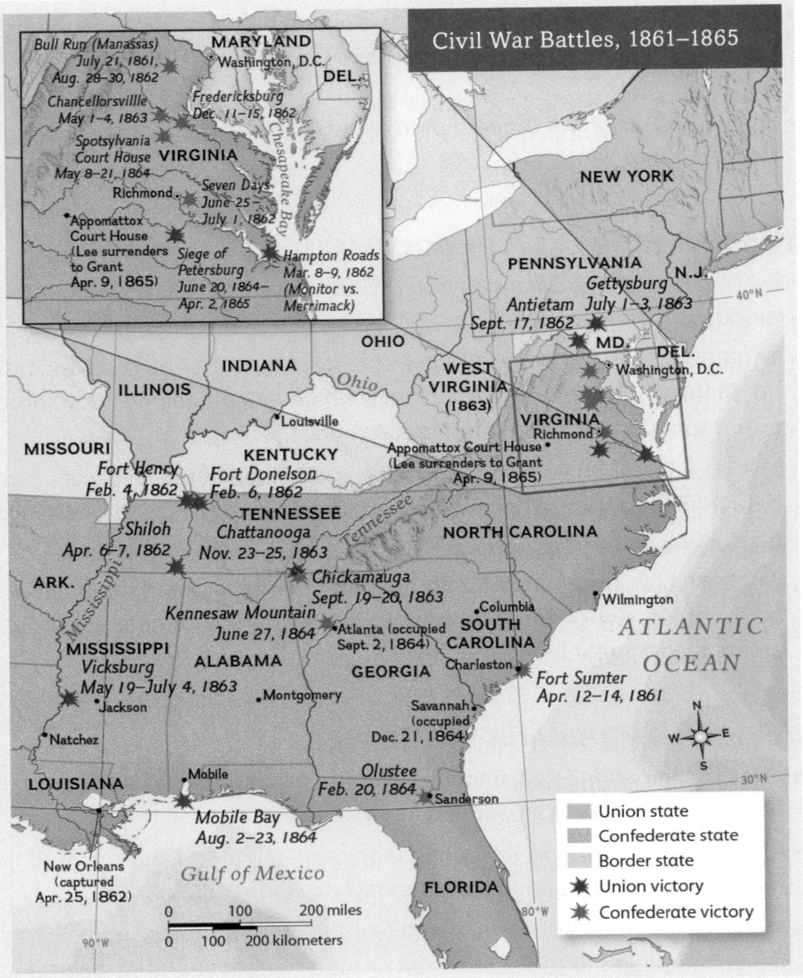

CONTROL OF THE MISSISSIPPI Vicksburg, Mississippi, a Confederate stronghold, sat high above the Mississippi River on its eastern shore. To seize control of the river, the Union Army first needed to conquer the city. General Grant's Union forces were stationed across the river, but attacking the city from the west proved impossible. One night in May, Grant secretly ferried his forces across the river at a point south of the city. From there, they marched toward Vicksburg, surrounding the city on the east. Cut off by Union troops for weeks, the residents of the city ran out of food. The Confederates surrendered on July 4, giving the Union command of the Mississippi Valley, which split the Confederacy into two parts.

THE TIDE TURNS AT GETTYSBURG Lee decided to invade the North again. He marched his troops into Pennsylvania with a goal to attack Philadelphia. At Gettysburg, the army encountered Union troops under **General George Meade**, who had replaced Joseph Hooker after the Chancellorsville disaster. The Union Army retreated until reinforcements arrived. Then they positioned themselves high on Cemetery Hill for a defensive advantage. Lee ordered **General George Pickett** and his men to charge the troops on the hill, which was a grave error. After suffering a huge number of casualties, the Confederate Army retreated, marking a turning point in the war.

LINCOLN SPEAKS AT GETTYSBURG A few months after the Battle of Gettysburg, Lincoln traveled to the battle site where crews had yet to bury all of the soldiers who had died there. He delivered a short—just three minutes—but powerful speech to dedicate a new military cemetery near where the fighting occurred. In his speech, he hailed the courage and sacrifice of the men who had died. He called for a "new birth of freedom" and referred to the principles of equality affirmed in the Declaration of Independence. He tied these ideas directly to the moral justification for the war. As time passed and the nation healed, the words of the Gettysburg Address gained force and resonance to become one of the most important speeches in American history.

KEY TAKEAWAYS

THE BATTLE OF VICKSBURG

- Capturing Vicksburg was necessary in order for the Union to gain control of the Mississippi River.
- On a long march to Vicksburg, Grant and his troops won five battles and captured thousands of Confederate soldiers.
- The Union troops then surrounded the city, cutting off shipments of food and other supplies to the city's defenders and residents. After several weeks, the siege of Vicksburg resulted in a Confederate surrender and a great Union victory.

SPLITTING THE CONFEDERACY

- After several other attempts to capture Vicksburg, Grant's decision to transport his troops across the river on vessels disguised as cargo boats proved successful.
- Grant's victory at Vicksburg allowed the Union to overtake the Mississippi Valley.
- With the Union in charge of the river, the Confederacy was split in two, putting the South at a severe disadvantage.
- The success at Vicksburg, after previous defeats, convinced Lincoln of Grant's outstanding military ability. Finally, Lincoln had a general on whom he could rely.

BATTLE OF GETTYSBURG

- Lee took his troops back to the North, and at Gettysburg, Pennsylvania, forced Union troops to retreat.
- Reinforced with new battalions and supplies, Union forces repositioned themselves on Cemetery Hill, where the high vantage point gave them a defensive advantage.
- Pickett's Charge, an attack on Union forces during the Battle of Gettysburg, proved disastrous for the Confederate Army. Led by Confederate General Pickett, the charge failed to break the Union line and resulted in thousands of men being killed or wounded.
- The following day, Lee and his troops retreated to Virginia. The Union victory was a turning point in the war.

GETTYSBURG ADDRESS

- The dedication of the Gettysburg battlefield on November 19, 1863, commemorated the massive loss of lives.
- Lincoln's address reinforced the moral principles of equality and freedom set out in the Declaration of Independence.
- Lincoln emphasized that the war was being fought for these moral principles and that the soldiers' deaths were not in vain.
- The Gettysburg Address set the tone for the end of the Civil War and the rebuilding of the nation that was to follow.

Confederate soldier's portrait

CURATING HISTORY

Confederate Memorial Hall

Photography was a new technology when the Civil War began. Many soldiers, like Sergeant Joseph Corneille of the 22nd Louisiana Infantry, shown here in 1861, had portraits made of themselves in full dress uniform before heading out to battle. Such portraits were expensive and dearly prized. They were often a family's only picture of a loved one. This photo is part of the collection at the museum in New Orleans.

HISTORICAL THINKING

1. **DETERMINE CHRONOLOGY** Describe the strategic troop movements that led to General Grant's victory at Vicksburg.
2. **EVALUATE** How did the Union's position on Cemetery Hill contribute to its victory at Gettysburg?
3. **DESCRIBE** In what way was the Gettysburg Address an attempt to realize the philosophy of government envisioned by the Founding Fathers?

8.10.4 Discuss Abraham Lincoln's presidency and his significant writings and speeches and their relationship to the Declaration of Independence, such as his "House Divided" speech (1858), Gettysburg Address (1863), Emancipation Proclamation (1863), and inaugural addresses (1861 and 1865); 8.10.6 Describe critical developments and events in the war, including the major battles, geographical advantages and obstacles, technological advances, and General Lee's surrender at Appomattox; 11.1 Students analyze the significant events in the founding of the nation and its attempts to realize the philosophy of government described in the Declaration of Independence.

REVIEW LESSON 4.9

UNION VICTORY

To commemorate the centennial anniversary of the end of the Civil War, the National Geographic Society commissioned Tom Lovell to paint *Surrender at Appomattox*. Lee, dressed in gray, signs the surrender terms while Grant (seated, center right) looks on.

In March 1864, President Lincoln named Ulysses S. Grant the commanding general of the Union Army. Grant had become a hero in the war for capturing two Confederate forts in Tennessee in 1862 and for securing victory at Vicksburg, Mississippi, for the Union in 1864. Both he and the president agreed to focus on defeating the Confederate Army rather than capturing Richmond.

TOTAL WAR As commander, Grant immediately initiated a series of widespread, relentless attacks against the Confederacy. He chose General Sherman to take Atlanta, Georgia, a railroad hub and an industrial center of the South. Following a victory there in September 1864, Sherman and his men proceeded to Savannah, Georgia, a port city on the Atlantic, and then north through the Carolinas. Along the way, the troops mercilessly destroyed property, crops, and other civilian and military targets. For instance, Sherman defeated Confederate troops in Fayetteville, North Carolina, and destroyed the arsenal there. Sherman's tactic of "total war"—breaching the rules of warfare in a concentrated attempt to defeat the enemy—achieved the intended result: it deeply demoralized the South.

GRANT FACES LEE Meanwhile, Grant took an offensive strategy against Lee. The two generals faced one another first in the May 1864 Battle of the Wilderness in northern Virginia. Despite heavy Union casualties, Grant pushed southward. At Spotsylvania, the armies waged a 12-day battle that cost many thousands of lives on both sides. Still, Grant marched to a final battle at Cold Harbor in southeastern Virginia, where he was defeated by Lee. The battles became known as the Overland Campaign.

END OF THE WAR Nearly five months after the re-election of President Lincoln, Grant's forces captured Richmond on April 3, 1865, but not before the Confederates set the city on fire. On April 9, Lee surrendered to Grant in **Appomattox Court House**, Virginia. The war was over. Just days later, Lincoln was assassinated and Andrew Johnson was sworn in as the new president. During Johnson's administration, Congress passed the 13th Amendment in December 1865, ending slavery in the United States. In the following years, Congress passed the 14th and 15th amendments, giving African Americans full citizenship and extending suffrage to African-American men.

8.10.5 Study the views and lives of leaders (e.g., Ulysses S. Grant, Jefferson Davis, Robert E. Lee) and soldiers on both sides of the war, including those of black soldiers and regiments; 11.1.4 Examine the effects of the Civil War and Reconstruction and of the industrial revolution, including demographic shifts and the emergence in the late nineteenth century of the United States as a world power.

KEY TAKEAWAYS

SHERMAN'S MARCH

- At Grant's command, General Sherman and his troops captured and burned Atlanta, the Confederacy's important industrial center.
- On the march to Savannah, Sherman's troops engaged in total war, burning property and crops.
- Sherman left Savannah standing, but then resumed the destruction on the way to Columbia, South Carolina.
- Sherman's march was a blow to southern morale and convinced northerners that the Union was winning the war.

GRANT AND LEE

- In the spring of 1864, Grant and his troops fought a series of battles known as the Overland Campaign during a march through Virginia.
- The Battle of the Wilderness in May was the first time Grant directly fought Lee. Suffering heavy casualties, Grant proceeded south.
- At Spotsylvania, Virginia, the two sides met again, suffering huge losses. Grant withdrew, defeated by the Confederates at Cold Harbor.
- The following spring, after Grant captured Richmond, Lee surrendered at Appomattox Court House, bringing the war to an end.

THREE CONSTITUTIONAL AMENDMENTS

- The 13th Amendment officially banned slavery across the nation. Governments in formerly Confederate states were required to write new state constitutions that acknowledged the law.
- The 14th Amendment defined citizenship to include anyone born or naturalized in the country regardless of race and guaranteed African Americans full equality.
- The 15th Amendment gave voting rights to African-American men.
- The amended Constitution gave the federal government increased power over the states, especially for the extension of equal rights and an inclusive definition of citizenship.
- The amendments laid the foundation for the legal phase of the 20th-century civil rights movement.

RE-ELECTION AND ASSASSINATION

- Convinced a Union victory in the war was inevitable, the North elected Lincoln in November 1864 to a second term to begin in March 1865.
- After the war, Lincoln prepared to rebuild, reconcile, and reunite the country—plans that came to be known as Reconstruction.
- On April 14, actor and Confederate sympathizer **John Wilkes Booth** shot Lincoln in Washington, D.C. Lincoln died the next day.
- Vice President Andrew Johnson was sworn in as the new president.

Lincoln's death bed

CURATING HISTORY

Chicago History Museum

After being shot at Ford's Theatre in Washington, D.C., Lincoln was carried to the Petersen House, a boarding house across the street. He died in this bed the next day.

Today, the Petersen House is a national museum, and the bed itself is displayed at the Chicago History Museum. Above the bed, *The Last Hours of Abraham Lincoln*, painted by Alonzo Chappel in 1868, shows Mary Todd Lincoln weeping on his chest.

HISTORICAL THINKING

1. **MAKE INFERENCES** How did Sherman demoralize southerners on his march through the south?
2. **EVALUATE** What impact did the 13th, 14th, and 15th amendments have on African Americans, and what role did they play in Reconstruction?
3. **MAKE PREDICTIONS** Having become president in the wake of Lincoln's death, what challenges were ahead for Andrew Johnson?

8.10.6 Describe critical developments and events in the war, including the major battles, geographical advantages and obstacles, technological advances, and General Lee's surrender at Appomattox; 8.11.5 Understand the Thirteenth, Fourteenth, and Fifteenth Amendments to the Constitution and analyze their connection to Reconstruction.

REVIEW LESSON 4.10

RECONSTRUCTION

The men in this print from 1872 are the first African Americans to serve in the U.S. Congress, representing five southern states. From left to right, the men are Senator Hiram Rhodes Revels, Congressman Benjamin S. Turner, Congressman Robert C. De Large, Congressman Josiah T. Walls, Congressman Jefferson F. Long, Congressman Joseph Rainey, and Congressman Robert B. Elliot.

President Andrew Johnson faced the monumental challenge of rebuilding the United States politically, socially, and economically. As a Democrat from Tennessee, Johnson had remained pro-Union throughout the war. Nevertheless, he was a southerner and a former slaveholder, and he quickly forgave most of the rebels. His prejudice against African Americans and his leniency toward former Confederates influenced his decisions as he directed the government in the process of reconstruction.

CONTROL OF RECONSTRUCTION Johnson decided to oversee Reconstruction himself. He required that Confederate states ratify the 14th Amendment and form new governments with new constitutions. But knowing Johnson's sympathies, some southern states refused to comply and wrote laws limiting African-American rights. Johnson himself opposed voting rights for African-American men. In an act of defiance, the Radical Republicans in Congress, wanting to punish the South and ensure complete equality, seized control of Reconstruction from the president. The power struggle eventually escalated to Johnson's impeachment trial.

AFRICAN AMERICANS IN RECONSTRUCTION Some African Americans took on leadership roles, particularly in government, religion, and education. African-American communities formed churches, particularly in the South, and education became a path to empowerment. African Americans elected representatives from their communities to state legislatures. Two men from Mississippi became the first African Americans to serve in the U.S. Senate. However, most African Americans' lives didn't change much. Opportunities were few, and groups including the Ku Klux Klan, an organization dedicated to terrorizing African Americans, encouraged racism. Many former slaves remained poor as they continued working on farms as sharecroppers.

RECONSTRUCTION COMES TO AN END
By 1869, Reconstruction was already losing steam with the American public. The Republicans successfully elected their candidate, **Ulysses S. Grant**, as president, and Congress passed the 15th Amendment. Even so, forces of resistance were rising. White Americans who opposed full equality created obstacles, such as charging a poll tax and committing acts of violence and intimidation to discourage African Americans from voting. The splintering of the Republican Party, an economic crisis, a corruption scandal, and Grant's poor political leadership further damaged the radical cause of civil rights. In 1876, Reconstruction came to an end with the election of **Rutherford B. Hayes** in a race so close that it required government intervention.

8.11.3 Understand the effects of the Freedmen's Bureau and the restrictions placed on the rights and opportunities of freedmen, including racial segregation and "Jim Crow" laws.

KEY TAKEAWAYS

PRESIDENTIAL RECONSTRUCTION

- Johnson required Confederate states to ratify the 13th Amendment, but he himself did not support equal rights for African Americans.
- Johnson quickly pardoned most Confederates who took an oath of loyalty to the Union, a move Radical Republicans thought too lenient.
- Congress created the Freedmen's Bureau to help the formerly enslaved as well as impoverished southern whites by providing aid, land, jobs, legal services, and educational opportunities.

RADICAL RECONSTRUCTION

- Radical Republicans were angered that some southern states refused to ratify the 13th and 14th amendments and passed black codes to limit African-American rights.
- Radical Republicans put themselves in charge of Reconstruction with the Reconstruction Acts of 1867.
- Radical Republicans required southern states to write new state constitutions that accepted the 14th Amendment.
- Congress passed the Tenure of Office Act, limiting the president's power, and when Johnson defied the act, Congress began the impeachment process to remove him from office. Johnson survived the impeachment trial by one vote.

AFRICAN AMERICANS

- African Americans eagerly participated in the political process, with many serving in public office.
- African-American communities formed new churches that focused on social justice issues and the importance of education.
- Many emancipated people labored on farms under the sharecropping system, which kept them poor and tied to the landowner's farm in a form of economic slavery called black peonage.
- White resistance to the goals of Reconstruction arose in the South and found powerful expression in the Ku Klux Klan, a terror organization aimed at preventing the advancement of African Americans.

END OF RECONSTRUCTION

- Civil War hero General Ulysses S. Grant became president in 1868. His election guaranteed that Reconstruction would continue, despite the Democratic Party's call to end it.
- Congress passed the 15th Amendment, but southern states passed laws, such as poll taxes, to restrict African-American voting rights.
- In a very close election requiring intervention by an electoral commission, Republican Rutherford B. Hayes became president in 1876.
- The Democrats and Republicans struck a deal, called the Compromise of 1877, awarding the presidency to Hayes if it would mean the end of Reconstruction.

8.11.5 Understand the Thirteenth, Fourteenth, and Fifteenth Amendments to the Constitution and analyze their connection to Reconstruction; 11.1.4 Examine the effects of the Civil War and Reconstruction and of the industrial revolution, including demographic shifts and the emergence in the late nineteenth century of the United States as a world power.

AMERICAN PLACES
Howard University

Howard University in Washington, D.C., was one of the first American universities dedicated to the education of African Americans. Established in 1867, it is named for one of its founders, General Oliver O. Howard, the first commissioner of the Freedmen's Bureau.

Today, the historically black university is a thriving institution with more than 10,000 students, and a campus of 89 buildings.

HISTORICAL THINKING

1. **DRAW CONCLUSIONS** Why did many legislators in Congress want to remove Johnson from the presidency?
2. **MAKE INFERENCES** For African Americans in the South, why might education have been a symbol of new freedom?
3. **FORM AND SUPPORT OPINIONS** Do you think Reconstruction was a success or a failure? Frame your answer in terms of how it affected particular groups in the United States.

REVIEW CHAPTER 4

CIVIL WAR AND RECONSTRUCTION

ASSESSMENT

MAIN IDEAS

Choose the best answer for each question from the choices available.

1. Why was a harsher version of the Fugitive Slave Act added to the Compromise of 1850? HSS 8.9.4

   A Northerners wanted to discourage enslaved people from trying to escape.
   B Northerners wanted to appease angry southerners who were threatening to secede.
   C The South's economy would collapse if escaped slaves were not returned.
   D The act would ensure that none of the western territories would adopt slavery.

2. Why did the Kansas-Nebraska Act of 1854 lead to violence in Kansas? HSS 8.9.5

   A The people of Kansas resisted voting on the question of slavery.
   B Kansas voted to be a free state, which outraged southerners and provoked attacks.
   C Settlers and outside agitators tried to influence the vote in Kansas.
   D The vote was too close to call, which increased tensions between the two sides.

3. Which of the following statements best describes the Underground Railroad? HSS 8.9.1

   A It was a secret network of tunnels through which fugitive slaves could safely travel north.
   B It was a network of freight trains that secretly carried escaping slaves.
   C It was a secret network of routes, transportation, and people who helped fleeing slaves.
   D It was a network of white abolitionists who encouraged enslaved people to escape.

4. What was the main point of Abraham Lincoln's "House Divided" speech? HSS 8.10.4

   A The country could not continue as a union of half-free and half-slave states.
   B If tensions were not resolved, a war was likely.
   C Free states and slave states must maintain an equal balance in the House of Representatives.
   D Only outlawing slavery would save the Union.

5. What was one of the South's strongest advantages over the North in the Civil War? HSS 8.10.6

   A African Americans could fight in the war, preventing many southern white deaths.
   B Southern soldiers were more properly trained than their northern counterparts.
   C Most of the battles took place in the South on territory that was unfamiliar to the northerners.
   D The South had a stronger economy.

6. What was the historic significance of the battle between the *Monitor* and the *Merrimack*? HSS 8.10.7

   A The use of ironclad ships heralded a new form of naval technology.
   B The battle was a decisive victory for the North.
   C Since neither side won the battle, the majority of the war thereafter was fought on land.
   D The ships blockaded the Hampton Roads harbor, thereby cutting off supplies to Virginia.

7. Why did the 54th Massachusetts Regiment lose the battle of Fort Wagner? HSS 8.10.5

   A The African-American soldiers of the regiment had been forced to fight against their will, which affected their determination.
   B The soldiers of the regiment were outnumbered by the Confederates.
   C The white commander of the regiment showed poor leadership of his troops.
   D The Confederate troops were more courageous than the soldiers of the 54th Massachusetts.

8. Why did Lincoln refer to the Declaration of Independence in his address at Gettysburg? HSS 8.10.4

   A He pointed out that the writers of the Declaration of Independence were opposed to slavery.
   B He saw a moral equivalency between the Civil War and the revolution against England.
   C He wanted to remind his audience that those who die in war do not die in vain.
   D He drew attention to the Declaration's assertion that "all men are created equal" as underscoring the moral basis for the Civil War.

9. How did the Union secure a victory at Vicksburg, Mississippi? HSS 8.10.6

A Union ships blocked all cotton exports.
B The Union attacked Vicksburg from the west side of the Mississippi River.
C Union troops surrounded Vicksburg, cutting off food supplies to the city.
D The Union gained control of the Mississippi River, dividing the Confederacy geographically.

10. Which right was not included in the three Reconstruction amendments to the Constitution? HSS 8.11.5

A equal protection under the law for women
B full citizenship rights for African Americans
C voting rights for women
D protection against being re-enslaved

11. What was the main goal of the Ku Klux Klan? HSS 8.11.4

A to reunify the nation after the war
B to improve the lives of formerly enslaved people and impoverished southern whites
C to stop the advancement of African Americans
D to impeach President Andrew Johnson

12. How did some southern states resist the goals of Reconstruction? HSS 11.1.4

A They imposed poll taxes and other obstacles to prevent African Americans from voting.
B They organized as southern Democrats and rewrote state constitutions.
C They actively intimidated, terrorized, and even killed African Americans who tried to take advantage of their new freedoms.
D all of the above

13. Why did the Democrats agree to the election of Rutherford B. Hayes, the Republican candidate, in the Compromise of 1877? HSS 11.1.4

A The Democrats agreed so that Hayes would end Reconstruction.
B The Democrats did not support their own candidate.
C The Democrats believed Hayes's election would prompt more southerners to join their party.
D The Democrats compromised with the Republicans to keep federal troops in the South to enforce the Reconstruction amendments.

ANALYZE SOURCES

In 1868, Congress passed the 14th Amendment to the U.S. Constitution, one of three Reconstruction amendments. It addresses citizenship rights and equal protection under the law.

> Section 1 of Amendment XIV:
>
> All persons born or naturalized in the United States, and subject to the jurisdiction thereof, are citizens of the United States and of the state wherein they reside. No state shall make or enforce any law which shall abridge the privileges or immunities of citizens of the United States; nor shall any state deprive any person of life, liberty, or property, without due process of law; nor deny to any person within its jurisdiction the equal protection of the laws.

14. What rights did this amendment extend to formerly enslaved people that they had previously been denied? HSS 8.11.5

15. How did the 14th Amendment relate directly to the goals of Reconstruction? HSS 8.11.5

WRITE ABOUT HISTORY

16. **EXPLANATORY** The Civil War succeeded in keeping the Union intact, but in many ways, the country was never the same again. How did the country change because of the Civil War and Reconstruction? HSS 11.1.4

TIPS

- Introduce the topic with a clear main idea statement.
- Develop the topic with relevant facts and concrete details.
- Recall what you have learned about the cause of the Civil War, and what Reconstruction was intended to accomplish.
- Provide a concluding statement that follows from the information you have presented.

ARCHAEOLOGY AND U.S. HISTORY

Fredrik Hiebert
Archaeologist-in-Residence, National Geographic Society

Dr. Hiebert directs archaeology projects around the world and recently curated an exhibition of more than 500 Greek artifacts in the National Geographic Museum.

Making sense of past events can be a complicated process. If history is the study of the past through written documents, such as firsthand accounts, letters, news reports, and inscriptions, then archaeology is the study of the human past through the **material record**—the buildings and objects that survive from a previous era. Archaeologists and historians are partners in preserving the human record.

Archaeology is the study of human-made objects, or **artifacts**, and the artifacts' context. An artifact tells a story by its style of manufacture, decoration, or inscription (words written on it). **Context** is the location of artifacts in the place of their last use or disposal. Context refers to where the artifacts were found, whether in the remains of buildings, in burial sites, on battlefields, or even in garbage pits.

This archaeological information sheds light on written histories that might tell only one side of the story. In fact, archaeology is one of the most important contributors to the interpretation of history here in the United States, from the original peopling of the continent right up to contemporary events.

For a look at American archaeology, start with the features on the opposite page. Then check out the map of U.S. archaeological sites that follows—archaeology may be just around the corner.

How does archaeology add to our understanding of U.S. history?

Pueblo Bonito (which means "beautiful town" in Spanish) was a great house in Chaco Canyon used by ancestral Puebloans between A.D. 850 and 1150. Built of sandstone blocks cemented with adobe mortar, this building once had hundreds of rooms—many of them round kivas, or ceremonial rooms—and in some areas was more than four stories high.

ARCHAEOLOGY AT A GLANCE

Archaeologists as First Responders

When disaster strikes, archaeologists are often among the first emergency personnel on the scene. Their expertise in proper excavation techniques is vital to the careful recovery of human remains and material evidence. The work of archaeologists, for example, sheds light on the real impact of the 9/11 devastation in New York City and the extent of the damage from Hurricane Katrina in New Orleans.

When the World Trade Center towers were destroyed, first responders included archaeologists. Instead of collecting artifacts such as ancient pottery, they collected wallets, briefcases, office supplies, and personal memorabilia of terrified workers forced to leave their belongings behind.

NatGeo Archaeology

National Geographic Society has a long history of archaeological exploration, including Hiram Bingham's work at the Inca site of Machu Picchu in the Andes in 1911. Today, Dr. Fredrik Hiebert is archaeologist-in-residence at National Geographic's headquarters in Washington, D.C. The Society has also been instrumental in conducting repatriations, the return of illegally excavated artifacts to their countries of origin.

National Geographic helps support ongoing excavation at Jamestown in Virginia, the site of the first permanent European settlement in North America.

State Archaeologist

Did you know that every state in the union has an official archaeologist? These experts help direct archaeological research and discovery on nonfederal land and bring that information to the public through stewardship and education.

Native American Graves Protection and Repatriation Act (NAGPRA)

This 1990 act provides protection for Native American burial sites and better control over the removal of Native American human remains and artifacts. The act requires federal agencies to return excavated cultural items, including human remains, funerary objects, sacred objects, and objects of cultural heritage, to descendants and culturally affiliated Indian tribes.

ARCHAEOLOGY SITES
ACROSS THE COUNTRY

The *Indiana Jones* movies put the academic study of archaeology on the map—the *world* map, that is. You might be surprised to learn about the range of archaeological projects right in your own backyard. Use the map on this page to get familiar with some of the exciting and important work underway in the United States, and go to *America Through The Lens* online to find archaeological sites in your state.

Ozette, Washington

A Makah village, excavated after a mudslide in 1970, yielded more than 55,000 artifacts, thousands of them wooden.

Little Bighorn River, Montana

Archaeology has changed historical accounts of the Battle of the Little Bighorn in 1876. There, Native Americans of the Great Plains engaged with U.S. Army troops under General George Custer. Analysis of artifacts and bones found there revealed this to be a major Native American victory, despite reports—and legend—to the contrary.

Pueblo Bonito, New Mexico

Archaeologists have found nearly 300,000 artifacts here, including wooden flutes, human effigy vessels, and cylindrical pottery jars. This site continues to draw archaeologists and other scientists hoping to uncover new information on the culture that thrived here.

Santa Rosa Island, California

This is the home of Arlington Man, possibly the oldest human remains found in North America, dating to 13,000 years ago. Additional sites suggest Paleo-Indian occupation dating to 8,000–11,000 years ago.

U.S.S. *Arizona*, Pearl Harbor, Hawaii

In 2016, National Park Service archaeologists and National Geographic photographers used an ROV (remotely operated vehicle) to explore this U.S. battleship, sunk on December 7, 1941. The team collected artifacts for analysis and took sediment and water samples for further study.

HREP 3 Students evaluate major debates among historians concerning alternative interpretations of the past, including an analysis of authors' use of evidence and the distinctions between sound generalizations and misleading oversimplifications.

Jeffers Petroglyphs, Minnesota

These rock carvings, some dating possibly to 9,000 years ago, include humans, elk, buffalo, turtles, and dragonflies. Archaeologists had to carefully remove lichen that covered the rocks in order to examine the carvings underneath. They speculate that the carvings were used for sacred ceremonies or to record events.

World Trade Center site, New York

A visit to the 9/11 Memorial Museum in New York City has been called an "archaeological walking tour." Archaeologists worked to recover human remains and artifacts from the tons of debris left after the towers collapsed.

Cahokia Mounds, Illinois

This 2,200-acre site of a pre-Columbian Native American city is the largest archaeological site in the United States. The roughly 80 mounds that remain today suggest a sophisticated urban Mississippian culture. Artifacts uncovered at Cahokia include pottery, tools, stones, shells, knives, arrowheads, and tattoo kits.

Mount Vernon, Virginia

The home of George and Martha Washington, Mount Vernon continues to yield a great deal of data that document life on an 18th-century plantation. One effort has focused on an archaeological survey of slave burials on the grounds.

Underwater Archaeological Preserves, Pensacola, Florida

The battleship U.S.S. *Massachusetts* from the Spanish-American War was towed to Pensacola in 1921 and eventually scuttled at the entrance to the harbor. Today, the ship is an artificial reef and home to an array of marine life in the Gulf of Mexico.

The Alamo, San Antonio, Texas

Once a fortress and mission, the Alamo is a moving reminder of the Texan forces who faced Santa Anna's Mexican troops there in 1836 as part of the Texas Revolution. Archaeologists are still excavating to identify the original structure's adobe walls and inventory thousands of artifacts.

2 GROWTH AND REFORM

Similar to today, New York City around 1900 was a bustling, congested place where cultures and social classes intermingled, influenced one another, and sometimes clashed. Rapid urban growth and the influx of immigrants contributed to some of the social challenges cities like Chicago, San Francisco, and New York faced. In this photo, children eagerly wait in line with empty tubs to collect free ice that could be used to keep food from spoiling.

UNIT 2 GROWTH AND REFORM

THE UNITED STATES

1877
Thomas Edison invents the phonograph.

1882
The Chinese Exclusion Act severely limits the immigration of Chinese laborers to the United States.

1890
Federal troops kill more than 150 Lakota Sioux at Wounded Knee Creek in South Dakota.

1892
Farmers form the Populist, or People's, Party to focus on issues such as better pay and working conditions.

1894
Railway workers for the Pullman Palace Car Company go on a strike that disrupts rail traffic throughout the country.

1896
In *Plessy* v. *Ferguson*, the Supreme Court rules that facilities for African Americans can be "separate but equal."

1870

1890

1884 AFRICA
European powers meet at the Berlin Conference to divide up Africa, triggering a race for territory on the continent.

1889 EUROPE
The Eiffel Tower is built in Paris, France, and becomes the world's tallest structure.

THE WORLD

HISTORICAL THINKING

DETERMINE CHRONOLOGY What two consecutive events indicated that the United States was expanding its influence?

1898
The Spanish-American War erupts after U.S. intervention in Cuba's war of independence against Spain.

1899 ASIA
The United States proposes the Open Door Policy in China.

1900

1900 ASIA
A secret society in China rebels against the spread of Western and Japanese influence during the Boxer Rebellion.

1906
President Theodore Roosevelt pushes Congress to pass the Meat Inspection Act and the Pure Food and Drug Act. (*uninspected medicine sold before the acts were passed*)

1909
W.E.B. Du Bois helps found the National Association for the Advancement of Colored People (NAACP). (*pin used during the anti-lynching movement*)

1910 AMERICAS
The Mexican Revolution begins.

1911
More than 140 workers—mostly young immigrant women—die in New York City's Triangle factory fire.

1913
Henry Ford uses the assembly line system to mass-produce his automobiles.

1914 EUROPE
World War I begins in Europe. (*helmet worn by German officers in the war*)

1917 EUROPE
The Russian Revolution begins.

1920

1920
The 19th Amendment is ratified, granting women the right to vote.

HI 1 Students show the connections, causal and otherwise, between particular historical events and larger social, economic, and political trends and developments.

CHAPTER 5

EXPANSION & CONFLICT IN THE WEST

1877–1900

HISTORICAL THINKING How did expansion alter the West and its native populations?

AMERICAN STORIES The Wild West

SECTION 1 **The Changing Frontier**

SECTION 2 **Broken Treaties and War**

AMERICAN GALLERY ONLINE The Battle of the Little Bighorn

National Geographic photographer Jim Brandenburg captured these wild American bison crossing the prairie near the Missouri River in South Dakota. In the first half of the 19th century, millions of bison roamed freely over North America. During the second half of the century, however, their numbers fell sharply, in part because settlers pushed westward, and farmers and ranchers killed off many of the animals. By the early 20th century, only a few hundred wild bison remained in North America.

> "These soldiers cut down my timber; they kill my buffalo; and when I see that, **my heart feels like bursting.**"
>
> —Chief Satanta of the Kiowa

THE WILD WEST

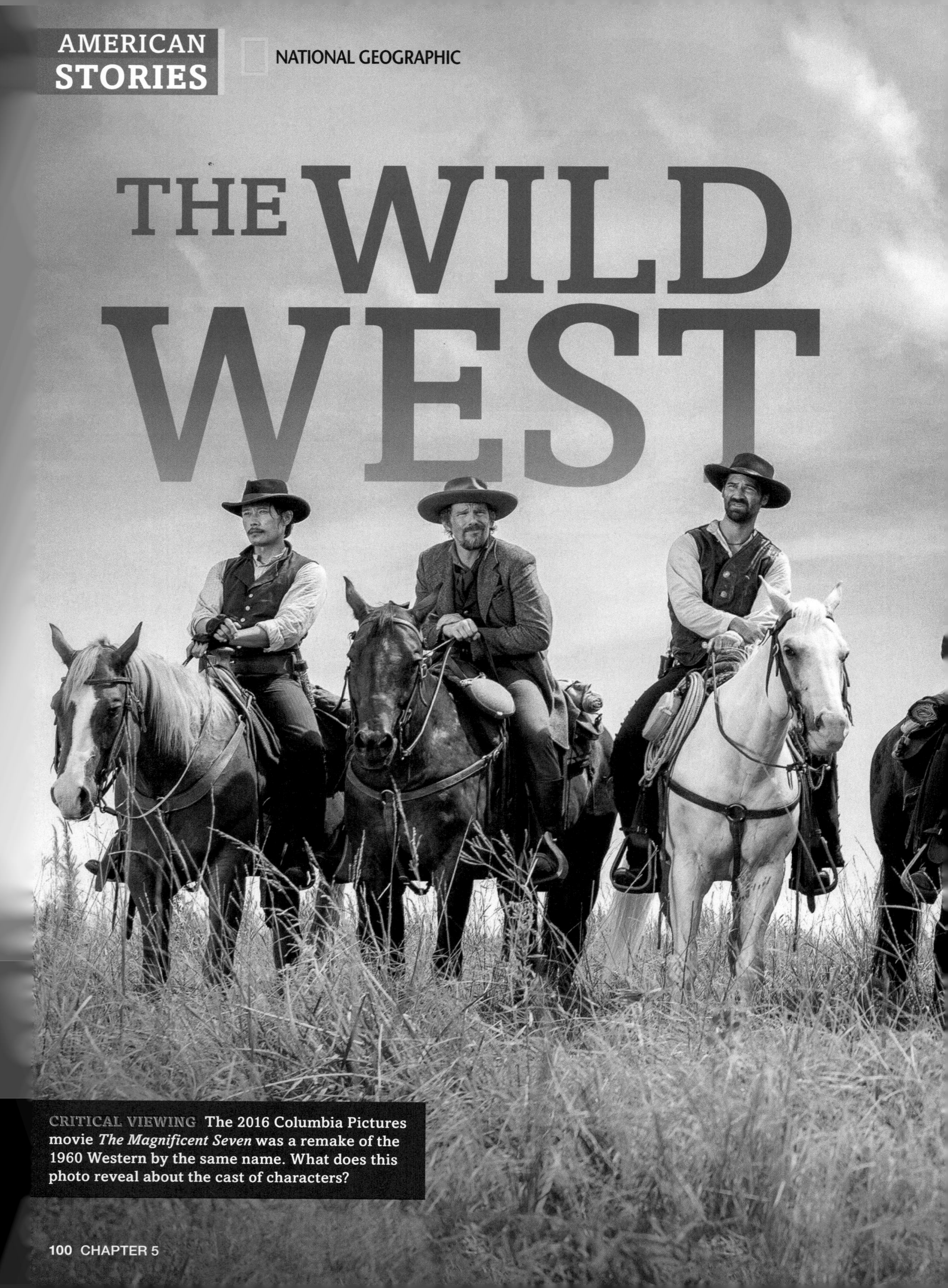

CRITICAL VIEWING The 2016 Columbia Pictures movie *The Magnificent Seven* was a remake of the 1960 Western by the same name. What does this photo reveal about the cast of characters?

In the 1950s and 1960s, you couldn't flip through the television channels during prime time without seeing at least one Western—a fictional series about the American West set in the late 1800s. Movie screens were also filled with images of scheming outlaws pursued by handsome, heroic lawmen, and cool, confident cowboys protecting herds from cattle thieves. In other words, the Wild West lived and breathed through the entertainment industry, and the American public loved it.

THE REAL WEST

The legend of the Wild West did not start with TV or the movies. First came the dime novels (pictured below): short, inexpensive paperback books that told thrilling tales of adventure, hardship, and daring rescues. Even as the real cowboys, outlaws, lawmen, and pioneers went about their business in the real West, dime novel writers were spinning the stories of these individuals into tall tales and wild adventures. At the same time, Buffalo Bill's Wild West show was touring the eastern states. This outdoor extravaganza featured mock shootouts, cowboys demonstrating their skills, buffalo, and other Wild West icons.

And so was born the larger-than-life image of the West as a place of theatrical violence, with masked bandits stalking every bank and frequent shootouts between the good guys and the bad guys. Life in the real West was by no means boring, and the West did have its colorful characters. But the day-to-day reality was not nearly as exciting as the stories on the pages and screens.

Two of the most popular "set" pieces from Westerns—the shootout between the sheriff and the villain in the town streets and the daring bank robbery—were extremely uncommon in real life. Historians have studied crime statistics for several western towns in the late 1800s. Using the information, these researchers estimated that the Wild West was no more violent than cities and towns today. Historian Larry Schweikart concluded

There are more bank robberies in modern-day Dayton, Ohio, in a year than there were in the entire Old West in a decade, perhaps in the entire frontier period!

—Historian Larry Schweikart

that fewer than a dozen bank robberies likely took place in the final decades of the 19th century. He remarked, "There are more bank robberies in modern-day Dayton, Ohio, in a year than there were in the entire Old West in a decade, perhaps in the entire frontier period!"

As for dramatic shootouts on Main Street, most of the life-altering disagreements in the West were over land, and people fought them out in court. In a book about the frontier, historian Patricia Nelson Limerick commented, "The showdowns would occur in the land office or the courtroom; weapons would be deeds and lawsuits, not six-guns."

DIME NOVELS

"Purple prose" is an expression used to describe writing that is elaborate, flowery, and over the top. It's also a good description of the style in which many dime novels were written. This 1910 novel features a dramatic image of Buffalo Bill in action. But the novel's title is relatively tame compared to more "purple" ones like *Adventures of Buffalo Bill from Boyhood to Manhood: Deeds of Daring, Scenes of Thrilling Peril*; and *Romantic Incidents in the Early Life of W. F. Cody, the Monarch of Bordermen.*

CALAMITY JANE

Men weren't the only real-life characters who found their way into the myth of the Wild West. Martha Jane Cannary was orphaned in 1867, soon after her family moved to Salt Lake City, Utah. The 12-year-old girl was uneducated and desperately poor, but she was tall, strong, and able to do the jobs that were mainly available to men. Dressing and working like a man, taking whatever jobs she could, the teenager acquired the nickname Calamity Jane.

We know for certain that Calamity Jane moved to Deadwood, South Dakota, in 1876 and met American frontiersman, army scout, and officer of the law, Wild Bill Hickok. At that point, the stories take over. Jane, an enthusiastic participant in the creation of her own tall tale, claimed that she had single-handedly caught the man who killed Hickok—a fact disproved by newspaper accounts of the time. She also claimed to have rescued a runaway stagecoach with its six passengers and driver.

In 1895, Jane joined Buffalo Bill Cody's Wild West show as a horseback rider and sharpshooter, further expanding both her legend and her fan base. Dime novels about Calamity Jane spun ever more fanciful tales of her adventures, including a marriage to Hickok. Though reports of a relationship between Calamity Jane and Hickok are highly suspect, she was buried next to him at Mount Moriah Cemetery in South Dakota.

An accomplished rider, Jane was often photographed on horseback. Here she poses in front of tepees and tents at the Pan-American Exposition in Buffalo, New York.

The life of the cowboy, too, was not exactly as portrayed in the Westerns. On-screen cowboys were almost exclusively white, and they seemed to spend their days with pistols drawn. In reality, of the approximately 40,000 cowboys on the Great Plains, 30 percent or more were African-American or Mexican. Several hundred were Native Americans. And the actual work of a cowboy? It was unromantic, poorly paid, and often revolved around the boredom of 14-hour days in the saddle herding cattle.

WILD BILL HICKOK: A CASE STUDY

The story of Wild Bill Hickok is a useful case study for examining how a real-life event was turned almost instantly into a Wild West legend. The tale begins with one of the few true instances of a quick-draw gun duel in the street. In 1865, James Butler Hickok, known as "Wild Bill," was a gambler and a drifter who made his temporary home in Springfield, Missouri. He got into a disagreement over a gambling debt with a man named Davis Tutt. It culminated on the evening of July 20, when both men drew their pistols and fired at each other in the town square. Tutt fell dead, with a bullet through the heart; Hickok was unharmed.

Within a few months, Hickok was on his way to Wild West stardom. Colonel George Ward Nichols started the process with an article about the showdown for *Harper's New Monthly Magazine*. Nichols's account of the shootout was mostly factual, but he went on to tell his readers that Hickok had once fought off 10 attackers on his own and that he had killed 100 men, among other fictions. The article was hugely popular and was soon followed by dime novels with titles such as *Wild Bill, the Indian Slayer*.

CRITICAL VIEWING American film stars Montgomery Clift (left), John Wayne (center), and Noah Beery, Jr., (right) endured long days of filming on the set of the 1948 Western *Red River.* What do you observe about the sets and process used to produce this film?

Hickok himself contributed to his legend by appearing in Buffalo Bill's Wild West show. It was as a gambler, however, that Hickok would meet an abrupt and unglamorous end, when a man crept up and shot him while he was playing poker. Even after his death, the dime novels continued to embellish the Wild Bill Hickok lore with titles such as *Wild Bill, the Pistol Prince.*

WHY THE LEGEND?

Why have the tall tales of the Wild West persisted for more than a century after the real American frontier began to fade from memory? Perhaps it is because the Old West embodies a spirit of toughness and independence that Americans admire. Perhaps, too, the legends recall a time when much of the country was untamed and new—to American settlers, at least. For the Native Americans of the West, many of the events of the frontier period are distinctly lacking in romance or nostalgia. For those who still enjoy the legends of the Wild West, however, and those who seek out the truth behind them, perhaps the greatest draw is the universal human love of a good story.

THINK ABOUT IT

How do films or TV shows you have seen that feature the Old West or the American frontier compare to the legends and realities you have learned about? What evidence of bias or historical inaccuracies have you observed?

11.5.6 Trace the growth and effects of radio and movies and their role in the worldwide diffusion of popular culture; HREP 2 Students identify bias and prejudice in historical interpretations.

THE LONE RANGER

"Hi-Yo Silver! Away!" was a call recognized by millions of Americans in the 1930s through the 1950s and beyond. It was the signature call of the Lone Ranger to his valiant horse, Silver, as he set off on another weekly adventure to bring order to the lawless West. Accompanied by his Native American sidekick, Tonto, the Lone Ranger protected the innocent and brought evildoers to justice. Unlike some heroes of Wild West tales, the Lone Ranger was entirely fictional and not based on a real-life individual.

The Lone Ranger began as a radio show in 1933, featuring the adventures of a mysterious masked man who fought for justice in the Wild West. In 1949, it debuted as a TV show and became wildly popular in its own right, running in syndication well after the series was canceled in 1957. The appeal of *The Lone Ranger* has continued into the 21st century. A TV movie with that title was made in 2003, and a new version was released in 2013.

Actor Clayton Moore took his job as a role model very seriously and made frequent public appearances as the Lone Ranger when he wasn't filming episodes.

PRIMARY SOURCE

Across the country in the 1930s, families would tune in their radios to hear the thrilling introduction to *The Lone Ranger* radio show, which many could recite by heart:

A fiery horse with the speed of light, a cloud of dust and a hearty Hi-Yo Silver! The Lone Ranger! With his faithful Indian companion Tonto, the daring and resourceful masked rider of the plains led the fight for law and order in the early western United States! Nowhere in the pages of history can one find a greater champion of justice! Return with us now to those thrilling days of yesteryear! From out of the past come the thundering hoofbeats of the great horse Silver!
The Lone Ranger rides again!

—from *The Lone Ranger*, by Fran Striker, 1933

Collectors love television memorabilia, and items from *The Lone Ranger* television series are no exception. This 1954 metal lunch box is a prized piece of pop culture.

1.1 **MAIN IDEA** Western settlement was spurred by economic opportunities in farming, ranching, and mining and by the federal government's goal of expanding the nation's boundaries.

FARMING, RANCHING, AND MINING

When there's a lot of open space, people tend to spread out. After the Civil War ended, Americans once again hitched their wagons and headed west of the Mississippi River, eager to settle the untamed land and begin their new lives.

MANIFEST DESTINY

Many of those who migrated west were inspired by the idea known as **manifest destiny**, the belief that Americans were intended to settle all the land between the Atlantic and Pacific coasts. While American communities were thriving in the East, many eastern farmers, hungry for greater stretches of land, moved westward. In 1860, the unsettled West included the grassland prairie region in the middle of North America, called the **Great Plains**, an area that was wide open for new settlement.

During the Civil War, the U.S. government had tried to make it easier for farmers to migrate to the Great Plains by passing the **Homestead Act** in 1862. The act offered plots of land in the region to American citizens or to those intending to become citizens. For a small filing fee, each person was eligible for 160 free acres as long as he or she lived on the land and cultivated it for five years. That may sound like a lot of land, but a settler had to purchase two or three times that acreage to grow enough crops for a reasonable profit. And the Homestead Act did not provide the money to go west, file a claim on the land, or purchase farming equipment.

Still, many pioneers left their homes and settled on the Great Plains. They were rewarded for their efforts when the transcontinental railroad opened in 1869. The railroad provided transportation for the settlers and brought new immigrants across the frontier. The lines also carried household goods, tools, and other merchandise to the homesteaders—items sometimes purchased through catalog companies such as Montgomery Ward.

After the Civil War, many African Americans also migrated west with the goal of seeking a life free from discrimination and establishing communities of their own. The settlers were called **Exodusters** because they made their exodus, or exit, from the South after Reconstruction had failed to end the racial oppression of African Americans. On the Great Plains, many became farmers, and some even established towns of their own. Many African-American men also worked as miners and cowboys. By 1890, about 520,000 African Americans lived west of the Mississippi River.

LIFE ON THE GREAT PLAINS

The settlers' lives weren't easy. The first order of business upon arrival on the Great Plains was building a house. Because there were no forests on the plains, and therefore no lumber, homesteaders cut thick blocks of earth, called "sod bricks," out of the prairie soil. It took about 3,000 sod bricks to construct a single sod house. The thick sod walls kept out the cold in the winter and the heat in the summer. Some homes were built right into a hill or ridge with only a single opening for a door and grass growing on the "roof." Lacking firewood, farmers burned buffalo chips—dry dung—or sunflower plants for fuel to cook their meals and provide warmth.

The arid climate and tough prairie soil proved challenging for farmers, but new technology in farming machines helped increase productivity. In 1837, an Illinois blacksmith named John Deere invented a plow tough enough to break through the prairie's dense soil. Cyrus McCormick's reaper, a

11.1.4 Examine the effects of the Civil War and Reconstruction and of the industrial revolution, including demographic shifts and the emergence in the late nineteenth century of the United States as a world power.

machine that helped harvest grain, was widely used by 1850. During the 1880s, inventors created steam-powered threshers to process wheat and machines that husked corn, or removed the ears' outer leaves. In 1873, Joseph Glidden devised a practical form of barbed wire for fencing. Soon a machine could produce this wire on a large scale, and it was used widely to keep livestock in and predators out.

Technology alone could not help the farmers cultivate crops. The region received little rain, and few rivers crossed the plains. Farmers who lived near the Rocky Mountains could build irrigation systems to bring water from mountain streams, but farther east, farmers came to rely on **dry farming** techniques to make the most use of what little rain did fall. They plowed widely spaced rows and planted their seeds between deep furrows so that rainwater would drain into the trench formed between the rows. They kept fields free of weeds to ensure that only food-producing plants received moisture.

One of the challenges of living on the Great Plains was dealing with its sheer size. On the vast prairie, tall grass stretched as far as the eye could see, and farms were far apart. The nearest neighbor was often miles away. Although families set up networks to meet socially and support each other during difficult times, homesteads were isolated. Loneliness was a fact of life.

THE LIFE OF A COWBOY

While lonely, the grasslands of the western plains were perfect for grazing cattle, and a number of wealthier settlers established ranches from Texas to Montana. At the same time, the once numerous herds of bison that had roamed the region were dwindling, victims

PRIMARY SOURCE

In 1880, former slave Benjamin "Pap" Singleton testified at congressional hearings regarding the migration of African Americans to the Great Plains. In this excerpt from the hearings, he states his reasons for promoting the exodus.

Well, my people, for the want of land—we needed land for our children—and their disadvantages—that caused my heart to grieve and sorrow; pity for my race, sir, that was coming down, instead of going up—that caused me to go to work for them. I sent out there perhaps in '66—perhaps so; or in '65, any way—my memory don't recollect which; and they brought back tolerable favorable reports; then I . . . went into Southern Kansas, and found it was a good country, and I thought Southern Kansas was congenial [agreeable] to our nature, sir; and I formed a colony there, and bought about a thousand acres of ground.

—from Benjamin "Pap" Singleton at congressional hearings, 1880

CRITICAL VIEWING In 1888, Solomon Butcher took this photograph of an African-American family posed in front of their sod house. What details in the photo suggest what their lives might have been like on the plains?

of overhunting and conflicts between the U.S. government and Native Americans. Their loss left even more land for cattle to roam.

Ranchers employed cowboys to round up their cattle and drive them to "cow towns" in Kansas, Nebraska, and Wyoming. From there the animals were loaded into boxcars and shipped by rail to the stockyards and meatpacking plants of Chicago. Improved slaughtering and packaging techniques as well as ice-cooled boxcars made beef more widely available throughout the nation. Americans developed a taste for beef, and its consumption soared.

Cattle drives took three to five months, depending on how far the ranch was from a cow town. More than 2,000 head of cattle were rounded up for a big cattle drive. Before the drive could begin, cowboys had to check each animal's brand—an identifying mark burned into its hide—to make sure that all the cattle belonged to the ranch they were working for. Cowboys also tamed horses, branded calves, herded the cattle safely across rivers, and prevented stampedes, or animals racing out of control.

Men of many different ethnicities worked as cowboys, but they all used the techniques and traditions developed by Mexican *vaqueros* (vuh-KAIR-ohz), or cattle drivers. These cowboys also adopted Mexican tools and apparel, such as spurs, chaps, and lariats. One of every seven cowboys was an African American. Although they were paid the same wages, African-American cowboys were not as likely to manage herds or hold other positions of authority on the cattle trail. Even so, some African-American cowboys became successful ranchers themselves when they retired from driving cattle.

When the use of barbed wire spread across the plains, and fences enclosed the once open range, the role of the cowboy faded. Today, as you know, many Western movies and novels portray cowboys as rugged heroes who led exciting lives, but wrangling cattle was hard work. Cowboys could easily work 14 hours or more every day. During cattle drives, cowboys worked in shifts to watch the herds through the night, rode throughout the day, and pocketed only about $30 or $40 per month for their labors.

IN SEARCH OF TREASURE

Farmers, ranchers, and cowboys worked hard for their money, but some people hoped to gain instant wealth. After the California gold rush of 1849, prospectors found gold and silver deposits in Colorado, Montana, and the Dakotas, as well as rich deposits of copper in New Mexico and Arizona.

The story was almost always the same. With the discovery of a **lode**, or vein of ore, a horde of hopeful miners rushed to the area, staked claims, and set up camp. Then the merchants arrived, bringing goods to sell to the miners at exorbitant, or very steep, prices. If the mineral lode was substantial, a wild and lawless mining camp might grow quickly into what was called a boomtown. Some boomtowns, such as Denver, Colorado, grew into large, prosperous cities. But most of the boomtowns went bust once the lode had been mined out. Abandoned as quickly as they sprang up, these boomtowns became ghost towns.

Initially, miners used **placer mining** techniques to search for gold, panning for gold nuggets and dust in riverbeds and streams with lightweight tools. They set up wooden runs called **sluices** to strain the water. But these techniques were not enough to eke, or obtain, every bit of precious metal from a rich lode. Soon mining companies stepped in and funded a much more intensive, aggressive process.

The companies used dynamite for **shaft mining**, blasting vertical channels into mountains. Once these dark passageways were carved out, men were lowered down shafts to mine for 10 to 12 hours a day using picks and shovels. Lack of oxygen, pockets of toxic gases, and cave-ins made these mines dangerous places to work. Other companies shot pressurized water onto the mountainsides to remove topsoil and gravel and expose the precious minerals beneath, a process known as **hydraulic mining**, or hydropower mining. Debris and the toxic chemicals used in the process—including mercury—flowed downstream, contaminating farmers' water sources. Farmers sued the mining companies and put an end to hydraulic mining, but it took decades for the land and water to recover.

Mining spawned many stories of fortune and failure. It also helped to spread the Union from coast to coast. People demanded law enforcement and government in the hastily organized, unruly mining camps. This eventually led to the creation of new territories and several new states, including Colorado in 1876. The Dakotas, Montana, and Washington were admitted to the Union in 1889.

Western expansion and advances in technology enriched the nation and made work more efficient, but this progress often came at a price—especially for farmers. Even as their farms became productive, many farmers found themselves falling into a cycle of debt. In time, they decided to get together and do something about it.

HI 1 Students show the connections, causal and otherwise, between particular historical events and larger social, economic, and political trends and developments; HI 5 Students analyze human modifications of landscapes and examine the resulting environmental policy issues.

Art Institute of Chicago

On a trip to Mexico in 1889, American artist Frederic Remington made sketches of the horsemen he saw there. He used this material to create many illustrations and paintings, including this one in 1890 called *A Mexican Vaquero.* The portrait of the *vaquero*, shown here sitting on his horse and looking directly at the viewer, was also made into a wood engraving for *Harper's New Monthly Magazine* in 1891.

HISTORICAL THINKING

1. **READING CHECK** What attracted settlers to the Great Plains after the Civil War?
2. **ANALYZE ENVIRONMENTAL CONCEPTS** In what ways were the byproducts of shaft mining and hydraulic mining detrimental to several natural systems?
3. **DRAW CONCLUSIONS** How was the establishment of new states and territories in the West connected to unruly behavior in mining camps?
4. **MAKE INFERENCES** What qualities did settlers need to survive on the Great Plains?

HOW GEOLOGY WATERS THE GREAT PLAINS

By Andrés Ruzo, National Geographic Explorer

Fresh water is one of our most rare and precious resources. We can't survive without it. Thanks to modern plumbing and water purification techniques, about 99 percent of Americans can get water right from the tap, but this ease of access is misleading. Only about 3 percent of Earth's water is fresh, and most of this water is locked away in ice caps and glaciers. Of all the water on Earth, less than 1 percent is available to humans as usable fresh water.

FROM THE GREAT AMERICAN DESERT

Most Americans get their fresh water from either surface or groundwater **reservoirs**, contained bodies of water that can be tapped. As rain flows over the land's surface, some of it collects in rivers and lakes, and some seeps into the earth. The water that soaks into the surface fills the space between soil particles and fractures in rock to become groundwater. Certain geologic formations have the right conditions below the surface to hold large groundwater reservoirs. These formations are called **aquifers**.

The water in some aquifers flows to the surface naturally. To get water from other aquifers, however, engineers must drill down and raise the water to the surface. Depending on the type of rock, an aquifer will produce different amounts and types of water. Fault zones, areas of easily dissolved rock, and expanses of gravel often result in productive aquifers. The groundwater can effectively flow through the fractures and spaces in the rock. Areas of rock that are solid and not porous or fractured usually do not form aquifers because water cannot penetrate.

In 1820, U.S. Army major Stephen H. Long dubbed the Great Plains, "the Great American Desert." He considered this dry, flat land, "almost wholly unfit for cultivation, and of course uninhabitable by a people depending upon agriculture for their subsistence." Despite this warning, settlers moved to the Great Plains in droves beginning in the 1860s and 1870s. While many did manage to make a living, it was tough. The thick sod of the plains had to be broken up before crops could be planted. And though farmers were able to use pumps powered by windmills to bring some underground water to the surface, this technique had its drawbacks. Farmers were not usually able to dig deep enough wells, and the pumping mechanisms did not work when the wind was not blowing. By the 1930s, drought and poor farming practices had so eroded parts of the Great Plains, they became known as the Dust Bowl because of the terrible dust storms that blew through the region.

Before pump technology improved in the 1950s, farmers struggled to create irrigation systems to water their fields, as shown in this photo of an Oklahoma farmer in the 1930s.

11.8.6 Discuss the diverse environmental regions of North America, their relationship to local economies, and the origins and prospects of environmental problems in those regions; CST 1 Students compare the present with the past, evaluating the consequences of past events and decisions and determining the lessons that were learned.

TO AMERICA'S BREADBASKET

Those settlers would never have believed that this same region would become part of America's breadbasket by the 1950s—all thanks to the **Ogallala Aquifer** (also called the High Plains Aquifer). For the past 15,000 years, water has been slowly collecting in the space between underground sand and gravel grains to form the Ogallala Aquifer. Spanning eight states, it's one of the world's largest aquifers.

Unfortunately, farmers didn't have access to this aquifer during westward expansion. In fact, full access to this reservoir wasn't available until the 1950s, when new technology made it economically viable to drill deep into the aquifer and access its water using powerful pumps. Today, Ogallala waters help grow nearly one-fifth of the wheat, corn, and beef cattle produced in the United States.

However, overuse has been drying up the Ogallala Aquifer. By the 1960s, geologists realized its water was limited, and natural processes refill it very slowly. Without rules for responsible groundwater extraction, some estimates indicate the aquifer will run dry as early as 2028. Once drained, it will take more than 6,000 years for it to naturally replenish.

THINK LIKE A GEOLOGIST

1. **IDENTIFY MAIN IDEAS AND DETAILS** Why are aquifers important to humans?
2. **DRAW CONCLUSIONS** Why is the fact that early settlers were unable to fully tap into the Ogallala Aquifer beneficial to farmers today?
3. **ANALYZE ENVIRONMENTAL CONCEPTS** What human practices in the 1950s altered the natural processes within the Ogallala Aquifer?

CRITICAL VIEWING Center-pivot irrigation systems, widely used to distribute water from the Ogallala Aquifer, operate equipment and sprinklers that rotate around a central point, or pivot, giving farm fields this circular pattern. How might this current form of irrigation be more efficient than others in this region?

CST 4 Students relate current events to the physical and human characteristics of places and regions.

1.3 **MAIN IDEA** Farmers joined together to try to solve their economic problems and address the political issues that most concerned them.

FARMERS AND THE POPULIST MOVEMENT

Staying afloat in any business is tough. In your own community, you've probably seen stores and restaurants close after they failed to thrive. Imagine, then, what it must have been like for small farmers in the late 19th century, who struggled against so many odds to make a profit. Some just didn't make it.

FARMERS STRUGGLE

Around 1870, farmers in the South, Midwest, and West all faced economic hardship. As a result of new technology, farms had become more productive, but the surplus of agricultural products caused the prices of the goods to fall. For example, the price of a bushel of wheat in 1865 was $1.50. By contrast, the price of that same bushel in 1894 was $0.49. In addition, the equipment and technology farmers had to invest in to remain productive—and competitive—cost a great deal of money. The prices of farm equipment and the shipping rates charged by the railroads continued to increase. Caught in a cycle of debt, many farmers faced financial ruin.

A boll weevil like this one grows to only about a half-inch long. It uses its anteater-like snout to devour the buds of cotton plants.

To keep out of debt, some farmers in the South turned to **tenant farming**, a system in which farmland—often including a house—was rented from a property owner. Tenant farmers decided what to plant and when, and they pocketed any profit they made from selling their crops. They used part of their profit to pay the rent on the land. During Reconstruction, many southern African Americans had intended to work as tenant farmers, but the majority of those who were newly freed from slavery lacked the financial means to start or operate a farm. So many African Americans became **sharecroppers**, working for a landowner who provided the basics: land, seeds, equipment, and meager shelter. In exchange, sharecroppers worked the land and turned over most of the crops to the landowners to sell. Sharecroppers could sell a small portion of the crops they grew, but they rarely sold enough to become independent farmers.

Tenant farmers and sharecroppers often bought seeds and tools on credit from furnishing merchants until their harvests were sold. These merchants placed **liens**, which were legal claims to the farmers' crops, home, and property if they failed to pay their debts. The interest rates the merchants charged were so exorbitant—as high as 60 percent—that many tenant farmers and most sharecroppers were trapped, unable to improve their economic condition. Ultimately, they worked just to pay off their debt—a system known as **debt peonage** or debt slavery.

To make matters even worse, disaster struck the South in 1892 in the form of the boll weevil, a beetle that ate the buds and flowers of the cotton plant. When this happens, the boll, or the rounded, fluffy seed capsule of the cotton, does not form. The boll is what is harvested, processed, and spun into

11.1.4 Examine the effects of the Civil War and Reconstruction and of the industrial revolution, including demographic shifts and the emergence in the late nineteenth century of the United States as a world power.

In this 1890 photo, African-American sharecroppers, including men, women, and children, harvest cotton in Georgia.

thread. Without the boll, there is no crop. Because the southern economy largely depended on cotton production, failed crops affected everyone's livelihood: landowners, sharecroppers, and merchants. When the cotton failed, many people were ruined financially and fled the South. Those who remained learned to diversify their crops, growing plants that weren't affected by the boll weevil. Eventually, the diversification of crops brought new agricultural industry and profits to the region.

FARMERS ORGANIZE

Dependent on merchants, railroads, and banks, which also charged high interest rates, farmers from many regions of the country started to organize and unite in protest. In the 1870s, a group of farmers in Texas formed the first **Farmers' Alliance**. By the 1880s, other alliances arose with millions of members in the South and the Midwest. These alliances served not only a social, cultural, and political purpose but also an economic one.

To help resolve their economic grievances, farmers in local Granges, or lodges within an alliance, banded together and formed cooperatives. **Cooperatives** are organizations run and funded by their members. Each farmer contributed funds into a pool of money, which the cooperative then used to buy seeds and equipment. The larger the order for goods or services, the easier it was to negotiate a good price. The cooperatives also demanded lower shipping and storage rates from railroads and loans at lower interest rates from banks.

One of the most significant problems farmers faced was selling crops at harvest time when there was an overabundance of agricultural products. As you've learned, this overabundance kept the prices of the goods low. To address this problem, Charles Macune came up with the **subtreasury system**, whereby the government set up storage silos, or subtreasuries, in urban centers. When a farmer deposited a crop in the silo, the government would loan the farmer a percentage of the crop's value to buy new seeds for the next season at a low interest rate. In 1889, Macune presented his system at a conference in St. Louis. However, some politicians questioned the constitutionality of having the government lend money to private citizens and refused to support Macune's plan. It was never put into practice.

African-American farmers, who were banned from joining the mostly white Farmers' Alliances, formed the **Colored Farmers' National Alliance** in 1886. At its peak, about 250,000 African-American farmers belonged to the alliance. However, in 1891, the Colored Alliance went on strike, refusing to pick cotton unless landowners increased their wages. Ben Patterson of Arkansas organized the strike, which resulted in the lynching of 15 strikers, including Patterson himself. After that incident, the Colored Alliance soon dissolved.

THE POPULIST PARTY

In time, the Farmers' Alliances began to push their ideas forward more forcefully on the political stage. But they wanted an alternative to the Republican and Democratic parties, both of which they believed had failed to support their interests. In 1892, Alliance leaders formed a third political party, known as the

A GLOBAL PERSPECTIVE Today, farmers' cooperatives, like those that arose in the late 1800s in the United States, have been established in countries all over the world. In this photo, African farmers belonging to the Orinde Farmers' Cooperative Society in Kenya sort coffee beans on a drying bed. About 700,000 small-scale farmers belong to more than 500 cooperatives in Kenya. These agricultural cooperatives help create jobs and provide training and financial help for members.

People's Party or the **Populist Party**. **Populism** is the belief that ordinary people should control government rather than a small group of wealthy, elite politicians. Populists called for a government that would serve "the plain people." While the populists' political platform promoted subtreasuries and called for regulations against businesses that charged farmers unreasonable rates for storage and shipping, it also supported workers' rights, specifically an eight-hour workday. A woman named Mary Elizabeth Lease became a powerful advocate for the Populist Party. Lease had gained prominence when she joined Kansas farmers in a revolt against high mortgage rates and railroad shipping costs, declaring that farmers should "raise less corn and more hell."

Although the farmers of the South and the West grew different crops and had different cultures, they had common concerns. For a time, they joined together in the Populist Party. The populists' most well-known concern revolved around the issue of silver coinage. At the time, American currency was backed by gold. The **gold standard** required the U.S. government to only print an amount of money equal to the total value of its gold reserves. Strictly following the gold standard kept a limited amount of currency in circulation, which, in turn, kept the economy from growing, even though the nation's population was rapidly expanding. The only way the United States could distribute more money was to obtain more gold. The limited number of dollars in circulation affected the value of each one. Farmers found they had to work harder to maintain the same level of income. As a result, they looked for ways to inflate the currency—that is, put more dollars into circulation—and help lift themselves out of debt.

With an abundant supply of silver from mines in the West, the Populist Party supported the **free silver movement**. According to the plan proposed, anyone holding silver could have it minted into U.S. coins for a small fee, and the coins could then be placed into circulation. Introducing free silver with the existing currency would increase the money supply and inflate prices substantially. In 1896, the Democratic nominee for president, **William Jennings Bryan**, supported the free silver platform. The Republican nominee, **William McKinley**, was for the gold standard. Although the populists had united farmers in the South and the West throughout the early 1890s, farmers threw their support behind the Democrats. When the Populist Party as a whole supported Bryan, its members joined the Democratic Party. The Populist Party came to an end.

PRIMARY SOURCE

At the Democratic Convention in 1896, William Jennings Bryan gave a fiery speech in support of free silver that came to be known as the "Cross of Gold" speech. In this excerpt from the speech, Bryan compares the gold standard to the crown of thorns Christians believe was placed on Jesus' head before he was crucified.

If they dare to come out in the open field and defend the gold standard as a good thing, we shall fight them to the uttermost, having behind us the producing masses of the nation and the world. Having behind us the commercial interests and the laboring interests and all the toiling masses, we shall answer their demands for a gold standard by saying to them, you shall not press down upon the brow of labor this crown of thorns. You shall not crucify mankind upon a cross of gold.

—from William Jennings Bryan's "Cross of Gold" speech, 1896

As it turned out, Bryan lost the 1896 election because of his free silver platform. Unlike farmers in other regions, those in the Northeast didn't pay high prices to warehouse their crops. Northeastern farmers lived near urban centers and shipped their crops short distances. Thus, these farmers did not support Bryan's economic ideas. Neither did the richest people in the nation. Proponents of free silver faced strong opposition from railroads, banks, and business owners who held almost all of the nation's wealth and who feared their interest rates would fall substantially with Bryan as president. The Republicans also convinced voters to turn against Bryan by fanning fears that free silver would lead to inflation. As a result, McKinley won the presidential election, and the gold standard remained in place until 1933.

HISTORICAL THINKING

1. **READING CHECK** How were farmers affected by industrialization?
2. **DRAW CONCLUSIONS** Why was sharecropping considered another form of slavery?
3. **MAKE INFERENCES** Why do you think Bryan used a biblical metaphor to argue his case in favor of free silver?
4. **ANALYZE CAUSE AND EFFECT** How did the free silver movement affect the Populist Party and the 1896 presidential election?

11.2.8 Examine the effect of political programs and activities of Populists; HI 4 Students understand the meaning, implication, and impact of historical events and recognize that events could have taken other directions.

1.4 THROUGH THE LENS AMERICAN PLACES

AMERICA'S BREADBASKET: THE GREAT PLAINS

For a long time, the term "breadbasket" referred literally to the basket that held your family's bread or rolls during meals. Today, it's a common name for a country's food-producing region, and in the United States, that's the Great Plains. Parts or all of 10 different states fall within the Great Plains, and most of them—Nebraska, Kansas, Iowa, Illinois, Indiana, and North Dakota, to name a few—are considered the breadbasket of North America because of the abundance of grains they produce.

The notion that an agricultural region could provide grain to cities that can't produce their own food isn't a new one. It dates back to the classical Greeks and Romans. In the United States, the farmers, fertile soils, and inexpensive available land of the Midwest have been growing reliable staple crops since the 1700s, and feeding not only Americans, but people across the world. Chances are great that the wheat, barley, corn, rice, or soybeans you eat each day are the product of your country's breadbasket.

Like other breadbasket states, Iowa is known for its cornfields. In 2015, the state's farmers grew 2.5 billion bushels of corn on 13 million sprawling acres of farmland. To preserve soil quality, corn is rotated with soybeans, growing here in front of the corn in the distance.

2.1 **MAIN IDEA** As more people settled in the West, Native Americans fought to hold on to their lands and resisted relocation to reservations.

Growing Pressures on Native Americans

When settlers pushed westward, the Native Americans in the region were forced to leave their homelands. Some went quietly, but many Native Americans chose to resist and fight back.

BATTLES AND RESERVATIONS

Approximately 325,000 Native Americans inhabited the lands west of the Mississippi River prior to white settlement. Each tribe or nation had its own culture and customs, and sometimes groups fought one another for land and access to resources. As migrants began to head west along the Oregon and Santa Fe trails and miners pursued gold in California in 1848, Native Americans in the region sometimes launched attacks on the settlers and miners who were pushing westward.

In an attempt to stop the violence, U.S. officials and Native Americans met in Wyoming in 1851 and signed the **Treaty of Fort Laramie**. The treaty guaranteed the Native Americans in the territory an annual cash payment. In exchange, the Native Americans agreed to remain within specified boundaries, end their attacks on settlers, and allow the U.S. military to build forts in the area. The treaty worked. Wagon trains filled with settlers passed safely through tribal lands, and the U.S. Army encountered no resistance as it built its forts.

However, conflicts arose once again when even greater numbers of American pioneers and homesteaders began to migrate to the West in the 1860s. The constant flow of white settlers and the expansion of the transcontinental railroad threatened to push the Native Americans off the lands they'd been guaranteed. In addition, the settlers' cattle, sheep, and horses competed for grazing land with the vast herds of bison that roamed the region, and commercial hunters slaughtered many of the huge animals. Native Americans living in the West relied on bison for food and supplies, using every part of the animal. Throughout the 1860s and 1870s, growing tensions over land and the bison erupted into frequent battles between Native Americans and U.S. forces.

The U.S. government tried to put an end to the conflicts by establishing reservations to confine Native Americans. A **reservation** is an area of land designated for and managed by a particular Native American tribe. However, most Native Americans found it hard to survive on reservations, which were typically located on undesirable land that was not good for farming. Most Native American cultures were based on a lifestyle of hunting and **foraging**, or searching for plants. The animals and plants Native Americans traditionally sought for food, medicines, and rituals were often scarce on reservations.

Native Americans were supposed to be safe on their reservations, but that was not always the case. In 1864, the governor of the Colorado Territory told the Cheyenne living there to gather near Fort Lyon on Sand Creek. He promised them protection from the battles raging in the region. Chief Black Kettle, leader of the Cheyenne, had his people set up camp along the creek. To show that the Cheyenne were friendly, he flew an American flag. Others in the village raised white flags, indicating their desire to communicate.

Ignoring these signs of peace, Colonel John Chivington, commander of a group of volunteer militiamen, swept into the camp after the able-bodied men had left to hunt. The militiamen slaughtered at least 150 unarmed women, children, and elderly men in the **Sand Creek Massacre**. In retaliation, the Cheyenne, Lakota, and Arapaho living in the territory conducted raids on unsuspecting settlers.

11.1.4 Examine the effects of the Civil War and Reconstruction and of the industrial revolution, including demographic shifts and the emergence in the late nineteenth century of the United States as a world power.

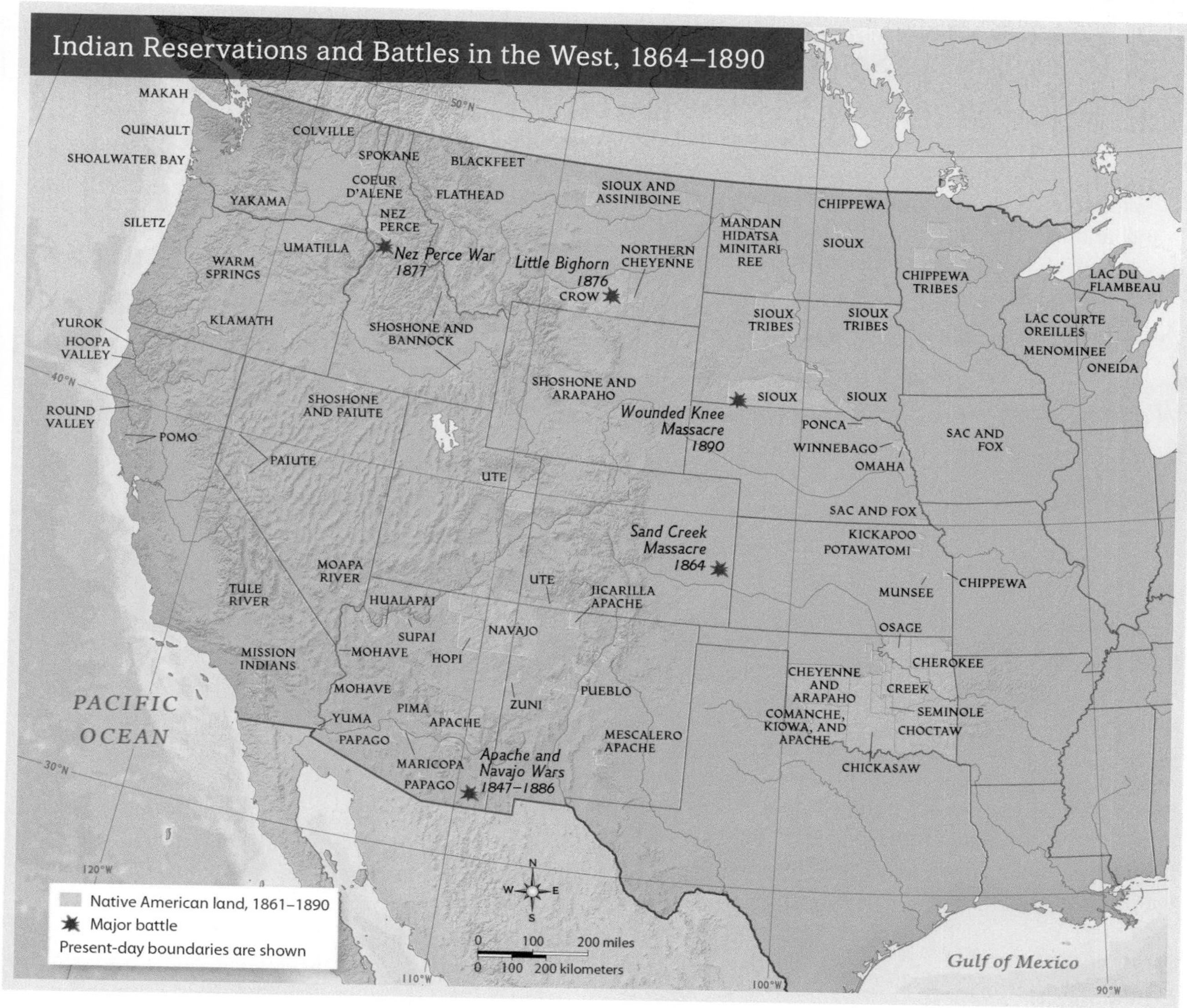

THE LITTLE BIGHORN

Few Native Americans liked being confined to a specific territory. But after the U.S. government promised the Lakota that miners and settlers would not encroach on their territory, they reluctantly agreed to settle on a reservation in the Black Hills in present-day South Dakota. When gold was discovered in the Black Hills, however, Colonel **George A. Custer** allowed miners to cross into Lakota hunting territory, in violation of a new Fort Laramie Treaty drawn up in 1868.

In 1874, the treaty was officially voided, and the commissioner of Indian affairs demanded that all Lakota leave the Black Hills by the end of January 1876. Sitting Bull, leader of the Lakota, refused to move, and troops arrived to force the relocation. Eventually Sitting Bull moved his band to a camp in the valley of the Little Bighorn River in Montana. There the Cheyenne, Lakota, and other Native Americans who had abandoned their reservations joined Sitting Bull in his fight.

On June 25, 1876, Colonel Custer and his 7th Cavalry entered Sitting Bull's encampment on the Little Bighorn River. The roughly 2,000 Native American warriors were in an advantageous position. Custer had only about 200 men, but the U.S. troops attacked anyway. The warriors killed nearly all of them, including Colonel Custer, in the **Battle of the Little Bighorn**. It marked the worst defeat for the U.S. Army in the Native American wars.

After their victory, the Lakota did not go on the offensive, but the U.S. government did. Fighting continued for another five years, and the U.S. Army ultimately forced the Lakota to relinquish their hunting grounds and relocate to reservations. The United States seized the Black Hills.

CST 3 Students use a variety of maps and documents to interpret human movement, including major patterns of domestic and international migration, changing environmental preferences and settlement patterns, the frictions that develop between population groups, and the diffusion of ideas, technological innovations, and goods.

AMERICAN PLACES

Black Hills of South Dakota

National Geographic photographer Anand Varma captured this scene overlooking a canyon in the Black Hills, a small mountain range that rises in South Dakota and extends into Wyoming. The Lakota—often called the Sioux—have refused offers of payment as compensation for the land from the U.S. government. The Lakota only want the Black Hills, which they consider their spiritual home.

CHIEF JOSEPH AND GERONIMO

A similar pattern of resistance played out in other regions as well. The Nez Perce (NEHZ PURSE), who had traditionally lived in the Pacific Northwest, refused to give up their territory and relocate to a small reservation in Idaho. Despite being outgunned and outnumbered, **Chief Joseph** fought U.S. troops while leading his band of about 700 Nez Perce in a retreat toward the Canadian border. The Nez Perce journeyed about 1,600 miles, climbing steep mountains and trudging across hot plains, but the U.S. Army apprehended them just 30 miles from the border.

PRIMARY SOURCE

Chief Joseph made his surrender speech at Bear Paw, Montana, in 1877. In this excerpt from the speech, Chief Joseph reflects the despair of all Native Americans whose efforts to resist the U.S. government had failed.

It is cold, and we have no blankets; the little children are freezing to death. My people, some of them, have run away to the hills, and have no blankets, no food. No one knows where they are—perhaps freezing to death. I want to have time to look for my children, to see how many I can find. Maybe I shall find them among the dead. Hear me, my chiefs! I am tired; my heart is sick and sad. From where the sun now stands, I will fight no more forever.

—from Chief Joseph's surrender speech, 1877

When Chief Joseph's band finally surrendered at Bear Paw Mountain in Montana, they were guaranteed settlement in Idaho, but the government broke that promise. Instead, the Nez Perce were sent to the Oklahoma Territory, where disease caused mass casualties. In 1884, after the public became aware of the tribe's plight, advocates pressured the government to allow the Nez Perce to return to their native lands. Today, they belong to a confederation of tribes in eastern Washington State.

In the Southwest, Apache chief **Geronimo** also resisted forced government confinement. In the 1870s, the Apache had been confined to a reservation in Arizona. Geronimo frequently left the reservation with a small band of followers to raid towns and settlements. In September 1886, Geronimo and 400 other Apaches were captured, exiled to Florida, and imprisoned there. Many of the prisoners died in Florida because the unfamiliar tropical environment made them susceptible to diseases. The U.S. government denied Geronimo's request to return his people to Arizona. Instead, in 1894, his band was transferred to Fort Sill in Oklahoma, where Geronimo died at the age of 80 in 1909.

Some people call the treatment of Native Americans **genocide**, or the deliberate killing of a large group of people and its culture. Many historians consider the Native American wars to have ended with Geronimo's capture. While in captivity, the Apache chief became a celebrity and sometimes appeared in public. When his autobiography was published in 1906, he dedicated the book to President Theodore Roosevelt. Geronimo believed Roosevelt was "fair-minded" and would treat the Apache people with justice in the future. However, on his deathbed, the chief told his nephew, "I should never have surrendered; I should have fought until I was the last man alive."

HISTORICAL THINKING

1. **READING CHECK** Why did the U.S. government break the Treaty of Fort Laramie?
2. **INTERPRET MAPS** Locate areas on the map with several reservations clustered together. What inferences can you make about the type of land in these areas and why tribes were placed there?
3. **MAKE PREDICTIONS** How might history have unfolded differently if the United States had not forced Native Americans to relocate to reservations?
4. **DRAW CONCLUSIONS** What did Chief Joseph mean when he said, "From where the sun now stands, I will fight no more forever"?

HI 4 Students understand the meaning, implication, and impact of historical events and recognize that events could have taken other directions.

2.2 **MAIN IDEA** Efforts by the U.S. government to assimilate Native Americans culminated in the massacre at Wounded Knee.

BROKEN PROMISES

Relations between the U.S. government and Native Americans were characterized by a trail of broken promises. No matter how many treaties Native Americans signed, their situation grew ever more desperate.

DAMAGE TO NATIVE CULTURES

The American public began to recognize the wrongs committed against Native Americans. In 1877, President Rutherford Hayes spoke out about how the nation had repeatedly broken its promises to them. Writer **Helen Hunt Jackson** also drew attention to the Native American plight in her 1881 book *A Century of Dishonor.* She submitted her work to Congress, hoping to stir its members to pass legislation that would improve Native American lives.

To that end, Congress passed the **Dawes Severalty Act** in 1887, which divided reservations into land **allotments**, or sections, of 160 acres. Native Americans who received an allotment were expected to establish farms. After 25 years, those who had successfully established a farm could become U.S. citizens. Sponsors intended the law as a positive alternative to the reservation system. However, the law also allowed the public to purchase any unoccupied allotments. Since most Native Americans of the Great Plains had lived as nomadic hunters and gatherers, few wanted to settle on the farms. So white settlers rushed to purchase the best reservation land. In the end, the allotments only weakened Native American communities.

THE TRAGEDY AT WOUNDED KNEE

By the 1880s, many Native Americans lived in poverty on reservations. They also suffered from illness, malnutrition, and despair. This was the case at the Pine Ridge Reservation on Wounded Knee Creek, to which Lakota leader Sitting Bull and his band had been sent. The United States considered Sitting Bull an agitator, or someone who seeks to rouse anger and stir rebellion as a means of forcing change. Sitting Bull refused to sign government treaties and boldly voiced his doubts over government promises. U.S. officials also believed Sitting Bull was the driving force behind the **Ghost Dance** movement.

Actually, the movement got underway in 1889 after a Northern Paiute named Wovoka had a vision of a rescuer destroying white men and restoring the world to Native Americans. Wovoka taught followers the ceremonial Ghost Dance, which would usher in this deliverer. Once every six weeks, the participants danced for five nights; on the final night, they danced until morning. The practice spread to many reservations in the West—including the Pine Ridge Reservation—giving demoralized Native Americans hope. Fearing the Ghost Dance would result in uprisings, the U.S. government tried unsuccessfully to ban it.

In autumn 1890, when government officials came to the Pine Ridge Reservation to distribute land allotments to the Lakota, Sitting Bull declared he and his followers would refuse them. This rebuff, as well as the fact that the officials believed Sitting Bull had instigated the Ghost Dance, led the government to issue a warrant for his arrest. On December 15, 1890, authorities tried to seize Sitting Bull. He resisted arrest and was fatally shot during the scuffle.

But his death did not end the Ghost Dance. Two weeks later, the U.S. Army confronted Lakota Ghost Dancers gathered at Wounded Knee Creek and demanded they hand over their weapons. During the tense transaction, a shot was fired—no one knows by whom—but U.S. troops immediately opened fire in return, killing about 300 Lakota. The **Massacre at Wounded Knee** failed to put an end to the Ghost Dance, but from then on, the ceremony was conducted in secret. However, the massacre did halt any further Native American resistance.

11.3.3 Cite incidences of religious intolerance in the United States (e.g., persecution of Mormons, anti-Catholic sentiment, anti-Semitism).

CRITICAL VIEWING In 1890, the U.S. government attempted to assimilate Native American children, or change their language, habits, and dress, by sending them to boarding schools to learn white values and culture. The Apache children shown in these two photos taken by John Choate were among those captured with Geronimo in Arizona in 1886. The children were sent to the Carlisle Indian Industrial School, a boarding school in Pennsylvania.

Choate took the top photo shortly after the children's arrival at the school. The bottom photo, showing the same children, was taken after four months at the school. What does the children's physical appearance reveal about the ways they were changed by the school?

HISTORICAL THINKING

1. **READING CHECK** What were the aim and results of the Dawes Severalty Act?
2. **MAKE INFERENCES** Why might U.S. officials have believed that Sitting Bull started the Ghost Dance movement?
3. **SYNTHESIZE** What series of misunderstandings led to the Massacre at Wounded Knee?
4. **DRAW CONCLUSIONS** What effect did assimilation have on the Native American community?

HI 1 Students show the connections, causal and otherwise, between particular historical events and larger social, economic, and political trends and developments.

The Field Museum of Natural History arose as a result of the World's Columbian Exposition, an international fair held in 1893 in Chicago. The fair celebrated the 400th anniversary of Christopher Columbus's landing in the so-called "New World" in 1492. Its exhibits showcased the development of civilization, with a focus on American culture.

Leading citizens of Chicago established the Field Museum in 1893 to commemorate the exposition and house its exhibits, which included an extensive collection of Native American artifacts. Over time, the Field Museum developed into a renowned natural history museum, covering such fields as anthropology, botany, zoology, and geology.

"The wonderful thing about museums is that you can **interact directly with other cultures**—ancient and modern—through their artifacts."

—Bill Parkinson, Associate Curator

The White City

This postcard from the Columbian Exposition shows the "White City," which showcased the fair's main exhibition buildings. Painted white, these buildings housed exhibits of industrial technology, agricultural production, and fine art. Running at a right angle to the White City was the Midway Plaisance, a mile-long avenue with live exhibits of indigenous people of many cultures. The Midway was intended to display humanity's progress toward the "ideal" civilization of the White City.

Columbian Exposition tickets cost 50 cents for adults and 25 cents for children under 12.

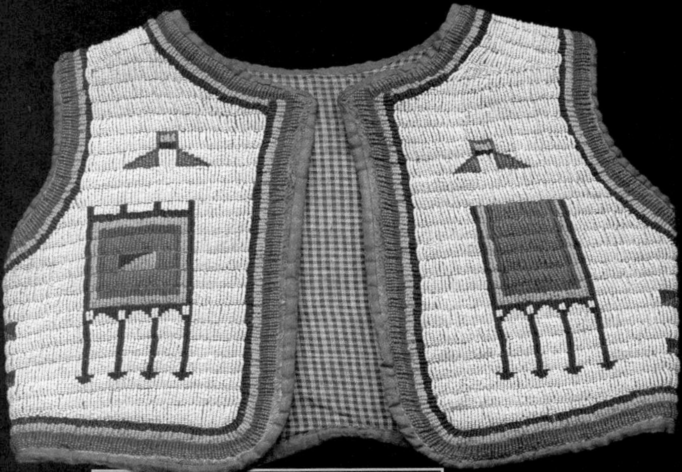

Sioux Beaded Vest

This Sioux beaded vest was worn by a child in a "live display" at the Columbian Exposition. At the fair, Native American performers lived in reconstructed villages to demonstrate their traditional life for fairgoers. The Sioux were one of the Plains Indian groups who lived in tepees and hunted bison. As this vest demonstrates, they were also highly skilled at beadwork.

How might a "live display" have been perceived differently by performers and spectators?

This mask was made before 1893 by a Kwakiutl artist named Xániyus.

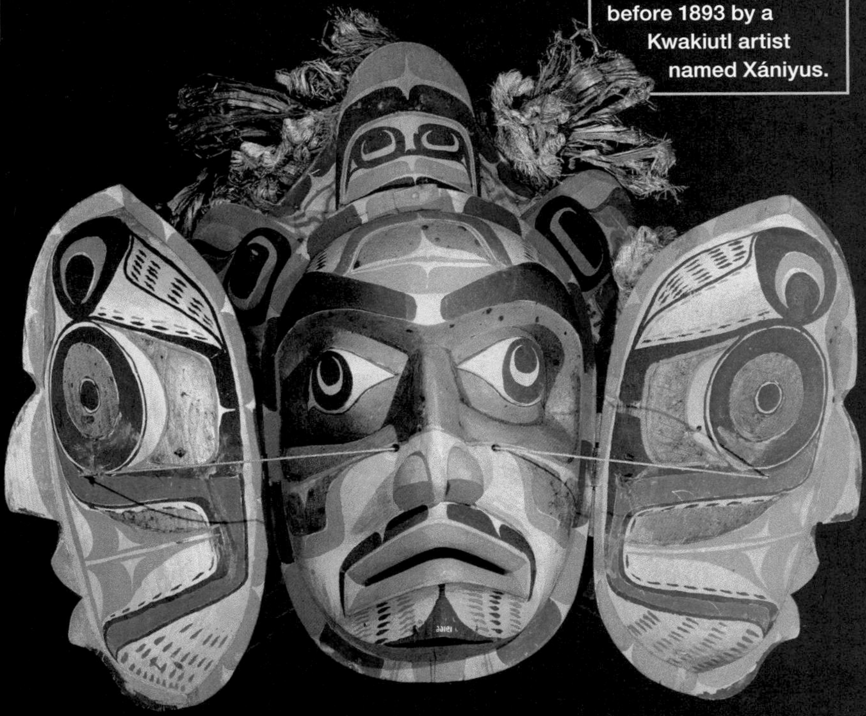

Kwakiutl Transformation Mask

Known for their painted carvings, the Kwakiutl originally lived in what is now British Columbia, Canada. This Kwakiutl carving is a transformation mask, which can be opened by strings to reveal another image. Shown in the open position, this mask represents a shaman, a priest believed to have magic powers. The Kwakiutl thought a transformation mask represented the inner change believed to occur when it was worn, such as a transformation from a human to a particular animal.

Formed from thin, flat copper, this fish model has characteristics of two different species native to the Mississippi River system.

Hopewell Copper Fish

The Field Museum has one of the world's largest collections of artifacts from the Hopewell culture, which flourished more than 2,000 years ago in what is now southern Ohio. Most of the museum's collection comes from an excavation that was undertaken specifically to obtain Native American artifacts for the Columbian Exposition. The Hopewell culture produced especially fine metalwork, as represented by this copper fish.

HREP 2 Students identify bias and prejudice in historical interpretations.

2.4 **MAIN IDEA** As the frontier disappeared, Americans became fascinated with the tales of those who had tamed it.

Closing the Frontier

Westerns, with their strong, quiet heroes and dastardly bad guys, have been a staple of films for more than 100 years. That tradition was born after the frontier vanished and stories of the rugged people who settled it took hold in people's imaginations.

TRANSFORMED BY THE FRONTIER

As the U.S. government forced Native Americans onto reservations, white settlers flooded deeper into western states and territories. By 1890, census data showed there was no longer a western region in which the population numbered fewer than two people per square mile. The frontier, once marked by open, unpopulated land, had ceased to exist.

In response to the census data, historian **Frederick Jackson Turner** developed a theory about the importance of the frontier. He presented his frontier theory in the paper "The Significance of the Frontier in American History," which he delivered to the American Historical Association in 1893. His views influenced generations of historians. Turner maintained that western settlement had shaped America's national identity. He portrayed the frontier as a place that encouraged individualism and the belief that a person's independence and self-reliance were more important than the rules and concerns of society as a whole. As each generation pushed farther west, it became more democratic and **egalitarian**, or equal. The people relied on themselves and their neighbors instead of institutions or government officials. For example, if a horse was stolen, the sheriff often gathered together a **posse**, or group of armed men formed to capture an outlaw.

Turner's characterization of the frontier and the people who conquered it became widely accepted. Like most Americans of the late 19th century, he ignored the stories of many groups of people who were an important part of western history: Native Americans, Latinos, African Americans, Asians, and women of all ethnicities. Turner's frontier was solely one of white settlement and expansion.

PRIMARY SOURCE

In this excerpt from one of William Cody's autobiographical writings, he explains why the Wild West show was important to him and popular with his audience.

It was because of my great interest in the West, and my belief that its development would be assisted by the interest I could awaken in others, that I decided to bring the West to the East through the medium of the Wild West show. I am sure the people enjoyed this spectacle, for they flocked in crowds to see it. There was never a day when, looking back over the red and white men in my cavalcade, I did not know the thrill of the trail, and feel a little sorry that my Western adventures would thereafter have to be lived in spectacles.

—from *Buffalo Bill's Own Story: An Autobiography of Buffalo Bill,* by Colonel W.F. Cody, 1920

THE WILD, WILD WEST

Incomplete though it may have been, Turner's characterization of the West began to be reflected in popular culture. Easterners and those living in urban areas developed a particular fascination with stories of the West, no matter how embellished, or exaggerated, they were. Novels, songs, plays—and, in time, films—portrayed bold characters and their adventures on the now vanished frontier.

One figure in particular captured the imagination of Americans from all walks of life: **Buffalo Bill Cody**. William Cody was born on the prairie in 1846, and he worked as a messenger, livestock wrangler, gold prospector, and Pony Express rider delivering mail

11.1.4 Examine the effects of the Civil War and Reconstruction and of the industrial revolution, including demographic shifts and the emergence in the late nineteenth century of the United States as a world power.

throughout the West. In 1867, he began hunting bison—which many people at the time referred to as *buffalo*—to feed railroad construction crews. He hunted and killed more than 4,000 buffalo in 17 months, but he actually earned his nickname by taking part in an 8-hour buffalo shooting match with another hunter named William. Cody also fought in numerous battles during the Native American wars.

Cody became the larger-than-life protagonist, or main character, of a series of novels penned by E.Z.C. Judson. Judson wrote **dime novels**, popular fiction that sold for 10 cents a book, that were made widely available through improved printing methods and shipping. Dime novels were the forerunners of modern paperback books. Judson, who published his books under the pen name Ned Buntline, created a Buffalo Bill character that became as iconic as American folk hero and frontiersman **Davy Crockett** had been to earlier generations.

In 1872, Judson encouraged Cody to portray his fictional character on stage. Cody discovered he was a natural showman, and his first performances were so well received that he launched Buffalo Bill's Wild West show, a traveling act that was part circus and part theater. In his Wild West show, Cody featured Native Americans and bison in different scenes, telling mostly true—but often sensationalized—stories. Besides Buffalo Bill himself, the indisputable star of the show was **Annie Oakley**, an excellent markswoman. She performed for crowds at the Wild West show for 16 years and is widely considered America's first female superstar. Lakota leader Sitting Bull also joined the show for a short time. The show toured for three decades throughout the United States and Europe.

Dime novels laid the foundation for Western films, which appeared at the dawn of the movie industry. The first Western, *The Great Train Robbery,* was a black-and-white film released in 1903. It was so successful that producers quickly made more films in the same genre. Initially, Westerns were filmed in eastern cities, but as plots grew more complicated, they required more authentic-looking scenery. Thus, producers moved to California-based studios, where Westerns became a significant percentage of the movies produced—and Hollywood was born. The public viewed cowboy characters as heroes. In the 1950s and early 1960s, Westerns were the most popular genre of television programming. Though tastes in entertainment have changed somewhat since then, Western stories continue to find eager audiences in movies, television, and novels.

Annie Oakley was born Phoebe Ann Moses in 1860. Her family had a small farm, and as a child, Annie helped support it by shooting small wild game to sell to grocery stores. At age 15, she won a shooting contest against a traveling marksman named Frank Butler, who was charmed by Annie. The two married and soon began performing together, with Annie using the name "Oakley." Sitting Bull saw their show and gave Annie the Lakota name *Watanya Cicilla*—"Little Sure Shot." In 1885, she joined the Wild West show. Oakley continued performing into her sixties.

HISTORICAL THINKING

1. **READING CHECK** According to Frederick Jackson Turner, how did western settlement shape America's national identity?
2. **MAKE INFERENCES** Why do you think city dwellers became especially entranced with tales of the West?
3. **FORM AND SUPPORT OPINIONS** Do you agree with Turner's theory about the impact of western settlement on American identity? Explain why or why not.

11.5.6 Trace the growth and effects of radio and movies and their role in the worldwide diffusion of popular culture; HREP 1 Students distinguish valid arguments from fallacious arguments in historical interpretations.

CHAPTER 5 EXPANSION AND CONFLICT IN THE WEST
REVIEW

VOCABULARY

Use each of the following vocabulary terms in a sentence that shows an understanding of the term's meaning.

1. shaft mining HSS HI 5
   Some companies used shaft mining to blast the passageways needed to reach the veins of gold deep within the mountain.
2. tenant farmer HSS 11.1.4
3. lode HSS HI 5
4. lien HSS 11.1.4
5. forage HSS 11.1.4
6. allotment HSS 11.1.4
7. cooperative HSS 11.2.8
8. dime novel HSS 11.1.4
9. egalitarian HSS 11.2.8

READING STRATEGY

DRAW CONCLUSIONS

When you draw conclusions, you make a judgment based on what you have read. You analyze the facts, make inferences, and use your own experiences to form your judgment. Use a diagram like this one to draw conclusions about the impact of expansion and conflict in the West.

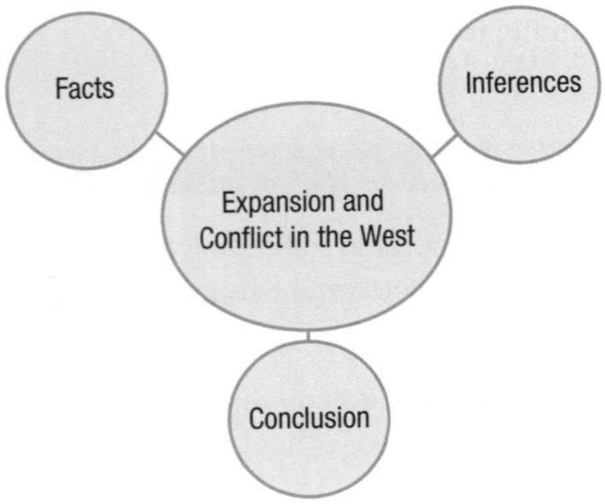

10. What impact did westward expansion and conflict with Native Americans have on American identity in the late 1800s? HSS HI 1

MAIN IDEAS

Answer the following questions. Support your answers with evidence from the chapter.

11. Why did Exodusters migrate west? LESSON 1.1 HSS 11.1.4
12. How did farmers respond to industrialization? LESSON 1.1 HSS 11.1.4
13. What is debt peonage? LESSON 1.3 HSS 11.2.8
14. What happened when William Jennings Bryan basically co-opted much of the Populist Party platform and ideology? LESSON 1.3 HSS 11.2.8
15. What contributed to the decline of the great bison herds? LESSON 2.1 HSS 11.1.4
16. What was the result of the Lakota victory at the Battle of the Little Bighorn? LESSON 2.1 HSS HI 1
17. Why did the U.S. government try to ban the Ghost Dance? LESSON 2.3 HSS HI 1
18. What piece of data clearly indicated that there was no longer a western frontier? LESSON 2.5 HSS 11.1.4
19. Who was left out of Frederick Jackson Turner's frontier theory, and why? LESSON 2.5 HSS HREP 2

HISTORICAL THINKING

Answer the following questions. Support your answers with evidence from the chapter.

20. **SYNTHESIZE** How did the federal government affect the country's growth in the years following the Civil War? HSS 11.1.4
21. **ANALYZE CAUSE AND EFFECT** How did the boll weevil infestation affect cotton production in the South? HSS HI 1
22. **EVALUATE** What impact—both good and bad—did settlement have on the Great Plains? HSS CST 3

23. **MAKE INFERENCES** How did Buffalo Bill Cody's life serve as inspiration for a character in a dime novel? HSS HI 1

24. **DRAW CONCLUSIONS** In the context of westward expansion, why did the U.S. government believe Native Americans would benefit from being assimilated into white culture? HSS HI 3

25. **COMPARE AND CONTRAST** In what ways were the lives of Chief Joseph and Geronimo both similar and different? HSS HI 1

INTERPRET VISUALS

This poster advertises land a railroad company sold on the Great Plains in 1872. Look at the poster and then answer the questions that follow.

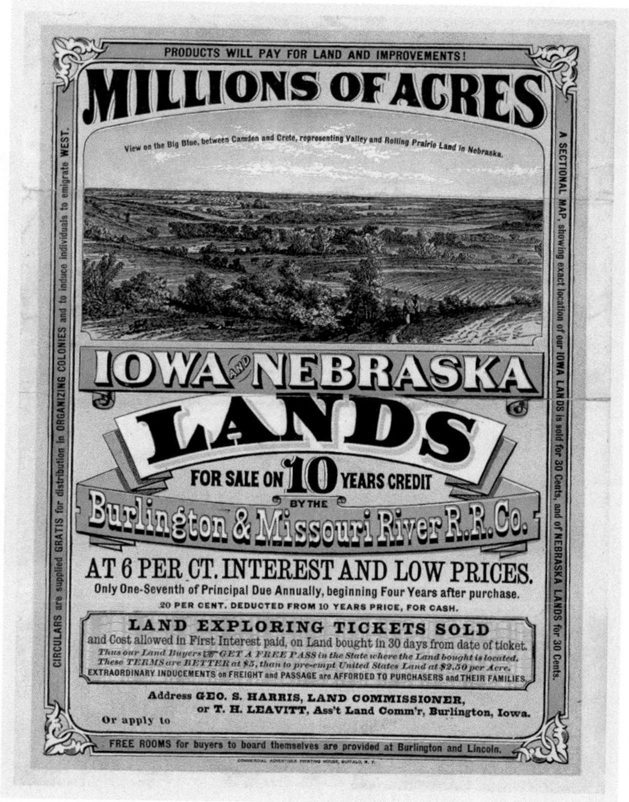

26. Based on what you've learned about the Great Plains, do you think the image in this poster of land in Iowa and Nebraska is an accurate depiction? Why or why not? HSS HREP 1

27. Why might those trying to sell this land use both valid and fallacious, or flawed, arguments in a poster like this one? HSS HREP 1

ANALYZE SOURCES

Helen Hunt Jackson was best known as a poet, but in 1881, she published *A Century of Dishonor*, a nonfiction book that exposed the injustice of U.S. government policies toward Native Americans. Read the excerpt from the book below and answer the question.

> There is not among these three hundred bands of Indians one which has not suffered cruelly at the hands either of the Government or of white settlers. The story of one tribe is the story of all, varied only by differences of time and place. Colorado is as greedy and unjust in 1880 as was Georgia in 1830, and Ohio in 1795, and the United States government breaks promises now as deftly [effortlessly] as then, and with the added ingenuity [inventiveness] from long practice.

28. What does the passage tell us about Jackson's historical interpretation of the U.S. government? HSS HREP 1

CONNECT TO YOUR LIFE

29. **ARGUMENT** You've read that westward expansion helped shape a new American identity. What do you think our identity is today, and what factors have shaped it? Write a paragraph in which you defend your ideas about what American identity means today. HSS CST 1

TIPS

- Think about how westward expansion shaped American identity in the late 1800s.
- Consider present-day events that have had a similar impact on our identity, including immigration and technology.
- Determine how these events have affected and changed our national identity.
- Write an opinion statement in which you state what you believe our American identity is today.
- Support your opinion with facts and reasons.

CHAPTER 6

INDUSTRIAL AMERICA 1877–1920

HISTORICAL THINKING What were the overall positive and negative effects of industrialization on America?

CRITICAL VIEWING In the 1880s, railroads were built to connect coal mines in the state of Washington with the port city of Seattle. Here a crew pauses during the final stages of building a railroad bridge over the Green River in western Washington. How does this scene convey the dynamic nature of the railroad industry?

“Make money—
honestly if you can—but make it.”

—Jay Gould, financier
and railroad executive

AMERICAN STORIES

NATIONAL GEOGRAPHIC

WORKING IN AMERICA

11.5.7 Discuss the rise of mass production techniques, the growth of cities, the impact of new technologies (e.g., the automobile, electricity), and the resulting prosperity and effect on the American landscape; 11.6.5 Trace the advances and retreats of organized labor, from the creation of the American Federation of Labor and the Congress of Industrial Organizations to current issues of a postindustrial, multinational economy, including the United Farm Workers in California.

CRITICAL VIEWING Workers build a truck engine on a General Motors assembly line in Flint, Michigan. What does this photograph reveal about the physical demands of a job like this and the skills a worker might need to have?

During the late 19th century, the nature of labor in the United States changed profoundly. In 1877, the country had 15 million non-domestic workers, with more than half in agriculture and another 4 million in manufacturing. In the decades that followed, the balance would shift as increasing numbers of Americans and new immigrants were attracted to factory work because it paid well. Manufacturing earnings went up about 50 percent between 1860 and 1890, prices of everyday goods fell, and wages increased. Earnings jumped again by 37 percent between 1890 and 1914.

Despite these improvements, working conditions weren't even close to what would be considered safe or even reasonable today. In 1890, the average pay rate for factory work was less than 16 cents per hour. The average workweek was 53 hours, and 2-day weekends were unheard of. In many industries, workers put in 12-hour workdays. At the same time, factory conditions were unsafe and largely unregulated by state or federal governments. At even greater risk than the adult workers—and earning lower wages—were the 1.75 million child laborers who were at work then.

The frustrations of the growing working class provided fertile soil for the seeds of the modern labor movement. Several large unions took up the cause of workers in industries such as steel, the railroads, and mining. Some of those unions no longer exist, but others, such as the American Federation of Labor, are still major forces today. In many ways, labor unions molded the 21st-century workplace. It is to their efforts that we owe reforms such as a 40-hour workweek and the end of child labor in factories and mines.

The story of American labor was shaped by a diverse group of charismatic activists, and it has influenced the lives of millions. This American Story focuses on a few of the many individuals who exemplify the diversity of labor in the United States.

MOTHER JONES

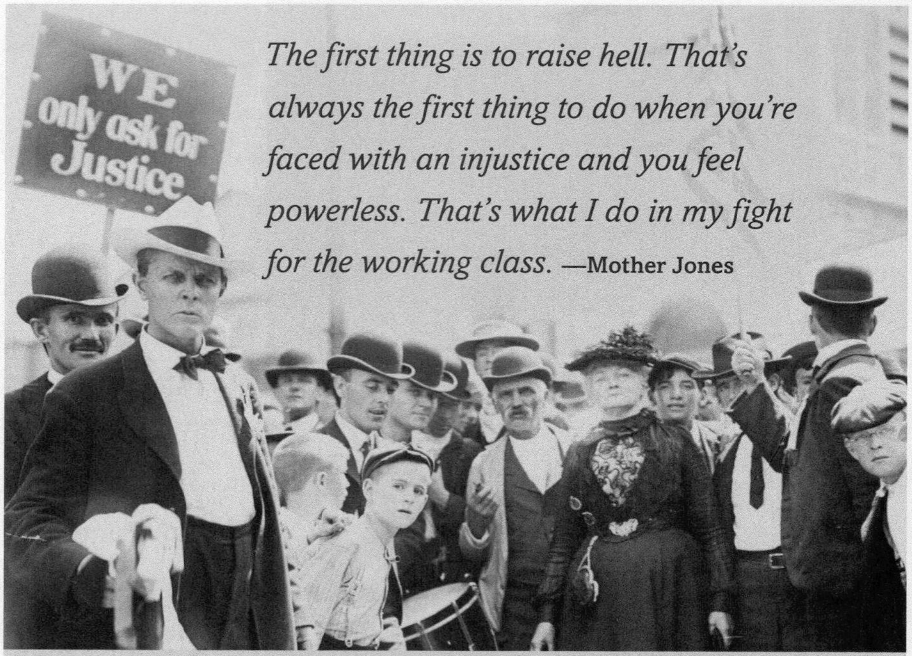

The first thing is to raise hell. That's always the first thing to do when you're faced with an injustice and you feel powerless. That's what I do in my fight for the working class. —Mother Jones

Mother Jones (center-right) and her army of striking textile workers are shown here descending upon New York City to protest unfair working conditions.

Round-faced, with a kindly expression and white hair in a messy bun atop her head, Mary Harris Jones looked like somebody's sweet elderly grandmother, and not the firebrand that she was in reality.

Born in Ireland around 1837, Harris and her family crossed the Atlantic to flee the devastation of the Great Irish Famine. In 1861, she married an American ironworker who was also a union supporter, but he and their children died in a yellow fever outbreak. Jones moved to Chicago and worked as a seamstress until she lost her home in the Great Chicago Fire of 1871. She then became a labor activist, campaigning for unions and workers' rights. In the 1870s, she traveled extensively, giving speeches to striking coal miners, railroad workers, and other laborers. The workers nicknamed her "Mother," a nod to her care for them. In 1905, Mother Jones helped found the Industrial Workers of the World union.

Mother Jones's efforts continued well into retirement age. While in her eighties, she actively supported a mine strike in West Virginia and traveled through Pennsylvania to encourage steel workers to vote in favor of a nationwide strike. She was arrested more than once for her activities but was never deterred. When one judge asked her who had given her a permit to speak on public property, she answered tartly, "Patrick Henry; Thomas Jefferson; John Adams!"

Unsurprisingly, Mother Jones elicited strong and varying reactions from workers, union organizers, factory owners, and government officials. Labor leader Eugene Debs called her the "heroine of a thousand battles." On the other side, one U.S. congressman condemned Mother Jones as a "notorious and troublesome woman" in a speech to the House of Representatives. One attorney for the government is said to have called her "the most dangerous woman in America," a label that is frequently used in biographies and other writings about the colorful activist.

THE JAPANESE-MEXICAN LABOR ASSOCIATION

Some early labor unions were exclusive, refusing to admit African Americans, women, or workers from certain ethnic groups. But others created bonds across ethnic groups as workers united to improve their conditions.

One such mixed union was the Japanese-Mexican Labor Association (JMLA), which was the first labor union formed by members of different racial backgrounds. The JMLA represented workers who had been hired by the Western Agricultural Contracting Company (WACC), a labor contractor, to work for a beet farming company in Oxnard, California. In February 1903, the JMLA presented a list of grievances to the WACC claiming workers were being paid less than they had been promised, and demanding that workers be allowed to shop in places other than the overpriced company store. When the JMLA went on strike, 90 percent of the laborers in the American beet industry stopped work to support them. Eventually, the WACC agreed to most of the JMLA's demands.

Justice is never given; it is exacted and the struggle must be continuous for freedom is never a final fact, but a continuing evolving process to higher and higher levels of human, social, economic, political, and religious relationship.

—A. Philip Randolph

A. Philip Randolph is considered one of the most important civil rights leaders to emerge from the labor movement.

A. PHILIP RANDOLPH

Asa Philip Randolph was born in Florida in 1889. In 1911, he moved to New York City, where he attended college at night and ran an employment agency. He attempted to organize black workers through his employment agency and later, during World War I, he advocated for more jobs for African Americans in the armed forces.

In 1925, Randolph became the founding president of the Brotherhood of Sleeping Car Porters, the first successful black trade union. At the time, long-distance travel within the United States often meant riding on a passenger train and, perhaps, spending the night in a sleeping car—a specialized railroad car with small bedroom compartments. Nearly all the porters who assisted sleeping-car passengers were African-American men. In 1937, the Brotherhood contracted with the Pullman Company, which manufactured and operated sleeping cars. Randolph's vision, however, extended well beyond any single union—he was determined to improve African Americans' job prospects overall.

In 1941, the American defense industry was rapidly expanding to provide arms and supplies to the country's European allies in World War II. Randolph observed that few African Americans were being hired to fill the new job openings, and the federal government was not taking action. Randolph began to plan a massive protest march on Washington, D.C., warning President Franklin D. Roosevelt that thousands of African-American workers would converge on the city. In response, Roosevelt issued an executive order forbidding defense contractors and the federal government from discriminating against African Americans. After the war, Randolph was instrumental in prompting President Harry S. Truman to eliminate segregation in the armed forces.

In 1955, Randolph became vice president of the American Federation of Labor and Congress of Industrial Organizations (AFL-CIO), where he continued to fight discrimination within the member unions. In 1963, he revived his plan for a giant protest in the country's capital, helping to organize the March on Washington for Jobs and Freedom. On August 28 of that year, around 200,000 people joined to support equal opportunities for African Americans—a goal that motivated A. Philip Randolph for decades.

AMERICAN STORIES

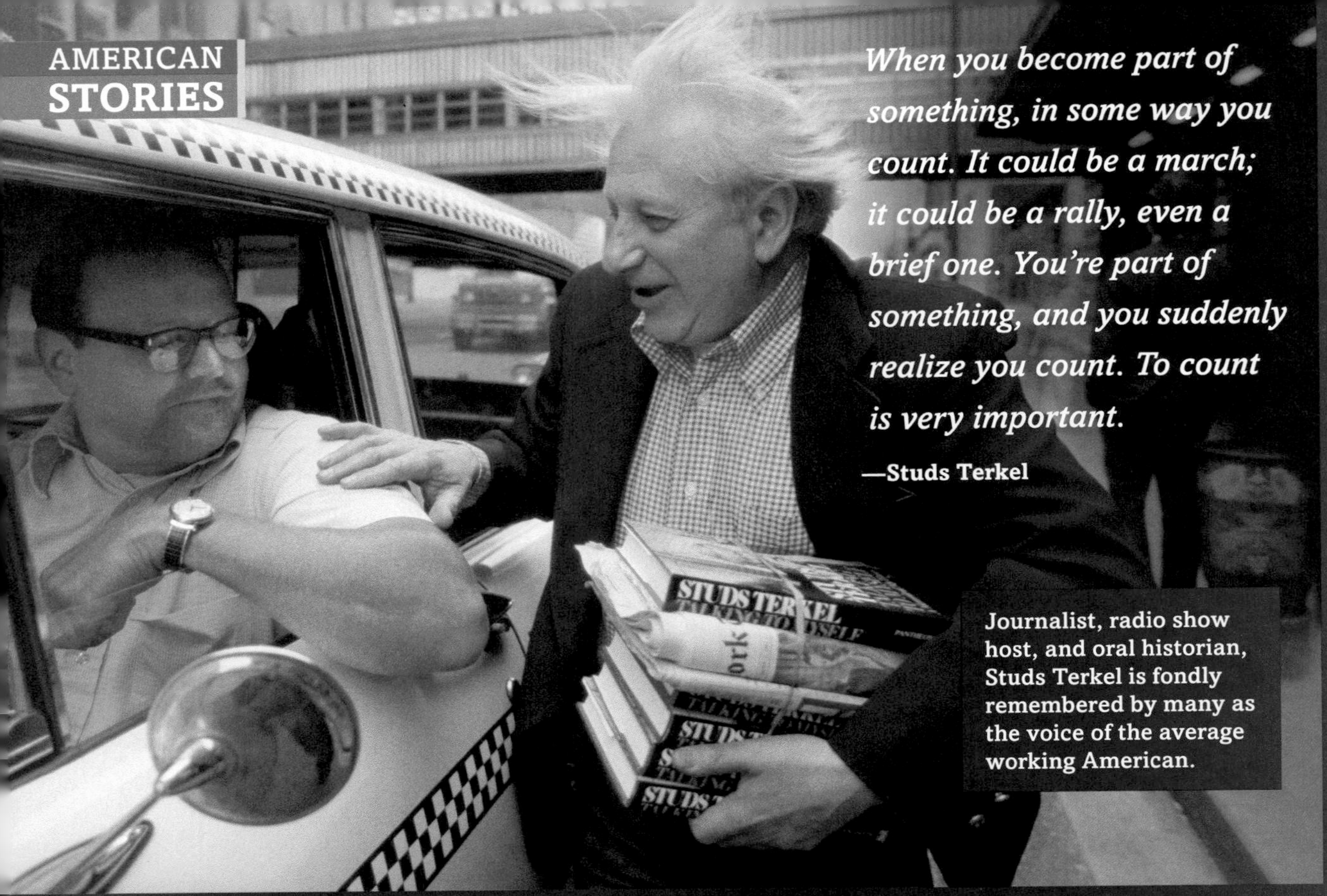

When you become part of something, in some way you count. It could be a march; it could be a rally, even a brief one. You're part of something, and you suddenly realize you count. To count is very important.

—Studs Terkel

Journalist, radio show host, and oral historian, Studs Terkel is fondly remembered by many as the voice of the average working American.

STUDS TERKEL

Louis Terkel was born in 1912, but later adopted the name "Studs" after the title character in a trio of books about a fictional youth growing into troubled manhood during the Great Depression.

Unlike the character in the book, Terkel was well educated, earning a law degree from the University of Chicago in 1934. After a varied career that included stints as a radio actor and writer and a period in the Air Force, he began hosting his own radio show in 1944. He found his voice in radio with a program that mixed music and interviews with Americans from all walks of life, both celebrities and everyday workers. Terkel's guests regularly opened up to him, revealing fascinating insights into their experiences, thoughts, and feelings. Of his gentle questioning style, he remarked, "The thing I'm able to do, I guess, is break down walls. If they think you're listening, they'll talk."

Terkel wrote books on many topics, including firsthand accounts of life during the Great Depression and World War II. In 1974, he published *Working*, a collection of interviews with dozens of people about their working lives. In the book, Terkel allowed individuals to tell their own stories. He took a broad view of the definition of labor, speaking with factory workers, farmers, office workers, stay-at-home mothers, business executives, musicians, and athletes, among many others.

One theme that runs through the book is workers' desire to find meaning in their work by taking pride in their jobs and asserting some control over their working conditions. According to Terkel, when that sense of purpose eludes them, they despair. Some of the people Terkel interviewed found meaning and satisfaction even in jobs that were poorly paid and sometimes perceived as menial. For example, waitress Dolores Dante described the highs and lows of her work to Terkel, explaining how she provided a special level of service. "I don't want to change the job," she told him during her interview.

Terkel once interviewed a union organizer who found his purpose in helping auto factory workers. These laborers often struggle to find meaning in their own jobs when they feel they have little or no say in their working conditions. The union organizer explained that workers "don't want to tell the company what to do, but simply have something to say about what *they're* going to do. They just want to be treated with dignity."

THE STATE OF THE UNIONS

The nature and power of labor unions have changed somewhat since the days of Mother Jones and A. Philip Randolph. Union density—the proportion of union members in the workforce—peaked in 1955, when it reached nearly 35 percent. Since then, union membership has declined steadily, especially in the private, or nongovernment, sector. Between 1970 and 1984, the number of private-sector union members dropped from 17 million to 11.6 million. By 2016, it dropped to 7.4 million. Public-sector unions representing teachers, police officers, and firefighters have had more success in keeping up their numbers, maintaining a density of around 35 percent between 1980 and 2016.

Various reasons may account for the decline in union membership. Many companies vigorously resisted attempts to unionize their workforces. Some moved the manufacturing of their products to factories in countries with lower labor costs. In the 1980s, the federal government enacted legislation that weakened unions' power. More recently, several state governments have also passed laws that make it harder for unions to organize workers and to bargain collectively for pay and benefits.

With the decline in private-sector unions, the face of union membership has changed. While the term "labor movement" often brings to mind gritty black-and-white images of 1930s factory strikes, a large proportion of 21st-century union members are white-collar workers. In fact, today, there are millions more unionized teachers than unionized truckers.

Nobody can predict with any certainty the future of labor unions in the United States. Some commentators believe the unions' influence will continue to be eroded by powerful corporations, government policies, and market forces such as globalization and the automation of workplaces. Others see hope in new ways of organizing and the increasing diversity of union membership. While the future is uncertain, unions will continue to search for ways to evolve as American workers confront the challenges of the 21st-century workplace.

THINK ABOUT IT

How do forces beyond workers' control affect union membership?

MEET LENNY RYBCZYK

In the present day, millions of workers still belong to unions. Lenny Rybczyk, who retired in 2016 after a 43-year career as a carpet installer, credits his union with his successful and satisfying work life.

Rybczyk has a family history of union membership. His mother belonged to the upholsterer's union in the 1950s and 1960s. His older brother apprenticed with the Chicago Carpenters Local Union 1185 in 1962, working four days a week and attending trade school (with pay) one day a week. When Rybczyk graduated from high school in 1973, he followed in his brother's footsteps, signing up as an apprentice to learn his trade. Recalling his early years, he says, "The work gave me structure as a young man, confidence, loyalty, equality, camaraderie, and also the ability to work independently with no supervisor."

Looking back on his career, Rybczyk takes pride in his work, which took him to such locations as Chicago's Sears Tower, the tallest building in the world at the time, and Argon National Laboratories, a high-level scientific research facility—in addition to banks, hospitals, and everyday office buildings. Without Local 1185, he believes, the story of his life would have been very different. "I have what I have only because of the union," he explains.

CRITICAL VIEWING Rybczyk takes tremendous pride in his union button collection. Based on what you have read about American laborers, what do you think fuels the intense pride many take in their unions?

1.1 **MAIN IDEA** During the 1870s and 1880s, the United States experienced a second Industrial Revolution distinguished by rapid industrialization and the development of the railroad, steel, and oil industries.

RAILROADS, STEEL, AND OIL

Being able to transport goods and people from coast to coast became a reality in the 1860s with the opening of the transcontinental railroad. This monumental achievement led to an explosion of business and technological innovations.

AN EXPANDING NATION

The invention of the steam engine and the cotton gin in the late 18th century sparked the first Industrial Revolution in the United States. Technological advances and the growth of railroad transportation brought about a second Industrial Revolution in the second half of the 19th century.

In 1862, two railroad companies began work on the nation's first transcontinental railroad, intent on making it easier to travel and move goods from the East Coast to the West Coast. The work crews of the Central Pacific, including thousands of Chinese immigrants, built eastward from California, and Union Pacific crews built westward from Nebraska. They blasted tunnels through mountains, constructed bridges over rivers, and laid 1,776 miles of track before connecting the railroad lines in Utah in 1869. The transcontinental railroad enabled overland commerce from coast to coast, accelerating industrialization and affecting every aspect of American society.

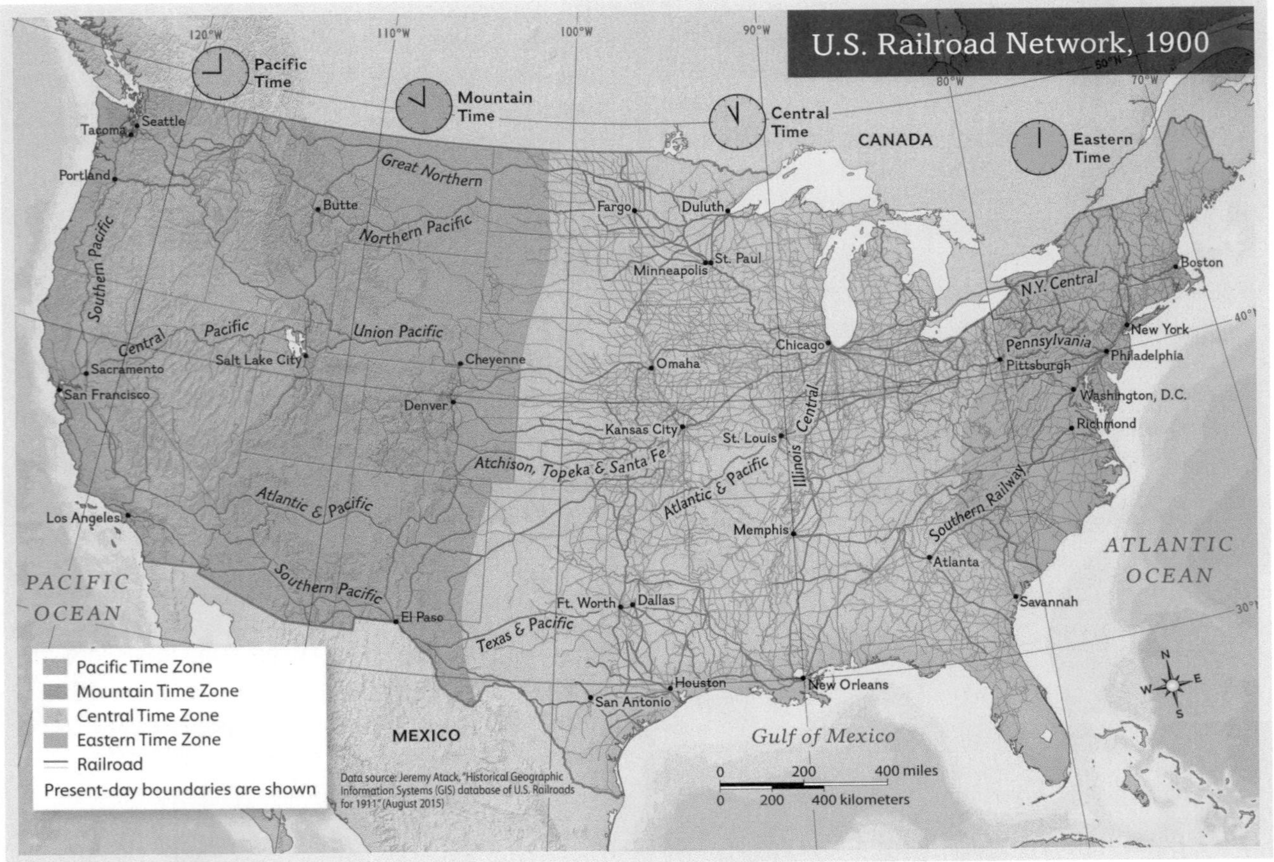

Over the next 25 years, the country added four more transcontinental rail lines, and railroad companies employed tens of thousands of employees. Goods such as coal and industrial machinery moved from one part of the country to another on a nationwide network of railroads. Special railroad cars transported food and livestock. Railroads became the nation's first big business.

CONSOLIDATING POWER

Entrepreneurs, or people who accept risk in starting a business, found that they could pool capital with partners to create security. As workers built the railroads, businessmen built **corporations**, companies or groups of people that invest in a business and then share its profits. The many investors that make up a corporation provide access to large amounts of capital. Such access is useful, and even necessary, for large industries. Large corporations were able to accumulate cash reserves, enabling them to weather a **depression** that began in the 1870s, as well as several **recessions** in the 1880s. A depression is a severe and long-term economic decline in which many businesses fail, industrial output is reduced, and unemployment is high. A recession, often part of a normal business cycle, is a shorter-lasting downturn.

While some business owners were largely immune to economic fluctuations, downturns affected workers substantially. As corporations hired more and more people, when the economy faltered, more workers lost their jobs. The perceived economic progress of the late 19th century was repeatedly disrupted by prolonged periods of decline as the country suffered a number of economic recessions during the intense boom-and-bust cycles.

Entrepreneurs generated levels of wealth not imagined before, even in spite of economic ups and downs. People began to question the practices of industry executives and owners. For example, railroad owners **Cornelius Vanderbilt** and **Jay Gould** had reputations for treating competitors ruthlessly. Their behavior earned them the negative description of "**robber barons**," or businessmen who sought to buy out their competitors and who conspired to set prices, enriching themselves, but often violating state laws. Such practices eventually enabled larger railroad companies to consolidate and control even more of the railroad business, forming the nation's first industrial giant.

In response, states set up commissions, or agencies composed of experts, to investigate the railroads' practices and settle issues of rates, finance, and service. Railroads rejected such oversight, and in the mid-1870s, the Illinois commission was challenged in the Supreme Court case *Munn* v. *Illinois* by a grain warehouse. The firm argued that it could set its own storage and railroad rates. Regulations that varied from state to state violated its 14th Amendment right to equal protection. But the court upheld the right of a state to regulate private industries that affect public interest and all railroads. In 1887, Congress passed the **Interstate Commerce Act**, establishing a commission to investigate complaints and sue companies that violated its regulations.

CARNEGIE'S EMPIRE

As the railroad industry grew, it created a demand for more steel for railroad tracks and train parts. As a result, the steel industry vastly increased its production between 1877 and 1880 alone. The main technology for steel production was the **Bessemer process**. In this process, workers forced air through molten pig iron to remove impurities. Doing this first made the process of adding carbon to transform the iron into steel cheaper and more efficient.

Andrew Carnegie became the dominant figure in the steel industry. To build his empire, Carnegie adopted the strategy used by Gustavus Swift in the meatpacking industry: **vertical integration**, or the control of all phases of production from start to finish. Carnegie purchased the mines to gather raw materials, bought boats and railroads to transport materials, built and controlled the steel mills, and developed a sales force to sell his products. By employing vertical integration, Carnegie maximized profits by not having to pay outside companies.

In dealing with his competition, Carnegie employed **horizontal integration**, which means he purchased other companies to reduce the number of competitors. Carnegie's use of horizontal integration allowed him to come close to achieving a **monopoly** on, or exclusive control over, the steel industry.

Carnegie believed the ability to create wealth came naturally for some people because the natural order of society determined that some people would be wealthy while others would be resigned to poverty. His assumption derived from a misapplication of Charles Darwin's theory of evolution, which states, in part, that the fittest animals and plants survive to reproduce and pass on their genes, while the less fit die off. British writer Herbert Spencer applied Darwin's theory to human society in a new philosophy. According to the ideas of **Social Darwinism**, wealthy individuals, who represented the fittest of humans, were destined to survive and succeed.

11.2.7 Analyze the similarities and differences between the ideologies of Social Darwinism and Social Gospel (e.g., using biographies of William Graham Sumner, Billy Sunday, Dwight L. Moody).

In an 1889 article "The Gospel of Wealth," Carnegie refined his ideas about wealth and Social Darwinism. He acknowledged his belief in a natural division between the wealthy and the poor, but Carnegie also believed that the wealthy were duty-bound to share that wealth with society. His philanthropy, or desire to promote the welfare of others through financial support, set an example for business leaders. Throughout his life, Carnegie donated millions of dollars to many causes, including educational institutions, libraries, and theaters. Between 1883 and 1929 he funded 2,509 libraries worldwide, 1,689 of them in the United States.

OIL TYCOON

In 1859, oil prospectors struck the first American oil near Titusville, Pennsylvania. The rise of the railroad and steel industries made oil more readily available nationwide. Railroads transported oil long distances, and the steel industry provided a strong material for constructing pipelines, drilling equipment, and tanks. Initially, oil's main purpose was to fuel lamps, but soon oil became necessary to lubricate the machinery that ran American industries. In the early 1900s, oil was an essential part of the new automobile industry and would later provide heat and electric power to the country as well.

AMERICAN PLACES

Carnegie Hall, New York City

Andrew Carnegie donated 90 percent of his wealth to worthy organizations and causes. He also supported educational institutions and promoted American arts and culture. One of his most long-lasting contributions is Carnegie Hall, which opened in New York City in 1891 as the "Music Hall." The first performances in the hall featured Peter Tchaikovsky, the Russian composer, conducting his own works.

Another successful and powerful business leader who shaped American industry was the oil tycoon, **John D. Rockefeller**. Rockefeller built his first oil refinery in Ohio in 1863 to convert crude, or raw, unprocessed oil into specialized oil products. Just a few years later, in 1870, he founded the **Standard Oil Company**. Rockefeller used tactics such as price-cutting to lure customers to his company. Like Carnegie, he also employed horizontal integration, taking over most of his competitors to ensure his company's dominance in the market.

Within a decade, Rockefeller controlled about 90 percent of the country's oil-refining capacity. But he had done so by engaging in secret deals to get railroad companies to charge him less than other producers for transportation costs. Regulators put a stop to that, so in 1881, he reestablished his corporation as a **trust**, or a company managed by members of a board rather than by owners or stockholders. These board members are called trustees. Unlike those who oversee the management of a company, trustees are not investors with a stake in profits. The switch allowed Rockefeller, through his trustees, to buy controlling amounts of stock in other oil companies, and to do so across various states.

Rockefeller's questionable business tactics did not go unnoticed by state and federal government or by the general public. Beginning in 1902, journalist **Ida Tarbell** wrote a series of articles called "The History of the Standard Oil Company" for *McClure's Magazine*. Tarbell's father had worked in the oil industry in Pennsylvania, and she learned firsthand the effects of Rockefeller's strategies. For example, the secret rebates Rockefeller had arranged with the railroad companies made the costs of transporting oil prohibitively high for independent producers like Tarbell's father, but generously low for Standard Oil. As a result, Tarbell's well-to-do family was soon living in poverty. Tarbell spent nearly two years researching Standard Oil before writing her articles exposing Rockefeller's unethical practices. Her reporting had a profound influence on the public's opinion of corporations and trusts in general. In fact, Tarbell and other investigative reporters became known as **muckrakers**, or journalists who expose misconduct by an organization or a person.

Still, despite Rockefeller's suspicious business strategies, he, like Carnegie, contributed enormous sums of money to philanthropic organizations, such as educational institutions and medical facilities. Additionally, in 1913 he established the Rockefeller Foundation, which for more than 100 years has supported research and initiatives to improve the well-being of people and the planet.

PRIMARY SOURCE

In the excerpt below, journalist Ida Tarbell evaluates John D. Rockefeller's takeover of oil producers in and around Cleveland, Ohio, by fixing transportation costs.

Mr. Rockefeller's capture of the Cleveland refineries in 1872 was as dazzling an achievement as it was a hateful one. The campaign . . . viewed simply as a piece of brigandage [piracy], was admirable. The man saw what was necessary to his purpose and he never hesitated before it. His courage was steady—and his faith in his ideas unwavering. He simply knew what was the thing to do, and he went ahead with the serenity of the man who knows.

—from "The History of the Standard Oil Company," by Ida Tarbell, in *McClure's Magazine*, 1903

The second Industrial Revolution profoundly changed Americans' relationships with work, transportation, and communication. As in the first Industrial Revolution, the development of new materials and new processes upended the roles of labor and attracted more people to jobs in cities. However, the second Industrial Revolution was characterized by government's increased role in social and business affairs. Ownership in company stocks became more common, unlike during the first Industrial Revolution. The trend toward groundbreaking inventions and the growth of big business continued throughout the late 19th century, ushering in the modern United States and a new American identity.

HISTORICAL THINKING

1. **READING CHECK** What strategies did leaders of different industries use to maximize profits and reduce competition?
2. **IDENTIFY PROBLEMS AND SOLUTIONS** What solution did the states and Congress create to investigate concerns about the railroad industry's practices?
3. **COMPARE AND CONTRAST** In what ways are vertical integration and horizontal integration similar and different?
4. **FORM AND SUPPORT OPINIONS** Do you think Ida Tarbell is biased in her assessment of John D. Rockefeller's practices in her articles? Use evidence from the text to support your opinion.

11.2.5 Discuss corporate mergers that produced trusts and cartels and the economic and political policies of industrial leaders; 11.2.6 Trace the economic development of the United States and its emergence as a major industrial power, including its gains from trade and the advantages of its physical geography; HREP 2 Students identify bias and prejudice in historical interpretations.

California State Railroad Museum, Sacramento

Home to 225,000 square feet of exhibits, restored railroad cars, and iconic engines, this museum brings railroad history in California and the West to life. One exhibit features early communication methods—the bells, whistles, flags, lanterns, and lights used by railroads before modern electronic communication methods existed. Another tells the story of Abraham Lincoln and his steadfast support of the railroad, highlighting the construction of the world's first transcontinental railroad, the Union Pacific Railroad, which has carried America through natural disasters, wars, and a changing transportation industry. There's even a train simulator for museum visitors who want to "pilot" a high-speed train.

Southern Pacific Motor Car

Completed in 1908 and retired in 1920, the Southern Pacific Railroad's McKeen Motor Car Number 9 operated along the railway's Sacramento Valley Lines. McKeen Motor Cars were the first steel self-propelled train cars in the world, and the first example of aerodynamic design in North America. This postcard, dated 1915, demonstrates the comfort of traveling via motor car.

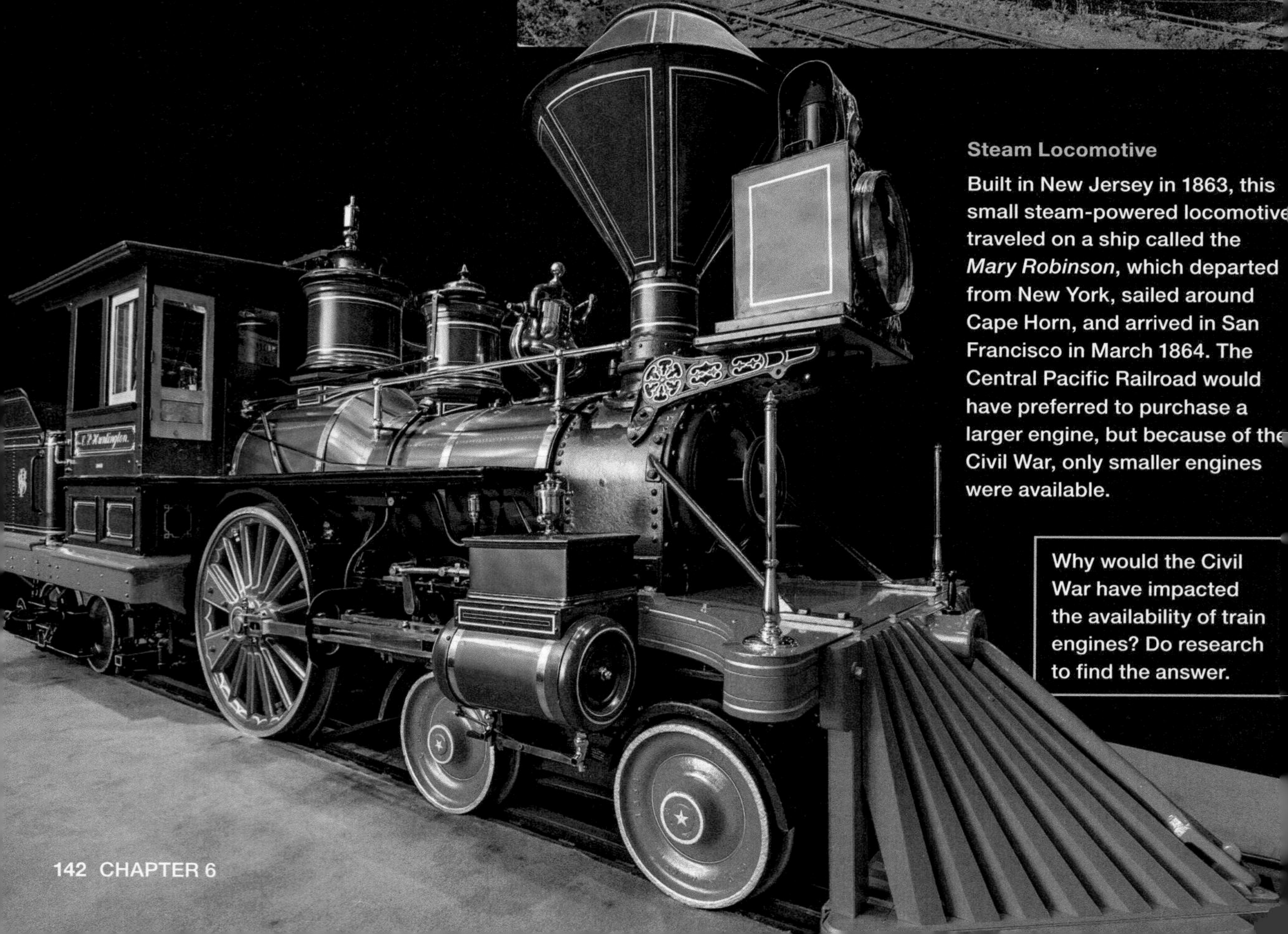

Steam Locomotive

Built in New Jersey in 1863, this small steam-powered locomotive traveled on a ship called the *Mary Robinson*, which departed from New York, sailed around Cape Horn, and arrived in San Francisco in March 1864. The Central Pacific Railroad would have preferred to purchase a larger engine, but because of the Civil War, only smaller engines were available.

Why would the Civil War have impacted the availability of train engines? Do research to find the answer.

Railroad companies proposed dividing North America into four time zones as a way to make rail transportation more efficient. Before the implementation of time zones in 1883, most towns in the United States kept their own local time based on the movement of the sun. As railroads made it easier and faster to move between cities, the fact that each city had its own local time made it impossible to track and set arrival and departure times. Major railroad companies collaborated on a plan to divide the country into four time zones, which greatly helped regulate their train schedules.

Station Clock

Train stations and their buildings, or depots, range in size tremendously, from the one-room country station to the grand union station serving more than one railroad line. But historically, most depots had some common features: benches, a clerk's office complete with a desk and safe, windows for selling tickets, and, of course, a traditional station clock hanging from the wall.

SPECIAL EXCURSION SEASON.

CENTRAL PACIFIC RAIL ROAD.

BIG TREES. GEYSERS. YOSEMITE. LAKE TAHOE.

CALIFORNIA PACIFIC RAILROAD. SOUTHERN EXTENSION SOUTHERN PACIFIC RAILROAD.

LOCAL TIME SCHEDULE, COMMENCING MAY 4th, 1873.

TRAINS AND BOATS WILL LEAVE AS FOLLOWS:

FROM SAN FRANCISCO:

7.00 A. M. (daily)—Atlantic Express Train (via Oakland) for Sacramento, Marysville, Redding and Portland (O.), Colfax, Reno, Ogden and Omaha.

7.30 A. M. (daily)—Cal. P. R. R. Steamer (from Broadway Wharf), connecting at Vallejo with Trains for Calistoga, Knight's Landing and Sacramento, *making close connection at Napa with Stages for Sonoma.*

2.00 P. M. (Sundays excepted)—Stockton Steamer (from Broadway Wharf), touching at Vallejo, Benicia and Landings on the San Joaquin River.

3.00 P. M. (daily)—San José Passenger Train (via Oakland), stopping at all Way Stations.

4.00 P. M. (Sundays excepted)—Passenger Train (via Oakland) for Lathrop, Merced, Visalia, Tipton and Los Angeles, Stockton and Sacramento.

4.00 P. M. (Sundays excepted)—Cal. P. R. R. Steamer (from Broadway Wharf), connecting at Vallejo with Trains for Calistoga, Knight's Landing and Sacramento.

4.00 P. M. (Sundays excepted)—Sacramento Steamer (from Broadway Wharf), touching at Benicia and Landings on the Sacramento River.

6.30 P. M. (daily)—Overland Emigrant Train (via Oakland): through Freight and Accommodation.

OAKLAND BRANCH.—Leave San Francisco: 7.00, 8.10, 9.20, 10.10 and 11.20 A. M.; 12.10, 1.50, 3.00, 4.00, 5.15, 6.30, 8.15, 9.20 and *11.30 P. M. (9.20, 11.20 and 3.00 to Oakland only).

ALAMEDA BRANCH.—Leave San Francisco: 7.20, 9.00 and 11.15 A. M.; 1.30, 4.00, 5.30 and 7.00 P. M. (7.20, 11.15 and 5.30 to Fruit Vale only).

*Sundays excepted.

FROM SACRAMENTO:

6.15 A. M. (Sundays excepted)—Local Passenger Train to Stockton, San José and San Francisco.

6.30 A. M. (Sundays excepted)—Accommodation Train to Marysville and Tehama.

6.45 A. M. (Sundays excepted)—Local Passenger Train (via Vallejo) for San Francisco.

7.00 A. M., or as soon thereafter as practicable (Sundays excepted)—San Francisco Boat, touching at all Way Ports on the Sacramento River.

9.45 A. M. (daily)—Overland Emigrant Train; Freight and Accommodation.

10.30 A. M. (Sundays excepted)—Accommodation Train to Davis and Knight's Landing.

1.20 P. M. (daily)—Express Train to Stockton, Lathrop, Merced and Tipton, San José and San Francisco.

2.10 P. M. (daily)—Overland Express Train to Colfax, Reno, Ogden and Omaha.

2.20 P. M. (daily)—Oregon Express Train to Marysville, Red Bluff and Redding.

3.40 P. M. (daily)—Express Train (via Vallejo) for San Francisco.

4.45 P. M. (daily)—Accommodation and Freight Train to Stockton and San Francisco.

7.15 P. M. (Sundays excepted)—Passenger Train to Davis and Knight's Landing.

[Record Printing House, Sacramento.]

Principal Through and Excursion Ticket Office,
2 NEW MONTGOMERY STREET, SAN FRANCISCO.

How might this 1873 schedule for the Central Pacific Railroad, which was based on local times, have contributed to confusion?

Moving Fresh Foods

By combining images, photographers and artists around the turn of the century created humorous scenes boasting of a region's agricultural capabilities. In this exaggeration or tall-tale postcard, a Southern Pacific flat car is loaded with six enormous California peaches.

HI 1 Students show the connections, causal and otherwise, between particular

1.3 **MAIN IDEA** In the late 1800s, Americans invented new devices and technologies that changed everyday life in dramatic ways and stimulated even more economic and industrial growth.

INVENTIONS AND NEW TECHNOLOGIES

Without even realizing it, you have been experimenting with and inventing things since you were young. During the late 19th century, men and women of varied backgrounds also experimented—and they created transformative technologies.

BELL'S TELEPHONE

The growth of the railroad, steel, and oil industries changed American life, but their rise was not the only economic development to transform the United States. At the same time, inventors were developing technologies and creating devices that would have profound impacts on daily life.

During the 19th century, people relied on the **telegraph**, a machine that transmitted messages along connected wires, to communicate over long distances. An operator tapped out the electric signals for a word with the telegraph key. The key completed an electric circuit and sent the message. In the 1870s, **Alexander Graham Bell**, a Scottish scientist, began to experiment with sending multiple messages at the same time. While trying out ways to subdivide a telegraph wire into many channels, Bell began transmitting musical tones over the telegraph. Ultimately, he hoped to transmit people's voices.

Bell devised a simple machine from which sounds were carried over wires—the first telephone. In February 1876, Bell filed a request for a **patent**, or a license that would give him the sole right to make and sell his new invention. He was just in time. Bell had submitted his patent request just two hours before another inventor

Surrounded by curious onlookers, Alexander Graham Bell speaks into his new invention. By the time the first telephone connection opened between Chicago and New York City in 1892, 950 miles of copper wire had been strung between the two cities to make telephone communication possible. Bell became president of the National Geographic Society in 1898. Under his leadership, photography became a central feature of the Society's magazine, *National Geographic*.

11.1.4 Examine the effects of the Civil War and Reconstruction and of the industrial revolution, including demographic shifts and the emergence in the late nineteenth century of the United States as a world power; 11.2.1 Know the effects of industrialization on living and working conditions, including the portrayal of working conditions and food safety in Upton Sinclair's *The Jungle.* HI 5 Students analyze human modifications of landscapes and examine the resulting environmental policy issues.

presented his own plans for a similar device. A few weeks later, the U.S. Patent and Trademark Office awarded Bell his patent. Within a week, Bell spoke the first words ever heard on a telephone, saying to his assistant: "Mr. Watson—come here—I want to see you."

Later that year, Bell demonstrated his invention at the Centennial Exposition in Philadelphia, and in 1877, he and two partners formed the Bell Telephone Company. In 1885, Bell created the American Telephone and Telegraph Company as a wholly owned **subsidiary**, or secondary business, of American Bell. The original purpose of American Telephone and Telegraph was to build and operate long-distance telephone lines, but its role expanded, and it eventually became the **parent company**, or controlling company, of the Bell System. The company, also known as AT&T, still exists today.

THE WIZARD OF ELECTRICITY

Not long after the debut of the telephone, another inventor unveiled one of the most important advancements of the 19th century. In 1880, **Thomas Edison** patented his most famous work: a practical electric light bulb. Just three years later, Edison put this invention to work by establishing the first electrical system in New York City. Within a year, 500 customers in the city had electric lights.

Although Edison's first career was as a telegraph operator, by the time he was in his 20s, he was an active inventor who had already patented some of his almost 1,100 inventions. His range of patents included both entirely new devices and improvements to existing ones, such as an efficient electrical generator, a motion picture projector, and an electric pen.

In 1876, Edison established an industrial research laboratory—the first of its kind—to work on his inventions. The lab, located in Menlo Park, New Jersey, became the site of many future discoveries. While there, Edison invented the **phonograph**, or record player, in 1877. The Menlo Park lab was also the site of Edison's experiments with electric lighting.

Edison's light bulbs relied on a direct electric current, which initially caused some problems. When the current traveled long distances, the amount of usable electric power decreased. A former colleague of Edison's, an immigrant named **Nikola Tesla**, developed a system for delivering electric power using an alternating current. Alternating current, or AC, electric power could travel longer distances than the direct current, or DC, power Edison and his team developed. Tesla sold his patent to industrialist **George Westinghouse**, who quickly embraced and marketed Tesla's new and improved method.

In 1886, Edison built a second research lab in West Orange, New Jersey, known as the Edison Laboratory. At this lab, Edison and his workers invented a motion picture camera and built the first motion-picture stage, launching the silent-film industry. They also improved his phonograph and developed an alkaline storage battery. For the wealth of contributions he made to technology, Edison became known as the "Wizard of Menlo Park."

A WAVE OF INVENTIONS

Although Bell and Edison undoubtedly produced some of the most important inventions of the late 19th century, many other inventors also introduced life-changing technologies. Products such as the cash register, the typewriter, and the linotype, which the newspaper industry used to set type, helped improve efficiency in the workplace. The Kodak Company's portable camera allowed anyone to become a photographer.

George Washington Carver was among the many African-American innovators who emerged during the late 19th century. Carver served as the head of the agriculture department at the Tuskegee Institute in Alabama, where he encouraged crop diversification in the South to address a major problem: soil quality. Because of decades of **monoculture**, or the practice of growing only one crop, the quality of soil in the South had diminished. Carver experimented with solutions by asking southern farmers to grow a variety of crops, such as peanuts and sweet potatoes. The problem was, however, that these crops didn't generate enough market demand. So Carver began developing new products derived from these crops, such as oils, flour, soap, and cosmetics. Peanuts eventually became one of the South's biggest cash crops.

Another African-American innovator was **Lewis Latimer**, who drew the blueprints for Alexander Graham Bell's telephone patent and also worked in the field of electric lighting. Latimer was a mechanical draftsman for the U.S. Electric Lighting Company, and in 1882, he invented an improved process for manufacturing the carbon filaments inside lamps. Latimer then went to work for Edison, first as an engineer and then as an inventor—the only African-American member of Edison's team.

PRIMARY SOURCE

Lewis Latimer was the youngest child of George Latimer, who had escaped from slavery. At Edison's urging, Latimer wrote a book about how electric lighting worked, but he also wrote about issues African Americans faced in the workplace. In the following excerpt, Latimer writes to a colleague planning a civil rights meeting in Detroit.

[O]ur history conclusively proves that the attempt to degrade any portion, class or race of common people, has always been fraught with more danger to the oppressor than to the oppressed.

If our cause be made the common cause, and all our claims and demands be founded on justice and humanity, recognizing that we must wrong no man in winning our rights, I have faith to believe that the Nation will respond to our plea for equality before the law, security under the law, and an opportunity by and through the maintenance of the law to enjoy with our fellow citizens of all races and complexions the blessings guaranteed us under the [Declaration of Independence], of "life, liberty and the pursuit of happiness."

—from a letter written by Lewis Latimer to be read at the National Conference of Colored Men, December 12–13, 1895

African-American inventor **Granville T. Woods** received many patents related to the field of transportation. One of his inventions was a telegraph system that enabled the transmission of messages to and from trains. Another was a safety feature that helped people avoid injury from accidental contact with electrical wires by running them above streetcars. Woods and his brother Lyates also received patents for emergency braking systems. In total, Woods patented more than 45 inventions during his lifetime, and he sold the rights to many of them to large companies.

Elijah McCoy was born in Canada to a family who had escaped slavery in Kentucky on the Underground Railroad. After studying mechanical engineering in Scotland, he returned to the United States and worked for the Michigan Central Railroad. Like Woods, McCoy also invented an important product related to transportation. Over the course of two years, McCoy experimented with a device to lubricate railroad engines automatically. In 1872, he patented the "lubricating cup," which continuously oiled a steam engine's gears.

During the late 1800s, enterprising women were also carving out a place as inventors, developing new labor-saving devices and safety-inspired products. **Margaret Knight** received patents for a variety of machines and products relating to both industry and the home. Some of Knight's patents were for shoe-manufacturing devices and rotary engines, while others related to sewing machines and clothing. By the time she died in 1914, Knight held a total of at least 27 patents for her inventions.

In 1886, **Josephine Garis Cochrane** patented the first dishwasher. As someone who entertained often, Cochrane wanted to find a way to wash dishes quickly and safely. She displayed her invention at the 1893 World's Columbian Exposition and later formed a company to sell the product, although the dishwasher did not become popular in American homes until the 1950s.

The number and variety of inventions developed during the late 19th century helped create factory and office jobs, and the country's workforce grew as a result. These innovations also enabled greater efficiency and constructive improvements in work, which led to greater economic gains and better working conditions for some, although not for all. The country's desire for inventions may have been motivated by practical considerations, but it also provided opportunities for resourceful and creative women and African Americans.

HISTORICAL THINKING

1. **READING CHECK** What contributions did Alexander Graham Bell and Thomas Edison make to American innovation in the late 19th century?
2. **MAKE INFERENCES** Why do you think the inventions of the women mentioned were oriented toward safety and efficiency?
3. **IDENTIFY PROBLEMS AND SOLUTIONS** What problem was George Washington Carver hoping to solve by diversifying crops in the South?
4. **ANALYZE CAUSE AND EFFECT** What factors contributed to the invention and innovation that occurred during the 19th century?

11.2.6 Trace the economic development of the United States and its emergence as a major industrial power, including its gains from trade and the advantages of its physical geography; 11.5.7 Discuss the rise of mass production techniques, the growth of cities, the impact of new technologies (e.g., the automobile, electricity), and the resulting prosperity and effect on the American landscape; CST 2 Students analyze how change happens at different rates at different times; understand that some aspects can change while others remain the same; and understand that change is complicated and affects not only technology and politics but also values and beliefs.

TWO PATHBREAKING INNOVATORS

Innovators and inventors throughout history share a common skill: problem-solving. George Washington Carver lived in the South and witnessed the effects of monoculture on southern farmers, so he innovated ways to improve soil nutrition. Margaret Knight was frustrated by slow and inefficient production in the factory where she worked, so she improved the process by inventing a machine.

GEORGE WASHINGTON CARVER

As an agricultural chemist, George Washington Carver spent a lot of time experimenting in his lab, as he is doing in the photo above. Carver's ideas about replenishing soil nutrients and growing more varied crops helped southern farmers, both in their harvests and their nutrition. His reputation earned him many invitations to work in other labs, but he declined, preferring to stay at Tuskegee.

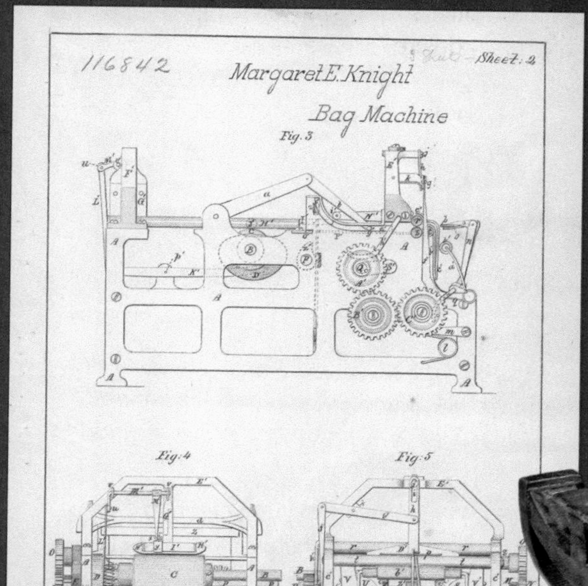

MARGARET KNIGHT

In 1870, Margaret Knight invented a machine that produced flat-bottomed paper bags by cutting, folding, and gluing paper together. In 1871, she submitted the drawing at the left with her patent application. Knight built her first paper-bag machine from wood and brass, and it produced more than 1,000 bags. It also served as the prototype, or example, for a stronger machine made with iron, which was used in mass production.

2.1 **MAIN IDEA** In the late 19th and early 20th centuries, the workforce and middle class grew, but so did job-related injuries and deaths.

THE STATE OF WORKERS

Rapid societal changes can have both positive and negative consequences. During the late 19th and early 20th centuries, many changes took place in the workforce—some for the better and some for the worse.

NEW INVENTIONS, NEW JOBS

Amid the explosion of technology in the late 1800s, the labor force expanded rapidly. In the 1870s alone, it increased by a whopping 29 percent. As new machines and office equipment made their way onto the market, factories and offices became common places of employment. This new work environment signaled a switch from work involving independent, skilled craftspeople to machine-driven jobs in large organizations—jobs that required little or no skill. Suddenly, many workers found themselves at the mercy of managers whose only concerns were maintaining order in the workplace and meeting profit expectations. Many workers had little chance of improving their circumstances.

When photographer Lewis Hine asked this cotton mill worker her age, she replied that she didn't remember, but that she knew she was too young to work. Hine took this 1908 photo in his role as an investigative photographer for the National Child Labor Committee.

11.2.1 Know the effects of industrialization on living and working conditions, including the portrayal of working conditions and food safety in Upton Sinclair's *The Jungle*; 11.2.2 Describe the changing landscape, including the growth of cities linked by industry and trade, and the development of cities divided according to race, ethnicity, and class; 11.2.7 Analyze the similarities and differences between the ideologies of Social Darwinism and Social Gospel (e.g., using biographies of William Graham Sumner, Billy Sunday, Dwight L. Moody).

People moving to urban areas as part of this workforce expansion included immigrants as well as native-born Americans. Workers experienced some benefits from the growth of factory and office work. Increased productivity made possible by technology created a surplus of goods, resulting in **deflation**, or a decrease in the prices of goods and services. Workers' buying power increased, and in many cases, employees could work fewer hours. Women's participation in the workforce also expanded, as they took positions as teachers, office workers, sales assistants, domestic workers, and factory workers. However, women earned less than men, and fewer opportunities were available to them.

DANGEROUS WORK

Though wages and work hours improved during the late 19th and early 20th centuries, safety conditions did not. Workers in the railroad, coal mining, steel, and meatpacking industries faced constant danger of mishaps and even death on the job. A 1906 novel by **Upton Sinclair**, *The Jungle,* described the deplorable working conditions in the meatpacking industry. In his novel Sinclair wrote that men "fell into the vats . . . sometimes they would be overlooked for days, till all but the bones of them had gone out to the world." In the coal mining industry, an estimated 3,242 miners died in job-related accidents in 1907. More than 350 of those deaths resulted from just one mine explosion in West Virginia. That same year, a journalist investigating a U.S. Steel plant in Chicago found that as many as 12 percent of its employees died or suffered injuries every year.

Factory managers often blamed the workers themselves for the accidents that caused their injuries. But many observers realized that the hazards workers faced in many industrial jobs were real. In response, states began providing **workers' compensation**, which meant that a worker who had been injured could receive assistance for medical care and loss of income. Wisconsin passed the first comprehensive workers' compensation law in 1911. By 1920, 43 states had passed some type of workers' compensation.

As the workforce expanded in the late 19th and early 20th centuries, child labor also peaked. Factory managers hired children because they were easier to control than adults, and they could be paid lower wages. Often, children worked to help support their families. In 1880, nearly 182,000 children younger than age 16 worked in such places as textile mills, glass factories, and even coal mines. Like adults, children endured long hours under dangerous conditions with few safety or health protections. Many children could not attend school because they had to spend their entire day at work.

PRIMARY SOURCE

In 1907, the Russell Sage Foundation brought investigators together to study industry in Pittsburgh, Pennsylvania, particularly the city's steel mills. One of these investigators was lawyer Crystal Eastman, whose survey of work accidents helped inspire workplace reforms.

The principal classes of fatalities which result, strictly speaking, from the process of making steel . . . are only 19 percent of the fatalities that occur in the mills where steel is made. It can be asserted that nearly twice as many men are killed in the process of transporting materials and finished product from place to place in mill and yard, as are killed in the actual process of making steel.

—from *Work-Accidents and the Law: The Pittsburgh Survey,* by Crystal Eastman, 1916

The nonregulatory approach to business that allowed practices such as child labor is called **laissez-faire economics**, in which the government rarely interferes in the free market and businesses choose how they will operate, with little or no oversight. An American sociologist named **William Graham Sumner** offered the ideas of Social Darwinism as justification for this approach, arguing that social reforms imposed a financial burden on the "forgotten men" of the middle class. However, despite the popularity of Social Darwinism—or indeed perhaps because of it—workers of the late 19th and early 20th centuries began to assert their rights and demand improvements and protections in their workplaces.

HISTORICAL THINKING

1. **READING CHECK** What changes took place in the workforce during the late 19th and early 20th centuries?
2. **ANALYZE CAUSE AND EFFECT** What larger social and economic issues did the large-scale use of child labor in 1880 impact?
3. **DRAW CONCLUSIONS** How common were injuries in the coal and steel industries in 1907?
4. **IDENTIFY MAIN IDEAS AND DETAILS** What protections did workers have during the late 19th and early 20th centuries? Support your answer with details from the text.

HI 1 Students show the connections, casual and otherwise, between particular historical events and larger social, economic, and political trends and developments.

2.2 **MAIN IDEA** Workers organized in the late 19th century to advocate for better working conditions in the midst of strikes and worker revolt.

ORGANIZING INTO UNIONS

Fighting for your rights takes a lot of perseverance, courage, and conviction. You could be putting your job or maybe even your life on the line. In the late 1800s, dangerous and unfair working conditions led many workers to fight for their rights—but not without a cost.

ORGANIZING FOR CHANGE

During the 1860s and 1870s, workers began to organize into **labor unions**, or groups of workers who band together to achieve better pay, safer working conditions, and other benefits. The first unions formed in the cigar manufacturing, shoemaking, and coal mining industries, but their popularity grew in other industries as well—most notably, the railroads. Strikes, or work stoppages, became a strategic tactic employed by unions when companies or bosses refused to negotiate with them. In industries with highly trained employees who performed specific jobs, such as a railroad brakeman, management struggled to replace workers when all of them walked off the job at once. Unionized workers knew they had a lot of leverage in this situation, and they used it.

PRIMARY SOURCE

The demand for an 8-hour workday dates from the early 1800s, but nearly 100 years later, it was not yet a reality. In this excerpt, Terence Powderly provides arguments in its favor.

Men who work short hours are better educated than those who do not; they have more time in which to study. A thinking, studious man will learn that overexertion shortens life, and he will guard against it. Thousands go to early graves through overwork every year, and until the struggle for existence is shortened by cutting down the hours of toil, this condition of affairs will continue.

—from "The Plea for Eight Hours," by Terence V. Powderly, 1890

What does Powderly imply will happen if workers' hours aren't reduced?

In July 1877, railroad workers launched a strike in Martinsburg, West Virginia, when the Baltimore and Ohio (B&O) Railroad Company announced it would immediately cut pay by 10 percent. Workers had already experienced one pay cut that year, and they balked at the company's decision. Soon the strike had spread to larger cities such as Baltimore, Pittsburgh, and Chicago. In total, about 100,000 workers across the country participated in what came to be known as the Great Railroad Strike. When management's attempt to break the strike resulted in rioting, federal troops arrived. Though the riots led to the deaths of about 100 people, the strike succeeded in sharpening the focus on workers' rights.

One of the first major unions was the **Knights of Labor**, founded in 1869. Like other unions at the time, the Knights of Labor sought an 8-hour workday to replace the more typical 10- to 12-hour workday. But the union also pressed for social reforms and equality. It offered membership to women and African Americans. Its inclusivity set the Knights of Labor apart from other 19th-century labor and trade unions.

In 1879, **Terence V. Powderly** assumed control of the Knights of Labor. After the Great Railroad Strike of 1877, the union's membership climbed from approximately 9,000 members in 1879 to more than 100,000 in 1885. Though Powderly himself did not generally support the practice of striking, the Knights of Labor mobilized a strike in 1885 against Jay Gould, an executive for the Union Pacific railroad known for his ruthless dealings with both employees and competitors. In 1886, the Knights of Labor called another strike against Gould's company—this one much more widespread than the first. Prompted by

11.1.4 Examine the effects of the Civil War and Reconstruction and of the industrial revolution, including demographic shifts and the emergence in the late nineteenth century of the United States as a world power.

Chicago History Museum

After witnessing the Haymarket Riot, Paul Hull, a reporter for the *Chicago Daily News,* wrote *The Chicago Riot: a Record of the Terrible Scenes of May 4, 1886.* In July and August of 1886, Hull and four other *Daily News* reporters also served as witnesses at the trial of those accused in the bombing. In addition to an account of the riot, Hull's book includes details of the bombing investigation that began on the day following the riot. This book is housed in the library of the Chicago History Museum.

the firing of a union member in Texas, the Great Southwest Strike spread to several states and halted railroads in the region, but Gould held fast, and the strike ended after a month and a half.

DESCENT INTO CHAOS

Meanwhile, Chicago experienced its own labor uprising in 1886. On May 3, striking union members at McCormick Works, a McCormick harvesting machine factory, were harassing **scabs**, or nonunion workers willing to cross strike lines in order to work, who were going into and out of the factory. The situation turned violent, and police killed one person and injured several others. In response, labor leaders called for a public protest rally in Haymarket Square the following day.

The May 4 rally began peacefully. In fact, Chicago's mayor, who lived only a mile away, even visited the event. Unconcerned that trouble might start, he returned home. However, the situation became chaotic when someone threw a bomb and police responded with gunfire. The blast was so powerful, the mayor heard it from his home. In the end, several police officers and protesters died, and dozens of people suffered injuries. Police blamed labor leaders for the bombing, giving rise to the argument that the labor movement supported terrorism and **anarchism**, or anti-government beliefs.

The event, later known as the **Haymarket Riot**, resulted in the arrests of eight people. Despite the fact that their guilt was questionable and the evidence flimsy, seven of those arrested were sentenced to death, and the eighth defendant was sentenced to life in prison. Though the Knights of Labor had no direct association with the events in Haymarket Square, many people nonetheless blamed the organization for what took place, and the union's membership declined.

In contrast, the **American Federation of Labor (AFL)**, which formed the same year that the Haymarket Riot occurred, suddenly drew many members to its ranks. Leader **Samuel Gompers,** a critic of the Knights of Labor, wanted to focus on labor's economic gains and less on social reform. He emphasized issues such as better wages, benefits, and working conditions rather than changing the structure of society. As labor unions gained strength in numbers, the steel and railroad industries faced increasing numbers of labor strikes.

HISTORICAL THINKING

1. **READING CHECK** In what way was the Knights of Labor a unique labor union in the late 1800s?
2. **IDENTIFY PROBLEMS AND SOLUTIONS** What problem did workers hope to solve by calling a strike? Explain by using information from the text.
3. **DETERMINE CHRONOLOGY** What was the order of the main events around the Haymarket Riot? Explain what happened before, during, and after the riot.

11.2.1 Know the effects of industrialization on living and working conditions, including the portrayal of working conditions and food safety in Upton Sinclair's *The Jungle*; HREP 2 Students identify bias and prejudice in historical interpretations.

2.3 **MAIN IDEA** Both the steel and railroad industries experienced major strikes in the 1890s as workers and management battled in Pennsylvania and Illinois.

LABOR CONFLICTS

Worker protests and union strikes might not seem newsworthy today, but in the late 1800s, they made headlines. When labor unions took on the giants of industry, they encountered the combined forces of police, the National Guard, and the U.S. government.

STRIKING AGAINST STEEL

Though union membership grew in the late 1800s, the public reactions to two major strikes—the **Homestead Strike** and the **Pullman Strike**—set the labor movement back in the 1890s. As you have read, Andrew Carnegie controlled much of the steel industry. Workers at his steel plant in Homestead, Pennsylvania, belonged to the Amalgamated Association of Iron and Steel Workers union, and their contract with Carnegie Steel was scheduled to expire on July 1, 1892. Carnegie, away in Scotland, gave permission to his operations manager, **Henry Clay Frick,** to break the union, or destroy its power, in advance of this date.

Frick strongly opposed the union—more so than Carnegie—and wasted no time. First, he tried cutting the workers' wages, a move the union rejected. Next, Frick locked the workers out of the mill, literally, by surrounding the mill with barbed wire so that workers could not get in. Then on July 2, he fired all of the union workers at the mill—a total of 3,800 employees.

Union workers knew that Frick would try to replace them with scabs, so the strikers charged the mill. Meanwhile, Frick had hired 300 security guards from the **Pinkerton Detective Agency**, whom industrialists often enlisted to break strikes, to guard the mill. In the battle that ensued, at least seven workers and three Pinkerton guards died. The workers took control of the mill for several days, but the National Guard advanced on July 12 and removed them. A few days later, scabs replaced union workers at the mill.

Neither labor nor Carnegie Steel fared well in the wake of the Homestead Strike. Union workers lost their jobs, and some also faced criminal charges for their roles in the violence. Public opinion of Carnegie Steel suffered because of the way the company had treated its workers.

THE PULLMAN STRIKE

In 1894, another major strike made headlines, this time in the railroad industry. Workers struck against the Pullman Palace Car Company near Chicago, Illinois. The company, owned by George Pullman, manufactured railway sleeper cars known as Pullman cars.

In 1881, Pullman had established a company town—Pullman, Illinois—near his factory to accommodate its workers. The town featured housing, shops, a library, parks, and other amenities for the workers. It might sound ideal, but it allowed Pullman great control over his workers. He did not allow free discussion, independent newspapers, or the observance of any religion other than Protestant Christianity. Pullman also charged a higher rent than landlords in nearby areas, enabling him to profit from his ownershp of the company town.

When an economic recession hit in 1893, Pullman cut his workers' wages and extended their work hours, but he still expected Pullman residents to pay the same amount in rent and other expenses. In response, angry workers joined the American Railway Union, a new union led by **Eugene V. Debs**.

The American Railway Union was the country's first union to consolidate workers across an entire industry. Before Debs succeeded in combining the many different railway unions, workers had organized themselves according to their individual crafts.

11.1.4 Examine the effects of the Civil War and Reconstruction and of the industrial revolution, including demographic shifts and the emergence in the late nineteenth century of the United States as a world power.

PULLMAN PORTERS

The Pullman company hired mostly southern African-American men to attend train passengers on their journeys. George Pullman supposed men who had previously been enslaved would be accustomed to a role of serving and would work for low wages.

For the Pullman porters, work shifts could be as long as 20 hours a day, and the pay was not enough to live on. On the plus side, however, porters received tips from passengers, they got to see the country, and the job didn't require heavy manual labor. In 1925, Pullman porters began fighting for better conditions by forming a union, called The Brotherhood of Sleeping Car Porters. The Brotherhood provided the first instance in which an African-American group negotiated terms with a powerful corporation.

The solidarity, or united purpose, of the American Railway Union turned a local strike into a national labor conflict.

When the Pullman union workers tried to discuss their grievances with their employer, he fired them. In response, the workers called for a strike. Debs coordinated a union boycott of Pullman cars on all rail lines. With members of the American Railway Union refusing to handle any Pullman cars, rail traffic in the Midwest screeched to a halt. Debs hoped the work stoppage would cause the railroads to discontinue their relationship with Pullman.

Instead, President Grover Cleveland sent federal troops to Illinois to facilitate train movement. Violence erupted, and members of the National Guard shot and killed several strikers. As a result of the bloodshed, Debs tried to end the strike, but his involvement with the boycott and strike led to his arrest. While in prison, Debs became interested in **socialism**, the political theory that advocates that the community as a whole should control the production, distribution, and exchange of goods and services. Debs later formed and became the leader of the Socialist Party of America.

Labor was not the only segment of society to experience change during the late 1800s. Greater transformations lay ahead for the United States as more immigrants began to arrive.

HISTORICAL THINKING

1. **READING CHECK** What actions led to the Homestead Strike and the Pullman Strike?
2. **IDENTIFY PROBLEMS AND SOLUTIONS** Describe solutions that indicate different directions events could have taken in the cases of the Homestead and the Pullman strikes.
3. **EVALUATE** What does the structure of the company town of Pullman say about George Pullman's attitude toward its residents? Use examples from the text to support your answer.

11.2.1 Know the effects of industrialization on living and working conditions, including the portrayal of working conditions and food safety in Upton Sinclair's *The Jungle*; 11.3.3 Cite incidences of religious intolerance in the United States (e.g., persecution of Mormons, anti-Catholic sentiment, anti-Semitism); HI 4 Students understand the meaning, implication, and impact of historical events and recognize that events could have taken other directions.

3.1 **MAIN IDEA** In the late 1800s, immigrants from Europe and Asia moved to the United States.

Ellis Island and Angel Island

Athlete. Artist. Gamer. Musician. Environmentalist. Your identity is a combination of traits and experiences, and it is likely to change as you grow. Likewise, the American identity was reshaped by the arrival of millions of new immigrants in the late 1800s.

THE NEW IMMIGRANTS

Until the early 1870s, most immigrants to the United States were from northern and western Europe. But between 1890 and 1920, immigrants began to arrive from southern and eastern European countries such as Italy, Greece, Hungary, Poland, Russia, and Czechoslovakia. Unlike many of their predecessors, few of these new immigrants were Protestant Christians, but instead were largely Catholic, Jewish, and Orthodox. They also typically did not speak English. Although seeking a better life, just as those who arrived before them, they were often treated with prejudice.

Like earlier groups of immigrants to the United States, southern and eastern European and Asian immigrants were motivated by several **push-pull factors**, or pressures that forced them from their home countries and drew them to a new one. The factors that pushed immigrants away from their home countries included a lack of economic opportunities, a shortage of farmland, too few educational opportunities, religious discrimination, and the threat of being drafted to fight in wars. For the Irish, the massive emigration that began with the Great Potato Famine of 1845–1849 stretched into the latter half of the century, as hunger and poverty continued to plague Ireland.

The pull factors that drew immigrants to the United States included the hope for greater economic opportunity, plentiful farmland available for purchase at affordable prices, political and religious freedom, and the absence of war. Following the Civil War, rapid industrial growth created an unprecedented demand for labor. Industries across the country needed both skilled and unskilled workers. Communities established by previous groups of immigrants in cities such as Chicago and New York welcomed the newcomers.

As the influx of non-English-speaking immigrants continued into the early 20th century, an **Americanization** movement emerged. Proponents of Americanization wanted to immerse immigrants in what they defined as American culture and transform them into "true" Americans. During the 1910s, schools, community organizations, and businesses offered immigrants English classes and lessons in American history and government. Some immigrants embraced Americanization efforts, but others rejected them, preferring instead to maintain their own languages and cultures.

Support for Americanization peaked during World War I and waned in the 1920s. In its place came a new appreciation by some for the coexistence of different groups, known today as pluralism. This new appreciation also applied to religious beliefs, as growing numbers of Catholics and Jews continued arriving from Europe.

WELCOME TO ELLIS ISLAND

Beginning in 1892, most of the European immigrants who arrived on the East Coast were processed through the immigration station at **Ellis Island** in New York Harbor. Before it opened, immigrants had arrived at a facility called Castle Garden in Lower Manhattan. Between 1855 and 1890, officials processed 8 million immigrants at the Castle Garden location, but the facility was no longer large enough to manage the large numbers of new immigrants. Ellis Island became the site of a new and more comprehensive immigration processing facility.

11.2.3 Trace the effect of the Americanization movement; 11.3.4 Discuss the expanding religious pluralism in the United States and California that resulted from large-scale immigration in the twentieth century.

THE FACES OF ELLIS ISLAND

Augustus Francis Sherman was the chief registry clerk at Ellis Island in the early 1900s. He took photographs of incoming immigrants, and in 1907, *National Geographic* magazine published some of them. In 2016, artist Jordan Lloyd digitally colorized many of these photos, including the four that appear below. The colorization specialists took care to reproduce historically accurate colors in order to bring to life the intricacies and beauty of the traditional clothing worn by immigrants who walked through the doors of Ellis Island.

Woman from Ruthenia, a region of present-day Ukraine and Belarus, wearing an embroidered linen blouse and sheepskin jacket

Bavarian man, wearing a trachtenjanker, or wool jacket, with horn buttons

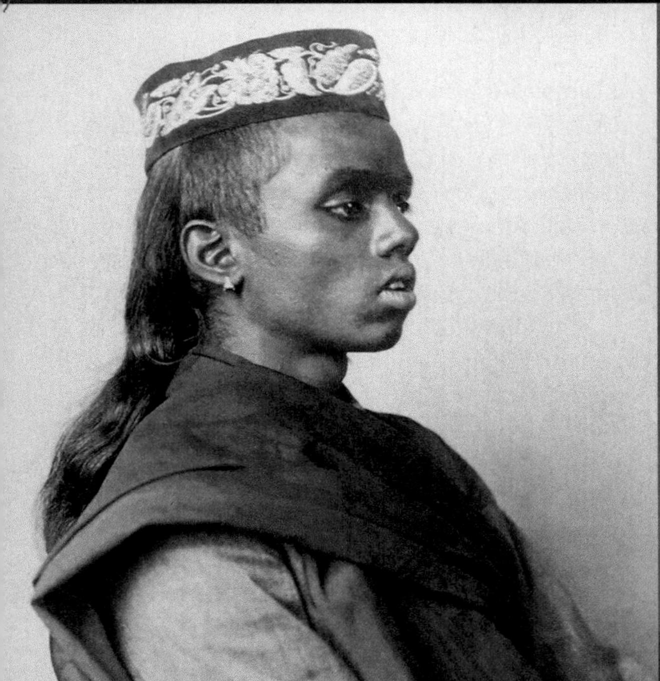

East Indian boy, wearing a topi (cap), homespun cotton cloth called khadi, and prayer shawl

Italian woman, wearing a traditional dress with blue shawl and veil

Once they arrived at Ellis Island, immigrants faced a series of examinations that generally took anywhere from three to seven hours. They answered questions about how they were going to support themselves in the United States and received medical exams to ensure they were free of contagious diseases. Aid workers and social workers also provided immigrants with other needs, such as clothing, counseling, or even money. Immigrants who were found to have a contagious disease or deemed unable to support themselves could be barred entry and sent back to their home countries. About 2 percent of immigrants met this fate. By the time Ellis Island stopped functioning as an immigration center in 1924, more than 12 million immigrants had passed through its doors.

Immigrants Arriving in the United States in 1900

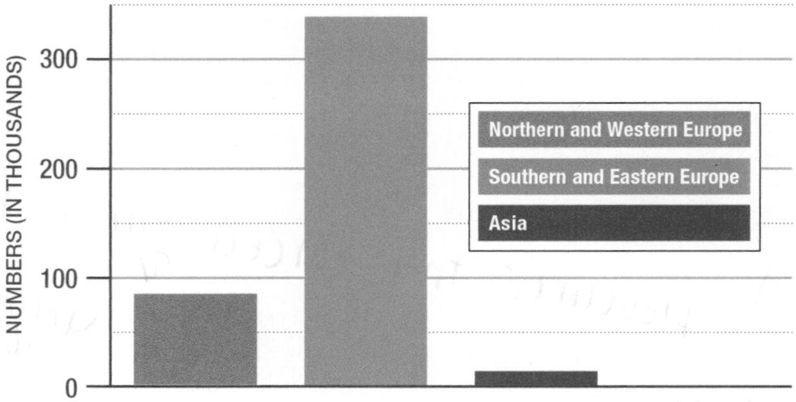

Source: U.S. Census Bureau

One experience shared by immigrants entering the United States through Ellis Island was seeing the **Statue of Liberty** as they arrived in New York Harbor. Unveiled on a wet and foggy day on October 28, 1886, with President Grover Cleveland in attendance, the statue was greeted with great celebration. The copper figure was designed and constructed as a gift from France, and the pedestal was built by the United States. Holding the torch of freedom in her upraised hand, "Lady Liberty" came to symbolize the welcoming spirit of the United States. **Emma Lazarus**'s poem "The New Colossus" was etched into a plaque at the base of the statue in 1903, reinforcing a message of inclusion: "From her beacon-hand / Glows world-wide welcome."

CONTROLLING IMMIGRATION

On the West Coast, immigrants arrived at **Angel Island,** a facility in San Francisco Bay that processed immigrants during the early 20th century. Unlike the mainly European immigrants who arrived at Ellis Island, those who arrived at Angel Island came from Asia, primarily China and Japan. Other Asian immigrants included Filipinos, Hindus, and Sikhs.

The Angel Island facility opened in 1910 not only to process immigrants but also to control the number of Chinese immigrants allowed into the country. Many native-born Americans harbored prejudices toward Chinese immigrants and believed Chinese laborers, who often worked for low wages, took jobs away from American workers. Anti-Chinese sentiment had intensified in the 1870s when unemployment ran especially high. In 1882, Congress passed the **Chinese Exclusion Act** to prevent Chinese immigrants from working in the United States. Although states had already passed their own versions of immigration laws, the Chinese Exclusion Act became the nation's first federal immigration law.

Immigration from Asia continued despite laws created to suppress it. Those who came for purposes other than work could still seek admission to the United States. However, they had to prove they were not laborers by providing certification from the Chinese government. Because the act included such a wide definition of who qualified as a laborer, proving their occupation was difficult for immigrants.

As a result, the act severely limited Chinese immigration for 10 years. Officials turned away more than 5 percent of Chinese immigrants who tried to enter the country—far more than the 2 percent of European immigrants turned away from Ellis Island. Even the Chinese people already living in the United States had to obtain certification to reenter the country if they traveled outside the United States and wanted to return. When the Chinese Exclusion Act expired in 1892, Congress enacted the **Geary Act**, which extended the restrictions on Chinese labor for an additional 10 years. When that act expired in 1902, Congress made the extension permanent. In fact, Congress did not finally repeal these exclusionary acts until the 1940s.

Chinese immigrants denied admission and detained at Angel Island could appeal, but they often had to endure difficult conditions while waiting to hear the results. The wait could last weeks, months, or

11.2.2 Describe the changing landscape, including the growth of cities linked by industry and trade, and the development of cities divided according to race, ethnicity, and class.

Japanese women aboard an incoming ship await processing at Angel Island in 1925. Between 1900 and 1925, more than 250,000 Japanese immigrated to the United States.

in some cases more than a year, and prospective immigrants had to submit to lengthy interrogations about their families and villages in China. To pass the time and express their feelings while waiting, some detainees carved poems in the walls. Facilities on Angel Island were often crowded, and some featured barbed wire and armed guards to prevent people from escaping. The island seemed more like a prison than an immigration center.

Also contributing to the diversity of the United States in the early 20th century was the openness of its southwestern borders. People crossed freely between the United States and Mexico. But the migration process could be difficult for new arrivals to the United States, and the struggle did not end there. Once admitted to the country, immigrants frequently faced prejudice and poverty as they settled into their new homes.

HISTORICAL THINKING

1. **READING CHECK** What were some of the push-pull factors that led immigrants to come to the United States during the late 19th and early 20th centuries?
2. **INTERPRET GRAPHS** From what region did the most immigrants to the United States come in 1900?
3. **IDENTIFY PROBLEMS AND SOLUTIONS** How could a Chinese person immigrate legally under the terms of the Chinese Exclusion Act?
4. **MAKE GENERALIZATIONS** Explain connections between the experiences of immigrants arriving in the late 19th and early 20th centuries with the larger issue of worldwide migration in the 21st century.

HI 1 Students show the connections, causal and otherwise, between particular historical events and larger social, economic, and political trends and developments.

Sikh immigrants from India, Angel Island, c. 1925

Japanese immigrant, Angel Island, c. 1925

Mexican immigrants at an immigration station in El Paso, Texas, 1938

3.2

THROUGH THE LENS

IMMIGRATION

As President John F. Kennedy famously acknowledged in the title of a book he published as senator in 1959, the United States is "a nation of immigrants." Except for those of us with Native American ancestry, we all can trace our heritage back to somewhere else. From English colonists seeking religious freedom on the shores of a distant land, to Asian, Latin American, and European immigrants eager for work opportunities and a chance to make a better life, the rich tapestry of this country is interwoven with the stories of many immigrants. How is immigration a piece of your American story?

European immigrants arriving at Ellis Island, 1921

Between 1870 and 1915, New York City's population more than tripled, and about 75 percent of its residents were immigrants and their children. Many Italian immigrants settled on or near Mulberry Street, the so-called Main Street of the neighborhood known as Little Italy, shown here.

Somalian immigrant outside the Mayo Clinic in Minnesota, where she works as a nurse

Little Havana, Miami, Florida

A Chinese shop owner uses an abacus in New York City's Chinatown.

3.3 **MAIN IDEA** Immigrants in the early 20th century often faced discrimination and poverty, but social welfare groups were ready to assist them in their new country.

DIFFICULT LIVES IN A NEW LAND

Adapting to a new country was especially difficult for newly arrived immigrants, whose languages, religions, food, and traditions often set them apart as they searched for shelter and work.

A PLACE TO LIVE AND WORK

Immigrants brought with them a hopeful optimism about a new future in a new country. At the same time, navigating daily life in an unfamiliar place sometimes brought a series of complex and frustrating encounters. For some, the language barrier was significant. In 1910, almost one-quarter of all immigrants spoke languages other than English. They were further isolated by their traditional dress, ethnic foods, and religious practices that were sometimes unfamiliar to the largely Protestant American population. Catholics and Jews, in particular, often faced religious prejudice, such as anti-Catholicism and **anti-Semitism**, or prejudice against Jewish people. For instance, throughout the late 19th century, American Jews were often barred from attending particular universities and conducting certain businesses.

Once settled, immigrants gained employment in a variety of jobs. Many immigrant men worked in construction. They dug tunnels and laid rails for the new subway system in New York, and they built steel mills in Pittsburgh. In Chicago, immigrants helped construct some of the world's first skyscrapers, or very tall buildings.

Some immigrant groups migrated toward specific types of work. For example, Italian women often sewed for the garment industry, Greek immigrants took jobs with the railroads, and Filipinos, Japanese, and Hindus and Sikhs from India, moved to California and other western states to work in the agriculture and service industries. Many immigrants started businesses.

The influx of new immigrants added to the population growth of cities across the country. In cities such as Chicago and New York, housing could not keep up with increased demand. Wealthier residents lived in spacious apartment buildings and townhomes, but working-class residents—including newly arriving immigrants—often found housing in structures called **tenements**. Most tenements were six- or seven-story, multi-resident buildings, constructed on narrow lots. They were typically poorly ventilated, crowded, and ill-maintained.

In New York City, tenements were designed to house as many people as possible. Individual residences featured small, narrow rooms and few windows. The space between the tenement buildings was often so narrow that people could reach out a window and touch someone living in the next building. Only the top floors actually received much light. Because of poor ventilation and substandard or nonexistent sanitation, diseases spread quickly in the tenements. The structures were also prone to fires because of overcrowding and poor construction.

STRENGTH IN NUMBERS

Many immigrants settled in neighborhoods that reflected their own ethnic backgrounds so their native languages and customs surrounded them. They built churches and synagogues and formed mutual aid, or self-help, societies to provide services and support for residents and incoming immigrants.

One of these societies was the Polish National Alliance, formed in Philadelphia and Chicago in 1880. Its purpose was to bring Polish immigrants together in support of Poland's independence and to help one another **assimilate**, or blend in with and adopt American ways of life in the United States. One year after forming, the alliance established a Polish-language newspaper. Later, it set up an insurance program for members and provided loans and scholarships to those seeking an education.

11.2 Students analyze the relationship among the rise of industrialization, large-scale rural-to-urban migration, and massive immigration from Southern and Eastern Europe.

CRITICAL VIEWING **Children play in the streets of New York City, amid traffic and trash. Lewis Hine captured this photograph in 1910. Based on details you notice in the photo, how would you describe this street and its tenements?**

The Hebrew Immigrant Aid Society, founded in 1881 on Manhattan's Lower East Side, originally formed to aid eastern European immigrants fleeing to the United States to escape religious persecution. The organization provided food, clothing, transportation, and employment to Jewish refugees. In 1904, it established a bureau on Ellis Island to assist newly arrived immigrants with translation and other services, such as loans for the $25 landing fee.

In addition to forming self-help societies, immigrants also contributed to their neighborhoods by constructing schools, theaters, and concert halls. These investments demonstrated the immigrants' commitment to their new country—an idea the Americanization movement promoted. The Polish National Alliance and the Hebrew Immigrant Aid Society still operate today, helping immigrants and others in need.

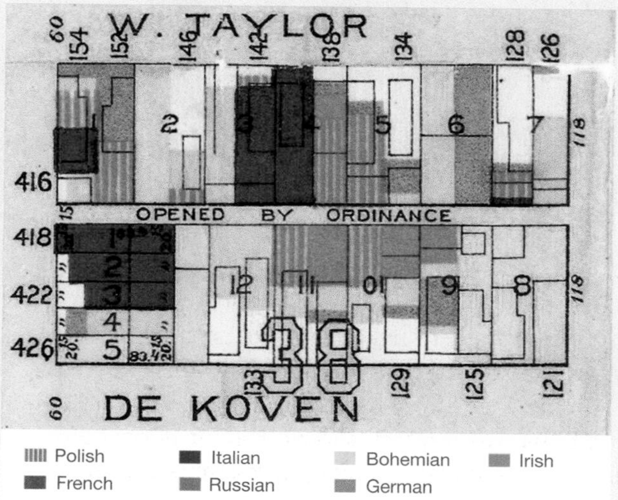

In 1895, Samuel Sewall Greeley created for Hull House a nationalities map of the Hull House neighborhood. The colors represent the ethnic diversity of this four-block area of Chicago.

ENCOUNTERING PREJUDICE

Despite many immigrants' attempts to assimilate into their new home, some Americans still harbored prejudices against them. Known as **nativists**, these citizens felt threatened by what they saw as changing cultural values and competition for employment. They vehemently opposed immigration and wanted to restrict it by using literacy tests and quotas based on national origin. Many nativist groups worked actively against immigrants, taking particular aim at certain religious groups, such as Catholics and Jews.

For example, in 1887, the American Protective Association formed in Iowa. In essence, this organization was a secret society of white, native-born Protestants that exploited Americans' fears about an unstable economy and what they perceived as a negative influence of immigrants in the country. The organization specifically targeted Catholic immigrants, spreading rumors and **propaganda**, or purposely misleading and usually negative information, to try to bar Catholics both from entering the United States and from serving in public office. In fact, the oath that members took included a pledge that they would not "vote for, or counsel others to vote for, any Roman Catholic." The organization boasted more than 2 million members in the 1890s, though by 1900, its membership had dwindled significantly, and it had little or no influence.

Of course, prejudice extended beyond anti-Catholic and anti-Semitic boundaries. Just as the

CRITICAL VIEWING **Anti-immigrant sentiment, though prevalent, was not unchallenged. This 1896 cartoon drawn by Frank Beard appeared in *The Ram's Horn*, a Social Gospel magazine. How does Beard portray both the United States and the immigrant trying to enter the country?**

11.2.2 Describe the changing landscape, including the growth of cities linked by industry and trade, and the development of cities divided according to race, ethnicity, and class; 11.2.3 Trace the effect of the Americanization movement.

Jukichi Harada, standing fifth from the left behind two of his children, immigrated with his family to southern California from Japan in 1905. He started a restaurant, which he named the "Washington Restaurant" in honor of America, his new home.

Chinese Exclusion Act of 1882 had barred many Chinese immigrants from entering the country, the **Gentlemen's Agreement of 1907** between the United States and Japan had a similar effect, though not quite as severe.

This understanding between President Theodore Roosevelt and the Japanese government affirmed that the Japanese would grant passports for Japanese emigration to the United States only to educated businessmen and other professionals and their direct family members—not to peasants (farmers) or laborers. In exchange, Roosevelt agreed that the San Francisco School Board would stop separating Japanese schoolchildren from white students. Californian nativists had drummed up the need for the Gentlemen's Agreement out of a fear that Japanese immigrants would ultimately control all the best farmland in the state. At the time, 1,000 Japanese immigrants were arriving in the state every month, and most of them were farmers.

Like the Chinese, most Japanese arrived at Angel Island in San Francisco Bay. But thanks to the Gentlemen's Agreement, Japanese immigrants rarely had to stay on the island beyond a couple of days. In the end, both Roosevelt and the Japanese government stuck to their promises, but the agreement did nothing to end discrimination against the Japanese in the United States.

Urban centers continued to expand as native-born Americans and newly arrived immigrants moved to the growing, crowded cities. At the same time, the gap between the wealthy and the poor continued to increase.

HISTORICAL THINKING

1. **READING CHECK** Who immigrated to the United States between 1877 and 1911, and why?
2. **DESCRIBE** Why did immigrants form self-help societies?
3. **EVALUATE** In what ways did the treatment of immigrants to the United States show both the strengths and weaknesses of American democracy at the turn of the 20th century?
4. **IDENTIFY PROBLEMS AND SOLUTIONS** Explain the problem that the Gentlemen's Agreement set out to address.

11.3.3 Cite incidences of religious intolerance in the United States (e.g., persecution of Mormons, anti-Catholic sentiment, anti-Semitism); 11.3.4 Discuss the expanding religious pluralism in the United States and California that resulted from large-scale immigration in the twentieth century.

JANE ADDAMS 1860–1935

"She is the truest American I have ever known, and there has been none braver."—Harold Ickes, United States Secretary of the Interior

In the late 1800s, Chicago was a tough place to live for the thousands of immigrants who came to work in the city's booming factories and stockyards. The journalist Lincoln Steffens described Chicago as "first in violence, deepest in dirt, loud, lawless, unlovely, ill-smelling. Criminally, it was wide-open; socially it was thoughtless and raw." Onto this grim and seemingly hopeless stage stepped an unlikely hero: Jane Addams.

In this photo taken in 1930, Jane Addams holds a little girl during the celebration of Hull House's 40th anniversary. The settlement house was located in a neighborhood that, at the time, had one of the city's highest infant mortality rates. In response, Hull House residents researched this problem as well as others that affected people in their neighborhoods. Their findings, often published in sociology journals, provided evidence for activists lobbying for reforms.

THE FOUNDING OF HULL HOUSE

Jane Addams was born into a financially comfortable family in the small town of Cedarville, Illinois—far from the poverty and bustle of Chicago. A bright and intellectually curious young woman, she attended college and went on to study medicine, although she did not complete her medical degree. Instead, she spent several years traveling in Europe and considering her choices for leading a meaningful life. During a visit to London, Addams and her friend Ellen Starr toured a settlement house—an urban community center that provided needed services to people in the neighborhood. There, Jane Addams discovered her purpose.

In 1889, Addams and Starr leased a house, called Hull House after the man who had built it, in a poor, immigrant neighborhood of Chicago. Hull House would be Addams's home for the rest of her life. Addams and her partner, Starr, moved into the house and immediately began renovating the space, creating programs to help the people in the neighborhood, and fundraising among wealthy Chicagoans to support their work.

11.2.9 Understand the effect of political programs and activities of the Progressives (e.g., federal regulation of railroad transport, Children's Bureau, the Sixteenth Amendment, Theodore Roosevelt, Hiram Johnson).

The well-used rocking chair (right) belonged to Addams and helped relieve the chronic back pain she suffered from for much of her life.

Hull House provided a generous range of desperately needed services, including a kindergarten, day care, afternoon clubs for older children, classes and activities for adults, a playground, a library, and a boarding house for girls. Addams crusaded for improvements throughout the city as well as in her own neighborhood. She served on the city's board of education and, at one point, worked as the garbage inspector in the ward where Hull House was located.

BEYOND HULL HOUSE

Addams's work at Hull House gained her respect and admiration from people throughout the country. However, when she took her activism onto the national scene, she was not afraid to take public stances she knew would make her deeply unpopular. She was opposed to war under any circumstance and spoke out against fighting in World War I, even after the United States had joined the war and most Americans strongly supported it. After the war, she continued to be critical of the military. She also supported labor unions and openly criticized elements of the American capitalist system. By the 1920s, J. Edgar Hoover, the director of the Federal Bureau of Investigation (FBI), was calling Jane Addams "the most dangerous woman in America"—the same description that had been applied to Mother Jones several years earlier by a U.S. attorney.

Then came the stock market crash of 1929 and the beginning of the Great Depression, a time of poverty and struggle for many Americans. Once again, Addams's efforts on behalf of the poor came to the forefront. She rose in the national esteem at the same time she received international recognition. In 1931, she was awarded the Nobel Peace Prize.

Jane Addams died only a few years later. Her legacy of support for all people continues today in the organizations she helped found, including the National Association for the Advancement of Colored People (NAACP), the American Civil Liberties Union (ACLU), and the Women's International League for Peace and Freedom. After 122 years of service, Hull House closed in 2012. However, the site now houses a museum dedicated to continuing Addams's vision through research, education, and social engagement.

HISTORICAL THINKING

1. **READING CHECK** Why was Jane Addams unpopular during World War I?
2. **IDENTIFY PROBLEMS AND SOLUTIONS** What are some of the problems that Jane Addams worked to solve during her lifetime?
3. **MAKE CONNECTIONS** Think of an issue of local, national, or international concern today. What do you think Jane Addams would say about it?

4.1 **MAIN IDEA** In the late 19th and early 20th centuries, cities across the country grew in size and number as people seeking opportunity and excitement moved to them.

GROWING URBANIZATION

Some people prefer the wide-open spaces of a rural environment, but others crave the energy of city life. In the late 19th and early 20th centuries, Americans moved to cities for a host of reasons, and the cities grew to accommodate them.

FROM COUNTRY TO CITY

Between 1860 and 1920, American cities grew immensely, especially in the Northeast and Midwest. For example, Chicago's population swelled from about 109,000 in 1860 to about 1.1 million by 1890. However, rapid urbanization was not confined to the Northeast and Midwest. In the 1890s, a new railroad connected south Florida, including Miami, with northeastern cities. By the following decade, the swampy land of southern Florida was drained to attract new residents with its affordable property and warm climate. Miami's expansion was so rapid that it acquired the nickname "Magic City."

Many factors contributed to American urbanization. The ever growing number of immigrants—more than 8 million between 1870 and 1890 alone—generally settled in the cities where they arrived. Increased industrialization and trade played a role as well. As a result of extensive railroad systems, cities such as Chicago could receive large shipments of food and other goods, which brokers then sold and transported to markets throughout the nation. Declining crop prices also drove people from rural areas into the cities when farming no longer provided them with a livable income.

Cities offered exciting opportunities for people to meet others, enjoy cultural events, and live independent lives. Many single men and women took advantage of these opportunities. Single women who moved to cities for work sometimes lived together in what were called "Boston marriages." The term, drawing on Henry James's novel *The Bostonians*, describes two women living together without a man in the household. The anonymity of the late 19th-century city provided a space in which individuals were able to seek out relationships with people of the same sex without fear of discovery by and disapproval from a society that didn't yet accept such attachments.

Cities also offered a wide variety of entertainments. Young and old Americans alike enjoyed amusement parks, dance halls, and **vaudeville** theaters. Vaudeville, a type of show featuring a variety of specialty acts such as singing and instrumental music, dancing, comedy, drama, and acrobatics, was popular with urban audiences.

Colorful posters like this one from 1894 advertised vaudeville productions and promised thrilling and exotic entertainment—including strongmen lifting humans high overhead.

11.1.4 Examine the effects of the Civil War and Reconstruction and of the industrial revolution, including demographic shifts and the emergence in the late nineteenth century of the United States as a world power.

CITY STRUCTURES

Busy, crowded, and growing cities need efficient forms of public transportation. In the 1880s, **streetcars** became the main form of transportation in urban centers, and cities that had streetcar systems, such as Boston, San Francisco, Chicago, and New York, became known as "streetcar cities." Streetcars helped foster the development of a city's central district because they gave people a means for traveling to and from the city to shop and work. At the same time, streetcars allowed people to travel easily to the outskirts of the city, so those who wanted to escape city living could move to emerging communities on the city's edge, called **suburbs**.

A city's central district featured businesses such as banks, railroad terminals, and the growth of new places to shop: **department stores**. First introduced in the United States in the mid-1800s, department stores offered a unique shopping experience by providing a wide variety of merchandise all under one roof. They drew shoppers from the suburbs. Chicago's Marshall Field & Company and New York's R.H. Macy & Company brought many customers into the big city.

As city populations grew, finding enough space to house all the residents quickly became a problem. When cities could not spread out, they found another solution: they built up. The revolutionary use of steel frameworks in construction allowed builders in Chicago to erect the first skyscraper—an incredible 10-story building—in the 1880s. Skyscrapers were soon standing 30 stories high or more in American cities, making efficient use of limited available urban space. Moreover, the development of the commercial electric passenger elevator just a few years after the first skyscraper's construction added to the practicality and usefulness of these tall buildings. But not everyone could afford to live in a roomy apartment in a skyscraper or move to the suburbs. Many city dwellers rented space in tightly packed, poorly ventilated tenements. The intense overcrowding in poor urban neighborhoods led to many public health problems that required solutions, and reformers ultimately took up the cause.

HISTORICAL THINKING

1. **READING CHECK** What factors contributed to urbanization between 1860 and 1920?
2. **ANALYZE CAUSE AND EFFECT** What effect did the use of steel have on building construction and the growth of cities?
3. **EXPLAIN** How and why did suburbs emerge in the late 19th century?

CRITICAL VIEWING Shoppers who patronized R.H. Macy & Company (center) in New York City in 1906 arrived by streetcar, horse-and-carriage, walking, or an elevated train line. How does the photo convey that commerce, transportation, and people are all interdependent?

11.2.1 Know the effects of industrialization on living and working conditions, including the portrayal of working conditions and food safety in Upton Sinclair's *The Jungle;* 11.2.2 Describe the changing landscape, including the growth of cities linked by industry and trade, and the development of cities divided according to race, ethnicity, and class; HI 4 Students understand the meaning, implication, and impact of historical events and recognize that events could have taken other directions.

4.2 **MAIN IDEA** In the 1890s, a new set of reformers addressed various problems stemming from urbanization and political corruption.

TACKLING URBAN PROBLEMS

When big problems are not solved by those in charge, sometimes ordinary citizens step up and become the agents of change. In the late 1800s, reformers took on social and political problems that had been brewing for several decades.

CITY PROBLEMS, CITY POLITICS

The growing density of urban populations during the late 19th century caused great concern among both public health officials and social reformers. Before 1895, effective departments of **sanitation**, or proper waste disposal and a system for providing clean water, did not exist in cities. Horse manure and garbage accumulated in the streets, while noxious factory smoke filled the air. Such unsanitary conditions made poor sections of cities particularly susceptible to outbreaks of illnesses such as cholera, a deadly disease that people sometimes contract after drinking contaminated water. Crowded conditions increased the amount of damage caused by fires and the likelihood of violent and criminal acts.

Corruption in big city governments was an accepted practice, and political machines were in charge. **Political machines**, or agreed upon, exclusive power structures, involved city officials bribing politicians, contractors, and constituents with all manner of favors to keep the city running. Bribes,

Butchers pause for a photo in Chicago's meatpacking district in 1904. Upton Sinclair exposed the ill treatment of workers and unsanitary and dangerous conditions in slaughterhouses. Through one of his characters in *The Jungle,* he asserts that "one of the consequences of civic administration by ignorant and vicious politicians, is that preventable diseases kill off half our population."

11.2.1 Know the effects of industrialization on living and working conditions, including the portrayal of working conditions and food safety in Upton Sinclair's *The Jungle*; 11.2.2 Describe the changing landscape, including the growth of cities linked by industry and trade, and the development of cities divided according to race, ethnicity, and class; 11.2.4 Analyze the effect of urban political machines and responses to them by immigrants and middle-class reformers.

promises, and favors were the oil that greased the political machine. In cities such as Chicago and New York, political machines were efficient but corrupt ways by which mayors and political bosses managed their cities.

New York's William Magear Tweed, or "Boss Tweed," ran one of the most notorious political machines. In the 1860s, Tweed led a Democratic Party committee called **Tammany Hall**, and he used his position to award city contracts to associates and supporters. Newspapers accused Tweed of corruption, but the inner-city residents, whom the machine depended on for votes, saw value in the services he provided. The contracts that Tweed awarded improved the residents' neighborhoods by paving roads, installing sewers and gas lines, and building parks and elevated train lines. Corruption charges eventually brought Tweed down in the early 1870s but did not disable political machines as a whole.

Because of the political corruption and gaudy excesses of the wealthy, the years between 1870 and 1900 became known as the **Gilded Age**. To gild something means to coat it with a thin layer of gold that can disguise what lies underneath. The phrase "Gilded Age" originated with the novel *The Gilded Age* by Mark Twain and Charles Dudley Warner. The authors used the term to highlight the way spectacular wealth masked the greed and corruption of industrialists and politicians.

REFORMING SOCIAL ILLS

Many Americans knew what was underneath the gilded layer, and they believed that governments did not do enough to solve the problems that stemmed from urbanization. In the 1890s, individuals organized a number of different reform movements to address social problems. These reformers were mostly native-born, middle class, white, and Protestant. They believed that society was responsible for the common good of all its citizens and that social ills resulting from industrial growth and political corruption had to be addressed.

Because one of the root values of these reformers was a belief in progress, the various reform movements became known as **progressivism**. Progressive reformers worked in many different capacities to achieve reforms. Some focused on improving urban living conditions. Some addressed the injustices of child labor, and others challenged big-city bosses and government corruption. While they may have focused on different issues, progressive reformers shared similar goals: addressing social problems such as poverty and exploitation, exposing corruption, reforming government, and expanding democracy.

Thanks to the writings of several novelists and journalists, even Americans who did not live in places like New York City or Chicago learned about the horrendous living conditions in these cities. As you have read, Upton Sinclair's 1906 novel *The Jungle* exposed the dangerous and filthy working conditions of Chicago's stockyards and the abusive treatment immigrant workers endured in the city. Like Ida Tarbell and other muckrakers, Sinclair shined a light on suffering and injustice and the need for reform.

The authors **Theodore Dreiser** and **Frank Norris** also highlighted social problems in their novels. Dreiser had grown up in poverty, and he used his experiences to inform his writing. He described urban poverty in *Sister Carrie* and targeted the legal system in *An American Tragedy*. Likewise, Frank Norris, in his novels *McTeague* and *The Octopus,* explored social issues such as the wheat industry's conflicts with railway monopolies.

Besides addressing social problems, progressive reformers aimed to clean up government by passing new laws that gave citizens the right to initiate **referendums**, or public votes on individual issues, and the right to recall, or remove, an elected official from office. These measures were one way to keep political figures and political machines from gaining too much power. Other progressive reforms included enforcing state regulation of industry and giving voters, instead of party officers, the chance to choose nominees for important political offices.

The late 1800s saw the beginning of many reforms in society and government. Even so, some deeply held prejudices still lurked in American society.

HISTORICAL THINKING

1. **READING CHECK** What steps did reformers take to try to improve citizens' lives and government practices?
2. **IDENTIFY PROBLEMS AND SOLUTIONS** In what ways did change in the late 19th and early 20th centuries affect politics, values, and beliefs?
3. **DESCRIBE** Why did poor city residents have positive feelings about political machines such as Tammany Hall?

11.2.9 Understand the effect of political programs and activities of the Progressives (e.g., federal regulation of railroad transport, Children's Bureau, the Sixteenth Amendment, Theodore Roosevelt, Hiram Johnson); CST 2 Students analyze how change happens at different rates at different times; understand that some aspects can change while others remain the same; and understand that change is complicated and affects not only technology and politics but also values and beliefs.

4.3 **MAIN IDEA** Discriminatory laws and violent hate groups threatened the rights and lives of African Americans, and African-American leaders struggled over the right approach to take against inequality.

JIM CROW AND SEGREGATION

Sometimes the struggle against injustice runs into obstacles, as personal and institutional prejudices get in the way of making laws that are fair for everybody. Although progressive reformers had made headway with social and political reforms, many African Americans still faced massive challenges.

SUPPRESSING THE VOTE

After the Civil War ended, the United States entered a period known as Reconstruction, when the country tried to rebuild the South, bring the former Confederate states back into the Union, and correct injustices resulting from slavery. As part of this effort, Congress proposed a series of amendments to the Constitution.

The **13th Amendment** (1865) abolished slavery. The **14th Amendment** (1868) guaranteed "equal protection of the laws" to African Americans and all citizens. Since its original passage, the 14th Amendment, which covers a broad range of rights, has also been cited in defense of both workers and corporations. The **15th Amendment** (1870) gave African-American males the right to vote.

CRITICAL VIEWING In 1874, this political cartoon by Thomas Nast appeared in *Harper's Weekly*. It depicts a Klansman and a member of the White League, another terrorist organization, formed in 1874 in Louisiana. What do the words "worse than slavery," which appear above the African-American family, suggest about life for African Americans during Reconstruction?

Despite these newly guaranteed constitutional rights, African Americans experienced what historians refer to as the "black nadir," or the lowest point since the end of the Civil War. Racial violence and legalized discrimination inhibited African Americans' economic opportunities and political participation. Southern communities and states passed laws meant to undermine many of the reforms enacted under Reconstruction. For example, white legislators tried to prevent African Americans from voting by instituting

11.1.4 Examine the effects of the Civil War and Reconstruction and of the industrial revolution, including demographic shifts and the emergence in the late nineteenth century of the United States as a world power.

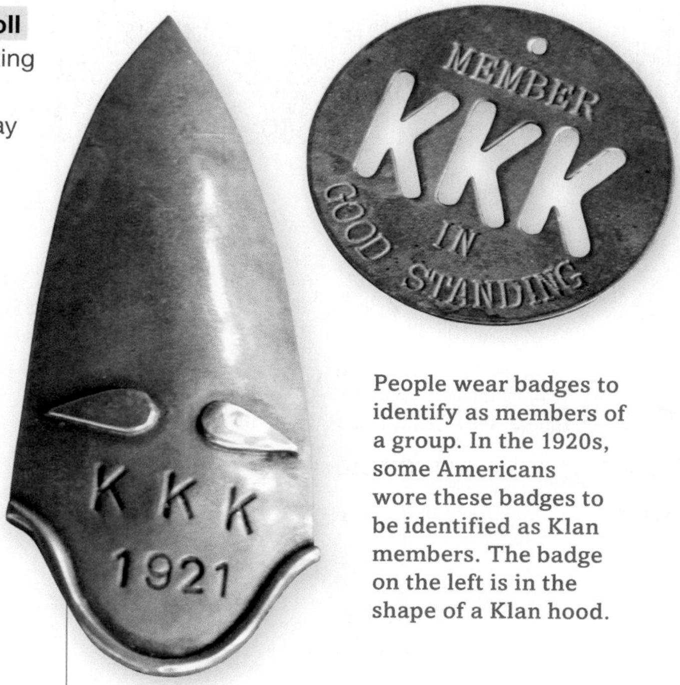

People wear badges to identify as members of a group. In the 1920s, some Americans wore these badges to be identified as Klan members. The badge on the left is in the shape of a Klan hood.

certain requirements, such as paying a special **poll tax** before being allowed to register to vote or taking a literacy test before being permitted to cast a ballot. If a prospective voter could not afford to pay the poll tax, then he could not vote. If an election judge decided a man did not understand a piece of writing or could not answer a set of questions correctly, then he could not vote, either.

By enforcing these measures, legislators claimed to prevent poor and uneducated people from voting, but their real aim was to keep African-American voters from the polls. The measures would also impact women after 1920, when women of all races won the right to vote. Although poll taxes and literacy tests technically applied to both white and African-American citizens, the measures were not applied equitably in practice. They prevented many more African-American citizens from voting than they did white citizens.

However, harassment of African Americans extended well beyond polling stations. In 1866 a group called the **Ku Klux Klan (KKK)** formed in Tennessee. Though originally established as a social club, the group soon began promoting white supremacy, mainly in reaction to the new freedoms and rights African Americans were legally entitled to enjoy. Klan members dressed in robes, masks, and hoods to conceal their identities and used threats and violence to intimidate African Americans who wanted to exercise their newly gained right to vote. Klan members and other hate groups assaulted and even murdered African Americans and their white supporters, often by lynching, or hanging, them. Klan activity peaked between 1868 and 1870. By the 1880s, membership had dwindled, but the racism that fueled the organization never died out. The Klan began to build its membership again in 1915. Despite the low profile of the Klan during the 1890s, the practice of lynching continued, and its members murdered on average 187 African Americans every year throughout the decade.

SEPARATION BASED ON RACE

Discrimination against African Americans was common practice throughout the United States, but it occurred most rampantly in the South. After the end of Reconstruction, southern politicians remained intent on enforcing **segregation**, or the separation of different groups of people, usually based on race. They passed a series of laws to ensure that African-American and white citizens attended separate schools and used separate public facilities, such as restrooms, theaters, restaurants, and public transportation. In states such as Florida, Louisiana, and Mississippi, whites enforced these laws, known as **Jim Crow laws**, to establish and maintain power in society. Jim Crow was an African-American character in minstrel shows of the day—a dim-witted, comic fellow, portrayed by a white actor in blackface, who was the target of ridicule and the butt of jokes. That the name of this character became associated with segregation laws is just one more affront to those to whom the laws applied.

One Jim Crow law had a particularly significant effect. In 1890, Louisiana passed the Separate Car Act, which required "equal but separate accommodations" for white and African-American train passengers. In other words, the railroads had to offer the same accommodations to whites and African Americans, but in separate rail cars.

A New Orleans committee that supported African-American rights decided to test the act's constitutionality. Because the act did not define the meaning of *white* or *African American*, the committee claimed the railroads could not consistently apply the act. To prove its point, in 1892, the committee enlisted Homer Plessy to purchase a train ticket in Louisiana. Plessy was one-eighth African American. When he purposely sat in the car reserved for whites, a conductor told Plessy to move to the African-American car. Plessy refused and was arrested.

11.5.2 Analyze the international and domestic events, interests, and philosophies that prompted attacks on civil liberties, including the Palmer Raids, Marcus Garvey's "back-to-Africa" movement, the Ku Klux Klan, and immigration quotas and the responses of organizations such as the American Civil Liberties Union, the National Association for the Advancement of Colored People, and the Anti-Defamation League to those attacks.

CRITICAL VIEWING **White bi-plane passengers tow a group of African-American passengers behind them in this 1913 cartoon from the New York humor magazine, *Puck*. What details in the cartoon demonstrate a northern critique of the "separate but equal" policies legalized by *Plessy* v. *Ferguson*?**

Plessy challenged the railroad company in the 1896 Supreme Court case *Plessy* v. *Ferguson*. The court decided that the Separate Car Act did not violate the 14th Amendment's guarantee of "equal protection of the laws" because the railroad company offered equal accommodations, even if they were separate. In a strong dissent from the majority of the court, Justice John Marshall Harlan wrote, "I am of the opinion that the statute of Louisiana is inconsistent with the personal liberties of citizens, white and black, in that State, and hostile to both the spirit and the letter of the Constitution of the United States." By ruling against Plessy, the Supreme Court upheld the practice of segregation, thereby allowing other businesses and institutions to apply a "**separate but equal**" treatment to African Americans for decades.

Public schools enforced "separate but equal" segregation policies. African-American and white students attended different schools, but they were rarely equal. Whites had much better access to schools and the public funding needed to pay for them. African Americans, on the other hand, often had to pay to build schools themselves and resort to using second-hand supplies, such as outdated textbooks that white schools gave them.

SELF-RELIANCE VS. SOCIAL REFORM

African-American leaders responded to segregation laws, but in very different ways. Some supported the idea of working to make changes from within the system. Others championed open protest because they believed that was the only route to securing their denied rights.

Booker T. Washington was an educator who founded the Tuskegee Institute in Alabama in 1881 to train African Americans to be teachers. Eventually, though, Washington incorporated vocational classes at the institute, teaching manual trades and developing students' agricultural skills. Washington also promoted self-reliance among

11.10.2 Examine and analyze the key events, policies and court cases in the evolution of civil rights, including *Dred Scot* v. *Sandford*, *Plessy* v. *Ferguson*, *Brown* v. *Board of Education*, *Regents of the University of California* v. *Bakke*, and California Proposition 209.

PRIMARY SOURCES

Our greatest danger is that in the great leap from slavery to freedom we may overlook the fact that the masses of us are to live by the productions of our hands, and fail to keep in mind that we shall prosper in proportion as we learn to dignify and glorify common labor and put brains and skill into the common occupations of life. No race can prosper till it learns that there is as much dignity in tilling a field as in writing a poem. It is at the bottom of life we must begin, and not at the top. Nor should we permit our grievances to overshadow our opportunities.

—from the "Atlanta Compromise" speech, by Booker T. Washington, 1895

How does Washington's speech reflect the Tuskegee Institute's goals?

The supplementary truths must never be lost sight of: first, slavery and race-prejudice are potent . . . causes of the Negro's position; second, industrial and common-school training were necessarily slow in planting because they had to await the black teachers trained by higher institutions . . . and, third, while it is a great truth to say that the Negro must strive and strive mightily to help himself, it is equally true that unless his striving be not simply seconded, but rather aroused and encouraged, by the initiative of the richer and wiser environing group, he cannot hope for great success.

—from *The Souls of Black Folk,* by W.E.B. Du Bois, 1903

What is Du Bois's main critique of Washington's theories?

African Americans, believing they should focus on hard work and personal development rather than on trying to reform entrenched, systemic racism. He thought the best way for African Americans to win the respect of whites was for them to prove themselves worthy of that respect. In 1895, Washington presented his ideas in a speech at the Cotton States and International Exposition in Atlanta, Georgia. In his speech, known as the "Atlanta Compromise" speech, Washington encouraged African Americans to refrain from openly and actively promoting social equality.

Washington's emphasis on self-reliance helped him raise money for the institute, especially from white donors. Although Washington did not publicly promote social reform, he did privately fund court challenges to segregation.

In contrast, historian, sociologist, and reformer **W.E.B. Du Bois** (doo-BOYS) believed that protest was the best path toward gaining equality and ending segregation. Du Bois charged that Washington's acceptance of discrimination helped promote bigotry rather than deter it. He critiqued the ideas of self-reliance in his book *The Souls of Black Folk*, and, in the process, motivated others to oppose Washington's approach.

By 1903, the year *The Souls of Black Folk* was published, eight years had passed since Washington's "Atlanta Compromise" speech. Little had improved in the daily lives of African Americans, however. Racial violence, discrimination, and segregation worked against African Americans' limited ability to participate in the political process, and the activism proposed by Du Bois gained favor.

In 1905, Du Bois founded a small organization called the Niagara Movement, which attacked Washington's ideas. The organization died out in 1909, but that same year Du Bois co-founded the **National Association for the Advancement of Colored People (NAACP)** with other African-American leaders and white supporters. DuBois served as the organization's director of research and edited its magazine, *The Crisis*. His hope was that the NAACP could be a force for change in ending segregation and discrimination against African Americans. In fact, reform did begin to attract greater attention as the nation entered a new period of rapid change.

HISTORICAL THINKING

1. **READING CHECK** What were Jim Crow laws, and why were they instituted?
2. **MAKE CONNECTIONS** How did changes to the Constitution and various court decisions affect the lives of African Americans during and after Reconstruction?
3. **EVALUATE** Regarding the events discussed in this lesson, evaluate what aspects of African Americans' lives changed and what aspects stayed the same.
4. **IDENTIFY PROBLEMS AND SOLUTIONS** What different solutions did Booker T. Washington and W.E.B. Du Bois propose as ways to fight discrimination against African Americans?

CST 2 Students analyze how change happens at different rates at different times; understand that some aspects can change while others remain the same; and understand that change is complicated and affects not only technology and politics but also values and beliefs.

CONFRONTING RACIAL VIOLENCE

Beginning in the 1870s, African Americans realized the freedoms they had gained following the Civil War were under attack. Many white people sought to manipulate laws to return African Americans to what, in effect, would be slavery.

CRITICAL VIEWING One way white southerners terrorized African Americans during the years after the Civil War—and well into the 20th century—was by burning down their houses and farms and destroying their crops and belongings. *Burned Out*, painted by William H. Johnson around 1943, depicts an African-American couple standing in front of their burning house with the few possessions they managed to rescue. How does the painting convey the vulnerability of African Americans in a hostile society?

Smithsonian American Art Museum Washington, D.C.

William H. Johnson grew up in South Carolina, left for New York at age 17, and studied art in Paris. He returned to New York, where he spent most of the rest of his life. Like many artists, Johnson brought his own life experiences into his art. From his studio in New York, Johnson recalled life in the South from his childhood, which he depicted in paintings and in works on paper. After his death in 1970, more than 1,000 of Johnson's paintings and drawings were discovered by friends. His work is now housed in the Smithsonian American Art Museum.

11.5.2 Analyze the international and domestic events, interests, and philosophies that prompted attacks on civil liberties, including the Palmer Raids, Marcus Garvey's "back-to-Africa" movement, the Ku Klux Klan, and immigration quotas and the responses of organizations such as the American Civil Liberties Union, the National Association for the Advancement of Colored People, and the Anti-Defamation League to those attacks; HREP 4 Students construct and test hypotheses; collect, evaluate, and employ information from multiple primary and secondary sources; and apply it in oral and written presentations.

DOCUMENT ONE

Primary Source: Newspaper Editorial
from "Mrs. Ida Wells-Barnett Calls on President McKinley," by Ida B. Wells-Barnett, 1898

Ida B. Wells-Barnett, an African-American journalist, wrote extensively about lynching. She traveled to England to speak about the topic and formed anti-lynching societies. Wells-Barnett devoted particular attention to the topic after mobs lynched three of her friends.

CONSTRUCTED RESPONSE How does Wells-Barnett characterize lynching in the United States?

> For nearly twenty years lynching crimes . . . have been committed and permitted by this Christian nation. Nowhere in the civilized world save the United States of America do men . . . go out in bands of 50 and 5,000 to hunt down, shoot, hang or burn to death a single individual. Statistics show that nearly 10,000 American citizens have been lynched in the past twenty years. To our appeals for justice the stereotyped reply has been that the governor could not interfere in a state matter. We refuse to believe this country, so powerful to defend its citizens abroad, is unable to protect its citizens at home.

DOCUMENT TWO

Primary Source: Document
from "Platform Adopted by the National Negro Committee," 1909

In response to racial violence, William English Walling and others, mostly whites, formed the National Negro Committee, which eventually became the NAACP. Written by the committee, the platform's signers include Ida B. Wells-Barnett and Jane Addams. This document emphasized that violence benefits no one.

CONSTRUCTED RESPONSE According to the statement, who is affected by violence against African Americans?

> The systematic persecution of law-abiding citizens . . . on account of their race alone is a crime that will ultimately drag down to an infamous end any nation that allows it . . . and it bears most heavily on those poor white farmers and laborers whose economic position is most similar to that of the persecuted race. Indeed persecution of organized workers, peonage, [and] enslavement of prisoners . . . already threaten large bodies of whites in many southern States.

DOCUMENT THREE

Secondary Source: Newspaper Article
from *Fort Worth Star-Telegram*, by Tim Madigan, 2011

In July 1910, a white mob, emboldened by rumors, randomly attacked African-American residents of Slocum, Texas. Anywhere from 20 to 200 people were killed. Newspaper accounts of the massacre were conflicting, and most articles falsely reported that it was begun by armed African Americans. Not until 2011 did the town officially acknowledge the massacre. This newspaper article relates what is known of the killings 100 years after they happened.

CONSTRUCTED RESPONSE What important information does this source provide about the 1910 events in Slocum?

> Some initial newspaper accounts erroneously reported that whites had also been killed, describing the Slocum incident as a race riot. But Slocum was no riot. "Men were going about killing Negroes as fast as they could find them, and, so far as I was able to ascertain, without any real cause," Anderson County Sheriff W.H. Black, a white from nearby Palestine, was quoted as saying. Seven white men were indicted on murder charges and had their cases transferred to Houston on a change of venue. But none ever came to trial.

SYNTHESIZE & WRITE

1. **REVIEW** Review what you have learned about racial violence from the passages and the painting.
2. **RECALL** On your own paper, write down some of the different reactions American citizens had to racial violence in the late 19th and early 20th centuries, as demonstrated in the passages.
3. **CONSTRUCT** Construct a topic sentence to answer this question: In what ways did African-American journalists and activists reveal the extent of racial violence?
4. **WRITE** Write an informative paragraph supporting your topic sentence in Step 3 by using evidence from the passages, the art, and the chapter.

CHAPTER 6 INDUSTRIAL AMERICA

REVIEW

VOCABULARY

Write a paragraph using each key vocabulary term from the chapter listed below in a way that conveys its importance. A sample beginning sentence is provided for the first term.

1. push-pull factors HSS 11.2
   Lack of opportunity in their home countries and opportunities in the United States were push-pull factors for immigrants.
2. muckraker HSS 11.2.1
3. tenement HSS 11.2.2
4. sanitation HSS 11.2.1
5. assimilate HSS 11.2.3
6. progressivism HSS 11.2.9

READING STRATEGY

IDENTIFY PROBLEMS AND SOLUTIONS

Identifying problems faced by individuals and nations and tracking their solutions can help readers understand the way history unfolds. Complete the Problem-and-Solution Chart to analyze several problems the United States faced as it continued to industrialize and solutions to those problems. Then answer the question.

Problem:

↓

Event 1:

Event 2:

Event 3:

↓

Solution:

7. Describe one problem the United States faced as industrialization grew, beginning in the 1890s. Then list events that led to a solution. HSS 11.1.4

MAIN IDEAS

Answer the following questions. Support your answers with evidence from the chapter.

8. How did expansion of the railroad industry help the steel industry grow? **LESSON 1.1** HSS 11.2.6
9. Why are Alexander Graham Bell and Thomas Edison considered significant inventors of the late 19th century? **LESSON 1.3** HSS 11.5.7
10. Why did states provide workers' compensation? **LESSON 2.1** HSS 11.2.1
11. Why did workers begin forming labor unions in the late 1800s? **LESSON 2.2** HSS 11.2.1
12. What was unique about the American Railway Union's structure? **LESSON 2.3** HSS 11.2.1
13. What did the Americanization movement hope to accomplish? **LESSON 3.1** HSS 11.2.3
14. Why did nativists oppose immigration? **LESSON 3.3** HSS 11.3.3
15. Why were fires and diseases especially deadly in large cities such as Chicago and New York? **LESSON 4.2** HSS 11.2.1
16. Why did many white southerners react the way they did to the reforms that took place during Reconstruction? **LESSON 4.3** HSS 11.5.2

HISTORICAL THINKING

Answer the following questions. Support your answers with evidence from the chapter.

17. **ANALYZE CAUSE AND EFFECT** What part did greed play in the growth of industry? HSS 11.2.5
18. **EVALUATE** In what ways did the late 19th and early 20th centuries represent both advancement and turmoil for African Americans? HSS 11.5.2
19. **SYNTHESIZE** How did writers in the late 19th and early 20th centuries help expose injustices in society, and why was it important? HSS HI 1

20. **IDENTIFY PROBLEMS AND SOLUTIONS** What problems did progressive reformers seek to solve? HSS 11.2.9

21. **DRAW CONCLUSIONS** How did Jim Crow laws and "separate but equal" treatment impact economic mobility and opportunity for African Americans? HSS 11.1.4

22. **FORM AND SUPPORT OPINIONS** What were positive effects of industrialization on living and working conditions? Support your opinion using evidence from the chapter. HSS 11.2.1

INTERPRET GRAPHS

Look carefully at the graph showing causes of death on the job for workers at steel mills in one Pennsylvania county. Then answer the questions that follow.

Steel Worker Deaths in Allegheny County, Pennsylvania, 1906–1907

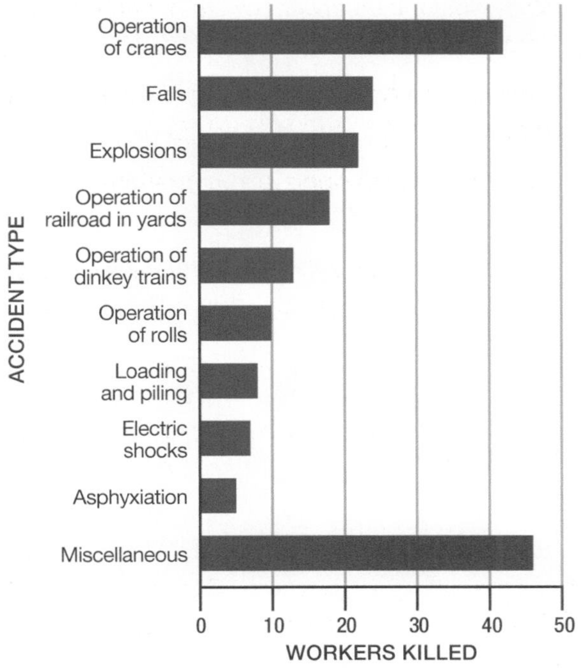

Source: Crystal Eastman, *Work-Accidents and the Law: The Pittsburgh Survey*, 1916

23. How many workers were killed by various causes not specified in the graph? HSS 11.2.1

24. How do the numbers of deaths from operating different types of equipment, such as cranes, the railroad in yards, dinkey trains, and rolls, compare? HSS 11.2.1

25. What were the causes of the third and fourth highest numbers of deaths? HSS 11.2.1

ANALYZE SOURCES

In 1900, writer and journalist Theodore Dreiser published *Sister Carrie*, a novel about a young woman who moves from rural Wisconsin to Chicago. In this scene, the narrator describes Carrie's visit to a department store, a new kind of consumer experience that arose in the late 1800s.

> Carrie passed along the busy aisles, much affected by the remarkable displays of trinkets, dress goods, stationery, and jewelry. Each separate counter was a show place of dazzling interest and attraction. She could not help feeling the claim of each trinket and valuable upon her personally, and yet she did not stop. There was nothing there which she could not have used—nothing which she did not long to own.

26. What was the effect of the department store on Carrie? HSS 11.1.4

CONNECT TO YOUR LIFE

27. **ARGUMENT** This chapter discusses the rise of cities and some of the benefits and drawbacks of city life. Is solving the problems of cities worthwhile, or should people just move out of cities? Write an argument supporting your position. HSS CST 4

TIPS

- Reread the chapter, listing the advantages and disadvantages of urban living.
- Look over your lists and add your own thoughts and experiences to them.
- Decide on a position to take. Then choose two or three of your strongest pros or cons to develop and support your argument.
- Include two or three vocabulary terms from the chapter in your argument.
- Address any opposing views you identify. Use your list to help in choosing an opposing view to challenge.
- Conclude with a summary that explains your arguments clearly and directly.

CHAPTER 7

THE PROGRESSIVE ERA AND EXPANSIONISM

1890–1920

HISTORICAL THINKING What reforms and expansion took place during the Progressive Era?

At the same time Americans were working to solve social, economic, and political problems at home, the United States was expanding its overseas territories. The island chain of Hawaii, where American companies operated pineapple plantations like the one pictured here, became a U.S. territory in 1900.

"A great democracy has got to be progressive, or it will soon **cease to be either great or a democracy.**"

—President Theodore Roosevelt

THE TRIANGLE WAIST COMPANY

FACTORY FIRE

March 25, 1911, was a normal day for the 500 workers at the Triangle Waist Company, a factory located on the 8th, 9th, and 10th floors of the Asch Building in New York City. That is to say, the workers, most of them immigrant women between the ages of 16 and 23, had put in several grueling hours sewing shirtwaists—a type of women's blouse—for a pay rate that came to around $15 for a week of 12-hour days.

In 1909, the Ladies Garment Workers Union had led a strike against New York clothing manufacturers. Their demands had included higher pay, shorter hours, and safer working conditions. Most of the smaller factories quickly agreed to the union's demands, but Isaac Harris and Max Blanck, the owners of the Triangle factory, resisted. Instead, they joined a group of manufacturers who fought back with dirty tactics, including paying police officers to beat or intimidate the striking workers. Eventually, Harris and Blanck relented, offering their employees higher wages and shorter working hours but refusing to allow them to unionize. Despite these improvements, work at the Triangle Waist Company was still exhausting, unsafe, and poorly paid. The factory remained a sweatshop with working conditions just as harsh as that name implies.

Around 4:40 p.m. on March 25, 1911, Isidore Abramowitz was preparing to go home from his job cutting fabric on the eighth floor, when he spotted sparks in a bin used for discarded scraps of fabric. At once, he seized one of the buckets of water placed throughout the factory in case of fires and dumped it on the flames. Abramowitz's fellow cutters rushed to throw water from other buckets onto the fire, but the workers were in a gigantic room filled with long wooden tables and piles of fabric scraps. They were surrounded by extremely flammable materials.

Within moments, the fire was out of control, and panicked employees were struggling toward the exits. Sylvia Kimeldorf, an 18-year-old who was working on the eighth floor that day, recalled, "The place was filling up with heavy black smoke, and we were all choking."

11.2.1 Know the effects of industrialization on living and working conditions, including the portrayal of working conditions and food safety in Upton Sinclair's *The Jungle*.

Limited firefighting technology, including short ladders and poor water pressure, made battling the Triangle factory fire and rescuing factory workers a serious challenge for firefighters.

In 1909, a fire insurance inspector recommended that Triangle factory owners keep the building's doors unlocked during the day and conduct fire drills with factory workers. Harris and Blanck did not follow through on either request. As a result, when Ladder Company 20 arrived on the scene of the horrific fire there two years later, there was little they could do. Fabric scraps provided fuel for what one fire captain called "a mass of traveling fire." Staircases were too few in number, and the fire escape didn't reach the ground. Short ladders and poor water pressure made putting out the fire and rescuing workers nearly impossible. All firefighters could do was mist the outside of the building.

The Asch Building had stairways and elevators located on the northeast and southwest corners, but the northeast corner was almost instantly consumed by flames. On the eighth and ninth floors, workers rushed for the stairway doors on the southwest side of the building but found them locked. It was company policy to lock the doors during working hours to prevent workers from stealing supplies or taking unauthorized breaks. On the eighth floor, one employee had a key, and most of the workers on that floor were able to escape.

Workers on the 10th floor managed to take the stairs up to the building's roof, from which they were rescued by a group of students at the neighboring New York University School of Law building, who placed ladders between the rooftops. Factory owners Isaac Harris and Max Blanck were able to escape the fire in this way. But for workers on the ninth floor, there was no escape via the staircases. They were unable to unlock or force the doors open, so their only hopes for survival were the southwest elevators or the fire escape.

Elevator operators Joseph Zito and Gaspar Mortillalo saved as many people as they could, making several trips to the burning floors before conditions became unbearable. Later, bodies of workers who had tried to escape down the elevator shaft but had fallen to their deaths were found piled on top of the elevators. A few people did survive the breakneck trip down the elevator shaft by gripping the cables. One of them, Sam Levine, recalled, "I can remember getting to the sixth floor. While on my way down, as slow as I could let myself drop, the bodies of six girls went falling past me."

The metal fire escape ladder on the outside of the building was not sufficiently strong to support the weight of the fleeing crowd, and it was further weakened by the fierce heat of the fire. Some workers were able to descend the fire escape to the sixth floor before the fragile ladder crashed to the ground. Nellie Ventura was one of those survivors. "At first I was too frightened to try to run through the fire," she recalled. "Then I heard the screams of the girls inside. I knew I had to go down the ladder or die where I was."

THE TRIANGLE FACTORY FLOOR

This diagram shows how the ninth floor of the Asch Building was laid out. The fire blocked access to the stairs and freight elevators on the Greene Street side of the building. Look at the spacing of the long tables and the location of the passenger elevators on the Washington Place side. One survivor described the space between the rows as "narrow and blocked by chairs and baskets." Other sources indicate that the stairs in the stairwells were 33 inches wide and the stairs of the fire escape were 17½ inches wide. In addition to the locked stairway door, what difficulties did the workers face in trying to escape the fire?

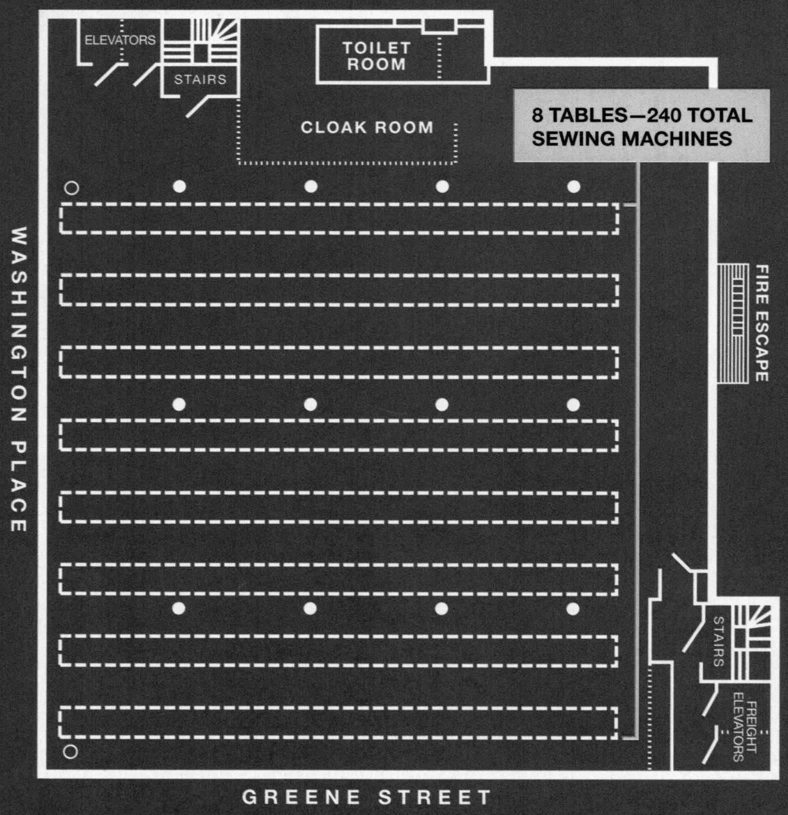

WHAT IS A SHIRTWAIST?

It is ironic that the shirtwaist, produced in sweatshops by an underpaid, mainly female workforce, was a symbol of social progress and women's growing empowerment. Popular in the late 19th and early 20th centuries, the shirtwaist was a style of blouse for women, featuring buttons down the front and modeled after men's shirts.

Practical and relatively comfortable, shirtwaists came to symbolize the modern working woman who earned her own wages and thus was not fully dependent on a man to support her. Women wearing shirtwaists as they demonstrated in the streets were the backbone of the women's movement around the turn of the 20th century.

As it gained in popularity, the shirtwaist also had a democratizing effect on fashion. Because the blouses were available in a range of prices, from 25 cents to 7 dollars, they were worn by women from every economic level, from salesclerks to wealthy socialites. According to the *Gimbel Brothers Illustrated 1915 Catalog*, "the women of other lands occasionally wear a shirtwaist—the American woman occasionally wears something else. Her daily apparel is a smart tailored skirt and neat blouse."

CRITICAL VIEWING What can you infer about women's fashions during the early part of the 1900s based on this 1905 shirtwaist and 1901 advertisement?

The Newest Shirt-Waists

DESIGNED AND DRAWN ESPECIALLY FOR THE JOURNAL

By KATHERINE VAUGHAN HOLDEN

CRITICAL VIEWING The Triangle factory fire caused extensive damage. What can you infer about the intensity of the fire from this photo?

CRITICAL VIEWING The bodies of the Triangle factory workers who did not survive the fire were taken to the New York City morgue to be identified by their loved ones. What does this photo reveal about the impact the fire had on New Yorkers?

11.5.7 Discuss the rise of mass production techniques, the growth of cities, the impact of new technologies (e.g., the automobile, electricity), and the resulting prosperity and effect on the American landscape; HI 4 Students understand the meaning, implication, and impact of historical events and recognize that events could have taken other directions.

Meanwhile, on the ground, the New York City fire department was trying desperately to quell the blaze, but the department's ladders reached only as high as the sixth floor of the Asch Building. Firefighters and onlookers watched helplessly as young women, trapped and in danger of burning to death, leapt from the factory windows.

Some firefighters tried to deploy safety nets to catch the falling workers, but all those who jumped died on impact. Sylvia Kimeldorf, who had managed to escape by the stairs, remembered reaching the ground floor of the building and being held back by firefighters: "The bodies were falling all around us and they were afraid to let us go out because we would be killed by the falling bodies." Within 40 minutes, all three floors of the Triangle factory had been destroyed by the blaze, and 146 workers were dead. Even seasoned police officers were appalled by the grim scene. "It's the worst thing I ever saw," one older officer told the *New York Times* that night.

Could the Triangle factory fire have been prevented, or could it at least have resulted in fewer fatalities? In the aftermath, angry New Yorkers and factory workers believed so. Outraged crowds took to the streets to protest dangerous factory working conditions. On April 5, 1911, a mourning parade of more than 100,000 factory workers marched along one of New York City's main streets as 300,000 spectators turned out to witness the event.

CRITICAL VIEWING **This household sewing machine from around 1900 didn't run on electricity. The user "powered" it by turning the crank to make the needle move up and down. What do you notice about the craftsmanship of this machine?**

SEWING MACHINES AT HOME AND AT WORK

The sewing machine is arguably one of the most influential American inventions in both the industrial and domestic domains. Before the sewing machine, garments were mostly stitched by women working at home. In New York City in 1850, around 5,000 women were employed hand-stitching shirts in their homes for very little pay. Beginning in the late 1800s, industrial sewing machines allowed entrepreneurs to hire women to work in factories, turning out clothing much more quickly and cheaply. Some sources touted the benefits of the new invention for "sewing girls," but as the Triangle story illustrates, the move from home to factory did not necessarily improve the situation for poor, immigrant working women.

In middle-class and wealthier homes, the sewing machine helped support the "cult of domesticity," the idea that a woman's home was her particular sphere of influence. In the words of an 1860 *New York Times* article, the sewing machine had "stitched its way onward as an agent of domestic economy." By acquiring a sewing machine—and perhaps a sewing room—a woman proved that she could master relatively complex machinery and produce and mend clothing for the family. Believers in the cult of domesticity conveniently overlooked the fact that the men in the home were usually in charge of the finances, and thus the decision to purchase a sewing machine.

Later that year, the New York state legislature formed a commission, which included union leader Samuel Gompers, to investigate ways to prevent disastrous workplace fires in the future. In 1912, the commission issued the first of a series of reports that resulted in numerous changes to health and safety laws in New York. Buildings were required to have fire alarms, fire extinguishers, well-built fire escapes, and sprinkler systems on higher floors. In addition, it became illegal to lock fire exits during working hours or to block stairways. Many of these laws were adopted in other states as well. Future Secretary of Labor Frances Perkins had been in New York on March 25, 1911, and had watched the tragedy unfold with gruesome swiftness. "Something must be done," she said, encapsulating the country's mood. "We've got to turn this into some kind of victory, some kind of constructive action."

THINK ABOUT IT

Do you think a workplace disaster like the Triangle factory fire could happen in the United States today? Why or why not?

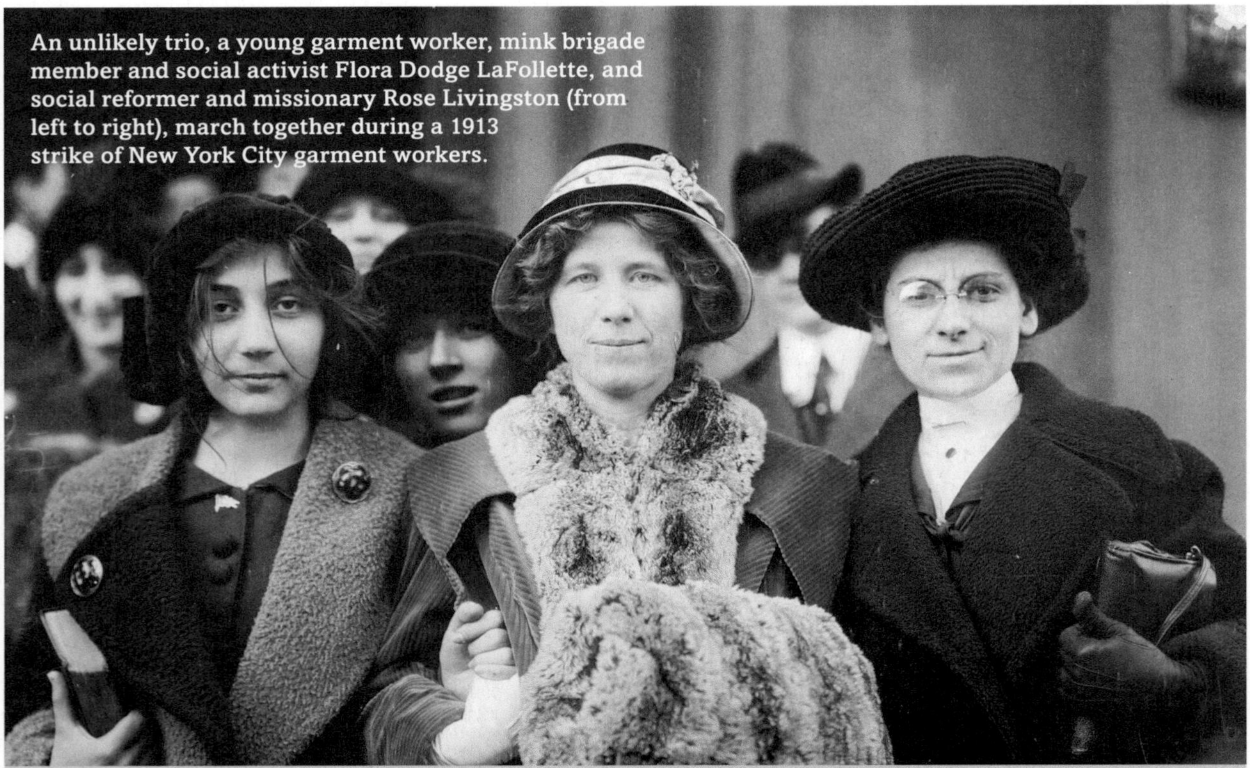

An unlikely trio, a young garment worker, mink brigade member and social activist Flora Dodge LaFollette, and social reformer and missionary Rose Livingston (from left to right), march together during a 1913 strike of New York City garment workers.

THE MINK BRIGADE

When female garment workers went on strike in 1909, prior to the Triangle factory fire, they garnered unlikely allies in wealthy, prominent women. Anne Morgan, daughter of the powerful financier J.P. Morgan, had never needed to earn a living—much less toil at a sewing machine for 12 hours a day. Still, she and her friends were moved by the plight of the young immigrant sweatshop workers. Morgan recruited other upper-class women, including social activist Flora Dodge LaFollette, to come to the workers' defense. The "mink brigade," as the women were mockingly called because of their extravagant furs, walked the picket lines, feeling less likely to be attacked due to their social status. The mink brigade also defended striking workers who had been arrested and paid their fines.

Women like Anne Morgan and Flora Dodge LaFollette engaged in other philanthropic projects and worked to advance women's rights. In a statement in 1927, Morgan pictured a time when women "will take their places beside men as partners, unafraid, useful, successful, and free." To what extent do you think this vision has been realized in the 21st century?

11.2.4 Analyze the effect of urban political machines and responses to them by immigrants and middle-class reformers; CST 1 Students compare the present with the past, evaluating the consequences of past events and decisions and determining the lessons that were learned.

MODERN-DAY TRIANGLES

In the 21st century, factory disasters in China, India, and Bangladesh have served as disturbing modern-day reminders of the Triangle factory fire. Bangladesh has become a world leader in garment manufacturing. The country's more than 5,000 factories, staffed with a largely female workforce, produce clothing for major international brands.

In November 2012, more than 100 people died in a fire at the Tazreen Fashions factory outside Dhaka, the capital of Bangladesh. The problems in the Tazreen factory—and other factories in Bangladesh—resembled those in the Triangle Waist Company factory: insufficient fire escapes, blocked exits, and poor safety measures. Then, in April 2013, the Rana Plaza building, in Savar, which is northwest of Dhaka, collapsed.

Rana Plaza had housed several garment factories. More than 1,100 workers were killed and 2,500 more injured in the catastrophe. The ensuing investigation revealed that the top four floors of the building had been built illegally, with no permits issued, and that the foundation was poorly constructed.

The disasters sparked a public outcry against the factory owners, the international brands that contracted the factories to make their garments, and the Bangladeshi government. Activists demanded improved safety measures and working conditions in the country's garment factories. The case of the Rana Plaza collapse resulted in criminal charges against the owners of the building and the factories housed inside. In addition to building code violations, charges in the case included murder.

CRITICAL VIEWING Workers in India stitch clothing in a garment factory in this 2012 photo. How would you describe working conditions in this factory?

1.1 **MAIN IDEA** Progressive reformers worked to address social, economic, and political problems in the United States in the early 1900s.

THE ROOTS OF PROGRESSIVISM

At the dawn of the 20th century, children as young as eight years of age helped support their families by working in dusty mines sorting coal. This situation was one of many that reformers at the time wanted to change.

GOALS OF PROGRESSIVISM

As you have read, the United States had quickly become more industrialized and urbanized after the Civil War, and its immigrant population had grown dramatically. These changes brought new social and economic problems that reformers pressured the government to address. The push for reform reached a peak during the **Progressive Era**, a period from about 1890 to 1920 in which reformers sought to correct many social, economic, and political inequalities and injustices in the United States. The era brought sweeping changes that had a lasting impact on American society. In fact, many laws, policies, and ideas that shape life in the United States today trace back to this period.

The Progressive Era featured numerous reform campaigns led by progressive-minded people who were primarily white, middle class, Protestant, and college educated. The various campaigns often shared the same general aims of helping the disadvantaged and making the United States a more equitable and democratic country. One of the progressives' major goals was to end the widespread corruption of political bosses and government officials. Progressives wanted government at all levels to be honest and more open, efficient, democratic, and responsive. The people, they felt, should have a stronger and more direct role in electing officials and creating laws.

Many progressives also sought reforms in business and labor. Rejecting the laissez-faire, or hands-off, approach to economic affairs that had prevailed previously, they called for the government to regulate business practices and to break up monopolies and trusts. They hoped to end child labor and bring about improved working conditions, higher pay, and better benefits for all workers, including immigrants.

Theodore Roosevelt was an avid horseback rider throughout much of his life. In this photo from 1902, Roosevelt jumps a horse over a fence on a friend's farm near Washington, D.C.

Women played a major role during the Progressive Era and fought for an equal voice in government. At the time, only a few states allowed women to vote in elections. Progressives sought an amendment to the U.S. Constitution guaranteeing women's suffrage.

SPREADING PROGRESSIVISM

Progressivism arose in response to a multitude of problems. These included poverty, the spread of urban slums, poor working conditions in factories and mines, corruption in government, and the power of large corporations over the economy and

11.2.7 Analyze the similarities and differences between the ideologies of Social Darwinism and Social Gospel (e.g., using biographies of William Graham Sumner, Billy Sunday, Dwight L. Moody); 11.3.1 Describe the contributions of various religious groups to American civic principles and social reform movements (e.g., civil and human rights, individual responsibility and the work ethic, antimonarchy and self-rule, worker protection, family-centered communities).

government. These problems gained the attention of most Americans through **exposés**, writings that publicize a scandal or injustice. You have read about Upton Sinclair and his book *The Jungle,* which exposed the horrors of working in the meatpacking industry. You have also read about Ida Tarbell and her exposé of Rockefeller's Standard Oil Company. Sinclair and Tarbell were just two of the many muckrakers who helped bring the nation's social ills to wide public attention.

Helen Hunt Jackson, who had achieved fame as a poet and novelist, became a fierce advocate for the rights of Native Americans. In her nonfiction book *A Century of Dishonor,* published in 1881, Jackson condemned the federal government and white settlers for their shameful and often brutal treatment of Native Americans. Her popular 1884 novel *Ramona* called attention to the struggles of Native Americans living on missions in the Southwest.

Journalist and photographer **Jacob Riis** drew public attention to the crime, disease, and squalor in New York City's slums, which he had experienced firsthand as a struggling immigrant and a police beat reporter. His influential book *How the Other Half Lives,* published in 1890, jolted readers with stark photographs, unsparing descriptions, and shocking statistics. The book helped bring about laws regulating tenements, and it strongly influenced then president-to-be Theodore Roosevelt.

Joseph Mayer Rice, a physician by training, became a leader in a movement to reform education. From 1891 to 1897, he authored a series of articles that appeared in a journal called *The Forum.* Rice's articles shocked Americans by revealing poor teaching methods, low achievement, and unhealthy conditions in the nation's public schools.

In his 1902 magazine article "Tweed Days in St. Louis," muckraker **Lincoln Steffens** revealed the destructive effect of corruption on the government of St. Louis, Missouri, then one of the country's largest cities. The popularity of that article led Steffens to report on the troublesome relationship between business and government in five other major cities. His articles were collected and published in 1904 in a book called *The Shame of the Cities*. They made a powerful impression on the American public.

The Lithuanian-born political activist and anarchist **Emma Goldman** spoke out in her writings and lectures for the rights of workers and the empowerment of women. When World War I erupted, she fought strongly against U.S. involvement in the war and against military **conscription**, in which the government requires men to enlist and serve in the armed forces. As a result of her antiwar activism, she was arrested and convicted of conspiracy against the conscription law. She spent two years in prison. After her release, she was deported to her home country.

SOCIAL GOSPEL AND FUNDAMENTALISM

Two distinct religious movements, Social Gospel and fundamentalism, took root during the Progressive Era. Social Gospel was based on Christian liberal theology, fundamentalism on a literal interpretation of the Bible. Two leading fundamentalists of the time were **Dwight L. Moody** and **Billy Sunday**. A former shoe salesman, Moody began preaching in the mid-1800s and devoted his life to winning souls and educating impoverished children in Chicago. Sunday left professional baseball to travel the country preaching against alcoholic beverages, declaring, "Whiskey and beer are all right in their place, but their place is in hell." Fundamentalists and followers of Social Gospel alike opposed the teachings of such Social Darwinists as William Graham Sumner, who portrayed the results of dire poverty as a natural mechanism to weed out the "unfit" in society.

The progressive movement coincided with and was strongly influenced by a religious movement known as **Social Gospel**, which originated around 1870 among Protestant ministers who sought to apply Christian liberal theology to societal problems. This theology emphasized helping others by following the moral and ethical example of Jesus. Like Social Darwinism, Social Gospel addressed the poverty in urban, industrial society. However, followers of Social Gospel rejected the tenet of Social Darwinism that people are engaged in a struggle for existence in which only the strong survive. In contrast, they believed that by creating a kinder and more equitable society, they could help build the kingdom of God on Earth. They worked for such reforms as an end to child labor, a living wage for workers, a shorter workday, and safer working conditions.

HISTORICAL THINKING

1. **READING CHECK** What were the goals of progressivism?
2. **ANALYZE CAUSE AND EFFECT** How did journalists help spread progressivism?
3. **COMPARE AND CONTRAST** How do the teachings of Social Gospel conflict with the theory of Social Darwinism?

11.3.2 Analyze the great religious revivals and the leaders involved in them, including the First Great Awakening, the Second Great Awakening, the Civil War revivals, the Social Gospel Movement, the rise of Christian liberal theology in the nineteenth century, the impact of the Second Vatican Council, and the rise of Christian fundamentalism in current times.

1.2 **MAIN IDEA** Women played leading roles in hard-fought battles for the right to vote and for other reforms during the Progressive Era.

WOMEN FIGHT FOR RIGHTS

When the Progressive Era began, the campaign to allow women to vote was about a half century old. How much longer would women have to fight before they gained something as basic as the right to cast a ballot?

MIDWEST LEADERS

In the early 20th century, American society still strongly restricted the roles of women. Women could not vote or hold office in most states, and many companies barred women from working in certain professions. For decades, American women had been working in support of social reforms, even as they began to demand that their own rights be expanded to include all the rights and responsibilities of citizenship. Women were the foot soldiers of progressive reform.

One of the best known foot soldiers was Jane Addams. As you have read, she founded Hull House in Chicago, one of the most famous settlement houses in the nation. Hull House provided many resources and services to struggling immigrants. Addams also fought for such progressive causes as workers' rights, **women's suffrage**, or women's right to vote, and the regulation of tenements. She helped bring about the first juvenile law court, and she played a role in the founding of the **American Civil Liberties Union (ACLU)**, an organization that fights to this day for the constitutional rights of all citizens.

Hull House became a magnet for bright, ambitious women who were dedicated to social work and reform. One such women was **Florence Kelley**. While residing at the settlement house, she investigated sweatshops and tenement conditions and conducted a thorough survey of Chicago's 19th Ward, a political district in the city. Her reports on the appalling conditions she observed helped bring about an Illinois law that banned child labor, limited working hours for women, and established regulations for sweatshops. Kelley's reports earned her an appointment as the state's chief factory inspector. In 1899, Kelley moved to New York City to become the general secretary of the newly created **National Consumers League**, an organization dedicated to defending the rights of consumers and workers. For the next 30 years, she led the league's fight for a minimum wage law for women, protection of in-home workers from exploitation, and restrictions on child labor.

Another social reformer drawn to Hull House was **Julia Lathrop**, who arrived in 1890. Lathrop worked to improve the lives of children, the disabled, and the mentally ill. In 1893, after becoming the first female member of the Illinois Board of Charities, Lathrop set out to inspect all of the state's poorhouses and "poor farms." These facilities housed, at state expense, people who could not support themselves, which included the mentally ill, physically ill, disabled, and aged—all mixed together. The inspections led her to push for separate facilities for the mentally ill. In 1912, President Taft appointed Lathrop as the first head of the **Children's Bureau**, the first federal agency dedicated to improving the lives of children and families. Lathrop worked to address the issues of child labor, infant and maternal mortality, juvenile delinquency, and the treatment of the mentally ill.

WEST COAST REFORMERS

On the West Coast, in San Francisco, women were working to solve other kinds of problems. The Chinese Exclusion Act of 1882 banned the immigration of Chinese laborers. As a result, Chinese men who had emigrated before the ban were cut off from their wives and families. Secret criminal societies called *tongs* arose in San Francisco's Chinatown, as well as in Chinese neighborhoods in other cities, to bring Chinese women to the United States. The tongs

11.2.9 Understand the effect of political programs and activities of the Progressives (e.g., federal regulation of railroad transport, Children's Bureau, the Sixteenth Amendment, Theodore Roosevelt, Hiram Johnson); 11.3.1 Describe the contributions of various religious groups to American civic principles and social reform movements (e.g., civil and human rights, individual responsibility and the work ethic, antimonarchy and self-rule, worker protection, family-centered communities).

Jane Addams Hull-House Museum, Chicago

Jane Addams appears with children at Hull House, the settlement house she established, in this photo from the collection of the Jane Addams Hull-House Museum. By 1907, Hull House consisted of 13 buildings occupying an entire block in Chicago. The museum is housed in one of the two original Hull House buildings.

kidnapped women and girls from China, smuggled them into California, and sold them as slaves to men or to brothels, or houses of prostitution. **Margaret Culbertson**, superintendent of the Occidental Mission Home for Girls, a Chinatown settlement house, was fearless in her efforts to rescue these women and girls. Once safe at the mission house, they received shelter, food, clothing, education, and security.

When Culbertson became too ill to continue her rescues, her assistant, **Donaldina Mackenzie Cameron**, took over. In the nearly 4 decades that she served as superintendent, Cameron rescued more than 3,000 women and girls from slavery, daring to run across rooftops and break down doors to carry out her work. The tongs hated and feared her, but those she rescued and sheltered called her *Lo Mo*, or "Beloved Mother."

COMBINING FORCES

In 1890, two competing women's rights organizations merged to form the **National American Woman Suffrage Association (NAWSA)**. Elizabeth Cady Stanton and Susan B. Anthony, pioneers in the women's suffrage movement, served as the new organization's first presidents. When Anthony retired in 1900, the presidency went to **Carrie Chapman Catt**, who stated that the enfranchisement of women would be the crowning glory of democracy. **Enfranchisement** is the act of granting full citizenship, including the right to vote. The right to vote is also referred to as the **franchise**.

For several decades, the strategy of **suffragists**, or people seeking the franchise for women, had been to push for a national constitutional amendment guaranteeing women the right to vote. By 1910, however, the movement had stalled. Southern Democrats in Congress opposed women's suffrage for fear it would include the enfranchisement of African-American women. In addition, companies that manufactured liquor worried that women's suffrage would strengthen the movement to prohibit the sale of alcohol. Faced with those roadblocks, suffragists began focusing their efforts at the state level. The result was a string of victories in western

CRITICAL VIEWING This print from 1874 depicts the actions of reformers who wanted to end the sale and consumption of alcohol. Why might the reformers' actions have been considered controversial?

HI 1 Students show the connections, causal and otherwise, between particular historical events and larger social, economic, and political trends and developments; 11.10.7 Analyze the women's rights movement from the era of Elizabeth Stanton and Susan Anthony and the passage of the Nineteenth Amendment to the movement launched in the 1960s, including differing perspectives on the roles of women.

states as well as several eastern states. Some of the victories were only partial—that is, women were granted the right to vote only in certain elections—but others fully enfranchised women. In California, women gained full voting rights in 1911.

Another important figure in the suffrage movement was **Alice Paul**, who led its radical wing. She had fought for the vote in England and now wanted to apply aggressive tactics, such as marches and protests, in the United States. Other women joined her, including Harriot Stanton Blatch, who was the daughter of Elizabeth Cady Stanton.

For a few years, Paul and her allies worked on NAWSA's congressional committee. NAWSA stressed that female voting would result in purer and more honest politics. The organization also played down the argument that women should have equal political rights. Instead, it argued that suffrage would offset the votes of immigrants and racial minorities in large cities. Thus, suffragists would be protecting traditional values against "alien" assaults. Frustrated with NAWSA's cautious tactics, Paul left the organization in 1913. Along with **Lucy Burns**, the suffragist known for spending the most time in jail for the cause, she formed the Congressional Union for Woman Suffrage.

In 1916, the Congressional Union for Woman Suffrage reorganized itself as a single-issue political party and adopted a new name: the **National Woman's Party (NWP)**. Although the NAWSA and the NWP were fighting for the same cause, their strategies could not have been more different. While the NAWSA continued to rely on lobbying, petition gathering, and state-level campaigns, the NWP opted for direct action. Its members staged marches, picketed the White House, went on hunger strikes, and committed acts of civil disobedience. The effort to win the vote for women would take several more years and a war to bring about victory.

THE PROHIBITION MOVEMENT

Women also took the lead in the **temperance movement**, which encouraged people to temper, or moderate, their consumption of alcohol, or to abstain from alcohol altogether. Temperance reformers pointed out that although men did much of the drinking, alcohol-related problems often hit women and children hardest. Some men, they argued, spent money on alcohol that could be used to provide for the needs of their families, such as food, shelter, clothing, and health care. Excessive alcohol consumption, reformers believed, often caused men to become abusive, abandon or neglect their families, turn to crime, or fall into poverty and homelessness.

The Anti-Saloon League, founded in 1893, became one of the leading national organizations in the crusade against alcohol. Through propaganda and educational materials that often focused on women, children, and families, the league developed a strong base, especially among devout Protestant Christians. Promoting the idea of **prohibition**, the league pressured local and state governments to create laws restricting or prohibiting the production, sale, and consumption of alcohol. Oklahoma was the first state to adopt prohibition in 1907, and by 1914, eight other states had done the same. Militant prohibitionists, however, were discouraged by the state-by-state approach. The Anti-Saloon League set its sights on a bigger goal: a constitutional amendment to ban the sale of alcohol in the United States.

PRIMARY SOURCE

Six feet tall and wielding a hatchet, temperance leader **Carry Nation** was famous for destroying bars and saloons to impede the selling and drinking of alcoholic beverages. Before she started using a hatchet, she collected bricks and stones—which she called "smashers"—to use as her weapons. Here, she describes her first experience "smashing" a saloon in Kiowa, Kansas, in 1899.

I threw as hard and as fast as I could, smashing mirrors and bottles and glasses and it was astonishing how quickly it was done. [The] men seemed terrified, threw up their hands and backed up in the corner. My strength was that of a giant. I felt invincible. God was certainly standing by me.

—from *The Use and Need of the Life of Carry A. Nation,* by Carry Nation, 1909

HISTORICAL THINKING

1. **READING CHECK** What reforms did Florence Kelley help bring about?
2. **FORM AND SUPPORT OPINIONS** What is your opinion of the NAWSA's claim that granting women the right to vote would offset the votes of immigrants and racial minorities? Give reasons for your opinion.
3. **COMPARE AND CONTRAST** How did the strategies of the NAWSA and the NWP differ?
4. **IDENTIFY PROBLEMS AND SOLUTIONS** What social problems did leaders in the temperance movement work to solve?

FOR OR AGAINST WOMEN'S SUFFRAGE?

From its beginnings in the 1840s to the start of the Progressive Era in the 1890s, the women's suffrage movement grew dramatically. Nevertheless, many Americans remained firmly opposed to the idea of extending the franchise to women. For every argument offered by suffragists, the anti-suffragists had a counterargument.

On November 2, 1915, voters in Massachusetts and New York—meaning men—cast ballots on whether to amend their state constitutions to grant the vote to women. The pennant shown below was part of the New York publicity campaign. In both states, the outcome was *No*: by a narrow margin of 175,000 votes in New York, but by 2 to 1 in Massachusetts. In another referendum 2 years later, voters in New York finally granted the franchise to women, becoming the 16th state to do so. Massachusetts women did not obtain the right to vote until the 19th Amendment was ratified in 1920.

CRITICAL VIEWING In 1910, this cartoon showing a male protester being arrested by two female police officers appeared on a *Life* magazine cover. Do you think this cartoon is satirical, or making fun of the idea of men's rights, or is it presenting that idea as a legitimate issue? What message does the cartoon convey about women's right to vote?

11.10.7 Analyze the women's rights movement from the era of Elizabeth Stanton and Susan Anthony and the passage of the Nineteenth Amendment to the movement launched in the 1960s, including differing perspectives on the roles of women; HREP 2 Students identify bias and prejudice in historical interpretations.

DOCUMENT ONE

Primary Source: Leaflet
from "Twelve Reasons Why Women Should Vote," by the National American Woman Suffrage Association, 1918

NAWSA produced posters, booklets, leaflets, and other printed materials that presented arguments in favor of women's suffrage. Local suffrage groups often purchased large quantities of the reading materials for rallies and women's suffrage campaigns.

CONSTRUCTED RESPONSE
Which of the 12 reasons do you think would have had the strongest impact on readers, and why?

Twelve Reasons Why Women Should Vote

1. BECAUSE those who obey the laws should help to choose those who make the laws.
2. BECAUSE laws affect women as much as men.
3. BECAUSE laws which affect WOMEN are now passed without consulting them.
4. BECAUSE laws affecting CHILDREN should include the woman's point of view as well as the man's.
5. BECAUSE laws affecting the HOME are voted on in every session of the Legislature.
6. BECAUSE women have experience which would be helpful to legislation.
7. BECAUSE to deprive women of the vote is to lower their position in common estimation.
8. BECAUSE having the vote would increase the sense of responsibility among women toward questions of public importance.
9. BECAUSE public spirited mothers make public spirited sons.
10. BECAUSE millions of women in the United States have become wage workers and the conditions under which they work are controlled by law.
11. BECAUSE the objections against their having the vote are based on prejudice, not on reason.
12. BECAUSE to sum up all reasons in one—IT IS FOR THE COMMON GOOD OF ALL.

DOCUMENT TWO

Primary Source: Pamphlet
from "Vote NO on Woman Suffrage," by the National Association Opposed to Woman Suffrage, c. 1915

As the women's suffrage movement gained strength, opposition groups, such as the NAOWS, sprang up. They often directed their messages at women. The anti-suffrage arguments below appeared on the back of a pamphlet offering household tips for women.

CONSTRUCTED RESPONSE What do you think is meant by "petticoat rule" in the fifth reason, and why would women consider it undesirable?

Vote NO on Woman Suffrage

BECAUSE 90% of the women either do not want it, or do not care.

BECAUSE it means competition of women with men instead of co-operation.

BECAUSE 80% of the women eligible to vote are married and can only double or annul their husbands' votes.

BECAUSE it can be of no benefit commensurate with the additional expense involved.

BECAUSE in some States more voting women than voting men will place the Government under petticoat rule.

BECAUSE it is unwise to risk the good we already have for the evil which may occur.

Vote "No" button, c. 1910

SYNTHESIZE & WRITE

1. **REVIEW** Review what you have learned about the women's suffrage movement.
2. **RECALL** Summarize the main arguments for and against women's suffrage presented in the two documents.
3. **CONSTRUCT** Construct a topic sentence that answers this question: How do the arguments for and against women's suffrage reflect different views of women's role in society?
4. **WRITE** Using evidence from this chapter and the documents, write an explanatory paragraph that supports your topic sentence.

1.4 **MAIN IDEA** During the Progressive Era, reform-minded Americans worked to make city and state governments more democratic, more efficient, and less corrupt.

REFORMING GOVERNMENT

If you were running for political office, how would you convince people to vote for you? Offer them money? Promise them jobs? Across the United States, candidates were using such tactics to gain and keep political offices in the late 1800s and early 1900s.

REFORMING CITY GOVERNMENT

The earliest push for political reform during the Progressive Era occurred at the level of city government. The city mayors and councils struggled to deal with expanding populations divided by ethnicity, race, religion, and economic class. Council members often traded favors with one another and blocked legislation that hurt their districts, which made city government ineffective.

This situation gave rise to "boss politics." You have read about Boss Tweed and his political machine, Tammany Hall, but Tweed was not an isolated example. Throughout many big cities, powerful bosses commanded hierarchical political party organizations that operated at the district, the neighborhood, and even the block level. These corrupt political machines provided services, jobs, and favors in exchange for votes.

Reformers worked to take city government out of the hands of corrupt officials. After a hurricane devastated Galveston, Texas, in 1900, the Texas legislature suspended Galveston's city council and established a five-member commission to temporarily oversee the city. This new form of **commission government**, dubbed the "Galveston plan," worked so well that it was made permanent. It quickly spread to Dallas, Fort Worth, and other Texas cities.

CRITICAL VIEWING Two boys explore the wreckage of St. Patrick's Church in Galveston, Texas, after a devastating hurricane in 1900. The city council handled the disaster so poorly that a new form of government was instituted, and a commission of experts took charge of the various city departments. What details in the photograph indicate the scale of the hurricane damage?

11.2.4 Analyze the effect of urban political machines and responses to them by immigrants and middle-class reformers; 11.2.9 Understand the effect of political programs and activities of the Progressives (e.g., federal regulation of railroad transport, Children's Bureau, Sixteenth Amendment, Theodore Roosevelt, Hiram Johnson).

In 1907, Des Moines, Iowa, became the first city outside Texas to adopt commission government, but it staged a vote so citizens could choose their own city commissioners. Des Moines became a model for cities around the United States that were seeking to overhaul their governments.

Staunton, Virginia, became another model. In 1908, Staunton's city council hired a professional manager to take charge of the city's struggling public services. The council-manager approach proved to be an effective way of taking politics out of city administration. Dayton, Ohio, adopted and popularized this form of government in 1913 following a devastating flood.

REFORMING STATE GOVERNMENT

The reform movement soon spread from the city level to the state level. Progressives, including future presidents Theodore Roosevelt and **Woodrow Wilson**, worked to make state government less corrupt, more efficient, and more democratic. Progressives instituted such structural changes as the **direct primary**, in which party candidates are nominated by a direct vote, and the direct election of U.S. senators.

At the time, party political bosses often controlled who was nominated to run for political offices. Direct primary elections gave this control to voters. In accordance with the U.S. Constitution, senators had always been elected by state legislatures, which often were strongly influenced by rich and powerful political supporters. In 1899, Nevada changed its law to allow voters to elect U.S. senators directly. Soon, other states did the same. Then, in 1913, progressive efforts helped pass and ratify the **17th Amendment**, which mandated that all U.S. senators be elected by popular vote.

Progressives also promoted such democratic reforms as the **initiative** and the referendum. An initiative enables citizens to bypass the legislature and propose new laws to be voted on. In a referendum, as you have learned, a proposal is submitted to voters directly for approval or rejection. During the Progressive Era, nearly 20 states adopted statewide processes for initiatives and referendums.

After he was elected New York's governor in 1898, Theodore Roosevelt worked with the state legislature to enact laws regulating tenements, corporations, and the civil service, and he fought against corruption and political machines. In 1906, New York gained another reform-minded governor with the election of Charles Evans Hughes. Hughes helped regulate public utilities, such as gas and water, and expanded the state's involvement in policing. He also pushed through laws that made political campaigns more open, honest, and democratic.

During his two-year tenure as governor of New Jersey beginning in 1911, Woodrow Wilson established a commission to oversee the state's public utilities and helped pass a workers' compensation law to help employees who were injured on the job. On the other side of the country, California governor **Hiram Johnson** led the charge for constitutional state amendments on the initiative, referendum, and **recall**, or the right of citizens to remove an elected official by direct vote.

But the leading symbol of state reform was **Robert M. La Follette**, a Republican who was elected governor of Wisconsin in 1900. During his two terms, he established direct primary elections, regulated Wisconsin's railroads, and levied higher taxes on corporations. He forged a close relationship between the state government and the University of Wisconsin faculty, who advised him on policy. This reliance on academic experts as government advisors was called the "Wisconsin Idea."

PRIMARY SOURCE

In his first inaugural address as governor of California, Hiram Johnson warned against corrupt business leaders and politicians who had only their own power and prosperity in mind.

I prefer, as less dangerous to society, the political thug of the waterfront to the smugly respectable individual in broadcloth of pretended respectability who from ambush employs and uses that thug for his selfish political gain.

—from Governor Hiram Johnson's first inaugural address, 1911

How can a corrupt politician be more dangerous than someone who uses physical violence to accomplish goals?

HISTORICAL THINKING

1. **READING CHECK** How did progressives give voters a larger voice in state government?
2. **MAKE CONNECTIONS** How did reforms instituted in city governments help shape reforms adopted in state governments?
3. **DRAW CONCLUSIONS** Why do you think Governor La Follette sought the advice of the faculty at the University of Wisconsin?

2.1 **MAIN IDEA** As the first progressive president, Theodore Roosevelt worked to promote fairer treatment of workers, regulate business, and protect natural resources.

Reform Under Roosevelt

Theodore Roosevelt had a strong commitment to reform, which fit perfectly with the mood of Americans at the start of the 20th century. He led the way in expanding the power of the federal government in order to carry out the reforms he thought were necessary.

ROOSEVELT BECOMES PRESIDENT

In November 1900, voters elected President William McKinley to a second term. McKinley's presidency was cut short, however. On September 6, 1901, a young Michigan-born anarchist, a person who opposes all government, shot the president at a world's fair in Buffalo, New York. The president died eight days later. His vice president, Theodore Roosevelt, took over as president.

At 42, Roosevelt was the youngest person ever to hold the office of president. Roosevelt was brash and energetic. He loved the outdoors, and he led an active lifestyle that included horseback riding, swimming, boxing, and hunting.

Roosevelt came to office at a time when there was strong momentum for social, economic, and political change in the United States. He became the first progressive president and took the lead in bringing about many reforms.

Since entering politics around 1880, Roosevelt had been either elected or appointed to a variety of government positions, including member of the New York State Assembly, assistant secretary of the U.S. Navy, and governor of the state of New York. He had earned a reputation for political independence and for commitment to eradicating, or getting rid of, political corruption.

After the deaths of his wife and his mother on a single day in 1884, Roosevelt had retreated to a cattle ranch he owned in the Dakota Territory and spent much of the next two years there. He became increasingly dedicated to **conservation**, or the management and protection of natural resources, as he saw how human activities were damaging the land and reducing the populations of such wildlife as bison, bighorn sheep, and elk.

The National Museum of American History, Washington, D.C.

Rose Michtom, the wife of a candy store owner, created the first Teddy bear in Brooklyn, New York, in 1902, after she and her husband saw a political cartoon involving President Theodore "Teddy" Roosevelt on a bear hunt. The couple put the bear on display in their store window, and many passers-by wanted to buy it. Rose and her husband, Morris, wrote to Roosevelt asking permission to use the name *Teddy* for the bear. On receiving the president's approval, Morris formed a toy company and began manufacturing Teddy bears.

An original Teddy bear

THE SQUARE DEAL

Nine months after taking office, President Theodore Roosevelt faced one of the first major challenges of his presidency. On May 12, 1902, the 140,000 members of the United Mine Workers union, an organization formed to protect the interests of workers, walked off their jobs in the coal fields of eastern Pennsylvania after the mine operators refused to meet with union representatives. The miners were seeking higher pay, shorter hours, and recognition of their union. The mine operators, who had lost a strike two years earlier, wanted to break the strike—and the union.

The drop in production caused coal prices to soar. As the walkout stretched into autumn, the threat of winter coal shortages loomed. Republicans worried that if voters' homes were cold, people might vote against the Republican Party in the congressional elections in November. Roosevelt, in a letter to Massachusetts's governor Winthrop Murray Crane, expressed concern that the shortages could cause "untold misery . . . with the certainty of riots which might develop into social war."

After much agonizing, Roosevelt decided to act. But he did not call in troops to break up the strike, as President Grover Cleveland had done in the Pullman Strike eight years earlier. Instead, he brought the two sides together and worked with them to negotiate a reasonable settlement. Roosevelt called his approach the **Square Deal** because he wanted to ensure fairness and balance to both sides. This approach in disputes between big business and labor would be a hallmark of Roosevelt's presidency.

Roosevelt believed that as president, he should take action to promote the general welfare of the people and to protect the country's natural resources. He saw the presidential office as a "bully pulpit," or a position of high authority and prestige from which he could promote his ideas and push his social and economic agenda more aggressively than presidents who came before him. For this reason, many historians consider Theodore Roosevelt the first modern president.

BUSTING THE TRUSTS

Corporations were a major source of concern for Roosevelt. Some of them were growing large and extremely powerful through **mergers**, in which two or more companies combine as one. One example was the 1901 merger of the Carnegie Steel Company with steel companies owned by J.P. Morgan, which created the mammoth United States Steel Corporation. Valued at more than $1.4 billion, it was the largest corporation in U.S. history. It had 168,000 employees, and it controlled 60 percent of the steel industry's production. By eliminating other employment opportunities, United States Steel used its size to drive down workers' wages, and so other steel companies were able to do the same.

In a cartoon entitled "The Lion Tamer," which appeared on the cover of *Harper's Weekly* in 1904, President Roosevelt is portrayed as taming the power of trusts in various industries.

11.2.1 Know the effects of industrialization on living and working conditions, including the portrayal of working conditions and food safety in Upton Sinclair's *The Jungle*; 11.2.5 Discuss corporate mergers that produced trusts and cartels and the economic and political policies of industrial leaders.

In 1903, President Theodore Roosevelt (left) went on a three-night camping trip with conservationist John Muir in the Yosemite region in California. Here the two men stand together atop Glacier Point, with Yosemite Falls in the distance behind and below them.

Roosevelt saw industrial mergers as unavoidable, but he thought that the federal government should play an active role in regulating business instead of sitting back and allowing corporations to do as they pleased. He believed in encouraging corporations to behave in a socially responsible way and in monitoring and controlling those that did not. Roosevelt's idea of a good company was one that paid a living wage to its employees, provided safe working conditions, did not overcharge its customers, and did not contribute to political corruption to gain an advantage.

In 1890, Congress had passed the **Sherman Antitrust Act**, which gave the federal government the power to prosecute and break up corporations and trusts that monopolized, or threatened to monopolize, specific markets and industries. Unlike previous presidents, Roosevelt used the act aggressively. His first target was the powerful Northern Securities Company, which controlled three railroads. In 1904, the Supreme Court ruled that the company had violated the Sherman Antitrust Act and ordered it to be dismantled. Americans saw Roosevelt as a **trustbuster**, someone who would fight to curb the power of big business by vigorously enforcing antitrust legislation.

REGULATING BUSINESS

Progressives had a strong belief in the power of government to do good and to promote a better society. They rejected laissez-faire economics, feeling the government's hands-off approach had allowed corporations to abuse their power at the expense of workers, consumers, and smaller businesses. Instead, progressives pushed the government to regulate business more closely. This work fell to agencies such as the **Federal Trade Commission (FTC)** and the **Interstate Commerce Commission (ICC)**, which employed experts on the industries they supervised.

The ICC was created in 1887 through the Interstate Commerce Act, which was intended to control corruption in the railroad industry. It required the railroad companies to offer reasonable and fair rates for transporting goods, and it prohibited them from offering preferred rates to certain customers. The act had not been strongly enforced, however, and the railroads and corporations still engaged in unfair practices. In 1903, Roosevelt took action. He signed the Elkins Act, which levied heavy fines on railroads that offered rebates, or partial returns on money paid, and on the companies that received them. Three years later, he signed the Hepburn Act, which gave the ICC the power to establish maximum transportation rates and review the accounts and records of the railroads.

Other industries also came under the watchful eyes of the Roosevelt administration. In late 1905, Congress began writing a bill intended to ensure the purity and safety of foods and drugs. Roosevelt strongly supported the bill, but it faced steep business opposition.

Then, in the winter of 1906, Upton Sinclair's muckraking novel *The Jungle* was published. As you have read, the book described the unsanitary practices of the meatpacking industry. Roosevelt was among the thousands of Americans who read the book and were shocked and disgusted by its revelations. He launched an investigation of the industry and supported legislation that established a federal program for meat inspection. Meanwhile, Sinclair's novel produced a public outcry that spurred the House to pass what would become the **Pure Food and Drug Act**, which Roosevelt signed into law in June of 1906.

RACE RELATIONS

While breaking up corporations and establishing food safety laws, Roosevelt also wanted to be seen as a friend to African Americans. In October 1901, he invited Booker T. Washington, who had built a political machine among black Republicans in the South, to dine with his family at the White House. Southerners were infuriated, and a Tennessee newspaper editor called the occasion "the most damnable outrage that has ever been perpetrated by any citizen of the United States." Roosevelt felt the backlash of his decision and never again invited another African American to dine at the White House. However, he appointed African Americans to positions in post offices and customs houses. The appointments could only help him win votes from black delegates in the upcoming election of 1904.

Beyond symbolic actions, however, Roosevelt did not challenge the racism that existed throughout the nation. Discrimination, segregation, poverty, and violence continued to be a scourge on the lives of African Americans.

THE CONSERVATION PRESIDENT

As a boy, Theodore Roosevelt had been frail and sickly, but he grew into a strong man who loved outdoor activities. As you have read, the two years he spent on a cattle ranch in the Dakota Territory helped transform him into a committed conservationist. He saw how human activities were ruining the land and destroying wildlife, and he felt an urgent need to protect the country's natural resources.

Conservation became one of the defining aspects of Roosevelt's presidency. He used his power as president to create 4 national game preserves, or areas set aside to protect wild animals, 51 refuges for wild birds, and 150 national forests. He also helped establish Crater Lake and Mesa Verde national parks. Through the Antiquities Act, he protected the Grand Canyon and many other areas of scenic or historical interest from destruction and development. He worked closely with Gifford Pinchot (PIN-show), head of the newly created National Forest Service, to create a policy that balanced the protection of natural resources with their industrial use. Because of his efforts, Roosevelt is remembered as the Conservation President.

HISTORICAL THINKING

1. **READING CHECK** Why did many Americans think of Theodore Roosevelt as a trustbuster?
2. **MAKE INFERENCES** What political reason might Roosevelt have had for inviting Booker T. Washington to the White House?
3. **ANALYZE ENVIRONMENTAL CONCEPTS** What actions did Roosevelt take to improve the viability of natural systems?

11.2.1 Know the effects of industrialization on living and working conditions, including the portrayal of working conditions and food safety in Upton Sinclair's *The Jungle*.

11.11.5 Trace the impact of, need for, and controversies associated with environmental conservation, expansion of the national park system, and the development of environmental protection laws, with particular attention to the interaction between environmental protection advocates and property rights advocates.

2.2 THROUGH THE LENS AMERICAN PLACES

THE GRAND CANYON NORTHWESTERN ARIZONA

One of the seven natural wonders of the world, the Grand Canyon is the most spectacular gorge on Earth. Over millions of years, the Colorado River carved the canyon, which displays through its layers of rock the most extensive record of geologic history on Earth. In fact, rocks at the bottom of the canyon date back 2.5 billion years. Still, the aesthetic and geologic value of the Grand Canyon have not been enough to ensure its protection. When mining and tourism interests posed a threat, President Theodore Roosevelt stepped in to safeguard the canyon by making it a national monument in 1908. Roosevelt expressed the hope that no human activity would "mar the wonderful grandeur, the sublimity, the great loneliness and beauty of the canyon." Congress established Grand Canyon National Park in 1919, but developers have not stopped devising plans to "mar" the canyon. Today, environmentalists affiliated with National Geographic and other organizations continue to battle against commercial groups who have proposed building a tram near the park's eastern edge to shuttle visitors to the canyon's bottom.

CRITICAL VIEWING Although mostly red, as revealed in this photo by National Geographic photographer Pete McBride, the Grand Canyon's rock layers also display hues of green, pink, gray, brown, and violet. What do you think motivates activists like McBride to protect the Grand Canyon from development?

2.3 **MAIN IDEA** Progressive reforms continued during the presidencies of William Taft and Woodrow Wilson.

PROGRESSIVISM UNDER TAFT AND WILSON

The description "a tough act to follow" could certainly be applied to Theodore Roosevelt. His popularity helped the Republicans retain the presidency in 1908, but his successor looked weak in comparison.

A MIXED COURSE

Theodore Roosevelt had stepped into the presidency early in McKinley's second term, so by 1908, he felt he had already served two terms in office. Citing George Washington's decision to limit his presidency to two terms, Roosevelt declined to run again. Instead he supported his secretary of war, **William Howard Taft**, as the next Republican candidate. Taft handily won the presidency against William Jennings Bryan, a Democrat who had run and been defeated twice before.

Roosevelt chose Taft as his successor because he believed Taft would carry on his progressive agenda. He did not realize that Taft disagreed with his expansive view of presidential power. Taft believed that the president should act within the strict constitutional boundaries of his office. Although he aggressively enforced antitrust legislation, Taft lacked the will to urge progressive policies on the more conservative members of the Republican Party. Roosevelt's progressive agenda continued under Taft, but it faced setbacks.

Taft started off on the wrong foot after he failed to name any progressives to his cabinet. Then he offended progressives again when he sided against Gifford Pinchot, the Forestry Service chief and Roosevelt's good friend, in a dispute over the commercial use of public lands in Alaska. Pinchot had barred the lands from development, but Richard A. Ballinger, Taft's secretary of the interior, opened the lands to coal-mining companies. Pinchot accused Ballinger of acting as a member of a **syndicate**, or group of criminals, trying to sell valuable coal lands for profit. Taft investigated the charges and publicly agreed with Ballinger. He fired Pinchot for insubordination, or defiance of authority. This incident led progressives to doubt Taft's commitment to conservation. Some even sent letters to Roosevelt, at the time on safari in Africa, saying as much.

As the president and the progressives argued, Americans struggled with major social issues. In 1910, some 200,000 youngsters below the age of 12 labored in mills and factories. Attempts to limit child labor in southern textile mills brought few results. In 1912, after a six-year struggle, progressive reformers succeeded in establishing the Children's Bureau. Its mission was to investigate and report on the conditions of children working in factories and living in orphanages. Unfortunately, Congress failed to pass any legislation that would have allowed reformers to take action against businesses that overworked child laborers. One such measure was a bill that would have prohibited interstate shipment of products made using child labor.

Another pressing social issue was immigration, which had nearly tripled from 1910 to 1914. Many of the immigrants were from southern and eastern Europe, and some Americans felt that their presence threatened traditional American values. The growing Americanization movement strongly encouraged immigrants to adopt American culture, including speaking and writing English instead of their native languages. While many immigrants quickly assimilated, others refused to give up their own languages and customs. By 1913, both houses of Congress had passed a bill to impose a literacy test on immigrants. President Taft, however, vetoed the bill as a largely anti-immigration measure.

11.2.3 Trace the effect of the Americanization movement; 11.2.9 Understand the effect of political programs and activities of the Progressives (e.g., federal regulation of railroad transport, Children's Bureau, the Sixteenth Amendment, Theodore Roosevelt, Hiram Johnson).

LABOR AND THE WORKPLACE

The progressive movement had made huge strides during Roosevelt's presidency, but it fell short in brokering deals between labor unions and corporations. During Taft's presidency, unions made progress in organizing workers and improving working conditions for their members. That progress was partly driven by a public outcry over workplace tragedies.

On March 25, 1911, a fire broke out near closing time on the top floors of the Triangle Waist Company in New York City. The company employed about 500 people, mostly young immigrant women, to produce fashionable blouses. The workers ran to the stairway doors, but they were locked. Many trapped, terrified women chose to jump out of the 10-story building, hoping to survive the fall. Tragically, 146 people died in the **Triangle Waist Company factory fire**, and an outraged American public cried out for factory reform.

PRIMARY SOURCE

As the Triangle Waist Company factory went up in flames, a reporter, who happened to be walking nearby, called his pressroom and narrated events as they occurred. Here is part of his story.

Two windows away two girls were climbing onto the sill; they were fighting each other and crowding for air. Behind them I saw many screaming heads. They fell almost together, but I heard two distinct thuds.

Suddenly the flame broke out from the windows below them and curled up into their faces.

—from an account of the fire by William Shepherd, United Press reporter, 1911

The intense heat of the factory fire at the Triangle Waist Company weakened the metal of the fire escape ladder. Some workers were able to descend to a lower floor before the ladder collapsed.

11.2.1 Know the effects of industrialization on living and working conditions, including the portrayal of working conditions and food safety in Upton Sinclair's *The Jungle*.

On March 4, 1913, Woodrow Wilson was inaugurated as the nation's 28th president. In this photograph taken at the White House just before the inauguration, Wilson appears on the left and his predecessor, President William H. Taft, is on the right.

Another outcry arose after soldiers moved in to clear a tent city in Ludlow, Colorado. For about seven months, mine workers had been striking against the Colorado Fuel and Iron Company for higher pay and better treatment in company camps. The company owner, John D. Rockefeller, had the governor call in the National Guard to end the strike, which resulted in clashes between soldiers and miners. On April 20, 1914, troops shot into the workers' camps and set fire to tents. As many as 20 people, including women and children, were shot or died in the fire.

Labor unions such as the American Federation of Labor (AFL) and the International Workers of the World (IWW) had existed prior to the turn of the 20th century, but their membership swelled between 1900 and 1914. The IWW grew, in part, because it aimed to unite workers of every industry, including unskilled and African-American workers. The IWW played a major role in a strike against textile mills in Massachusetts. Workers walked out of the mills in January 1912 after company owners announced pay reductions. Strikers sang of "bread and roses," symbolizing both a living wage and hope for the future. With production at a standstill, company owners were eager to negotiate. By March 1, 1912, with the IWW's help, the workers won a raise in pay.

As labor unions made important gains for workers, company owners looked at ways to make their businesses more efficient. A mechanical engineer named **Frederick Winslow Taylor** developed **scientific management**, a method of running factories and other workplaces efficiently. Taylor studied individual tasks and determined the best way to complete them in the shortest amount of time. Taylor's findings resulted in sweeping changes in many industries. Factory managers expected workers to perform one specific activity for hours at a time, which made many workers feel like little more than machines. As workers in other countries attained benefits such as **social security**, a program in which the government provides money to the elderly, disabled, and unemployed, Americans continued their fight for improved working conditions and higher pay.

HI 4 Students understand the meaning, implication, and impact of historical events and recognize that events could have taken other directions.

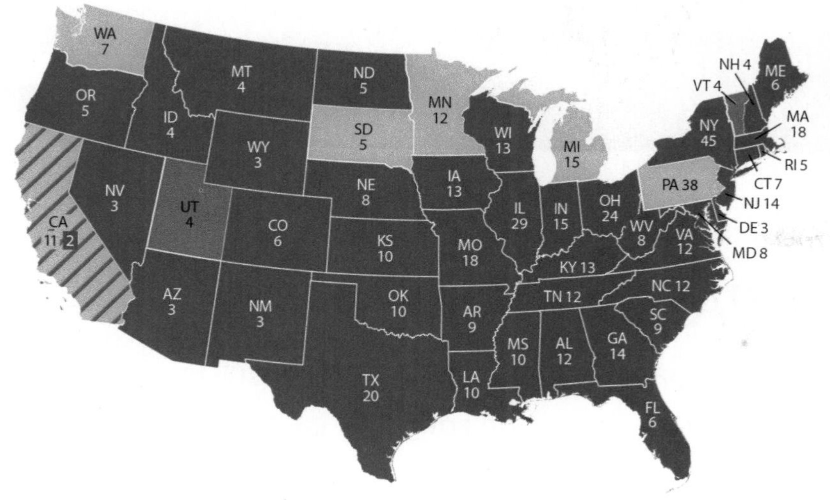

The 1912 Election

Woodrow Wilson, Democrat

Electoral Vote: 435 votes, 81.9%

Popular Vote: 6,294,327 votes, 41.8%

Theodore Roosevelt, Progressive

Electoral Vote: 88 votes, 16.6%

Popular Vote: 4,120,207 votes, 27.4%

William H. Taft, Republican

Electoral Vote: 8 votes, 1.5%

Popular Vote: 3,486,343 votes, 23.2%

Eugene Debs, Socialist

Popular Vote: 900,370 votes, 6.0%

A PROGRESSIVE DEMOCRAT

As Taft neared the end of his first term in office, many Americans viewed him as a weak president. Political divisions in the country became apparent during the 1912 election. Theodore Roosevelt, apparently forgetting his pledge not to seek another presidential term, started his own party, the Progressive Party, to run against Republican Taft. The Democrats nominated Woodrow Wilson, then the governor of New Jersey.

Another candidate, Eugene Debs, ran as the Socialist candidate. With the Republican vote split, Woodrow Wilson won the election by a landslide. Taft won only 8 electoral votes to Wilson's 435.

President Wilson set to work immediately on his pet project: lowering tariffs, or taxes imposed on imported goods. This issue was important to progressives because tariffs added to the price of imported household items. Cutting tariffs would cut prices for consumers. Wilson fought hard to persuade Congress to pass the Revenue Act of 1913 to reduce tariffs. However, there was a glaring problem: how to make up for the income lost by reducing tariffs.

To remedy this shortfall, Congress added another provision to the bill: an **income tax**, or money paid to the government based on how much a person earns. Earlier in the year, the states had ratified, or approved, the **16th Amendment**, which granted Congress the power to collect income taxes nationwide. Wilson's success with the Revenue Act helped build his image as an effective leader.

The Wilson administration then turned its attention to banking and trustbusting, or breaking up monopolies. The country needed a central bank to control the money supply and make sure it was adequate to meet the demands of the growing economy. Wilson's solution was to form the **Federal Reserve System**, a system of 12 banks located around the country and overseen by board members appointed by the president. The Federal Reserve System functioned as the nation's central bank.

Wilson also urged Congress to strengthen the nation's antitrust laws. As you have read, the Sherman Antitrust Act, passed in 1890, gave the government the right to break up monopolies and illegal trusts. However, it did not forbid businesses from engaging in some questionable practices, such as allowing one person to direct two or more "competing" companies. The **Clayton Antitrust Act**, passed in 1914, closed many of the loopholes, or ways around the law, not specifically prohibited by the Sherman Antitrust Act.

While Wilson made significant contributions to the progressive movement, he opposed African-American causes. In addition, like Taft, he did not support women's suffrage, at least initially. Of the three progressive presidents, only Roosevelt supported women's right to vote.

HISTORICAL THINKING

1. **READING CHECK** How did Taft and Wilson further the progressive agenda?
2. **INTERPRET MAPS** If Roosevelt and Taft had not split the Republican vote, is it likely that the Republican candidate would have won the election? Use electoral and popular vote data from the map to explain your answer.
3. **ANALYZE CAUSE AND EFFECT** How did the Revenue Act of 1913 affect American consumers?
4. **MAKE INFERENCES** Why did many Americans view Taft as a weak president?

11.6.1 Describe the monetary issues of the late nineteenth and early twentieth centuries that gave rise to the establishment of the Federal Reserve and the weaknesses in key sectors of the economy in the late 1920s

3.1 **MAIN IDEA** In the late 1800s, the United States expanded its territory and embarked on a new course in foreign policy.

AMERICAN EXPANSIONISM

For more than a hundred years, the United States grew in size until it stretched from coast to coast. Then, in the late 1800s, the nation sought to gain a foothold in distant lands.

THE ROOTS OF IMPERIALISM

As Americans struggled with social issues at home, the United States began to take an interest in expanding its influence overseas. For most of its short history, the nation had kept a low profile in world affairs. While European powers pursued **imperialism**, a policy of exerting economic, political, or military control over weaker nations, Americans had followed the course of **isolationism**, avoiding entanglements in foreign countries. By the 1880s, however, the United States had begun to look beyond its borders.

Trade played a big role in this new outlook. American business was booming, and one of the results was a surplus of American-made goods. Business leaders wanted to increase opportunities to sell these goods overseas. Their desire to do so led many of them to endorse **expansionism**, a policy similar to imperialism. Expansionism focuses on increasing a country's territory. Such a policy would open up new markets for American products and provide access to more raw materials.

American leaders had watched closely as European powers carved up territories in Africa and Asia, adding colonies and **protectorates**, or countries that are partly controlled by a stronger country. Americans worried about being left behind. One expansionist leader, Captain **Alfred T. Mahan** of the U.S. Navy, proposed an international network of naval bases, a powerful battleship fleet, and an aggressive foreign policy that would make the United States a competitive world power.

More than a hint of racism ran through the aims of the imperialists and expansionists. They believed in the superiority of white, English-speaking people and thought the rest of the world should bend to their will.

PRIMARY SOURCE

After losing her throne in 1893, Queen Liliuokalani of Hawaii continued to demand that the United States give her country back to her. Here she presents her case to the U.S. government.

Therefore, supplementing my protest of June 17, 1897, I call upon the President and the National Legislature and the People of the United States to do justice in this matter and to restore to me this property, the enjoyment of which is being withheld from me by your government under what must be a misapprehension [misunderstanding] of my right and title.

—from Queen Liliuokalani's letter of protest addressed to the House of Representatives, 1898

EYES ON ALASKA AND HAWAII

Americans had already taken the first steps toward expansion years earlier. In 1867, the United States paid $7.2 million to purchase Russia's territory in Alaska. Most Americans believed the land was useless, but the discovery of gold there in the 1880s and 1890s lured prospectors to the territory, and the population began to grow. At the same time, the Alaskan salmon fishing industry began to thrive. When Alaskans discovered copper in 1898, Americans started to recognize the great deal they had made with the Russians.

The Hawaiian Islands, an **archipelago**, or island chain, in the midst of the Pacific Ocean, attracted American interest even earlier than Alaska did. American missionaries began preaching in the islands in the early 1800s, and by the 1850s,

11.1.4 Examine the effects of the Civil War and Reconstruction and of the industrial revolution, including demographic shifts and the emergence in the late nineteenth century of the United States as a world power; 11.2.6 Trace the economic development of the United States and its emergence as a major industrial power, including its gains from trade and the advantages of its physical geography.

Kennecott Mines National Historic Landmark, shown here, preserves the main buildings and land of Kennecott, Alaska, a historic mining town. In 1900, copper was discovered near this site. Its mining and processing gave rise to a multinational company, the Kennecott Copper Corporation. The Kennecott mines closed in 1938, and the site fell into disrepair.

Americans were establishing businesses there, primarily growing and exporting sugarcane and pineapples. As early as the 1870s, the United States had recognized the strategic value of a naval base in Hawaii for protecting the Pacific Coast in wartime.

As more Americans came to the islands, their growing influence on the local economy and government soon sparked conflict with the Hawaiian monarchy. When **Queen Liliuokalani** came to power in 1891, she dismissed the legislature, which she felt was too sympathetic to Americans, and she presented a constitution that stripped white settlers of the powers they had secured for themselves. Most native Hawaiians agreed with the new constitution. But by this time, there were enough Americans and pro-American Hawaiians—including 150 U.S. Marines—living on the islands to stage a revolt against the queen. They overthrew the queen, established their own government, and requested that the United States **annex**, or take possession of, the islands.

President Benjamin Harrison agreed to sign a treaty with the pro-American, and mostly white, rebels to annex the islands, effective on February 14, 1893. But in the meantime, he lost the 1892 election to Grover Cleveland, who did not approve of the rebels' actions. Cleveland put the treaty on hold.

The fate of the islands remained unsettled until 1898, when the United States annexed Hawaii. By then, the islands were viewed as an essential naval asset in the Spanish-American War. In the "Organic Act" of 1900, Congress established a government for Hawaii, and the islands became an official U.S. territory. Meanwhile, the United States had set its sights on securing trading deals in Asia.

HISTORICAL THINKING

1. **READING CHECK** What were some reasons that the United States began an expansionist course in foreign policy in the late 1800s?
2. **EVALUATE** How did the acquisitions of Alaska and Hawaii benefit the United States?
3. **COMPARE AND CONTRAST** How are imperialism and expansionism alike and different?

11.4 Students trace the rise of the United States to its role as a world power in the twentieth century; 11.4.2 Describe the Spanish-American War and U.S. expansion in the South Pacific.

3.2 **MAIN IDEA** After establishing trade with Japan, the United States tried to gain a foothold in China in the late 1800s.

EXTENDING INFLUENCE IN ASIA

Near the end of the 19th century, Japan and several of the most powerful European nations had secured exclusive trading deals in China. The United States wanted to trade in China as well. How did the Americans open the door to trade in China? They simply made a proposal.

OPENING THE DOOR TO CHINA

The United States successfully established a diplomatic and trading presence in Asia after Naval Commodore Matthew C. Perry negotiated the Treaty of Kanagawa with Japan in 1854. For centuries, Japan had a policy of isolation and limited trade with other countries. In 1853, Perry was sent to negotiate diplomatic relations and trade between Japan and the United States. As a result of the treaty the two countries signed, Japan opened its ports to American ships for the first time in more than 200 years. As the 19th century came to a close, the United States had begun to turn its attention to Japan's neighbor: China.

At that time, Great Britain had the strongest presence of any foreign power in China. But other countries, such as France, Germany, Italy, Russia, and Japan, had also carved out **spheres of influence**, or claims of exclusive economic and trading authority, in parts of the country. Within each sphere of influence, the controlling nation made deals with local banks and businesses that allowed it exclusive economic benefits within the community. The United States wanted a part of this economic action.

In 1900, U.S. Secretary of State **John Hay** proposed the **Open Door Policy** to all of the countries with spheres of influence in China. Hay suggested that all Chinese ports accept ships from every nation, not just those with which China had brokered deals. The plan honored the trading arrangements China had already made, but it extended those same provisions to other nations as well, giving the United States a foothold in China. The policy also calmed Chinese fears that the competition between the foreign powers would change the spheres of influence into colonies and tear China apart. While the nations affected by this policy may not have agreed with the American proposal, they did not openly oppose it either.

Meanwhile, many Chinese were fed up with foreign interference in their country. Their discontent was about to erupt into open rebellion.

THE BOXER REBELLION

A secret society in China called the Righteous and Harmonious Fists had long opposed the presence of so many Westerners and Japanese in the country. Members of the society particularly resented the influence of Christian missionaries, who questioned the teachings of traditional religions. Bands of rebels started wandering the countryside outside Beijing, attacking foreigners, mostly Christian missionaries. The rebels were dubbed "the Boxers" because they exercised by sparring in a boxing ring. The Boxers also attacked Chinese leaders whom they believed were responsible for the preferential treatment that foreigners received. The attacks were called the **Boxer Rebellion**.

In 1898, forces within the Chinese government also began calling for an end to foreign meddling. The Boxers then changed the group's name to the Righteous and Harmonious Militia, and the government enlisted the militia and encouraged its violent actions.

The Boxers began burning Christian churches and buildings that housed foreign businesses. By the spring of 1900, the Boxers were staging attacks in the capital city of Beijing. An international relief force arrived in the city in June to stop the violence. China's empress dowager Cixi—the emperor's adoptive

11.2.6 Trace the economic development of the United States and its emergence as a major industrial power, including its gains from trade and the advantages of its physical geography; 11.4.1 List the purpose and the effects of the Open Door policy.

CIXI, EMPRESS DOWAGER OF CHINA

Yehenara, a middle-class Chinese girl, started her political career by giving birth to a son in 1856. A mistress of the Chinese emperor, she became known as Cixi, meaning "kind and virtuous." Her son was the emperor's only male heir. When the emperor died, the six-year-old boy took the throne. Cixi became one of the regents, or officials who govern in place of a child monarch.

Cixi gave up the regency when her son became 17 years old. But he died two years later, and her three-year-old nephew, whom Cixi had adopted, ascended to the throne. Cixi again became a regent.

She ruled China until 1889, when she retired to a palace she had built near Beijing. However, Chinese officials returned her to power in 1898 after the country suffered a major defeat in a war with Russia and Japan. She fled Beijing during the Boxer Rebellion but returned in 1902 and continued to rule until her death in 1908.

A bright and ambitious woman, Cixi ruled China for almost half a century. She ranks as one of the most powerful women in Chinese history.

mother and the person who actually ruled China—sent troops to fight the relief force and declared war on the United States, the United Kingdom, France, Germany, Italy, Russia, Japan, and Austria-Hungary.

Another international force of 20,000 soldiers captured Beijing in August 1900. The empress dowager and her court escaped the city, and she had little to do with the negotiations that followed. In September 1901, China signed the treaty that officially ended the Boxer Rebellion. The treaty forced China to pay **reparations**, or forced compensation, to the foreign powers for damages and lost lives. Payment of these reparations had a disastrous effect on the Chinese economy, fueling a resentment that resurfaced later in the 20th century.

HISTORICAL THINKING

1. **READING CHECK** How did the United States gain a foothold in China in the late 1800s?
2. **ANALYZE CAUSE AND EFFECT** What were the causes of the Boxer Rebellion?
3. **DRAW CONCLUSIONS** Why do you think John Hay proposed the Open Door Policy instead of negotiating directly with China?
4. **COMPARE AND CONTRAST** How did the political system in China differ from that in the United States in the 1800s? Support your answer with evidence from the text.

3.3 **MAIN IDEA** As a result of the Spanish-American War of 1898, the United States acquired territories in the Caribbean and in the Pacific.

THE SPANISH-AMERICAN WAR

At the same time the United States was seeking to expand its territory, Spain was losing hold on its empire. In the late 1800s, the paths of the two nations collided.

SPANISH HOLDINGS

By the late 1800s, Spain had lost most of its once vast colonial empire stretching around the world. It still retained a few colonies, including Cuba and Puerto Rico in the Caribbean and the Philippines in the Pacific. Yet people in these lands had begun to demand their independence from Spanish rule.

In Cuba, a revolt against Spanish rule broke out in February 1895. The Cuban rebels waged a strong campaign, and Spain responded with brutal tactics. When the Spanish could not defeat the rebels in direct combat, they herded the civilian population into fortified camps so the people could not aid the rebels. In these disease-ridden and overcrowded camps, more than 100,000 Cubans died, many of them from starvation.

For a number of reasons, Americans took a keen interest in events in Cuba. One reason was the island's proximity—it lies only about 90 miles south of the tip of Florida. Another factor was economic interest. American companies had millions of dollars invested in sugarcane plantations on the island. In 1894, the United States accounted for 85 percent of Cuba's exports, while Spain was responsible for only 6 percent. Thus, Cuba was an economically valuable neighbor of the United States. In addition, Americans identified with the Cubans' desire for independence. Spain's brutal measures to end the Cuban rebellion, which American newspapers graphically portrayed, aroused the sympathy of the American public.

REMEMBER THE *MAINE*

By the time William McKinley was inaugurated as president in 1897, many Americans were calling for the United States to intervene in Cuba and aid the rebels. At first, McKinley attempted to negotiate a peace settlement between the Cuban rebels and the Spanish. The president succeeded in getting Spain to offer the Cubans limited self-government.

CRITICAL VIEWING This print, published in 1898 by the printmakers Kurz and Allison, shows the explosion of the U.S.S. *Maine*. The men featured at the top of the print are American naval officers Admiral Montgomery Sicard (left) and Captain Charles Sigsbee (right). What kind of reaction might this print have aroused in Americans at the time it was published?

Then a dramatic event changed the course of American involvement. The United States had sent a battleship, the U.S.S. *Maine*, to Havana, Cuba, to protect American citizens and property there. On February 15, 1898, the ship exploded in the Havana harbor, killing more than 250 men, or about two-thirds of the crew. Modern research suggests that naturally occurring chemical reactions in one of the ship's coal bunkers caused the explosion. At the time, however, a naval board of inquiry, along with the American public, blamed Spain.

Though they lacked any evidence, American newspapers claimed that Spain had blown up the battleship. The *New York Journal and Advertiser*, owned by newspaper publisher William Randolph Hearst, printed such unfounded headlines as "Destruction of the War Ship *Maine* Was the Work of an Enemy!" and "Spanish Treachery!" This type of sensationalized newswriting, using exaggeration, melodrama, and outright lies to attract readers, became known as **yellow journalism**.

While a Navy investigation never pinned blame on Spain, many Americans readily believed that the Spanish had caused the explosion. Proponents of U.S. military intervention in Cuba used the slogan "Remember the *Maine*!" to rally public support. As public opinion in the United States increasingly favored war, Spain tried to avert it by conceding to many U.S. demands. But then the U.S. Congress authorized the president to use force to gain the withdrawal of Spain's armed forces from Cuba.

PRIMARY SOURCE

In an article entitled "Naval Officers Think the *Maine* Was Destroyed by a Spanish Mine," the *New York Journal and Advertiser* led Americans to believe that the U.S.S. *Maine* was deliberately blown up.

Assistant Secretary of the Navy Theodore Roosevelt says he is convinced that the destruction of the Maine *in Havana Harbor was not an accident. The* Journal *offers a reward of $50,000 for exclusive evidence that will convict the person, persons or government criminally responsible for the [destruction] of the American battleship and the death of 258 of its crew. The suspicion that the* Maine *was deliberately blown up grows stronger every hour. Not a single fact to the contrary has been produced.*

—from the *New York Journal and Advertiser*, February 17, 1898

Spain responded by declaring war on the United States on April 24, and the United States in turn declared war on Spain the next day, on April 25.

WAR IN THE PACIFIC

Although events in Cuba led the United States into war, the first battle of the Spanish-American War actually took place in the Philippines. The U.S. Navy believed their superior forces could easily disable the Spanish fleet in the Philippines, where Spain was also battling rebels. Because they wanted freedom from Spain, the Filipino rebels joined forces with the Americans.

On May 1, 1898, a U.S. naval squadron under the command of Commodore **George Dewey** attacked the Spanish navy at Manila Bay. Within hours, the Spanish fleet was destroyed in an uneven fight.

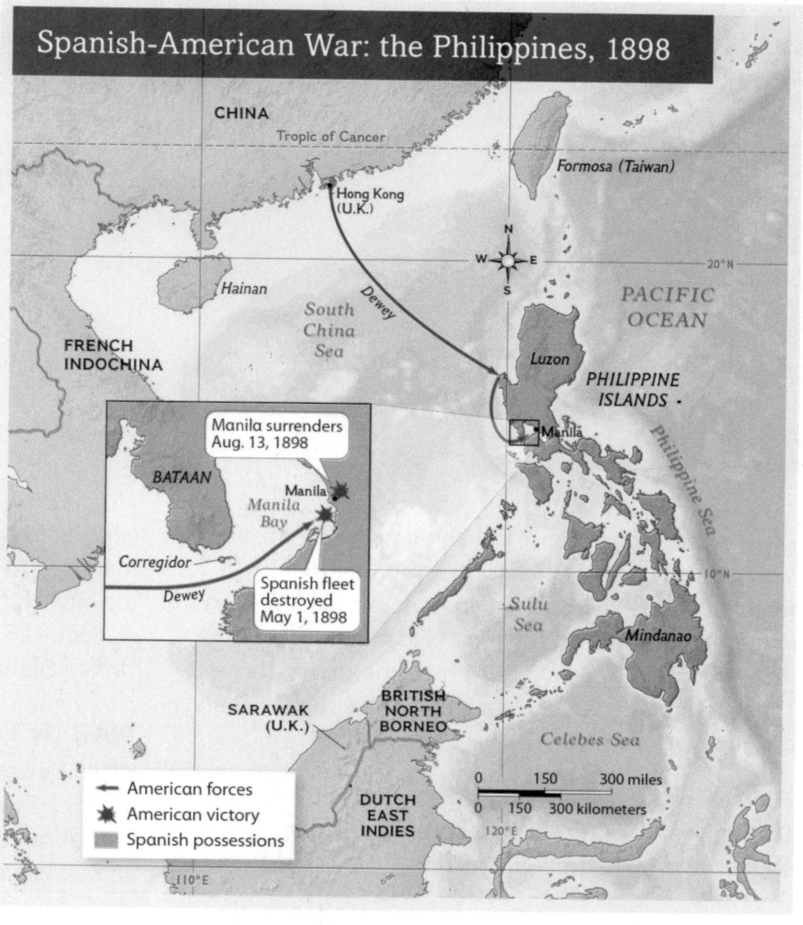

Spanish-American War: the Philippines, 1898

11.4.2 Describe the Spanish-American War and U.S. expansion in the South Pacific.

Theodore Roosevelt appears near the center in this 1898 photograph of the Rough Riders, a volunteer cavalry unit. The photograph was taken at the top of Kettle Hill, which the Rough Riders captured as part of the Battle of San Juan Hill. The battle became legendary, due largely to Roosevelt's fame. Although the Rough Riders trained as cavalry, they never fought on horseback because their horses did not arrive in Cuba in time.

Dewey had brought six steel ships to the battle, while the Spanish fleet consisted of seven unarmored wooden ships. The Spanish lost more than 350 men in the battle, while no Americans lost their lives. After the battle, Dewey reported to his superior officer: "There were . . . only seven men in the squadron very slightly wounded."

Dewey's victory was widely celebrated in the United States, even though it was incomplete. Though his squadron had control of Manila Bay, Dewey lacked enough troops to take Manila itself. He estimated that he would need 5,000 additional troops to seize the city. He soon received twice that number, and by August, U.S. troops occupied Manila. However, the United States still had to battle the Spanish in Cuba.

WAR IN THE CARIBBEAN

While Dewey's victory demonstrated the superiority of U.S. naval forces, the U.S. Army consisted of only about 25,000 troops, too small a force for the scale of fighting that was anticipated. The United

CST 3 Students use a variety of maps and documents to interpret human movement, including major patterns of domestic and international migration, changing environmental preferences and settlement patterns, the frictions that develop between population groups, and the diffusion of ideas, technological innovations, and goods.

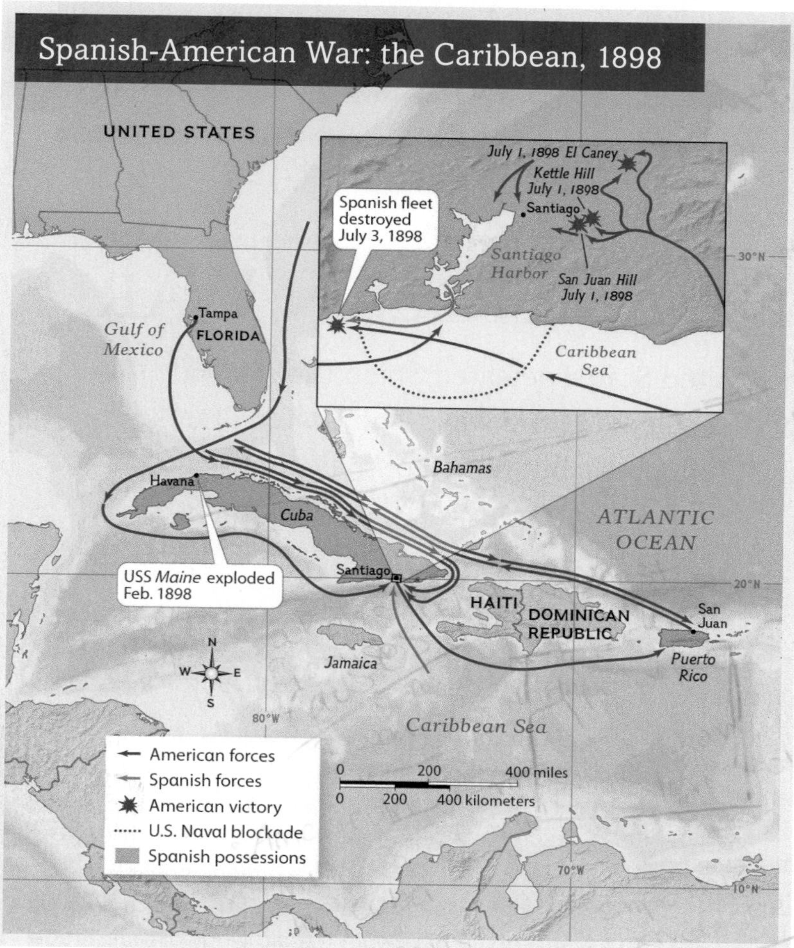

States had to turn to volunteers to fight the war. With enthusiasm for the war running high, about 1 million men volunteered, which was far more than the army could handle. About 280,000 men actually saw active duty in the war.

The war in the Caribbean began in late June 1898 with U.S. troops landing at Guantanamo Bay in Cuba and additional forces converging on the harbor city of Santiago. The most famous land battle in Cuba, the Battle of San Juan Hill, was fought near Santiago on July 1. A volunteer cavalry regiment called the Rough Riders and two African-American regiments, the Ninth and Tenth Cavalries, charged up Kettle Hill while other units attacked San Juan Hill. The Rough Riders were commanded by Leonard Wood and Theodore Roosevelt, who had resigned as assistant secretary of the Navy to lead the regiment. American newspapers portrayed Roosevelt as a hero in the battle, which contributed to his success in his future campaign for president.

At the time the war broke out, the U.S. Army included four regiments of African-American soldiers who had been headquartered in the West and on the northern plains. When they were ordered to Cuba and traveled through the southern United States, they encountered segregation and racial threats. Despite such unfair treatment, they fought fiercely in Cuba and earned numerous citations for bravery, including five Congressional Medals of Honor.

The war in the Caribbean came to an end after the U.S. Navy destroyed the Spanish fleet as it attempted to escape from the harbor at Santiago. The Spanish surrendered on July 16. American troops then invaded and took control of Puerto Rico on July 25, meeting with no opposition. On August 12, Spain and the United States signed a cease-fire agreement. From the first battle in the Pacific to the cease-fire agreement, the entire war had lasted just 16 weeks.

Representatives of the two countries met in Paris on December 10, 1898, to agree on a peace treaty. In the **Treaty of Paris**, Spain granted independence to Cuba, gave Puerto Rico and Guam to the United States, and allowed the United States to buy the Philippines for $20 million. The United States later convinced the new Cuban government to lease land for the Guantanamo Bay Naval Base. As the United States gained new territory, Spain's 400-year run as a colonial power in the Americas ended.

HISTORICAL THINKING

1. **READING CHECK** Why did the United States fight in the Spanish-American War, and what did the country gain from it?
2. **INTERPRET MAPS** Which American fleet had to travel farther, the one sailing from Hong Kong to Manila in the Philippines or the one departing from Tampa, Florida, to fight in Cuba? Use the scale of miles on the maps to determine your answer.
3. **ANALYZE CAUSE AND EFFECT** How did yellow journalism help drive the United States into war with Spain?
4. **MAKE CONNECTIONS** Describe a recent example of yellow journalism, and compare its effect with the effect of the reporting about the *Maine* explosion.

CST 1 Students compare the present with the past, evaluating the consequences of past events and decisions and determining the lessons that were learned; HREP 2 Students identify bias and prejudice in historical interpretations.

3.4 **MAIN IDEA** Between 1899 and 1902, Americans fought to gain control of the Philippines as Filipino rebels protested Spain's sale of their country to the United States.

THE PHILIPPINE-AMERICAN WAR

After just 16 weeks of fighting, the United States defeated Spain in what the American secretary of state dubbed "a splendid little war." The United States gained Puerto Rico, Guam, and the Philippines, but not all of the countries involved felt "splendid" about it.

AN OPPORTUNITY TO EXPAND

Once Spain signed the Treaty of Paris in 1898, its empire dwindled to almost nothing. The United States, on the other hand, had become an imperialist nation at the stroke of a pen, claiming control over three island territories in two oceans. Americans were divided about McKinley's diplomatic success in acquiring those lands, however. The Americans who favored manifest destiny believed acquiring foreign territories was the next logical step for the nation. Many others, however, disapproved of such expansion, recalling how American colonists felt about British rule many years before.

As the Treaty of Paris was being negotiated, President McKinley headed to the Midwest in October 1898 to convince his fellow citizens that annexing the Philippines was in the nation's best interests. The president gave many speeches stating his case for a more expansive foreign policy. A territory in the South Pacific would bolster trade

A GLOBAL PERSPECTIVE In the Umbrella Revolution of 2014, tens of thousands of people took to the streets of Hong Kong to protest attempts by mainland China to control the island's elections. After police tried to break up the protests, the people used colorful umbrellas to protect themselves from pepper spray, as shown in this photo. Although Hong Kong became part of mainland China in 1997, the people were promised their autonomy for 50 years. How does the reaction of the people of Hong Kong compare to the reaction of many Filipinos when the United States claimed control of the Philippines?

with China, he argued, and the Philippines could supply certain goods that Americans needed, such as sugar. McKinley explained that the Germans and the Japanese had positioned ships around the Philippines, waiting for a chance to occupy the archipelago. He reasoned that it was better for the Filipinos to be taken under the wing of the United States than to be governed by any other nation. In Iowa, McKinley told his audience, "We do not want to shirk a single responsibility that has been put upon us by the results of the war."

Many Filipinos, however, did not agree with McKinley's reasoning. **Emilio Aguinaldo**, one of the leaders of the rebellion against Spain before and during the Spanish-American War, believed the United States had promised the Filipinos their independence. Now he felt that Filipinos had battled one colonial power only to be handed over to another. Aguinaldo and his men readied themselves to fight yet again.

A BRUTAL WAR

Only two days after ratifying the treaty ending the Spanish-American War, the United States became embroiled in the Philippine-American War. Aguinaldo and his troops took control of the largest island in the Philippines and proclaimed it a republic, prompting a swift U.S. reaction. President McKinley sent a fleet of ships to put down the rebellion.

During 1899, the U.S. Army defeated the Filipinos in conventional battles. However, when faced with the highly organized and fully supplied American army, Aguinaldo and his men switched strategies. They started a **guerrilla war**, a war fought by unconventional means, such as sabotage, ambushes, and unexpected raids. Aguinaldo's troops were a grassroots group—untrained and assembled from local residents—but they had some advantages. They knew the geography of their island, and they looked like the civilian population. They could hit selected targets and then escape by blending in with the crowd. Individual soldiers slipped into the American troops' camps at night and sabotaged or stole equipment. Faced with this new threat, the American military responded by killing and torturing Filipino prisoners to gain information about the rebels' plans. American troops also looted and burned down villages, moving the inhabitants into camps that they then failed to supply with food.

The American press reported the soldiers' brutality, and enthusiasm waned in the United States for pursuing further expansion. People who opposed imperialism began to organize. The **American Anti-Imperialist League** became a voice against McKinley's foreign policy decisions. By 1900, many Americans believed the existing empire should be retained and protected—but not increased.

PRIMARY SOURCE

Why do the Imperialists wish to subjugate us? What do they intend to do with us? Do they expect us to surrender—to yield our inalienable rights . . . to the absolute control of the United States? What would you do with our nine millions of people? Would you permit us to take part in your elections? Or, would you tax us without representation?

—from a letter to the American people, by Galicano Apacible, Filipino political leader, 1899

Even some of the soldiers fighting in the Philippines struggled with their purpose in the war. One soldier wrote, "I am not afraid, and am always ready to do my duty, but I would like someone to tell me what we are fighting for." A Minnesota general lamented, "It seems to me that we are doing something that is contrary to our principles in the past."

American troops captured Aguinaldo in 1901, effectively ending the rebellion. Some minor uprisings occurred through the next summer, but without Aguinaldo, who took an oath of allegiance to the United States, the rebel forces slowly disbanded. On July 4, 1902, President Theodore Roosevelt forgave the Filipino nationalists and proclaimed the end of the war. The fighting had claimed the lives of 4,200 American soldiers and more than 20,000 Filipino rebels. In addition, some 200,000 Filipino civilians perished in the warfare or from starvation and disease. The Philippines would not become an independent nation until more than four decades later, in 1946.

HISTORICAL THINKING

1. **READING CHECK** What were the reasons for the Philippine-American War, and what were the results?
2. **ANALYZE CAUSE AND EFFECT** How did the Philippine-American War affect some Americans' views on expansionist foreign policy?
3. **ANALYZE LANGUAGE USE** The word *guerrilla* means "little war" in Spanish. How does this meaning help you understand the difference between conventional and guerrilla warfare?
4. **MAKE CONNECTIONS** How did the Spanish-American War lead to the Philippine-American War?

11.2.6 Trace the economic development of the United States and its emergence as a major industrial power, including its gains from trade and the advantages of its physical geography; 11.4.2 Describe the Spanish-American War and U.S. expansion in the South Pacific; CST 1 Students compare the present with the past, evaluating the consequences of past events and decisions and determining the lessons that were learned.

3.5 **MAIN IDEA** In the early 1900s, the United States used its military strength to expand its involvement and gain territory in Latin America.

INVOLVEMENT IN LATIN AMERICA

Have you ever felt overshadowed by a stronger opponent in an athletic contest? In the early 1900s, the United States cast such a shadow over Latin America.

ACQUIRING PUERTO RICO

As you have read, the United States gained control of Puerto Rico at the end of the Spanish-American War in 1898. Before the war, many Puerto Ricans had long sought independence from Spanish rule. **Luis Muñoz Rivera,** a leader of the Puerto Rican independence movement, had worked with the Spanish government to negotiate for the island's independence. By 1897, Puerto Rico had won the right to self-governance, though it remained a Spanish colony. When the United States acquired Puerto Rico, Muñoz Rivera continued to advocate for independence. But the U.S. government had its own ideas.

After gaining control of Puerto Rico, the United States initially appointed military officers to govern the island. But on April 12, 1900, Congress ratified the Foraker Act, which established the island's first House of Representatives and Supreme Court. The act reserved for the U.S. president the authority to appoint a governor and an executive council, but it gave some political power to Puerto Ricans as well.

Control of high government positions in Puerto Rico was important to U.S. interests for a number of reasons. The tropical island could supply goods, such as sugar, to the United States, and it served as a new market for American goods, such as coal, a natural resource Puerto Rico lacked. The United States could enjoy exclusive rights to trade. In addition, Puerto Rico would become the site of an important U.S. naval base.

BIG STICK DIPLOMACY

In 1901, Theodore Roosevelt became president. By then, in addition to the territories discussed, the United States possessed the previously uninhabited Wake Island as well as part of the island chain of Samoa, which became American Samoa. Earlier, in 1867, the United States had annexed Midway Islands. Roosevelt began making plans to extend American influence worldwide, especially in Latin America. He relied on recommendations made by Alfred T. Mahan years before: build a strong navy, adopt an aggressive foreign policy, and connect the Atlantic and Pacific oceans by digging a canal through Central America.

In terms of foreign policy, Roosevelt said the United States should "speak softly and carry a big stick," meaning the nation should negotiate peacefully while

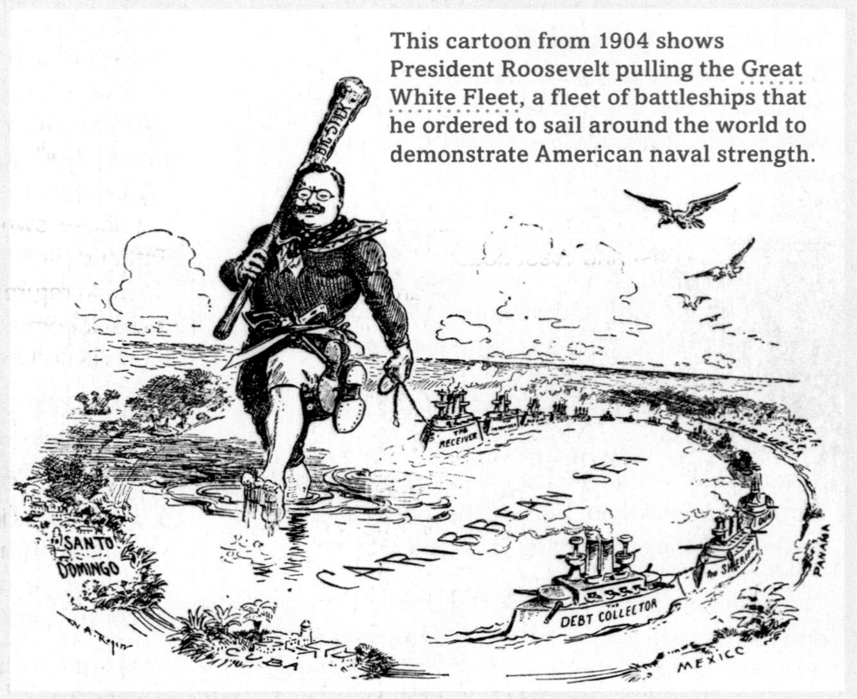

This cartoon from 1904 shows President Roosevelt pulling the Great White Fleet, a fleet of battleships that he ordered to sail around the world to demonstrate American naval strength.

11.4 Students trace the rise of the United States to its role as a world power in the twentieth century; 11.4.3 Discuss America's role in the Panama Revolution and the building of the Panama Canal.

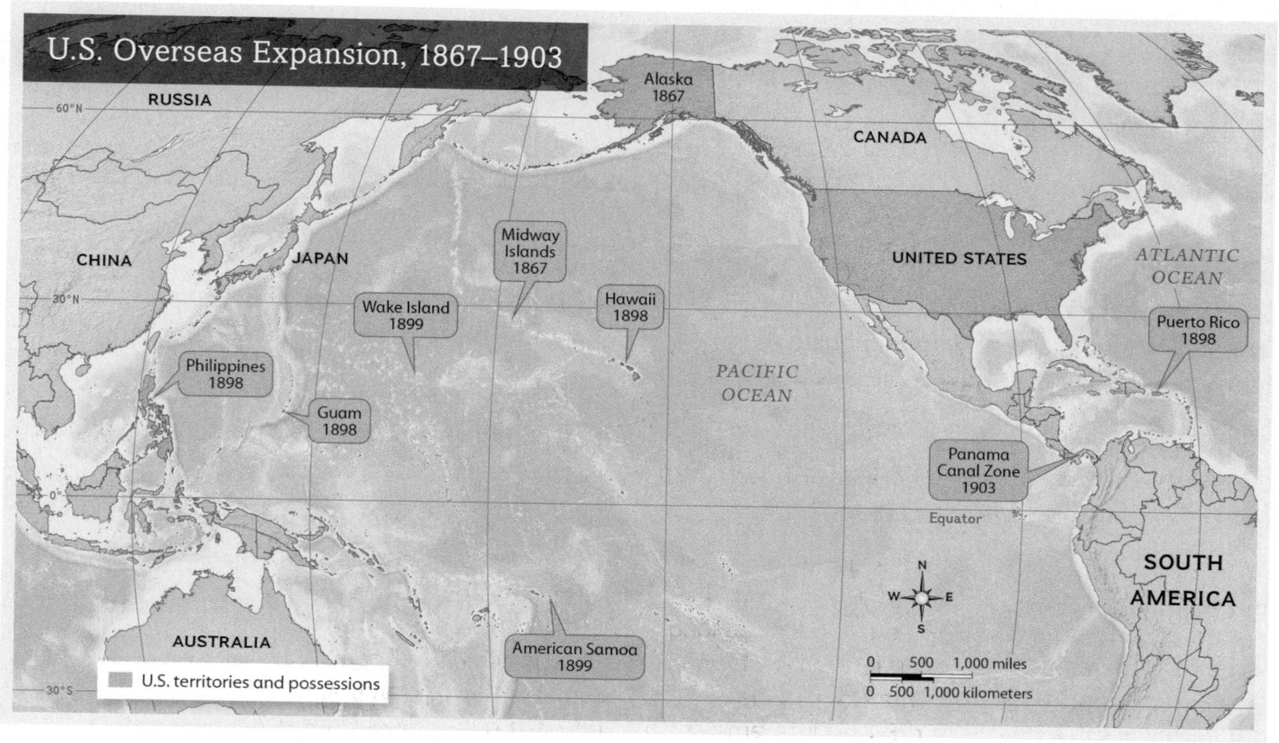

flexing its military strength. Roosevelt employed his **Big Stick Diplomacy** early in his presidency during an incident involving Venezuela. In 1902, German and British ships destroyed the Venezuelan economy by blockading its ports in order to collect debts owed to them. The event forced the president to act. Roosevelt "spoke softly" by negotiating a deal to end the crisis, and he "carried a big stick" by writing a declaration that, when necessary, the United States would intervene in the affairs of Latin American nations. The declaration, called the **Roosevelt Corollary**, amended the Monroe Doctrine, a much earlier U.S. declaration that opposed European interference in the Americas.

The Roosevelt Corollary came into play later as Roosevelt set out to build a canal in Central America. The canal would dramatically cut shipping times between the East and West coasts of the United States. Ships at the time had to sail around all of South America to complete this journey. In 1902, Congress pursued a treaty to lease a tract of land for the canal on an **isthmus**, or strip of land between two bodies of water, in Colombia. When the Colombian government refused, Roosevelt gently encouraged the people who lived on the isthmus to start an **insurrection**, or rebellion, against the Colombian government. The presence of American ships around the isthmus discouraged the Colombians from putting down the insurrection, which in turn allowed the newly formed nation of Panama to quickly claim its independence.

The Panamanians agreed to lease a 10-mile tract of land to the United States, giving it control over the area. On March 3, 1904, construction began on the **Panama Canal** and continued long after Roosevelt's presidency. The canal opened in 1914. With the Panama Canal Zone, the United States added another foreign territory to its collection. Technically, the acquisitions had all taken place by treaty and not by force, but that did not stop people around the world from calling the United States an empire.

Roosevelt passed the responsibilities of his administration to President Taft in 1909. Taft generally followed Roosevelt's diplomatic techniques, although when opportunities to invest in China arose, he replaced Roosevelt's "big stick" with money. For instance, when the Chinese asked for help to buy Japanese-owned railroads in their country in 1909, Taft and other world leaders loaned the money to them. In return, Taft requested that the Chinese be more accommodating to American trade. American journalists dubbed this approach "Dollar Diplomacy."

HISTORICAL THINKING

1. **READING CHECK** How did President Roosevelt apply Big Stick Diplomacy in gaining land for the Panama Canal?
2. **INTERPRET MAPS** Which territories did the United States acquire in 1898?
3. **FORM AND SUPPORT OPINIONS** What do you think were the pros and cons of Big Stick Diplomacy?

11.4.4 Explain Theodore Roosevelt's Big Stick diplomacy, William Taft's Dollar Diplomacy, and Woodrow Wilson's Moral Diplomacy, drawing on relevant speeches.

CHAPTER 7 THE PROGRESSIVE ERA AND EXPANSIONISM

REVIEW

VOCABULARY

Use each of the following vocabulary words in a sentence that shows an understanding of the term's meaning.

1. Progressive Era HSS 11.2.9
   As a result of Progressive Era initiatives, fewer children worked as laborers in factories.
2. temperance movement HSS 11.3.1
3. conservation HSS 11.2.9
4. initiative HSS 11.2.9
5. syndicate HSS 11.2.9
6. isolationism HSS 11.4.2
7. reparations HSS 11.4.1
8. yellow journalism HSS 11.4.2
9. guerrilla war HSS 11.4.2
10. insurrection HSS 11.4.2

READING STRATEGY

ANALYZE LANGUAGE USE

Complete the Word Map to analyze the meaning of the quotation from Theodore Roosevelt that appears at the beginning of the chapter. Then answer the question.

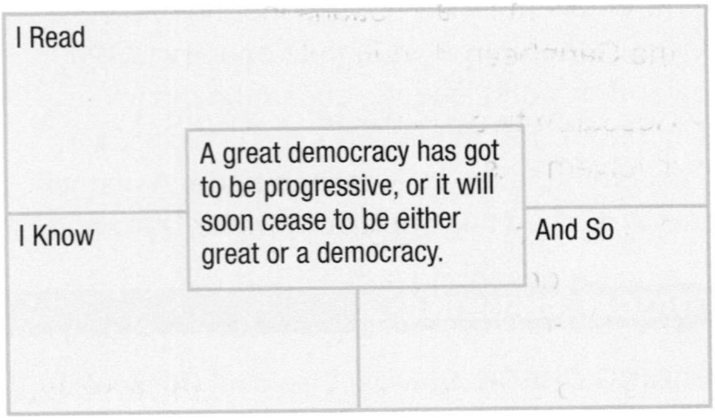

11. How did Roosevelt's progressivism impact the future of American democracy? HSS 11.2.9
12. Where did women's suffrage fit within the progressive movement? HSS 11.2.9

MAIN IDEAS

Answer the following questions. Support your answers with evidence from the chapter.

13. Why did the constitutional amendment guaranteeing women the right to vote become stalled? **LESSON 1.2** HSS 11.10.7
14. Why were direct primaries considered a progressive idea? **LESSON 1.4** HSS 11.2.9
15. Why is Theodore Roosevelt's presidency so strongly associated with the Progressive Era? **LESSON 2.1** HSS 11.2.9
16. Why did progressives reject laissez-faire economics? **LESSON 2.1** HSS 11.2.9
17. What problem did the Federal Reserve System solve? **LESSON 2.3** HSS 11.6.1
18. What were some of the factors that changed Americans' minds about the purchase of Alaska from the Russians? **LESSON 3.1** HSS 11.4
19. Why did the United States seek to replace China's spheres of influence with the Open Door Policy? **LESSON 3.2** HSS 11.4.1
20. What territories did the United States gain at the end of the Spanish-American War? **LESSON 3.3** HSS 11.4.2
21. Why did some Americans oppose the United States' actions during the Philippine-American War? **LESSON 3.4** HSS 11.4.2
22. How did President Roosevelt apply Big Stick Diplomacy in Latin America? **LESSON 3.5** HSS 11.4.4

HISTORICAL THINKING

Answer the following questions. Support your answers with evidence from the chapter.

23. **MAKE GENERALIZATIONS** What methods did reformers use to achieve their goals during the Progressive Era? HSS 11.2.9

24. **EVALUATE** In what way was President Roosevelt's Square Deal an innovative approach to labor disputes? HSS 11.2.9

25. **MAKE INFERENCES** How did the United States' role in the world change after the Spanish-American War? HSS 11.4.2

26. **SYNTHESIZE** What were the purpose and effects of the Open Door Policy? HSS 11.4.1

27. **COMPARE AND CONTRAST** How did Roosevelt's Big Stick Diplomacy differ from Taft's Dollar Diplomacy? HSS 11.4.4

28. **DRAW CONCLUSIONS** What was the impact of the Children's Bureau? HSS 11.2.9

INTERPRET GRAPHS

Study the line graph below, which shows the results of censuses conducted on the Hawaiian Islands. Then answer the questions.

Hawaii's Changing Population 1853–1920

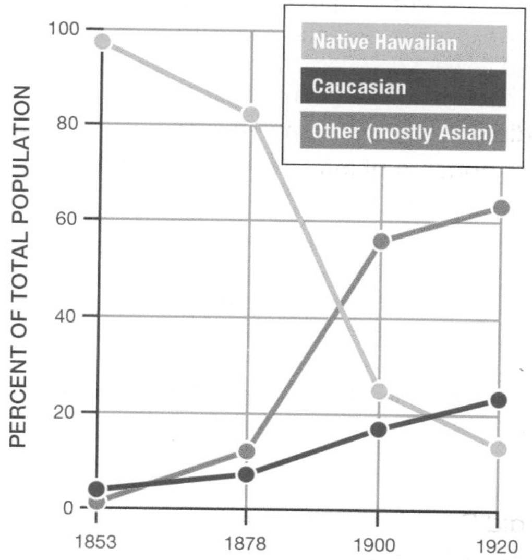

Source: Robert C. Schmitt, Demographic Statistics of Hawaii, 1778–1965

29. Which population group declined the most and which increased the most during the time period covered on the graph? HSS CST 3

30. What does the graph reveal about the non-native population of Hawaii during that time period? HSS CST 3

ANALYZE SOURCES

In 1917, Carrie Chapman Catt delivered an address to Congress explaining why women's suffrage was inevitable and essential. Read the excerpt from the speech and answer the question that follows.

> Behold our Uncle Sam floating the banner with one hand, "Taxation without representation is tyranny," and with the other seizing the billions of dollars paid in taxes by women to whom he refuses "representation." Behold him again, welcoming the boys of twenty-one . . . to "a voice in their own government" while he denies that fundamental right of democracy to thousands of women public school teachers from whom many of these men learn all they know of citizenship and patriotism.

31. What point is Catt making about the United States government? HSS HREP 1

CONNECT TO YOUR LIFE

32. **ARGUMENT** Once the West was settled in the late 1800s, the United States turned its sights to the world outside its borders. American involvement in world affairs has increased ever since. Write an essay arguing whether or not the United States should have so much global influence, citing examples from the chapter and your own research. HSS CST 1

TIPS

- Review American actions in the Pacific and the Caribbean discussed in the chapter.
- Research two or three current U.S. foreign involvements.
- Develop your topic by comparing U.S. actions described in the chapter with the present-day situations you researched.
- Use two or three vocabulary words from the chapter in your argument.
- End your essay with a recommendation on the role you believe the United States should have in world affairs.

Nature for Everyone

by Gary Strauss

Adapted from "Biologist Wants Nature for Everyone—Including Prisoners," by Gary Strauss, news.nationalgeographic.com, September 2016

National Geographic Explorer Nalini Nadkarni developed a reputation as "queen of the forest canopy," thanks to her extensive research among the towering branches of the forests of Costa Rica. On solid ground, she brings her knowledge of the natural world to unconventional settings. It's a long way from the Costa Rican rain forest to a U.S. prison, but Nadkarni navigates both environments with ease.

As a forest ecologist, Nadkarni spent her early career enmeshed in tree canopies. But after years of fieldwork and university life, she decided that her efforts needed a broader audience than scientists, academics, and natural history buffs. "I was preaching to the choir, so I began to ask myself how can I bring my message to others," says Nadkarni. "Rather than saying you need to read my articles or attend my lectures to understand my science, I took the approach of appealing to people in their own venues."

Nadkarni coordinated with rap artists to develop nature programs for at-risk youth, created a fieldwork outfit for a Barbie doll, and organized eco-fashion shows. She hoped that these entertaining yet educational initiatives would better connect people to trees and forests. Her work bringing science and nature programs to prisons could have that impact.

While teaching at Washington's Evergreen State College, she studied the movement of tree branches by attaching a paint brush to twigs. Measuring wind-aided changes and calculating them over 12 months, she found that a tree can sway back and forth up to 186,540 miles in a single year. "I began to think of other entities that are perceived to be static and stuck," she explains. "Prisoners are also stuck. But whether you're a CEO or an inmate stuck in solitary confinement, what we have in common is humanity and a connection to nature."

She put her observations into action by developing science and nature programs at Washington's Cedar Corrections Center. There, inmates working with biologists raised threatened Oregon spotted frogs. They also grew mosses in an effort to help replace what had been commercially harvested in old growth forests.

Those efforts evolved into the Sustainability in Prisons Project, funded in part by the National Science Foundation. The project spread to 10 Washington state prisons and facilities in Oregon, California, Ohio, and Maryland. The group's efforts include recycling programs, beekeeping, organic vegetable farms, tree planting, and flower nurseries. Inmates develop skills for future employment and gain a sense of purpose, responsibility, and teamwork. Nadkarni asserts that prisoners who participate are less likely to return to criminal activity after their release.

Now a biology professor and head of the University of Utah's Center for Science and Mathematics Education, Nadkarni has also brought nature to inmates housed in solitary confinement. She beamed images and videos of forests, oceans, mountains, and skies into their recreation rooms. While limited in scope, the impact has been dramatic. Some inmates housed for violent crimes or tendencies in the isolation unit at Oregon's Snake River Correctional Institution were shown nature videos. Those shown recordings of nature scenes committed 26 percent fewer violent infractions, according to a study presented in August 2016 to the American Psychological Association.

"We can't bring nature programs to maximum security," Nadkarni says. "But what we've found is that exposing violent offenders to images of nature for an hour a day brings down their stress and anxiety levels and reduces violent tendencies." She wants to bring her successes to other prisoners as well to further demonstrate her simple but profound approach.

For more from National Geographic check out "21st Century Cowboys" online.

UNIT INQUIRY: Produce a Documentary

In this unit, you learned about the changes that occurred in the United States in the late 1800s and early 1900s. From the displacement of Native Americans on the western frontier to the influx of immigrants into the growing industrial cities of the Northeast and Midwest, these changes produced a wide range of social, political, and economic problems. Writers and photographers documented the problems to call public attention to them.

ASSIGNMENT

Assume the role of a reporter and produce a short documentary that examines an important problem in American life between 1877 and 1920. Topics include poverty, child labor, substandard housing, unsafe working conditions, and political corruption in city governments. Explain the causes and effects of the problem and outline attempted solutions. Be prepared to present your documentary to the class.

Plan Review the social, economic, and political problems covered in this unit and choose one to investigate. Reread the text's description of the problem and make a list of questions you have about its causes, effects, and solutions. Use library and online resources to research multiple points of view on the issue. Evaluate each source's explanation of the cause of the problem. Determine which explanation best agrees with the text evidence provided to include in your documentary. Take notes using a graphic organizer like this one.

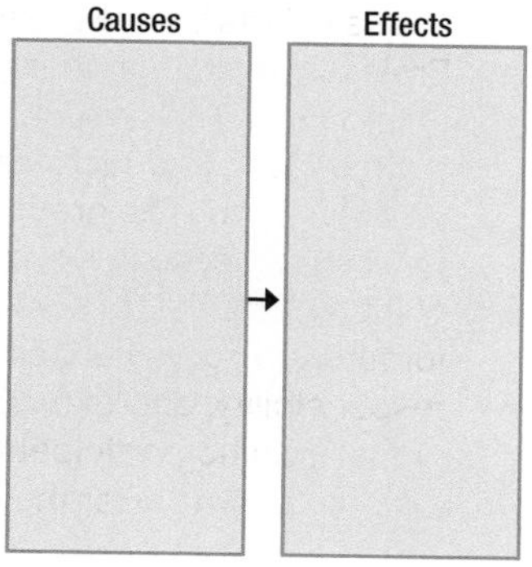

Produce Create an outline for your documentary. Then write a script in which you introduce the problem, identify its causes and effects, describe attempted solutions, and conclude by stating the outcome of the events. Revise the script as necessary. Consider your audience, and make sure to address the most significant points of the problem and solution. Choose photographs and other graphics from books and online sources to help convey your main points. Make a video of the narration and graphics.

Present Show your documentary to the class. You might consider one of these options:

- Post the documentary on a class website and invite your classmates and friends to view it. Invite viewers to share their feedback and questions with you. Respond to the feedback and questions you receive.
- Work with your teacher to schedule a class viewing of the documentary. After the viewing, ask classmates for their reactions and lead a class discussion of the issue.

NATIONAL GEOGRAPHIC | LEARNING FRAMEWORK ACTIVITIES

Write a Position Statement

ATTITUDE Responsibility

SKILL Communication

In the late 1800s and early 1900s, disadvantaged groups of Americans struggled to gain rights and improve their situations. These groups included farmers, Native Americans, laborers, immigrants, African Americans, and women. Choose one of these groups and research the group's struggles. Write a position statement addressed to a government official or agency of the time in which you detail your concerns and demands. Present your position statement to the class and discuss possible reactions of the government official or agency, taking into account historical context.

Plan a Protest

ATTITUDE Empowerment

KNOWLEDGE Critical Species

The settlement of the West and the expansion of farming had a negative impact on the natural environment in the late 1800s and early 1900s. A prime example of this negative impact was the fate of the American bison, which were hunted to the point of near extinction. Working with a partner or small group, research the bison's decline and plan a protest to persuade the government to take action to protect current and future herds. Create a slogan and protest signs. Outline where you will stage the protest and how you will draw participants. Present your plan to the class and solicit their reactions.

HREP 4 Students construct and test hypotheses; collect, evaluate, and employ information from multiple primary and secondary sources; and apply it in oral and written presentations; HI 3 Students interpret past events and issues within the context in which an event unfolded rather than solely in terms of present-day norms and values.

3 From the Great War to the New Deal

CRITICAL VIEWING Artist Franz Kline painted *Lower East Side Market Scene* (detail) around 1938, soon after moving to New York City. It shows an open-air market likely inspired by the artist's Greenwich Village neighborhood, with its older buildings and working-class residents. What does the painting reveal about American culture?

THE UNITED STATES

1920
Henry Ford produces more than 1 million cars, called Model Ts, and sells each one for $335.

1919
Congress passes the 19th Amendment, which, once ratified, grants women the right to vote.

1917
The United States enters the war under President Woodrow Wilson. *(More than 4 million copies of this poster featuring "Uncle Sam" were printed between 1917 and 1918 to recruit soldiers.)*

1918
The Allies defeat Germany, bringing an end to the war.

1914
The assassination of Archduke Franz Ferdinand of Austria-Hungary triggers the start of World War I.

1910

1920

1919 EUROPE
The Treaty of Versailles is signed in France, which officially brings World War I to a close.

THE WORLD

1916 AMERICAS
Mexican military leader Pancho Villa leads a raid in New Mexico, killing about 17 Americans.

1917 EUROPE
The Russian Revolution begins.
(Vladimir Lenin, who led the revolution)

HISTORICAL THINKING

DETERMINE CHRONOLOGY What other conflict began the year the United States entered World War I?

1929
The stock market crashes, marking the start of the Great Depression. *(men wearing signs in downtown Chicago advertising their qualifications, 1934)*

1933
To address the Great Depression, Roosevelt enacts a series of domestic programs called the New Deal. *(mural created by Charles Wells under the New Deal's Works Progress Administration)*

1940
Roosevelt signs into law an act creating the first peacetime draft in U.S. history.

1931
As a result of drought and overplowed land, terrible dust storms sweep across the Great Plains states, a region some call the Dust Bowl.

1932
Franklin Delano Roosevelt is elected to his first term as president.

1937 ASIA
Japan goes to war with China and occupies Chinese cities including Shanghai, Beijing, and Nanjing.

1933 EUROPE
Adolf Hitler becomes dictator of Germany. *(postage stamp of Hitler made by the Nazi regime)*

1922 AFRICA
Egypt gains independence from Great Britain.

HI 1 Students show the connections, causal and otherwise, between particular historical events and larger social, economic, and political trends and developments.

CHAPTER 8

THE GREAT WAR

1914–1920

HISTORICAL THINKING How did World War I affect the United States politically, economically, and socially?

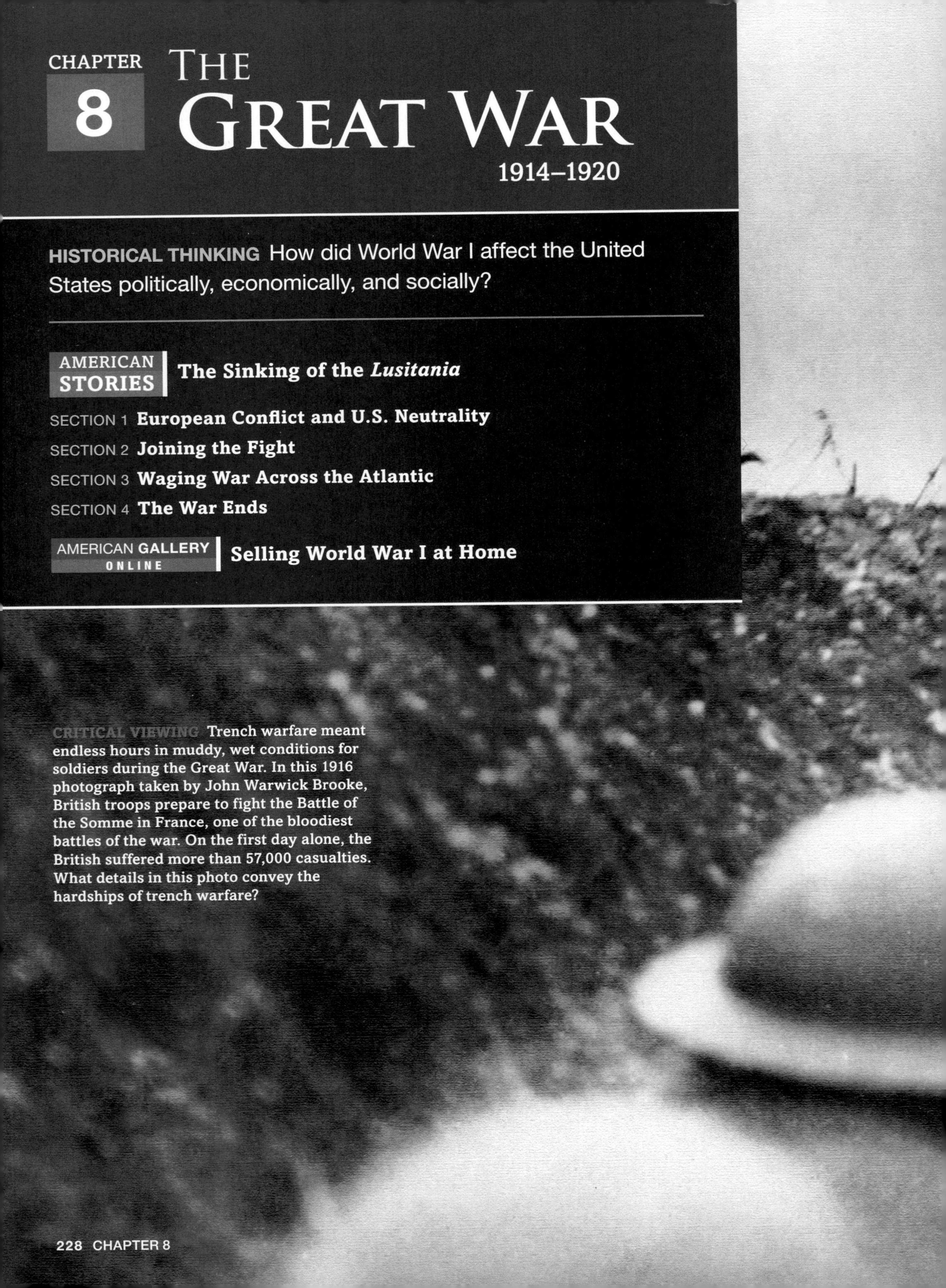

CRITICAL VIEWING Trench warfare meant endless hours in muddy, wet conditions for soldiers during the Great War. In this 1916 photograph taken by John Warwick Brooke, British troops prepare to fight the Battle of the Somme in France, one of the bloodiest battles of the war. On the first day alone, the British suffered more than 57,000 casualties. What details in this photo convey the hardships of trench warfare?

“It is a fearful thing to lead this great peaceful people into war . . . **civilization itself seeming to be in the balance.**”

—President Woodrow Wilson

CRITICAL VIEWING The luxury ocean liner *Lusitania* departed for her last voyage from Pier 54 in New York City on May 1, 1915. Why do you think a crowd would have gathered to see the *Lusitania* off on its voyage?

11.4.5 Analyze the political, economic, and social ramifications of World War I on the home front.

THE SINKING OF THE LUSITANIA

Today you can board a plane anywhere in the continental United States and arrive in Europe in less than a day. In 1915, the only option for trans-Atlantic travel was by ship, and the fastest crossing you could expect to make was 4 days, 11 hours, and 42 minutes—a record set by the British passenger liner R.M.S. *Lusitania*, the swiftest and possibly the most luxurious ship afloat at that time.

A DISTANT WAR

On May 1, 1915, the *Lusitania* was set to depart New York for England with approximately 2,000 passengers and crew aboard, including nearly 200 Americans. The ship was also carrying war material, including ammunition, for the British war effort. Great Britain and its allies had been at war with Germany for nearly a year. Germany had taken the battle to the seas, deploying submarines to attack not only naval vessels but also civilian ships suspected of carrying ammunition or other war materials to Britain.

This cork life ring covered in yellow fabric bears the name of the ill-fated passenger ship.

On the morning the *Lusitania* sailed, the German Embassy in the United States placed an advertisement in several newspapers stating, rather ominously, that Germany considered the seas around Great Britain to be a war zone, and that "vessels flying the flag of Great Britain . . . are liable to destruction in these waters."

CROSSING THE ATLANTIC

The *Lusitania*'s passengers represented all walks of life, from the extremely wealthy who took up residence in the most glamorous cabins, to the third-class passengers who shared dormitory-type rooms. One of the most celebrated passengers aboard the *Lusitania* was the American millionaire Alfred Gwynne Vanderbilt, who had inherited a lavish fortune from his father, the railroad baron Cornelius Vanderbilt. Before the ship sailed, a reporter asked Alfred about the German newspaper threat. He replied, "I don't take much stock in it myself. What would they gain by sinking the *Lusitania*?"

Other notable American passengers included Theodate Pope, one of the first female architects in the United States, and Charles Lauriat, a well-known Boston book dealer. Pope spent the six-day Atlantic crossing reading and chatting with her traveling companion, Edwin Friend. Lauriat was transporting an extremely rare book by British writer Charles Dickens, and a priceless set of drawings.

Among the younger passengers was an American named Dorothy Conner, who found the uneventful trip across the Atlantic to be frustratingly dull. She remarked to a dinner companion, "I can't help hoping that we get some sort of thrill going up the [English] Channel." Later, when a friend remarked that she'd had her thrill, Conner replied, "I never want another."

AMERICAN STORIES

A DISASTROUS COURSE

Captain William Turner appears to have sailed the *Lusitania* in a straight line through the dangerous waters of the Irish Sea. A zig-zag course would have made the ship a more difficult target for the U-boat torpedoes. Turner was later heavily criticized for his decision. How might a different course have changed history?

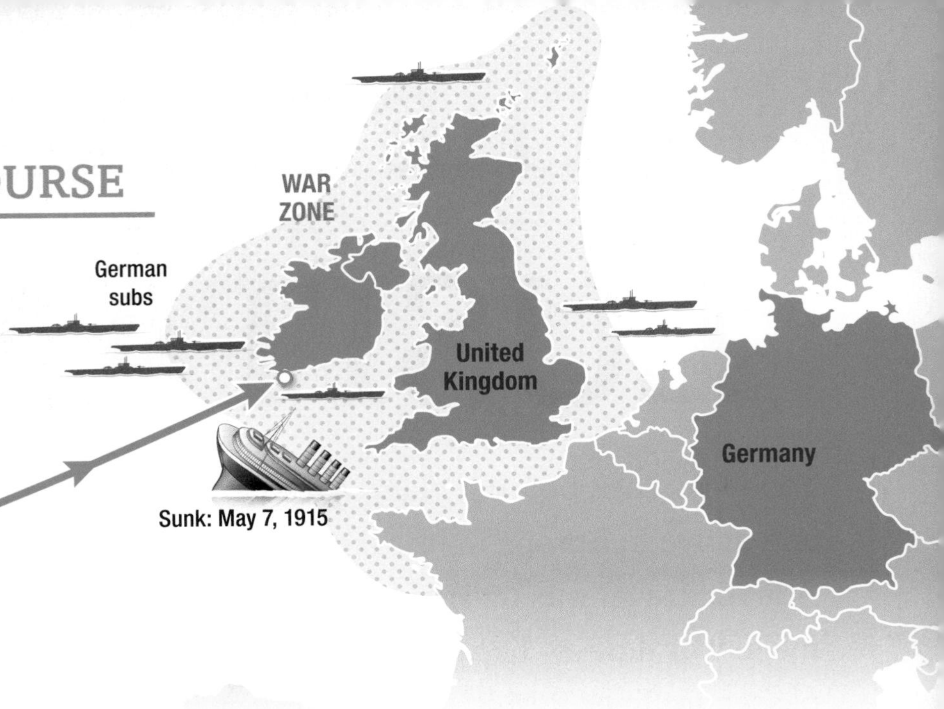

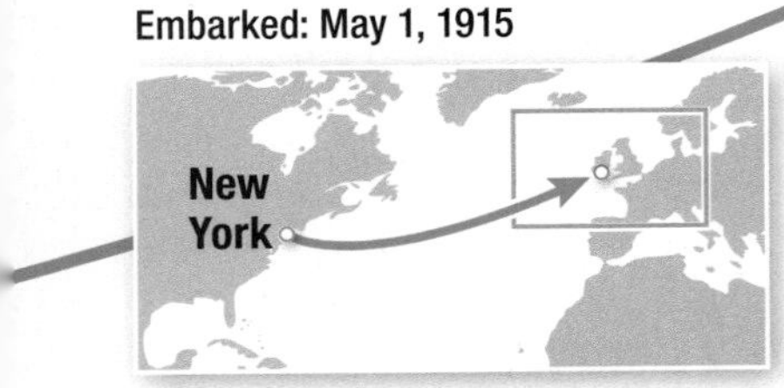

ATTACK NEAR IRELAND

At a little after 2 p.m. on May 7, the *Lusitania* was steaming into the Irish Sea, about 20 miles from the Irish Coast. Lurking in the same waters was the U-20, a German submarine with a mission to target British ships. The *Lusitania*'s captain ordered a turn to starboard, unknowingly placing the liner directly within the submarine's sights.

Passengers and crew alike watched, transfixed, as a German torpedo streaked toward the helpless ship. One passenger described himself as "spellbound" by the sight, adding, "I felt absolutely sick."

This moment of fearful anticipation ended when the torpedo slammed into the *Lusitania*'s side, blasting a hole in the hull. Immediately, seawater began to pour into the vessel at an estimated rate of 100 tons per second. The *Lusitania* began to list—or tilt—at an extreme angle, making it nearly impossible for passengers to clamber into the lifeboats. Panicked passengers and crew members scrambled to find and put on their life vests, and parents desperately searched for their children in the crowds. Some people leaped into the sea while others clung to the sinking ship. Within 18 chaotic minutes, the *Lusitania* had disappeared beneath the surface of the sea.

"All the News That's Fit to Print."

The New York Times.

NEW YORK, SATURDAY, MAY 8, 1915.—TWENTY-FOUR PAGES. ONE CENT

LUSITANIA SUNK BY A SUBMARINE, PROBABLY 1,000 DEAD; TWICE TORPEDOED OFF IRISH COAST; SINKS IN 15 MINUTES; AMERICANS ABOARD INCLUDED VANDERBILT AND FROHMAN; WASHINGTON BELIEVES THAT A GRAVE CRISIS IS AT HAND

SHOCKS THE PRESIDENT

Washington Deeply Stirred by Disaster and Fears a Crisis.

BULLETINS AT WHITE HOUSE

Wilson Reads Them Closely, but Is Silent on the Nation's Course.

HINTS OF CONGRESS CALL

CAPITAL FULL OF RUMORS

SOME DEAD TAKEN ASHORE

Several Hundred Survivors at Queenstown and Kinsale.

STEWARD TELLS OF DISASTER

One Torpedo Crashes into the Doomed Liner's Bow, Another into the Engine Room.

SHIP LISTS OVER TO PORT

ATTACKED IN BROAD DAY

The Lost Cunard Steamship Lusitania

Cunard Office Here Besieged for News; Fate of 1,918 on Lusitania Long in Doubt

Loss of the Lusitania Fills London With Horror and Utter Amazement

Newspapers, including this May 8, 1915, edition of the *New York Times*, spread word of the event across the world.

ONE SHIPWRECK: TWO PERSPECTIVES

There are many survivor accounts of the sinking of the *Lusitania*, and it is valuable to compare these primary sources to better understand the event. The captain of the German U-boat that sank the ship offers a different perspective entirely from that of the survivors. Read and compare the two accounts below.

PRIMARY SOURCE

A SURVIVOR'S STORY

Dwight Harris, a young New Yorker, was carrying an engagement ring when he boarded the *Lusitania,* planning to propose to his beloved in England. He also brought with him a custom-made life preserver he had bought the day before. Pacing anxiously on deck on the day of the attack, he saw the torpedo: "a white and greenish streak in the water!" Harris hurried to his room to locate his life preserver, failed to get into a lifeboat, and jumped overboard.

Floating in the sea, he witnessed the *Lusitania's* plunge toward the bottom. He later described, "A terrible mass of iron, wood, steam, and water! And worst of all, human forms!—A great swirling greenish white bubble formed where the ship went down, which was a mass of struggling humanity and wreckage!" The ring Harris carried survived the catastrophe and he later offered it to Aileen Cavendish Foster, whom he married on July 2, 1915.

This illustration of survivors fleeing in lifeboats from the sinking of the *Lusitania* appeared in an Italian weekly newspaper.

PRIMARY SOURCE

THE SUBMARINE CAPTAIN'S STORY

The submarine that sank the *Lusitania* was the U-20, under the command of Captain Walther Schwieger. The U-20 left Germany on April 30 with a mission to destroy shipping vessels destined for Liverpool, England. It was a successful cruise: by May 7, the submarine had already sunk three vessels off the coast of Ireland. That morning, Captain Schwieger decided to turn for home, since the U-20 was running low on both fuel and torpedoes. Then, at 1:20 p.m., an officer at the periscope spotted the distinctive shape of the *Lusitania.*

In his ship's log, Schwieger provided one of the clearest eyewitness accounts of the torpedo's aftermath. He recorded, "There was a terrific panic on her deck. Overcrowded lifeboats, fairly torn from their positions, dropped into the water. Desperate people ran helplessly up and down the decks. Men and women jumped into the water and tried to swim to empty, overturned lifeboats. It was the most terrible sight I have ever seen."

The "terrible sight" did not dampen Schwieger's enthusiasm for his job. On a single cruise in September 1915, he sank 11 ships, including the passenger ship *Hesperian*, which was carrying home the body of a Canadian passenger who had been killed on the *Lusitania.* By the time the war in Europe was over, German submarines had sunk more than 4,000 ships, around one-fourth of the world's shipping vessels.

AFTERMATH

During the hours and days immediately following the disaster, the main concern for family and friends of the victims was the frantic search for survivors—or for the bodies of those who had perished. Alfred Vanderbilt had last been seen helping others escape the wreckage. His body was never found. Dorothy Conner survived the sinking and went on to serve in France, supporting the troops. Charles Lauriat also survived, but his irreplaceable book and drawings were lost in the icy Irish Sea. When rescuers pulled Theodate Pope aboard their boat, they believed she was dead and left her on deck with the other bodies. Fortunately, another rescued passenger realized she was alive and called for help to revive her. Her companion, Edwin Friend, was among those who disappeared.

It is believed that 1,191 people died in the sinking of the *Lusitania*. Of those, 129 were Americans. Exact totals have remained elusive because of the difficulty in identifying stowaways and last-minute changes to crew and passenger lists. Naturally, the news of the sinking sparked shock and horror in the United States. In private, President Wilson expressed his fury to his secretary. "In God's name, how could any nation calling itself civilized purpose [plan] so horrible a thing?" he asked. In public, however, he made speeches counseling a restrained response to the German aggression.

Despite their anger, most Americans agreed with Wilson; they opposed the idea of the United States entering the war in Europe. Still, the sinking of the *Lusitania* can be seen as the first in a series of events that did finally engage the United States in the conflict that would engulf the world. By the time Wilson declared war in 1917, American public opinion had turned firmly against Germany.

THINK ABOUT IT

1. What factors likely contributed to the sinking of the *Lusitania*?
2. If the ship hadn't been sunk, do you think the United States would have been drawn into the war? Why or why not?

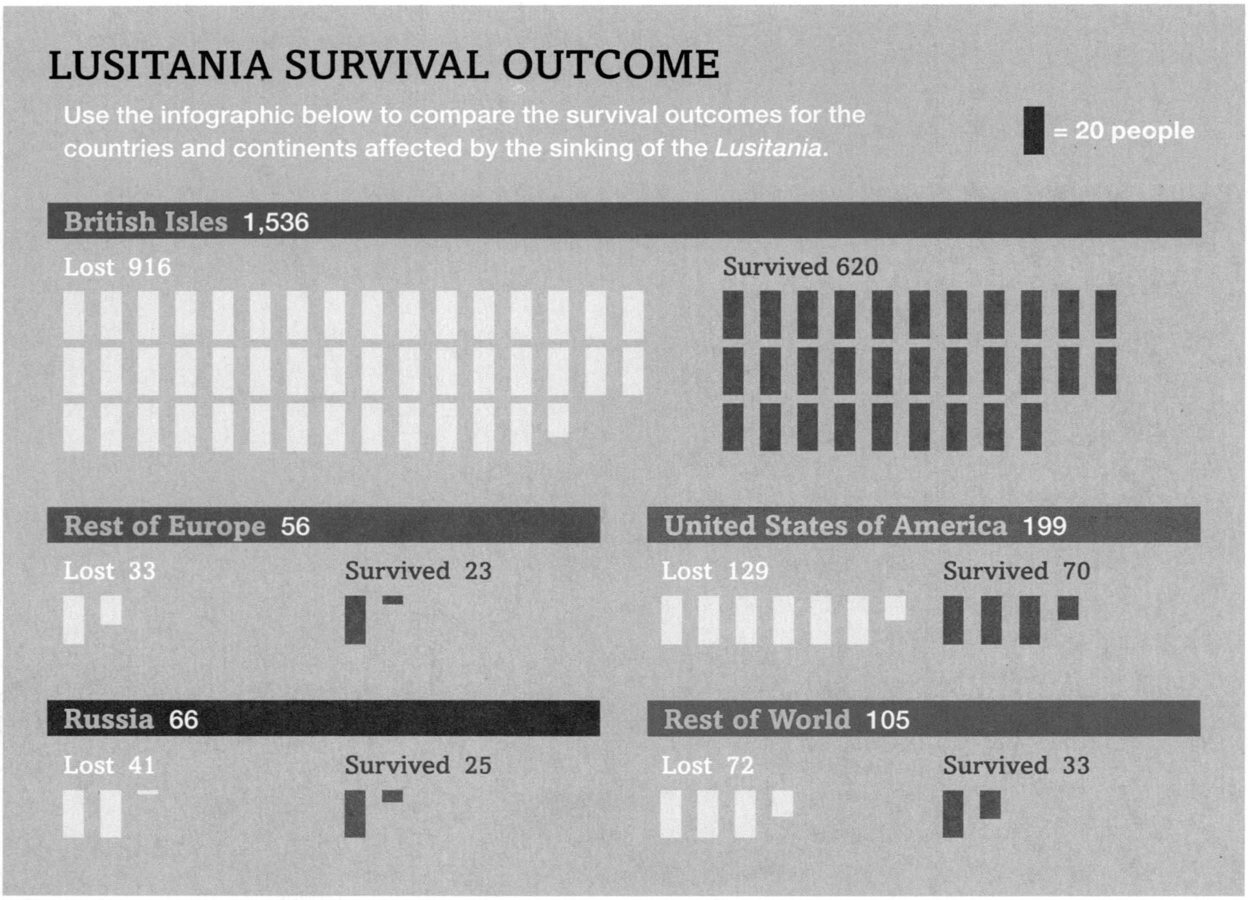

SOURCE: Merseyside Maritime Museum

HI 2 Students recognize the complexity of historical causes and effects, including the limitations on determining cause and effect.

The *Lusitania* was a well-constructed ship, designed to survive the flooding of one or two of its internal compartments. Why, then, did it sink almost instantly after just one torpedo strike? Many witnesses claimed that a second explosion followed the torpedo strike, and several theories have been used to explain this blast, but none have been proven.

Some have claimed that the *Lusitania* was secretly carrying explosives for Britain's military and that these were ignited by the torpedo strike. As you have read, the ship was in fact carrying rifle ammunition and other war supplies, but none of these materials would have caused a massive explosion.

National Geographic Explorer-in-Residence Robert Ballard explored the *Lusitania's* wreck in 1993 and proposed the theory that the ship's coal bunkers exploded. The coal bunkers were enormous compartments that stored the 5,690 tons of coal needed to fuel the engines. By the end of the long voyage, only highly combustible coal dust remained in those spaces, but the dust may have been too damp to explode.

During hearings after the sinking, the *Lusitania's* captain proposed that the torpedo could have ruptured the line that carried steam from the boiler rooms to power the propellers. Tests conducted by a National Geographic team in 2012 seem to support this explanation, but definitive proof remains elusive. The wreck of the *Lusitania* guards its secrets.

Says Robert Ballard of the *Lusitania* wreckage: "She is now a faint ghost of the ocean greyhound she once was, one of the saddest wrecks I've ever seen. But when I visualize her upturned bow, I can imagine the pride of those who once sailed on the swiftest ship in the world."

A small submersible called *Delta* took Ballard to the *Lusitania* for a firsthand look at the wreckage.

1.1 **MAIN IDEA** In 1914, Europe was overtaken by war when an assassination triggered a complex web of treaties and agreements among countries.

WAR BREAKS OUT IN EUROPE

Have you ever built a house of cards? Each card must be placed perfectly in order to support the delicate structure. Nudge just one card, and the whole building collapses. In 1914, Europe was a house of cards, just waiting for the nudge that would lead to fighting and chaos.

EUROPE AT THE EDGE OF WAR

In 1914, Europe was divided into hostile nations and poised for war. At the heart of the tension was lingering animosity between France and Germany in the wake of the Franco-Prussian War. In 1870, Germany had conquered France and then demanded $1 billion. Germany also seized the eastern French provinces of Alsace and Lorraine. For Germany, the acquisition of the provinces was the final step in unification. German leaders brought together several regions under the control of the kingdom of Prussia and declared a German Empire in 1871.

Frustrated by the military loss and determined to reclaim the lost provinces, the French worked to rebuild their economy and military. To further strengthen its position against Germany, France also formed **alliances**, or agreements of mutual support, with Russia and Great Britain. The German government had similar understandings with Austria-Hungary and the Ottoman Empire. Italy had been part of an earlier alliance with Germany and Austria-Hungary, but those ties had become frayed by 1914.

Because of these complex and delicate networks of treaties and alliances, an attack on one country could—and did—trigger retaliation by others and plunge all of Europe into a state of war. The conflict would come to be called "the Great War" because of the enormous number of casualties that resulted from it and the large number of nations involved in it. As war once again loomed in Europe in the 1930s, many historians began to refer to the conflict that began in 1914 as "World War I."

THE THREE *-ism's*

Alongside the alliances, three cultural attitudes helped push Europe down the path to conflict. **Nationalism** is a strong belief in one's own country and its superiority to others. In Europe, nationalism often conflicted with individuals' ethnic ties to a certain region or group of people.

Imperialism is the drive to conquer or colonize other territories and form an empire. Great Britain, Germany, and France were imperial powers, competing for colonies in Africa and Asia and the raw materials and markets that the colonies provided.

Militarism is the belief that a government must create a strong military and be prepared to use it to achieve the country's goals. By 1914, Germany was a major military power, and France was working to catch up. Britain did not have a strong military presence on the ground, but it did have a large and powerful navy and felt threatened by Germany's push to expand its own seagoing forces.

AN ASSASSINATION SPARKS WAR

On June 28, 1914, **Archduke Franz Ferdinand** of Austria-Hungary and his wife were **assassinated**, or murdered for political reasons, during a parade in the capital city of Bosnia. Their killer was a Serbian nationalist. Serbia was allied with Russia and had a history of conflict with Austria-Hungary.

One after another, European alliances were activated. The Austrians, supported by the Germans, made harsh demands of the Serbs to punish them for the assassination. Russia came to Serbia's defense, and France declared its support for its ally Russia.

CST 3 Students use a variety of maps and documents to interpret human movement, including major patterns of domestic and international migration, changing environmental preferences and settlement patterns, the frictions that develop between population groups, and the diffusion of ideas, technological innovations, and goods.

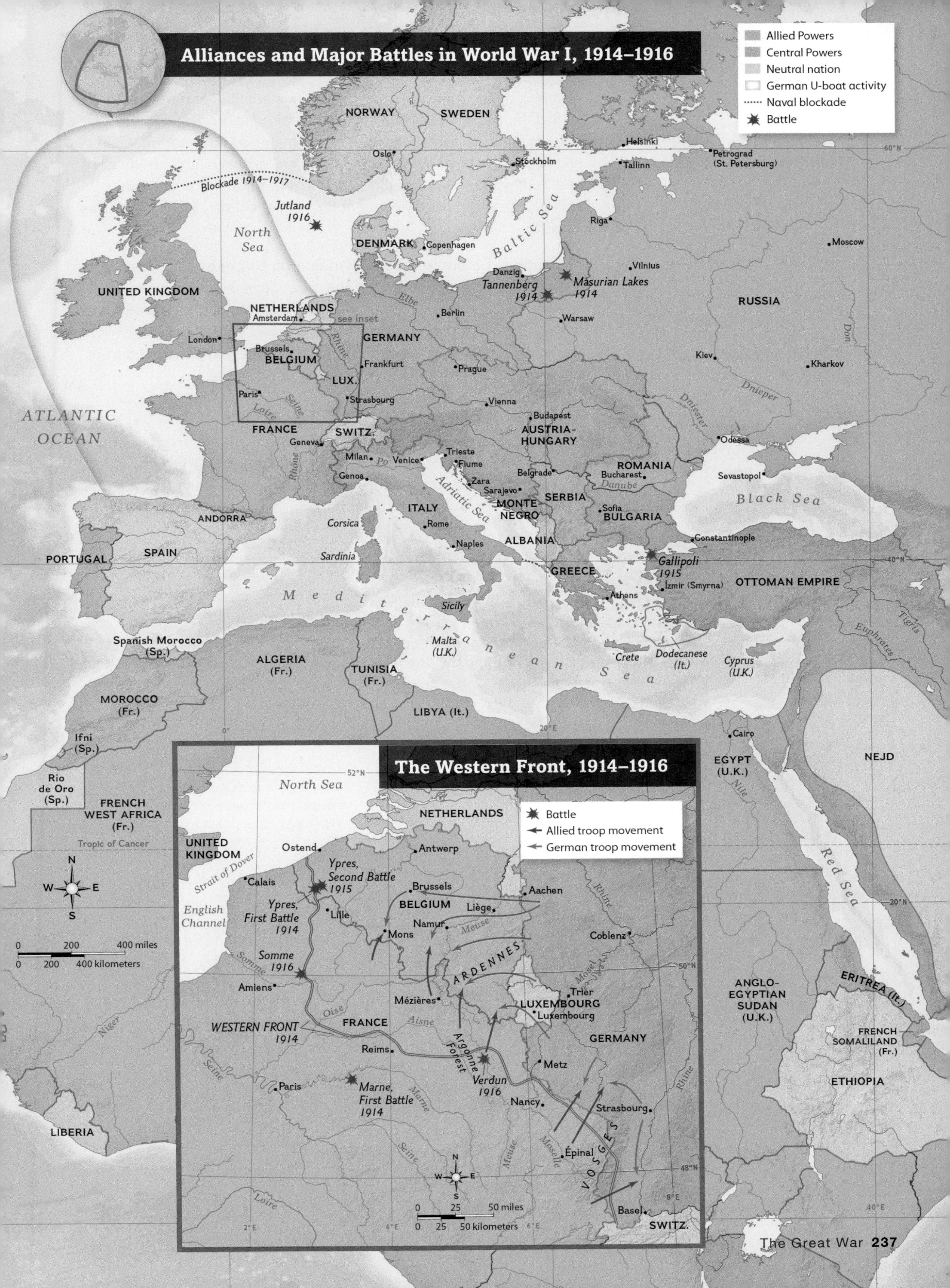
Alliances and Major Battles in World War I, 1914–1916
Allied Powers
Central Powers
Neutral nation
German U-boat activity
Naval blockade
Battle
NORWAY
SWEDEN
Oslo
Stockholm
Helsinki
Tallinn
Petrograd (St. Petersburg)
60°N
Blockade 1914–1917
Jutland 1916
North Sea
Baltic Sea
Riga
Moscow
DENMARK
Copenhagen
Danzig
Tannenberg 1914
Masurian Lakes 1914
Vilnius
UNITED KINGDOM
NETHERLANDS
Amsterdam
see inset
Elbe
Berlin
Warsaw
RUSSIA
Don
London
Brussels
BELGIUM
Rhine
GERMANY
Frankfurt
Prague
Kiev
Kharkov
LUX.
Paris
Seine
Loire
Strasbourg
Vienna
Dnieper
Dniester
ATLANTIC OCEAN
FRANCE
SWITZ.
Budapest
AUSTRIA-HUNGARY
Geneva
Odessa
Trieste
Fiume
Milan
Po
Venice
Rhône
Genoa
Zara
Belgrade
ROMANIA
Bucharest
Danube
Sevastopol
Adriatic Sea
Sarajevo
SERBIA
MONTE-NEGRO
Black Sea
ITALY
Sofia
BULGARIA
ANDORRA
Corsica
Rome
Naples
ALBANIA
Constantinople
PORTUGAL
SPAIN
Sardinia
Gallipoli 1915
40°N
GREECE
İzmir (Smyrna)
OTTOMAN EMPIRE
Mediterranean Sea
Athens
Sicily
Tigris
Euphrates
Spanish Morocco (Sp.)
Malta (U.K.)
Crete
Dodecanese (It.)
Cyprus (U.K.)
ALGERIA (Fr.)
TUNISIA (Fr.)
MOROCCO (Fr.)
LIBYA (It.)
0°
20°E
Ifni (Sp.)
Cairo
Rio de Oro (Sp.)
EGYPT (U.K.)
NEJD
Nile
FRENCH WEST AFRICA (Fr.)
Tropic of Cancer
Red Sea
20°N
N
W
E
S
0 200 400 miles
0 200 400 kilometers
Niger
ANGLO-EGYPTIAN SUDAN (U.K.)
ERITREA (It.)
FRENCH SOMALILAND (Fr.)
ETHIOPIA
LIBERIA
40°E
The Western Front, 1914–1916
52°N
North Sea
NETHERLANDS
Battle
Allied troop movement
German troop movement
UNITED KINGDOM
Ostend
Antwerp
Strait of Dover
Ypres, Second Battle 1915
Calais
Brussels
Aachen
Ypres, First Battle 1914
BELGIUM
Liège
English Channel
Lille
Namur
Meuse
Mons
Coblenz
Rhine
Somme 1916
Somme
ARDENNES
50°N
Amiens
Mosel
Trier
Mézières
LUXEMBOURG
Luxembourg
Oise
FRANCE
Aisne
WESTERN FRONT 1914
Argonne Forest
GERMANY
Reims
Metz
Seine
Verdun 1916
Paris
Marne, First Battle 1914
Marne
Nancy
Rhine
Strasbourg
VOSGES
Épinal
Moselle
Meuse
N
W
E
S
48°N
Loire
0 25 50 miles
0 25 50 kilometers
8°E
Basel
SWITZ.
2°E
4°E
6°E

> **PRIMARY SOURCE**
>
> *We entered the trenches about midnight, we found them very uncomfortable, as there was only one dug-out for our company. . . . I spent six hours making myself a shelter in a communication trench, a sort of sofa with a waterproof sheet above it, cut out of one side of a five-foot trench. I worked most of the night throwing earth up to shield my bed, as the Germans were sniping at our parapet all day long. Meals were wretched, as we had nowhere decent to eat them, and we also lost our principal ration bag, containing tinned fruits and other joys.*
>
> —from the personal account of British Lieutenant William Andrew Turnbull, regarding the trenches near Hooge, France, 1915

In early August, Germany declared war on both Russia and France, invading Belgium in a push to reach France's northern border.

Alarmed by the actions of belligerent, militaristic Germany, which lay just across the English Channel, Britain declared war on the country. Within months, Europe was consumed by a war between two alliances: the **Central Powers** (primarily Germany, Austria-Hungary, and Turkey) and the **Allies** (primarily Great Britain, France, and Russia). Italy remained neutral at first but eventually joined the Allies in 1915.

The sudden outbreak of fighting in Europe surprised Americans. Although the arms race among the great powers had seemed potentially dangerous, it had been a century since a war involving all of the major European countries had erupted. Additionally, American faith in progress and the betterment of humanity, a principal part of the Progressive Era's creed, made war unthinkable.

TRENCH WARFARE ON TWO FRONTS

For years before the events of 1914, Germany had been preparing to wage war on France and Russia. **The Schlieffen Plan**, devised by a German army officer and completed in 1906, called for a rapid conquest of France, so that German troops could then turn east and

IN THE TRENCHES

The Great War is known for its trench warfare. Troops fighting for the Allies and Central Powers dug trenches fairly close to each other to attack and defend from below ground level. Trench warfare is typically used when the troops defending themselves from an attack have superior firepower, forcing the opposition to give up their mobility by digging trenches for protection.

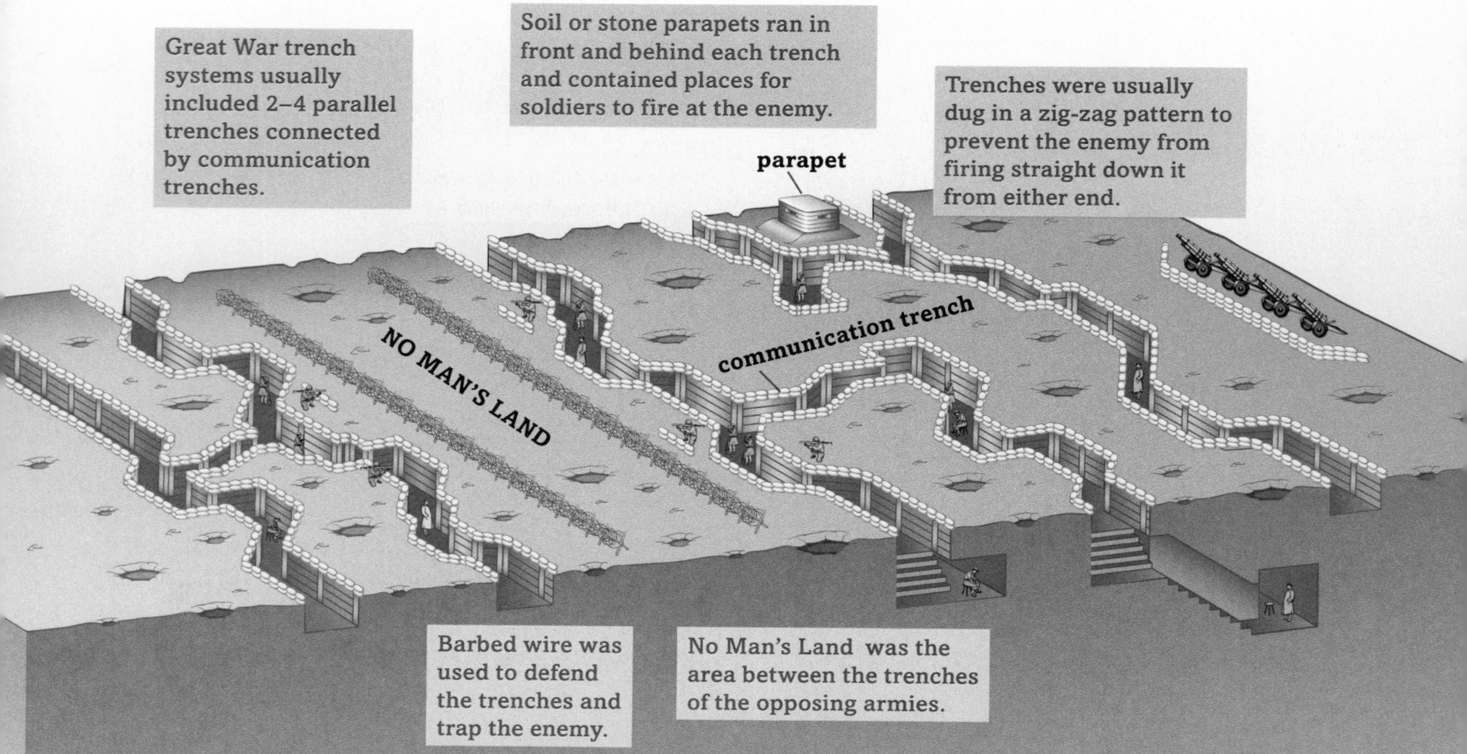

CRITICAL VIEWING This colorful 1917 postcard features the flags of the Allies in the Great War. From left: Portugal, Serbia, Belgium, Italy, France, Great Britain, the United States, Romania, Russia, and Japan. What might have been the goal behind the creation of artwork like this during the Great War?

march on Russia. This strategy failed, however, when the British Army joined France in stalling the advance of the German Army before it reached Paris. By the end of 1914, Germany found itself fighting enemies on two **fronts**, or battle lines. On the Western Front in northern France, German troops battled French and British forces; on the Eastern Front, Germany faced off with Russia.

On both fronts, a type of fighting called **trench warfare** prevailed. To shelter from enemy artillery fire, troops would dig complex networks of trenches into the ground, often starting with simple foxholes that could hold one or two soldiers. The holes were then deepened and connected by shallow crawling trenches. From there, the trenches were excavated further underground to strengthen them, and lined with boards to ease movement along the passageways. The boards also helped troops avoid potential diseases caused by mud and dirty water.

Fighting between the trenches took a brutal toll on all sides. One army might take an enemy trench at the cost of thousands of lives, only to lose it again within a matter of weeks. In one battle along the Somme River in France, more than a million soldiers were killed or wounded in order for the Allies to advance a meager six miles. The space between enemy trenches, called "No Man's Land," had an average width of 150 to 250 yards, but the distance could vary from just a few yards to miles across. Once productive farm fields or lush open meadows, No Man's Land quickly turned into a nightmarish dead landscape filled with rubble, bomb craters, and the bodies of soldiers killed by artillery or machine-gun fire. Sometimes wounded soldiers suffered for days there before they died.

HISTORICAL THINKING

1. **READING CHECK** Why was trench warfare so costly in human lives?
2. **ANALYZE CAUSE AND EFFECT** How did the conclusion of the Franco-Prussian war lead to hostilities between Germany, France, and Britain?
3. **MAKE GENERALIZATIONS** How do militarism and nationalism affect a country's attitude toward going to war?
4. **MAKE INFERENCES** Based on the diagram of trench warfare and what you have read in the chapter, what can you infer about the effectiveness of this type of fighting?

HI 1 Students show the connections, causal and otherwise, between particular historical events and larger social, economic, and political trends and developments.

1.2 **MAIN IDEA** When war broke out in Europe, President Wilson declared that the United States would not take sides, and most Americans supported this decision.

WILSON'S NEUTRALITY

In 1914, Americans were eagerly following the baseball pennant race between the New York Giants and the Boston Braves and flocking to the movies to escape into the world of silent films. The guns of war in Europe seemed like distant and muffled thunder.

WILSON'S MORAL DIPLOMACY

In 1914, when the war began in Europe, the United States began to supply the Allies with weapons and goods. However, President Woodrow Wilson firmly declared the country would follow a policy of **neutrality**, or refusal to support either side in the war. He asked his fellow citizens to "be neutral in fact as well as in name" and "impartial in thought as well as in action." Elected president in 1912, Wilson had wanted to concentrate on a domestic policy of economic reform. In 1913, he remarked to a friend, "it would be the irony of fate if my administration had to deal chiefly with foreign affairs." When confronted with the question of whether to support one of the warring sides in Europe, Wilson left no doubt of his opinion. "Our whole duty for the present . . . is summed up in the motto America First," he said. "Let us think of America before we think of Europe."

In fact, however, Wilson did actively pursue matters of foreign policy even before being confronted with the war in Europe. Wilson believed in a concept called **moral diplomacy**, which required that the

Woodrow Wilson, shown here giving a speech after his 1912 nomination for president of the United States, had been elected New Jersey's governor in 1910 and was elected U.S. president just two years later.

11.4.4 Explain Theodore Roosevelt's Big Stick diplomacy, William Taft's Dollar Diplomacy, and Woodrow Wilson's Moral Diplomacy, drawing on relevant speeches; 11.4.5 Analyze the political, economic, and social ramifications of World War I on the home front; HI 3 Students interpret past events and issues within the context in which an event unfolded rather than solely in terms of present-day norms and values.

United States drastically reduce its intervention in the affairs of other countries. Wilson felt that the role of the United States should be to act as an example of democracy and to support the efforts of other peoples to elect their own governments. Wilson contrasted his philosophy to the "dollar diplomacy" practiced by his predecessor. Dollar diplomacy was a theory used to justify U.S. interference with the governments of countries in which American companies stood to make a profit. Pursuing the ideal of moral diplomacy, Wilson tried to lessen U.S. involvement in the Philippines and Latin America.

AMERICAN PUBLIC OPINION

Most Americans were solidly in agreement with Wilson's stance on the war in Europe. Still, many expressed sympathy for one or more of the countries embroiled in the fighting. The United States was home to more than five million German Americans, who tended to favor the Central Powers. The three million-plus Irish Americans strongly resented England and cheered for its enemies. Russia, with its authoritarian government, was generally regarded with suspicion. On the other hand, many Americans felt a kinship with Britain and France, which were both democracies and had a great deal of shared history with the United States.

Germany initiated an extensive propaganda campaign to sway American public opinion in its favor. The campaign was conducted principally through pamphlets and newspaper advertisements. At the same time, the German government used **espionage**, or spying, and sabotage to harm the Allied war effort by preventing American goods from being shipped to Britain. German agents would find ways to destroy the goods in the United States before they could be loaded onto ships, costing American businesses a great deal of money and sometimes injuring or killing civilians. When instances of sabotage were eventually discovered, they helped turn American public opinion against Germany.

American public opinion of the Central Powers was further soured by stories appearing in the *New York Times* in December 1915, reporting the killing or forced deportation of millions of Armenian civilians by the Turkish government. This campaign by the Turks became known as the **Armenian genocide**.

ECONOMIC TIES

While Americans were divided in their emotional loyalties to the European powers, the U.S. government had close economic ties to the Allies. In 1914, exports to Britain and France totaled $754 million. In contrast, that same year Germany received $190 million worth of imported products from the United States. As the war continued, the economic difference widened. In 1916, exports from the United States to Britain and France stood at $2.75 billion, while trade with Germany had dwindled to practically nothing because the British Navy was blockading German ports.

The United States had other growing financial ties to the Allies. In order to pay for American goods used in their war efforts, the Allies borrowed billions of dollars from the U.S. government, as well as from American banks and investors. Thus, a victory for the Allies would benefit many American investors.

This political cartoon draws attention to the U.S. government's conflicting attitude toward the war. It portrays Uncle Sam advertising peace on the front of his two-sided "sandwich board" and promoting the sale of ammunition to warring countries on the back.

HISTORICAL THINKING

1. **READING CHECK** Why did some Americans favor the Central Powers while others favored the Allies?
2. **COMPARE AND CONTRAST** What are the differences in the principles behind moral diplomacy and dollar diplomacy?
3. **MAKE INFERENCES** Why might a military defeat for the Allies cause a loss to American investors?

2.1 **MAIN IDEA** Germany's aggressive actions posed an increasing threat to American lives and business, leading the United States to declare war with Germany in 1917.

PRESSURES TO ENTER THE WAR

In 1914, the war in Europe seemed remote. Its violence was taking place on the far side of the ocean and was hardly relevant to life in the United States. By 1917, the war was on America's doorstep, and American blood had been shed.

GERMAN ATTACKS AT SEA

Since colonial times, the U.S. government had generally followed a policy of isolationism by declining to become involved in politics or wars in Europe. Even though certain groups within the United States sympathized with either the Allies or the Central Powers, the American public as a whole saw no reason to depart from the centuries-old policy. Even so, two strong forces were slowly pushing the United States toward engagement in the war: the economic ties with Britain and France that have already been discussed and the risk posed to American lives by the fighting.

This 1916 campaign button reflected Wilson's isolationist platform.

American civilians were mainly at risk when they were at sea. Germany was confronted with a British naval blockade that prevented imported goods such as food and ammunition from reaching German ports. In 1914, the German Navy turned to a new weapon to combat the blockade: submarines, also called **U-boats** (short for *unterseeboot*, the German word for "submarine"). German submarines targeted not only enemy warships but also merchant ships that might be carrying war-related supplies from the United States to British or French ports. Even trans-Atlantic passenger ships, which often carried U.S. citizens, were not safe from the U-boats, since they were often suspected of also carrying cargo destined for the Allied war effort.

As you have read, on May 1, 1915, the passenger ship *Lusitania* left New York harbor for Liverpool, England. The *Lusitania* was huge, luxurious, and the fastest ship afloat. Its legendary speed offered no protection, however, when a German submarine encountered the ship in the Irish Sea on May 7 and sank it with a torpedo. Wilson and the nation were angered by the deaths of 129 Americans aboard the ship. The president demanded an apology from the German government, as well as a pledge to limit submarine warfare. Eventually, Germany agreed to stop attacking civilian ships without warning.

GERMAN U-BOAT

The German U-boat was less than 150 feet long and only 12 feet in diameter. The crew of 35 were packed into a tiny space no bigger than a double-decker bus.

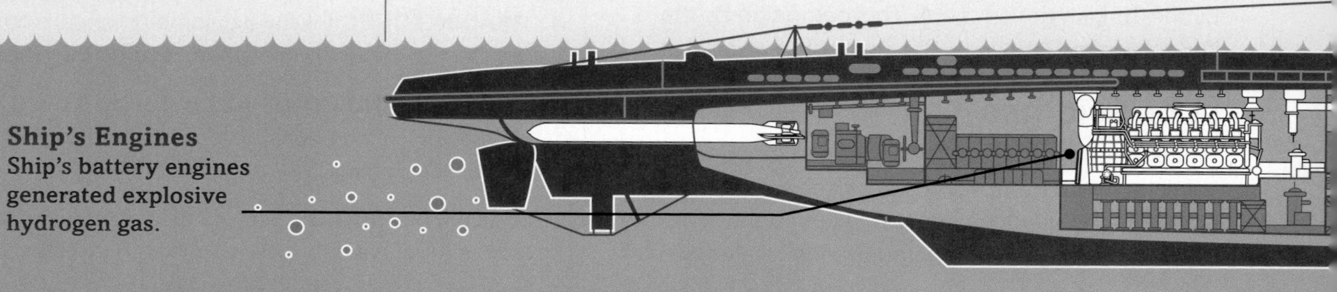

11.4.5 Analyze the political, economic, and social ramifications of World War I on the home front.

GERMANY BREAKS ITS PROMISE

Despite the sinking of the *Lusitania* and the deaths of American citizens in other submarine attacks, Wilson refused to join the war. In the 1916 election, he ran on a platform of prosperity, progressivism, and peace. He won re-election after a campaign that featured the slogan "He kept us out of the war." Wilson then proposed ending the war through negotiation, but both Britain and Germany rejected his offer to broker a peace treaty. In response, Wilson addressed the Senate in January 1917 with a speech that called for a "Peace Without Victory" in which he argued that "only a peace among equals can last." The warring powers remained unwilling to cooperate, convinced that the only place to find a solution was the battlefield.

By 1917, the British naval blockade was successfully starving Germany of much-needed war supplies. On land, the Central Powers' armies were bogged down in the trenches and making no progress in either the east or the west. Becoming desperate, Germany decided to resume unrestricted submarine attacks to choke off the stream of supplies arriving in Great Britain by sea. The German military commanders knew this move would enrage Wilson and the American public, but they gambled that all-out submarine warfare would bring down the Allies before the United States could declare war and send troops to Europe.

THE ZIMMERMANN TELEGRAM

At the same time, another incident helped propel the country toward war. British intelligence had intercepted and decoded a secret telegram from the German foreign minister, Arthur Zimmermann, to Germany's ambassador in Mexico. The **Zimmermann Telegram** laid out a plan to ally with Mexico and offer financial aid to the country if it attacked the United States. The telegram promised that Arizona, Texas, and New Mexico would be returned to Mexico as part of this deal. Wilson released this diplomatic bombshell to the public on March 1, 1917.

PRIMARY SOURCE

The world must be made safe for democracy. Its peace must be planted upon the tested foundations of political liberty. We have no selfish ends to serve. We desire no conquest, no dominion [control over another country]. We seek no indemnities [promises to pay for any damages] for ourselves, no material compensation for the sacrifices we shall freely make. We are but one of the champions of the rights of mankind. We shall be satisfied when those rights have been made as secure as the faith and the freedom of nations can make them.

—from President Woodrow Wilson's Joint Address to Congress Leading to a Declaration of War Against Germany, April 2, 1917

From that point, events moved quickly to bring the United States to war. On March 18, the Germans sank three American ships. On April 2, Wilson called Congress to a special session and asked for a **declaration of war** against Germany. He pledged to fight for "the ultimate peace of the world and for the liberation of its peoples, the German peoples included." In many ways, Wilson's war declaration was also an effort to continue promoting America's vision for the world. Congress agreed and declared war on Germany on April 6, 1917.

HISTORICAL THINKING

1. **READING CHECK** What events led President Wilson to ask Congress to formally declare war on Germany?
2. **IDENTIFY PROBLEMS AND SOLUTIONS** Why did Germany choose to launch unrestricted submarine warfare in 1917?
3. **EVALUATE** For Germany, what were the advantages and disadvantages of submarine warfare?

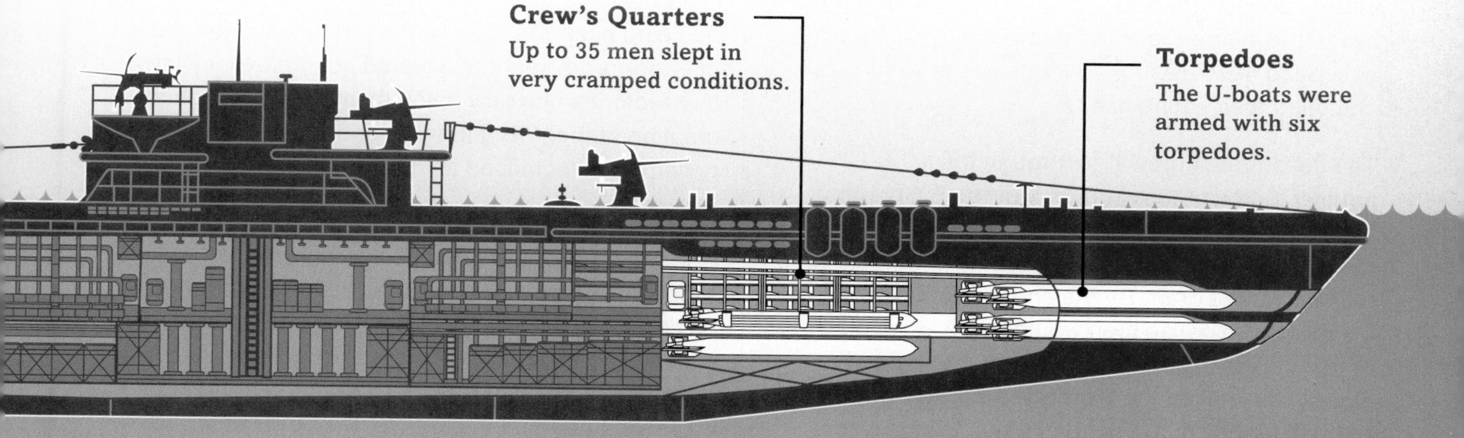

HI 3 Students interpret past events and issues within the context in which an event unfolded rather than solely in terms of present-day norms and values.

2.2 **MAIN IDEA** As the United States prepared for war, the government acted to increase the production of war goods, recruit soldiers and sailors, and gain Americans' support, but efforts to raise morale also eroded important liberties.

America Enters the War

On every public surface, colorful posters encouraged young men to join the armed forces. Factories converted their assembly lines to make uniforms instead of children's clothes. Americans were asked to have a "meatless" and a "wheatless" day each week so that more food could be sent to Europe. The United States was going to war, and life was changing for everyone.

BUILDING A MILITARY—AND FAST

By 1917, both Germany and the Allies were battle weary, and the number of casualties on both sides was staggering. On the Western Front, where the Allies and the Germans confronted each other in France, more than 1.4 million French soldiers had been killed or wounded in 1915 alone. In a single battle at the French town of Verdun in 1916, both sides lost more than 300,000 men. Gigantic battles also occurred on the Eastern Front between the Russians and the Germans and their Austrian allies.

Although American entry into the Great War came later than the Allies had hoped, they greatly welcomed the help. Unfortunately, in 1917, the United States was in a poor position to supply desperately needed soldiers to the Allies; together, the regular U.S. Army and National Guard numbered only 379,000 troops. The power of the federal government began to increase in response to the need to mobilize people for war. In fact, the war initiated a century-long growth of the federal government. Average citizens found they had to respond to government programs in strange and unfamiliar ways, including accepting new rules for their businesses and changing their eating habits.

The government grew first through the administration of the draft. In May 1917, Congress adopted the **Selective Service Act**, which required all men between the ages of 21 and 30 to register for the draft. By the end of World War I, 3.7 million American men would serve as soldiers or sailors. The corps of soldiers sent to fight in Europe was called the **American Expeditionary Forces (AEF)**. At the head of these troops was General **John J. Pershing**, an experienced military leader who had commanded troops in Cuba, Mexico, and the American West.

THE WARTIME ECONOMY

As the United States entered into the most extensive conflict it had ever faced in terms of dollars, American businesses were also caught unprepared for war. The war effort would require the manufacturing of ships, airplanes, guns, and ammunition, but after a decades-long peacetime economy, American factories were accustomed to producing items like cars, bicycles, and kitchen stoves. They too would need to be readied for war.

To help solve this problem, the government undertook the organization of the war at home. Wilson began by establishing the **War Industries Board (WIB)**. The WIB oversaw manufacturing in the United States, finding ways to make factories more efficient as they converted to wartime production. Some labor unions threw their support behind the war effort and the WIB. In exchange for a voice in deciding economic policy, the American Federation of Labor promised that it would not strike or insist that factories hire only union members. Through the creation of the WIB and other agencies, the federal government increased its role in the U.S. economy.

Outside of the workplace, the government also promoted civilian support for the war. All Americans were asked to support the war effort by buying **Liberty Bonds**. Purchasing a bond was, in essence, loaning money to the U.S. government. The government would repay the cost of the bond after 30 years, and in the meantime, the buyer received

11.4.5 Analyze the political, economic, and social ramifications of World War I on the home front.

CRITICAL VIEWING During the war, women were recruited into jobs vacated by men who had gone off to fight. New factory jobs, especially in munitions factories like the ones shown above, were also created as part of the war effort and became the largest employers of women in 1918. How might the work women did during the war have related to their quest for suffrage?

annual interest at a rate of 3.5 percent. Those who failed to buy war bonds were deemed unpatriotic and said to be helping the Germans. Ultimately, the total cost of the war to the United States exceeded $35 billion. The United States had loaned over $11.2 billion to the Allies, most of which was never repaid. Yet President Wilson counted on the Allies' financial dependence on the United States to leverage achieving the goals he had for postwar diplomacy.

WARTIME FOOD

In addition to financial support, the Allies needed food. To mobilize the agricultural resources of the United States, Congress passed the Lever Act, which established the Food Administration. Wilson named **Herbert Hoover** to head the agency. A mining engineer from California, Hoover had gained international fame through his work to feed the starving people of Belgium. He asked Americans to observe days without meat and wheat because "wheatless days in America make sleepless nights in Germany." Additionally, families planted "victory gardens" to grow fruits and vegetables. With the price of wheat rising higher, farmers were induced to expand their production, increasing the wheat crop from 637 million bushels in 1917 to 921 million bushels a year later.

PRIMARY SOURCE

Internationally, the Great War led to many important advances for women, including increased support for women's suffrage in the United States.

If the women in the factories stopped work for twenty minutes, the Allies would lose the war.

—Joseph Joffre, French Field Marshall, 1916–1918

What does this quote reveal about the global perspective on the role women played in the Great War?

HI 3 Students interpret past events and issues within the context in which an event unfolded rather than solely in terms of present-day norms and values.

DISSENT AND CIVIL LIBERTIES

Americans on the home front had mixed reactions to the war. Some were vocal in expressing their **dissent**, or disagreement, with the government's official opinion. Many men proclaimed themselves **conscientious objectors**—people who refuse to fight in a war for religious reasons—while others simply failed to register for the draft. Opposition to the war was especially prevalent among German Americans and Irish Americans.

To counter possible dissent and raise the country's enthusiasm for the war, the government established the **Committee on Public Information (CPI)**, which launched a massive campaign of advertising and propaganda. George Creel, the head of the committee, declared that its task was to create a spirit of "[brotherhood], devotion, courage, and deathless determination." The CPI used pamphlets, posters, billboards, movies, and dynamic public speakers to spread its message. This was no easy task for Creel, who called it "the world's greatest adventure in advertising."

The campaign stirred up strong feelings of patriotism but also hostility toward everything German. Hamburgers, named after the German town of Hamburg, came to be called "Salisbury steak" or "liberty steak." Sauerkraut was renamed "liberty cabbage," and the people in some cities gave up pretzels. German literature vanished from library shelves, and schools stopped teaching the German language. More alarming, German Americans experienced prejudice and extreme nativism, or a policy that favors the interests of native inhabitants over those of immigrants, and became the targets of suspicion, threats, and even violence.

The government had legitimate reasons to be concerned about German espionage, but the measures taken to combat it during the war were excessive. The government began a campaign against radicals and progressives, a position that Wilson had opposed during his run for re-election in 1916. This reversal of policy undermined public support for the president in domestic politics. In his eagerness to win the war, Wilson alienated part of his own political base.

ENSURING PATRIOTIC BEHAVIOR

The Wilson administration and Congress enacted a number of laws designed to place limits on the rights of Americans to criticize the government or the war effort. National Security concerns led to the passage and enforcement of the Espionage Act of 1917. The act was designed to prevent sabotage and spying, but simply speaking out against the war could be considered illegal. The Trading with the Enemy Act authorized the postmaster general to suspend the delivery of foreign-language publications or any material he believed might be offensive to the government.

The Sedition Act of 1918 prohibited "uttering, printing, writing, or publishing any disloyal, profane, scurrilous [slanderous], or abusive language" about either the government or the armed forces. Thus, nearly any public criticism could be deemed punishable by law in an attempt to prevent **sedition**, the criminal act of trying to persuade individuals to undermine the government. These acts severely encroached on Americans' **civil liberties**—the right to engage in legal activities such as free expression without being hindered by the government. People were even jailed for making negative comments about Woodrow Wilson or calling the conflict a "rich man's war."

ARE YOU A SLACKER?

Nobody likes to be called a slacker, but nowadays acting like one will only get you in trouble with a teacher, parent, or boss. In 1917 and 1918, the term "slacker" referred to a man who failed to register for the draft or declare a conscientious objection. At first, the government tried using publicity to shame slackers into registering. Then, in 1918, the Justice Department took more serious steps. Agents began raiding restaurants and ballparks or just approaching groups on street corners. Any man who could not show draft registration papers was promptly arrested and taken to jail.

HISTORICAL THINKING

1. **READING CHECK** What steps did the U.S. government take to prepare for war?
2. **ANALYZE CAUSE AND EFFECT** How did entering the war affect the organization of the economy of the United States?
3. **DRAW CONCLUSIONS** How did the government's actions both unite and divide Americans?
4. **INTERPRET VISUALS** Select one of the propaganda posters (right) and consider its purpose. Who was its intended audience and what techniques were used to make the poster effective?

HI 1 Students show the connections, causal and otherwise, between particular historical events and larger social, economic, and political trends and developments; HREP2 Students identify bias and prejudice in historical interpretations.

National World War I Museum and Memorial Kansas City, Missouri

The National World War I Museum in Kansas City, Missouri, is positioned beneath the Liberty Memorial, a 217-foot granite monument to the veterans of World War I. The museum opened in 2006 to national acclaim and was recognized by Congress in 2014 as the National World War I Museum and Memorial. More than one million people have visited the museum, including presidents and American veterans like Frank Buckles, the country's last surviving Great War veteran.

The museum houses a vast collection of World War I-era propaganda posters, including those pictured here. Their high-interest, colorful graphics and thought-provoking messages called Americans to action and attempted to inspire great patriotism.

Shortly after the start of the war, the poster was recognized as an effective way to distribute national propaganda to a wide audience cheaply, vividly, and quickly. In almost every country involved in the war, posters like these played a significant role in spreading patriotism.

This poster features Uncle Sam and Germany's ruler, Kaiser, or emperor, Wilhelm II.

Posters encouraged people to plant victory gardens at home to provide food for soldiers.

Prominent studios produced short propaganda films to foster pro-war public sentiments.

3.1 **MAIN IDEA** Millions of American soldiers arrived in Europe and engaged in fighting made more deadly than ever before by advanced weapons technology and unsanitary conditions in the trenches.

A Brutal War

The trainee pilots were young and hopeful. They were eager to engage in daring aerial duels against the Germans, just like the glamorous Allied flying aces they idolized. Within weeks of their arrival in Europe, at least half of these young flyers died in action.

LETHAL TECHNOLOGY

When they arrived in France, American troops entered a war unlike any fought before. New technologies, as well as improvements to existing military machines, led to enormous numbers of casualties in every battle. **Machine guns**, for example, had existed since the late 1800s, but they were refined and improved over the course of World War I. Mounted atop trenches and able to fire hundreds of bullets per minute, machine guns could mow down attacking soldiers much more efficiently than single-shot rifles.

To counter the machine gun, the British invented the **tank**, an armored, heavily armed vehicle that used treads instead of wheels. Tanks could cross No Man's Land in the face of intense machine-gun fire and plow directly into enemy trenches. By the end of the war, both sides were using tanks to assault enemy lines.

This rotary engine came from the red Fokker Dr.1 Triplane of German ace pilot, the Red Baron.

For the first time ever, war also took to the skies. Only 11 years after the Wright brothers' first flight, airplanes were transformed into fighting machines and deployed over the battlefield. Pilots used cameras to take photos of enemy troop movements on the ground. German and Allied pilots engaged in one-on-one battles in the air, guiding their planes through acrobatic maneuvers high above the ground. At first, the pilots shot at each other with pistols, but eventually guns were installed on the planes themselves.

Being a pilot was extremely dangerous. On average, a new pilot survived three to six weeks in combat conditions. The most famous flyer on the Allied side was American ace fighter pilot, Eddie Rickenbacker, who was credited with shooting down 26 enemy planes. His impressive attack on 7 German aircraft in September 1918 earned him the U.S. Medal of Honor. On the opposing side, German Manfred von Richtofen, known as the Red Baron, was considered the ace of aces and credited with shooting down 80 Allied planes.

Nowhere near as nimble as airplanes, but also useful, were airships—also called dirigibles—whose cockpits were held aloft by gigantic rigid balloons filled with lighter-than-air gas. Airships could conduct aerial surveillance of enemy troop movements. Countering both planes and airships was the **antiaircraft gun**, a piece of heavy artillery modified so that it could be pointed skyward.

At sea, the Allies used a new strategy to end the threat of German submarines to Allied shipping. Convoys of destroyers and other warships—whose torpedoes, guns, and depth charges (bombs designed to explode under water) could easily sink a German submarine—surrounded and protected vulnerable merchant ships as they crossed the Atlantic. Escorted across the Atlantic by destroyers and other patrol vessels, these otherwise defenseless merchant vessels could move safely in groups.

WARBIRDS OF WORLD WAR I

The first aircraft used in World War I were extremely basic. Vulnerable pilots sat in open cockpits using unsophisticated and sometimes nonfunctional instruments. Navigation devices didn't exist, so they relied on paper maps and glimpses of the railway signs down below them. Sometimes lost pilots even landed in fields and asked directions! But air technology advanced throughout the war, and increasingly effective aircraft replaced the simple machines that took to the skies in 1914, transforming the airplane into a war machine.

BRITISH SOPWITH CAMEL BIPLANE
This plane's unusual name came from the slight hump in front of the cockpit. It shot down more German aircraft than any other Allied plane using twin machine guns that easily destroyed its flimsy opponents.

NIEUPORT 28
War hero Eddie Rickenbacker and many other American pilots flew these biplanes, which had a distinctive pair of machine guns mounted on their left sides.

SPAD XIII
Known as one of the most successful fighter planes of the Great War, this plane was widely used by French, American, and other Allied squadrons. Nearly 8,500 of them were produced.

FOKKER D VII
This popular German biplane was one of the best World War I fighters and was considered easy to fly, highly maneuverable, and safe. The Red Baron endorsed it wholeheartedly.

NORTH SEA 6 AIRSHIP
Along with the NS7, this airship became one of the more famous North Sea Class airships of the Great War. It could fly for 30 hours or more, escorting convoys and hunting for submarines.

AMERICANS ON THE WESTERN FRONT

In 1917, the situation for Britain and France took a dangerous turn when a revolution overturned the monarchy in Russia. The country's new government pulled out of the war, which freed the German troops from the Eastern Front to go fight in the west. At the same time, few American troops had arrived to reinforce the Western Front.

But in 1918, millions of American soldiers poured into France to turn the tide against Germany and eventually helped bring an end to the war. In contrast to the Allied troops, who were exhausted after years of brutal fighting, the Americans were fresh and well fed. In May 1918, one million American troops helped stop the German advance at the town of Cantigny.

Many members of minority groups who experienced discrimination at home served with distinction on the battlefields of Europe. A number of Asian Americans chose to serve in the armed forces and received U.S. citizenship as a result. Many Hispanic Americans from Texas and New Mexico also fought, although some refused to register for the draft to protest the discrimination they faced in everyday life. African-American leaders debated the merits of serving in the armed forces of a country that did not grant them equal rights. Still, thousands of black men did serve in segregated army units in Europe. With the exception of three exclusive fighting divisions, most African Americans were assigned behind-the-scenes duties instead of combat roles with white soldiers. But their wartime experience broadened the soldiers' views. Young men serving abroad found European ideas about race and sexuality very liberating.

The National Portrait Gallery, Washington, D.C.

W.E.B. Du Bois (doo-BOYS) was an African-American historian and author and is pictured here in artist Winold Reiss's 1925 drawing. In 1909, Du Bois helped found the National Association for the Advancement of Colored People (NAACP), which fought for equal rights for African Americans. He supported the war effort but believed the patriotism and heroism of African-American soldiers was not appropriately acknowledged or rewarded.

HAZARDS FOR SOLDIERS

Charging into a barrage of machine-gun fire wasn't the only danger to soldiers fighting in the trenches. Poison gas was first used by the Germans in 1915, but eventually both sides employed this fearsome weapon. Tossed into enemy trenches, the gas caused agonizing pain and killed soldiers by suffocation. After the Great War, most countries banned the use of poison gas. In addition, exposure to intense bombardment while in the trenches sent some soldiers home with physical injuries and others with a new syndrome known as "shell shock," a disorder brought on by the stress of war.

The trenches themselves posed other dangers to soldiers. Heavy rains filled the trenches with water and mud, leading to diseases such as trench foot, which was caused by standing for hours in cold water with no possibility of changing into dry socks or boots. A severe case of trench foot could require amputation. Even the mud that filled the trenches could pose a drowning hazard for wounded soldiers waiting for medical assistance.

Among the lesser-known heroes of World War I who helped rescue and care for injured soldiers, many were women. Women and men drove ambulances, ferrying the sick and wounded from the front to hospitals behind the lines. Women were also the majority of the corps of nurses who treated the injured and comforted the dying. **Julia C. Stimson**, an American nurse, arrived at an army hospital in France just weeks after the United States joined the war. She was later appointed chief nurse of the Red Cross in France, and then head of the nursing services of the American Expeditionary Forces. After the war, Stimson was awarded medals by the United States, Britain, and France for her bravery and life-saving service.

11.5.2 Analyze the international and domestic events, interests, and philosophies that prompted attacks on civil liberties, including the Palmer Raids, Marcus Garvey's "back-to-Africa" movement, the Ku Klux Klan, and immigration quotas and the responses of organizations such as the American Civil Liberties Union, the National Association for the Advancement of Colored People, and the Anti-Defamation League to those attacks.

CRITICAL VIEWING The African-American soldiers of the 369th Infantry from New York City, nicknamed the "Harlem Hellfighters," fought with the French and were the first Americans to receive the French Croix de Guerre (War Cross) for Gallantry. What questions does this image—and what you've learned in this lesson—raise for you about the experiences African Americans had in the Great War?

PRIMARY SOURCE

The day has been tremendous, and the first in which I have not lost a life. We soldiers are hard pressed these days. The wounded pour in day and night by trains, by American autos too, but I can't take a minute to run out to salute my countrymen [American ambulance drivers]. We discharge our patients as fast as we can, and bury dozens a week. It is all like a weird dream, laughter (for they laugh well, the soldiers) and blood and death and funny episodes, and sublime also, all under the autumn stars.

—from *Mademoiselle Miss,* letters from an American nurse in France, entry dated October 27, 1915

HISTORICAL THINKING

1. **READING CHECK** How did women and minorities contribute to the war effort in Europe?
2. **DRAW CONCLUSIONS** Why did the Great War have more casualties than previous wars?
3. **ANALYZE CAUSE AND EFFECT** What effect does war have on the development of technology?
4. **EVALUATE** In 1918, W.E.B. Du Bois wrote in the NAACP's monthly journal that "while the war lasts [we should] forget our special grievances and close our ranks shoulder to shoulder with our white fellow citizens and allied nations that are fighting for democracy." This was viewed by some as puzzling, given his views on racial equality. What do you think about Du Bois's statement, based on what you know about the civil rights movement?

11.4.5 Analyze the political, economic, and social ramifications of World War I on the home front.

CRITICAL VIEWING Stairs lead from the relative safety of an underground quarry to the trenches. What sorts of challenges might soldiers have faced while living below ground?

French officer

German infantryman

Carving of “the disasters of the 20th century”

German military leader Field Marshal Paul von Hindenburg

3.2

THROUGH THE LENS

JEFFREY GUSKY

During World War I, some troops took refuge in centuries-old underground cities in northeastern France. They left their mark in the soft limestone in the form of signatures, sketches, carvings, and relief sculptures. National Geographic photographer Jeffrey Gusky captured the intimate stories of these soldiers, many of whom never made it out from the trenches.

U.S. troops of the 26th “Yankee” Division did around 500 carvings during the 6 weeks they spent in an underground quarry in France in 1918.

3.3 **MAIN IDEA** The war abroad and reform movements at home combined to bring about changes in social and economic conditions for many Americans. At the same time, the world confronted a massive, deadly outbreak of a familiar disease.

THE HOME FRONT

Life didn't come to a halt in the United States while the young men fought overseas. The war accelerated far-reaching social changes that had already begun in America's cities, workplaces, and among the voting public. When the soldiers returned, they would find that home was not exactly the way they had left it.

The Phillips Collection, Washington, D.C.

Jacob Lawrence is considered one of the most influential visual artists of the 20th century. The painting above is Panel 1 of his 1941 series, *The Migration of the Negro*. This 60-painting collection pays tribute to southern African Americans, including his parents, who fled to cities in the American North and West during the Great Migration. To escape racial inequality, many migrants landed in cities like New York, St. Louis, and Chicago, transforming the culture, music, and politics of these locations.

11.4.5 Analyze the political, economic, and social ramifications of World War I on the home front; 11.5.2 Analyze the international and domestic events, interests, and philosophies that prompted attacks on civil liberties, including the Palmer Raids, Marcus Garvey's "back-to-Africa" movement, the Ku Klux Klan, and immigration quotas and the responses of organizations such as the American Civil Liberties Union, the National Association for the Advancement of Colored People, and the Anti-Defamation League to those attacks.

THE WAR'S IMPACT AT HOME

Nearly every racial or ethnic group in the United States was affected by economic and cultural changes brought about by the war. As you've read, German Americans were viewed with suspicion by their fellow citizens. German Americans lost connections with their culture, as German-language newspapers were shut down, and speaking German in public was banned in half the states. Dissenters of any national background suffered a similar fate, being viewed with hostility by other Americans and persecuted by the government.

Some minority groups saw more positive changes. Jewish Americans had formerly been grouped according to their country of origin in Europe. Now they united to play a stronger international role by forming charities and donating millions to help victims of the war. Mexican American workers living in the southern and southwestern states moved north to follow job opportunities that opened up in factories when young men enlisted. Many women, too, left their traditional roles to take paying jobs in factories, offices, or loading docks.

For African Americans, the war years brought enormous changes. In the South, a variety of natural disasters crippled southern agriculture, which resulted in increasingly poor job prospects for black farm workers. African Americans had begun leaving the South for cities in the North around 1910, a mass movement known as the **Great Migration**. The outbreak of the war played a key role in this process. As immigration from Europe ended and white American factory workers enlisted, thousands of jobs opened up in industrial centers in northern cities. Between 1914 and 1920, more than 600,000 African Americans moved north.

African Americans who moved to these centers, however, were often met with hostility. And even after the war, the prospect of improved rights for African Americans remained bleak. The Wilson administration and the Democratic Party resisted efforts to reduce racism, and harsh policies toward black Americans persisted in many states.

PROHIBITION

At the start of the 20th century, saloons could be found in cities throughout the United States. They not only served beer and other alcoholic drinks, they offered places where working men could gather to socialize. Women were not permitted to enter a saloon—and many didn't want to. Reform organizations, such as the Anti-Saloon League and the Women's Christian Temperance Union, believed saloons encouraged drunkenness and overspending by men. Feeling that they were defending their families, many women supported **Prohibition**—making the sale of liquor illegal.

During the war, the Prohibition movement gained ground because the grain used to make beer was needed for food, and because most brewers (beer makers) were German. In December 1917, Congress approved the **18th Amendment** to the Constitution, prohibiting the sale of alcohol in the United States. The amendment was ratified after the war, in January 1919. Congress also passed the **Volstead Act**, which contained measures to enforce Prohibition.

In 1910, the National Woman's Christian Temperance Union (NWCTU) produced this "Vote No" Prohibition postcard. "Vote no" refers to localized "no license" campaigns that attempted to deny the license renewals of taverns in order to protect children and preserve family unity and values.

11.3.1 Describe the contributions of various religious groups to American civic principles and social reform movements (e.g., civil and human rights, individual responsibility and the work ethic, antimonarchy and self-rule, worker protection, family-centered communities).

Suffragists align with Woodrow Wilson during his 1916 re-election campaign. While Wilson's political platform favored women's suffrage, the president didn't fully support it until 1918.

PRIMARY SOURCE

Do you realize that when you ask women to take their cause [suffrage] to state referendum . . . you drive women of education, refinement, achievement, to beg men who cannot read for their political freedom?

Do you realize that such anomalies as a college president asking her janitor to give her a vote are overstraining the patience and driving women to desperation? Do you realize that women in increasing numbers indignantly resent the long delay in their enfranchisement?

Your party platforms have pledged women suffrage. Then why not be honest, frank friends of our cause, adopt it in reality as your own, make it a party program, and "fight with us"? As a party measure —a measure of all parties—why not put the amendment through Congress and the legislatures? We shall all be better friends, we shall have a happier nation, we women will be free to support loyally the party of our choice, and we shall be far prouder of our history.

—from Carrie Chapman Catt's address to the U.S. Congress, November 4, 1917

WOMEN GAIN THE VOTE

Women had been demanding the right to vote since the 1840s, and by 1914, they could vote in several states. However, after Wilson's re-election, his support for a constitutional amendment giving women suffrage seemed lukewarm at best to those in the movement. In 1917, women picketed the White House, and many were imprisoned. Still, they continued to demonstrate, in spite of the threat of increasingly long jail terms.

World War I finally provided the context in which women's activism to secure the vote could finally succeed. Women saw the opportunity to strengthen their argument. Carrie Chapman Catt, a leader of the National American Woman Suffrage Association, claimed that women were patriotic voters. According to her argument, giving women the right to vote would counteract the potential influence of dissenters at the polls. At the same time, the pickets in front of the White House continued.

The combined impact of these tactics pushed the House of Representatives to pass the **19th Amendment**, granting suffrage to women in January 1918. The Senate took another year to approve the amendment, and the states ratified it in August 1920. Beyond the success of women's suffrage, however, the war did not produce lasting changes in the everyday lives of American women. As soon as the war ended, women were expected to relinquish their office and factory jobs to the returning soldiers and resume their traditional roles at home.

11.5.4 Analyze the passage of the Nineteenth Amendment and the changing role of women in society; CST 2 Students analyze how change happens at different rates at different times; understand that some aspects can change while others remain the same; and understand that change is complicated and affects not only technology and politics but also values and beliefs.

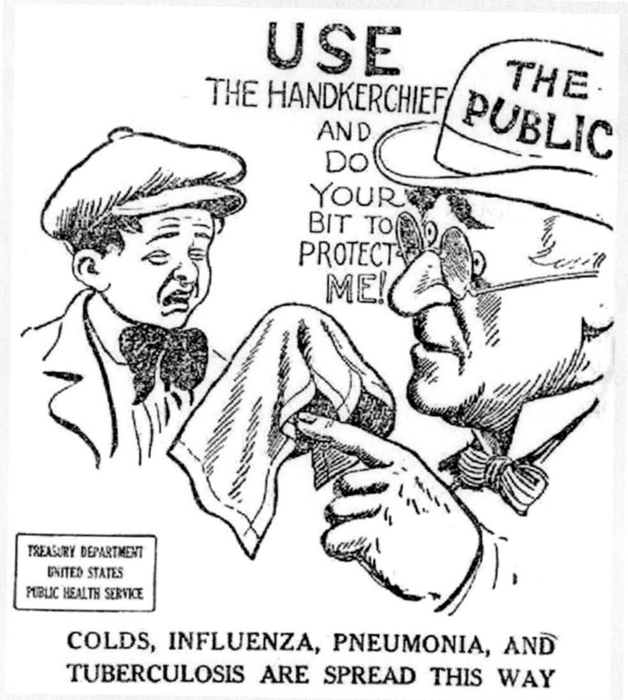

Flu Epidemic 1918–1919

First cases reported at U.S. military bases
August 1918

September 1918 total U.S. deaths
12,000

October 1918 total U.S. deaths
195,000

Total U.S. deaths 1918–1919
600,000

Total deaths worldwide 1918–1919
50,000,000

Sources: PBS, U.S. National Library of Medicine

Despite attempts at public health education, like displaying this 1919 poster, the 1918 influenza pandemic was widespread and deadly. Scientists have since learned the virus was H1N1, which has resurfaced at various times throughout history.

THE FLU STRIKES

At the end of 1918, a particularly powerful strain of **influenza**, the contagious virus we now call "the flu," struck with dramatic suddenness and spread rapidly throughout the U.S. population. Scientists were not able to develop a vaccine quickly enough against the Spanish flu, as it was called. Antibiotics did not come into widespread use until around 1940, so they were not yet available to fight secondary infections, such as pneumonia, that could accompany the flu. More than 600,000 Americans died of the disease in 1918 and 1919, overwhelming the funeral facilities of many major cities. It was most deadly for people aged 20–40, which was unusual, since influenza is typically more likely to be fatal among the very young and the very old. As a result, soldiers and officers were in the most vulnerable age group.

The outbreak was a **pandemic**—a sudden spread of disease that covers a very large geographic area and affects a major portion of the population. By the time it receded in 1920, the flu had killed more than 50 million people worldwide. It is estimated that one-third of the world's population became infected. The pandemic sapped the strength of the Allied forces who had already lived through brutal trench warfare and had been tasked with enforcing the peace treaty at the end of the war. The outbreak also diverted attention from important social problems, and illustrated how vulnerable humanity was to infectious diseases.

PRIMARY SOURCE

1918 has gone: a year momentous as the termination of the most cruel war in the annals of the human race; a year which marked the end, at least for a time, of man's destruction of man; unfortunately a year in which developed a most fatal infectious disease causing the death of hundreds of thousands of human beings. Medical science for four and one-half years devoted itself to putting men on the firing line and keeping them there. Now it must turn with its whole might to combating the greatest enemy of all—infectious disease.

—from the *Journal of the American Medical Association,* 1918

HISTORICAL THINKING

1. **READING CHECK** What changes were reform movements able to bring about during and immediately after the war?
2. **MAKE GENERALIZATIONS** In what ways can a war help bring about social changes on the home front?
3. **EVALUATE** In Catt's appeal to Congress, what details suggest her frustration with having to beg for women's suffrage?
4. **FORM AND SUPPORT OPINIONS** Do you believe women and African Americans made large strides toward civil rights during the war years? Explain.

HREP 4 Students construct and test hypotheses; collect, evaluate, and employ information from multiple primary and secondary sources; and apply it in oral and written presentations.

4.1 **MAIN IDEA** After the American forces helped end the war and defeat Germany, President Wilson met with the leaders of the countries embroiled in the fighting to negotiate a peace treaty and try to impose his vision for Europe's future.

ROAD TO VICTORY

As you know, many people referred to the fighting as the Great War because it consumed so many countries in its fires. By the end, they were calling it "the war to end all wars" because the bloodshed and ruin were unlike anything that had gone before. But the participation of American troops in the war helped establish the United States as a global power.

Major Battles of World War I, 1917–1918

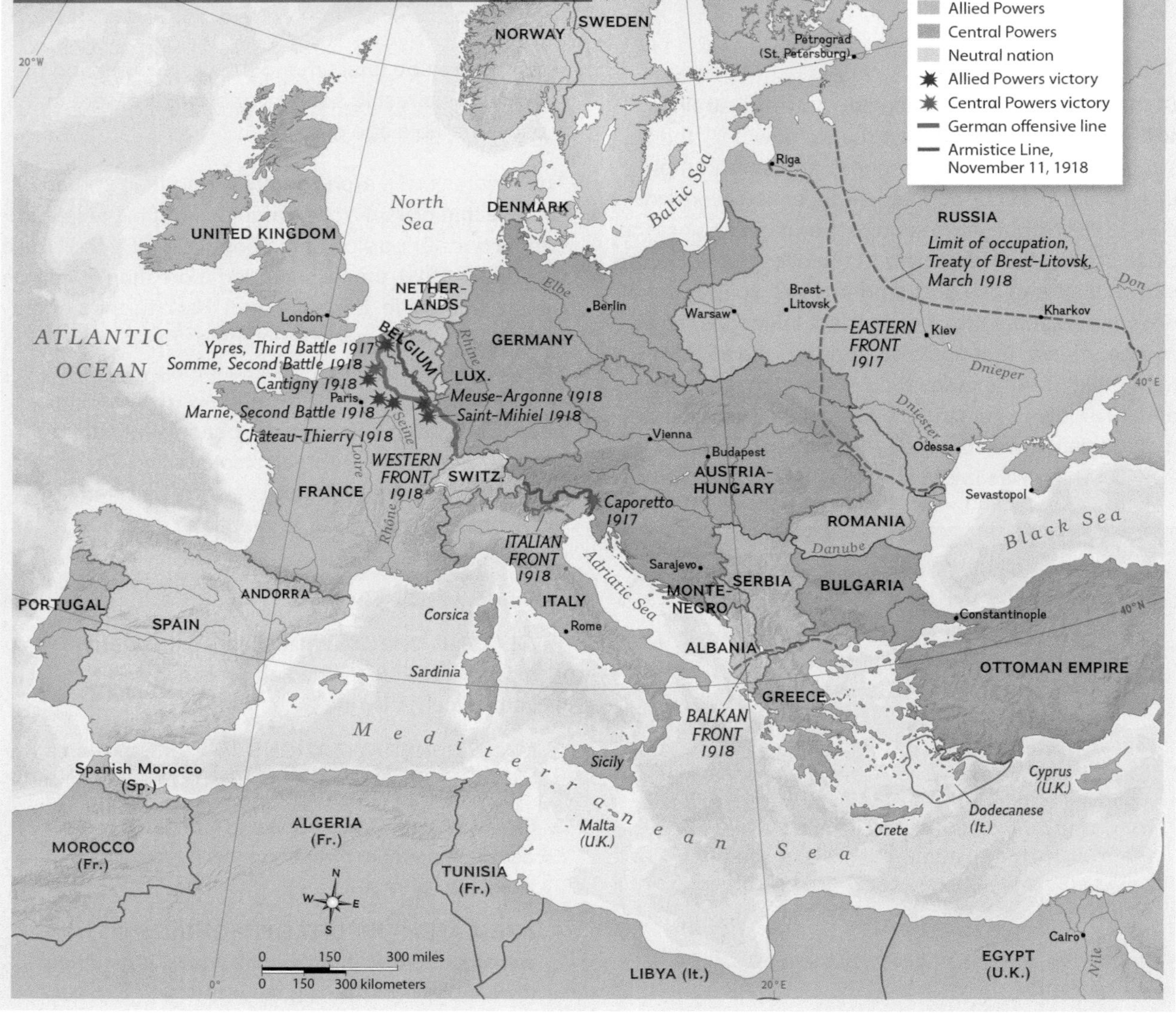

CST 3 Students use a variety of maps and documents to interpret human movement, including major patterns of domestic and international migration, changing environmental preferences and settlement patterns, the frictions that develop between population groups, and the diffusion of ideas, technological innovations, and goods.

ATTACK AND COUNTERATTACK

During the late winter of 1918, the Allies faced a dangerous military crisis. As you may recall, by November 1917, revolution had erupted in Russia, and the second of two revolutions had taken that nation out of the Allied coalition. The revolutionaries placed the Bolsheviks, a party of communist extremists, in power and overthrew the Russian imperial government. This turmoil enabled the Germans to move troops to the Western Front. Berlin hoped to achieve victory before the Americans could reinforce the Allies.

On March 21, 1918, the German Army launched a renewed offensive to conquer France and end the war before large numbers of American forces landed in Europe. Over the next two months, the Germans gained ground in Belgium and France, only to be stopped in May by the American counterattack at Cantigny, France. With millions of U.S. soldiers now in France, the German drive for a quick victory had failed. The following month, the American Expeditionary Forces (AEF) stopped Germany from advancing in battles near Belleau Wood and Château-Thierry. In addition to their strategic value, these victories provided a tremendous morale boost to the flagging Allied armies.

The Germans made one more offensive push in July, but the British, French, and American troops repelled it. After that, the Allies went on the offensive, driving the German forces back, trench by trench. In September, the Allies began an operation called the **Meuse-Argonne offensive**, in which American divisions cut off the railroads that were bringing supplies to the German Army. As part of the offensive, General Pershing led AEF troops in the bloody and decisive **Battle of Argonne Forest** in October 1918. Looking back on the offensive years later, German general Erich Ludendorff wrote, "America thus became the most decisive power in the war." Still, American casualties in the Battle of Argonne were staggering, reaching 117,000, including 26,000 killed. French casualties totaled 70,000, and German casualties came to 100,000 soldiers.

WILSON'S PEACE PROGRAM

As the war ground toward its end, Wilson proposed a program for peace that he called the **Fourteen Points**. Among the key provisions of this plan were freedom of the seas, free trade among countries, and no more secret treaties. Wilson also advocated national self-determination, the idea that countries should reflect the national origins of the people who lived within their boundaries.

PRIMARY SOURCE

President Wilson's **Fourteen Points** were presented in a speech to Congress on January 8, 1918.

Points 1–5 dealt with diplomatic issues that Wilson believed were essential for preventing further war:

1. Open covenants [binding agreements] of peace, openly arrived at, after which there shall be no private international understandings of any kind but diplomacy shall proceed always frankly and in the public view.

2. Absolute freedom of navigation upon the seas, outside territorial waters, alike in peace and in war, except as the seas may be closed in whole or in part by international action for the enforcement of international covenants.

3. The removal, so far as possible, of all economic barriers and the establishment of an equality of trade conditions among all the nations consenting to the peace and associating themselves for its maintenance.

4. Adequate guarantees given and taken that national armaments [weaponry] will be reduced to the lowest point consistent with domestic safety.

5. A free, open-minded, and absolutely impartial adjustment of all colonial claims, based upon a strict observance of the principle that in determining all such questions of sovereignty, the interests of the populations concerned must have equal weight with the equitable [fair] claims of the government whose title is to be determined.

[Points 6–13 are not included here. These points dealt with boundary changes and called for ensuring the sovereignty of several nations. They also included a request for the break-up of the Ottoman Empire and the development of an independent Polish state.]

Point 14 called for the creation of an assembly of nations that would help safeguard the sovereignty of all countries:

14. A general association of nations must be formed under specific covenants for the purpose of affording mutual guarantees of political independence and territorial integrity to great and small states alike.

Which of the Fourteen Points do you think might have been controversial in the context of the war? Explain your answer.

CRITICAL VIEWING A wave of ceramic poppy flowers appears to tumble from the Tower of London in England as part of an evolving art installation called "Blood-Swept Lands and Seas of Red," created in 2014 by artists Paul Cummins and Tom Piper. Flowers were added daily from July 17 until November 11, 2014—the 100th anniversary of Britain's first full day of involvement in the Great War—until they reached the number of British fatalities in the war: 888,246. Beginning in the 1920s, the poppy, which grew in many of the war's battlefields, became a symbol of the sacrifice made by the soldiers. How does the name of this exhibition connect to the Great War?

The Fourteen Points would not be easy to achieve. Britain and France objected to the proposal because it did not include heavy sanctions on Germany. After four years of slaughter, these European nations wanted to punish Germany and cripple its ability to wage war in the future. They also disliked Wilson's interference with European policies. For the desperate Germans, however, the Fourteen Points seemed much more appealing than direct negotiations with Britain and France.

In early October, the German government asked Wilson to arrange an **armistice**, an end to the fighting, based on the provisions of the Fourteen Points. Britain and France objected to this proposal. However, by threatening to make a separate peace between the United States and Germany, Wilson convinced the two European nations to accept the Fourteen Points in general terms and attend a peace conference with Germany.

The fighting officially ended on November 11, 1918, at 11:00 a.m.—the 11th hour on the 11th day of the 11th month, or Armistice Day, as it would be called. Earlier that morning, Germany, lacking supplies and manpower and facing invasion at any moment, had signed an armistice, or peace agreement, with the Allies in a railroad car outside Compiégne, France. The details of the peace treaties among the formerly warring nations would be decided over the next year, but the relief that day was evident. British prime minister David Lloyd George stated, "This is no time for words. Our hearts are too full of gratitude to which no tongue can give adequate expression."

Nine million soldiers died in the Great War, and 21 million were wounded. France, Germany, Russia, Austria-Hungary, and Great Britain each lost nearly a million or more soldiers, and at least five million more civilians died from factors such as exposure, starvation, and disease. The Great War killed more people, involved more countries, and cost more money than any previous war in history. Its technology transformed the nature of modern warfare, introducing newer, deadlier, more effective weapons onto the battlefield.

The impact of the war was staggering, and many major global events that took place later in the 20th century can be tied to this first World War. The Russian Revolution, World War II, the Holocaust, and the creation of the atomic bomb, which you will read about later in this book, are all directly linked to the Great War. Even the Great Depression and the Cold War are connected to it in significant ways.

THE PARIS PEACE CONFERENCE

Breaking with the tradition that presidents did not travel outside the country, Wilson decided to attend the Paris Peace Conference. By the time he left for the conference, which began in January 1919, Wilson's political position at home had weakened considerably. He had alienated Republicans by keeping them out of the highest levels of his government and angered progressives with his harsh repression of dissent. In the October 1918 congressional elections, Americans voted Republican majorities into both the Senate and House of Representatives. This situation promised to make it difficult for a peace treaty negotiated by Wilson to be ratified.

In Europe, however, Wilson was heralded as a hero when he traveled to the Paris Peace Conference. The people greeted him with lavish applause and the nickname "Wilson the Just." Wilson, David Lloyd George, Georges Clemenceau, the president of France, and Italy's prime minister, Vittorio Orlando, made up the "Big Four" who directed the conference. The European leaders were hard-headed realists who did not share Wilson's idealism, and they were skeptical of the Fourteen Points. "God gave us the Ten Commandments and we broke them," said Clemenceau. "Wilson gives us the Fourteen Points. We shall see."

Notably absent from the Paris Peace Conference was one of the original Allies—Russia. As a result of the Russian Revolution, Russia's monarchy had given way to **communism**, a form of government in which all the means of production and transportation are owned by the state. The revolutionaries changed Russia's name to the Union of Soviet Socialist Republics (U.S.S.R.), or the **Soviet Union** for short. Its leader was Vladimir Ilyich Lenin. In March 1918, the Russian revolutionary party had made its own peace treaty with Germany.

HISTORICAL THINKING

1. **READING CHECK** What effect did the arrival of American troops have on the outcome of the war?
2. **MAKE INFERENCES** Why did Germany prefer to negotiate the terms of peace with Wilson rather than with France and Britain?
3. **EVALUATE** How did Wilson's Fourteen Points serve as a justification for America's entry into the war?
4. **MAKE PREDICTIONS** How might a later event in history, such as World War II or the Great Depression, be connected to the Great War?

CST 1 Students compare the present with the past, evaluating the consequences of past events and decisions and determining the lessons that were learned; HI 2 Students recognize the complexity of historical causes and effects, including the limitations on determining cause and effect.

4.2 **MAIN IDEA** Wilson successfully negotiated a peace treaty between the Allies and Germany, but the Senate refused to ratify the treaty, and the end of the war brought social and economic turmoil to the United States.

VICTORY AND WILSON'S PEACE

Woodrow Wilson had a lofty dream of a world at peace and a great gathering of nations. It was a vision that blinded him to the necessities of everyday politics. In the end, the nations gathered, but the United States was not among them.

THE TREATY OF VERSAILLES

The **Treaty of Versailles**, which officially brought the war to a close, was signed in the Hall of Mirrors at the Palace of Versailles outside of Paris, France, on June 28, 1919. Although Wilson had a significant role in designing the Versailles Treaty, the negotiations over peace terms with Germany had produced both victories and defeats for the American president. Against his wishes, the final wording of the treaty included a clause assigning Germany the "guilt" for starting the war in 1914. The treaty also exacted severe financial penalties from Germany in the form of reparations, payments to make up for damages and casualties caused by the war, that eventually amounted to $33 billion. Both of these provisions fueled bitter resentment in Germany that would only deepen in the decades that followed.

With regard to self-determination for nations, Wilson was somewhat more successful. In the aftermath of the war, the Austro-Hungarian Empire was dissolved, and new boundaries were drawn. It was not possible to fully align national borders with the ethnic origins of the groups within each country. Still, borders in postwar Europe did more closely follow ethnic divisions than the prewar boundaries.

THE LEAGUE OF NATIONS

Wilson's main goal in the negotiations was to establish a **League of Nations**, a general assembly of countries that would stabilize relations among countries and help preserve peace. The final Treaty of Versailles included the league's charter. Each member country would have an equal voice in the general assembly, and the league would have an international court of justice. For Wilson, the "heart of the covenant" of the League of Nations was Article X, which required member nations to take unified action when any member country was attacked.

Because Democrats were in the minority in the Senate, Wilson would need some Republican votes to ratify the Treaty of Versailles. Many Republicans, however, objected to establishing the League of Nations, believing it infringed on U.S. **sovereignty**,

Three global powerhouses, British prime minister David Lloyd George (left), French prime minister Georges Clemenceau (center), and American president Woodrow Wilson (right), take a stroll during the Versailles Peace Conference in June 1919.

11.4.5 Analyze the political, economic, and social ramifications of World War I on the home front.

or freedom from external control. Senator **Henry Cabot Lodge**, a Republican and chair of the Senate Foreign Relations Committee, was especially vocal in his opposition. Lodge and Wilson had been political enemies for a long time and disliked each other personally. Wilson did not help matters when he indicated that since the treaty's critics had offered no alternate plan, "it is a case of 'put up or shut up'."

In the political battle over the treaty, Lodge focused on Article X and the issue of whether Congress should be able to approve American participation in any actions taken by the league to defend its members from aggression. By September 1919, with the treaty in trouble, Wilson decided to take his case to the American people in a series of speeches in the Midwest and on the West Coast. The grueling schedule—32 major speeches in 22 days—exhausted him, and the heart and blood disorders that had bothered him for years became aggravated. He was rushed back to Washington where he suffered a massive stroke that left his left side paralyzed.

The president's wife and his doctors did not reveal how sick Wilson was. As the first lady screened his few visitors and decided what documents he would see, Wilson became a shell of a president, and the government drifted. The Treaty of Versailles came up for a vote in the Senate in November 1919 and March 1920, and both times it was defeated. Wilson ultimately could not convince Congress to join the League of Nations. He died in 1924.

THE DECLINE OF PROGRESSIVISM

As you have read in this chapter, many goals of progressivism, including women's suffrage, a stronger labor movement, and Prohibition, had been attained by 1919. Enough states had ratified the 18th

CST 3 Students use a variety of maps and documents to interpret human movement, including major patterns of domestic and international migration, changing environmental preferences and settlement patterns, the frictions that develop between population groups, and the diffusion of ideas, technological innovations, and goods.

Mounted Chicago police officers escort African Americans to a safety zone during the Chicago Race Riots of 1919. Thirty-eight people, most of them black, were killed, and another 500 were injured over the course of five violent days.

PRIMARY SOURCE

As revealed in this account of the Chicago Race Riots of 1919, racial tension and social unrest reached a boiling point that year across the United States.

The fury spread like wildfire. Workers in the stockyards, 10,000 or more of whom are [African American], were at first guarded as they entered and left, but few of them could get to their work when rioting made passage through the streets unsafe. Gangs of white and black hoodlums appeared and ran amuck [wild]. Armed men of either color dashed through the district in automobiles and beyond, firing as they flew. Two white men, wounded while shooting up the district, were found to carry official badges, one being thus identified as . . . a Chicago policeman.

—from *The Survey*, August 9, 1919

Amendment (the Prohibition amendment) by January 1919 to make it part of the Constitution. Additionally, thanks to the 19th Amendment, women could "take their appropriate place in political work," according to Carrie Chapman Catt. Americans began to turn their attention away from progressive ideas as they faced the switch from a wartime to a peacetime economy.

The end of the war created an uncertain situation for American businesses. Orders for guns, ammunition, and other wartime goods were canceled, leaving factories with a pressing need to retool themselves once again, this time to produce peacetime consumer items. When the war had broken out, the WIB had stepped in to help American industry remake itself, but now the government retreated from its earlier organizational role. At the same time, inflation raised prices considerably. By 1920, the government's cost of living index had gone up 105 percent over prewar levels, making goods more expensive. As returning

STRIKE CALLED

ALL UNIONS TO GO OUT

Seattle Union Record

SIXTY THOUSAND TO RESPOND TO CALL

NO CONSTRUCTIVE LEGISLATION YET

ANNOUNCEMENT OF STRIKE

35,000 SILK MILL WORKERS STRIKE

CLUB TO HEAR PROF. SCHOLZ

JACKSON GANG FEARS PROBE

The photograph on the left shows a large crowd gathering at the entrance of the Skinner and Eddy Shipbuilding Corporation on Seattle's central waterfront during the nation's first citywide general strike. It began in the shipyards in January 1919, paralyzing the city for several days. On the right is the front page of the *Seattle Union Record* announcing the strike.

soldiers began to seek jobs, unemployment soared, reaching nearly 12 percent by 1921.

In the midst of economic hardship, social unrest also flared. In early 1919, labor unions staged major strikes demanding higher wages at shipyards in Seattle and steel mills across the country. The Industrial Workers of the World called for a general strike to support the shipyard and steel strikers. When 60,000 laborers took part in the strike, the mayor of Seattle, Ole Hanson, mobilized police and soldiers, earning himself the nickname "the Savior of Seattle." Inflammatory newspaper articles depicted the strike as a precursor to a communist revolution.

The largest industrial strike of the year was the Great Steel Strike of 1919. The American Federation of Labor tried to rally all steelworkers to end the grueling 7-day workweek and the 12-hour workday. In September 1919, 350,000 midwestern steelworkers left the mills. Steel manufacturers refused to recognize the union and replaced striking workers with unemployed minority workers and immigrants to keep their factories running during the strike. They waited for the strike to break due to police harassment and internal divisions within the unions themselves. Striking workers held their position for months, but could not withstand the financial and political pressure being exerted on them by management. The strike failed in early 1920.

Racial tensions also flared up in the turbulent postwar atmosphere. There were frequent lynchings in the American South. In the North, the flow of African-American migrants produced confrontations with angry whites. This tension erupted into race riots in Washington, D.C., Elaine, Arkansas, and Chicago, Illinois, during the summer of 1919, which one black leader came to call "the red summer." Racism and antilabor sentiments fueled each other during these tense months.

With Wilson ill and the government leaderless, the Republicans expected Theodore Roosevelt to be their nominee in 1920, but he died in 1919. The party then turned to Senator **Warren G. Harding**, who promised frustrated voters a "return to normalcy." By *normalcy* he meant reducing government's role in business and stepping back into a more isolationist stance. Harding was elected by a large majority over the Democratic candidate, James M. Cox of Ohio. Voters wanted to turn the Democrats out of office because of their anger over big government, high taxes, and labor unrest. Americans were also prepared to let Europe grapple on its own with its new postwar realities. Although World War I transformed America into a world leader, the aftermath of the war ushered in a decade of isolationism. By the end of the 1920s, this policy would have serious consequences for the world economies.

HISTORICAL THINKING

1. **READING CHECK** How did the end of the war affect the U.S. economy?
2. **COMPARE AND CONTRAST** Compare the social climate of the United States at the beginning of the Great War to the social climate at the end of the war. How did they differ?
3. **FORM AND SUPPORT OPINIONS** Should the Senate have ratified the Treaty of Versailles? Support your opinion.
4. **MAKE INFERENCES** Why did some newspapers compare the steelworkers' strike to the beginning of a communist revolution?

11.5.1 Discuss the policies of Presidents Warren Harding, Calvin Coolidge, and Herbert Hoover; 11.6.5 Trace the advances and retreats of organized labor, from the creation of the American Federation of Labor and the Congress of Industrial Organizations to current issues of a postindustrial, multinational economy, including the United Farm Workers in California.

CHAPTER 8 THE GREAT WAR REVIEW

VOCABULARY

For each pair of vocabulary words, write one sentence that explains the connection between the words.

1. **sedition; civil liberties** HSS 11.4.5
   In its quest to suppress possible sedition, the U.S. government enacted laws that curtailed civil liberties.
2. **militarism; nationalism** HSS 11.4.5
3. **neutrality; declaration of war** HSS 11.4.4
4. **machine gun; tank** HSS 11.4.5
5. **armistice; Fourteen Points** HSS 11.4.5
6. **assassinate; alliance** HSS 11.4.5

READING STRATEGY

DRAW CONCLUSIONS

When you draw conclusions, you make a judgment based on what you have read. You analyze evidence, make inferences, and use your own experiences to form your judgment. Use a chart like this one to draw a conclusion about how the war changed the perception of the United States in the world. Then answer the question.

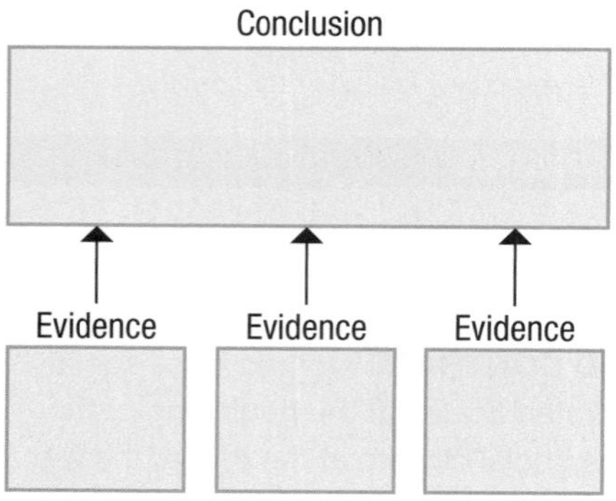

7. In what ways did World War I mark the beginning of a new role for the United States on the world stage? HSS 11.4.5

MAIN IDEAS

Answer the following questions. Support your answers with evidence from the chapter.

8. How did the networks of alliances in Europe lead to the beginning of World War I? **LESSON 1.1** HSS HI 2
9. Why did President Wilson declare a policy of neutrality toward the war in Europe? **LESSON 1.2** HSS 11.4.4
10. What German actions eventually led the United States to declare war? **LESSON 2.1** HSS 11.4.5
11. In what ways did the U.S. government support the war effort? **LESSON 2.2** HSS 11.4.5
12. How were members of minority groups treated during the war ? **LESSON 3.1** HSS 11.4.5
13. What effect did the flu pandemic of 1918–1919 have on the Allied forces? **LESSON 3.3** HSS 11.4.5
14. In what ways did Wilson and the Allies disagree about a peace treaty for Europe? **LESSON 4.1** HSS 11.4
15. Why did the United States refuse to ratify the Treaty of Versailles? **LESSON 4.2** HSS HI 4

HISTORICAL THINKING

Answer the following questions. Support your answers with evidence from the chapter.

16. **MAKE GENERALIZATIONS** What general statement could you make about the power and usefulness of propaganda? HSS HREP 1
17. **DRAW CONCLUSIONS** How did Wilson's view of the United States' role in the world change during the war? HSS 11.4
18. **IDENTIFY MAIN IDEAS AND DETAILS** What advantages made the United States instrumental in helping the Allied side win the war? HSS 11.4.5

19. **SYNTHESIZE** How did the United States change its policies, both at home and abroad, because of World War I? HSS 11.4.5

20. **MAKE CONNECTIONS** In what ways is the flu pandemic of 1918–1919 similar to modern disease outbreaks you have heard of? In what ways is it different? HSS CST 1

21. **FORM AND SUPPORT OPINIONS** What do you think is the most important lasting effect of World War I on life in the United States? Explain your answer. HSS CST 1

INTERPRET VISUALS

Study this propaganda poster created by the U.S. Food Administration during the war. Then answer the questions that follow.

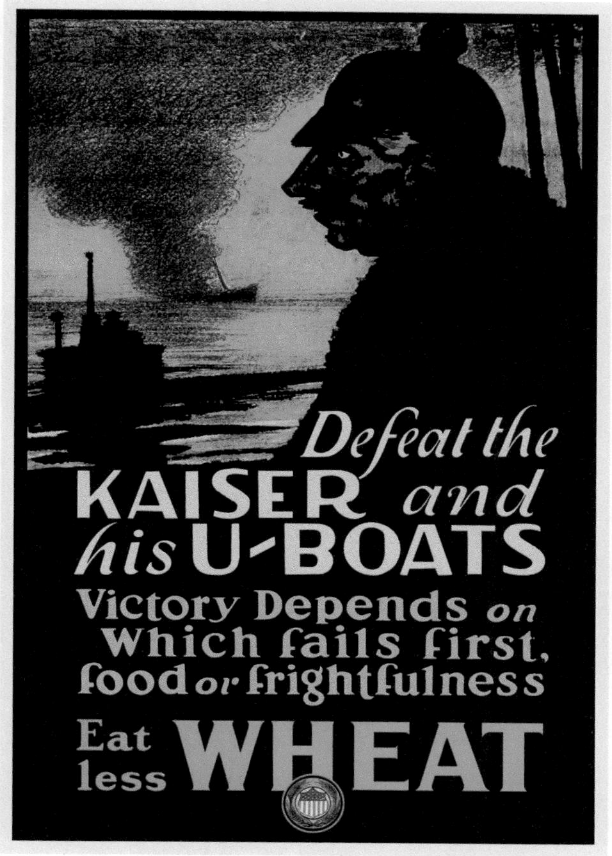

22. How do the poster's visuals and artistic details inspire fear? HSS 11.4.5

23. What does the poster's slogan, "Victory depends on which fails first, food or frightfulness," mean? HSS 11.4.5

ANALYZE SOURCES

Supporters of women's suffrage stood outside the White House day after day carrying signs and hoping to influence President Wilson. Often, the signs would elicit angry, or even violent, responses. Read the text of one such sign below. Then answer the question that follows.

> Kaiser Wilson
> Have you forgotten your sympathy with the poor Germans because they were not self-governed? 20,000,000 American women are not self-governed.
>
> —banner of the National Woman's Party, 1917

24. Why does the writer of this sign use the term "Kaiser Wilson"? HSS HREP 2

CONNECT TO YOUR LIFE

25. **EXPOSITORY** Imagine the year is 1919, and you spent the war working on the home front. The war has ended, and you are writing a letter to a friend explaining how events during and just after the war have changed your feelings about what it means to be an American. HSS 11.4.5

TIPS

- Consider how the war affected all Americans, including the government's efforts to influence citizens' thoughts.
- Determine your identity as the letter writer. Are you male or female? Are you white, African American, a recent immigrant, or a member of a different group?
- Develop your topic by discussing ways in which your circumstances and your attitudes changed—and did not change.
- Use two or three vocabulary terms from the chapter in your letter.
- End the letter with a brief summary statement about how you feel at the current point in time.

CHAPTER 9

THE JAZZ AGE AND MASS CULTURE

1921–1929

HISTORICAL THINKING How did the Roaring Twenties both divide and unite Americans?

The 2013 film version of F. Scott Fitzgerald's novel *The Great Gatsby* portrayed the Jazz Age as a swirl of activity. Director Baz Luhrmann interpreted the extravagant, self-indulgent world of the wealthy Jay Gatsby with vibrant party scenes like this one.

"Everybody's
youth is a dream."

—F. Scott Fitzgerald, author

ALL THAT JAZZ

11.8.8 Discuss forms of popular culture, with emphasis on their origins and geographic diffusion (e.g., jazz and other forms of popular music, professional sports, architectural and artistic styles).

CRITICAL VIEWING The Preservation Hall Jazz Band is a contemporary jazz ensemble formed in 1963 with the aim of preserving the original spirit of New Orleans jazz. The band takes its name from Preservation Hall, a music venue located in New Orleans' French Quarter. Based on this photograph, what musical instruments appear in a typical jazz band?

It seems that every generation chooses to rebel against previous ones, partly through the rhythms and melodies of new styles of music. In the 1950s and 1960s, the rebellious music of choice was rock and roll, described as "savage music" in an advertisement by the Citizens' Council of Greater New Orleans. In the 1980s and 1990s, rap and hip-hop came on the scene, once again rattling the sensibilities of older generations.

Though they are each unique, rock, rap, and hip-hop are cousins, bearing family resemblances because they are all descended from an earlier musical and social revolution—the birth of jazz and the blues.

THE ORIGINS OF JAZZ

New Orleans is generally considered to be the birthplace of jazz. A city like no other in the late 1800s, New Orleans was home to an extremely diverse population of whites, African Americans, and people of mixed races.

In this cultural whirlwind could be heard the sounds of music that had originated with enslaved people who worked in the cotton fields. The music was based on traditional African work songs and "field hollers." Work songs often had a call-and-response structure, with one person singing a line and other people singing a response. Field hollers were high-pitched calls used by individuals working alone to communicate with workers in other fields.

Late in the 19th century, New Orleans also hosted a lively European classical music scene, with several well-attended opera houses. At this time, new kinds of sounds emerged that blended various African and European influences. By the turn of the 20th century, the strains of jazz could be heard in the

CRITICAL VIEWING This 1943 oil painting by Chicago artist Archibald J. Motley, Jr., called *Nightlife*, depicts a crowded nightclub in a Chicago South Side neighborhood. What kind of mood does the painting convey?

streets of New Orleans. Two key features stood out as hallmarks of the jazz style: syncopation and improvisation. Syncopation is the temporary placement of stress on normally weak beats in a piece of music to create a complex rhythm. Improvisation is the act of composing and performing music on the spot. Modern-day jazz styles still feature catchy syncopated rhythms and dizzying original riffs improvised by performers.

NEXT STOP: CHICAGO

If New Orleans was the birthplace of jazz, Chicago was its nursery. In the 1910s and 1920s, many African Americans migrated north in search of better economic opportunities. Jazz musicians were part of this trend, and some of the most notable musicians landed in Chicago. Joe "King" Oliver was one of the best-known New Orleans transplants, playing with King Oliver's Creole Jazz Band on Chicago's South Side.

Today, Oliver is remembered not only for his own musical accomplishments but also for hiring one of jazz's legendary greats for his band. Trumpet player Louis Armstrong, also originally from New Orleans, brought the art of improvisation to new heights. Ron David, the author of *Jazz for Beginners*, describes Armstrong this way: "He built his improvisations like songs within a song, and his trumpet sound glowed." Also a singer, Armstrong had a distinctive vocal style and specialized in scatting, or singing improvised melodies in meaningless syllables.

The jazz craze spread like wildfire among diverse audiences in the 1920s, a decade now known as the Jazz Age. Young people flocked to nightclubs in Chicago, New York, Los Angeles, and other cities to hear jazz and to dance in ways their elders considered immodest. One of the most popular dances of the Jazz Age was the fast-paced, energetic Charleston, which featured quick kicking steps.

11.5.5 Describe the Harlem Renaissance and new trends in literature, music, and art, with special attention to the work of writers (e.g., Zora Neale Hurston, Langston Hughes); 11.5.6 Trace the growth and effects of radio and movies and their role in the worldwide diffusion of popular culture.

Jazz singer Ella Fitzgerald performs with Duke Ellington's band in this 1964 photograph.

THE WOMEN OF JAZZ

The female jazz musicians who have received the most acclaim are the great vocalists of the swing era and later, such as Ella Fitzgerald, Billie Holiday, and Lena Horne. Fitzgerald was a master of scatting, using her voice to weave complex improvised melodies around the beat of the band. Holiday, nicknamed "Lady Day," was known for her soulful and moving ballads. Horne, a dancer, singer, and actress, became one of the top African-American performers of her time, appearing in theater and movies and on television. She refused to accept any acting roles that stereotyped African-American women, and she became an activist in the civil rights movement.

A 1922 photograph shows Lil Hardin (center) performing with King Oliver's Creole Jazz Band in California.

Other lesser known but equally talented female jazz musicians include Lil Hardin and Mary Lou Williams. Born in 1898, Hardin was a pianist and composer. She started her career in New Orleans, where she played, wrote, and arranged music for several bands. After moving to Chicago, she played for King Oliver's Creole Jazz Band. She was married to Louis Armstrong from 1924 to 1938 and collaborated with him on a number of recordings. Williams was born in 1910 and was a composer, arranger, pianist, and bandleader whose work spanned several musical genres. During the swing era, she wrote and arranged pieces for Duke Ellington's band. Later, she worked in the style called bebop, which grew out of swing.

PRIMARY SOURCE

In a 1974 interview conducted by Canadian broadcast journalist Brian Linehan, Ella Fitzgerald was asked to explain her previous claim that she had "stolen from the horns" to create her singing style. In her reply, she spoke about the interaction between a singer and a musician, especially as she experienced it in jazz music.

You know, I think everybody steals from each other. I think that's the only way that we keep alive. As far as learning, it's just like going to school and learning history or learning anything. Actually when you're learning in school you're stealing something from another . . . from something from years back, but you add something to it, and that's the way people are.

We all learn something—the horns learn from another musician, and singers learn from another singer. And I like to try to sing like a horn sometimes in some of my songs, because to me, that's a great accomplishment, to try to feel like I'm playing what I hear a musician play.

—from Ella Fitzgerald, as interviewed by Brian Linehan on *City Lights*, a Canadian television show, 1974

SWINGING ON

A style of jazz called swing, which had a lively rhythm and was played by larger ensembles called big bands, became popular during the 1930s and 1940s. Some music scholars consider the swing era the golden age of jazz, and many would nominate Duke Ellington as the king of swing. Ellington was a bandleader, pianist, and composer. His songs, such as "It Don't Mean a Thing," are still recorded today.

During the swing era, most big bands were segregated. The white bandleader Benny Goodman was one of the few who hired both black and white musicians. Like many other successful bandleaders, Ellington was African American. Even though his band toured nationally and played to both black and white audiences, Ellington and his musicians continually faced the possibility of being turned away from a gig because of the color of their skin.

THE COTTON CLUB

If you were trendy, fashionable, famous, or just hoping to hear some stellar jazz in 1920s New York City, the Cotton Club was the place to go. In this legendary nightclub, white audiences displayed a strange mix of admiration and disdain toward the conventionally African-American art form of jazz and those who performed it.

Located in Harlem, the Cotton Club had its heyday between 1922 and 1935. All workers and entertainers at the club were African Americans, but the clientele were exclusively white. The club's decor reflected a "stylish plantation environment," and the staff were dressed to reflect management's idea of enslaved people or plantation workers.

Despite the segregation and offensive depiction of African Americans, some of the greatest African-American jazz artists of the period played at the Cotton Club. Duke Ellington's orchestra performed as the house band between 1927 and 1931, after which the orchestra of another jazz great, Cab Calloway, took over. Cotton Club guest performers included Louis Armstrong, Ethel Waters, Lena Horne, and many other outstanding African-American musicians. Weekly radio broadcasts from the club brought their music to a national audience.

The Cotton Club moved to a new location after the Harlem riots of 1935, but it never regained its ranking as the premier New York nightclub. In 1940, it closed its doors for good.

How do you think the Cotton Club both helped and harmed the cause of African Americans?

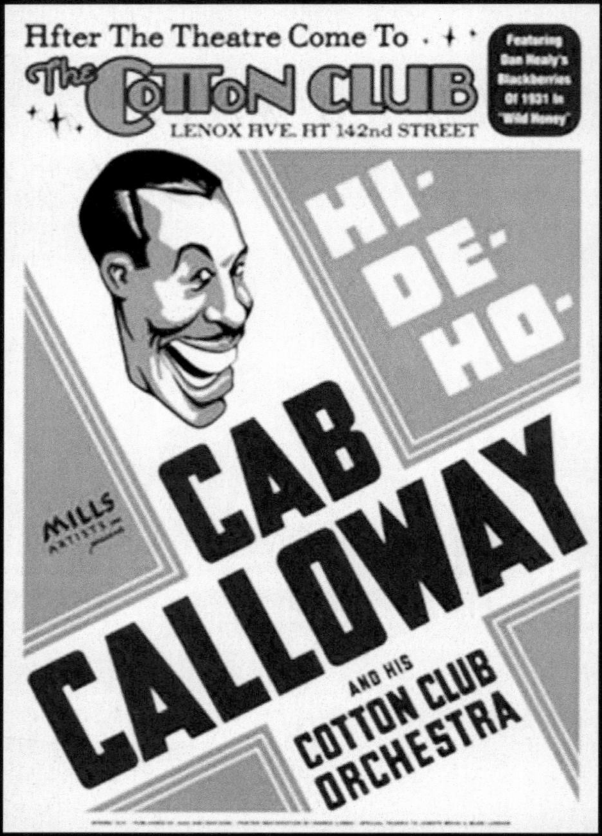

A Cotton Club poster from the 1930s publicizes the orchestra of Cab Calloway, a popular jazz singer and bandleader.

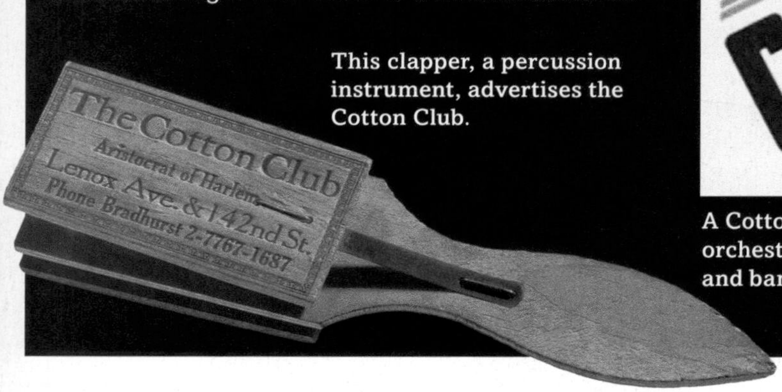

This clapper, a percussion instrument, advertises the Cotton Club.

11.5.6 Trace the growth and effects of radio and movies and their role in the worldwide diffusion of popular culture; HI 1 Students show the connections, causal and otherwise, between particular historical events and larger social, economic, and political trends and developments.

Bobbed hair and shorter skirts were hallmarks of a flapper.

JAZZ AND THE FLAPPER

One popular image of the Jazz Age is the flapper, a young woman who bobbed her hair, sported a wide, lipstick-outlined smile, and wore a short, straight-waisted dress. Often, she was portrayed dancing.

Flappers were generally young white working women living in cities. As the economy improved in the 1920s, more jobs began opening up for women in offices, in department stores, and on telephone switchboards. At the same time, women had gained the right to vote. These changes helped produce a generation of newly independent-minded young women. Flappers abandoned the restrictive clothing of earlier times and adopted higher hemlines, bright colors, and cosmetics. In the evenings after work, they could be found dressed in daring new clothing styles and dancing to jazz music in nightclubs. They also engaged in smoking and drinking, activities formerly associated almost exclusively with men.

Not surprisingly, the flappers and their culture drew the condemnation of an outraged older generation. The president of the Christian Endeavor Society, for example, called jazz dancing “an offense against womanly purity.” Nevertheless, even though the flappers’ signature style faded away after the 1920s, their spirit of independence and youthful energy was passed on to the generations that followed.

11.5.4 Analyze the passage of the Nineteenth Amendment and the changing role of women in society.

JAZZ TODAY

The popularity of jazz declined after the swing era, but the genre still has many dedicated fans and has evolved in a variety of directions. Some musicians have fused elements of jazz with the sounds of Latin and Caribbean music, while others have incorporated electronic instruments, such as synthesizers, and digital technology to move jazz into new realms. Still others continue to explore new ways to perform the classics of Duke Ellington, Louis Armstrong, Benny Goodman, and other jazz greats. Jazz in the 21st century is as diverse as those who perform it and those who listen to it.

THE EVOLUTION OF THE BLUES

Like jazz, the blues originated in the South, developing from such African roots as work songs and field hollers. The blues started out in rural areas rather than cities, sometime after the Civil War. Blues tunes principally expressed the singer's own feelings and struggles, and the instrument of choice was the guitar.

Even more than jazz, the blues featured improvisation, with singers making up both the words and melody as they played. Lyrics were often structured with one line being repeated two or three times, followed by a final line. Most of the early blues players were self-taught, and many could not read music. "The blues didn't come out of no book," the 1930s bluesman Big Bill Broonzy once remarked.

In the 1920s, blues musicians joined the northward migration to Chicago and other cities. Some of the most famous blues singers during this period were women, including Mamie Smith, who made the first blues record in 1920, and Bessie Smith, who became famous internationally. Born around 1898 to a poor family in Tennessee, Bessie Smith came to be known as the Empress of the Blues.

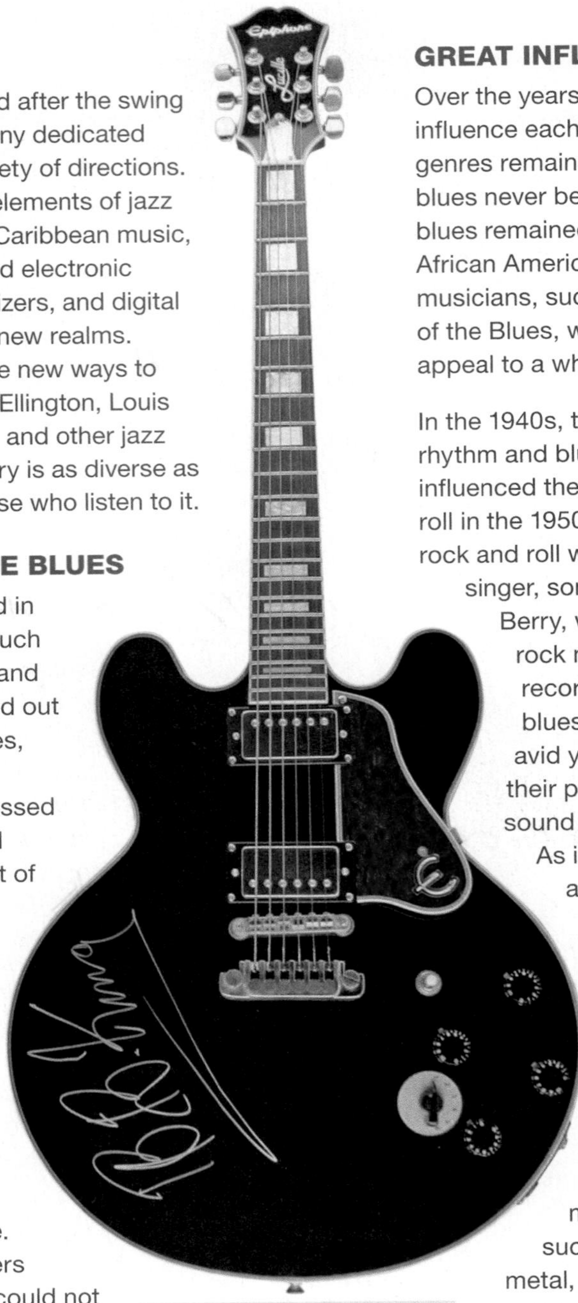

B.B. King named each of his trademark Gibson guitars Lucille. King also wrote a song called "Lucille," which is about his guitar and his music.

GREAT INFLUENCERS

Over the years, jazz and the blues would influence each other's sounds, but the two genres remained distinct. Unlike jazz, the blues never became a national craze. The blues remained popular mainly among African Americans. However, a few blues musicians, such as B.B. King, the King of the Blues, were able to cross over and appeal to a white audience.

In the 1940s, the blues branched out into rhythm and blues (R & B), and both genres influenced the development of rock and roll in the 1950s. Among the pioneers of rock and roll was the African-American singer, songwriter, and guitarist Chuck Berry, who influenced many later rock musicians. Elvis Presley recorded rock songs based on blues tunes, thrilling millions of avid young fans and scandalizing their parents with his energetic sound and his dance moves. As in the Jazz Age, parents and churches and other institutions sounded the alarm that the new music would surely warp young minds. Some of the criticisms were even racist in tone.

In later decades, rock and roll developed into rock music, which has gone in such diverse directions as heavy metal, alternative, and punk. In rap and hip-hop, listeners can trace the enduring blues elements of protest, personal expression, and irresistible rhythms. At the same time, jazz and the blues are still going strong in clubs, recording studios, and the hearts of fans.

THINK ABOUT IT

Why do you think young people turn to music to express their differences from their parents' generation?

JAZZ AND COMPANY

This chart shows the musical styles that blended to become jazz and blues, and many of the genres that evolved from jazz and blues. How many of the genres do you recognize? Which ones do you listen to?

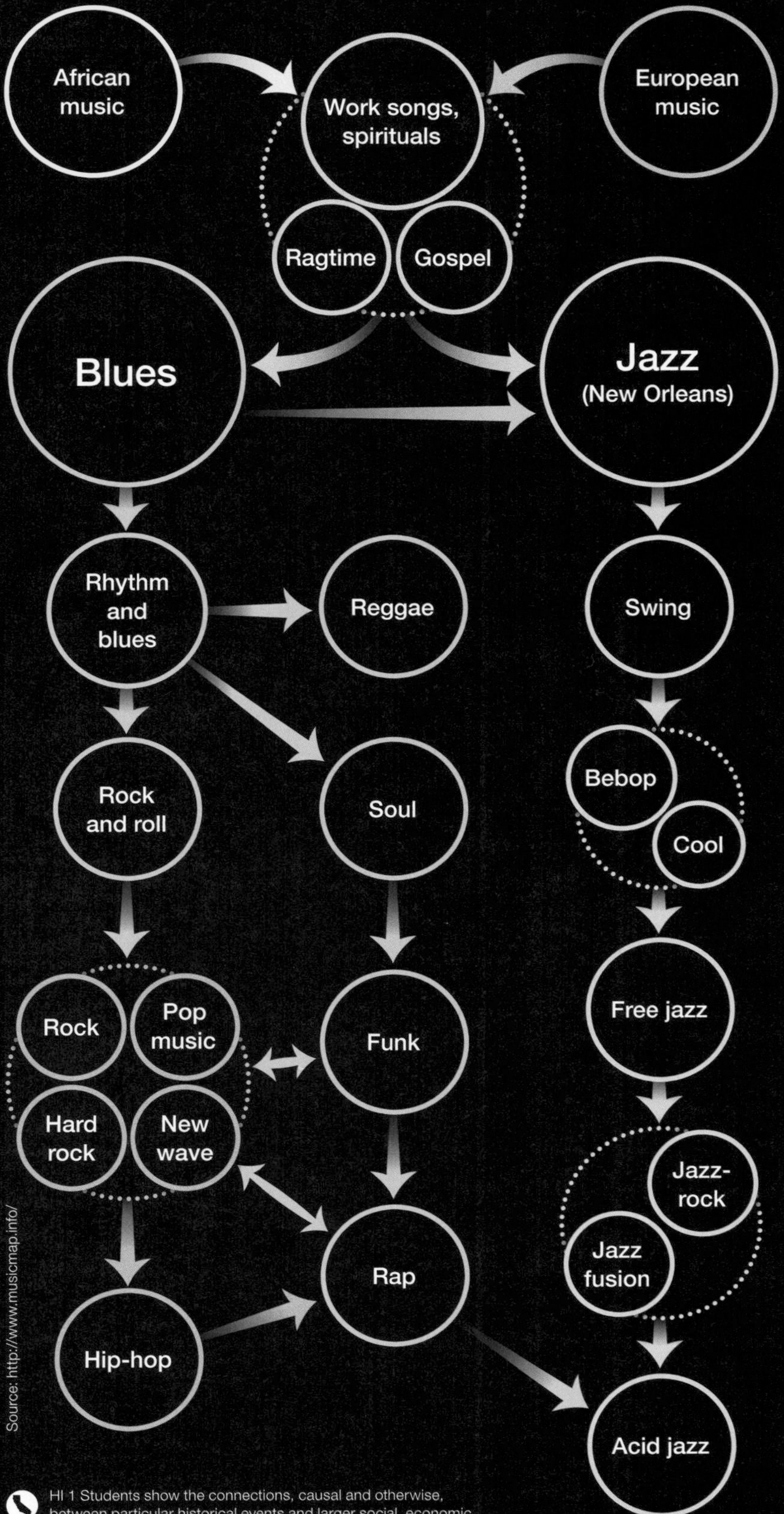

Source: http://www.musicmap.info/

HI 1 Students show the connections, causal and otherwise, between particular historical events and larger social, economic, and political trends and developments.

The influence of a great musician often spans generations and can spark the development of new genres. Blues giant B.B. King influenced the guitar playing of hard rock musician Jimi Hendrix, who in turn influenced funk musician Prince.

B.B. King

influenced

Jimi Hendrix

influenced

Prince

1.1 **MAIN IDEA** In the years following World War I, a fear of communism gripped the United States and led to tensions between individual rights and the power of government.

THE RED SCARE

Think about something that scares you. What makes it so frightening? Following World War I, the threat of communism spreading to the United States frightened many Americans and put the nation on edge.

CONCERNS ABOUT COMMUNISM

The 1920s would eventually become a decade of prosperity in the United States. But as you have read, the economy stumbled right after World War I as it shifted from wartime to peacetime. Production declined as the federal government canceled war contracts for the manufacturing of defense materials, such as rifles, bullets, and bombs. These slowdowns led to large-scale layoffs just as some 4 million soldiers were returning home in need of jobs, contributing to a two-year postwar recession.

The postwar economic slowdown spurred social unrest, from racial tensions to large strikes. During these anxious times, American leaders worried that the ideas of communism might spread to the United States. As you have learned, the Russian Revolution in 1917 resulted in the formation of the Soviet Union under communist-style rule, in which the government controls all business and the distribution of goods and food. As the United States struggled economically, some Americans viewed communism as fairer and more equitable than **capitalism**, an economic system in which private individuals or groups own the resources and produce goods for a profit.

FEAR GRIPS THE NATION

The emotions sparked by postwar unrest fueled the **Red Scare** of 1919 and 1920, a time when the federal government targeted suspected communists, anarchists,

CRITICAL VIEWING Americans wrote songs such as "We'll Never Change the Blue and White to Red" after World War I amid growing fears of communism. What would "anarchy" lead to according to the cover of this sheet music?

11.5.1 Discuss the policies of Presidents Warren Harding, Calvin Coolidge, and Herbert Hoover; 11.5.2 Analyze the international and domestic events, interests, and philosophies that prompted attacks on civil liberties, including the Palmer Raids, Marcus Garvey's "back-to-Africa" movement, the Ku Klux Klan, and immigration quotas and the responses of organizations such as the American Civil Liberties Union, the National Association for the Advancement of Colored People, and the Anti-Defamation League to those attacks.

and **radicals**, or people who hold extreme political views. After these groups were blamed for a series of mail bombs, officials went on the offensive. Attorney General **A. Mitchell Palmer** obtained funding from Congress to establish a division in the Justice Department to hunt for radicals, naming **J. Edgar Hoover** as its head. In November 1919, officials working under Palmer's direction conducted what were known as the **Palmer Raids**. Police broke into the homes and offices of suspected radicals, including labor union leaders and Russian immigrants. They made scores of arrests, often without obtaining search warrants. By January 1920, authorities had deported some 300 Russian immigrants to the Soviet Union under suspicion of communist activities.

Union leaders of the Industrial Workers of the World (IWW) "Big Bill" Haywood (seated, left) and George Speed (seated, right) appeared in court after their arrests during the Palmer Raids.

Throughout the country, Americans' civil liberties came under assault. Officials outlawed the Communist Party, and state legislatures imposed restrictions on groups and ideas they deemed radical. The Supreme Court upheld most of the laws restricting civil liberties during this time. In *Schenck* v. *United States* (1919), Charles Schenck faced espionage charges for handing out flyers encouraging citizens to resist the military draft. He claimed his arrest violated the First Amendment. However, Justice Oliver Wendell Holmes, Jr., argued that the flyers posed a "clear and present danger" to American society and were not protected by the amendment. Schenck served 10 years in prison for the flyers. In 1927, the Court reaffirmed the verdict in *Whitney* v. *California*. That case involved a Communist Party leader convicted for making a speech that some people interpreted as encouraging violence against the government.

PRIMARY SOURCE

My best judgment of America's needs is to steady down, to get squarely on our feet, to make sure of the right path. Let's get out of the fevered delirium of war, with the hallucination that all the money in the world is to be made in the madness of war and . . . its aftermath. Let us stop to consider that tranquility at home is more precious than peace abroad, and that both our good fortune and our eminence [greatness] are dependent on the normal forward stride of all the American people.

—from Warren G. Harding's campaign speech, 1920

Concern that the Red Scare was weakening freedoms protected by the Constitution led to the founding of the **American Civil Liberties Union (ACLU)** in 1920. The organization dedicated itself to defending the individual rights and freedoms of all Americans. The **Anti-Defamation League (ADL)** also worked to expose and counter the violence of extremist groups, including the Ku Klux Klan, which spread anti-Semitic and anticommunist propaganda. By late 1920, the Red Scare had lost momentum. Palmer had predicted ongoing violence, which never occurred, and his credibility was damaged.

The unrest and anxiety that immediately followed the war influenced the 1920 presidential election. Warren G. Harding easily won the election on his promise to "return to normalcy." He spoke of returning to an era of peace, wealth, and conservative values by reducing the power of government, lowering taxes, and reining in labor unions. Despite Harding's victory, the years ahead would be anything but normal. The 1920s would be a decade of extremes in the United States, combining broad cultural leaps toward modernity with deep anxiety about the country changing too fast and for the worse.

HISTORICAL THINKING

1. **READING CHECK** How did the end of World War I lead to a postwar recession?
2. **COMPARE AND CONTRAST** How was communism different from capitalism?
3. **EVALUATE** Why might the Palmer Raids be considered unconstitutional?

HI 1 Students show the connections, causal and otherwise, between particular historical events and larger social, economic, and political trends and developments.

1.2 **MAIN IDEA** During the 1920s, Americans who embraced modern ideas about science and society clashed with those holding more traditional beliefs.

DIVISIONS IN SOCIETY

Sometimes it's hard to let go of old ideas, especially ideas that make you feel comfortable and secure. During the 1920s, changes in society challenged traditional ways and sparked anxiety and division.

POINTING FINGERS

After a few difficult years following World War I, the nation's economy began to recover. This triggered a wave of immigrants from around the world. More than 430,000 people sought entry to the United States in 1920, and another 805,000 immigrants came in 1921. Competition with immigrants for jobs—along with the Red Scare—contributed to a rise in **nativism**. This ideology favored people born in the United States over more recent immigrants. Nativists especially targeted immigrants from southern and eastern Europe, who were more willing to work for low wages. Adding to the anti-immigrant sentiment was a rise in the popularity of **eugenics**, the belief that some races are superior to others. Eugenicists thought that the more "desirable" race, which was usually western European and Protestant, should populate and grow.

The rise of nativists and eugenicists—who warned of the "degradation" of the population—prompted U.S. lawmakers to take action. Congress approved an emergency quota law in 1921 that limited immigration from Europe to 600,000 people per year. Three years later, lawmakers passed the **National Origins Act**, which reduced annual legal immigration from Europe to about 150,000 people. The act gave preference to people arriving from western and northern European countries and blocked Asian immigrants entirely.

The courts often supported anti-immigrant legislation. One case that highlighted the courts' view involved an immigrant named Bhagat Singh Thind. Thind arrived in the United States from India in 1913 and began studying at the University of California at Berkeley. He volunteered for service in the U.S. Army during World War I. In 1920, he applied for U.S. citizenship, but he was denied under a 1917 law that barred all

PRIMARY SOURCES

Madison Grant was a nativist and a eugenics advocate. Franz Boas was an anthropologist and an opponent of such beliefs. The two held opposite views on immigration and diversity.

These immigrants adopt the language of the native[-born] American, they wear his clothes, they steal his name and they are beginning to take his women, but they seldom adopt his religion or understand his ideals and while he is being elbowed out of his own home the American looks calmly abroad and urges on others the suicidal ethics which are exterminating his own race.

—from *The Passing of the Great Race*, by Madison Grant, 1916

The fear of continued segregation of European national groups is not founded on facts, but on vague impressions obtained from the massing of immigrants in congested city quarters. It does not take into consideration the dispersion of the second and third generation, who become so thoroughly Americanized that in many cases it is quite impossible to obtain exact information in regard to the provenience [origin] of individuals.

—from "This Nordic Nonsense," by Franz Boas in *The Forum*, 1925

11.5.2 Analyze the international and domestic events, interests, and philosophies that prompted attacks on civil liberties, including the Palmer Raids, Marcus Garvey's "back-to-Africa" movement, the Ku Klux Klan, and immigration quotas and the responses of organizations such as the American Civil Liberties Union, the National Association for the Advancement of Colored People, and the Anti-Defamation League to those attacks.

CRITICAL VIEWING Syracuse University is home to artist Ben Shahn's 1967 mosaic mural *The Passion of Sacco and Vanzetti* (above). The detail of the mural (right) shows the men who upheld the death sentence standing before Sacco's and Vanzetti's coffins. The trial judge is in the background. Shahn, like many people, thought the men hadn't received a fair trial. What does the artist suggest about the judge and these men by including them in this mural?

immigration from India. He took his case to the U.S. Supreme Court. In the 1923 case, *United States* v. *Bhagat Singh Thind*, the Court ruled that "Hindus" were "aliens ineligible to citizenship." In effect, the ruling established that the federal government could deny citizenship based merely on race or country of origin.

Concerns about immigration played into another prominent court case—a highly controversial murder trial that grabbed global headlines. In 1920, a robbery and murder took place in South Braintree, Massachusetts. Police arrested two Italian immigrants who were also known anarchists, Nicola Sacco and Bartolomeo Vanzetti. Despite claims that authorities had framed the two men, a jury found them guilty and sentenced them to death. People around the world protested against this trial, which came to be called the **Sacco-Vanzetti case**. Many believed that bias against immigrants and radical political beliefs had led to an unfair trial. During the next several years, the men's attorneys filed appeals to overturn the verdict. The American Civil Liberties Union even aided in their defense. However, by 1927, their appeals had run out, and the state of Massachusetts executed the men.

THE RISE OF THE KLAN

Nativist sentiments led to the re-emergence of the Ku Klux Klan. The Klan, as you have read, opposed Catholics, Jews, Asians, women, African Americans, and other minorities. The group, known for its white hoods, regained popularity in the 1920s and spread its beliefs of white supremacy into northern states. Its members often used violence and terrorist tactics to intimidate those they opposed. Despite its reputation for brutality, including lynching and even torture, the Klan influenced many local and state leaders. Both Democrats and Republicans adopted some of the Klan's language to appeal to voters concerned about the rise of immigration.

The Klan claimed it had 3 million members by the early 1920s, but the organization's national influence began to decline around 1925 after scandals exposed widespread corruption. Meanwhile, groups such as the NAACP fought back against Klan violence through lawsuits and efforts to pass anti-lynching legislation. Despite ongoing racism, African Americans continued to make their voices heard during the 1920s, demanding more opportunities in all aspects of American society. In particular, African-American veterans of World War I expressed their beliefs that people who had risked their lives for their country should not be discriminated against.

To enforce prohibition, agents, often in disguise, identified places where alcohol was being served and confiscated it. In this photo from 1921, agents pour a barrel of beer down a sewer in New York City.

MOBSTERS AND BOOTLEGGERS

As you have read, the 18th Amendment and the Volstead Act had outlawed the sale of alcohol by 1920. Many progressives believed that these laws would decrease alcohol abuse in the United States. Overall, the laws achieved this goal. National consumption of alcohol declined significantly and rates of alcoholism dropped in the first few years of Prohibition.

However, Prohibition also had unintended consequences. In cities across the United States, **bootleggers**, or people who made, transported, or supplied alcohol illegally, sold their products to saloons or **speakeasies**, illegal drinking clubs where people secretly gathered in the evenings. Eventually, millions of middle-class Americans regularly broke the law by continuing to frequent speakeasies and purchase or make alcoholic beverages. Meanwhile, mobsters and their gangs became involved in the sale of illegal liquor, leading to a wave of violence and killing among rival crime organizations. Prohibition did not create organized crime. In fact, the 1920s was not a decade of rising crime rates overall. However, the nation became more aware of crime as a social problem due to the well-publicized activities of gangsters such as **Alphonse "Al" Capone**. In the later years of the decade, Capone ran a huge and notorious organization of illegal saloons, gambling houses, and other shady businesses in Chicago.

DISCOVERIES IN SCIENCE

The anxiety and unrest that emerged during the early 1920s was also fueled by new scientific theories that challenged traditional beliefs. Scientists like **Albert Einstein** argued that space, time, and mass

11.3.2 Analyze the great religious revivals and the leaders involved in them, including the First Great Awakening, the Second Great Awakening, the Civil War revivals, the Social Gospel Movement, the rise of Christian liberal theology in the nineteenth century, the impact of the Second Vatican Council, and the rise of Christian fundamentalism in current times; 11.5.3 Examine the passage of the Eighteenth Amendment to the Constitution and the Volstead Act (Prohibition); HREP 2 Students identify bias and prejudice in historical interpretations.

Albert Einstein won the Nobel Prize for Physics in 1921 for his work on relativity. Here, he was photographed while lecturing in Vienna, Austria, in 1921. That same year, Einstein, a German, visited the United States. He was impressed during his visit by what he called Americans' "joyous, positive attitude to life."

were all relative rather than absolute. This caused people to question traditional ideas about the nature of the universe. Psychologist **Sigmund Freud** suggested that the unconscious mind controlled much of an individual's behavior, an idea that opposed established notions about the causes of mental illness and emotional distress.

These new concepts spurred passionate debates among some American Christians over the proper position to take on scientific matters. Some Christians looked for ways to incorporate new scientific and social ideas into their traditional belief systems, but conservative church leaders preached about the dangers of moving away from the strict teachings of the Bible. This led to the rise of **fundamentalism**, a movement that promoted the idea that every word of the Bible was the literal truth. Fundamentalists criticized many aspects of modern thinking. In particular, they targeted Charles Darwin's theory of evolution, which, as you will remember, stated that diverse species originated from common ancestors and only the strongest species have adapted and changed in order to survive. Fundamentalists argued that the theory undermined the Bible's teaching that God created all life, including human life, at one fixed point in time. Lawyer and politician William Jennings Bryan emerged as a leading opponent of evolution. "It is better to trust the Rock of Ages," he said, "than to know the age of rocks." In a dozen states, lawmakers introduced bills to ban the teaching of evolution in public schools. A group called the Anti-Evolution League formed to challenge Darwin's theory. Its members hoped to ban the teaching of evolution throughout the nation.

In 1924, Tennessee passed a law that prohibited spending public money "to teach any theory that denies the story of the Divine Creation of man as taught in the Bible." The next year, authorities arrested and tried teacher **John T. Scopes** for talking about evolution in his high school classroom in Dayton, Tennessee. The Scopes trial attracted national attention, with many viewing it as a clash between traditional and modern ideas.

Bryan agreed to help prosecute Scopes. The ACLU brought in noted trial lawyer **Clarence Darrow** to defend the teacher. The judge refused to let Darrow call in scientists to defend evolution, so Darrow called Bryan as an expert witness on the Bible. Bryan defended the literal interpretation of the Bible. However, under Darrow's cross-examination, Bryan came across as contradictory and uncertain. The jury found Scopes guilty and assessed him a small fine. Although Scopes lost the trial, many Americans believed that Bryan's fundamentalism had lost the battle to science and reason.

HISTORICAL THINKING

1. **READING CHECK** What prompted the wave of immigration to the United States in the early 1920s?
2. **MAKE INFERENCES** How did nativist and eugenic beliefs fuel opposition to immigrants?
3. **ANALYZE CAUSE AND EFFECT** What effect did Prohibition have on alcohol consumption in the United States?
4. **DRAW CONCLUSIONS** Why was the Scopes trial viewed as both a victory and a defeat for fundamentalism?

MAIN IDEA Caves provided shelter for early humans and served another role thousands of years later: a place to locate speakeasies during Prohibition.

How Geology Kept the '20s Roaring

By Andrés Ruzo, National Geographic Explorer

A cave may not be where you choose to hang out with friends, but in the 1920s, caves had their attractions. For one thing, they made good hiding places. For another, in some of them, alcohol was served.

FINDING THE PERFECT SPEAKEASY

For many people during the 1920s, hiding out and drinking were both important considerations. As you have read, the 18th Amendment, popularly known as Prohibition, had passed, making the sale, production, importation, and transportation of alcoholic beverages illegal. Household consumption of the beverages was still legal, but unless people made their own, they had no way of getting a drink—except illegally, of course.

One of the best places to buy illegal alcoholic drinks was at a speakeasy. The word *speakeasy* suggests the need to whisper, and that's just what people often had to do to get into one of these establishments. Some required a password, others a secret knock or handshake. But these precautions didn't stop the determined. People flocked to speakeasies to drink, dance, enjoy music, and just have a good time.

Still, no one wanted to be arrested, so it was important to find the right speakeasy. Privacy, comfort, seclusion, safety, and getaway routes were all factors to consider. Speakeasies promising all these things popped up everywhere: in cities and in the country as well as in homes and businesses. Some were even in caves.

HUNKERING DOWN IN CAVES

In prehistoric times, early humans took refuge from their often hostile environment in caves. Geology was also on the side of Prohibition-era Americans who sought out caves because they provided shelter from the law. Caves form over hundreds or even millions of years in rocks as water drips through their cracks, eventually hollowing out underground channels. These make for perfect hideouts and even allow for secret passageways to be carved into the rock. And, with their thick walls, caves are insulated from the weather and so maintain near-constant temperatures all year round. As a result, speakeasies in caves were cool in the summer and relatively warm in the winter.

During Prohibition, these amenities attracted customers to the speakeasy at the Longhorn Cavern in Burnet, Texas, not far from the state capital of Austin. With its spacious dance room and dining area, the speakeasy provided a fairly respectable setting. In contrast, the speakeasy at the De Soto Cavern near Birmingham, Alabama, was known for its violence. Fights and shootings earned the speakeasy the nickname "the bloody bucket." Drunken patrons sometimes shot at the cave's **stalactites** and **stalagmites**—mineral deposits hanging from its ceiling or rising from its floor—and bullet holes can still be seen in the rock.

In 1933, Congress repealed the 18th Amendment—the only amendment to be entirely reversed—and liquor flowed freely once more. But Prohibition had forced people to think geologically and seek refuge in caves. The decade may have started on a dry note, but caves helped keep the '20s roaring.

THINK LIKE A GEOLOGIST

1. **READING CHECK** What factors did people look for in a speakeasy?
2. **ANALYZE ENVIRONMENTAL CONCEPTS** How did the formation of caves lead some people to benefit from this natural process during Prohibition?
3. **FORM AND SUPPORT OPINIONS** Would you like to explore a cave? Why or why not?

11.5.3 Examine the passage of the Eighteenth Amendment to the Constitution and the Volstead Act (Prohibition).

CRITICAL VIEWING The top photo shows the Longhorn Cavern in Burnet, Texas, which was converted into a speakeasy during Prohibition, complete with a wooden dance floor. The bottom photo shows the cavern today. What geologic elements shown in these pictures reveal why a cave would make an effective speakeasy?

HI 5 Students analyze human modifications of landscapes and examine the resulting environmental policy issues.

MAIN IDEA The postwar recession soon gave way to a prosperous economy built on consumer spending, but not all segments of society benefited from the boom.

A New Consumer Society

The camera follows a gleaming red sports car as it races down a highway. Inside, we see its slick leather interior as the driver shifts gears. Americans today are accustomed to these irresistible images, but in the 1920s this form of advertising was just developing.

Tangee lipstick—which changed color for each individual wearer—combined new technology, modern advertising, and the flapper's look to become a symbol of the Jazz Age. Young women of the 1920s carried their makeup in small compacts, like the one below, designed in the elaborate art deco style.

Art deco makeup compact

A NEW WORLD OF ADVERTISING

Despite the social anxiety and turmoil of the postwar years, the U.S. economy began to recover during the 1920s. Factory output returned to its prewar levels, and the unemployment rate fell from 12 percent of the labor force in 1922 to only 4 percent in 1927. A good portion of the recovery was stimulated by a new consumer culture, built on an expanding middle class continually encouraged to buy new products.

Advertising boomed during the 1920s. Ad agencies developed effective ways to persuade Americans to buy the many goods produced in the nation's factories. New means of communication, such as the radio, helped advertisers spread their messages and contributed to the development of **mass markets**, or large numbers of consumers to whom manufacturers can sell goods. Before World War I, about $400 million was spent on advertising annually. That number soared to $2.6 billion by 1929. "Advertising," said one industry specialist, "literally creates demand for the things of life that raise the standard of living, elevate the taste, changing luxuries into necessities."

As advertising was coming into its own, so was a new mass audience: the youth market. The growing economy made households more secure, so fewer children were expected to work to help support the family. As a result, many young people had greater freedom and more leisure time. The teen years came to be seen as a distinct phase in the development of young Americans, and the youth culture became linked with seeking fun, excitement, and novelty. Appealing images of cars, cosmetics, motion pictures, fashions, and other attractions in advertisements gave young people ideas about how to have fun and where to spend their parents' money.

Advertisers also focused on the growing number and variety of home products, including electrical appliances. The electric power industry expanded rapidly during the 1920s. By 1928, two-thirds of American families had electricity in their homes. This boosted the market for a host of appliances, from refrigerators and vacuum cleaners to electric irons and washing machines. Advertisers promised these products would make housework easier than ever and give families more time for leisure and fun.

AN AUTOMOBILE CULTURE ARISES

Among the mass consumer goods that emerged during the 1920s, none had a bigger impact on American society than the automobile. Cars became affordable to more and more Americans, thanks in large part to people like carmaker **Henry Ford**. Ford developed a simple and affordable vehicle, the **Model T**, and he devised an efficient way to mass-produce it. In his **assembly line** system, stationary workers each added a part to a vehicle as it moved along a conveyer belt. Ford's factories were soon turning out a car every 24 seconds, and millions of Americans were getting behind the wheel of the Model T. Ford shocked industry leaders by paying his workers five dollars a day—an unusually high rate for the time. But such wages ensured loyalty and limited turnover among his employees. Higher wages also pushed his factory workers into the middle class, and they, in turn, could afford to buy his cars.

The Model T was popular, affordable, and practical, but not particularly attractive. The Ford Motor Company's lack of varied car models was an opportunity for its competitor, General Motors (GM). Under the leadership of Alfred P. Sloan, Jr., GM introduced innovations that appealed to consumers, such as self-starters, fuel gauges, and reliable headlights. The constant flow of GM's new models and features led customers to want a fresh vehicle every few years. The General Motors Acceptance Corporation made it easy to acquire a car on credit, boosting profits for GM.

As car sales increased, so did the need for good roads throughout the nation. The Federal Highway Act of 1921 left road construction to the states, but it set national standards for concrete surfaces and access to roads. Gasoline taxes brought in revenues, enabling the state governments to build roads and highways. The national network of roads grew from 7,000 miles at the end of the World War I to 50,000 miles by 1927, and more than 20 million cars drove on them. A new category of businesses popped up along the roads to cater to travelers. Motels offered overnight accommodations, roadside restaurants provided food, and gas stations sold fuel and made car repairs. Even the advertising companies got in on the scene, erecting billboards along the roadways to promote local goods and services.

Other forms of transportation expanded as well during the decade. By 1927, there were more than 3 million trucks and buses on the roads. Glenn Curtiss, a champion bicycle racer, had made tremendous advances in motorcycle technology. After one of his early models tested at more than 136.3 miles per hour, he gained a reputation as the "fastest man on earth." Curtiss wasn't content to stick with motorbikes, however. He also helped advance the field of aviation, developing airplanes that set ever-increasing distance records.

11.5.6 Trace the growth and effects of radio and movies and their role in the worldwide diffusion of popular culture; 11.5.7 Discuss the rise of mass production techniques, the growth of cities, the impact of new technologies (e.g., the automobile, electricity), and the resulting prosperity and effect on the American landscape.

Automakers like Henry Ford recognized that more efficient car manufacturing processes would allow them to make less expensive cars. In 1913, Ford pioneered the first large-scale moving manufacturing assembly line, and by the mid-1920s, the auto manufacturing process had achieved large-scale uniformity. In this 1914 photo, Model Ts move continuously along a Ford assembly line in Detroit, Michigan.

> **PRIMARY SOURCE**
>
> During the 1920s, the advertising industry grew rapidly as the proliferation of newspapers, magazines, and radios gave it greater access to consumers. But the public became wary of fraudulent product claims, so advertisers promoted the Truth-in-Advertising Movement, a self-regulating program that later became the Better Business Bureau.
>
> *Truth in advertising is not only an asset, but brings business. Untruth in advertising is not only a liability, but it does not bring business in any lasting form. It may thrive for a time on the poor prey . . . [but] How absurd to commit a crime for minnows when whales are to be had for the catching! Truth is the best form of advertising.*
>
> —from "Just Why Implicit Truth Is the Business Man's Greatest Asset" by Ed Wolff in *Associated Advertising*, March 1921

STRUGGLES AND SCANDALS

Even as prosperity returned, some Americans still struggled. The postwar recession continued to hit farmers hard. As European agriculture recovered from the war, many overseas markets closed for American farm products. American farmers' incomes generally leveled off after 1919, and the gap between farm earnings and urban wages widened. As a result, most farmers could not afford the modern appliances and conveniences that city dwellers enjoyed.

Not everyone in the cities flourished, either. Labor unions had lost some of their popularity during the Red Scare, and many factory workers struggled to get ahead. Increasingly, government officials and business owners, citing the cost of supporting labor, worked to weaken the power of unions.

On the positive side, some prosperous companies, such as General Electric, International Harvester, and Bethlehem Steel, offered their workers recreational facilities, benefit plans, and even profit-sharing opportunities, through which workers were paid a portion of profits when their company performed well. These extras, which would become known as **welfare capitalism**, were meant to satisfy workers' demands without relying on unions. But as the decade wore on, many of these programs stalled. The weakening of organized labor had removed the incentive for employers to make concessions to workers.

Away from the emerging mass consumerism, the nation's leadership struggled with corruption and scandal. An indecisive leader and a poor judge of people, President Warren Harding had allowed cronies and crooks to infest his administration. Attorney General Harry Daugherty was a political ally of the president, and his weak oversight of the Justice Department had allowed corruption to flourish.

The Harding administration's most serious scandal was called the **Teapot Dome scandal**. Secretary of the Interior Albert B. Fall leased federal oil reserves in Teapot Dome, Wyoming, to private oil companies. Soon after, Fall received $400,000 from his friends in the oil industry in what many taxpayers interpreted as payoffs for his leasing decisions. The Teapot Dome scandal exposed Harding's presidency as one of the more corrupt administrations in American history. The president himself did not make it to the end of his term. During a tour of the West Coast, Harding fell ill in San Francisco and died of heart disease on August 2, 1923.

Calvin Coolidge, Harding's vice president and the former governor of Massachusetts, became the nation's next president. Coolidge promised to continue growing the economy and to promote Harding's return to "normalcy." Coolidge was even more committed to conservative Republican principles than Harding had been. He proclaimed that "the chief business of the American people is business," and he endorsed policies designed to promote free enterprise. He extended tax-cutting policies and appointed pro-business individuals to head the regulatory agencies and departments that progressives had established a generation earlier.

President Coolidge used modern public relations techniques to bolster his image as the embodiment of old-time virtues of morality and frugality, or thrift. In addition, Coolidge succeeded in cleaning up much of the corruption that had plagued Harding's term in the White House.

HISTORICAL THINKING

1. **READING CHECK** How did advertising drive mass markets in the 1920s?
2. **IDENTIFY MAIN IDEAS AND DETAILS** How did Henry Ford's assembly line increase mass marketing of automobiles?
3. **ASK AND ANSWER QUESTIONS** What other questions do you have about the consequences of the new consumer economy in the 1920s, and where can you find the answers?
4. **MAKE GENERALIZATIONS** Why was the farming industry not as prosperous as other industries during the early 1920s?

11.5 Students analyze the major political, social, economic, technological, and cultural developments of the 1920s; 11.5.1 Discuss the policies of Presidents Warren Harding, Calvin Coolidge, and Herbert Hoover.

2.1 **MAIN IDEA** In the 1920s, a distinct form of African-American music known as jazz emerged and gained popularity in the United States and parts of Europe.

THE BIRTH OF JAZZ

What do many of today's musicians have in common? They have been inspired by jazz artists. In fact, many rock and roll, hip-hop, and rhythm and blues musicians have been heavily influenced by jazz.

THE MUSIC OF NEW ORLEANS

After World War I, the music that came to be called **jazz** grew in popularity beyond its origins among African-American musicians in New Orleans. Jazz contains lively rhythms, sounds from a variety of instruments, and improvisation—the act of creating and playing music without prior rehearsal or reliance on a written score. Jazz is a uniquely American art form, and from its beginnings it brought together black and white musicians. The term *jazz* came into wide use after a New Orleans group, the Original Dixieland Jazz Band, produced a best-selling record album with mass appeal.

In the 1920s, radio stations broadcast live jazz concerts almost every night, making jazz singers and bandleaders famous. A leading jazz artist, **Joe "King" Oliver**, took his band on the road to cities such as Chicago and New York. Oliver trained many new artists in jazz techniques, and these

CRITICAL VIEWING Jazz and blues artists Ma Rainey (center) and her Georgia Jazz Band (from left), Gabriel Washington, Albert Wynn, Dave Nelson, Ed Pollack, and Thomas A. Dorsey, brought old country blues and new jazz to sold-out crowds in the 1920s. The innovative Ma Rainey was the first singer to record "See See Rider," a song still popular today. What image of jazz and the blues is projected by the musicians in this photo?

11.5.6 Trace the growth and effects of radio and movies and their role in the worldwide diffusion of popular culture; 11.8.8 Discuss forms of popular culture, with emphasis on their origins and geographic diffusion (e.g., jazz and other forms of popular music, professional sports, architectural and artistic styles).

artists took what they learned and added their own variations and innovations. Jazz trumpeter **Louis** (LOO-ee) **Armstrong** was one of the musicians who worked with Oliver early in his career. Armstrong was nicknamed Satchmo, for "Satchel Mouth," because his cheeks puffed out like a bag when he played. Armstrong became one of the world's most successful musicians, and throughout his career, he helped spread American culture and goodwill through his talent.

JAZZ FROM COAST TO COAST

Modern forms of communication, such as record players and radio, helped spread the popularity of jazz from coast to coast and throughout the world. The music traveled from major American cities to smaller urban centers, such as Kansas City and Denver, and across the ocean to Britain, France, and even Russia. Part of the music's appeal lay in its fast-paced, unpredictable style. Many younger Americans looking for entertainment started attending nightclubs to dance to jazz music. The rhythms and sounds of jazz gave the 1920s its enduring title: the Jazz Age.

Trumpeter and singer Louis Armstrong is pictured on the cover of the sheet music for "Saint Louis Blues," an iconic jazz song written in 1914 by W.C. Handy. Armstrong first recorded the song in 1929.

Jazz also helped increase the crossover appeal of other African-American musical forms, especially the blues, the roots of which reach back to slave spirituals. Unlike upbeat jazz music, blues songs speak of sadness and heartache, sometimes covering adult themes such as alcoholism and drug abuse. Blues artists **Gertrude "Ma" Rainey** and **Bessie Smith** often drew upon their personal experiences in singing their sad, soulful tunes. Early in her career, a young Bessie Smith sang with Rainey and one of her bands. Both women performed and recorded songs with Armstrong. By the end of the 1920s, Smith was the highest paid performer in the world.

Some older, more conservative Americans considered jazz shocking. They associated the music with illegal drinking and other illicit activities. Jazz and the blues became one more point of generational conflict in the divide between traditional and modern cultural norms. Eventually, jazz gained widespread appeal and respect, particularly from Armstrong's global popularity and stars such as singer and bandleader **Cab Calloway**, dancer and singer **Josephine Baker**, and pianist and bandleader **Edward Kennedy "Duke" Ellington**.

The multitalented Calloway turned down a chance to play with the famous Harlem Globetrotters basketball team and left law school to sing with a band. He became a popular bandleader at the Cotton Club in Harlem, a composer, a scat singer (someone who sings jazz using only syllables instead of words), and a Broadway and film actor. Pianist, composer, and bandleader Duke Ellington is probably the most well-known American jazz musician. He is noted particularly for writing to showcase the talent of each member of his band. In describing his inspiration to write jazz, or what he liked to call "American music," Ellington said, "My men and my race are the inspiration of my work. I try to catch the character and mood and feeling of my people."

HISTORICAL THINKING

1. **READING CHECK** What were the origins of jazz?
2. **DESCRIBE** What are some characteristics of jazz music?
3. **FORM AND SUPPORT OPINIONS** Why do you think jazz was so popular in the 1920s?
4. **IDENTIFY** Through what methods was jazz music diffused across the United States and throughout the world?

2.2 **MAIN IDEA** The 1920s saw the rise of popular entertainment and sports along with a flourishing literary culture.

Popular Culture and Artistic Achievement

Consider some of the things you like to do today, from watching videos on a computer or phone to going to movies, sporting events, or concerts. It all began in the 1920s, as mass forms of entertainment emerged and Americans began to enjoy the shared experience of popular culture.

MOVIES AND RADIO

With money to spend and more free time than ever, Americans found many ways to entertain themselves. One of the most popular activities was going to the movies. From uncertain beginnings at the turn of the century, motion picture studios had developed into large enterprises employing hundreds of people. Studio heads, including Adolph Zukor of Paramount Pictures and Louis B. Mayer of Metro-Goldwyn-Mayer (MGM), also controlled theater chains in order to show the films they had made on a tight schedule to maximize profits.

These posters, from the golden age of silent movies, advertise the films *It* (1927) with Clara Bow and *The Sheik* (1921) with Rudolph Valentino. In bright, bold colors, the posters feature the names and portraits of the stars, whose popularity drew the public into the movie "palaces," or theaters.

11.5.6 Trace the growth and effects of radio and movies and their role in the worldwide diffusion of popular culture; 11.5.7 Discuss the rise of mass production techniques, the growth of cities, the impact of new technologies (e.g., the automobile, electricity), and the resulting prosperity and effect on the American landscape.

AN ORIGINAL AMERICAN ARCHITECTURE

During the 1920s, creative building designs flourished and became the basis of 20th century architecture. Among the most innovative architects of that time was **Frank Lloyd Wright**, who developed the Prairie style, a uniquely American design. Wright was influenced by the natural world, as represented here in his Fallingwater House, which was built in the mid-1930s in Bear Run, Pennsylvania. Today, skyscrapers and city centers throughout the world reflect aspects of Wright's distinctive Prairie style, which emphasizes geometric shapes and openness.

At the motion picture industry's peak during the 1920s, 20,000 theaters screened films attended by some 100 million people each week. Ticket prices were relatively affordable—admission was usually about 50 cents. Until the end of the decade, all the movies were silent. Live musicians in the theaters provided background music and sounds. Large urban movie palaces boasted entire orchestras to accompany silent films, but most smaller movie houses simply hired a pianist to put sound to the picture. Title cards in the films provided limited dialogue. The movie actors had to depend on their ability to convey emotions through facial expressions and actions, and actors who mastered the craft often became stars.

The movies provided a model for what young people wore, the slang they used, and even how they behaved. Women copied the fashions and bobbed haircuts of popular actresses, such as **Clara Bow**, nicknamed the "It Girl" for her on-screen appeal. Fans closely followed the personal lives of Hollywood celebrities, such as **Mary Pickford**, the biggest box office star of the decade and a leader in the film industry. Some historians consider Pickford and her husband, dashing action star **Douglas Fairbanks**, to have been the first Hollywood "supercouple." Comic actor **Charlie Chaplin** and mysterious, handsome **Rudolph Valentino** also attracted a huge following of adoring fans.

In 1926, when Valentino died suddenly at the age of 31, many of his shocked fans became hysterical. Because they had seen him on-screen and read magazine articles about him, fans felt as if they had lost someone they knew. Thousands of people paid their respects at his funeral as hundreds of thousands stood on the street outside. It was the first time a celebrity was the object of such a public outpouring of grief. The reaction to Valentino's death reflected the growing influence movie stars had on American culture.

By the end of the decade, the film industry developed the technology to synchronize sounds with the actions of actors. Sound films, or "talkies," replaced silent pictures. The first major sound film, *The Jazz Singer* (1927), starred well-known entertainer **Al Jolson**. Fans loved the possibilities sound offered to enhance the film-going experience.

Radio technology, made possible by the expansion of electricity, added to entertainment options at home. The first radio station, KDKA in Pittsburgh, went on the air in 1920. In 1923, New York station WBAY began selling airtime to advertisers, who quickly

11.8.8 Discuss forms of popular culture, with emphasis on their origins and geographic diffusion (e.g., jazz and other forms of popular music, professional sports, architectural and artistic styles).

saw the potential of radio to spread their messages. Radios soon became popular consumer items, and by 1923, they were in 400,000 households.

HEROES OF SPORT AND DARING FEATS

Another pastime that took off during the 1920s was following sports. During the decade, football grew into a national obsession. Large stadiums sprang up at colleges on the West Coast and in the Midwest. The most famous football player of the era was **Harold "Red" Grange** of the University of Illinois. When he scored 4 touchdowns in 12 minutes against the University of Michigan in 1924, his picture appeared on the cover of *Time*, a new magazine featuring news and popular culture. After he left college, Grange joined the newly formed National Professional Football League, a predecessor of today's National Football League, where he was paid $12,000 per game at the start. In contrast, the average worker in 1925 made 65 cents an hour.

Although football attracted millions of followers, baseball best captured the excitement and passion of the 1920s, especially after a phenomenal player named **George Herman "Babe" Ruth** emerged.

The National Museum of American History Washington, D.C.

Popular for his dramatic home runs and generosity to fans, Babe Ruth (1895–1948) signed this baseball for a Pennsylvania fan. The Sultan of Swat played ball at St. Mary's Industrial School for Boys before joining the Red Sox and then the Yankees, the team he led to seven American League pennants and four World Series titles.

Babe Ruth was a pitcher for the Boston Red Sox when they traded him to the New York Yankees for $400,000 in 1918. Ruth was the first of the celebrity sluggers. He belted out 54 home runs during the 1920 season alone. His team constructed Yankee Stadium ("The House That Ruth Built") to hold the growing number of fans who flocked to New York City to watch him play. Baseball fans were captivated in 1927 when Babe Ruth hit 60 home runs, helping the New York Yankees capture the American League pennant and win the World Series in four games. Other sports heroes of the time included **Gertrude Ederle**, the first woman to swim the English Channel, and heavyweight boxing champion **Jack Dempsey**.

Athletes were not the only people who gained fans through their extraordinary feats. **Charles A. Lindbergh** secured his fame and fortune by making a historic, groundbreaking flight across the Atlantic Ocean. Lindbergh, an airmail pilot for the government, took up a challenge that offered a $25,000 prize to the pilot who could make the first solo nonstop flight between New York City and Paris, France, a distance of 3,610 miles. Lindbergh raised money to have a new plane built—the *Spirit of St. Louis*. On May 10, 1927, Lindbergh took off from Roosevelt Field in New York, headed across the Atlantic Ocean to Paris. When he landed in the French capital 33 hours and 30 minutes later, he was an international celebrity. Lucky Lindy, as he came to be known, was celebrated with a parade in New York City in his honor, medals from foreign nations, and a lifetime in the public eye. To the generation growing up in the 1920s, Lindbergh's laudable feat symbolized the ability of a single person to overcome any obstacle by sheer determination.

THE "LOST GENERATION" OF WRITERS

Not all artists and entertainers tried to appeal to popular tastes. Many leading authors of this time had come of age during World War I, and the horror of that war darkened their views of society. Their writing often struck a hard and realistic tone, a style that later became known as **modernism**.

The list of influential authors of the 1920s is long and distinguished. The most popular novelist of the early 1920s was **Sinclair Lewis**, whose books *Main Street* (1920) and *Babbitt* (1922) examined small-town life in the Midwest with brutal honesty. Novelists such as **Edith Wharton**, **Willa Cather**, and **William Faulkner** produced bodies of work that examined the lives of aristocratic women (Wharton), prairie pioneers (Cather), and life in the Deep South (Faulkner) with unflinching frankness rather than rosy nostalgia.

11.8.8 Discuss forms of popular culture, with emphasis on their origins and geographic diffusion (e.g., jazz and other forms of popular music, professional sports, architectural and artistic styles).

National Air and Space Museum, Washington, D.C.

The Ryan Airlines NYP *Spirit of St. Louis* plane hangs high above visitors in a flight hall at the National Air and Space Museum. In 1927, pilot Charles Lindbergh flew the monoplane across the United States and set a transcontinental record of 21 hours and 40 minutes for the flight. Eight days later, he made the 3,610-mile flight from New York to France. His risky venture brought immediate attention and financial support to the U.S. aeronautical industry. Upon his return, Lindbergh toured the United States, Mexico, and other countries in the Americas in the *Spirit of St. Louis* and had the flags of those countries painted around the plane's nose.

Two of the most popular fiction writers of the decade were **Ernest Hemingway** and **F. Scott Fitzgerald**. World War I and its aftermath greatly shaped the works of both authors. They were among a group of artists whom fellow writer **Gertrude Stein** nicknamed the "lost generation." The phrase refers to the uncertainty and despair many artists felt after the war. Influenced by writer **Ezra Pound**, Hemingway wrote in a sharp, understated style in best sellers such as *The Sun Also Rises* (1926) and *A Farewell to Arms* (1929), which spoke of the pain and doubt suffered by those who had fought in World War I. In *The Great Gatsby* (1925), Fitzgerald told the story of young Jay Gatsby, who tried to use his wealth to impress a lost love—with tragic consequences.

PRIMARY SOURCE

Toward the end of *The Great Gatsby*, the narrator, Nick Carraway, reflects on the life of a wealthy couple with whom he had once been friends but now concludes are partly responsible for Gatsby's untimely death.

They were careless people, Tom and Daisy—they smashed up things and creatures and then retreated back into their money or their vast carelessness, or whatever it was that kept them together, and let other people clean up the mess they had made.

—from *The Great Gatsby*, by F. Scott Fitzgerald, 1925

HISTORICAL THINKING

1. **READING CHECK** How did people spend their leisure time and money in the 1920s?
2. **ANALYZE VISUALS** Based on the 1920s movie posters, what ideas do you think motion picture studios were trying to sell to their audiences?
3. **COMPARE AND CONTRAST** What was different and similar about the heroes of sports and the heroes of daring feats?
4. **ANALYZE LANGUAGE USE** What does Fitzgerald's description of his characters imply about values of the Jazz Age?

11.5 Students analyze the major political, social, economic, technological, and cultural developments of the 1920s.

3.1 **MAIN IDEA** In the 1920s, many women experienced newfound freedoms to express themselves, socialize, and enter the workforce.

CHANGING ROLES FOR WOMEN

Do you remember how you felt when you got your driver's license or your first job? That new sense of freedom and respect was similar to what a number of women felt in the 1920s as they gained greater independence in society.

EMBRACING NEW FREEDOMS

As it did for many people in America, World War I and its aftermath changed the lives of women. Having aided in the war effort and having won the right to vote, many younger women entered the postwar era with expectations very different from those of previous generations. Rather than moving straight from their parents' home to marriage and child-rearing, as was traditional before the war, more women sought to gain greater control over their lives by exercising personal choice in the timing of their education, career, marriage, and motherhood. After World War I, it became more common for a woman to postpone marriage or motherhood, in part because of access to new health care options, including family planning.

Standards for acceptable public behavior in the 1920s were changing for everyone, including young women. Dating young men without the presence of a chaperone and drinking in public—even though it was illegal—became commonplace. The most famous expression of these new social freedoms was conveyed through fashion. Many young women embraced a freer style of dress, and the media dubbed them "**flappers**." This name came from an illustration in a magazine showing a fashionable young woman whose rubber rain boots were open and flapping, but the real hallmarks of a flapper were her bobbed hair, her short dresses, and—perhaps most shocking of all—her use of cosmetics.

In 1925, a group of high school girls posed as flappers. The image of the flapper caught on as a symbol of a spontaneous approach to life.

AMELIA EARHART

Nicknamed Lady Lindy because she, too, was a record-breaking flier like celebrity pilot Lucky Lindy (Charles Lindbergh), aviator **Amelia Earhart** was a famous trendsetter of the 1920s. She was as skillful a flier and as knowledgeable about planes as any male pilot, and quickly established a huge fan following.

In 1928, Earhart became the first woman to fly across the Atlantic Ocean, and she was the first pilot of either gender to fly over both the Atlantic and Pacific oceans. Her dream was to become the first pilot to fly around the world. She set out on her journey in 1937, but she vanished with her navigator over the Pacific Ocean, more than 22,000 air miles into her trip. Her fate remains a mystery.

The flapper became associated with fun and fashion, and advertisers took notice. Magazines promoted this image to sell clothing and cosmetics to mass markets. As many young women looked to assert their independence, mass media pushed them to conform to the latest ideals of glamour and physical beauty. Many older suffragists scolded the younger generation for focusing on fun and glamour rather than on bringing about political and social changes. Most young women, however, were excited to break with traditional ideals, and to do it in their own ways.

ENTERING THE WORKFORCE

Women also wielded greater economic power, thanks to their increasing entry into the workforce. As the 1920s began, 8.3 million women worked outside the home, representing about 24 percent of the national workforce. Ten years later, the number of working women stood at 10.6 million, or 27 percent of the workforce. Despite this increase, the kinds of work available to women remained limited. A few occupations accounted for 85 percent of female jobs. One-third of employed women worked in clerical positions, one-fifth as domestic servants, and another third in factory jobs. And women were still paid less than men; on average, they made about half of what men earned for doing the same jobs.

In addition, not all women advanced equally. For the majority of working-class women, the barriers to opportunity remained high. Poor white women in the South often worked at dead-end jobs in textile mills or agricultural processing plants. Due to racial discrimination, African-American women found it difficult to secure nondomestic jobs in either the North or the South. Even upper- and middle-class white women faced formidable obstacles in the workplace. Many school districts forced newly married female schoolteachers to resign. The medical and legal professions employed more women than in the past, but men in power made it difficult for women to advance in these careers. In government, male employees regularly received favorable treatment. What's more, women were still expected to take care of all household duties—which made managing a full-time job all the more difficult.

HISTORICAL THINKING

1. **READING CHECK** In what ways did women's lives change in the 1920s?
2. **DESCRIBE** How did women exercise their new freedoms and increased independence after World War I?
3. **IDENTIFY MAIN IDEAS AND DETAILS** How did Amelia Earhart represent the changing roles of women in the 1920s?
4. **COMPARE AND CONTRAST** How were women's experiences in the workforce in the 1920s different from and similar to those of men and to those of women today?

11.5.4 Analyze the passage of the Nineteenth Amendment and the changing role of women in society; 11.10.7 Analyze the women's rights movement from the era of Elizabeth Cady Stanton and Susan B. Anthony and the passage of the Nineteenth Amendment to the movement launched in the 1960s, including differing perspectives on the roles of women; HI 3 Students interpret past events and issues within the context in which an event unfolded rather than solely in terms of present-day norms and values.

3.2 **MAIN IDEA** Although women in the 1920s could now exercise their right to vote and become more active in government, they did not have as immediate an impact on politics as some had expected.

WOMEN IN POLITICS

Hearing about women running for and being elected to prominent government positions is not uncommon today, but this is a relatively new development in the United States. It was only in the 1920s, after passage of the 19th Amendment, that women slowly began to enter politics.

WOMEN IN ELECTED OFFICE

As you have read, the 19th Amendment to the U.S. Constitution guaranteed women throughout the country the right to vote. Both supporters and opponents of women's suffrage had expected the amendment to change politics dramatically after it was ratified in 1920. It soon became apparent, however, that a majority of women tended to vote for the same candidates as the men in their lives. The notion of a unified bloc of female voters did not materialize.

Although women's suffrage did not usher in the sweeping political change some observers had predicted, increasing numbers of women served in political office in the 1920s. Two states, Wyoming and Texas, were the first to elect female governors. When Governor William Ross of Wyoming died shortly before votes were cast in his 1924 campaign for re-election, political leaders persuaded his widow, **Nellie Tayloe Ross**, to take his place on the ballot. Despite campaigning very little, Ross easily defeated her male opponent to become the United States' first female governor. She proved an excellent leader, remaining independent and refusing to bow to special interest groups. She narrowly lost her bid for re-election in 1926, after powerful business leaders backed her opponent. Ross went on to work for the federal government in Washington, D.C., as the first female director of the United States Mint, a position she held for more than 20 years.

The same year of Ross's election, **Miriam Amanda "Ma" Ferguson**, a housewife with no previous political experience, won the Texas governor's seat. The legislature had impeached and convicted her husband, the popular but corrupt James "Pa" Ferguson, and barred him from holding state office. Ma Ferguson ran with the goal of carrying on her husband's work and clearing his name. Like Ross, she easily defeated her male opponent. Ferguson took office 15 days after Ross, making her the country's second female governor. Surrounded by the same cronies who had corrupted her husband's administration, Ferguson faced her own scandals, which kept her from winning re-election. Ferguson remained active in politics, however, and she made a comeback in 1932 when voters elected her as governor again. During her second term, a much more politically experienced Ferguson proved an

Governor Nellie Tayloe Ross, c. 1925

11.5.4 Analyze the passage of the Nineteenth Amendment and the changing role of women in society.

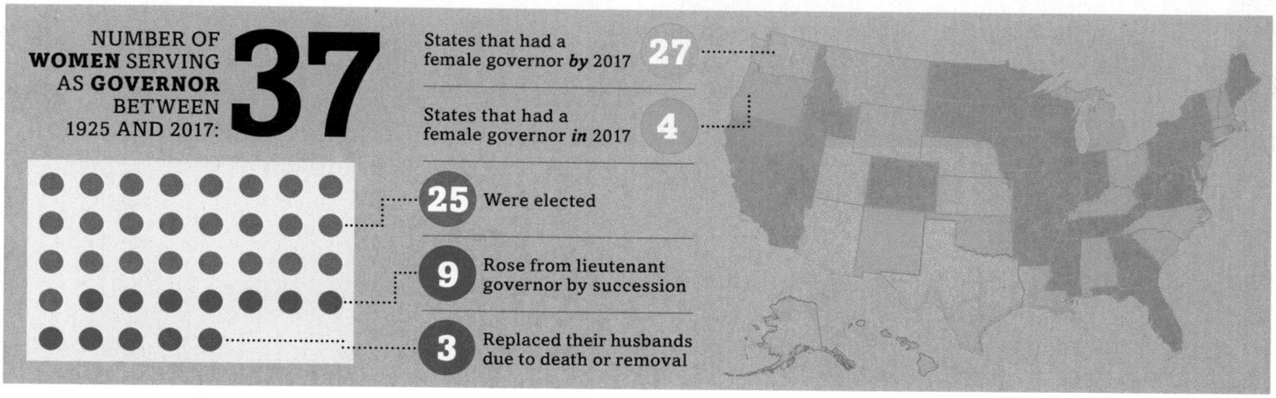

effective leader to her **constituency**, or those who elected her, during tough economic times.

During the 1920s, voters elected 11 women to the House of Representatives, many of them as political heirs of their husbands. Many more women won seats in state legislatures and held local offices. Other women, such as **Eleanor Roosevelt**, the wife of a rising Democratic politician in New York, built up a network of support for women's causes and careers. In 1924, Roosevelt accepted a position as chair of the National Democratic Party's platform committee on women's issues. After male party leaders refused to allow the women of the committee to participate in the final party platform decisions, Roosevelt pressed for the inclusion of more female party delegates. In 1928, she organized one of New York's most successful campaigns ever to encourage women's political participation. "Women must learn to play the game as men do," she wrote.

EQUAL RIGHTS FOR WOMEN

Having achieved the vote, a more militant, or activist, wing of the suffragists campaigned to add an **Equal Rights Amendment (ERA)** to the U.S. Constitution. The purpose of the amendment was to end gender discrimination, which primarily affected women. Examples of discrimination, according to ERA proponents, ranged from women earning less than men for the same work to being excluded from various activities and jobs. Originally proposed by Alice Paul in 1923, the amendment states, "Equality of rights under the law shall not be denied or abridged by the United States or by any state on account of sex." Paul viewed the amendment as the next logical step in bringing "equal justice under law" to all U.S. citizens.

The amendment's language seemed simple and straightforward, but in reality it left much to interpretation. Some female reformers, such as Florence Kelley and Carrie Chapman Catt, opposed the ERA. They regarded it as a threat to hard-won laws that protected women in the workplace, such as maximum hours, minimum wage, and safe working conditions. Despite the lobbying efforts of Paul's National Woman's Party, the ERA did not gain wide support during the 1920s. Even so, the amendment was introduced in every session of Congress until it was approved in slightly modified form in the early 1970s.

A WOMAN RUNS FOR PRESIDENT

Nellie Ross and Ma Ferguson weren't the first women to run for office. At least one woman aspired to the highest position in the land decades before women were even allowed to vote. On April 2, 1870, the country's first female stockbroker, Victoria C. Woodhull, announced her candidacy for president. Her platform included an eight-hour workday, divorce laws that treated men and women equally, and support for social welfare—all issues that would come up in future decades. "I am quite well aware that in assuming this position I shall evoke more ridicule than enthusiasm at the outset," she wrote. Woodhull was disqualified for the candidacy due to her age. Presidents must be at least 35 years old; Woodhull was 34.

HISTORICAL THINKING

1. **READING CHECK** In what ways were Nellie Ross and Miriam Ferguson effective role models?
2. **MAKE INFERENCES** Why did some women see the need for an equal rights amendment?
3. **ANALYZE CAUSE AND EFFECT** Why didn't the ratification of the 19th Amendment bring about sweeping changes in American politics?
4. **INTERPRET CHARTS** Based on the chart, how many women became governor without initially running for the office?

11.10.7 Analyze the women's rights movement from the era of Elizabeth Cady Stanton and Susan B. Anthony and the passage of the Nineteenth Amendment to the movement launched in the 1960s, including differing perspectives on the roles of women; HI 2 Students recognize the complexity of historical causes and effects, including the limitations on determining cause and effect.

4.1 **MAIN IDEA** The 1920s saw a major migration from the rural South to the urban North as African Americans sought new economic and political opportunities in large cities.

THE GREAT MIGRATION

As industry continued booming in the steel and car manufacturing cities of the North, thousands of African Americans arrived seeking better jobs and new lives. Most were not disappointed. One migrant to Chicago declared in a letter to his southern family, "Nothing here but money, and it is not hard to get."

DISCRIMINATION IN THE NORTH

During World War I, the need for northern factory workers led to the Great Migration, in which African Americans and other minority groups moved from the South to the North and West. The migration continued during the 1920s, as the economy boomed and industries expanded. In all, 1 million African Americans—about 13 percent of the South's entire black population—moved to cities such as Chicago, Detroit, New York, Los Angeles, and San Francisco.

Within their segregated neighborhoods, the migrants created vibrant communities. As African-American neighborhoods grew in the North, their residents gained greater local political influence. In addition, community magazines and newspapers, such as the *Chicago Defender*, focused on issues of local concern. Some publications gained national and international reputations, making it more difficult in some cases for political leaders to ignore the concerns of African-American citizens.

While African Americans found greater opportunity in the North and West, they still confronted racism. Whites who did not want the ethnic makeup of their cities to change or who feared economic competition, initiated conflicts with African-American migrants. In 1917, racial tensions boiled over in East

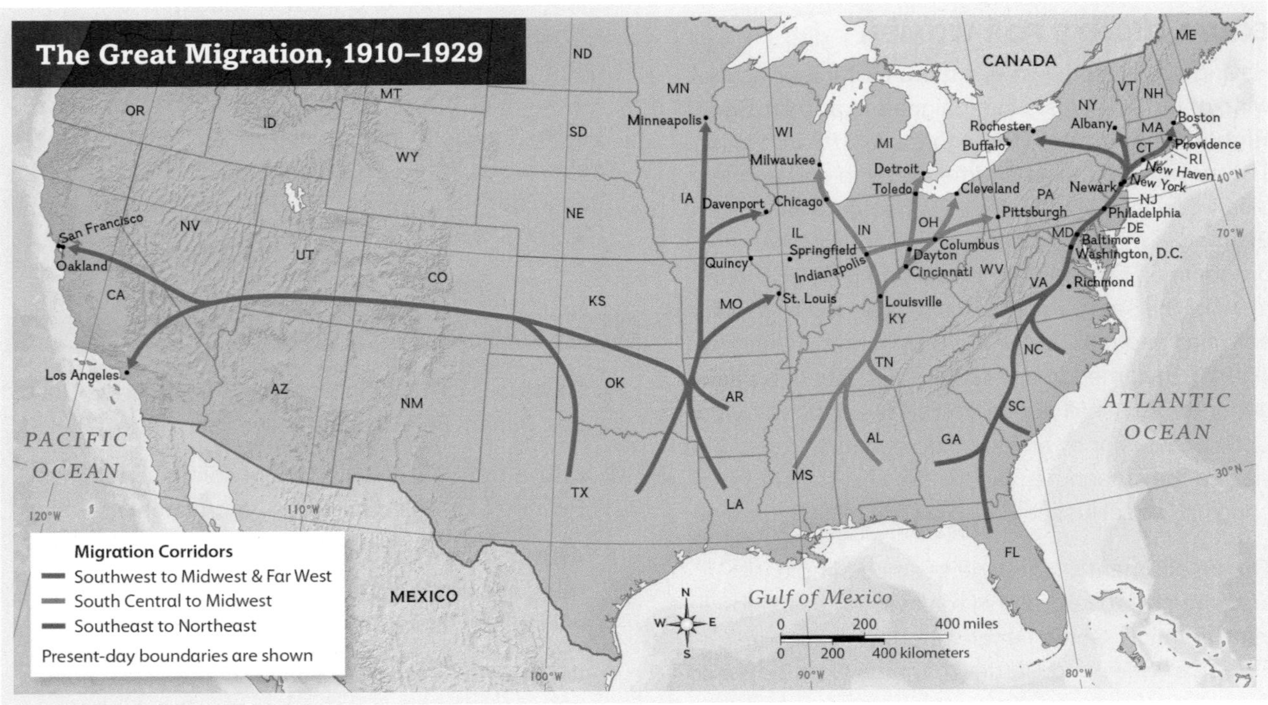

11.5.2 Analyze the international and domestic events, interests, and philosophies that prompted attacks on civil liberties, including the Palmer Raids, Marcus Garvey's "back-to-Africa" movement, the Ku Klux Klan, and immigration quotas and the responses of organizations such as the American Civil Liberties Union, the National Association for the Advancement of Colored People, and the Anti-Defamation League to those attacks.

St. Louis, Illinois, across the Mississippi River from St. Louis, Missouri. Many migrants had moved to the area for work. Following rumors that a black man had killed a white man, roving bands of whites attacked African Americans, killing between 39 and 100 African Americans. They also destroyed $400,000 worth of property. The number of race riots increased during the postwar recession, as white workers saw African Americans as economic competitors.

In the face of growing violence and discrimination, many African Americans in the North looked to the NAACP for assistance. Since it began in 1909, the NAACP, which, as you have read, W.E.B. Du Bois helped found, had worked to build a network of local branches in cities across the country. Between 1917 and 1919 alone, the organization's membership jumped tenfold, from about 9,000 to 90,000 people.

Responding to the violence of the 1920s, civil rights leaders altered their strategies for overcoming segregation and discrimination. Focusing on the long view, the NAACP organized a team of lawyers to challenge segregationist laws in court and influence legislation. But change came slowly. It took more than 30 years for the organization to achieve one of its main goals: persuading Congress to pass a federal anti-lynching law.

A NEW HOMELAND

A number of African Americans believed the NAACP's methodical approach to combating racism and segregation was far too slow. As a result, they turned to more militant civil rights leaders who promised faster results. **Marcus Garvey**, who had immigrated to the United States from Jamaica in 1916, was among the most powerful of those leaders.

In part, Garvey followed Booker T. Washington's beliefs that African Americans should focus more on improving their personal economic conditions than on ending legal segregation. Garvey urged African Americans to support black-owned businesses and organizations to empower their communities. He also boosted the self-esteem of many followers by encouraging conversations about African pride.

The charismatic Garvey preached the doctrine of **Pan-Africanism**, a movement that sought to unify people of African descent. Many of Garvey's followers hoped to establish settlements in Africa so that African Americans could move there and live together. Garvey led this **back-to-Africa movement** and promised to "organize the 400,000,000 Negroes of the World into a vast organization to plant the banner of freedom on the great continent of Africa." He created a group called the Universal Negro Improvement Association (UNIA) to establish such settlements in areas of Africa that were not controlled by imperialist nations.

At what he called the "First International Convention of the Negro Peoples of the World" in 1920, Marcus Garvey was elected the "Provisional President of Africa." This photo captured Garvey in his self-styled presidential uniform as he rode in a Harlem parade.

Pan-African rallies in New York and other cities often drew 25,000 people and raised funds for the UNIA. Ultimately, however, poor management caused Garvey's venture to fail. His health, finances, and political power gradually declined until his death in 1940. However, Garvey's ideas continued to influence generations of African Americans. Many civil rights groups throughout the 20th century adopted Garvey's message that urban blacks should band together to wield economic and political power.

HISTORICAL THINKING

1. **READING CHECK** Why did the Great Migration continue into the 1920s?
2. **SYNTHESIZE** What approach did the NAACP take to fight segregation and discrimination?
3. **INTERPRET MAPS** What generalization can you make about where African Americans migrated to and from?

CST 3 Students use a variety of maps and documents to interpret human movement, including major patterns of domestic and international migration, changing environmental preferences and settlement patterns, the frictions that develop between population groups, and the diffusion of ideas, technological innovations, and goods.

4.2 **MAIN IDEA** As large numbers of African Americans settled in the North, they banded together to influence culture and the arts.

THE HARLEM RENAISSANCE

It feels good to be part of a group where everyone gets along and shares similar interests. This is how many African Americans felt as they settled in the New York City neighborhood of Harlem and built a flourishing community.

In November 1934, Zora Neale Hurston went to Chicago to give a performance of African-American stories and songs she had collected in the South. Harlem Renaissance photographer Carl van Vechten captured this shot of Hurston.

AN ERA OF CREATIVE REBIRTH

One of the vibrant communities that emerged from the Great Migration is the neighborhood of Harlem in New York City. Located on the northern part of Manhattan Island, for decades the neighborhood attracted a variety of working-class immigrants from different ethnic groups. Starting around 1904, the Afro-American Realty Company began recruiting African-American families to move to the area.

Over time, Harlem became a majority African-American neighborhood. By the 1920s, it was the premier African-American community in the United States, a place where black culture thrived. African-American writers, artists, and musicians who lived there led a wave of creativity known as the **Harlem Renaissance**, which spread across the country.

Major figures in the Harlem Renaissance included poets **Countee Cullen** ("Yet Do I Marvel," a famous sonnet) and **Claude McKay** (*Harlem Shadows*, a collection of his celebrated poetry) as well as the memoirist and songwriter **James Weldon Johnson** (*God's Trombones*). Many artists crossed over into multiple genres, such as anthropologist and writer **Zora Neale Hurston** (*Their Eyes Were Watching God*) and poet, playwright, and novelist **Langston Hughes** (*The Weary Blues*). Then as now, their work provided readers with vivid descriptions of life during segregation. "For various reasons, the average, struggling . . . Negro is the best-kept secret in America," Hurston wrote. "His revelation to the public is the thing needed to do away with the feeling of difference which inspires fear, and which ever expresses itself in dislike."

Some writers and artists, such as painter **Archibald J. Motley, Jr.**, who was born in New Orleans and spent most of his life in Chicago, found inspiration in the sights and sounds of the jazz and blues scenes. The music inspired young people and artists of all ages, and the venues were places for creative thinkers to socialize and share ideas. Writers and artists gathered at clubs, speakeasies, parties, and balls that welcomed diversity and embraced nontraditional gendered behavior, unlike other parts of society. In Harlem, white, black, lesbian, gay, and bisexual performers and patrons could mingle together, forming what we now refer to as the **lesbian, gay, bisexual, and transgender (LGBT)** community. Prominent Harlem Renaissance artists, including Hughes, Hurston, and Johnson, were thought to be part of this community.

11.5.5 Describe the Harlem Renaissance and new trends in literature, music, and art, with special attention to the work of writers (e.g., Zora Neale Hurston, Langston Hughes).

In 1936, artist Jacob Lawrence painted *Ice Peddlers*, a vivid portrayal of the daily journey of ice sellers on a Harlem street. Lawrence was still a teen when he created this sophisticated streetscape of the peddlers at the forefront of the bustling city that surrounds them. As one of the first young men trained by other artists in the African-American community during the Harlem Renaissance, Lawrence drew on the life around him to chronicle African-American experiences and the effects of the Great Migration.

Although excluding all but white customers, the Cotton Club featured largely African-American performers. The headliners on this night in 1930 included Avis Andrews, Ann Lewis, Bill Robinson, and Cab Calloway.

11.5.5 Describe the Harlem Renaissance and new trends in literature, music, and art, with special attention to the work of writers (e.g., Zora Neale Hurston, Langston Hughes).

The hottest nightclub in Harlem was the **Cotton Club**, originally opened as the Club Deluxe by African-American boxing champion Jack Johnson in 1920. The club featured the biggest names in jazz at the time, including Duke Ellington, Cab Calloway, and Louis Armstrong. In 1923, a white gangster named Owney Madden bought the club, expanded it, and remodeled it into a swanky, segregated venue he renamed as the Cotton Club. Although most of the Cotton Club's performers were African-American, only whites were allowed in the audience. The exclusive nature of the club enhanced its appeal among wealthy white club-goers while reinforcing racism and segregation. In many ways the Cotton Club served as a symbol of the limits of African-American success, even within black neighborhoods.

The Harlem Renaissance reached its peak in 1925. The neighborhood boasted an exciting nightlife filled with intellectuals, artists, and wealthy white patrons. A national magazine's special feature, titled "Harlem: Mecca of the New Negro," included an article describing the importance of the Harlem Renaissance for African Americans and the country:

> *It has attracted the African, the West Indian, the Negro American. [Harlem] . . . has brought together the Negro of the North and the Negro of the South; the man from the city and the man from the town and village; the peasant, the student, the business man, the professional man, artist, poet, musician, adventurer and worker, preacher and criminal, exploiter and social outcast. Each group has come with its own separate motives and for its own special ends, but their greatest experience has been the finding of one another.*

In the same year, Howard University professor **Alain Locke** published *The New Negro: An Interpretation*, a collection of works by Harlem Renaissance writers. The stories, essays, and poems in the book revealed a shift in how African Americans defined themselves. The work of many of the authors featured in the book has since been incorporated into American culture.

ON STAGE AND SCREEN

African Americans made advances in a variety of performing arts during the 1920s. As jazz and the blues wowed popular audiences, some African-American performers excelled in other musical forms. Opera singer **Roland Hayes** became an international star with his sensitive renditions of songs in multiple languages. He was the first African-American man to perform with a major American orchestra when he sang with the Boston Symphony.

PRIMARY SOURCE

In his introduction to *The New Negro*, Alain Locke states that his purpose was to "register the transformations of the inner and outer life of the Negro in America that have so significantly taken place in the last few years." This excerpt from an essay in the book describes life in Harlem.

> *[Harlem] has many unique characteristics. It has movement, color, gayety, singing, dancing, boisterous laughter and loud talk. One of its outstanding features is brass band parades. Hardly a Sunday passes but that there are several of these parades of which many are gorgeous with regalia and insignia.*

—from "Harlem: The Culture Capital," an essay by James Weldon Johnson, in *The New Negro*, 1925

Actress **Ethel Waters** started her career singing the blues and jazz but soon branched out as a popular performer in Broadway and film musicals. Her signature song was the lively tune "Heat Wave." One of her occasional costars was **Paul Robeson**, the most popular African-American stage and film actor of his generation. Robeson's skills as a star student and football player in his youth led to the rare opportunity to earn college and law degrees. Discouraged by racism in the legal profession, the multitalented Robeson turned to acting. His physical stature, good looks, and booming bass voice cut an imposing figure in stage and film versions of the hit musical *Show Boat*, especially during the legendary scene in which he sang "Ol' Man River." He used his celebrity status to draw attention to human rights and civil rights concerns.

HISTORICAL THINKING

1. **READING CHECK** What was the Harlem Renaissance?
2. **CATEGORIZE** Which arts did the Harlem Renaissance influence?
3. **COMPARE AND CONTRAST** How did the Cotton Club represent both opportunities and limitations for African Americans?
4. **DRAW CONCLUSIONS** Why do you think many African-American poets and other authors in the 1920s wrote about life under segregation?

11.5.2 Analyze the international and domestic events, interests, and philosophies that prompted attacks on civil liberties, including the Palmer Raids, Marcus Garvey's "back-to-Africa" movement, the Ku Klux Klan, and immigration quotas and the responses of organizations such as the American Civil Liberties Union, the National Association for the Advancement of Colored People, and the Anti-Defamation League to those attacks.

LANGSTON HUGHES 1902–1967

"I, too, sing America. . . . I, too, am America." —Langston Hughes

Langston Hughes wasn't the first writer to "sing America" in his poetry. In fact, in the poem "I, Too," quoted above, he may have taken his cue from poet Walt Whitman, who celebrated the speech of ordinary Americans as a great symphony of song. For his part, Hughes sang about America to the strains of jazz and the blues. He infused his poetry with the rhythm and structure of these musical forms to speak to all African Americans. They, too, he affirms in his poems, are America.

This 1958 photo shows Langston Hughes on the streets of New York, a setting he often explored in his poetry.

YOUNG WRITER

Hughes was the first African American to make his living as a writer. But then, he came from a family of firsts. His grandmother was the first African-American woman to graduate from Oberlin College in Ohio. His great-uncle was the first African American elected to public office. Great things were expected of young Langston.

But what his father, at least, didn't expect was that his son would want to be a poet. When Hughes was a child, his parents divorced, and his father moved to Mexico. Hughes was raised first by his grandmother and then by his mother and stepfather. After Hughes graduated from high school, he spent a year with his father in Mexico. It was there that Hughes told his father he wanted to make his living as a writer.

The pair argued bitterly over Hughes's career choice. Then, a poem Hughes had written while traveling to Mexico, "The Negro Speaks of Rivers," was published in *The Crisis*, the official magazine of the NAACP. The poem connects the

African-American experience with the dawn of civilization ("I bathed in the Euphrates when dawns were young") and the struggle for equality in America ("I heard the singing of the Mississippi when Abe Lincoln went down to New Orleans"). Impressed, Hughes's father agreed to pay for his son's education at Columbia University in New York City—as long as he studied engineering. As fortune would have it, though, when Hughes entered Columbia in 1921, the Harlem Renaissance was in full force.

He was hooked. The writers, artists, musicians, and thinkers of the movement fueled his passion for poetry and for creating a new African-American cultural identity. As a gay man, Hughes also felt a sense of belonging in 1920s Harlem, where LGBT life had expanded. As you have read, rules for acceptable gendered behavior seemed more flexible for black and white Americans in Harlem than in other parts of society at that time. Hughes soon became a central figure in Harlem's literary community. After just two semesters at Columbia, he dropped out.

THE VOICE OF HARLEM

Hughes solidified his reputation in the Harlem Renaissance movement with the publication of his first volume of poetry, *The Weary Blues*. It was hailed a masterpiece—even by the white press. For many, Hughes became the poetic voice of Harlem. But some African Americans criticized his work. Fearing that his poems reinforced racial stereotypes, they claimed Hughes should represent African Americans in the best possible light. Angrily, they dubbed him the "poet low-rate" of Harlem. In response to the criticism, Hughes said, "I felt that the masses of our people had as much in their lives to put into books as did those more fortunate ones."

Throughout his career, Hughes wrote poetry and prose that often angered both his black and white critics. But he continued to write about ordinary African Americans and their suffering and common experiences. These black Americans became his most devoted audience because he reflected their culture back to them through their language and music. Arguably more than any other African-American poet or writer, Hughes diligently captured the small details and frustrations of black life during the early part of the 20th century.

Hughes sang of struggles and dreams deferred, but he tempered his themes with humor, affection, and optimism. In "I, Too," Hughes writes about being denied a place at the table with white America. At the end of the poem, however, he envisions a time when there will be a place there for him and all African Americans: "They'll see how beautiful I am / And be ashamed."

HISTORICAL THINKING

1. **READING CHECK** Who was the subject of and intended audience for Hughes's poetry?
2. **MAKE INFERENCES** Why do you think Hughes often used the rhythm and structure of jazz and the blues in his poetry?
3. **FORM AND SUPPORT OPINIONS** Do you think Hughes's critics were right when they said that he should portray African Americans in the best possible light? Explain why or why not.

11.5.5 Describe the Harlem Renaissance and new trends in literature, music, and art, with special attention to the work of writers (e.g., Zora Neale Hurston, Langston Hughes).

THE ART OF THE COVER
The books of Langston Hughes were works of art, both inside and out. For his book covers (shown from top to bottom), Hughes collaborated with the famous painters Miguel Covarrubias and Aaron Douglas and popular illustrator Cliff Roberts, all of whom conveyed the spirit of the time in stylized silhouettes.

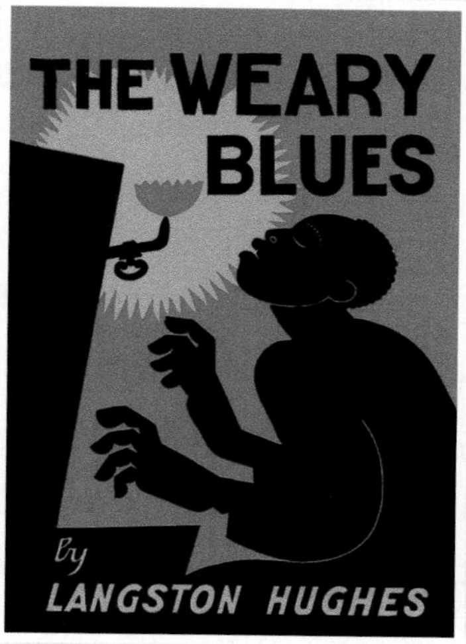

CHAPTER 9 THE JAZZ AGE AND MASS CULTURE

REVIEW

VOCABULARY

For each pair of vocabulary words, write one sentence that explains the connection between the words.

1. radical; Red Scare HSS 11.5.2
   During the Red Scare, many Americans were afraid of people who had radical political ideas.
2. nativism; eugenics HSS 11.5.2
3. assembly line; mass market HSS 11.5.7
4. jazz; flapper HSS 11.5.6
5. bootlegger; speakeasy HSS 11.5.3
6. Pan-Africanism; back-to-Africa movement HSS 11.5.2
7. American Civil Liberties Union; Anti-Defamation League HSS 11.5.2

READING STRATEGY

COMPARE AND CONTRAST

Comparing and contrasting concepts in a chart can help readers better understand the similarities and differences between people, events, and movements in history. In your chart, list traditional versus modern practices that emerged in major areas during the 1920s. Then answer the question.

Comparison Chart

	Traditional	Modern
Industry	Factories	Assembly line
Music		
Science		
Women's roles		

8. Which modern change had the most impact on a traditional practice, process, or idea? Explain your answer. HSS 11.5

MAIN IDEAS

Answer the following questions. Support your answers with evidence from the chapter.

9. What factors led to the Palmer Raids? **LESSON 1.1** HSS 11.5.2
10. What role did anti-immigration feelings play in the Sacco-Vanzetti case? **LESSON 1.2** HSS 11.5.2
11. How did the Teapot Dome scandal affect Warren Harding's presidency? **LESSON 1.3** HSS 11.5.1
12. How did new communications technology help popularize jazz? **LESSON 2.1** HSS 11.5.6
13. What forms of entertainment grew popular during the 1920s? **LESSON 2.2** HSS 11.5.6
14. How did the image of the flapper reflect the changing status of women? **LESSON 3.1** HSS 11.5.4
15. Why did the passage of the 19th Amendment fail to have the immediate impact some people thought it might? **LESSON 3.2** HSS 11.5.4
16. What factors made Marcus Garvey's back-to-Africa movement attractive to some African Americans? **LESSON 4.1** HSS 11.5.2
17. Why did so many African Americans move to Harlem in the 1910s and 1920s? **LESSON 4.2** HSS 11.5.5

HISTORICAL THINKING

Answer the following questions. Support your answers with evidence from the chapter.

18. **MAKE GENERALIZATIONS** How did culture change in the United States during the 1920s? HSS 11.5
19. **ANALYZE CAUSE AND EFFECT** What were the main effects of the 18th Amendment and the Volstead Act? HSS 11.5.3

20. **MAKE GENERALIZATIONS** What strides in politics did women make after passage of the 19th Amendment? HSS 11.5.4

21. **DRAW CONCLUSIONS** Why do you think the NAACP worked to change laws even if it might take years to accomplish? HSS 11.5.2

22. **FORM AND SUPPORT OPINIONS** Were the 1920s a "return to normalcy"? Support your opinion with evidence from the text. HSS HI 3

INTERPRET VISUALS

The August 1927 cover of *McClure's* magazine features a vision of the Jazz Age by the artist John Held, Jr. Look at the cover (at right) and answer the questions that follow.

23. What do you think the portrait of the flapper symbolizes, and why? HSS 11.8.8

24. In what ways does this illustration reflect the characteristics of the 1920s? HSS 11.8.8

ANALYZE SOURCES

Colleen Moore was an actor during the 1920s and 1930s famous for playing flappers in numerous movies. Moore talked to author Joshua Zeitz about how she was influenced by the free-spirited young women of the 1920s during an interview for his 2006 book *Flapper: A Madcap Story of Sex, Style, Celebrity, and the Women Who Made America Modern*. Read the excerpt, which is a quotation from Moore. Then answer the question.

> They were smart and sophisticated, with an air of independence about them, and so casual about their looks and clothes and manners as to be almost slapdash. I don't know if I realized as soon as I began seeing them that they represented the wave of the future, but I do know I was drawn to them. I shared their restlessness, understood their determination to free themselves of the Victorian shackles of the pre–World War I era and find out for themselves what life was all about.

25. What were the attributes that Moore admired in flappers? HSS 11.10.7

CONNECT TO YOUR LIFE

26. **ARGUMENT** Movies had a huge impact on fashion and other aspects of popular culture in the 1920s, and they still drive fashion and popular culture today. Then, as now, some people embraced this influence, and some people saw it as a threat to society and the status quo. Examine the influence of movies both now and in the 1920s, and write an argument that the art form exerts either a positive or a negative influence. HSS HI 4

TIPS

- Use textual evidence from the chapter in your argument.
- Clearly state your point of view, briefly including the reasons for your stance.
- Acknowledge the opposite viewpoint by providing one or two valid alternative ideas.
- Provide examples from the text and your own understanding and experience to support each reason for your argument.
- Provide a conclusion that restates your argument, making your stand on the matter clear.
- Use two or three vocabulary terms from the chapter in your response.

CHAPTER 10

THE GREAT DEPRESSION

1929–1939

HISTORICAL THINKING What impact did the Great Depression have on the American people, culture, economy, and spirit?

Walker Evans's photography during the Great Depression captured the essence of Americans' despair and worry. Here, the focus of his lens lands on the plates and bowls people are holding while they stand in line at a soup kitchen in Arkansas in 1937.

“Brother, can you spare a dime?”

—Yip Harburg, songwriter

THE DUST BOWL

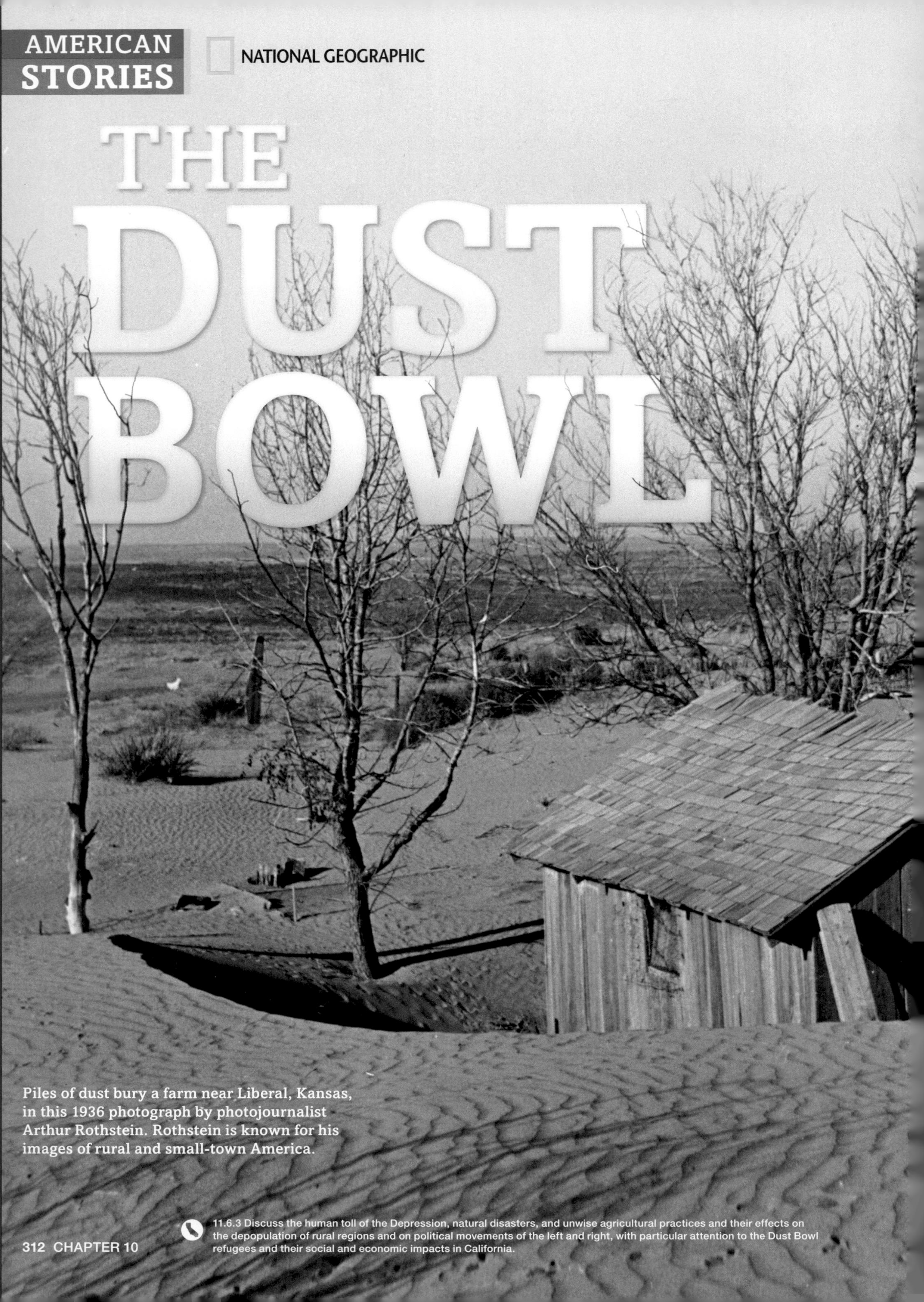

Piles of dust bury a farm near Liberal, Kansas, in this 1936 photograph by photojournalist Arthur Rothstein. Rothstein is known for his images of rural and small-town America.

11.6.3 Discuss the human toll of the Depression, natural disasters, and unwise agricultural practices and their effects on the depopulation of rural regions and on political movements of the left and right, with particular attention to the Dust Bowl refugees and their social and economic impacts in California.

Between 1931 and 1939, so-called "black blizzards"—dangerous dust storms—were frighteningly common across the Great Plains, especially in Texas, Oklahoma, Colorado, Kansas, and New Mexico. Journalist Robert Geiger coined the nickname "Dust Bowl" for this drought-stricken region in 1935. The name stuck because it was such an apt description for a bleak time and place, and possibly the worst environmental disaster ever to strike the United States.

When a black blizzard came howling into town, it looked and felt like the end of the world. One witness described one of these traumatizing storms after it assaulted a Texas town in 1935, writing, "The front of the cloud was a rolling, bumbling, boiling mass of dust and dirt about two hundred feet high, almost vertical, and as black as an Angus bull. . . . After the front passed, the darkness rivaled the darkness inside a whale resting on the bottom of the ocean at midnight." Lorena Hickok, a newspaper reporter, was in a car when a black blizzard hit. It was "[like] driving in a fog, only worse because of the wind that seemed as if it would blow the car right off the road," she recalled. "It was as though we were picked up in a vast, impenetrable black cloud which was hurling us right off the earth."

CAUSES AND REMEDIES

To a great extent, the Dust Bowl was a human-caused catastrophe. The Great Plains region has a semiarid climate, which means it receives light annual rainfall and is prone to occasional droughts. In the 1880s and 1890s, however, when millions of European settlers were arriving on the plains, the weather was exceptionally rainy, leading the new arrivals to the comfortable assumption that the bountiful rainfall would continue.

In the decades between 1880 and 1930, agricultural technology improved, allowing farmers to plow up increasingly wide swathes of native prairie grasses in order to plant their crops. These native plants had deep roots that anchored the soil when strong winds blew across the wide-open prairies, and they were perennials, which means they would survive from year to year. In contrast, wheat and other crops had shallow roots and were annuals, or plants that die after their growing season. Thus, in 1931, when heat and drought dried up the soil, there was nothing to hold it down when the turbulent winds blew. Wendell Berry, a writer and environmental activist, observed, "We plowed the prairie and never knew what we were doing, because we did not know what we were undoing." One perceptive Texas sheepherder put it more plainly when he asserted, "Grass is what holds the earth together."

A black blizzard could carry unimaginable quantities of dirt. In 1934, one storm traveled clear across the continent, deposited 12 million tons of former prairie soil on the city of Chicago, then carried dust so far east it darkened the sky in New York City and even reached ships 300 miles from shore in the Atlantic Ocean. On what became Black Sunday, April 14, 1935, another storm ripped up an estimated 300 million tons of topsoil from the Great Plains, trapping people who were caught outside in biting winds and absolute blackness.

The end of the Dust Bowl came about through both human solutions and nature's intervention. A federal agency called the Soil Conservation Service was established to introduce new farming techniques that would help retain the soil. The agency encouraged farmers to use contour plowing, a method of plowing furrows that follow the shape of the land, rather than plowing in a straight line regardless of hills or dips in the terrain. When occasional rains did fall, the contoured furrows would catch the water as it flowed downhill rather than channeling it through the parched land. The agency also suggested planting soybeans, sweet clover, and other crops that would help anchor the soil.

President Franklin Roosevelt also promoted his own plan, known as the Shelterbelt Project. According to the plan, the government would pay farmers to plant a broad line of trees from Texas to the Canadian border. This "shelterbelt" was intended to break the momentum of winds sweeping eastward across the plains and provide cooling to nearby areas. In the end, Roosevelt's shelterbelt was never completed, but it did help publicize the importance of taking action to reduce the negative effects of farming on the environment. By 1938, the drought continued unabated, but the tonnage of soil carried aloft by storms was reduced almost by half. In 1939, nature stepped in and rainfall resumed, putting an end to the lengthy drought.

CRITICAL VIEWING This poster from the late 1930s promotes the planting of trees on the Great Plains in order to combat wind erosion. How does the poster visually convey its message, and what audience do you think the poster was targeting?

11.6.4 Analyze the effects of and the controversies arising from New Deal economic policies and the expanded role of the federal government in society and the economy since the 1930s (e.g., Works Progress Administration, Social Security, National Labor Relations Board, farm programs, regional development policies, and energy development projects such as the Tennessee Valley Authority, California Central Valley Project, and Bonneville Dam).

CRITICAL VIEWING Thousands of migrant families in California carried their belongings from one farm to the next as they worked harvesting crops. How might this way of life have impacted children's social and educational lives?

THOSE WHO LEFT

When the long drought began, the United States was already in the throes of the Great Depression. Farmers were struggling to make a living after a drastic fall in crop prices. For many, the arrival of the first severe dust storms in 1933 turned a difficult situation into a desperate one. Crops and livestock were already suffering from the lack of moisture, and now the black blizzards were carrying the soil away. Homes and buildings were half buried, while animals trapped outside in the storms sickened and died from the dirt they inhaled. One grim joke of the time told of a farmer applying for a loan to support his farm, and then looking out the window of the bank to see that same farm blowing past in the wind.

Feeling they had no options, about one quarter of the people affected by the Dust Bowl decided to abandon their homes. Many of them packed their families and belongings into their cars and headed west for California, where they believed they would find work.

HI 1 Students show the connections, causal and otherwise, between particular historical events and larger social, economic, and political trends and developments.

SEEMS LIKE ANOTHER COUNTRY

As the black blizzards raged and bread lines stretched along city streets, some Depression-era artists sought to imagine the country in more promising times. A group of American painters known as Regionalists aimed to create a purely American style, distinct from the styles of their contemporaries in Europe, and several used the American countryside as their subject. Instead of the ravaged scenery of the Dust Bowl, they painted idealized Midwestern farms that appeared green, fertile, and prosperous. Among the most prominent Regionalists were Grant Wood, Thomas Hart Benton, and John Steuart Curry. The painting below by Grant Wood is entitled *Young Corn*.

How does the image of rural life portrayed in this painting by Grant Wood differ from the image shown in the photographs in this article?

"THE NIGHTMARE IS BECOMING LIFE"

Many people who lived through the Dust Bowl wrote horrifying accounts of black blizzards. Avis D. Carlson, of Kansas, wrote the following description in 1935 for the magazine *The New Republic.* How does the line, "It is becoming Real," contribute to the excerpt?

PRIMARY SOURCE

The impact is like a shovelful of fine sand flung against the face. People caught in their own yards grope for the doorstep. Cars come to a standstill, for no light in the world can penetrate that swirling murk. . . . The nightmare is deepest during the storms. But on the occasional bright day and the usual gray day we cannot shake from it. We live with the dust, eat it, sleep with it, watch it strip us of possessions and the hope of possessions. It is becoming Real. The poetic uplift of spring fades into a phantom of the storied past. The nightmare is becoming life.

The rich California farm fields could not have looked more different to the exhausted migrants streaming into the state. The area of California known as the Inland Empire was home to large farms growing lemons, oranges, lettuce, grapes, and many other varieties of produce. Jobs, however, were not so plentiful, and the agricultural work was back-breaking. In addition, the farm owners used the influx of migrants to force down the already low wages for all workers, including native Californians and immigrants from Mexico.

As a result, local workers intensely resented the newcomers, whom they called "Okies." The term was short for Oklahoma, although most of the migrants were not from that state. Singer Woody Guthrie, who was well acquainted with the sufferings of Dust Bowl refugees, described the connotations of the name "Okie." According to him, the term "means you ain't got no home. Sort of meant, too, that you're out of a job. Or owe more than you can rake or scrape [up]."

Thousands of Okies found themselves living in roadside camps that were collections of ramshackle huts. There was little or no sanitation or privacy. Eventually, the federal government stepped in to help provide better conditions for the migrants, but for many, life did not noticeably improve until the end of the Great Depression.

11.6.3 Discuss the human toll of the Depression, natural disasters, and unwise agricultural practices and their effects on the depopulation of rural regions and on political movements of the left and right, with particular attention to the Dust Bowl refugees and their social and economic impacts in California; CST 1 Students compare the present with the past, evaluating the consequences of past events and decisions and determining the lessons that were learned.

THOSE WHO STAYED

The people who remained in the Dust Bowl learned to endure nearly unbearable heat, extreme dryness, and inescapable dust. It was impossible to keep dirt out of the houses, no matter how tightly the doors and windows were sealed. One woman described sheltering in her home during a dust storm: "All we could do was just sit in our dusty chairs, gaze at each other through the fog that filled the room and watch the fog settle slowly and silently, covering everything—including ourselves—in a thick, brownish gray blanket." At night, people slept uncomfortably on gritty sheets. When setting the table, women placed plates and glasses upside-down until it was just time to serve the food, to avoid dirt settling onto the dishes.

It was impossible to avoid breathing in some dust, which could cause a variety of illnesses. Among the worst was silicosis, nicknamed "dust pneumonia," which was caused by sharp dust particles gradually scraping the lungs until the sufferer died.

People caught outside on foot or in cars during storms were at risk of becoming lost in the darkness and being suffocated by the violently blowing dirt. Some died just a few feet away from shelter that they could not glimpse through the black blizzard. One farmer recalled stretching a wire between his house and barn so that he could navigate his way home if a dust storm hit while he was in the barn.

Asked why people stayed on their farms, one woman from Kansas replied, "In part . . . we hope for the coming of moisture, which would change conditions so we can again have bountiful harvests. And in great part, because it is home. We have reared our family here and many have precious memories of the past. We have our memories. We have faith in the future, we are here to stay."

THINK ABOUT IT

What lessons about land use or management can be drawn from the Dust Bowl?

To get an overview of a field or a camp that she wanted to photograph, Dorothea Lange would often climb up on the roof of her car.

DUST BOWL PHOTOGRAPHER: DOROTHEA LANGE

Dorothea Lange was not planning to become an influential documentary photographer when she moved to San Francisco. Born into a wealthy family in 1895, she studied photography at Columbia University in New York City and then worked as an apprentice to several photographers before moving west to set up a successful portrait studio.

When the Great Depression hit San Francisco, it brought the same scenes of human misery as in other cities: homelessness, unemployment, and bread lines. Disturbed by the suffering she saw daily in the streets, Lange turned her camera to the people and events outside of her studio. Soon, she was working for the federal government, tasked with a mission to document the predicaments of people forced from their land by the Dust Bowl.

From 1935 to 1939, Lange traveled throughout the western United States photographing Dust Bowl refugees in settlement camps, in their cars, and at work. She used her skills as a portrait photographer to capture faces in unguarded moments of exhaustion, worry, and occasional relaxation. Paul Taylor, who accompanied Lange on her travels, explained her technique for putting her subjects at ease. "Her method of work," he recalled, "was often to just saunter up to the people and look around, and then when she saw something that she wanted to photograph, to quietly take her camera, look at it, and if she saw that they objected, why, she would close it up and not take a photograph, or perhaps she would wait until . . . they were used to her."

The photo on the bottom of the next page is part of a series of images that became symbolic of the Great Depression, capturing the poverty, misery, and stress endured by migratory farmworkers in the 1930s. The main subject of the "Migrant Mother" photographs was 32-year-old Florence Owens Thompson, who was the sole supporter of her seven children. Lange claimed Thompson had sold her car's tires to buy food for her children and that the family had been surviving on vegetables that had frozen in a nearby field, but Thompson's children said Lange must have confused their mother with someone else.

Lange's images from the 1930s leave an indelible impression on viewers to this day. She and other Depression-era photographers helped ensure that all Americans would know about the struggles of those impoverished and left homeless by the upheavals of the time. After the Depression ended, Lange continued her work as a documentary photographer until her death in 1965.

In these photographs taken in California in the 1930s Dorothea Lange captured rural people at work and at rest. The photo on the top left shows two workers loading cotton. The one on the right shows Dust Bowl refugees stopped along a highway. The bottom photograph from Lange's 1936 "Migrant Mother" series features mother Florence Owens Thompson sitting in a tent with two of her seven children.

1.1 **MAIN IDEA** The United States enjoyed widespread prosperity in the 1920s, but economic problems in Europe and an uneven distribution of wealth at home threatened to undermine the stability.

A Deceptive Prosperity

The saying "All that glitters is not gold" is an apt description of the 1920s. When President Calvin Coolidge began his first full term in office, he believed the United States was prosperous and secure. But economic troubles lurked beneath the sparkling surface.

COOLIDGE IN THE WHITE HOUSE

In 1924, after serving out Harding's remaining term in office, Calvin Coolidge ran for and won the presidency. Strongly pro-business and against government intervention, his policy goals were modest. When Coolidge asked Congress for a cut in taxes, lawmakers responded with a measure that lowered taxes for people who made more than $100,000 a year. However, most married couples made less than $3,500 a year, so the tax cuts affected only the wealthiest Americans. The president also promoted laws to oversee the expansion of the new airline industry and to regulate the growing radio business. At the same time, Coolidge did little to help farmers and people living in rural areas. He twice vetoed a bill to aid farmers and did not support a federal government initiative to build dams on the Tennessee River that would provide affordable electric power to that region of the country.

In foreign policy, Coolidge opposed the use of military force, but he also believed the United States had an obligation to help countries in need. In 1924, the Coolidge administration had endorsed a plan to help a struggling Germany meet its huge war reparation debt. During the next four years, Germany borrowed almost $1.5 million from the United States. Similarly, when the Soviet Union faced a famine in the early 1920s, Americans sent large amounts of food and monetary aid. But when revolution and civil war took place in China, the U.S. government did not get

PRIMARY SOURCE

Coolidge focused on cutting taxes that were already low for most Americans and viewed taxation as funding "extravagance" in government.

We must have tax reform. We cannot finance the country, we cannot improve social conditions, through any system of injustice, even if we attempt to inflict it upon the rich. Those who suffer the most harm will be the poor. This country believes in prosperity. It is absurd to suppose that it is envious of those who are already prosperous. The wise and correct course to follow in taxation and all other economic legislation is not to destroy those who have already secured success but to create conditions under which everyone will have a better chance to be successful.

—from Calvin Coolidge's Inaugural Address, March 4, 1925

11.3.3 Cite incidences of religious intolerance in the United States (e.g., persecution of Mormons, anti-Catholic sentiment, anti-Semitism); 11.5.1 Discuss the policies of Presidents Warren Harding, Calvin Coolidge, and Herbert Hoover.

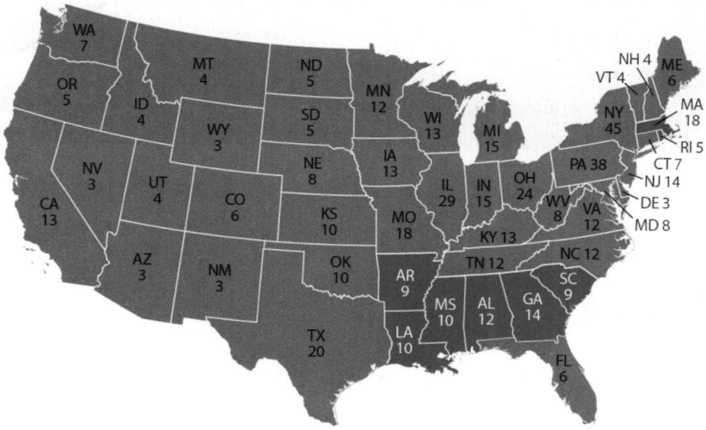

The Election of 1928

Herbert Hoover, Republican

Electoral Vote: 444 votes, 83.6%

Popular Vote: 21,391,381 votes, 58.8%

Al Smith, Democrat

Electoral Vote: 87 votes, 16.4%

Popular Vote: 15,016,443 votes, 41.2%

involved. In fact, the State Department preferred the idea of outlawing war altogether, an idea that peace groups supported. The resulting **Kellogg-Briand Pact** was a multinational agreement in which the signing countries agreed to renounce, or reject, war. Coolidge was among those who signed the pact in 1928, and it was ratified in 1929. However, there was no way to enforce the pact worldwide.

Believing that it would be difficult for anyone to be effective in the office for more than eight years, Coolidge declined to run for a second full term. Herbert Hoover, Coolidge's secretary of commerce, beat out his political rivals to win the Republican nomination for president. Hoover faced off against the Democratic candidate, Governor Alfred E. Smith of New York, who was Roman Catholic. In the general election, Hoover benefited from the religious intolerance many Protestants held against Smith's faith. Hoover won the electoral vote in a landslide.

A TROUBLED ECONOMY

When Hoover took office, the future looked bright, but the surface prosperity of the 1920s hid some serious economic problems. The most pervasive of these was the dramatically uneven distribution of income. Agricultural overproduction had driven down crop prices throughout the decade, so farmers did not benefit from the nation's general prosperity. Furthermore, by 1929, the economy was characterized by a lopsided distribution of income. At the top level, 5 percent of Americans received 33 percent of the total annual personal income, while half of all Americans received about 16 percent of the total. More than half of American families lived near or below the poverty line even though unemployment was low. More than 21 million families, or 80 percent of the national population, did not have any savings at all. But in order to expand, the economy relied on people purchasing consumer goods. If most ordinary Americans lacked **disposable income**—or spending money—and purchasing power, it would have a big impact on the national economy.

Other warning signs signaled the economy was in trouble, including a recession in 1927. Wholesale prices fell nearly 4.5 percent, the production of goods slowed, and consumer spending dropped. The global economy was also fragile. Germany continued to struggle with its reparation payments, even after the United States reduced the burden of German war debts in 1924. In 1929, an international committee proposed another plan that further reduced Germany's total debt and established a longer period for repayment. These concessions eased economic pressures, but only temporarily. Weakness in the German economy continued to grow as banks closed and markets disintegrated.

Yet, despite multiple national and global warning signs, the U.S. banking system continued to expand credit. Americans increasingly speculated in the **stock market**, or the buying and selling of shares in companies. Earnings from stocks could be higher than interest paid by banks, but an investor could also lose money, especially over the short term. For the average American, though, it looked like the economy would grow forever.

HISTORICAL THINKING

1. **READING CHECK** What role did religion play in the presidential race between Hoover and Smith?
2. **ANALYZE LANGUAGE USE** How did President Coolidge's use of the phrase "any system of injustice" help his argument for tax reform?
3. **IDENTIFY MAIN IDEAS AND DETAILS** What warning signs suggested that the U.S. economy was not as prosperous as it appeared?

11.6.1 Describe the monetary issues of the late nineteenth and early twentieth centuries that gave rise to the establishment of the Federal Reserve and the weaknesses in key sectors of the economy in the late 1920s; 11.6.2 Understand the explanations of the principal causes of the Great Depression and the steps taken by the Federal Reserve, Congress, and Presidents Herbert Hoover and Franklin Delano Roosevelt to combat the economic crisis.

1.2 **MAIN IDEA** The phenomenal rise in stock prices came to a catastrophic end when the stock market crashed on October 29, 1929.

PANIC ON WALL STREET

We all know that what goes up must eventually come down. Investors in the 1920s didn't realize that old saying also applied to the stock market. On October 29, 1929, they learned just how wrong they were.

INVESTMENT FEVER

In the 1920s, Americans pointed to the growth of the stock market as an indication of the nation's growing prosperity. The market grew so quickly that many Americans saw it as the ideal place to make a fast buck. The U.S. Treasury's sale of Liberty Bonds during World War I had shown citizens that investments could lead to wealth.

More and more, corporations offered their stocks for sale to obtain cash to finance business growth. During the prosperous Harding and Coolidge years, generous government tax policies allowed the very wealthy to pay little or no income taxes, giving them extra money to invest in the stock market.

When this New York investor lost everything in the 1929 stock market crash, he put his car up for sale for less than 10 percent of its value.

Smaller investors often bought stocks on **margin**. That is, they purchased stocks on credit, paying only 10 or 15 percent of the actual price up front. Buying on margin is a risky strategy because the investor is betting on being able to sell the stock at a higher price, pay off the stockbroker—the person who buys and sells stocks for his or her clients—and pocket a substantial profit. The lure of making easy money in the market was so great that people borrowed money to buy on margin. Banks happily loaned American investors that money, in spite of the Federal Reserve's warnings against the practice, which consequently gave rise to the establishment of weaknesses in the economy.

Buying stocks on margin is a form of **speculation**. The buyer assumes, or speculates, that stock prices will always go up, even though there is no guarantee that they will. But in the 1920s, this looked like a sure bet. On September 3, 1929, the **Dow Jones Industrial Average (DJIA)**—a leading measure of general stock market trends—hit 381.17, a high for the decade, driven up in part by speculation and margin buying. Few suspected that the weakening market was headed for collapse.

11.6.1 Describe the monetary issues of the late nineteenth and early twentieth centuries that gave rise to the establishment of the Federal Reserve and the weaknesses in key sectors of the economy in the late 1920s; 11.6.2 Understand the explanations of the principal causes of the Great Depression and the steps taken by the Federal Reserve, Congress, and Presidents Herbert Hoover and Franklin Delano Roosevelt to combat the economic crisis.

OCTOBER 29, 1929

The problem began in September 1929. At the beginning of that month, the market hit its record high, but then stock prices declined. They regained some strength but began drifting downward again. Since there had been no abrupt collapse, many on Wall Street, their confidence unshaken, saw these events as one of the normal and temporary "corrections" that typically preceded another big increase in the stock market. A few people warned that problems lay ahead, but they were dismissed as chronic naysayers who had been wrong before.

Dow Jones Industrial Average Daily Index

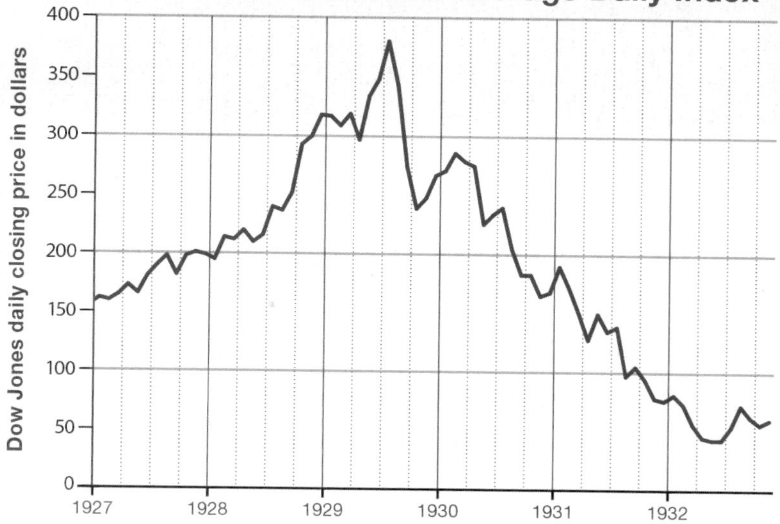

Source: The Dow Jones Averages (1885–1995)

But prices did not rise. On October 24, 1929, the day that became known as **Black Thursday**, stock trading began as usual, but few investors were willing to buy. Prices collapsed as investors, many of whom had bought on margin, tried to sell their stocks before prices fell even more. Nearly 13 million stocks were traded that day, which was then an all-time record. Stockholders absorbed, by some estimates, a $9 billion loss in the value of their stocks. During the afternoon, a large banking group led by bank executive J.P. Morgan, Jr., urged investors to be calm. Morgan even purchased some stocks himself. The market seemed to settle, leading to the hope that normal trading might recover.

Recovery was not in the cards. On the following Monday, the market fell sharply—around 13 percent—and the DJIA plummeted to 260.64. Then the hammer fell on October 29, a day that is still known as **Black Tuesday**. When trading began, the sell-off continued, with more than 16 million shares changing hands in a single day. The DJIA fell to 230.07 and continued to drop for nearly three years.

The consequences of the crash were immediate and striking. The prices of individual stocks continued on their downward slide. The DJIA reached a low of 41.22 on July 8, 1932. Within a few months of the crash, General Electric's stock had dropped from $403 a share to $168, and Standard Oil shares fell from $83 to $48. During the next year, the **gross national product (GNP)**—the total goods and services produced by the nation plus the income earned by its citizens—shrank from nearly $88 billion to $76 billion. With the already existing difficulties in agriculture and the large debt crisis, the U.S. economy slumped into a long and severe decline, resulting in an economic catastrophe that became known as the **Great Depression**, the deepest and most prolonged economic downturn in American history with a substantial human toll.

PRIMARY SOURCE

Oral historian Studs Terkel interviewed people who lived through the Great Depression. In 1970, he published their stories in his book, *Hard Times*. In the following excerpt, composer Alec Wilder is speaking to Terkel of his losses in the stock market.

I knew something was terribly wrong because I heard bellboys, everybody, talking about the stock market. About six weeks before the Wall Street Crash, I persuaded my mother in Rochester to let me talk to our family adviser. I wanted to sell stock which had been left me by my father. He got very sentimental: "Oh your father wouldn't have liked you to do that." He was so persuasive, I said O.K. I could have sold it for $160,000. Four years later, I sold it for $4,000.

—from *Hard Times: An Oral History of the Great Depression*, by Studs Terkel, 1970

HISTORICAL THINKING

1. **READING CHECK** What effect did speculation and buying on margin have on stock prices?
2. **DRAW CONCLUSIONS** If trading reached record highs on October 24 and 29, why are these days called Black Thursday and Black Tuesday?
3. **INTERPRET GRAPHS** According to the graph, what were the highest and lowest averages in the DJIA in 1929, and how does the graph illustrate the cost and benefit of investing in the stock market?

HI 6 Students conduct cost-benefit analyses and apply basic economic indicators to analyze the aggregate economic behavior of the U.S. economy.

2.1 **MAIN IDEA** The stock market crash of 1929 marked the beginning of the Great Depression, but many factors caused the economy to collapse.

THE DEPRESSION BEGINS

The reaction in a domino chain starts with the fall of the first domino, but it's the structure of the chain that causes the other dominos to fall. That principle applied to the economy during the Great Depression.

A WEAK FOUNDATION

The stock market crash of 1929 signaled the start of the Great Depression of the 1930s, the deepest and most prolonged economic downturn in American history. But the Depression was caused by broad underlying weaknesses more deeply rooted than falling stock values. The apparent prosperity of the 1920s hid the fact that the U.S. and world economies rested on an unsound foundation. Four main factors contributed to the problem: overproduction resulting in oversaturated markets, unequal income distribution, lack of proper banking regulations, and a weak worldwide financial system.

After World War I, American farmers continued to maintain high levels of wartime production, even though Europe was once again producing its own food or buying from U.S. competitors. Soon, the surplus of American crops and meat drove down prices on the global market. In the manufacturing sector—especially in one of the nation's leading industries, the automotive industry—new machinery and assembly lines led to increased productivity, and output jumped almost 32 percent between 1923 and 1929. Similarly, the other leading U.S. industry, construction, far outpaced demand for new houses. But by 1929, growth in the auto, housing, and consumer goods industries had begun to decline. Innovations that had enabled producing those items affordably meant that many people had already purchased what they needed. As demand decreased, workers were laid off.

Income inequality, or the unequal distribution of income and wealth between the few wealthiest Americans and the rest of the population, made the problem of overproduction worse, especially in the automobile and housing construction markets.

Similarly, the uneven distribution of wealth, or the value of what a household owns minus debts, factored into an unstable economy. The small percentage of wealthy Americans purchased only so many houses, cars, and luxury goods. To keep the consumer economy growing, the majority of the population needed to purchase newly built houses and to buy cars and consumer goods. Though unemployment was low, wages did not rise as fast as production, and soon more goods existed than people could afford to buy. As businesses accumulated profits rather than increasing workers' wages, demand weakened, prices and profits actually fell, and businesses laid off workers. By 1929, more than half of American families could not meet their basic needs with their income.

A lack of regulation in the banking and financial industries was another cause of the Depression. While the Federal Reserve regulated banking, district banks often had difficulty agreeing on regulation. For example, they could not decide on how best to rein in margin buying and overspeculation. Investors formed **trading pools**, groups formed to buy and sell large amounts of stocks. They made stocks appear active by buying and selling among themselves. This drove up the price of the stock artificially, and after they had sold off their stock at high prices, other investors' shares had little value. Lack of regulation also kept the Federal Reserve from acting quickly and decisively when, as the Depression deepened, American banks began to fail.

The fragile state of the global economy also contributed to the Depression. Internationally, the world stock market, international loans, economic policies, and World War I reparations formed a web of interconnected factors that helped lead to a

11.4.6 Trace the declining role of Great Britain and the expanding role of the United States in world affairs after World War II; 11.6.1 Describe the monetary issues of the late nineteenth and early twentieth centuries that gave rise to the establishment of the Federal Reserve and the weaknesses in key sectors of the economy in the late 1920s.

THE GREAT DEPRESSION BY THE NUMBERS

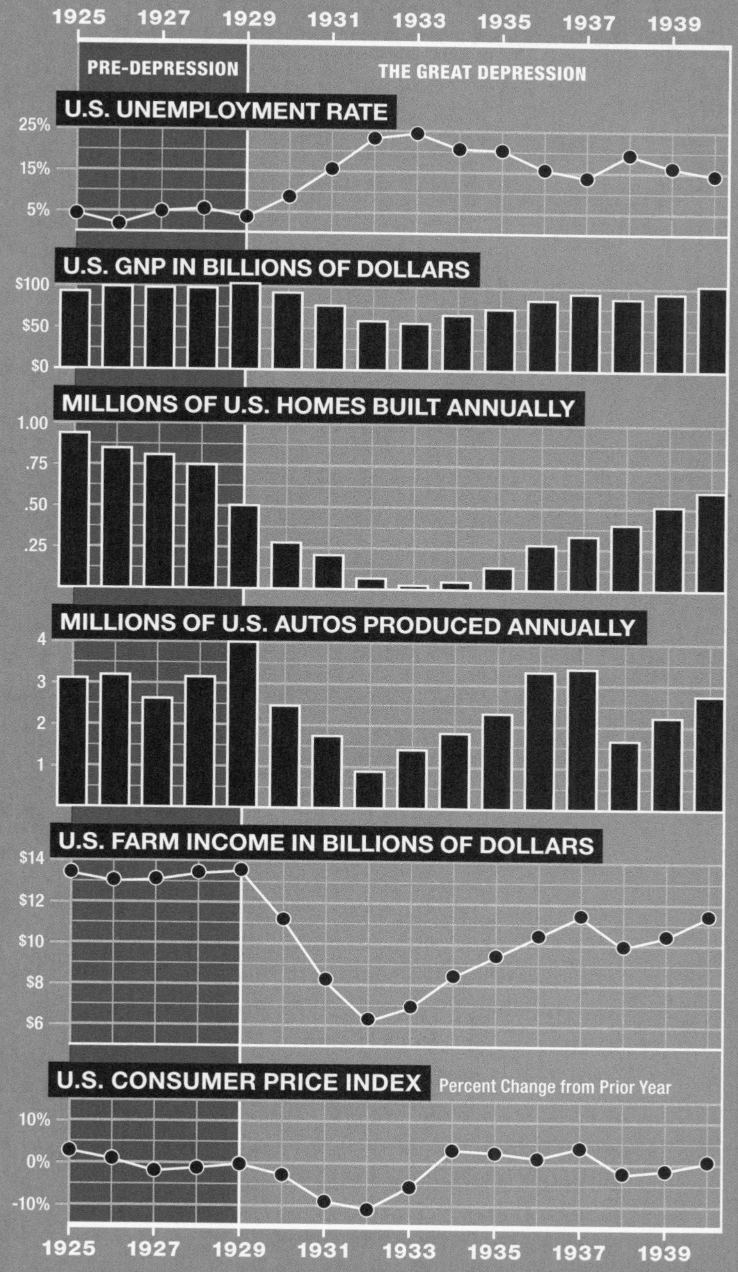

SOURCES: National Bureau of Economic Research, 1937, 1957, 1965; CQPress http://cqpress.com, 2017; U.S. Census Bureau; U.S. Department of Labor, 2014; U.S. Internal Revenue Service, 1925, 1934.

ANALYZE ECONOMIC INDICATORS

Study these economic indicators to analyze economic trends from 1925 to 1939. Use the data to expand your understanding of the economic behaviors that led to the Great Depression. Then do the following:

Describe the relationship between two or more of the economic indicators shown here, and explain how those indicators contributed to the Great Depression.

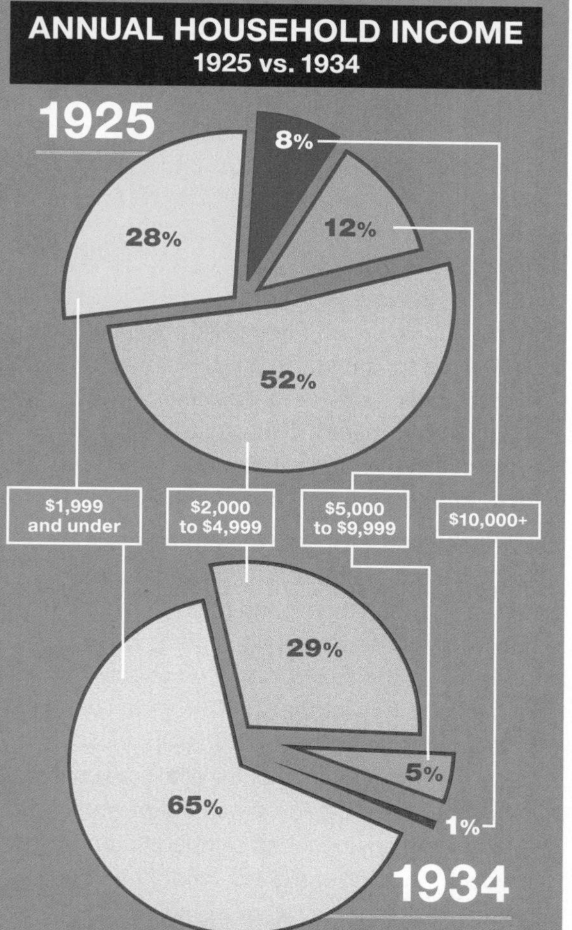

worldwide downturn. Europe was already weakened by Germany's inability to pay its war reparations. The United States had overtaken Britain after World War I as the world's financial leader and now passed protective tariffs it believed would enable American agriculture and industry to rebound. But the **Smoot-Hawley Tariff Act** of 1930, which raised customs duties to high levels, made it more difficult for European businesses to sell goods in the United States and obstructed the flow of capital, goods, and services in the world economy. Dozens of countries responded by passing retaliatory tariffs that made it harder for the United States to export goods. International trade declined sharply, triggering international bank failures and adding to the suffering at home and abroad.

HI 6 Students conduct cost-benefit analyses and apply basic economic indicators to analyze the aggregate economic behavior of the U.S. economy.

THE DEPRESSION DEEPENS

When the DJIA rose for a few months in early 1930, President Hoover told the nation, "I am convinced we have passed the worst and with continued effort shall rapidly recover." But as 1930 continued, it was clear the situation was only getting worse. Bank failures soared from 659 in 1929 to 1,350 a year later.

CRITICAL VIEWING In May 1933, New York City police evicted inhabitants of 80 shacks between 9th and 10th streets along the East River. What can you infer about what life was like for the people in this photo, taken shortly before their eviction?

Businesses closed, investment declined, and profits fell. Industrial production was 26 percent lower at the end of 1930 than it had been 12 months earlier. Automobile manufacturing, a prime driver of the economy in the 1920s, operated at only 20 percent of capacity. By October 1930, 4 million people were jobless (almost 9 percent of the labor force), and the trend worsened each month. Within a year, nearly 16 percent of the labor force was out of work, and by 1932, unemployment had climbed to more than 23 percent. An additional 33 percent of Americans were underemployed: they were working but not earning enough to support themselves and their families.

The stock market crash left banks in a fragile position. Rural banks were particularly vulnerable, and many failed when farmers could not repay their loans. Small local banks also shut down, leaving their communities without functioning banks. Some of these banks had contributed to their own failure by providing loans for buying stocks on margin. When stock prices fell, investors and stockbrokers could not repay their loans. In addition, some banks had placed their own assets at risk by investing their deposits directly in the stock market.

When bank failures began, the Federal Reserve took a wait-and-see attitude. Some believed the failures would weed out weaker banks and strengthen the system, helping to combat the economic crisis. By the time larger banks began to fail, it was too late for action. Bank deposits were not insured by the government, so individual banks were vulnerable when customers requested to withdraw their money. Stronger banks called in loans they had made to smaller banks to save themselves, further damaging weaker banks. When a bank failed, its customers lost their savings with no hope of recovering the funds.

ECONOMIC REALITIES

For most Americans, there was no single moment after 1929 when they knew the economy was in trouble. But in the months following October 1929, families began making lifestyle changes as workers' hours were cut and the human toll became evident. People began postponing purchases and asking their children to contribute to the household's income. Job losses had a dramatic impact on families. Savings could help tide the family over for a while, but if a family had lost its savings in a bank failure or if its

11.6.2 Understand the explanations of the principal causes of the Great Depression and the steps taken by the Federal Reserve, Congress, and Presidents Herbert Hoover and Franklin Delano Roosevelt to combat the economic crisis; 11.6.3 Discuss the human toll of the Depression, natural disasters, and unwise agricultural practices and their effects on the depopulation of rural regions and on political movements of the left and right, with particular attention to the Dust Bowl refugees and their social and economic impacts in California.

savings ran out, the family would have to put its home up for sale or wait for the bank to foreclose on, or take possession of, its mortgaged property.

Some responses to the economic crisis revealed underlying ideas about civil liberties and gender in the workforce. Many female workers were pressured to give up their jobs to men in an attempt to end the unemployment crisis. Men were considered to be the main "breadwinners," or the principal sources of income for the family, and working women were accused of taking their jobs away from men. Some corporations fired all married female employees, and southern school districts dismissed married female teachers. While the Depression did hinder women's participation in the workforce and slowed their economic progress, unemployment rates were lower for women than for men because women continued to work at their clerical and domestic jobs.

For already economically vulnerable Americans, the Depression presented still greater challenges. In the South, whites seeking work forced African Americans out of the low-paying service jobs they had traditionally filled. Sometimes this process was violent. Native Americans already trapped in a life of neglect and poverty fared even worse during the Depression. The infant mortality rate among Native Americans far exceeded the rate for the white population because of poverty, lack of healthcare facilities, and inadequate sanitation. The Bureau of Indian Affairs (BIA) did not address the many social problems that the people under its jurisdiction faced.

Like African Americans and Native Americans, immigrants faced serious challenges to their civil liberties during the Depression. Theirs were in the form of backlash. In an attempt to combat economic crisis, the Hoover administration instituted immigration quotas, or limits, to reduce the number of people looking for jobs and receiving government services. While potential restrictions applied to all immigrants, these efforts targeted Mexicans and Mexican Americans. Between 1930 and 1940, in a coordinated governmental effort known as the **Mexican Repatriation Program**, about 1 million people of Mexican descent were either **deported**, or forcibly removed from the country, or pressured to leave. An estimated 400,000 of those deported had been living in California. **Repatriation** means returning or being returned to the country of one's citizenship, but an astonishing 60 percent of those who returned to Mexico were actually U.S. citizens, and their deportation violated their civil rights.

PRIMARY SOURCE

In the 1980s, historian Vicki L. Ruiz interviewed Mexican women who had worked in California's canneries in the 1930s and 1940s. Carmen Escobar recounts an interaction with her foreman about how she was being paid.

When I caught the foreman cheating me, he said, "I love you like a daughter, Carmen, but who's the foreman, me or you?" "You are, but I came here to make money, not to stand around and not get my due." And then he would tell me, "Look, the poor bosses are losing money. One hour is nothing." "What do you mean one hour is nothing?" "Be quiet, Carmen."

—from *Cannery Women, Cannery Lives*, by Vicki Ruiz, 1987

Filipinos were also pressured to leave the United States. The Filipino Repatriation Act of 1935 provided transportation funds for Filipinos who agreed to move back to their home country permanently.

On the nation's farms, where many Mexican Americans worked, produce rotted in the fields because few people could afford to buy it. The Federal Farm Board was established in 1929 to stabilize farm prices. However, when farm surpluses around the world flooded grain markets in 1930, nothing could keep crop prices from plummeting. As banks foreclosed on farm mortgages, many former landowners became tenant farmers. All economic indicators, including GNP, consumer price index, and farm income, were in decline. And now an environmental disaster was about to deliver a crushing blow.

HISTORICAL THINKING

1. **READING CHECK** How did overproduction lead to weakness in key sectors of the economy?
2. **ANALYZE CAUSE AND EFFECT** What were the unintended consequences and complexities of the Smoot-Hawley Tariff Act of 1930?
3. **SYNTHESIZE** Why was there a Great Depression? State how individuals affected the U.S. economy.
4. **MAKE CONNECTIONS** How were African Americans, married women, Mexicans, and Mexican Americans hurt by the unemployment of white male workers?

11.5.2 Analyze the international and domestic events, interests, and philosophies that prompted attacks on civil liberties, including the Palmer Raids, Marcus Garvey's "back-to-Africa" movement, the Ku Klux Klan, and immigration quotas and the responses of organizations such as the American Civil Liberties Union, the National Association for the Advancement of Colored People, and the Anti-Defamation League to those attacks; HI 2 Students recognize the complexity of historical causes and effects, including the limitations on determining cause and effect.

CRITICAL VIEWING Safety liaison Jamison Walsh, photographed by Chin, climbs the spire of 1 World Trade Center after leading Chin's ascent. How are New York's skyscrapers symbols of the 1920s?

2.2

THROUGH THE LENS

Jimmy Chin

National Geographic adventure photographer Jimmy Chin is used to extreme heights. He's skied down Mount Everest, photographed free climbers on Yosemite, and conquered the granite Shark Fin's wall of Meru Peak in the Himalayas. So 1,776 feet—the height of New York's 1 World Trade Center—is no big deal. In this shoot, Chin focused on capturing the great city of New York, a city of skyscrapers, many of which rose up around the Great Depression, from the spire of the building constructed where the World Trade Center once stood.

2.3 **MAIN IDEA** A lack of rain and unwise agricultural practices transformed the Great Plains into the Dust Bowl in the 1930s, forcing many farmers off their land.

THE DUST BOWL

Sometimes nature and human actions mix in deadly and destructive ways. On the Great Plains, farmers had planted millions of acres of croplands with one main crop—wheat. When prolonged drought struck in the 1930s, the golden fields of wheat turned to dust, resulting in ecological disaster and human misery.

THE DIRTY THIRTIES

Farmers, already hit hard after World War I by falling crop and livestock prices, suffered a devastating blow in the early 1930s. Record high temperatures and **drought**, a prolonged period of low rainfall, gripped the Great Plains. In addition to the drought, strong winds whipped through the region, causing terrifying dust storms that swept through the plains and stripped nutrients from the dry soil.

Drought is a natural occurrence on the Great Plains, as are high winds and extreme temperatures. But the dust storms that plagued the region during the 1930s were unexpected and worsened by unwise agricultural methods and human modification of the landscape. Farmers had plowed millions of acres of grasslands on the Great Plains in order to plant wheat. After the crops were harvested, farmers used new machinery, such as disc plows pulled by small gas-powered tractors, to turn up the fields again. They then left them unplanted for months. Ranchers on the plains allowed their cattle and other livestock to overgraze what grassland remained. Without the deep roots of the prairie grasses, there was nothing to keep the soil in place. The wind picked up the dry soil and carried it for hundreds of miles.

CRITICAL VIEWING On April 14, 1935, a black blizzard hit the panhandles of Texas and Oklahoma. What details in this photo convey how threatening the cloud seems as it approaches a Texas town?

11.6.3 Discuss the human toll of the Depression, natural disasters, and unwise agricultural practices and their effects on the depopulation of rural regions and on political movements of the left and right, with particular attention to the Dust Bowl refugees and their social and economic impacts in California.

PRIMARY SOURCE

John Steinbeck's novel *The Grapes of Wrath* tells the story of an "Okie" family on its way to California from Oklahoma along "Route 66." That remains the popular name for U.S. highway 66, which ran from Chicago to Los Angeles before the interstate highway system was built beginning in 1956.

[Route] 66 is the path of a people in flight, refugees from dust and shrinking land, from the thunder of tractors and shrinking ownership, from the desert's slow northward invasion, from the twisting winds that howl up out of Texas, from the floods that bring no richness to the land and steal what little richness is there.

—from *The Grapes of Wrath,* by John Steinbeck, 1939

Some of the dust storms were caused by low-level winds that blew sand into huge drifts. Others were massive storms—black blizzards—with rolling dust clouds thousands of feet high that crackled with electricity, carried precious soil away to neighboring states, and turned daylight into dark. "This is the ultimate darkness," a Kansas woman wrote in her diary. "So must come the end of the world."

The blowing dust of a black blizzard destroyed crops and sickened and killed livestock and people. Dirt permeated everything, even the inside of houses, despite people's best efforts to seal every crack, window, and door. After the storm passed and light returned, farmers found their cattle and horses buried alive. The storms turned millions of acres of cultivated land in parts of Kansas, Colorado, Oklahoma, Texas, and New Mexico into a barren desert that became known as the **Dust Bowl**. The dust storms continued as the 1930s wore on—14 in 1932, then 38 in 1933—earning the decade the nickname the "Dirty Thirties."

HITTING THE ROAD

Many people living in the Dust Bowl region stuck it out because of pride, determination, or hope. Others stayed because they were simply too poor or too beaten down to leave. But a quarter of the population fled the region, some pushed off their land as they could not pay their mortgages. In one of the largest internal migrations in the nation's history, more than 3 million "Dust Bowl refugees" in Oklahoma, Kansas, the Dakotas, and other states abandoned their farms in the 1930s. Many set out for California seeking work and opportunity. The fortunate found low-wage work there, picking fruit, boxing vegetables, and baling hay. Others went to cities to work as laborers. But few "Okies," as the Californians called them, found relief from the economic turmoil they had fled. Once in California, most lived in squatter camps along roads, often contracting diseases such as intestinal worms, typhoid, and dysentery as a result of the polluted water and lack of sanitation. The **Farm Security Administration (FSA)**, a federal agency charged with combating rural poverty, built camps to house families temporarily in somewhat improved conditions, but life was still difficult.

Okies were generally treated poorly, and they experienced discrimination at the hands of many native Californians. The Los Angeles police set up a task force called the "bum brigade" to turn Okies away at the border between California and Arizona. Residents complained about the tent communities, called "Okievilles," growing around the edges of Los Angeles, so sheriffs would ask the migrants to pack up and move on. In some towns, residents beat up the Okies and set fire to their camps.

Photographer **Dorothea Lange** documented the plight of the Okies as they traveled to California and tried to eke out a living there. Author **John Steinbeck** did the same in his 1939 novel, *The Grapes of Wrath*. His story chronicled the lives of the Joads, a sharecropper family from Oklahoma, who migrated to California in search of work. Steinbeck and Lange, along with many other writers and photographers in the 1930s, captured the struggles of ordinary people weighed down by circumstances.

HISTORICAL THINKING

1. **READING CHECK** Why did many people living in the Dust Bowl region stay during the 1930s?
2. **ANALYZE ENVIRONMENTAL CONCEPTS** How did the scale and duration of human actions, including modifying the landscape, affect the natural systems of the Great Plains during the Dust Bowl?
3. **MAKE INFERENCES** How might the social and economic impacts of the Dust Bowl refugees have influenced the reception the Okies received in California?
4. **ANALYZE LANGUAGE USE** How did Steinbeck characterize Route 66?

CST 3 Students use a variety of maps and documents to interpret human movement, including major patterns of domestic and international migration, changing environmental preferences and settlement patterns, the frictions that develop between population groups, and the diffusion of ideas, technological innovations, and goods; HI 5 Students analyze human modifications of landscapes and examine the resulting environmental policy issues.

2.4 **MAIN IDEA** In spite of widespread poverty and suffering, the Great Depression inspired artistic creativity and a vibrant popular culture.

CULTURE DURING THE DEPRESSION

Maybe you take in a good movie or watch your favorite television show to cheer up when you're feeling down. Many people during the Great Depression tuned into their favorite radio shows, went to theaters to watch movies, and listened to music to escape reality—at least for a few minutes.

FORGETTING TROUBLES

Amid the challenges of the Depression, Americans found diversion in popular entertainment and **mass media**, or forms of communication such as radio, film, and musical recordings designed to reach large numbers of people. By the 1930s, radios had become more affordable, and they began to play a significant role in the worldwide diffusion of popular culture. Listening to a favorite radio show was a vital part of the daily lives of many families. Many listeners preferred daytime dramas such as *One Man's Family* or *Mary Noble, Backstage Wife*, which were quickly dubbed "soap operas" after the detergent companies that sponsored them.

Comic books also became popular during the Depression. The first comic books were collections of newspaper comic strips, and their heroes provided a sense that everything was going to be okay during a time of uncertainty. Among the most popular comic strip heroes were a police detective named Dick Tracy, a frontier lawman called the Lone Ranger, and Buck Rogers, a courageous space explorer living in the 25th century.

With ticket prices low and audiences hungry for a break from the stress of the Depression, movie theaters presented a wide choice of Hollywood films. Movies with sound had replaced the silent pictures of the 1920s, and people regularly went to the movies to forget their own troubles for a while.

Audiences enjoyed movie musicals and laughed at the Marx Brothers, W.C. Fields, and a new genre called screwball comedy, named for the unpredictable baseball pitch. Characterized by rapid-fire dialogue, social satire, and a blend of wacky situations and sophisticated settings, examples of screwball comedy include such hits as *It Happened One Night* (1934) and *My Man Godfrey* (1936). Not all films were pure escapism, however. Gangster films such as *The Public Enemy* and *Little Caesar* (both from 1931) were entertaining, but they also exposed viewers to the urban crime and corruption that existed in cities like Chicago and New York City.

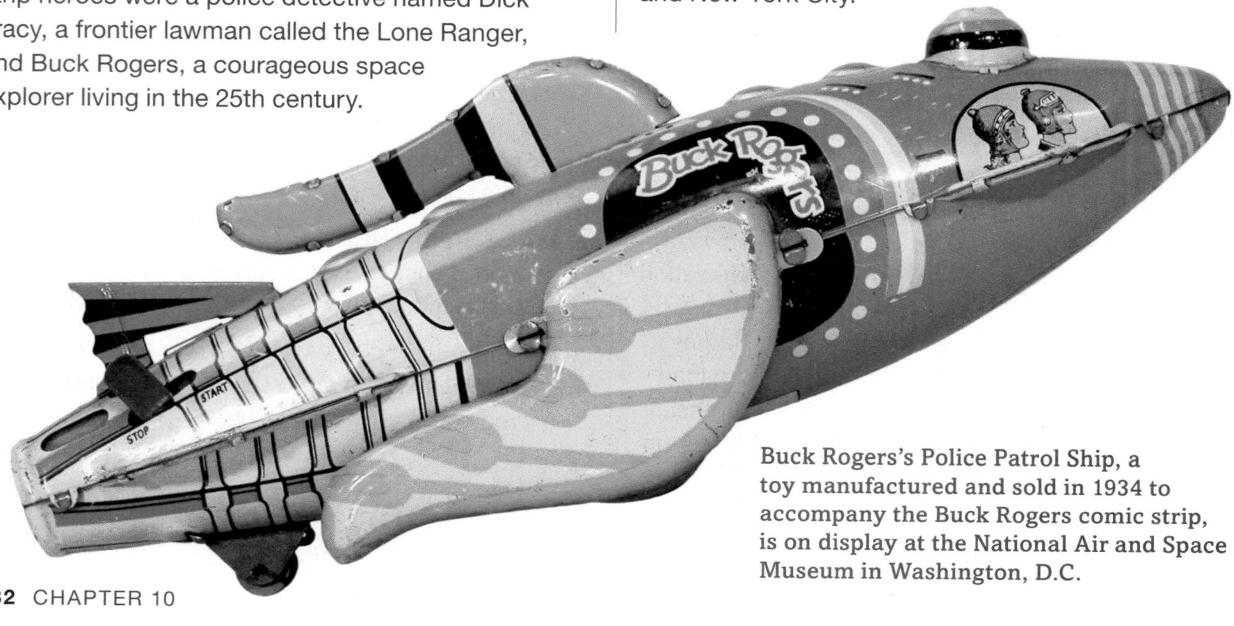

Buck Rogers's Police Patrol Ship, a toy manufactured and sold in 1934 to accompany the Buck Rogers comic strip, is on display at the National Air and Space Museum in Washington, D.C.

The Depression was also a vibrant period for music. In Kansas City and other midwestern cities, African-American musicians developed a new jazz style known as "swing." Marked by complicated but compelling rhythms, swing was energetic and loud. As swing grew more popular, white musicians added elements of more sedate musical genres, such as classical music, to make swing more commercial. Many swing bands evolved into big bands with percussion, woodwind, and horn sections. **Benny Goodman**, from Chicago, led a big band that made swing popular with young people.

In 1943, *Life* magazine photographer Eric Schaal accompanied Woody Guthrie as he gave on-the-spot performances around New York City, where Guthrie lived from 1940 on.

Not all music was flamboyant and brassy, however. Folk singers such as **Woody Guthrie**, Pete Seeger, and Huddie Ledbetter caught the public's attention by singing about the lives of the people hit hardest by the Dust Bowl and the Depression. Guthrie, an "Okie" who migrated to California, lived the life he sang about, riding the rails and sleeping in migrant camps. He sang on the streets for money and took whatever small jobs he could find to survive. Some of Guthrie's songs, such as "(If You Ain't Got That) Do Re Mi," describe the struggles of the Okies seeking a new beginning in California. But Guthrie also wrote the anthem "This Land Is Your Land," celebrating the beauty and diversity of the country while also commenting on the disparity between rich landowners and those who could not afford land.

Similarly, Huddie Ledbetter—nicknamed Lead Belly—chronicled the troubles of African Americans during the Depression through his songs. Lead Belly bridged a gap between folk music and the blues. He sang old folk standards of the rural South, gospel songs, the blues, and protest songs. He also composed his own music, including "Goodnight, Irene," which became a hit after his death in 1949.

CAPTURING THE DEPRESSION

Other artists joined musicians in telling Americans' stories during the Great Depression. As you have read, photographer Dorothea Lange captured images of Dust Bowl refugees. Photographer **Walker Evans** traveled throughout the South during the Depression, photographing rural life. Lange and Evans both worked for the Resettlement Administration, which later became the Farm Security Administration. Evans's photographs helped reveal the challenges faced by the rural poor. Evans also worked with writer **James Agee** to document the lives of three sharecropper families trying to farm on a dry hillside in the 1930s. In 1941, they published their text and photographs in *Let Us Now Praise Famous Men*.

Writer **John Dos Passos**, part of the "lost generation" you read about earlier, exposed the divisions in American society in his trilogy *U.S.A.*, which combined fiction, biographies of famous people, newsreels, and newspaper headlines to paint a picture of what he saw as the two halves of society: rich and poor. Novelist **Richard Wright** portrayed the discrimination and struggles faced by African Americans in his novel *Native Son*. The novel is about a young African-American man who lives in poverty on Chicago's South Side during the 1930s.

HISTORICAL THINKING

1. **READING CHECK** How did mass media trends help people cope with the Great Depression?
2. **MAKE CONNECTIONS** How did folk music, photography, and literature help recount the plight of the poor during the Great Depression?
3. **EVALUATE** Why is it important that artists document significant historical events through their art?

11.5.6 Trace the growth and effects of radio and movies and their role in the worldwide diffusion of popular culture; 11.6.3 Discuss the human toll of the Depression, natural disasters, and unwise agricultural practices and their effects on the depopulation of rural regions and on political movements of the left and right, with particular attention to the Dust Bowl refugees and their social and economic impacts in California; HI 1 Students show the connections, causal and otherwise, between particular historical events and larger social, economic, and political trends and developments.

3.1 **MAIN IDEA** President Hoover's policies did little to protect Americans from the devastating effects of the Great Depression.

HOOVER'S INITIATIVES

President Hoover's assumption that private citizens and businesses could work together to solve the ills created by the Great Depression reflected a faith in human decency. But the problems were too big to solve without government intervention.

VOLUNTARY ACTION AND SELF-HELP

President Hoover's life experiences influenced how he handled the Great Depression. Raised as a Quaker, he believed in the power of individual effort and the obligation for all citizens to help one another. His success as a mining engineer and business leader reinforced his belief in the rewards of individual effort. His success in running relief programs during and after World War I convinced him of the effectiveness of voluntary action—private citizens and businesses working together to solve problems without government prompting or legal requirements. Hoover believed the traditional self-reliance and volunteer spirit of the American people provided the most dependable means of combating the economic crisis of the Great Depression.

Toward this end, Hoover set up presidential committees to coordinate volunteer relief efforts for the unemployed, such as the **President's Organization of Unemployment Relief (POUR)**. In an effort to keep the banking system afloat, he persuaded bankers to set up the National Credit Corporation, a private agency that would **underwrite**, or buy up the assets of, banks that had failed. That action was meant to safeguard the deposits of bank customers. Unfortunately, bank managers were reluctant to do this. Since that experiment was a failure, Hoover tried again with the Reconstruction Finance Corporation (RFC), a government agency to loan money to troubled banks that did not belong to the Federal Reserve System. During the year Hoover was to remain in office, the RFC was not particularly successful either.

Hoover's attempts to ease the misery that Americans were facing every day also failed. His programs were unable to deal with the scale of the unemployment situation. Eight million workers were jobless by 1931, a number that overwhelmed the resources of existing charitable agencies. The POUR program coordinated relief agencies and urged people to help their neighbors, but these efforts did little to alleviate the human toll of the Great Depression that gripped the country.

Millions of Americans were feeling desperate and hopeless. The homeless and unemployed took to the roads and rails, looking for work, better opportunities, or a simple meal along the way. Migrant workers moved through the farmlands of California, picking produce for whatever they could earn. Others traveled from city to city, doing their best to survive on the charity of relief stations and church groups. Homeless Americans lived in and around cities in shantytowns dubbed **Hoovervilles**. The name "Hooverville" mocked the president's failure to provide for the American people.

Yet when politicians begged the federal government to find a solution to the unemployment problem, Hoover refused to budge. His response to the drought that caused the Dust Bowl provided yet

PRIMARY SOURCE

Any lack of confidence in the economic future and the basic strength of business in the United States is simply foolish. Our national capacity for hard work and intelligent cooperation is ample [promise] of the future of the United States.

—from President Herbert Hoover's press conference, November 15, 1929

11.5.1 Discuss the policies of Presidents Warren Harding, Calvin Coolidge, and Herbert Hoover; 11.6.2 Understand the explanations of the principal causes of the Great Depression and the steps taken by the Federal Reserve, Congress, and Presidents Herbert Hoover and Franklin Delano Roosevelt to combat the economic crisis.

CRITICAL VIEWING One of the largest and longest-lasting Hoovervilles covered 9 acres outside of Seattle, Washington, and had a population of 1,200. Based on details you see in the photo, what were living conditions like in Hoovervilles?

another example of the administration's failures. Congress proposed to allocate $60 million to help disaster victims buy fuel and food. Hoover offered money to feed animals, but he rejected the idea of feeding farmers and their families. This concern for animals over starving citizens conveyed a lack of empathy on the president's part, and additional derogatory references to the president circulated. A pocket turned outward to show it was empty of money was called a "Hoover flag." A newspaper unfolded and used to cover oneself for warmth was a "Hoover blanket." In 1931, in Minneapolis and Oklahoma City, crowds stormed into grocery stores and took food for themselves, and more protests against Hoover's lack of help were to come.

TURMOIL ABROAD

As the U.S. economy deteriorated, so did the international economy, inspiring some Europeans to look to strong but authoritarian leaders for relief. Such a leader had already risen to power in Europe. Playing on the social unrest and economic turmoil of the postwar years, dictator **Benito Mussolini** had seized control of Italy in 1922. Mussolini was a proponent of **fascism**, a political movement that involves extreme nationalism, militarism, and racism. As the supreme leader, or *Duce*, Mussolini destroyed Italian labor unions, censored the press, abolished all political parties but his own, and relied upon a secret police force to silence his critics. Global economic insecurity opened the door for fascism to grow in Europe. As people slid into poverty, many were willing to give up some of their rights on the basis of their authoritarian leader Mussolini's promises to bring back prosperity.

Asia was also affected. A 30 percent decrease in trade worldwide caused drops in income and productivity throughout the world. Japan, an island nation, needed raw materials for its industry and saw China as a likely source. Extreme nationalism provided a rationale for expanding its empire, and in 1931, Japan launched a war to occupy Manchuria, in China. Ultimately, Japan sought military, political, and economic control over the Pacific.

HISTORICAL THINKING

1. **READING CHECK** Why did President Hoover rely on voluntary action of citizens to try to address the economic crisis of the Great Depression?
2. **MAKE INFERENCES** Why was Hoover's response to drought victims in the Midwest unwise from a political standpoint?
3. **SYNTHESIZE** How did citizens and politicians try to deal with the effects of widespread unemployment?

11.6.3 Discuss the human toll of the Depression, natural disasters, and unwise agricultural practices and their effects on the depopulation of rural regions and on political movements of the left and right, with particular attention to the Dust Bowl refugees and their social and economic impacts in California.

3.2 **MAIN IDEA** President Hoover became less popular with Americans after he handled a growing protest movement poorly.

The Bonus Army

President Hoover was quickly reminded that sometimes things go from bad to worse. As unemployment rose, Hoover's popularity with Americans plummeted. As a result, the Democrats made progress in the 1930 elections and set their sights on victory in the 1932 presidential election.

HOOVER'S WANING POPULARITY

Hoover already had a low favorability rating with his constituents because of his policies to battle unemployment. Because Hoover was a Republican, many Americans assigned blame for the nation's struggles to his party. In the 1930 election, the Democrats picked up 8 seats in the Senate and 49 in the House. Neither gave the Democrats a majority, but by the time Congress next convened, Democrats had a majority in the House due to special elections held to replace representatives who had died.

To deal with a growing budget deficit, Congress passed the **Revenue Act of 1932**, the greatest peacetime increase in taxes in the nation's history. At a time when the economy needed Americans to have more buying power to keep factories and businesses open, the tax measure drew money out of the hands of potential consumers. Raising taxes in an election year contributed to Hoover's decreasing popularity. On the other hand, Congress also passed the **Norris-LaGuardia Act of 1932**, which extended to workers "full freedom of association" in unions and labor representation. The law restricted the use of federal **injunctions**, or court orders, to stop labor strikes, boycotts, and picketing and barred actions that prevented workers from joining unions. This legislation strengthened the power of labor, and it was popular among many American workers.

Tents and shacks burned as the U.S. Army drove the Bonus Army out of Washington, D.C., in July 1932.

To make matters worse, Congress introduced bills to provide direct assistance to the unemployed, but a coalition of Republicans and southern Democrats blocked their passage. Finally, as public pressure for action intensified, Congress passed the **Emergency Relief and Construction Act of 1932**. The act allocated federal funds to states for building public structures that could generate income, such as toll bridges, if the states proved they could not raise any money themselves. Although the law limited the kinds of construction projects that could be funded, it represented a symbolic step toward a greater federal role in combating the economic crisis and meeting the needs of desperate Americans.

THE BONUS MARCH

As the Depression worsened, economic distress triggered social protests, including one by war veterans. In 1931, a veterans organization passed a resolution demanding from Congress immediate payment of the cash bonus scheduled to be paid to World War I veterans in 1945. Veterans argued the early payment would not only help them but would also stimulate the economy. In December 1931, a bill authorizing this payment was introduced in the House. In May 1932, veterans began traveling to Washington, D.C., to show their support for the bill.

By June, more than 15,000 veterans calling themselves the Bonus Expeditionary Force, or the **Bonus Army**, had arrived in Washington to listen to Congress debate the bonus bill. While some slept in government buildings, most members of the Bonus Army camped out in makeshift tents and sheds on the banks of the Anacostia River. The Washington, D.C., police superintendent and the police captain in charge of Anacostia helped the veterans by providing food, medical care, and supplies for building their shacks. Hoover, on the other hand, ignored them. On June 17, the bill was rejected by the Senate. In July, the Hoover administration urged the Bonus Army to leave Washington and even allocated $100,000 to pay the men's transportation costs home. But many stayed on, hoping for a change in government policy.

On July 28, 1932, the secretary of war ordered the police to remove marchers from government buildings. Veterans resisted, and fighting broke out. When a police pistol went off, other officers began shooting, and soon two veterans lay dead. The president ordered the federal troops in Washington, commanded by Army Chief of Staff General **Douglas MacArthur**, to restore order. MacArthur took his men, armed with tanks and machine guns, across the Anacostia River into the Bonus Army's camp. His troops hurled tear gas canisters and burned tents and shacks as the veterans fled in terror. Documentary filmmakers captured the events, and moviegoers across the nation saw newsreels of MacArthur in full military dress directing the attack, cavalry soldiers charging veterans, and flames and smoke billowing from the camp. By the next day, the camp was a ruin and all the veterans had left. Many Americans were shocked. "If the Army must be called out to make war on unarmed citizens," wrote one newspaper editor, "this is no longer America." The public outrage spelled trouble for Hoover as the 1932 presidential election approached.

PRIMARY SOURCE

A 1932 editorial in the magazine *The New Republic* described the violence directed against the Bonus Army in Washington, D.C.

The orders which sent the soldiers to Anacostia, routing men, women and children out of bed, drenching them with tear gas, ruthlessly burning their poor shelters and whatever personal property they could not carry on their backs, then driving all of them, cripples, babies, pregnant women, up a steep hill at the point of a bayonet—these were the orders of a furious child who has been thwarted and is raging for revenge. It is profoundly humiliating to every decent American that he must see his government thus persecuting and stealing from these hungry and ragged men whom, fourteen years ago, it did not hesitate to send into the trenches at the risk of death.

—from "Bullets for the B.E.F.," *The New Republic*, August 10, 1932

HISTORICAL THINKING

1. **READING CHECK** Why did veterans organize the Bonus Army?
2. **IDENTIFY PROBLEMS AND SOLUTIONS** What problem was the Emergency Relief and Construction Act of 1932 meant to solve?
3. **ANALYZE CAUSE AND EFFECT** How did public pressure and opinion affect the political actions of Hoover and his administration?
4. **DISTINGUISH FACT AND OPINION** Does the phrase "these were the orders of a furious child" convey a fact or an opinion? Explain your answer.

11.6.3 Discuss the human toll of the Depression, natural disasters, and unwise agricultural practices and their effects on the depopulation of rural regions and on political movements of the left and right, with particular attention to the Dust Bowl refugees and their social and economic impacts in California; HI 1 Students show the connections, causal and otherwise, between particular historical events and larger social, economic, and political trends and developments.

CHAPTER 10 THE GREAT DEPRESSION

REVIEW

VOCABULARY

Write a paragraph about the topic using all the words in each group of words. A sentence is provided as a sample beginning.

1. Topic: the stock market crash HSS 11.6.1
   Dow Jones Industrial Average
   margin speculation
   trading pool stock market
   Speculation was one factor impacting the Dow Jones Industrial Average.

2. Topic: effects of the Depression HSS 11.6.3
   Dust Bowl drought Bonus Army
   Hooverville deportation

3. Topic: remedying the Depression HSS 11.6.2
   underwrite Smoot-Hawley Tariff Act
   Revenue Act of 1932 injunction

READING STRATEGY

ANALYZE CAUSE AND EFFECT

Analyzing cause and effect can help you understand how situations develop throughout history. Complete the Cause-and-Effect Chain to identify the factors that led to the stock market crash in 1929 and the Great Depression that followed. Then answer the question.

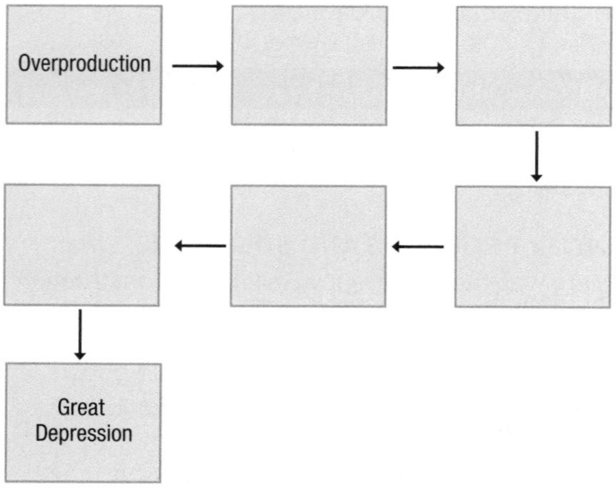

4. Describe the chain of causes and effects that resulted in the Great Depression. HSS 11.6

MAIN IDEAS

Answer the following questions. Support your answers with evidence from the chapter.

5. What was the Kellogg-Briand Pact? **LESSON 1.1** HSS 11.5.1
6. Why did intervention fail to stop the stock market slide between Black Thursday and Black Tuesday? **LESSON 1.2** HSS 11.6.2
7. How did income inequality and overproduction in manufacturing work together to create problems during the 1920s? **LESSON 2.1** HSS 11.6.2
8. In what ways did new farm machinery contribute to the conditions that caused the Dust Bowl? **LESSON 2.3** HSS HI 5
9. Why was Woody Guthrie's music so important to people facing poverty during the Depression? **LESSON 2.4** HSS 11.6.3
10. Why did Hoover's plan to help the banking system stay afloat fail? **LESSON 3.1** HSS 11.6.2
11. How did worldwide economic problems influence the emergence of fascism? **LESSON 3.1** HSS HI 1
12. How did the passage of the Revenue Act of 1932 hurt Hoover's popularity? **LESSON 3.2** HSS 11.6.2

HISTORICAL THINKING

Answer the following questions. Support your answers with evidence from the chapter.

13. **ANALYZE CAUSE AND EFFECT** How did international loans and World War I reparations contribute to the Great Depression? HSS 11.6.2
14. **MAKE CONNECTIONS** How did the Dust Bowl contribute to the depopulation of rural areas in the Great Plains? HSS 11.6.3
15. **EVALUATE** In what ways did ordinary people respond to the Great Depression? HSS 11.6.3

16. **ANALYZE CAUSE AND EFFECT** Did panic help cause the stock market crash, or was panic an effect of that crash? Explain your answer and describe how determining historical causes and effects can be complicated. HSS HI 2

17. **FORM AND SUPPORT OPINIONS** How would you rate Hoover's handling of the Great Depression? Support your position with evidence from the text. HSS 11.6.2

18. **ASK AND ANSWER QUESTIONS** Write a question you could ask about causes of the Great Depression, and describe how you could research the answer. Then explain the challenges of determining the causes and effects of a historical event like this. HSS HI 2

ANALYZE VISUALS

Look closely at the political cartoon from 1929 depicting Herbert Hoover saying to a farmer, "It may not be perfect, but I'm sure it'll help quite a bit." Then answer the questions that follow.

19. What do each of the characters depicted in the cartoon represent? HSS 11.6.2

20. What solution is Hoover offering the farmer, and what do the expressions of the scarecrow and crow convey about the solution? HSS 11.6.2

ANALYZE SOURCES

California Industrial Scenes is a 1934 fresco by John Langley Howard depicting unemployed workers during the Great Depression.

21. How does the painting reflect the larger social and economic developments of the Depression era? HSS HI 1

CONNECT TO YOUR LIFE

22. **EXPLANATORY** The Dust Bowl was an ecological disaster that may have been prevented if farmers had better understood the impact of their farming methods on the land. Find information about an ecological problem of today. Using the Dust Bowl as an example, write a short essay explaining why it is important that we understand problems before we can begin to solve them. HSS CST 4

TIPS

- Think about the physical and human characteristics of the region.
- Use textual evidence from the chapter in your explanation.
- Make a connection between the Dust Bowl and the problem of today, and explain how being more informed can prevent ecological problems from turning into disasters.
- Use two or three vocabulary terms from the chapter in your response.

CHAPTER **11**

THE NEW DEAL

1933–1940

HISTORICAL THINKING In what ways were Franklin Roosevelt's policies during the Great Depression groundbreaking?

This mural, titled *Agriculture in California*, appears in Coit Tower in San Francisco. Created in 1934 by American artist Maxine Albro, it was commissioned under a federal program to fund the visual arts. In an attempt to end the Great Depression, President Franklin Roosevelt initiated programs to help workers in all occupations, including artists and farmers.

"We are helping, **and shall continue to help** the farmer."

—President Franklin D. Roosevelt

AMERICA'S FAVORITE PASTIME

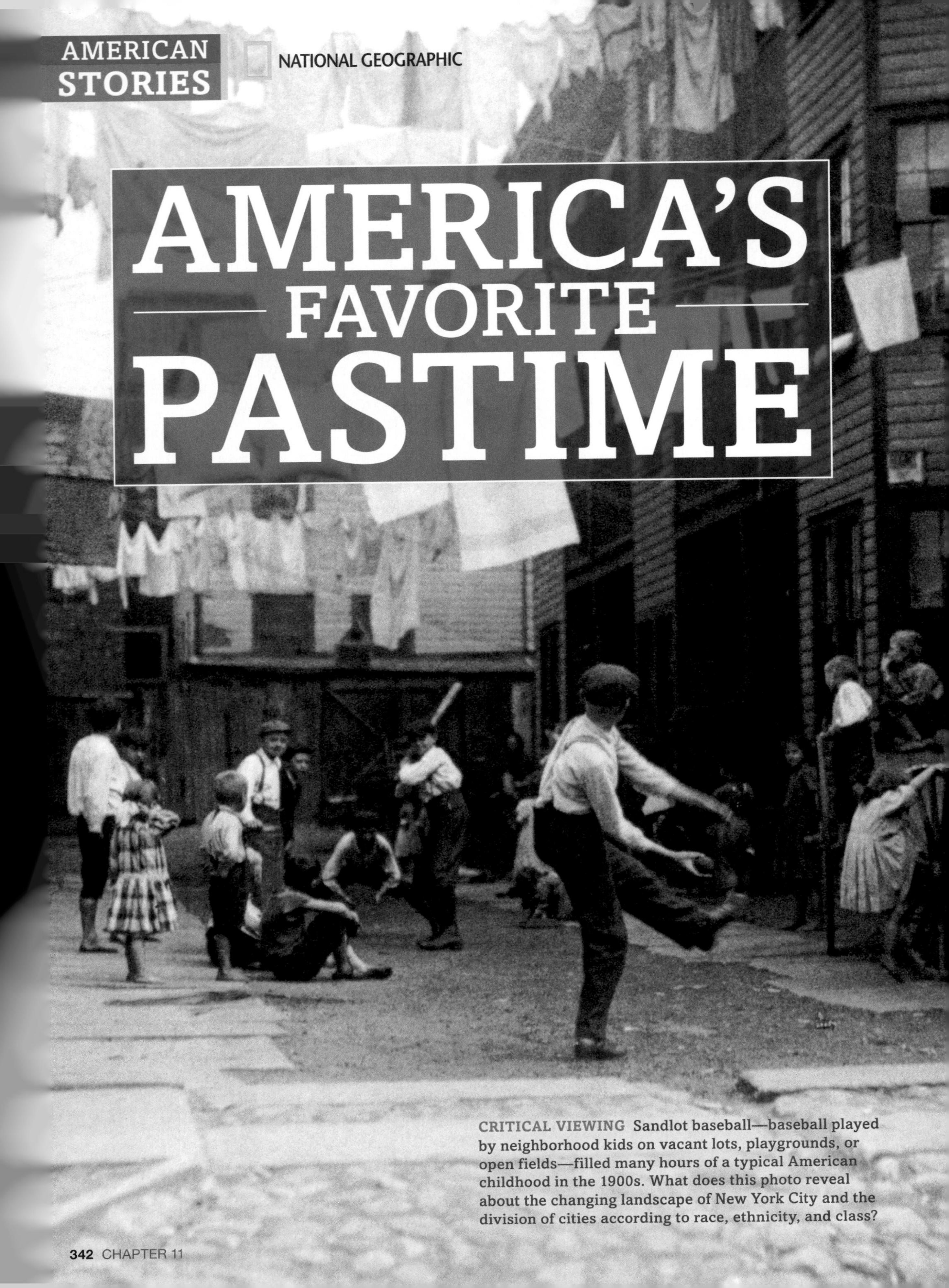

CRITICAL VIEWING Sandlot baseball—baseball played by neighborhood kids on vacant lots, playgrounds, or open fields—filled many hours of a typical American childhood in the 1900s. What does this photo reveal about the changing landscape of New York City and the division of cities according to race, ethnicity, and class?

In our sundown perambulations of late, through the outer parts of Brooklyn, we have observed several parties of youngsters playing "base," a certain game of ball. . . . Let us go forth awhile and get better air in our lungs. Let us leave our close rooms. . . . The game of ball is glorious.

—American poet Walt Whitman, 1846

Opening day ticket for the Cincinnati Baseball Club, April 18, 1895

When you hear the expression "America's pastime," you know the topic is baseball. Although some other popular sports, such as basketball and football, also developed in the United States, there's something about baseball that uniquely symbolizes the American identity. Russell Lewis, Chief Historian of the Chicago History Museum, has this theory about the sport in the early 1900s: "Baseball was . . . extremely popular, and I think it really cut across the ethnic groups. I think a lot of minorities found baseball one of the ways they could participate in being an American."

IN THE STADIUM AND ON THE RADIO

During the 1930s, the United States was in the grip of the Great Depression, and its human toll was widespread, touching nearly every household. Struggling to make ends meet, many Americans could not afford the cost of a ticket to the ballpark, so attendance at major league fields suffered. Between 1930 and 1933, the number of spectators at games decreased by 40 percent. Still, many people made room in their budgets for an escape to the ballpark when they could. Writer Ray Robinson, who was a child in New York City during the Depression, remembered people would "go to the ballpark to get away from the economic horrors of empty wallets and ice boxes."

Those who couldn't get to the ballpark could follow the games on the radio. The World Series was first broadcast "live" in 1921 by a studio announcer who read the play-by-play descriptions relayed to him from a news feed printed on a strip of paper called ticker tape. In some early radio broadcasts, a special effects operator provided sounds of an imaginary ballpark. By the 1930s, announcers were broadcasting from actual stadiums—no special effects needed. Not all team owners permitted radio coverage of the games, fearing that fans would stay home to listen and ballpark attendance would drop.

Listening to baseball on the radio in the 1930s was more challenging than it is today. Radios, cumbersome and far from portable, resided in the family living room, and often produced scratchy or static-filled sound. Sportswriter Robert Creamer wrote about listening to the World Series during the 1930s: "As a nine-year-old boy, I heard those World Series games on our living-room radio, which my mother, who was not even a fan, turned on and tuned in before I came home from school. Those old radios took a long time to warm up, and tuning to the right station took patience and a deft hand." Still, the role of radio in terms of popularizing baseball within American culture was profound.

11.5.6 Trace the growth and effects of radio and movies and their role in the worldwide diffusion of popular culture; 11.6.3 Discuss the human toll of the Depression, natural disasters, and unwise agricultural practices and their effects on the depopulation of rural regions and on political movements of the left and right, with particular attention to the Dust Bowl refugees and their social and economic impacts in California.

Toward the end of the 1930s, ballpark attendance began to rebound as the Depression lifted with the start of World War II. After the war ended and the soldiers returned, game attendance would return to—and even exceed—its pre-Depression levels. In the meantime, an intriguing new way to enjoy baseball made its debut during a game between the Brooklyn Dodgers and Cincinnati Reds on August 27, 1939. That day, station W2XBS in New York City broadcast live television coverage of the game to the fortunate TV owners who lived within 50 miles of the station. A *New York Times* sportswriter reported delightedly, "At times it was possible to catch a fleeting glimpse of the ball as it sped from the pitcher's hand toward home plate."

CRITICAL VIEWING Yankees hero Babe Ruth showed a group of attentive young boys in New York City how to grip a baseball bat. How might the relationship between professional athletes and their fans during the 1920s and 1930s compare to that of today?

BASEBALL LEGENDS

One name drew eager fans to the ballparks more than any other: that of legendary power hitter George Herman "Babe" Ruth of the New York Yankees. Ruth broke the single-season home run record in three consecutive seasons, hitting 29 in 1919, 54 in 1920 and 59 in 1921. In the early 1920s, he drew such a crowd that Yankees owner Jacob Ruppert built a new stadium to fit more spectators. Completed in 1923, Yankee Stadium was immediately given the nickname "The House that Ruth Built."

During the 1927 season, Ruth smashed 60 home runs, setting a record that remained unbroken until Roger Maris, who played in an era when the baseball season was 8 games longer, came along in 1961 and hit 61 home runs.

National Baseball Hall of Fame and Museum Cooperstown, New York

Baseball legend Babe Ruth hit three home runs with this 36-inch wooden bat—a bat worthy of a museum collection—in Game Four of the 1926 World Series.

11.8.8. Discuss forms of popular culture, with emphasis on their origins and geographic diffusion (e.g., jazz and other forms of popular music, professional sports, architectural and artistic styles).

During his stellar 1927 season, Ruth hit more home runs than most major league teams—only the St. Louis Cardinals, Chicago Cubs, New York Giants, and his own team, the Yankees, managed to out homer him. To the dismay of his opponents, he hit home runs in every stadium of the American League.

In the 1930s, even though his home run stats were in decline, Ruth remained a force to be reckoned with. In the 1932 World Series, he helped the Yankees to victory over the Cubs with a three-run homer and a single in the third game of the series. Ruth hit his last major league home run at Forbes Field in Pittsburgh, Pennsylvania, on May 25, 1935. Aging and out of shape, he nonetheless hit three homers in a single game. The last of these, described by the Pittsburgh pitcher as "the longest cockeyed ball I ever saw in my life," was the first ball ever hit completely out of that park. It was Babe Ruth's 714th and final home run.

While all eyes were on Babe Ruth, his teammate Lou Gehrig was quietly setting a major league record of his own. Between May 1925 and May 1939, he played in 2,130 consecutive games, earning the nickname "The Iron Horse." When asked why he wouldn't take a rest, Gehrig replied, "There's no point to it. I like to play baseball." Gehrig's record remained unbroken for 56 years, until Cal Ripken, Jr., of the Baltimore Orioles played his 2,131st consecutive game.

Gehrig was not far behind Ruth in slugging abilities, nearly equaling Ruth's record with 47 home runs of his own in 1927. In 1932, he surpassed one of Ruth's accomplishments by hitting four home runs in a single game. Perhaps because of Ruth's fame and flamboyant personality, Gehrig spent the first half of the 1930s in Ruth's shadow, even though he was scoring runs at a faster pace than the aging star.

The 1930s saw the birth of new baseball legends as well as the passing of an earlier golden age. Center fielder Joe DiMaggio made his debut with the New York Yankees in 1936, introducing himself to the major leagues by hitting 29 home runs and batting in 125 runs during his rookie year. DiMaggio helped lead the Yankees, without Ruth, to four consecutive World Series championships between 1936 and 1939.

Also in 1939, Ted Williams, playing for the Boston Red Sox, had possibly the best major league rookie year in all of baseball: 31 home runs, 145 runs batted in, and a batting average of .327. Both DiMaggio and Williams would become dominant players in the major leagues in the 1940s. In 1941, DiMaggio went on a spectacular hitting streak, racking up hits in 56 consecutive games. That same year, Williams achieved an unheard-of batting average of .406. No player since then has ever approached either of these feats.

Ted Williams was chosen three times (in 1954, 1957, and 1958) by baseball card manufacturer Topps as the "leadoff man," meaning his was the first card in the set.

It seems appropriate that the Baseball Hall of Fame in Cooperstown, New York, was established in 1939. That year marked the end of a decade filled with legendary players, whose names are familiar to nearly all Americans. Babe Ruth was in the first group of inductees, along with greats from earlier eras, such as Ty Cobb and Honus Wagner. Lou Gehrig was elected to the Hall of Fame later that year, even though there is normally a waiting period between a player's retirement and his induction.

THINK ABOUT IT

What connections can you make between the popularity of baseball and the Great Depression?

HI 1 Students show the connections, causal and otherwise, between particular historical events and larger social, economic, and political trends and developments.

AMERICAN STORIES

THE NEGRO LEAGUES

Although such teams as the New York Yankees and St. Louis Cardinals dominated sports headlines throughout the 1930s, the all-white major leagues were not the only game in town. Prevented by prejudice and segregation from participating in the major leagues, African-American team owners and players formed their own leagues in the early 20th century. In 1920, Andrew "Rube" Foster, owner of the Chicago American Giants, organized the Negro National League, which consisted of eight teams in the Midwest. Other leagues soon followed, including the Negro Southern League later in 1920 and the Eastern Colored League in 1923.

Facing the same financial difficulties as the white major leagues during the Great Depression, Rube Foster's league disbanded after the 1931 season. It was soon replaced by a new Negro National League organized by Gus Greenlee, owner of the Pittsburgh Crawfords. From 1933 to 1949, Greenlee's league dominated the African-American baseball scene.

The best-known player in the Negro leagues was Leroy "Satchel" Paige, a tall, gangly pitcher with an unusual, high-legged windup and a spitfire delivery. Paige played for a number of teams, including the Pittsburgh Crawfords and the Kansas City Monarchs. There is little doubt that Satchel Paige would have been a star in the major leagues if teams had been integrated. Negro league teams did play

In a Negro league game in 1940, the Homestead Grays played the New York Black Yankees at Griffith Stadium in Washington, D.C.

11.10.5 Discuss the diffusion of the civil rights movement of African Americans from the churches of the rural South and the urban North, including the resistance to racial desegregation in Little Rock and Birmingham, and how the advances influenced the agendas, strategies, and effectiveness of the quests of American Indians, Asian Americans, and Hispanic Americans for civil rights and equal opportunities.

The 1935 Pittsburgh Crawfords, shown here in front of their team bus, were one of the best teams in the Negro leagues.

exhibition games against major league teams, and Paige struck out some of the toughest white hitters. Hack Wilson, a major leaguer, gave this description of Paige's fastball: "It starts out like a baseball, but when it gets to the plate it looks like a marble." Paige, known for his dazzling self-confidence and showmanship, gave this response: "You must be talking about my slowball. My fastball looks like a fish egg."

For all his brilliance, Paige may not have been the best pitcher in the Negro leagues. Some sportswriters and former players have suggested that Smokey Joe Williams or Bullet Joe Rogan may have been even better. Because the Negro leagues did not keep consistent records, it is difficult to compare players' statistics.

Despite their talent and popularity, even the top Negro league players were not allowed in most white-owned hotels and restaurants while they were on the road. However, by the end of the 1930s, some people were beginning to question the segregation of baseball. A group of African-American sportswriters was joined by the CIO labor union in calling for an end to the practice. Team owners in the major leagues ignored the calls, even though they were passing up the chance to sign extremely talented players. Over the course of the Negro leagues' existence, African-American teams played white teams in at least 438 exhibition games, and the Negro league teams won 309 times.

The racial barrier finally fell in 1947, when African-American player Jackie Robinson stepped up to the plate for the Brooklyn Dodgers. After that, the Negro leagues gradually dissolved as their best talent was hired by the now-integrated major leagues. In their later years, the Negro leagues were inclusive in a way that is not often recognized. Three women—Toni Stone, Connie Morgan, and Mamie "Peanut" Johnson—played on regular Negro league teams in the early 1950s.

This Negro leagues souvenir key chain from about 1940 features pitcher Satchel Paige.

WORTH THE WAIT

Much of baseball history focuses on traditionally dominant teams, such as the New York Yankees and the St. Louis Cardinals. Often overlooked are the teams that struggle a little—or a lot. One of those struggling teams—the Chicago Cubs—gained the limelight in 2016. When the opening pitch of the 2016 World Series was thrown, it had been 108 years since the Cubs had won baseball's most coveted prize. Teams like the Chicago White Sox and the Boston Red Sox hadn't fared much better.

The Cubs and the Red Sox had one other quirk in common: each team carried a famous curse. In the case of the Cubs, it was the so-called Curse of the Billy Goat. The tale goes that tavern owner William Sianis tried to bring his goat, named Murphy, to Game Four of the 1945 World Series at Wrigley Field, the Cubs' ballpark. When Murphy was turned away, Sianis supposedly proclaimed that the Cubs would lose that World Series and would never win another. The Cubs did in fact lose the 1945 World Series.

For all three long-suffering teams, the World Series drought ended in the 21st century. The Red Sox took the championship in 2004, and the White Sox in 2005. And in 2016, the Cubs won the World Series in a hotly contested, seven-game series against the Cleveland Indians. Lifelong fans across the country rooted for the team to break its epic losing streak, and after what may be the greatest World Series in history, it did. The score of the final game: Cubs 8, Indians 7.

Chicagoans welcomed their beloved Cubbies home after the win with a parade and rally that drew larger crowds than the city had ever seen. And longtime journalist Dan Rather posted his thoughts on the Cubs' historic win, reflecting at the same time on what baseball means to many Americans:

> In a world of nanosecond news cycles, baseball is measured in what by comparison is geologic time. It ties us to those who came before us—the many generations. And it stretches to those yet unborn. Fans of the future will hear about a curse and the 2016 Cubbies without fully understanding the full import of the moment. A cosmic quirk in the law of averages has been reconciled.
>
> But the sun will rise tomorrow. The calendar will turn to winter and then spring. And hope on the diamond always springs eternal.

Unprecedented crowds of emotional fans took to the streets surrounding Wrigley Field after the Cubs' 2016 World Series win.

First baseman Anthony Rizzo leapt into the air with Kris Bryant alongside Mike Montgomery, Javier Báez, and Addison Russell seconds after the Cubs made the winning out in the 2016 World Series.

1.1 **MAIN IDEA** Franklin Delano Roosevelt won the presidency in 1932 by promising to take action to end the Great Depression.

FDR AND THE 1932 ELECTION

When a baseball team isn't doing well, sometimes the solution is to replace the manager. That's what happened in 1932 when the country was struggling through the Great Depression. Americans decided it was time for a new leader.

NOMINATING ROOSEVELT

In the years leading up to the 1932 presidential election, Republican Herbert Hoover, who was set to run for a second term, gradually lost public support. He had failed to ease the Great Depression, and many Americans had grown to resent him and wealthy people in general. The Democrats saw an opportunity to take back the presidency and began looking for an appealing and experienced candidate. **Franklin Delano Roosevelt**, popularly known as FDR, fit the bill. He was the distant cousin of a well-respected former president, Theodore Roosevelt, and he was married to Theodore's niece, Eleanor Roosevelt. Her political opinions and support of such causes as women's rights and labor had a great influence on her husband. Roosevelt was elected to

While campaigning for the presidency, Franklin Roosevelt greets a coal miner in West Virginia in this photograph from October 1932. Although he came from a wealthy, privileged background, Roosevelt was able to connect with ordinary Americans and convince them he cared.

the New York State Senate in 1910, and he served as assistant secretary of the Navy under President Wilson. In 1920, he ran as the Democratic candidate for vice president but did not win the election.

Unfortunately, in 1921, Roosevelt contracted an infectious disease called **polio** and lost the use of his legs. The public knew about his disability, though the press did not focus on his condition. Roosevelt assumed his bout of polio and the disability it caused meant the end of his political career, but Eleanor encouraged him to carry on. After taking time off to recover, Roosevelt worked hard to reenter politics. His determination paid off in 1928 when he narrowly won the governorship of the state of New York. As governor, he earned a reputation as a strong, reform-minded leader who actively worked to address such problems as unemployment and poverty.

FDR's forceful personality and "can-do" attitude impressed Democratic Party members. The Democrats felt Roosevelt's confidence and optimism would inspire hope in the many Americans who were struggling. They also believed his friendly, easy way of connecting with people would appeal to all Americans, rich and poor. At the party's national convention in Chicago, Roosevelt secured the presidential nomination, and John Nance Garner, a senator from Texas, was chosen as his running mate.

THE ELECTION OF 1932

The 1932 presidential race was not just a choice between Roosevelt and Hoover, however. The Socialist and Communist parties also nominated presidential candidates, hoping to appeal to Americans by proposing that their respective political systems offered the best solution to the Great Depression.

By October 1932, Hoover's public image was so unfavorable that Roosevelt's advisors assured the Democratic candidate that there was no need to campaign vigorously. FDR disagreed. Sensing that a passive campaign would not appeal to voters, he crisscrossed the country, giving speeches that convinced Americans their lives would improve if they elected him president.

On election day, November 8, 1932, Roosevelt won in a landslide, securing 57 percent of the popular vote and an overwhelming 89 percent of the electoral vote. Democratic candidates benefited from FDR's popularity, gaining 90 seats in the House and 13 in the Senate. The election proved a major disappointment to both the Socialist and Communist parties. The Socialist candidate received fewer than 1 million votes, and the Communist candidate collected only about 100,000. Herbert Hoover was now a **lame duck**, an outgoing elected official soon to be replaced by a successor. For many Americans, his exit could not come soon enough. In fact, Congress was in the process of ratifying the **20th Amendment**, which would move up the presidential inauguration from March to January.

Meanwhile, the Great Depression continued to deepen. By the morning of Roosevelt's inauguration on March 4, 1933, many banks in New York City, the nation's financial capital, were closing. Roosevelt took the presidential oath of office in a steady, chilling rain. "Only a foolish optimist can deny the dark realities of the moment," he told the huge crowd in attendance and the millions who listened on the radio. "This nation asks for action, and action now," he declared.

Roosevelt offered few specific solutions that day. His objective was to persuade a dispirited people to have faith in him and in themselves. Standing straight in his leg braces, he stressed four major themes: sacrifice, discipline, compassion, and hope.

PRIMARY SOURCE

This is preeminently the time to speak the truth, the whole truth, frankly and boldly. Nor need we shrink from honestly facing conditions in our country today. This great Nation will endure as it has endured, will revive and will prosper. So, first of all, let me assert my firm belief that the only thing we have to fear is fear itself.

—from Franklin Delano Roosevelt's First Inaugural Address, March 4, 1933

HISTORICAL THINKING

1. **READING CHECK** Why did Democrats believe Franklin Roosevelt was a good candidate for president?
2. **DETERMINE CHRONOLOGY** Review Roosevelt's political career before the 1932 election. How did the positions he held and the order in which he held them prepare him for the presidency?
3. **MAKE INFERENCES** Why do you think the press did not focus on FDR's disability?
4. **DRAW CONCLUSIONS** What did FDR mean when he said "the only thing we have to fear is fear itself"?

11.6.2 Understand the explanations of the principal causes of the Great Depression and the steps taken by the Federal Reserve, Congress, and Presidents Herbert Hoover and Franklin Delano Roosevelt to combat the economic crisis.

1.2 **MAIN IDEA** As president, Franklin Roosevelt took immediate action to address the problems of the Great Depression and thus expanded the federal government's role in the nation's economy.

AN ACTIVIST GOVERNMENT

As the old saying goes, sometimes you have to spend money to make money. Roosevelt and his advisors believed that the best way to move the United States toward economic recovery was to spend government money, so they emptied the nation's wallet and invested in the thousands of desperate Americans in need of work.

THE FIRST HUNDRED DAYS

As soon as Roosevelt stepped into the White House, things began to change. Roosevelt asked several university professors, whom journalists called the "**brain trust**," to offer ideas on how to fix the still-floundering economy. With their help, he generated within his first few months in office 15 effective laws that fortified the nation's economy. This time of frenzied lawmaking was later dubbed the **First Hundred Days**.

The brain trust advised Roosevelt to proclaim a holiday for all the country's banks to prevent people from withdrawing their money in a panic. The **bank holiday**, which Roosevelt declared on March 6, 1933, stopped all banking operations nationwide. Roosevelt also called Congress back into a special session, so he could present laws designed to restore public confidence in the nation's banking industry. Americans were understandably anxious about the financial industry after many of them had lost their money when numerous banks closed throughout the nation. With both the House and the Senate now under firm Democratic control, Roosevelt had little trouble getting these bills passed.

The brain trust based their advice on theories developed by **John Maynard Keynes**, a leading British economist. Years before, Keynes had proposed that the best way for a government to jump-start an economy was to invest all of its money back into the country, a strategy he called "priming the pump." The solution was risky because it created a **deficit**, or negative balance, in the national treasury. Basically, the idea was to print more money and give it to individual citizens, who would then stimulate the economy by spending it. The Federal Reserve Bank soon began printing more money. The brain trust also suggested a plan to regulate the banks. They called for the federal inspection of all banks, after which the banks with cash on hand would be allowed to reopen. The remaining banks would be reorganized, if possible, or closed for good.

Roosevelt then decided to address America's concerns about the banking industry directly. On March 12, 1933, he gave his first **fireside chat**, a radio broadcast that became a tradition throughout the rest of his presidency. More than 60 million Americans tuned in to listen. In the days that followed, as the stronger banks reopened, people began depositing money again. By the end of March, almost $1 billion had been returned to bank vaults. The banking crisis was over.

Roosevelt's strategy revealed his pragmatism, or practicality, and his belief in an activist government. Instead of taking a radical

The National Museum of American History Washington, D.C.

Instead of sitting before a fire for his chats, President Roosevelt sat before an array of microphones, including the first one used for the National Broadcasting Company (NBC). Carleton Smith, who set up the RCA type 50-A microphone for NBC and introduced the radio broadcasts, donated it to the museum.

11.5.6 Trace the growth and effects of radio and movies and their role in the worldwide diffusion of popular culture.

In the 1930s, President Roosevelt was photographed as he delivered one of his 30 fireside chats. He began the practice 8 days after his inauguration in 1933 and continued it until 1944.

approach—giving the government control of all the nation's banks, for example—he demonstrated that his primary mission was to preserve capitalism. Roosevelt was willing to experiment with a wide array of ideas to save capitalism from its own excesses.

The special session of Congress continued meeting. In that time, the president established government agencies with the aim of creating jobs. One such agency was the **Civilian Conservation Corps (CCC)**, which combined the president's enthusiasm for conservation with his belief in national service. The corps provided outdoor jobs to young men ages 17 to 24. They worked on soil-erosion and flood-control projects and developed many state parks by paving roads, building cabins, and planting trees. Popular and successful, the CCC eased unemployment, lowered urban crime rates, and helped countless families.

Roosevelt chose a social worker and one of his closest advisors, **Harry Hopkins**, to help him manage the **New Deal**, a group of laws, agencies, and programs designed to combat the economic crisis. They coined the name of their plan from Theodore Roosevelt's Square Deal, and they hoped it would be as successful.

SUPPORT FOR RURAL AREAS

Roosevelt wanted to help all Americans through the Depression, including those who lived in rural areas. His New Deal featured programs designed to help poor farming families. Two major programs were in Tennessee and California.

The Tennessee River drained land in seven states. The 4 million people who lived there were some of the country's poorest farmers. Their communities were isolated and lacked doctors, proper schools, electricity, and paved roads. In May 1933, Roosevelt established a federal agency called the **Tennessee Valley Authority (TVA)** to construct dams and power plants along the river and its tributaries. Within a decade, 16 dams and hydroelectric plants operated along the river, providing thousands of jobs and bringing electrical power to residents.

In California, the New Deal funded the **Central Valley Project (CVP)**, a plan to irrigate the arid San Joaquin Valley, a portion of the state's vast Central Valley. Like the TVA, the CVP involved the construction of dams to create reservoirs for storing and delivering water.

Throughout the country, most farmers' incomes had been falling since the 1920s. In 1932, for instance,

11.6.2 Understand the explanations of the principal causes of the Great Depression and the steps taken by the Federal Reserve, Congress, and Presidents Herbert Hoover and Franklin Delano Roosevelt to combat the economic crisis.

PRIMARY SOURCE

The Southern Tenant Farmers' Union began during a meeting of 27 African-American and white sharecroppers held in a schoolhouse in eastern Arkansas in 1934. One man spoke up to convince the white farmers to join an integrated union.

We live under the same sun, eat the same food, wear the same kind of clothing, work on the same land, raise the same crop for the same landlord who oppresses and cheats us both. For a long time now [we] have been fighting each other and both of us has been getting whipped all the time. We don't have nothing against one another but we got plenty against the landlord.

—from a speech by African-American tenant farmer Isaac Shaw, given at an Arkansas schoolhouse, 1934

farmers were earning less than one-third of their 1929 incomes, even though the introduction of tractors and high-grade fertilizer allowed farms to produce more crops than ever.

The **Agricultural Adjustment Act (AAA)** was the New Deal's solution to declining farm incomes. Passed in 1933, the act limited the quantity of such staple crops as cotton, wheat, and corn that farmers could grow. It also paid farmers who voluntarily stopped growing crops on some of their land. The AAA was based on a theory called **planned scarcity**, in which the government lowers the supplies of certain products in order to create a high demand for them and raise their prices. The government also offered generous loans to farmers who stored their crop surpluses in government warehouses. Roosevelt funded the AAA by taxing businesses that processed farm goods, such as flour millers, cotton gin operators, and meatpackers. The plan worked. Within a year, more than 3 million farmers had signed individual contracts with the AAA. Farm incomes shot up almost 60 percent between 1932 and 1935.

In 1941, workers completed the construction of a turbine to generate hydroelectric power from water falling over the Cherokee Dam in Tennessee. The Cherokee Dam was one of 16 dams the TVA built between 1933 and 1943.

11.6.4 Analyze the effects of and the controversies arising from New Deal economic policies and the expanded role of the federal government in society and the economy since the 1930s (e.g., Works Progress Administration, Social Security, National Labor Relations Board, farm programs, regional development policies, and energy development projects such as the Tennessee Valley Authority, California Central Valley Project, and Bonneville Dam).

In the 1930s, members of the Civilian Conservation Corps could show their pride in the work they did for the CCC by purchasing and displaying items like this decorative pennant.

The AAA helped countless farm families, yet the system barely reached desperately poor tenant farmers, who did not own the land they farmed but rented it. Some tenant farmers were sharecroppers, who gave part of their harvest as rent. Tenant farmers made up almost one-half of the nation's white farm families and three-quarters of its African-American farm families. Under AAA regulations, tenants were supposed to get a fair share of the government payments, but this rarely occurred. Few landlords obeyed the rules, and some evicted their tenants in order to take even more land out of production.

In response, sharecroppers and other tenant farmers formed their own organization, the **Southern Tenant Farmers' Union**, to fight for their rights. But those who joined the union were evicted from their homes, ignored by potential employers, and denied credit at banks and stores. The union's organizers were beaten and jailed, and the union soon collapsed.

NATIONAL INDUSTRIAL RECOVERY ACT

The president's brain trust soon expanded to include such advisors as Eleanor Roosevelt and Harry Hopkins. The group experimented with centralized **economic planning**, or management of the economy by the federal government. The chief way Roosevelt centralized economic planning was through the **National Industrial Recovery Act (NIRA)**, enacted in June 1933. The act created two federal agencies: the **Public Works Administration (PWA)** and the **National Recovery Administration (NRA)**.

The Public Works Administration provided jobs for the unemployed and also generated new orders for factories in the steel, glass, rubber, and cement industries. It worked differently from most other New Deal agencies because it helped individual contractors hire and pay their own workers, instead of having the federal government pay the employees' wages. Roosevelt selected his Secretary of the Interior, **Harold Ickes**, to run the agency. Ickes managed hundreds of PWA projects, including the construction of the Hoover Dam in Nevada, the Golden Gate Bridge in San Francisco, the Bonneville Dam between Washington and Oregon, and the Lincoln Tunnel in New York City.

The National Recovery Administration, led by General Hugh S. Johnson, established codes of fair business practices for individual industries. The idea was to set clear expectations for both business owners and workers in order to reduce labor strikes and allow the economy to stabilize. The NRA's main goals were to abolish child labor and give labor unions the right to organize and negotiate contracts. Johnson signed up major industries first—coal, steel, oil, automakers, and shipbuilders—and then moved on to smaller businesses. By the end of 1933, the NRA had 746 agreements in place.

But the NRA ran into trouble when small business owners complained that the codes encouraged monopolies and drowned them in paperwork. Labor leaders claimed that employers ignored the wage and hour expectations and continued to discourage union activity. To cover the cost of implementing the standards, manufacturers charged more for their products. Then consumers began to blame the NRA for rising prices.

During a court case in 1935, the Supreme Court declared the NRA unconstitutional on the grounds that Congress had delegated too much legislative authority to the president. Relieved, Roosevelt confided to an aide, "It has been an awful headache. I think perhaps NRA has done all it can do."

HISTORICAL THINKING

1. **READING CHECK** Describe the ways in which President Franklin Roosevelt used his increased presidential powers in response to the Great Depression.
2. **ANALYZE CAUSE AND EFFECT** In what ways did the expanded role of the federal government affect society and the economy in the 1930s?
3. **DRAW CONCLUSIONS** How does the Southern Tenant Farmers Union symbolize the advance and retreat of organized labor?

11.6.5 Trace the advances and retreats of organized labor, from the creation of the American Federation of Labor and the Congress of Industrial Organizations to current issues of a postindustrial, multinational economy, including the United Farm Workers in California; 11.8.5 Describe the increased powers of the presidency in response to the Great Depression, World War II, and the Cold War.

The New Deal

In the 1930s, the United States faced an enormous economic crisis. Many Americans, citizens and leaders alike, disagreed about how the federal government should respond to massive unemployment, business failures, labor strikes, and social unrest. It was a frightening time for the country.

Political cartoons during FDR's administration depicted Roosevelt in a variety of ways. Some painted him as strong, caring, and affable, while others characterized him as a sneaky politician, out for power. This cartoon from 1934 shows FDR surrounded by happy, dancing children who represent the various agencies established by the New Deal.

CRITICAL VIEWING Do you think this cartoon presents a positive, negative, or neutral characterization of FDR? Support your opinion with details from the cartoon.

11.6.4 Analyze the effects of and the controversies arising from New Deal economic policies and the expanded role of the federal government in society and the economy since the 1930s (e.g., Works Progress Administration, Social Security, National Labor Relations Board, farm programs, regional development policies, and energy development projects such as the Tennessee Valley Authority, California Central Valley Project, and Bonneville Dam); HI 3 Students interpret past events and issues within the context in which an event unfolded rather than solely in terms of present-day norms and values; HREP 4 Students construct and test hypotheses; collect, evaluate, and employ information from multiple primary and secondary sources; and apply it in oral and written presentations.

DOCUMENT ONE

Primary Source: Speech
from Franklin D. Roosevelt's first fireside chat, March 12, 1933

In his first fireside chat to the nation, President Roosevelt outlined his plans to restore confidence in banks. He faced a daunting challenge: how to rally a downtrodden citizenry from the depths of economic despair.

CONSTRUCTED RESPONSE What challenge does FDR present Americans in place of "rumors or guesses" about the failing financial system?

> After all, there is an element in the readjustment of our financial system more important than currency, more important than gold, and that is the confidence of the people themselves. Confidence and courage are the essentials of success in carrying out our plan. You people must have faith; you must not be stampeded by rumors or guesses. Let us unite in banishing fear. We have provided the machinery to restore our financial system, and it is up to you to support and make it work. It is your problem, my friends, your problem no less than it is mine. Together we cannot fail.

DOCUMENT TWO

Primary Source: Letter
from an anonymous letter to Senator Robert F. Wagner, March 7, 1934

Some Americans were wary of FDR's plans to get the country back on its feet. Many wrote letters to members of Congress and to the president himself, warning of the dire threats that the New Deal and other Roosevelt policies posed to the American social, political, and economic system.

CONSTRUCTED RESPONSE According to the author of this letter, what specific factors will lead to "disaster to all classes"?

> My Dear Senator:
>
> It seems very apparent to me that the Administration at Washington is accelerating its pace towards socialism and communism.
>
> Everyone is sympathetic to the cause of creating more jobs and better wages for labor; but, a program continually promoting labor troubles, higher wages, shorter hours, and less profits for business, would seem to me to be leading us fast to a condition where the Government must more and more expand its relief activities, and will lead in the end to disaster to all classes.

DOCUMENT THREE

Primary Source: Newspaper article
from "The Roosevelt Record," *The Crisis*, November 1940

Roy Wilkins was one of the civil rights movement's most important figures. He was the editor of *The Crisis*, the official publication of the NAACP, from 1934 to 1949. From the 1940s through the 1960s, he helped organize legal efforts to overturn "separate but equal" segregation in public schools, participated in marches and protests, and served as the executive director of the NAACP.

CONSTRUCTED RESPONSE According to Wilkins, what problem could not be solved by the New Deal?

> It is foolish to deny the imperfections and shortcomings of the New Deal. . . . The New Deal could not perform miracles. It could not overturn entrenched prejudices. The poor and the underprivileged, among whom are to be found most Negroes, need not look for comparison to the days of Herbert Hoover. They need only glance about them to see who is against the present administration. We are all Americans. We all seek security, justice, liberty, peace. But by what methods? And for whom?

SYNTHESIZE & WRITE

1. **REVIEW** Review what you have learned about the events surrounding the development and implementation of New Deal policies.
2. **RECALL** List the main ideas about the New Deal expressed in the three documents above.
3. **CONSTRUCT** Construct a topic sentence that answers this question: How did the federal government respond to the Great Depression, and what were the reactions to the New Deal?
4. **WRITE** Using evidence from this chapter and the documents, write an informative paragraph that supports your topic sentence in Step 3.

2.1 **MAIN IDEA** Roosevelt launched the second part of the New Deal while facing difficult challenges at home and abroad.

THE SECOND NEW DEAL

In 2007, the American economy almost collapsed, and more than 8 million people lost their jobs as a result. Double that number and you have some idea of the need that overwhelmed the country during the Great Depression.

JOBS, JOBS, JOBS

The progress made by Roosevelt's administration in its first hundred days was enough for Roosevelt to earn the American voters' loyalty. The economy was rebounding, and things were looking up. But the Roosevelt administration knew that too many citizens were still dealing with the persistence of poverty. When the Democrats gained even more seats in the House and Senate after the midterm elections of 1934, Roosevelt was confident Congress would pass more relief legislation. He presented Congress with a new set of reforms, the **Second New Deal**.

Despite the progress, millions of Americans remained unemployed. Roosevelt decided once again to rely on his pragmatic and activist government to address this problem. His administration launched the **Works Progress Administration (WPA)** in 1935, which provided jobs on small construction projects in communities around the country. WPA regional development projects ranged from building new schools, bridges, and landing fields for airplanes to improving more than 650,000 miles of roads. The WPA also funded projects that employed writers, teachers, musicians, and artists. Most of the WPA jobs were temporary and relatively low-paying, so as not to compete directly with private businesses. Nonetheless, the WPA, headed by Harry Hopkins, employed more than a quarter of the entire United States' workforce by 1936.

A separate division of the WPA, inspired by Eleanor Roosevelt, provided part-time jobs specifically for high school and college students. The agency, called the **National Youth Administration (NYA)**, employed several million young people.

SOCIAL SECURITY

In addition to promoting job opportunities, Secretary of Labor **Frances Perkins** urged the government to provide for those who could not work. The war years had led Americans to value independence, hard work, and sacrifice for the sake of their country. People were expected to be financially responsible for themselves. But the Depression changed that attitude. The crash proved that even the hardest workers could face financial setbacks created by economic forces over which they had no control.

In response to Perkins's request, Roosevelt proposed the **Social Security Act**, a law that would provide old-age insurance, unemployment insurance, and financial aid to the disabled and others in need. The program established a **pension fund**, or a pool of money used to pay people a small, established income after they retire. The Social Security Act was passed in 1935 and was funded by taxes paid by both employees and employers beginning in 1937.

Although the Social Security Act provided many benefits, it had some flaws and provoked controversies. It excluded millions of people, including the self-employed, farmers, and domestic workers. Benefits were not high—between $20 and $30 a month—but they were better than what those in need had been receiving: nothing. Some retired and disabled people were literally starving.

THE FASCIST CHALLENGE

While President Roosevelt labored to right the economic ship at home, some other countries were reacting to the Great Depression in very different, and in some cases, disturbing ways.

11.6.4 Analyze the effects of and the controversies arising from New Deal economic policies and the expanded role of the federal government in society and the economy since the 1930s (e.g., Works Progress Administration, Social Security, National Labor Relations Board, farm programs, regional development policies, and energy development projects such as the Tennessee Valley Authority, California Central Valley Project, and Bonneville Dam); 11.11.6 Analyze the persistence of poverty and how different analyses of this issue influence welfare reform, health insurance reform, and other social policies.

Artists working for the Works Progress Administration Federal Art Project designed posters that publicized WPA initiatives in such areas as education, recreation, safety, and health. WPA artists created the posters shown above between 1936 and 1941.

The changing face of European politics in the 1930s would challenge the United States' foreign policy as brutal authoritarian leaders emerged in several nations, particularly in Germany and Italy.

As you have read, Benito Mussolini had risen to power in the 1920s, instituting a fascist government in Italy that was based on extreme nationalism and militarism. A few years later, **Adolf Hitler** began his rise to power in Germany when he helped form the National Socialist German Workers Party. Also known as the **Nazi Party**, this organization was one of the many extremist groups that developed after World War I. Hitler modeled himself, to some degree, on Mussolini. Both were fascist dictators who established **totalitarian** regimes, in which the government relies on force to exert complete control over a country. Hitler's philosophy of **National Socialism** promoted the superiority of Germany and the German people, rejected communism, and carried anti-Semitism—hatred of Jewish people—to extreme levels. Both Hitler and Mussolini wanted to spread their power, which stirred fears of conflict in Europe and beyond.

PRIMARY SOURCE

Out of our first century of national life we evolved the ethical principle that it was not right or just that an honest and industrious man should live and die in misery. He was entitled to some degree of sympathy and security. Our conscience declared against the honest workman's becoming a pauper, but our eyes told us that he very often did.

—from *People at Work,* by Frances Perkins, 1934

Some leaders with fascist tendencies also gained popularity in the United States. **Huey P. Long**, the fiery governor of Louisiana, was a champion of the poor but acted ruthlessly in gaining power in his state. He abolished local government and took control of job appointments in education, police, and fire departments throughout the state. He also controlled the state militia, the judiciary, and the election system. In 1936, shortly after he announced that he would run for the presidency, he was assassinated in Baton Rouge, Louisiana.

Father Charles E. Coughlin, a Roman Catholic priest and an influential radio host from Michigan, also gained a loyal following by championing the poor. However, he began expressing anti-democratic and anti-Semitic views, which resulted in the Catholic Church ordering him to stop broadcasting in 1942. He went on to help form a new political group called the Union Party. Both Long and Coughlin were considered **populists**, or politicians who claim to represent the concerns of ordinary people.

Midway into the construction of the Golden Gate Bridge in California, Frances Perkins (center) came to observe the work in March 1935.

11.6.2 Understand the explanations of the principal causes of the Great Depression and the steps taken by the Federal Reserve, Congress, and Presidents Herbert Hoover and Franklin Delano Roosevelt to combat the economic crisis.

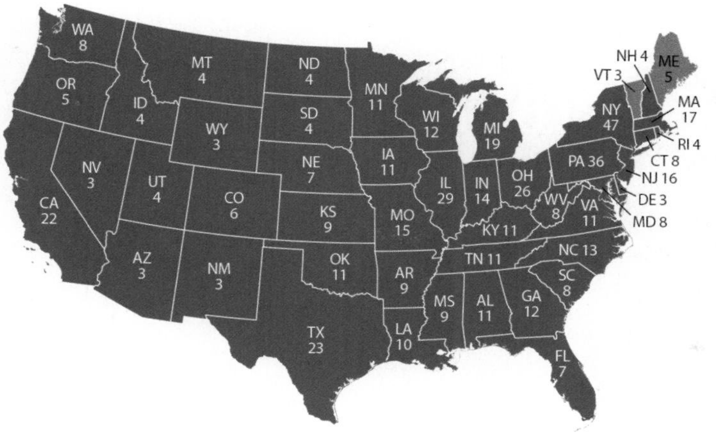

The 1936 Election

Franklin D. Roosevelt, Democrat

Electoral Vote: 523 votes, 98.5%

Popular Vote: 27,750,866 votes, 60.8%

Alfred M. Landon, Republican

Electoral Vote: 8 votes, 1.5%

Popular Vote: 16,679,683 votes, 36.5%

Union and Other Parties

Popular Vote: 1,216,442 votes, 2.7%

THE 1936 ELECTION

As the 1936 election approached, FDR had reason to be concerned about his political future. Although personal income and industrial production had risen dramatically, the country's unemployment rate was still very high. Some of his fellow Democrats argued that he needed to do more to ease Americans' suffering. In addition, more than 80 percent of the nation's newspapers and most of the business community remained loyal to the Republican Party, which meant that Roosevelt's major presidential opponent could count on strong editorial and financial support.

A **coalition**, or alliance, of Republican and Democratic opponents of the New Deal had formed an organization in 1934 called the **American Liberty League**. Members of the League claimed that some New Deal programs were unconstitutional because they gave increased power to the president to regulate the economy rather than to the judicial and legislative branches. League members were intent on defeating Roosevelt in the 1936 election.

But the Democrats had hope. Roosevelt's policies appealed to workers, farmers, African Americans, southern whites, and educated northerners. Many members of such religious groups as Catholics and Jews also backed the New Deal. This coalition had a good chance of keeping FDR in the White House.

The Republicans chose Kansas governor Alfred M. Landon to head their ticket, and Frank Knox, a Chicago publisher, as the vice presidential nominee. Landon, a political moderate, promised "fewer radio talks, fewer experiments, and a lot more common sense." However, Landon lacked the compassion and confidence that made Roosevelt so popular with many Americans.

Once again, Roosevelt faced presidential challenges from the Communist and Socialist parties. Both ran spirited campaigns in 1936, demanding more federal aid for the poor. Roosevelt was also opposed by the newly formed Union Party, which nominated William "Liberty Bill" Lemke, an obscure North Dakota congressman, as its presidential candidate.

Roosevelt's strategy in the 1936 election was to present himself as a champion of the common people, as opposed to the wealthy. In his final campaign speech in New York, he declared that the wealthy had "met their match" in the Roosevelt administration. If the rich and powerful hated him for that, he thundered, "I welcome their hatred."

On November 3, 1936, FDR crushed his opponents in the most one-sided election in over a century. The final totals showed Roosevelt with 27,750,866 popular votes, Landon with 16,679,683, and Lemke with about 890,000. The Socialist and Communist parties together won less than 270,000 votes. Roosevelt won every state except Maine and Vermont, securing 98.5 percent of the electoral vote. The Democratic Party added 9 seats each to its already huge majorities in the two houses of Congress.

HISTORICAL THINKING

1. **READING CHECK** In what ways did the Second New Deal improve people's lives?
2. **DRAW CONCLUSIONS** Why might people be drawn to fascist or ruthless leaders who promote extreme nationalism during difficult economic times?
3. **MAKE GENERALIZATIONS** What segments of American society did the Second New Deal target?
4. **COMPARE AND CONTRAST** How were Roosevelt's New Deal policies criticized by both Democrats and and Republicans?

11.8.5 Describe the increased powers of the presidency in response to the Great Depression, World War II, and the Cold War.

Milwaukee Public Museum
Milwaukee, Wisconsin

The Milwaukee Public Museum is the largest natural and human history museum in the state of Wisconsin, and one of the largest in the Midwest. Chartered in 1882, its collection contains more than 4 million objects, and its exhibits feature world cultures, life-size dioramas, walk-through villages, dinosaurs, a rain forest, and a live butterfly garden.

The museum's WPA Milwaukee Handicraft Project collection (MHP) contains artifacts and photographs that tell the story of one of the first national welfare programs. During the Great Depression, it employed more than 5,000 women and minorities in Milwaukee and broke gender and color barriers, while bringing fame to the city.

Integrated Workforce

Workers on the Milwaukee Handicraft Project were paid by the federal government to create handmade goods such as toys, dolls, furniture, coverlets, and books. The products were then sold to public institutions such as schools, for the cost of the materials alone. As shown in the photo above, the MHP was racially integrated while most WPA projects were segregated. The MHP also hired women, though most WPA projects were structured to provide work for the male head of a household.

This giraffe pull-toy, which was cut from wood and painted by project workers, was sold to schools.

Original Designs

Although its focus was on providing work, the MHP produced beautiful, original, high-quality products that were sold throughout the United States. MHP products were designed by trained art educators and artists who taught basic crafting skills to the workers. The workers in the photograph above are printing designs onto fabric using linoleum blocks. This fabric would then be made into draperies or sold by the yard.

This coverlet is made of appliquéd cotton, with a design called "Horse." It was sold to nursery schools for children's napping cots.

"The Milwaukee Public Museum's unique WPA collection **reflects the artistic focus** the WPA had in Milwaukee."

—Ellen Censky
Senior Vice President

This upholstered chair represents the variety of skills taught on the MHP: woodworking for the frame, weaving for the fabric, and upholstery for the chair seat and back.

Skills Training

Many of the female workers who came to the MHP had never worked outside of their homes. The impact of the Great Depression caused many women to seek jobs for the first time to help support their families. The MHP trained the women to produce handicrafts that gave them skills they could apply to work outside of the WPA, sewing as seamstresses, repairing books, and working in factories.

11.6.4 Analyze the effects of and the controversies arising from New Deal economic policies and the expanded role of the federal government in society and the economy since the 1930s (e.g., Works Progress Administration, Social Security, National Labor Relations Board, farm programs, regional development policies, and energy development projects such as the Tennessee Valley Authority, California Central Valley Project, and Bonneville Dam).

2.3 **MAIN IDEA** With the backing of progressives and New Deal legislation, American workers won the right to organize and improve their salaries and working conditions.

SUPPORTING LABOR

When you are used to having no car at all, you might be thrilled to finally own an old vehicle that still runs. But once you have that, you might wish for a nicer car. As Americans' lives got better under the New Deal, their acceptance of hardship and struggle gave way to a desire for more improvements in their lives.

GAINS BY LABOR

Despite his progressive leanings, Franklin Roosevelt never fully supported organized labor. He felt uneasy when the head of the United Mine Workers, **John L. Lewis**, tripled his labor union's membership by announcing to workers, "The president wants you to join a union!" When other major labor leaders began using the same tactic to increase membership numbers, Roosevelt became irritated.

Unions needed large memberships to maintain the authority to stand up to corporate managers. As you have read, one effective labor tactic was to organize strikes to persuade management to listen to workers' demands. The more people involved in a strike, the greater the impact.

Unions used strikes to fight for the right of **collective bargaining**, or negotiation between

New laws passed during FDR's first term guaranteed workers the right to organize and strike. The practice continues today. In this photo from April 2016, members of a janitors' union march peacefully in downtown Los Angeles to publicize their campaign for higher pay and benefits.

11.6.5 Trace the advances and retreats of organized labor, from the creation of the American Federation of Labor and the Congress of Industrial Organizations to current issues of a postindustrial, multinational economy, including the United Farm Workers in California.

an employer and union leaders on behalf of all union members. Union members had become aware that pay rates and benefits were not uniform for workers doing the same job. Because workers negotiated their wages and benefits individually and secretly with factory managers, two workers hired for the same position could be offered different hourly wages. Before collective bargaining, employees might complain to management, but their complaints had little effect. Union organizers used collective bargaining to negotiate employment contracts that guaranteed standard pay ranges and equal benefits for all workers.

Unfortunately, labor disputes resulted in violence on numerous occasions as scabs—workers brought in to replace those on strike—and police fought with striking workers. In 1933, for example, 60 workers at the Spang-Chalfant Seamless Tube Company, which produced steel tubing and was located near Pittsburgh, went out on strike after management increased their work hours. As the strikers were protesting on a **picket line**, 200 armed police officers arrived. A picket line is a group of strikers who form a barrier to keep scabs, or strikebreakers, from entering a building to work in their place. When the strikers refused to leave the picket line, the police began firing tear gas. When that tactic failed, the police fired bullets, killing 1 bystander and injuring 15 strikers and onlookers. The strike finally ended after three weeks when the workers agreed that the company could make changes to the work schedule. In return, the company agreed to consult union leaders about shift changes and increases or decreases in work hours.

In response to this kind of violence, Senator Robert Wagner of New York wrote a bill to protect the rights of striking workers. His legislation, later called the **Wagner Act**, passed in 1935. A portion of the act—the **National Labor Relations Act**—required employers to allow unions to collectively bargain for wages and benefits. It also prohibited employers from engaging in a wide range of "unfair labor practices," such as discriminating against a worker because of union membership and punishing workers for filing complaints against an employer. In addition, it created the **National Labor Relations Board** to supervise union elections and assign union representatives to advocate for workers. This board still meets today.

The Wagner Act made forming unions easier, but its enforcement revealed deep racial divisions when workers in non-unionized factories attempted to organize. At the 1935 convention of the American Federation of Labor (AFL), an organization of labor unions, John Lewis pleaded with fellow union leaders to begin serious membership drives in the steel mills, automobile plants, and rubber factories. These industries employed many African Americans and immigrants from eastern and southern Europe. But most AFL leaders, who represented such skilled trade workers as masons and carpenters, had little interest in organizing such unions.

Determined, Lewis joined with like-minded labor leaders who agreed with him to form the **Congress of Industrial Organizations (CIO)**. The goal of the CIO was to create powerful unions in mass-production industries, such as auto manufacturing and steel.

CONFLICT OVER THE SUPREME COURT

In his second inaugural address, which he delivered at the Capitol on January 20, 1937, Roosevelt emphasized the New Deal's unfinished business. "I see one-third of a nation ill-housed, ill-clad, ill-nourished," he declared. His landslide election had provided him with a strong popular **mandate**, or authority to act. In addition, he enjoyed huge Democratic majorities in the House and Senate, enabling him to continue his political agenda.

PRIMARY SOURCE

In 1937, President Franklin Roosevelt proposed changes to the Supreme Court, which had opposed some of his New Deal legislation. In a fireside chat, he explained to the American people his view of the conflict.

Last Thursday I described the American form of Government as a three-horse team provided by the Constitution to the American people so that their field might be plowed. The three horses are, of course, the three branches of government—the Congress, the Executive and the Courts. Two of the horses are pulling in unison today; the third is not. Those who have intimated that the President of the United States is trying to drive that team, overlook the simple fact that the President, as Chief Executive, is himself one of the three horses.

It is the American people themselves who are in the driver's seat.

It is the American people themselves who want the furrow plowed.

It is the American people themselves who expect the third horse to pull in unison with the other two.

—from a fireside chat given by President Franklin Roosevelt, March 9, 1937

The only branch of government not on FDR's side was the judicial branch—specifically, the Supreme Court.

The Supreme Court was dominated by elderly, conservative justices who strongly opposed the New Deal legislation. Roosevelt knew that in the coming months the justices would be reviewing two of the New Deal's most important accomplishments—the National Labor Relations Act and the Social Security Act. He took action to save his programs.

In February 1937, without consulting Congress, Roosevelt ordered a complete reorganization of the federal court system. Under his plan, the Supreme Court would gain six new members, raising the total number of justices to fifteen. Roosevelt would be able to fill these new positions with judges who shared his political views. This **court-packing plan** was legal; the Constitution set no limits on the size of the Supreme Court.

Roosevelt had miscalculated the power of his mandate, however. Some politicians worried that expanding the judicial branch would throw off the balance among the three branches of government. As opposition to the plan grew stronger, aides urged Roosevelt to withdraw it. The Senate later defeated it.

As it turned out, the president did not need to pack the court. In the spring of 1937, the Supreme Court changed course. By a vote of 5 to 4, the court upheld both the National Labor Relations Act and the Social Security Act. Then, one by one, the old conservative justices decided to retire, making FDR's plan unnecessary. Roosevelt—the only president in American history to make no Supreme Court appointments during his first four-year term—filled five vacancies over the next three years. The liberal justices he chose—especially Hugo Black, Felix Frankfurter, and William O. Douglas—would steer the court for decades to come.

Autoworkers at a General Motors plant in Flint, Michigan, staged a strike by sitting in the seats made to be installed in cars, as shown in this 1936 photograph.

11.6.2 Understand the explanations of the principal causes of the Great Depression and the steps taken by the Federal Reserve, Congress, and Presidents Herbert Hoover and Franklin Delano Roosevelt to combat the economic crisis.

Protected by state-of-the-art safety gear in 2016, a welder performs detailed work on aluminum for a lighting manufacturer. Welding has always been a hazardous occupation. Welders first began to wear modern safety gear in the 1930s, when factories invested in goggles and face shields at the urging of workers and unions.

CONFLICT OVER UNIONS

Away from Washington, new battles raged in the automobile plants of Michigan, the textile mills of North Carolina, and the coal mines of Kentucky. Workers in such major industries demanded union recognition under the banner of the CIO, but management ignored their demand.

On November 12, 1936, a small group of autoworkers at a General Motors (GM) plant in Flint, Michigan, staged a **sit-down strike**. Instead of leaving their jobs, the workers stayed in the plant, refusing to work. They thus prevented management from bringing in scabs to continue production and shut down the plant. Unlike the Spang-Chalfant strike, the Flint strike was effective and mostly peaceful.

In addition to seeking recognition for the CIO, the sit-down strikers wanted higher wages and safer working conditions. At the time, the average autoworker earned $900 a year, far below the $1,600 the government deemed necessary to support a family of four. In addition, hundreds of workers had died in auto plants in Michigan because of dangerous working conditions. Soon, the strike spread as workers at other General Motors plants began sitting down at their jobs. Journalists called this first major labor dispute between autoworkers and management "the strike heard 'round the world."

The 44-day Flint sit-down strike ended when GM recognized the CIO's United Automobile Workers (UAW) union as the bargaining agent for its employees and raised wages. The success of the strike motivated other autoworkers to protest as well. Within a few weeks after the strike, 87 more sit-down strikes occurred in the Detroit area alone. Chrysler came to terms with strikers a few months later. Other industry leaders followed suit after the UAW victory, including Firestone, General Electric, and RCA.

Some industry leaders were not so quick to give in to unions, however. Henry Ford hired an army of thugs to rough up union organizers and disrupt strikers on picket lines. The worst violence, however, occurred outside Republic Steel's South Chicago mill on Memorial Day 1937, when heavily armed police battled rock-throwing strikers on a picket line. Casualties included 10 workers killed by gunfire, and dozens more injured. Under pressure from the National Labor Relations Board, Ford and Republic Steel gradually accepted unions as a legitimate force in American manufacturing. With a membership approaching 3 million, the CIO had come a long way since its break with the conservative, trades-oriented American Federation of Labor a few years before.

The Supreme Court battle and the sit-down strikes slowed the political momentum that followed FDR's re-election landslide in 1936. In addition, a serious recession in 1937 eroded public confidence in the New Deal. Other problems loomed in Europe, where fascism continued to gain strength. For President Roosevelt, the road ahead appeared even steeper and rockier than before.

HISTORICAL THINKING

1. **READING CHECK** What gains did American labor make during the 1930s?
2. **EVALUATE** Why were unions important to American workers in the 1930s?
3. **FORM AND SUPPORT OPINIONS** Was the Wagner Act effective? Support your opinion with evidence from the text.
4. **DETERMINE CHRONOLOGY** What sequence of events made Roosevelt's court-packing plan unnecessary?

11.6.4 Analyze the effects of and the controversies arising from New Deal economic policies and the expanded role of the federal government in society and the economy since the 1930s (e.g., Works Progress Administration, Social Security, National Labor Relations Board, farm programs, regional development policies, and energy development projects such as the Tennessee Valley Authority, California Central Valley Project, and Bonneville Dam); HI 3 Students interpret past events and issues within the context in which an event unfolded rather than solely in terms of present-day norms and values.

2.4 THROUGH THE LENS AMERICAN PLACES

Golden Gate Bridge San Francisco, California

The iconic Golden Gate Bridge extends across the Golden Gate Strait and connects the city of San Francisco to Marin County, California. Opened in 1937, this steel suspension bridge is the product of thousands of hours of backbreaking, dangerous labor by hundreds of American workers. It was built during the Great Depression, a time when one out of four Americans were unemployed. Those who worked on it were grateful for their jobs. Bridge workers were hired through local unions, such as the Ironworkers Local Union 377, and included people from a wide range of backgrounds: farmers, lumberjacks, cowboys, and taxicab drivers. It took nerves of steel to work on the Golden Gate Bridge. Workers faced many physical challenges, including water, wind, and blinding fog. But creating this gateway to the "Golden City" during one of the lowest points in American economic history gave union workers financial stability and pride. "It was never just a job to me. I loved the work," said bridge worker Harold McClain.

CRITICAL VIEWING Measuring 1.7 miles long, the Golden Gate Bridge weighs nearly 900,000 tons. Two towers support two enormous carbon-steel cables, which are secured at each end by giant anchorages. Based on what you notice in the photograph, what challenges did workers probably face while building the bridge?

3.1 **MAIN IDEA** Eleanor Roosevelt led the way in gaining opportunities and benefits for women under the New Deal.

WOMEN DURING THE NEW DEAL

You probably take for granted that women hold important jobs and contribute to their families' financial security. But many jobs might still be closed to women if not for the efforts of pioneers like Eleanor Roosevelt.

OPPORTUNITIES FOR WOMEN

When the stock market crashed in 1929, men were not the only ones to lose their jobs. By 1933, about 2 million women were unemployed as well. In some families, the women were the main **breadwinners**, or contributors to a family's income. These women—in fact, all American women—had a powerful ally in Eleanor Roosevelt. The first lady was among the president's chief advisors, and her progressive beliefs strongly influenced him. An advocate for child welfare and equal rights for women and minorities, she traveled the country and reported to FDR on the social conditions she observed.

Eleanor worked to persuade those in charge of implementing the New Deal to include positions for women in their relief programs. She quoted girls and women who had written her letters telling how the Great Depression had affected them and their families. She pointed out that many women were earning their college degrees and entering the workforce with fresh ideas that the nation urgently needed. Influential leaders like Harry Hopkins listened.

Hopkins headed one of the first New Deal agencies designed to put people back to work, the Federal Emergency Relief Administration (FERA). He established a division in FERA called the Civil Works Administration (CWA), which was committed to finding jobs for women. Hopkins appointed his assistant and former Mississippi legislator, **Ellen Woodward**, to lead the CWA. Woodward required that each state hire a woman to direct the program.

As first lady of New York State, Eleanor Roosevelt took time from her political activities to serve as a volunteer. In this photo, she serves soup to unemployed women in New York in 1932.

11.6.2 Understand the explanations of the principal causes of the Great Depression and the steps taken by the Federal Reserve, Congress, and Presidents Herbert Hoover and Franklin Delano Roosevelt to combat the economic crisis.

PRIMARY SOURCES

Eleanor Roosevelt received hundreds of letters from Americans asking for help during the Great Depression. After leaving the White House in 1945, she continued to fight for social change and to champion human rights.

I hope to complete my education, but I will have to quit school I guess if there is no clothes can be bought. Mrs. Roosevelt, don't think I am just begging, but that is all you can call it I guess. There is no harm in asking I guess [either]. Do you have any old clothes you have throwed back. The clothes may be too large but I can cut them down so I can wear them. Not only clothes but old shoes, hats, hose, and under wear would be appreciated so much.

—from a letter written to Eleanor Roosevelt by a 15-year-old girl from Alabama, 1936

Where, after all, do universal human rights begin? In small places close to home—so close and so small that they cannot be seen on any map of the world. Such are the places where every man, woman, and child seeks equal justice, equal opportunity, equal dignity without discrimination. Unless these rights have meaning there, they have little meaning anywhere.

—from a speech given to the United Nations by Eleanor Roosevelt, March 27, 1958

Women were also hired to renovate buildings, conduct public surveys, help develop museums, and carry out a variety of other projects. Job opportunities were far from equal, however. Women held only 7 percent of the jobs created by the CWA, and they were paid less than their male counterparts. The situation improved when FDR established the Works Progress Administration in 1935, replacing FERA. By 1938, more than 13 percent of the people working in the agency were women.

WOMEN LEAD THE WAY

Eleanor Roosevelt and Ellen Woodward were not the only influential women in the Roosevelt administration. Others included Frances Perkins, Josephine Roche, and Hilda Smith.

Frances Perkins, a labor rights activist from New York, was appointed secretary of Labor by FDR. She was the first woman in American history to hold a cabinet-level post. As secretary, she drew on her experiences inspecting working conditions in textile mills and advocating for working-class immigrants and African Americans. She outlined her goals for the president, including a 40-hour workweek, unemployment insurance, a minimum wage, and an end to child labor. FDR incorporated so many of Perkins's ideas that she was later called "the architect of the New Deal." As a member of the Special Board for Public Works, Perkins ensured that government funds were spent on roads, schools, and post offices. As chair of the Committee on Economic Security, she helped develop the Social Security Act, which provided aid for the elderly and workers who had been laid off and grants to states for maternal and child healthcare.

Roosevelt appointed **Josephine Roche**, Colorado's first policewoman and heir to a fuel company, as the assistant secretary of the Treasury in 1934. She had previously advocated for fair wages and health benefits for Colorado mine workers and had used her own money to establish unions in her family's mines.

Before joining the Roosevelt administration as the director of Workers' Education in FERA, **Hilda Smith** was a dean at Bryn Mawr College in Pennsylvania and had been active in social work and women's suffrage. As director, Smith ran FERA and WPA camps and schools for unemployed women. The camps provided food and clothing, and the schools taught such classes as literacy and typing. Unlike the men's camps, however, the women's camps failed to provide work. The women's camps were closed down after three years when New Deal opponents began complaining about the cost. "As so often the case," Smith wrote, "the boys get the breaks, the girls are neglected."

HISTORICAL THINKING

1. **READING CHECK** How did the New Deal affect the role of women in society?
2. **IDENTIFY MAIN IDEAS AND DETAILS** Why was Frances Perkins called the "architect of the New Deal"?
3. **DESCRIBE** How did Eleanor Roosevelt influence the appointment of women to important positions in New Deal agencies?
4. **ANALYZE CAUSE AND EFFECT** Why did the camps for unemployed women fail?

11.11.3 Describe the changing roles of women in society as reflected in the entry of more women into the labor force and the changing family structure.

Mixed Progress on Civil Rights

Perhaps the greatest challenge of American democracy has been making equal rights for all a reality. Every generation has faced this challenge.

AFRICAN AMERICANS AND THE NEW DEAL

President Roosevelt crafted his New Deal policies to apply to all Americans, no matter their ethnicity. African Americans appreciated this effort, and many of them supported him at the ballot box. As you have read, the Great Migration brought many African Americans to northern cities, where they often formed a **voting bloc**, or a large group of citizens who share a common concern and tend to vote the same in elections.

Historically, most African Americans had supported the Republican Party, an allegiance that dated back to Abraham Lincoln and the Civil War. With the New Deal, however, many African Americans shifted to the Democratic Party. This massive switch occurred because the Roosevelt administration provided jobs and relief benefits to all Americans, regardless of race.

Federal assistance was especially welcome in African-American communities, where the human toll of the Great Depression was especially evident. By 1933, unemployment among African Americans had reached 50 percent. Fortunately, the two New Deal administrators most responsible for creating jobs were sympathetic to minority needs. At the

AMERICAN PLACES

Lincoln Memorial, Washington, D.C.

On a chilly Easter Sunday in 1939, world-renowned opera singer Marian Anderson performed at the Lincoln Memorial in Washington, D.C., before a crowd of about 75,000 people. Previously, the Daughters of the American Revolution had refused to allow Anderson to perform at Constitution Hall because of her skin color. Anderson began her performance with a moving rendition of "My Country 'Tis of Thee."

11.6.3 Discuss the human toll of the Depression, natural disasters, and unwise agricultural practices and their effects on the depopulation of rural regions and on political movements of the left and right, with particular attention to the Dust Bowl refugees and their social and economic impacts in California.

Public Works Administration (PWA), Harold Ickes insisted that African Americans receive equal pay on all construction projects. Although local officials often ignored this rule, the PWA provided thousands of jobs for African Americans and built African-American schools and hospitals throughout the segregated South. At the Works Progress Administration, African Americans received a share of the work in northern cities. Many African Americans welcomed an administration that showed some interest in their well-being. They particularly admired the efforts of First Lady Eleanor Roosevelt, who took strong stands in favor of equal rights for minorities and women.

Eleanor Roosevelt's interest in civil rights had been fueled in large measure by her friendship with prominent African Americans, including **Mary McLeod Bethune,** founder of Bethune-Cookman College in Florida. In 1936, Eleanor Roosevelt recommended Bethune to head the National Youth Administration's Office of Negro Affairs. As the New Deal's highest-ranking African-American appointee, Bethune presided over the administration's "black cabinet," an informal group of African-American leaders who advised the White House on minority issues. Bethune went on to play an important role many years later as one of the original U.S. representatives to the United Nations and its first black female delegate.

In 1939, Eleanor Roosevelt further demonstrated her commitment to African-American rights when she resigned from a historically all-white organization called the Daughters of the American Revolution. The group had refused to allow **Marian Anderson**, a gifted African-American opera singer, to perform at Washington's Constitution Hall. A few months later, Harold Ickes arranged for Anderson to sing at the Lincoln Memorial on Easter Sunday. An integrated audience of about 75,000 gathered to hear her stirring performance.

Yet the progressive work of Eleanor Roosevelt and others could not make up for larger New Deal failures in the field of civil rights. Throughout his presidency, for example, Franklin Roosevelt made no effort to dismantle segregation or to enable African Americans to vote. He remained on the sidelines as federal anti-lynching bills were narrowly defeated in Congress. Roosevelt argued that he could not support civil rights legislation without alienating southern Democrats, who controlled the most important committees in Congress. "They will block every bill I [need] to keep America from collapsing," Roosevelt said. "I just can't take that risk." The president's position did not prevent African Americans from supporting him in 1936, however. Roosevelt received 76 percent of their votes—the same percentage that Herbert Hoover, the Republican candidate, had won four years before.

THE SCOTTSBORO BOYS

In March 1931, nine young African-American men, ages 12 to 20, hopped aboard a freight train in northern Alabama to ride the rails as "hoboes," or homeless wanderers in search of work. A fight broke out between them and two white men. In the fray that followed, two white women, also riding the same train, accused the young black men of rape. Police arrested the nine African-American men and locked them up in the Scottsboro, Alabama, jail. From that point on, the nine were known as the Scottsboro Boys.

Over the course of the next seven years, the Scottsboro Boys would attend trials and retrials, which were marred by lies, bribes, and racial bias on the part of the accusers, the prosecuting attorney, and the judges. The victims gave vastly different accounts of the crime, and one even took back her accusation, admitting it was a lie. Even so, a series of all-white juries convicted and sentenced the young men to death several times. Each time, the defense appealed. The case went all the way to the U.S. Supreme Court, finally ending with five convictions and four dismissals. By 1950, all of the convicted Scottsboro Boys had been either pardoned or paroled.

MEXICAN AMERICANS AND THE NEW DEAL

As African Americans struggled with racism and discrimination, both Mexican immigrants and American citizens of Mexican descent, or Mexican Americans, faced their own challenges during the Depression.

CST 3 Students use a variety of maps and documents to interpret human movement, including major patterns of domestic and international migration, changing environmental preferences and settlement patterns, the frictions that develop between population groups, and the diffusion of ideas, technological innovations, and goods.

Despite being recruited to work on American farms just 10 years before, Mexican immigrants met with deep resentment from white Americans who felt jobs were being taken away from them. In response to this resentment, in 1929, the federal government began the Mexican Repatriation Program, which, as you've read, deported hundreds of thousands of people of Mexican descent. In this context, repatriation is the act of sending an immigrant back to his or her home country to live. Some people left the United States voluntarily, accepting the government's free train fares. Others were coerced or tricked into leaving.

Many Mexican Americans were also deported to Mexico simply because authorities did not trust their claims of nationality or did not care. Of those who remained in the United States, many experienced unemployment because farm owners were hiring fewer migrant workers and giving jobs to white workers first. Farmers in various ethnic groups had begun working as migrant farm laborers after losing their farmland in bank foreclosures during the Great Depression. Many Mexican American farmers were among those who had lost their land and become migrant laborers.

Fortunately, the New Deal provided some relief. The Farm Security Administration (FSA), a New Deal agency, established camps to provide food and shelter for migrant workers and their families. Several camps were specifically for Mexican American workers. Farmworkers who lived in the camps were able to discuss labor issues among themselves. These discussions led to the formation of Mexican-American farm labor unions, which fought for higher wages and better working conditions.

In 2005, the California State Legislature passed the "Apology Act," a long-overdue response to the deportations that took place during and after the New Deal. California senator Joe Dunn wrote the act on behalf of his constituency to acknowledge the mistreatment Americans had suffered since the 1930s simply for being of Mexican descent.

However, Mexican Americans were not the only target of federal repatriation acts. In 1935, Congress passed a repatriation act targeting Filipinos. The act encouraged both Filipino immigrants and Americans of Filipino descent to return voluntarily to the Philippines, but the Filipino American community

CRITICAL VIEWING In 1930, a group of Filipino American farmworkers posed with tomatoes they harvested on California's Central Coast. The migrant workers followed the crops from the Mexican border to Alaska. Although migrant work was rough and the workers were often mistreated, why do you think these men mostly look happy in the photograph?

11.6.4 Analyze the effects of and the controversies arising from New Deal economic policies and the expanded role of the federal government in society and the economy since the 1930s (e.g., Works Progress Administration, Social Security, National Labor Relations Board, farm programs, regional development policies, and energy development projects such as the Tennessee Valley Authority, California Central Valley Project, and Bonneville Dam).

ENCOURAGING AN APPRECIATION OF NATIVE AMERICAN ART

As Commissioner of Indian Affairs from 1933 to 1945, John Collier worked to foster the economic independence of Native Americans, partly by promoting the work of Native American artists and craftspeople. This poster is one of a series designed by Native American artists to advertise a special exhibition held at the Museum of Modern Art in New York City from January to April of 1936. The goal of the exhibition was to expose white Americans to Native American cultures and encourage them to purchase works of art to decorate their homes.

resisted. One Filipino told an interviewer, "I would rather go hungry and die here than go home with an empty hand." At the end of the first year, only about 150 people had chosen to return to the islands, and by 1941 just 2,064 Filipinos had left the United States under the act.

NATIVE AMERICANS AND THE NEW DEAL

The New Deal brought major changes in federal policy toward Native Americans. As you have read, in 1871 the federal government had passed a law stripping Native Americans of their national sovereignty and making them wards of the state. The government had forced Native American children to attend "Indian schools," where all efforts focused on eliminating their languages and cultures. The goal was to assimilate Native Americans into mainstream American culture. The Dawes Act of 1887 attempted to turn Native Americans into farmers by dividing their reservation lands into plots intended for individual farms. However, most of the land was unsuitable for farming, and outsiders quickly bought up the best land.

When Roosevelt took office, he chose **John Collier**, a sociologist and author, as Commissioner of Indian Affairs. Collier was outraged by the effects of the Indian schools and the Dawes Act, and he set about making changes. He made sure that employers working on projects authorized by the CCC, NYA, WPA, and PWA hired Native American workers. He also encouraged Congress to authorize the **Indian Emergency Conservation Program (IECP)**. The IECP was similar to the CCC, but it employed Native Americans to work on physical improvements to reservations. Through the IECP, the government employed more than 85,000 Native Americans.

Collier worked to repeal the Dawes Act through Congressional passage of the 1934 **Indian Reorganization Act (IRA)**. The IRA provided tribes with federal funds to buy back some reservation lands. It also repealed laws that prohibited Native Americans from speaking their languages and practicing their customs. In addition, it provided for federal government recognition of tribal constitutions. Collier instituted a major shift in federal policy away from assimilation and toward autonomy.

HISTORICAL THINKING

1. **READING CHECK** How did the New Deal improve the lives of minorities in the United States?
2. **COMPARE AND CONTRAST** How did the Mexican Repatriation Program differ from the government program to repatriate Filipinos?
3. **SYNTHESIZE** What did the Scottsboro Boys case demonstrate about racism and discrimination in the United States at the time?
4. **DETERMINE CHRONOLOGY** Trace government treatment of Native Americans between 1871 and 1934. What changed and when?

11.9.7 Examine relations between the United States and Mexico in the twentieth century, including key economic, political, immigration, and environmental issues.

4.1 **MAIN IDEA** The New Deal helped many people survive the Great Depression, but as the decade and the depression wore on, its effectiveness started to fade.

THE NEW DEAL WINDS DOWN

The New Deal featured many ambitious, expensive programs. It had its successes and its failures, its staunch advocates and its fierce critics. By 1937, President Roosevelt had to make some hard decisions about the New Deal.

THE ECONOMY STUMBLES AGAIN

As 1937 approached, the United States' national income and production rose nearly to the levels of 1929, before the stock market crash. However, the stock market itself had yet to reach its peak levels of 1929, even though stocks had enjoyed a minor boom over the preceding five years.

Roosevelt knew that government spending on programs such as the WPA had helped combat the economic crisis and fueled this recovery, and he knew that following John Maynard Keynes's economic guidance had been effective. Still, he was uncomfortable with the huge amount of government spending his programs had required. He worried that the ever-increasing national debt would cause inflation, or rising prices for goods and services, and that federal welfare programs would diminish the recipients' initiative and self-respect. Indeed, Roosevelt had never intended for these programs to continue for the long term.

In 1937, the new Social Security payroll tax took effect, cutting into workers' take-home pay and removing billions of dollars of purchasing power from the economy. That same year, Roosevelt slashed funding for both the PWA and WPA, resulting in a loss of almost 2 million jobs. The new tax, combined with the program cuts, caused a recession. Unemployment began to rise, production plummeted, and people with no other choice began returning to breadlines and soup kitchens. The stock market fell yet again. Something had to be done, and quickly.

PRIMARY SOURCES

Elected to four terms, Franklin Roosevelt is still one of the most popular presidents in American history. But many people disagreed with his policies. For example, former president Herbert Hoover did not believe the New Deal had much chance for success.

The country is going sour on the New Deal, despite the heroic efforts of the Press. Unless there is a halt, the real question will be that, having cast off all moorings, will we swing to the "right" or to the "left." I fear first the "left," and then when the great middle class (80% of America) realizes its ruin, it will drive into some American interpretation of Hitler or Mussolini.

—from a letter written by Herbert Hoover, 1933

Four years after Hoover made his prediction, FDR was still promoting New Deal policies. In a speech to Congress, he introduced the Fair Labor Standards Act.

Our Nation so richly endowed with natural resources and with a capable and industrious population should be able to devise ways and means of insuring to all our able-bodied working men and women a fair day's pay for a fair day's work. All but the hopelessly reactionary will agree that to conserve our primary resources of man power, government must have some control over maximum hours, minimum wages, the evil of child labor and the exploitation of unorganized labor.

—from President Franklin Roosevelt's message to Congress, May 24, 1937

11.6.4 Analyze the effects of and the controversies arising from New Deal economic policies and the expanded role of the federal government in society and the economy since the 1930s (e.g., Works Progress Administration, Social Security, National Labor Relations Board, farm programs, regional development policies, and energy development projects such as the Tennessee Valley Authority, California Central Valley Project, and Bonneville Dam).

As the Fair Labor Standards Act took effect, it became the norm for teenagers to be in high school rather than in the workforce. In a 1941 photograph, energetic high school cheerleaders in Springfield, Pennsylvania, practice their routines.

TRIMMING THE NEW DEAL

Starting in October of 1937, Roosevelt and Congress took steps to approve $5 billion in federal funds for relief and public works programs. The economy in crisis responded positively, but Roosevelt's public image suffered because people felt he relied on government spending to solve economic problems.

By 1938, the New Deal had clearly lost momentum. Harry Hopkins, one of the architects of the New Deal, lamented that the public was "bored with the poor, the unemployed, the insecure." Congressional Republicans and conservative Democrats—in other words, Roosevelt's political opponents—gained control of the legislature in that year's midterm elections. Without a majority in Congress supporting him, Roosevelt could not enact any more progressive programs. On top of that, Roosevelt's court-packing scheme had taken a toll on his reputation. Many members of Congress had turned against him.

The passage of the Fair Labor Standards Act was among Roosevelt's few legislative achievements in 1938. The act stipulated a minimum hourly wage and a maximum 40-hour workweek. It immediately raised the wages of almost a million American workers and shortened the work hours of millions as well. The act also finally abolished child labor in most industries. As you have read, prior to the passage of the Fair Labor Standards Act, child labor was a common practice. In 1900, for example, 18 percent of American workers were under age 16. Now American children could concentrate on their education rather than on helping to support their families.

Without the support of Congress, most of the New Deal programs came to an end from a lack of funding in 1939. However, the nation's economic battle was not completely won. More than 8 million Americans were still unemployed. Roosevelt's critics pointed out that the New Deal strategy may have offered a measure of protection for unemployed and vulnerable workers, but it had not restored the nation to the prosperity of the 1920s. As it turned out, it would take another world war—and the full **mobilization**, or enlistment of soldiers, that followed—to bring back prosperity.

HISTORICAL THINKING

1. **READING CHECK** Why were most New Deal programs discontinued?
2. **MAKE CONNECTIONS** What types of economic indicators contributed to a recession in 1937?
3. **DRAW CONCLUSIONS** Why do you think a ban on child labor passed during the time of the New Deal?
4. **SUMMARIZE** What controversies and negative effects was Roosevelt concerned about in terms of the New Deal?

HI 6 Students conduct cost-benefit analyses and apply basic economic indicators to analyze the aggregate economic behavior of the U.S. economy.

4.2 **MAIN IDEA** The New Deal expanded the role and the reach of the federal government in ways that are still evident today.

THE NEW DEAL'S IMPACT

Without realizing it, you've probably encountered the New Deal in your everyday life. If you have a part-time job, you may be paying Social Security tax. If you have a bank account, your money is safe because it's insured by an agency that was part of the New Deal.

AN EXPANDED GOVERNMENT ROLE

When the Great Depression began, some people believed restricting government spending was the best way to make the economy bounce back. But President Roosevelt did just the opposite. As you have read, he took an active role in combatting the economic crisis by enacting the New Deal and following a policy of **deficit spending**, or spending more money than the government receives from taxes.

The New Deal pumped millions of dollars into the economy by creating federal jobs. It regulated banking and investment activities and increased the government's participation in the settlement of labor disputes. The New Deal also set the precedent of providing federal aid to farmers.

As you have read, the Supreme Court nullified some New Deal legislation, claiming programs were unconstitutional because they gave the executive branch of the government too much authority. Because of the new powers assumed by the executive branch, some historians have labeled the New Deal as the beginning of the **Imperial Presidency**, a presidency that exercises more power than the Constitution allows.

Some New Deal programs, such as the National Industrial Recovery Act and the WPA, reflected the principle that government has a responsibility for its citizens' welfare. Such New Deal innovations as unions' right to collective bargaining, a minimum wage, a 40-hour workweek, and Social Security also reflected that principle. Thus, the New Deal contributed to the idea of the modern **welfare state**, a system in which the government provides for the health and well-being of its citizens.

CONSERVATIVE RESPONSES

Conservatives had criticized Roosevelt's New Deal policies from the start. They believed the New Deal expanded the size and power of the federal government too much, while curbing free enterprise. They also argued that the New Deal had not reached its goals. Pointing to continuing unemployment and poverty, they claimed the New Deal had been no kind of deal at all. Some liberals, who felt the New Deal could do more to remedy social and economic problems, joined the conservatives in this criticism.

Among the New Deal's most vocal critics was Ohio senator **Robert A. Taft**, the son of former president William Howard Taft. Although he supported some New Deal programs, such as unemployment insurance, he opposed big government and thought the New Deal exhibited some of its worst aspects, from wasteful spending to excessive interference in business. The New Deal's overregulation and high taxes hurt business, Taft asserted, accusing its supporters of attacking "individual opportunity, initiative, and freedom." He continued to be a thorn in progressives' sides throughout his career.

LASTING PROGRAMS

Today, supporters and critics agree on one aspect of the New Deal: its lasting impact on the United States. Many Americans still depend on government agencies and programs that began with the New Deal. For example, most Americans take advantage of Social Security at some time. Although never intended to provide a full pension, Social Security does grant senior citizens a measure of security and a hedge against poverty. It also aids workers who have become disabled or temporarily unemployed.

11.6.2. Understand the explanations of the principal causes of the Great Depression and the steps taken by the Federal Reserve, Congress, and Presidents Herbert Hoover and Franklin Delano Roosevelt to combat the economic crisis.

AMERICAN PLACES

The Hoover Dam Arizona and Nevada

Designed to control flooding of the Colorado River and to provide water to western states, the Hoover Dam was built during the Great Depression and employed more than 21,000 workers. Its construction was a huge and dangerous undertaking, claiming more than 90 lives.

The **Federal Deposit Insurance Corporation (FDIC)**, which insures the savings accounts of individual bank depositors, was part of the Glass-Steagall Banking Act of 1933. The FDIC continues to protect bank customers, insuring their deposits for up to $250,000 against loss in the event of a bank failure. After decades of urging from the big banks, Congress repealed most of the Glass-Steagall Banking Act in 1999, but it left the FDIC in place.

Another New Deal agency that still exists is the **Securities and Exchange Commission (SEC)**, created in 1934. As you have read, the economic crash in 1929 that caused the Great Depression was driven by the collapse of the stock market. Roosevelt created the SEC to protect investors in the stock market in ways similar to how the FDIC insures bank depositors. The SEC continues to oversee the stock market today, regulating stock-trading procedures and managing the nation's economic growth.

The National Labor Relations Board also continues to meet to this day. The board mediates labor disputes between unions and employers. Under the New Deal, workers gained protection of their right to organize and negotiate collectively with employers.

Thousands of bridges, dams, highways, schools, and other construction projects that remain today are another major legacy of the New Deal. Large public works projects, including the Hoover Dam, the Bonneville Dam, the California Central Valley Project, and the Tennessee Valley Authority, changed the lives of millions of Americans, providing them with flood control, irrigation, and electrical power.

HISTORICAL THINKING

1. **READING CHECK** How did the New Deal expand the role of the federal government in the nation's economy?
2. **DETERMINE CHRONOLOGY** What sequence of events led to the establishment of the Securities and Exchange Commission, and what is its function today?
3. **FORM AND SUPPORT OPINIONS** Do you agree or disagree with conservative critics of the New Deal? Give reasons for your opinion.

11.6.4. Analyze the effects of and the controversies arising from New Deal economic policies and the expanded role of the federal government in society and the economy since the 1930s (e.g., Works Progress Administration, Social Security, National Labor Relations Board, farm programs, regional development policies, and energy development projects such as the Tennessee Valley Authority, California Central Valley Project, and Bonneville Dam).

CHAPTER 11 THE NEW DEAL REVIEW

VOCABULARY

Use each of the following vocabulary words in a sentence that shows an understanding of the term's meaning.

1. lame duck HSS 11.6.2
   Once Roosevelt won the 1932 presidential election, President Hoover was a lame duck.
2. economic planning HSS 11.6.2
3. First Hundred Days HSS 11.6.2
4. New Deal HSS 11.6.2
5. court-packing plan HSS 11.6.4
6. coalition HSS 11.6.4
7. collective bargaining HSS 11.6.5
8. mobilization HSS 11.6.4
9. deficit spending HSS 11.6.2

READING STRATEGY

DETERMINE CHRONOLOGY

Use a time line like the one below to organize the major events of the 1930s. Include dates and notes on the events. Then answer the question.

Time Line

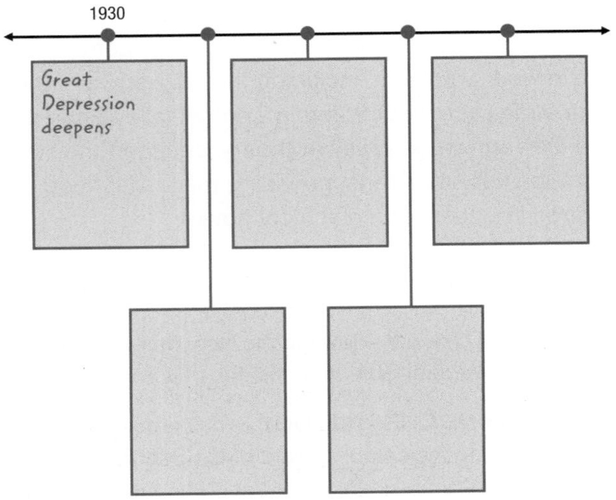

10. How did New Deal policies change the lives of ordinary Americans? HSS 11.6.4

MAIN IDEAS

Answer the following questions. Support your answers with evidence from the chapter.

11. In what way did Franklin Roosevelt's 1932 election indicate a change in direction for the country? **LESSON 1.1** HSS HI 1
12. What did President Roosevelt accomplish in the First Hundred Days? **LESSON 1.2** HSS 11.6.2
13. How did planned scarcity help the nation's economy recover? **LESSON 1.2** HSS 11.6.2
14. What was the purpose of the Social Security Act? **LESSON 2.1** HSS 11.6.4
15. What was the main goal of the Wagner Act? **LESSON 2.3** HSS 11.6.2
16. How did Eleanor Roosevelt serve as the "conscience" of the Roosevelt administration? **LESSON 3.1** HSS 11.6.4
17. Who was Mary McLeod Bethune? **LESSON 3.2** HSS 11.6.4
18. Why did President Roosevelt view his New Deal programs as short-term solutions? **LESSON 4.1** HSS 11.6.2
19. What New Deal programs still exist today? **LESSON 4.2** HSS 11.6

HISTORICAL THINKING

Answer the following questions. Support your answers with evidence from the chapter.

20. **SYNTHESIZE** How did the New Deal attempt to remedy problems created by the Great Depression? HSS 11.6.2
21. **MAKE INFERENCES** Why do you think President Roosevelt gathered the advisers known as the brain trust around him during the beginning of his presidency? HSS 11.6.2

22. **COMPARE AND CONTRAST** How were the AFL and the CIO alike and different? HSS 11.6.5

23. **MAKE PREDICTIONS** What direction might the country have taken during the Depression if FDR had not been elected president? HSS HI 4

24. **DETERMINE CHRONOLOGY** What events led to increased labor union membership and activity in the 1930s? HSS 11.6.5

25. **FORM AND SUPPORT OPINIONS** Was the development of an activist government during the 1930s positive or negative? Support your opinion with evidence from the chapter. HSS 11.6.4

ANALYZE VISUALS

On February 11, 1937, the *Buffalo* [New York] *Evening News* ran a cartoon by Billy Warren portraying FDR walking up some steps with a cane. Study the cartoon and answer the questions that follow.

26. What actions do the steps on the stairs represent? HSS 11.6.2

27. What does the cartoon reveal about the artist's bias toward FDR's actions? HSS HREP 2

ANALYZE SOURCES

In 1998, the National Parks Service interviewed men about their work for the CCC during the Depression. In the transcript that follows, Reed Engle (RE) interviews Arthur Emory (AE), a former CCC worker. Read the excerpt and answer the question.

> RE: What do you think was the best thing about the CCC experience?
>
> AE: The chance for learning. You see most of the people that went in there had dropped out of school. And they were just allowed to roam the street. Which was bad—that'd get you in a heap of trouble. It kind of gave them a chance to get their feet on the ground. So they could learn if they wanted to, which most of them did. It was actually the best thing that ever happened to kids our age at that time. Because you actually earned your way in it. They learned to do so many different things. Like, nobody wants to use a shovel, I don't believe. But they had to learn to use a shovel, and everybody learned something.
>
> —from an interview with Arthur Emory, former CCC employee, 1998

28. How might this employee's experiences and personal biases have shaped his views toward the benefits of working for the CCC? HSS HREP 2

CONNECT TO YOUR LIFE

29. **INFORMATIVE** Research a New Deal artifact in your state, such as a WPA building or work of art. Write an essay describing the artifact and explaining how it reflects the New Deal. HSS 11.6.4

TIPS

- Revisit the Curating History feature in this chapter. Then find more WPA artifacts at the Milwaukee Public Museum website.
- Organize your research in a two-column chart. In the first, write notes about the artifact. In the second, indicate how that information reflects the New Deal.
- Be sure to identify the New Deal agency that produced the artifact, the agency director, and who worked on the artifact, if possible. Cite information from the chapter describing the purpose of the agency.
- Conclude the essay with a paragraph that sums up what the artifact reveals about the New Deal's effects on American life.

NATIONAL GEOGRAPHIC | CONNECTION

The Hidden World of the Great War

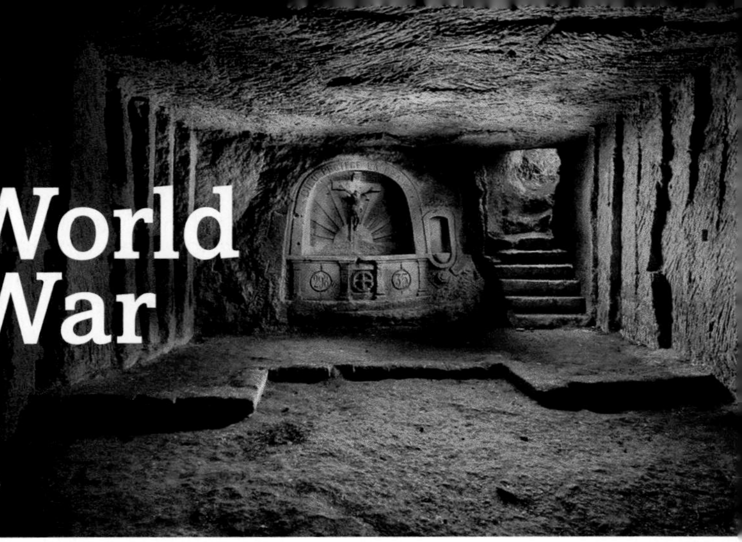

BY EVAN HADINGHAM

Adapted from "The Hidden World of the Great War," by Evan Hadingham, in ***National Geographic***, August 2014

The entrance is a small hole in the earth in northeastern France. I'm following Jeff Gusky, a photographer and physician from Texas who has explored dozens of underground spaces like this one. Here, shortly after the outbreak of the First World War, German military engineers would take turns listening for the slightest sound of enemy tunnelers. Muffled voices or the scraping of shovels meant that a hostile mining team might be only yards away. The danger grew if the digging stopped and you heard the sounds of the enemy laying high explosives at the end of the tunnel. Most nerve-racking of all was the silence that followed. At any moment the charges might detonate and blow you apart or bury you alive.

Nearby, on one of the tunnel walls, our headlamps illuminate graffiti left by the German engineers who manned this listening post. The pencil marks appear as if they were written yesterday. The soft chalk and limestone bedrock of France's Picardy region was ideal for World War I soldiers to record their presence in penciled signatures, sketches and caricatures, carvings, and even intricate relief sculptures.

The conflict began with confidence on all sides that the fighting would be over by Christmas. By the end of 1914, the German advance had stalled, the armies had dug in, and an extensive network of trenches stretched from the North Sea coast to the Swiss border. In the grip of this deadly stalemate, the Germans, French, and British resorted to siege-warfare techniques that had changed little over the centuries. The goal was to dig under key enemy strongpoints and blow them up.

But the underground war was not confined to narrow tunnels. Beneath Picardy's fields and forests are centuries-old abandoned quarries, some of which could shelter thousands of troops. One morning, we explore one such site, led there by the owner of the property. In one cavern, we peer at an array of finely engraved badges and memorials proclaiming the French regiments that had sheltered here. Then we encounter several chapels elaborately carved and painted with religious symbols, army insignia, and the names of notable French victories.

Life in the quarries was vastly preferable to the muddy hell of the trenches above. A journalist visiting one of the caverns in 1915 noted that "a dry shelter, straw, some furniture, a fire, are great luxuries for those returning from the trenches."

The quarries kept an even temperature year-round, but as one French soldier wrote home, "vermin devour us, and it's teeming with lice, fleas, rats and mice." To pass the time, the exhausted men would daydream. Images of women proliferate on the quarry walls, including many sentimental and idealized portraits.

Both sides converted the largest quarries into underground cities, many of them remarkably intact today. Not far from the landowner's property, we find ourselves in an astonishing quarry that stretches for more than seven miles, with twisting passageways and high ceilings. In 1915, the Germans connected this network to their frontline trenches. They installed electric lights and telephones, command posts, a bakery, a butcher's shop, a machine shop, a hospital, and a chapel.

The original diesel generator and barbed wire defenses are still in place. So are dozens of street signs neatly stenciled on every corner. On the cavern walls, German troops have inscribed their names and regiments, religious and military icons, elaborately sculpted portraits and caricatures, and sketches of dogs and other cartoons.

Safe underground from the inhuman chaos of the battlefield above, the men of the First World War left these personal expressions of identity and survival. Gusky's images bring to light the subterranean world soldiers inhabited and endured while sheltering from constant shellfire.

The traces they left behind reveal a forgotten world of World War I. They also connect us to individual soldiers, many of whom would not survive the nightmare of trench warfare.

For more from National Geographic check out "1918 Flu Pandemic" online.

UNIT INQUIRY: Create a Conflict Resolution Strategy

In this unit, you learned about conflicts the United States confronted on global, national, and local levels. From fighting in World War I to addressing political and labor unrest, embracing rights for women, and managing a massive economic downturn, American leaders and citizens alike had to navigate through new territories. Based on your understanding of the text, which conflict resolution strategies worked best? Which failed? How important were leaders' approaches in producing a positive or negative outcome?

ASSIGNMENT

Create a strategy you think could have been successful in resolving a conflict that took place in the United States between 1914 and 1940. Take into account factors that led to the conflict. Be prepared to present and defend your strategy to the class.

Plan As you create your conflict resolution strategy, think about the context in which the conflict unfolded, including the clash of old and new ideas of nationalism, government, and individual human rights. Also consider the impact of war, migration, and expanded citizenship. List the factors that sparked conflict, and address the most significant ones in your strategy. Use a graphic organizer to organize your thoughts.

Goals	Obstacles	Outcome
Summary		

Produce Use your notes to produce a detailed description of your conflict and design a solid conflict resolution strategy. Write your descriptions in outline or paragraph form.

Present Present your strategy to the class. You might consider one of these options:

- Host a debate on a conflict that you have learned about in this unit. Select volunteers to represent both sides of the conflict. Provide a short summary of the conflict to remind the audience of the main issues. Then have an appointed moderator pose prepared questions for the debaters. Allow time for the audience to pose questions as well. Conclude with a vote by the audience on which debaters proposed the best resolution to the conflict.
- Launch a campaign. Create election posters that summarize a conflict and its causes and that propose viable resolutions to the problem. Include a name for your campaign, slogans, and information that communicates the core issues.
- Write a speech that describes the origins of and proposes a resolution for the conflict through use of relevant factual evidence and sound reasoning.

NATIONAL GEOGRAPHIC | LEARNING FRAMEWORK ACTIVITIES

Write a Conflict Negotiator Profile

ATTITUDE Curiosity

KNOWLEDGE Our Human Story

Choose a historical figure you read about in this unit who demonstrated good conflict resolution skills. Research primary and secondary sources to gather evidence about his or her role in negotiating a resolution to a conflict. Note discrepancies among sources. Then write a profile for this individual or create something more visual, such as a poster or digital presentation. Your profile should include information such as birth and death dates, where the person lived, and the work she or he did. Your profile must also highlight a specific resolution to a conflict this person helped negotiate. Consider exploring what you think might have happened if she or he had not taken proactive action in negotiating a resolution.

Settle a Dispute

ATTITUDES Empowerment, Responsibility

SKILLS Collaboration, Problem Solving

Collaborate with a small group to research a dispute in your school or community. Assign roles to group members, such as researcher, interviewer, writer, and presenter. Scan the news and other diverse sources to gather evidence about the dispute, including people or groups on both (or all) sides of the conflict and important dates or events. Then, as a group, create a document or set up a poster or whiteboard on which you can chart the evidence you gather. Hold a meeting to discuss how your group might settle the dispute. Use the evidence you have gathered to put together a viable proposal. Once your group has settled on a solution, present both the dispute and your solution to the class.

HI 3 Students interpret past events and issues within the context in which an event unfolded rather than solely in terms of present-day norms and values.

UNIT 4

1931–1960

A New World Power

As you will learn in this unit, World War II involved countries on almost every continent. After the major Allied powers, the United States and Great Britain, liberated North Africa from the Axis powers of Italy and Germany, they set out to defeat the Italian and German forces in Europe. The Allies' Italian campaign began with the invasion in July 1943 of the island of Sicily, where they successfully drove out German and Italian troops and prepared to assault the Italian mainland. Just outside the city of Palermo, Sicilian civilians (shown below) rejoice at the sight of American troops, cheering as the soldiers' jeeps and trucks navigate the rubble of the city's streets.

UNIT 4

A New World Power

THE UNITED STATES

1945
The United States drops two atomic bombs on Japan; Japan and Germany surrender, ending World War II. *(an atomic bomb similar to those dropped on Japan)*

1941
Japan attacks the naval base at Hawaii's Pearl Harbor, and the United States enters World War II. *(newspaper announcing the attack)*

1942
Roosevelt issues Executive Order 9066, authorizing the internment of Japanese Americans in relocation centers.

1947
President Harry Truman signs a bill that would give rise to the Truman Doctrine, pledging support to democratic countries threatened by communist aggression.

1932
Franklin D. Roosevelt is elected to the first of his four terms as president.

1935
Roosevelt signs the first Neutrality Act in an effort to avoid involvement in future wars.

1930

1940

THE WORLD

1944 EUROPE
Allied forces invade Normandy, a region in France, and liberate western Europe from German control.

1933 EUROPE
Adolf Hitler is appointed chancellor of Germany.

1931 ASIA
Japan invades and conquers Manchuria, a northern province of China. *(Japanese naval flag)*

1949 ASIA
Communists defeat nationalist forces in China, and Mao Zedong becomes the leader of the new communist nation. *(poster featuring Mao Zedong)*

HISTORICAL THINKING

DETERMINE CHRONOLOGY What world events might have prompted the passage of the Neutrality Act in 1935?

1956
Congress passes the Interstate Highway Act, which calls for the construction of an extensive interstate highway system.
(car from the 1950s)

1960
John F. Kennedy becomes the youngest man ever elected president.
(profile of Kennedy on a half-dollar coin)

1953
Julius and Ethel Rosenberg are executed after being convicted of spying for the Soviet Union.

1954
Wisconsin senator Joseph McCarthy's campaign to expose communist subversion in government comes to an end when he accuses U.S. Army personnel.

1952
Dwight D. Eisenhower is elected president.

1950

1960

1959 AMERICAS
Fidel Castro leads a band of revolutionaries in Cuba and overthrows military dictator Fulgencio Batista.
(Castro and his fellow revolutionaries celebrate their victory.)

1957 EUROPE
The Soviets launch *Sputnik 1*, the first artificial satellite to orbit Earth, and trigger the space race between the United States and the U.S.S.R.

1952 AFRICA
The Mau Mau, a militant nationalist group in Kenya, revolts against British rule.

1950 ASIA
The Korean War begins.

HI 1 Students show the connections, causal and otherwise, between particular historical events and larger social, economic, and political trends and developments.

CHAPTER 12

A THREATENING WORLD 1931–1941

HISTORICAL THINKING What ideas and events brought about World War II?

AMERICAN STORIES ONLINE | **Combat Artists of World War II**

AMERICAN GALLERY ONLINE | **The Battle of Britain**

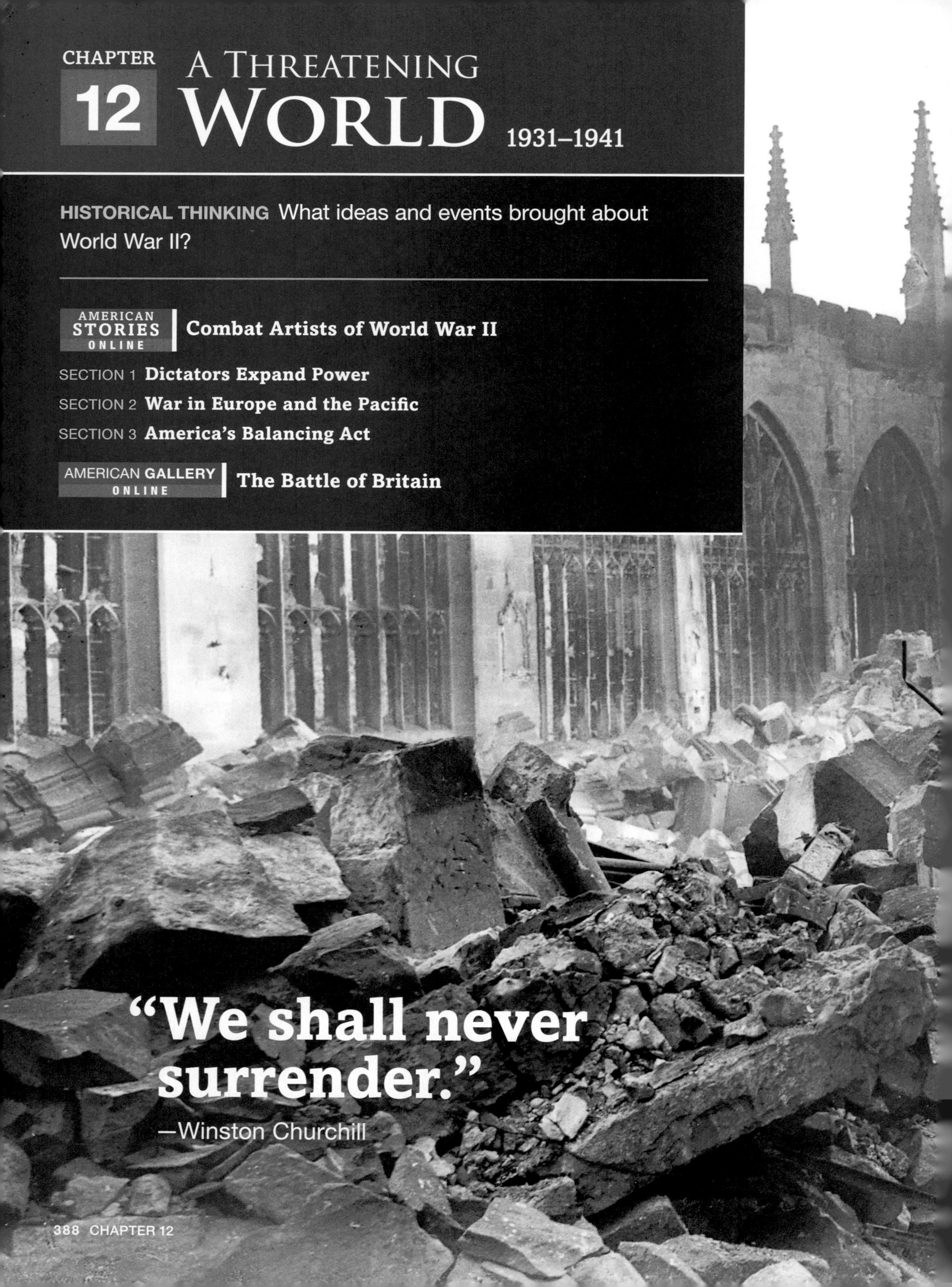

"We shall never surrender."

—Winston Churchill

The medieval cathedral and city center of Coventry, England, were leveled by German bombings on November 14, 1940. Coventry's munitions factories were a target, but the destruction of the city center, along with the killing of hundreds of civilians, was perceived as an act of terrorism to demoralize the British.

1.1 **MAIN IDEA** In the 1930s dictators established military regimes in Italy, Germany, the Soviet Union, and Spain.

FASCISM SPREADS IN EUROPE

Would you give up any of your personal freedoms to be more economically secure or more physically safe? Some people might say they would protect freedom at all costs, but history proves that security often comes first. That was certainly true in Europe in the 1930s.

TOTALITARIANISM TIGHTENS ITS GRIP

As the United States worked to pull itself out of the Great Depression, the nations of Europe were undergoing dramatic political change. With many European economies also suffering during the 1930s, great anxiety and unrest spread across the continent. Authoritarian leaders took advantage of the turmoil and uncertainty to seize power in several countries. They took control of government, built powerful armies, and looked to expand their territory.

As you have read, Adolf Hitler and his Nazi Party seized control in Germany. Hitler had risen to power as the German economy collapsed under the weight of the global depression. Millions listened as Hitler promised to create jobs, restore what he perceived as Germany's past glory, and avenge the "humiliation" of the Treaty of Versailles, which ended World War I. Nazi representation in the Reichstag, the German parliament, rose from 12 members in 1928 to 230 by 1932. A year later, Hitler became Germany's chancellor, or the head of its government.

Hitler's regime, which the Nazi Party dubbed the **Third Reich**, suspended constitutional rights and banned all competing political parties. *Reich* means "empire," and the term Third Reich acknowledged two powerful German states of the past while envisioning a strong, prosperous state that would endure into the future. The Nazis transformed German police departments into the **Gestapo**, a brutal secret police force that went after Hitler's political opponents and anyone else whom the Nazis deemed an enemy of the Reich.

Hitler began a massive **rearmament**, a rebuilding of Germany's stockpile of weapons. By 1934, German factories were churning out tanks and military aircraft at an ever-increasing rate. Hitler then began building an army by instituting a draft that forced men 20 or older to join the military. In 1936, in clear violation of the Treaty of Versailles, Nazi forces marched into the Rhineland, a region of Germany that had been occupied by the French after World War I. German soldiers conquered it without firing a shot.

THE CROOKED CROSS

Before it became associated with the Nazis, the swastika (pictured on the flags in the photo on the next page) was known as an ancient symbol of good fortune. In the ancient Asian language of Sanskrit, the word *swastika* means "well-being." At the beginning of the 20th century, many in the West saw it as a good luck symbol. The Boy Scouts adopted it, and the Girls' Club of America called their official magazine *Swastika*. The Nazis interpreted the cross as a symbol of racial superiority and adopted it as their party logo. After World War II, the swastika was banned in Germany and today is almost universally seen as a symbol of hate.

Meanwhile, Benito Mussolini—the fascist dictator who had risen to power in Italy in the early 1920s—had dreams of recreating the Roman Empire by conquering territory in Africa. In October 1935, Mussolini invaded Ethiopia, a nation in east-central Africa. The League of Nations condemned the act, but that did little to stop Mussolini. Italian forces took the capital, Addis Ababa, in May 1936 and annexed Ethiopia to Italy. Several months later, in October, Mussolini signed a pact of friendship with Hitler,

HI 2 Students recognize the complexity of historical causes and effects, including the limitations on determining cause and effect;
HI 4 Students understand the meaning, implication, and impact of historical events and recognize that events could have taken other directions.

In 1934, Hitler walks up the steps to the speaker's platform at a harvest festival staged by the Nazis. A crowd of 700,000 attended this rally on Bückeberg, a hill in the farmland of northern Germany.

known as the **Rome-Berlin Axis**. Germany, Italy, and later Japan, would become known as the **Axis Powers**. The countries eventually opposing them would be referred to as the **Allied Powers**.

While Italy and Germany were hardening into dictatorships, **Joseph Stalin** was tightening his totalitarian grip on the Soviet Union. Stalin had come to power in 1924, and he steadily transformed his country from a peasant society into an industrial and military superpower. He ruled by terror during his brutal reign. Stalin expanded the powers of his secret police force, encouraged citizens to spy on one another, and had millions of people executed or sent to labor camps.

THE SPANISH CIVIL WAR

In 1936, civil war broke out in Spain, and Europe's dictators were eager to get involved. Spanish military officers led by **General Francisco Franco** attempted to overthrow the recently elected Spanish government, called the Republicans. Franco represented the Nationalists, a fascist group, and Hitler and Mussolini provided him with military aid, such as tanks, planes, and other weapons. Mussolini also sent 70,000 troops. Meanwhile, Stalin aided the Republicans, who represented a coalition of left wing groups, including communists, socialists, and liberal democrats, by sending weapons and money to help the government in its fight against Franco and the Nationalists.

CRITICAL VIEWING Pablo Picasso (1881–1973), born in Spain, was one of the best-known artists of the 20th century. The large painting *Guernica*, completed in 1937—two years before Franco's victory—was the artist's reaction to the bombing of a northern Spanish coastal village by the German and Italian air forces in support of Franco's Nationalists. The title of the painting is the name of the village they destroyed, including its homes and shops, killing an estimated 1,650 people. Perhaps most disturbing, the attack was a terrorist bombing whose primary target was the civilians of the town. The first bomb fell on the center of the town on a market day.

Picasso used black, white, and gray shades of paint, depicting distorted human and animal forms and anguished facial expressions. Also shown are symbols of transition from a traditional to a modern world—a light bulb inside the sun and shapes filled with newsprint. According to Picasso's wishes, the painting was kept in New York's Museum of Modern Art until Spain restored its democracy. In 1981, the painting returned to Spain. At about 11 feet high by 25 feet wide, the painting occupies an entire wall in Madrid's Reina Sofia Museum. In applying the techniques he used, what do you think Picasso wanted visitors to feel as they viewed the painting?

Pablo Picasso, "Guernica", credit: © 2017 Estate of Pablo Picasso / Artists Rights Society (ARS), New York

CST 1 Students compare the present with the past, evaluating the consequences of past events and decisions and determining the lessons that were learned; HI 3 Students interpret past events and issues within the context in which an event unfolded rather than solely in terms of present-day norms and values.

Many international volunteers joined the war, including some from the United States. Some Americans praised Franco as an enemy of communism. However, many viewed him as a fascist thug trying to overthrow an elected government.

A group of several thousand Americans known as the **Abraham Lincoln Brigade** fought alongside the Spanish government. The famous American writer Ernest Hemingway, who covered the war as a reporter, summed up the anti-Franco view: "There is only one way to quell a bully and that is to thrash him." The fighting was widespread and brutal, with more than 500,000 killed. The war ended in 1939 with a complete victory for General Franco and his forces. Another dictator had taken power in Europe.

The riots of Kristallnacht, ordered indirectly by Goebbels and intended to appear as spontaneous expressions of rage, took place throughout Germany. This Jewish-owned shop in Berlin was one of more than 7,000 businesses destroyed during the two days.

PERSECUTION OF JEWS

As Europe's dictators engaged in military actions outside their borders, they also tightened their grip on the home front. Their regimes silenced critics and oppressed people whom they deemed "undesirable." In Germany, the Nazis sought to reshape society according to their vision of a pure German "master race." The Nazis believed all other races and ethnicities to be inferior, and they targeted one group in particular: Jews.

In Europe, anti-Semitism, or hostility toward and discrimination against Jewish people, had deep historical roots. Many Europeans accused Jews of working to remain a separate social and religious group that refused to adopt the values of the countries in which they lived. After Germany's defeat in World War I, many Germans believed the German Army was betrayed by politicians, especially Jewish politicians. In addition, a number of Jews worked in the banking and money-lending industries, making them easy scapegoats for Germany's financial problems.

When the Nazis gained power, the persecution of Jews became government policy. Nazis began to exclude Jews from public life. At the annual Nazi rally in 1935, Hitler announced laws denying Jewish people citizenship and prohibiting marriage between Jews and people of "German or related blood." Three years later, under Hitler's personal orders, the Nazis destroyed the Great Synagogue in Munich.

On November 7, 1938, a 17-year-old Polish Jew, Hershel Grynszpan (GRIHNZ-pan), shot and killed Ernst vom Rath, a German diplomat in France. Joseph Goebbels (GEH-buhlz), the Nazi propaganda minister, immediately seized on the assassination to whip up rage against Jews. What followed became known as the **Kristallnacht**—the Night of Broken Glass. Between November 9 and November 10, 1938, Nazis destroyed Jewish homes, schools, and businesses, burned synagogues, and killed nearly 100 Jews. Officials arrested 30,000 Jewish men and sent them to concentration camps. Shortly after the attacks, U.S. president Franklin D. Roosevelt denounced the rising tide of anti-Semitism and violence in Germany. He also recalled Hugh Wilson, the U.S. ambassador to Germany. Nonetheless, the persecution of Jews in Germany continued.

HISTORICAL THINKING

1. **READING CHECK** What measures did Hitler take against Germany's Jews?
2. **ANALYZE CAUSE AND EFFECT** Why is it difficult to determine a single cause for four dictators all coming to power at about the same time in Europe?
3. **FORM AND SUPPORT OPINIONS** Do you think dictators and fascist regimes would have risen to power if Europe hadn't been so economically depressed after World War I? Explain your answer.
4. **MAKE CONNECTIONS** What similarities do you see among Hitler, Mussolini, and Stalin and one of today's world leaders?

11.7.5 Discuss the constitutional issues and impact of events on the U.S. home front, including the internment of Japanese Americans (e.g., *Fred Korematsu* v. *United States of America*) and the restrictions on German and Italian resident aliens; the response of the administration to Hitler's atrocities against Jews and other groups; the roles of women in military production; and the roles and growing political demands of African Americans.

1.2 **MAIN IDEA** Amid the growing possibility of another large-scale war, many Americans wanted the United States to remain neutral and to isolate itself from foreign conflict.

Isolationism and Neutrality

Maybe you have been in situations where you had your own conflicting opinions about an issue. In the 1930s, many Americans did not like what was happening in Europe, but they had concerns about the United States getting involved.

AVOIDING INVOLVEMENT IN EUROPE

As authoritarian leaders rose to power in Europe, U.S. president Franklin Roosevelt watched with increasing alarm. Roosevelt felt very early on that Hitler posed a threat to the world unlike any other. However, a majority of Americans did not feel the same way. Many had no wish to get involved in the turmoil they saw threatening Europe.

Americans voiced many reasons for wanting to stay out of the growing conflict. In the Great Plains and Upper Midwest, some were suspicious of international bankers and arms manufacturers, believing such businesspeople were responsible for pushing the United States into World War I for their own financial gain. Americans of German descent supported isolationism because they remembered how badly German Americans were treated during World War I. Americans of Irish descent opposed any kind of aid to Great Britain because of conflicts between Ireland and Great Britain, while many Americans of Italian descent admired Mussolini, due to a propaganda campaign by the dictator meant to win over Italian Americans. Furthermore, **pacifism**, the belief that war is morally wrong, appealed to clergy, peace groups, and many college students.

Following the will of the American public, the U.S. Congress passed a series of Neutrality Acts. The first act, passed in 1935, banned the export of "arms, ammunition, and implements of war" from the United States to any foreign nation at war. President Roosevelt opposed the act, but bowed to pressure from Congress and the public to maintain neutrality. Congress renewed the act in 1936 and 1937, and expanded it. U.S. citizens were now forbidden from traveling on ships owned by nations at war, and the United States could bar any warring ships from entering U.S. waters. In a compromise with Roosevelt, the act did allow the United States to sell European nations materials and supplies—just not ammunition and arms. This enabled America to provide its allies with critical resources, such as oil. In an effort to limit the interaction, European nations had to arrange to pick up the materials and pay immediately in cash. The provision thus became known as "cash-and-carry."

ROOSEVELT CHALLENGES THE NATION

Standing in direct opposition to the American people and Congress, President Roosevelt continued to push for greater American involvement in Europe. He felt the United States could not remain strictly neutral, and the time would come when the democratic countries of Europe, especially Great

PRIMARY SOURCE

On October 5, 1937, President Roosevelt traveled to Chicago to speak at the dedication of a bridge completed under a New Deal program. Expected to praise the accomplishment of the bridge's construction, Roosevelt instead used the occasion to make his case for opposing tyranny in Europe. His speech at the bridge dedication became known as the **Quarantine Speech**.

The political situation in the world, which of late has been growing progressively worse, is such as to cause grave concern and anxiety to all the peoples and nations. Innocent peoples, innocent nations, are being cruelly sacrificed to a greed for power and supremacy which is devoid of all sense of justice and humane considerations. If those things come to pass in other parts of the world, let no one imagine that America will escape.

—from the Quarantine Speech, by Franklin D. Roosevelt, 1937

11.7.1 Examine the origins of American involvement in the war, with an emphasis on the events that precipitated the attack on Pearl Harbor; 11.7.4 Analyze Roosevelt's foreign policy during World War II (e.g., Four Freedoms speech).

A GLOBAL PERSPECTIVE Refugees still flee dangerous situations and oppressive regimes to this day. In 2016, millions of men, women, and children fled a brutal civil war in the country of Syria. Hoping to find a better life in Europe, large numbers of these refugees packed into overcrowded boats and made a dangerous voyage across the Mediterranean Sea. Many died along the way. Those who made it struggled to fit in across Europe, as many nations opposed the influx of so many immigrants. For a single day in September 2016, at Parliament Square in London, international aid organizations displayed 2,500 life jackets worn by the refugees to help bring attention to their plight.

Britain, would need help from the United States. Roosevelt gave a speech in which he compared war with a disease, saying it was the responsibility of peace-loving nations to "quarantine" countries that threatened world peace.

In that speech, Roosevelt mentioned people and nations who were being "cruelly sacrificed," referring partly to the Jews suffering under the Nazi regime. But Roosevelt's speech did not go over well with the public, and the United States refused to ease the immigration restrictions that kept large numbers of German Jews from the safety of American shores. Each year between 1935 and 1941, the United States took in an average of 8,500 Jewish **refugees**, or people seeking shelter and protection from persecution. This was far below the annual quota of 30,000 for German immigrants set by the National Origins Act of 1924. Most Americans were still feeling the sting of the Depression and did not want foreigners competing with them for jobs and resources. A combination of economics, anti-Semitism, and isolationism in the United States kept the "golden door" shut to most Jewish refugees.

Isolationists strongly criticized the president for trying to violate neutrality, while many average Americans remained opposed to deeper U.S. involvement in Europe's troubles. As Europe moved closer to war, the United States remained neutral.

HISTORICAL THINKING

1. **READING CHECK** Why did many Americans wish to remain neutral and not take sides in the growing conflicts in Europe?
2. **COMPARE AND CONTRAST** Compare the refugee crisis described in the lesson with what you know about the status of refugees today.
3. **MAKE INFERENCES** How do you think the American experience in World War I affected the country's attitude toward international events in the 1930s?

11.7.5 Discuss the constitutional issues and impact of events on the U.S. home front, including the internment of Japanese Americans (e.g., *Fred Korematsu v. United States of America*) and the restrictions on German and Italian resident aliens; the response of the administration to Hitler's atrocities against Jews and other groups; the roles of women in military production; and the roles and growing political demands of African Americans; CST 1 Students compare the present with the past, evaluating the consequences of past events and decisions and determining the lessons that were learned.

2.1 **MAIN IDEA** Germany's invasion of Poland prompted Britain and France to declare war.

WAR ENGULFS EUROPE

Is it better to reason with a bully to achieve a compromise, or let the fight begin? The nations of Europe tried to compromise with Hitler as he rose to power and looked to conquer his neighbors. But in the end, they decided they had to fight.

THE MUNICH AGREEMENT

One of Adolf Hitler's main goals was to unite all German-speaking people into a "Greater Germany," or "Grossdeutschland." As you have read, Germany took its first steps toward this goal in 1936, when it reoccupied the Rhineland. In 1938, German troops marched into neighboring Austria. Hitler announced the "Anschluss" (AHN-shloos), or union, of Germany and Austria, adding six million German speakers to greater Germany.

With each aggressive step Hitler took, the nations of Western Europe made little attempt to confront him. Instead, Great Britain and France took an approach

CST 3 Students use a variety of maps and documents to interpret human movement, including major patterns of domestic and international migration, changing environmental preferences and settlement patterns, the frictions that develop between population groups, and the diffusion of ideas, technological innovations, and goods.

BLITZKRIEG

In invading Poland, the Germans demonstrated for the first time a new and seemingly unstoppable type of warfare—blitzkrieg (BLIHTS-kreeg), or "lightning war." Blitzkrieg was characterized first by bombing—to cripple the target's air capacity, railroads, and communication lines—followed by fast moving tanks, artillery, and waves of troops.

Using this new tactic of speed and overwhelming force, the Germans conquered Poland in a matter of weeks. In this photo, a German gunner fires from a plane attacking a Polish town.

known as **appeasement**—a policy of making political compromises in order to avoid conflict. Neither country had forgotten the horrors of World War I, and they sought to maintain peace at any price. In addition, many British politicians believed that Germany had genuine grievances, as the Treaty of Versailles had left hundreds of thousands of German-speaking people under the control of other countries in Europe. What's more, a number of Western leaders viewed communism, not fascism, as the greatest threat to Europe. Thus, they saw Hitler as a potential safeguard against Soviet expansion.

Facing little resistance, Hitler continued to invade and annex. After absorbing Austria, the German leader turned his attention to Czechoslovakia. He insisted that the Czechs surrender the Sudetenland (soo-DAY-tehn-land), a region of western Czechoslovakia where three million ethnic Germans lived. In September 1938, Hitler met with British Prime Minister Neville Chamberlain, French Premier Edouard Daladier, and Italian dictator Benito Mussolini in Munich. Under the **Munich Agreement**, the leaders agreed to Hitler's demand for the Sudetenland. In return, Hitler promised he would not occupy any more territory in Czechoslovakia. Daladier pressured the Czechs to accept the agreement and give the Sudetenland to Germany. Meanwhile, Chamberlain claimed the agreement had brought "peace in our time." Less than a year later, on March 15, 1939, Hitler violated the pact and sent German troops to seize the rest of Czechoslovakia.

GERMANY ATTACKS POLAND

In August 1939, the world was shocked to learn that two sworn enemies, fascist Nazi Germany and the communist Soviet Union, had signed a **nonaggression pact**. Under the pact, the two countries agreed to take no military action against each other for 10 years. The agreement also contained a secret section that detailed how the Soviets and Germans planned to divide up Eastern Europe. The first country targeted under their plan: Poland.

On September 1, 1939, Hitler sent the Wehrmacht—the German Army—across the German border into Poland. (The Soviets would invade weeks later and claim their share of Polish territory.) Hitler, it appeared, had finally gone too far. Two days after the German attack, Britain and France declared war on Germany. **World War II** had begun. What followed were months of quiet, known as the "phony war." During this time, the French and British hunkered down on one side of the French-German border, behind a series of fortifications known as the **Maginot** (MAJ-ih-noh) **Line**, and the Germans settled in on the other side.

GERMANY INVADES FRANCE

In April 1940, the calm came to an explosive end when German forces invaded Denmark and Norway, quickly conquering both nations and defeating British forces stationed in Norway. The defeat brought down Chamberlain's government, and he was replaced as prime minister by British statesman

Winston Churchill. Meanwhile, German forces rolled on, pushing into Belgium, Holland, and Luxembourg.

Next, Germany invaded France, and German forces seized Paris in June 1940. The French signed an armistice that divided France into two regions, one under German occupation and one under French authority, with the town of Vichy (VISH-ee) as its capital. Although French leaders oversaw Vichy, the Germans controlled the region—one of the most significant strategic outcomes of the war.

Despite the German victory, some of the French decided to fight on. The French general **Charles de Gaulle** set up headquarters in Britain to allow "Free French" forces to continue fighting as a resistance force. In the autumn of 1940, a number of French colonies in Africa declared their loyalty to de Gaulle, but they were a small force compared to the German enemy. The French resistance fighters did what they could to thwart the Nazis as the war progressed.

THE NAZIS TARGET GREAT BRITAIN

The Nazis had conquered most of Western Europe in less than two months. Now they targeted Britain. Winston Churchill rallied the British to fight on against Germany's overwhelming power, despite some calls for Britain to negotiate peace with Hitler. "We shall defend our island, whatever the cost may be," Churchill declared. "We shall fight on the landing grounds, we shall fight in the fields and in the streets, we shall fight in the hills; we shall never surrender."

From June through October 1940, British and German forces fought the **Battle of Britain**. It was primarily an air war, as Britain's Royal Air Force (RAF) and Germany's air force, the Luftwaffe (LOOFT-vahf-uh), clashed over the skies of Great Britain. Germany's attempts to bomb Britain into surrender met with stiff resistance. While German attacks inflicted heavy damage on British cities, the RAF continued fighting back and eventually forced Germany's air force to retreat. Unable to achieve victory, Hitler suspended further attacks on Britain and moved on. Referring to the RAF fighters who turned back the Germans, Churchill said, "Never in the field of human conflict was so much owed by so many to so few."

The British people suffered greatly during the Battle of Britain. Families were split up, as Londoners put their children on trains for the countryside, sending them as refugees to willing rural homes in hopes of keeping them safe from the nightly bombing. All too many children never saw their parents again, as the bombing campaign known as the London Blitz claimed the lives of nearly 17,500 civilians in London. Thousands more were killed nationwide. Relentless German raids destroyed whole neighborhoods of London and other cities as the British took cover deep beneath ground in London's tube, or subway stations, or in other designated bunkers and shelters. One of the more deadly attacks toward the end of the campaign killed nearly 1,500 civilians in a single night of bombing.

PRIMARY SOURCE

Hitler knows that he will have to break us in this Island or lose the war. If we can stand up to him, all Europe may be free. But if we fail, then the whole world, including the United States . . . will sink into the abyss of a new Dark Age made more sinister, and perhaps more protracted, by the lights of perverted science. Let us therefore brace ourselves to our duties, and so bear ourselves that, if the British Empire and its Commonwealth last for a thousand years, men will still say, 'This was their finest hour.'

—from a speech before the House of Commons (British legislature), by Winston Churchill, 1940

Across the Atlantic Ocean, Americans watched the onset of World War II with interest and alarm. Isolationists continued to argue that the country should stay out of the conflict. Interventionists insisted the United States must enter the fight to halt Hitler's march of conquest. President Roosevelt, in particular, felt that the United States should do more to help Britain. On September 21, 1939, soon after the war had begun, Roosevelt called Congress into special session. He pressed lawmakers to amend the Neutrality Act to lift the ban on arms sales and allow the United States to provide weapons to the nations threatened by Germany, specifically Great Britain. After much debate, Congress approved the amendment. The United States was slowly moving toward greater involvement in the war.

HISTORICAL THINKING

1. **READING CHECK** Explain the theory of appeasement. Why do you think it led to war in Europe?
2. **INTERPRET MAPS** From a geographical standpoint, why was it important that Germany capture France before battling with Britain?
3. **ANALYZE CAUSE AND EFFECT** How might events have taken a different turn if the world had not underestimated Hitler's intentions?

11.7.1 Examine the origins of American involvement in the war, with an emphasis on the events that precipitated the attack on Pearl Harbor; HI 4 Students understand the meaning, implication, and impact of historical events and recognize that events could have taken other directions.

CRITICAL VIEWING British children of farmworkers take cover in a trench in southeastern England in 1940. In this photo, which appeared in *Life* magazine, the children watch an aerial fight between a British and a German fighter plane. What does the photo reveal about the children's reactions to what is happening in the sky above them?

2.2 **MAIN IDEA** As World War II spread in Europe, Japan attacked its neighbors in Asia and elevated tensions with the United States.

JAPAN INVADES CHINA

By the time the nations of Europe went to war in the fall of 1939, another military power had risen on the other side of the globe. Japan was carving out an empire of its own, giving the world—and the United States—another serious threat to confront.

CHINA IN TURMOIL

China had been ruled as an empire for 2,000 years, and at the turn of the 20th century, it was poverty-stricken and underdeveloped. In 1911, a group of revolutionaries led by **Sun Yat-sen** overthrew the ruling Qing (CHING) Dynasty and established the Republic of China. Sun was elected China's first president, but he struggled to maintain control of the country—in reality ruled by a number of warlords, or local military leaders. After Sun's death in 1925, power passed to **Chiang Kai-shek** (jee-AHNG ky-SHEHK). Chiang soon faced an armed resistance from the growing **Chinese Communist Party (CCP)**, led by **Mao Zedong** (MOW dzuh-DUNG).

In 1927, fearful of the CCP's increasing power, Chiang ordered a **purge**, or elimination, of CCP members in Shanghai and other Chinese cities. Chiang's troops, known as the Kuomintang, or KMT, killed tens of thousands of communists. By 1931, the KMT had

Mao Zedong arrives in Shaanxi Province in northern China in 1935, near the end of the Long March. Most officers rode horses, but all others walked on foot.

11.7.1 Examine the origins of American involvement in the war, with an emphasis on the events that precipitated the attack on Pearl Harbor; CST 3 Students use a variety of maps and documents to interpret human movement, including major patterns of domestic and international migration, changing environmental preferences and settlement patterns, the frictions that develop between population groups, and the diffusion of ideas, technological innovations, and goods.

almost completely defeated Mao's forces. Some 700,000 KMT troops encircled communist positions in southeast China, preventing supplies from entering their territory. Hundreds of thousands of soldiers and peasants loyal to Mao were killed or died of starvation.

Facing almost certain defeat, the remaining Chinese communists decided to retreat to a more remote part of China. There, Mao hoped, the CCP could regroup and build its military power. In October 1934, at the beginning of what became known as the **Long March**, 86,000 communist troops and around 15,000 civilians marched out of southeast China, attempting to escape Chiang's KMT forces. They faced almost daily battles and skirmishes with KMT troops and local warlords, and they even were the targets of aerial bombardment. Many were killed in the fighting, and others died of starvation and exposure. Only 7,000 of the approximately 100,000 who had begun the Long March the year before survived the journey. After the Long March, Chiang Kai-shek planned to wipe out the remaining communist forces, but by then a more serious threat had emerged from the neighboring nation of Japan.

JAPAN TAKES ACTION

By the early 20th century, Japan was a strong country with developed industries and a powerful military. In 1904, its forces had soundly defeated Russia in a war over several disputed territories in Asia. The easy victory had surprised observers and signaled that Japan was a rising world power. But as an island nation, it lacked the land and natural resources necessary for economic growth. Ambitious military leaders such as **Tojo Hideki** urged the young Japanese emperor **Hirohito** to seek out and conquer new land and build an empire. To achieve this goal, the Japanese turned their attention to China, their large neighbor to the west.

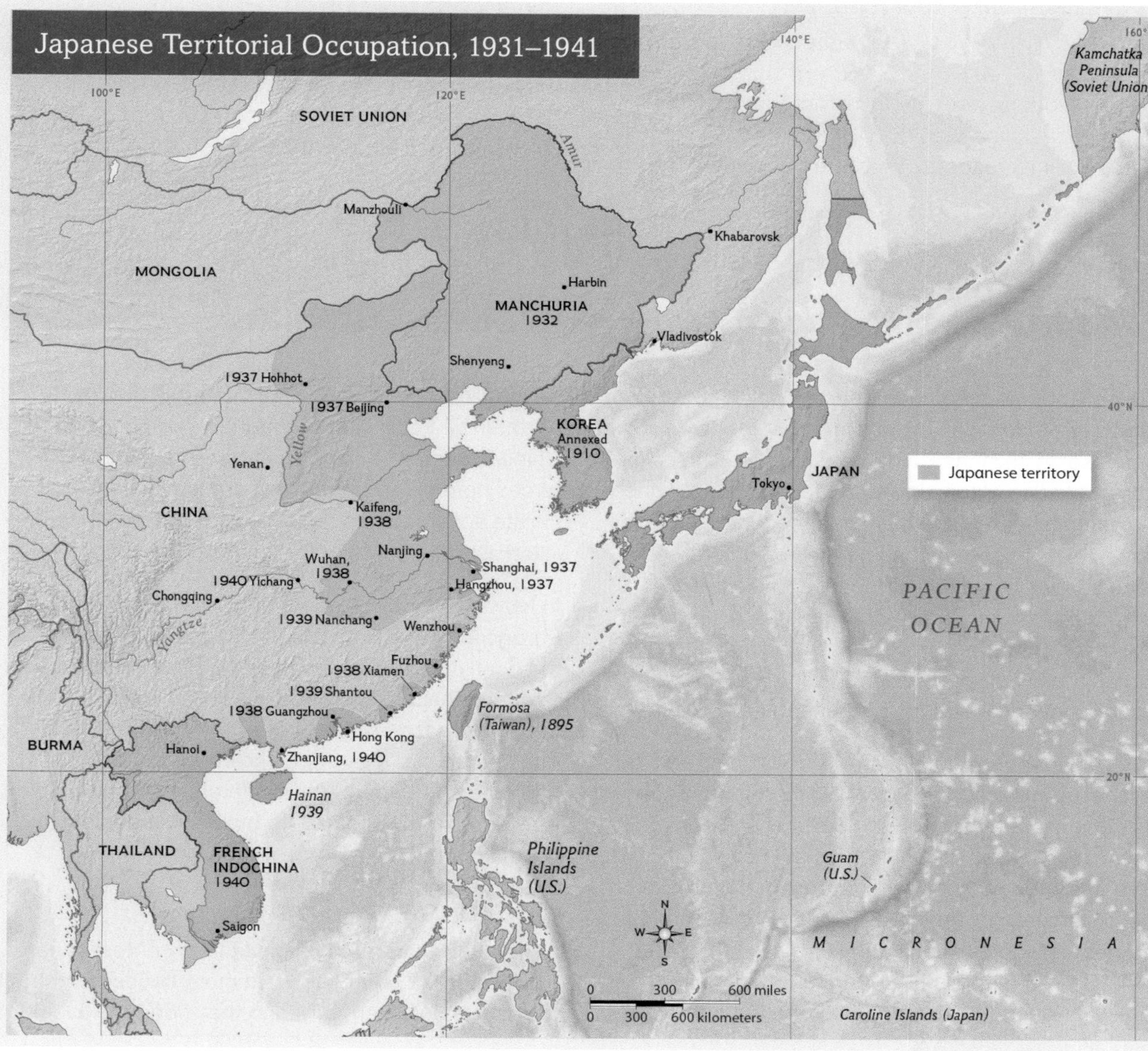

CRITICAL VIEWING **The Memorial Hall of the Victims in the Nanjing Massacre was built in 1985 in Nanjing, China. In 2015, students from the Nanjing University for the Arts painted huge Chinese violet cress flowers on the walkway before a Chinese holiday called "Tomb-Sweeping Day," when people honor their ancestors. How do the flowers contrast with other aspects of the Memorial?**

China's land and resources—and its political instability—made it an attractive target to the Japanese. In 1931, as China was troubled with internal fighting, Japan invaded the Chinese province of Manchuria and made it an independent Japanese state, which it controlled completely. China turned to the League of Nations for help, and the League demanded that Japan withdraw its troops. Japan refused and withdrew from the League. By 1936, the Japanese military was in full control of Japan's government and intent on conquering new territory.

In 1937, Japan renewed its attack on China. Japanese Ambassador Hiroshi Saito defended the assault as an attempt to bring political and social order to the region. "If China's house were in order there would be no need for the presence of these foreign forces," he declared. "What our government and people want is peace and security in the Far East." Chiang reluctantly agreed to form a united front with Mao to fight the new threat, but just six months later, Japanese forces controlled all of northern China, including Beijing, Shanghai, and the Chinese capital of Nanjing. In Nanjing, Japanese forces committed horrific war crimes, actions that violate accepted international rules of war, when they killed as many as 300,000 Chinese civilians.

In November 1937, leaders of 18 nations met in the European city of Brussels to discuss ways of ending the conflict between Japan and China. The **Brussels Conference**, as it was known, ended with a call for Japan to cease all hostilities against its neighbor. The decree had little effect, however, as Japan had refused to attend the conference and claimed that western nations had no business meddling in its affairs.

TENSIONS RISE

At first, the United States did little to contest Japan's aggression. U.S. leaders were more concerned about the rise of Nazi Germany, and they hoped to avoid

> ## PRIMARY SOURCE
>
> Captain Frank Roberts was aboard the *Panay* during the attack. He recalled how he narrowly escaped death.
>
> *I had only taken a couple of steps when a shower of fragments [bomb pieces] hit me in the back and knocked me to my hands and knees. At the same time, I heard the sound of a machine gun and the splatter of bullets against the ship's side. Almost simultaneously, another bomb exploded to port, knocking down some of the bunks and breaking more glass. Being dazed and dizzy, I remained on the floor for some moments while two other bombs exploded somewhere near. Later I discovered that a bullet or a metal fragment had torn a three-inch rip in my left trouser leg at the top of the pocket. Still later, I found holes in my coat, the largest at the left shoulder, and there was a severe bruise, although the bullet or fragment did not penetrate.*
>
> —from *The Panay Incident*,
> by Hamilton Darby Perry, 1969

a crisis with Japan. In December 1937, Japanese warplanes sank the U.S. gunboat *Panay* on China's Yangtze (yang-tsee) River, killing 3 Americans and wounding nearly 30. President Roosevelt condemned the attack, but Japan apologized and the two nations settled the matter peacefully.

Japan, however, continued to expand its empire. In 1938, Japanese forces annexed European colonies in Southeast Asia and the Western Pacific. U.S. Secretary of State Cordell Hull warned that "Japan definitely contemplates securing domination over as many hundreds of millions of people as possible in eastern Asia." The United States responded to Japan's continued conquests by pulling back on trade. Japan purchased the bulk of its oil, steel, and machinery from America. In an effort to slow Japanese expansion, President Roosevelt declared an **embargo**, barring U.S. companies from selling a number of strategic industrial goods, such as oil and copper, to Japan. In May 1940, the president moved the headquarters of the U.S. Pacific Fleet from San Diego, California, to Pearl Harbor, Hawaii. The move was intended to enable the U.S. Navy to keep a closer watch on Japan. The United States had a base in the Philippines, but it was not prepared for war.

Relations grew more strained in September 1940, when Japan signed a war agreement with Germany and Italy, forming the Axis powers. They agreed to assist one another if any one of them were attacked by a nation not already involved in the war. Roosevelt retaliated by freezing all Japanese assets in the United States and blocking shipments of scrap iron and aviation fuel to Japan. Japanese Foreign Minister Teijiro Toyoda declared, "Commercial and economic relations between Japan and third countries, led by England and the United States, are gradually becoming so horribly strained that we cannot endure it much longer." The United States and Japan were now openly at odds, and tensions were mounting.

HISTORICAL THINKING

1. **READING CHECK** Who were the opposing sides in China's civil war?
2. **INTERPRET MAPS** Based on the information on the map, why was conquering China so appealing to Japan?
3. **EVALUATE** What led to the growing tensions between Japan and the United States?

11.7.6 Describe major developments in aviation, weaponry, communication, and medicine and the war's impact on the location of American industry and use of resources.

3.1 **MAIN IDEA** At the onset of World War II, U.S. foreign policy reflected a struggle between Americans who wanted to maintain neutrality and those who favored greater involvement in the widening conflict.

SUPPORTING THE ALLIES

The question on every American's mind was, "Should the United States go to war, or should it stay neutral?" Even as Americans continued to debate this issue, the nation took greater steps to support the Allies.

A THIRD TERM FOR FDR

As the 1940 presidential election approached, the leading campaign issue was the war raging in Europe. France had fallen, and Great Britain was fighting alone against the Axis Powers. In this atmosphere of turmoil, President Roosevelt took the unprecedented step of running for a third term in the White House. No American president had ever served a third term. Roosevelt felt it was his duty to continue to lead the United States through the current world crisis, so he allowed himself to be drafted by the Democratic National Convention in 1940 as their candidate. Meanwhile, the Republicans nominated lawyer and businessman Wendell Willkie of Indiana as their presidential candidate.

The 1940 presidential campaign intensified the debate over U.S. neutrality. Roosevelt favored greater intervention, while Willkie took a more isolationist stance. "The President's attacks on foreign powers have been useless and dangerous," Willkie declared. "He has courted a war for which the country is hopelessly unprepared—and which it emphatically does not want."

As you have read, Roosevelt had persuaded Congress to amend the Neutrality Act in 1939 to lift the ban on arms sales to U.S. allies and continue cash-and-carry. American ships, however, were still barred from transporting goods to ports of **belligerents**, or the countries already fighting in the war. In September 1940, at Britain's request, and without informing Congress, Roosevelt took the step of supplying the British with 50 old but usable destroyers. In return, the United States obtained the rights to establish naval bases in various British territories. The agreement outraged isolationists, who viewed it as a clear violation of American neutrality.

Nonetheless, Roosevelt easily defeated Willkie in the November election, with about 27 million votes to 22 million votes (449 electoral votes to 82 electoral votes). Although many Americans were opposed to involvement in the war, most were rooting against Germany. A national poll in 1940 found that 83 percent of U.S. citizens favored a British victory. Many Americans believed that if Britain fell to the Nazis, the United States would be on its own and potentially Germany's next target.

AN "ARSENAL OF DEMOCRACY"

After his re-election, Roosevelt continued nudging the United States toward greater involvement in the war. In December 1940, the president declared the nation must devote its industrial might to helping Britain. "We must be the great **arsenal** of democracy," Roosevelt proclaimed. "For us this is an emergency as serious as war itself." An arsenal is a place where weapons are stored. In his declaration, Roosevelt indicated he envisioned the United States as the major supplier of arms for its allies. He went on to say, "No dictator . . . will weaken [our] determination."

Even before Roosevelt's declaration, the nation had begun ramping up its war effort. In August 1940, Congress passed the first peacetime draft in U.S. history. Like the original Selective Service Act from World War I, the **Selective Service and Training Act** again required able-bodied young men to register for potential military service. Congress also allocated $10.5 billion for defense spending. American factories began working around the clock to build weaponry, including tanks, warplanes, and warships. Unemployment virtually disappeared. The United States' urgent push to build up its arsenal had finally ended the Great Depression.

11.7.1 Examine the origins of American involvement in the war, with an emphasis on the events that precipitated the attack on Pearl Harbor; 11.7.4 Analyze Roosevelt's foreign policy during World War II (e.g., Four Freedoms speech); 11.7.6 Describe major developments in aviation, weaponry, communication, and medicine and the war's impact on the location of American industry and use of resources.

The "arsenal of democracy" included U.S.-made aircraft. In this 1940 photograph, a worker in a Los Angeles aircraft plant completes tail-fin assemblies for warplanes built for the Allies.

THE LEND-LEASE ACT

As the United States increased its military production, Winston Churchill sent a plea for help to Roosevelt. Churchill told the president that Great Britain was in deep financial trouble and unable to pay for arms from the United States. Roosevelt responded by crafting the **Lend-Lease Act**, which enabled countries to receive American military aid without immediately paying for it.

Proposed in late 1940 and passed on March 11, 1941, the Lend-Lease Act allowed the president to deliver arms and other defense materials to "the government of any country whose defense the President deems vital to the defense of the United States." The act enabled the United States to more directly aid nations at war against the Axis powers, while technically remaining neutral. Isolationists, such as Republican senator Robert Taft from Ohio, strongly opposed Lend-Lease as a violation of neutrality. FDR's isolationist opponents also included Henry Ford and Charles Lindbergh, who organized the America First Committee (AFC). The AFC opposed every effort by the president to move away from neutrality, and it strongly contested Lend-Lease. Despite Taft's and the AFC's opposition, Lend-Lease proceeded, allowing the United States to supply weapons to the Allied powers.

Lindbergh argued that by supporting one side or another, the United States was being used to aid in that country's domination of the continent. He did not evaluate the countries of Europe in terms of their ideology or aggressiveness, but viewed them all as equally seeking advantage over the others. In his mind, there was no justification for sending Americans to further those causes. Some perceived Lindbergh's position as support for the Nazis.

HISTORICAL THINKING

1. **READING CHECK** Why did Franklin Roosevelt want to run for a third term as president?
2. **COMPARE AND CONTRAST** How did cash-and-carry and Lend-Lease differ, and which was more beneficial to the Allies?
3. **ANALYZE CAUSE AND EFFECT** How did Roosevelt's push to be an "arsenal of democracy" affect technology, the U.S. economy, and people's values and beliefs?

CST 2 Students analyze how change happens at different rates at different times; understand that some aspects can change while others remain the same; and understand that change is complicated and affects not only technology and politics but also values and beliefs.

MAIN IDEA Germany expanded the war by invading the Soviet Union and clashing with U.S. ships on the Atlantic Ocean.

A New Alliance

Sometimes no matter how much you try to stay out of a fight, circumstances force you to take action. When German warships began patrolling the Atlantic Ocean in order to stop supplies from reaching Great Britain, they targeted and tried to sink American ships. This brought the United States to the brink of battle.

THE ATLANTIC CHARTER

In the summer of 1941, the war in Europe took a dramatic turn. On June 22, Hitler pointed his army to the east and invaded the Soviet Union. The invasion was named Operation Barbarossa after the 12th-century Holy Roman Emperor, Frederick Barbarossa, and it ended the nonaggression pact between the two nations. Hitler had two objectives in mind: he wanted control of the oil supply in the Caucasus Mountains between the Black Sea and the Caspian Sea, and he wanted to conquer more territory for the expansion of Germany's population. More than 3 million German soldiers and 3,000 tanks plunged deep into Soviet territory. The German army defeated Soviet forces, captured more than 1 million prisoners, and moved toward Moscow and Leningrad.

Operation Barbarossa prompted many Americans to rethink their isolationist stance. The Nazis were becoming a true global threat. Following the German invasion, President Roosevelt offered Lend-Lease support to Soviet leader Joseph Stalin. While many Americans did not favor aiding a communist dictator, Roosevelt believed Hitler must be stopped at all costs. Over the next four years, Stalin received more than $11 billion in Lend-Lease aid from the United States to fight the Nazis.

In August 1941, two months after Germany marched on the Soviets, President Roosevelt and British prime minister Winston Churchill met aboard naval ships in Placentia Bay off the coast of Newfoundland in Canada. Even though the United States had not yet entered the war, the two leaders discussed their mutual aims and principles around fighting and winning the war. They drafted what became known as the **Atlantic Charter**. Under the eight-point charter, the two leaders agreed to such principles as freedom of the seas, greater trade among nations, and the right of people to choose the kind of government they

11.7.1 Examine the origins of American involvement in the war, with an emphasis on the events that precipitated the attack on Pearl Harbor; 11.7.4 Analyze Roosevelt's foreign policy during World War II (e.g., Four Freedoms Speech).

desire. The charter stated the two countries would not wage war to gain territory, and they would oppose all changes in territory brought about by any war the people who lived there opposed. They would restore self-government to any nation that had lost it in the war, they would work together with other nations to improve living and working conditions throughout the world, and—perhaps most importantly—they stated that all countries should give up the use of force against one another.

By January 1942, 26 nations of North and South America, Europe, Asia, and Africa, along with Australia and New Zealand, had allied against the Axis Powers and pledged their support to the principles of the Atlantic Charter.

A FRIENDSHIP THAT CHANGED HISTORY
As the world plunged into war, the personal friendship between Winston Churchill and Franklin Roosevelt helped cement the historically strong bonds between the United States and Great Britain. The friendship helped lead to the Lend-Lease Act and the Atlantic Charter. In all, the two leaders met nine times. After one of these meetings, Roosevelt wrote to Churchill, saying, "It is fun to be in the same decade with you." After Roosevelt's death, Churchill wrote, "I felt I was in contact with a very great man, who was a warm-hearted friend, and the foremost champion of the high causes which we served."

HOSTILITIES INCREASE

In the fall of 1941, tensions flared between the United States and Germany over activities in the Atlantic Ocean. German U-boats, or submarines, were targeting ships on the Atlantic sea-lanes. Roosevelt responded by authorizing U.S. destroyers—a type of warship—to hunt down the German subs. This policy was called **active defense**. On September 4, 1941, Germany fired on the U.S. destroyer *Greer*. The Germans claimed it was a case of mistaken identity, as they believed the ship to be a British vessel. President Roosevelt warned that any Axis ships that attacked American vessels in the North Atlantic would "do so at their own peril."

By October, U.S. Navy ships were providing escorts for civilian cargo vessels carrying war materials to Great Britain. This angered the Germans, who clearly saw the United States as aiding and supporting their enemy. In the early morning of October 31, a German U-boat sank the U.S.S. *Reuben James*, killing 115 crewmen. Americans were outraged. The United States appeared to be on the brink of entering the war. However, it would take a shocking attack from the other side of the world to ultimately push the United States into battle.

HISTORICAL THINKING

1. **READING CHECK** How did Germany's attack on the Soviet Union affect Roosevelt's foreign policy and American public opinion about the war?
2. **INTERPRET MAPS** Along which German troop path were frictions and fighting the fiercest? Why do you think this was the case?
3. **EVALUATE** How did the Atlantic Charter seek to promote global peace?
4. **DETERMINE CHRONOLOGY** What events on the Atlantic Ocean heightened U.S.-German tensions to near-conflict?

CST 3 Students use a variety of maps and documents to interpret human movement, including major patterns of domestic and international migration, changing environmental preferences and settlement patterns, the frictions that develop between population groups, and the diffusion of ideas, technological innovations, and goods.

CHAPTER A THREATENING WORLD

12 REVIEW

VOCABULARY

For each pair of vocabulary words, write a sentence that explains the connection between the words.

1. **rearmament; pacifism** HSS 11.7.1
   Germany moved toward rearmament, while pacifism was strong in the United States.
2. **Third Reich; Gestapo** HSS 11.7.1
3. **Munich Agreement; appeasement** HSS 11.7.1
4. **nonaggression pact; belligerent** HSS 11.7.1
5. **embargo; arsenal** HSS 11.7.1
6. **purge; Long March** HSS 11.7.1

READING STRATEGY

COMPARE AND CONTRAST

Comparing and contrasting can help readers form a deeper understanding of concepts and events. Both Nazi Germany and Japan disrupted world peace in the 1930s and 1940s. Complete a Venn diagram to compare and contrast Nazi Germany and Japan. Include the following features:

single charismatic leader
desire for territorial conquest
disregard for established international laws
resentment over the outcome of World War I
lack of natural resources
policy of anti-Semitism
buildup of armed forces

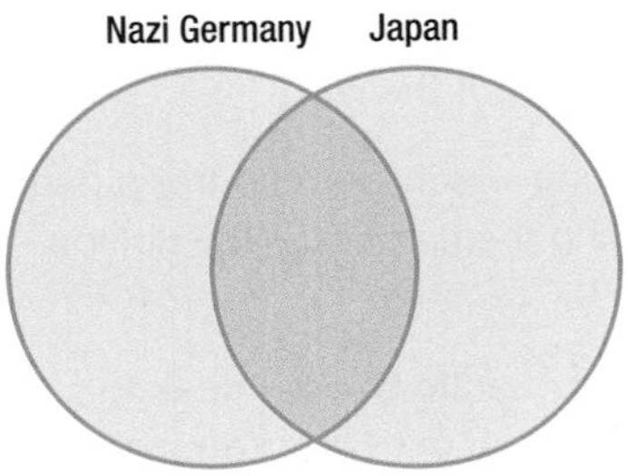

7. In what way do you think Nazi Germany and Japan were most alike? Support your opinion with details. HSS 11.7.1

MAIN IDEAS

Answer the following questions. Support your answers with evidence from the chapter.

8. What complex historical causes led to the rise of Adolf Hitler in Germany during the 1930s? **LESSON 1.1** HSS HI 2
9. How did the views of President Roosevelt and a majority of Americans differ regarding involvement in the war? **LESSON 1.2** HSS 11.7
10. How did the German-Soviet nonaggression pact contribute to the outbreak of World War II? **LESSON 2.1** HSS HI 2
11. Why did Japan look upon China as a desirable target for invasion? **LESSON 2.2** HSS 11.7.1
12. How did President Roosevelt intend to make America an "arsenal of democracy"? **LESSON 3.1** HSS 11.7.1
13. How did the breaking of the German-Soviet nonaggression pact impact the debate between isolationists and interventionists in the United States? **LESSON 3.2** HSS HI 4

HISTORICAL THINKING

Answer the following questions. Support your answers with evidence from the chapter.

14. **DETERMINE CHRONOLOGY** What 1940 military events preceded the Battle of Britain? HSS HI 1
15. **EVALUATE** How did changes to the Neutrality Act over the years lead to greater U.S. involvement in the war effort? HSS 11.7.1
16. **SYNTHESIZE** How did the onset of World War II help bring about the Atlantic Charter? HSS 11.7.1
17. **DRAW CONCLUSIONS** Why do you think so many dictators were able to rise to power during the years before World War II? HSS HI 4
18. **FORM AND SUPPORT OPINIONS** What events helped President Roosevelt build his case that Hitler posed a threat to the world unlike any other? Support your opinion. HSS 11.7.1

INTERPRET VISUALS

During the Battle of Britain, many Londoners took shelter in the subway stations of the London Underground as Nazi bombs rained from the sky over their city. Study this photograph and then answer the questions.

19. A slogan during the bombing of London was "Your courage, your cheerfulness . . . will bring us victory." How does this photo reflect that philosophy? HSS CST 3

20. What potential challenges do you see in living in these conditions for an extended period? HSS CST 3

ANALYZE SOURCES

The Atlantic Charter, drafted in 1941 by Roosevelt and Churchill, consisted of eight general principles. Read the text of the eighth principle below. Then answer the questions that follow.

> Eighth, they [President Roosevelt and Prime Minister Churchill] believe that all of the nations of the world, for realistic as well as spiritual reasons must come to the abandonment of the use of force. Since no future peace can be maintained if land, sea or air armaments continue to be employed by nations which threaten, or may threaten, aggression outside of their frontiers, they believe, pending the establishment of a wider and permanent system of general security, that the disarmament of such nations is essential. They will likewise aid and encourage all other practicable measures which will lighten for peace-loving peoples the crushing burden of armaments.

21. What does the charter argue is "essential" to helping secure world peace? HSS HREP 1

22. Describe the complex cause and effect relationships between disarmament and peace. Support your answer with evidence from the text. HSS HI 2

CONNECT TO YOUR LIFE

23. **NARRATIVE** Reread the summary of the Atlantic Charter from the chapter. Sum up the ideals Churchill and Roosevelt expressed to the world. To what extent have those ideals become reality since the charter was written? Think of what you know about the world today. Choose one or more of the principles of the Atlantic Charter, and describe the state of that principle in the world today. HSS CST 1

TIPS

- Read the summary of the charter's principles, and state in your own words the principles and ideals expressed there.
- State the principle or principles you will compare with today's world—for example, the principle of not expanding territory, or of open trade among nations.
- Describe some aspect of the state of the world in terms of that principle.
- Use two or three vocabulary terms from the chapter in your narrative, if possible.
- Conclude your narrative with a summary of what exists now and how it could be changed to achieve the principle or principles you named.

CHAPTER 13

AMERICA IN WORLD WAR II

1941–1945

HISTORICAL THINKING How did World War II and the Holocaust impact Americans and the world?

CRITICAL VIEWING During the Battle of Iwo Jima, an island near the Japanese coast, U.S. Marines took control of Mount Suribachi, the highest point of the island. In celebration, soldiers raised the U.S. flag at the top of the peak—twice. The second time, Joseph Rosenthal captured this image of the flag-raising, which won him a Pulitzer Prize and became one of the most iconic photos of World War II. What do you think the photo symbolized to Americans on the home front?

"War is a grim, cruel business,

. . . justified only as a means of sustaining the forces of good against those of evil."

—General Dwight D. Eisenhower

CRITICAL VIEWING Navajo Code Talkers working with a U.S. Marine signal unit operate a portable radio in the jungles of Bougainville Island in the South Pacific. What does this photo reveal about the conditions of this military campaign?

The Code Talkers of WORLD WAR II

When U.S. Marines disembarked onto Japanese-occupied beaches in the Pacific Islands during World War II, the battle scenes were unimaginable. Fighting their way inch by inch through firestorms of artillery, the "bullets fell like deadly sleet," reported one Marine of his landing on Guam. Bombs nicknamed "daisy cutters" rained down, spraying shrapnel outward in all directions to cause maximum damage to vulnerable human bodies.

DEVELOPING THE NAVAJO CODE

Amidst the chaos, it was essential for different military units to maintain communication. Messages had to be passed quickly, accurately, cryptically, in a way the Japanese could not interpret. To do this job, the Marines relied on an elite group of fighters—the Code Talkers.

The idea of using a Native American language as a wartime code originated during World War I. By transmitting messages in Choctaw, U.S. forces were able to orchestrate a successful surprise attack against the German army. In the years following World War I, scholars from Germany, Japan, and other countries visited the United States and studied various Native American languages including Cherokee, Choctaw, and Comanche. Few people in the United States or Europe spoke or understood the Navajo language. Navajo is complex in both its structure and its pronunciation. It is a tonal language, meaning that the tone used to pronounce a word can completely change its meaning. In addition, Navajo was almost never written down—both the language and its wealth of traditional stories were passed along orally.

NAVAJO CODE WORDS

The Navajo language did not have words for the technology of 20th-century warfare. When devising the code, the men first thought of an object that could symbolize the word they wanted to encode, then they chose the Navajo word for that object. These are some of the words for engines of war in the Navajo code.

ENGLISH	NAVAJO	MEANING
dive bomber	gini	chicken hawk
observation plane	ne-ahs-jah	owl
aircraft carrier	tsidi-ne-ye-hi	bird carrier
bombs	a-ye-shi	eggs
amphibious vehicle	chal	frog
submarine	besh-lo	iron fish

One non-native speaker who did have a basic understanding of Navajo was Philip Johnston, a civil engineer who had lived on a Navajo reservation as a child with his missionary parents. It was Johnston who suggested to the Marines that the Navajo language could form the basis of a wartime code.

In 1942, the Marines launched the Navajo code project with 29 Native American recruits. They gathered at a base in California, where they were charged with creating the code. The team devised a system of word substitutions in which a different Navajo word would stand for each letter of the English alphabet. To avoid spelling every word out, commonly used military terms were assigned their own Navajo words. For example, "fighter plane" became *da-he-tih-hi*, or "hummingbird" in Navajo. To make the code even more unbreakable, it was not written down.

The men, who came to be known as Code Talkers, memorized every single word of the code and practiced until they could quickly translate messages from English into Navajo code and back again. Chester Nez, one of the original 29, claimed that the Navajo tradition of oral storytelling helped the Code Talkers hone their memorization skills.

In an early test of the Navajo code, a message was sent over the radio from one post to another using the coding machines that were in common use. Simultaneously, one Code Talker relayed the same message orally to another. The Marine officers estimated the message would take four hours to transmit and decode using the machine method. The Code Talkers did it in under three minutes.

CODE TALKERS AT WAR

The Navajo were the largest group of Code Talkers, with around 420 members. They fought in the Pacific. Members of the Comanche, Cherokee, Chippewa, Kiowa, Pawnee, Lakota, and other tribes served as Code Talkers in Europe and other war zones. Code Talkers worked in pairs as battlefield radio officers. They carried a 30-pound radio that had to be cranked to generate electricity. As one man cranked the radio, the other transmitted coded messages to another pair of Code Talkers elsewhere on the battlefield or on a transport ship. Working under the deafening tumult of battle, the Code Talkers had to maintain enough focus to quickly translate and transmit messages, and be prepared to take part in the fighting.

The Code Talkers served with courage and distinction wherever they were assigned. In the Pacific, the Navajo Code Talkers were instrumental in several U.S. victories, including the famous battle for the island of Iwo Jima. According to one Marine officer, "The entire operation was directed by Navajo code. During the two days that followed the initial landings I had six Navajo radio nets working around the clock. They sent and received over 800 messages without an error. Were it not for the Navajo Code Talkers, the Marines never would have taken Iwo Jima."

COMING HOME

The return to civilian life after the war was difficult for many soldiers, including the Code Talkers. In their fighting units they had been respected by their fellow soldiers and treated as equals. Back in

11.7.2 Explain U.S. and Allied wartime strategy, including the major battles of Midway, Normandy, Iwo Jima, Okinawa, and the Battle of the Bulge; 11.7.3 Identify the roles and sacrifices of individual American soldiers, as well as the unique contributions of the special fighting forces (e.g., the Tuskegee Airmen, the 442nd Regimental Combat team, the Navajo Code Talkers).

the United States, however, old prejudices were still in force. When Chester Nez returned to his home state of New Mexico after serving in the Marines, for example, he was not allowed to vote. Native Americans were not given the right to vote in that state until 1948.

Many of the returning Native American soldiers were also troubled by their experiences during the war, especially those that went against the traditions of their tribes. In his autobiography, Nez recalled being plagued with nightmares until he underwent a traditional ceremony called the Enemy Way that helped him return to the Right Way—a sense of balance between the physical and spiritual worlds.

The situation was made worse by the fact that the Code Talkers could not reveal the pivotal role they had played in so many hard-fought battles. The existence of Native American codes was kept secret until 1968, because the government did not want to reveal any possible keys to the only unbroken oral code from World War II.

After the work of the Code Talkers was declassified, or no longer declared an official secret, the soldiers were finally recognized for their true contributions to the war effort. In July 2001, the four surviving Code Talkers of the original 29 received the Congressional Gold Medal in a ceremony in Washington, D.C.

Navajo Code Talker Chester Nez was the last living member of the U.S. Marine Corps 382nd Platoon, comprised of 29 Navajo Code Talkers. A proud recipient of a Congressional Gold Medal (shown below) from President George W. Bush in 2001, Nez passed away in 2014, but the story of the Code Talkers lives on.

PRIMARY SOURCE

Today we mark a moment of shared history and shared victory. We recall a story that all Americans can celebrate and every American should know. It is a story of ancient people called to serve in a modern war. It is a story of one unbreakable oral code of the Second World War, messages traveling by field radio on Iwo Jima in the very language heard across the Colorado plateau centuries ago.

—President George W. Bush, 2001

OTHER CODES IN WORLD WAR II

While the Navajo worked to create a unique American code, others in the U.S. military were racing to break the German and Japanese codes. Like the non-Navajo codes used by the United States, the German and Japanese forms of encryption were machine-based.

The Germans used a machine known as the Enigma to create their coded messages. An operator would type a message in plain text on the Enigma's keyboard, and a series of notched wheels, or rotors, within the machine would turn, encoding the message into a seemingly random jumble of letters. The message would then be sent via radio to another operator who would use an Enigma machine to decode it. The second operator would have to know the exact sequence of rotor settings in order to correctly decrypt the message. The rotor settings for each day—called the daily key—were listed in codebooks that each Enigma operator possessed. Not surprisingly, these codebooks were some of the most closely guarded items of the war. The Enigma code was eventually penetrated by British code breakers building on earlier work by Polish intelligence.

American code breakers focused their efforts on the Japanese code known as Purple. The Japanese had purchased an Enigma machine from the Germans in the early 1930s, then added refinements to make it easier to use and harder to decrypt. Like the Enigma, the Purple machine required a daily key. Over the course of the war, U.S. code breakers were able to identify certain patterns in the way the Japanese daily keys were determined, and by the end of the war, Purple was broken.

World War II also saw the beginning of the digital age of encryption. The Allies quickly recognized the need for a way to communicate securely via telephone between the United States, London, and other locations. In cooperation with the U.S. Army Signal Corps, Bell Laboratories devised a digital method of encoding voice signals traveling over telephone wires. The code, called Sigsaly, was in use from 1943 to 1946, but it was not declassified until 1975. It was never broken.

CRITICAL VIEWING Introduced on German U-boats sailing in the Atlantic Ocean in February 1942, the code produced by the MK 4 Enigma was not broken until December 1942. The cracking of German cypher codes by Allied intelligence was a major achievement in cryptanalysis, or code breaking, and played an important role in the outcome of the North Atlantic U-boat engagements during World War II. How might the course of the war have been different if the Enigma's code had not been broken?

THINK ABOUT IT

How did developments in communication during World War II affect its participants and outcome?

11.7.6 Describe major developments in aviation, weaponry, communication, and medicine and the war's impact on the location of American industry and use of resources; HI 4 Students understand the meaning, implication, and impact of historical events and recognize that events could have taken other directions.

Intelligent, rebellious, and quirky, Alan Turing, represented here by actor Benedict Cumberbatch in the 2014 movie *The Imitation Game*, was also gay. British law at the time made same-sex relationships illegal, which prevented Turing from being open about his personal life. But he found social acceptance at Kings College in Cambridge. In 1952, however, Turing was arrested and charged with "indecency" after a brief relationship with a man. He did not deny the charges.

According to Andrew Hodges, a mathematician and author of the Turing biography that inspired *The Imitation Game*, "When [Turing] was arrested, the first thing he said was he thought that this shouldn't be against the law." Defiantly mocking the absurdity of his arrest, Turing traveled to Norway and the Mediterranean, where the gay rights movement was beginning to gain momentum. However, 1950s British law considered homosexuality a security risk, and Turing's arrest and conviction cost him his job and the ability to travel. Hodges believes these consequences ultimately led Turing to suicide at the age of 41.

Homosexuality was not fully decriminalized for adults in Great Britain until the 1980s. In 2009, British Prime Minister Gordon Brown publicly apologized for Turing's "utterly unfair" treatment on behalf of the British government. Four years later, Queen Elizabeth II granted him a royal pardon.

FROM CODES TO COMPUTERS

The history of code breaking is entwined with the history of computers. Alan Turing, the mathematician in charge of Britain's cryptanalysis department during World War II, is viewed by many as the father of the modern computer. He played a key role in cracking the Enigma code by helping to develop an electromechanical machine called the bombe. An improvement on a pre-war Polish machine, the bombe greatly sped up the rate at which codes could be deciphered. In 1943, British code breakers designed another machine called the Colossus, which, like early computers, used vacuum tubes to control electric current. The Colossus could do basic mathematical calculations. It could also quickly perform the repetitive operations necessary to identify the patterns found in encrypted messages.

Interest in Britain's code-breaking operation, and in Alan Turing, has been awakened in recent years by historical accounts, novels, and the popular 2014 film *The Imitation Game*. It is less well known that by the end of the war, the U.S. Navy had developed electronic machines that were similar to the Colossus but had a greater number of vacuum tubes—and thus greater computing power. Also like the Colossus, these lacked the memory of a digital computer.

Further advancements in computer technology would come as researchers developed vacuum-tube computers that could work more quickly and run a greater variety of programs. Eventually, of course, digital technology would rapidly make computers much more powerful, versatile, and accessible to users outside the military and scientific communities.

A Devastating Attack

Which of the freedoms you enjoy as an American citizen do you value the most? In 1941, President Franklin Roosevelt identified four freedoms he felt were the most essential—and worth fighting for. After an unprovoked attack, Americans would be doing just that.

FOUR FREEDOMS

In his annual address to Congress in January 1941, President Roosevelt named and discussed "four essential human freedoms" that were at stake in World War II. As a result, Roosevelt's address became known as the "Four Freedoms" speech.

> *In the future days, which we seek to make secure, we look forward to a world founded upon four essential human freedoms.*
>
> *The first is freedom of speech and expression—everywhere in the world.*
>
> *The second is freedom of every person to worship God in his own way—everywhere in the world.*
>
> *The third is freedom from want—which, translated into world terms, means economic understandings which will secure to every nation a healthy peacetime life for its inhabitants—everywhere in the world.*
>
> *The fourth is freedom from fear—which, translated into world terms, means a world-wide reduction of armaments to such a point and in such a thorough fashion that no nation will be in a position to commit an act of physical aggression against any neighbor—anywhere in the world.*
>
> —President Franklin D. Roosevelt, Annual Address to Congress, January 6, 1941

Roosevelt used his speech to frame the war as a conflict about fundamental values. After the United States entered the conflict, his words inspired artist Norman Rockwell to create four illustrations (at right) for the *Saturday Evening Post*, a popular weekly magazine, that translated the war aims into scenes of everyday American life.

A DAY OF INFAMY

Within a year of Roosevelt's speech, the United States would go to war against Japan to defend the freedoms he described. Relations between the two countries had long been strained. The United States had watched Japan's aggression and expansion into China with growing concern. This apprehension had increased when Japan signed the Tripartite Pact with Germany and Italy in September 1940. In an effort to put a halt to Japan's expansionism, Roosevelt froze Japanese business interests in the United States in 1941. He also established an embargo on essential goods such as oil to Japan. Many believed war between the United States and Japan was imminent. But most U.S. military analysts expected the Japanese would probably attack a European colony in the South Pacific, with an outside chance they would attack the United States in the Philippines. The U.S. military never imagined the Japanese would be bold enough to strike Hawaii.

The Japanese had planned their attack for months, and their goal was to destroy the U.S. Pacific fleet. So, in late November, a large convoy of Japanese battleships, destroyers, aircraft carriers, and cruisers headed toward the U.S. naval base at Pearl Harbor on the island of Oahu in Hawaii. On the morning of December 7, 1941, the fleet was within 200 miles of Pearl Harbor, and Japanese bomber planes took off from the aircraft carriers to launch the attack. Military personnel in Pearl Harbor had no idea they were in danger until the planes appeared on radar. And even then, they thought the planes were American fighters. In addition, the Japanese had deliberately attacked on a Sunday morning, when security at the base was likely to be more relaxed.

11.7.1 Examine the origins of American involvement in the war, with an emphasis on the events that precipitated the attack on Pearl Harbor; 11.7.4 Analyze Roosevelt's foreign policy during World War II (e.g., Four Freedoms speech).

Norman Rockwell's paintings of the Four Freedoms appeared in the *Saturday Evening Post* in March and April 1943. The U.S. government printed and sold posters of the popular paintings in a campaign that raised more than $132 million for the war effort

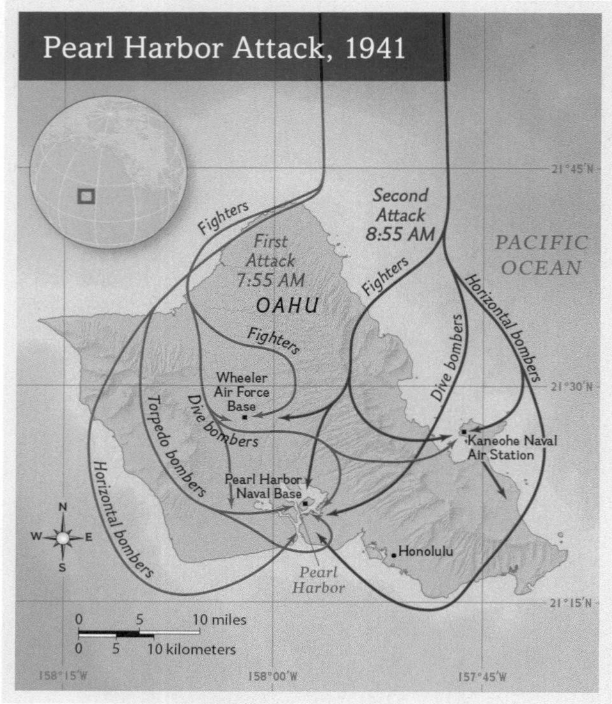

Smoke billows from U.S. battleships anchored in Pearl Harbor following the Japanese attack on December 7, 1941. The map on the left shows the two waves of the attack carried out by 353 fighter, dive bomber, torpedo bomber, and horizontal bomber planes. The planes launched the assault from 6 aircraft carriers north of Pearl Harbor.

The assault came in two waves, with the first bombers arriving shortly before 8 a.m., and the second wave arriving an hour later. The planes rained their bombs and bullets down on U.S. battleships anchored in the harbor and American military aircraft sitting on the ground. Battleships, including the U.S.S. *Arizona*, were completely destroyed in the attack. In the end, the Japanese demolished or damaged nearly 20 American warships and about 200 planes. Far worse, more than 2,300 Americans were killed. The Japanese lost fewer than 100 men.

Roosevelt addressed Congress and the American people by radio the next day saying, "Yesterday, December 7, 1941—a date which will live in infamy—the United States of America was suddenly and deliberately attacked by naval and air forces of the Empire of Japan." **Infamy** refers to an extremely shameful or evil act. Roosevelt called for a declaration of war, and Congress—with only one dissenting vote—agreed. On December 8, Congress declared war on Japan. Three days later, Germany and Italy honored their allegiance to Japan and declared war on the United States. As you know, many Americans had been opposed to joining the war. But the bombing of Pearl Harbor had stunned the nation and instantly turned the tide of American opinion in favor of the war. Americans took their place among the Allied powers—including Great Britain, the Soviet Union, and China—in the fight against the Axis powers Germany, Italy, and Japan.

BATAAN DEATH MARCH

Within hours of the attack on Pearl Harbor, Japanese forces struck the Philippines, which was designated a commonwealth, or territory, of the United States in 1935. The United States Armed Forces in the Far East (USAFFE) had been mobilized earlier in case of attack and headquartered in the Philippines under the command of American general Douglas MacArthur. You may remember that President Hoover called on MacArthur to restore order when World War I veterans marched on Washington, D.C., in 1932.

The majority of the forces were Filipinos, but American troops also made up the ranks. However, the troops were unprepared for the full-scale attack the Japanese had planned. The Japanese air force bombed airfields, bases, harbors, and shipyards, and approximately 56,500 soldiers from the Japanese Army came ashore at Luzon, the largest island of the Philippines. By January 2, 1942, Japanese troops had taken Manila, the country's capital. Unable to defend the territory, the USAFFE strategically retreated to the jungles of the Bataan Peninsula.

11.7 Students analyze America's participation in World War II.

Despite suffering from disease and starvation and fighting without any air support, the USAFFE troops defended Bataan for 99 days. Then, in March 1942, Roosevelt ordered MacArthur to leave the Philippines. The official story was that Roosevelt wanted MacArthur to go to Australia to coordinate the war effort. The truth was that MacArthur was too valuable an officer for the United States to lose, especially at the beginning of a war, so he was brought to safety. The general left the Philippines but vowed, "I shall return." Despite constant bombardment, the soldiers continued to fight under General Edward P. King, Jr., the Commanding General of the Luzon Force.

Finally, on April 9, King and his 75,000 Filipino and American troops surrendered to the Japanese. The troops were forced to march some 60 miles to their prison at Camp O'Donnell with no provisions for food, water, or shelter. Those who could no longer go on were beaten, bayoneted, shot, and in some cases, beheaded by their Japanese captors. Approximately 10,000 Filipinos and 750 Americans perished in what became known as the **Bataan Death March**.

Once imprisoned in Camp O'Donnell, another 20,000 Filipinos and 1,600 Americans died. A majority of the American prisoners were later transported in the hulls of unmarked vessels, known as "Hell Ships," to Japan, China, Formosa (present-day Taiwan), and Korea, where they worked as slave laborers. Thousands died on the ships and while in servitude. U.S. involvement in World War II had just begun, but Americans quickly realized it would take a lot of strength and resources to fight their formidable enemies.

HISTORICAL THINKING

1. **READING CHECK** What events brought on Japan's attack on Pearl Harbor?
2. **ANALYZE SOURCES** In Roosevelt's Four Freedoms speech, how did he frame American beliefs on both a personal and international level?
3. **DETERMINE CHRONOLOGY** What order of events took place within days of the attack on Pearl Harbor?
4. **INTERPRET MAPS** Based on the map, what conclusions can you draw about the attack?

CST 3 Students use a variety of maps and documents to interpret human movement, including major patterns of domestic and international migration, changing environmental preferences and settlement patterns, the frictions that develop between population groups, and the diffusion of ideas, technological innovations, and goods.

1.2 **MAIN IDEA** Americans in the military and at home contributed to the war effort during World War II.

GEARING UP FOR WAR

Once the United States entered the war, the country mobilized to prepare for it. World War II would require a massive buildup of resources to fight on both the Asian and European fronts.

THE WAR EFFORT

In order to gather the materials the country would need, President Roosevelt established the **War Production Board** in 1942. He called on automobile companies, such as Ford and General Motors, to build tanks and warplanes instead of passenger cars. Roosevelt knew these large corporations could fill the military's needs quickly and gave them the bulk of the work orders. He also offered the companies low-interest loans so they could convert their factories to war production and assured factory owners they would make a profit.

To help pay for the war supplies, Congress passed the **Revenue Act of 1942**, which increased taxes on individuals and corporations. However, this measure only provided about 45 percent of the funds needed to meet expenses. So the government issued **war bonds**. Citizens could purchase a bond for 75 percent of its face value and later cash it in with interest. To induce Americans to buy war bonds, the government appealed to people's emotions. Remember the illustrations Norman Rockwell created after Roosevelt's Four Freedoms speech? These illustrations became a centerpiece of the bond drive. By the war's end, about half of the nation's population had purchased bonds.

New developments in various fields also aided the war effort. In aviation, the powerful B-24 bomber helped the Allies defend against German submarines. **Napalm**, a thick, flammable substance used in bombs to cause and spread fires, first appeared in World War II. Strides in medical technology and, in particular, the development of penicillin, helped save soldiers' lives. **Penicillin** is an antibiotic, or bacteria killer, made from mold and used to treat infections and disease.

Industrial demands fueled by wartime needs helped end the Depression and set a model for an expanded governmental role in regulating the economy after the war. The defense-related industries became especially critical to California's economy, helping drive other developments in the manufacturing sector and in science and technology. The state played a huge role in America's successful war effort and built more military installations than any other state. The number of military bases in California increased from 16 to 41, more than those of the next 5 states combined.

MILITARY SUPPORT

New military bases were definitely needed. Six million Americans volunteered for service between 1942 and 1945, and the country drafted another 10 million men. The draft also conscripted conscientious objectors—those who opposed the war on religious grounds. However, COs, as they were sometimes called, were allowed to participate in public works projects or serve in other nonmilitary ways.

General **George Marshall**, the chief of staff of the U.S. Army in 1939, was largely responsible for training the troops and selecting commanders for the war. He put Lesley J. McNair in charge of the Army Ground Forces once the United States entered the war. McNair dedicated himself to ensuring the troops received the most realistic combat training possible. He staged huge mock battles and simulated real wartime situations.

Though the military training the troops received was similar, men from minority groups did not fight with white soldiers. Instead they were placed in segregated troops. Nevertheless, these troops made great sacrifices and demonstrated valor and

11.7.6 Describe major developments in aviation, weaponry, communication, and medicine and the war's impact on the location of American industry and use of resources; 11.8.5 Describe the increased powers of the presidency in response to the Great Depression, World War II, and the Cold War.

Tuskegee Airmen National Historical Museum Detroit, Michigan

Toni Frissell photographed a group of Tuskegee Airmen receiving instructions for a mission at the Ramitelli airfield in Italy in 1945. Throughout the war, the Airmen played an important role, escorting allied bombers with one of the lowest loss records among escort fighter groups. They also flew about 15,500 combat missions. In recognition of their outstanding record and sacrifices, the Tuskegee Airmen received more than 150 Distinguished Flying Crosses.

distinction. The **Tuskegee Airmen** was a squadron of African-American pilots who trained in Tuskegee, Alabama, and shot down a dozen Nazi planes during an invasion in Italy in 1943. That same year saw the formation of the **442nd Infantry Regimental Combat Team**, a military unit that consisted entirely of Japanese Americans. The 442nd successfully fought in Europe in 1944 and rescued a regiment of Texas soldiers surrounded by German forces.

In April 1941, the U.S. government formed American Volunteer Groups to help the Nationalist government of China in its struggle against Japan. The "**Flying Tigers**" was the only American Volunteer Group to take part in combat. It sprang into action to help defend Burma and China against the Japanese after the attack on Pearl Harbor. Volunteer pilots from the American and Chinese air forces made up the Flying Tigers.

As you know, the Navajo provided an indispensable service to American forces during World War II. After it became clear the Japanese were intercepting and deciphering coded U.S. messages, the Marines enlisted Navajo men to transmit and translate messages using their native language. The men became known as the **Navajo Code Talkers**. The Navajo language was so difficult—and so few people spoke it—that the Japanese could not decode the messages. The Code Talkers were a major factor in the eventual Allied victory.

The military didn't welcome all Americans. Officials screened out and rejected homosexuals, though gay

11.7.3 Identify the roles and sacrifices of individual American soldiers, as well as the unique contributions of the special fighting forces (e.g., the Tuskegee Airmen, the 442nd Regimental Combat team, the Navajo Code Talkers).

men and women still served in the armed forces in significant numbers. Some were tolerated because of the war effort, and their fellow soldiers often came to appreciate their service. However, many other gays were imprisoned or dishonorably discharged when their sexual orientation was discovered. That persecution set the stage for increased postwar oppression and organized resistance.

ON THE HOME FRONT

At home, World War II had many long-lasting effects. Increased production made employment skyrocket, resulting in 17 million new jobs—including jobs for women and minority groups. Income for the average American nearly doubled as well, largely as a result of the overtime factory workers logged in. The new jobs drew enormous numbers of migrants from all over the country to urban areas and eventually spurred the creation of expansive suburbs, highways, and shopping complexes.

The war also drew immigrants to the United States. In 1942, the government sponsored the **Bracero Program**, which continued until 1964 and was designed primarily to import Mexican laborers to replace native-born agricultural and transportation industry workers who were mobilizing for war. California particularly benefited from the braceros, which means "strong armed ones." Importing more than 40,000 workers in 1942 alone, the state came to depend on the agricultural laborers who came through the program. By the end of the war, California had the fastest population growth of any state—and an increasingly diversified society.

Meanwhile, Americans at home faced many everyday challenges. In 1942, Roosevelt enacted the **Office of Price Administration** to help limit inflation and **ration**, or control, the supply of goods made available to the public. The military desperately needed items such as gas, rubber, and certain foods, so civilians were urged to cut back on driving and consume less sugar, coffee, and meat. To supplement their food supplies, the government encouraged people to plant victory gardens, or plots of land on which they could grow their own food. Almost 20 million Americans planted victory gardens during the war. The gardens made people on the home front feel as if they were contributing to the war effort—much as the purchase of war bonds did.

Buying war bonds and planting victory gardens made people feel patriotic, but the stress of war was hard to avoid. Popular films and radio programs provided much needed distraction from the war. Diversions such as baseball games helped take people's minds off their worries as well. Some politicians had called for the suspension of major league baseball during the war, but Roosevelt disagreed. He explained that the game helped keep up people's morale. The **Office of War Information**, formed in 1942, also boosted Americans' spirits. The agency produced posters, photos, and films that celebrated the troops and encouraged Americans' support for the war.

Dorothy Harrell of the Rockford Peaches, 1944

THE ALL-AMERICAN GIRLS PROFESSIONAL BASEBALL LEAGUE

As young men were drafted into the armed services during the war, minor league baseball lost most of its players. Philip Wrigley, owner of the Chicago Cubs, decided that a female ball league might bring fans to the parks and help keep the sport in the public eye. The result was the All-American Girls Professional Baseball League. After the athletes had been recruited and teams organized, the League first stepped up to the plate in 1943. The players were accomplished pitchers, batters, and hitters, but organizers insisted that they also be "lady-like." They attended charm school and wore make-up, even on the field. The League was an enormous success, and the women kept playing until 1954, nearly a decade after the war ended.

11.7.5 Discuss the constitutional issues and impact of events on the U.S. home front, including the internment of Japanese Americans (e.g., *Fred Korematsu* v. *United States of America*) and the restrictions on German and Italian resident aliens; the response of the administration to Hitler's atrocities against Jews and other groups; the roles of women in military production; and the roles and growing political demands of African Americans; 11.7.6 Describe major developments in aviation, weaponry, communication, and medicine and the war's impact on the location of American industry and use of resources.

STRUGGLES AT HOME

As you've read, wartime factory work created new and higher-paying job opportunities for African Americans and other minorities. However, opening up the wage-labor market raised their expectations about what else they might be able to achieve. The contrast between the ideology of the war effort and the racial segregation of the armed forces sparked multiple efforts at minority equality and, in time, for civil rights activism after the war.

In 1941, a letter printed in the African-American newspaper, the *Pittsburgh Courier*, launched the "Double V" campaign. The campaign called on African Americans to fight for victory against fascism abroad and victory against racism at home. That same year, **A. Philip Randolph**, the head of the largely African-American **Brotherhood of Sleeping Car Porters** union, planned a march in Washington, D.C., to focus international attention on the hypocrisy of undemocratic practices at home while the country was poised to fight for democracy abroad. The march ultimately prompted Roosevelt to sign **Executive Order 8802** in 1941 to desegregate military-related industries.

But wartime racial discrimination went beyond the military and the workplace. In 1943, white shipyard workers attacked African-American workers in Mobile, Alabama, and a race riot between whites and blacks in Detroit resulted in more than 30 deaths and 700 injuries. That same year, Mexican Americans dressed in zoot suits also came under attack in Los Angeles, California. A zoot suit is a flamboyant man's suit that features wide-legged trousers and long jackets with wide lapels. The outfits were a fad among many African Americans and Mexican Americans. Many people considered those who wore zoot suits to be thugs.

The white American sailors who arrived in Los Angeles on leave in 1943 particularly objected to zoot suits—and the young Mexican Americans dressed in them. Tensions had long been growing between the two groups, who often fought and exchanged insults. Finally, the **Zoot Suit Riots** erupted in May when mobs of sailors attacked the zoot-suiters, beating the young men and tearing off their suits. Similar attacks continued for more than a week. During this time, the police sometimes stood by while the servicemen rampaged through the city. After the riots died down, a commission investigated the riots and identified racism as their central cause.

This photograph captured a couple of young African-American men, dressed in zoot suits, in 1943. During the war, the zoot suit became a part of the jazz world. Some people of color—including women—wore the suit to make a bold statement.

HISTORICAL THINKING

1. **READING CHECK** What measures did the U.S. government take to help pay for the war?
2. **SYNTHESIZE** What were some of the different ways in which civilians helped contribute to the war effort?
3. **MAKE INFERENCES** Why do you think African Americans, Japanese Americans, and Native Americans wanted to fight in the war?
4. **DRAW CONCLUSIONS** Why did Randolph call the treatment of African Americans at home hypocritical?

11.10.1 Explain how demands of African Americans helped produce a stimulus for civil rights, including President Roosevelt's ban on racial discrimination in defense industries in 1941, and how African Americans' service in World War II produced a stimulus for President Truman's decision to end segregation in the armed forces in 1948.

1.3 **MAIN IDEA** Women's participation in the workforce and the military greatly increased during World War II.

WOMEN AND THE WAR EFFORT

Throughout American history, women had stepped up in times of crisis but never in the numbers seen during World War II. Their reward was satisfaction in a job well done and pride in serving their country.

NEW OPPORTUNITIES

World War II provided women with an unprecedented opportunity to enter the workforce. Many men left their jobs to fight in the war, and women filled their places in factories and offices. The defense industries, particularly in aircraft and munitions, needed workers. These businesses employed 6 million women as welders, electricians, and assembly line workers during the war.

Some women also decided to join the military and served in the few branches the military allowed women to join. The establishment of the **Women's Auxiliary Army Corps (WAAC)** in 1942 offered women a chance to participate in noncombat roles as radio operators and air-traffic controllers, for example. Women who joined the WAAC earned a salary but were not given all the benefits men in the military received. However, within just a few months of the corps's establishment, more than 25,000 women had signed up. As a result, the army dropped the "auxiliary" designation in 1943, and members of the Women's Army Corps (WAC) received full U.S. Army benefits, comparable to those of male soldiers. A total of about 150,000 women served all over the world, including in war zones.

The navy equivalent of the WAC was the **Women Accepted for Volunteer Emergency Service (WAVES)**, which was also established in 1942. About 27,000 women joined in its first year. Unlike WACs, WAVES received full benefits from the beginning as well as the same salary as men. However, WAVES were not allowed to serve abroad. Members worked in fields such as aviation, medicine, intelligence, science, and technology. About one-third of WAVES were involved with naval aviation, while others performed duties such as calculating bomb trajectories or paths, and working as meteorologists. A total of about 100,000 women served as WAVES during the war.

By enabling women to fill noncombat roles, WACs and WAVES helped free up additional men for combat duties. These branches of the service also allowed women to take on vital and complicated responsibilities in the war effort. Though male officers at first anticipated that their female counterparts would only perform clerical duties, the women's dedication and capability soon changed the male officers' minds.

UNFAIR TREATMENT

Even as women sacrificed and worked hard for the war effort, they experienced unfair treatment in their new jobs. Some employers didn't even want to hire them. They didn't believe women had the strength or ability to do the jobs. Furthermore, many employers feared the women would distract male workers and prevent them from doing their work.

Another form of unfair treatment was **wage discrimination**, or receiving lower pay for the same job based on gender, race, or ethnicity. Though women who worked in defense industries generally made more money than they did working in other jobs, they still made far less than their male coworkers. In 1945, for example, a woman working in a factory earned an average of $32 a week, while a man made an average of $55—even though a law required equal pay for equal work. Some companies dodged the law by reclassifying higher-paying jobs into a lower pay scale or assigning women to lower-level positions.

11.7.5 Discuss the constitutional issues and impact of events on the U.S. home front, including the internment of Japanese Americans (e.g., *Fred Korematsu* v. *United States of America*) and the restrictions on German and Italian resident aliens; the response of the administration to Hitler's atrocities against Jews and other groups; the roles of women in military production; and the roles and growing political demands of African Americans.

In 1943, the Women Airforce Service Pilots (WASP) program formed to train women to fly military aircraft for noncombat purposes. The WASP in this photo is about to take off.

After **demobilization**, or the release of soldiers from military duty, more women remained in the workforce than had done so following World War I. Still, most were forced to leave. Employers notified women they would have to give up their jobs to the returning soldiers. Employers—and society as a whole—still believed a woman's place was in the home. Advertisers also promoted a return to traditional women's roles.

As a result, even though the majority of women wanted to keep their jobs after the war, most either had to return to their roles as homemakers or take lower-paying jobs. By 1947, women's presence in blue-collar jobs had sunk to its prewar level. Nevertheless, women had briefly enjoyed a degree of liberation and financial security in their newfound workplace roles. Unfortunately, not all segments of American society would experience as much freedom as women had.

PRIMARY SOURCE

You have just made the change from peacetime pursuits to wartime tasks—from the individualism of civilian life to the anonymity of mass military life. You have given up comfortable homes, highly paid positions, leisure. You have taken off silk and put on khaki. And all for essentially the same reason. You have a debt and a date—a debt to democracy and a date with destiny.

—from Director Oveta Culp Hobby's remarks to the first WAAC officer training class, 1942

HISTORICAL THINKING

1. **READING CHECK** What new opportunities were available to women during World War II, and how do those opportunities compare to those woman have today?
2. **COMPARE AND CONTRAST** How were the jobs of WACs and WAVES alike and different?
3. **MAKE INFERENCES** Why do you think women wanted to keep their jobs in the defense industries after the war ended?
4. **EVALUATE** What tone did Hobby use in her remarks to the WAACs, and why did she use that tone?

HI 3 Students interpret past events and issues within the context in which an event unfolded rather than solely in terms of present-day norms and values.

ROSIE THE RIVETER 1942–1945

"She's making history, / working for victory / Rosie the Riveter."
— from "Rosie the Riveter," a song by Redd Evans and Jacob Loeb, 1943

Rosie the Riveter came to life in a song—some of its lyrics are quoted above. The song was a hit, and its title came to represent the millions of American women who took on the industrial jobs that were vacated as more and more men joined the war effort during World War II. Rosie became part of a U.S. government campaign to recruit women into the workforce. The campaign worked, and the women excelled in their new jobs. As the song says, "That little frail [woman] can do more than a male / will do."

Mary Doyle Keefe, the model for Rockwell's illustration, was actually a petite young woman. Rockwell wanted to portray his Rosie as strong and powerful. Still, he apologized to Keefe for making her so brawny.

A TALE OF TWO ROSIES

The face of Rosie the Riveter that most people were familiar with during the war was the one featured on the cover of the *Saturday Evening Post*. But this Rosie is no "little frail." In Norman Rockwell's painting, she's a muscular, monumental figure, based on the style Italian Renaissance artist Michelangelo used to depict biblical prophets in Rome's Sistine Chapel.

Apparently on her lunch break, Rosie holds a sandwich aloft and balances her riveting gun and lunchbox, etched with her name, on her lap. Her foot rests squarely on *Mein Kampf*, or *My Struggle*, Adolf Hitler's autobiography, in which he outlined his anti-Semitic views. Rosie's contempt for the German dictator and confidence that he will be defeated—with her help—are clear.

11.7.5 Discuss the constitutional issues and impact of events on the U.S. home front, including the internment of Japanese Americans (e.g., *Fred Korematsu* v. *United States of America*) and the restrictions on German and Italian resident aliens; the response of the administration to Hitler's atrocities against Jews and other groups; the roles of women in military production; and the roles and growing political demands of African Americans.

This real-life Rosie is working on an A-31 Vengeance dive bomber at a plant in Tennessee. She's adjusting the wheel well preparatory to installing the plane's landing gear, one of many tasks that made up the assembly-line production of the bombers.

Rockwell fashioned his subject after a 19-year-old neighbor named Mary Doyle Keefe. The model for another iconic image of Rosie is unknown or, at least, contested. This image was one of a series of posters created for the Westinghouse Electric Corporation in 1942 and designed to boost workers' morale. The poster of a young woman in a red-and-white bandana, flexing her arm, and exclaiming, "We can do it!" only appeared in the Westinghouse factory and only for a couple of weeks. Now fast-forward to 1982, when the poster was rediscovered and became a symbol of the movement to expand women's rights. Although the woman in the poster wasn't given a name in the 1940s, for many people today, she is Rosie the Riveter.

REAL-LIFE ROSIES

Of course, behind the song, painting, and poster were millions of women eager to do their part for the war effort. As you've read, many of these real-life Rosies worked in the aircraft and munitions industries. In some cases, they apparently did their jobs too well. A foreman in one plant told the women not to work so fast because when the war ended, the men would get their jobs back. And the men, he said, weren't nearly as productive as they were.

Many of the women came to California to find jobs during the war. One named Bettye worked the graveyard shift—which began at midnight—building B-17 bomber planes. She entered the enormous plant through a tunnel covered in camouflage. Once there, Bettye and another woman worked as a team to install rivets into the part of the plane from which the turret gun, or multishot firearm, would be fired. Her teammate stood on the outside of the compartment and drove in the rivet, which is a permanent metal fastener that looks something like a thick screw. Bettye stood on the inside and bucked the end of the rivet, pounding and flattening it. But she insisted that the process "wasn't as easy as it looked." The "skin" of the plane was fairly thin. If the operator of the rivet gun didn't hold it steady, the gun would drill a bigger-than-desired hole in the plane, and a larger rivet would have to be installed. And that, Bettye said, would weaken the whole plane.

For many of the real-life Rosies, the work provided an experience of the world they may never have had otherwise. They met and worked alongside women from many different backgrounds and ethnicities. And the work gave them independence, an income—which was certainly welcome after the deprivations of the Depression—and a sense of pride and patriotism. As one Rosie named Bonnie remarked, "I wouldn't have missed the experience for anything. And we did do good. We won the war."

HISTORICAL THINKING

1. **READING CHECK** What purpose did Rosie the Riveter serve during World War II?
2. **MAKE INFERENCES** Why do you think the women's rights movement adopted the Westinghouse Rosie poster as a symbol?
3. **DRAW CONCLUSIONS** What did Bonnie suggest when she said, "We won the war"?

11.7.6 Describe major developments in aviation, weaponry, communication, and medicine and the war's impact on the location of American industry and use of resources.

1.5 **MAIN IDEA** Responding to the attack on Pearl Harbor and fears of invasion from the Pacific, the U.S. government forcibly moved thousands of Japanese Americans to camps for the duration of the war.

JAPANESE AMERICAN INTERNMENT

Have you ever been unfairly accused of something? During World War II, the U.S. government viewed Japanese Americans as a threat and removed them from their homes.

EXECUTIVE ORDER 9066

Entry into the war drew most Americans together in their support for the Allied cause, but others quickly discovered their heritage marked them as objects of fear. On December 8, 1941—the day after the Pearl Harbor attack—President Roosevelt issued a series of executive orders that established the **Enemy Alien Control Program**. An **enemy alien** is someone whose loyalty to the nation is suspect. Many persons of Italian and German origin who were in the United States when World War II began were classified as enemy aliens and had their rights restricted. Thousands were **interned**, or confined in prisons or camps for military or political reasons, while many others were sent back to Germany or Italy.

Photographer Ansel Adams took this image of Japanese Americans waiting for lunch at California's Manzanar Camp in 1943.

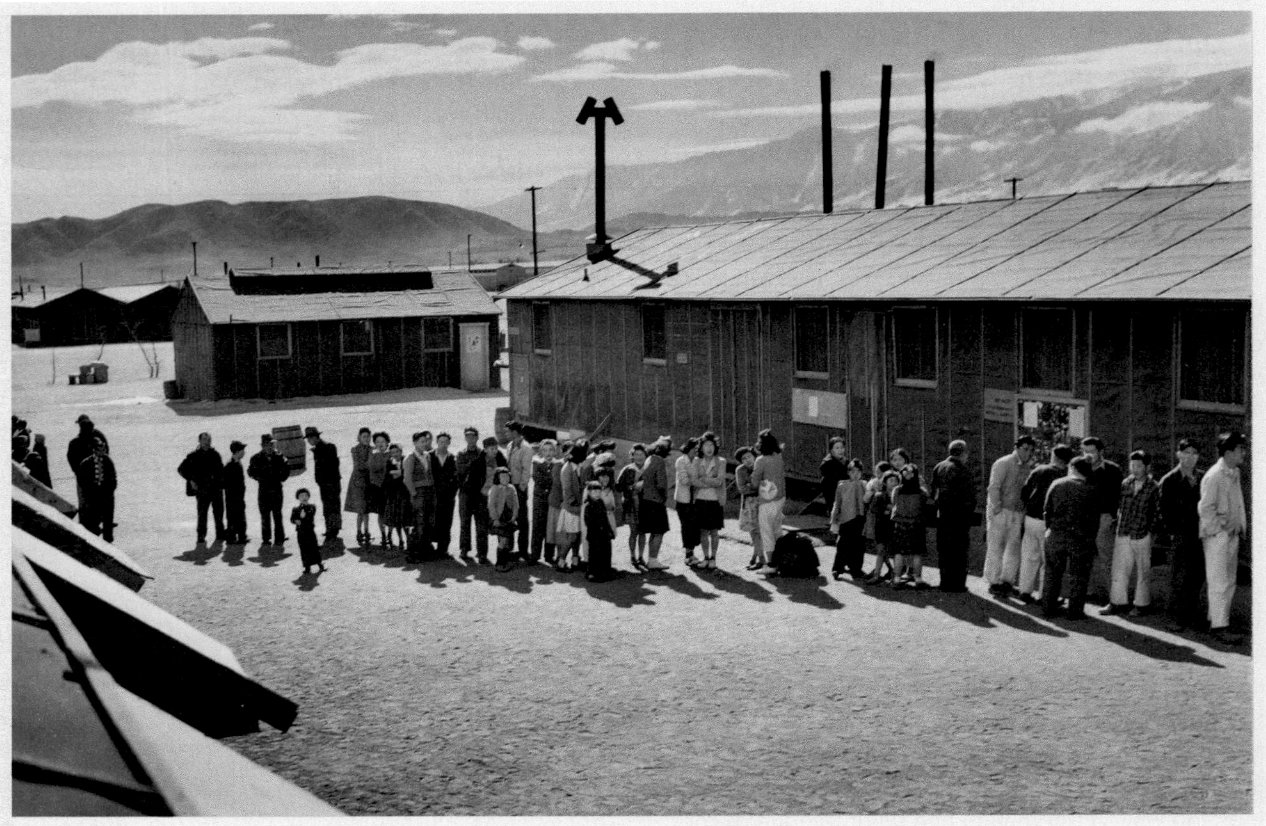

11.7.5 Discuss the constitutional issues and impact of events on the U.S. home front, including the internment of Japanese Americans (e.g., *Fred Korematsu* v. *United States of America*) and the restrictions on German and Italian resident aliens; the response of the administration to Hitler's atrocities against Jews and other groups; the roles of women in military production; and the roles and growing political demands of African Americans.

Japanese Americans were also classified as enemy aliens and interned. Public opinion had turned sharply against Japanese Americans after the attack on Pearl Harbor. Unlike the Italians and Germans who were interned, more than 60 percent of those with Japanese ancestry who were relocated to camps were **Nisei** (nee-SAY). Nisei are people born in the United States whose parents emigrated from Japan. The general population and the military believed Japanese Americans were a threat, even though the FBI did not consider them a danger. Military leaders feared the close proximity of Japanese American communities to American military bases and aircraft plants on the West Coast, and the public associated Japanese Americans with the actions of Japan's armed forces.

In response to the perceived threat, President Roosevelt signed **Executive Order 9066** in 1942, which authorized the relocation and internment of 110,000 Japanese Americans and "resident aliens" living within 60 miles of the West Coast and in parts of Arizona on grounds of national security. An **executive order** is a directive issued by a president that has the force of law.

Nearly all Japanese Americans lived on the West Coast, in California, Washington, and Oregon. The order violated their constitutional and human rights. However, the Supreme Court, in a decision heavily criticized today, upheld its implementation in ***Korematsu* v. *United States***, arguing that, "When under conditions of modern warfare our shores are threatened by hostile forces, the power to protect must be commensurate with [in proportion to] the threatened danger." The government removed Japanese Americans to **internment camps** in military zones, where they lived in prison-like surroundings until the war's end.

INTERNMENT

Ten internment camps were set up in California, Arizona, Wyoming, Utah, Arkansas, and Colorado. Japanese American families were forced to sell whatever belongings they could not carry and relocate to the camps. Japanese American merchants had to sell their businesses in a matter of just days or weeks. By June 1942, the government had moved 120,000 Japanese Americans into the camps. The first camp to open, in March of that year, was Manzanar in California's Owens Valley. The largest of the camps was Tule Lake, also in California, which housed more than 18,000 internees by 1944.

This military dog tag, or ID, belonged to Jack Wakamatsu. While his family lived behind barbed wire at Manzanar, Wakamatsu fought in the 442nd Infantry Regimental Combat Team, the all Japanese American military unit.

Families at the camps were housed in army barracks surrounded by barbed wire and towers where armed guards kept watch. The barracks themselves were not insulated, and residents had to rely on coal-burning stoves for heat. Families slept on cots and shared bathrooms with other internees. Guards were authorized to shoot residents who tried to escape. Nonetheless, Japanese Americans tried to make the camps as much like communities as possible. They established schools, churches, newspapers, and farms, and children stayed active by playing sports. And even though their government had imprisoned them, many young Japanese American men volunteered to fight for their country. They were released from the camps to do so.

After the war ended, Japanese Americans were at last allowed to return to their homes. They lost personal property, businesses, farms, and homes as a result of their forced removal. After many years of campaigning for redress, or compensation, Japanese Americans finally obtained justice. Congress formally apologized for their internment and allocated funds to compensate the survivors in 1988.

HISTORICAL THINKING

1. **READING CHECK** Why were Japanese Americans relocated to internment camps?
2. **DESCRIBE** What constitutional issues were involved in *Korematsu* v. *United States*, and how did the case impact events on the U.S. home front?
3. **FORM AND SUPPORT OPINIONS** Given the circumstances of the war, do you think the U.S. government was justified in interning Japanese Americans? Explain your opinion.

HI 3 Students interpret past events and issues within the context in which an event unfolded rather than solely in terms of present-day norms and values.

JAPANESE AMERICAN NATIONA MUSEUM, LOS ANGELES

apanese American National Museum in Los es, California, presents over 150 years of ese American history and culture. It aims to e appreciation for America's ethnic and cultural ity by sharing the struggles and triumphs of cans of Japanese ancestry. The museum s a permanent collection of over 60,000 items, ing movies, photographs, artwork, letters, oral es, textiles, and other artifacts that tell the s of this group of Americans.

Many of those stories focus on the experiences Japanese Americans whose lives were abruptly uprooted during World War II when they were relocated to internment camps. For example, the museum's collection of letters written by childre the camps to a sympathetic librarian in San Dieg describe their living conditions and experiences. museum also exhibits artwork by adults, includi the pieces shown here, that document the fears monotony of everyday life at the camps.

Hisako Hibi, Painter

In this oil painting titled *Morning*, female artist Hisako Hibi (1907–1991) depicts a scene at an internment camp in Topaz, Utah, in 1942. The painting shows U.S. soldiers marching into the camp at dawn to construct more barracks for internees. Two Japanese Americans watch the soldiers from behind a water tower.

Hibi was imprisoned at the Topaz camp along with her husband—who was also an artist—and their two young children. The Japanese Americans set up schools at the camps, and the Hibis both taught in an art school at the camp in Topaz. What does Hibi's painting suggest about the relationship between the internees and soldiers?

George Hoshida, Sketch Artist

A self-educated artist, George Hoshida (1907–1985) created a visual record of internment camp life in a series of notebooks in which he sketched portraits of inmates and painted scenes of everyday activities. In the watercolor at top right, Hoshida depicts two men playing a board game while others watch. The men in the ink drawing at bottom right are making pipes. The two ink portraits below are of internees Sawaichi Fujita (left), a tinsmith, and store owner Keizo Takata (right). Initially separated from his wife and daughters, Hoshida shared his drawing skills with other internees to pass the time and preserve history.

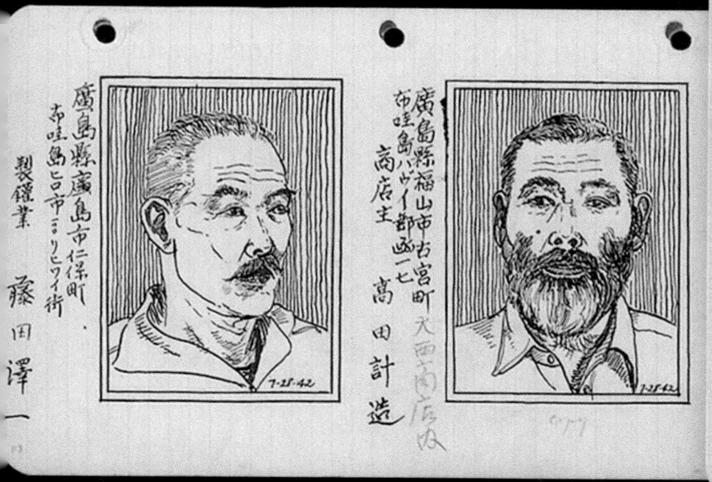

Jack Iwata, Photographer

Born in Seattle, Washington, professional photographer Jack Iwata (1912–1992) was forcibly relocated to an internment camp at Manzanar, California, along with his wife. Iwata and a fellow photographer established a photo lab at the camp and began documenting life there. In the photo at right, Iwata captured a group of internees arriving with their luggage at Manzanar.

In December 1944, the U.S. government announced the internment camps would be closed. Japanese Americans began leaving the camps in early 1945, and the last camp shut down in 1946. Upon release, former inmates had to rebuild their lives. In 1948, a law was passed to reimburse some of the property losses sustained by internees. And then in 1988, Congress passed the Civil Liberties Act, which awarded $20,000 to each camp survivor.

11.7.5 Discuss the constitutional issues and impact of events on the U.S. home front, including the internment of Japanese Americans (e.g., *Fred Korematsu* v. *United States of America*) and the restrictions on German and Italian resident aliens; the response of the administration to Hitler's atrocities against Jews and other groups; the roles of women in military production; and the roles and growing political demands of African Americans.

2.1 **MAIN IDEA** While the United States and Britain fought in North Africa and Italy, the Soviet Union battled the Nazis in Russia.

CAMPAIGNS IN EUROPE AND AFRICA

The Soviet Union received economic aid and supplies from the United States, but Stalin did not like how the war was being fought in Europe. While some of the Allies invaded Africa, Stalin's army battled the bulk of the German forces in Russia alone.

INVADING NORTH AFRICA

As the United States mobilized for war in the Pacific and in Europe, President Roosevelt and British prime minister Winston Churchill planned a course of action against Hitler in Europe and North Africa. But Soviet premier Joseph Stalin did not agree with the other two leaders on the best strategy to use against the Germans. Stalin wanted Allied help in battling the Germans and defending the Soviet Union. As you have read, Hitler's troops launched an invasion of the Soviet Union in 1941, and Stalin wanted the Allies to establish a second front, or line of battle, in western Europe to help the Soviets combat the Germans. Britain and the United States, however, preferred invading French North Africa and reclaiming Nazi-controlled areas there. The North African attack

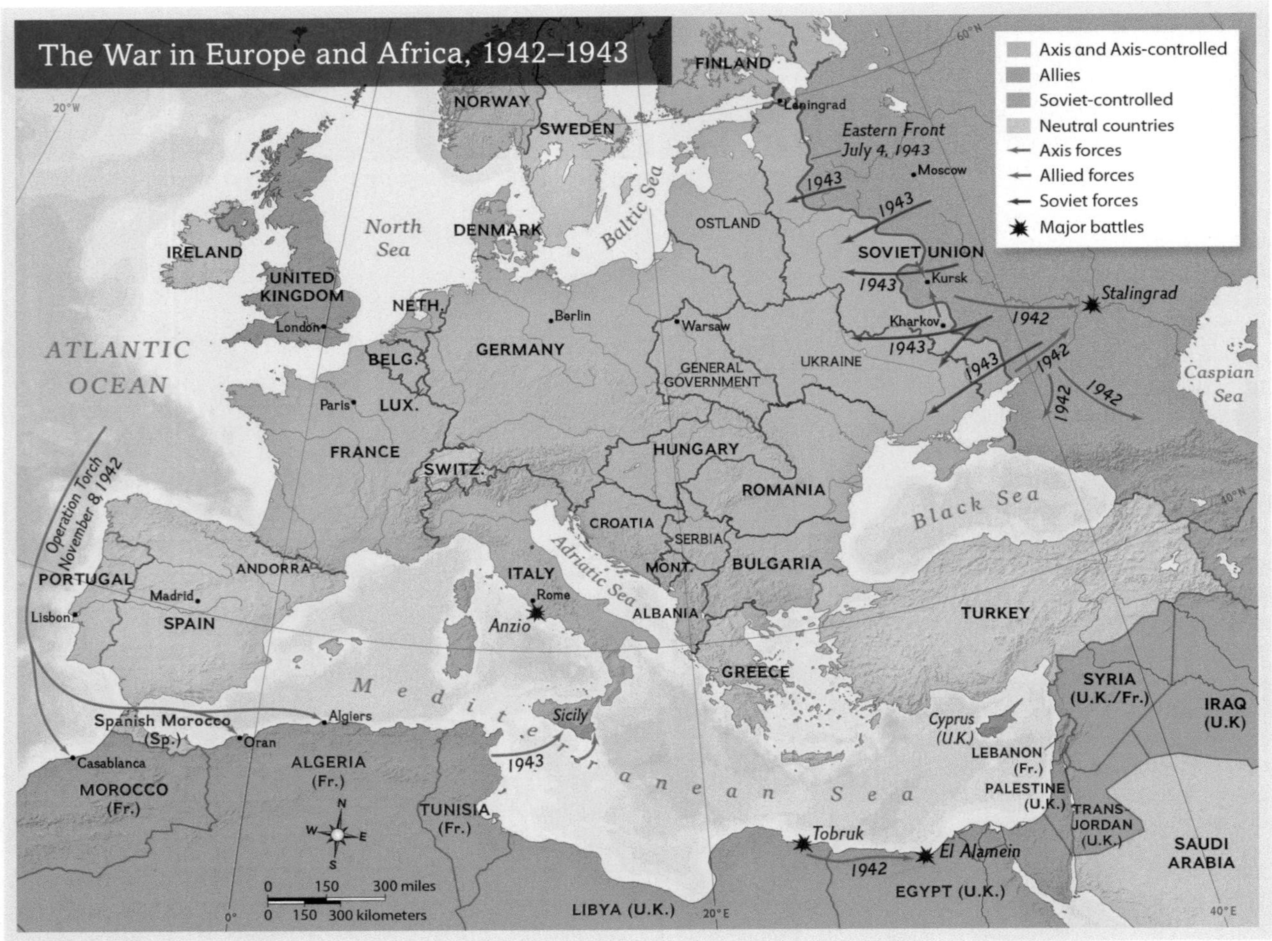

The War in Europe and Africa, 1942–1943

CST 3 Students use a variety of maps and documents to interpret human movement, including major patterns of domestic and international migration, changing environmental preferences and settlement patterns, the frictions that develop between population groups, and the diffusion of ideas, technological innovations, and goods.

would be on a smaller, more manageable scale for the Americans, who were just entering the fight.

However, the first step toward victory in this campaign was for the United States to seize control of the Atlantic Ocean and ensure the safe mobilization of Allied troops in Africa. During the first few months of 1942, German submarines had been prowling the Atlantic, regularly sinking Allied ships. Eventually, new antisubmarine technologies and weapons such as radar and **depth charges**, underwater bombs that are programmed to explode at certain depths, enabled the Allies to strike back. By mid-1943, the German submarine threat in the Atlantic had been neutralized.

In November 1942, U.S. Army general **Dwight D. Eisenhower** led the Allied forces in an invasion of North Africa called **Operation Torch**. Eisenhower had been supreme commander of the Allied forces in Europe before taking charge of Operation Torch. By May 1943, the British and American forces had successfully recaptured Morocco and Algeria and defeated the army under German general **Edwin Rommel**, capturing more than 250,000 Nazi prisoners in Tunisia. Once they were firmly established in North Africa, the Allied forces planned to use it as a base of operations against Italy.

Germany's success in the first years of the war had been due in part to its superior fleet of tanks, known as **panzers**, which the Germans arranged in massed formations. Manufactured in Germany from the mid-1930s to the mid-1940s, the panzers were thickly armored and boasted impressive firepower, but their size and weight kept them from being speedy or easy to maneuver. The German panzers had a distinct advantage over the relatively older British tanks, but U.S. troops arrived in Europe and North Africa with American-built Sherman tanks, which could often outmaneuver the panzers. Sherman tanks had less substantial armor and firepower, but they were more agile. As a result, the British forces traded in their tanks for the Sherman tanks in 1943 and 1944.

GERMANY VERSUS THE SOVIET UNION

When Hitler's forces undertook their invasion of the Soviet Union in June 1941, they believed they could defeat the Soviet army in a matter of months. The Germans had caught the Soviets off guard, sending

ANTISUBMARINE TECHNOLOGY

The barrel-shaped depth charge was filled with explosives and contained a fuse set to detonate at a specific depth, based on water pressure. Depth charges were deployed in three major ways.

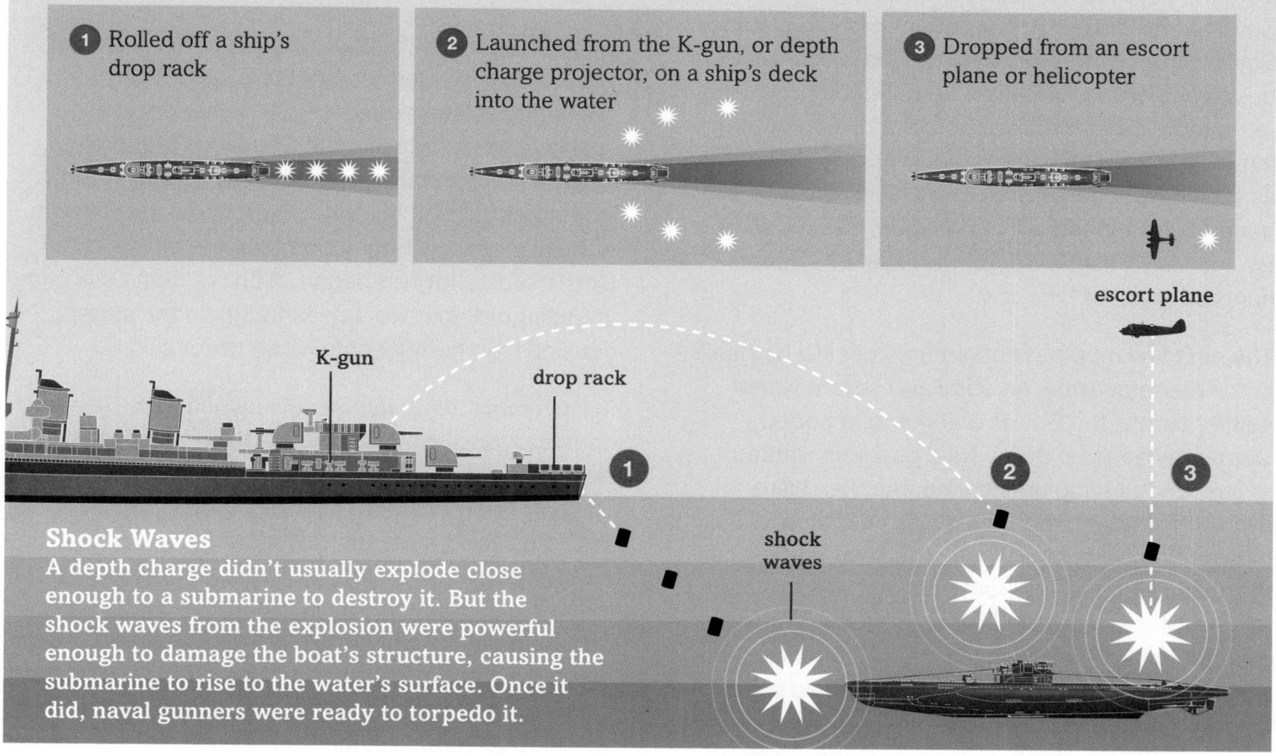

11.7.2 Explain U.S. and Allied wartime strategy, including the major battles of Midway, Normandy, Iwo Jima, Okinawa, and the Battle of the Bulge; 11.7.6 Describe major developments in aviation, weaponry, communication, and medicine and the war's impact on the location of American industry and use of resources.

In October 1942, the Soviets sometimes sought defensive positions inside industrial buildings, including the Red October factory, while battling the Germans at Stalingrad. The factory protected the soldiers but was destroyed in the Battle of Stalingrad. In this photo taken by *Life* magazine photographer Thomas D. McAvoy, Soviet soldiers march German prisoners of war past the ruins of Red October.

200 divisions with 10,000 to 20,000 soldiers each to attack along a front stretching nearly 2,000 miles from the Baltic to the Black seas. Nonetheless, the Soviet army, or Red Army, put up strong resistance. Soviet forces employed a "scorched-earth" policy, destroying crops, bridges, and railroad cars as they retreated deeper into their homeland. This strategy left the German soldiers without food or shelter as they advanced east. Still, the Germans took hundreds of thousands of prisoners along the way. By mid-July, Hitler's troops were within a couple hundred miles of Moscow.

The next few months brought unexpected hardship to the German Army. An early and severe winter settled across the Soviet Union and impeded German advances. Some Nazi generals wanted to suspend fighting until spring, but they were overruled, and the army pressed on to Moscow. Both the German troops and their machinery suffered in the cold. Because the Germans had not expected the Soviet resistance to last so long, they had not brought enough supplies to last through the winter. By November 1941, 700,000 Germans had died. The following month, the Soviets launched an organized attack on the Germans, but Hitler would not allow his army to retreat. As a result, the Germans held on to most of the ground they had captured earlier in the year.

By the summer of 1942, Soviet casualties stood at about 4 million. German numbers were high but not nearly as staggering. In July, Hitler decided to split his forces between the Caucasus Mountains near the Turkish border and the city of Stalingrad, located about 500 miles north on the Volga River. In August, Germany began bombing the city, and the **Battle of Stalingrad** began. With residents still living in Stalingrad, the two armies fought in the streets, causing high numbers of civilian casualties.

In November 1942, the Soviets launched a counteroffensive attack against the now freezing, starving, and poorly supplied German troops. Once again, Hitler refused to allow his army to retreat from the Volga River, ordering them to fight to the death. As the Nazis weakened, the Soviets surrounded them. The German troops surrendered at the end of January 1943. But battle resumed between the two armies about six months later in Kursk, a city to the west of Stalingrad. In the largest tank battle ever fought, the German Army was dealt a crushing defeat

A landing craft with General George Patton (wearing a helmet) aboard leaves the North African country of Tunisia for Sicily, in the combined British and American invasion of the island in 1943.

and suffered about 500,000 casualties. The Battle of Kursk was the last major offensive launched by the Nazis in the Soviet Union.

THE ITALIAN CAMPAIGN

In the summer of 1943, not long after the Allied victory in North Africa and the Soviet triumph in Stalingrad, the Allies turned their attention to Italy. The Soviets, still calling for a second front in Western Europe, were not happy with this turn of events, especially after the extreme losses they had suffered battling the Germans without the support of other Allied troops. Roosevelt tried to appease Stalin by promising him a second front the following year, but Stalin remained displeased.

In July 1943, Allied forces, led by American lieutenant general **George S. Patton** and British general Bernard Montgomery, began the Italian campaign by storming the island of Sicily. The invasion represented the biggest **amphibious assault** that had ever taken place. An amphibious assault uses naval support to protect military forces invading by land and air. The assault also demonstrated the cohesion of the American and British forces led by Patton and Montgomery, who successfully worked together to secure the island. The Allies conquered Sicily in about a month, and their invasion indirectly forced a regime change in Italy. The Italian government removed, arrested, and eventually executed its leader, Benito Mussolini. Meanwhile, approximately 100,000 Axis troops retreated from Sicily and headed for Italy's mainland, having suffered many more casualties than the Allies in the battle over the island.

The Allies followed closely behind, landing on the southern coast of Italy in early September. Not long after their arrival, the new Italian government secretly agreed to sign an armistice with the Allies and help them fight against Germany. Additional Allied landings followed at Salerno and Naples along Italy's western coast, and by mid-October, Italy had officially changed sides and declared war against Germany. But Germany still occupied much of Italy. In November 1943, German troops began establishing defensive lines about halfway up the Italian peninsula to prevent the Allies from reaching Rome. Exhausting battles, the treacherous mountain terrain, and a lack of supplies slowed the Allied advance. It took four months for the Allies to move forward just 70 miles, and they were still 80 miles from Rome, Italy's capital.

For months, the Allies continued advancing up the peninsula. Then, in May 1944, they broke through one of the Germans' defensive lines and reached Rome about a month later. Fighting continued during the summer and into the fall and winter, leaving the Germans short of supplies—especially fuel. They were forced to use oxen to tow their tanks. In contrast, the Allies had received new reinforcements and weapons. German forces finally surrendered in May 1945, but the campaign had been costly on both sides. Allied casualties numbered around 300,000, while German casualties were about 434,000.

HISTORICAL THINKING

1. **READING CHECK** What strategy did Stalin want the Allies to follow against Germany?
2. **DETERMINE CHRONOLOGY** What events led to the German surrender at the Battle of Stalingrad in 1943?
3. **INTERPRET MAPS** Why did it make sense, geographically, for the Allied forces to invade Sicily and Italy's mainland after fighting in North Africa?
4. **DRAW CONCLUSIONS** Why did the Italian government switch to the Allied side during the Italian campaign?

11.7.2 Explain U.S. and Allied wartime strategy, including the major battles of Midway, Normandy, Iwo Jima, Okinawa, and the Battle of the Bulge.

2.2 **MAIN IDEA** The Allies fought Japan in the Pacific to prevent the nation from seizing new territory and to take back control of Japanese-occupied islands.

WAR IN THE PACIFIC

If you've ever played a game of war strategy, you know that different types of battles require different plans of action. The Allies knew this as they fought Japan in the war in the Pacific.

BATTLING BY SEA AND AIR

The Americans were the primary fighting force in the Pacific and were supported by Allied troops from Australia, New Zealand, Canada, and Britain. The troops were led by General Douglas MacArthur, who, as you may recall, was ordered to leave his troops in the Philippines early in the war, and Admiral **Chester Nimitz** of the U.S. Navy. Their mission had four goals: maintain communication between the United States and Australia, where the Americans had established bases; defend North America against the Japanese; prevent the Japanese from venturing outside of the Pacific; and plan amphibious counteroffensives against them.

In spring 1942, the Japanese sought to take control of the sea north of Australia by establishing air bases in New Guinea and the Solomon Islands. From these bases, the Japanese planned to destroy U.S. naval bases along the eastern coast of Australia. However, Allied code breakers had uncovered their plan and alerted U.S. officials, who launched a preemptive attack. Over the course of several days in May, the two enemies battled by air and sea off the coast of New Guinea in what is known as the **Battle of the Coral Sea**. It was the first air-sea battle in history. Japanese forces sank one U.S. aircraft carrier and damaged another, and the Allies destroyed many Japanese planes and badly damaged a Japanese carrier.

During the war, Allied forces used the North American Mitchell B-25 bomber, shown here, to fight battles in the Pacific and in Europe. James Doolittle flew the bomber in his raid on Tokyo. You will read about his raid and see a photo of his plane taking off for Japan later in this lesson.

11.7.2 Explain U.S. and Allied wartime strategy, including the major battles of Midway, Normandy, Iwo Jima, Okinawa, and the Battle of the Bulge; 11.7.6 Describe major developments in aviation, weaponry, communication, and medicine and the war's impact on the location of American industry and use of resources.

But the Japanese remained determined. In June 1942, they tried to seize Midway Island, located 1,400 miles west of Hawaii, in an attempt to destroy a U.S. carrier fleet. Once again, the Allies had intercepted Japan's battle plans. Though the Japanese fleet far outnumbered the U.S. fleet during the three-day-long **Battle of Midway**, the Americans used the intelligence they'd received to stay one step ahead of their enemy.

On June 3, U.S. bombers attacked the Japanese fleet when it was still 500 miles from its destination. Undeterred, Japan attacked Midway the following morning, a decision it came to regret. The battle greatly reduced Japan's naval forces, including the destruction of four carriers and the loss of hundreds of planes and pilots. After its defeat at Midway, Japan canceled plans for several subsequent invasions.

James Doolittle's B-25 taking off from the aircraft carrier, the U.S.S. *Hornet*

TOKYO RAIDERS

Since Japan's attack on Pearl Harbor in December 1941, the United States had wanted revenge. So in April 1942, Lieutenant Colonel James Doolittle led a squadron of B-25 bomber pilots on a surprise attack on the Japanese mainland.

As the planes flew over Tokyo, some citizens below waved to the pilots, believing the aircraft were Japanese. They were shocked when Doolittle and his raiders dropped their bombs, striking industrial and military facilities as well as civilian areas before retreating to free China, where most of them crash-landed.

Japanese casualties were relatively light, but the attack devastated Japanese morale and proved the nation was vulnerable. On the other hand, the raid gave the Americans new confidence and helped set the stage for the war in the Pacific.

ISLAND HOPPING

Having established control of the Pacific, the Allies' next move involved a two-pronged approach. Admiral Nimitz would travel west from Hawaii, and General MacArthur would travel north from Australia, carrying out a campaign of **island hopping**. This strategy was designed to capture and control islands in the Pacific one by one. The Allies planned to establish bases on the islands along a path to the Japanese homeland in preparation for an Allied attack on Japan.

The offensive began on the island of **Guadalcanal**, northeast of Australia in the Solomon Islands chain. In July 1942, the Japanese had begun constructing an air base there. A month later, the U.S. Marines were sent in to fight the Japanese and force them off Guadalcanal. As the battle dragged on, additional troops arrived to replenish both sides. By mid-October, the Japanese and the Americans each had more than 20,000 troops engaged in battle on the island. By January 1943, however, the Americans had managed to block the stream of Japanese reinforcements, while allowing the American troop strength to nearly double. The Japanese suffered many more casualties and, with their fewer numbers, soon evacuated the island. After six grueling months of battle, the Americans finally held Guadalcanal.

More Pacific victories soon followed for the Allies. In November 1943, Nimitz led his forces west of Guadalcanal to the Gilbert Islands, where they also defeated the Japanese. Nimitz and MacArthur continued island hopping throughout 1944. MacArthur overpowered the Japanese in parts of New Guinea and the Philippines. Nimitz took control of the Marshall and Marianas islands in February and August, respectively. From there, the two commanders set their sights on the islands of Japan, only about 1,200 miles away. Meanwhile, the Allied forces in Europe were planning an invasion they hoped would turn the tide of war against Germany.

HISTORICAL THINKING

1. **READING CHECK** What was the Allied mission in the Pacific war?
2. **MAKE INFERENCES** What might have happened if the American military hadn't learned about Japan's plans for the battles of the Coral Sea and Midway?
3. **IDENTIFY PROBLEMS AND SOLUTIONS** Why was island hopping a good strategy for an Allied attack on Japan?

HI 4 Students understand the meaning, implication, and impact of historical events and recognize that events could have taken other directions.

3.1 **MAIN IDEA** The invasion of Normandy, France, marked the beginning of the end of the war in Europe.

VICTORY IN EUROPE

When faced with a daunting task, you are never sure whether you have prepared well enough, and you don't know how it will turn out. As the Allied forces advanced on Europe, they met many challenges—both expected and unexpected.

OPERATION OVERLORD

With the war in the Pacific going well, the Allies began to make plans to drive the Nazis back to Germany. In November 1943, Roosevelt, Churchill, and Stalin gathered at the **Tehran Conference** in Iran in southwest Asia. It would be the first time Roosevelt had met Stalin. At the conference, the three leaders discussed their plans to invade western Europe—the second front in the west that Stalin had been pressing for—the following spring.

The plan was for General Eisenhower to lead an Allied invasion, code-named **Operation Overlord**, from Britain. Eisenhower organized 3 million soldiers for the invasion and stockpiled plenty of supplies, including food, planes, and smaller ships. To prevent the Nazis from learning their plans, the Allies deliberately planted false information indicating they intended to invade near Calais, France, directly across the English Channel from Dover, England. In addition, in the weeks leading up to the invasion, the Allied air forces kept the Nazis distracted by dropping bombs on German airfields, military bases, and bridges over the main rivers in France. The deception ultimately helped isolate and draw the Nazis away from the invasion's actual target: the French coastal province of Normandy.

Operation Overlord was originally planned to take place in May 1944, but naval vessels called **amphibious landing craft** were not assembled until June. A departure planned for June 5 was delayed by bad weather. At last, on June 6, 1944, thousands of amphibious landing craft, airplanes, and an armada, or fleet of warships, departed from several British ports. Eisenhower's huge force headed toward five different Normandy beaches, code-named Utah, Omaha, Gold, Juno, and Sword. By sundown that day, on what came to be known as **D-Day**, 150,000 American, British, and Canadian troops stormed the beaches.

American troops under the command of Major General **Omar Bradley** at Omaha, the largest assault area, endured some of the worst conditions. Many Americans drowned as they tried to reach the beach. The troops also faced heavy resistance from German soldiers who turned their machine-gun fire on the Americans as soon as they set foot on the beach. By the next morning, more than 2,000 American soldiers lay dead in the sand. Despite such difficult battles, the Normandy invasion was successful, and Allied forces soon began to move inland. Within two months of the initial landing, more than 1 million Allied troops were fighting to take back France.

BATTLE OF THE BULGE

It took Allied troops only about two months to reach Paris, France's capital, which was controlled by the Nazis. On August 19, 1944, Parisians—aware that the Allies would soon reach them—rose up against the occupying Germans. By the time the Allied forces arrived on August 25, the Nazis were ready to surrender. The liberation of Paris was complete. But the war was still far from over.

In early September, Allied troops advanced from northern France and captured Antwerp, Belgium, an important supply port. From there, they set out toward the German border. At this point, most people believed the end of the war was close. But as the Allies marched farther east, Nazi defenses strengthened. In mid-October, Hitler required all males between the ages of 16 and 60 to fight on behalf of the Third Reich. In mid-December,

11.7.6 Describe major developments in aviation, weaponry, communication, and medicine and the war's impact on the location of American industry and use of resources.

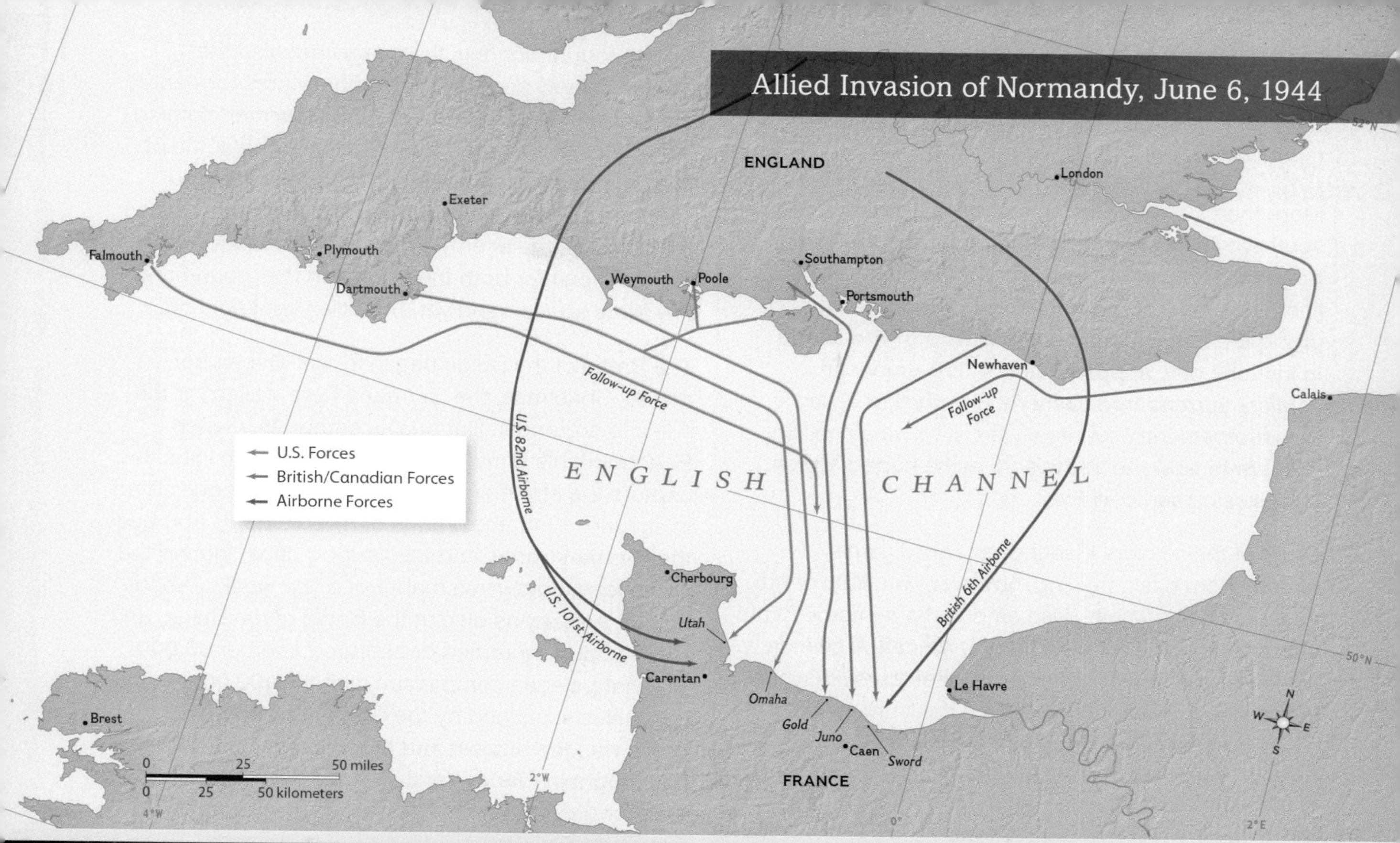

U.S. soldiers jump off their amphibious landing craft into the water and prepare for battle on the beach at Normandy on D-Day.

reinforced with fresh soldiers, the Germans launched an unexpected attack on the Allies in southern Belgium's Ardennes region. Their goal was to split up the Allied troops and retake Antwerp.

More than 200,000 German soldiers advanced into southern Belgium, greatly outnumbering the Allied troops there, and broke through the Allied front line. This break in the front line created a "bulge," giving the battle its name: the **Battle of the Bulge**. In just one day, approximately 4,000 American soldiers surrendered. General Eisenhower called in reinforcements, eventually enlisting a half million soldiers to fight the battle and, as he hoped, move the Allies closer to victory.

Many of the soldiers Eisenhower called came directly from basic training, however, with little or no experience in combat. Also among the reinforcements called to action were about 2,500 African-American soldiers, who fought shoulder-to-shoulder with white soldiers at Ardennes. An all-black tank unit also rolled in to fight in the battle. It was the first time desegregated troops had fought in a U.S. war.

Troops fought not only the enemy but also the weather. Snow and freezing temperatures tormented the soldiers, who lacked appropriate winter clothing. Many soldiers suffered from frostbite, and some of the wounded froze to death in their foxholes, the holes they dug in the ground to shield themselves as they fired on the enemy. Thick fog also made warfare more difficult for both the troops on the ground and the pilots above—and yet, the Allies kept fighting.

The Battle of the Bulge began in mid-December, and by Christmas, the Germans were calling for the Allies to surrender. But on December 26, General Patton and his army broke through German lines to capture the strategic Belgian town of Bastogne. Then in January 1945, thousands of Allied aircraft bombed the German troops and their supply lines, forcing the Nazis to withdraw in a matter of a few weeks. About 20,000 Americans died in the Battle of the Bulge, and the Germans wounded or captured another 60,000. But that paled in comparison with the 100,000 casualties sustained by the German troops. The battle was the biggest and bloodiest the U.S. Army had fought in World War II.

General Dwight D. Eisenhower (center) and Pierre Koenig (left), leader of the French resistance, take a symbolic walk under the Arc de Triomphe in Paris on August 27, 1944, two days after the Germans surrendered the city to the Allies.

11.7.2 Explain U.S. and Allied wartime strategy, including the major battles of Midway, Normandy, Iwo Jima, Okinawa, and the Battle of the Bulge.

END OF THE THIRD REICH

Meanwhile, the Soviet army was advancing toward the western front. Throughout January 1945, the Soviets had moved west across Poland toward Germany. By the end of the month, they were within 40 miles of Berlin. At the same time, more Allied forces pressed east from France and Belgium, while those involved in the Italian campaign continued to push German troops north along the Italian peninsula. To prepare the way for the ground-force invasion of Germany, the Allies intensified their aerial assault on the country in February 1945. Much of this strategic bombing targeted both industrial and civilian areas.

In 1945, Churchill, Roosevelt, and Stalin (from left to right) attend the Yalta Conference.

By late March, Allied ground troops began crossing the Rhine River into western Germany. Hitler ordered his retreating troops to destroy the country's industrial plants and power and water facilities, along with any food or clothing stores. He wanted to use the scorched-earth policy, much as the Soviets had done against the Germans. But Hitler's minister of war production refused, knowing it would lead to the suffering and deaths of many German citizens—a prospect that did not concern Hitler.

On April 11, Allied troops arrived at the Elbe River, within 60 miles of Berlin. Within two weeks, the Soviet troops joined them, and together they encircled the German capital. On April 30, with the Soviets closing in on his bunker, Hitler committed suicide. With their leader gone and their cause lost, the Nazis surrendered. The war in Europe officially ended on May 8, 1945. The Third Reich had fallen.

THE YALTA CONFERENCE

Before Germany surrendered, Roosevelt, Churchill, and Stalin met at Yalta, a Russian town in the Crimea, in February 1945. With the war turning in the Allies' favor, the leaders spent a week drawing up postwar plans for Europe. The decisions they made came to be called the **Yalta Accords**. The three leaders decided to divide Germany into different occupation zones controlled by the United States, the Soviet Union, Britain, and France. They also agreed to take control of or destroy German arms industries, try German war criminals in a court of law, and establish a commission in Moscow to decide on the reparations Germany would need to make. Stalin particularly pressed for reparations. German soldiers had killed or injured about 20 million Soviet citizens during the war and destroyed many Soviet towns and businesses. Stalin wanted to ensure the Soviet Union received appropriate compensation.

In addition, the leaders discussed Poland's geographic boundaries and political future as well as the establishment of a new international body called the United Nations. At the conference, Stalin agreed to respect free elections in Poland and elsewhere in the eastern European region of the Soviet Union. However, just weeks later, he ordered the arrest of Polish anti-communist leaders and the murder of political dissidents in Romania and Bulgaria.

The war in Europe was over, but the war in the Pacific dragged on. Japan refused to quit, even after crushing defeats. Nevertheless, the Allies hoped to bring a quick end to the war in the Pacific.

HISTORICAL THINKING

1. **READING CHECK** What was Operation Overlord?
2. **INTERPRET MAPS** Why might it have made sense to the Germans that the Allied forces would stage their invasion in Calais rather than in Normandy?
3. **MAKE INFERENCES** Why do you think defeat at the Battle of the Bulge made Hitler realize he might lose the war?
4. **EVALUATE** What did Stalin's actions after the Yalta Conference reveal about the Soviet leader?

CST 3 Students use a variety of maps and documents to interpret human movement, including major patterns of domestic and international migration, changing environmental preferences and settlement patterns, the frictions that develop between population groups, and the diffusion of ideas, technological innovations, and goods.

3.2 **MAIN IDEA** The Allies won key battles against the Japanese but felt they had to resort to atomic warfare to bring the war in the Pacific to a close.

VICTORY IN ASIA

The Allies found themselves up against a determined and relentless enemy in the Japanese. A strong sense of honor prevented Japanese soldiers from surrendering, even when the odds were heavily stacked against them. Faced with defeat, some even chose suicide.

LIBERATING THE PHILIPPINES

As the Allies gained ground and fought to secure victory in Europe, war continued to rage in the Pacific. In mid-September 1944, President Roosevelt and General MacArthur decided that the Philippines—which Japan had seized early in 1942—should be the next target of an Allied invasion, with American naval forces taking the lead. In preparation for the liberation, Filipino and American troops had formed guerrilla groups on the ground.

On October 20, 1944, General MacArthur led an amphibious landing on the island of Leyte, southeast of Luzon, where the Philippine capital, Manila, is located. The Allies had judged correctly that the Japanese did not have a strong defense on Leyte. In fact, the Japanese used a decoy ship to draw some of the U.S. naval fleet away from the island. They also sent forces to attack the American fleet at the landing. But the U.S. Navy had anticipated Japan's strategy and, on October 23, used submarines to sink two Japanese cruisers as they approached Leyte. The next day, American aerial attacks sank a Japanese battleship, and the fighting began in earnest.

The **Battles of Leyte Gulf** took place between October 23 and October 26, 1944, during which time the Japanese suffered heavy losses—far more than the Americans. Japanese losses were due, in part, to Japan's decision to deploy suicide bomber pilots called **kamikaze**, meaning "divine wind." These Japanese pilots volunteered to crash their planes, loaded with explosives, into American ships. Over the course of the rest of the war, the kamikaze destroyed 34 U.S. ships, but about 2,800 Japanese pilots sacrificed their lives in the process.

Though the United States did not achieve total control over Leyte until the end of December, the battles destroyed the Imperial Japanese Navy. The United States finally liberated the Philippines in March 1945. Filipino soldiers played an important role in the war effort, but the conflict had taken a terrible toll on their island nation. Manila became the second most devastated city in the world after Warsaw, Poland. By the end of the war, as many as 1 million civilians in the Philippines had died.

CLOSING IN ON JAPAN

Once the Philippines was under American control, the Allies turned their attention to Japan itself. The Allied forces wanted to establish a base for their B-29 bombers close to the Japanese mainland to conduct aerial attacks. They chose the Japanese island of Iwo Jima, located 760 miles southeast of Tokyo.

On February 19, 1945, the Allies, made up mostly of U.S. Marines, landed on Iwo Jima to confront the roughly 20,000 Japanese troops they believed were stationed there. Before the landing, however, the Allies had bombarded the island with napalm bombs and rockets. When the Marines set foot on the devastated island, they saw no sign of life and thought, for a moment at least, that they were going to take the island without a fight. Then suddenly, machine-gun fire erupted, seemingly out of nowhere. The Japanese were firing from a network of hidden natural caves and tunnels they had carved out all over Iwo Jima. And once again, they used kamikaze air raids, crashing their planes into American vessels, sinking one U.S. carrier and damaging many other ships. Fighting was intense, but eventually the Allies prevailed. About 6,000 Americans died while fighting

11.7.2 Explain U.S. and Allied wartime strategy, including the major battles of Midway, Normandy, Iwo Jima, Okinawa, and the Battle of the Bulge.

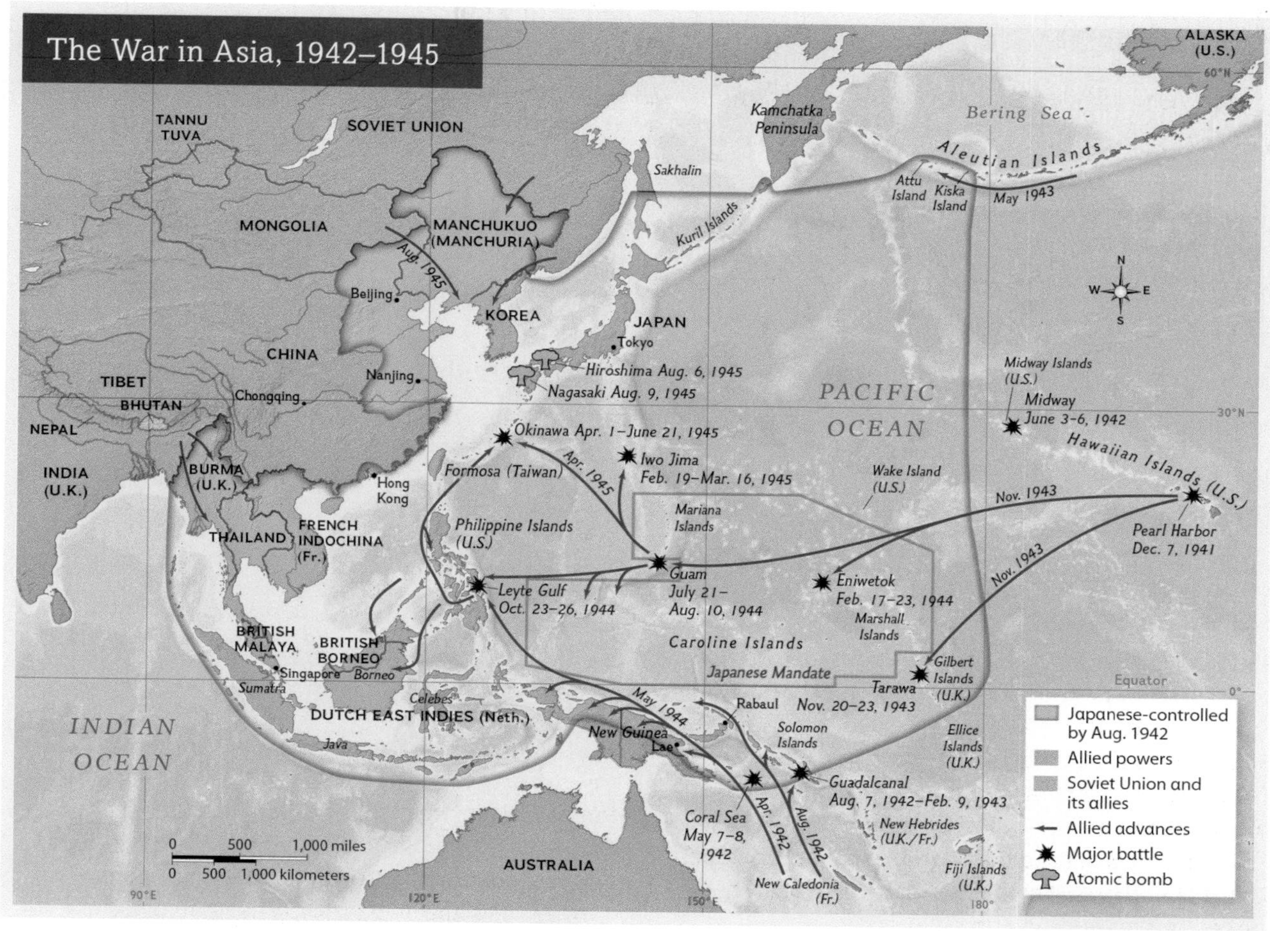

The War in Asia, 1942–1945

the **Battle of Iwo Jima**, and nearly all the Japanese soldiers and civilians on the island perished. The Marines took Iwo Jima on March 16, and the United States staged about 2,000 B-29 bombers there.

That same month, just before the Marines secured Iwo Jima, the Allies used a new bombing technique on Tokyo, Japan: nighttime napalm firebombs. The first drop destroyed 25 percent of Tokyo's buildings and killed tens of thousands of people—most of them civilians. The Allies then used a similar technique on several other Japanese cities, hoping that the bombing campaigns would avoid the necessity of sending ground troops into Japan and force the Japanese to surrender.

On April 1, Allied troops landed on the island of Okinawa, located about 400 miles south of Honshu, Japan's main island, where Tokyo is located. Admiral Nimitz and 180,000 troops, most of his carriers, and 18 battleships faced off against 110,000 Japanese soldiers in the **Battle of Okinawa**. Nimitz's troops captured Okinawa's airfields, but the Japanese refused to back down. A few days later, Japan launched a counterattack that involved hundreds of kamikaze raids against the Allied fleet and a successful attack on a U.S. destroyer.

As a result of the kamikaze strategy, American casualty rates skyrocketed. And as on Iwo Jima, a maze of natural caves lay beneath the surface of Okinawa. Japanese soldiers hunkered down in the caves and in pillboxes, small concrete fortifications used to house weapons. American troops were forced to go from one hiding place to another and destroy them with dynamite. Fighting did not officially end on Okinawa until July 2. By then, 7,000 U.S. troops had died on land, and 5,000 more had died at sea. In addition, 40,000 American troops had sustained injuries. More than 100,000 Japanese died in the battle. The overwhelming losses on both sides would play a big role in the U.S. government's decision to use a new strategy to end the war.

A NEW PRESIDENT

Meanwhile, back on the home front, Roosevelt won an unprecedented fourth term in office. During his campaign, Roosevelt chose a new running mate for vice president, Senator **Harry S. Truman** of Missouri. When Roosevelt suddenly died of a massive stroke on April 12, 1945, just a few weeks after his inauguration, Truman became president. Truman was born in Missouri and had fought in World War I. He was an experienced politician, having served

The atomic bomb explodes over Hiroshima on August 6, 1945. In addition to the deaths caused by the explosion, tens of thousands of Japanese in both Hiroshima and Nagasaki died from radiation sickness.

first as a county judge and later as U.S. senator. But as the new president, he struggled to manage operations during the war.

President Truman was receiving conflicting advice about how to end the war and how to deal with Stalin, who was going back on promises he made at the Yalta Conference. Roosevelt's former vice president, Henry Wallace, encouraged Truman to negotiate with Stalin. The U.S. ambassador to the Soviet Union, however, urged the president to demand Stalin's compliance with the Yalta Accords. Truman took the ambassador's advice and pressed the Soviet foreign minister to convince Stalin to comply with the agreements, threatening that the United States would otherwise withdraw economic aid.

In mid-July 1945, Truman met with Churchill and Stalin in Potsdam, Germany, near Berlin. At the **Potsdam Conference**, the leaders agreed to the terms of peace for Germany and the procedure for bringing Nazi war criminals to trial, among other issues. The defeat of Churchill's Conservative Party interrupted the conference, as Churchill had to return to Britain to pass on his role as prime minister to a new leader. When the Potsdam Conference resumed, the friction between Truman and Stalin was apparent. Stalin brushed aside Truman's concerns about Poland and Eastern Europe, while Truman opposed Stalin's demand for reparations from Germany.

THE ATOMIC BOMB

Another talking point the leaders discussed at the Potsdam Conference was the possibility of using an **atomic bomb**, a type of nuclear bomb whose violent explosion is triggered by splitting atoms, which releases intense heat and radioactivity. Armed with this powerful weapon, Truman warned Japan about the disaster that would befall if the nation refused to surrender without conditions. But for the Japanese, any surrender would be a great dishonor to their country and to their emperor, Hirohito.

11.7.6 Describe major developments in aviation, weaponry, communication, and medicine and the war's impact on the location of American industry and use of resources; 11.7.7 Discuss the decision to drop atomic bombs and the consequences of the decision (Hiroshima and Nagasaki).

Truman had only learned of the atomic bomb's existence after he took office in April 1945. Roosevelt had decided to build the bomb after he was advised the Nazis were taking steps to build one themselves. The U.S. effort, known as the **Manhattan Project**, included top-secret facilities in Washington state, New Mexico, and Tennessee, where scientists designed, built, and tested the new weapon.

Truman formed committees to advise him on how best to deploy the atomic bomb. One of the committees recommended that the United States drop the bomb on four Japanese cities: Kokura, Niigata, **Hiroshima**, and **Nagasaki**. The president decided that although using atomic weapons would cause horrendous loss of life, it would also end the war more quickly, saving more lives in the long run.

In the end, Truman had two Japanese cities bombed. On August 6, 1945, a B-29 bomber called the *Enola Gay* dropped an atomic bomb on Hiroshima. At least 100,000 civilians died in the explosion and the firestorm that followed. A second atomic bomb was dropped on Nagasaki on August 9. Between 35,000 and 40,000 people died, and a similar number of Japanese were injured.

Photographer Alfred Eisenstaedt captured this moment of celebration in Times Square, New York, on August 14, 1945, the day the Japanese surrendered.

On August 15, Japan accepted the terms of surrender. World War II officially ended on September 2, 1945, when the Japanese signed the formal document of surrender aboard the battleship U.S.S. *Missouri* in Tokyo Bay. After the Japanese surrendered, the Allies occupied Japan, but they allowed the emperor to remain in power to restore order to the country. The Allies also conducted trials against Japanese military and government officials accused of war crimes.

Although American war casualties were small in comparison with those suffered by other nations, more than 400,000 Americans lost their lives. But in Europe as well as Japan, not only soldiers died in the war. The Allies would soon confront murder of civilians on a scale never seen before.

HISTORICAL THINKING

1. **READING CHECK** What strategies did the Americans and the Japanese use in the Battles of Leyte Gulf?
2. **COMPARE AND CONTRAST** In what ways were the Battles of Iwo Jima and Okinawa similar, and how did they differ?
3. **DETERMINE CHRONOLOGY** How soon after the Potsdam Conference were atomic bombs deployed over Japan?
4. **FORM AND SUPPORT OPINIONS** Do you think Truman was justified in dropping the atomic bomb on Hiroshima and Nagasaki? Explain your answer.

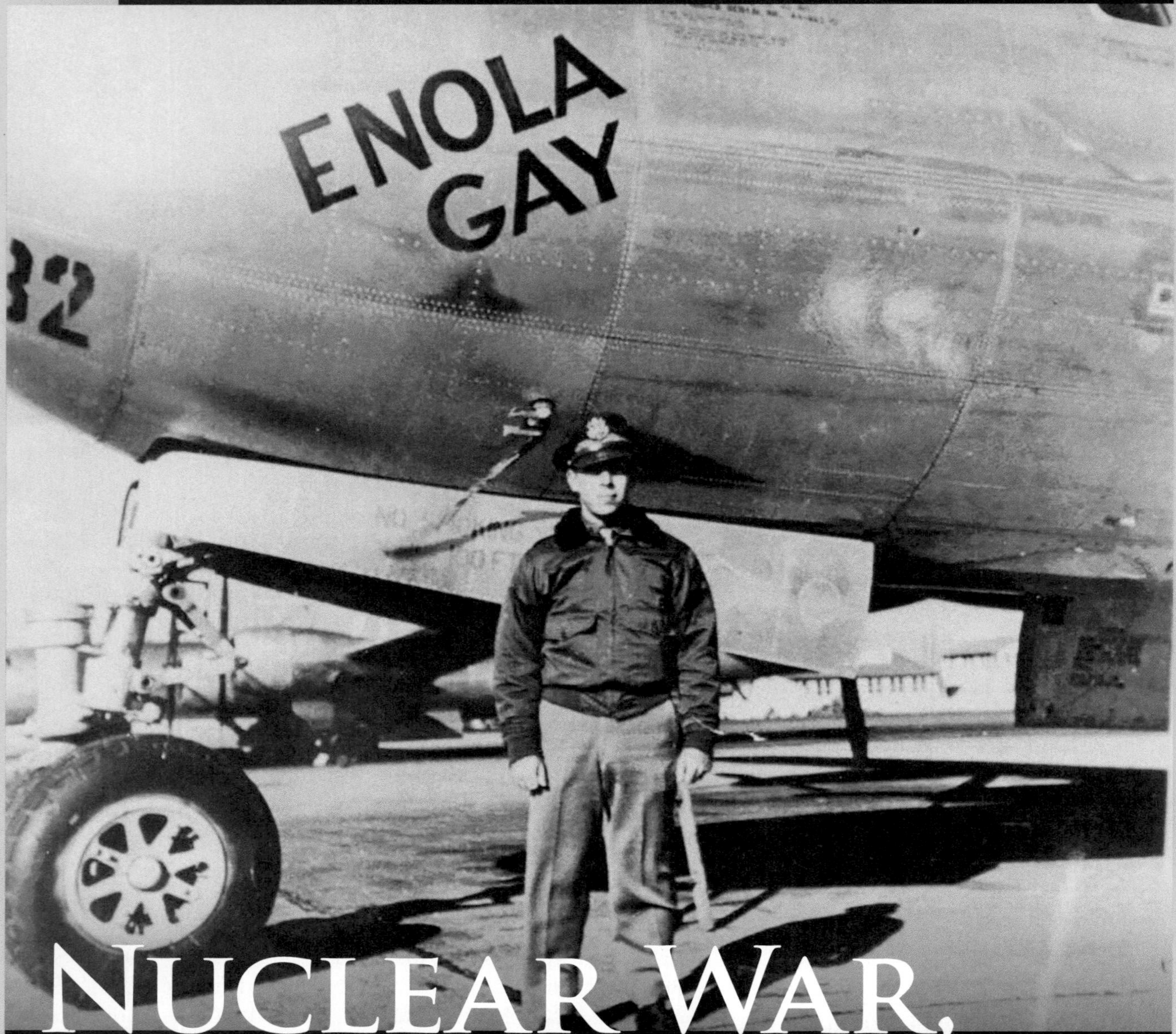

NUCLEAR WAR, NUCLEAR PEACE

**"There is no one truth when it comes to World War II."
—Ari Beser**

Ari Beser should know. His paternal grandfather was the only person to have flown in both of the planes that dropped atomic bombs on the Japanese cities of Hiroshima and Nagasaki. His maternal grandfather had employed a young Japanese woman who survived the bombing of Hiroshima. Spurred by this dual connection to these 1945 events, Beser set out to document his paternal grandfather's story, along with those of the survivors. "This is not just an American story or a Japanese story. It's a human story," he says.

^ Ari Beser's grandfather, Lieutenant Jacob Beser, poses in front of the B-29 bomber, *Enola Gay*. This photo was taken before the plane dropped the first atomic weapon ever used in combat on the city of Hiroshima, Japan, on August 6, 1945.

MAIN IDEA American scholar Ari Beser investigates the stories of atomic bomb survivors to promote peace and reconciliation.

Ari Beser (left) poses with Clifton Truman Daniel (right), grandson of President Harry Truman, who ordered the use of atomic weapons against Japan in 1945. They are joined by survivors of the bombs and their family members in Hiroshima.

ATOMIC HERITAGE

Growing up, Ari Beser had long heard tales of his grandfather's crucial role in the most historic of events. An engineer, Lieutenant (Lt.) Jacob Beser modified radar systems to suit the unique needs of the bombing mission. He was unapologetic about his part. He viewed the bombings as a necessary step in ending the war with Japan. Nonetheless, he expressed the wish that no such tragedy should ever happen again and made a point of ensuring that his grandchildren were aware of his story.

Lt. Beser left behind a technical memoir about his time on the Manhattan Project, the research and development initiative during World War II that produced the first atomic weapons. From the memoir, Ari Beser gained a wealth of firsthand information about his grandfather and his perspective on World War II. To better understand the perspective of the Japanese impacted by the bombing, Beser set out to talk to some of the remaining *hibakusha*—survivors of the bombs.

TRUTH AND RECONCILIATION

Through projects that aimed to raise awareness of the events at Hiroshima and Nagasaki, Beser did just that. A Fulbright–National Geographic Digital Storytelling Fellowship allowed him to travel to Japan in 2015 for the 70th anniversary of the bombings. The bombs together had killed some 200,000 people. Thousands more suffered radiation sickness. Beser has interviewed more than 50 *hibakusha* about their experiences during and in the wake of the bombings.

Despite the horrors they experienced, many *hibakusha* were eager to talk to Lt. Beser's grandson. The survivors bore no ill will toward the family of the man who had participated in the bombing missions. Ari Beser's frank but respectful approach gained him the trust of his interviewees. "How do you always get me to say things I've never said before?" asked a relative of Sadako Sasaki, who gained international renown for folding over 1,000 paper cranes as she battled leukemia caused by radiation exposure.

11.7.7 Discuss the decision to drop atomic bombs and the consequences of the decision (Hiroshima and Nagasaki); CST 1 Students compare the present with the past, evaluating the consequences of past events and decisions and determining the lessons that were learned.

Gaining that trust was a necessary step. The accounts of the *hibakusha* are universally awful. They recount vividly the bright flash, the heat, and the wind generated by the bomb. And they all have tales of the carnage they witnessed in the aftermath. The rivers were choked with human remains, and horribly injured survivors wandered in search of help. Many were burned and stripped of skin. Even those who recovered endured years of chronic pain and wounds that wouldn't heal. As painful as reliving these memories is, the *hibakusha* insist that recording them is essential. Remarkably, many suspend judgment of the actions taken by the United States. Beser concurs. "We are each other's history," he says. "We all have a relative somewhere that fought in some war. This just happens to be my family's story."

It is his hope—and the hope of the *hibakusha*—that the exchange of these stories will put an end to nuclear warfare once and for all.

HISTORICAL THINKING

1. **READING CHECK** What does Beser hope to accomplish by talking to bomb survivors?
2. **EVALUATE** Compare the 1945 bombing of Japan to a similar recent event. What were the consequences of both events? What lessons were learned from them?
3. **MAKE GENERALIZATIONS** How do most survivors view the bombings?

4.1 **MAIN IDEA** The Nazis rounded up Jews and other persecuted groups and imprisoned them in concentration camps, where millions were murdered.

THE HOLOCAUST

In the haze of war, Americans knew about Hitler's hatred of the Jews, but few allowed themselves to imagine the full extent of his anti-Semitic fervor. After the war in Europe was over, the world learned what the Nazis were capable of.

NAZI PERSECUTION OF JEWS

When the Allies invaded Germany and Poland in the spring of 1945, they encountered scenes of horror: **concentration camps** full of starving and dying prisoners. Most were Jews, but there were also non-Jewish Poles; Roma, or Gypsies; homosexuals; and political dissidents.

The nightmare began when Hitler became Germany's chancellor in January 1933. You've learned that Hitler considered Jews an inferior race, and he began almost immediately to devise a plan for their extermination. On Hitler's command, the Nazis began to systematically restrict the civil and political rights of Jews. They removed Jews from German schools and universities and banned them from many public areas. Businesses were taken away from their Jewish owners, and Jewish doctors and lawyers were not allowed to practice. In time, the Jewish people lost their right to vote.

Persecution of the Jews escalated with Kristallnacht on November 9, 1938, when, as you have read, rioters attacked and killed about 100 Jews and destroyed Jewish shops and synagogues. Many German Jews sought refuge in other countries, but the Nazis made travel outside of Germany difficult. Soon, Jews were forbidden to leave the country at all.

Jews in the Netherlands were forced to wear a Star of David, like this one, with the Dutch word *Jood*, meaning "Jew." Any Jew in a German-occupied territory who refused to wear a star faced severe punishment or even death.

Germany invaded Poland in 1939, and the Nazis subjected both Jewish and non-Jewish Poles to brutal treatment. They made Poles perform hard labor and seized their property. They also created about 400 confined areas in Polish cities, called ghettos, forcing huge numbers of Jews to live in them. Barbed wire, thick walls, and armed guards surrounded the ghettos to prevent residents from escaping. Jews older than the age of six in Poland and in all German-occupied territories eventually were forced to wear a yellow Star of David with *Jew* written in the region's

After putting up a fight in 1943, the Jews in Poland's Warsaw ghetto who survived were captured and deported to concentration camps. The Nazis systematically destroyed the city and blew up Warsaw's Great Synagogue. This photo is one of many taken by a Nazi photographer to document the Jews' removal.

language on it. With so many people living in such tight quarters, food was scarce, and disease spread quickly. In 1941, the Nazis rounded up others they had imprisoned as "undesirables" and sent them to the Polish ghettos. But the ghettos were just holding places until the Nazis came up with a plan to solve what they called "the Jewish question."

"THE FINAL SOLUTION"

When Germany invaded the Soviet Union, special military units accompanied the German Army. Their sole responsibility was to kill Jews, Gypsies, and Soviet heads of government departments. By 1943, these mobile killing units had executed an estimated 1 million Jews. This was the first step in what the Nazis called the "final solution." "Final solution" was code for the plan to murder all the Jews in Europe—approximately 11 million in all. Hitler had made it known that this was his goal. In January 1942, **Reinhard Heydrich**, head of the Gestapo, called a meeting of high-ranking Nazis in Wannsee, a suburb of Berlin. Heydrich had gathered the men together at the **Wannsee Conference** to explain how the rest of the plan would be carried out.

Heydrich told the men that concentration camps would be constructed in eastern Europe. Jews would be sent to the camps, where the able-bodied among them would build roads and do other work. The work would be so hard that many Jews would die due to "natural reduction." Those who put up any resistance would be executed. But Jewish genocide, or the systematic destruction of a racial, cultural, or ethnic group and its culture, was the real purpose of the camps. The Nazis equipped most of the camps with facilities for carrying out the killings. The camps became known as extermination or death camps.

CRITICAL VIEWING These survivors of Buchenwald, one of the largest concentration camps inside Germany, were photographed as U.S. forces arrived at the camp in April 1945. Among them is Elie Wiesel, whose face appears farthest to the right in the second bunk from the bottom. Wiesel would describe his experiences in concentration camps in his memoir *Night*. What does the survivors' appearance suggest about their treatment in the camp?

Anne Frank, 1942

PRIMARY SOURCE

The most famous Jew who went into hiding from the Nazis is Anne Frank, a young girl who hid with her family in a secret attic apartment in Amsterdam, the Netherlands. Not long before the Nazis found the Franks and deported Anne to Auschwitz, she wrote the following in her famous diary.

In spite of everything I still believe that people are really good at heart. I simply can't build up my hopes on a foundation consisting of confusion, misery, and death. I see the world gradually being turned into a wilderness, I hear the ever approaching thunder, which will destroy us too, I can feel the sufferings of millions and yet, if I look up into the heavens, I think that it will all come right, that this cruelty too will end, and that peace and tranquility will return again.

—from *The Diary of a Young Girl*, by Anne Frank, published in 1947

From 1942 until early 1945, the Nazis rounded up millions of Jews all across Europe. Jews were often ordered to gather in a town square, where Nazi officers terrorized them and then packed them into trains for "deportation," or transport, to the death camps. The overcrowded train cars were hot in the summer and freezing in the winter, and passengers did not receive food or water during the journey. Some died before they reached their destinations.

A number of Jews went into hiding or resisted rather than board the trains. The most famous example of resistance took place in 1943, when Jews in the Polish ghetto of Warsaw fought back against the Nazis. Armed with weapons they had managed to smuggle into the ghetto, the group held off the Nazis for a time. But in the end, the far better-equipped German troops overpowered the Jews. About 7,000 of those in the Warsaw ghetto were shot immediately. The rest—about 50,000—were sent to the camps.

DEATH CAMPS

The most notorious death camps were located in Poland and included Chelmno, Treblinka, and **Auschwitz** (OWSH-vits), the largest of the camps. Auschwitz consisted of three main camps. All were labor camps, and one included a killing center. Because Auschwitz was at a junction where several railways converged, the camp served as a convenient place for the Nazis to transport prisoners from all across Europe. In 1944, for example, Nazis transferred more than 400,000 Hungarian Jews there.

When prisoners first arrived, a doctor would review them, sending certain groups of people to their death, including pregnant women, young children, the elderly, the disabled, and the ill. Most of these people were killed immediately in specially prepared gas chambers, where they were told they would simply be taking a shower. Then the victims' bodies were burned in **crematoria**, or ovens. Those who were in good physical shape were put to work, often in factories in the area. When the laborers could no longer work due to malnutrition, illness, or exhaustion, the Nazis sent them to the gas chambers. An estimated 1.1 million Jews died at Auschwitz, including those who had been subjected to terrible medical "experiments" performed by the camp's chief doctor, Josef Mengele.

Even when the end of the war in Europe—and the end of the Third Reich—was in sight, the killings at Auschwitz and other death camps continued. But as the Soviets and other Allies advanced across eastern Europe, the Nazis who ran the camps abandoned them and fled. First, however, they tried to destroy any evidence of what had happened in the camps. They dismantled the barracks where prisoners had lived, burned down buildings that housed crematoria, and destroyed warehouses containing prisoners' clothing and personal items. Nonetheless, plenty of evidence remained of the murders that had been committed in the camps. In all, about 6 million Jews died in the **Holocaust**, which is what the systematic genocide carried out by the Nazis came to be called.

HISTORICAL THINKING

1. **READING CHECK** What was the "final solution"?
2. **MAKE INFERENCES** Why do you think the Nazis forced Jews to wear a yellow Star of David?
3. **DRAW CONCLUSIONS** In what ways did the initial restrictions placed on the civil and political rights of the Jews impact the events of the holocaust?

HI 4 Students understand the meaning, implication, and impact of historical events and recognize that events could have taken other directions.

4.2 **MAIN IDEA** The War Refugee Board was created late in the war to rescue Jews, and Nazi war criminals were tried at Nuremberg after the war.

REFUGEES AND JUSTICE

When American troops discovered the concentration camps and their starved, tortured inmates, they could scarcely believe what they saw. For the first time, many of the soldiers understood what they'd been fighting for.

PLIGHT OF THE REFUGEES

While most Americans were unaware of the existence of the Nazi concentration camps, the Allied leaders of the United States, Britain, and the Soviet Union did know about them. In December 1942, Roosevelt, Churchill, and Stalin issued a declaration officially recognizing the mass murder of European Jews and vowing to bring those responsible to justice. Even so, the Allies did not make bombing death camps and the railroad tracks that carried the prisoners a priority. Thousands of Jews fleeing Europe were admitted to the United States, but many thousands more were turned away. The U.S. State Department claimed that some of the refugees could be spies and therefore posed a national security risk.

Finally, pressured by American Jewish organizations and officials in his own government, President Roosevelt created the **War Refugee Board** in January 1944 to rescue Jews. In its most ambitious effort, the board helped finance the work of Swedish diplomat **Raoul Wallenberg** to save tens of

United States Holocaust Memorial Museum Washington, D.C.

When Masha Kessler and her 17-year-old daughter, Esther, arrived at the Kaiserwald concentration camp in the northern European country of Latvia, one of the two Polish women was issued this striped uniform coat. The rectangular patch at the top of the coat once contained the prisoner's ID number, and the yellow triangle beneath the patch indicated the prisoner was Jewish. Prior to their transfer to Kaiserwald, the mother and daughter had been forced to live in a Jewish ghetto. The pair worked as slave laborers in several concentration camps before Soviet troops liberated them in January 1945. Masha or Esther continued to wear the coat throughout their imprisonment in the camps. The Holocaust Memorial Museum displays this coat and other artifacts worn by Holocaust victims in their permanent collection.

thousands of Hungarian Jews from the death camps. Wallenberg traveled to Nazi-occupied Hungary and set up hospitals, soup kitchens, and safe houses for Jews in Budapest. He and his colleagues also distributed certificates of protection and Swedish passports to the Jews. During World War II, Sweden remained neutral, which meant the Nazis could not legally harm citizens holding a Swedish passport.

THE NUREMBERG TRIALS

The world learned about the extent of Nazi **atrocities**, or extremely cruel and shocking acts of violence, when the International Military Tribunal charged and tried former Nazi officials, military officers, industrialists, and others as war criminals. A **tribunal** is a court with authority over a specific matter. The series of trials, known as the **Nuremberg trials**, took place in Nuremberg, Germany, beginning in 1945. The tribunal determined that defendants could be charged with any of the following: crimes against peace, for having waged a war of aggression; crimes against humanity, for having exterminated groups of people; and war crimes, for having violated common and agreed-upon laws of war. Members of the tribunal represented the United States, Great Britain, the Soviet Union, and France and had the authority to determine the guilt of any individual or group. As evidence, the prosecution presented Nazi propaganda films, footage filmed at concentration camps by Allied troops, and ghastly artifacts taken from the camps. Survivors of the camps also testified, describing what they had witnessed and experienced.

Trials for 22 major Nazi war criminals were held in 1945 and 1946. Several of the leading figures in the party could not be tried, however. Hitler and two of his top officers, Heinrich Himmler and Joseph Goebbels, committed suicide before they could be brought to justice. Most of those charged did not deny or apologize for their actions. In their defense, many said they were "just following orders." On October 1, 1946, the tribunals issued their verdicts. While the tribunals acquitted some of the major war criminals and sent others to prison, they sentenced 12 to death by hanging. One of the 12 was Hermann Goering, whom Hitler had designated as his successor. However, Goering evaded execution by committing suicide. He swallowed a tablet of cyanide, which he had hidden in his cell, the day before he was to hang.

The Nuremberg trials attempted to bring Nazi war criminals to justice. But for many of those who survived the Nazi atrocities, their experiences would continue to haunt them throughout their lives. Some survivors, including the Romanian-born writer **Elie Wiesel**, wanted to bring the horrors of the Holocaust to the world's attention. Wiesel was 15 years old when he was sent to Auschwitz along with his parents and sister. He was later transferred to Buchenwald. After the war, Wiesel wrote *Night*, an account of the violence and abuse he experienced and witnessed in the camps. He did not want the world to forget what happened.

Holocaust museums created after the war have the same mission. By telling the stories of the victims and survivors, these museums show that those affected were not numbers but real people. The museums also stress the responsibility of citizens to speak out against hatred and prejudice to help prevent genocide from happening again.

PRIMARY SOURCE

In 1986, Elie Wiesel was awarded the Nobel Peace Prize. In this excerpt from his acceptance speech, Wiesel explains our role in the face of suffering and oppression.

There is much to be done, there is much that can be done. One person—a Raoul Wallenberg . . . one person of integrity, can make a difference, a difference of life and death. As long as one dissident is in prison, our freedom will not be true. As long as one child is hungry, our lives will be filled with anguish and shame. What all these victims need above all is to know that they are not alone; that we are not forgetting them, that when their voices are stifled we shall lend them ours, that while their freedom depends on ours, the quality of our freedom depends on theirs.

—from Elie Wiesel's Nobel Peace Prize acceptance speech, December 10, 1986

HISTORICAL THINKING

1. **READING CHECK** What did Raoul Wallenberg do to try to save Hungarian Jews in Budapest?
2. **MAKE INFERENCES** Why do you think it was important to bring Nazi war criminals to trial instead of simply executing them?
3. **DRAW CONCLUSIONS** What did Wiesel mean when he said, "their [the victims'] freedom depends on ours, the quality of our freedom depends on theirs"?

11.7.5 Discuss the constitutional issues and impact of events on the U.S. home front, including the internment of Japanese Americans (e.g., *Fred Korematsu* v. *United States of America*) and the restrictions on German and Italian resident aliens; the response of the administration to Hitler's atrocities against Jews and other groups; the roles of women in military production; and the roles and growing political demands of African Americans.

CHAPTER 13 AMERICA IN WORLD WAR II

13 REVIEW

VOCABULARY

Use each of the following vocabulary words in a sentence that shows an understanding of the term's meaning.

1. atomic bomb HSS 11.7.7
   The atomic bomb caused firestorms and released radioactivity in Hiroshima and Nagasaki, resulting in thousands of casualties.
2. wage discrimination HSS 11.7.5
3. Holocaust HSS 11.7.5
4. war bond HSS 11.7.5
5. ration HSS 11.7.5
6. concentration camp HSS 11.7.5
7. kamikaze HSS 11.7.2
8. internment camp HSS 11.7.5

READING STRATEGY

DETERMINE CHRONOLOGY

When you determine chronology, you place events in the order in which they occurred and note correlations between events. Use a time line like this one to order the key events in America's involvement in World War II. Then answer the question.

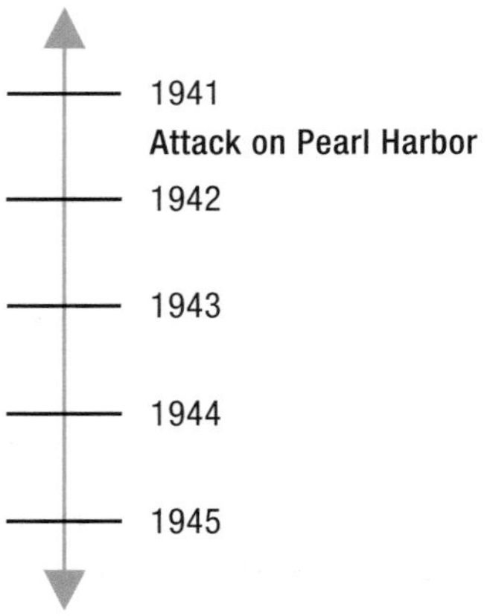

9. What events in 1945 led the United States to drop two atomic bombs on Japan? HSS 11.7.7

MAIN IDEAS

Answer the following questions. Support your answers with evidence from the chapter.

10. Why did President Roosevelt order General MacArthur to leave the Philippines? LESSON 1.1 HSS 11.7.2
11. How did the experience of war impact California demographically, economically, socially, and politically? LESSON 1.2 HSS 11.7.5
12. What advantages did American-built Sherman tanks have over German panzers? LESSON 2.1 HSS 11.7.6
13. What unique impact did James Doolittle's raid on Tokyo have on Americans and the Japanese? LESSON 2.2 HSS 11.7.3
14. What postwar plans for Europe did Roosevelt, Churchill, and Stalin draw up at the Yalta Conference? LESSON 3.1 HSS 11.7.4
15. How did America win the war in the Pacific? LESSON 3.2 HSS 11.7.2
16. How did Roosevelt respond to Hitler's atrocities against Jewish people? LESSON 4.2 HSS 11.7.5

HISTORICAL THINKING

Answer the following questions. Support your answers with evidence from the chapter.

17. **MAKE INFERENCES** Why do you think Norman Rockwell chose to illustrate the four freedoms from Roosevelt's speech as scenes from everyday life? HSS 11.7.4
18. **SYNTHESIZE** How did World War II serve to advance movements for equality at home and abroad? HSS 11.7.5
19. **DRAW CONCLUSIONS** How did the American government change because of World War II? HSS 11.7.5

20. **COMPARE AND CONTRAST** How was the war mobilized and fought differently in the Atlantic versus the Pacific? HSS 11.7.2

21. **FORM AND SUPPORT OPINIONS** Do you think President Roosevelt and the Allies should have bombed death camps and railroads in Poland, or were they right to prioritize ending the war quickly? Explain your answer. HSS 11.7.5

INTERPRET VISUALS

In 1942, the U.S. War Production Board published this poster to encourage Americans to contribute scrap—in this case, discarded pieces of metal, rubber, and clothing—to the war effort. Study the poster, and then answer the questions that follow.

22. According to the poster, what did contributions of scrap bring down? HSS 11.7.5

23. Why might the poster have inspired Americans to contribute scrap? HSS 11.7.5

ANALYZE SOURCES

Lawson Inada's collection, *Only What We Could Carry*, provides firsthand accounts of the Japanese American experience during World War II, including oral histories of Japanese servicemen. The collection includes *Citizen 13660* by Miné Okubo, a Japanese American who was relocated during the war. In this excerpt from *Citizen 13660*, Okubo describes the train ride from the assembly center near San Francisco to the internment camp.

> The trip was a nightmare that lasted two nights and a day. The train creaked with age. It was covered with dust, and as the gaslights failed to function properly we traveled in complete darkness most of the night. All the shades were drawn and we were not allowed to look out of the windows. Many became train sick and vomited. The children cried from restlessness.

24. What details does Okubo use to convey the frightening journey? HSS 11.7.5

CONNECT TO YOUR LIFE

25. **ARGUMENT** Before the attack on Pearl Harbor, many Americans did not want to get involved in World War II. Do you think the United States was ultimately right to go to war? Or do you believe that war is never justified? Write a paragraph in which you make an argument for or against going to war. HSS 11.7.1

TIPS

- State your position about whether the country was right to go to war.
- Explain what, if any, circumstances make war justifiable.
- Use information from the chapter to help support your ideas.
- Address any counterarguments.
- Conclude your argument with a sentence summarizing your position.

CHAPTER 14

THE COLD WAR AND KOREA 1945–1960

HISTORICAL THINKING What impact did communism have on the United States and the rest of the world?

CRITICAL VIEWING The Korean War Veterans Memorial on the National Mall in Washington, D.C., dedicated in 1995, includes 19 stainless steel figures representing all branches of the U.S. armed forces. The ponchos they are wearing indicate the extreme weather conditions the soldiers faced in Korea. How do the statues convey the tension and uncertainty the soldiers experienced?

"Peace must be built upon **power.**"

—President Harry S. Truman

1.1 **MAIN IDEA** After World War II, the United States and its allies set out to rebuild Europe and promote lasting peace through greater international cooperation.

EUROPE REBUILDS

When a powerful storm destroys buildings, people rebuild and try to make them stronger. Following the war, the United States and its allies worked to rebuild war-torn Europe and to strengthen international cooperation in order to keep the horrors of World War II from happening again.

THE UNITED NATIONS

In the autumn of 1945, the world sighed with relief. The guns were silent. Peace had arrived. As World War II ended, the Allies turned their attention to building a lasting peace. As you have read, early in the war, a number of nations signed on to the Atlantic Charter, which promoted the ideals of democracy and mutual respect among nations. The Allies acted on these ideals to create the **United Nations (UN)**, a global organization promoting cooperation among nations and working together to resolve conflicts peacefully. On October 24, 1945, the required 28 nations had ratified the organization's charter, and the United Nations became a reality. By the end of the year, it had a total of 52 member nations.

While the main focus of the United Nations was to promote international peace, it also worked proactively to help promote economic development, social progress, and human rights around the world. Officials created a number of smaller organizations within the UN to support these goals. The **United Nations Educational, Scientific, and Cultural Organization (UNESCO)** was created in 1945 to rebuild schools, libraries, and museums that had been destroyed during World War II. The **UN Commission on Human Rights**, established in 1946, aimed to protect fundamental human rights and freedoms around the world. And in 1948, the United Nations established the **World Health Organization (WHO)** to promote health worldwide.

A GLOBAL PERSPECTIVE

In 2016, the World Health Organization worked with local authorities in Angola and the Democratic Republic of the Congo (DRC) to vaccinate 30 million citizens against yellow fever.

In this photo, a nurse vaccinates a young woman at a clinic in Kinshasa, the capital of the DRC. Yellow fever causes severe flu symptoms and in some cases can be fatal. Nearly 1,000 cases of the disease had been confirmed in the 2 countries before the end of the outbreak was declared in July 2016.

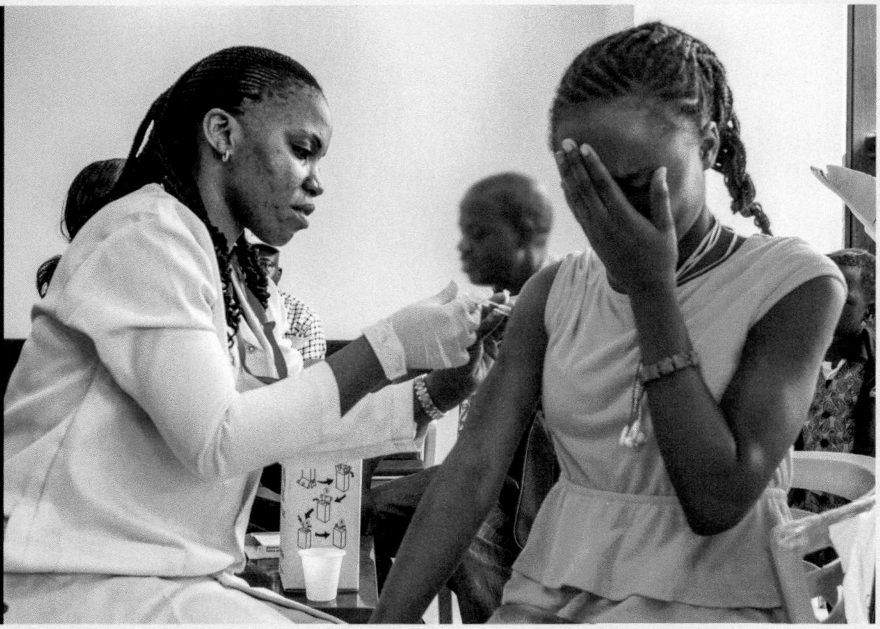

11.7.8 Analyze the effect of massive aid given to Western Europe under the Marshall Plan to rebuild itself after the war and the importance of a rebuilt Europe to the U.S. economy; 11.9 Students analyze U.S. foreign policy since World War II; 11.9.1 Discuss the establishment of the United Nations and International Declaration of Human Rights, International Monetary Fund, World Bank, and General Agreement on Tariffs and Trade (GATT) and their importance in shaping modern Europe and maintaining peace and international order.

In addition to establishing a much-needed structure of organizations to rebuild and promote peace, the United Nations also formally documented basic human rights. In 1948, the UN adopted its **Universal Declaration of Human Rights**, which set out the fundamental rights of all people of all nations. These rights include freedom of thought and religion as well as freedom of expression and the right to assemble peacefully.

Several other organizations were created after the war to help battle-scarred nations recover economically. Proposed in 1944, the **International Monetary Fund** was officially established in 1945 to standardize worldwide financial relations and rates of exchange between countries. Its purpose is to safeguard and stabilize the global monetary system. The **World Bank** was founded in 1944 to provide financial support to countries that needed to rebuild after World War II. The **General Agreement on Tariffs and Trade (GATT)** was launched in 1947 and created rules for world trade.

In addition to working toward a lasting peace, the United States and its allies also sought to make any future wars more humane and just. In 1949, a number of nations agreed to the **Geneva Conventions**. This was the collective name of a revised set of three earlier treaties establishing rules for the humane treatment of prisoners of war as well as wounded or sick soldiers. Nations created and agreed to a fourth treaty that called for fair treatment and protection of civilians living in and around war zones.

THE MARSHALL PLAN

Across Europe, from Germany to Poland and the Soviet Union, the destruction from World War II was immense. Rail lines lay in ruin, roads were impassable, and major parts of cities were piles of rubble. Economies were no longer functioning, and the threat of mass starvation hung over the continent. In contrast, the United States had emerged from the war as the world's strongest economic and military power. The United States was determined to rebuild Europe and keep its economy from collapsing.

In June 1947, U.S. Secretary of State George C. Marshall proposed a massive financial aid plan he called the **European Recovery Program**. Marshall assured Europeans that it was a helping hand and not a way for the United States to control the continent. "Our policy is not directed against any country or doctrine," Marshall said, "but against hunger, poverty, desperation, and fear." Most Americans agreed and broke from their isolationist past. As citizens of the wealthiest and most powerful nation, they accepted the idea that they had some responsibility to keep the peace and help countries rebuild. Congress granted the billions of dollars needed to fund the proposal, which became known as the "**Marshall Plan**," and committed more than 10 percent of the U.S. federal budget to restore Europe's economic health.

The Marshall Plan

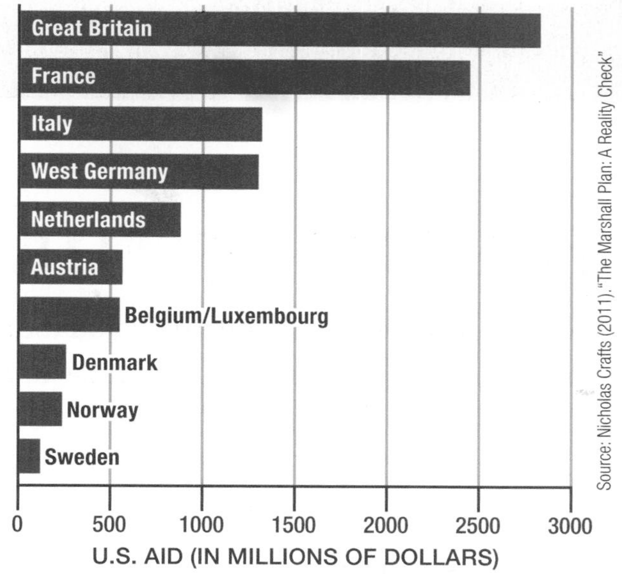

As the Marshall Plan came together, the nations of Europe, including the Soviet Union, met to assess their common needs. But the Soviets soon walked out. They objected to giving critical Soviet economic information to outsiders. The Soviets also believed that accepting aid from capitalist countries might undermine their communist system. With the Soviets out, the Marshall Plan targeted mainly Western Europe. In the end, the program proved to be a tremendous success. It helped to rebuild Britain, Germany, and France and restore economic confidence to many European nations. Helping rebuild Europe also increased American trade and investment in Europe, creating new markets for U.S. goods.

HISTORICAL THINKING

1. **READING CHECK** What are the main goals of the United Nations?
2. **DRAW CONCLUSIONS** What might the Soviet Union's response to the Marshall Plan meeting have indicated about the potential for tension with the United States?
3. **INTERPRET GRAPHS** In total, how much did the Marshall Plan give to the top three aid recipients?

11.9.3 Trace the origins and geopolitical consequences (foreign and domestic) of the Cold War and containment policy, including the following: • The era of McCarthyism, instances of domestic Communism (e.g., Alger Hiss) and blacklisting • The Truman Doctrine • The Berlin Blockade • The Korean War • The Bay of Pigs invasion and the Cuban Missile Crisis • Atomic testing in the American West, the "mutual assured destruction" doctrine, and disarmament policies • The Vietnam War • Latin American policy.

1.2 **MAIN IDEA** Sharp divisions between Western capitalist countries, led by the United States, and communist countries, led by the Soviet Union, created a new threat to world peace.

THE SOVIET THREAT

Did you ever work with someone you didn't like in order to win a game or complete a project? The United States and the Soviet Union put aside their differences to help win World War II—but then their differences re-emerged and ushered in a new struggle.

THE DIVISION OF EUROPE

The Allies had fought hard together to defeat Nazi Germany and Imperial Japan, and the Soviet Union had been essential to that effort. Soon, however, relations between the Soviets and the West began to decline. As you have read, President Franklin Roosevelt, Soviet Premier Joseph Stalin, and British Prime Minister Winston Churchill met at Yalta in 1945 to make plans for postwar Europe. The leaders had difficulty reaching any agreements. Underlying the rift was a vast difference between the political and economic structures of the United States and Soviet Union.

The disagreement was based on differing visions of government and economic policy. The United States and Great Britain wanted capitalist democratic governments established throughout Europe. Capitalism is an economic system in which private individuals or groups own the resources and produce goods for a profit. In contrast, Stalin wanted the Soviet Union to dominate the internal affairs of its Eastern European neighbors, controlling them under a communist regime, where all economic resources are owned by the state. In addition, the Soviets wanted to spread communism to other nations. The fundamental differences between communism and capitalism would shape the relationship between the United States and the Soviet Union for decades to come.

By the war's end, Soviet forces had occupied much of Eastern Europe, creating suspicion of communism among Western countries. Instead of withdrawing, the Soviet Army stayed, and Stalin installed communist rule throughout the region.

"Glory to the Russian people—the *bogatyr* people, the creator people!" is the message on this Soviet propaganda poster created by Viktor Ivanov in 1947. The man in front is a Russian engineer, a symbol of Soviet postwar industrial growth, and the towering figure standing behind him is a *bogatyr*, a Russian medieval hero. The intention of the poster is to motivate the working masses, the new "heroes" of Soviet nationalism.

11.9.3 Trace the origins and geopolitical consequences (foreign and domestic) of the Cold War and containment policy, including the following: • The era of McCarthyism, instances of domestic Communism (e.g., Alger Hiss) and blacklisting • The Truman Doctrine • The Berlin Blockade • The Korean War • The Bay of Pigs invasion and the Cuban Missile Crisis • Atomic testing in the American West, the "mutual assured destruction" doctrine, and disarmament policies • The Vietnam War • Latin American policy.

By 1947, Stalin had created a ring of communist "satellite states" around the Soviet Union that became known as the **Eastern Bloc**. These Soviet-style communist governments suppressed political opposition, using the brutal methods employed by Stalin and his Soviet secret police. When the slightest stirrings of political independence arose in Eastern Europe, Soviet officials removed key people from power, imprisoned opponents, and in some instances, executed perceived "rebels."

The defeated nation of Germany was a special case. In the summer of 1945, the victors—the United States, Great Britain, France, and the Soviet Union—split Germany into four allied **occupation zones**. The eastern part of Germany became an occupation zone ruled by the Soviet Union. The western part was split into three occupation zones, with the United States, Great Britain, and France each controlling a zone. Berlin, Germany's capital, was entirely within the Soviet occupation zone, but it was governed by a joint agency of all four nations.

In 1946, the Americans and British combined their two sections of Berlin into a single section: West Berlin. In May 1949, the occupation zones of Germany controlled by the United States, Britain, and France merged into a single zone and, on May 23, this zone became the sovereign nation of the **Federal Republic of Germany**, or West Germany. The Soviets reacted to the formation of West Germany by creating the **German Democratic Republic**, or East Germany, in October 1949.

CONTAINMENT AND THE TRUMAN DOCTRINE

While visiting the United States in 1946, former British prime minister Winston Churchill addressed the growing concern over Soviet expansion. Speaking at Westminster College in Missouri, Churchill summed up the division of Europe. "From Stettin in the Baltic to Trieste in the Adriatic," he declared, "an **iron curtain** has descended across the Continent." The term "iron curtain" became shorthand for the divide in Europe between Western capitalist and Eastern communist countries. Churchill insisted the Soviets must be dealt with from a position of strength, and the United States must take a leading role in preventing the further expansion of communism.

By the time Churchill had spoken, the United States was already mapping out a plan for confronting the Soviets. The plan's architect was George F. Kennan, a foreign service officer stationed at the U.S. embassy in Moscow. In early 1946, Kennan laid out the doctrine of **containment**, or control of Soviet influence, that would shape American foreign policy for the next 40 years. Under containment, the

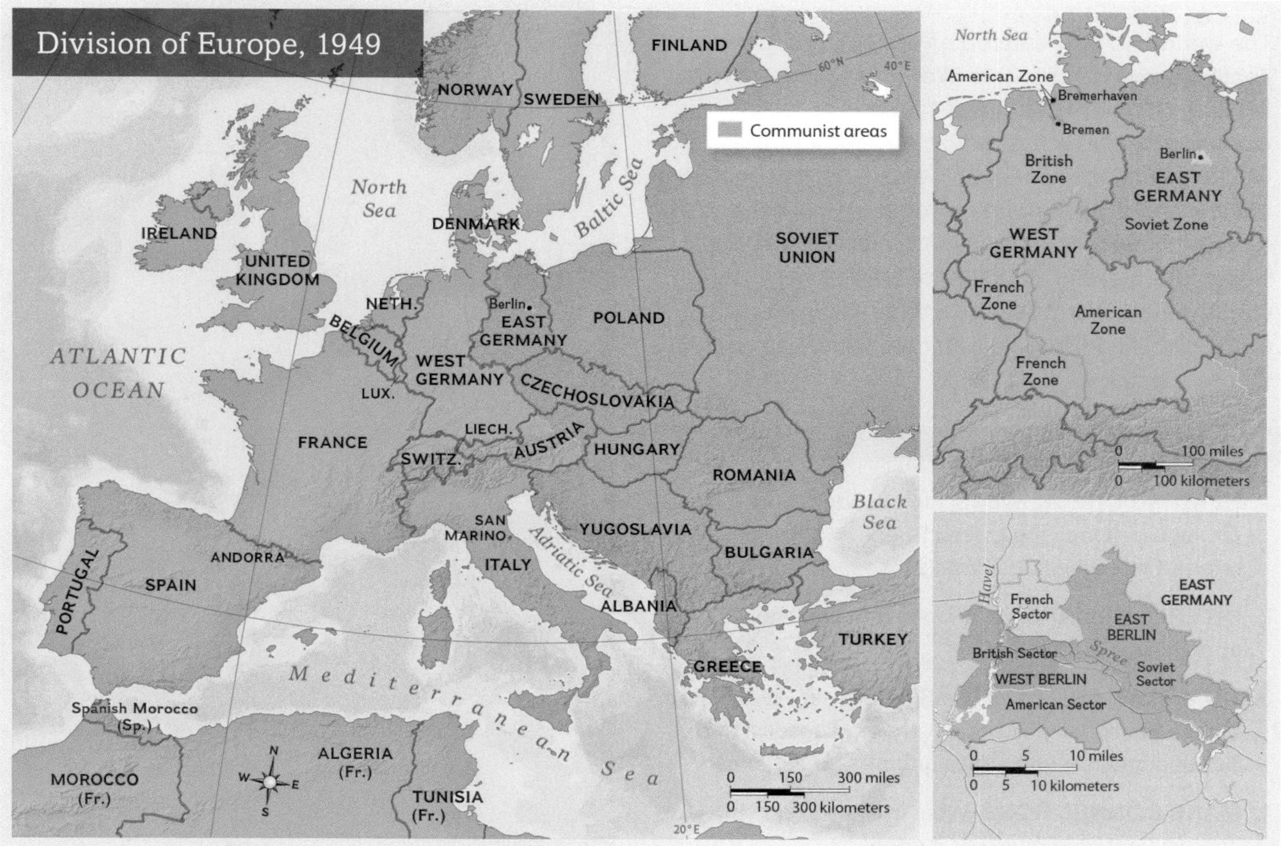

United States would focus on keeping communism from expanding. American forces, Kennan said, would employ "the adroit [skillful] and vigilant [watchful] application of counterforce at a series of constantly shifting geographical and political points, corresponding to the shift and maneuvers of Soviet policy." President Truman firmly supported the policy of containment and its goal of blocking the Soviets from spreading communism to other countries. "Unless Russia is faced with an iron fist and strong language, another war is in the making," Truman predicted. "I am tired of babying the Soviets."

In 1947, the United States acted on its containment policy as it entered a conflict in the Mediterranean region. The Soviet Union was threatening to take land in Turkey, while in Greece, communist-led guerrillas were battling the government in a bloody civil war. Great Britain, which controlled the area, warned the United States that Britain could no longer afford to offer military and economic aid to Greece and Turkey. In response, Truman told Congress that "Great Britain finds itself under the necessity of reducing or liquidating its commitments in several parts of the world." He then proposed that the United States provide economic and military aid to all countries threatened by a communist takeover. This proposal became known as the **Truman Doctrine**. The president asked for and received from Congress $400 million in aid for Greece and Turkey.

The world had now entered an era of U.S.-Soviet conflict known as the **Cold War** that would last from the late 1940s to 1991. It was termed the "cold" war because the United States and Soviet Union would never engage in open warfare against each other. Instead, each country would try to weaken the other's influence around the world, and each country would take sides in a number of smaller wars. In the end, the Cold War would be a massive ideological and geopolitical struggle with consequences rippling across the globe.

HISTORICAL THINKING

1. **READING CHECK** Why is the decades-long struggle between the United States and Soviet Union referred to as the "Cold War"?
2. **INTERPRET MAPS** What does the map show about Berlin in 1949?
3. **COMPARE AND CONTRAST** Following WW II, how did the economic policies of Western capitalist and Soviet communist countries differ from each other?
4. **MAKE CONNECTIONS** What is the doctrine of containment, and how was it applied?

THE BERLIN AIRLIFT

The Soviet Union resented having a democratic West Berlin in the middle of its occupation zone. In June 1948, the Soviets began a blockade of the city, cutting off land access and hoping to starve out the British and Americans. Unwilling to use military force to end the blockade, the Western allies devised another way to get food, fuel, and other supplies to West Berlin.

In what became known as the Berlin Airlift, allied cargo planes used open air corridors over the Soviet occupation zone to drop the supplies into West Berlin. By the spring of 1949, it was clear that the Soviet blockade had failed, and it was lifted by the middle of May.

While on their way to school in 1948, West Berlin children and adults turned to watch an inbound U.S. C-47 cargo plane heading for Tempelhof Airport with food and other supplies.

11.4.6 Trace the declining role of Great Britain and the expanding role of the United States in world affairs after World War II; CST 3 Students use a variety of maps and documents to interpret human movement, including major patterns of domestic and international migration, changing environmental preferences and settlement patterns, the frictions that develop between population groups, and the diffusion of ideas, technological innovations, and goods.

THE COLD WAR BEGINS

The years following the end of World War II saw the onset of the Cold War, as the United States and the Soviet Union battled each other for global dominance.

The notion of an "Iron Curtain" across Europe symbolized the Cold War and the deep division between the free West and the communist world. Not surprisingly, it was a favorite subject of cartoonists. British cartoonist Leslie Illingworth sketched this cartoon the day after Winston Churchill's famous speech in Missouri in 1946. He depicts Churchill peeking under a curtain that carries a message signed by "Joe," a reference to Soviet leader Joseph Stalin. The cartoon also features several symbols of the division of Europe.

CRITICAL VIEWING Look closely at the cartoon. Which symbols of the division of East and West does the cartoonist include?

11.9.3 Trace the origins and geopolitical consequences (foreign and domestic) of the Cold War and containment policy, including the following: • The era of McCarthyism, instances of domestic Communism (e.g., Alger Hiss) and blacklisting • The Truman Doctrine • The Berlin Blockade • The Korean War • The Bay of Pigs Invasion and the Cuban Missile Crisis • Atomic testing in the American West, the "mutual assured destruction" doctrine, and disarmament policies • The Vietnam War • Latin American policy.

DOCUMENT ONE

Primary Source: Speech
from Winston Churchill's speech, delivered at Westminster College in Fulton, Missouri, March 5, 1946

In this famous speech, Churchill condemned the Soviet Union's policies in Europe and coined the phrase "Iron Curtain." The speech ends with a strong plea for a unified international front against communist expansion.

CONSTRUCTED RESPONSE A metaphor is a figure of speech that directly compares two unlike things. What does the metaphor "iron curtain" help you understand about the situation Churchill describes in his speech?

> An *iron curtain* has descended across the Continent. Behind that line lie all the capitals of the ancient states of Central and Eastern Europe. Warsaw, Berlin, Prague, Vienna, Budapest, Belgrade, Bucharest and Sofia, all these famous cities and the populations around them lie in what I must call the Soviet sphere, and all are subject . . . not only to Soviet influence but to a very high and, in some cases, increasing measure of control from Moscow.

DOCUMENT TWO

Primary Source: Speech
from President Harry S. Truman's speech, delivered March 12, 1947, before a joint session of Congress

How should the United States react to the advance of communism in Europe? In a dramatic speech to a joint session of Congress, President Truman asked Congress to appropriate money to stop communist aggression in Greece and Turkey. The president first articulated the Truman Doctrine in this speech.

CONSTRUCTED RESPONSE Truman's speech is considered the opening "shot" of the Cold War. Why do you think it is regarded as such?

> At the present moment in world history nearly every nation must choose between alternative ways of life. The choice is too often not a free one. . . . I believe that it must be the policy of the United States to support free peoples who are resisting attempted subjugation [control] by armed minorities or by outside pressures. I believe that we must assist free peoples to work out their own destinies in their own way. I believe that our help should be primarily through economic and financial aid which is essential to economic stability and orderly political processes.

DOCUMENT THREE

Secondary Source: Newspaper Article
from "Truman Acts to Save Nations From Red Rule," by Felix Belair, Jr., March 12, 1947, the *New York Times*

The *New York Times* journalist Felix Belair covered the speech in which President Truman announced the Truman Doctrine.

CONSTRUCTED RESPONSE What are two important points the newspaper reporter has gathered from Truman's speech?

> President Truman outlined a new foreign policy for the United States. He proposed that this country intervene wherever necessary throughout the world to prevent the subjection of free peoples to Communist-inspired totalitarian regimes. . . . Although the President refrained from mentioning the Soviet Union by name, there could be no mistaking his identification of the Communist state as the source of much of the unrest throughout the world.

SYNTHESIZE & WRITE

1. **REVIEW** Review what you have learned about the events that led to the Cold War and the division of Europe.
2. **RECALL** On your own paper, write the main differences between the views of Stalin and other Soviet leaders and the views of Western leaders toward the postwar situation.
3. **CONSTRUCT** Construct a topic sentence that answers this question: How did President Truman respond to the advance of communism in Europe?
4. **WRITE** Using evidence from this chapter and the documents, write an informative paragraph that supports your topic sentence in Step 3. Include information about Truman's and Churchill's views of the Soviet Union.

HREP 4 Students construct and test hypotheses; collect, evaluate, and employ information from multiple primary and secondary sources; and apply it in oral and written presentations.

1.4 **MAIN IDEA** After the 1948 election, President Truman proposed a progressive plan that extended the New Deal.

TRUMAN'S FAIR DEAL

Imagine being a soldier returning home after fighting on the front lines of World War II. You have no job waiting for you. What do you do? Can you count on the government to help you?

THE POSTWAR ECONOMY

In addition to the foreign policy challenges of the impending Cold War, President Truman's domestic challenges proved demanding as well. When millions of soldiers came back from overseas, ready to resume their lives as civilians, the U.S. economy struggled to accommodate them. With no more military orders to fill, factories closed, causing widespread layoffs. There was little work for returning soldiers. In addition, home construction had been on hold during the war, which caused a major housing shortage for veterans and their families. Homelessness spiked in major cities—Chicago had more than 100,000 homeless veterans and Washington, D.C., had 25,000.

CRITICAL VIEWING The longest lasting and most popular feature of the GI Bill was the guaranteed loan for veterans. How might the poster above encourage a World War II veteran and his family to apply for a loan?

Fortunately, the United States was entering a period where both the Democrats and Republicans saw the benefit of working together to solve many of the nation's problems. They agreed that the welfare state that began during the New Deal should be continued and even expanded. Legislators supported the development of a national security system to fight communism within the country. And they believed a strong central government with a powerful executive branch could help achieve these goals. Historian Godfrey Hodgson called this agreement between parties the **liberal consensus**.

11.8 Students analyze the economic boom and social transformation of post-World War II America; 11.8.1 Trace the growth of service sector, white collar, and professional sector jobs in business and government.

For example, in 1944 both parties in Congress worked together to pass the Servicemen's Readjustment Act, commonly known as the **GI Bill**. "GI," short for "Government Issue," is a military term that refers to U.S. armed forces. The GI Bill provided long-term, low-interest loans to veterans; funds to help pay college tuition; and a $2,000 bonus toward the purchase of a new home. As a result, millions of new homes popped up around the country, and newly educated veterans joined the nation's growing **white-collar**, or professional, workforce.

Not all domestic efforts went so smoothly. In June 1946, Truman lifted the price controls on consumer goods previously imposed during the war to prevent inflation, even though he feared the cost of food and other necessities would skyrocket without the controls. They did. In just weeks, the cost of meat doubled. Faced with higher prices and no increase in wages, unions across the country began to strike.

The United Auto Workers went on strike for 113 days, demanding a pay increase. Large railroad and mine workers' unions also went on strike for higher pay, bringing U.S. transportation and energy industries to a standstill. Although the strikes were resolved, Congress passed the **Taft-Hartley Act** in 1947 to limit strikes in the future. The act allowed the president to impose an 80-day federal injunction to temporarily stop strikes that threatened national safety or health and required unions to give their employers a 60-day notice before staging a strike. Truman vetoed it, but Congress overrode his veto.

TRUMAN'S PLAN

Truman also faced the problem of racial conflict in the United States after the war, and he took a strong stand for civil rights. He authorized a special task force to investigate racial discrimination in the country. The task force recommended the desegregation of the armed forces, the creation of a civil rights division in the federal government, and the end of segregation and lynching in the United States. After Congress failed to pass any civil rights laws, Truman ordered the armed forces to be desegregated in 1948.

As the 1948 election approached, President Truman was on shaky ground. His stance on racial equality had caused a group of southern Democrats to split from the party, demanding "complete segregation of the races." He had a rocky relationship with other members of Congress as well, some of whom urged him not to run for re-election. And he faced a strong Republican opponent, New York Governor **Thomas E. Dewey**.

PRIMARY SOURCE

We cannot afford to float along ceaselessly on a postwar boom until it collapses. It is not enough merely to prepare to weather a recession if it comes. Instead, government and business must work together constantly to achieve more and more jobs and more and more production—which mean more and more prosperity for all the people.

—from President Harry Truman's State of the Union speech in reference to the "Fair Deal," 1949

As the election neared, Dewey held the lead in opinion polls and was widely predicted to become the next president. However, Truman launched a vigorous campaign, traveling by train across the country attacking the "do-nothing" Congress. In a surprising upset, Truman won the election. The *Chicago Tribune* newspaper even ran the mistaken headline "Dewey Defeats Truman."

At his inauguration on January 20, 1949, Truman introduced a plan he called the **Fair Deal**, after Roosevelt's New Deal. The Fair Deal included such progressive ideas as expanding Social Security, increasing the minimum wage, continuing subsidies to support crop prices, instituting national health care, and passing an anti-discrimination law. He also called for expanding the Tennessee Valley Authority and providing funds for **rural electrification** in farm communities that did not yet have electricity.

The Fair Deal was a mixed success. By the end of his term, Truman had managed to expand Social Security and raise the minimum wage, but many of his other proposals were blocked by a conservative Congress. Also, the national debt grew in order to cover the government programs that boosted the postwar economy. In turn, the federal government had to pay higher interest rates on that debt, although neither the vital programs nor the nation's economy were in jeopardy. Still, the Fair Deal set the stage for future administrations to push a progressive agenda with the help of the liberal consensus.

HISTORICAL THINKING

1. **READING CHECK** What did Truman propose in the Fair Deal, and how did Congress respond?
2. **MAKE GENERALIZATIONS** How did the GI Bill improve the lives of soldiers returning from the war?
3. **IDENTIFY MAIN IDEAS AND DETAILS** What were the goals of the liberal consensus?

11.8.3 Examine Truman's labor policy and congressional reaction to it; 11.8.4 Analyze new federal government spending on defense, welfare, interest on the national debt, and federal and state spending on education, including the California Master Plan; 11.11.2 Discuss the significant domestic policy speeches of Truman, Eisenhower, Kennedy, Johnson, Nixon, Carter, Reagan, Bush, and Clinton (e.g., with regard to education, civil rights, economic policy, environmental policy).

2.1 **MAIN IDEA** The United States and the Soviet Union established themselves as opposing superpowers as they built up their arms and formed protective alliances.

ESCALATING TENSIONS

One of the benefits of being part of a group of friends is a feeling of security and knowing that people "have your back." As the Cold War began, nations joined sides with either the United States or the Soviet Union, seeking that same feeling of protection in a world of new dangers.

THE SOVIETS UNVEIL THE BOMB

On August 29, 1949, a little more than four years after the United States dropped the first atomic bomb on Hiroshima, the Soviet Union stunned the world by conducting a test explosion of its own atomic bomb. Americans were shocked. Few believed the Soviets could have developed such a weapon. After all, the Soviet Union was considered a backward nation struggling to rebuild its destroyed **infrastructure**—roads, buildings, and public utilities—after the war. A number of officials accused the Soviets of espionage, or obtaining the bomb plans through theft or spying.

The development of the Soviet bomb set off a nuclear **arms race** between the United States and the Soviet Union that would last for decades. As the two countries continued their competitive buildup of nuclear weapons, the odds that they might use them kept rising. However, the complete destructive potential of both stockpiles ultimately acted as a deterrent to using them.

The onset of the arms race led to rapid growth for the U.S. defense industry. Factories geared up to design and build planes, rockets, and satellites. Southern California, in particular, became the booming center of the U.S. **aerospace industry**. The availability of land and a favorable climate made southern California an attractive location, and more than half of the nation's 25 largest aerospace companies would

NATO and the Warsaw Pact 1955

Sources: NATO and U.S. State Department

Nuclear Stockpiles 1945–1991

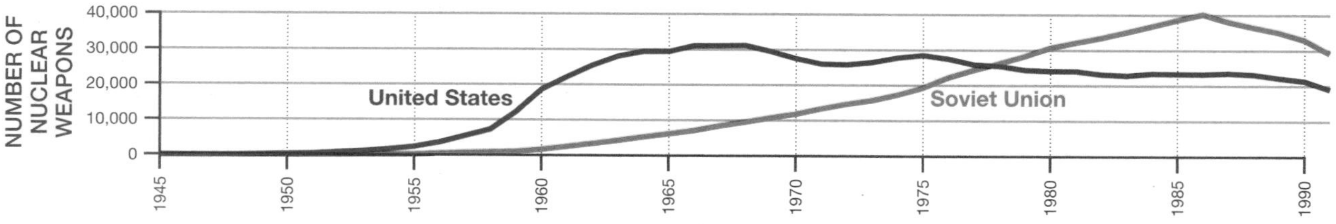

Source: Hans M. Kristensen & Robert S. Norris, "Global nuclear weapons inventories, 1945–2013," 2013

Rows of new F-4 Phantom fighter jets designated for the U.S. Navy and Air Force in the 1960s

PRIMARY SOURCE

Many years after the arms race began, President Dwight D. Eisenhower (elected in 1952) gave a speech in which he warned against the close relationship that had grown between the military and the aerospace industry, a relationship he called the **military-industrial complex**.

In the councils of government, we must guard against the acquisition of unwarranted influence, whether sought or unsought, by the military-industrial complex. The potential for the disastrous rise of misplaced power exists and will persist. . . . Only an alert and knowledgeable citizenry can compel the proper meshing of the huge industrial and military machinery of defense with our peaceful methods and goals, so that security and liberty may prosper together.

—from President Dwight D. Eisenhower's Farewell Address, 1961

come to reside there. Between 1952 and 1962, the U.S. government funneled more than $50 billion into California, twice the amount received by any other state. For decades, the aerospace industry would be a major driving force of the California economy.

CREATING ALLIANCES

In addition to stockpiling arms, the United States and the Soviet Union formed alliances to keep each other in check. In 1949, the United States, Canada, and 10 Western European nations formed the **North Atlantic Treaty Organization (NATO)**. Member nations agreed to aid each other should one of the countries be attacked. To counter NATO, the Soviets created the **Warsaw Pact**, a collective defense treaty of communist countries that included the Soviet Union, Albania, Poland, Romania, Hungary, East Germany, Czechoslovakia, and Bulgaria. Similar to NATO, the Warsaw Pact stated that the member countries would defend each other against attack. Several years later, the United States would help establish a similar alliance among Asian countries, known as the **Southeast Asia Treaty Organization (SEATO)**.

As the United States built global alliances, the nation also moved to strengthen its own security and defense. In 1947, lawmakers passed the National Security Act, which unified all of the armed forces under a single **Department of Defense.** The act also created the **National Security Council (NSC)** to gather and provide foreign policy information to the president. In addition, the act established the **Central Intelligence Agency (CIA)** to collect classified information overseas and uncover what other nations were doing behind the scenes. The CIA was similar to wartime intelligence agencies that had since been disbanded.

In 1950, Secretary of State Dean Acheson wrote a secret document known as National Security Council Paper 68 (NSC68), which called for a steep increase in peacetime military spending—from $13 billion to $50 billion per year. It also called for the construction of a "thermonuclear device," a **hydrogen bomb**, that would be even more powerful than the atomic bomb. Truman never showed NSC68 to Congress, but when the document was declassified, or made public, in 1975, it provided a look at how U.S. defense policy was shaped.

HISTORICAL THINKING

1. **READING CHECK** How was the establishment of international alliances in the 1950s tied to the arms race?
2. **ANALYZE CAUSE AND EFFECT** How did the development of a Soviet atomic bomb affect the economy of southern California?
3. **INTERPRET GRAPHS** During which decade did the Soviets begin to surpass the United States in number of nuclear weapons?

11.8.4 Analyze new federal government spending on defense, welfare, interest on the national debt, and federal and state spending on education, including the California Master Plan; 11.9.2 Understand the role of military alliances, including NATO and SEATO, in deterring communist aggression and maintaining security during the Cold War; HI 1 Students show the connections, causal and otherwise, between particular historical events and larger social, economic, and political trends and developments.

2.2 **MAIN IDEA** Communist governments were established in Asia, including in China, as the Cold War spread across the globe.

COLD WAR AROUND THE GLOBE

Have you ever seen a video of hundreds of dominoes falling in a chain reaction? During the Cold War, some feared that might happen with countries: if one became communist, its neighbors might quickly follow.

THE CHINESE REVOLUTION

As the United States and its allies confronted the Soviet Union, another communist power was emerging—China. As you have read, communist forces had been active in China since the 1920s. By the 1930s, the Chinese Communist Party (CCP), led by Mao Zedong, was battling Chiang Kai-shek and his Chinese Nationalist Party, which ruled the country.

When World War II broke out, the two sides joined together to help defeat Japan. After the war, however, their civil war resumed. On paper, Chiang and his forces had better resources. But Chiang's government had grown increasingly corrupt, ineffective, and unpopular during World War II. Meanwhile, Mao had become an inspiring leader. He attracted many people, and his Communist Party gained a reputation for supporting the common man. Chiang responded to communist attacks with increased violence and repression, which only made him more unpopular.

Despite strong U.S. support for Chiang in the Chinese civil war, the tide turned in favor of Mao's communist army, now called the People's Liberation Army (PLA). The PLA captured the city of Beijing in January 1949 and occupied, or took over, Nanjing and Shanghai soon after. In late 1949, Mao claimed victory. He announced the formation of the **People's Republic of China** and declared his communist solidarity with the Soviet Union.

Chiang and his remaining forces fled to the island of Taiwan, where they set up a **government-in-exile**, or a government that has been deposed and attempts to rule from another land. Chiang claimed to lead the only legitimate Chinese government. The United States strongly backed this claim. Now, mainland China, once a loyal U.S. ally, had become a clear enemy to the United States. With the world starkly divided into American and Soviet spheres of influence, or areas

The Andy Warhol Museum Pittsburgh, Pennsylvania

The 5-foot wide by 7-foot tall image of Mao by artist Andy Warhol suggests the enormous scale of the images of communist leaders publicly displayed in their countries. Warhol made hundreds of silk screens of Mao, each altered in a different way by adding paint. The Mao series of work comments on communist propaganda and popular culture in the United States. Warhol was a leading practitioner of pop art.

11.8.8 Discuss forms of popular culture, with emphasis on their origins and geographic diffusion (e.g., jazz and other forms of popular music, professional sports, architectural and artistic styles).

PRIMARY SOURCE

In 1945, Ho Chi Minh declared Vietnam's independence from France using rhetoric from the French Declaration of the Rights of Man and the Citizen and from the American Declaration of Independence.

The Declaration of the French Revolution made in 1791 on the Rights of Man and the Citizen also states: 'All men are born free and with equal rights, and must always remain free and have equal rights.' Nevertheless for more than 80 years, the French imperialists . . . have built more prisons than schools. They have mercilessly slain our patriots; they have drowned our uprisings in rivers of blood. They have . . . impoverished our people, and devastated our land. They have robbed us of our rice fields, our mines, our forests.

—from Declaration of Independence of the Democratic Republic of Vietnam, by Ho Chi Minh, 1945

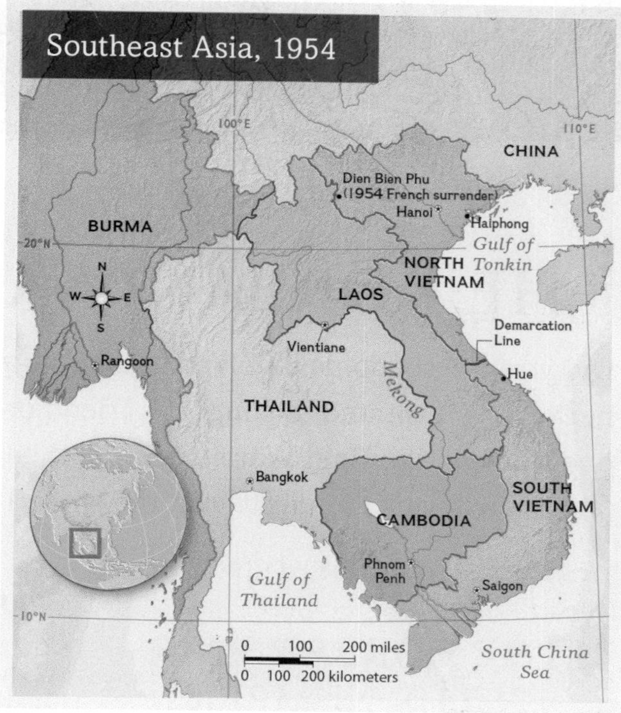

of authority, China's shift was seen as a serious loss for the West. A debate raged in Washington about who was to blame for "losing China" to communism. Opponents of President Truman portrayed Mao's victory as an "avoidable catastrophe" that the president failed to prevent by focusing too much on Eastern Europe and not enough on China.

FROM CHINA TO SOUTHEAST ASIA

The policy of containment, as you have read, was based on a fear that communism would spread. Western leaders reinforced this idea with the **domino theory**. They argued that just like rows of dominoes knocking each other down, communist countries—especially those in Asia—would "knock over" their neighbors and make them communist as well.

After World War II, the French controlled much of Southeast Asia, including Vietnam, Laos, and Cambodia, a region known as Indochina. In Vietnam, France soon faced a revolt led by communist leader **Ho Chi Minh**. Ho led a group known as the Viet Minh. In September 1945, the Viet Minh announced their independence from France, seized control of the northern part of the country, and declared the **Democratic Republic of Vietnam (North Vietnam)** with Ho as president.

Financial backing and military supplies from the United States helped France secure control of the southern region and set up the **State of Vietnam (South Vietnam)**. For the next five years, France fought the Viet Minh, who were supported by the Soviet Union and China, for control of Vietnam. Ho and his troops realized it was impossible to win large-scale battles against the French. Instead, they conducted a guerrilla war in the countryside, attacking the French and then retreating into Vietnam's mountains and jungles.

In March 1954, the Viet Minh defeated a large French force at the **Battle of Dien Bien Phu**. The two sides negotiated a peace agreement that officially divided Vietnam into two countries: communist North Vietnam and democratic South Vietnam. However, the situation remained unstable and battles continued to erupt. By the end of the 1950s, the United States would increase its direct involvement in the Vietnam conflict. But before that, the United States focused on stopping the spread of communism in another Asian country—Korea.

HISTORICAL THINKING

1. **READING CHECK** Why did the United States support Chiang's Chinese government-in-exile?
2. **INTERPRET MAPS** What war advantage did North Vietnam have, considering its location next to China?
3. **DRAW CONCLUSIONS** How might breaking Vietnam into two separate countries lead to conflict later on? Use evidence from the text to support your prediction.
4. **FORM AND SUPPORT OPINIONS** Does it make sense to compare countries to game pieces that might fall in a chain reaction as the domino theory did? Why or why not?

11.9.3 Trace the origins and geopolitical consequences (foreign and domestic) of the Cold War and containment policy, including the following: • The era of McCarthyism, instances of domestic Communism (e.g., Alger Hiss) and blacklisting • The Truman Doctrine • The Berlin Blockade • The Korean War • The Bay of Pigs invasion and the Cuban Missile Crisis • Atomic testing in the American West, the "mutual assured destruction" doctrine, and disarmament policies • The Vietnam War • Latin American policy.

2.3 **MAIN IDEA** The first major conflict of the Cold War broke out in Korea, as U.S. troops joined UN forces to help battle communist forces for control of the country.

THE KOREAN WAR

Did you ever become involved in an argument or debate between two people because you wanted to support a friend or because you strongly supported one side? As the Cold War heated up, the United States became involved in a far-off civil war in order to halt the spread of communism.

THE KOREAN WAR BY THE NUMBERS

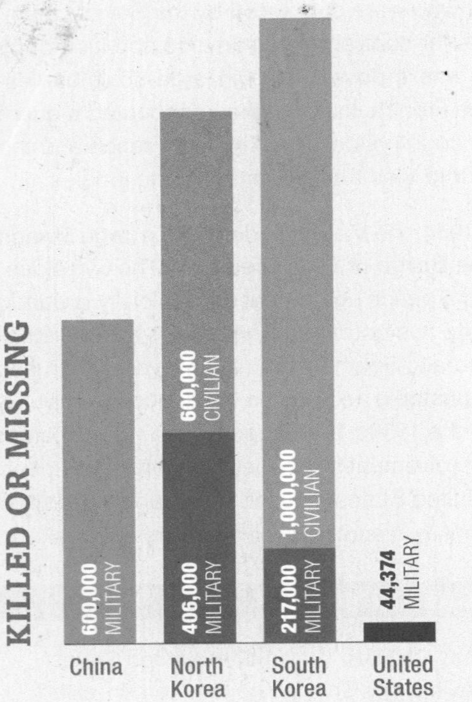

1,789,000 Total number of U.S. troops serving

36,574 U.S. soldiers killed in action

>7,800 American soldiers still unaccounted for as of June 2016

Sources: CNN and the Department of Veterans Affairs

WAR ERUPTS IN KOREA

The nation of Korea lies on a peninsula that borders northeastern China. Japan had ruled the land since the late 1800s. In 1945, after Japan's defeat in World War II, the Allies took control. They divided the Korean Peninsula roughly in half at the **38th parallel**, which is 38 degrees latitude north of the equator. Soviet troops controlled North Korea, while American-backed troops controlled the Republic of Korea, also called South Korea. With Soviet backing, a communist government was set up in North Korea, while the United States helped establish democratic rule in the south. Both sides claimed to be the legitimate ruler of the entire peninsula, and skirmishes along the border were common. In 1948, the United Nations moved to unify the country through national elections. But the Soviets refused to let UN officials into North Korea, preventing the elections from taking place.

On June 25, 1950, North Korean troops crossed the 38th parallel and invaded South Korea, taking everyone by surprise. It was clear that, although North Korea was the immediate aggressor, it attacked with the approval of the Soviet Union. This situation—where a major power starts a war in which it does not become directly involved—is called a **proxy war**. A proxy is a person or nation that acts as a substitute for or on behalf of another.

President Truman viewed the invasion as a test of his containment policy aimed at preventing the Soviets from spreading communism further. At Truman's urging, the United Nations condemned the attack and ordered North Korea to withdraw. North Korea refused, and the UN dispatched a multinational military force to South Korea. Meanwhile, Truman ordered American troops stationed in Japan to provide additional military support to the UN forces, including those U.S. troops already stationed on the Korean peninsula. He also sent an American naval fleet into the waters between China and Taiwan.

11.9.2 Understand the role of military alliances, including NATO and SEATO, in deterring communist aggression and maintaining security during the Cold War.

The Korean War, 1950–1954

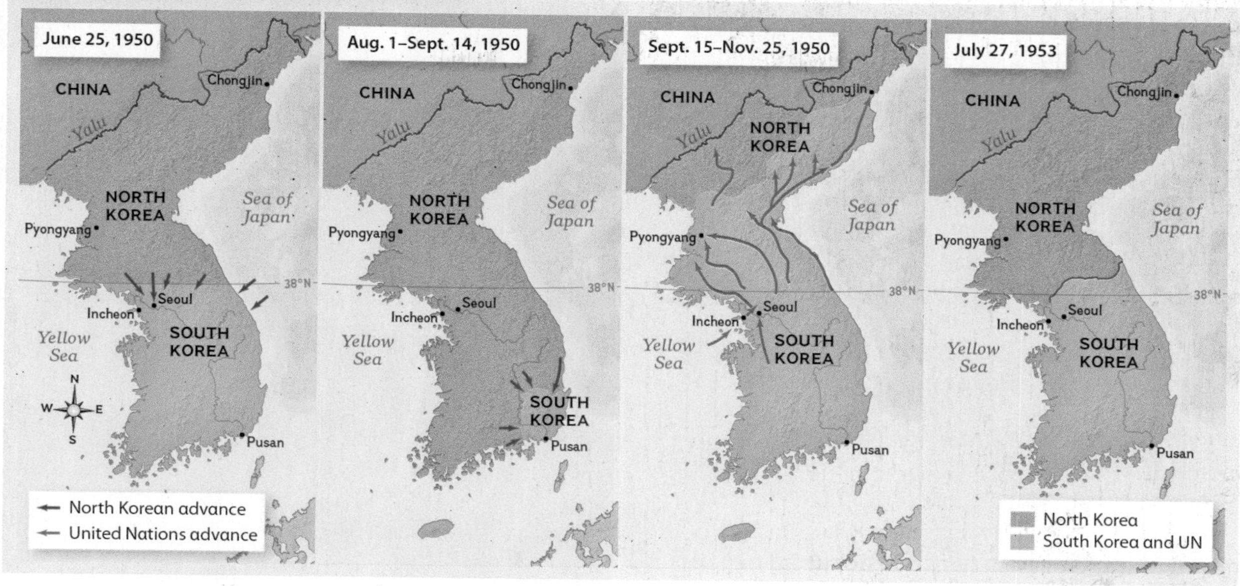

A BACK-AND-FORTH BATTLE

North Korean forces had moved swiftly, and within weeks they had captured the South Korean capital of Seoul (sohl). The army continued to push south. By the end of July 1950, North Korea had pushed UN troops to the southern tip of the peninsula, into a small region around the city of Pusan. The defenders, however, dug in and fought off one furious attack after another as they waited for reinforcements.

As North Korea seemed poised to win, U.S. commander General Douglas MacArthur executed a bold plan. He sent UN and U.S. troops by sea to the port of **Incheon**, 150 miles behind North Korean lines. MacArthur intended to surprise and overwhelm the enemy by attacking from the rear. It worked. With their communications cut and under heavy bombardment, the North Koreans fled back north across the 38th parallel. Sensing an opening, MacArthur chased the enemy over the border, deep into North Korea. Surrounded and under siege, the North Koreans pressed for peace and a return to the old border at the 38th parallel. The United States and South Korea, however, had set their sights on controlling all of Korea. Then China stepped in.

CHINA JOINS THE WAR

In November 1950, China staged a massive attack across its border into Korea. While the Chinese had initially stayed out of the conflict, they were not about to let their fellow communists in North Korea suffer a defeat. More than 300,000 Chinese troops overwhelmed American and South Korean forces. MacArthur, who had assured President Truman the Chinese would not enter the fight, now admitted, "We face an entirely new war." Scores of troops retreated to the south by sea. Meanwhile, several U.S. Marine and Army divisions trapped inland battled ferociously to escape. U.S. and UN forces withdrew south of the 38th parallel, and in January 1951, abandoned Seoul for a second time. After several months of intense fighting, the retreating forces held their ground just south of Seoul along the 37th parallel. MacArthur launched attack after attack, slowly pushing the Chinese and North Koreans back up the peninsula and eventually back over the 38th parallel.

TRUMAN FIRES MACARTHUR

China's entry into the war caused tensions between Truman and MacArthur. The general wanted to strike China with nuclear weapons, but President Truman strongly rejected the idea. Any attempt to widen the war, Truman reasoned, would alarm other UN partners and perhaps provoke the Soviets into starting a larger, more deadly war.

MacArthur, however, refused to be silent. He sent a letter to Congress criticizing Truman's refusal to meet force "with maximum counterforce" and ended with his oft-quoted phrase: "There is no substitute for victory." MacArthur also leaked information to the press, warning of a crushing defeat for UN forces if nuclear bombs were not used. On his own, MacArthur issued a warning to China, threatening to expand the war into Chinese territory. Truman was furious. In April 1951, the President

11.9.3 Trace the origins and geopolitical consequences (foreign and domestic) of the Cold War and containment policy, including the following: • The era of McCarthyism, instances of domestic Communism (e.g., Alger Hiss) and blacklisting • The Truman Doctrine • The Berlin Blockade • The Korean War • The Bay of Pigs invasion and the Cuban Missile Crisis • Atomic testing in the American West, the "mutual assured destruction" doctrine, and disarmament policies • The Vietnam War • Latin American policy.

PRIMARY SOURCE

With deep regret I have concluded that General of the Army Douglas MacArthur is unable to give his wholehearted support to the policies of the United States Government and of the United Nations in matters pertaining to his official duties. In view of the specific responsibilities imposed upon me by the Constitution of the United States and the added responsibility which has been entrusted to me by the United Nations, I have decided that I must make a change of command in the Far East. I have, therefore, relieved General MacArthur of his commands and have designated Lt. Gen. Matthew B. Ridgway as his successor.

—from a statement by President Harry Truman, April 11, 1951

removed MacArthur from his post, accusing him of insubordination, or refusal to obey orders. Truman replaced MacArthur with General Matthew Ridgway.

MacArthur returned to the United States to public acclaim as a hero who symbolized old military values in a world complicated by the threat of nuclear war. Letters poured into the White House, and the vast majority—21 to 1—were against his firing. Angry groups of citizens even burned President Truman in effigy. An effigy is a crude model of a person, made to be damaged in protest. MacArthur gave a farewell address to a joint session of Congress. His closing words were: "Old soldiers never die; they just fade away. And like the old soldier of that ballad, I now close my military career and just fade away—an old soldier who tried to do his duty as God gave him the light to see that duty."

THE KOREAN WAR ENDS

As the Truman-MacArthur drama unfolded on the home front, the war in Korea settled into a standoff. By spring of 1951, both sides seemed willing to accept the prewar border of the 38th parallel. Truce talks began that summer but dragged on for two more years due to continuous disagreements. In July 1953, both sides finally signed a truce that stopped the fighting without formally ending the war.

The truce called for both sides to pull back from the battle line and designated the space between them along the 38th parallel as a **demilitarized zone**. No army could enter the zone without breaking the truce. The demilitarized zone, often referred to as the DMZ, still stretches across the entire width of the Korean Peninsula—a 148-mile border—from which hundreds of thousands of troops remain ready for conflict to erupt. South Korean troops, joined by U.S. troops, face North Korean troops across this fenced and guarded wasteland, which has now become a haven for vegetation and wildlife.

The toll from the first "hot" conflict of the Cold War was high, resulting in hundreds of thousands of lives lost, hundreds of cities and villages destroyed, and a ruined countryside, but it did not change the postwar division of Korea into two countries. War is always brutal, but the devastation of the

CST 3 Students use a variety of maps and documents to interpret human movement, including major patterns of domestic and international migration, changing environmental preferences and settlement patterns, the frictions that develop between population groups, and the diffusion of ideas, technological innovations, and goods.

North Korea today remains a communist-ruled country and is isolated from much of the rest of the world. In this 2012 photo, North Korean soldiers carry a large portrait of late leader Kim Il Sung in a military parade in Kim Il Sung square in Pyongyang, the capital city of North Korea. North Korea follows a policy of "Songun Chong'chi," or "Military First," and its army of more than 1 million is one of the largest in the world.

Korean War is unparalleled. The demilitarized zone continues to separate families and stifle the culture of a once united nation. But in defining their Korean identity, many South Koreans see themselves as a united community. North Korea presents itself as a united country, but its people have experienced long famines and much poverty. The armies still poised on either side of the DMZ ready to fight at any moment keep the two countries and the rest of the world on edge. After the North Korean government tested nuclear missiles in March 2013, South Korean officials called the act "an unforgiveable threat to the Korean peninsula's peace and safety."

HISTORICAL THINKING

1. **READING CHECK** What were the two major turning points in the Korean War?
2. **EVALUATE** North Korea was the Soviet Union's proxy in the Korean War. Was South Korea a proxy for the United States? Explain your answer.
3. **INTERPRET MAPS** According to the map, how did the war affect territory controlled by each side?
4. **FORM AND SUPPORT OPINIONS** Was President Truman right to fire MacArthur? Explain your opinion.

3.1 **MAIN IDEA** As the Cold War intensified, fear of communism once again gripped the home front, and Americans accused each other of disloyalty.

THE RED SCARE CONTINUES

Everyone knows fear can be contagious, and there was plenty of fear to go around in the years following World War II. Many people were afraid communism could gain a foothold in the United States, and that fear led to a period of suspicion and accusations, some of which implicated ordinary, innocent Americans.

A SECOND RED SCARE

As you have read, fear of communism seized America following World War I in what became known as the Red Scare. After World War II, a second Red Scare swept the nation. Americans watched with alarm as the Soviet Union imposed its communist rule across Eastern Europe and successfully tested an atomic bomb. In Asia, Mao Zedong's communist army toppled the pro-American government of Chiang Kai-shek in China, and the United States sent troops overseas to battle communist forces in Korea. As communism appeared to be on the march everywhere, Americans started to look for signs of the enemy at home, even among their friends and neighbors.

Congress led the attack on suspected communists through its **House Un-American Activities Committee (HUAC)**. The committee had originally been established to investigate Nazi propaganda in the United States in the 1930s. After World War II, HUAC began targeting suspected communists. Officials used the **Alien Registration Act**, also called the Smith Act, to prosecute alleged communist activity. The 1940 act, written in part by Democratic congressman Howard W. Smith, made it illegal to discuss overthrowing the government and required immigrants to register with authorities. Fewer than 200 people were charged under the legislation. When civil rights organizations spoke out against such practices, they too were targeted as possible communist sympathizers.

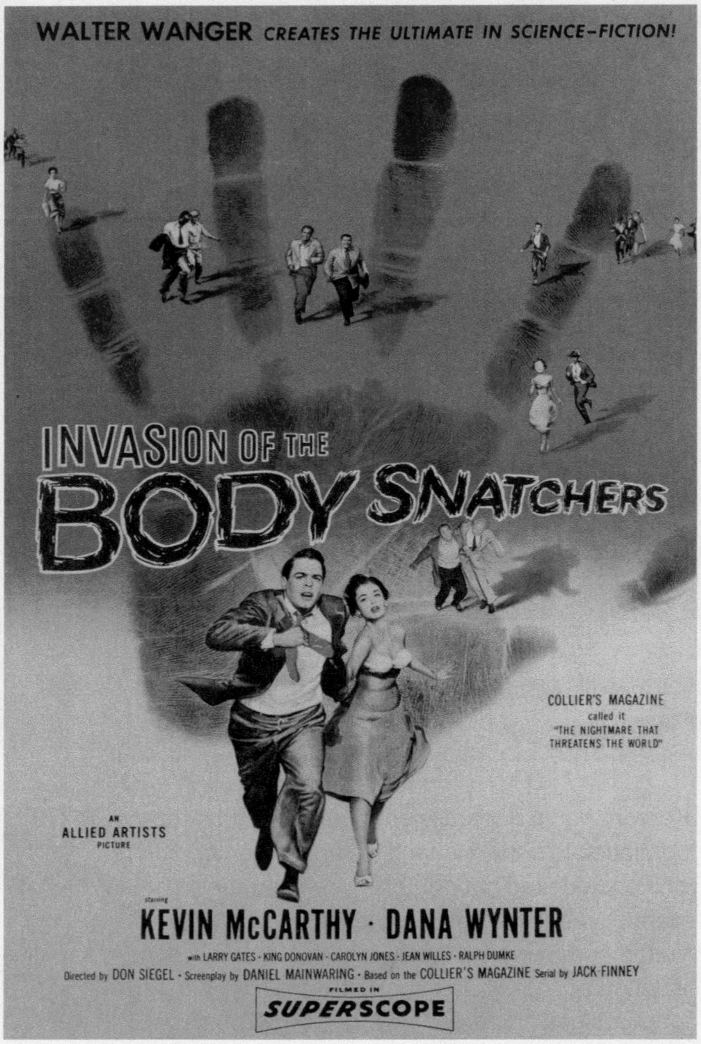

The 1956 Hollywood movie *Invasion of the Body Snatchers* tells the story of aliens who take over the bodies of humans. Many viewed the film as a commentary on the nation's postwar, anticommunist hysteria. The official movie poster released by the studio, Allied Artists Pictures, highlights the fear of the postwar years.

THE HOLLYWOOD TEN

In 1947, HUAC launched a highly publicized anticommunist investigation into the American motion picture industry. The committee accused ten screenwriters and film directors of creating pro-communist films and materials. Committee members issued the writers and directors a subpoena, or formal request to appear before them. During their hearings, the writers and directors refused to answer questions about their political beliefs and associations. Judges charged the "**Hollywood Ten**," as they became known, with contempt of Congress and sent them to jail. In addition, the group was blacklisted in the entertainment industry, which meant no one was willing to do any further work with them.

In the years that followed, many people found themselves in communism-related Supreme Court cases. The film industry became so linked to communism that its labor union, the Screen Actors Guild (SAG), required its members to take a **loyalty oath**, a sworn statement that they did not belong to various organizations including those identified as communist. Some universities, school districts, and school boards also started requiring their members to take loyalty oaths. In 1950, as part of a newly enacted state law, leaders of the University of California required its employees to take a loyalty oath and reject radical beliefs. A number of university professors lost their positions when they refused to sign loyalty oaths. In 1952, the California Supreme Court ruled in favor of the professors, but not until 1967 did federal courts rule the law unconstitutional.

SPY CASES GRIP THE NATION

The growing fear of communism at home sparked two prominent spy cases that captivated Americans. In 1948, American writer **Whittaker Chambers** testified before HUAC and claimed to have once been part of a "communist cell" in Washington, D.C. Chambers added that the cell included **Alger Hiss**, a former government official who had advised President Roosevelt in foreign affairs. Hiss denied the allegations in testimony before HUAC. When Chambers repeated the charge on a national radio broadcast, Hiss sued him for **libel**, the crime of making unsubstantiated negative claims about someone.

Chambers struck back by producing dozens of classified State Department documents from the 1930s that suggested Hiss was a spy for the Russians. The evidence included photographs and summaries of confidential reports Hiss had written in longhand or typed on a unique typewriter he once owned. **Richard M. Nixon**, a young California congressman, made a name for himself by pushing hard for Hiss's indictment, or formal charge of a criminal offense. Hiss could not be charged with espionage, as the alleged crime occurred too long ago. Instead, a federal grand jury indicted him for perjury, or lying, before HUAC. Hiss's first trial ended in a hung jury, or a jury that can't agree on a verdict. His second trial ended with a guilty verdict and a jail sentence for Hiss.

Another stunning trial involved **Julius and Ethel Rosenberg**, a New York couple who were active in the Communist Party. The case began in 1950, when the FBI discovered a spy network of American and British communists who were passing the Soviets information about U.S. atomic bomb development. After authorities arrested a German-born nuclear physicist for espionage, they discovered that Julius and Ethel Rosenberg were part of the same network of spies.

The Rosenbergs were arrested and convicted, in part on the testimony of Ethel Rosenberg's brother, David Greenglass, an engineer working on the Manhattan Project, which developed the American atomic bomb. A number of people viewed the Rosenbergs as innocent victims of anticommunist hysteria. However, numerous appeals and pleas for clemency, or mercy, failed. In 1953, the Rosenbergs were executed for treason.

Decades later, after the fall of the Soviet Union, information concerning the case was made public, including a number of radio messages. These messages were gathered and decrypted by the Venona Project, a code-breaking operation run by the U.S. Army. The messages, known as the Venona Papers, bolstered HUAC's claims of a communist threat in the United States. For years, the Rosenbergs' sons worked to prove their parents' innocence. By 2016, new evidence confirmed their father's guilt, but cast doubt on their mother's involvement.

HISTORICAL THINKING

1. **READING CHECK** What international events sparked the second Red Scare?
2. **DESCRIBE** Who were the prime targets of the House Un-American Activities Committee, and why were they targeted?
3. **MAKE INFERENCES** Why do you think the Screen Actors Guild agreed to blacklist members of its own union?

11.9.3 Trace the origins and geopolitical consequences (foreign and domestic) of the Cold War and containment policy, including the following: • The era of McCarthyism, instances of domestic Communism (e.g., Alger Hiss) and blacklisting • The Truman Doctrine • The Berlin Blockade • The Korean War • The Bay of Pigs invasion and the Cuban Missile Crisis • Atomic testing in the American West, the "mutual assured destruction" doctrine, and disarmament policies • The Vietnam War • Latin American policy; 11.9.4 List the effects of foreign policy on domestic policies and vice versa (e.g., protests during the war in Vietnam, the "nuclear freeze" movement).

3.2 **MAIN IDEA** A U.S. Senator named Joe McCarthy emerged as the leading figure in the hunt for suspected communists, creating an atmosphere of hysteria and fear in the United States.

THE RISE OF MCCARTHYISM

Have you ever been afraid to speak your mind out of fear that others will attack you or accuse you of something? That is the way many people felt during Senator Joseph McCarthy's hunt for communists within the U.S. government during the early 1950s.

McCARTHY'S LIST OF COMMUNISTS

On a bleak February evening in 1950, Senator **Joseph R. McCarthy**, a little-known politician from Wisconsin, delivered a speech to a Republican women's club in Wheeling, West Virginia. The topic of the speech was communist subversion in the federal government. **Subversion** is the act of secretly undermining something in an attempt to destroy it. "I have here in my hand," McCarthy told his audience, "a list of 205 Communists that were made known to the secretary of state and who are still working and shaping the policy of the State Department." The message was clear. The United States was losing the Cold War to the evil forces of communism because the U.S. government was filled with "traitors."

Among the politicians who targeted suspected communists at home during the Cold War, none stood out more than Joe McCarthy. Wisconsin's junior senator was an erratic, or unpredictable, politician, known for his reckless ambition and rowdy behavior. He knew little about communists in government or anywhere else. But as he spoke out about alleged sympathizers of communism within the U.S. government, the public listened. McCarthy had struck a nerve in a country growing more anxious about Soviet aggression and communist expansion. As the nation searched for explanations, McCarthy provided a simple answer. Disloyal Americans, especially those working in Washington, D.C., were the real enemy.

PRIMARY SOURCES

In an attack on President Truman's foreign policy in February 1950, Senator Joseph McCarthy claimed to have a list of hundreds of communists employed by the federal government, but he never publicly revealed any of those names. In June 1950, Senator Margaret Chase Smith went before the Senate to deliver a personal rebuttal to McCarthyism in her "Declaration of Conscience."

While I cannot take the time to name [them], I have in my hand 205 cases of individuals who would appear to be either card carrying members or certainly loyal to the Communist Party, but who nevertheless are still helping to shape our foreign policy.

One thing to remember in discussing the Communists in our government is that we are not dealing with spies who get thirty pieces of silver to steal the blueprints of a new weapon. We are dealing with a far more sinister type of activity because it permits the enemy to guide and shape our policy.

—from a speech in West Virginia by Senator Joseph R. McCarthy, 1950

The United States Senate has long enjoyed worldwide respect as the greatest deliberative body in the world. But recently that deliberative character has too often been debased to the level of a forum of hate and character assassination sheltered by the shield of congressional immunity.

The American people are sick and tired of being afraid to speak their minds lest they be politically smeared as "Communists" or "Fascists" by their opponents. Freedom of speech is not what it used to be in America. It has been so abused by some that it is not exercised by others.

—from a speech in the Senate by Senator Margaret Chase Smith, 1950

11.9.3 Trace the origins and geopolitical consequences (foreign and domestic) of the Cold War and containment policy, including the following: • The era of McCarthyism, instances of domestic Communism (e.g., Alger Hiss) and blacklisting • The Truman Doctrine • The Berlin Blockade • The Korean War • The Bay of Pigs invasion and the Cuban Missile Crisis • Atomic testing in the American West, the "mutual assured destruction" doctrine, and disarmament policies • The Vietnam War • Latin American policy.

Senator Joseph McCarthy points to a map while questioning Joseph Welch, the lawyer for the army in Senate committee hearings in 1954. McCarthy's accusations of communist infiltration of the army led to diminishing support for his investigations.

RECKLESS ACCUSATIONS

McCarthy's charges of treason in high places made him an instant celebrity. Prominent Republicans, sensing the political benefits of the "communist issue," embraced his attacks, which became known as **McCarthyism**. As he gained fame, McCarthy's assertions grew bolder. He called former secretary of state George C. Marshall a traitor, mocked the current secretary of state, Dean Acheson, as the "Red Dean of fashion," and described President Truman as a drunkard, saying that he should be impeached. Yet Republican colleagues continued to encourage McCarthy, who they thought could turn public distrust into votes for their party.

During the 1952 national elections, Republicans won control of Congress. McCarthy became chairman of the Senate Subcommittee of Investigations. He used the power of his committee to force government officials to testify and defend their loyalty. He also began to target other groups he believed were suspicious, including homosexuals who might hold sensitive positions in the government with access to classified information. During the 1950s, many gay men and women kept their sexual orientations secret due to the prejudice and discrimination they would face. McCarthy and others believed this made them more vulnerable to blackmail and more willing to do anything—including revealing national secrets—to keep from being exposed.

As a result, Congress held closed-door hearings on the threat homosexuals posed to the nation. The State Department fired 91 homosexuals, claiming they were security risks. In what became known as the **Lavender Scare,** federal agencies began firing or forcing out suspected homosexuals and selecting new hires on the basis of their sexual orientation. This wave of discrimination resulted in thousands of homosexuals being forced out of federal government service, and it didn't end there. Throughout the nation, suspected lesbians and gay men were targeted for surveillance and persecution, and many were forced out of career positions in state and local government, education, and even private industry.

MCCARTHY'S FALL

Eventually, McCarthy went too far. In 1954, his committee attempted to uncover suspected communists within the ranks of the army. During televised hearings, the senator repeatedly bullied respected army officials. He quickly lost his credibility. The public turned away from him, and the Senate openly criticized him for bringing it into "dishonor and disrepute." The darkest days of McCarthyism soon ended, but the effects of the "witch hunts" and the alarm over communism followed the country into the next decade.

HISTORICAL THINKING

1. **READING CHECK** How did Joseph McCarthy increase suspicion of government officials?
2. **SYNTHESIZE** How might the Lavender Scare have affected attitudes toward the larger LGBT community?
3. **ANALYZE LANGUAGE USE** What did Senator Smith mean when she said that freedom of speech had "been so abused by some that it is not exercised by others"?

HI 1 Students show the connections, causal and otherwise, between particular historical events and larger social, economic, and political trends and developments.

CHAPTER 14 THE COLD WAR AND KOREA
REVIEW

VOCABULARY

Write a paragraph to answer each question. Use all the words that appear below each question in your paragraph.

1. How were American politics and culture shaped by the Cold War? HSS 11.9.3

   subversion, hydrogen bomb, domino theory, containment, McCarthyism

2. What effect did the Cold War have on jobs in business and government sectors? HSS 11.8.1

   infrastructure, aerospace industry, white-collar, arms race, GI Bill

READING STRATEGY

SYNTHESIZE

When you synthesize, you identify the most important information in a text, look for evidence that connects the facts, and think about what you already know about the topic. Then you use the evidence, explanations, and your prior knowledge to form an overall understanding of what you have read. Use the chart below to help you synthesize the information presented in this chapter. Then answer the question.

The Roots of McCarthyism

Evidence:

↓

Supporting Explanation:

↓

Synthesis:

3. How did world events following the Allied victory in World War II lead to distrust and suspicion within the United States? HSS 11.9.3

MAIN IDEAS

Answer the following questions. Support your answers with evidence from the chapter.

4. Name two organizations formed by the United Nations in the 1940s and the purposes of those organizations. **LESSON 1.1** HSS 11.9.1
5. How did American foreign policy shift after World War II? **LESSON 1.2** HSS 11.9
6. What caused the arms race between the United States and the Soviet Union? **LESSON 2.1** HSS 11.9.3
7. How was the Chinese Communist Party able to win the support of the Chinese people following World War II? **LESSON 2.2** HSS HI 3
8. Why did President Truman remove General Douglas MacArthur from command of the American troops in Korea? **LESSON 2.3** HSS 11.9.3
9. How were the Alger Hiss and the Rosenberg spy cases similar and different? **LESSON 3.1** HSS 11.9.3
10. What other groups, besides communists, were singled out by Joseph McCarthy as a threat to the United States, and why? **LESSON 3.2** HSS 11.9.3

HISTORICAL THINKING

Answer the following questions. Support your answers with evidence from the chapter.

11. **IDENTIFY MAIN IDEAS AND DETAILS** How did the United Nations originate, and what purpose was it intended to serve? HSS 11.9.1
12. **DRAW CONCLUSIONS** How did the Cold War and fear of communism affect ordinary Americans? HSS 11.9.3
13. **ANALYZE CAUSE AND EFFECT** What triggered the larger conflict in Korea? HSS HI 1

14. **ANALYZE LANGUAGE USE** Why did the historian Godfrey Hodgson refer to the postwar interaction of Republicans and Democrats as a "liberal consensus"? HSS 11.9.3

15. **SUMMARIZE** What threats did the United States face from the expansion of communism throughout Eastern Europe and parts of Asia? HSS 11.9.3

16. **MAKE INFERENCES** Why do you think the National Security Council Paper 68 called for an increase in military spending? HSS 11.9

17. **FORM AND SUPPORT OPINIONS** How did the Cold War affect American politics? HSS HI 1

INTERPRET VISUALS

Look carefully at this comic book cover created during the Cold War. Then answer the questions that follow.

18. What elements in the image convey the fear that arose from the Cold War? HSS 11.9.3

19. Is the message of this image based on opinion or fact? Explain your response. HSS 11.9.3

ANALYZE SOURCES

Not everyone trusted Senator Joseph McCarthy or believed his accusations. The excerpt below is from a letter President Truman wrote in 1950, but never sent, in response to a telegram he had received from the senator.

> This is the first time in my experience . . . that I ever heard of a Senator trying to discredit his own Government before the world. Your telegram is not only not true and an insolent approach to a situation that should have been worked out between man and man—but it shows conclusively that you are not even fit to have a hand in the operation of the Government of the United States.

20. Based on the excerpt, how would you describe the president's attitude toward McCarthy's accusations? HSS 11.9.3

CONNECT TO YOUR LIFE

21. **NARRATIVE** You have considered how the Cold War affected ordinary American citizens between 1945 and 1960. Judging a person's response to historical events is often easier than knowing how you might behave in the same situation without the advantage of hindsight. Write a story in which you are a main character and explore what you may have thought or done in the midst of the Cold War as events occurred. HSS HI 3

TIPS

- Focus on one or two historical events that present a conflict for you and describe them.
- Identify your character's thoughts and feelings as world events unfolded.
- Use vivid language to describe the location of the story and the other characters in it.
- Include realistic dialogue in your story.
- Use two or three vocabulary terms from the chapter in your narrative.
- End the narrative by stating a moral, or a lesson one or more of the characters learned.

CHAPTER 15

POSTWAR PROSPERITY

1945–1960

HISTORICAL THINKING How did the prosperity of the post–World War II period shape American society?

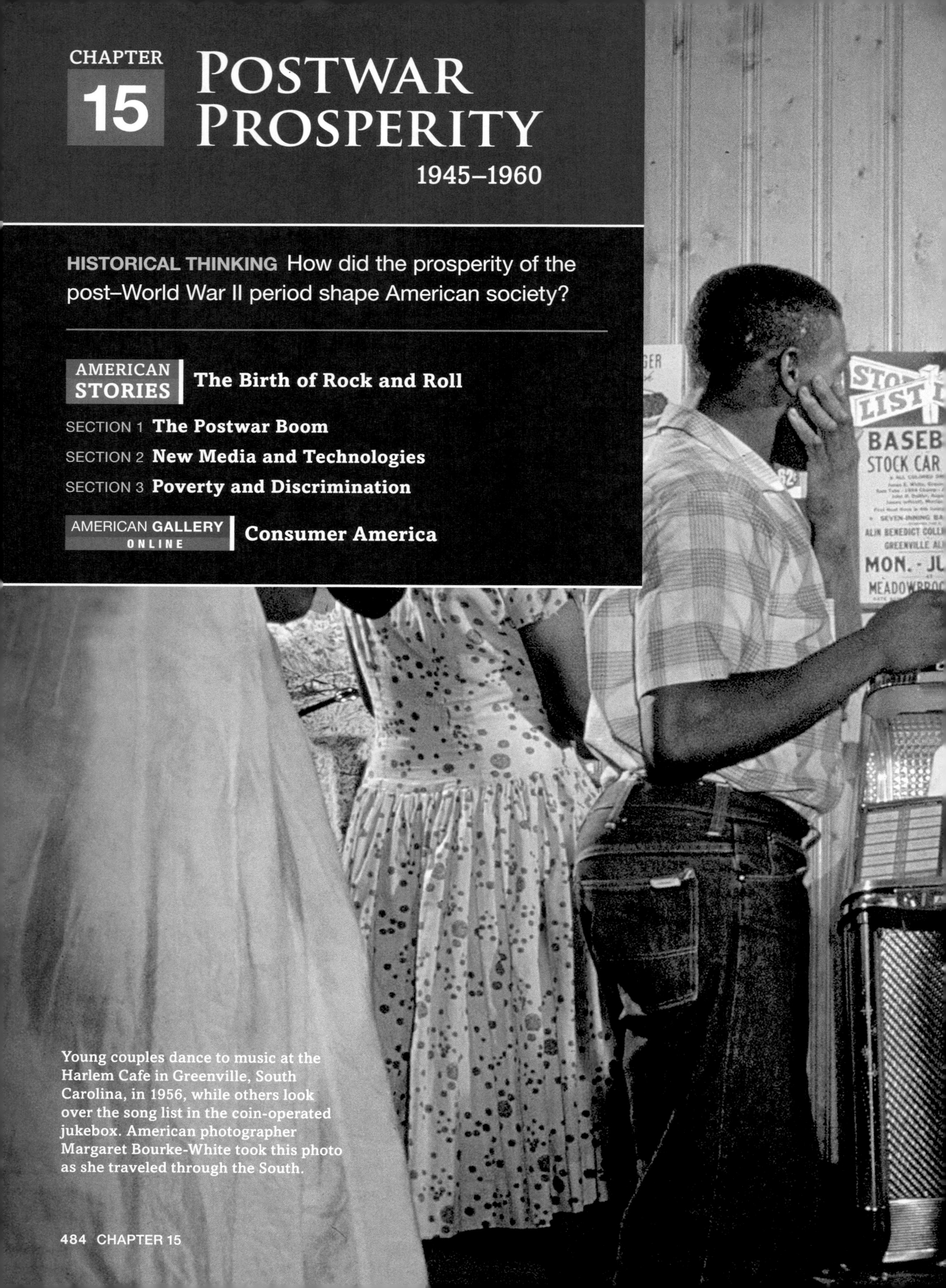

Young couples dance to music at the Harlem Cafe in Greenville, South Carolina, in 1956, while others look over the song list in the coin-operated jukebox. American photographer Margaret Bourke-White took this photo as she traveled through the South.

"I don't care what people say, **rock and roll is here to stay."**

—Danny and the Juniors

THE BIRTH OF ROCK AND ROLL

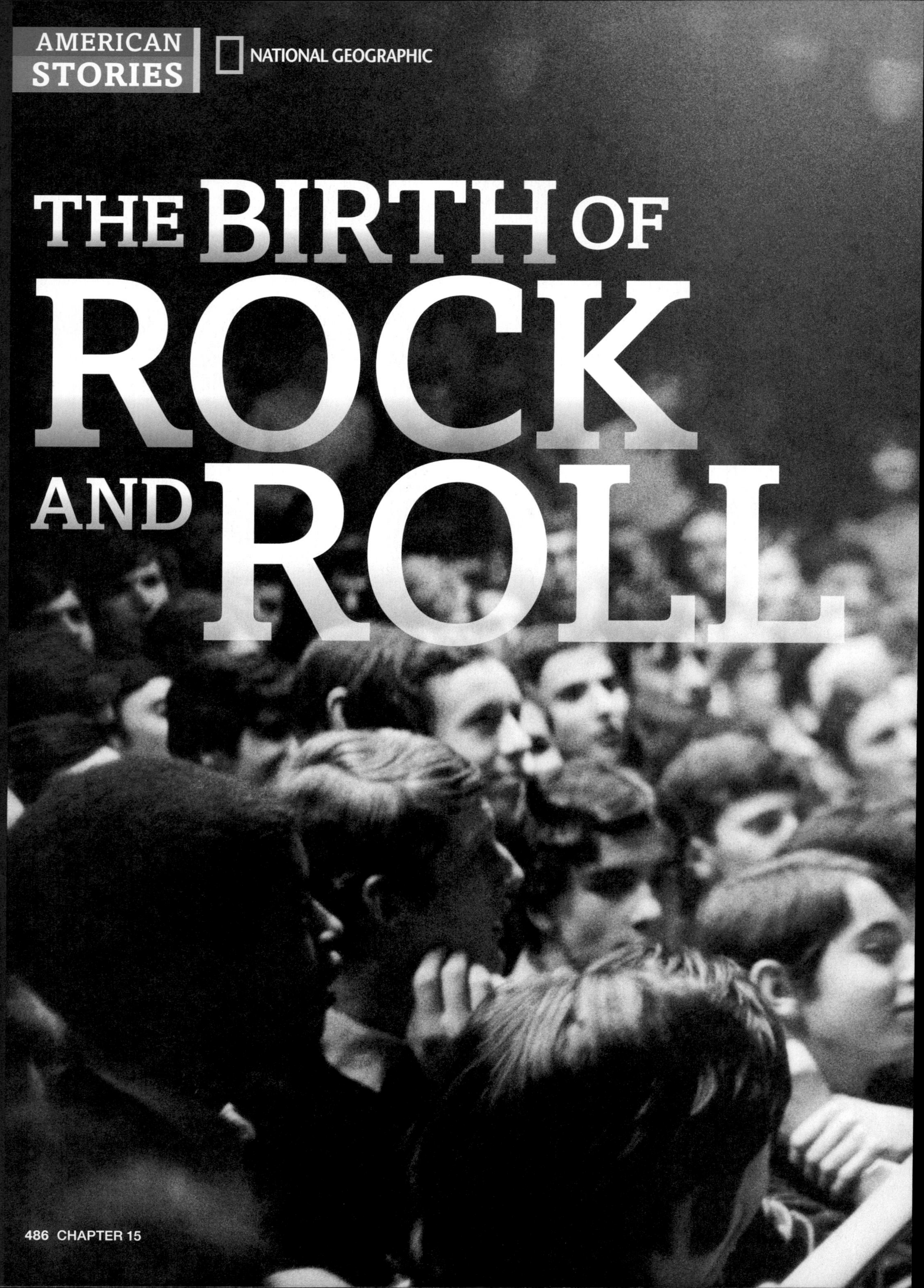

CRITICAL VIEWING Rock and roll pioneer Chuck Berry performs before an enthusiastic audience in 1966. What do you observe about the demographics of the crowd?

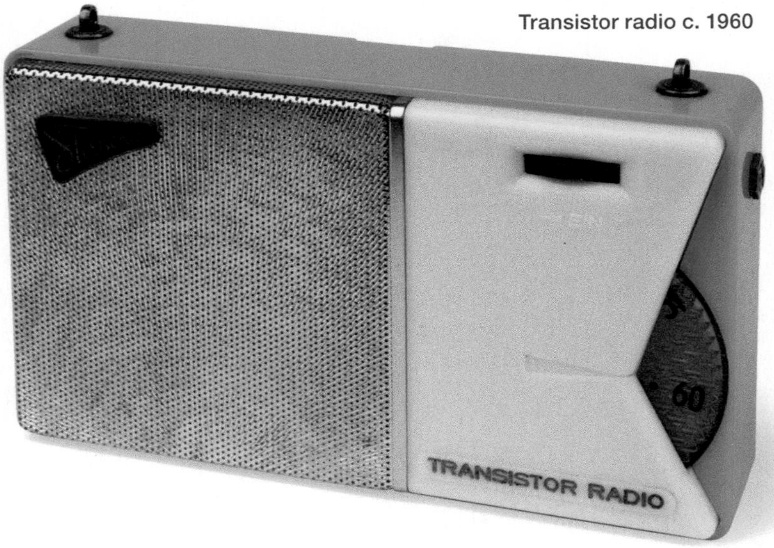

Transistor radio c. 1960

It's the rhythm that gets to the kids—they're starved for music they can dance to, after all those years of crooners.

—disc jockey Alan Freed, 1956

Since the dawn of humanity, there have been teenagers. The word *teenager*, however, didn't come into existence until sometime during World War II. At the time, there was nothing new about young people coming of age and seeking ways to rebel against society's norms. In the 1920s' Jazz Age, youths in their twenties defined themselves through music, clothing, and behavior that their elders found scandalous. In the 1940s and 1950s, the rebels were a little younger—high-school age—but they too sought their own social identity. And, like the jazz fans of the 1920s, they were looking for a new kind of music to serve as the soundtrack to their rebellion.

As the 1950s dawned, the tunes playing on America's pop radio stations weren't exactly exciting to a teenage audience. A record producer of the era later recalled, "Big fiddle-faddle orchestras . . . played lush mood music for relaxing, cocktails, and vacationing in far-away places." Such singers as Frank Sinatra and Bing Crosby—known as "crooners" because of their deep voices and smooth, romantic styles—dominated the airwaves, appealing to mainly white audiences.

American teenagers, however, were looking for something different in the way of entertainment, and they had the money to spend on it in the prosperous postwar economy. Teens also had access to new technology that made it easier to buy and listen to music independently from their parents. Transistor radios like the one shown above were small, portable units, unlike the large console radios that squatted somberly in a family's living room. Advancements in recording technology allowed teens to buy inexpensive "singles," small vinyl records that featured just one song on each side.

While the crooners serenaded white listeners, many African Americans were drawn to "race records," songs with strong, syncopated beats and a sound directly derived from jazz and the blues. Around 1950, the term *race records* was replaced by the more accurate—and less offensive—*rhythm and blues*, or R & B.

One record store owner in Cleveland, Ohio, noticed his white teenage customers purchasing R & B records in large numbers. When he shared this information with local disc jockey Alan Freed, a rock and roll phenomenon was born. Freed debuted *The Moondog Show* on WJW radio in June 1951 in an exuberant, unheard-of style. As the records spun, Freed would leave his microphone on and accompany the music with cries of "Ho, now!" and "Go! Go! Gogogogogogogo!" while pounding madly on a phone book he kept in the studio. Music critic Ed Ward later wrote, "It was just what a very large number of teenagers had been waiting all their lives to hear." Freed is credited with first using the term *rock and roll* to describe the music that was emerging from R & B in the 1950s.

11.5.6 Trace the growth and effects of radio and movies and their role in the worldwide diffusion of popular culture; 11.8.8 Discuss forms of popular culture, with emphasis on their origins and geographic diffusion (e.g., jazz and other forms of popular music, professional sports, architectural and artistic styles).

Guitar wizard Les Paul plays in the New York City nightclub called Fat Tuesday's.

LES PAUL

New technologies helped create the distinctive sounds of rock and roll both onstage and in the recording studios. One of rock's most influential early innovators was Les Paul, an inventor and popular, well-respected guitarist.

Paul was a pioneer in the use of overdubbing—recording a performance, and then replaying it and layering additional instruments or voices onto the recording. Using overdubbing, Paul sped up the sound of his guitar to create new and unusual effects. In 1952, he invented the eight-track tape recorder, which facilitated overdubbing and became standard in the recording industry. Today, music recording has gone digital, but the complex, layered sounds listeners are accustomed to hearing owe much to Paul's experiments.

Paul is perhaps best known for the solid-body electric guitar he designed, which was also released in 1952. He had worked for years to perfect an electric guitar that could sound and sustain a note without distortions. Paul's was not the first solid-body guitar on the market; the Fender Broadcaster had been introduced in 1948. However, the Les Paul Standard, sold by the Gibson guitar company, quickly rose in popularity and was adopted by many legendary rock guitarists.

Throughout his inventing career, Paul remained an accomplished, Grammy-winning performer. He was inducted into the Rock and Roll Hall of Fame in 1988 and continued both tinkering and performing until his death in 2009.

1952 Gibson Les Paul Goldtop

1968 Prototype Gibson Les Paul Custom Recording Model

Freed moved to New York in 1954 and began to organize R & B concerts that drew enthusiastic audiences of both white and African-American teens. He drew criticism from those who considered rock and roll obscene and from those who objected to people of different races mixing socially, but his popularity expanded throughout the 1950s.

Who were the artists making the new music that enthralled American teens and horrified many of their elders? In the early 1950s, most of the hit-makers were male, with roots in R & B or country and western music. Bill Haley, for example, started his career playing in a country band called the Saddlemen, but he loved the blues and experimented with combining many musical traditions. In 1953, the Saddlemen became Bill Haley & His Comets. In 1954, they released the single "Rock Around the Clock," which was featured in the 1955 film *Blackboard Jungle* and became a wildly successful anthem for the new rock generation, selling a record-setting 6 million copies.

Meanwhile, in Memphis, Tennessee, record producer Sam Phillips was frustrated because he was recording tracks by talented black musicians, but white radio stations would not give them airtime. "If I could find a white man with the Negro sound and Negro feel, I could make a million dollars," he told his assistant. Enter Elvis Presley, soon to become a rock star of unprecedented fame and teen idol to millions worldwide.

Presley's signature sound was strongly influenced by the African-American blues and gospel singers he had listened to in his youth, and he gratefully acknowledged their contributions throughout his career. In addition to having a versatile singing voice, Presley was handsome and charismatic, had a dazzling smile, and performed energetic, provocative dance moves. Presley once remarked, "Rock and roll music, if you like it, if you feel it, you can't help but move to it. That's what happens to me. I can't help it." Not everyone agreed that Presley's way of moving was a good thing. When he appeared on a popular television variety show, he was filmed from the waist up because his hip shimmy was considered too suggestive for viewers. One Catholic cardinal accused Presley of promoting a "creed of dishonesty, violence, lust, and degeneration" among teens. Presley's best-selling singles of the 1950s include "Hound Dog," "Jailhouse Rock," "Heartbreak Hotel," "Love Me Tender," and "Don't Be Cruel."

Rock and roll singer Elvis Presley leans toward his screaming fans during an outdoor concert around 1957.

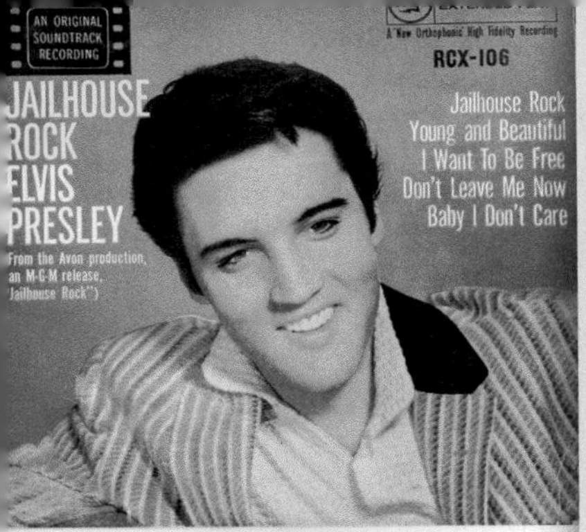

TOP OF THE LIST

In the 1950s, *Billboard* was a magazine that tracked the popularity of individual musicians and songs, publishing weekly charts of top sellers. From 1950 through 1954, the number one songs on the *Billboard* charts were mostly swing songs and ballads, with frequent appearances by such crooners as Tony Bennett and Frank Sinatra. Les Paul and his wife Mary Ford appeared on the 1953 list with a slow song called "Vaya Con Dios" (May God Be With You).

In July 1955, "Rock Around the Clock" by Bill Haley and His Comets took the number one spot, opening the door for rock and roll to dominate the charts. Chuck Berry and Little Richard also had hit records in 1955, and by 1957, rock and roll musicians were regular top sellers.

Excerpt from *Billboard's* Top 50 Best Sellers in Stores, November 18, 1957

Position In List	TITLE	ARTIST
1	JAILHOUSE ROCK	Elvis Presley
2	WAKE UP LITTLE SUSIE	The Everly Brothers
3	YOU SEND ME	Sam Cooke
4	SILHOUETTES	The Rays
5	BE-BOP BABY	Ricky Nelson
6	LITTLE BITTY PRETTY ONE	Thurston Harris
7	MY SPECIAL ANGEL	Bobby Helms
8	APRIL LOVE	Pat Boone
9	CHANCES ARE	Johnny Mathis
10	HONEYCOMB	Jimmie Rodgers
15	KEEP A KNOCKIN'	Little Richard
19	ROCK AND ROLL MUSIC	Chuck Berry
25	PEGGY SUE	Buddy Holly
30	WAIT AND SEE	Fats Domino
39	WHOLE LOTTA SHAKIN' GOIN' ON	Jerry Lee Lewis
40	THAT'LL BE THE DAY	The Crickets (Buddy Holly)

Joel Whitburn's Top Pop Playlists 1955–1969, 2014

AMERICAN STORIES

While performing with his band in 1956, rock and roll star Little Richard props his foot on top of the piano, a signature move.

COVERING UP

Today, when a song has potentially offensive lyrics, radio stations play it with the problematic words edited out. In the 1950s, a cover artist would record the song with alterations to make it appealing to different markets. Many R & B hits, for example, were recorded in "sanitized" versions that were more acceptable to the decision-makers at pop radio stations. It was not uncommon for several versions of a hit song to be in circulation at the same time.

Pat Boone was one of the most successful of the cover artists, with an enthusiastic following of mostly white teenagers and a string of hit songs. His clean-cut, wholesome image presented a contrast to the raucous and raw performances of Elvis Presley, Little Richard, and other early rockers. In 1956, rock and roll music reached a milestone when Little Richard's sensual recordings of "Long Tall Sally" and "Rip It Up" outsold Pat Boone's covers of the same tunes. Parents and conservative radio station owners may have preferred the white cover artist's cleaned-up version, but the younger generation had voted with their dollars.

Rock and roll is the most brutal, ugly, degenerate, vicious form of expression—lewd, sly, in plain fact, dirt. —singer Frank Sinatra, 1957

Several African-American stars also rose to fame on the rock and roll tide. Little Richard burst onto the scene with a flamboyant splash and was one of the first African-American rock and roll musicians to play to integrated audiences. A brilliant pianist, Little Richard fixed his audiences with an intense, wide-eyed gaze and astonished them with irrepressible dance moves, sometimes planting a foot on top of the piano as he played. In the words of music writer Donald Clarke, "In two minutes [Little Richard] used as much energy as an all-night party." Little Richard's hit songs "Tutti Frutti" and "Good Golly Miss Molly" were hugely popular, but because his lyrics were suggestive, he received relatively little airplay.

Chuck Berry, another African-American musician, was an early master of the instrument that came to define the sound of rock and roll—the electric guitar. His dexterous playing and unforgettable guitar licks, or short patterns of notes, influenced generations of players. Berry engaged his listeners with songs that told a story. His first hit, "Maybellene," narrated the comic miseries of a man chasing after his unfaithful girlfriend. "Sweet Little Sixteen" spoke directly to the teenagers in his audience.

By the end of the 1950s, some people felt, and perhaps hoped, rock and roll was a fad that would quickly fade away. Instead, it not only endured but evolved into a musical scene more diverse than even Alan Freed might have imagined. Later rock stars have acknowledged the debt they owe to the musicians who pioneered the genre. In fact, singer-songwriter John Lennon of the Beatles, one of the best-selling rock bands of all time, introduced Chuck Berry on a 1972 television show by saying, "If you had to give rock and roll another name, you might call it Chuck Berry."

THINK ABOUT IT

How did the introduction of rock and roll serve as a means for social change?

HI 1 Students show the connections, causal and otherwise, between particular historical events and larger social, economic, and political trends and developments.

THE DAY THE MUSIC DIED

Ritchie Valens, the first Latino rock and roll star, added a distinctive Mexican flavor to the R & B beat of his songs. Born in California, the Mexican American singer had a number of hits in his short career, including "Donna," which reached number two on the pop charts in 1959. Today, he is best remembered for "La Bamba," a Mexican folk tune with a rock and roll beat. Since its first release in 1958, the song has been recorded by several bands, including Los Lobos.

While still a teenager, Valens appeared on national television and on Alan Freed's radio show. In 1959, Valens went on tour with a group of fellow rock sensations, including Buddy Holly, whose 1957 song "That'll Be the Day" had reached number one on the charts in both the United States and Great Britain. On February 3, Valens, Holly, and J. P. "the Big Bopper" Richardson boarded a small plane for their next stop on the tour. The plane crashed near Clear Lake, Iowa, killing everyone aboard. Valens was just 17 years old, and Holly just 22. In 1971, singer Don McLean wrote a popular song about the crash and called it "American Pie." In the song, McLean referred to the tragedy as "the day the music died."

A self-taught musician, Ritchie Valens joined his first band at age 16.

MASON CITY GLOBE-GAZETTE

"The Newspaper That Makes All North Iowans Neighbors"

VOL. 97 — Associated Press and United Press International Full Lease Wires — MASON CITY, IOWA, WEDNESDAY, FEBRUARY 4, 1959 — No. 108

Rock 'n' Roll Idols Among Lake Crash Dead

Bodies of two victims (arrows) lie near the demolished plane in stubble field

Plane Piloted by Clear Lake Man Plows Into Field

Four persons, three identified as nationally famous rock 'n' roll singers, died early Tuesday in a plane crash five miles north of Clear Lake.

The three singers were Buddy Holly, 22, Texas, Ritchie Valens, 21, Los Angeles, and J. P. Richardson, 24, of Louisiana, known professionally as the "Big Bopper."

Also killed was the pilot of the plane, Roger Peterson, 21, Clear Lake.

The entertainers had appeared at the Surf Ballroom Monday night and were to appear at Fargo, N.D., Tuesday night.

Other members of the troupe which appeared at Clear Lake left after the show by chartered bus for Fargo. They are Dion and the Belmonts, Frankie Sardo and the Crickets, of which Holly was the singing star.

APPARENTLY HOLLY, Valens and Richardson decided to fly in order to arrive ahead of the troupe and make advance preparations.

The single-engine, four-place Beechcraft Bonanza left the Mason City Municipal airport shortly after 1 a.m. It crashed about

Russ Hold

Iowa's Right-to-Work Law

'3 Reasons'

An Iowa newspaper reports the plane crash that killed a local pilot and musicians Ritchie Valens, Buddy Holly, and J. P. Richardson on February 3, 1959.

1.1 **MAIN IDEA** As a moderate Republican, President Eisenhower continued many of Truman's domestic policies but introduced a new approach in foreign policy.

EISENHOWER AS PRESIDENT

Have you ever found it hard to choose sides in a political debate? Dwight D. Eisenhower didn't fit neatly on either the Democratic or the Republican side. But when he ran for president, he had to choose.

THE ELECTION OF EISENHOWER

The Cold War affected not only the nation's foreign policy but also the lives of everyday Americans. The United States enjoyed great prosperity and stability in the post–World War II period, made possible in part by the growth of industries that provided the technology needed to fight the Cold War. Not all Americans shared in the general prosperity, however. Minorities continued to face discrimination that made it more difficult to achieve the American dream of a secure job, a comfortable home, and a healthy family. As the Cold War continued, Americans turned to a strong general to lead the country's government and maintain stability.

In preparation for the 1952 presidential election, Democrats and Republicans searched for candidates to nominate. Both parties approached the same person—General Dwight D. Eisenhower, a celebrated World War II general and former commander of NATO forces. Until this time, Eisenhower had never declared allegiance to a particular political party.

In this photograph from September 1956, President Eisenhower (left) escorts Vice President Nixon (right) to the airplane that would take Nixon on a campaign tour for their re-election.

11.8.1 Trace the growth of service sector, white collar, and professional sector jobs in business and government; 11.8.6 Discuss the diverse environmental regions of North America, their relationship to local economies, and the origins and prospects of environmental problems in those regions; 11.8.7 Describe the effects on society and the economy of technological developments since 1945, including the computer revolution, changes in communication, advances in medicine, and improvements in agricultural technology.

In January 1952, he chose to run for president as a Republican, probably to distance himself from Truman and the Democratic Party, which had been losing popularity.

The Republican Party had problems as well. The party was split between moderates and conservatives, who fought each other for control. Eisenhower, a moderate, had to face off against a conservative Republican leader, Ohio senator Robert A. Taft. Eisenhower's fame as a dynamic leader won him the nomination and unified the party. The Democrats nominated the governor of Illinois, **Adlai Stevenson**. While Stevenson was a distinguished diplomat and had helped found the United Nations, he lacked the popularity that bolstered Eisenhower's election campaign.

Eisenhower did not wage a typical Republican campaign. He supported many of Truman's Fair Deal programs, which conservative Republicans threatened to revoke, and he vowed to support the U.S. soldiers who were fighting in the Korean War. But he purposefully left out specific details about his goals as president. He stated he was "pro-business" and practiced "modern Republicanism," which he defined as economic conservatism paired with social liberalism. Eisenhower and his running mate, Richard Nixon, beat Stevenson in a landslide, 442 electoral votes to 89.

Eisenhower immediately assigned several business leaders to his Cabinet. He chose the former president of General Motors, Charles E. Wilson, to serve as secretary of defense and a former steel company president, George Humphrey, to serve as secretary of the treasury. In 1953, he appointed Oveta Culp Hobby, the first commander of the Woman's Army Corps (WACs), to run the newly created Department of Health, Education, and Welfare. Eisenhower took measures to continue Social Security and unemployment insurance but otherwise cut government spending whenever he could. And due to the liberal consensus, which you have read about, Congress was usually willing to follow his lead.

PROSPERITY UNDER EISENHOWER

Postwar prosperity continued through the 1950s for the majority of Americans. This ongoing economic success was due largely to the position of the United States as a dominant world power, which enabled the nation to negotiate advantageous trade deals worldwide, and its embrace of **consumerism**. According to the theory of consumerism, the economy flourishes when people buy, or consume, a lot of goods and services.

The country's new role as a world leader meant the United States had to be on the cutting edge of technology. Military defense, electronics, and aerospace industries, essential to fighting the Cold War, flourished. Many of these industries were located in the **Sunbelt**, the southern region of the country that enjoys warm weather year-round. As a result, people from the **Frostbelt**, the north-central and northeastern region that has cold winters, migrated to Georgia, Florida, Texas, and California, where manufacturing jobs were on the rise.

Labor unions grew stronger and helped expand the middle class by ensuring that their members, who worked in these booming industries, received competitive pay, health insurance, paid vacations, and retirement benefits. Additionally, the number of service-sector, white-collar, and professional-sector jobs in business and government increased.

The growing middle class had more money to spend on consumer goods, such as food and automobiles. New industries developed to meet consumers' demands. Railroad, bank, and meatpacking companies created **agribusiness**—or the commercial business of agriculture—by buying up small family farms and creating huge, efficient factory farms. The companies converted the relatively humble occupation of farming into lucrative businesses. They opened supermarkets that offered middle-class shoppers a much wider variety of foods than was available at small corner markets.

As more people bought cars, the demand for highways and gasoline grew. Oil companies expanded their exploration programs and refineries and quickly became dominant businesses. Gas stations and auto repair shops flourished.

The growth of industries had some negative effects, however. Throughout the 1950s and into the 1960s, industrial waste products polluted the air and the lakes and rivers of major cities. **Smog**, a noxious combination of fog and smoke from factories, began to blanket such cities as Gary, Indiana, and Pittsburgh, Pennsylvania. The beaches of Lake Erie, the smallest and shallowest of the Great Lakes, were often covered in dead fish, killed by industrial pollutants that poisoned the water.

COLD WAR DEVELOPMENTS

Just as he supported many of Truman's domestic policies, Eisenhower also supported Truman's containment policy, aimed at preventing the spread of communism in the world. However, Eisenhower believed he could prevent any communist advance

11.11.7 Explain how the federal, state, and local governments have responded to demographic and social changes such as population shifts to the suburbs, racial concentrations in the cities, Frostbelt-to-Sunbelt migration, international migration, decline of family farms, increases in out-of-wedlock births, and drug abuse.

WORLD EVENTS, 1953–1956

1953

January 20, 1953
Dwight D. Eisenhower is sworn in as the 34th president of the United States. *(Campaign button of Dwight "Ike" Eisenhower, 1952)*

February 1953
President Eisenhower appoints Allen Dulles, the brother of Secretary of State John Foster Dulles, to head the CIA.

July 27, 1953
China signs a truce establishing North and South Korea, thus ending the Korean War.

August 19, 1953
The United States restores the shah of Iran to power after his prime minister had successfully overthrown him a few days before. *(Reza Shah Pahlavi's honor guard salutes him upon his return to Iran in 1953.)*

1954

June 18, 1954
The CIA stages a coup in Guatemala, replacing the recently elected president with a military dictator who supports United States' interests.

PRIMARY SOURCE

As the threat of nuclear war loomed in 1953, President Eisenhower addressed the United Nations about his nuclear deterrence policy.

I know that the American people share my deep belief that if a danger exists in the world, it is a danger shared by all—and equally, that if hope exists in the mind of one nation, that hope should be shared by all. . . . Atomic bombs today are more than 25 times as powerful as the weapons with which the atomic age dawned, while hydrogen weapons are in the ranges of millions of tons of TNT equivalent. . . . But the dread secret, and the fearful engines of atomic might, are not ours alone.

—from President Eisenhower's "Atoms for Peace" address to the United Nations, December 8, 1953

by using the threat of a nuclear attack rather than by mobilizing an army. Eisenhower's plan was called **nuclear deterrence**. It involved placing enough nuclear weapons in numerous safe places to guarantee that an enemy could not destroy all the weapons at once. Supposedly, nations would not risk war because both sides would be annihilated. Nuclear deterrence resulted in a world constantly on the brink, or the edge, of nuclear war. Secretary of State **John Foster Dulles** called this tension "**brinkmanship**," claiming that "the ability to get to the verge without getting into the war is the necessary art." Critics of nuclear deterrence claimed it was too dangerous. Still, the production of nuclear warheads increased, while the number of soldiers in service decreased and overall defense spending was actually cut by 20 percent between 1953 and 1955.

Meanwhile, the importance of strategic military bases in Hawaii and Alaska helped move these two U.S. territories toward full statehood. Near the end of Eisenhower's terms of office, in 1959, first Alaska and then Hawaii became the 49th and 50th states.

U.S. INVOLVEMENT OVERSEAS

As part of his containment program, Eisenhower gave the Central Intelligence Agency (CIA) new authority to investigate communism in other countries. In 1953, Eisenhower appointed **Allen Dulles** to head the CIA. Under Dulles, the CIA practiced **covert action**, gathering intelligence and secretly getting involved in the politics and internal affairs of other nations. In opposing communism, the United States came to support some authoritarian and corrupt governments.

For example, in 1953 in Iran, a new, duly elected government led by Prime Minister **Mohammad Mossadegh** (MOH-sah-dehk) deposed

11.8.4 Analyze new federal government spending on defense, welfare, interest on the national debt, and federal and state spending on education, including the California Master Plan; 11.8.5 Describe the increased powers of the presidency in response to the Great Depression, World War II, and the Cold War.

July 26, 1956
President Nasser takes control of the Suez Canal in Egypt. *(Container ship in the modern Suez Canal)*

November 4, 1956
Soviets crush the Hungarian revolt.

November 6, 1956
Eisenhower is re-elected to a second term as president.

1955

1956

October 23, 1956
Hungarian citizens revolt against Soviet troops in Budapest. *(Hungarians burn a portrait of Stalin in 1956.)*

November 6, 1956
Egypt, Israel, Britain, and France sign a cease-fire in the Suez Canal conflict. *(United Nations peacekeeping troops in Port Said, Egypt, in 1956)*

the shah, or king, named **Reza Shah Pahlavi** (rih-ZAH shah PAH-luh-vee). The U.S. government feared Mossadegh was a communist. Eisenhower did not want a communist heading the country from which the United States received most of its oil, so he commanded the CIA to work with the secret services of other nations to topple Mossadegh and return the shah to power. In exchange, the shah's government granted American companies 40 percent of Iran's oil production. Reacting to similar communist suspicions, in 1954 the CIA ousted the newly elected president of Guatemala, **Jacobo Árbenz Guzmán**, and replaced him with a military dictator who protected American business interests in that Central American nation.

In 1956, two major world events captured Americans' attention. In Budapest, Hungary, citizens revolted against the communists that governed their country. Street battles soon escalated into all-out war. The Soviet Union sent troops to help the Hungarian government. Eisenhower refused to send American troops for fear of triggering a war between the United States and the Soviet Union. Soviet troops crushed the revolt within a month.

In Egypt, President **Gamal Abdel Nasser** seized control of the **Suez Canal**, the British-controlled waterway that lay between Africa and Asia, connecting the Red and Mediterranean seas. Two months later, Israeli troops advanced on Egypt, followed by French and British paratroopers who worked together to retake the canal. Tensions heightened when the Soviet Union threatened nuclear war on Western Europe if Israel, Britain, and France did not withdraw from Egypt. A cease-fire resolved the situation, but the canal remained a source of conflict.

Meanwhile, the Cold War continued. As you've read, the Truman Doctrine supported free people and nations resisting communist takeovers. Although Eisenhower had failed to live up to this doctrine in Hungary, he continued to funnel money and American soldiers to Turkey and Greece, the **bulwarks**, or protective defenses, against Soviet expansion into the Middle East and Africa.

HISTORICAL THINKING

1. **READING CHECK** Which of Truman's domestic policies did President Eisenhower continue?
2. **DESCRIBE** How did technological development affect society and the economy in the United States during the 1950s?
3. **INTERPRET TIME LINES** How did the United States interfere in foreign governments during Eisenhower's first term in office?
4. **EVALUATE** What were some advantages of Eisenhower's nuclear deterrence plan?

11.9.3 Trace the origins and geopolitical consequences (foreign and domestic) of the Cold War and containment policy, including the following: • The era of McCarthyism, instances of domestic Communism (e.g., Alger Hiss) and blacklisting • The Truman Doctrine • The Berlin Blockade • The Korean War • The Bay of Pigs invasion and the Cuban Missile Crisis • Atomic testing in the American West, the "mutual assured destruction" doctrine, and disarmament policies • The Vietnam War • Latin American policy.

1.2 **MAIN IDEA** The Cold War period brought many economic and social changes to the lives of ordinary Americans.

American Society

If you had more money than you needed, what would you do with it? Would you save it? Spend it? Share it? Many Americans had this choice to make as they confronted social changes during the Cold War years.

THE COLD WAR'S EFFECTS

The Cold War shaped the daily lives of Americans in numerous ways. Its economic effects were especially significant. To fight the Cold War, the government made heavy investments in the defense and aerospace industries, which became major American employers in such states as California and Missouri. In addition, millions of veterans took advantage of the GI Bill of Rights and received a college education. Many of them then contributed to building the nation's technology industries. Thus, the livelihoods of many Americans depended on Cold War government investments and goals.

A growing group of educated, white-collar Americans strengthened the nation's industrial base, earned more money, and enjoyed a steady increase in their standard of living. With their new affluence, these Americans began to consume more goods and services, adding to the general prosperity.

PRESSURES ON AMERICAN WOMEN

It happened after World War I, and again after World War II. After each war, employers pressured the women who had stepped in to keep industries and businesses running to leave their jobs and make room for the returning soldiers. Between 1945 and 1947, more than 2 million women dropped out of the workforce, either by choice or by force. Women were also pressured to drop out of college to make room for men. The graduation rate for college women fell from 40 percent during the war to 25 percent by 1950. Married and single women generally returned to **domesticity**, or home life. Many women, especially those who enjoyed working or were college-educated, found the transition from self-sufficiency to dependence on male breadwinners difficult and disappointing. Those who remained in the workforce, often out of financial necessity, were typically paid 53 percent less than men performing similar tasks.

The return of soldiers after World War II brought other changes as well. Americans were longing for life to return to normal after years of war. As families were being reunited, many more couples were marrying and starting new families. Immediately following the war, the U.S. marriage rate spiked dramatically before leveling off slightly. The high marriage rate led to a 20-year surge in the number of babies born in the United States, a phenomenon called the **baby boom**. An estimated 75 million Americans were born between 1946 and 1964.

ATTITUDES ABOUT GENDER AND SEXUALITY

The changes brewing in postwar America were not limited to family life. A shift occurred in the way people spoke about and understood sexuality—a topic that had long been taboo. Publicity surrounding the research of biologist **Alfred Charles Kinsey** helped create this shift by sparking discussions about sexuality. Dr. Kinsey's books on human sexuality, *Sexual Behavior in the Human Male* (1948) and *Sexual Behavior in the Human Female* (1953), are collectively known as the **Kinsey Reports**. They feature the transcripts of thousands of interviews about sexual behavior that Dr. Kinsey and his research team conducted with both men and women.

Dr. Kinsey's research helped shine a light on the lives of lesbian, gay, and bisexual people in the United States. In 1950, activist **Harry Hay** founded the **Mattachine Society** in Los Angeles. One of the

11.8.1 Trace the growth of service sector, white collar, and professional sector jobs in business and government; 11.10.7 Analyze the women's rights movement from the era of Elizabeth Cady Stanton and Susan B. Anthony and the passage of the Nineteenth Amendment to the movement launched in the 1960s, including differing perspectives on the roles of women; 11.11.3 Describe the changing roles of women in society as reflected in the entry of more women into the labor force and the changing family structure.

first gay rights organizations in the United States, it provided a safe place for gay men to talk openly about the issues they faced. In 1955, a group of women formed the **Daughters of Bilitus** in San Francisco, one of the first social clubs where lesbians could meet without facing hostility and discrimination. These organizations offered much needed support to a community whose sexual behaviors were widely considered immoral and, in the eyes of the law, illegal.

Amid this period of sexual upheaval, a woman named **Christine Jorgensen** made international headlines when she announced that she had undergone surgery to change her gender from male to female. At a time when the term *transgender* did not exist, Jorgensen became a role model and a symbol of hope for other people whose gender identity differed from their biological sex at birth.

Birth and Marriage Rates in the Baby Boom Era (1945–1965)

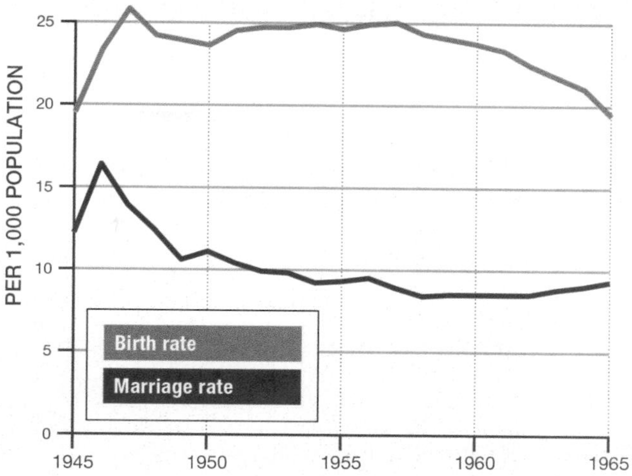

Source: CDC/National Center for Health Statistics

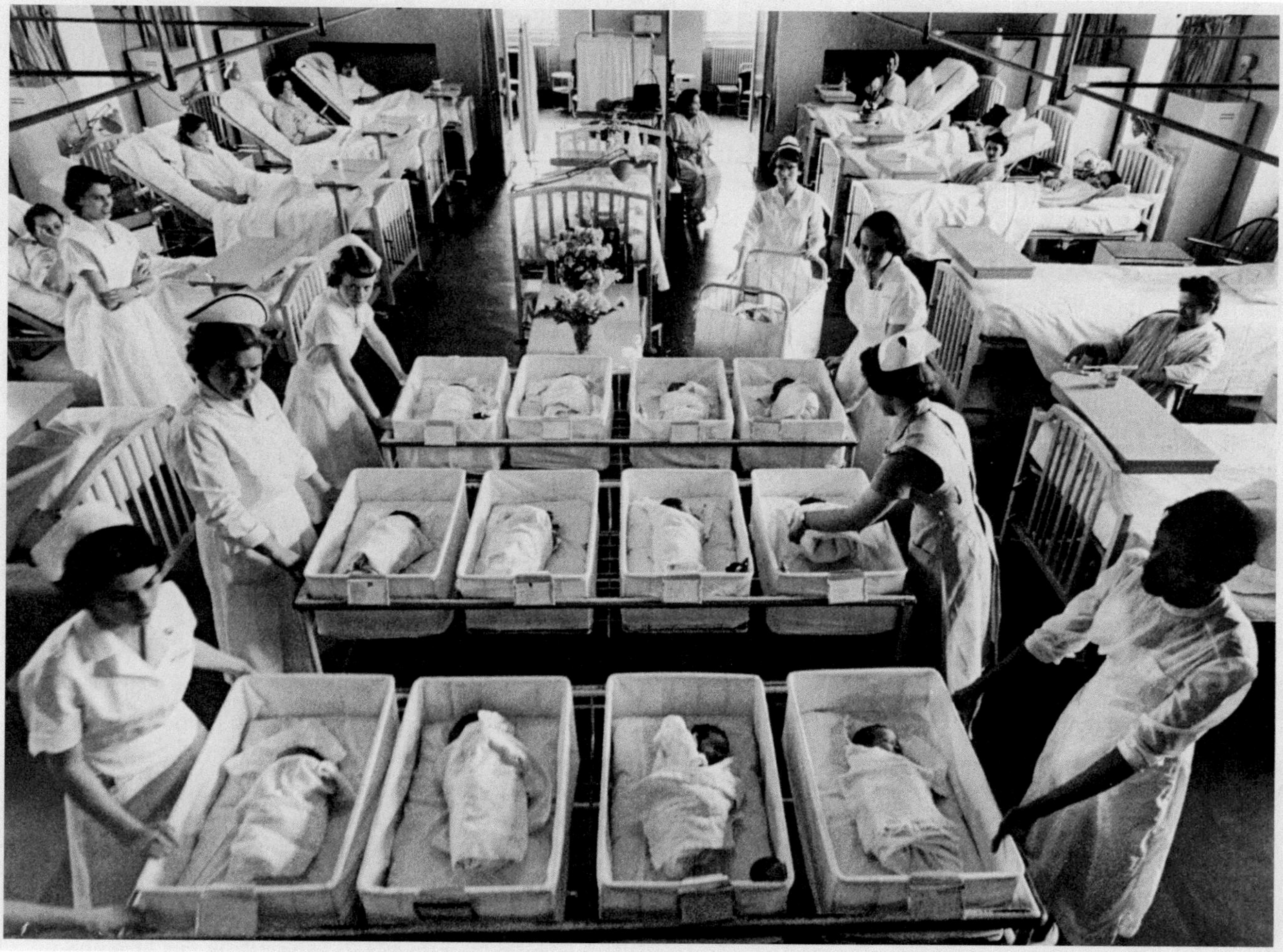

In 1958, nurses deliver a group of infants to their mothers in a hospital dormitory room. During the baby boom, a shortage of rooms for mothers and babies overwhelmed hospitals, which were designed for fewer births. In addition, home births declined and hospital births rose from 37 percent of all births in 1935 to 88 percent in 1950. The baby boom led to a growth in hospitals and a dramatic increase in the demand for many products and services.

Customers listen as a salesperson points out the new features of a television set at an appliance store in Silver Spring, Maryland, in 1950.

THE CONSUMER SOCIETY

During the Cold War years, many Americans had more money to spend and more goods to buy. Thanks to strong labor unions negotiating for regular working hours and personal time off, they also had more free time in which to shop. Consumer spending was now considered a patriotic way to build the nation's economy. Between 1946 and 1950, this new **consumer society** purchased over 21 million automobiles, 20 million refrigerators, 5.5 million electric stoves, and more than 2 million dishwashers. Shopping became an important part of the American lifestyle.

The consumer society was supported by easy access to credit—buying now and paying later, in installments. In 1950, a financial company called Diners Club issued the first credit cards in the United States. Department stores soon followed, offering charge accounts with easy payment plans.

Televisions became a popular item to charge to credit accounts. By the 1950s, televisions were no longer a luxury item that only upper-class families could afford. Most American homes had a TV; in fact, stores were selling millions of televisions every year. Television provided advertisers easy access to millions of consumers. Enticing television commercials promoted shiny new appliances and unique gadgets guaranteed to make life easier for Americans. Much of this advertising was directed specifically at women. Commercials told women they could be more efficient and effective wives and mothers if they owned the newest washing machine, dishwasher, and vacuum. In addition to encouraging consumer spending, these advertisements also reinforced women's traditional domestic roles.

MEDICINE, SCIENCE, AND EDUCATION

The Cold War years also featured major advances in medicine, science, and education. One of the most important medical breakthroughs was the development of a vaccine against polio, an infectious, crippling disease. Between the late 1940s and early 1950s, doctors had reported 35,000 new cases of the disease in the United States. In 1952, the nation experienced its worst polio outbreak—58,000 cases. Three years later, in 1955, **Jonas Salk**, an American physician and medical researcher, introduced the **Salk vaccine**. The incidence of polio quickly fell, and the disease is no longer a threat in the United States.

11.8.4 Analyze new federal government spending on defense, welfare, interest on the national debt, and federal and state spending on education, including the California Master Plan; 11.8.7 Describe the effects on society and the economy of technological developments since 1945, including the computer revolution, changes in communication, advances in medicine, and improvements in agricultural technology.

A young girl looks apprehensively at the needle before receiving a lifesaving Salk polio vaccine in the 1950s. Health departments and schools vigorously publicized the free vaccination program with public service posters, newspaper ads, and radio announcements. An oral vaccine developed by Alfred Sabin was also developed in the 1950s and given in drops placed on a sugar cube.

In the late 1940s, three American physicists invented the **transistor**, an electronic device used to control the flow of electricity in electronic equipment. Transistors became available for public purchase during the 1950s and were commonly used in small, portable radios and hearing aids. Today, transistors are components of the microchips found in computers and many other electronic devices.

One of the first commercial computers designed for processing business data was the **Universal Automatic Computer (UNIVAC)**. Developed in the late 1940s, the room-size UNIVAC was put into use by various businesses and organizations. For example, the **Bureau of the Census**, the government agency that counts the nation's population, used the UNIVAC to count and record part of the 1950 population.

Scientists also explored ways to produce cheaper energy to meet the nation's growing energy demands. Using the same science behind the atomic bomb, scientists working in the United States developed a way to capture the heat released during nuclear fission, which is the reaction that occurs when atoms split apart. The steam from this heat can be used to turn turbine blades to power generators and make electricity. The energy created from this process is called **nuclear power**. In 1957, the first large-scale American nuclear power plant started operating in Shippingport, Pennsylvania.

Advances in the sciences were not limited to earthbound endeavors. Scientists studied planetary satellites, or bodies in space that orbit other bodies of a larger size. On October 4, 1957, the Soviet Union sent the first mechanical, or human-made, satellite, called ***Sputnik 1***, into space to orbit Earth. Americans worried that such satellites might enable the Soviets to direct nuclear missiles toward the United States. President Eisenhower responded by establishing the **National Aeronautics and Space Administration (NASA)**, which oversees the U.S. space program. NASA worked to match and exceed the Soviets' accomplishments in space exploration.

After being caught off guard by *Sputnik*, the American public demanded improvements to their educational systems. Eisenhower responded by signing the National Defense Education Act (NDEA) into law on September 2, 1958. The purpose of NDEA was to improve schools through government funding, encourage students to attend college, and promote education in science, engineering, math, and foreign languages. In California, educators used NDEA funding to reorganize the state's higher education system. The **California Master Plan**, adopted in 1960, joined the state's universities and community colleges into one accessible and affordable system governed by a framework that promoted academic excellence.

HISTORICAL THINKING

1. **READING CHECK** How did the Cold War affect the lives of ordinary Americans?
2. **ANALYZE CAUSE AND EFFECT** Explain how the return of World War II veterans had complex effects on women in the workforce, and identify the types of data that could be used in determining these effects.
3. **IDENTIFY MAIN IDEAS AND DETAILS** What factors contributed to the development of a consumer society in the United States?

HI 1 Students show the connections, causal and otherwise, between particular historical events and larger social, economic, and political trends and developments. HI 2 Students recognize the complexity of historical causes and effects, including the limitations of determining cause and effect.

1.3 **MAIN IDEA** During the Cold War years, government programs encouraged many Americans to move out of crowded cities and into suburbs.

SUBURBS SURROUND CITIES

Where would you most like to live—in a city, suburb, small town, or rural area? During the Cold War years, many Americans chose to move to suburbs. Why might the suburbs have appealed to them?

MOVING TO THE SUBURBS

As populations were increasing in Sunbelt states in response to the expansion of aerospace and other industries in the region, another major demographic change was also taking place. **Suburbanization**, or a population shift from cities to outlying communities, was rapidly transforming the American landscape.

In 1950, about 1.7 million new houses were built in the United States, and more than 80 percent were built in suburbs. A home in the suburbs offered relief from crowded cities. Suburbs often had larger homes, better schools, and lower crime rates. By 1950, more than 18 million people, or 1 in every 8 Americans, had moved from cities to suburbs.

The GI Bill, which offered loans to World War II veterans to purchase houses, helped make suburbanization possible. So did two federal government agencies. The **Veterans Administration (VA)**, which serves the needs of veterans, and the **Federal Housing Administration (FHA)**, which provides financing for housing, worked together to manage the GI Bill program. From 1944 to 1952, the government issued nearly 2.4 million low-interest home loans as a benefit of the GI Bill, accelerating the movement of families to the suburbs.

All over the country, veterans paid building contractors to construct affordable, single-family homes. **William Levitt**, a New York contractor, purchased several thousand acres of farmland in Hempstead, New York, 25 miles east of Manhattan, for the mass production of private homes. Levitt based his building operation on Henry Ford's assembly lines. His company manufactured precut building materials in his factories, delivered them using his trucking company, and assembled the homes using his builders. On the construction site, each worker performed a single task, such as framing or pouring concrete, to complete each house. Levitt's builders constructed as many as 180 houses in a week. When completed in 1951, **Levittown, Long Island**, boasted 17,000 houses plus dozens of parks, ball fields, swimming pools, churches, and shopping areas for its 82,000 residents.

Levitt's system of mass-produced neighborhoods was duplicated across the country. Linking Cold War thinking and home ownership, Levitt declared, "No man who owns his own house and lot can be a communist."

Meanwhile, new expressways improved access between suburbs and cities. President Eisenhower viewed road improvement as vital to the national defense during the Cold War. When he signed the **Federal-Aid Highway Act of 1956**, launching one of the greatest public works projects in history, he stated, "In case of atomic attack on our key cities, the road net must permit quick evacuation of target areas." Better roads would also benefit the economy by creating jobs, making it easier and cheaper for industries to transport goods, and allowing Americans to live farther away from their workplaces. In fact, state and local governments often covered the entire cost of highway segments in response to local commuting demand. The resulting **Interstate Highway System** linked towns, cities, and suburbs nationwide with limited access, multilane highways.

IMPACT OF SUBURBANIZATION

Suburbanization dramatically transformed American culture. The American dream of owning one's home became a reality for millions. The first house sold in Levittown, Long Island, came with a free television and appliances, prompting Levitt to call it "the best house in the U.S."

11.8.4 Analyze new federal government spending on defense, welfare, interest on the national debt, and federal and state spending on education, including the California Master Plan.

But social observers criticized these developments, mocking the uniform design of the "little boxes." Far more troubling was the **homogeneity**, or sameness, of the residents. Many mass-produced neighborhoods, or **subdivisions**, refused to admit minorities, especially African Americans. Levittown's standard sales contract stated that homes could not be "used or occupied by any person other than members of the Caucasian race." Nearly 10 years after the U.S. Supreme Court ruled in 1948 against such discrimination, not a single African American lived in Levittown. Social observers also deplored the homogeneity of the suburbanites' lives. The men commuted from their uniformly designed houses to work in offices that were also mostly alike, and the women cleaned house, cooked, and raised children.

Suburbanization and discrimination changed the makeup of American cities. African Americans and the less wealthy remained in the cities, where making a living became more difficult. Many businesses and factories also moved to the suburbs, taking jobs and services with them. Fewer residents and businesses meant lower revenues for city or local governments, but as taxes were raised to cover the shortfall, even more people moved to the suburbs. In just a few years, many American cities lost a large portion of their upper- and middle-class residents.

Suburbanization also affected rural communities and natural environments. The relentless demand for subdivisions and the expansion of interstate highways pressured farmers near cities to sell their land. In 1930, more than 30 million Americans lived on farms. By 1960, that number had fallen to 15.6 million, and nearly one in three Americans lived in a suburb. Suburbs and highways also disrupted wildlife habitats, a process that continues to this day.

HISTORICAL THINKING

1. **READING CHECK** What motivated many Americans to move to suburbs during the Cold War years?
2. **MAKE INFERENCES** What did William Levitt mean when he said "No man who owns his own house and lot can be a communist"?
3. **IDENTIFY PROBLEMS AND SOLUTIONS** What do you consider the greatest problem to have resulted from the growth of suburbs?

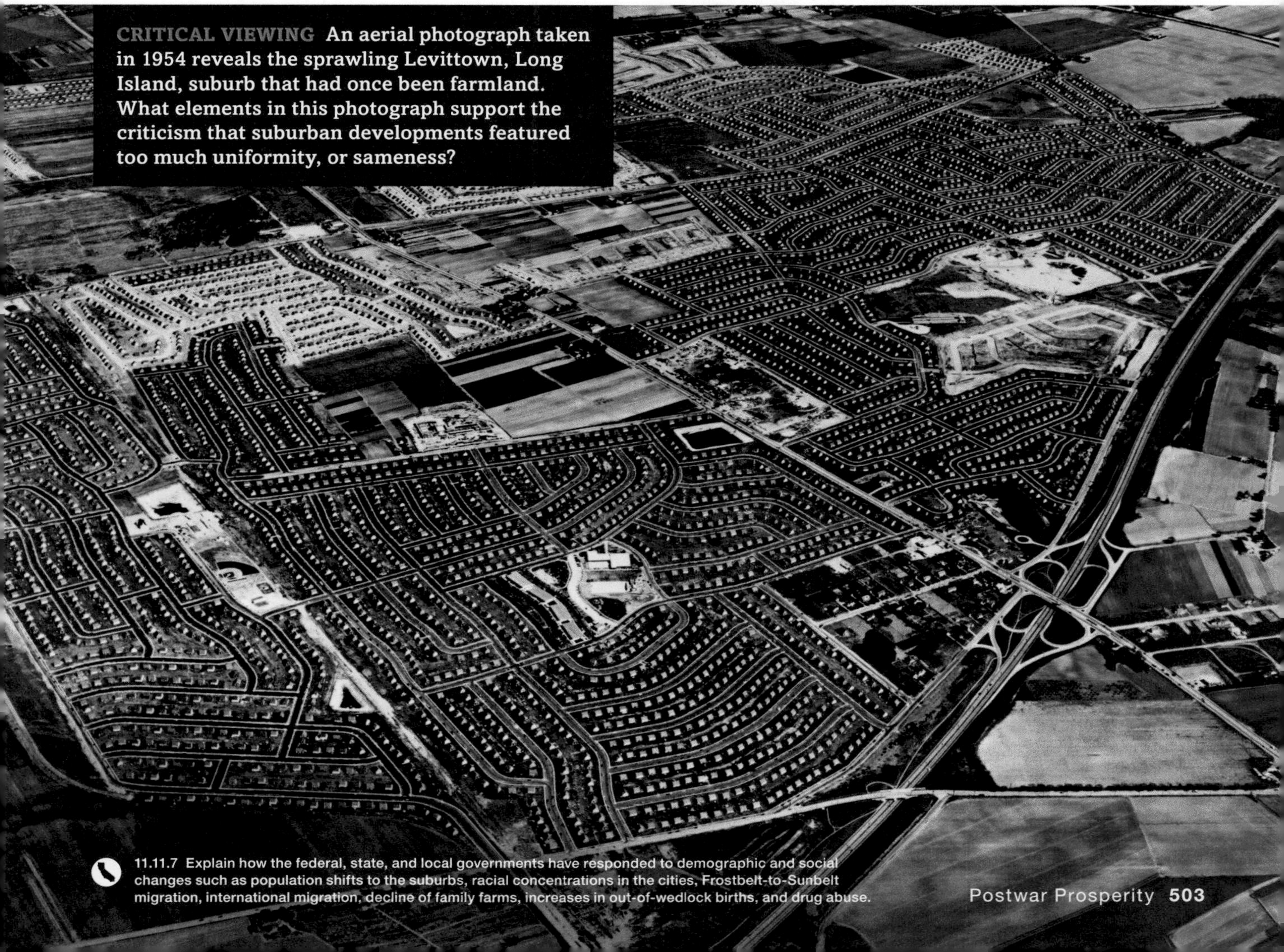

CRITICAL VIEWING **An aerial photograph taken in 1954 reveals the sprawling Levittown, Long Island, suburb that had once been farmland. What elements in this photograph support the criticism that suburban developments featured too much uniformity, or sameness?**

11.11.7 Explain how the federal, state, and local governments have responded to demographic and social changes such as population shifts to the suburbs, racial concentrations in the cities, Frostbelt-to-Sunbelt migration, international migration, decline of family farms, increases in out-of-wedlock births, and drug abuse.

2.1 **MAIN IDEA** The Cold War years gave rise to an automobile-based culture in the United States.

AUTOMOBILE MANIA

Can you imagine never using a car? If not, you're in step with the majority of Americans who rely on cars for transportation at least part, if not most, of the time. That dependence developed during the 1950s.

CRITICAL VIEWING In 1948, The Track, an innovative drive-in restaurant in Los Angeles, used technology to entice hungry drivers. Instead of employing carhops, or waiters, to serve people at their cars, The Track installed a conveyor belt. How do you think this system worked, and to whom might it appeal?

11.8.7 Describe the effects on society and the economy of technological developments since 1945, including the computer revolution, changes in communication, advances in medicine, and improvements in agricultural technology; HI 5 Students analyze human modifications of landscapes and examine the resulting environmental policy issues.

GROWING RELIANCE ON AUTOMOBILES

The growth of suburbs during the Cold War years made Americans more dependent on automobiles. Many workers had to commute from the suburbs to jobs in the city each day. As the demand for automobiles increased, American production quadrupled from 2 million cars in 1946 to 8 million in 1955. Between 1945 and 1960, new technologies cut by half the time it took to manufacture a car. As a result, the nation's gross national product (GNP), the total value of goods and services produced during a year, skyrocketed from $212 billion to $503 billion. The business of making cars became the most important contributor to the U.S. economy.

During the Cold War years, the automobile industry employed a large percentage of the country's population. By 1960, one out of six Americans earned paychecks by contributing to the production of cars, either directly by assembling vehicles or indirectly by working for a company that supplied automotive parts and equipment. Factory employees rolled out close to 58 million new cars during the 1950s.

The United Automobile Workers (UAW), an industrial union representing automotive workers, had grown in size and become a powerful force in the automotive industry by the 1950s. The UAW, in partnership with other labor unions, successfully organized strikes for better wages and benefits and negotiated paid vacation days, pensions, and medical care for union members.

A CAR CULTURE

The growth of the car culture rapidly transformed the American landscape. Entire industries blossomed along the increasing network of roads and highways lined with gas stations. Restaurants adjusted their operations so drivers could buy food "to go" or even eat meals without leaving their cars. One of the first restaurant owners to adopt this "fast food" model was Ray Kroc. He opened the first McDonald's restaurant in 1955 in Des Plaines, Illinois, a suburb of Chicago. Motor hotels, or motels, were built along busy roads to accommodate the growing number of travelers taking road trips. The American car culture also prompted the development of drive-in movie theaters and shopping malls. All these businesses added to **suburban sprawl**, or the spread of suburban developments over more and more land.

As the car culture spread, the economies of the United States and other Western nations became increasingly dependent on oil, which is the source of gasoline, diesel fuel, and many other products.

ROUTE 66

Completed in 1926, this famous highway ran 2,448 miles between Chicago and Los Angeles. Over the years, Route 66 became a symbol of the open roads in the United States. Okies, or migrant farm workers from Oklahoma, used it during the Great Depression to travel west, seeking a better life in California. Families traveled the highway to visit the American heartland, the canyons and deserts of the Southwest, and the Pacific Ocean. Some stores and restaurants along the route are now historic landmarks. But Eisenhower's Interstate Highway System threatened its existence in the 1950s. Many travelers chose the newer, more direct highways over the often meandering Route 66.

Between 1945 and 1960, U.S. oil production rose by nearly 50 percent, and annual oil imports increased from 74 million to 371 million barrels. The need for oil—not only to power automobiles but also to meet other energy needs—would affect American foreign and domestic policy for decades to come.

The large number of gas-guzzling cars on American roads led to rising air pollution in cities. By 1966, motor vehicles contributed more than 60 percent of the pollutants discharged into the nation's air, amounting to 86 million tons out of 146 million tons. In 1955, the U.S. Congress passed the Air Pollution Control Act, the first law to address air pollution. The act was amended in 1963 to provide funding to study the effects of automobile exhaust on people's health.

Other environmental problems resulted from the extraction, refining, and transportation of oil. During the 1960s and beyond, oil spills and the dumping of oil wastes damaged wildlife habitats and polluted streams, lakes, and other bodies of water.

HISTORICAL THINKING

1. **READING CHECK** Why did many Americans become dependent on automobiles during the Cold War years?
2. **MAKE INFERENCES** How might the need for oil affect American foreign policy?
3. **ANALYZE ENVIRONMENTAL CONCEPTS** How did its increased oil production help the United States, and what environmental problems were caused by Americans' growing dependence on oil?

1950s hot rod

Music fan driving to Woodstock, 1969

2.2

THROUGH THE LENS

CARS & AMERICAN CULTURE

It's surprising that a brutish industrial-age machine has maintained its status as a cultural icon amid the buzz of technology in the digital age. Decades ago, owning a car was about horsepower, status, and youthful rebellion. Cars inspired movies, songs, and literature. They were a driver's ticket to the freedom and glory of the open road. Do you think concerns about pollution, gridlock, and gas prices will cause the American car obsession to subside?

American World War II soldier in a seagoing Jeep, Europe, c. 1946

Tail fins on a 1959 Cadillac Eldorado

Architect Frank Lloyd Wright's 1930 Cord L-29

American actor and car enthusiast James Dean pushes his cousin in a homemade roadster in Indiana, 1955.

Dressed in their Sunday best, boys strike a serious pose on the hood of a car in a Chicago South Side neighborhood, 1941.

In 1977, Janet Guthrie was the first woman to drive in the Indianapolis 500 and the Daytona 500.

Electric vehicle charging at a Detroit, Michigan, auto show

2.3 **MAIN IDEA** During the 1950s, Americans enjoyed new forms of entertainment that became part of mainstream culture.

CULTURE OF THE FIFTIES

The next time you're watching your favorite TV show or listening to your favorite music, consider that much of what we now consider American pop culture came into being during the 1950s.

THE GOLDEN AGE OF TELEVISION

You have read about the important role television played in American consumer culture, both as an item for consumers to purchase and as a way for advertisers to sell their products. In 1948, less than one percent of American households could boast of owning a TV set. Back then, television's fuzzy black-and-white images were anything but "must-see." The first televised baseball game was filmed using only one camera. The first TV actors sweated under hot lights and wore black lipstick and green makeup just to show up on screen. But by 1959, more than 83 percent of homes in the United States had one or more televisions.

Television evolved by modeling itself on another medium—radio. In the 1930s and 1940s, radio offered a variety of entertainment to more than 60 percent of U.S. households and was available in nearly 2 million cars. Some radio programs were so popular that many movie theaters did not bother opening for the evening until after the top programs had aired. Early television programs just couldn't compete with the witty dialogue and skillfully achieved sound effects of radio, but television continued to improve.

Among the major changes in television technology was the introduction of color in 1950. In the early 1950s, special cables were used to link both coasts, marking a significant change in communication and allowing millions of viewers to watch the same program simultaneously. In 1949, a TV set appeared for the first time in the Sears department store catalog. Its price was $149.95. Only a year later, Americans were buying 20,000 television sets a day.

By 1954, three national television networks—ABC, CBS, and NBC—were broadcasting regularly. These networks were also the major radio broadcasters, and they boasted better technology and greater talent than their competitors. They also had two other advantages. Their profits from radio broadcasting enabled them to invest in new television programming. They could also move their most popular radio programs, including *Jack Benny, Burns & Allen*, and *Amos 'n' Andy*, over to television.

Television in the 1950s introduced or reinvented many genres, including variety shows, quiz shows, informational programming, and high-quality dramas. Among the most popular genres was the **situation comedy**, or sitcom, a weekly series that featured a familiar setting and a group of characters who faced amusing problems. These shows reflected traditional elements of American society, often with a twist. For example, on the popular sitcom *I Love Lucy*, the title character was a woman who stayed at home while her husband, Ricky, worked as a musician. Money was never an issue for the couple and their young son, and no one stayed angry for long. The show's humor came from crazy schemes Lucy developed to make her life more interesting. *I Love Lucy* introduced techniques that revolutionized the television industry, including taping in front of a live studio audience and using multiple cameras to film scenes from different angles. The show became so popular that more people tuned in to watch *I Love Lucy* on January 19, 1953—a staggering 44 million—than would watch President Eisenhower's inauguration the following day.

Though racial minorities rarely appeared in the 1950s sitcoms, they did play major—if stereotypical—roles in several popular shows. The most popular was *Amos 'n' Andy*, an adaptation of a radio comedy created by two white men and featuring an all-black cast. The NAACP angrily denounced *Amos 'n' Andy*

11.8.7 Describe the effects on society and the economy of technological developments since 1945, including the computer revolution, changes in communication, advances in medicine, and improvements in agricultural technology.

Wearing a TV-inspired Davy Crockett T-shirt, cowboy boots, and coonskin cap, a young boy reads about the legendary American frontiersman at his school desk in the 1950s. The 1950s pin-back button shown below pictures Crockett carrying his rifle and wearing a deerskin shirt and coonskin cap.

for portraying blacks as "clowns" and "crooks," but others praised the performers for transforming racist stereotypes into humor that authentically portrayed the African-American experience.

By the mid-1950s, TV networks were mining the riches of children's programming. American film producer Walt Disney struck gold with his three-part series about the historical American frontiersman Davy Crockett, which aired nationally in December 1954. In the months that followed, millions of schoolchildren began wearing coonskin caps just like the one Crockett wore on the program. Stores soon began selling other Davy Crockett merchandise, including shirts, blankets, toothbrushes, and lunch boxes. One department store chain sold 20,000 surplus tents in less than a week simply by printing "Davy Crockett" on a flap.

Television and marketing businesspeople noted the new media's power to sell products. Important advertisers started sponsoring entire programs. The television industry expanded with each new program, providing work for hundreds of performers and technicians at a time and taking business away from the motion picture industry. By the mid-1950s, the "golden age" of television was in full swing.

A NEW KIND OF MUSIC

In the 1950s, a distinctive teenage culture emerged, rooted in the prosperity and population boom that followed World War II. While the threat of nuclear war was ever-present, teenagers had little experience of the grim events of the previous two decades. They were raised in relative affluence, surrounded by ads that ignored the traditional value of thrift. Fewer were employed than in prewar years, but close to half had summer jobs, and many had their own money. By 1956, teenagers bought $9 billion worth of products a year; a typical teen spent as much on entertainment as the average family had spent in 1941.

Many teens chose to spend their money on the popular music of the time. Known as **rock and roll**, this musical genre grew out of rhythm and blues, the music brought north by African-American musicians during the Great Migration. Most rock and roll songs were originally written or performed by African-American artists. Because African-American music was not considered appropriate for white audiences, music studio executives rerecorded versions of these songs using white "cover artists" so that white radio stations would play them.

The wildly popular Elvis Presley (1935–1977) sings and dances at the Olympia Theater in Miami, Florida, in 1956. Presley had an exceptional vocal range.

11.8.8 Discuss forms of popular culture, with emphasis on their origins and geographic diffusion (e.g., jazz and other forms of popular music, professional sports, architectural and artistic styles).

PRIMARY SOURCE

In this passage from the novel *On the Road* (1957) by Jack Kerouac, the narrator describes the kind of people he admires.

[T]he only people for me are the mad ones, the ones who are mad to live, mad to talk, mad to be saved, desirous of everything at the same time, the ones who never yawn or say a commonplace thing, but burn, burn, burn like fabulous yellow roman candles exploding like spiders across the stars.

—from *On the Road,* by Jack Kerouac, 1957

That situation began to change in 1951, after an American disc jockey named **Alan Freed** learned that white teens in Cleveland were buying up records featuring African-American rhythm and blues artists. Freed began playing the hard-edged music on the air. Suddenly, teens could discover new music just by turning a radio dial.

In 1955, African-American rhythm and blues artist **Chuck Berry** (1926–2017) recorded one of the first rock and roll songs, "Maybellene," which quickly became a hit. Berry followed up with "Roll Over Beethoven" (1956), "Rock and Roll Music" (1957), and "Johnny B. Goode" (1958). A rock and roll pioneer, Berry played guitar in an infectious, rhythmic style and wrote songs about cool cars and dances to appeal to teenagers. Berry's showmanship on stage—playing guitar between his legs and behind his head and performing a movement called the "duckwalk"—influenced many rock and roll guitarists.

In 1955, a 21-year-old truck driver from Memphis named **Elvis Presley** exploded onto the popular music scene. Born in rural Mississippi, Presley grew up singing country music, gospel, and blues. Tall and handsome with long sideburns and slicked-back hair, he was a riveting performer. His music was strongly rooted in the southern music of his childhood.

Presley quickly became a national sensation. In less than a year, he recorded 8 number one songs and 6 of the all-time top 25 records of music company RCA. However, Presley had many critics, including teachers and members of the clergy, who complained that his unique way of dancing and shaking his hips proved that rock and roll posed a moral danger to the country's youth. This criticism only increased Presley's popularity among young people.

In 1956, rock and roll reached a milestone when an African-American singer named **Little Richard** outsold tamer versions of his songs that had been rerecorded by Pat Boone, a leading white cover artist. The success of Little Richard and other rock and roll musicians led major record companies to start recording more of the genre, performed by both black and white musicians. Music sales tripled during the 1950s, aided by such technological advances as portable transistor radios and vinyl records.

THE BEAT GENERATION

While rock and roll was changing the American music scene, another youth rebellion transformed American writing. The **Beat Generation** was a group of young writers and poets in San Francisco and New York City who attacked the values and beliefs of mainstream American society. They called themselves "beat" because they were tired of living in the homogenous, or uniform, society they felt was taking hold in the United States. They despised politics, consumerism, and technology, and they valued creative expression.

Poet **Allen Ginsberg** expressed the Beats' disgust for the conventions of the time in his long, free verse poem "Howl" (1955). Its opening line—"I saw the best minds of my generation destroyed by madness"—sets a mood of anger and despair. Ginsberg's work demonstrated his belief that a mass audience could relate to an individual's thoughts and experiences, no matter how outside the norm they might be.

The Beats equated happiness and creativity with total freedom of expression. Their model of authentic living was Dean Moriarty, the hero of *On the Road* (1957) by Beat author **Jack Kerouac**. Loosely based on an actual road trip that Kerouac and some friends took, the book tells of the cross-country adventures of a group of young Americans trying to escape from middle-class life. *On the Road* became a national best seller and a cult book on college campuses. Like Presley, Little Richard, and Ginsberg, Kerouac appealed to the young people dissatisfied with conventional American culture of the 1950s.

HISTORICAL THINKING

1. **READING CHECK** What forms of entertainment that developed in the 1950s became part of mainstream American culture?
2. **ANALYZE CAUSE AND EFFECT** How did racism affect television programming in the 1950s?
3. **MAKE CONNECTIONS** How do you think the historical story of rock and roll influenced social trends in today's popular music?

HI 1 Students show the connections, causal and otherwise, between particular historical events and larger social, economic, and political trends and developments.

NATIONAL BASEBALL HALL OF FAME AND MUSEUM COOPERSTOWN, NEW YORK

he National Baseball Hall of Fame and Museum in ooperstown, New York, celebrates and preserves he history of America's favorite pastime. Dedicated n June 12, 1939, the museum houses the bronze laques of more than 300 inductees elected to the lall of Fame, the sport's highest honor. Exhibits eature trophies, baseballs, gloves, jerseys, and other artifacts associated with legendary players a managers, from Ted Williams to Ken Griffey, Jr. The museum also tells the history of African Americans baseball—as well as the story of women in the gam Each year, about 300,000 visitors tour the museum relive the greatest moments in baseball history anc learn more about the heroes of the sport.

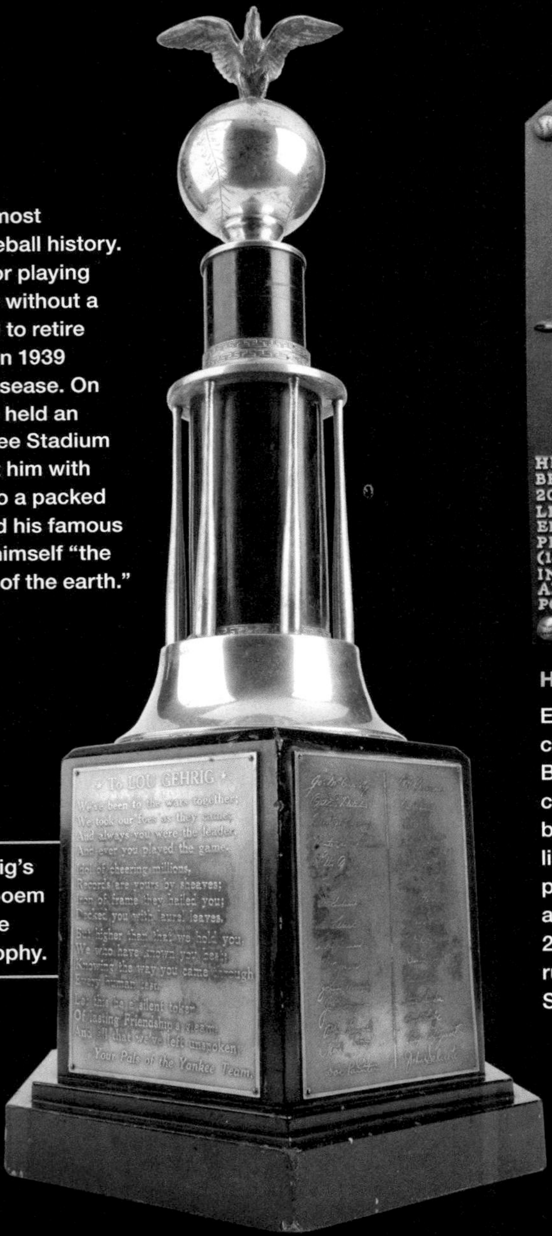

ou Gehrig's Trophy

ou Gehrig is one of the most espected players in baseball history. Called the "Iron Horse" for playing 2,130 consecutive games without a reak, Gehrig was forced to retire when he was diagnosed in 1939 with an incurable, fatal disease. On July 4, 1939, the Yankees held an appreciation day at Yankee Stadium o honor him and present him with he trophy shown here. To a packed stadium, Gehrig delivered his famous arewell speech, calling himself "the uckiest man on the face of the earth."

The names of Gehrig's teammates and a poem honoring Gehrig are inscribed on the trophy.

Hank Aaron's Plaque

Each year, baseball writers vote on candidates for induction into the National Baseball Hall of Fame. In addition, a specia committee periodically elects inductees. A bronze plaque is made for each inductee, like this one for Hank Aaron, identifying the person's accomplishments. Aaron reigned as baseball's home run king from 1974 unti 2007, when his career record of 755 home runs was surpassed by Barry Bonds of the San Francisco Giants.

11.8.8 Discuss forms of popular culture, with emphasis on their origins and geographic diffusion (e.g., jazz and other forms popular music, professional sports, architectural and artistic styles).

Which other major league players served in the World Wars? Do research to find out.

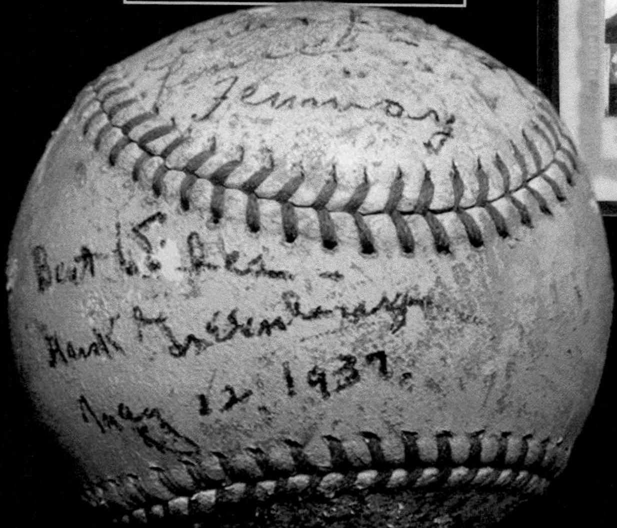

Hank Greenberg's Baseball and ID Card

One of the best hitters in baseball, Henry "Hank" Greenberg won two Most Valuable Player awards with the Detroit Tigers before his career was interrupted by World War II. Like many other major league players, Greenberg served in the war from 1941 to 1945. His War Department ID card appears above. When Greenberg returned to the major leagues in 1945, he helped the Tigers win the World Series by driving in 7 runs in 7 games. The next year, he led the American League in home runs and RBIs.

"I love that baseball is timeless. I love that it's traditional, but that it has adapted over the years. . . . **There's nothing better than sitting at a ballgame."**

—Jeff Idelson, President, National Baseball Hall of Fame and Museum

Catcher's mitts lack individual fingers, like mittens, and have heavy padding.

Yogi Berra's Mitt

A colorful baseball icon, New York Yankees catcher Yogi Berra was a 10-time World Series champion. He used this mitt to catch a perfect game thrown by pitcher Don Larsen in the World Series on October 8, 1956. The game was played at Yankee Stadium in New York City against the Brooklyn Dodgers. In a perfect game, a pitcher allows no hits or walks through at least 9 innings. A perfect game is a rare accomplishment. In major league history through 2016, only 23 pitchers had achieved the feat.

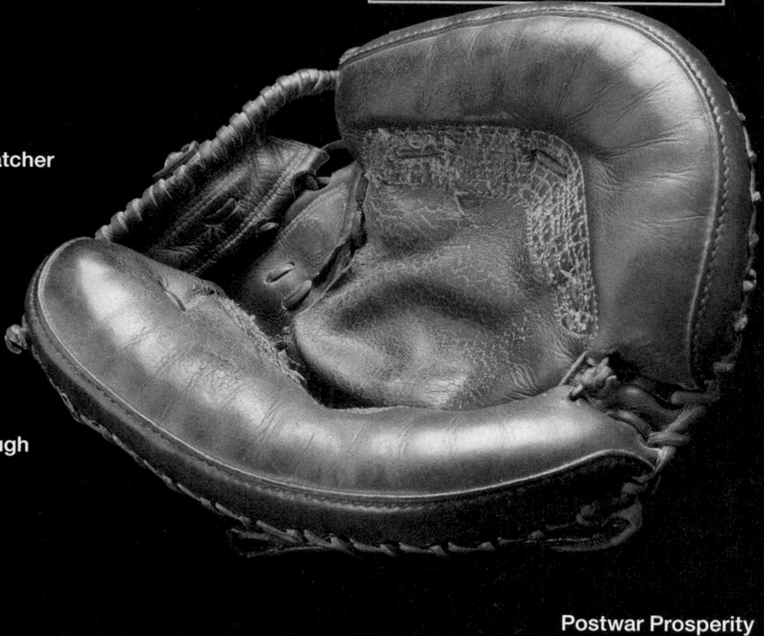

3.1 **MAIN IDEA** Although many Americans enjoyed increased prosperity during the 1950s, a significant portion of the population lived in poverty.

URBAN AND RURAL POVERTY

If you don't experience something yourself, you may find it hard to imagine it even exists. In the 1950s, middle-class suburbanites lived sheltered from the poverty that plagued inner cities and rural areas.

PERSISTENT POVERTY

The 1950s were a prosperous time for the United States as a whole, but the nation's wealth was not distributed equally. While the total amount of wealth in the country increased, the economic gap between the wealthy and the poor remained the same. In the late 1950s, the **poverty rate**, or the percentage of the population living in poverty, was 22.4 percent, which amounted to about 39.5 million people.

American journalists and writers of the early 1960s worked to expose the pervasive poverty in the United States. In 1960, journalist Edward R. Murrow revealed the harsh living conditions of migrant farm workers in a nationally aired documentary for CBS, *Harvest of Shame*. Television viewers witnessed families who could barely afford food for themselves as they harvested crops for the wealthiest, best-fed country in the world. In the book *The Other America*, published in 1962, author Michael Harrington portrayed the persistence of poverty among such groups as the working poor, the elderly, and the mentally ill. The book became required reading in college courses and prompted government officials to address some of the problems it had exposed.

PRIMARY SOURCE

The American city has been transformed. The poor still inhabit the miserable housing in the central area, but they are increasingly isolated from contact with, or sight of, anybody else. Middle-class women coming in from Suburbia on a rare trip may catch the merest glimpse of the other America on the way to an evening at the theater, but their children are segregated in suburban schools. The business or professional man may drive along the fringes of slums in a car or bus, but it is not an important experience to him. The failures, the unskilled, the disabled, the aged, and the minorities are right there, across the tracks, where they have always been. But hardly anyone else is.

— from *The Other America*,
by Michael Harrington, 1962

URBAN POVERTY

As you have read, many middle-class Americans and businesses moved to the suburbs in the 1950s. This population shift lowered the taxes collected by cities, decreased municipal budgets, and influenced the racial concentrations in cities. Those departing for new homes in the suburbs were mostly white, while those who remained in the cities were more often members of minority groups. This difference was due both to economic factors and to discriminatory practices that prevented members of minorities from moving to largely white suburban neighborhoods.

President Truman's Fair Deal had included the American Housing Act of 1949. The act provided mortgage assistance for Americans buying homes and began the process of **urban renewal**, which involved clearing slums to replace them with large, publicly funded housing projects. Federal and state government urban renewal programs continued into the 1960s. Although the original intent of the plan was good, the huge projects destroyed existing communities, were too large to manage efficiently, and often isolated the residents from affordable services. Instead of alleviating problems, many of the housing projects became centers of despair and unemployment. Out-of-wedlock births increased, as did criminal activity and drug abuse. By the late 1960s, the urban renewal effort was largely deemed a failure.

11.8.6 Discuss the diverse environmental regions of North America, their relationship to local economies, and the origins and prospects of environmental problems in those regions; 11.11.6 Analyze the persistence of poverty and how different analyses of this issue influence welfare reform, health insurance reform, and other social policies.

American photographer Wayne Miller took this photograph of tenements in Chicago in 1948 as part of a project documenting the lives of African Americans who were left out of the postwar economic boom.

RURAL POVERTY

Poverty in the United States was not confined to the inner cities in the 1950s. As you have read, suburbanization affected rural areas as well. The loss of farmland, the rise of agribusiness, and increased mechanization meant fewer farming jobs. Many rural communities slowly declined, especially as young people left in search of job opportunities.

Some rural areas were extremely poor. **Appalachia**, a part of the Appalachian Mountain region that stretches from northern Alabama to southern New York, had one of the most severe poverty rates in the United States in the late 1950s and early 1960s. In 1960, when the overall United States poverty rate was 22 percent, the poverty rate in Appalachia averaged more than 31 percent.

Appalachia was mountainous and hard to farm, but it had an abundance of coal. With little else to sustain the local economy, the region became dependent on coal mining. But mining was hard, dirty, and dangerous work. It stripped forests and polluted the air, land, and water, contributing to a variety of environmental problems. By the mid-20th century, the introduction of machinery that could do the work of many miners in a much shorter time frame put many miners out of work. Logging provided some temporary jobs, but the process scarred the Appalachian landscape.

Over time, efforts to reduce poverty in many places in the United States were successful, but Appalachia saw little economic improvement. In a decade, the region had lost 1.5 percent of its jobs, even as the nation's total employment grew by 17 percent. Its rugged landscape was unattractive to most industries, and re-education and job training programs were well intentioned but ineffective. Between 1945 and 1965, approximately 3.5 million people left Appalachia, seeking better lives and work opportunities in larger cities in the Midwest.

HISTORICAL THINKING

1. **READING CHECK** How did suburbanization contribute to urban and rural poverty in the 1950s?
2. **ANALYZE CAUSE AND EFFECT** Why did many urban renewal projects of the 1950s and 1960s fail?
3. **IDENTIFY PROBLEMS AND SOLUTIONS** Why did attempts to reverse Appalachian poverty fail?

11.11.7 Explain how the federal, state, and local governments have responded to demographic and social changes such as population shifts to the suburbs, racial concentrations in the cities, Frostbelt-to-Sunbelt migration, international migration, decline of family farms, increases in out-of-wedlock births, and drug abuse.

3.2 **MAIN IDEA** Many Native Americans and Mexican Americans struggled against poverty and discrimination during the 1950s.

NATIVE AMERICANS AND MEXICAN AMERICANS

The 1950s were great years to be a white, middle-class American. But if you were Native American or Mexican American, it was a different story.

DEMANDING A PLACE AS CITIZENS

In the years following World War II, Native Americans, many of whom had volunteered and fought bravely during the war, found themselves shut out of both the postwar economic boom and the political system. On reservations, they faced high rates of poverty and unemployment, poor access to government assistance and services, and inadequate schools. Many Native Americans did not even have the right to vote, despite the fact that, in 1924, Congress had granted citizenship to all Native Americans born within the United States. In addition, for decades, the federal government's policy toward Native Americans' sovereignty, or self-government, was inconsistent.

Some states refused to grant suffrage to Native Americans. The states took the position that Native Americans living on reservations were not citizens of the state, but rather citizens of their individual tribes or nations. Native Americans turned to the courts.

In 1948, Miguel Trujillo, a U.S. Marine war veteran and member of the Isleta Pueblo in New Mexico, was denied when he attempted to register to vote. He filed suit against the registrar and the state. A panel of three federal judges ruled in *Trujillo* v. *Garley* that the portion of New Mexico's constitution that prohibited Native American reservation residents from voting violated the 14th and 15th amendments of the U.S. Constitution.

Their decision backed up a similar case, *Harrison and Austin* v. *Laveen*, which had been brought by two Mojave-Apache men in Arizona that same year. These two cases effectively granted all Native American citizens the right to vote throughout the United States; however, Maine did not officially grant this right until 1953, and Utah held out until 1957.

Another major issue in the postwar era was poor government management of reservations. The Meriam Report, a government study released in 1928, had documented the problems and suggested specific reforms. The Indian Reorganization Act, passed in 1934, was an attempt to address the problems. The act sought to decrease federal control of Native American affairs and to encourage Native American self-government. It ended the government practice—adopted with the Dawes Act in 1887—of selling off the best reservation lands to white land speculators and homesteaders. It recognized the authority of tribal governments and promoted their self-government by urging them to adopt constitutions drafted by the Bureau of Indian Affairs.

But the reorganization was not a success. The act did not give Native Americans full control over their lands and governments. Instead, the reservations remained under the management of the Bureau of Indian Affairs, and little progress was made in solving the problems detailed in the Meriam Report.

Hoping to restore their tribal sovereignty and take control of their own future, Native Americans from 50 tribes and associations met in Denver, Colorado, to establish the National Congress of American Indians in 1944. In one year, membership rose to about 800 tribes and nations, representing nearly every Native American group in the United States. The organization began working to protect treaty rights, maintain Native American traditions, and push for self-determination and self-government.

11.8.6 Discuss the diverse environmental regions of North America, their relationship to local economies, and the origins and prospects of environmental problems in those regions; 11.11.7 Explain how the federal, state, and local governments have responded to demographic and social changes such as population shifts to the suburbs, racial concentrations in the cities, Frostbelt-to-Sunbelt migration, international migration, decline of family farms, increases in out-of-wedlock births, and drug abuse.

Protester George Pletnikoff, Jr., a member of the Unangax (Aleut) tribe, helps train protesters in nonviolent methods.

Krystal Two Bulls, a member of the Northern Cheyenne and Oglala Lakota tribes, raises her fist in protest at right.

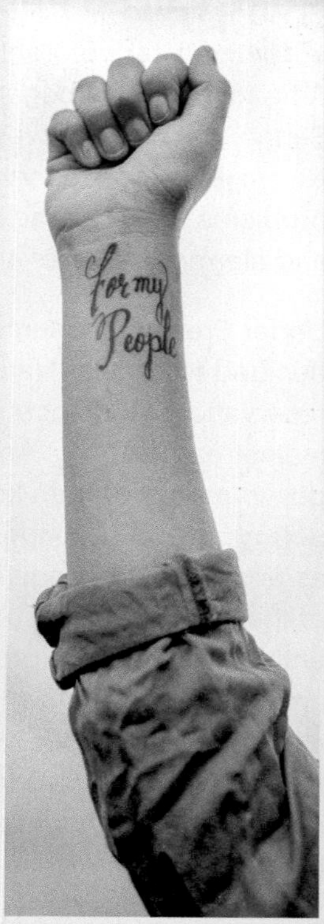

Nailed to a signpost at the main protest camp are the names of participating tribes and the distances to their homelands.

Protester Ray Curtis Yazzie, a member of the Blackfeet tribe, displays a Blackfeet Nation flag.

STANDING ROCK PROTEST

The struggle by Native Americans to protect their rights has continued into the 21st century. Beginning in April 2016, the Standing Rock Sioux led a 10-month protest in North Dakota against construction of the Dakota Access oil pipeline, designed to travel along the Missouri River and connect North Dakota oil fields with pipeline networks in Illinois. Seeking to protect their freshwater source and the diverse environmental regions crossed by the pipeline from potential oil leaks, the Standing Rock Sioux were joined by people from hundreds of indigenous tribes, including those shown above. In late February 2017, police cleared the main protest camp, following an executive order by President Donald Trump to advance approval of the pipeline's construction.

MORE FAILED POLICIES

In 1943, a year before the National Congress of American Indians began to organize, the U.S. Senate decided to investigate living conditions on Native American reservations. They found serious problems: poverty, racism, abuse by police officers, and alarming rates of alcoholism and suicide.

Under President Eisenhower, the federal government decided to remove Native Americans from reservations and encourage them to assimilate into mainstream society. And so began the disastrous government program known as the **termination policy**. In 1953, Congress set a goal to "as rapidly as possible make Indians within the territorial limits of the United States subject to the same laws and entitled to the same privileges and responsibilities as are applicable to other citizens of the United States." Under this policy, the government terminated all benefits and services to reservations, withdrawing its responsibility to maintain reservations and ending the limited sovereignty of individual tribes and nations.

Among the first tribes to be terminated were the Agua Caliente, who owned the land around Palm Springs, California, and the Klamath, whose land in Oregon was rich in lumber. The federal government took over their lands, as well as the land belonging to 107 other tribes between 1953 and 1964. Much of the land was sold to non–Native Americans.

Under this policy, Native Americans were expected to assimilate quickly into the mainstream of American society. To aid in this process, the Bureau of Indian Affairs set up a relocation program to move Native Americans from reservations to cities, where they were expected to find higher-paying jobs. The bureau set up relocation centers in Los Angeles, San Francisco, San Jose, Denver, Dallas, Cincinnati, Cleveland, St. Louis, and Chicago to help Native Americans find work, housing, and community resources. But not everyone found employment, and adjustment was difficult. Families were often separated, and tribal affiliations severed. In addition, a large number of Native Americans remained in poverty, and alcoholism continued to be a problem among many relocated populations.

Ultimately, the termination policy and the relocation program were failures. Federal termination efforts ended in 1963, and some of the affected tribes have been successful in regaining their lands through a number of lawsuits. The relocation era lasted for nearly two more decades, with as many as 750,000 Native Americans migrating to cities between 1950 and 1980.

THE THREAT OF DEPORTATION

During President Truman's eight years in office, from 1945 to 1953, about 127,000 undocumented immigrants were deported and more than 3.2 million left in fear of deportation. In 1954, under President Eisenhower, the government responded to an economic recession and a large U.S. labor pool with a program called "Operation Wetback," a reference to an offensive name for Mexicans who crossed the Rio Grande illegally. Intended to deport undocumented workers, the program mistreated many Mexicans and indiscriminately deported U.S. citizens as well. Officially, 2.1 million people of Mexican descent were deported through this aggressive, military-like campaign between 1954 and 1958.

MEXICAN AMERICAN WORKERS

In the 1950s and 1960s, the Latino population in the United States was relatively small. In 1960, about 6 million Latinos lived in the country. Many had first entered the United States to take part in the Bracero Program, an organized labor program that invited Mexican agricultural workers to replace U.S. farmworkers who were serving in World War II.

The government extended the Bracero Program after the war, and the number of braceros entering the United States increased. Most of the workers arrived from Mexico, but some came from Jamaica and the Bahamas. When the program was terminated in 1964, nearly 5 million worker contracts had been issued. Although President Truman had signed legislation to protect the rights of legal migrant workers in the United States, he also proposed legislation to stop employers from hiring undocumented immigrants. Congress did not approve it.

After the Bracero Program ended, many workers maintained connections with friends and families by continuing to cross the border informally and to return at will. Still others, knowing they would find fewer opportunities back at home, remained in the United States illegally after they were no longer in the program. Businesses were happy to hire these workers, paying them even lower wages than other migrant laborers. These low-paid workers contributed much to the economy of California and the Southwest, yet they lived in poverty and faced the constant threat of deportation.

THE LONGORIA INCIDENT

Even though they aided the United States during World War II, Mexican Americans faced

11.6.5 Trace the advances and retreats of organized labor, from the creation of the American Federation of Labor and the Congress of Industrial Organizations to current issues of a postindustrial, multinational economy, including the United Farm Workers in California; 11.8.2 Describe the significance of Mexican immigration and its relationship to the agricultural economy, especially in California.

Braceros registering to enter the United States to work are fingerprinted and given documents at the Monterrey Processing Center in Mexico in 1956.

discrimination in the Southwest and elsewhere in the nation, whether they were citizens or undocumented immigrants. The Longoria incident was a prime example. Felix Longoria, a Mexican American war hero, was killed in the Philippines during World War II. When his body was returned to his family in 1948, his widow attempted to hold a wake in his honor at the only funeral home in Three Rivers, Texas. The owner of the funeral home refused her, saying, "The whites wouldn't like it."

The incident became front-page news across the country. **Dr. Hector P. Garcia**, a Mexican American and the president of the American GI Forum, a Latino veterans' civil rights organization, gathered more than 1,000 people to protest. He also sent a telegram directly to influential Texas senator **Lyndon B. Johnson**, who would later rise to the presidency. By the next afternoon, Johnson replied with an offer to bury Private Longoria at Arlington National Cemetery. The funeral was held there on February 16, 1949. The incident inspired many Mexican Americans to unify in their quest for civil rights and equal opportunities.

As early as the 1920s, Mexican Americans had organized to address discrimination. The **League of United Latin American Citizens (LULAC)**, formed in 1929, was one such organization. In 1945, LULAC sued the segregated Orange County, California, school system for openly discriminating against Latino children. LULAC also protested the Longoria incident. In the 1960s, the organization actively supported the United Farm Workers, a labor union representing California farmworkers, most of whom were Latino. LULAC grew in the following decades, and today it provides college scholarships and other kinds of support to the Latino community.

Inspired by the agendas, strategies, and effectiveness of the civil rights movement elsewhere in the country, another Mexican American organization, the **Unity League,** was launched in California in 1947. The league campaigned against blatant acts of discrimination in housing, cemeteries, theaters, schools, and public administration. The league won lawsuits in the 1950s in cases involving segregation in schools and public swimming pools.

HISTORICAL THINKING

1. **READING CHECK** What kinds of discrimination did Native Americans and Mexican Americans face during the 1950s?
2. **IDENTIFY MAIN IDEAS AND DETAILS** Why did the United States open its borders to Mexican workers during World War II?
3. **IDENTIFY PROBLEMS AND SOLUTIONS** What actions did Mexican Americans take to gain civil rights during the 1950s?

11.9.7 Examine relations between the United States and Mexico in the twentieth century, including key economic, political, immigration, and environmental issues; 11.10.5 Discuss the diffusion of the civil rights movement of African Americans from the churches of the rural South and the urban North, including the resistance to racial desegregation in Little Rock and Birmingham, and how the advances influenced the agendas, strategies, and effectiveness of the quests of American Indians, Asian Americans, and Hispanic Americans for civil rights and equal opportunities.

CHAPTER 15 POSTWAR PROSPERITY

REVIEW

VOCABULARY

Use each of the following vocabulary terms in a sentence that shows an understanding of the term's meaning.

1. suburbanization HSS 11.11.7
   As a result of suburbanization, subdivisions replaced large tracts of land.
2. nuclear deterrence HSS 11.9.3
3. brinkmanship HSS 11.9.3
4. consumer society HSS 11.8
5. suburban sprawl HSS 11.11.7
6. situation comedy HSS 11.8.8
7. urban renewal HSS 11.11.7
8. poverty rate HSS 11.11.6
9. termination policy HSS 11.11

READING STRATEGY

MAKE INFERENCES

Complete a graphic organizer like the one below to make an inference about the postwar effects of the GI Bill of Rights. Tell what you know about the subject in the "I Know" section. Write your inference in the "And So" section. Then answer the question that follows the graphic organizer.

Make Inferences

I Read *Millions of veterans gained a college education through the GI Bill of Rights, and many became employed in technology industries.*	
I Know	And So

10. Why might some Americans today idealize the 1950s? HSS 11.8

MAIN IDEAS

Answer the following questions. Support your answers with evidence from the chapter.

11. How did Eisenhower present his political ideas during his campaign for president in 1952? **LESSON 1.1** HSS HI 3
12. How did women's wages compare with men's wages after the end of World War II and during the 1950s? **LESSON 1.2** HSS 11.11.3
13. How was the system used to build houses in Levittown similar to production on an assembly line? **LESSON 1.3** HSS 11.8
14. In what ways did Americans' obsession with cars affect other industries during the 1950s? **LESSON 2.1** HSS 11.8.7
15. What aspects of American life did the Beat poets rebel against? **LESSON 2.3** HSS 11.8.8
16. Why did Appalachia suffer from a high poverty rate in the 1950s? **LESSON 3.1** HSS 11.8
17. How did Dr. Hector P. Garcia help resolve the Longoria incident? **LESSON 3.2** HSS 11.8.2

HISTORICAL THINKING

Answer the following questions. Support your answers with evidence from the chapter.

18. **EVALUATE** What were some drawbacks of Eisenhower's nuclear deterrence plan? HSS 11.9.3
19. **MAKE CONNECTIONS** What effects of the suburbanization of the 1950s do you notice in your life today? HSS CST 1
20. **IDENTIFY** What were some long-lasting effects of the Bracero Program? HSS 11.8.2
21. **FORM AND SUPPORT OPINIONS** Based on the results of the urban renewal projects of the 1950s and 1960s, what advice would you give an urban planner who wants to replace decaying neighborhoods in a city? HSS 11.8

22. **MAKE INFERENCES** How do you think voters in Guatemala reacted when the United States ousted their elected president in 1954? HSS 11.9.3

23. **DETERMINE CHRONOLOGY** What sequence of events led the federal government to establish the termination policy and relocation programs for Native Americans? HSS 11.11

INTERPRET VISUALS

With the baby boom in full swing in the 1950s, toy manufacturers had a ready market for their products. Study the toy advertisement and answer the questions that follow.

24. What is the manufacturer's purpose in offering a space man and jet rocket for free? HSS 11.8.8

25. What does it tell you about the growing consumer society that the manufacturers chose a space rocket as the perfect toy to offer kids? HSS 11.8.8

ANALYZE SOURCES

In the 1950s, William H. Whyte, a magazine editor, wrote a book about the culture of large corporate organizations and the suburbs where the employees—the "organization men"—lived. He found the suburbs alarming rather than blissful.

> At Levittown, Pennsylvania, residents are very much aware of who has what "modification" of the basic ranch-house design, and one house on which the owner mounted a small gargoyle became so famous a sight that many residents used to drive out of their way to show it to visitors. People have a sharp eye for interior amenities also, and the acquisition of an automatic dryer . . . or any other divergence from the norm is always cause for notice. Those who lack such amenities, conversely, are also noted.
>
> —from *The Organization Man*, by William Whyte, 1956

26. What is Whyte implying about people's values and attitudes in the suburbs? HSS 11.11.7

CONNECT TO YOUR LIFE

27. **EXPLANATORY** You have read about American life and culture during the 1950s. Some historians think the postwar era laid the foundation for our current American identity. Review the chapter and research the lives of teenagers in the 1950s. Then write a short essay comparing their lives and experiences with yours. HSS 11.8.8

TIPS

- Use a Venn Diagram or a T-Chart to make notes about similarities and differences between your experiences and those of a teenager in the 1950s.
- Choose two or three of the most interesting items on your chart to write about.
- Conduct an Internet or library search to find more information on the topic.
- Use two or three vocabulary words from the chapter in your essay.
- End the essay with a generalization about the similarities and differences.

NATIONAL GEOGRAPHIC | CONNECTION

America's Propaganda Machine

BY BECKY LITTLE

Adapted from "Inside America's Shocking WWII Propaganda Machine," by Becky Little, news.nationalgeographic.com, December 2016

The United States was about six months into World War II when it founded the Office of War Information (OWI). Its mission: to disseminate political propaganda. The office spread its messages through print, radio, and film. But perhaps its most striking legacy is its posters with bright colors and sensational language. They encouraged Americans to ration their food, buy war bonds, and basically perform everyday tasks in support of the war effort. In one, a woman carrying her groceries is compared to soldiers carrying weapons. The poster implies that by walking instead of driving she is doing her patriotic duty. By not driving, people extended the lives of their cars and reduced the use of rubber and metal, which were instead needed to make tanks and weapons for the war.

LOOSE LIPS SINK SHIPS

Both the Allies and the Axis powers feared that leaked information could undermine their troops. With that in mind, the OWI produced posters urging people to keep sensitive information to themselves so enemies wouldn't overhear it. According to Stephen G. Hyslop, co-author of the National Geographic book *The Secret History of World War II*, the OWI struggled to find the best way to convey this message. As an example, he points to a poster that depicts a mysterious figure in a German helmet and warns "He's Watching You."

"The point of the poster is it's a German soldier" who could overhear what you say, Hyslop explains, but its message was too subtle. Consequently, the United States began to favor posters that got right to the point. In one of these, a woman's image appears alongside the words "WANTED! FOR MURDER. Her careless talk costs lives." This very clear message was still a bit strange. Most civilians didn't have access to sensitive military information, yet the images telling them to zip their lips were pretty aggressive and sometimes created the feeling of "Are the authorities on my side or are they after me?"

The OWI's propaganda was made for people at home and abroad, and it was always clear that these messages came from the U.S. government. However, the United States had another propaganda arm that produced messages specifically for the enemy and made it look like this propaganda was coming from inside the enemy's country.

ATTACKING ENEMY MORALE

Creating propaganda that hid or misrepresented its source wasn't only done by the United States. Germany transmitted radio messages to France, Britain, and other countries that appeared to originate from inside those nations.

The American Office of Strategic Services (OSS) responded with its own "black propaganda," as the practice was known. One mission, called Operation Cornflakes, involved dropping mailbags into Germany containing fake newspapers that looked as if they were made by Nazi resisters. Some of the mail had stamps with a picture of a deathly, skeletal-looking Hitler with the words *Futsches Reich* ("Ruined Empire").

The Allies also transmitted radio messages that appeared to come from inside Germany. This was an easier way to get information into the country than by dropping mailbags, Hyslop says.

Three-quarters of a century later, technological advances have made it even easier to sneak information into a country. As an example, Hyslop points to Russia's use of the Internet to spread propaganda during the 2016 U.S. election. Could future history books about our current era be illustrated with Internet political memes, just as today's history books are with propaganda posters? It's not unthinkable.

For more from National Geographic, check out "Dogs at War" online.

UNIT INQUIRY: Persuade an Audience

In this unit, you learned about a watershed event in which the United States became a major actor on the global stage: World War II. The Second World War placed tremendous demands on Americans, both those who fought abroad and those who remained at home. In public speeches and informal talks, Franklin Roosevelt and other leaders of the time worked to inspire citizens to make huge personal sacrifices in support of the war effort. How important were the rhetorical skills of the major leaders of this period? What kinds of persuasive language and appeals did they use? As you read quotes from their addresses, think about the way in which they crafted their messages to reach people's minds and hearts.

ASSIGNMENT

Choose an audience of the World War II era—such as newly enlisted soldiers, factory workers, farmers, or high school students—and write a speech persuading them to contribute to the war effort in a specific way. For example, you might research victory gardens and encourage high school students to plant one at their school to supplement the nation's food supply. Be prepared to present your speech to the class.

Plan Think about the reasons that success in World War II was vital to Americans and the way that Allied leaders like Roosevelt and Churchill inspired people to go all out to win the war. Then consider your audience and the contribution you're asking them to make. You might want to use a graphic organizer to outline your argument.

I. ____________
  A. ____________
  B. ____________
II. ____________
  A. ____________
  B. ____________
III. ____________
  A. ____________
  B. ____________

Produce Use your outline to write a persuasive speech that will inspire your audience to support the war effort in the way you've identified. Incorporate persuasive language and appeals directed specifically to your audience. Use words and phrases that clarify the relationship between your reasons and evidence. Provide a concluding statement that supports your argument.

Present Share your speech with the class. You might consider one of these options:

- Record a "fireside chat" audiotape. Play the audiotape in class, and then play a portion of one of Roosevelt's fireside chats. Invite students to compare and contrast your oratory style with Roosevelt's style.
- Create notes of your speech, then practice the speech and deliver it to the class. Ask students to identify the persuasive techniques you used and rate their effectiveness.

NATIONAL GEOGRAPHIC | LEARNING FRAMEWORK ACTIVITY

Write About a Cold War Advance

SKILLS Observation, Communication

KNOWLEDGE Our Human Story

Major advances in medicine, science, and technology occurred during the Cold War years. Identify and research a Cold War development that improved Americans' lives, like the use of nuclear power as an energy source, or the development of new vaccines or commercial computers. Write a narrative incorporating real or imagined experiences during the Cold War, focusing on how the advancement affected a particular character's life. Use dialogue, description, and reflection to express the importance of the advancement on society.

Debate the Origins of the Cold War

ATTITUDE Curiosity

SKILL Collaboration

Work with a small group to research the major debates among historians concerning the origins of the Cold War. Read excerpts from *Origins of the Cold War* by Arthur M. Schlesinger, Jr., and excerpts from *The Tragedy of American Diplomacy* by William A. Williams. Evaluate each historian's use of evidence, looking for sound generalizations or misleading oversimplifications. Choose a creative way to present both sides of the argument, and have a class debate about the roles the United States and the Soviet Union played in the start of the Cold War.

HREP 3 Students evaluate major debates among historians concerning alternative interpretations of the past, including an analysis of authors' use of evidence and the distinctions between sound generalizations and misleading oversimplifications.

UNIT 5

1954–1975

YEARS OF TURBULENCE

CRITICAL VIEWING U.S. National Guard troops block Beale Street in Memphis, Tennessee, on March 29, 1968, as civil rights marchers pass by. The activists held a number of marches over several days. Martin Luther King, Jr., participated in one of them. It was one of the last public appearances he would make before he was assassinated on April 4. What message are the protesters trying to convey with their signs?

I AM
A MAN
I AM
MAN

THE UNITED STATES

1960
John F. Kennedy is elected president. *(Kennedy campaign button)*

1964
After a North Vietnamese torpedo boat allegedly fires on an American destroyer in Southeast Asia's Gulf of Tonkin, the United States greatly expands its role in the Vietnam War.

1955
African Americans in Montgomery, Alabama, boycott the city's buses shortly after Rosa Parks is arrested for refusing to give up her seat on one of them to a white man. *(bus Rosa Parks was riding when she refused to give up her seat)*

1963
Martin Luther King, Jr., leads the March on Washington and delivers his "I Have a Dream" speech; Kennedy is assassinated, and Lyndon Johnson assumes the presidency.

1954
The ruling in *Brown* v. *Board of Education of Topeka, Kansas*, ends the legal segregation of public schools.

1950

1960

1954 ASIA
After the overthrow of France, Vietnam is divided into North Vietnam and South Vietnam.

1959 AMERICAS
Fidel Castro becomes the communist leader of Cuba.

1962 EUROPE
The Soviet Union places missiles in Cuba, triggering the Cuban Missile Crisis. *(political cartoon depicting Soviet leader Nikita Khrushchev as a dentist pulling out Fidel Castro's teeth, which are shaped like missiles)*

THE WORLD

1957 AFRICA
Ghana gains its independence from Britain. *(Ghana's Independence Arch)*

HISTORICAL THINKING

DETERMINE CHRONOLOGY What happened two years after the United States withdrew from Vietnam?

1965
Johnson sends the first U.S. ground troops to Vietnam.

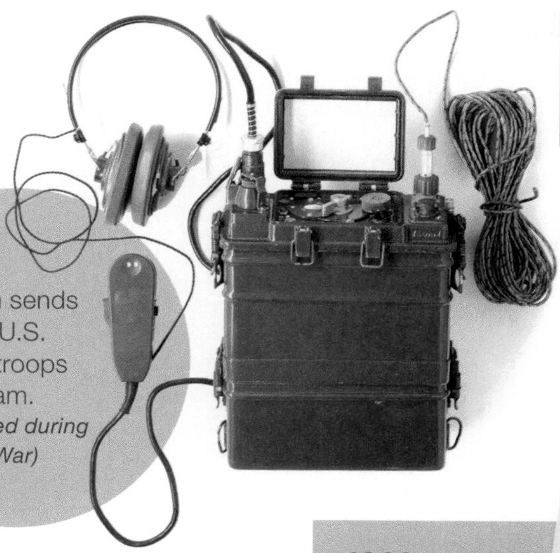

(radio used during Vietnam War)

1966
César Chávez leads a march to Sacramento, California's capital, to protest the low wages and poor working conditions of the state's farmworkers.

1968
Martin Luther King, Jr., is assassinated at the age of 39; Richard Nixon is elected president.

1969
American astronauts are the first to land and walk on the moon.

FINAL
DAILY NEWS
NEW YORK'S PICTURE NEWSPAPER
8¢

MEN WALK ON THE MOON

'One Small Step for Man, One Giant Leap for Mankind'

1970

1972
The American Indian Movement occupies the Bureau of Indian Affairs to protest broken treaties; the Equal Rights Amendment for women passes Congress but fails to be ratified.

1973
The United States pulls its troops from Vietnam, ending its involvement in the war in Southeast Asia.

1975

1975 ASIA
South Vietnam falls to the communists, ending the civil war in Vietnam.

1967 AFRICA
Civil war breaks out in Nigeria after the Republic of Biafra secedes from the African nation.
(flag of Biafra)

1968 ASIA
North Vietnamese forces launch the Tet Offensive and attack many cities and towns in South Vietnam.
(Troops battle in Saigon following the Tet Offensive.)

HI 1 Students show the connections, causal and otherwise, between particular historical events and larger social, economic, and political trends and developments.

CHAPTER 16

THE CIVIL RIGHTS MOVEMENT

1954–1964

HISTORICAL THINKING How did the civil rights movement redefine American identity?

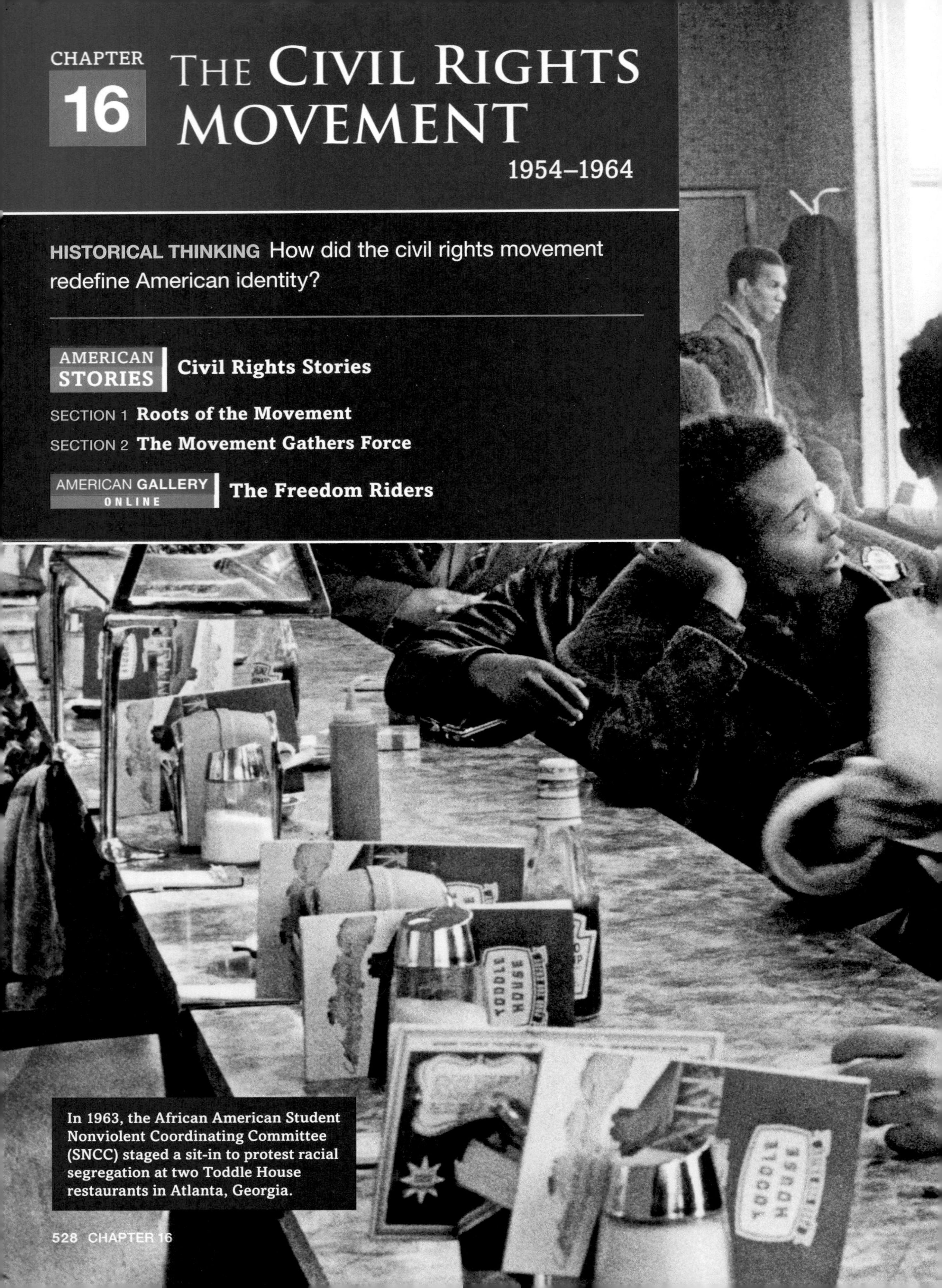

In 1963, the African American Student Nonviolent Coordinating Committee (SNCC) staged a sit-in to protest racial segregation at two Toddle House restaurants in Atlanta, Georgia.

"Nobody's free until **everybody's free.**"

—Fannie Lou Hamer, civil rights leader

CIVIL RIGHTS STORIES

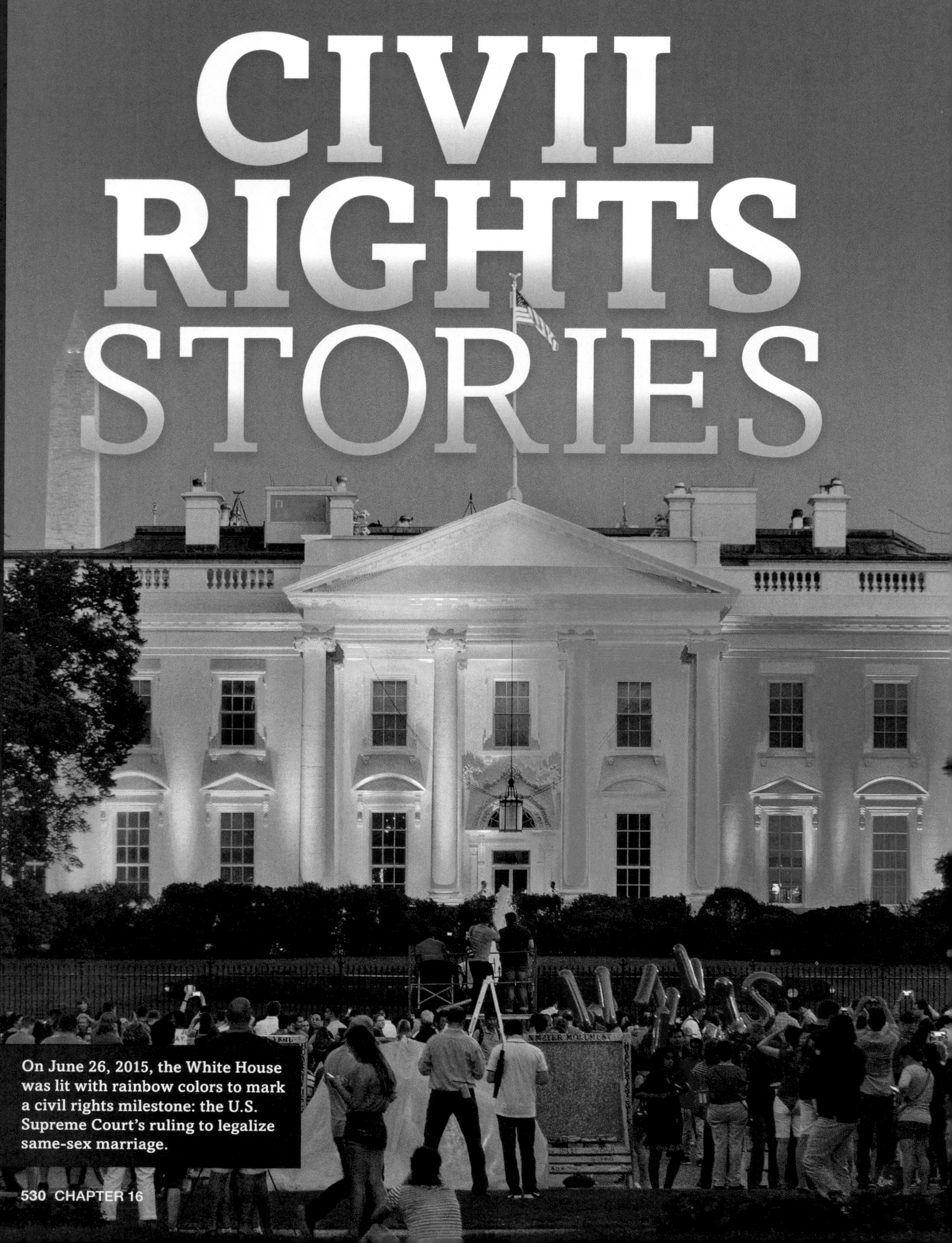

On June 26, 2015, the White House was lit with rainbow colors to mark a civil rights milestone: the U.S. Supreme Court's ruling to legalize same-sex marriage.

The struggle for civil rights in the 1950s and 1960s evokes powerful images in the minds of Americans: Dr. Martin Luther King, Jr., delivering his "I Have a Dream" speech; young African-American children facing angry crowds of protesters trying to keep them out of school; citizens marching to demand equal voting rights or school desegregation. These images represent the long and ongoing process of establishing and defending civil rights for all citizens. This American Story highlights the stories of some of the key people, places, and events in the civil rights movements, from the 1930s to the present day.

THE MARCH ON WASHINGTON

One familiar image from the civil rights movement shows Dr. Martin Luther King, Jr., standing on the steps of the Lincoln Memorial in Washington, D.C., delivering his most famous speech to a crowd of more than 200,000 people. It was a day of true unity—civil rights organizations, religious leaders, and men and women of all races came together to protest the inequalities African Americans still faced even 100 years after Abraham Lincoln's Emancipation Proclamation.

The 1963 March on Washington for Jobs and Freedom was not the first-ever march to the capital planned to support the rights of African Americans. You may recall that in 1941, A. Philip Randolph proposed a march on Washington to protest racial discrimination in the context of federal jobs. Randolph canceled the march, however, when President Franklin D. Roosevelt issued an executive order barring discrimination in the growing defense industry.

In 1963, President John F. Kennedy proposed a sweeping civil rights bill, but it was mired in a divided Congress. In an attempt to demonstrate public support for the bill and encourage Congress to act, Randolph and other civil rights leaders decided it was time to organize an even larger march on Washington. About 100,000 participants were expected to flood the city. Organizations such as the National Association for the Advancement of Colored People (NAACP) and the Southern Christian Leadership Conference planned the event, encouraging African Americans and whites from all states to come to Washington in a display of unified support for equal rights. And on August 28, 1963, around 200,000 people gathered peacefully in front of the Lincoln Memorial.

At the 1963 march, a multiracial crowd listened to songs by popular performers, prayers by prominent clergymen, and speeches by activists, including Dr. Martin Luther King, Jr.

11.10.1 Explain how demands of African Americans helped produce a stimulus for civil rights, including President Roosevelt's ban on racial discrimination in defense industries in 1941, and how African Americans' service in World War II produced a stimulus for President Truman's decision to end segregation in the armed forces in 1948; 11.10.4 Examine the roles of civil rights advocates (e.g., A. Philip Randolph, Martin Luther King, Jr., Malcolm X, Thurgood Marshall, James Farmer, Rosa Parks), including the significance of Martin Luther King, Jr.'s "Letter from Birmingham Jail" and "I Have a Dream" speech.

CRITICAL VIEWING The Obama family, members of Congress, former President George W. Bush, and civil rights leaders cross the bridge in Selma to commemorate the 50th anniversary of Bloody Sunday, a 1965 civil rights march that turned violent. How might this photo reflect the progress of the civil rights movement in the United States?

COLLABORATING TO DESEGREGATE EDUCATION

As you will read in greater detail later in this chapter, well into the 1950s, many parts of the United States, especially the South, had racially segregated schools. School segregation had been made legal in 1896 by the *Plessy* v. *Ferguson* court case, which held that having separate public facilities for African Americans and whites was constitutional as long as the facilities were equal to each other.

For many decades, African-American and white civil rights lawyers worked together to challenge this "separate but equal" ruling. In 1930, the NAACP hired Nathan Margold, a white lawyer from New York. Margold conducted a study and found that African-American and white schools were not funded equally. This violated the equal protection rights provided for by the 14th Amendment. He recommended suing segregated public schools.

In 1934, Charles H. Houston, a prominent African-American lawyer, began directing the NAACP's legal campaign against segregation and focused on higher education programs. One case involved African-American student Lloyd Gaines who was denied admission to the University of Missouri's law school because of his race. At the time, no law school in the state accepted African-American students. Although Gaines was offered a scholarship to attend a school out of state, he sued the university with the help of Houston, who argued that the state must either admit Gaines or provide an equal facility in Missouri. The courts agreed.

Through numerous other cases and victories, the NAACP's lawyers worked to protect civil rights. By the 1950s, a young African-American lawyer named Thurgood Marshall made it his mission to end segregation. He won many cases, preparing him for a historic legal battle in Topeka, Kansas.

In Kansas, segregation still existed in public schools. Linda Brown was denied enrollment in

11.10.3 Describe the collaboration on legal strategy between African American and white civil rights lawyers to end racial segregation in higher education.

AMERICAN PLACES

The Edmund Pettus Bridge

Some places will forever remain in the national consciousness as symbols of the fight for African-American civil rights in the 1950s and 1960s. One such place is the Edmund Pettus Bridge in Selma, Alabama. Completed in 1940, the bridge was named after a Confederate general and leader of the racist Ku Klux Klan in Alabama.

On March 7, 1965, a group of 600 protesters set out from Selma on a march to the state capital of Montgomery, to protest restrictions on voting rights for African Americans. On the Edmund Pettus Bridge just outside of town, local law enforcement officers waited with clubs and tear gas. They attacked the demonstrators and forced them back into Selma in an outbreak of violence that came to be known as Bloody Sunday. The marchers tried again on March 9 and were again turned away at the bridge. On March 21, after a federal judge had ruled in favor of the protesters' right to march along a public highway in order to "petition . . . government for redress of grievances," a new Selma-to-Montgomery march began. This time, 3,200 people set out from Selma and 25,000 arrived in the state capital. You will read more about these three marches in the next chapter.

Today, the Edmund Pettus Bridge is part of the Selma to Montgomery National Historic Trail administered by the National Park Service. On March 7, 2015, President Barack Obama and his family joined thousands of Americans at the bridge to commemorate the courage of the Bloody Sunday protesters. Among the 2015 marchers were some who had been present on Bloody Sunday, including Representative John Lewis of Georgia and Amelia Boynton Robinson, one of the original march's organizers.

the all-white school in her neighborhood. She had to walk more than a mile, cross a dangerous railroad yard, and then take a bus, to attend a school that accepted African Americans. Represented by Thurgood Marshall, the Brown family and other families decided to sue the school system, and in 1954, they won what would become one of the most important Supreme Court cases of all time, *Brown* v. *Board of Education of Topeka*.

While the landmark Brown ruling legally ended segregation, it did not erase it from the United States. Today, few schools and neighborhoods are truly racially integrated.

THINK ABOUT IT

Why might it have been advantageous for African-American and white lawyers to collaborate on cases to end racial discrimination in schools?

Linda Brown, shown here in front of the all-white Sumner Elementary School in 1953, lived only a few blocks away from this school but couldn't attend it.

11.10.2 Examine and analyze the key events, policies, and court cases in the evolution of civil rights, including *Dred Scott* v. *Sandford*, *Plessy* v. *Ferguson*, *Brown* v. *Board of Education*, *Regents of the University of California* v. *Bakke*, and California Proposition 209.

THE RIGHTS OF THE DISABLED

Ehlena Fry, 12, of Michigan, sits with her service dog Wonder outside the Supreme Court in Washington, D.C. Fry, who has cerebral palsy, is fighting to bring Wonder to school with her for assistance.

In 1990, the Americans With Disabilities Act (ADA), a bipartisan effort, was passed by Congress and signed into law by President George H. W. Bush. It banned job discrimination against people with disabilities and required buildings, businesses, and public transportation to be accessible to all. "The ADA was a response to an appalling problem: widespread, systemic, inhumane discrimination against people with disabilities," explains Robert Burgdorf, Jr., a disability rights legal advocate.

In 1971, according to Burgdorf, a "judge described people with disabilities as 'the most discriminated [against] minority in our nation.'" He was not alone in believing this. State-run residential treatment centers were "primitive and often unsanitary, dangerous, overcrowded and inhumane," states Burgdorf. Many children with disabilities were routinely prevented from attending public schools and therefore did not have access to an adequate education. Very few public transportation systems or private vehicles accommodated the disabled, making taxis, buses, trains, and ferries virtually unusable by people with physical impairments. Accessibility aids, such as flat entrances, ramps, sidewalk curb cuts, or Braille elevator signs, were not included in parks, stores, and office buildings.

Additionally, individuals with disabilities were often excluded from rights most Americans count on, from applying for a driver's license, to voting, to running for public office. In some states, people with developmental disabilities could not legally marry or enter into a contract. Even cities, such as Columbus, Ohio, and Chicago, practiced discrimination by enacting "ugly laws" to keep people whose physical conditions were perceived as "unpleasant" from public places.

Crucial victories in the courts during the 1970s and 1980s led to gains for people with disabilities in the fight for equal access to public schools and improved conditions in live-in facilities. As activists and protesters tackled the unfair treatment of individuals with disabilities, the courts ruled against discrimination in housing, transportation, voting, contracts, and medical services.

Since its passage, the ADA has had a positive impact on the lives of people with disabilities and their families. Accessible entrances, now the norm rather than the exception, assist those with mobility limitations as they enter buildings, cross streets, and visit public parks. Conveniently located parking spaces for people with disabilities are set aside in garages and parking lots to give people better access to public and private buildings. Mass transit accessibility in cities has also progressed, even if improvements to public transportation systems under the ADA have occurred more slowly and less consistently than many would like.

Yet not all equality issues for people with disabilities have been resolved, and people see tremendous disparities in how the ADA is enforced among business owners, school districts, and communities. In fact, according to Burgdorf, "Some . . . have taken an I-won't-do-anything-until-I'm-sued attitude toward the obligations imposed on them" by the act. Although there are many battles yet to be fought, the passing of the ADA was an inarguably significant milestone for ensuring equal rights for the disabled.

MARRIAGE EQUALITY

The question of marriage as a civil rights issue for same-sex couples garnered much attention in the 2010s, but the legal struggle began decades earlier. In 1970, Jack Baker and Michael McConnell applied for a marriage license in Minneapolis, Minnesota. When the men were refused a license, they took the case to court. Baker, a lawyer, made the case that prohibiting same-sex marriage was unconstitutional and a form of discrimination. He drew parallels to the 1967 case *Loving* v. *Virginia*, in which the Supreme Court ruled that it was unconstitutional to forbid interracial marriage. When Baker and McConnell's case was sent to the Supreme Court in 1972, however, the court refused to hear it.

The next legal test for same-sex marriage rights took place in Hawaii in 1996. There, a judge ruled that the state had no reason to prevent same-sex couples from marrying. A national backlash soon followed. Congress passed and President Bill Clinton signed the Defense of Marriage Act, which defined marriage as existing solely between a man and a woman in federal law. Several states, Hawaii among them, proposed and enacted constitutional amendments prohibiting same-sex marriage.

With the majority of both legislators and public opinion against same-sex marriage, gay activists and their supporters began a long campaign to change the minds of individual Americans. They also worked to bring the question to courtrooms and ballot boxes throughout the country. Gay marriage advocacy groups launched extensive advertising campaigns and engaged lobbyists to meet with lawmakers. Over time and despite staunch opposition, their efforts began to pay off. In 2004, the Massachusetts Supreme Court ruled in favor of same-sex marriage, and this time, the ruling was not reversed by a constitutional amendment. By 2011, the majority of the public supported same-sex marriage.

In 2015, when the United States Supreme Court agreed to rule on the issue it had turned down in 1972, gay marriage was legal in 36 states. On June 26, 2015, the nation's highest court ruled that the Constitution guarantees the right to marriage for same-sex couples. In the decision, Justice Anthony Kennedy wrote, "Their hope is not to be condemned to live in loneliness, excluded from one of civilization's oldest institutions. They ask for equal dignity in the eyes of the law. The Constitution grants them that right."

In what ways were the campaigns for same-sex marriage and other civil rights campaigns similar and different?

Now-married activists and parents Theresa Volpe and Mercedes Santos celebrate the results of a 2013 vote by the Senate Executive Committee on same-sex marriages in Illinois, prior to the 2015 Supreme Court ruling.

11.10.2 Examine and analyze the key events, policies, and court cases in the evolution of civil rights, including *Dred Scott* v. *Sandford, Plessy* v. *Ferguson, Brown* v. *Board of Education, Regents of the University of California* v. *Bakke*, and California Proposition 209; 11.11.7 Explain how the federal, state, and local governments have responded to demographic and social changes such as population shifts to the suburbs, racial concentrations in the cities, Frostbelt-to-Sunbelt migration, international migration, decline of family farms, increases in out-of-wedlock births, and drug abuse.

BLACK LIVES MATTER

The civil rights movement of the 1950s and 1960s achieved notable advancements for African Americans, such as desegregation and bans on many forms of discrimination. Yet many issues remain, such as poverty and lack of jobs in African-American neighborhoods, and the disproportionate numbers of African Americans who are jailed.

Present-day organizations such as Black Lives Matter (BLM) utilize social media and public protests to make their voices heard. Black Lives Matter began in July 2013, when Alicia Garza wrote a Facebook post that she called “a love letter to black people” after a white man named George Zimmerman was acquitted of the shooting death of black teenager Trayvon Martin. In the post she wrote, “I continue to be surprised at how little Black lives matter.” Patrice Cullors, a friend of Garza’s, was struck by that sentence and created the hashtag #BlackLivesMatter. Another friend built a social-media platform around the hashtag.

Many Americans became aware of Black Lives Matter in 2014, after a black teenager named Michael Brown was shot and killed by a white police officer in Ferguson, Missouri. People from all parts of the country used the media platform to express their outrage and to plan protests in Ferguson and other cities. Black Lives Matter groups continue to stage protests following other police shootings of African Americans and to strongly advocate for reform.

Black Lives Matter is sometimes described as “not your grandfather’s civil-rights movement.” It utilizes social media—not an option years ago. Unlike groups such as the Student Nonviolent Coordinating Committee, which had clear, centralized leadership, Black Lives Matter chapters operate independently to plan local events and protests. BLM also pursues civil rights for women, gays, and transgender people, while earlier civil rights groups often marginalized female leaders and put men at the forefront.

Some believe that Black Lives Matter’s methods are most effective for today’s civil rights issues. Others feel modern civil rights groups should more closely follow the structures and techniques that succeeded in the 1950s and 1960s. Ongoing changes in communications technology and American thinking are likely to influence today’s civil rights movements, which will continue to evolve as they pursue the goal of true equality for all.

On September 15, 1963, a bomb exploded at the predominantly black 16th Street Baptist Church in Birmingham, Alabama, killing four young girls. This stained-glass rosette was part of the rubble.

THE NATIONAL MUSEUM OF AFRICAN AMERICAN HISTORY AND CULTURE

On September 24, 2016, the Smithsonian Institution in Washington, D.C., opened a new museum. Standing alongside the other Smithsonian buildings on the National Mall, the National Museum of African American History and Culture (NMAAHC) offers a unique perspective on U.S. history and national identity. “This museum will tell the American story through the lens of African-American history and culture,” explained Lonnie G. Bunch, III, the NMAAHC’s Founding Director. “This is America’s Story and this museum is for all Americans.”

The galleries on the lower levels of the NMAAHC display collections of original artifacts that recount African-American history from the earliest years of

Photojournalist Eli Reed has documented the lives of people throughout the world for publications including *National Geographic*. One of his best-known projects is a book of photos called *Black in America*, which includes this 1999 photograph of members of the Minority Achievement Committee at Shaker Heights High School in Ohio. In *Black in America*, Reed captures the diversity of the African-American experience, the consequences of prejudice, and the continuing efforts to secure a better life for all.

the country to the present day. The dark times of slavery are represented by the manacles, whips, and other items used by slaveholders to control their prisoners. The museum also gives a voice to enslaved Americans by displaying items they created to express themselves. One such object is an embroidered pillowcase given by an enslaved mother to her nine-year-old daughter when the girl was sold. The pre-emancipation collection also includes Harriet Tubman's hymn book and Frederick Douglass's cane.

Other collections in the historical galleries illustrate the Reconstruction period, the struggle for civil rights, and recent events such as the election of the first African-American president of the United States in 2008 and the controversy over the shooting of Trayvon Martin in 2012.

The upper-level Culture and Community galleries of the museum focus on the diverse African-American communities within the United States. Exhibits highlight achievements in the arts and sports, and ongoing efforts to bring about positive social change.

PRIMARY SOURCE

At the opening of the National Museum of African American History and Culture in Washington, D.C., President Barack Obama struck a hopeful note in a speech about the need for continuing progress on civil rights and the museum's role in the quest for equality.

This national museum helps to tell a richer and fuller story of who we are. . . . Hopefully this museum can help us talk to each other. And more importantly, listen to each other. And most importantly, see each other—Black and White and Latino and Native American, and Asian American—see how our stories are bound together. And bound together with women in America, and workers in America, and entrepreneurs in America, and LGBT Americans.

—President Obama, September 24, 2016

1.1 **MAIN IDEA** After World War II, the Truman administration, the NAACP, and African-American authors helped bring civil rights to the forefront of American society.

PROGRESS AFTER THE WAR

The struggle for civil rights in America spans many decades, many presidents, and across many states, and it continues today. Change has come slowly. But with each court ruling and protest, more people have seen the need for all Americans to have the same rights. This chapter highlights some of the key events and people who have inspired racially based social changes throughout the mid-20th century in America.

CHANGE DRIVEN BY THE PEOPLE

In many ways, World War II changed race relations in the United States and gave momentum to the civil rights movement. Millions of African Americans, Native Americans, and Mexican Americans had contributed to the U.S. war effort through military service or work in the defense industry. Having served their country in a war often framed as being against two racist empires (Germany and Japan), they were determined to claim their rights as guaranteed by the Constitution. Minority groups began fighting against laws that prevented them from voting and kept their children from attending public schools. Some Native American veterans filed lawsuits challenging these practices. Furthermore, many minorities did not want to lose the economic foothold they had gained from their wartime jobs.

Individuals engaged in **grassroots activism** to bring about the equality they desired. Grassroots activism refers to political movements driven by people who individually do not have much power, but who, working together, can be very effective. Churches in the rural South and urban North played important roles in the grassroots diffusion of the civil rights movement. Church leaders stressed the value of equality and communal support, which inspired church members to make sacrifices for racial justice. Groups also used churches as meeting places. The NAACP, a grassroots group, began with 60 members in 1909. By 1946, it had 600,000 members and was working to persuade Congress to pass federal anti-lynching laws. NAACP leaders, including **Walter White**, **Thurgood Marshall**, and the writer James Weldon Johnson, organized lawsuits against people accused of civil rights violations and used those cases to command the public's attention.

A. Philip Randolph and **Bayard Rustin** were also notable civil rights leaders. As you've read, Randolph, a journalist and labor organizer, established the country's first African-American trade union, the Brotherhood of Sleeping Car

PRIMARY SOURCES

Today, the American people enjoy more freedom and opportunity than ever before. Never in our history has there been better reason to hope for the complete realization of the ideals of liberty and equality.

We shall not, however, finally achieve the ideals for which this Nation was founded so long as any American suffers discrimination as a result of his race, or religion, or color, or the land of origin of his forefathers.

—from "Special Message to the Congress on Civil Rights," by President Harry S. Truman, February 2, 1948

Mr. Speaker, not since the first gun was fired on Fort Sumter . . . has any message of any President of these glorious United States provoked so much controversy . . . as did President Truman's so-called civil-rights message. Not only did that message provoke serious racial controversies, but it raised anew the issue of the rights of the sovereign States as against a strong centralized government and drove a devastating wedge into the unity of the Democratic Party at a time when that party was riding high on a wave of popularity in the entire country.

—from Mississippi Representative William M. Colmer's response to President Truman's "Special Message to Congress on Civil Rights," April 8, 1948

11.10.1 Explain how demands of African Americans helped produce a stimulus for civil rights, including President Roosevelt's ban on racial discrimination in defense industries in 1941, and how African Americans' service in World War II produced a stimulus for President Truman's decision to end segregation in the armed forces in 1948; 11.10.4 Examine the roles of civil rights advocates (e.g., A. Philip Randolph, Martin Luther King, Jr., Malcolm X, Thurgood Marshall, James Farmer, Rosa Parks), including the significance of Martin Luther King, Jr.'s "Letter from Birmingham Jail" and "I Have a Dream" speech.

At a press conference in New York City in 1964 (from left) Norman Hill, Frederick D. Jones, and Bayard Rustin called for New York City to desegregate its public schools or face a series of coordinated boycotts. The three civil rights leaders were lifelong anti-violence activists who orchestrated demonstrations and boycotts and negotiated with government officials.

Porters. Rustin became a leader in movements for civil rights and nonviolence beginning in the 1940s and for gay rights in the 1950s. He would eventually become a close advisor to Dr. Martin Luther King, Jr. In 1941, Randolph and Rustin threatened to lead tens of thousands of people in a march on Washington, D.C., to protest employment discrimination in the federal government. President Franklin D. Roosevelt averted the march by issuing an executive order prohibiting discriminatory hiring in government jobs. The order also established the Fair Employment Practices Committee, whose mission was to investigate violations of the new policy.

In 1942, civil rights activist **James Farmer** helped to found the interracial **Congress of Racial Equality (CORE)**. The organization fought discrimination through nonviolent acts of protest. It would play a crucial role in future decades of the civil rights movement. Activist and NAACP member **Mary Church Terrell** led the antidiscrimination struggle in deeply segregated Washington, D.C. In 1950, she entered a restaurant and ordered lunch, knowing the owners would refuse to serve her. In a lawsuit, she cited laws from the 1870s that guaranteed equal rights to African Americans in all "places of public accommodation." Her case reached the Supreme Court, which ruled unanimously in her favor.

TRUMAN'S SUPPORT FOR CIVIL RIGHTS

After Franklin D. Roosevelt's death in 1945, his vice president Harry Truman became the 33rd president. Truman was the grandchild of slave owners and had grown up in a segregated town in Missouri. But Truman proved to be a strong supporter of civil rights. In 1946, he established the **President's Committee on Civil Rights (PCCR)**. Its mission was to protect all Americans' civil rights. The PCCR report, "To Secure These Rights," detailed widespread discrimination and recommended 34 immediate actions, including desegregating the U.S. military. Truman sent to Congress a plan for stronger civil rights statutes, better protection of the right to vote, and federal protection against lynching. But Republicans and conservative southern Democrats blocked the plan.

At the 1948 Democratic National Convention, Senate candidate Hubert Humphrey implored his fellow Democrats to strongly support the civil rights movement. Moderates, including aides to Truman, favored a weaker stance on civil rights, fearing the loss of votes in the South. In the end, Humphrey got his way. Shortly after the convention, Truman abolished segregation in the U.S. military and prohibited discriminatory hiring practices in the federal civil service. When Americans cast their ballots in 1948, Truman won re-election, thanks in part to the support of African-American voters.

HISTORICAL THINKING

1. **READING CHECK** How did World War II stimulate the civil rights movement?
2. **DRAW CONCLUSIONS** How can grassroots activism cause change? Use examples from the text.
3. **SYNTHESIZE** How does Truman's message to Congress and William Colmer's response reflect the idea that change is complicated?

11.10.5 Discuss the diffusion of the civil rights movement of African Americans from the churches of the rural South and the urban North, including the resistance to racial desegregation in Little Rock and Birmingham, and how the advances influenced the agendas, strategies, and effectiveness of the quests of American Indians, Asian Americans, and Hispanic Americans for civil rights and equal opportunities; CST 2 Students analyze how change happens at different rates at different times; understand that some aspects can change while others remain the same; and understand that change is complicated and affects not only technology and politics but also values and beliefs.

1.2 **MAIN IDEA** Artists of every medium created works to draw public awareness to the civil rights movement.

RESISTANCE THROUGH THE ARTS

Looking at a painting, listening to a song from another culture, and reading a book can help us understand how another person views the world. With that idea in mind, artists, musicians, and writers use their art to influence public opinion.

FREEDOM THROUGH ART AND SONG

The civil rights movement wasn't limited to nonviolent student and political organizations or the leadership of individual activists, such as Martin Luther King, Jr. Other forms of social advocacy sprang up around the country, notably in its art and music scenes. Activists took ideas from earlier artists and musicians and incorporated them into their own works as a way to express the connections between generations of African-American creativity.

The folk-inspired style of artist **William H. Johnson**, who painted from roughly 1920 to 1945, showed scenes of African-American soldiers and people doing everyday activities. His expressionistic subjects and use of bright colors are reflected in the paintings of **Jacob Lawrence** and **Charles Henry Alston**, artists working at the beginning of the civil rights movement.

Billie Holiday, shown here performing in New York City in 1947, is considered by many to be the best jazz vocalist of all time. She sought inspiration from such artists as Louis Armstrong and Bessie Smith, and flatly refused to be silent about racism, using music as a way to explore the issue.

Some artists working in the 1960s saw the civil unrest happening around them and found ways to incorporate their passion and solidarity with the protesters into their art. The subject matter of many African-American artists became more political. For example, artist **Norman Lewis** chose to use red, white, and blue in his work. Sculptor **Elizabeth Catlett** posed her figures in defiant positions, with crossed arms or a fist to the sky.

Musicians also built public awareness about civil rights. In 1939, jazz singer **Billie Holiday** recorded "Strange Fruit," a song about lynching in the South. It was the first time a popular African-American singer had spoken out against racism through music. She inspired other

11.8.8 Discuss forms of popular culture, with emphasis on their origins and geographic diffusion (e.g., jazz and other forms of popular music, professional sports, architectural and artistic styles).

PRIMARY SOURCE

Recipient of the 1953 National Book Award for fiction, Ralph Ellison wrote *Invisible Man* in an experimental style, hoping to portray a truth about the human condition, race, and identity.

I am an invisible man. No, I am not a spook like those who haunted Edgar Allan Poe; nor am I one of your Hollywood-movie ectoplasms [ghosts]. I am a man of substance, of flesh and bone, fiber and liquids—and I might even be said to possess a mind. I am invisible, understand, simply because people refuse to see me.

—from *Invisible Man* by Ralph Ellison, 1952

singers to do so as well. Throughout her career, jazz singer **Nina Simone** performed songs protesting lynching, segregation, and the Vietnam War. **Harry Belafonte**, a singer famous for a style of Caribbean music called calypso, was a social activist who donated time and money to civil rights efforts.

Many African-American musicians incorporated the spirituals and gospel songs that arose out of the slavery era to help fuel the civil rights movement. African-American folk singer **Odetta** taught her audiences the lyrics to spirituals as a way to unite the protesters. Odetta knew the old work songs, such as "We Shall Overcome" and "Go Tell It on the Mountain," from her childhood in Birmingham, Alabama. The spirituals inspired white folk singers, including Pete Seeger, **Bob Dylan**, and **Joan Baez**, to perform them at concerts and raise money and popular support for the civil rights cause.

Other activist musicians fought racism not with the words they sang but through the concert halls where they performed. In 1955, Marian Anderson became the first African-American opera singer to perform at New York's Metropolitan Opera. People flocked to hear the well-respected artist. "Men as well as women were dabbing at their eyes," reported the *New York Times*. Anderson's success at the Met was considered an important step toward racial equality because she proved African-American artists could draw large and diverse crowds.

THE POWER OF THE WRITTEN WORD

African-American authors bolstered the civil rights movement with words. In his 1940 novel *Native Son*, **Richard Wright** explored poverty and oppression in the lives of African Americans. Another novel, *Invisible Man* by **Ralph Ellison**, told of an unnamed African-American civil rights worker who moves from the South to New York City to escape segregation. The civil rights worker in the novel feels **dehumanized**, no longer regarded as a person, after he encounters racism in the city.

Playwright **Lorraine Hansberry** examined racial harassment as experienced by a working-class African-American family in the groundbreaking 1959 play *A Raisin in the Sun*. The character Beneatha decides to wear her hair in the natural style of people living in Africa, instead of in the straightened style of white women. Her decision symbolized a shift in African-American identity because Beneatha embraced her African heritage.

Civil-rights activist and influential African-American author **James Baldwin** released a book of two essays in 1963 called *The Fire Next Time*. In the book, he uses his personal experiences to explain what it was like to live in the United States as an African American. "[White people] have had to believe for many years, and for innumerable reasons, that black men are inferior to white men," he wrote. "Many of them, indeed, know better, but, as you will discover, people find it very difficult to act on what they know."

HISTORICAL THINKING

1. **READING CHECK** How did artists raise awareness of the civil rights movement among the public?
2. **ANALYZE LANGUAGE USE** What does Ralph Ellison mean when he writes, "I am an invisible man"?
3. **MAKE INFERENCES** How might spirituals and gospel songs from the slavery era help fuel the civil rights movement?

11.10.4 Examine the roles of civil rights advocates (e.g., A. Philip Randolph, Martin Luther King, Jr., Malcolm X, Thurgood Marshall, James Farmer, Rosa Parks), including the significance of Martin Luther King, Jr.'s "Letter from Birmingham Jail" and "I Have a Dream" speech.

1.3 **MAIN IDEA** In the 1950s, civil rights activists successfully challenged segregation and discrimination in public education.

CHALLENGING SCHOOL SEGREGATION

Third-grader Linda Brown lived just a short walk from an elementary school in Topeka, Kansas. But because she was an African American, she was forced to walk to a school farther from her home. This injustice became the focus of a landmark civil rights case.

CHALLENGING "SEPARATE BUT EQUAL"

In the 1940s, civil rights activists such as Thurgood Marshall and **William Hastie** began to mount legal attacks on *Plessy* v. *Ferguson*, the 1896 case that established the doctrine of "separate but equal." Marshall was chief of the NAACP's Legal Defense and Education Fund, a group of lawyers who pursued inequality and segregation lawsuits against educational institutions. In 1946, a federal lawsuit known as ***Mendez* v. *Westminster*** successfully challenged "separate but equal." Five Mexican American families sued their local school board in California for forcing their children to attend schools for Mexican students only. The court ruled in favor of the families, declaring that the segregation of Mexican American, Native American, and Asian American students was unconstitutional. This case provided a basis for further challenges.

On September 4, 1957, 15-year-old Elizabeth Eckford was followed by an angry mob as she tried to enter Central High School. Eckford was one of the Little Rock Nine, a group of African-American students who desegregated the school in Little Rock, Arkansas.

11.10 Students analyze the development of federal civil rights and voting rights; 11.10.2 Examine and analyze the key events, policies, and court cases in the evolution of civil rights, including *Dred Scott* v. *Sandford*, *Plessy* v. **Ferguson**, *Brown* v. *Board of Education*, *Regents of the University of California* v. *Bakke*, and California Proposition 209; 11.10.3 Describe the collaboration on legal strategy between African American and white civil rights lawyers to end racial segregation in higher education.

In 1946, Thurgood Marshall took the case of Heman Marion Sweatt, an African American seeking admission to the University of Texas School of Law. The university rejected Sweatt because of his race, but to comply with the "separate but equal" doctrine, it established a law school solely for African Americans. In 1950, the U.S. Supreme Court ruled in ***Sweatt* v. *Painter*** that the university must admit Sweatt to the original law school under the 14th Amendment. That same day, the Supreme Court ruled against segregation in ***McLaurin* v. *Oklahoma State Regents***. Because of these decisions, college classes throughout the nation were to be **integrated**, meaning they would have to allow the free association of people of all races and ethnicities.

By 1953, five civil rights lawsuits had reached the Supreme Court, including ***Brown* v. *Board of Education of Topeka***. That year, President Eisenhower had appointed **Earl Warren** as the court's Chief Justice, even though Warren's political views were more liberal than his own.

BROWN v. *BOARD OF EDUCATION*

Remember that *Brown* v. *Board of Education* centered on a Kansas law permitting cities to segregate their public schools. The case began when a team of six NAACP lawyers—five black, one white—represented the Reverend Oliver Brown in suing the Topeka school board. The lawyers argued that Brown's 8-year-old daughter should not have to attend a segregated school 21 blocks from her home when a white public school was much closer. One of the lawyers' strategies was to present social science studies showing that segregated schools had a negative effect on the self-esteem of African-American children, especially that of girls.

Eventually, the Supreme Court agreed to hear the case. The African-American and white lawyers collaborated on finding documented evidence of unequal education in several states. In a unanimous decision delivered on May 17, 1954, the Supreme Court ruled that the doctrine of "separate but equal" had no place in public education. Chief Justice Warren wrote, "Separate educational facilities are inherently [essentially] unequal." The court ordered the speedy integration of the nation's public schools. Because of the decision, the definition of *equal rights* included the equal opportunity for education and inspired a new generation of civil rights activists.

Many white southerners were outraged and reacted violently to **desegregation** efforts, or stopping the practice of separating groups of people in public spaces. To them, the ruling was an example of the federal government misusing its power. President Eisenhower was quiet about the issue. When asked directly about the *Brown* decision, he replied: "The Supreme Court has spoken . . . and I will obey."

In 1956, about 100 members of Congress from former Confederate states issued a document called "The Southern Manifesto on Integration." Vowing to use "all lawful means" to resist the *Brown* decision and court-ordered integration, they claimed *Brown* was a misinterpretation of the 14th Amendment and that the government was forcing states to carry out a law no one had voted for.

In 1957, this conflict over federal authority and states' rights erupted in Little Rock, Arkansas, when nine African-American students who tried to integrate a local high school were denied access to the school by the governor, the National Guard, and local citizens. President Eisenhower finally sent federal troops to escort the **Little Rock Nine** to their classes and to restore order. That month, he signed the **Civil Rights Act of 1957**, which protected the voting rights of African Americans. To remedy the act's shortcomings, he later signed the **Civil Rights Act of 1960**. Neither act proved to be effective.

PRIMARY SOURCE

Segregation of white and colored children in public schools has a detrimental effect upon the colored children. The impact is greater when it has the sanction of the law, for the policy of separating the races is usually interpreted as denoting the inferiority of the negro group. A sense of inferiority affects the motivation of a child to learn. Segregation with the sanction of law, therefore, has a tendency to [retard] the educational and mental development of negro children and to deprive them of some of the benefits they would receive in a racial[ly] integrated school system.

—from *Brown* v. *Board of Education of Topeka*, Supreme Court Decision, May 17, 1954

HISTORICAL THINKING

1. **READING CHECK** How did many white southerners, including those in Congress, react to desegregation?
2. **ANALYZE CAUSE AND EFFECT** How did the court decisions in *Mendez*, *Sweatt*, and *McLaurin* affect the Brown ruling?

11.10.4 Examine the roles of civil rights advocates (e.g., A. Philip Randolph, Martin Luther King, Jr., Malcolm X, Thurgood Marshall, James Farmer, Rosa Parks), including the significance of Martin Luther King, Jr.'s "Letter from Birmingham Jail" and "I Have a Dream" speech; 11.10.5 Discuss the diffusion of the civil rights movement of African Americans from the churches of the rural South and the urban North, including the resistance to racial desegregation in Little Rock and Birmingham, and how the advances influenced the agendas, strategies, and effectiveness of the quests of American Indians, Asian Americans, and Hispanic Americans for civil rights and equal opportunities.

THURGOOD MARSHALL 1908–1993

"To protest against injustice is the foundation of all our American democracy."—Thurgood Marshall

Fighting for justice and the rights of others became Thurgood Marshall's life's work. In his first case as a lawyer, he helped defend Donald Murray, a young African American who had been denied admission to the University of Maryland School of Law in 1935 because of his race. The case hit home. In 1930, Marshall himself had been refused entry to the school because he was black. He took on the Murray case to battle against the school's blatant discrimination and won. The young man became the first African American admitted to the law school.

In his early years as chief counsel of the NAACP, Marshall successfully challenged the practice in several southern states of holding "white primaries" and preventing African Americans from voting.

CIVIL RIGHTS LAWYER

Instead of Maryland's law school, Marshall attended the Howard University School of Law in Washington, D.C., the oldest historically black law school in the United States. There he found a mentor in Charles Hamilton Houston, the school's vice-dean from 1929 to 1935 and an early civil rights lawyer. After graduating in 1933 from Howard—*cum laude*, or "with distinction"—Marshall eventually followed Houston to New York City. In time, Marshall became the chief counsel of the NAACP Legal Defense and Education Fund, a position he held for 21 years.

During his career at the NAACP, Marshall took on cases involving segregation and discrimination and, as you know, helped to successfully overturn the entire legal basis of "separate but equal." Sometimes his work took him to the Deep South where he experienced firsthand the racism his clients suffered. After winning one case in Tennessee, Marshall was nearly lynched. Many of his cases went to the Supreme Court, including the one for which he is most famous, *Brown* v. *Board of Education*. Of the 32 cases he argued before the Court, Marshall won 29. In fact, over his career, he won more Supreme Court cases than any other lawyer in American history.

Those who witnessed him in action said that Marshall's oratorical style was not flowery and emotional. Rather, he spoke eloquently and with great dignity, often addressing the moral and social implications of a case. Most of all, he conveyed his deep respect for the law and the Constitution, which he had been forced to memorize as punishment for

11.10.2 Examine and analyze the key events, policies, and court cases in the evolution of civil rights, including *Dred Scott* v. *Sandford*, *Plessy* v. *Ferguson*, *Brown* v. *Board of Education*, *Regents of the University of California* v. *Bakke*, and California Proposition 209.

Marshall is sworn in as U.S. solicitor general while his family (front left) and Johnson (behind left) look on. The solicitor general is often called the 10th justice because he or she works closely with Supreme Court justices.

misbehaving when he was a high school student in Baltimore. When asked by a journalist why he had become a lawyer, Marshall (who had once wanted to be a dentist) replied that he didn't know. "The nearest I can get," he said, "is that my dad, my brother, and I had the most violent arguments you ever heard about anything. I guess we argued five out of seven nights at the dinner table."

JUDGE AND JUSTICE

In recognition of his brilliance, Marshall was appointed to high-level judicial positions during the 1960s. In 1961, President John Kennedy nominated him to the U.S. Court of Appeals. Four years later, President Lyndon Johnson made Marshall the first African-American U.S. solicitor general, the lawyer representing the federal government before the Supreme Court. Finally, in 1967, Johnson appointed Marshall as a justice on the Court, claiming that it was "the right thing to do, the right time to do it, the right man and the right place." And so the great-grandson of a slave became the first African American on the Supreme Court.

During Marshall's first years there, the Court, headed by Chief Justice Earl Warren, was decidedly liberal. Most of the justices agreed on such issues as racial discrimination and immigration. However, after Johnson, a Democrat, left the White House, Republican presidents picked the next eight justices. When President Richard Nixon made Warren Burger chief justice in 1969, the Court became more ideologically conservative, and Marshall grew more and more marginalized. As the Court's rulings chipped away at abortion rights, limited affirmative action laws, and reinstated the death penalty, Marshall voiced his disagreement with these decisions in forceful dissents.

Marshall retired from the Supreme Court in 1991 and was replaced by Clarence Thomas, a conservative African American. Though Marshall was less celebrated than Martin Luther King, Jr., and Malcolm X—an African-American civil rights activist in the 1960s—he arguably had the greatest impact on the civil rights movement of the three. As one obituary declared after Marshall died in 1993, "We make movies about Malcolm X, we get a holiday to honor Dr. Martin Luther King, but every day we live with the legacy of Justice Thurgood Marshall."

HISTORICAL THINKING

1. **READING CHECK** What was particularly meaningful about Marshall's first case?
2. **MAKE INFERENCES** Why do you think it was important to Marshall to express his disagreement with some of the Supreme Court decisions made under Warren Burger?
3. **DRAW CONCLUSIONS** What did the writer of the obituary mean by the statement: "every day we live with the legacy of Justice Thurgood Marshall"?

2.1 **MAIN IDEA** A yearlong bus boycott by African Americans in Montgomery, Alabama, led to a landmark Supreme Court decision against segregation on city buses.

WOMEN TAKE A STAND

Sometimes people have to break the rules to prove a point. A woman stepped onto a city bus in Montgomery, Alabama, one fateful evening in 1955 to do just that. Her action sparked a national debate over civil rights.

A BOYCOTT BEGINS

A year and a half after the Supreme Court's ruling in *Brown* v. *Board of Education*, its decision continued to rock the nation. Meanwhile, in Montgomery, Alabama, another major civil rights development was taking shape.

Segregation and discrimination were firmly established and strictly enforced in Montgomery, "the cradle of the Confederacy." African Americans were expected to tip their hats to whites, stand in the presence of whites unless told to sit, and address whites with titles of respect. City buses were segregated, and the first four rows of seats were reserved for whites, according to a Montgomery ordinance. African Americans had to pay their fares in the front, then get off the bus and enter the designated "colored section" through the rear door. They could also sit in the middle rows of the bus, but they had to relinquish their seat to white passengers when the front section filled up.

One regular bus rider was **Rosa Parks**, an African-American woman and longtime civil rights activist who worked as an assistant tailor at a downtown Montgomery department store. She also served as secretary for the Montgomery chapter of the NAACP, which she had joined in 1943. In the summer of 1955, the 42-year-old Parks traveled to the Highlander Folk School in Tennessee for a two-week interracial conference focused on leadership in the struggle against segregation. She later revealed that through this experience, she "gained strength to persevere in my work for freedom, not just for [African Americans] but for all oppressed people."

Rosa Parks holds up the identification number in her booking photo after being arrested during the Montgomery Bus Boycott in 1956.

PRIMARY SOURCE

Four months after refusing to give up her bus seat, Rosa Parks spoke to an interviewer about that fateful evening.

I felt that I was not being treated right, and that I had a right to retain the seat that I had taken as a passenger on the bus. The time had just come when I had been pushed as far as I could stand to be pushed, I suppose. They placed me under arrest. No, I wasn't frightened at all. I don't know why I wasn't, but I didn't feel afraid. I had decided that I would have to know once and for all what rights I had as a human being and a citizen, even in Montgomery, Alabama.

—from a transcript of a radio interview with Rosa Parks, April 1956

11.10.4 Examine the roles of civil rights advocates (e.g., A. Philip Randolph, Martin Luther King, Jr., Malcolm X, Thurgood Marshall, James Farmer, Rosa Parks), including the significance of Martin Luther King, Jr.'s "Letter from Birmingham Jai" and "I Have a Dream" speech.

During the Montgomery Bus Boycott, many people chose to carpool rather than take the bus, as shown in this 1956 photo. The empty bus in the background is a sign of the boycott's success.

Earlier in 1955, other African-American women had refused to give up their bus seats in Montgomery. In March, 15-year-old Claudette Colvin was arrested after refusing to give up her seat in the black section of the bus for a white woman. "It's my constitutional right to sit here as much as that lady. I paid my fare!" she yelled as the policemen dragged her off the bus. Rosa Parks was one of the volunteers who raised money for Colvin's court hearing, but in addition to segregation violations, police charged Colvin with assaulting the officers, so civil rights activists decided not to pursue her case. In October, police arrested 18-year-old Mary Louise Smith for violating the same segregation policies. Civil rights leaders deemed Smith an unsympathetic plaintiff because she was poor and young.

Knowing that the NAACP was looking for a lead plaintiff in a case to test Montgomery's segregated bus law, Parks boarded a bus on December 1, 1955. She took a seat in the middle section of the mostly empty bus, but after a few stops, the white section of the bus filled up. When more white passengers stepped aboard, the driver asked Parks and three other African-American passengers sitting in the same row to move to the back of the bus, where they would have had to stand. The others reluctantly complied, but Parks refused to give up her seat. The driver called the police, who arrested Parks for violating the ordinance.

Parks's **civil disobedience**, or act of purposely breaking a law in protest, and her arrest galvanized Montgomery's African-American community. **Jo Ann Robinson**, the president of a local political group called the Women's Political Council, organized volunteers who distributed 50,000 flyers declaring a one-day boycott of the city's buses. The initial **Montgomery Bus Boycott** was so successful that Robinson and other civil rights leaders decided to extend it to a long-term campaign. Activists, including Robinson's Women's Political Council and members of the NAACP, joined with a group of local ministers at the Holy Street Baptist Church to form the Montgomery Improvement Association (MIA). For its president, the MIA chose an eloquent, energetic young minister named **Martin Luther King, Jr.**, who had just arrived in Montgomery the previous year.

11.10.5 Discuss the diffusion of the civil rights movement of African Americans from the churches of the rural South and the urban North, including the resistance to racial desegregation in Little Rock and Birmingham, and how the advances influenced the agendas, strategies, and effectiveness of the quests of American Indians, Asian Americans, and Hispanic Americans for civil rights and equal opportunities.

THE MURDER OF EMMETT TILL

While some women fought for civil rights through activism, staging and engaging in boycotts and marches, others took very personal stands that led to national action. In August of 1955, Mamie Till-Mobley sent her 14-year-old son Emmett on a train to visit relatives in Mississippi. A few days after Emmett had left his home in Chicago, Mrs. Till-Mobley received a phone call. Two white men had killed her child. The men claimed Emmett had flirted with a white woman in a local grocery store. They beat Till, shot him, and hung a 75-pound metal fan around his neck to keep his body hidden at the bottom of the Tallahatchie River.

A jury quickly released the white men. It wasn't until 2008 that the woman who claimed Till had physically and verbally attacked her admitted that she had made up those accusations.

Mrs. Till-Mobley brought Emmett's body back home to Chicago. The condition of Emmett's maimed body would usually call for a closed casket, but Mrs. Till-Mobley insisted on keeping his casket open during the funeral. "Let the people see what I've seen," she said. *Jet* magazine published photos of Mrs. Till-Mobley mourning over her son's body and forced the American public to witness the glaring brutality of racism in their country. Till's casket is now at the Smithsonian National Museum of African American History and Culture in Washington, D.C.

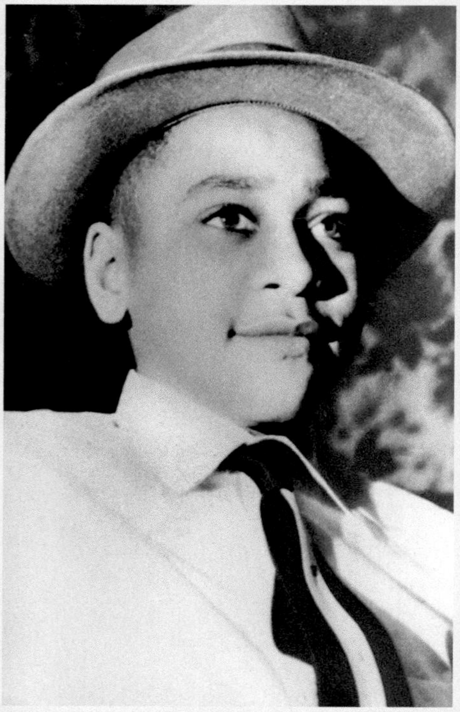

An undated photograph shows the young Emmett Till before his murder in 1955.

Mamie Till-Mobley mourns for her son as she leans against his glass-covered coffin. Following Emmett's funeral, she helped form a campaign for justice and civil rights.

THE BOYCOTT GAINS MOMENTUM

Boycott organizers knew their protest would be effective because African Americans accounted for roughly three-quarters of Montgomery's bus ridership. Losing most of these riders would have harsh economic consequences for the city's bus company. The organizers also knew that since few African Americans owned cars, the boycott would be difficult to sustain. However, the community was determined to keep the protest going. Friends, coworkers, and neighbors formed carpools to get people to their jobs and other destinations. Churches hosted boycott-related meetings and raised money for fuel, and African-American-owned garages did auto repair work free of charge. Many people rode bicycles or simply walked.

Days stretched into weeks, weeks into months, and still the boycott continued. It pushed the bus company to the brink of bankruptcy and dealt a severe financial blow to white-owned businesses in downtown Montgomery. Some whites retaliated by firing or threatening to fire African-American workers, and others threw bombs into churches and homes, including King's home.

On June 5, 1956, a federal district court, citing the *Brown* v. *Board of Education* decision as precedent, ruled that Alabama state statutes and Montgomery city ordinances requiring segregation on buses were unconstitutional. The Supreme Court affirmed this ruling on November 13 of that year, and on December 20, a U.S. marshal delivered a court order to Montgomery City Hall requiring the integration of the city's buses. King immediately called off the boycott and urged African Americans to begin riding the buses again the following day. The 381-day boycott had demonstrated both the power of collective action and the possibility of social change.

Coretta and Martin Luther King, Jr., leave the courthouse after his arrest for conspiring to boycott Montgomery city buses in 1956.

HISTORICAL THINKING

1. **READING CHECK** How did the African-American community work together to sustain the bus boycott?
2. **DESCRIBE** How might historical events have taken a different direction if Claudette Colvin, Mary Louise Smith, and Rosa Parks had not taken a stand?
3. **MAKE INFERENCES** What personal traits do you think Rosa Parks and other civil rights activists must have had in order to work for the freedom of all people?

HI 4 Students understand the meaning, implication, and impact of historical events and recognize that events could have taken other directions.

2.2 **MAIN IDEA** In the mid-1950s, the struggle for civil rights developed into a mass movement, and Martin Luther King, Jr., emerged as its leader.

MARTIN LUTHER KING, JR., AND A GROWING MOVEMENT

When he was 15 years old, Martin Luther King, Jr., left the segregated South for the first time and spent the summer in Connecticut. Seeing African Americans and whites eating in the same restaurants, shopping in the same stores, and worshiping in the same churches shaped his vision of what the United States could be: a multiracial, peaceful society.

THE EMERGENCE OF DR. KING

King was born on January 15, 1929, in Atlanta, Georgia. His parents were college educated, and the family lived in a middle-class neighborhood known for its thriving African-American businesses and churches. His father was a pastor at the highly regarded Ebenezer Baptist Church, a position his maternal grandfather had also held.

In 1944, King graduated from high school and entered Atlanta's Morehouse College. His studies there focused on medicine and law, but by the time of his graduation, he had decided to follow the example of his father and join the ministry. His spiritual and intellectual mentor, Morehouse president Benjamin Mays, also influenced his decision. Mays was not only an influential educator and minister, but also a strong voice for racial equality. King enrolled at the liberal-leaning Crozer Theological Seminary in Pennsylvania and graduated three years later with a bachelor's degree in divinity. He then earned a doctoral degree in theology from Boston University.

While completing his studies, King accepted a position in Montgomery, Alabama, as pastor at Dexter Avenue Baptist Church. The following year, in 1955, he led the Montgomery Bus Boycott, which helped bring an end to segregation on the city's buses. In the wake of that successful protest, King joined with other African-American ministers and civil rights activists to form the **Southern Christian Leadership Conference (SCLC)** in 1957. This organization, whose strength came from the leadership of African-American churches, promoted racial justice through peaceful means and provided assistance and guidance to local protest groups.

Official signs enforcing segregated seating were common, particularly across the South, during the first half of the 20th century.

King was convinced that nonviolent civil disobedience was the best way for African Americans to fight injustice and bring about social change. His philosophical and religious dedication to nonviolence took shape while he was in the seminary where his studies exposed him to the teachings of **Mohandas Gandhi**. A lawyer, politician, writer, and civil rights activist, Gandhi advocated peaceful protest and noncooperation in the struggle against colonial injustice in India. Through this approach, Gandhi had helped free his country from British imperial rule. King applied Gandhi's use of nonviolent methods throughout his career as a civil rights activist.

11.10.1 Explain how demands of African Americans helped produce a stimulus for civil rights, including President Roosevelt's ban on racial discrimination in defense industries in 1941, and how African Americans' service in World War II produced a stimulus for President Truman's decision to end segregation in the armed forces in 1948.

A MASS MOVEMENT FORMS

The Supreme Court's *Brown* v. *Board of Education* decision and the success of the Montgomery Bus Boycott profoundly altered race relations in the United States. Thanks to the extraordinary courage of ordinary African-American men, women, and children who joined the battle, the call for civil rights transformed into a mass movement that included Americans of all races.

Developments in North Carolina in 1960 ushered in a new phase in the movement. On February 1, four African-American college students entered a Woolworth's store and restaurant in Greensboro, took seats at the lunch counter marked "For Whites Only," and politely attempted to order lunch. The waitstaff refused to serve them and the manager asked them to leave, but they stayed until closing time. The next day, they returned with 25 fellow students. On the third day, the number of student protesters rose to 63, and by the fifth day it exceeded 300.

News outlets around the country reported the story, and soon more people in many other cities were staging **sit-ins**, coordinated protests in which people occupy seats or floor space in places that are the targets of protest. There also were other "ins." African-American churches organized kneel-ins at segregated churches and wade-ins at segregated pools. These protests were remarkably effective. In the following months, segregation began to yield to integration in cities across the South. On July 25, nearly six months after the first day of the Greensboro sit-in, the four original protesters were finally served at the Woolworth's lunch counter.

The success of the sit-ins and similar nonviolent protests inspired a group of African-American students to create their own political organization, the **Student Nonviolent Coordinating Committee (SNCC)**. A cofounder of SCLC, **Ella Baker**, had become frustrated with its cautious approach and hierarchical nature, so she left that organization to become an advisor to SNCC. Baker had also served as a national director for the NAACP and had co-founded an organization called In Friendship, which raised money to fight Jim Crow laws in the South. While serving at SCLC, Baker helped to organize a "prayer pilgrimage" to Washington, D.C., and an ambitious voter registration campaign called the Crusade for Citizenship.

North Carolina A&T College students (left to right) Ronald Martin, Robert Patterson, and Mark Martin joined the second day of the sit-in at the Greensboro lunch counter.

11.10.4 Examine the roles of civil rights advocates (e.g., A. Philip Randolph, Martin Luther King, Jr., Malcolm X, Thurgood Marshall, James Farmer, Rosa Parks), including the significance of Martin Luther King, Jr.'s "Letter from Birmingham Jail" and "I Have a Dream" speech.

Barely escaping alive from their burning bus, a group of Freedom Riders waits on the roadside outside Anniston, Alabama. The 13 men and women who set out on an interstate trip to test desegregation laws were assaulted by Ku Klux Klan members before they were rescued several hours later. News of this and other vicious attacks led hundreds of people to join the Freedom Riders throughout 1961.

Another prominent leader of SNCC was a woman named **Fannie Lou Hamer**. Hamer had been born into poverty and oppression in the Mississippi Delta, the 20th child of sharecropper parents, and her education had ended at the 6th-grade level. Her background made her later accomplishments all the more remarkable.

As a SNCC field secretary whose job was to assist in building membership, Hamer fought to end segregation and protect the rights of African Americans. Angered that Mississippi's conservative, white-dominated Democratic Party did not allow African Americans to participate in meetings, she helped to establish the **Mississippi Freedom Democratic Party**, a grassroots political group established as an alternative to the larger, more conservative state arm of the Democratic Party. The Mississippi Freedom Democratic Party was dedicated to encouraging African-American voter registration. Hamer earned the respect of many, and in 1964, she delivered a powerful speech at a Democratic National Convention about the intimidation and violence that African Americans in her state faced when they attempted to register to vote. Because of their strong leadership, Baker and Hamer joined Rosa Parks as influential women in the civil rights movement.

THE FREEDOM RIDERS

In November 1960, **John F. Kennedy** was elected president of the United States. (Read more about Kennedy's election and presidency in the next chapter.) Although he was more sympathetic to the civil rights cause than Eisenhower had been, Kennedy wanted change to come slowly, without the mass protests and violent incidents that had made headlines around the world. He worried, too, that White House support for immediate desegregation would cost him the goodwill of powerful southern Democrats in Congress.

In December 1960, the Supreme Court had ruled in a case called *Boynton* v. *Virginia*, finding that racial segregation was illegal in bus terminals, restrooms, and other facilities serving passengers traveling

11.10.2 Examine and analyze the key events, policies, and court cases in the evolution of civil rights, including *Dred Scott* v. *Sandford*, *Plessy* v. *Ferguson*, *Brown* v. *Board of Education*, *Regents of the University of California* v. *Bakke*, and California Proposition 209.

across state lines. Shortly thereafter, CORE, which you read about earlier in this chapter, announced plans to test that court decision to see if local police were upholding the law. CORE's stated objective was "to provoke the southern authorities into arresting us and thereby prod the Justice Department into enforcing the law of the land."

In May 1961, seven African-American and six white "**Freedom Riders**" left Washington, D.C., on two buses bound for New Orleans. At stops along the way, they ignored "white" and "colored" signs that hung by the restrooms, lunch counters, and waiting rooms in defiance of federal law. Trouble erupted in Anniston, Alabama, when white segregationists firebombed one of the buses. As the passengers escaped, a mob beat them with fists and clubs. Riders on the second bus suffered a similar attack in Birmingham. Local police in these and other cities made little effort to stop the attacks. The continuing violence finally compelled Attorney General **Robert F. Kennedy**, who was President Kennedy's younger brother and close aide, to send U.S. marshals to protect the riders. CORE, with assistance from SNCC, continued to organize freedom rides until September of that year, when the federal government banned interstate buses and trains from using any terminal that segregated people by race.

Meanwhile, another key development in the civil rights movement unfolded in Mississippi. After repeatedly being denied admission to the all-white University of Mississippi, an African-American student named James Meredith filed a discrimination lawsuit against the university. Supported by the NAACP, Meredith took his case all the way to the Supreme Court, which ruled in his favor. When he attempted to register at the university, however, state troopers, acting on the orders of Mississippi governor Ross Barnett, turned him away. U.S. marshals accompanied Meredith during several more attempts to register, but large numbers of protesters and state troopers blocked him. Riots broke out as the situation escalated. After the federal government sent hundreds of agents to the scene, Meredith was finally able to register and attend classes as the university's first African-American student.

This period in Mississippi's civil rights movement is memorably captured in *Coming of Age in Mississippi*, an autobiography by activist and writer Anne Moody. With bracing honesty, she tells of growing up desperately poor in rural southern Mississippi, of the brutal racism that she and her family faced, and of fighting for the rights of African Americans.

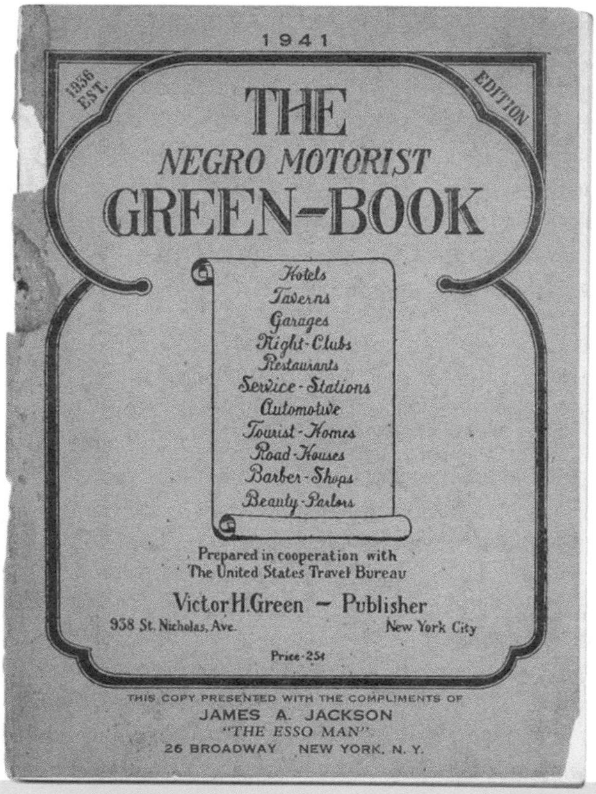

THE GREEN BOOK

In 1936, publisher Victor Green saw the need for a national guide for African-American travelers. Titled *The Negro Motorist Green Book*, the book listed restaurants, rooming houses, barbers, and tourist activities that welcomed African Americans in the time of segregation, particularly in areas with strict Jim Crow laws. Unlike most book publishers, Green looked forward to the time when his Green Book was not necessary. "That is when we as a race will have equal opportunities and privileges in the United States," he wrote in an introduction to his book.

HISTORICAL THINKING

1. **READING CHECK** What legal action did the federal government take in response to the Freedom Rides?
2. **FORM AND SUPPORT OPINIONS** Do you think nonviolent civil disobedience proved to be a good strategy for bringing about social change? Support your opinion with evidence from the text.
3. **MAKE INFERENCES** Why do you think Fannie Lou Hamer focused her efforts on African-American voter registration?
4. **ANALYZE CAUSE AND EFFECT** What caused the sit-in protest in Greensboro, and what effect did the protest have on the larger civil rights movement?

11.10.5 Discuss the diffusion of the civil rights movement of African Americans from the churches of the rural South and the urban North, including the resistance to racial desegregation in Little Rock and Birmingham, and how the advances influenced the agendas, strategies, and effectiveness of the quests of American Indians, Asian Americans, and Hispanic Americans for civil rights and equal opportunities; HI 1 Students show the connections, causal and otherwise, between particular historical events and larger social, economic, and political trends and developments.

2.3 **MAIN IDEA** In 1963, a brutal police response to peaceful protests in Birmingham, Alabama, prompted President John F. Kennedy to propose strong new civil rights legislation.

PROTESTS IN BIRMINGHAM

In Kelly Ingram Park in Birmingham, Alabama, vicious police dogs lunge at peaceful protesters. Children cower before a powerful water cannon. Church ministers kneel in prayer. These scenes, depicted in sculptures, tell of a dark time in the city's history.

CONFRONTATION IN BIRMINGHAM

In December 1962, three months after James Meredith's lawsuit to be admitted into the University of Mississippi was successful, President Kennedy received a telegraph from Dr. Martin Luther King, Jr., with this message: "A virtual reign of terror is still alive in Birmingham, Alabama. It is by far the worst big city in race relations in the United States."

The previous day, Birmingham's Bethel Baptist Church had been bombed for the third time in 6 years. For 15 years, white segregationists had committed numerous other acts of intimidation and violence against African Americans, including the 1961 attack on the Freedom Riders. The police, under the command of **Eugene T. "Bull" Connor**, the Commissioner of Public Safety, strictly enforced segregation ordinances. Connor was an active white segregationist with close ties to the Ku Klux Klan.

The following spring, King and other leaders of SCLC developed plans for an all-out campaign to confront segregation in Birmingham. They scheduled the campaign to coincide with the busy Easter shopping season. The organizers kicked off the campaign in early April 1963 with mass meetings, lunch-counter sit-ins, a boycott of downtown merchants, and marches, each intended to provoke confrontation and sympathy for the civil rights cause. As days passed, more people joined in the protests, and the police made more arrests.

"LETTER FROM BIRMINGHAM CITY JAIL"

On April 12, 1963, King himself was arrested. That same day, the *Birmingham News* published a letter from eight white ministers titled "A Call for Unity." The ministers appealed to African Americans to withdraw their support for the demonstrations, and they denounced King and others for inciting hatred and violence. From his jail cell, King responded with what would become known as his "Letter from Birmingham City Jail." The letter eloquently rebutted the ministers' arguments and defended the morality of nonviolent civil disobedience. King was released from jail after eight days of **solitary confinement**, being locked in an enclosed cell alone.

As support for the protests began to fade, King and the other organizers seized upon the idea of bringing local students into the campaign in order to re-energize it. On May 2, more than 1,000 students, some as young as 6, marched from the 16th Street Baptist Church to City Hall. Police arrested and held 969 students, among others, packing the city's jails.

Abandoning restraint, Bull Connor ordered the police and fire departments to use police dogs and high-pressure fire hoses to break up the protest. News outlets across the United States and around the world carried shocking images of Birmingham police officers striking peaceful protestors with batons, vicious dogs attacking children and adults alike, and officials blasting people with powerful fire hoses.

On May 10, the campaign's organizers announced that they had worked out an agreement with Birmingham city leaders to end the public demonstrations. The agreement established specific steps and a timetable for ending segregation in Birmingham's public facilities and for creating an employment program for African Americans.

Once again Alabama was headlined in national newspapers when, on June 11, 1963, its segregationist governor **George Wallace**, flanked

11.10.1 Explain how demands of African Americans helped produce a stimulus for civil rights, including President Roosevelt's ban on racial discrimination in defense industries in 1941, and how African Americans' service in World War II produced a stimulus for President Truman's decision to end segregation in the armed forces in 1948; 11.10.4 Examine the roles of civil rights advocates (e.g., A. Philip Randolph, Martin Luther King, Jr., Malcolm X, Thurgood Marshall, James Farmer, Rosa Parks), including the significance of Martin Luther King, Jr.'s "Letter from Birmingham Jail" and "I Have a Dream" speech.

By 1963, major news media sent reporters and photographers to cover the unfolding civil rights demonstrations that targeted the segregated city of Birmingham, Alabama. As the Birmingham fire department turned high velocity water hoses on peaceful demonstrators, a photographer recorded one of the assaults that shocked Americans.

by state troopers, physically blocked two African-American students from registering at the University of Alabama in Tuscaloosa. President Kennedy and Attorney General Robert Kennedy responded to Wallace's symbolic action by authorizing the Alabama National Guard to physically remove the governor and by allowing the students to register.

On national television that evening, President Kennedy delivered an impassioned speech on civil rights. He spoke of the "moral crisis" facing the country and declared that "The events in Birmingham . . . have so increased the cries for equality that no city or state or legislative body can prudently choose to ignore them." Just hours after the broadcast, a white segregationist in Mississippi shot and killed civil rights activist **Medgar Evers** in front of his home.

The following week, Kennedy expanded the role of the federal government as a guarantor of civil rights by sending Congress a proposal for a civil rights bill that was far stronger than the civil rights bills that had passed in 1957 and 1960. In fact, it was the most sweeping civil rights bill since Reconstruction.

The turmoil in Alabama had a powerful impact on race relations in the United States, as well as on the perception of how protesters were being treated. Many white Americans had been indifferent to the plight of African Americans. But because the violence and brutality in Birmingham was widely televised, most Americans, no matter what their backgrounds, were horrified by the violence. They began to pay attention to and support the civil rights movement.

HISTORICAL THINKING

1. **READING CHECK** What was the goal of the Birmingham campaign, and what caused the organizers to end the campaign?
2. **EXPLAIN** How did the television footage of police officers attacking protesters contribute to the diffusion of the civil rights movement?
3. **FORM AND SUPPORT OPINIONS** What effect do you think President Kennedy's address about the events in Birmingham had on the nation?
4. **IDENTIFY** What was the role of Martin Luther King, Jr., in the Birmingham protests?

11.10.5 Discuss the diffusion of the civil rights movement of African Americans from the churches of the rural South and the urban North, including the resistance to racial desegregation in Little Rock and Birmingham, and how the advances influenced the agendas, strategies, and effectiveness of the quests of American Indians, Asian Americans, and Hispanic Americans for civil rights and equal opportunities; 11.11.2 Discuss the significant domestic policy speeches of Truman, Eisenhower, Kennedy, Johnson, Nixon, Carter, Reagan, Bush, and Clinton (e.g., with regard to education, civil rights, economic policy, environmental policy).

Demanding Reform

African-American civil rights activists worked through the nation's judicial and legislative systems to win the rights of full citizenship, but they also turned to nonviolent protest to raise awareness of their cause and win support for their movement. Sometimes that meant paying a legal cost.

CRITICAL VIEWING In 1967, four years after he wrote "Letter from Birmingham City Jail," Martin Luther King, Jr., returned to the Alabama jail to complete serving his sentence for participating in the 1963 civil rights demonstration. In 10 years, King was arrested more than 10 times for conducting peaceful protests. Why do you think this photo of King in an Alabama jail cell has become a symbol of the civil rights movement?

11.10.2 Examine and analyze the key events, policies, and court cases in the evolution of civil rights, including *Dred Scott* v. *Sandford*, *Plessy* v. *Ferguson*, *Brown* v. *Board of Education*, *Regents of the University of California* v. *Bakke*, and California Proposition 209.

DOCUMENT ONE

Primary Source: Speech
from *Speech at the March on Washington*, by John Lewis, August 28, 1963

John Lewis, the son of Alabama sharecroppers, helped organize the March on Washington for Jobs and Freedom and was its youngest speaker. His speech focused on the need for civil rights legislation that would address how the economy affected African Americans and the nation's poor and homeless.

CONSTRUCTED RESPONSE What does Lewis mean when he says "we will not and cannot be patient"?

We march today for jobs and freedom, but we have nothing to be proud of. While we stand here, there are sharecroppers in the Delta of Mississippi who are out in the fields working for less than three dollars a day, twelve hours a day.

We must have legislation that will protect the Mississippi sharecropper who is put off of his farm because he dares to register to vote. We need a bill that will ensure the equality of a maid who earns five dollars a week in a home of a family whose total income is $100,000 a year. . . . For we cannot stop, and we will not and cannot be patient.

DOCUMENT TWO

Primary Source: Newspaper Article
from "A Call for Unity," by eight Alabama clergymen, April 12, 1963

During the campaign in Birmingham, as you have learned, local newspapers printed a letter titled "A Call for Unity," which was signed by eight white religious leaders. The men agreed that segregation was wrong, but believed King's tactics were "unwise and untimely."

CONSTRUCTED RESPONSE What evidence in the text suggests the clergymen are sympathetic to the protesters?

We are now confronted by a series of demonstrations by some of our Negro citizens, directed and led in part by outsiders. We recognize the natural impatience of people who feel that their hopes are slow in being realized. But we are convinced that these demonstrations are unwise and untimely.

DOCUMENT THREE

Primary Source: Letter
from "Letter from Birmingham City Jail," by Martin Luther King, Jr., April 16, 1963

In this excerpt from the letter he wrote in response to "A Call for Unity," King addresses the ministers' assertion that the demonstrations were "directed and led in part by outsiders."

CONSTRUCTED RESPONSE What is King's response to the label of "outsider"?

I cannot sit idly by in Atlanta and not be concerned about what happens in Birmingham. Injustice anywhere is a threat to justice everywhere. We are caught in an inescapable network of mutuality, tied in a single garment of destiny. Whatever affects one directly affects all indirectly. Never again can we afford to live with the narrow, provincial "outside agitator" idea. Anyone who lives inside the United States can never be considered an outsider anywhere in this country.

SYNTHESIZE & WRITE

1. **REVIEW** Review what you have learned about the civil rights movement from the *Speech at the March on Washington*, the Birmingham campaign, and other strategies.
2. **RECALL** On your own paper, write the main idea expressed in each of these documents: John Lewis's speech, the "A Call for Unity" letter, and the "Letter from Birmingham City Jail."
3. **CONSTRUCT** Construct a topic sentence that supports this question: In what ways did the different forms of protest work together to bring about change?
4. **WRITE** Using evidence from this chapter and the documents, write an informative paragraph that supports your topic sentence in Step 3.

11.10.4 Examine the roles of civil rights advocates (e.g., A. Philip Randolph, Martin Luther King, Jr., Malcom X, Thurgood Marshall, James Farmer, Rosa Parks), including the significance of Martin Luther King, Jr.'s "Letter from Birmingham Jail" and "I Have a Dream" speech; HREP 4 Students construct and test hypotheses; collect, evaluate, and employ information from multiple primary and secondary sources; and apply it in oral and written presentations.

2.5 **MAIN IDEA** The 1963 March on Washington demonstrated the unity of the civil rights movement and featured one of the most famous speeches in American history.

THE MARCH ON WASHINGTON

Important speeches tend to include memorable and often-quoted words. Take, for example, Patrick Henry's "Give me liberty or give me death!" Without question, the most famous speech of Martin Luther King, Jr., became a rallying point for justice, freedom, and a better world.

JOBS AND FREEDOM

As you have read, in July 1963 President Kennedy sent Congress a proposal for a sweeping civil rights bill. Recent events in Birmingham and Tuscaloosa, Alabama, had convinced him of the urgent need for strong legislation protecting the rights of African Americans. The legislation faced stiff opposition in Congress, and the bill stalled there.

Meanwhile, plans were underway for a major rally in the nation's capital in support of civil rights and the civil rights bill. The demonstration took place on August 28, 1963, and was called the **March on Washington for Jobs and Freedom**. Its chief organizer was Bayard Rustin. Starting in 1941, Rustin and A. Philip Randolph had built an alliance of civil rights, labor, and religious organizations, bringing unity to the movement.

Rustin expected 100,000 people to take part in the 1963 March on Washington, but more than twice that number arrived. They came from every region of the country and every walk of life. Most were African American, but roughly one-fourth were white. After assembling on the grounds of the Washington Monument, the participants sang "We Shall Overcome" and marched down Constitution and Independence avenues. They ended at the Lincoln Memorial for the day's main program. It featured prayers, a performance by gospel singer **Mahalia Jackson**, and speeches by civil rights leaders.

DR. KING'S DREAM

The last and most highly anticipated speaker at the March on Washington was King. The eloquent and uplifting speech he delivered that afternoon is considered one of the greatest orations in American history. King began by reminding his listeners that although almost 100 years had passed since President Lincoln emancipated enslaved people, "the Negro is still sadly crippled by the manacles of segregation and the chains of discrimination. Now is the time," he proclaimed, "to rise from the dark and desolate valley of segregation to the sunlit path of racial justice." Putting aside his prepared notes, King spoke of his dream for a brighter future:

> *I have a dream that one day this nation will rise up and live out the true meaning of its creed: "We hold these truths to be self-evident, that all men are created equal."*
>
> *I have a dream that my four little children will one day live in a nation where they will not be judged by the color of their skin but by the content of their character.*

The March on Washington demonstrated the growing power and unity of the civil rights movement. Just weeks later, however, a horrific event in Alabama was a reminder of the gulf between King's dream and the harsh reality that African Americans still faced. On Sunday morning, September 15, a bomb planted by the Ku Klux Klan killed four young African-American girls at Birmingham's 16th Street Baptist Church.

In the fall of 1963, SNCC and CORE launched a **voter registration drive** in Mississippi to sign up as many eligible African-American voters as possible. Expanded in 1964, the program was called the Mississippi Summer Project, or **Freedom Summer**. More than 700 student volunteers, most of whom were white, came from colleges in the North

CRITICAL VIEWING Martin Luther King, Jr., waves to the diverse crowd following the March on Washington for Jobs and Freedom. From the Lincoln Memorial, King began what became known as his "I Have a Dream" speech. As he spoke, his friend, gospel singer Mahalia Jackson, eagerly called out to him "Tell them about the dream." From your view of King and the crowd in the photograph, what do you think was the effect of King's message about his dream?

to work with local civil rights organizations in Mississippi. On June 21, 1964, two white workers, Andrew Goodman and Michael Schwerner from New York, and one local African-American worker, James Chaney, disappeared after investigating the burning of an African-American church. Six weeks later, acting on a tip, authorities uncovered the bodies of the workers. All three had been shot at close range. It was clear that the nonviolent civil rights movement still faced dangerous opposition.

HISTORICAL THINKING

1. **READING CHECK** In what ways did the March on Washington demonstrate the power and unity of the civil rights movement?
2. **MAKE GENERALIZATIONS** How does the fact that students volunteered to travel to Mississippi after the violence of the Birmingham campaign speak to larger developments in the civil rights movement?
3. **ANALYZE LANGUAGE USE** What was the impact of King's deliberate repetition of the phrase "I have a dream" in his speech?

11.10.2 Examine and analyze the key events, policies, and court cases in the evolution of civil rights, including *Dred Scott* v. *Sandford, Plessy* v. *Ferguson, Brown* v. *Board of Education, Regents of the University of California* v. *Bakke*, and California Proposition 209; 11.10.4 Examine the roles of civil rights advocates (e.g., A. Philip Randolph, Martin Luther King, Jr., Malcolm X, Thurgood Marshall, James Farmer, Rosa Parks), including the significance of Martin Luther King, Jr.'s "Letter from Birmingham Jail" and "I Have a Dream" speech; HI 1 Students show the connections, causal and otherwise, between particular historical events and larger social, economic, and political trends and developments.

CHAPTER 16 THE CIVIL RIGHTS MOVEMENT

REVIEW

VOCABULARY

Use each of the following vocabulary terms in a sentence that shows an understanding of the term's meaning.

1. desegregation HSS 11.10.2
   The Supreme Court ruled against "separate but equal" education, which led to the desegregation of public schools.
2. Freedom Riders HSS 11.10.5
3. integrate HSS 11.10.2
4. civil disobedience HSS 11.10.2
5. sit-in HSS 11.10.4
6. grassroots activism HSS 11.10.5
7. dehumanized HSS 11.5.2
8. solitary confinement HSS 11.10.2

READING STRATEGY

MAKE INFERENCES

Use a chart like the one below to make inferences about ways Americans reacted to key events in the civil rights movement. Then answer the question.

The Civil Rights Movement

Key Events	American Reactions	Inferences

9. How did the civil rights movement redefine American identity? HSS 11.10.2

MAIN IDEAS

Answer the following questions. Support your answers with evidence from the chapter.

10. How did the issue of civil rights divide Democrats at their 1948 convention? **LESSON 1.1** HSS 11.10
11. By writing about his own experience of living in the United States as an African-American man, what did James Baldwin hope to accomplish? **LESSON 1.2** HSS 11.10.4
12. How did the definition of equal rights change after the Supreme Court issued the *Brown* decision? **LESSON 1.3** HSS 11.10
13. How did the Montgomery African-American community react to the arrest of Rosa Parks, and what was the arrest's effect? **LESSON 2.1** HSS 11.10.4
14. In what ways do the teachings of Gandhi still affect the civil rights movement today? **LESSON 2.2** HSS CST 1
15. What impact did the Greensboro sit-in have across the South? **LESSON 2.2** HSS 11.10.5
16. How did Dr. King respond to the letter titled "A Call for Unity" written by white ministers in Birmingham? **LESSON 2.3** HSS 11.10.4
17. How was the March on Washington a key event in the evolution of the civil rights movement? **LESSON 2.5** HSS 11.10.2

HISTORICAL THINKING

Answer the following questions. Support your answers with evidence from the chapter.

18. **IDENTIFY PROBLEMS AND SOLUTIONS** What was the role of various civil rights organizations in influencing public opinion and achieving civil rights legislation? HSS 11.10
19. **DESCRIBE** Who were some of the leaders of the civil rights movement, and what were their contributions? HSS 11.10.4

20. **SYNTHESIZE** Why was the civil rights movement able to gain momentum during the 1950s and into the 1960s? HSS 11.10.5

21. **EVALUATE** What were the goals and strategies of the civil rights movement, and how did change affect those goals? HSS CST 2

22. **DRAW CONCLUSIONS** Describe the strategy civil rights lawyers used to end segregation in education. HSS 11.10.3

INTERPRET VISUALS

Pulitzer Prize-winning cartoonist Bill Mauldin drew this cartoon in 1960, six years after the Supreme Court's *Brown* v. *Board of Education* decision and five years after the court ordered that desegregation of public schools should proceed "with all deliberate speed."

INCH BY INCH

23. What point is the cartoonist making about segregation in schools? HSS 11.10.2

24. What details from the cartoon support this point of view? HSS 11.10.2

ANALYZE SOURCES

In his January 1963 inaugural speech, Alabama governor George Wallace defied the civil rights movement and federal efforts to end discrimination and segregation in his state.

> Today I have stood, where once Jefferson Davis stood, and took an oath to my people. It is very appropriate then that from this Cradle of the Confederacy, this very Heart of the Great Anglo-Saxon Southland, that today we sound the drum for freedom as have our generations of forebears before us done, time and time again down through history. Let us rise to the call of freedom-loving blood that is in us and send our answer to the tyranny that clanks its chains upon the South. In the name of the greatest people that have ever trod this earth, I draw the line in the dust and toss the gauntlet before the feet of tyranny and I say: segregation today, segregation tomorrow, segregation forever.

25. What is Wallace referring to when he says "the tyranny that clanks its chains upon the South," and does this statement show bias? HSS HREP 2

CONNECT TO YOUR LIFE

26. **EXPOSITORY** The civil rights protesters you've read about risked their safety to achieve equal rights. Write a short paragraph describing a cause you would march for, and explain why the cause is important. HSS HREP 4
    - List causes that are important to you, and if necessary, research them online.
    - Decide which cause you listed is most important by evaluating how society would be affected if the cause were not supported.
    - State your main idea clearly at the beginning of the paragraph.
    - Provide a concluding sentence that summarizes the importance of the cause.

CHAPTER 17

REFORM IN THE 1960S

1960–1968

HISTORICAL THINKING What challenges did Americans face during the 1960s?

In October 1960, three weeks before being elected the 35th president of the United States, Senator John F. Kennedy campaigned in a parade in New York City. Kennedy and his wife, Jacqueline, charmed voters with their friendliness and energy. The couple were known as Jack and Jackie.

"Ask not what your country can do for you—
ask what you can do for your country."

—President John F. Kennedy

1.1 **MAIN IDEA** John F. Kennedy won the race for president in 1960 and quickly turned his attention to foreign policy and confronting the spread of communism.

KENNEDY'S EARLY CHALLENGES

When you commit to something, you know how important it is to follow through. In 1960, both presidential candidates promised to fight communism aggressively. John Kennedy won the election and had to act quickly on his commitment.

THE 1960 ELECTION

In the previous chapter, you read about John F. Kennedy's fight for the civil rights movement. Before that battle, he had fought hard to become president. In the 1960 election, both presidential candidates were tough, hard-driving campaigners. The Republicans ran Eisenhower's vice president Richard M. Nixon against then-Senator John Kennedy, the Democratic candidate. The men were the first two presidential candidates born in the 20th century, and both had entered Congress in 1946 after serving as junior naval officers during World War II.

But that was where the similarities ended. Nixon, 47, had grown up in modest circumstances. His Quaker parents ran a grocery store in Whittier, California, near Los Angeles, where Nixon worked as a boy. After his service in the Navy, Nixon's political rise was swift, helped by his strong stance against communism. Nixon then went on to win a U.S. Senate seat in 1950 after accusing his Democratic opponent, Helen Gahagan Douglas, of being "soft on communism." From 1953 to 1960, Nixon served as vice president, where he emerged as a vocal leader of the Republican Party.

John Kennedy, on the other hand, grew up in Boston, a child of wealth and privilege. A Catholic, Kennedy attended the finest private schools and graduated from Harvard University. Though he was elected to Congress in 1946 and to the Senate in 1952, Kennedy did not really stand out as a legislator. Nonetheless,

CRITICAL VIEWING On September 26, 1960, Kennedy and Nixon met in the first-ever televised presidential debate. What details in the photos convey how the two men might have come across to voters watching on television?

11.9.3 Trace the origins and geopolitical consequences (foreign and domestic) of the Cold War and containment policy, including the following: • The era of McCarthyism, instances of domestic Communism (e.g., Alger Hiss) and blacklisting • The Truman Doctrine • The Berlin Blockade • The Korean War • The Bay of Pigs Invasion and the Cuban Missile Crisis • Atomic testing in the American West, the "mutual assured destruction" doctrine, and disarmament policies • The Vietnam War • Latin American policy.

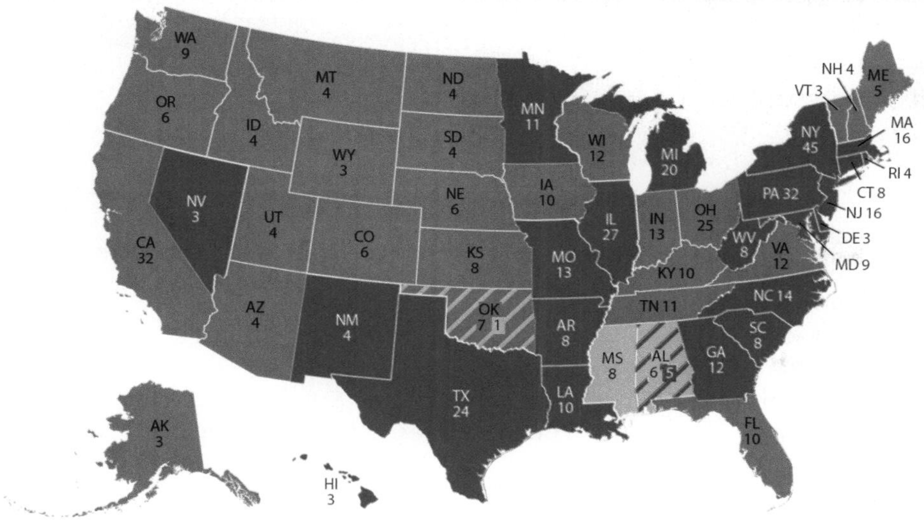

The 1960 Election

John F. Kennedy, Democrat

Electoral Vote: 303 votes, 56.5%

Popular Vote: 34,227,096, 49.7%

Richard M. Nixon, Republican

Electoral Vote: 219 votes, 40.75%

Popular Vote: 34,107,646, 49.6%

Harry Byrd, Democrat*

Electoral Vote: 15 votes, 2.75%

Popular Vote: 0, 0%

*Although he was not formally a candidate, electors in three states cast votes for Democratic Senator Harry Byrd.

he showed a desire to run for higher office. In 1956, he was nearly chosen to be the Democratic vice presidential candidate. Over the next four years, Kennedy traveled the country with his wife, Jacqueline, to build support for a 1960 presidential run. The couple drew crowds wherever they went.

For his running mate, Nixon chose Henry Cabot Lodge, Jr., a respected politician who served in the Senate and as U.S. ambassador to the United Nations. Like Kennedy, Lodge was from Massachusetts, and Nixon hoped his roots in the Northeast would help make the Republican ticket competitive in Kennedy's home region. Meanwhile, Kennedy surprised almost everyone by selecting Senator Lyndon Johnson, a longtime rival, as his running mate. Johnson was a Texan who held liberal political views. Kennedy felt Johnson, as a Texan, could help win votes in the conservative South without losing votes in the more liberal North.

Nixon campaigned largely on Eisenhower's record, reminding Americans that the United States was prosperous and at peace. Kennedy attacked that record without criticizing the popular Eisenhower directly. He portrayed the United States as reacting too slowly to a changing world and promised new leadership "to get the country moving once again." Kennedy had two main obstacles to overcome: a prejudice against Catholics that ran through U.S. history, and his inexperience—he was 43 years old. Kennedy addressed the religion issue in a powerful speech in the fall of 1960 in which he vowed to uphold the constitutional separation of church and state. He dispelled much doubt about his inexperience during a series of debates with Nixon.

For the first time in a presidential election, the debates were televised, which benefited Kennedy. The first debate had the greatest impact, as more than 80 million Americans watched on television or listened by radio. Though both candidates spoke well, the handsome, well-groomed Kennedy radiated confidence and charm on the TV screen, while Nixon appeared awkward and ill at ease.

Kennedy won the election, but the popular vote was the closest since the presidential election of 1888. A difference of several thousand votes in Texas and Illinois, where there were charges of **voter fraud**, or illegal manipulation of ballots, would have given the election to Nixon.

TROUBLE IN CUBA

President Kennedy charged into office in 1961 with ambitious plans both at home and abroad, and with increased powers in response to the Cold War. He immediately had to focus on a growing foreign policy crisis. The threat of communism had emerged on the small island nation of Cuba, just 90 miles south of Florida. In 1959, a year before Kennedy's election, communist revolutionaries led by **Fidel Castro** had overthrown Fulgencio Batista, the dictator of Cuba. Castro seized control of most of the country's industries and drove out foreign investors. Those investors, many of whom were Americans, lost millions of dollars. Thousands of Cubans who had supported Batista fled to the United States, mostly to Florida. They settled largely around Miami, where they would help shape the culture and politics of the region for years to come.

Castro quickly joined the Soviet bloc, establishing economic and military ties with the Soviet Union. Americans responded with alarm, as they now faced an ally of the Soviet Union located just off their shores. Soviet leader **Nikita Khrushchev** (nih-KEE-tuh KROOsh-chehf) warned the United

11.8.5 Describe the increased powers of the presidency in response to the Great Depression, World War II, and the Cold War.

States not to interfere with Cuba, promising to defend his new ally with nuclear weapons, if necessary. In response, the United States issued a trade embargo against Cuba.

THE BAY OF PIGS

As tensions grew between the United States and Cuba, Kennedy put into action a plan developed by the Eisenhower administration to overthrow Castro's government. The covert, or secret, plan called for anti-Castro exiles, trained and equipped by the CIA, to invade Cuba and trigger an anticommunist revolution. On April 17, 1961, 1,500 exiles waded ashore at the **Bay of Pigs**, on Cuba's southern coast. The attack fell apart almost immediately. The landing site contained sharp coral reefs and swampy terrain, making it hard to unload supplies and move out from the beaches. In addition, Cuban intelligence already knew of the plan from gossip among Cuban exiles in Miami. Cuban forces fired on the invaders as they came ashore. More than 100 of the anti-Castro exiles were killed, and most of the rest were captured.

The invasion was a humiliating defeat for the United States. American aggression in the region angered Cubans and other Latin Americans and drove Castro even closer to the Soviet Union. After reviewing the events with his advisors, Kennedy took a walk on the White House lawn. It was "the first time in my life," a friend recalled, "that I ever saw tears come to his eyes." Nonetheless, the president continued trying to overthrow Castro. During his administration, he approved a top-secret program, code-named Operation Mongoose, intended to topple the Cuban government and assassinate its leaders. U.S. officials also devised plans to destroy Cuba's vital sugar crop and even send a box of exploding cigars to Castro. The plans never materialized. In hindsight, one Kennedy aide called the overall effort against Cuba "an expensive and embarrassing failure."

THE BERLIN WALL

Shortly after the Bay of Pigs, Kennedy faced another communist challenge, this time in Europe. As you have read, following World War II, Germany was divided into democratic West Germany and communist East Germany. Berlin, the capital of Germany and its largest city, was located entirely within East Germany and itself was divided into three Western-occupied zones that made up West Berlin, and East Berlin, a Soviet-occupied zone. By the early 1960s, the division of Berlin was proving an embarrassment to Khrushchev. West Berlin thrived as a model of democracy and capitalism, while East Berlin was communist. Each day, more than 1,000 refugees from East Berlin poured into West Berlin seeking a better life. As a result, East Germany was losing many skilled workers to the West.

In August 1961, East German officials constructed a wall of concrete that encircled West Berlin. Intended to stop the migration from East Berlin and from surrounding East Germany to West Berlin, the **Berlin Wall** stretched 27 miles and divided the city in two. It stopped the flow of refugees across the border and for decades would stand as a symbol of the division between the **Western bloc** and the **Soviet bloc** nations of Europe. The presence of the wall heightened the anxiety of the Cold War.

Kennedy chose not to challenge the building of the Berlin Wall, but he did make a historic visit to the site in June 1963. Thousands of West Berliners greeted him with flowers and confetti. In a brief speech to a crowd of 120,000 people, Kennedy praised the city and declared his solidarity with its citizens. "Today," he declared, "Ich bin ein Berliner (I am a Berliner)!"

PRIMARY SOURCE

There are many people in the world who really don't understand, or say they don't, what is the great issue between the free world and the communist world. Let them come to Berlin. There are some who say that communism is the wave of the future. Let them come to Berlin. And there are some who say in Europe and elsewhere we can work with the communists. Let them come to Berlin. And there are even a few who say that it is true that communism is an evil system, but it permits us to make economic progress. Lass' sie nach Berlin kommen. *Let them come to Berlin.*

—from President John F. Kennedy's "Ich bin ein Berliner" speech, June 26, 1963

HISTORICAL THINKING

1. **READING CHECK** Why did the United States launch the Bay of Pigs invasion? Why did the mission fail?
2. **EVALUATE** Using text evidence, explain how you think historical events influenced Kennedy's decision not to challenge the building of the Berlin Wall.
3. **DRAW CONCLUSIONS** What did the Berlin Wall seem to say about life under communism?
4. **INTERPRET MAPS** Examine the 1960 election map. Why would Nixon have won the election if he had won Illinois and Texas?

HI 1 Students show the connections, causal and otherwise, between particular historical events and larger social, economic, and political trends and developments; HI 3 Students interpret past events and issues within the context in which an event unfolded rather than solely in terms of present-day norms and values; HI 4 Students understand the meaning, implication, and impact of historical events and recognize that events could have taken other directions.

CRITICAL VIEWING Built around 1790, the Brandenburg Gate served as a monument at an entry point to the city of Berlin. When Berlin was divided, the gate was on the border, barely within East Berlin, as shown in the top photo from around 1965. In the 1981 photo below, a West Berlin policeman patrols in front of a sign that reads, "Caution: You are leaving West Berlin." What do the photos reveal about people's feelings about the division of East and West Berlin?

1.2 **MAIN IDEA** President Kennedy's plans for moving the nation forward met with successes and setbacks.

KENNEDY EMBRACES PROGRESS

"The Best and the Brightest" was the nickname some observers gave to John Fitzgerald Kennedy's administration. Young, well-educated, and full of new ideas, his team was eager to make its mark and continue moving the nation forward.

THE NEW FRONTIER

Kennedy's ambitious presidential agenda became known as the **New Frontier**, a reference to a new decade and new opportunities awaiting the nation. Kennedy believed that creative problem solving could help the United States win friends overseas, resolve economic challenges at home and abroad, and achieve scientific and technological feats only imagined by others.

Kennedy's administration shared the president's optimism and confidence in problem solving. The new secretary of state, Dean Rusk, came from the Rockefeller Foundation, while the new defense secretary, Robert McNamara, had resigned as president of the Ford Motor Company so he could help restructure the nation's armed forces. You might recall that Kennedy chose his younger brother Robert Kennedy to serve as his attorney general.

SUCCESS AND SETBACK

A key domestic priority for Kennedy and his team was re-energizing the U.S. economy. Economic growth in the Eisenhower years had been steady but increasingly slow. Real wages for an average family rose a remarkable 20 percent in the 1950s. However, a series of recessions toward the end of Eisenhower's second term prompted a drop in factory production and a rise in unemployment. By the time Kennedy took office, more Americans were out of work than at any other time since the end of World War II. In 1961, Kennedy devised an economic plan that called for a major tax cut for consumers and businesses. He hoped the tax cut would boost the economy by encouraging both individuals and businesses to spend more. The plan successfully achieved low unemployment, stable prices, and steady growth. He pushed through Congress increases in various Social Security benefits, including an increase in the minimum monthly retirement benefit from $33 to $40. Kennedy also asked for and received a raise in the minimum wage, from $1 to $1.25 an hour.

Congress did not support all of Kennedy's plans, however. It defeated a number of the president's proposals, including an effort to increase education spending for school construction and higher teacher salaries. For the most part, Kennedy moved cautiously in pushing his domestic agenda, including the push for civil rights, as you have read. Since he had won the election by a slim margin, he lacked the widespread popularity that might have enabled him to do more.

In addition, Republicans and conservative southern Democrats in Congress were largely opposed to expanding the power and reach of the federal government. Kennedy understood this, so he picked his battles carefully and only pushed on those proposals he thought were most critical. One of them was a civil rights bill designed to strengthen the weak bills that had passed in 1957 and 1960. The new bill would eventually pass and would become an important step toward achieving equal rights for all.

STRENGTHENING FRIENDSHIPS

President Kennedy bypassed Congress to implement one of his most famous and lasting programs. On March 1, 1961, Kennedy issued an executive order, or a legally binding directive from a president, to create the **Peace Corps** and named R. Sargent Shriver, the husband of Kennedy's sister Eunice, as its director. The first group of 51 Peace Corps volunteers arrived

11.8.5 Describe the increased powers of the presidency in response to the Great Depression, World War II, and the Cold War; 11.9.3 Trace the origins and geopolitical consequences (foreign and domestic) of the Cold War and containment policy, including the following: • The era of McCarthyism, instances of domestic Communism (e.g., Alger Hiss) and blacklisting • The Truman Doctrine • The Berlin Blockade • The Korean War • The Bay of Pigs Invasion and the Cuban Missile Crisis • Atomic testing in the American West, the "mutual assured destruction" doctrine, and disarmament policies • The Vietnam War • Latin American policy.

A GLOBAL PERSPECTIVE **The Peace Corps proved to be one of Kennedy's most successful and long-lasting endeavors. By 2016, the Peace Corps had sent more than 220,000 volunteers to 140 nations throughout the world. In Cambodia in 2014, a volunteer helps villagers develop safe and nutritious food practices, including managing gardens and preparing healthy meals.**

in Accra, the capital of the African nation of Ghana, in August 1961, to serve as teachers. Within 6 years, the Peace Corps sent thousands of American volunteers to 55 underdeveloped nations, or nations with a low standard of living compared with other nations, to provide educational and technical assistance.

With a tiny budget, the Peace Corps became one of Kennedy's great triumphs, showcasing American idealism and know-how throughout the world. A geopolitical consequence of the Cold War, American leaders viewed the Peace Corps as not only a humanitarian program, but also a vital tool in the fight against communism. By spreading American goodwill and improving living conditions in underdeveloped nations, the president and others hoped the Peace Corps would help prevent countries from embracing communism.

With this same goal in mind—winning more allies and undermining communism—the Kennedy administration worked to strengthen its Latin American policy. During the 1940s and 1950s, the United States had focused primarily on assisting Europe and confronting the Soviet Union, resulting in a weakening of relationships with Latin American countries. After seeing Cuba turn communist, however, American leaders moved to improve relations with the larger Latin American world. In 1961, Kennedy persuaded Congress

PRIMARY SOURCE

In his inaugural address, Kennedy outlined a progressive agenda that included a pledge to help the citizens of poverty-stricken nations—a pledge from which the Peace Corps grew.

To those peoples in the huts and villages of half the globe struggling to break the bonds of mass misery, we pledge our best efforts to help them help themselves, for whatever period is required—not because the communists may be doing it, not because we seek their votes, but because it is right. If a free society cannot help the many who are poor, it cannot save the few who are rich.

—from John Kennedy's Inaugural Address, January 20, 1961

With John Glenn standing beside him, President Kennedy (left) looks inside *Friendship 7* in 1962, after Glenn's historic mission to orbit the earth.

to fund the **Alliance for Progress**, an aid program to improve education, health, and economic conditions in Latin America. During its first year alone, the program provided more than $1 billion in aid to various countries. The effort achieved mixed results. Some corrupt leaders misspent the money, and communism ultimately gained a foothold in some Latin American countries. In the end, however, houses, schools, electrical grids, roads, and hospitals were built, and children fed.

THE SPACE RACE

One of Kennedy's boldest proposals involved expansion of the space program. Shortly after taking office, the president declared the United States would put a man on the moon before the end of the decade, and he persuaded Congress to allocate between $7 billion and $9 billion for space research.

As with many of his other initiatives, the Cold War drove Kennedy's push for technological development in space travel. In addition to their arms race, the United States and Soviet Union engaged in a **space race**, or the Cold War rivalry between the United States and the Soviet Union to see who would dominate in its ability to travel in and collect data from space.

The competition had begun in the late 1950s, after the Soviets launched the first satellite, *Sputnik 1*, and President Eisenhower responded with the creation of NASA to advance space exploration. In 1959, NASA carefully selected seven men for the first class of American astronauts, or space travelers. These astronauts trained for nearly two years as part of Project Mercury. The scientists' primary goal for Project Mercury was to send a manned spacecraft into orbit around the earth. Doing so naturally entailed the astronauts returning to Earth unharmed, with their spacecraft intact. While in space and afterward, scientists closely monitored the physical effects of space travel on the astronauts' bodies, gathering data to improve safety and technology for future launches.

By the time Kennedy took office, both countries were making bold advances into space—and captivating the world. In April 1961, Soviet cosmonaut—the Russian term for *astronaut*—Yuri Gagarin orbited Earth in less than two hours. A month later, American Alan Shepard rocketed 300 miles from Cape Canaveral into space. In February 1962, American John Glenn achieved the historic feat of orbiting Earth three times aboard *Friendship 7* before splashing down in the Caribbean Sea. Glenn became a national hero, celebrated with ticker-tape parades and a televised address before a joint session of Congress.

Throughout the 1960s, astronauts were cheered as heroes and celebrities as the media closely followed space-race developments. The space race would have a huge impact on the world, producing dramatic scientific and technological advances with far-reaching applications in a surprisingly short amount of time.

HISTORICAL THINKING

1. **READING CHECK** What important roles did the Peace Corps serve in the context of the Cold War?
2. **DRAW CONCLUSIONS** Why might some people consider the Alliance for Progress a failure despite its successes?
3. **FORM AND SUPPORT OPINIONS** How was Kennedy both bold and cautious in promoting his presidential agenda? Support your opinion with evidence from the text.
4. **MAKE CONNECTIONS** What effects did the space race have on society and the economy?

11.8.7 Describe the effects on society and the economy of technological developments since 1945, including the computer revolution, changes in communication, advances in medicine, and improvements in agricultural technology; HI 3 Students interpret past events and issues within the context in which an event unfolded rather than solely in terms of present-day norms and values.

Sputnik 1

THE SPACE RACE

The original NASA logo

SOVIET UNION	Year	UNITED STATES
OCT. 4 *Sputnik 1*, the first satellite, launches into orbit. **NOV. 3** *Sputnik 2* launches "space-dog" Laika, who died during the mission, into orbit.	1957	**DEC. 6** America attempts to launch the Vanguard TV3 satellite, but the rocket explodes on the launchpad.
MAY 15 *Sputnik 3* is successfully launched, after a failed attempt in April of that year.	1958	**JAN. 31** *Explorer 1* becomes the first American satellite to reach orbit. **JULY 28** The National Aeronautics and Space Administration (NASA) is established.
JAN. 4 *Luna 1* becomes the first satellite to reach heliocentric orbit. **SEPT. 14** *Luna 2* is the first man-made object to reach the moon.	1959	**FEB. 17** *Vanguard 1*, the first solar-powered satellite, is launched.
AUG. 19 *Sputnik 5* launches "space-dogs" Strelka and Belka into orbit; they are the first living creatures to survive a space voyage.	1960	**APRIL 1** *TIROS 1*, the first weather observation satellite, is put into orbit.
APRIL 12 Cosmonaut Yuri Gagarin becomes the first human in space.	1961	**MAY 5** Alan Shepard becomes the first American astronaut in space. **MAY 25** President Kennedy announces the United States will land a man on the moon by the end of the decade.
APRIL 12 Cosmonaut Andriyan Nikolayev orbits Earth 64 times aboard *Vostok 3* to test the endurance of humans and spacecraft.	1962	**FEB. 20** Astronaut John Glenn becomes the first American to orbit Earth.
JUNE 16 Cosmonaut Valentina Tereshkova becomes the first woman in space.	1963	**JULY 19** *X-15*, the first reusable piloted spacecraft, is launched. The craft goes on to complete 15 successful missions.
OCT. 12 With 3 cosmonauts aboard, *Voskhod 1* becomes the first spacecraft to carry a multiperson crew into orbit.	1964	**AUG. 19** *Syncom 3*, the first satellite to achieve geostationary orbit, is launched.
MARCH 18 Cosmonaut Alexey Leonov takes the first spacewalk.	1965	**JUNE 3** Astronaut Ed White becomes the first American to perform a spacewalk.
FEB. 3 The *Luna 9* probe achieves the first soft landing on the moon, and sends back the first photographs from the moon's surface.	1966	**JUNE 2** *Surveyor 1* lands on the moon, sending back photos and data.
OCT. 30 *Cosmos 186* and *Cosmos 188* are successfully docked in space via Earth-based remote control.	1967	**JAN. 27** Project Apollo is temporarily paused when astronauts Gus Grissom, Ed White, and Roger Chaffee are killed by a fire during prelaunch testing.
SEPT. 15 *Zond 5* orbits the moon with worms, insects, and two tortoises aboard. It returns to Earth with all its "passengers" alive and healthy.	1968	**DEC. 21** *Apollo 8* launches; astronauts Frank Borman, James Lovell, and William Anders become the first humans to orbit the moon and return to Earth.
JAN. 16 *Soyuz 4* and *Soyuz 5* dock in space and exchange crew members via spacewalk.	1969	**JULY 20** Astronauts Neil Armstrong and Buzz Aldrin are the first humans to walk on the moon, while Michael Collins pilots the capsule in moon orbit.

Astronaut Buzz Aldrin sets up an experiment on the lunar surface.

MAIN IDEA President Kennedy successfully navigated his most serious foreign policy crisis before his tragic death shocked the nation.

THE CUBAN MISSILE CRISIS

Do you remember a time when you were involved in a compromise—when each side gave up something to avoid a fight or some other negative outcome? In 1962, the United States and the Soviet Union engaged in a tense standoff, and only a compromise would be able to save the world from an impending nuclear war.

THE MISSILES OF OCTOBER

By 1962, Americans were in good spirits. A growing economy and Kennedy's optimism were inspiring the nation. But ongoing Cold War tensions between the United States and the Soviet Union continued to be a threat. In October 1962, those tensions erupted and would put the world at the brink of nuclear war.

The trouble began with rumors, confirmed by American U-2 spy plane photos, that the Soviets were establishing intermediate-range **ballistic missiles**, or rocket-propelled, self-guiding nuclear weapons, in Cuba. In the eyes of Cuban leader Fidel Castro, this was simply a means of defending his nation. As a communist country in the middle of the Western Hemisphere, Cuba felt increasingly isolated and under siege. The Kennedy administration had imposed an economic embargo on Cuba and arranged for Cuba's expulsion from the **Organization of American States (OAS)**, an alliance of Western Hemisphere nations established in 1948, whose purpose is to keep peace among the nations of North and South America. What's more, the United States had already attacked Cuba at the Bay of Pigs in early 1961. Whatever his reasons, Castro was stockpiling nuclear weapons capable of reaching dozens of American cities. U.S. leaders would not stand for such a threat.

A TENSE STANDOFF

Kennedy demanded the Soviets remove the missiles in Cuba. In addition, the president ordered a **naval quarantine**, or blockade of ports, of Cuba to stop the Soviets from delivering more missiles. On October 22, 1962, the president went on television to reassure an increasingly tense nation. The entire world watched anxiously as Soviet ships headed toward Cuba and the U.S. warships enforcing the quarantine. On October 26, Kennedy received a note from Soviet leader Nikita Khrushchev suggesting a settlement. "There is no intention to . . . doom the world to the catastrophe of thermonuclear war," he wrote. "Let us take measures to untie [the] knot."

Khrushchev promised to remove his missiles if the United States pledged never to invade Cuba. Before Kennedy could respond, he received a second note, demanding the United States also remove its missiles on the Soviet border with Turkey. Attorney General Robert Kennedy advised his brother to respond to the first note and ignore the second. On October 27, the president vowed not to invade Cuba if the Soviets removed the missiles. In private, Robert Kennedy assured the Soviets the United States would remove its missiles from Turkey in the near future.

On October 28, Khrushchev accepted the deal. In the end, he had miscalculated the stern American response to the placement of offensive missiles so close to U.S. shores. In fact, many of the president's advisors had recommended a military strike, but Kennedy rejected their advice. Secretary of State Dean Rusk summed up the feelings of everyone in the Kennedy administration: "We [were] eyeball to eyeball, and I think the other fellow just blinked." The **Cuban Missile Crisis**, as it came to be known, had ended, but it left a deep impression. For those two weeks, the world had seemed headed for nuclear war and the real possibility of annihilation for both sides.

PEACEFUL RESOLUTION

Throughout the 1950s, the U.S. government developed a civil defense system to keep American

11.9.3 Trace the origins and geopolitical consequences (foreign and domestic) of the Cold War and containment policy, including the following: • The era of McCarthyism, instances of domestic Communism (e.g., Alger Hiss) and blacklisting • The Truman Doctrine • The Berlin Blockade • The Korean War • The Bay of Pigs Invasion and the Cuban Missile Crisis • Atomic testing in the American West, the "mutual assured destruction" doctrine, and disarmament policies • The Vietnam War • Latin American policy; 11.9.4 List the effects of foreign policy on domestic policies and vice versa (e.g., protests during the war in Vietnam, the "nuclear freeze" movement).

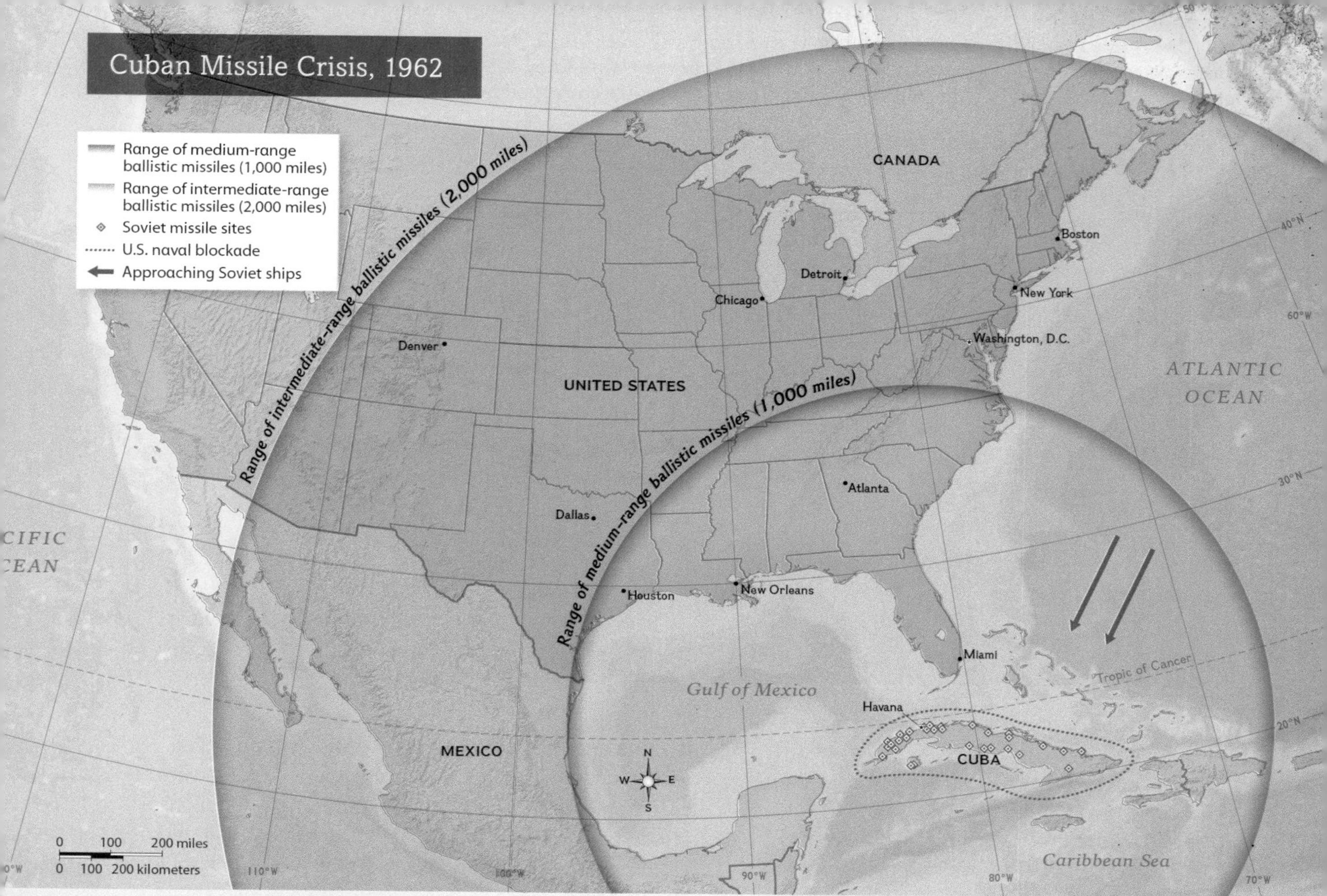

A year before the Cuban Missile Crisis, President Kennedy urged Americans to build fallout shelters for their homes. Promotional photos show the features of one model available commercially in 1955.

CRITICAL VIEWING Attorney General Robert Kennedy was one of the closest advisors to his brother, President John F. Kennedy. Here the two meet in the Oval Office of the White House in October 1962, during the Cuban Missile Crisis. What feelings are conveyed by the two men?

THE SECOND VATICAN COUNCIL

On October 11, 1962, 10 days before President Kennedy went on television to explain to the nation the crisis around the presence of Soviet missiles in Cuba, Pope John XXIII (the 23rd) announced the principles of the Second Vatican Council in Rome. The Council called for a new openness in the Catholic Church and for the Church to take a role in promoting peace and social justice worldwide.

As news of the crisis became known, a priest from the Vatican attending a conference on peace in Massachusetts suggested asking the pope to intervene. The White House approved the suggestion, and the pope broadcast a message on Vatican radio begging the two leaders to consider all of humanity and find a peaceful solution to the crisis.

The pope also sent a message personally to Khrushchev asking him to be "the man of peace." Khrushchev agreed to do so and ordered the missiles withdrawn. The Soviet leader was reported to say the pope's message was the only "gleam of hope" in the crisis. In 1963, partly in response to the crisis now past, the pope issued a statement calling for "Peace on Earth," reinforcing that principle of what came to be called Vatican II (2).

leaders and as many American civilians as possible safe in case of nuclear war. Civil defense plans were communicated throughout the nation, through signs in public places and a broadcast communications network that was established to keep people informed should an attack occur. Plans to build large-scale public shelters, however, were put forth and rejected. In their place were signs in public buildings indicating evacuation areas.

But the Cuban Missile Crisis frightened U.S. and Soviet leaders into changing their relationship from brinkmanship to one in which they would work together to manage tensions. The reality of mutual assured destruction seemed to inspire the leaders to consider more peaceful options. In July 1963, officials installed a direct telephone link, known as the "hotline," between the White House and the Kremlin, the residence and office of the Soviet leader. Shortly after, the United States and the Soviet Union joined other nations in agreeing to limits on future development of nuclear weapons. The United States and the Soviet Union began seeking ways to coexist peacefully. While no one denied that significant differences existed between them, the countries both mutually recognized that they could not risk the type of confrontation that could destroy civilization.

Nonetheless, the nation's civil defense system remains active in protecting citizens. When natural disasters such as hurricanes and floods strike, the people affected depend on clear communication and effective evacuation plans and routes. In addition, since the early years of

11.3.2 Analyze the great religious revivals and the leaders involved in them, including the First Great Awakening, the Second Great Awakening, the Civil War revivals, the Social Gospel Movement, the rise of Christian liberal theology in the nineteenth century, the impact of the Second Vatican Council, and the rise of Christian fundamentalism in current times.

the 21st century, concerns about terrorism have emerged, and civil defense practices appropriate to the new types of threats have been developed.

TRAGEDY IN DALLAS

By 1963, President Kennedy had positioned himself well to run for re-election. He had moved the country forward economically and had proved himself on the world stage. However, not all Americans were behind him. Kennedy's support for the growing civil rights movement particularly angered white southern Democrats. In an attempt to win southern votes, President and Jacqueline Kennedy traveled to Texas—the southern state with the most electoral votes—to campaign in late November 1963. On November 22, as the Kennedys' motorcade passed through Dealey Plaza in Dallas, shots rang out from a window on the sixth floor of a nearby building—a textbook depository, or warehouse, near the motorcade route. Kennedy suddenly slumped in his seat, shot in the head. The motorcade raced to Parkland Hospital, where doctors pronounced the president dead.

Within hours, the police arrested a 24-year-old suspect named **Lee Harvey Oswald**, whom witnesses identified as fleeing the book depository after Kennedy's assassination. Two days later, on November 24, as law enforcement officers were moving Oswald between jails, Dallas nightclub owner Jack Ruby stepped forward and shot and killed him. Ruby claimed he killed Oswald out of a sense of patriotism and extreme distress over Kennedy's death. Ruby died in prison four years later.

With the murder of the prime suspect in Kennedy's assassination, many people suspected the events were all part of a larger conspiracy. The federal government immediately assembled a special group led by Chief Justice Earl Warren to investigate. After spending almost a year sifting through every bit of evidence available on the murders, the **Warren Commission** report concluded that both Oswald and Ruby had acted alone. Despite this conclusion, alternative interpretations of this event are still debated as various theories of the assassination have been proposed. Some blame Fidel Castro, others the Mafia, the Ku Klux Klan, or the CIA. To some, the simple explanation that a deranged man had committed a senseless act of violence and met a violent end himself did not explain sufficiently the death of a president so young and full of life.

Such doubts reflected the depth of shock over Kennedy's assassination. Few other events in the nation's history produced so much bewilderment and grief. Even Khrushchev felt a deep loss, calling Kennedy's death "a heavy blow to all people who hold dear the cause of peace and Soviet-American cooperation." Kennedy had seemed an ideal president: a charming, handsome war hero with a glamorous wife. The reality was different, of course. Kennedy's three years in office saw failures as well as successes, and after his death, evidence emerged of personal shortcomings that raised questions about his character. Still, Kennedy's final months were his most productive, and many supporters felt he would have accomplished even more in a second term.

Three-year-old John Kennedy, Jr., salutes his father, President Kennedy, one last time at the president's funeral, November 25, 1963.

HISTORICAL THINKING

1. **READING CHECK** What were the origins and geopolitical consequences of the Cuban Missile Crisis?
2. **DETERMINE CHRONOLOGY** Identify in order three major events that occurred between November 22 and November 24, 1963.
3. **INTERPRET MAPS** Based on the map, what part of the United States would be safe from a missile attack from Cuba?

HREP 3 Students evaluate major debates among historians concerning alternative interpretations of the past, including an analysis of authors' use of evidence and the distinctions between sound generalizations and misleading oversimplifications; HI 1 Students show the connections, causal and otherwise, between particular historical events and larger social, economic, and political trends and developments.

JOHN FITZGERALD KENNEDY 1917–1963

"Let the word go forth from this time and place, to friend and foe alike, that the torch has been passed to a new generation of Americans."—John F. Kennedy

John F. Kennedy, who is often referred to by his initials, JFK, spoke these words at his inaugural address on January 20, 1961. The words were probably meant to energize his supporters and send a warning to his enemies. JFK heralded a new era of youth, vigor—one of his favorite words—and confidence. He embodied all three. Kennedy was the youngest U.S. president ever elected, and he seemed the picture of health. (He wasn't; more on that later.) His confidence was very likely a quality instilled by his family.

In September 1962, JFK addressed a crowd of 40,000 at Rice University in Houston, Texas, with his now-famous speech in which he boldly announced, "We choose to go to the moon."

THE KENNEDY CLAN

Kennedy, as you know, grew up amid great wealth in Boston, Massachusetts. His father, Joseph (Joe) Kennedy, Sr., was a highly successful businessman and held several political positions, including U.S. ambassador to Great Britain. However, Joe, Sr., always felt he had been prevented from achieving higher office as a result of the anti-Catholic animosity in the United States. He vowed his children would overcome that prejudice. Rose Kennedy, the family matriarch, was "the glue that always held the family together," as John once said about his mother. She devoted herself to her brood of four boys and five girls.

The brothers and sisters were close-knit but extremely competitive, especially in sports. Any visitor to the family's summer home in Hyannis Port on Cape Cod had to be ready to take part in a game of touch football. And the game could get rough. John's wife, Jacqueline (Jackie), once broke her ankle while playing—and she was pregnant at the time. After that, she refused to play touch football again. John threw himself into the family games, but the physical activity was often hard on him. He had been a sickly child and suffered from ill health all his life. Nevertheless, Joe, Sr., liked to pit John and his older brother, Joe, Jr., against each other. On a bicycle race organized by their father, the brothers collided, and John had to have 28 stitches. Joe, Sr., wanted his boys to be tough.

The entire Kennedy clan gathered for this 1935 photo taken at Hyannis Port. Seated from left to right: Patricia, Robert, Rose, John, Joseph, Sr., with Edward on his lap; standing from left to right: Joseph, Jr., Kathleen, Rosemary, Eunice (rear), Jean

During World War II, both brothers served in the U.S. Navy. As a lieutenant, John commanded a patrol torpedo boat, PT-109. One night, a Japanese destroyer rammed into the boat in the Pacific Ocean. Two crew members were killed, but 11 others survived the collision, including John. Despite suffering from a bad back, he swam for 4 hours to an island while tugging an injured man with him. They ending up swimming to yet another island in search of food and fresh water. There, John carved a message on a coconut shell and sent it with two scouts in a canoe to the Australian Coast Guard. John was awarded a medal for gallantry. Later, when someone asked Kennedy how he came to be a hero, he replied, "It was involuntary. They sank my boat."

Joe, Jr., flew combat missions over Europe in the war. Then he volunteered to take part in a secret and highly dangerous mission that involved flying a drone loaded with explosives to Normandy, France. The explosives unexpectedly detonated before Joe, Jr., could parachute out of the plane. His death at age 29 was the first in a series of tragedies that plagued the Kennedy family. Some called it a curse. Kathleen, the second-eldest daughter of the clan, died in a plane crash three years later. Before his son's death, Joe, Sr., had hoped to fulfill his political ambitions through Joe, Jr. Now he pinned his hopes on John.

THE CAMELOT PRESIDENCY

John Kennedy may have succeeded beyond his father's wildest dreams. During the 1,037 days of his presidency, as you know, JFK experienced both successes and failures. But he remained a charismatic leader throughout his time in office. His idealism inspired people to believe they really could make their country and the world a better place. The handsome president and his beautiful wife enchanted Americans, who followed their trips and social engagements on television and in the news with avid interest. Women admired Jackie and tried to imitate her sophisticated taste in fashion. When the first lady gave the first-ever televised tour of the White House in 1962 to show the restorations she'd had done, a record 56 million people tuned in to watch.

Americans were also charmed by JFK's wit, which he often directed toward himself. After naming his inexperienced 36-year-old brother, Robert, as attorney general, JFK joked, "I don't see anything wrong with giving Bobby a little legal experience before he goes out on his own to practice law." On a visit to Paris in 1961, as it became clear Jackie was the one the crowds had come out to see, he said, "I do not think it altogether inappropriate to introduce myself. I am the man who accompanied Jacqueline Kennedy to Paris, and I have enjoyed it."

Kennedy commanded PT-109, which was split in two by a Japanese destroyer on August 1, 1943. He and his crew salvaged what they could from the boat, including a wood plank they used to tow two men—who couldn't swim—to safety.

JFK's children, Caroline and John Jr., often had the run of the White House. Here, John Jr., peeks out from what he called the "secret door" of his father's desk in the Oval Office.

Kennedy's presidency would come to be called "Camelot," suggesting that it brought the romantic legend of King Arthur to life. But this characterization masks the anguish that lay beneath the surface. JFK had chronic back pain and suffered from a rare disorder called Addison's disease, which causes severe fatigue and muscle weakness. Jackie had her own pain while she endured her husband's unfaithfulness. Most tragically of all, they both mourned the death of their infant son, Patrick, who died 39 hours after his birth in August 1963.

TRAGEDY AND LOSS

Of course, just a few months later, John Kennedy himself would be dead. Widowed at 34, Jackie planned her late husband's funeral and modeled it on that of Abraham Lincoln. She had a horse-drawn wagon carry Kennedy's flag-draped casket to the White House. Then the mourners followed a riderless horse, with boots symbolically reversed in the stirrups, to the church where the service was to be held. Jackie's strength and dignity throughout the funeral helped the nation cope with its own sorrow.

At the Democratic National Convention held in August 1964, Robert Kennedy took the floor to introduce a short film on his brother's legacy. But every time he tried to speak, the delegates erupted into applause. This went on for more than 20 minutes. Just about 4 years later, Robert would be cut down by an assassin's bullet, too. John Kennedy's son, John F. Kennedy, Jr., died in 1999 at age 38 in a plane crash. To many, the Kennedy family certainly seemed to be cursed.

In defiance of the curse, however, more than 50 years after his death, John Kennedy remained the most popular president of the post–World War II era. The young president's ideals still capture people's imaginations and hearts. As JFK once said, "A man may die, nations may rise and fall, but an idea lives on."

HISTORICAL THINKING

1. **READING CHECK** How was John Kennedy shaped by his early years?
2. **MAKE INFERENCES** What do the quotations by JFK in this lesson reveal about the man?
3. **ANALYZE CAUSE AND EFFECT** Describe the complex effects the death of Joseph Kennedy, Jr., had on JFK and the country.
4. **EVALUATE** What limitations might prevent you from determining the effects referred to in question 3?

HI 2 Students recognize the complexity of historical causes and effects, including the limitations on determining cause and effect.

People thronged the streets of Dallas to see JFK and Jackie riding in this limousine on November 22, 1963. John Connally, Jr., the governor of Texas, and his wife, Nellie, rode in the seat in front of them. Moments before JFK was shot, she said to Kennedy, "Mr. President, you certainly cannot say that Dallas does not love you."

President Kennedy's flag-draped coffin moves slowly past mourners on November 25, 1963. The president was buried in Arlington Cemetery, where an eternal flame marks his grave.

1.5 NATIONAL GEOGRAPHIC EXPLORER LESLIE DEWAN

REINVENTING CLEAN ENERGY

"I think I can save the world with nuclear power."
—Leslie Dewan

Leslie Dewan stands out from the crowd—a visionary woman in a male-dominated field. With guidance and input from her female teachers and mentors, and with a nod to history and its lessons, Dewan is determined to develop a cleaner form of nuclear power that will reinvent the definition of clean energy. This carbon-free energy will power the world, and—as a side note—will greatly decrease the production of nuclear waste. It's ambitious, but if it can be done, this National Geographic Explorer will figure out how.

^ As one of the only women in her graduate school classes at the Massachusetts Institute of Technology (MIT), Leslie Dewan, shown here on the MIT campus, learned to take the lead.

MAIN IDEA Leslie Dewan is developing a safer, cleaner alternative to traditional nuclear power.

In 1979, the Three Mile Island nuclear power station in Pennsylvania had the most serious accident in U.S. history. Luckily, the small amount of radioactive material released had no health effects on plant workers or the public.

A NEW SOURCE OF ENERGY

From the beginning of history, humans have used fire to generate power. In fact, as early as 2000 B.C., people burned coal for energy. They later discovered the usefulness of natural gas and petroleum. But as you know, fossil fuels like coal, oil, and natural gas are nonrenewable energy sources. Burning them is believed to have negative impacts on our planet, including air, land, and water pollution. Utilizing cleaner energy sources is a must for the environment.

Although fossil fuels are still widely in use, we now harness the power of the sun, wind, water, and geothermal sources more than ever before to generate power and electricity. Leslie Dewan, an MIT-trained nuclear engineer, National Geographic Explorer, and environmentalist, would like to add nuclear power to that list, but others disagree. The impact on people and the environment that resulted from nuclear disasters at power plants, including Three Mile Island in the United States, Chernobyl in the Ukraine, and Fukushima in Japan, leaves many uneasy. They feel nuclear power is just too dangerous.

Scientists first figured out how to generate nuclear power about 70 years ago. It was exciting at first, imagining nuclear-powered cars, planes, and weapons, and nuclear reactors to generate electricity. At that time, the focus was not on reducing carbon dioxide emissions, but on gaining energy independence from other countries.

As you have read, nuclear technology was used during the Cold War to create weapons of mass destruction. The Cuban Missile Crisis brought the world to the brink of nuclear war. After World War II, Americans were acutely aware of the destructive power of nuclear weapons, so the fear of "being nuked" during the Cold War led people to build bomb shelters and practice nuclear attack drills.

Decades later, highly publicized nuclear disasters gave people the impression that nuclear power was more dangerous than useful. Serious failures did occur, and they were disastrous—in the case of Chernobyl, a whole continent was affected. There were also serious concerns about technology and safety. In its rush to develop reactors, the United States built reactors similar to those designed for nuclear submarines instead of developing ones better suited for land. Nearly all of the reactors still in use in this country today are submarine-style reactors.

SAFER NUCLEAR REACTORS

That's where Dewan comes in. She's designing a safer, more efficient alternative to today's nuclear reactors, and says, "I want to come up with new technology that keeps the good elements of nuclear power but solves the bad aspects." Dewan and her colleague, Mark Massie, developed a new design for a molten salt reactor, initially intended for nuclear-powered airplanes. Ideally, their reactors would leave behind less than half as much nuclear waste as existing reactors, and produce enough energy to power the world for decades. Dewan hopes to develop a prototype by 2020 and a commercial reactor by the 2030s.

Currently, nuclear power provides 10 percent of the world's electricity and 45 percent of the world's fossil-free electricity. Dewan believes nuclear energy will move the world away from fossil fuels and offer dramatic reductions in carbon dioxide emissions. She notes, "I think the world needs nuclear power, alongside solar, wind, hydro, and geothermal, if we want to have any hope of reducing fossil fuel emissions and preventing global climate change."

HISTORICAL THINKING

1. **READING CHECK** What problem is Dewan attempting to solve with her development of new nuclear reactor technology?
2. **ANALYZE ENVIRONMENTAL CONCEPTS** How might nuclear technology affect the environment in both positive and negative ways?

11.7.6 Describe major developments in aviation, weaponry, communication, and medicine and the war's impact on the location of American industry and use of resources.

CRITICAL VIEWING How does Cuba's history with the United States relate to the abundance of classic American cars on the historic streets of Havana?

1.6

THROUGH THE LENS

DAVID GUTTENFELDER

In May 2016, **National Geographic photographer David Guttenfelder** set sail from Miami, Florida, on the first cruise ship to sail from the United States to Havana, Cuba, in nearly 50 years. His images capture Cuba's colorful culture and identity, but also its infrastructure, much of which hasn't been updated since the 1960s when the United States cut off ties. Guttenfelder's photos reveal how, in many ways, time has stood still on this island country until recently.

2.1 **MAIN IDEA** President Lyndon Johnson led the nation through a smooth transition following Kennedy's death and worked to get important legislation passed.

JOHNSON'S STRONG START

"All I have, I would gladly have given not to be standing here today," Lyndon Johnson said in his first address to Congress. But the job was his, and, while determined to carry on the work started by Kennedy, he still blazed his own path forward.

A SMOOTH TRANSITION

On the night of November 22, 1963, just hours after President Kennedy's assassination, Vice President Lyndon Johnson took the presidential oath of office aboard Air Force One. Lyndon Baines Johnson—popularly called LBJ—was born in a small house in the hills of south-central Texas in 1908. He belonged to a lower social class and an older political generation than Kennedy. And with his down-home style and earthy language, he seemed rather crude to the East Coast newscasters and journalists compared with the media-savvy Kennedy. Yet few people knew more than LBJ about how to get things done in Washington.

Lyndon Johnson was sworn in as president aboard Air Force One before it left Dallas, only 90 minutes after Kennedy was pronounced dead. Crowded into the plane's stateroom, and photographed by White House photographer Cecil Stoughton, were Johnson, Judge Sara Hughes, Jacqueline Kennedy, Johnson's wife Lady Bird, reporters, and Kennedy's staff.

PRIMARY SOURCES

Senator Richard Russell, Jr., a Democrat from Georgia, opposed civil rights legislation for decades and joined the Senate filibuster against the civil rights bill. Illinois senator Everett M. Dirksen, a Republican and a strong supporter of the bill, spoke out to end the long filibuster and debate and move it to a vote.

We will resist to the bitter end any measure or any movement which would have a tendency to bring about social equality and intermingling and amalgamation [mixture] of the races in our [Southern] states.

—from a speech by Senator Richard Russell, Jr., during the Senate filibuster, March 30, 1964

There is another reason why we dare not temporize with [delay] the issue which is before us. It is essentially moral in character. It must be resolved. It will not go away. Its time has come.

—from a speech in the Senate by minority leader Everett M. Dirksen, June 10, 1964

Johnson entered the White House with three decades of political experience in hand. After running the Texas division of the National Youth Administration, a New Deal program, he won a seat in Congress in 1937. By 1949, Johnson had become a master of Texas politics, and used all his savvy to win election to the U.S. Senate. Elected Senate majority leader in the 1950s, he worked with the Eisenhower White House to craft important legislation on defense spending, highway construction, and civil rights. Johnson proved to be such an effective Senate majority leader that some even referred to him as the "Master of the Senate."

He became president under tragic circumstances but moved quickly to restore public confidence through a smooth transition of power. Johnson told Congress, "The ideas and ideals which [Kennedy] so nobly represented must and will be translated into effective action." To provide continuity, he kept Kennedy's team largely intact, persuading Secretary of State Dean Rusk, Secretary of Defense Robert McNamara, and other key cabinet members to stay on.

THE CIVIL RIGHTS ACT

With his political expertise, Johnson was able to win early legislative victories. One of his first presidential acts was to work for the stalled tax cut Kennedy had supported. Like Kennedy, Johnson believed lower taxes would encourage economic growth and reduce unemployment. In February 1964, he signed a measure that cut taxes by $10 billion over the following two years. The economy responded. The GNP rose by 7 percent in 1964 and 8 percent in 1965. Unemployment fell below 5 percent for the first time since World War II. As Johnson predicted, the resulting economic growth also generated greater federal revenues.

Johnson also set about achieving some of Kennedy's civil rights goals. Both Kennedy and Johnson were supporters of civil rights and believed the federal government needed to create laws to help promote greater equality in the United States. As Senate majority leader, Johnson had steered the Civil Rights Acts of 1957 and 1960 through Congress. Just weeks after taking office, Johnson met with Martin Luther King, Jr., and other African-American leaders to assure them of his commitment to a stronger civil rights act—the one Kennedy had proposed in 1963.

At great political risk, Johnson immediately took up the battle for Kennedy's stalled bill. "No memorial oration or eulogy," Johnson said in a speech to Congress on November 27, 1963, "could more eloquently honor President Kennedy's memory than the earliest possible passage of the civil rights bill for which he fought so long." Johnson then successfully persuaded Congress to enact federal programs in civil rights, education, and social welfare.

In early 1964, the House of Representatives, by a vote of 290 to 130, approved Kennedy's civil rights bill, but it hit a wall in the Senate. Southern senators had formed a bloc to oppose the bill. They used the **filibuster**—a strategy in which a small group of senators take turns speaking and refuse to stop the debate or allow the bill to come to a vote—against it. A number of Democratic and Republican senators gathered **bipartisan** support to ultimately end what had grown to an 83-day filibuster. The Senate passed the bill, proving Congress's commitment to civil rights.

On July 2, President Johnson signed the **Civil Rights Act of 1964** into law. The seven-part act was one of the most comprehensive civil rights laws Congress

11.10 Students analyze the development of federal civil rights and voting rights; 11.10.6 Analyze the passage and effects of civil rights and voting rights legislation (e.g., 1964 Civil Rights Act, Voting Rights Act of 1965) and the Twenty-Fourth Amendment, with an emphasis on equality of access to education and to the political process.

ver enacted. It expanded the role of the federal ment in the fight for civil rights by enforcing egation in public schools and prohibiting discrimination in federally funded public programs and in such facilities as restaurants, parks, libraries, and movie theaters. The new law made discrimination in the workplace based on gender illegal, and it created the **Equal Employment Opportunity Commission (EEOC)** to monitor and protect workplace rights. The act prohibited employment discrimination based on race, creed, national origin, and gender. As a result of the Civil RIghts Act, women and minorities who faced workplace discrimination could seek assistance from the EEOC.

RESISTANCE IN THE SOUTH

The Civil Rights Act of 1964 met with stiff resistance in the South. One of the most notable examples occurred in Atlanta, Georgia, within a few days of the act's signing. A segregationist restaurant owner named Lester Maddox refused to serve food to three African-American college students, calling them "dirty devils" and "dirty communists" and pointing a gun at them. Some of the white customers in the restaurant threatened the students with ax handles that Maddox kept on hand. A month later, Maddox decided to close his restaurant rather than obey a court order to desegregate it. Maddox went on to become governor of Georgia in 1966.

Dr. Martin Luther King, Jr., stands behind President Lyndon Johnson (seated) to witness the signing of the Civil Rights Act of 1964. Others in the room include Republican and Democratic representatives who voted for the most far-reaching civil rights legislation enacted since Reconstruction.

11.10.1 Explain how demands of African Americans helped produce a stimulus for civil rights, including President Roosevelt's ban on racial discrimination in defense industries in 1941, and how African Americans' service in World War II produced a stimulus for President Truman's decision to end segregation in the armed forces in 1948.

CRITICAL VIEWING In the South, African Americans were still being kept from voting even after the Civil Rights Act was passed. On September 7, 1963, SNCC organized more than 350 African Americans to come to register to vote at the county courthouse in Selma, Alabama. What appears to be taking place on the courthouse steps?

Voting rights gained additional protection in August 1964 when the states ratified the **24th Amendment**, which banned poll taxes. Southern states had required citizens to pay fixed voter registration fees, a strategy used to discourage African Americans from voting. With these landmark laws, the federal government re-established a commitment to providing people of all races, ethnicities, religious groups, and sexes with the rights of full citizenship.

December 1964 brought yet another victory for the civil rights movement. Dr. Martin Luther King, Jr., was awarded the Nobel Peace Prize for his leadership in the movement against discrimination and segregation and his commitment to nonviolence in the effort. In his acceptance speech, he said, "I refuse to accept the view that mankind is so tragically bound to the starless midnight of racism and war that the bright daybreak of peace and brotherhood can never become a reality."

King celebrated the 1964 Civil Rights Act as a tremendous advance in the struggle for racial equality, but believed it fell short in some areas, especially voting rights. The act restricted, but did not prohibit, literacy tests and other tricks white segregationists used to **disenfranchise** African Americans, or take away their right to vote. The tricks proved effective: in many areas of the Deep South, only a small percentage of the African-American population was registered to vote. King and other civil rights leaders chose establishing hard and fast voting rights as their next battle, while Johnson turned to other social and international issues.

HISTORICAL THINKING

1. **READING CHECK** Why did Johnson want members of Kennedy's Cabinet to stay in their current roles?
2. **COMPARE AND CONTRAST** Examine the primary source excerpts in this lesson. How do the senators' points of view differ on the issue of civil rights?
3. **DRAW CONCLUSIONS** How do you think Johnson's experiences in Congress may have helped him get legislation passed as president?
4. **DETERMINE CHRONOLOGY** How did the Civil Rights Act of 1964 build on previous legislation and civil rights activism?

HI 4 Students understand the meaning, implication, and impact of historical events and recognize that events could have taken other directions.

2.2 **MAIN IDEA** After winning the presidential election in 1964, Lyndon Johnson drove an ambitious agenda to improve American life.

The Great Society

Do you know someone who can walk into a room and make his or her presence felt right away? To many people, that was President Lyndon Johnson. The president had energy and determination to spare, and he relied on it to work toward many lofty goals.

LANDSLIDE IN 1964

Lyndon Johnson achieved legislative success early on as he worked to accomplish some of Kennedy's goals. Johnson hoped to build on this momentum and enact his own sweeping presidential agenda. First, he would have to hold on to the presidency by winning the 1964 election. Johnson chose as his running mate Senator Hubert H. Humphrey of Minnesota, a likable leader nicknamed "the Happy Warrior," who shared Johnson's goals.

For Republicans, things did not line up so easily. By 1964, the party was facing deep divisions between moderates, who supported the civil rights movement and agreed with a limited expansion of government, and conservatives, who favored smaller government and the use of force to stop communism.

PRIMARY SOURCE

The Great Society is a place where every child can find knowledge to enrich his mind and to enlarge his talents. It is a place where the city of man serves not only the needs of the body and the demands of commerce but the desire for beauty and the hunger for community.

But most of all, the Great Society is not a safe harbor, a resting place, a final objective, a finished work. It is a challenge constantly renewed, beckoning us toward a destiny where the meaning of our lives matches the marvelous products of our labor.

—from a speech at the University of Michigan by President Lyndon B. Johnson, May 22, 1964

After intense debate, Republicans nominated conservative senator **Barry Goldwater** of Arizona for president and Representative William Miller of New York as his running mate. Goldwater's vision for the country couldn't have been further from those of Johnson and Kennedy. In the Senate, he had voted against Social Security increases, the Nuclear Test Ban Treaty of 1963, and the Civil Rights Act of 1964. In accepting the nomination, Goldwater promised a "spiritual awakening" for the United States. He declared: "Extremism in the defense of liberty is no vice. Moderation in the pursuit of justice is no virtue."

The Johnson campaign focused on some of Goldwater's most extreme views to portray him as a dangerous and unpredictable candidate. In one of the most famous television campaign commercials ever, a three-year-old child was shown counting the petals of a daisy, out of order. Her counting turned into an ominous male voice counting down to a launch. The girl disappeared as the viewer saw a missile being launched, followed by the blast and mushroom cloud of a nuclear explosion. The "Daisy" ad, the name by which it became known, implied that Goldwater would destroy innocent lives by leading the nation into a nuclear war. Viewers found the commercial so disturbing that it ran only once.

On Election Day, Johnson won 61 percent of the popular vote and 44 of the 50 states, which translated to 486 electoral votes. Johnson's lopsided margin of victory helped the Democrats increase their substantial majorities in both houses of Congress. Although the Republicans lost ground, the election returns showed that a new coalition was forming in their ranks. The party was gaining strength

11.8.4 Analyze new federal government spending on defense, welfare, interest on the national debt, and federal and state spending on education, including the California Master Plan; 11.11.2 Discuss the significant domestic policy speeches of Truman, Eisenhower, Kennedy, Johnson, Nixon, Carter, Reagan, Bush, and Clinton (e.g., with regard to education, civil rights, economic policy, environmental policy).

among middle-class white voters in the South and Southwest. Furthermore, Goldwater attracted thousands of young recruits determined to reshape the Republican Party along more conservative lines. For the growing number of Republicans, 1964 was a beginning rather than the end.

WAR ON POVERTY

President Johnson viewed his landslide victory as a mandate for change. He spoke of creating "a great society" for Americans, one free of poverty, ignorance, and discrimination, where the spirit of "true community" would prevail. Together, his sweeping set of programs became known as the **Great Society**. The centerpiece of Johnson's agenda was what he called his **War on Poverty**—an all-out effort to address the persistence of poverty and create a decent standard of living for all Americans. Despite a strong economy, about 20 percent of the nation still lived in poverty in 1964. "We shall not rest until [this] war is won," Johnson insisted. "The richest nation on Earth can afford to win it. We cannot afford to lose it."

Some War on Poverty programs aimed to help children. **Head Start**, for example, was an educational program designed to better prepare low-income preschoolers for primary school. Title I of the

Federal spending on education in 1966 funded this Head Start program in Clarksdale, Mississippi, providing both jobs for teachers and learning opportunities for children.

Food stamps help people pay for meals, but low-income neighborhoods often lack supermarkets with affordable healthy foods. In response, a nonprofit organization in Chicago has pioneered the use of buses to bring fresh produce to communities where there are no markets residents can reach easily.

Elementary and Secondary Education Act of 1965 provided extra federal funding to public schools that served a high percentage of low-income students. In addition, the Food Stamp program helped families afford nutritional meals. Johnson himself had experienced poverty and hunger as a child, and those memories drove his desire to help relieve the suffering of others.

As another part of his antipoverty effort, Johnson pushed the **Economic Opportunity Act** through Congress in 1964. The act established a range of programs aimed at creating jobs and battling poverty. The War on Poverty focused attention on community action, which led to an increase of minority participation in local affairs. Johnson named Peace Corps director R. Sargent Shriver to coordinate the numerous work programs created by the act. These work programs included the Job Corps, an education and training program for young people; the Neighborhood Youth Corps, which provided employment, job counseling, and additional education to low-income youth; and Volunteers in Service to America (VISTA), a domestic service program modeled on the Peace Corps.

Overall, the War on Poverty achieved considerable success. It did not eradicate poverty, and some critics have argued that it made impoverished people dependent on the federal government. Nonetheless, poverty declined dramatically in the late 1960s—the result of both the expanding economy and the federal programs aimed directly at alleviating poverty. By 1970, the number of Americans living below the poverty line had dropped from more than 40 million (about 20 percent of the population) to around 24 million (about 12 percent). Over the years, Congress continued to renew many of these anti-poverty programs, most of which are still in place today.

HEALTH CARE AND IMMIGRATION

In addition to tackling the issue of poverty, Johnson believed medical care for all was an essential part of the Great Society. When Johnson took office in 1963, a majority of older Americans, as well as the one-fifth of the nation living below the poverty line, were without health insurance. The American Medical Association (AMA) and private insurers strongly opposed the idea of lower-cost or even free health care, calling it "socialized medicine." The president, however, was determined. After months of intense lobbying, Congress passed landmark legislation that Johnson had requested to fund medical insurance for the neediest Americans. The legislation created two federal programs. **Medicare** provided federal health care assistance to the elderly. **Medicaid** extended medical coverage to welfare recipients.

11.11.6 Analyze the persistence of poverty and how different analyses of this issue influence welfare reform, health insurance reform, and other social policies; CST 3 Students use a variety of maps and documents to interpret human movement, including major patterns of domestic and international migration, changing environmental preferences and settlement patterns, the frictions that develop between population groups, and the diffusion of ideas, technological innovations, and goods.

IMMIGRATION AND CITIZENSHIP, 1960–2015

Source: Migration Policy Institute

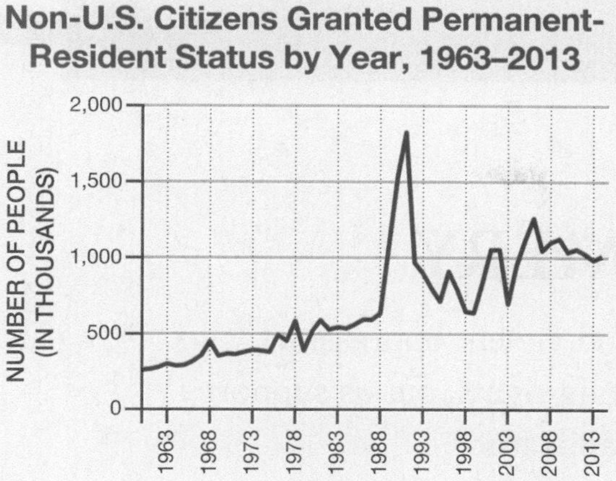

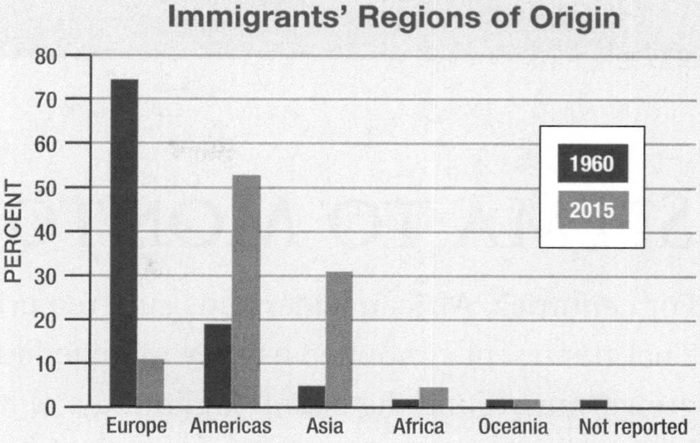

Both programs grew rapidly, reaching as many as 40 million Americans by 1970. Supporters pointed to statistics showing an increase in life expectancy and a drop in infant mortality as a result of the programs. However, opponents argued the programs led to high costs and gaps in coverage, while the quality of care patients received through the programs was low.

The Great Society also included an important new immigration law that went largely unnoticed at the time. In one bold sweep, the **Immigration Act of 1965** removed the national origins quotas as well as the ban on Asians, which dated back to 1924. Although it capped the number of immigrants allowed into the country at about 300,000 per year, the law permitted many foreign family members of American citizens to enter the United States without limit. Immigration from Asia and Latin America grew rapidly. By the mid-1970s, the majority of legal immigrants came from seven Asian and Latin American countries: Korea, Taiwan, India, the Philippines, Cuba, the Dominican Republic, and Mexico. The law had a dramatic impact on the **demographic composition** of the United States, which refers to the number and concentration of a variety of ethnic groups within the nation.

THE DOMINICAN INTERVENTION

The challenges faced by President Johnson and his administration were not confined to domestic issues, however. In 1965, the United States intervened in a civil war in the nearby **Dominican Republic**. The Dominican Republic lies slightly southeast of Cuba and shares the island of Hispaniola with the nation of Haiti.

Until he was assassinated in 1961, General **Rafael Trujillo** (troo-HEE-yoh) had ruled over the Dominican Republic as a dictator for more than 30 years. Although a brutal leader, he opposed communism, earning U.S. support. His death created a power vacuum, and the government was unstable for several years. In 1965, civil war broke out. In April of that year, Johnson sent in thousands of U.S. Marines, who joined troops from the Organization of American States in an attempt to bring the chaotic situation under control. The official reason for Johnson's action, which became known as the **Dominican Intervention**, was to rescue Americans on the island. However, the actual reason for the intervention was to keep communism from spreading to other Caribbean nations.

The strategy worked. The troops put down the rebellion within a few weeks, and the OAS restored a democratically elected government to the Dominican Republic. While the outcome was positive, Johnson was widely criticized for using American military might to interfere in the government of another nation. This criticism grew as the United States became involved even more deeply in a fight against communism in Vietnam, half a world away.

HISTORICAL THINKING

1. **READING CHECK** What was the Great Society?
2. **ASK AND ANSWER QUESTIONS** Read about cost-benefit analysis in the online Financial Literacy Handbook. Generate a list of questions you could ask to help determine how society benefits economically from the reduction of poverty.
3. **INTERPRET GRAPHS** Which region of the world experienced the largest decrease in immigration to the United States from 1960 to 2015?

11.11.1 Discuss the reasons for the nation's changing immigration policy, with emphasis on how the Immigration Act of 1965 and successor acts have transformed American society; HI 6 Students conduct cost-benefit analyses and apply basic economic indicators to analyze the aggregate economic behavior of the U.S. economy.

 MAIN IDEA Dr. Martin Luther King, Jr., led marches in the South that resulted in the Voting Rights Act of 1965.

SELMA TO MONTGOMERY

For centuries, African Americans suffered cruel and violent oppression. That treatment continued as they marched for voting rights, but as support grew from around the country, glimmers of hope appeared.

MARCHING FOR EQUALITY

As you have read, Dr. Martin Luther King, Jr., viewed the 1964 Civil Rights Act as a victory for racial equality, but he felt it fell short in terms of voting rights. Securing equal voting rights for all, King and other civil rights leaders believed, was the next battle to wage. One place where the fight was already underway was Selma, Alabama, where in 1963 SNCC and other local activists had organized a "Freedom Day." Lines formed around the block as 350 African-American people appeared at the courthouse to register to vote. Facing strong white resistance, the activists asked King and SCLC for support.

In the first of a series of 1965 voting rights marches, Alabama police gave demonstrators two minutes to turn around at the Edmund Pettus Bridge. The marchers paused, but the police advanced anyway and beat the demonstrators, sending more than 50 people to the hospital on what became known as Bloody Sunday.

11.10 Students analyze the development of federal civil rights and voting rights; 11.10.4 Examine the roles of civil rights advocates (e.g., A. Philip Randolph, Martin Luther King, Jr., Malcom X, Thurgood Marshall, James Farmer, Rosa Parks), including the significance of Martin Luther King, Jr.'s "Letter from Birmingham Jail" and "I Have a Dream" speech.

Freedom Day led to the Selma voting rights campaign that began early in 1965. Local African Americans marched daily to the courthouse, where Sheriff Jim Clark—wearing a huge button bearing the single word *NEVER*—turned them away with force. Thousands were beaten with clubs, shocked with cattle prods, and arrested for attempting to register with the local election board.

On March 7, a day that would be remembered as **Bloody Sunday**, 700 people set out to walk 50 miles to the state capital on the first of 3 **Selma-to-Montgomery marches**. Leading the procession was a key organizer of the march, **John Lewis**, a representative of SNCC. Upon crossing the Edmund Pettus Bridge at the edge of Selma, Lewis and the marchers found their way blocked by a large contingent of Sheriff Clark's deputies and Alabama state police. When the peaceful marchers refused orders to disperse, the police attacked them with clubs, whips, and tear gas. The police officers forced the marchers to retreat while white onlookers cheered. Dozens of marchers were injured, and some required hospitalization. News crews captured the assault on film. That evening, television stations aired the shocking footage into millions of American homes, sparking national outrage and calls for government action to protect voting rights.

On March 9, a crowd of 2,000 people gathered with King for the second march. Roughly a third were religious leaders who had rushed to Selma to show their support. When they crossed the Edmund Pettus Bridge and again faced a roadblock, the marchers knelt in prayer. Then, instead of attempting to continue on to Montgomery, they turned back. That night in Selma, a group of white segregationists attacked three white Unitarian Universalist ministers who had participated in the march. One of the ministers, James Reeb, died from his injuries two days later.

On March 21, a third attempt at the march to Montgomery got underway, with King leading roughly 3,200 marchers out of Selma. Under the terms of a ruling by a federal judge, more than 1,800 members of the Alabama National Guard under federal command, as well as roughly 2,000 U.S. soldiers, federal marshals, and FBI agents, protected the marchers. The protesters walked about 12 miles each day and slept in fields along the highway at night. Their numbers grew along the way, and on the fifth day, 25,000 marchers arrived at the steps of the state capitol for a final rally.

VOTING RIGHTS ACT OF 1965

In early August 1965, less than five months after the Selma-to-Montgomery marches, Congress passed the **Voting Rights Act of 1965**, and President Johnson signed it into law. The act outlawed literacy tests and other discriminatory tactics used by segregationists to deny African Americans and other minorities the right to vote. It also required states with a history of voting discrimination to obtain approval from federal authorities for any changes, even minor ones, to their voting laws or practices. The act did not ban poll taxes, but it directed the U.S. attorney general to challenge their constitutionality wherever they were found to be in use in local and state elections.

It did not take long for the impact of this **landmark legislation**, or important and historic law, to be felt. By the end of 1965, as many as 250,000 new African-American voters had been registered, and within three years, the registration rate of African Americans in the South had climbed to more than 60 percent. Although challenged in the courts because it changed the relationship of the federal and state governments, the Supreme Court upheld the act's constitutionality in 1966 and in 1968. With the Civil Rights Act of 1964 and the Voting Rights Act of 1965, the civil rights movement had been the most important stimulus in moving the federal government to ensure and protect African-American civil rights, including voting rights.

The movement used grassroots activism to mobilize the government into defending those rights for all citizens. Through the efforts of grassroots organizations and the leadership of presidents Kennedy and Johnson, the civil rights movement made great strides in the 1960s in the South. Discrimination was most visible and dramatic there, but African Americans also faced obstacles in the North, where there was still much work to be done.

HISTORICAL THINKING

1. **READING CHECK** How did the passage of the Civil Rights Act of 1964 and the Voting Rights Act of 1965 affect the nation?
2. **MAKE CONNECTIONS** Describe the role of the government, citizens, and religious leaders in the civil rights movement.
3. **SYNTHESIZE** How did the Selma marches represent the role of civil rights advocates in ensuring the ability of African Americans to vote in elections?

11.10.6 Analyze the passage and effects of civil rights and voting rights legislation (e.g., 1964 Civil Rights Act, Voting Rights Act of 1965) and the Twenty-Fourth Amendment, with an emphasis on equality of access to education and to the political process.

2.4 **MAIN IDEA** Between 1956 and 1968, new African-American leaders emerged who favored militancy and separatism over nonviolence and integration, and King shifted the focus of the civil rights movement to the North.

NEW LEADERS AND CHALLENGES

By the mid-1960s, many African Americans were growing increasingly impatient with the slow pace of racial progress in the United States. Was it time to abandon the nonviolent tactics preached by King in favor of a more militant approach?

SEGREGATION OUTSIDE THE SOUTH

From its beginnings in the early 20th century, the civil rights movement had focused on the South, where African Americans faced blatant discrimination and ***de jure* segregation**—separation enforced by law. In other regions of the country, however, African Americans and other minorities also confronted discrimination, though it was perhaps less extreme than in the South. Northern states had not passed laws mandating racial separation, but it existed anyway. ***De facto* segregation**, or segregation that is present in society despite there being no laws to enforce it, greatly affected urban areas. Many African Americans lived in public housing where crime was rampant, public services were poor, and schools were inferior. Banks often refused home loans to African Americans who sought to buy houses outside their traditional neighborhoods. Many people self-segregated simply to avoid ugly conflicts. And yet conflicts arose and anger was building.

One catalyst for frustration was police targeting of and violence against African Americans. For instance, in August 1965, a white police officer pulled an African-American motorist over on suspicion of impaired driving in the predominantly African-American section of south central Los Angeles known as Watts. African-American drivers were often pulled over and cited for traffic infractions, founded or not. The incident escalated into an argument, which in turn sparked a riot. Rioters looted stores and burned down hundreds of buildings. When police officers clashed with the rioters, at least 34 people died and more than 1,000 were injured. The violent clashes between residents and police, which became known as the **Watts Riots**, continued for 6 days. The following year, similar conflicts rocked Chicago, Detroit, Cleveland, Newark, and other U.S. cities.

THE BLACK POWER MOVEMENT

At the time of these riots, King's leadership in the civil rights movement was coming under increasing criticism due to a split between generations. On one side were "old" civil rights groups, such as King's and the NAACP, which saw racial integration and nonviolent resistance as the keys to African-American advancement. On the other side were "new" movement groups, such as SNCC, who embraced more forceful and even violent strategies.

At a 1966 rally in Mississippi, an activist named **Stokely Carmichael** who had just served time in jail for peacefully protesting, set out to fire up the crowd by yelling about "Black Power." The phrase became a rallying cry for many younger African Americans. To some, it meant group strength and independent action. To the more radical **black separatists**—those like Carmichael who believed in the political and cultural division of African Americans and whites—it meant taking extreme measures to claim their rights and maintain their freedoms. The radicals felt that African Americans should work together to gain economic power in order to create a separate nation within the United States. As you have read, these ideas were central to black nationalism, a movement Marcus Garvey originally embraced in the early 20th century.

One of the most extreme of the "new" movement groups was the **Black Panther Party**, founded in Oakland, California, in 1966 by **Huey Newton** and **Bobby Seale**. Its original mission was to conduct heavily armed patrols to protect African-American neighborhoods from police brutality and harassment. It also began an effective free-lunch program for children, but as the party grew, it evolved into a revolutionary movement that fiercely opposed

CRITICAL VIEWING Black Panther Party members hold a vigil outside a New York City courthouse on April 11, 1969, to protest the arrest of party members accused of criminal activities related to terrorism. The arrested men were acquitted more than one year later. Why do you think the photographer included the Abraham Lincoln quote "the ultimate justice of the people" in the photograph of the Black Panthers?

American society. The Black Panthers demanded that the government release all African Americans from prison and pay reparations for slavery. They won modest support for their community work but lost influence when a few members were jailed for committing crimes such as extortion, or obtaining money through forceful coercion, and drug-dealing. The Panthers became a feared enemy and primary target of local, state, and federal law enforcement. While they never received the mainstream support that the general civil rights movement did, their emphasis on racial pride, their celebration of black culture, and their powerful criticisms of racism continue to influence American culture today.

MALCOLM X AND THE NATION OF ISLAM

Newton and Seale had been strongly influenced by **Malcolm X**, one of the most controversial African-American activists of the 1960s. Malcolm X, born Malcolm Little and later known as el-Hajj Malik el-Shabazz, adopted the "X" to replace Little, the slave name imposed on his ancestors by their slave master. In the late 1940s, while serving in prison for robbery, Malcolm X became a member of the **Nation of Islam**, a religious black nationalist movement founded in Detroit in 1930. The organization preached a doctrine of self-help, moral discipline, and complete separation of the races. Members of the Nation of Islam, also called Black Muslims, were forbidden to smoke, drink alcohol, or eat pork.

11.10.4 Examine the roles of civil rights advocates (e.g., A. Philip Randolph, Martin Luther King, Jr., Malcolm X, Thurgood Marshall, James Farmer, Rosa Parks), including the significance of Martin Luther King, Jr.'s "Letter from Birmingham Jail" and "I Have a Dream" speech.

While at a New York City rally, Malcolm X held up the *Muhammad Speaks* newspaper, emphasizing his consistent message: "Our Freedom Can't Wait!"

Malcolm X quickly rose to a position of prominence within the Nation of Islam and helped it to achieve explosive growth. In fiery speeches, he denounced white American society for the injustices it inflicted on African Americans. He also scorned King's tactics of nonviolence and civil disobedience. He preached self-defense, saying that African Americans must protect themselves "by any means necessary" and that "killing is a two-way street." Malcolm X's intense philosophy made it easy to interpret the Nation of Islam's message as one of violence and hate.

In 1963, tensions developed between Malcolm X and **Elijah Muhammad**, the leader of the Nation of Islam, and in early 1964 Muhammad expelled Malcolm from the religion. After making a pilgrimage to the Muslim holy city of Mecca, Malcolm renounced some of the more extreme ideas he had espoused in the past, including racial separatism. Upon returning to the United States, Malcolm continued to speak out against racism and work for change, despite threats against his life from members of the Nation of Islam. In February 1965, they followed through with their threats, assassinating Malcolm X as he gave a speech in Harlem.

THE MOVEMENT MOVES NORTH

As rioting shook northern cities and the Black Power movement grew, Dr. King decided to take the civil rights movement to the North and broaden its scope. He focused his efforts on fighting poverty among African Americans and on opposing U.S. military involvement in the Vietnam War. Speaking in New York City in April 1967, he pointed out the contradiction of sending young African-American men 8,000 miles away "to guarantee liberties in Southeast Asia which they had not found in southwest Georgia and East Harlem."

On April 3, 1968, King led a peaceful march in Memphis in support of a strike by sanitation workers. The following day, while King was standing on the balcony of the Lorraine Motel, a white segregationist named James Earl Ray shot and killed him. The nation mourned the assassination of the civil rights movement's most famous leader. But King's words would have enduring effects on American life as his legacy continued with the work of other supporters, including President Johnson.

The rioting and segregation that had troubled King also troubled President Johnson. Johnson had established the National Advisory Commission on Civil Disorders in 1967, also known as the Kerner Commission, to study the causes of urban riots. He appointed Illinois governor Otto Kerner to lead it. In its report, the commission concluded that the United States was "moving toward two societies, one black, one white—separate and unequal." The report criticized the media for failing to cover the violent

11.10.1 Explain how demands of African Americans helped produce a stimulus for civil rights, including President Roosevelt's ban on racial discrimination in defense industries in 1941, and how African Americans' service in World War II produced a stimulus for President Truman's decision to end segregation in the armed forces in 1948; 11.10.2 Examine and analyze the key events, policies and court cases in the evolution of civil rights, including *Dred Scot* v. *Sandford*, *Plessy* v. *Ferguson*, *Brown* v. *Board of Education*, *Regents of the University of California* v. *Bakke*, and California Proposition 209.

This iconic photograph by South African photographer Joseph Louw was taken immediately after Martin Luther King, Jr.'s assassination on April 4, 1968. King lies on the hotel balcony, bleeding from a neck wound, while aides point to the opposite rooftop where they had seen the shooter, James Earl Ray, fleeing after firing at King.

protests from the rioters' perspective and concluded by stating "the press has too long basked in a white world, looking out of it, if at all, with white men's eyes and a white perspective."

As you have read, Johnson's administration developed strategies for expanding the welfare state and providing a broader safety net for vulnerable Americans as part of his Great Society program. One of these strategies demonstrated the government's commitment to providing education to all Americans. You have read about the Elementary and Secondary Education Act, which Johnson signed into law in 1965. This act provided federal funding to ensure that all children regardless of race, ethnicity, religion, or sex received equal educational opportunities.

Still, schools remained unequal because of *de facto* segregation, so courts ordered **busing**, or transporting students of all races to schools outside their school districts or neighborhoods to assure integration and therefore equal opportunity. Busing sparked controversy and legal challenges. In the 1971 case ***Swann* v. *Charlotte-Mecklenburg Board of Education***, the Supreme Court unanimously upheld busing programs. Three years later, however, in ***Milliken* v. *Bradley*** (1974), the Court struck down a plan to desegregate schools in Detroit by busing students between the predominantly African-American city and its predominantly white suburbs.

Supreme Court rulings continued to expand the government's role in supporting civil rights. In the 1967 case ***Loving* v. *Virginia***, the Court cited a violation of the 14th Amendment when it overturned Virginia state laws prohibiting **miscegenation**, or marriage between people of different races. The Court's decision abolished anti-miscegenation laws around the country.

Another strategy of the Johnson administration was **affirmative action**, a government policy that institutes racial quotas to favor groups that suffer from discrimination. The goal of supporters of affirmative action was to improve educational and employment opportunities for all Americans. Like school busing, affirmative action ignited controversy and was challenged in court. In the 1978 case, ***Regents of the University of California* v. *Bakke***, the Supreme Court ruled that affirmative action programs were constitutional in some circumstances but that quotas based solely on race were not.

HISTORICAL THINKING

1. **READING CHECK** In the 1960s, what were some of the challenges African Americans faced in the North?
2. **COMPARE AND CONTRAST** On which issues did the "old" and "new" civil rights activists disagree?
3. **INTERPRET VISUALS** In addition to the headline, what message do you think Malcolm X wanted to convey when he held up the newspaper?
4. **IDENTIFY MAIN IDEAS AND DETAILS** What were the Johnson administration's strategies for fighting segregation and poverty?

11.10.5 Discuss the diffusion of the civil rights movement of African Americans from the churches of the rural South and the urban North, including the resistance to racial desegregation in Little Rock and Birmingham, and how the advances influenced the agendas, strategies, and effectiveness of the quests of American Indians, Asian Americans, and Hispanic Americans for civil rights and equal opportunities; 11.10.6 Analyze the passage and effects of civil rights and voting rights legislation (e.g., 1964 Civil Rights Act, Voting Rights Act of 1965) and the Twenty-Fourth Amendment, with an emphasis on equality of access to education and to the political process.

NATIONAL CIVIL RIGHTS MUSEUM MEMPHIS, TENNESSEE

The National Civil Rights Museum has a fascinating ocation: the grounds of the Lorraine Motel, where Dr. Martin Luther King, Jr., was assassinated in 1968 while staying in Memphis, Tennessee. Visitors reflect upon this important historical site while viewing the museum's impressive collection of historic objects, documents, and photographs spanning five centuries of African-American history—from the beginning of the resistance to slavery through the Civil War, Reconstruction, the rise of Jim Crow, and the civil rights movement. The National Civil Rights Museum's exhibits center around African-American history and the quest for racial equality in the United States, but also feature the culture of slavery and international human rights. The museum's mission is clear: to educate, inform, and inspire.

The museum's four-acre site includes the Lorraine Motel (shown below) and its related buildings and the nearby Young and Morrow Building, from which James Earl Ray fired the shot that killed Dr. King.

oom 306

r. Martin Luther King, Jr., was a frequent guest at the orraine Motel in downtown Memphis. He stayed there in pril 1968 while in town to support a strike by sanitation orkers. On April 4, he spent the day at the motel with his rother and aides. When Dr. King stepped onto the balcony utside his room to talk to friends, he was shot in the neck om across the street. Motel owner Walter Bailey never ented room 306 again, turning it instead into a memorial. s part of the museum's collection, room 306 has been reserved exactly as it looked on that tragic night.

11.10.4 Examine the roles of civil rights advocates (e.g., A. Philip Randolph, Martin Luther King, Jr., Malcolm X, Thurgood Marshall, James Farmer, Rosa Parks), including the significance of Martin Luther King, Jr.'s "Letter from Birmingham Jail"

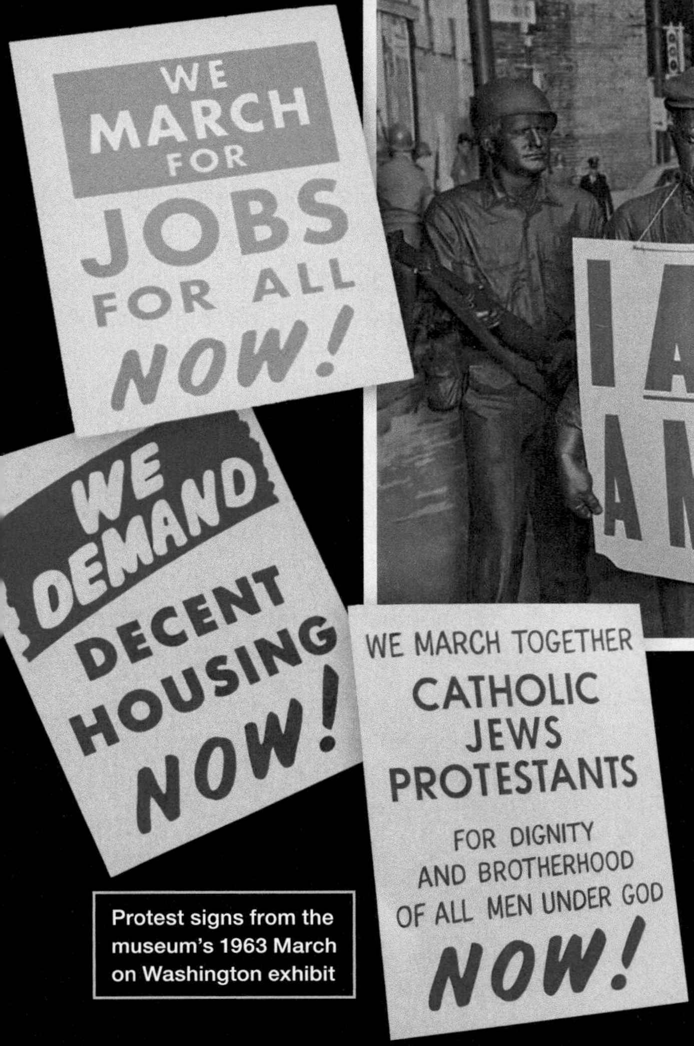

Protest signs from the museum's 1963 March on Washington exhibit

"I Am a Man" Exhibit

This museum exhibit tells the story of the 1968 sanitation strike that drew Dr. King to Memphis during what would become his final days. Represented in bronze statues, strikers holding iconic "I am a man" signs—designed to humanize the protesters—appear in front of National Guard troops, while footage from the strike is projected onto a garbage truck. The exhibit also features footage from Dr. King's famous "I've Been to the Mountaintop" speech, which he gave in Memphis the day before his assassination.

Black Panther Jacket

The museum's Black Power exhibit highlights the rise and fall of one of the most influential movements in civil rights history: the Black Panther Party.

The black leather jacket shown here was worn in the late 1960s by Cyril Innis, Jr., of the Corona, New York, chapter of the Black Panthers. The museum's collection also includes a beret and a crossed fist necklace worn by party members. Black Panther Party founders Huey P. Newton and Bobby Seale encouraged members to dress neatly in a uniform consisting of a light blue shirt under a black leather jacket, black pants and shoes, a black beret, and black gloves.

What impact do you think historical events such as the assassination of Dr. King and the fall of the Black Power movement had on the civil rights movement?

HI 4 Students understand the meaning, implication, and impact of historical events and recognize that events could have taken other directions.

REVIEW

VOCABULARY

Use each of the terms below in a sentence that expresses an understanding about an event or topic from the chapter.

1. affirmative action HSS 11.10.2
2. ballistic missiles HSS 11.9.3
3. bipartisan HSS 11.10.6
4. disenfranchise HSS 11.10
5. *de facto* segregation HSS 11.10.6
6. miscegenation HSS 11.10.2
7. Medicare HSS 11.11.6
8. New Frontier HSS 11.8.5
9. space race HSS 11.8.7

READING STRATEGY

DRAW CONCLUSIONS

Drawing conclusions can help a reader make connections and better understand the text. Complete the following chart to draw conclusions about how the domestic policies of Kennedy and Johnson affected the United States.

Text Clues	What I Know	My Conclusions
"optimism and confidence in problem solving"	Kennedy developed new programs and approaches.	Kennedy looked forward to the future in responding to problems.

10. How did Kennedy's and Johnson's domestic policies impact the United States? HSS 11.8

MAIN IDEAS

Answer the following questions. Support your answers with evidence from the chapter.

11. What were Kennedy's first two challenges? **LESSON 1.1** HSS 11.9.3
12. Why did the Soviet Union build the Berlin Wall? **LESSON 1.1** HSS 11.9.3
13. What was the purpose of the international treaty the United States and the Soviet Union signed in 1963? **LESSON 1.2** HSS 11.9.3
14. What event sparked the Cuban Missile Crisis? **LESSON 1.3** HSS 11.9.3
15. What is the main function of the Equal Employment Opportunity Commission? **LESSON 2.1** HSS 11.10.6
16. How did southern members of Congress try to kill the Civil Rights Act? **LESSON 2.1** HSS 11.10.6
17. What was the collective name of Johnson's reform policies designed to relieve economic inequality in the United States? **LESSON 2.2** HSS 11.11
18. What did the Immigration Act of 1965 eliminate? **LESSON 2.2** HSS 11.11.1
19. How was the Civil Rights Act of 1964 different from previous civil rights legislation? **LESSON 2.3** HSS 11.10. 2
20. What was the goal of the Selma-to-Montgomery marches? **LESSON 2.3** HSS 11.10. 2
21. In what ways did Stokely Carmichael's phrase "Black Power" divide the civil rights movement? **LESSON 2.4** HSS 11.10.4

HISTORICAL THINKING

Answer the following questions. Support your answers with evidence from the chapter.

22. **FORM AND SUPPORT OPINIONS** Using information from the chapter, explain whether and why you think a cost-benefit analysis would have supported continuing the Alliance for Progress program. HSS HI 6
23. **ANALYZE CAUSE AND EFFECT** How did the Cuban Missile Crisis ultimately make the world safer, and how could events surrounding it have taken a different direction? HSS HI 4

24. **FORM AND SUPPORT OPINIONS** Would you have agreed with senators supporting the Immigration Act of 1965 or with those opposing the bill? Write a brief paragraph explaining your response. HSS 11.11.1

25. **COMPARE AND CONTRAST** How were the presidencies of Kennedy and Johnson similar and different in terms of their accomplishments, problems, and impact on larger social, economic, and political trends? HSS HI 1

INTERPRET GRAPHS

Look closely at the graph below. Use information from the chapter and in the graph to answer the questions that follow.

U.S. National Spending and Debt, 1960–1968

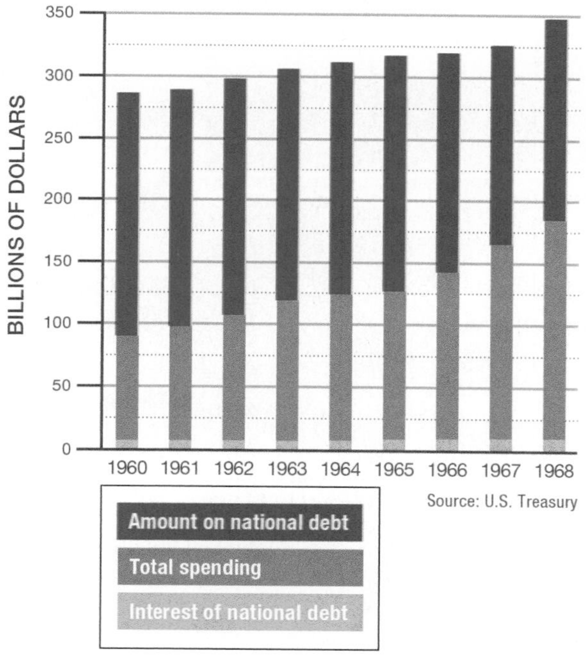

26. Based on what you know about programs and issues during the Kennedy and Johnson administrations, how would you explain the trend in government spending shown in the graph? HSS 11.8.4

27. According to the graph, how are changes in spending reflected in changes in the national debt, or the amount of money the government has borrowed, and in the interest on that debt? HSS 11.8.4

ANALYZE SOURCES

The space race was both an idealistic vision and important to national security. Here, in interviews, two of the seven Mercury astronauts, Wally Schirra and Scott Carpenter, express different thoughts about the meaning of the effort.

> The challenge was that Kennedy had made a mess in Cuba at the Bay of Pigs, and he had to do something to look good. The . . . concept of going to the moon and back before the decade was out was quite a goal, which we all accepted, because we loved the man. —Wally Schirra, 2007
>
> I am so overjoyed that the competition has now [changed] into cooperation. Space is not an enterprise that belongs to the United States or to Russia or to China—it is a human endeavor.
> —Scott Carpenter, 2012

28. What different messages do Schirra and Carpenter convey about the American space program, and what evidence do you see of bias and prejudice in the historical interpretations of these individuals? HSS HREP 2

CONNECT TO YOUR LIFE

29. **ARGUMENT** Many people questioned President Kennedy's proposal to spend billions of dollars to put a man on the moon within 10 years. Suppose a president of the United States proposed to commit trillions of dollars to colonizing Mars within 10 years. Write a short argument stating reasons why you would or would not support such an endeavor. HSS CST 1

TIPS

- Evaluate the consequences of Kennedy's plan and determine the lessons that were learned.
- Summarize your viewpoint and your reasoning clearly before you present your points in more depth.
- Use textual evidence from the chapter in supporting your argument.
- Include reasons why the United States should or should not invest in such a goal.
- Counter the strengths of the opposing viewpoint with your own position.

CHAPTER 18

THE VIETNAM WAR

1954–1975

HISTORICAL THINKING How did the Vietnam War affect Americans at home and on the battlefield?

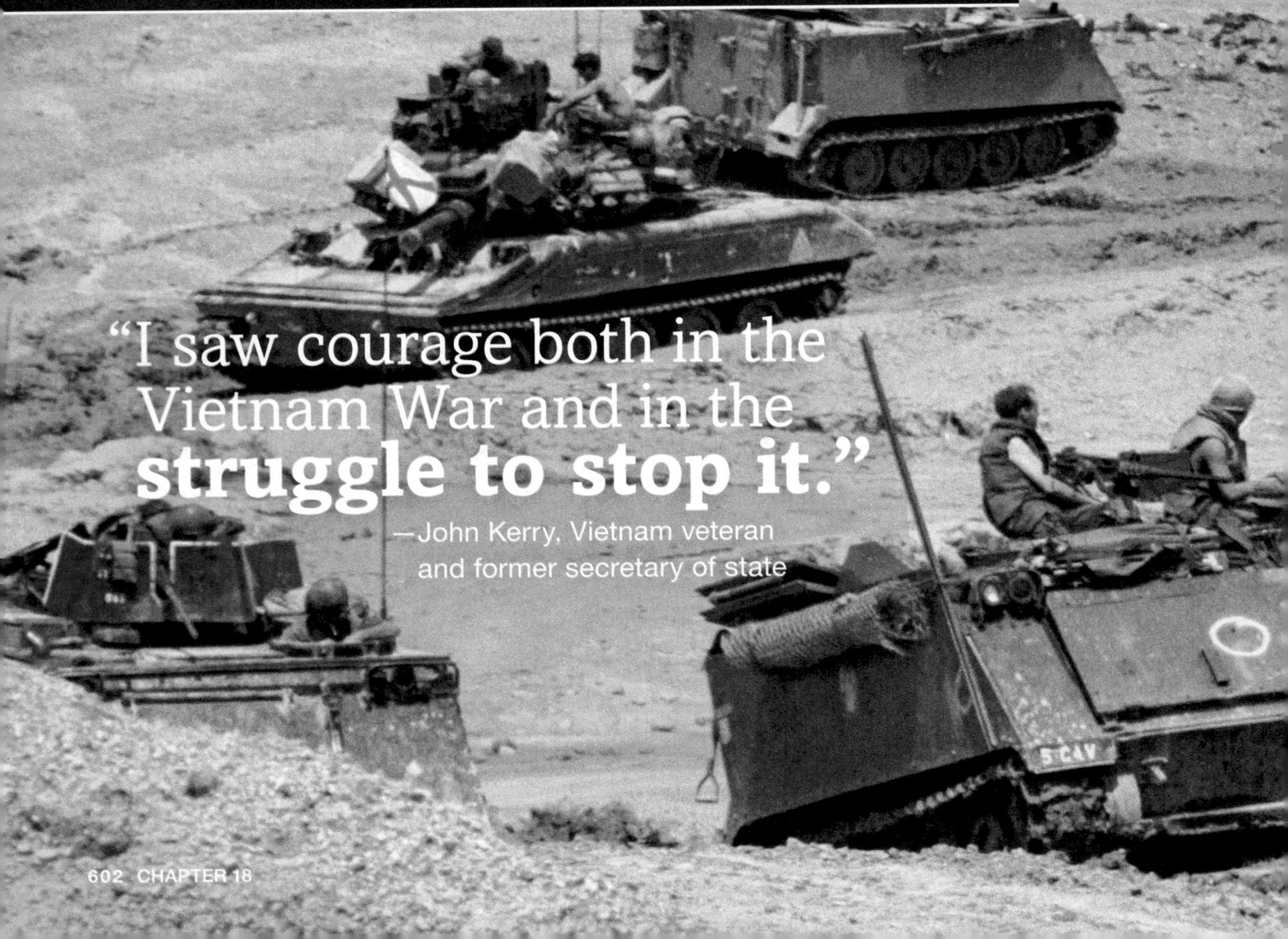

"I saw courage both in the Vietnam War and in the **struggle to stop it.**"

—John Kerry, Vietnam veteran and former secretary of state

In this photo taken in 1971, U.S. soldiers maneuver their tanks through the rugged, mountainous terrain of Quang Tri Province. At the time of the Vietnam War, the South Vietnamese province bordered communist North Vietnam and was the site of several fierce battles. Vietnam's mountains, jungles, and dense forests posed a challenge for American troops throughout the war.

1.1 **MAIN IDEA** The United States supported the anticommunist government that arose in South Vietnam, but the South Vietnamese leader proved to be a tyrant.

THE COLD WAR IN THE THIRD WORLD

If you've ever fought for a cause you believed was just, you probably encountered some obstacles along the way. The United States would run into quite a few as it tried to halt the spread of communism in Southeast Asia.

After Ngo Dinh Diem formed South Vietnam and made himself its president in 1955, tribesmen from the country's mountains and plateaus came to pledge their loyalty to him. Here, President Diem (seated) receives gifts from the tribesmen.

CONFRONTING COMMUNISM IN ASIA

In the 1950s and 1960s, the U.S. government focused to a large extent on domestic policy, particularly on civil rights for African Americans. But foreign policy and events in Southeast Asia also claimed the attention of several presidents during this period, beginning with Dwight Eisenhower. Remember reading about the victory of Ho Chi Minh's communist forces against the French in the Southeast Asian country of Vietnam? After the decisive Battle of Dien Bien Phu in 1954, a peace agreement negotiated in Geneva, Switzerland, temporarily divided the country roughly in half.

According to the **Geneva Accords**, which detailed the terms of the agreement, Vietnam was split along the 17th parallel. Ho and the Viet Minh governed the northern part of the country, while the French colonial government remained in the south. The accords also called for free democratic elections in 1956, the withdrawal of the French from Indochina, and the reunification of Vietnam under a national government. In 1955, however, **Ngo Dinh Diem** (ungh-oh dihn zih-EHM), the prime minister of the southern part of the country, founded the Republic of Vietnam, or South Vietnam, and proclaimed himself its president. During Ho's anti-imperialist revolution against the French, Diem had lived for a time in the United States.

The United States fully backed Diem and his new government. Eisenhower embraced President Harry Truman's containment policy to prevent the spread of communism throughout Asia. To achieve that goal, Eisenhower believed that an anticommunist government had to be established in South Vietnam, which was considered a "third world" country. During the Cold War, a country that was not aligned with either the United States or the Soviet Union was called a **third world** country. Communist and democratic forces struggled to gain influence over third world countries. The United States used the Southeast Asia Treaty Organization (SEATO) to justify its increasing involvement in Southeast Asia after the French conceded to the Vietnamese in 1956. You may recall that the United States and other countries, including France, Great Britain, Thailand, and the Philippines, formed SEATO in 1955 to help prevent communist expansion in Southeast Asia. The United States claimed Vietnam as a whole to be a territory that fell under SEATO protection.

DIEM'S GOVERNMENT

Diem had declared that he would uphold democratic principles as stipulated by the Geneva Accords. However, with Eisenhower's support and encouragement, he refused to allow free elections to take place in 1956. Instead, he ruled

This North Vietnamese poster shows two soldiers and a worker standing in front of the Thang Hoa Bridge. In 1945, the Viet Minh destroyed the bridge (nicknamed Ham Rong, or "Dragon's Jaw") to prevent the French from transporting arms across it. The bridge was rebuilt in 1957.

11.9.2 Understand the role of military alliances, including NATO and SEATO, in deterring communist aggression and maintaining security during the Cold War.

On July 17, 1963, police set up barbed wire to block a demonstration at the Giac Minh pagoda in Saigon during the Buddhist crisis. In this photo, demonstrators try to pull down the barbed wire. The police beat and arrested some of the protesters.

as an **autocrat**, a tyrant with absolute power, and appointed members of his own wealthy family to serve in the highest levels of his government. For example, Diem's younger brother was his chief advisor.

Furthermore, even though the majority of Vietnamese people were Buddhist, Diem, a Roman Catholic, strongly favored those of his own faith. He filled his government with Catholics and retained the anti-Buddhist laws the French had put in place. On the positive side, Diem provided refuge in his country for the hundreds of thousands of Vietnamese fleeing communist rule in the north. However, he dealt harshly with **insurgents**, or rebels, within his country who belonged to the National Liberation Front, or **Viet Cong**. These insurgents tried to spread communism among the South Vietnamese and wage war against Diem's government. Diem put his younger brother in charge of a special army unit that tracked down communists and imprisoned or killed them. Even those who were only suspected of aiding the rebels—often with little or no evidence—were likely to meet the same fate.

Diem's heavy-handed tactics against the insurgents and his treatment of Buddhists made him increasingly unpopular among the people of South Vietnam. Nonetheless, presidents John Kennedy and Lyndon Johnson continued to support President Eisenhower's domino theory, formulated in 1954. As you may recall, this theory states that if one Southeast Asian country were to become communist, all the rest would follow like falling dominoes. Kennedy and Johnson used the domino theory to explain the presence of the U.S. military in South Vietnam.

THE BUDDHIST CRISIS

Eisenhower began to send military personnel and aid to South Vietnam in 1955. By the time Kennedy became president in January 1961, however, this aid effort had decreased. An anticommunist, Kennedy revitalized the effort and sent 500 Special Forces troops as military advisors to South Vietnam in May. Kennedy ignored the advice of French general Charles de Gaulle, who warned him that war in Vietnam would drag the United States into "a bottomless military and political swamp." The American president continued to send military advisors to South Vietnam until their numbers totaled about 16,000 in 1963.

PRIMARY SOURCE

For Lam Quang Thi, the years from 1950 to 1975 were the most important of the 20th century. He spent that time serving in South Vietnam's army. Thi wrote about his experiences as a soldier and general in his memoir, *The Twenty-Five Year Century*. In this excerpt from the memoir, Thi recalls the pagoda raids in August 1963.

We heard the news of the raids on the pagodas in Saigon by armed troops. More than 1,400 monks had been arrested and some of them had been beaten. This brutal act of repression . . . sealed the fate of the regime and marked the beginning of its downfall. Washington . . . was stunned by the pagoda raids. President Kennedy . . . authorized the suspension of economic subsidies for South Vietnam's commercial imports and a cutoff of financial aid to the Vietnamese Special Forces. The financial assistance would resume only under the specific condition that the Special Forces be put under the control of the Joint General Staff . . . who were plotting against the regime.

—from *The Twenty-Five Year Century*, by Lam Quang Thi, 2001

Meanwhile, Diem's discrimination against Buddhists reached a critical point. On May 7, 1963, government forces angered Buddhists by tearing down the religious flags they hung on homes and buildings in the city of Hue (HWAY). Diem had passed a law against such displays, but up to that point, the law had not been enforced. In protest, a crowd of more than 3,000 Buddhists gathered the next day—on the Buddha's birthday—and marched to the center of town. Later that evening, as the protests continued, soldiers fired bullets and tossed grenades at the crowd, killing 8 people and seriously injuring another 4. Diem blamed the Buddhists for the violence.

Seeking nonviolent solutions, Buddhist clergy presented a list of demands to the government. They asked the government to grant Buddhists the right to display their flags, worship freely, and enjoy the same rights as Catholics. Some Buddhists also staged hunger strikes. Kennedy encouraged Diem to reform his policy toward the Buddhists, but Diem ignored his advice. Finally, in June, 500 monks and nuns gathered in Saigon, South Vietnam's capital. They watched while a monk immolated himself, or burned himself to death, to protest Diem's treatment of Buddhists. A photographer captured the event, drawing worldwide attention to the Buddhists' plight in South Vietnam.

Protests continued throughout the summer, and more Buddhist monks and nuns immolated themselves. Then, on August 21, Diem declared martial law, giving military forces, rather than the police, the authority to enforce order. That night, the military raided Buddhist pagodas in cities throughout South Vietnam. When monks and nuns used sticks and stones to resist the soldiers, many were arrested on charges of possessing weapons.

As the Buddhist crisis continued, the United States began to distance itself from Diem and withdraw its support from his government. When officers in the South Vietnamese Army approached U.S. officials about staging a **coup** (KOO), or an illegal overthrow of the government, the Americans stated they would do nothing to prevent it. According to some accounts, in fact, the U.S. officials even encouraged the action. As a result, Diem was arrested on November 1, 1963, and assassinated the next day.

Diem's death caused political instability in South Vietnam. A series of military leaders followed who, like Diem, never actually instituted a democratic government. As you know, President Kennedy was also assassinated in November 1963. Under President Johnson, U.S. engagement in South Vietnam increased. As in Korea, the United States conducted a proxy war in Vietnam.

HISTORICAL THINKING

1. **READING CHECK** Why did the United States back Ngo Dinh Diem's government?
2. **DRAW CONCLUSIONS** Why did Kennedy suspend financial aid to South Vietnam after the Buddhist pagoda raids?
3. **MAKE INFERENCES** Why do you think the U.S. government did nothing to prevent the coup against Diem?
4. **ANALYZE CAUSE AND EFFECT** What complex string of events led to the assassination of Diem?

HI 2 Students recognize the complexity of historical causes and effects, including the limitations on determining cause and effect.

1.2 **MAIN IDEA** After an incident between the United States and North Vietnam in the Gulf of Tonkin, the war in Vietnam expanded.

GULF OF TONKIN

A challenge by one side in wartime often results in an increase in hostilities by the other side. That's exactly what happened when a perceived threat occurred in the waters off the coast of Vietnam.

UNOFFICIAL DECLARATION OF WAR

When Lyndon Johnson assumed the presidency after John Kennedy's assassination in 1963, he had little foreign policy experience. As a result, he chose to continue the former president's course of action in Southeast Asia. But he also decided to make Vietnam a priority. Determined not to lose South Vietnam to the communists, Johnson intensified the effort there. For example, he authorized the U.S. military to carry out covert operations in North Vietnam and gather information on communist activity. However, Johnson was opposed to sending American ground forces to Vietnam. As he said, "We are not about to send American boys nine or ten thousand miles away from home to do what Asian boys ought to be doing for themselves." Johnson insisted the ultimate responsibility for resolving the conflict lay with the Vietnamese.

Soon, though, several events made him re-evaluate his position. On August 2, 1964, the USS *Maddox* reported that it had been attacked by a North Vietnamese torpedo boat while patrolling off the coast of northern Vietnam in the Gulf of Tonkin. The U.S. destroyer fought off the attack, and the torpedo boat retreated. Then, on August 4, the *Maddox* and another destroyer, the USS *C. Turner Joy*, reported renewed unprovoked attacks. In response, Johnson ordered an air attack on North Vietnamese naval bases and put the **Gulf of Tonkin Resolution** before Congress. The resolution would give the president the power to take any action necessary to repel armed aggression and defend South Vietnam.

Congress passed the resolution within days. Although the resolution was not an official declaration of war against North Vietnam, it came to be considered as such. Almost immediately, however, some people questioned whether the second attack had actually occurred. After reviewing the often contradictory tape recordings from the incident, even Johnson said that the Vietnamese in the boats were probably just "sailors shooting at flying fish!" Others even believed the attack had been provoked by American forces. Nevertheless, the Johnson administration publicly stuck to its official line, claiming the Vietnamese had been the aggressors.

WAR EXPANDS

Johnson's secretary of defense, Robert McNamara, who strongly championed war, made many of the decisions related to the conflict in Vietnam. In fact, over the next few years, the war would come to be called "McNamara's War." As you may remember, McNamara had been part of Kennedy's Cabinet and continued to serve Johnson after the latter won re-election in November 1964. The secretary favored **escalation**, or

11.9.3 Trace the origins and geopolitical consequences (foreign and domestic) of the Cold War and containment policy, including the following: • The era of McCarthyism, instances of domestic Communism (e.g., Alger Hiss) and blacklisting • The Truman Doctrine • The Berlin Blockade • The Korean War • The Bay of Pigs invasion and the Cuban Missile Crisis • Atomic testing in the American West, the "mutual assured destruction" doctrine, and disarmament policies • The Vietnam War • Latin American policy.

On March 8, 1965, about 3,500 Marines landed in Da Nang to protect its airbase. They were the first U.S. combat troops in South Vietnam. Although both the United States and South Vietnam had wanted the troops to come ashore without fanfare, the Marines were greeted by a cheering crowd.

an increase in intensity, of the war. Under McNamara's advice, Johnson increased the number of military advisors in Vietnam to 23,000 and ordered limited air raids on the Ho Chi Minh Trail, a series of connected paths linking North Vietnam with South Vietnam by way of neighboring Laos and Cambodia.

The war escalated further in February 1965. The Viet Cong attacked a U.S. air base at Pleiku (PLAY-koo), South Vietnam, killing eight Americans. Johnson countered by initiating a sustained air bombing campaign of North Vietnam, known as Operation Rolling Thunder. The campaign involved a series of gradually intensified bombings designed to decrease the flow of supplies from North Vietnam to the Viet Cong and force the communists to negotiate a lasting peace. Operation Rolling Thunder would continue for more than three years. During this period, bombs dropped by air strikes on the Ho Chi Minh Trail and other targets in Southeast Asia would be twice the number of those dropped during World War II.

Soon after Rolling Thunder began, Johnson sent the first ground troops to South Vietnam—even though, as you know, he had vowed he would not do so. In the beginning, the troops were instructed to protect U.S. air bases, not to fight. But before long, American soldiers would be drawn into combat as the U.S. military embarked on an air and ground war that aimed to eliminate the communist threat from South Vietnam.

PRIMARY SOURCE

In a televised address on August 4, 1964, Johnson informed the nation about the attacks in the Gulf of Tonkin and the retaliation that would be taken against North Vietnam. In this excerpt from the address, the president paints a frightening picture of the situation.

Aggression by terror against the peaceful villagers of South Vietnam has now been joined by open aggression on the high seas against the United States of America. The determination of all Americans to carry out our full commitment to the people and to the government of South Vietnam will be redoubled [increased all the more] by this outrage. Yet our response, for the present, will be limited and fitting. We Americans know, although others appear to forget, the risks of spreading conflict. We still seek no wider war.

—from President Lyndon B. Johnson's report on the Gulf of Tonkin Incident, August 4, 1964

HISTORICAL THINKING

1. **READING CHECK** What authority did the Gulf of Tonkin Resolution give Johnson?
2. **EVALUATE** Identify examples of bias in Johnson's televised address used to sway the American people into thinking that retaliation against North Vietnam was justified.
3. **FORM AND SUPPORT OPINIONS** Do you think Johnson was right to escalate the war? Cite evidence from the text to support your opinion.

HREP 2 Students identify bias and prejudice in historical interpretations.

2.1 **MAIN IDEA** In Vietnam, the U.S military used strategies against a determined enemy whose own methods proved highly successful.

War Strategies

Imagine running onto a field with a game plan in hand for playing a soccer match only to find you're actually playing baseball. Something like that happened to the U.S. military forces when they came to fight in Vietnam.

HEARTS AND MINDS

The United States employed two key strategies to win the war in Vietnam. First, it planned to use its superior military technology and weaponry to defeat the enemy through both air strikes and ground force operations. Second, it set out to gain the complete support of the South Vietnamese people—to win their hearts and minds. The United States particularly wanted their help in defeating the Viet Cong. But many South Vietnamese believed life under their U.S.-supported government was no better than life under the North Vietnamese communists.

The increasing influx of American troops arriving in South Vietnam did not help win the people's hearts and minds. General **William Westmoreland**,

CRITICAL VIEWING U.S. Army paratroopers wade across a river in the rain, searching for Viet Cong in a jungle area of South Vietnam in September 1965. Paratroopers are military personnel who parachute into a war zone. What details in the photo convey the conditions the soldiers had to deal with?

who had begun commanding the American forces in Vietnam in June 1964, persuaded leaders in Washington to increase the number of ground troops in Vietnam. By the end of 1965, nearly 185,000 American troops had landed. The American soldiers were originally supposed to train the South Vietnamese troops of the Army of the Republic of Vietnam (ARVN). The idea was that, once they were transformed into a strong fighting force, the ARVN would be equipped to combat the communists from the north. Unfortunately, many of the South Vietnamese troops—and their generals—were ineffectual. While some ARVN soldiers were well trained, disciplined, and dedicated to the cause, others were not. In some cases, they were reluctant to fight against those they considered their countrymen. As a result, American troops soon found themselves engaged in actual combat.

Still, Westmoreland hoped to weaken and wear down the North Vietnamese and Viet Cong through a **war of attrition**. The American general thought he could win the war by inflicting heavy losses on the enemy through fighting many small battles that would add up, ultimately, to victory. But the communists refused to back down, no matter how many casualties they suffered. They were engaged in what they considered a national struggle for independence. Men from the North and the South were willing to take the place of fallen soldiers and reoccupy areas that the Americans and ARVN had cleared. The communist forces in Vietnam also benefited from the weapons and other supplies they received from the Soviet Union and China.

A GUERRILLA WAR

General Westmoreland underestimated his enemy's determination. He and other military leaders were also not prepared for the type of war the Vietnamese fought. The United States was supremely ready to fight a conventional war against another industrialized country. But Vietnam was not industrialized, and the Viet Cong and others opposing U.S. forces engaged in unconventional warfare. Bands of trained and untrained Viet Cong soldiers fought a guerrilla war against the ARVN and the U.S. military. Their arsenal included guns, grenades, and **mortars**, or short range, muzzle-loaded cannons. They also manufactured their own bombs and set booby traps.

Helicopters like this one, nicknamed "Huey" for their early "HU-1" designation, were used to transport soldiers to and from war zones and airlift the wounded in Vietnam. Hueys carried U.S. troops to South Vietnam's Ia Drang Valley in November 1965, where the American soldiers engaged in the first major battle of the war with North Vietnamese forces.

11.9.3 Trace the origins and geopolitical consequences (foreign and domestic) of the Cold War and containment policy, including the following: • The era of McCarthyism, instances of domestic Communism (e.g., Alger Hiss) and blacklisting • The Truman Doctrine • The Berlin Blockade • The Korean War • The Bay of Pigs invasion and the Cuban Missile Crisis • Atomic testing in the American West, the "mutual assured destruction" doctrine, and disarmament policies • The Vietnam War • Latin American policy.

The war in Vietnam did not have official fronts and battles like conventional wars. More often, the Viet Cong launched ambushes and carried out hit-and-run attacks against the U.S. troops and the ARVN, taking off before they could be captured. And American soldiers couldn't always tell enemies apart from friends. The Vietnamese villagers who smiled in welcome when the soldiers arrived were sometimes hiding hand grenades ready to be tossed.

Fighting often took place in jungle terrain, where the dense foliage made it easy for the Viet Cong to camouflage both themselves and their bases. Often soldiers on both sides had to slog through swamps, submerged up to their waists in the mosquito-infested waters. In areas closer to Saigon, where the terrain provided less cover, the Viet Cong traveled through an extensive system of underground tunnels. Local villagers had helped build the tunnels, which stretched for thousands of miles and served not only as shelters where soldiers could retreat, but also as bases of operation.

As they launched their surprise attacks—sometimes firing from concealed bunkers within the tunnels—the Viet Cong entered and exited through well-hidden entryways. The tunnels contained chambers where the Viet Cong stored their weapons, water, and food, and even housed sleeping chambers and kitchens, enabling the soldiers to live in the tunnels for weeks at a time. American and South Vietnamese troops known as "tunnel rats" crawled through the narrow passages, searching for Viet Cong and setting off explosives in an attempt to collapse the tunnels. In the process, however, they had to be careful not to trigger any of the booby traps planted by the Viet Cong, such as bamboo spikes or trip wires that set off grenades.

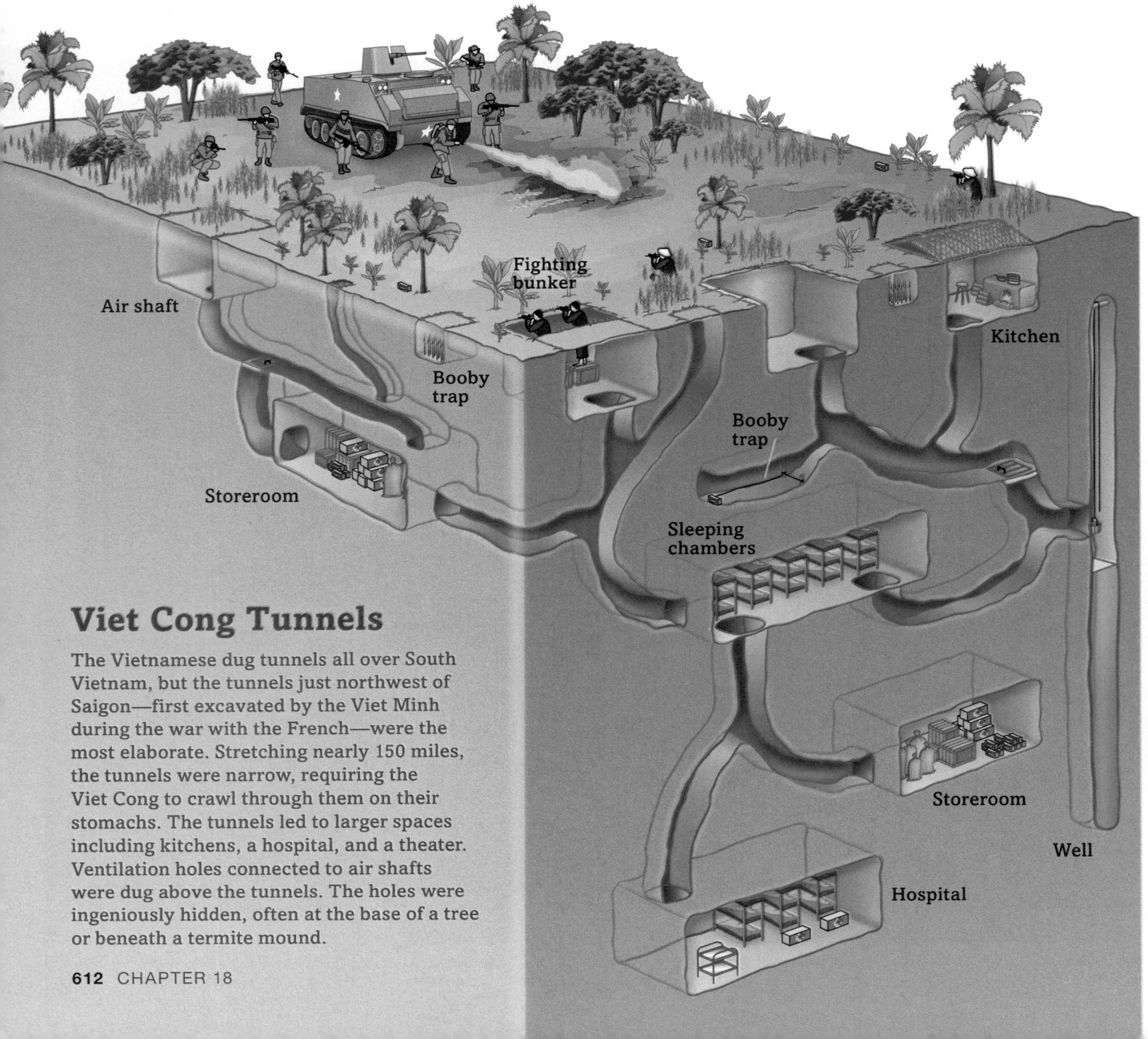

Viet Cong Tunnels

The Vietnamese dug tunnels all over South Vietnam, but the tunnels just northwest of Saigon—first excavated by the Viet Minh during the war with the French—were the most elaborate. Stretching nearly 150 miles, the tunnels were narrow, requiring the Viet Cong to crawl through them on their stomachs. The tunnels led to larger spaces including kitchens, a hospital, and a theater. Ventilation holes connected to air shafts were dug above the tunnels. The holes were ingeniously hidden, often at the base of a tree or beneath a termite mound.

SEARCH-AND-DESTROY MISSIONS

To combat the Viet Cong and North Vietnamese Army, General Westmoreland used search-and-destroy missions in villages and along the Ho Chi Minh Trail. First, low-flying helicopters sprayed an area with gunfire, and then ground troops moved in to search out enemies, destroy them, and get away quickly. Though these missions often resulted in the eradication of Viet Cong bases and the confiscation of their arms and supplies, such attacks could also devastate entire villages and kill hundreds of civilians.

To deal with the thick growth in the jungles that so effectively concealed the Viet Cong, the U.S. Air Force began spraying **Agent Orange**, a potent herbicide, or chemical substance used to kill vegetation. Agent Orange destroyed foliage, but doctors discovered later that the herbicide caused serious health issues, for both the Vietnamese and U.S. soldiers. American troops also frequently used napalm, a flammable jellied gasoline that, like Agent Orange, helped clear foliage and undergrowth. When it came into contact with skin, however, napalm caused severe burns, leaving some people with long-lasting injuries. Together, the search-and-destroy missions and use of chemical agents did little to win the hearts and minds of the South Vietnamese or turn them against the communists. The chemicals harmed many South Vietnamese civilians and burned their villages and farms.

The American cause wasn't helped by the rise to power of **Nguyen Cao Ky** (NWIHN KOW KAY), who became prime minister of South Vietnam following a military coup in 1965. The Vietnamese people viewed Ky, who prohibited criticism of his government and imprisoned his opponents, as an autocrat similar to Diem. The United States supported Ky, even though his corrupt regime was anything but democratic.

Meanwhile, by the end of 1965, great numbers of soldiers had deserted the ARVN, with many joining the North Vietnamese army. The Viet Cong had gained control, to some degree, of about 50 percent of the countryside in South Vietnam. As Westmoreland's war of attrition failed to discourage the communist forces in Vietnam, American casualties started to mount over the course of that first year of the war. Progress seemed elusive, and methods of calculating success were muddled and hard to measure. American troops fought bravely, but the stress of combat in Vietnam led many soldiers to suffer from low morale and depression. As the war dragged on, the conflict also became the subject of growing criticism at home.

In 1963, the Ca Mau Peninsula at the southern tip of South Vietnam was almost completely covered with forests. As a stronghold of the Viet Cong, this stretch of Ca Mau was heavily sprayed with Agent Orange and defoliated in 1968. This photo was taken four years later and, as you can see, the forests showed no signs of recovery.

HISTORICAL THINKING

1. **READING CHECK** How did the U.S. military hope to win the war in Vietnam?
2. **MAKE INFERENCES** Why do you think guerrilla warfare was so effective against American troops?
3. **ANALYZE ENVIRONMENTAL CONCEPTS** How did Agent Orange and napalm affect the natural systems and resources in the jungles of South Vietnam?
4. **DRAW CONCLUSIONS** How did the U.S. military strategy undermine the campaign to win the hearts and minds of the South Vietnamese?

HI 5 Students analyze human modifications of landscapes and examine the resulting environmental policy issues.

2.2 **MAIN IDEA** As Americans followed the progress of the Vietnam War on television, many began to oppose U.S. involvement in the conflict.

GROWING OPPOSITION TO THE WAR

You're no doubt used to the 24/7 coverage of world events available on TV, the Internet, and social media. But in the 1960s, information wasn't so easily accessed. So when reports on the Vietnam War filled the television airwaves, people watched—and thought about what they saw.

THE TELEVISION WAR

The Vietnam War became the first in the nation's history to be broadcast regularly on television. Journalists and photographers covered the war from the jungles and battlefields of Vietnam and brought it into people's homes, night after night. As a result, the Vietnam War became known as the "television war" or "living-room war." Recording their accounts in the haze of war, American journalists reported on television what urban warfare and guerrilla fighting entailed. Film clips of fighting, bombings, and dead or wounded soldiers appeared on nightly newscasts. The public's daily exposure to the horrors of war kept people informed about events. In time, it would also begin to influence their opinion of the war.

However, despite what television reports revealed about casualties and conditions in Vietnam, government and military officials made announcements about the war's progress. The Johnson administration launched a "success

An American television news crew interviews U.S. soldiers in South Vietnam in 1967. The Vietnam War was a dangerous assignment. During the course of the war, nine television personnel were killed, and many more were wounded.

11.9.3 Trace the origins and geopolitical consequences (foreign and domestic) of the Cold War and containment policy, including the following: • The era of McCarthyism, instances of domestic Communism (e.g., Alger Hiss) and blacklisting • The Truman Doctrine • The Berlin Blockade • The Korean War • The Bay of Pigs invasion and the Cuban Missile Crisis • Atomic testing in the American West, the "mutual assured destruction" doctrine, and disarmament policies • The Vietnam War • Latin American policy.

offensive," a campaign to convince the public that the United States was defeating the communists in Vietnam.

In 1967, General Westmoreland made three trips to the United States to promote this idea, appearing before Congress to present his positive assessments of the war. But Westmoreland manipulated the numbers of enemy losses and claimed that U.S. forces had won every battle. He told Congress that "your continued strong support is vital to the success of our mission . . . over the communist aggressor!" In truth, neither the bombing campaign nor the ground war in Vietnam was having any measurable effect on the enemy.

Americans became increasingly aware of the difference between the optimistic reports they heard from the government and what they saw for themselves on television. This contrast resulted in a **credibility gap**, an increasing skepticism about what the government told them about the war. In this context, Americans eventually started to call into question the principles upon which the war was being fought. Why, many wondered, was the United States involved in Vietnam at all?

AMERICAN WOMEN IN VIETNAM
Women could not serve in combat during the conflict, but thousands of female members of the military took on other roles in Vietnam. The vast majority worked as nurses. The number and severity of war casualties—and the rate at which the wounded arrived to be treated—meant that the nurses had to make quick decisions about whom to treat first. They also had to determine the treatment on their own, without much advice from doctors, who were often busy with their own patients. Thousands of civilian women also worked in Vietnam, many of them serving with the American Red Cross or working as journalists, like the woman in this photo.

Some members of Congress also began to take issue with the U.S. involvement in Vietnam. Senator George McGovern of South Dakota expressed his opposition in 1963. In 1966, Arkansas senator J. William Fulbright, chairman of the Senate Foreign Relations Committee, also voiced his opposition to the bombing of North Vietnam. That same year, Fulbright published a book called *The Arrogance of Power* in which he criticized the government's goal in Vietnam. He wrote, "We are trying to remake Vietnamese society, a task which certainly cannot be accomplished by force and which probably cannot be accomplished by any means available to outsiders. The objective may be desirable, but it is not feasible [practical]."

CONTROVERSY OVER THE DRAFT

While some people voiced their objection to the war, many others opposed the idea of conscription, commonly known as the draft. With the escalation of the war, more young men were needed to fight it. Hundreds of thousands of American men volunteered for or were drafted to serve in the war, which government and military leaders portrayed as an extension of broader Cold War struggles. The Selective Service System, a federal agency, administered the draft. On turning 18 years old, all young men were required to register with their local draft board, but some could be granted a **deferment**, or official permission to delay conscription. For example, men enrolled full-time in college could claim a student deferment for as long as they remained in school.

However, the agency did not always act fairly in its selection process. Draft board members could show favoritism to friends, family members, and others by granting their sons special deferments. Many of the men who received deferments also came from wealthy and educated families. As a result, most of the draftees came from poor and working-class families. A substantial percentage of these men belonged to minority groups. In the first few years of the war, once it became clear that American minorities were fighting and dying in numbers that were disproportionate to their representation in the country, many activist rights groups loudly protested the war. They objected to the war on the grounds that, to them, it represented one more form of oppression—oppression for minorities at home and abroad.

More moderate voices also spoke out against the war, including civil rights leader Martin Luther King, Jr., who called it "a white man's war, a black man's fight." Most famously, in a 1967 speech, King criticized the war both for its expense and for the large number of poor men of all races who were fighting it. He pointed out that the money the government spent on the war could have been used to fight poverty in the United States. He also objected to the devastation the war was bringing to the Vietnamese people and their land. The response to King's speech was largely negative. Newspaper editorials attacked him for his stance on the war. And even the NAACP criticized King for linking what the organization considered two separate issues: civil rights and the Vietnam War. However, King did not back down and continued to speak out against the war and the draft.

INCREASING PROTESTS

In 1964, other civil rights advocates began the **Free Speech Movement** in response to a ban on distributing political flyers at the University of California at Berkeley campus. When police arrested a student for handing out civil rights pamphlets and put him in their patrol car, other students sat down around the car to prevent it from being driven away. A young man named Mario Savio jumped on top of the car and addressed the crowd. Savio emerged as the movement's leader, and the students sitting around the police car passed around a hat to collect money to repair the vehicle. They wanted to show that they were good citizens. The protest continued for more than 30 hours until authorities dropped the charges, and the student was released.

Then, on December 1, 1964, Savio and other movement leaders led a rally, exhorting students to take part in a sit-in at Sproul Hall, Berkeley's administration building. As a result, thousands of students occupied the building and remained there for many hours. Finally, the police moved in and arrested about 800 people. As the police ushered them away, some of the officers physically assaulted the students. Eventually, the university lifted its ban of on-campus political activity, and the Free Speech Movement declared victory.

The Free Speech Movement soon turned its focus on the Vietnam War. Students at Berkeley and other college campuses throughout the country organized protests against the war. These antiwar protests, provoked by the expansion of the war in Vietnam, reflected and contributed to a deep rift within American society and culture. Americans became divided into **hawks**, who supported the war, and **doves**, who opposed it.

Another movement, called the **New Left**, arose out of student activism. One New Left group, the **Students for a Democratic Society (SDS)**, originated at the University of Michigan at Ann Arbor in the early 1960s and soon spread to other colleges. The SDS promoted socialist principles and denounced racism, militarism, and in time, U.S. involvement in Vietnam. In April 1965, the SDS sponsored the first major antiwar rally in Washington, D.C.

PRIMARY SOURCE

Just before the 1964 sit-in, Mario Savio delivered a speech on the steps of Berkeley's Sproul Hall. In this excerpt from the speech, Savio refers to the university as a "machine" that may need to be actively stopped.

There's a time when the operation of the machine becomes so odious [hateful]—makes you so sick at heart—that you can't take part. You can't even passively take part. And you've got to put your bodies upon the gears and upon the wheels, upon the levers, upon all the apparatus, and you've got to make it stop. And you've got to indicate to the people who run it, to the people who own it that unless you're free, the machine will be prevented from working at all.

—from a speech in Berkeley, by Mario Savio, 1964

11.10.4 Examine the roles of civil rights advocates (e.g., A. Philip Randolph, Martin Luther King, Jr., Malcolm X, Thurgood Marshall, James Farmer, Rosa Parks), including the significance of Martin Luther King, Jr.'s "Letter from Birmingham Jail" and "I Have a Dream" speech.

During the March on the Pentagon, this young woman offered a flower to the soldiers guarding the building with bayoneted M-14 rifles. At one point, a group of demonstrators tried to levitate, or lift, the Pentagon and used spells to drive "the evil war spirits" out of the Defense Department headquarters.

About two weeks earlier, President Johnson had pledged to continue military operations in Vietnam. The event drew tens of thousands of people calling for U.S. withdrawal from South Vietnam. Protesters picketed the White House and carried signs saying "No more war." At the Capitol, people delivered speeches, and performers such as activist and folk-singer Joan Baez (BY-ehz) led the crowd in song.

While the 1965 protest rally was largely peaceful, the March on the Pentagon, which took place in the capital in October 1967, was far more confrontational. The demonstration, organized by the National Mobilization Committee to End the War in Vietnam—a coalition of antiwar groups—sought to shut down the Pentagon. By this point in the war, about 13,000 Americans had died in Vietnam, and more than half of the population disapproved of the president's handling of the war. An estimated 100,000 people rallied first at the Lincoln Memorial and then marched to the Pentagon. When the protesters arrived, they found about 2,500 troops and U.S. marshals guarding the Pentagon. Some of the protesters placed flowers in the barrels of the soldiers' rifles, but a small group of demonstrators managed to gain access to the building. Soldiers and marshals used tear gas and force to clear them out. In the end, nearly 700 people were arrested.

Despite the protests at home, the war in Vietnam continued. But in 1968, a military campaign launched by North Vietnam and the Viet Cong would mark a turning point in the war and the beginning of American withdrawal from the conflict.

HISTORICAL THINKING

1. **READING CHECK** Why was the Vietnam War called the "television war"?
2. **DRAW CONCLUSIONS** How did the war in Vietnam affect the larger trend toward equality at home?
3. **MAKE INFERENCES** Why did Mario Savio compare the University of California at Berkeley to a machine?
4. **FORM AND SUPPORT OPINIONS** Do you think peaceful antiwar protests in the 1960s were more effective than more confrontational protests? Why or why not?

HI 1 Students show the connections, causal and otherwise, between particular historical events and larger social, economic, and political trends and developments.

3.1

MAIN IDEA In 1968, the North Vietnamese and Viet Cong launched a series of attacks in South Vietnam, hoping to provoke a popular uprising among its people.

THE TET OFFENSIVE

The element of surprise can be key in a battle. An attack by communist forces in South Vietnam surprised the U.S. military and stunned the American people, who began to cry "Enough!" in ever greater numbers.

A SURPRISE ATTACK

It all began on Tet, the celebration of the Lunar New Year and the most important holiday in Vietnam. In other years, hostilities on both sides of the war had been suspended during the holiday. But early on the morning of January 31, 1968, about 80,000 North Vietnamese and Viet Cong forces initiated a coordinated and unexpected attack on dozens of locations throughout South Vietnam. The sites of the **Tet Offensive** included cities and towns, military bases, General Westmoreland's headquarters, and even the U.S. embassy in Saigon. In launching their attack, communist forces hoped to provoke a popular uprising against U.S. and ARVN troops and persuade the United States to pull out of Vietnam.

A few months before the Tet Offensive, the communists had begun a campaign to distract the Americans and ARVN from the real targets. First, the communists attacked a couple of towns in South Vietnam, and then a U.S. Marine base located in the northwest corner of the country. Johnson and Westmoreland sent 50,000 troops to protect the besieged Marine base as well as other bases in the country. Once the troops had been diverted and the communists' true targets stood nearly undefended, the Tet Offensive began.

Initially, the communist forces scored a few successes, including invading the embassy grounds in Saigon, but the U.S. and ARVN troops soon defeated the communists there and managed to retake most of the other targeted locations. However, fighting in the city of Hue raged on for nearly a month. As you may remember, Hue was the site of a major Buddhist protest against Diem in 1963. Hue was also once the capital of Vietnam and the home of its emperor. It was a symbolic target for the communists and poorly defended. On the morning of the Tet Offensive, communist forces quickly seized control of the city. The U.S. and ARVN troops fought fiercely, going from house to house in the city to root out the communist occupiers before finally winning the Battle of Hue.

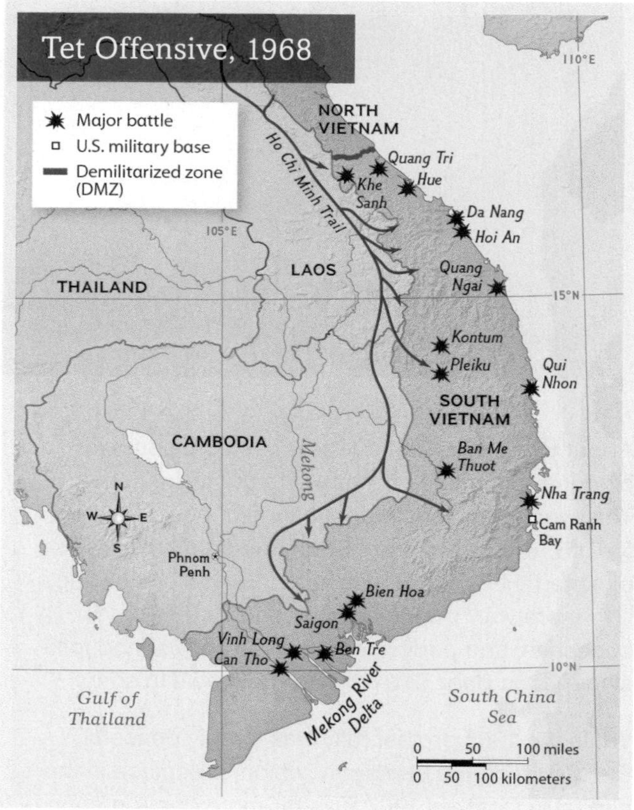

It would be one of the longest and bloodiest battles of the war. After taking control of the city, the Americans discovered mass graves filled

11.9.3 Trace the origins and geopolitical consequences (foreign and domestic) of the Cold War and containment policy, including the following: • The era of McCarthyism, instances of domestic Communism (e.g., Alger Hiss) and blacklisting • The Truman Doctrine • The Berlin Blockade • The Korean War • The Bay of Pigs invasion and the Cuban Missile Crisis • Atomic testing in the American West, the "mutual assured destruction" doctrine, and disarmament policies • The Vietnam War • Latin American policy.

Journalist Walter Cronkite, popularly called "the most trusted man in America" for the integrity of his reporting, went to Vietnam to cover the aftermath of the Tet Offensive. For two weeks, he reported from battle sites, and his commentary influenced public opinion.

with thousands of Hue civilians murdered by the communists. Before the battle, the North Vietnamese and Viet Cong had executed those they believed were sympathetic to the American cause. The Battle of Hue also resulted in heavy losses, with about 5,000 dead on the communist side and around 500 on the American and South Vietnamese side. Thousands more died or were wounded in other battles of the Tet Offensive. The communists were defeated militarily, and they didn't win more South Vietnamese to their side, but they did score a strategic victory. Television crews had captured scenes of the fighting. To many viewers, it didn't look as though the United States was about to win the war, as the government had led them to believe.

DISILLUSIONMENT WITH THE WAR

After the Tet Offensive, an overwhelming number of Americans called for an end to the war. Few now really believed the United States was winning the conflict. From Saigon, American broadcast journalist Walter Cronkite reported that the Tet Offensive made "more certain than ever that the bloody experience of Vietnam is to end in a **stalemate**." In other words, Cronkite believed neither side would be able to claim a clear victory.

In February 1968, Secretary of Defense Robert McNamara resigned from his position. He, too, had become disillusioned with the war and realized he had misjudged the resolve of the North Vietnamese. Like McNamara, the American public had grown weary of the war. They no longer believed the government's positive assessment of it or Westmoreland's optimistic claim after the Tet Offensive that there was now "light at the end of the tunnel."

Just a few weeks after Tet, General Westmoreland requested an additional 206,000 troops in Vietnam. About 550,000 American troops were already stationed there. Clark Clifford, who replaced McNamara as secretary of defense, advised Johnson to deny the request. He also recommended that the United States reduce its bombing raids over North Vietnam and take steps to end the war.

Johnson took Clifford's advice and refused to send Westmoreland all the troops he'd requested, approving only an additional 13,500 soldiers. The president also informed the South Vietnamese leadership that its army would have to assume a greater role in the fight. But to many Americans, Johnson's actions were too little, too late. After the Tet Offensive, his approval ratings dropped by more than 10 percentage points. The unpopular war had taken a severe toll on Johnson's presidency.

HISTORICAL THINKING

1. **READING CHECK** How did the communists devise and carry out their surprise attack?
2. **ANALYZE CAUSE AND EFFECT** What does the Tet Offensive—which North Vietnam lost—suggest about the complexity of historical causes and effects?
3. **DRAW CONCLUSIONS** Why was the Tet Offensive a major turning point in the war?

HI 2 Students recognize the complexity of historical causes and effects, including the limitations on determining cause and effect.

3.2 **MAIN IDEA** Divisions in the Democratic Party and acts of violence characterized the chaotic year of 1968.

1968: VIOLENCE AND DIVISION

When Walter Cronkite said after the Tet Offensive that the war was mired in stalemate, Johnson reportedly said, "If I've lost Cronkite, I've lost Middle America." Soon, Johnson would make a decision that would rock the nation.

A DIVIDED DEMOCRATIC PARTY

Johnson's unpopularity among Middle America, or average middle-class Americans, weakened his chances in the 1968 presidential race. At the end of November 1967, Senator **Eugene McCarthy** of Minnesota announced he would seek the nomination of the Democratic Party. McCarthy opposed the Vietnam War and won strong support for his position, especially among young people. He also performed surprisingly well against Johnson in the first Democratic primary election in New Hampshire in March 1968. Johnson won the primary with 49 percent of the vote—but McCarthy was a close runner-up. He captured 42 percent of the vote. As you may know, in a primary election, voters in a particular state choose the candidate they'd like to see on the ballot in the general election.

Just a few days after the primary, John Kennedy's brother and former attorney general, Senator Robert Kennedy of New York, also joined the race. Kennedy had stated before that he would not run, but McCarthy's success in New Hampshire made

A protester in Chicago bends to pick up a tear gas canister and throw it back at the police during the Democratic National Convention. Nearly 600 people were arrested in the riots, and more than 200 were injured, including both police and protesters.

11.9.3 Trace the origins and geopolitical consequences (foreign and domestic) of the Cold War and containment policy, including the following: • The era of McCarthyism, instances of domestic Communism (e.g., Alger Hiss) and blacklisting • The Truman Doctrine • The Berlin Blockade • The Korean War • The Bay of Pigs invasion and the Cuban Missile Crisis • Atomic testing in the American West, the "mutual assured destruction" doctrine, and disarmament policies • The Vietnam War • Latin American policy.

him change his mind. Like McCarthy, Kennedy ran as an antiwar candidate. Kennedy's decision to run upset some voters because they believed his candidacy might undermine McCarthy's campaign. Others, however, acknowledged that Kennedy, with his money and connections, had a better prospect of winning the Democratic nomination.

On March 31, faced with the likelihood of losing the primary in Wisconsin, Johnson dropped a bombshell by announcing that he would not seek a second term as president. During his televised address, Johnson also revealed his intentions to scale back the bombings in North Vietnam and engage in peace talks with the North Vietnamese. A few weeks later, Johnson's vice president, Hubert Humphrey, joined the race for president. Humphrey, who received Johnson's endorsement, decided not to campaign or run in the state primaries against McCarthy and Kennedy. Instead, he hoped to receive enough votes from **delegates**, or people representing their states, to win the nomination at the Democratic National Convention.

Meanwhile, peace talks began with the North Vietnamese in Paris, but negotiations were short-lived. The North Vietnamese demanded that Johnson scale back the bombing everywhere, not just in North Vietnam, but Johnson resisted. With the talks at an **impasse**, or standstill, heavy combat continued in South Vietnam throughout the spring of 1968. And American troops continued to fight and die in Southeast Asia.

VIOLENCE AND CHAOS

Less than a week after Johnson's startling announcement, Martin Luther King, Jr., was assassinated in Memphis, Tennessee. His violent death touched off a series of riots in more than 100 cities across the country, including Washington, D.C., Baltimore, San Francisco, and Chicago. Rioters set fires and looted stores. In some cities, officials called in the military to establish order. The police made thousands of arrests across the country, and dozens of people died. And the violence was just beginning. In fact, 1968 would become one of the most chaotic years in American history.

Throughout the turbulent spring, McCarthy and Kennedy continued battling in the primaries. Kennedy drew greater support from African Americans and Latinos, while McCarthy had more success with white college students. But on June 5, the contest between the two came to an abrupt and horrifying end. Only moments after Kennedy delivered a victory speech in Los Angeles celebrating his California primary win, an assassin shot him. Kennedy died the following day. For the second time in just two months, the nation was shocked and heartbroken over the death of a major national leader.

McCarthy remained in the race after Kennedy's assassination, but Hubert Humphrey was the strong favorite going into the Democratic National Convention, which was held in Chicago during the last week of August. Chicago mayor Richard J. Daley had prepared for the internal divisions among delegates inside the convention hall. He was also ready for any confrontations that might take place outside the hall. Daley had turned the convention center into a fortress, bulletproofing its doors and surrounding it with fencing and barbed wire. Police patrolled the area inside the fence, poised for the worst. And that's just what happened.

As many as 15,000 antiwar protesters flooded the city, intent on making their voices heard. The plan was for their protest to be peaceful but loud. Instead, violence erupted when protesters refused to leave a nearby park. The mayor sent about 27,000 police officers and members of the National Guard into the park to confront the crowds. There, the officers lobbed tear gas at the protesters and beat them with clubs. Clashes continued as protesters tried to approach the convention site. Innocent bystanders, including doctors and reporters, got caught in the mayhem. And once again, America watched the violence on television.

In the end, the delegates nominated Humphrey, who was backed by moderates in the Democratic Party. The young people who supported McCarthy felt betrayed. And they saw Humphrey's candidacy as a continuation of Johnson's pro-war policies. Disillusioned with American values, some young people would simply withdraw from traditional society and adopt an unconventional lifestyle.

HISTORICAL THINKING

1. **READING CHECK** What divided the Democratic Party in 1968?
2. **EVALUATE** How did the protests against the Vietnam War affect domestic issues and policies?
3. **MAKE INFERENCES** Given the social and political climate of 1968, how do you think Americans reacted to the images of the Democratic National Convention they saw on television?

11.9.4 List the effects of foreign policy on domestic policies and vice versa (e.g., protests during the war in Vietnam, the "nuclear freeze" movement); HI 3 Students interpret past events and issues within the context in which an event unfolded rather than solely in terms of present-day norms and values.

3.3 **MAIN IDEA** During the 1960s, young people developed a counterculture in reaction to conventional society.

THE COUNTERCULTURE

"Power to the people." "Don't trust anyone over 30." "Flower power." These are just a few of the slogans adopted by groups of young people who rejected middle-class values, the war, and what came to be called "the establishment."

ANTIESTABLISHMENT

From within the antiwar and rights protest movements of the New Left, a **counterculture** emerged, promoting a way of life that was in opposition with American society's established rules and behavior. Those who participated in the counterculture, often called "hippies," were frustrated with the war, politics, and discrimination in America. They believed that true equality and peace could only be realized through a revolution of cultural values.

Thus, hippies decided to "check out" from mainstream society as a way of rebelling against middle-class American values and seeking true happiness. They embraced pacifism and demonstrated against the conflict in Vietnam, declaring that waging war anywhere in the world was wrong. "Make love, not war" and "Give peace a chance" were popular hippie slogans. These members of the counterculture rebelled by calling into question Cold War values and even long-standing American principles.

The counterculture had its own distinctive style of music, dress, language, and films, all of which influenced mainstream social and cultural sensibilities. Both men and women in the counterculture typically let their hair grow long, dressed in tie-dyed shirts and bell-bottom pants, and adorned themselves with strings of beads.

They also had liberated attitudes toward sexuality and the use of psychedelic drugs, which produced hallucinations and an altered state of consciousness. In 1960, Harvard psychologist and researcher Timothy Leary had begun studying the effects of psychedelic drugs and became a folk hero of the counterculture. Leary promoted the use of such drugs with his slogan "Tune in, Turn On, Drop Out." Counterculture music used electronically distorted sounds to try to reproduce the experience of using these drugs. And films about the counterculture, such as *Easy Rider* and *Wild in the Streets,* were shown in theaters across the country.

To create a sense of family, some hippies formed communes, where they shared living arrangements, food, and possessions. Communes were often founded in rural areas where members longed to get "back to the land." They rejected the consumerism of modern life, grew their own food, and reconnected with nature. Many other members of the counterculture settled in urban areas, such as San Francisco's Haight-Ashbury neighborhood, where they lived in the company of like-minded hippies. More than 75,000 young people migrated to the neighborhood in 1967 alone.

WOODSTOCK NATION

Perhaps the high point of the counterculture came in August 1969 when the Woodstock Music Festival took place on a farm in Bethel, New York. Billed as "Three Days of Peace and Music," Woodstock drew a crowd of about 400,000 people—twice the number expected. They came to see some of the biggest musical acts of the day, including Jimi Hendrix, Janis Joplin, the Grateful Dead, and the Who. Many of these singers performed songs that were critical of the Vietnam War—to the delight of their audience.

The organizers of the festival had planned to use the profits from it to build a recording studio, but they were unprepared for the masses that thronged the festival. Unable to handle the crowds, the organizers let everyone in for free. Though plagued by rain, Woodstock was a great success and, remarkably, largely peaceful. Only two deaths occurred at the festival: one from an accident involving a tractor and the other from a drug overdose. The term

In this photo, audience members at the Woodstock festival stand and perch on top of cars and buses to watch the show. The enormous crowds created a food shortage. When people in the area heard about the situation, they donated food, including 10,000 sandwiches. Others served rice, vegetables, and granola, which came to be associated with hippies. In an effort to feed everyone, thousands of cups of granola were passed through the audience.

"Woodstock Nation" would be used to describe the youth counterculture of the 1960s.

By the end of the decade, however, the hippies' hopes for a world filled with peace and love were fading. The rampant drug use was taking its toll. Some of the musicians who had performed at the Woodstock festival had died from drug overdoses. Partly in response to the counterculture's drug abuse, the federal government declared a "war on drugs" in the early 1970s. Agencies were created to provide treatment for drug abusers and to establish federal and local task forces to fight the drug trade.

Meanwhile, many mainstream Americans, who had been scandalized by the counterculture and troubled by the protests, longed for an end to the unrest. They saw the counterculture's emphasis on "free love" and rejection of consumerism as a threat to the American way of life. They wanted a leader who could re-establish order and end the war in Vietnam. They believed they had found such a leader in former vice president Richard Nixon.

HISTORICAL THINKING

1. **READING CHECK** What values set members of the counterculture apart from members of traditional American society?
2. **MAKE INFERENCES** Why did the emergence of the counterculture coincide with the Vietnam War?
3. **MAKE CONNECTIONS** What characteristics of the counterculture described in the lesson do you see around you today? Explain the similarities.

11.9.4 List the effects of foreign policy on domestic policies and vice versa (e.g., protests during the war in Vietnam, the "nuclear freeze" movement); 11.11.7 Explain how the federal, state, and local governments have responded to demographic and social changes such as population shifts to the suburbs, racial concentrations in the cities, Frostbelt-to-Sunbelt migration, international migration, decline of family farms, increases in out-of-wedlock births, and drug abuse; CST 4 Students relate current events to the physical and human characteristics of places and regions.

4.1 **MAIN IDEA** Richard Nixon vowed to end the Vietnam War and bring Americans together, but the war dragged on for more than four years after he became president.

VIETNAMIZATION UNDER NIXON

Many Americans wanted peace in Vietnam and on their streets. They thought Republican Richard Nixon could deliver on both.

AN HONORABLE PEACE

Republican Richard Nixon narrowly beat Democrat Hubert Humphrey in the presidential election, winning the popular vote by less than one percent. You may remember that Nixon was involved in the campaign against communism when he was a congressman in the 1940s. He also served for eight years as Dwight Eisenhower's vice president. To sway voters, Nixon had appealed to more conservative Americans—those who conformed to social norms, unlike the members of the counterculture. The social unrest the country had experienced made many people long for law and order. Nixon would later refer to these Americans as "the silent majority."

During his campaign, Nixon had promised he could bring about a quick victory in Vietnam, but he didn't provide any details. He also referred to seeking "an honorable peace." A reporter called this vague promise Nixon's "secret plan." Once Nixon assumed the presidency in January 1969, he and his National Security Advisor **Henry Kissinger** discussed what to do about Vietnam. They knew the United States could not win the war, but they didn't want to pull their forces out of South Vietnam, leaving it vulnerable to invasion from communist North Vietnam. And Nixon didn't want the war to destroy his presidency as it had Lyndon Johnson's. Soon he came up with a plan to end the war.

Nixon proposed a strategy called **Vietnamization**, which allowed for the gradual replacement of U.S. troops with ARVN troops. Under this plan, all American troops would be out of Vietnam by 1972. Nixon began the process of Vietnamization in June 1969 with the withdrawal of 25,000 U.S. troops. He announced more withdrawals that September. In April 1970, Nixon expressed his intention of pulling an additional 150,000 troops out of Vietnam within a year. General Creighton Abrams, who had replaced General Westmoreland as commander in Vietnam, expressed concern about the American troops' ability to train additional ARVN troops in such a short time, but Nixon was determined to follow through with his Vietnamization plan.

U.S. Troops in Vietnam, 1960–1972

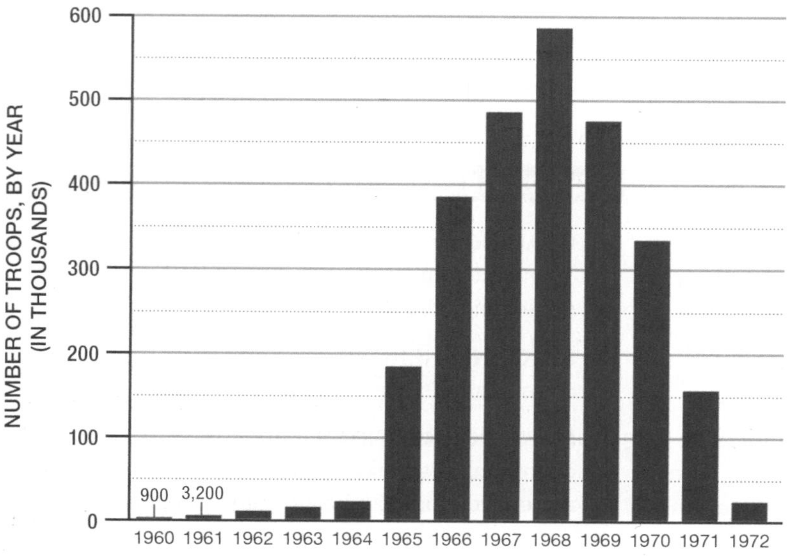

Source: U.S. Department of Defense

Nixon also proposed a change to the conscription process. During the early years of the war, the Selective Service had drafted any eligible man between the ages of 18 and 26, with the oldest men drafted first. This system was replaced with a draft lottery, which had last been used in 1942. On December 1, 1969, the Selective Service placed 366 plastic capsules—one for every day of the year, including February 29—into a

11.9.4 List the effects of foreign policy on domestic policies and vice versa (e.g., protests during the war in Vietnam, the "nuclear freeze" movement).

Some men, like these protesters in New York's Central Park in 1967, publicly burned their draft classification cards to protest the draft and the Vietnam War.

jar and drew them out by hand. The first capsule drawn was September 14. This meant that all men born between 1944 and 1950 on that date were assigned the number 1 and would be the first to be considered for the draft. The drawing continued until all the dates had been assigned numbers. The higher your number, the less likely you would be chosen for **induction**, or being drafted into the military.

COVERUPS AND SECRETS

In the midst of what appeared to be positive news about the war, Americans learned about an incident in South Vietnam that had occurred the year before. In March 1968, U.S. troops led by Lieutenant William Calley entered the tiny village of My Lai (MEE LYE) in search of Viet Cong. The troops didn't find any Viet Cong, but they rounded up the unarmed civilians—mostly women, children, and elderly men—and brutally murdered them. Approximately 500 people died in the **My Lai Massacre**, almost the entire population of the village.

The U.S. Army covered up the mass killing, but a soldier who had heard of the massacre eventually spoke to the press, which broke the story to the public in November 1969. Outraged people from around the world demanded justice. In the end, only Calley was punished for the incident. He was put under house arrest and released within four years.

Nixon also tried to keep some secrets of his own. The United States had suspected Vietnam's neighbors, Cambodia and Laos, of sheltering Vietnamese communists. The government also knew that communists transported supplies along the Ho Chi Minh Trail, which passed through those countries. General Abrams suggested carrying out heavy bombing raids on Cambodia and Laos to root out the communist forces, and Nixon and Kissinger agreed to the plan. The United States had conducted air attacks over Cambodia and Laos for several years, but Nixon chose to "carpet bomb" the countries, or attack them with large numbers of missiles.

By showing the communists in Vietnam the lengths to which he was willing to go, Nixon hoped to force them into negotiations. The secret bombing of Cambodia and Laos began in March 1969—not even Congress knew about it. But in May 1969, the *New York Times* reported on the attacks. Furious with the newspaper's revelation, Nixon had the FBI discover the source of the leak in the name of national security. In spite of the leak, the president continued carpet bombing Cambodia and Laos until 1973.

TRAGEDY AT KENT STATE

After several days of student protest at Kent State, classes resumed on May 4. When students gathered for an unauthorized demonstration that day, the National Guard fired tear gas canisters into the crowd to disperse it. Some students picked up the canisters and other items and threw them back at the soldiers, who responded by firing their guns into the crowd. Two of the students killed were walking to class, including Jeffrey Miller, shown lying on the ground in this photo. The image, taken by photojournalism student John Filo, shows Mary Ann Vecchio kneeling by Miller, screaming in anguish. The photo won the Pulitzer Prize and became a symbol of the protest movement.

11.9.3 Trace the origins and geopolitical consequences (foreign and domestic) of the Cold War and containment policy, including the following: • The era of McCarthyism, instances of domestic Communism (e.g., Alger Hiss) and blacklisting • The Truman Doctrine • The Berlin Blockade • The Korean War • The Bay of Pigs invasion and the Cuban Missile Crisis • Atomic testing in the American West, the "mutual assured destruction" doctrine, and disarmament policies • The Vietnam War • Latin American policy

Then in April 1970, Nixon sent 20,000 U.S. and ARVN ground troops into Cambodia to find and destroy what he and the military thought were secret Viet Cong headquarters there. When the White House announced the Cambodian ground invasion, protests broke out. Some of the protests turned violent. On May 4, the National Guard shot into a crowd of student demonstrators at Kent State University in Ohio, killing four students and injuring several others. On May 15, at Jackson State, a predominantly black university in Mississippi, two African-American students were killed and 12 were injured following protests of U.S. policy in Cambodia and Vietnam and demonstrations against racial discrimination. Nixon pulled ground troops out of Cambodia in June.

The release in 1971 of what came to be known as the **Pentagon Papers** revealed more embarrassing secrets. In 1967, then Secretary of Defense Robert McNamara commissioned a study on U.S. activities and policies in Vietnam between 1947 and 1967. The 7,000-page work was never meant for the public eye. Daniel Ellsberg worked on the study and, at that time, was a strong supporter of the Vietnam War. As the war escalated, however, Ellsberg came to oppose it, and he turned the classified document over to the *New York Times*.

The Pentagon Papers revealed that U.S. involvement in Vietnam during the administrations of Truman, Eisenhower, Kennedy, and Johnson had been far greater than the American public had been led to believe. Although Nixon wasn't mentioned in the study, he was enraged by its publication. He considered the Pentagon Papers an attack on his presidency and his handling of the war. Nixon unsuccessfully used both legal and illegal means to incriminate Ellsberg.

THE END OF THE WAR

By 1972, only about 24,000 American troops remained in Vietnam as Nixon continued his gradual withdrawal plan. However, that spring, North Vietnam launched attacks on South Vietnam, prompting Nixon to bomb North Vietnam. Once again, he was trying to force North Vietnam to negotiate a peace agreement. The bombing continued into the next presidential election, which Nixon won in a landslide. In December, one month after Nixon's re-election, the United States dropped more bombs on the North Vietnamese cities of Hanoi and Haiphong than they had dropped in the previous two years. The bombing devastated North Vietnam, destroying harbors, railway lines, and factories.

PRIMARY SOUR

On January 23, 1973, Nixon addressed th on television and radio, announcing an agree to bring an end to the war in Vietnam. In this excerpt from his address, Nixon echoes the "honorable peace" he'd promised.

Your steadfastness in supporting our insistence on peace with honor has made peace with honor possible. Now that we have achieved an honorable agreement, let us be proud that America did not settle for a peace that would have betrayed our allies, that would have abandoned our prisoners of war, or that would have ended the war for us but would have continued the war for the 50 million people of Indochina. Let us be proud of . . . those who sacrificed, who gave their lives so that the people of South Vietnam might live in freedom and so that the world might live in peace.

—from an address by President Nixon, 1973

On January 27, 1973, North Vietnam, South Vietnam, and the United States negotiated an agreement calling for U.S. troop withdrawal from South Vietnam in exchange for the release of prisoners of war. But Nixon declared the United States would attack North Vietnam again if it committed acts of aggression against South Vietnam. About two months after the signing, the last American troops departed South Vietnam: U.S. involvement in the war was over.

In direct violation of the agreement they signed, the communists began planning their attack on South Vietnam in October 1974. North Vietnamese troops moved into the nation in March 1975. Congress denied requests to send emergency aid to South Vietnam. In late April, Saigon fell to the communists. With the communist victory, the Vietnam War was finally over, but its memory and legacy would haunt the United States for years to come.

HISTORICAL THINKING

1. **READING CHECK** What was Vietnamization?
2. **ANALYZE CAUSE AND EFFECT** What social and political developments occurred as a result of the Cambodian ground invasion?
3. **DRAW CONCLUSIONS** In his 1973 address, what did Nixon mean by "peace with honor"?
4. **FORM AND SUPPORT OPINIONS** Do you think the U.S. involvement in Vietnam was justified? Explain why or why not.

HI 1 Students show the connections, causal and otherwise, between particular historical events and larger social, economic, and political trends and developments.

he Vietnam War left a legacy of damaged veterans and
ocial change.

LE Y OF THE WAR

Many American veterans came home to a country they hardly recognized and where they seemed to be regarded as living symbols of an unpopular war. It would be difficult for everyone to adjust to the post-war world.

CASUALTIES OF WAR

Before 2010, the Vietnam War was the longest conflict in U.S. history. It claimed the lives of almost 60,000 Americans and about 2 million Vietnamese. As agreed, about two weeks after they signed the January 1973 peace agreement, the North Vietnamese began releasing American prisoners of war, or POWs. The POW camps freed 120 prisoners every two weeks, with the sick and injured leaving first, followed by those who had been imprisoned the longest. Some soldiers had been prisoners for more than 8 years, during which time many endured torture and isolation. Prisoners referred to one of the worst prison camps as the "Hanoi Hilton," a sarcastic reference to a famous hotel chain. At this camp in North Vietnam's capital, American soldiers were tortured and interrogated for information. It took about two months for all of the nearly 600 POWs to return home.

In 1973, about 2,500 American troops remained missing in action, or MIA. The Vietnamese landscape, with its thick jungles and swamps, made it difficult to locate the soldiers' remains. The military could not search the area for missing or dead soldiers because the United States never occupied North Vietnam. Though some of those who were MIA later returned to the United States and others were discovered to have died in POW camps, 1,600 men were still designated MIA in 2015.

Once veterans returned from Vietnam, they faced a new set of problems. Unlike soldiers of other wars, Vietnam veterans were not given a hero's welcome when they came home. No parades or celebrations awaited them. The country was still deeply divided over the war. For the most part, Americans didn't

Vietnam Veterans Memorial Washington, D.C.

The Vietnam Veterans Memorial consists of three parts: The Three Soldiers statue, the Vietnam Women's Memorial, and the Vietnam Veterans Memorial Wall, which lists the names of all the servicemen and women who died in the war. Men and women who served in Vietnam sometimes leave mementos of their war experience in front of the three memorials—especially boots. The National Park Service collects these items and stores them. Many are put on display at the Smithsonian Museum of American History.

want to hear about the veterans' experiences in the war. At best, the returning soldiers were ignored; at worst, they were despised. While most veterans made a successful return to civilian life, some struggled with physical injuries, mental health problems, and drug addictions that had begun while they were in Vietnam.

Some of the physical problems veterans suffered from were due to exposure to Agent Orange. The herbicide contained dioxin, a toxic compound that could cause a host of problems, such as cancer and birth defects. The government was slow to acknowledge the relationship between exposure to Agent Orange and the various health problems soldiers reported.

Other veterans experienced **post-traumatic stress disorder (PTSD)**, a condition brought on by injury or psychological trauma. Symptoms of PTSD can include flashbacks—vivid, realistic memories of horrific events—sleeping disorders, and sudden, often irrational bursts of anger. When they didn't receive adequate support or treatment for their physical and emotional problems, many veterans turned to substance abuse, and some committed suicide. Long after the troops had returned home, the effects of their time in Vietnam lingered, sometimes for many years.

LESSONS OF WAR

Attitudes at home about the war often reflected peoples' political viewpoints. Conservatives fumed because the United States had lost the war, while liberals thought the country should never have waged the war. As one veteran said, "The left hated us for killing, and the right hated us for not killing enough." Over time, though, conservatives learned that Vietnam veterans had fought valiantly under very challenging circumstances, and liberals learned that the veterans, too, were victims of the war.

The American public also collectively realized that forcing democracy on an unstable country such as Vietnam was a recipe for disaster. As a result of the war, Americans became more critical of their government. In fact, the escalation of the Vietnam War and the secret bombings of Laos and Cambodia proved to be the culmination, or conclusion, of Cold War strategies. Ultimately, Vietnam caused Americans to question the underlying assumptions of the Cold War era and protest against their government's policies abroad.

In the 1990s, the United States began to normalize relations with Vietnam. In 1994, President William Clinton lifted a trade embargo that the United States had imposed on North Vietnam in 1964 and on the newly reunited Vietnam in 1975. Veterans' groups

After Saigon fell to North Vietnam in April 1975, the United States evacuated Americans and many South Vietnamese by helicopter. In this photo, U.S. Marines help a long line of South Vietnamese board a helicopter on a lawn near the U.S. Embassy, seen in the background at the left. The helicopters made many trips, but not all those desperate to leave could be evacuated.

initially opposed this decision. However, Clinton lifted the embargo largely due to Vietnam's cooperation in tracking down and supplying information about American MIAs. Finally, in 1995, Clinton re-established diplomatic relations with Vietnam. In 1997, he named Douglas Peterson, a former American POW who had been imprisoned in Vietnam for six years, as the country's ambassador from the United States. Today, Vietnam is still a communist nation, but it has also embraced elements of capitalism and has a growing economy.

POLITICAL AND SOCIAL CHANGE

The impact of the Vietnam War extended to the U.S. Constitution. The document mandated that citizens had to be 21 years old to vote. But during the war, some people began to support lowering the voting age to 18. Arguing in favor of the age reduction in 1970, Senator Edward Kennedy of Massachusetts pointed out that about one-third of the troops fighting in Vietnam—and about one-half of those who died—were under the age of 21. Kennedy said, "At the very least, the opportunity to vote should be granted in recognition of the risks an 18-year-old is obliged to assume when he is sent off to fight and perhaps die for his country." Senator Kennedy also pointed out that many other countries, including South Vietnam, gave 18-year-olds suffrage. The **26th Amendment**, which reduced the voting age to 18, was ratified in 1971.

Another important political change took place a couple of years later. In 1973, Congress passed the War Powers Resolution, also known as the War Powers Act. The act required the president to notify Congress about any American troops sent overseas within 48 hours of their deployment. After 60 days, the president had to obtain congressional approval for the troops to remain in a state of armed conflict or make a formal declaration of war. Legislators intended the act as a check on the president's power to send troops into battle without the consent of Congress. Many believed the act was also passed to avoid future Vietnams.

The reunification of Vietnam brought about social change to the United States in the form of a significant influx of Southeast Asian immigrants. When Saigon fell to the North Vietnamese in April 1975, crowds of South Vietnamese fled to the U.S. Embassy and other buildings in the city, hoping to escape the communist invasion. Though U.S. pilots managed to evacuate 7,000 South Vietnamese in less than 24 hours—making the effort the largest

PRIMARY SOURCE

In 1975, John Tenhula began interviewing refugees from Vietnam, Cambodia, and Laos who immigrated to the United States. In this excerpt from an interview, Heng Mui, a South Vietnamese woman, talks about becoming an American citizen.

I became a citizen last year; I am now an American. I do not especially feel like an American, but I don't know if there is any special way I should feel. For some refugees, becoming an American is not an easy thing to do. It means you give up that final thing that is yours, your nationality. But after it happened, I never thought about it. There is something exciting about holding my new blue passport and knowing that I will vote next year for the president.

—from *Voices from Southeast Asia*, by John Tenhula, 1991

National Geographic photographer Michael S. Lewis captured the lights and activity of Lam Son Square in modern Ho Chi Minh City, formerly known as Saigon. Today, Vietnam's economy is one of the fastest-growing in the world, and the country boasts a developing middle class.

11.9.3 Trace the origins and geopolitical consequences (foreign and domestic) of the Cold War and containment policy, including the following: • The era of McCarthyism, instances of domestic Communism (e.g., Alger Hiss) and blacklisting • The Truman Doctrine • The Berlin Blockade • The Korean War • The Bay of Pigs invasion and the Cuban Missile Crisis • Atomic testing in the American West, the "mutual assured destruction" doctrine, and disarmament policies • The Vietnam War • Latin American policy; 11.9.4 List the effects of foreign policy on domestic policies and vice versa (e.g., protests during the war in Vietnam, the "nuclear freeze" movement); CST 1 Students compare the present with the past, evaluating the consequences of past events and decisions and determining the lessons that were learned.

helicopter airlift in history—hundreds more were left behind in the embassy. About one month before the fall of Saigon, however, the U.S. government had ordered Operation Babylift. The government airlifted about 3,000 Vietnamese orphans from Saigon to the United States throughout April and placed them with adoptive parents.

Many Vietnamese, Cambodian, and Laotian refugees would arrive as immigrants to the United States in the coming decades, however. The greatest numbers of immigrants arrived between 1980 and 2000. Though the immigrant flow has since decreased, the Vietnamese still made up the sixth largest immigrant population in the United States as of 2014. Most settled in California, Texas, Washington, and Florida. Like other groups that have immigrated to the United States, the Vietnamese have become part of the country's rich diversity, and they now embrace their own American identities.

HISTORICAL THINKING

1. **READING CHECK** What problems did Vietnam veterans face when they returned home from the war?
2. **FORM AND SUPPORT OPINIONS** What do you think is the most important legacy of the Vietnam War? Support your opinion with evidence from the text.
3. **IDENTIFY** What domestic policies changed as a result of the Vietnam War?
4. **MAKE INFERENCES** Explain the meaning behind the Vietnam veteran's statement, "The left hated us for killing, and the right hated us for not killing enough," and describe how people's viewpoints toward Vietnam veterans could be so different.

CHAPTER 18 THE VIETNAM WAR

REVIEW

VOCABULARY

Use each of the following vocabulary words in a sentence that shows an understanding of the term's meaning.

1. stalemate HSS 11.9.3
   The two sides were at a stalemate, with neither side able to claim victory.
2. hawk HSS 11.9.4
3. post-traumatic stress disorder HSS 11.9.3
4. coup HSS 11.9.3
5. induction HSS 11.9.4
6. escalation HSS 11.9.3
7. deferment HSS 11.9.4
8. counterculture HSS 11.9.4

READING STRATEGY

FORM AND SUPPORT OPINIONS

When you form an opinion, you determine and assess the importance and significance of something. Your opinion is your personal judgment, not a fact, so you should support your opinion with examples and facts. Use a chart like this one to form and support an opinion about protesters during the Vietnam War. Then answer the question.

Role of Protesters		
Example/Fact	Example/Fact	Example/Fact
Opinion		

9. Do you think Vietnam War protesters played a positive or a negative role in the conflict? HSS 11.9.4

MAIN IDEAS

Answer the following questions. Support your answers with evidence from the chapter.

10. Who were the Viet Cong? LESSON 1.1 HSS 11.9.3
11. Why was President Johnson initially opposed to sending American ground troops to Vietnam? LESSON 1.2 HSS 11.9.3
12. What was the purpose of General Westmoreland's war of attrition? LESSON 2.1 HSS 11.9.3
13. How did hawks and doves differ in their views of the war in Vietnam? LESSON 2.2 HSS 11.9.4
14. Why did the communists choose to begin their offensive on Tet? LESSON 3.1 HSS 11.9.3
15. Why did Johnson choose not to run for a second term as president? LESSON 3.2 HSS 11.9.4
16. What happened at My Lai? LESSON 4.1 HSS 11.9.3
17. What right did the 26th Amendment guarantee? LESSON 4.2 HSS 11.9.4

HISTORICAL THINKING

Answer the following questions. Support your answers with evidence from the chapter.

18. **ANALYZE CAUSE AND EFFECT** How did American journalists affect the war in Vietnam? HSS HI 1
19. **EVALUATE** What did Martin Luther King, Jr., mean when he called the Vietnam War "a white man's war, a black man's fight"? HSS 11.9.4
20. **MAKE INFERENCES** Why did the U.S. government present positive assessments of the war, even when it was going badly? HSS 11.9.4
21. **DRAW CONCLUSIONS** How was the Tet Offensive a strategic victory for the communists in Vietnam? HSS 11.9.3

22. **COMPARE AND CONTRAST** How was the war in Vietnam similar to and different from other Cold War struggles? HSS 11.9.3

23. **ANALYZE CAUSE AND EFFECT** How did the Vietnam War cause Americans to question the assumptions behind Cold War policy? HSS 11.9.3

24. **SUMMARIZE** What turned American public opinion against U.S. involvement in Vietnam? HSS 11.9.3

25. **FORM AND SUPPORT OPINIONS** How do you think American society changed as a result of the Vietnam War? HSS CST 2

26. **SYNTHESIZE** What combination of factors caused the United States to end its involvement in the Vietnam War? HSS 11.9.3

27. **MAKE CONNECTIONS** What similarities do you detect between the Vietnam War and more recent conflicts in Southwest Asia? HSS CST 1

INTERPRET GRAPHS

Study the graph below, which shows the Vietnamese immigrant populations in the United States between 1980 and 2010. Then answer the questions that follow.

Vietnamese Immigrant Population in the United States, 1980–2010

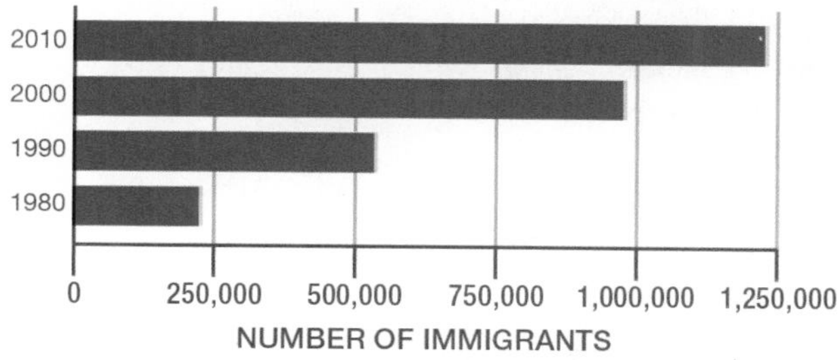

Sources: U.S. Census Bureau and American Community Surveys

28. Why do you think the number of Vietnamese immigrants more than quadrupled between 1980 and 2000? HSS CST 3

29. How might Vietnam's growing economy explain why the number of immigrants coming to the United States had tapered off by 2010? HSS CST 3

ANALYZE SOURCES

Tim O'Brien wrote about his experiences as a soldier in the Vietnam War. In this excerpt from his 1973 autobiographical story "If I Die in a Combat Zone," which appears in *The Vietnam Reader*, O'Brien discusses the summer he was drafted.

> The summer of 1968, the summer I turned into a soldier, was a good time for talking about war and peace. Eugene McCarthy was bringing quiet thought to the subject. Lyndon Johnson was almost forgotten. Robert Kennedy was dead but not quite forgotten; Richard Nixon looked like a loser. With all the tragedy and change that summer, it was fine weather for discussion. And, with all of this, there was an induction notice tucked into a corner of my billfold.

30. What details in the excerpt convey O'Brien's bias toward the politicians he names? HSS HREP 2

CONNECT TO YOUR LIFE

31. **ARGUMENT** Service in the armed forces today is voluntary. Do you think the draft should be reinstated? If so, do you think it should apply to both men and women? Write a paragraph in which you make an argument for or against the draft. HSS 11.9.4

TIPS

- State your position on the draft.
- List arguments for and against the draft.
- Explain why you think either voluntary or required military service is more fair or just.
- Use information from the chapter to help support your ideas.
- Address the counterarguments you listed.
- Conclude your argument with a sentence summarizing your position.

CHAPTER 19

CHANGES IN SOCIETY 1960–1975

HISTORICAL THINKING How did new calls for equality and the space race impact American society?

AMERICAN STORIES **One Giant Leap**

SECTION 1 **Latinos Organize**

SECTION 2 **Native Americans and Asian Americans**

SECTION 3 **Movements for Equality**

SECTION 4 **From Earth to the Moon**

AMERICAN GALLERY ONLINE **The Women's Movement**

Taking a cue from Susan B. Anthony and the suffragists as well as the civil rights movement, women of the 1960s and 1970s used nonviolent resistance and marched for equal treatment. In the 21st century, women once more took to the streets for equality. More than 400,000 people joined the 2017 Women's March on Washington, D.C., declaring, "women's rights are human rights."

"The fact that you can build and you can make nonviolent change through organization; that's what I would want my legacy to be."

—Dolores Huerta, civil rights activist

AMERICAN STORIES

NATIONAL GEOGRAPHIC

ONE GIANT LEAP

Astronauts Buzz Aldrin (shown here) and Neil Armstrong set up scientific experiments near their landing site on the moon. One of the experiments used seismometers powered by solar panels to measure lunar shock waves caused by seismic activity—moonquakes. It also measured the impact of meteoroids or other objects on the lunar surface.

On the evening of July 20, 1969, most Americans were fixated on a television screen, witnessing one of the greatest feats of engineering and technology in history: the first landing of a human on the moon. Years later in an interview, Neil Armstrong shared the credit for his lunar landing with a team of hundreds of thousands of men and women whose feet never left Earth, remarking, "Every guy that's setting up the tests, cranking the torque wrench, and so on, is saying—man or woman—'if anything goes wrong here, it's not going to be my fault.'"

Apollo 11 mission patch

THE SPACE RACE

Much of the technology needed to put Neil Armstrong and Buzz Aldrin on the moon was developed in a remarkably short span of time. One of the motivations for inventing that technology—competition—is as old as humanity.

As you have read, in 1957, the United States and the Soviet Union were engaged in a period of mutual distrust and hostility—the Cold War. Each country worried about the other developing more advanced weaponry or spying capabilities. When the Soviet Union launched *Sputnik* on October 4 of that year, Americans fretted that if the Soviets were more advanced in space technology, they might be ahead in weapons technology as well.

The American public was not reassured when, in December 1957, the U.S. Navy attempted to launch a satellite aboard a Vanguard rocket that caught fire upon take-off and crashed, earning the nickname "flopnik" from the press. A month later, however, the first U.S. satellite reached space atop a Jupiter rocket launched by the army. The space race between the Americans and Soviets was on.

HUMAN COMPUTERS

In May 1961, President Kennedy set out an ambitious goal in a speech before Congress, telling legislators, "I believe that this nation should commit itself to achieving the goal, before this decade is out, of landing a man on the moon and returning him safely to the earth." It was time to get to work.

Neil Armstrong's estimate of "hundreds of thousands" of people needed to place him on the moon was not an exaggeration. By one account, around 36,000 employees from NASA and 376,700 from universities or private industry worked on aspects of the lunar landing.

Armstrong was also correct to note that both men and women were involved in the massive effort. During the early years of space exploration, digital computers were not very advanced and could not perform the complex mathematics of placing a satellite, or a human being, in orbit or on the moon. That job fell to humans who held the job title of "computer" at NASA facilities such as Jet Propulsion Laboratory (JPL) in California and the Langley Research Center in Virginia. Most of the human computers were women.

11.8.7 Describe the effects on society and the economy of technological developments since 1945, including the computer revolution, changes in communication, advances in medicine, and improvements in agricultural technology.

AMERICAN STORIES

Both Langley and JPL had started hiring female computers in the 1940s, before they became part of NASA, to calculate the trajectories of rockets and missiles being developed for World War II. Later, the women turned their superb math skills to plotting trajectories and calculating fuel loads for rockets that would carry satellites and humans into space.

The computers were a diverse group. At JPL, Helen Ling was an immigrant from China, and Janez Lawson was the first African American hired for a professional position at the laboratory. At Langley, many of the computers were African-American women who were forced to use a separate workspace and bathroom until the facility was officially desegregated in 1958.

As digital computers began to outpace humans' ability to perform calculations, the human computers became NASA's first programmers. In 1962, however, when preparing for his orbital flight, astronaut John Glenn was not ready to trust the new machines. He wanted Katherine Johnson, one of the African-American computers at Langley, to do the math. "Get the girl to do it," he said. "I want this human computer to check the output of the electronic computer, and if she says they're good, you know, I'm good to go."

On September 12, 1962, President John F. Kennedy gave a speech at Rice University about the quest for the moon. In it, he expressed his optimism and enthusiasm for the space program.

PRIMARY SOURCE

The exploration of space will go ahead, whether we join in it or not, and it is one of the great adventures of all time, and no nation which expects to be the leader of other nations can expect to stay behind in the race for space.

We mean to be a part of it—we mean to lead it. For the eyes of the world now look into space, to the moon and to the planets beyond, and we have vowed that we shall not see it governed by a hostile flag of conquest, but by a banner of freedom and peace. We have vowed that we shall not see space filled with weapons of mass destruction, but with instruments of knowledge and understanding.

Yet the vows of this Nation can only be fulfilled if we in this Nation are first, and, therefore, we intend to be first. In short, our leadership in science and in industry, our hopes for peace and security, our obligations to ourselves as well as others, all require us to make this effort, to solve these mysteries, to solve them for the good of all men, and to become the world's leading space-faring nation.

—from President John F. Kennedy's speech at Rice University, September 12, 1962

The 2016 film *Hidden Figures* tells the story of the African-American "computers" at Langley who helped put astronauts on the moon. Here, actor Taraji P. Henson (right), in the role of Katherine Johnson, does mathematical calculations in front of an impressed audience.

11.11.2 Discuss the significant domestic policy speeches of Truman, Eisenhower, Kennedy, Johnson, Nixon, Carter, Reagan, Bush, and Clinton (e.g., with regard to education, civil rights, economic policy, environmental policy).

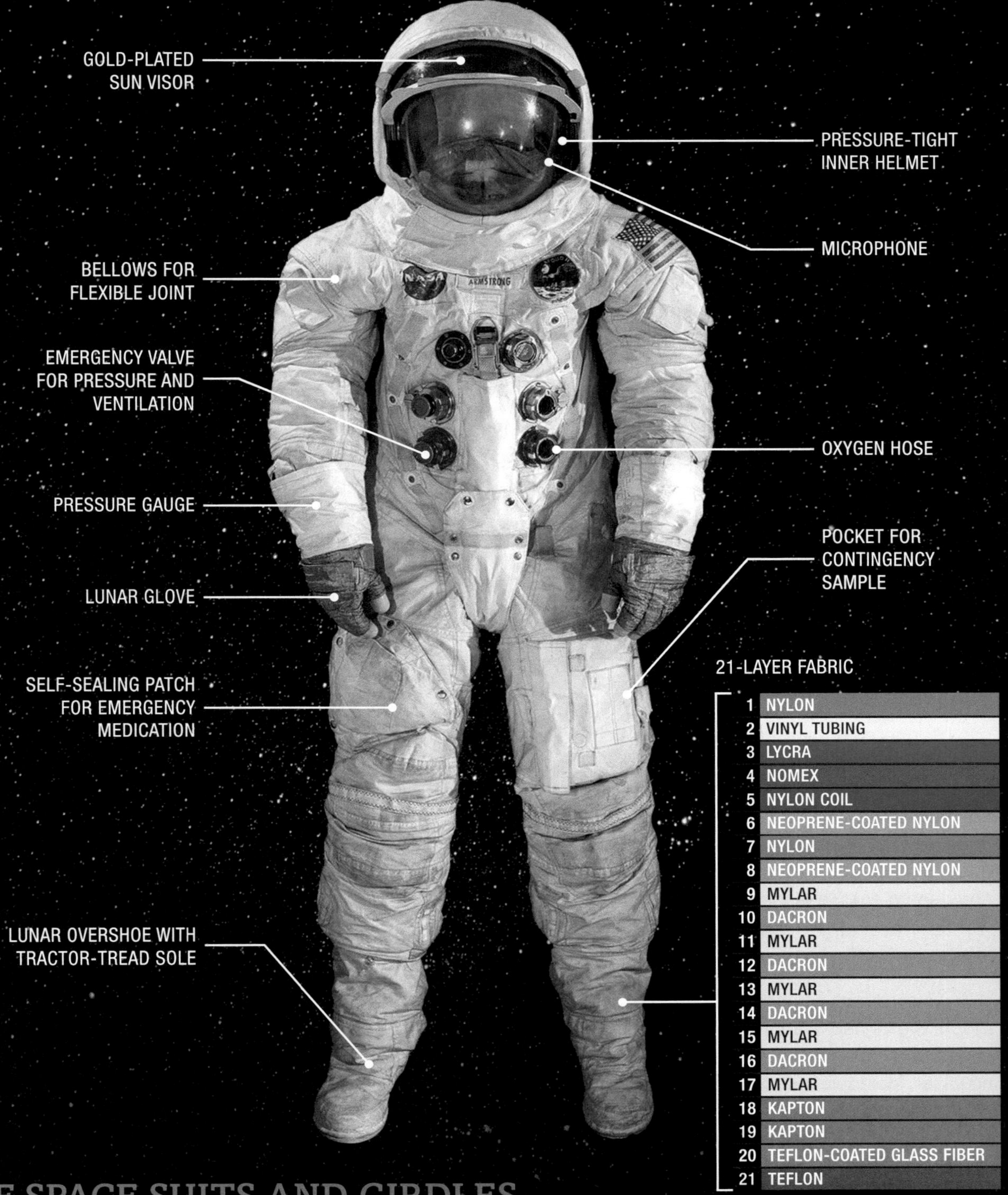

OF SPACE SUITS AND GIRDLES

Before Sally Ride went into space aboard NASA's space shuttle in 1983, all American astronauts were men. And yet, the maker of the first space suits was best known for its popular lines of bras and girdles—attire not commonly associated with male pilots. The International Latex Corporation, known as Playtex, had experience and expertise in working with latex and other tough, stretchy fabrics—just the materials needed to make a space suit.

Skilled Playtex seamstresses had to meticulously assemble 21 layers of material into a space suit tailored to fit each astronaut. Neil Armstrong described the suit he wore on the moon as a "spacecraft," and it did indeed have to function as a one-man habitat, providing air and a constant temperature as he walked on the moon's inhospitable surface. In the 1970s, the division of Playtex that designed and made space suits split off to become a separate company called ILC Dover that continues to make space suits today.

How were the 1960s a period of rapid change? Explain your answer in the context of space technology, social values and norms, and politics.

CST 2 Students analyze how change happens at different rates at different times; understand that some aspects can change while others remain the same; and understand that change is complicated and affects not only technology and politics but also values and beliefs.

AMERICAN **STORIES**

TO THE MOON AND BACK

While the computers worked on the math, engineers and other specialists were laboring to develop the technology that could carry humans into space, keep them alive there, and bring them back to Earth. They invented a spacecraft called a command module that would launch atop a powerful Saturn V rocket, which would place it in orbit around the moon. A lunar module would detach from this spacecraft to land on the moon. For the return trip, the lunar module would blast off from the moon's surface to dock with the command module for the return to Earth. Every part of the rocket and modules had to be engineered to perfection. There would be no rescue if a key component malfunctioned in the airless cold of space.

Even packing food for the trip required enormous amounts of planning. NASA researchers had to consider what would happen to a sandwich in orbit. As author Mary Roach noted, "A crumb in zero gravity does not drop to the floor where it can be ignored and ground into the flooring until the janitor comes around." Instead, it can float into delicate equipment and cause real damage. Foods had to be devised that would be light, easily packed into tight spaces, and neat to eat. Sadly for the early astronauts, deliciousness wasn't a top requirement of space food.

When Neil Armstrong set foot on the moon, the United States won the space race. The prizes for winning, however, included benefits for all countries. Between 1969 and 1972, 12 astronauts walked on the lunar surface, gathering evidence that advanced our understanding of the solar system. These missions also spurred the growth of computer technology and led to numerous product advancements, from fireproof clothing to better navigation systems for airplanes.

THINK ABOUT IT

How did the space program affect the U.S. economy and society?

HOW TO PLANT A FLAG ON THE MOON

The American flag that was planted on the moon by the Apollo 11 astronauts symbolizes both a victory for the United States and the complexity of performing simple tasks without Earth's gravity.

Because there is no wind on the moon, but just enough gravity to pull a flag down into a droop, a special flagpole had to be designed with a hinged crossbar at the top from which the flag would hang. Next came the problem of how to transport the flagpole, as there was not enough room inside the lunar module. It had to be mounted on the outside of the vehicle in a specially engineered case that could withstand the 2,000-degree Fahrenheit heat produced by the module's descent engine.

Setting up the flag wearing gloves that limited their range of motion would be tricky for the astronauts once they reached the moon, so they conducted several practice sessions on Earth to make sure they could plant the flag while wearing space suits. As this photo reveals, all their planning and practice paid off.

EXPLORING ALTERNATIVE VIEWS

After the lunar landing, conspiracy theorists insisted the event was actually an elaborate hoax created by the U.S. government to appear to have beaten the Soviets to the moon. They claimed Armstrong and Aldrin acted out their space mission on a secret film set, citing evidence to support their theories.

One piece of so-called evidence is video footage of Aldrin planting a waving American flag on the moon. Conspiracy theorists claimed the moving flag reveals the presence of wind, which is impossible in space. NASA says Aldrin was twisting the flagpole to penetrate the lunar soil, causing the flag to wave.

Decades later, some still support the lunar landing conspiracy theory. Conduct research about the conspiracy theorists' alternative interpretation of the historic event. Analyze their evidence and consider why many experts and historians dispute it. **As you research, do the following:**

- Distinguish valid arguments from fallacious ones in the conspiracy theorists' historical interpretation.
- Identify any evidence of bias and/or prejudice in the conspiracy theorists' historical interpretation.
- Distinguish between sound generalizations and misleading oversimplifications in both the conspiracy theory and in the more widely accepted account of the lunar landing.

HREP 1 Students distinguish valid arguments from fallacious arguments in historical interpretations; HREP 2 Students identify bias and prejudice in historical interpretations; HREP 3 Students evaluate major debates among historians concerning alternative interpretations of the past, including an analysis of authors' use of evidence and the distinctions between sound generalizations and misleading oversimplifications.

LIFE BEYOND EARTH?

National Geographic Explorer Kevin Hand wants to know if there is life beyond Earth. Working at JPL, the astrobiologist is helping to plan a NASA mission to Europa, a moon of Jupiter located about 600 million miles from Earth. In the 1990s, NASA's Galileo probe flew past the ice-covered moon and detected hints of a vast subsurface ocean. This led researchers to speculate about the possibility of life there. In 2013 and 2016, scientific teams using NASA's Hubble Space Telescope spotted what they believed were plumes of water erupting from beneath Europa's surface, raising hopes that a Europa probe might fly through a plume and analyze its chemistry.

To gain an understanding of the extreme conditions that might be found on other planets and their moons, Kevin Hand has explored such remote Earth locations as Alaska's north slope, Antarctica, and the depths of the ocean. "I'm trying to understand extremes of life here, so we can better assess and investigate habitable environments on alien worlds like Europa," he says.

Hand is as concerned about life on Earth as he is about possible life on a distant moon. He founded Cosmos Education, a foundation that helps educate and empower some of Africa's poorest children through science, health, and environmental education. "When I think about the desire to connect with life elsewhere in the universe," he reflects, "it gives me an incredible sense of the fragility of life here on Earth and how crucial it is to protect our collective home."

National Geographic's Kevin Hand prepares to deploy a rover beneath the ice of Alaska's Sukok Lake.

MISSIONS TO MARS

For some, the obvious next step in space exploration is Mars. NASA is exploring the possibility of sending astronauts to Mars and has already landed several unmanned vehicles on the planet. In September 2016, Elon Musk, owner of the private space contractor SpaceX, announced his goal to land a spaceship with humans aboard on Mars within a decade, establish a colony there, and ensure that humanity becomes a "multiplanetary species." Many are skeptical Musk can make this dream a reality in the foreseeable future, but his goals prove Mars exerts a strong pull on human imagination.

SpaceX's Falcon 9 rocket makes its first successful upright landing on a droneship in April 2016, 200 miles offshore in the Atlantic Ocean after launching from Cape Canaveral, Florida.

In the meantime, NASA missions are studying the sun and our solar system, expanding our understanding of the universe, and developing technology that also benefits humans on Earth. Whether we reach Mars in a decade or a century, it seems certain that our drive to explore space will continue to expand human knowledge and lead to new technologies we can only imagine today.

11.8.7 Describe the effects on society and the economy of technological developments since 1945, including the computer revolution, changes in communication, advances in medicine, and improvements in agricultural technology.

1.1 **MAIN IDEA** As the Latino population grew in the United States during the 1950s and 1960s, many Latinos endured poverty and discrimination.

LATINO LIVES IN THE UNITED STATES

Once an idea takes hold, it tends to spread. The advances of the African-American civil rights movement encouraged other minority groups to mount their own campaigns for legislative and judicial recognition of their civil rights.

LATINOS IN THE 1950s AND 1960s

As you have read, the term *Latino* refers to someone whose heritage is Latin American. In the mid-20th century, the Latino population of the United States consisted of three main groups. The largest group of Latinos were Mexican Americans, who began coming to the United States in significant numbers during World War II as part of the Bracero Program, a government program created to fill the nation's need for agricultural workers. Most Mexican Americans settled in California and the Southwest. Cuban Americans, many of whom fled Cuba after communist leader Fidel Castro seized power, settled mainly in Florida. And about 900,000 Puerto Ricans lived in the United States at that time, the vast majority of them in New York City.

By 1960, almost 6 million Latinos lived in the United States. Within the next 10 years, the population had increased to over 9 million Latinos. Immigration rose largely because of the Immigration Act of 1965, which raised immigration quotas and eased restrictions on settling in the United States.

World War II generated opportunities for Mexican Americans, along with others, to serve on the battlefield and to support the war effort in a variety of ways. However, in the years following the war, Mexican Americans, like other minority groups, continued to face discrimination and bias. In 1948, the **American GI Forum (AGIF),** a newly formed Hispanic veterans' group, and other Mexican American organizations, such as the Unity League and the League of United Latin American Citizens (LULAC), mobilized during the postwar years to fight for Latinos' civil rights.

Aided by these organizations, Latinos pushed for greater equality in education. In 1948, organizers challenged the segregation of Latino children in Bastrop, Texas, and three other Texas school districts in the case *Delgado* v. *Bastrop Independent School District*. The suit maintained that the children were being separated and provided with substandard facilities because of their race and without any legal or educational basis. The court agreed and ordered an end to the segregation. This case was similar to *Mendez* v. *Westminster*, which, as you have read, preceded *Brown* v. *Board of Education* and paved the way to ending public school segregation nationwide.

Latinos also succeeded in advancing their legal rights, including a significant victory in the 1954 case *Hernandez* v. *Texas*. Supporters of farmworker Pete Hernandez sued the state of Texas after Hernandez was convicted of murder by an all-white jury. For many years, counties in Texas—including the county where Hernandez was tried—systematically kept Mexican Americans from serving as jurors. The Latino attorneys representing Hernandez argued that, because the jury had not been made up of Hernandez's **peers**, or equals, their client had been denied equal protection under the law as guaranteed by the 14th Amendment. The case, *Hernandez* v. *Texas*, went all the way to the U.S. Supreme Court. The Court ruled unanimously in favor of Hernandez, stating that the 14th Amendment guaranteed protection not only on the basis of race, but also on the basis of ethnicity. *Hernandez* v. *Texas* set a **precedent**, or a basic legal standard, for many of the civil rights cases that followed.

11.8.2 Describe the significance of Mexican immigration and its relationship to the agricultural economy, especially in California; 11.9.3 Trace the origins and geopolitical consequences (foreign and domestic) of the Cold War and containment policy, including the following: • The era of McCarthyism, instances of domestic Communism (e.g., Alger Hiss) and blacklisting • The Truman Doctrine • The Berlin Blockade • The Korean War • The Bay of Pigs invasion and the Cuban Missile Crisis • Atomic testing in the American West, the "mutual assured destruction" doctrine, and disarmament policies • The Vietnam War • Latin American policy.

The *Arte de las Americas* mural runs along busy Calle Ocho, or Southwest 8th Street, in the Little Havana neighborhood, the heart of Cuban American life in Miami, Florida. Among the cultural icons portrayed on the wall are musicians, including world-famous salsa singer Celia Cruz.

A STRUGGLE FOR MANY

As Latinos pushed for greater civil rights, some made strides in achieving success. A number of Latinos joined the middle class. They also made notable achievements in the scientific fields. Latino biochemist Severo Ochoa received the Nobel Prize in medicine in 1959 for his research into the enzymes associated with DNA and RNA. Luis Alvarez received the Nobel Prize in physics in 1968 for his research into the basics of particle physics. Baseball star Roberto Clemente thrilled fans throughout the 1960s, while Cuban-born Desi Arnaz earned fame on the hit show *I Love Lucy* and became a successful television actor and producer.

For the vast majority of Latinos, however, success was a distant dream. In fact, life for the many Mexican American migrant workers was a struggle. Although migrant farm labor was vital to the success of the agricultural economy, in the mid-20th century migrant workers were not treated as the important human resource they were. They were paid poorly, earning an average of about $1,500 a year when the median U.S. income was about $6,200. They worked long hours with few breaks, and most lived in shacks, if they had housing at all. Because migrants continuously moved from farm to farm, most migrant children only occasionally attended school, and some received no education at all. And because they were poor and not well represented, farmworkers had been unable to organize or form a union, although they had been trying to improve their conditions since the end of World War II. Building upon the civil rights efforts of African Americans, a new generation of Latino leaders began an organized campaign to achieve greater equality and rights for farmworkers.

HISTORICAL THINKING

1. **READING CHECK** How did the Immigration Act of 1965 change the process for immigrating to the United States and transform American society?
2. **MAKE INFERENCES** How would serving in World War II affect the expectations of Latinos returning to the United States after the war?
3. **EVALUATE** How did the living and working conditions of migrant farmworkers make it difficult for them to demand greater equality and rights?

11.10.2 Examine and analyze the key events, policies, and court cases in the evolution of civil rights, including *Dred Scott* v. *Sandford*, *Plessy* v. *Ferguson*, *Brown* v. *Board of Education*, *Regents of the University of California* v. *Bakke*, and California Proposition 209; 11.10.5 Discuss the diffusion of the civil rights movement of African Americans from the churches of the rural South and the urban North, including the resistance to racial desegregation in Little Rock and Birmingham, and how the advances influenced the agendas, strategies, and effectiveness of the quests of American Indians, Asian Americans, and Hispanic Americans for civil rights and equal opportunities. 11.11.1 Discuss the reasons for the nation's changing immigration policy, with emphasis on how the Immigration Act of 1965 and successor acts have transformed American society.

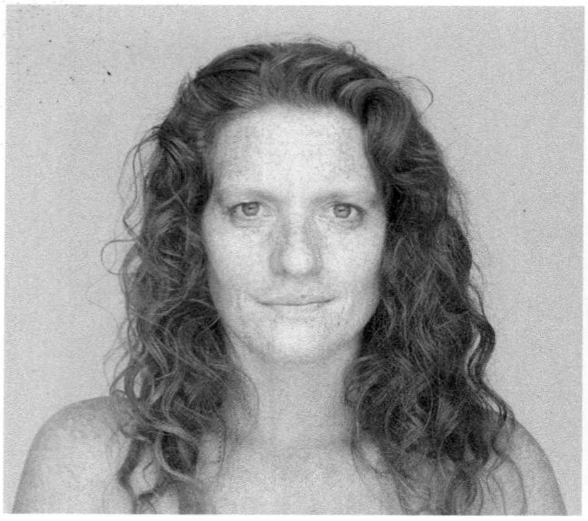

PANTONE® 58-7 C

PANTONE® 323-1 C

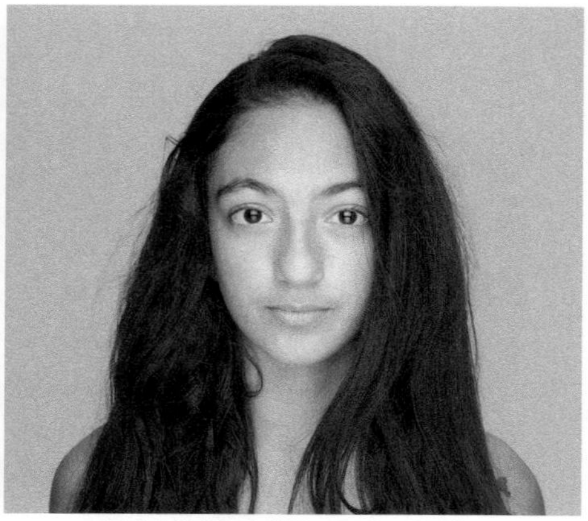

PANTONE® 51-6 C

1.2

THROUGH THE LENS

ANGÉLICA DASS

Humanæ, by the Brazilian artist Angélica Dass, is a photographic work intended to illustrate our similarities as global citizens. By identifying people with a Pantone color based on the actual color of their skin rather than by their nationality, gender, race, social class, or religion, Dass challenges us to think about how we see one another. Her portraits have been exhibited worldwide in museums and as public art installations.

PANTONE® 77-9 C

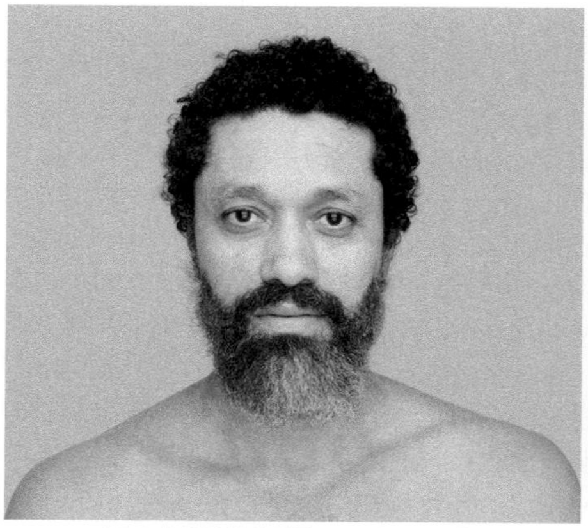

PANTONE® 58-6 C

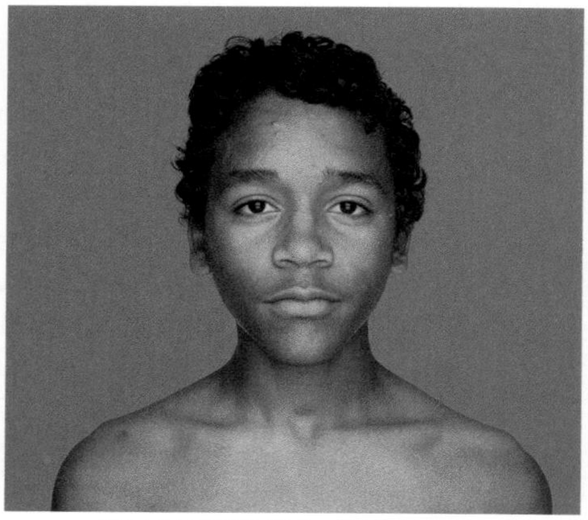

PANTONE® 66-5 C

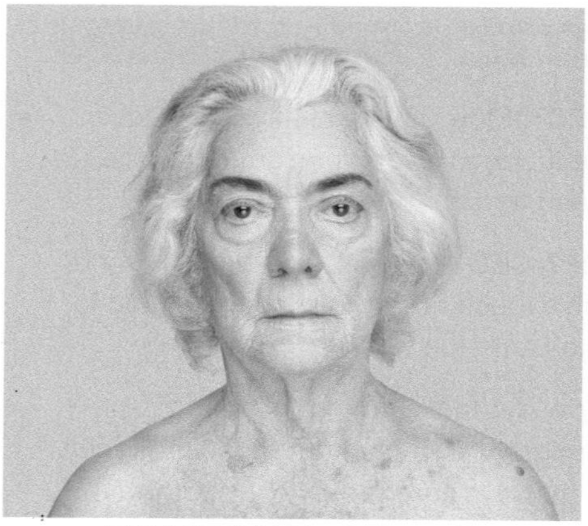

PANTONE® 97-7 C

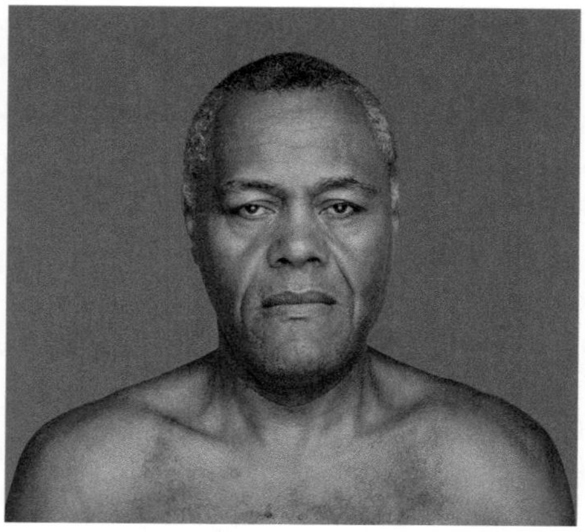

PANTONE® 317-5 C

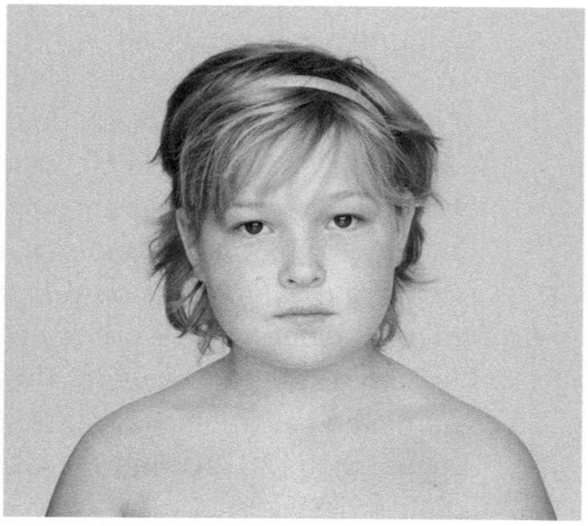

PANTONE® 58-7 C

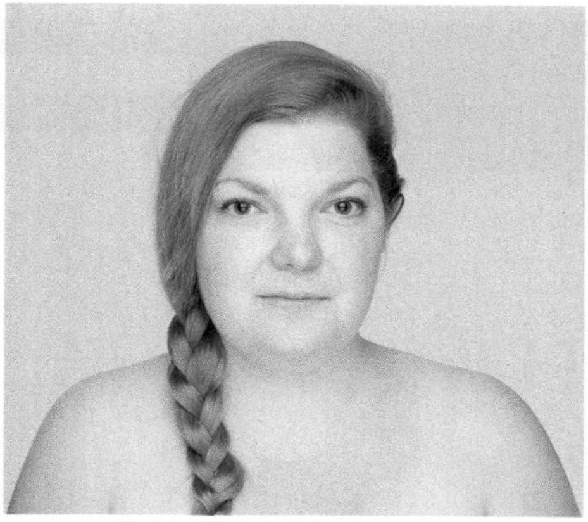
PANTONE® 99-9 C

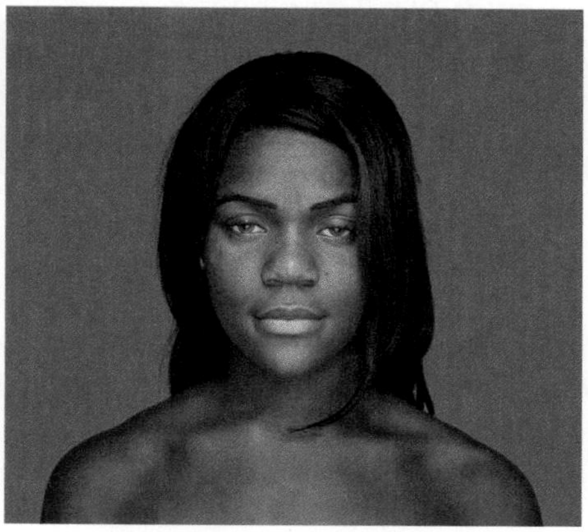
PANTONE® 321-6 C

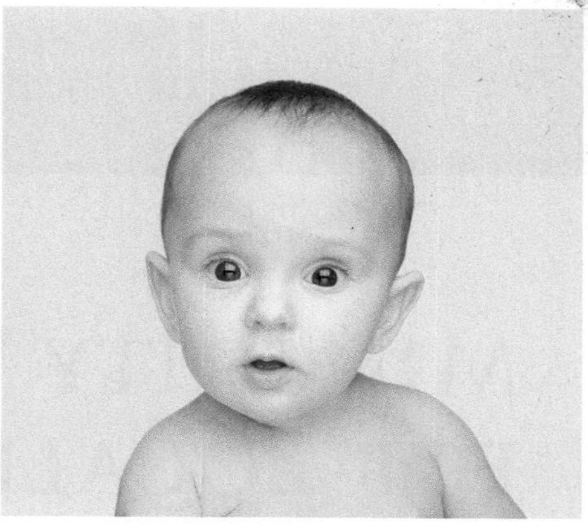
PANTONE® 95-9 C

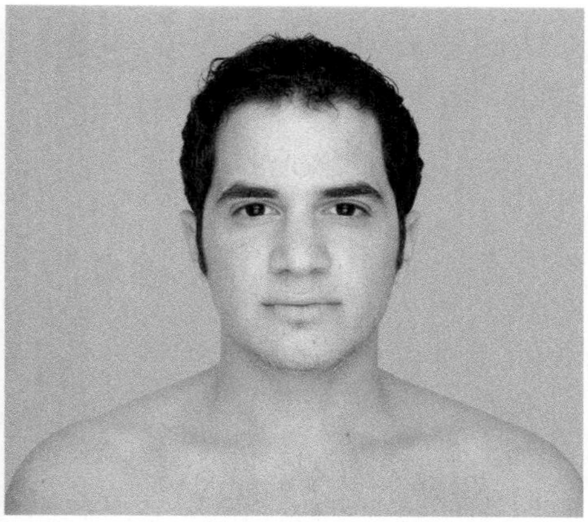
PANTONE® 62-6 C

PANTONE® 116-5 C

PANTONE® 7522 C

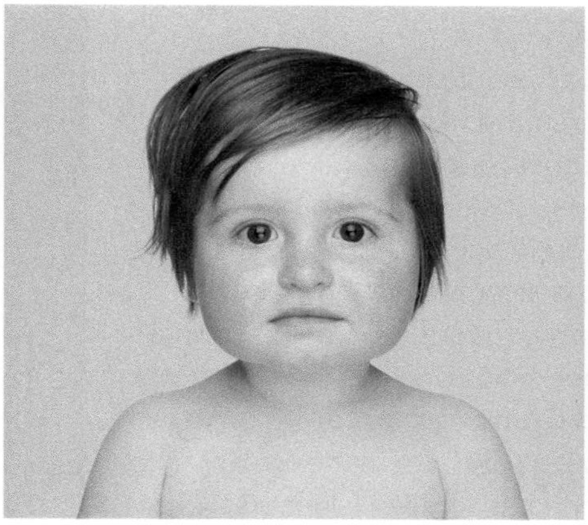
PANTONE® 92-9 C

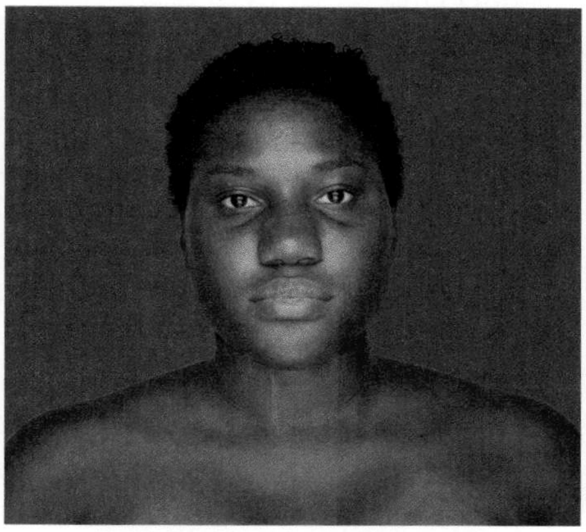
PANTONE® 319-2 C

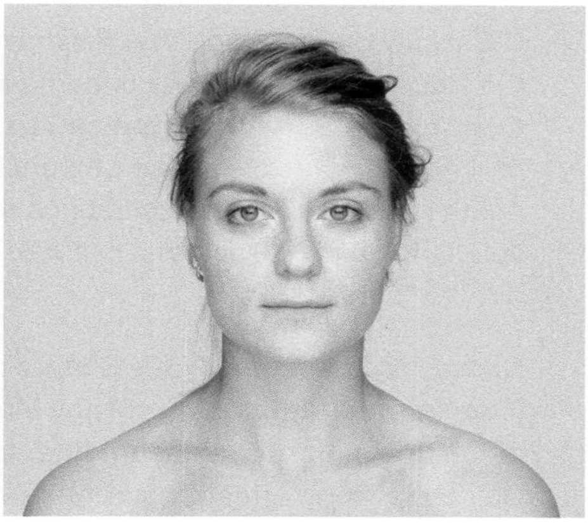
PANTONE® 57-7 C

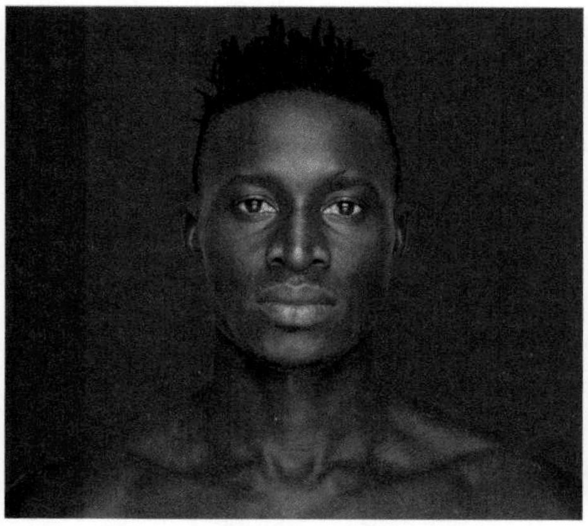
PANTONE® 322-1 C

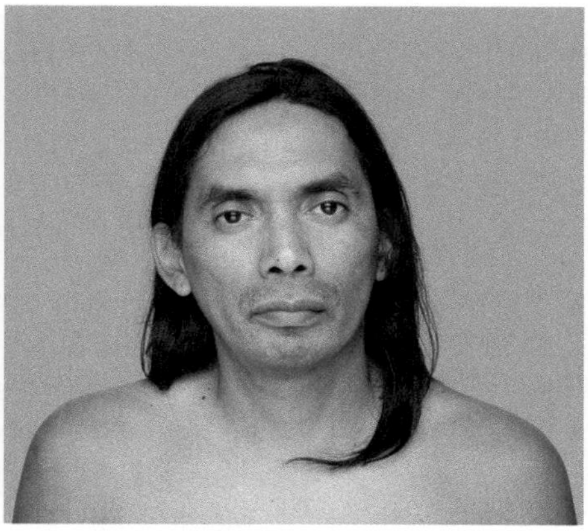
PANTONE® 71-5 C

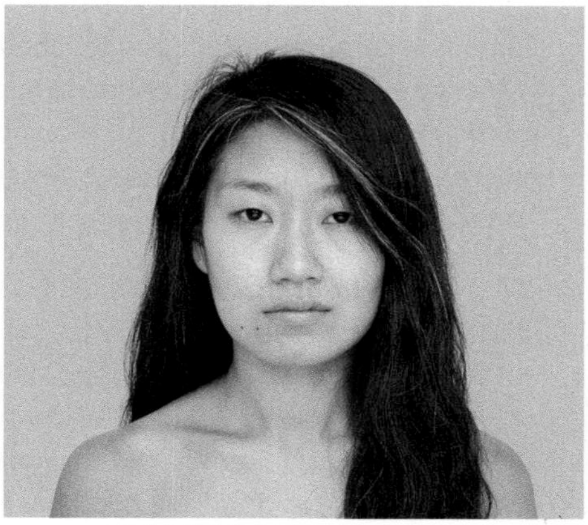
PANTONE® 53-7 C

1.3 **MAIN IDEA** During the 1960s, minority workers mobilized for improved wages and working conditions and more civil rights.

MINORITY WORKERS FIGHT FOR EQUALITY

Do you remember a time you felt ignored or treated unfairly? This was how a large number of Mexican American and Filipino American farmworkers felt during the 1960s. Latino and Filipino leaders joined forces to organize a historic campaign to win more rights for workers by drawing on strategies diffused from the African-American civil rights movement.

ORGANIZING FARMWORKERS

César Chávez was born in Yuma, Arizona, in 1927. His family owned a ranch and a grocery store, but they lost their property during the Great Depression. They moved to California, where they became migrant farmworkers. After serving two years in the U.S. Navy during World War II, Chávez returned to the fields. In 1952, Chávez became involved in the **Community Service Organization (CSO)**, a Latino civil rights group. He spoke on behalf of workers' rights and helped organize Latinos to register and vote in their local elections. In 1958, Chávez became director of the CSO.

During his time at the CSO, Chávez met **Dolores Huerta**. Huerta was born in New Mexico and moved at the age of three with her mother to Stockton, California, soon after her parents divorced. Growing up, Huerta was bright, talented, and a good student, but she often experienced discrimination because she was a Latina. After college, she became a teacher in an impoverished farming community. The difficult living situations of so many of her students—the children of migrant workers—inspired her to become an activist.

Chávez and Huerta quickly realized that they shared a common goal of helping better the lives and wages of farmworkers. Chávez left the CSO and formed the Farm Workers Association (FWA) while Huerta left to form the Agricultural Workers Association (AWA). In 1962, they merged their organizations to form the **National Farm Workers Association (NFWA)**. Their goal was to unionize farmworkers and help them seek better wages and more rights. The two activists were a powerful combination—Huerta was usually the negotiator and Chávez, an inspirational speaker and recruiter.

THE GRAPE BOYCOTT

Chávez and Huerta were dedicated to nonviolent protest. Chávez admired the work of Mohandas Gandhi and Martin Luther King, Jr., both of whom used nonviolent means—including boycotts and marches—to protest prejudice and injustice. These methods took time to deliver results, and Chávez knew that patience and cooperation were essential to success. In September 1965, Chávez and the NFWA joined a strike started by the **Agricultural Workers Organizing Committee (AWOC)**, made up largely of Filipino American grape packers in Delano, California. These farmworkers, led by labor leader **Larry Itliong**, were protesting a pay cut and demanding to be paid the legal minimum wage. On September 16, Mexican Independence Day, NFWA grape pickers walked out in solidarity with the AWOC strikers. It would be the beginning of *La Causa*, a five-year struggle to win a fair wage for the farm laborers.

Chávez organized a nationwide boycott of any grapes that did not bear a union label. To help build recognition for the strikers and the boycott, Chávez and Huerta led a peaceful 340-mile march from Delano, California, to the state capitol at Sacramento in March 1966. They began with only 100 people.

11.10.5 Discuss the diffusion of the civil rights movement of African Americans from the churches of the rural South and the urban North, including the resistance to racial desegregation in Little Rock and Birmingham, and how the advances influenced the agendas, strategies, and effectiveness of the quest of American Indians, Asian Americans, and Hispanic Americans for civil rights and equal opportunities.

THE GREAT GRAPE STRIKE

For years, attempts to organize farmworkers were defeated, often by growers who had played one race against the other. But change began in 1965, when Larry Itliong and 1,000 mostly Filipino grape laborers walked off their jobs, demanding better pay. Within days, Itliong asked Dolores Huerta and César Chávez of the NFWA to join the strike. Dismayed at some growers' brutal treatment of the strikers, Chávez, Huerta, and 1,200 Latino farmworkers joined the strike. By working together, these three leaders brought new life to the nonviolent fight to gain equality for all farmworkers.

Dolores Huerta

César Chávez

Larry Itliong

A boycott poster depicts farm-labor families gathered before a lettuce field as the setting sun displays the United Farm Workers symbol and its motto in Spanish and English. Immediately after the grape strike settlement, the UFW led a nationwide boycott of non-union lettuce to help improve lettuce pickers' wages and living conditions.

"We, as Filipinos, are not alone anymore. We have brothers among the Mexicans and the Blacks and in the conscience of the American people." —Larry Itliong

11.6.5 Trace the advances and retreats of organized labor, from the creation of the American Federation of Labor and the Congress of Industrial Organizations to current issues of a postindustrial, multinational economy, including the United Farm Workers in California.

They finished the trek with more than 1,000. The pilgrimage drew national attention to the situation farmworkers faced. A few months later, in August, the NFWA and AWOC merged and became the United Farm Workers Organizing Committee, which later became the **United Farm Workers (UFW)**, a full-fledged union.

The union's combined strength enabled it to expand its protest movement and target all California grape growers. The UFW organized strikes and picket lines at farms across the state. Other unions offered their support. In the San Francisco Bay Area, for example, longshoremen refused to load grapes onto ships, instead leaving tons of grapes to rot on the docks. Meanwhile, a growing number of consumers in North America supported the workers by refusing to buy grapes. The campaign did not always go smoothly, and at one point Chávez went on a 24-day water-only fast to protest against some of his own union members who were advocating more violent forms of opposition. As grape growers watched their profits decline, they eventually gave in to the UFW. In 1970, the boycott ended as growers agreed to a collective bargaining agreement with at least 10,000 laborers, as well as better wages, union recognition, a health clinic, a health plan, and a credit union.

FIGHTING FOR CHICANO RIGHTS

As Latino civil rights efforts gained greater attention, a growing number of Mexican Americans in California and the Southwest began raising their voices. Throughout the 1960s, scores of activists and young people mobilized to protest a variety of issues—including the Vietnam War, police brutality, and economic and social inequalities—as well as to promote cultural pride. Many activists began identifying with the term "Chicano," another name for Mexican American, and their different protests and campaigns became known collectively as the **Chicano Civil Rights Movement**, or "El Movimiento."

A leading voice in the movement was **Rodolfo "Corky" Gonzales**, a poet and activist in Denver who called on Chicanos to take greater control over their own destinies. He argued that the white establishment could not provide adequate education, economic stability, or social acceptance, and that Chicanos should look for alternatives. Under his leadership, Denver's Chicano community developed its own school, newspaper, and credit bureau, and it continued to fight for better economic and housing opportunities. Gonzales became the voice of the Chicano movement when his epic poem *I Am Joaquín* became widely read. It is an elegant statement of the complex history of Mexican Americans and their lives in the United States.

Gonzales also convened the first Chicano Youth Liberation Conference in Denver in 1969, which was attended by many activists and artists. At the conference, attendees drafted the *El Plan Espiritual de Aztlán*, more commonly known as **El Plan de Aztlán**. This **manifesto**, or declaration, called for a new nationalism among Chicanos. It spoke to the dream of gaining back the land Mexico surrendered to the United States—including California and much of the Southwest—in the Treaty of Guadalupe Hidalgo in 1848.

In California, Chicano students became increasingly engaged in El Movimiento. In 1968, approximately 15,000 high school students protested racial discrimination and low-quality education by walking out of their classrooms in five East Los Angeles high schools in a series of protests they called "blowouts." At that time, schools in Los Angeles received funding based on how many students attended per day. By walking out of their homerooms before attendance was taken, the students made their point both actively and financially. Although the blowouts did not bring about immediate change, they empowered the Chicano community and built unity and solidarity for the cause. Chicano activists also drafted the **El Plan de Santa Bárbara: A Chicano Plan for Higher Education**, a document that called for the creation of Chicano Studies programs throughout the California state college system. In a victory for the Chicano movement, state officials adopted the plan in April 1969.

PRIMARY SOURCE

I am Joaquín,
Lost in a world of confusion,
Caught up in a whirl of a gringo society,
Confused by the rules,
Scorned by attitudes,
Suppressed by manipulation,
And destroyed by modern society.
My fathers
have lost the economic battle
and won
the struggle of cultural survival.

—from the epic poem *I Am Joaquín*, by Rodolfo "Corky" Gonzales, 1967

What do you think the poet means when he says "My fathers have lost the economic battle and won the struggle of cultural survival"?

©Herald-Examiner Collection/Los Angeles Public Library

THE LOS ANGELES BLOWOUTS
During a walkout at Belmont High School in East Los Angeles, police in riot gear handcuff a member of the Brown Berets (left) and a press photographer (right). The **Brown Berets**, a group within the Chicano movement, arose in East Los Angeles in 1968 to agitate for the Chicano community. A militant group modeled on the Black Panthers, they focused on educational and employment opportunities and against police harassment and brutality. They also established a free clinic organized by Chicana feminist Gloria Arellanes. Following the blowouts across East Los Angeles, 13 of the activist leaders were arrested and charged with "conspiring to disrupt education," which was punishable by up to 66 years in jail. The charges were dropped for violating the Bill of Rights, but only after 2 years of legal battles.

As part of their fight for greater equality and rights, some Chicano activists publicly protested the Vietnam War, claiming that a disproportionately high number of Mexican Americans were being drafted, wounded, and killed in the conflict. Across the country, Chicanos engaged in a series of antiwar protests, which became known as the Chicano Moratorium. This movement culminated in a major protest in Los Angeles in August 1970. The protest proceeded peacefully enough, as more than 30,000 people marched through East Los Angeles. Although it inspired more Hispanics to become involved in the movement for Chicano rights, it ended in tragedy as protesters were met with a heavy-handed police response. In the resulting violence, three people were killed.

In Texas in 1968, the **Mexican American Legal Defense Education Fund (MALDEF)** was founded specifically to protect and promote Latino civil rights. Modeled on the NAACP's Legal Defense Fund and LULAC, the organization's role was to provide the legal expertise for the grassroots Latino community. Throughout the 1960s, Chicanos increased their political activity, and by the end of the decade they had organized their own political party. José Angel Gutiérrez, later an attorney and college professor, founded the **La Raza Unida Party** in response to many Chicanos' dissatisfaction with the mainstream political parties. La Raza Unida promoted Chicano nationalism and was most influential in Texas and southern California. The party experienced its greatest successes at the local level in southwest Texas, where its members won seats on a number of city councils and school boards. But the party failed to gain widespread support, and by the late 1970s, it had faded away. However, Hispanic Americans around the country would continue to organize politically and work to promote their causes at the local, state, and national levels of government.

HISTORICAL THINKING

1. **READING CHECK** What were the goals of the National Farm Workers Association?
2. **DRAW CONCLUSIONS** Why was the cooperation of Chávez, Huerta, and Itliong vital to maintaining a five-year, nonviolent strike and boycott?
3. **ANALYZE CAUSE AND EFFECT** What were some of the actions that finally forced the grape growers to agree on a fair contract with farmworkers?
4. **MAKE GENERALIZATIONS** Why did Chicanos protest the war in Vietnam as a civil rights issue?

HI 1 Students show the connections, causal and otherwise, between particular historical events and larger social, economic, and political trends and developments.

2.1 **MAIN IDEA** In the 1960s, Native Americans mobilized to protest against assimilation and fight for greater rights and opportunities.

NATIVE AMERICANS MOBILIZE

What are the things you like most about where you live? Why do you consider your neighborhood a special place? Many Native Americans considered their ancient homelands special and sacred. They did not want to move from their lands. Instead, they wanted greater rights and opportunities to improve their living conditions.

THE DECLARATION OF PURPOSE

In the 1960s, Native Americans were one of the nation's smallest minority groups, but collectively, they continued to suffer greatly. Many lived in poverty and faced discrimination and neglect from the nation at large.

As you have read, the U.S. government enacted the termination policy in the early 1950s in an effort to better assimilate Native Americans into mainstream society. Officials ended federal support for reservations—many of which had become isolated, poverty-stricken places—and tried to urge Native American families to move to the cities, where more jobs were available. The effort was largely a failure.

Many Native Americans did not wish to assimilate. Instead, they began to seek greater rights and opportunities as they insisted on preserving their distinct culture and staying on their land. **Ben Nighthorse Campbell**, a member of the Northern Cheyenne tribe and later a U.S. senator from Colorado, spoke for many Native Americans in criticizing the

PRIMARY SOURCE

After the American Indian Chicago Conference, President Kennedy met with delegates from 90 Native American tribes, including (from left) Eleanor Red Fawn Smooth, Mohawk and Cherokee Nations, Connecticut; Calvin W. McGhee, Atmore, Alabama, representing the Creek Nation east of the Mississippi; and Kathitha Addison, of the Narragansett Nation. They spoke on the lawn of the White House, where Kennedy acknowledged the plight of Native Americans and promised his support.

I hope that this visit here, which is more than ceremonial, will be a reminder to all Americans of the number of Indians whose housing is inadequate, whose education is inadequate, whose employment is inadequate, whose health is inadequate, whose security and old age is inadequate—a very useful reminder that there is still a good deal of unfinished business.

—John F. Kennedy, August 15, 1962

termination policy. "If you can't change them [Native Americans], absorb them until they simply disappear into the mainstream culture," he declared with irony. "In Washington's infinite wisdom, it was decided that tribes should no longer be tribes, never mind that they had been tribes for thousands of years."

Rather than assimilate, Native Americans pushed to preserve their identity and demanded greater support from the federal government in helping them improve their lives. In 1961, some 700 Native Americans from 64 tribes met in Chicago to draft a common agenda and call to action. During the weeklong conference, the group created the **Declaration of Indian Purpose**, a document listing the major issues facing Native Americans and calling for a policy of greater self-determination. "We, the Indian People, must be governed in a democratic manner with a right to choose our own way of life," the statement declared. "We believe we have the responsibility of preserving our precious heritage." The declaration urged the federal government to move away from its termination policy and instead help Native Americans to better thrive on their own. "What we ask of America," the declaration stated, "is that the nature of our situation be recognized and made the basis of policy and action."

SLOW PROGRESS

By the early 1960s, U.S. officials began pulling back from the termination policy and instead promoted greater self-determination for Native Americans. Activists found sympathetic supporters in both President Kennedy and President Johnson. Kennedy secured funding to build adequate public housing on a prominent Native American reservation, and he worked during his short time as president to set the groundwork for later legislation promoting greater rights and federal support for Native Americans.

When Lyndon Johnson assumed the presidency after Kennedy's death, he pledged to help Native Americans as part of his War on Poverty. As you have read, this program sought to create a decent standard of living for all Americans. Early in his term Johnson stated, "Both in terms of statistics and in terms of human welfare, it is a fact that America's first citizens, our Indian people, suffer more from poverty than any other group in America." In 1968, Johnson gave a speech titled "The Forgotten American" to Congress, in which he stressed the need to raise Native American living standards to the same level as that of other American citizens. He said that Native Americans should be able to live wherever they pleased, whether it was on a reservation or in a city, and that any Native American policy should stress self-help, self-development, and self-determination for the minority group. "For two centuries," Johnson told Congress, "he [the Native American] has been an alien in his own land."

Despite such commitment at the highest level, progress proved slow. Among Native Americans, younger activists began to express frustration—both with the federal government and their own tribal leaders—over what they viewed as too little action and too few results. A group of younger leaders eventually broke away and formed the **National Indian Youth Council (NIYC)**. The NIYC included members of diverse tribes, yet they shared the same agenda: to draw greater attention to the cause of Native Americans through stronger mobilization and protest. The NIYC **charter**, or founding document, declared, "We, the younger generation, at this time in the history of the American Indian, find it expedient [practical] to band together on a national scale in meeting the challenges facing our Indian people."

NIYC priorities included reclaiming Native American hunting and fishing rights on their traditional lands. Diffusing the African-American civil rights movement model of sit-ins, NIYC held "fish-ins" by occupying areas around rivers and disrupting the commercial fishing activity there. Members of the group also protested at museums that displayed sacred artifacts taken from their tribes. They challenged movies and other media to present more honest portrayals of Native Americans and asked colleges and universities to create Indian Studies programs. These efforts revealed a younger generation of Native Americans ready to advance its agenda through bolder protest strategies. In the years ahead, they would engage in even more disruptive and confrontational tactics in their quest to gain greater rights.

HISTORICAL THINKING

1. **READING CHECK** What was the thinking behind the Declaration of Purpose?
2. **ANALYZE LANGUAGE USE** Why do you think President Kennedy kept repeating the word "inadequate" in the primary source quotation?
3. **EVALUATE** Why did young Native American leaders start the National Indian Youth Council?
4. **COMPARE AND CONTRAST** How were the federal policies and actions toward Native Americans in the 1960s different from those of the past, and why?

11.10.5 Discuss the diffusion of the civil rights movement of African Americans from the churches of the rural South and the urban North, including the resistance to racial desegregation in Little Rock and Birmingham, and how the advances influenced the agendas, strategies, and effectiveness of the quests of American Indians, Asian Americans, and Hispanic Americans for civil rights and equal opportunities; CST 1 Students compare the present with the past, evaluating the consequences of past events and decisions and determining the lessons that were learned.

2.2 **MAIN IDEA** In their fight for greater rights, some Native Americans moved away from peaceful demonstrations and turned to more confrontational protests.

NATIVE AMERICAN ACTIVISM

The advances of the African-American civil rights movement helped breathe new life into Native Americans' fight for their own rights, but the way forward proved to be more difficult. Native Americans were few in number and saw little public attention paid to their cause. As a result, they began taking more extreme measures to make their voices heard.

THE AMERICAN INDIAN MOVEMENT

In 1968, a group of Native American activists in Minneapolis founded the **American Indian Movement (AIM)**. The group's founders, including **George Mitchell, Dennis Banks**, and others, were members of the Ojibwe (oh-JIHB-way) tribe. Their goal was to help fellow Native Americans displaced during the years of the termination policy and to call attention to their substandard living conditions. AIM established urban centers where Native Americans could meet to give and receive help finding jobs, housing, and transportation. The organization grew and set up chapters in Cleveland, Chicago, Milwaukee, Denver, and San Francisco.

As AIM expanded, its leaders' strategies took an increasingly active and **militant**, or forceful, turn in promoting Native American rights. In November 1969, AIM members occupied the abandoned federal prison on Alcatraz Island in San Francisco Bay as a protest against the city's refusal to let Native Americans use the site as a cultural and heritage center. AIM initially received an outpouring of support in the form of donated funds, food, and clothing, but the protest eventually lost momentum and effectiveness. The occupiers included a number of local college students who returned to school and were replaced by people less interested in the cause than in living rent-free. By June 1971, the number of occupiers had dwindled, and U.S. marshals removed them from the island.

A "Remember Wounded Knee" embroidered patch from the American Indian Movement

A year later, a week before the 1972 presidential election, AIM organized the "Trail of Broken Treaties," a march on Washington, D.C., involving about 1,000 protesters. It ended with the occupation of the **Bureau of Indian Affairs (BIA)** headquarters. AIM protesters seized large numbers of files from the BIA offices and caused more than $2 million in damage to the building. They also presented President Nixon with 20 demands for immediate action. Government officials eventually negotiated a peaceful end to the occupation.

Meanwhile, in Minnesota, AIM leaders helped parents establish Native American "survival schools" to avoid the biases of local child welfare and legal systems. As the schools multiplied, they engaged adults and students with issues of Native American language, culture, spirituality, and identity.

PROTESTS AT WOUNDED KNEE

In February 1973, AIM engaged in what would become one of its best-known and most violent protests. About 200 members of the Oglala Lakota tribe along with AIM leaders seized and occupied the town of Wounded Knee, South Dakota, on the Pine Ridge Reservation. The occupiers were protesting the failure to impeach tribal president Richard Wilson, whom they accused of corruption and abuse of opponents. They were also protesting the U.S. government's failure to fulfill promises made in treaties with Native Americans, and they

11.10.5 Discuss the diffusion of the civil rights movement of African Americans from the churches of the rural South and the urban North, including the resistance to racial desegregation in Little Rock and Birmingham, and how the advances influenced the agendas, strategies, and effectiveness of the quests of American Indians, Asian Americans, and Hispanic Americans for civil rights and equal opportunities.

CRITICAL VIEWING In 1969, the members of various Native American tribes held a vigil, or watchful protest, on the dock at Alcatraz Island as other members negotiated with the U.S. government over the island's fate. What alterations were made to the sign behind the occupiers, and what do you think was the purpose of the alterations?

demanded the reopening of treaty negotiations. The activists chose the site of the 1890 Wounded Knee Massacre, where federal troops had killed more than 150 Lakota. A tense standoff ensued for 71 days, in which two AIM members were shot and killed and a U.S. marshal was shot and paralyzed. Ultimately, a truce was negotiated and federal officers agreed to review a number of treaties made with Native Americans. Dennis Banks and another prominent AIM leader, **Russell Means**, were charged with crimes for their role in the event, but the charges were later dismissed.

Despite their largely symbolic protests, the strategies and effectiveness of Native Americans led to some gains. In 1975, Congress passed the **Indian Self-Determination and Educational Assistance Act**, which boosted funds for Native American education and gave Native Americans greater control in administering local programs. In 1978, Congress passed the **Indian Religious Freedom Act**, which allowed Native Americans to practice their traditional religions freely. Native Americans also gained greater representation within the Bureau of Indian Affairs, a federal organization they had long criticized for not being fully attentive to their needs.

In addition, Native Americans used the courts to accomplish what protests could not. They sued state and federal governments to force compliance with old treaties that had been ignored and took legal action to win back numerous land and water rights. The Pueblo in New Mexico, for example, regained rights to their land, as did several tribes in Maine. Court decisions also enabled Native Americans to receive millions of dollars for their land claims, while other rulings allowed Native Americans to impose taxes on businesses on their reservations and take greater control of their economic futures.

HISTORICAL THINKING

1. **READING CHECK** Why did the American Indian Movement take more drastic actions than other civil rights movements?
2. **ANALYZE CAUSE AND EFFECT** What effect did the passage of the Indian Self-Determination and Education Assistance Act have on the Native American community?
3. **DRAW CONCLUSIONS** How effective were the lawsuits brought by Native Americans to establish their basic civil rights? Support your response with evidence from the text.

11.10.6 Analyze the passage and effects of civil rights and voting rights legislation (e.g., 1964 Civil Rights Act, Voting Rights Act of 1965) and the Twenty-Fourth Amendment, with an emphasis on equality of access to education and to the political process.

2.3 **MAIN IDEA** Asian Americans faced discrimination for many years, and as their population grew during the 1960s and 1970s, they demanded better treatment.

ASIAN AMERICAN CIVIL RIGHTS

Asia, the world's largest continent, encompasses many diverse countries and cultures. As a result, the term "Asian American" refers to all Americans of Asian origin. They share a desire for equal opportunities in the United States.

DISCRIMINATION AGAINST ASIAN AMERICANS

Like other groups seeking equal civil rights, the story of Asian Americans has been one of exclusion, discrimination, and the gradual gaining of rights and respect. The decision by Congress to pass the Chinese Exclusion Act in 1882 was based largely on complaints that Chinese immigrants were taking labor union jobs. The measure denied any Chinese person the opportunity to immigrate to the United States. The Immigration Act of 1924 expanded the law and excluded all Asians. It wasn't until World War II, when the United States and China became allies, that restrictions against Chinese immigration were eased. During the war, as you learned, it was Japanese Americans who suffered discrimination, and worse. Thousands of Japanese Americans were confined to internment camps based on fears they were disloyal and dangerous.

Internment robbed many Japanese Americans of their homes, land, and livelihoods, and racist discrimination made it hard for many of them to recover their property. For example, in California, an Alien Land Law passed in 1913 prohibited Asian immigrants who were noncitizens—usually because of immigration restrictions—from owning agricultural land. Kajiro Oyama had moved to the United States as a teenager. In 1934, he bought six acres of farmland, registering the property in the name of his son, Fred,

Protesters surrounded the San Francisco State College administration building, demonstrating against alleged racism and political harassment by college administrators.

11.10.5 Discuss the diffusion of the civil rights movement of African Americans from the churches of the rural South and the urban North, including the resistance to racial desegregation in Little Rock and Birmingham, and how the advances influenced the agendas, strategies, and effectiveness of the quests of American Indians, Asian Americans, and Hispanic Americans for civil rights and equal opportunities.

who had been born in the United States and thus was an American citizen. During World War II, the Oyama family took part in a "voluntary evacuation," relocating to Utah rather than being forced into an internment camp. When they returned to California after the war, they found that their farm had been seized. With the help of the **Japanese American Citizens League**, Kajiro sued to get his land back. *Oyama* v. *California* reached the U.S. Supreme Court, which ruled in 1948 that Fred Oyama's rights as an American citizen had been violated. The Oyama family retained ownership of the land, but the Court did not overturn the Alien Land Law until 1952.

Other Asian American groups also endured discrimination. As you have read, Filipino Americans worked largely as farm laborers and collaborated with Latino workers to push for better pay and more rights. Pacific Islanders struggled in their relations with the United States. The natives of Guam became Americans overnight when the United States acquired their island after winning the Spanish-American War in 1898. But Americans did little to acknowledge and support the island's culture. Similarly, when the United States annexed the Hawaiian Islands in 1898, land was taken from native Hawaiians and their culture suffered from the imposition of American values in the territory.

PROGRESS ON CIVIL RIGHTS

As a result of the Immigration Act of 1965, which raised quotas on immigrants from outside Europe, the number of Asian Americans grew steadily through the second half of the 20th century. In the 1950s, Asians represented 6 percent of all immigrants to the United States, and by 1980, that number had climbed to 42 percent. Like other groups that had to fight for their civil rights, Asian Americans and Pacific Islanders also vary widely in their backgrounds and cultures, and as they grew in numbers, they united to fight for greater rights and recognition.

In 1968, students at the University of California, Berkeley, started the **Asian American Political Alliance (AAPA)** to advocate on behalf of Asian Americans. The group fought for many issues, from improved housing for poor Asians to use of the term "Asian American" rather than widely used derogatory terms. That same year, Asian American students went on strike at San Francisco State College (renamed San Francisco State University in 1974). Forming a coalition with other student groups, including the Black Student Union and the Third World Liberation Front (a group that included Native Americans, African Americans, and Latinos), the students demanded establishment of an Ethnic Studies program. The strike lasted five months until the university acquiesced, agreeing to add the program. In 1969, students and activists in Seattle, Washington, founded the **Asian Coalition for Equality (ACE)**, which protested police brutality and worked to desegregate the region's industries and open up clubs and organizations to minorities.

Meanwhile, Japanese Americans began pressuring the federal government to issue an apology for the World War II internment camps. In 1976, the government responded. President Gerald Ford signed **Proclamation 4417**, formally apologizing for the internment program. Twelve years later, President Reagan signed the **Civil Liberties Act of 1988**, which paid each living internee $20,000 in **reparations** for what they had experienced in the camps. Today, some 18 million Asian Americans and Pacific Islanders live in the United States. That is about 5.8 percent of the country's population. Their population continues to grow, and while they continue to face prejudice, they also continue to achieve success and help to shape and build the American identity.

PRIMARY SOURCE

Born on a U.S. military base in Japan in 1948, Merilynne Hamano Quon came to adulthood in the turbulent 1960s. As an activist, she drew on her own experiences of racism as well as on those of her parents and grandparents during World War II.

While American society saw Japanese Americans as the model minority, many in the Japanese American community suffered quietly, on their own, with problems that could be traced directly back to racism and what happened in our community during World War II. My mother's mother died while sharecropping in Utah after her father "voluntarily" evacuated his family to Utah during World War II.

—from a memoir by Merilynne Hamano Quon in *Asian Americans: The Movement and the Moment*

HISTORICAL THINKING

1. **READING CHECK** What kinds of discrimination have Asian Americans faced?

2. **IDENTIFY** What were the reasons given for American immigration policies, and how did bias or prejudice contribute to the policies' transformation of society?

3. **COMPARE AND CONTRAST** How are Asian Americans similar to and different from other groups seeking equal rights?

11.11.1 Discuss the reasons for the nation's changing immigration policy, with emphasis on how the Immigration Act of 1965 and successor acts have transformed American society); HREP 2 Students identify bias and prejudice in historical interpretations.

3.1 **MAIN IDEA** Inspired by the civil rights movement, the women's movement grew stronger in the 1960s.

NEW VOICES FOR WOMEN

Did you ever expect a streak of good fortune to continue, and then it didn't? After World War II, the professional opportunities American women had grown accustomed to decreased, and women were strongly discouraged from working outside the home.

THE WOMEN'S MOVEMENT REAWAKENS

Like other groups, women had done their fair share during World War II. They worked in factories and served in the military, although they were not officially allowed to fight in combat. Yet, as you have read, after the war many women found themselves back in the midst of domestic life. They were often discouraged from pursuing careers, and those still in the workforce generally received lower pay than men doing the same jobs.

Even so, in the post-war years the nation made some attempts to address the problem of limited opportunities for women. In 1961, President Kennedy created the **President's Commission on the Status of Women**, a 20-member committee chaired by Eleanor Roosevelt, that developed recommendations for overcoming employment discrimination and establishing services "which will enable women to continue their role as wives and mothers while making a maximum contribution to the world around them." The committee recommended paid maternity leave, affordable child care, and equal employment opportunities. Its report led to the **Equal Pay Act of 1963**, which prohibited wage discrimination based on sex. Two years later, in 1965, President Johnson established the Equal Employment Opportunity Commission (EEOC) to help give women greater security in the workplace. The EEOC, for example, declared that employers who fired a woman for such acts as getting married or having a baby were in violation of federal law.

Despite these actions, progress for women was slow. Just like other groups, women realized they could not rely solely on the federal government. They would have to push for greater equality themselves. Like their predecessors in the early 1900s, women in the 1960s began to mobilize. In the eyes of many, the effort began with the publication of a groundbreaking book.

A National Organization for Women pin-back button from the 1970s

In 1970s' New York City, three young women donned Equal Rights Amendment (ERA) buttons to march for the ERA and celebrate a day for women's rights.

11.10.7 Analyze the women's rights movement from the era of Elizabeth Cady Stanton and Susan B. Anthony and the passage of the Nineteenth Amendment to the movement launched in the 1960s, including differing perspectives on the roles of women.

Its author was **Betty Friedan**, a graduate of Smith College who worked as a reporter. When Friedan and her husband Carl were expecting their second child, she lost her job, so she stayed home to raise her children. But she experienced a growing sense of restlessness and frustration with the limits imposed on her by society. She talked to other Smith graduates and discovered that many felt the same way.

Friedan compiled what she learned into a book called *The Feminine Mystique*. The word *mystique* means "an air of mystery," and in this context, referred to the silent unhappiness, or "problem that had no name," that many women dealt with. Published in 1963, *The Feminine Mystique* challenged the assumption that all women wanted to be mothers and homemakers. The book encouraged women to seek their own paths.

Response to the book was overwhelming, and it became a bestseller. Women across the country began voicing their dissatisfaction and their demands. The idea of "choice," implicit in the book, captured what many women wanted: the opportunity to make choices that weren't limited to domestic roles or by other people. While the book's ideas may seem less controversial now than they did in 1963, *The Feminine Mystique* is still considered one of the most influential books of its time. Inspired, women wanted their contributions and importance acknowledged, and began working to promote the ideals of **feminism**, or greater political, economic, social, and cultural rights for women. **Gloria Steinem** was another writer and feminist who used communication to unite women in the fight for equality. In 1971, she and several other feminists founded *Ms.*, a successful magazine that focused on life and politics from women's perspectives.

FEMINISM IN ACTION

The civil rights movements of the 1960s helped fuel women's push for greater equality. Women were obviously inspired by the efforts of African Americans and other minorities in their quest for equality, and many women became part of and worked hard for civil rights causes. Ironically, however, many women who joined the larger civil rights movements reported feeling like second-class citizens, restricted to unimportant tasks and largely kept out of any policy decisions. Just as in their personal lives, women found that their contributions were not as highly valued as those of men. It was clear that in order to achieve success in their quest for equality, women needed to form their own movement and promote their agenda.

In 1966, Friedan and other women leaders gathered together to form the **National Organization for Women (NOW)**. This grassroots association of activist feminists included not only straight women and lesbians, but also men. NOW's goals extended beyond fair pay: it wanted to guarantee women's access to health care, including reproductive rights, affordable child care, and the passage of equal rights legislation at the state and national levels. Similar to the NAACP, NOW pursued legal equality for women in the public sphere. The group lobbied Congress to pass laws emphasizing equality for women, raised awareness about women's issues, and reached out to women in all walks of life to promote feminism.

Led by NOW, feminists pushed for significant changes in society, and while their fight ahead would be a difficult one, they would achieve a number of groundbreaking victories. A major victory for women occurred in 1968 when **Shirley Chisholm** was elected the first African-American Congresswoman. She represented her Brooklyn, New York, district for seven terms, building a reputation as a "people's politician" and "Fighting Shirley" from her advocacy for inner-city poor people.

PRIMARY SOURCE

The problem lay buried, unspoken, for many years in the minds of American women. It was a strange stirring, a sense of dissatisfaction, a yearning that women suffered in the middle of the twentieth century in the United States. Each suburban wife struggled with it alone. As she made the beds, shopped for groceries, matched slipcover material, ate peanut butter sandwiches with her children, chauffeured Cub Scouts and Brownies, lay beside her husband at night—she was afraid to ask even of herself the silent question—"Is this all?"

— from *The Feminine Mystique,* by Betty Friedan, 1963

What information in the source leads you to understand why Friedan and others decided to form a women's rights organization?

HISTORICAL THINKING

1. **READING CHECK** Why did women want a larger role in society?
2. **DRAW CONCLUSIONS** Why was *The Feminine Mystique* so much more controversial when it first appeared than it is today?
3. **ANALYZE CAUSE AND EFFECT** What lesson did women learn from their early participation in the civil rights movements of the 1960s?

11.11.3 Describe the changing roles of women in society as reflected in the entry of more women into the labor force and the changing family structure;
CST 1 Students compare the present with the past, evaluating the consequences of past events and decisions and determining the lessons that were learned;
HI 3 Students interpret past events and issues within the context in which an event unfolded rather than solely in terms of present-day norms and values.

3.2 **MAIN IDEA** During the 1960s and 1970s, women began seeking legal remedies to the discrimination they faced because of their gender.

WOMEN SEEK EQUALITY

The fight for equality sometimes proceeds at an uneven rate, with breakthroughs and advances alternating with long periods where progress is difficult or impossible. Half a century after securing the right to vote, women were still struggling for fair wages, attention to women's health issues, and an end to discrimination based on gender.

BATTLES FOR GENDER EQUALITY

NOW leaders and women activists pushed for a number of reforms. One area they focused on was long-standing **gender bias**, or the preference for one gender over another, against women in education. In particular, activists targeted the area of women's sports, which schools and colleges viewed as an afterthought. Women's teams often received little funding and support. As a result, women had fewer opportunities to earn scholarships or play collegiate sports. Feminists pushed for federal legislation banning gender discrimination in education. In 1972, Congress passed a law known collectively as the **Education Amendments**. One section, **Title IX**, prohibited federally funded schools from discriminating against girls and women in nearly all areas, from admissions to athletics. Title IX helped to bolster women's athletics as well as to give women and girls the chance to obtain athletic and academic scholarships formerly reserved only for men.

Women also made advances on social and cultural fronts. Throughout the 1970s, feminists promoted women's health clinics and opened shelters for victims of domestic abuse. They tackled day-to-day sexism with the mantra "the personal is political"—meaning they were willing to fight against laws that restricted their personal and private lives.

One such area was women's health, particularly reproductive rights. When the Food and Drug Administration approved the use of an oral birth control pill in 1960, women finally had access to a discreet, extremely effective **contraceptive**, or means of preventing pregnancy. But some states still made it difficult for women to use birth control. In Connecticut, birth control had been outlawed in 1879. Women's groups claimed the law unconstitutionally denied women a right to privacy. The case, ***Griswold* v. *Connecticut***, went to the U.S. Supreme Court. In a victory for women, the Court agreed, ruling in 1965 that a ban on contraceptives violated privacy rights. The debate over forms of birth control continued, especially among Catholics. In the Second Vatican Council (Vatican II), held in 1962, the Church had an impact on civil rights and other human rights movements by encouraging its members to participate in them. But the Church was less supportive of women's rights when, in 1968, it condemned "artificial" birth control, defying a growing consensus among its parishioners.

In 1973, feminists achieved victory for a woman's right to make personal choices again, in a landmark case that remains controversial even today: ***Roe* v. *Wade***. During the 1950s and 1960s, abortion, or the purposeful termination of a pregnancy, was illegal in most states. Two Texas attorneys sued on behalf of "Jane Roe," an unnamed defendant, arguing that the inability to obtain a safe abortion violated Roe's constitutional right to privacy. The Supreme Court agreed, saying that a woman's decision to end her pregnancy lay within the "zone of privacy" that is protected by the Constitution. Since this decision, *Roe* v. *Wade* has been a target of conservatives, who argue against it on religious and moral grounds. For those who agree with the Court's decision, it supports a woman's right to make choices about her own reproductive health and to choose when and if to have children.

11.3.2 Analyze the great religious revivals and the leaders involved in them, including the First Great Awakening, the Second Great Awakening, the Civil War revivals, the Social Gospel Movement, the rise of Christian liberal theology in the nineteenth century, the impact of the Second Vatican Council, and the rise of Christian fundamentalism in current times.

University of Tennessee Head Coach Pat Summitt (left) and guard Shanna Zolman (5) evaluate the play during a basketball game in 2004. Summitt retired from coaching at Tennessee having achieved the highest National Collegiate Athletic Association (NCCA) overall win record at that time of 1,098–208. The passage of Title IX gave many hardworking and talented women like Coach Summitt and her players the opportunity to compete at exceptionally high levels.

EQUAL RIGHTS AMENDMENT

Another primary goal of the women's movement was the long-overdue passage of the Equal Rights Amendment (ERA) to the Constitution, which would guarantee protection from gender-based discrimination or even from **misogyny**, a hatred of women. As you learned, the ERA was proposed in 1923, three years after the 19th Amendment granted women the right to vote. The ERA lacked support among several groups and stalled for years on Capitol Hill. Finally, in 1972, Congress passed the ERA and sent it to the states for ratification, with 38 states (three-quarters) needed to ratify, or vote "yes," and make the amendment part of the Constitution.

A coalition of fundamentalist religious groups, states' rights advocates, and political conservatives opposed the ERA. They claimed that it would have unintended consequences, such as forcing women into combat and destroying conventional marriage. Among women leaders opposing the ERA was **Phyllis Schlafly**, a lawyer and activist, who argued that the ERA would subject women to the military draft and force them to lose federal benefits they received as "dependents." The ERA's opponents eventually helped to defeat the measure and keep it from becoming law. It had been ratified by 35 states—3 states short of approval.

By the end of the 1970s, women's lives had changed dramatically. Their career options had grown and were no longer limited to traditional professions, such as nurse, secretary, or teacher. More women's health-care clinics, rape crisis centers, and shelters for domestic abuse victims were available. More women enrolled in medical and law schools. Colleges once closed to women, including the U.S. military academies, opened their doors to female students. The changing roles of women in society, especially as more women entered the labor force, were accompanied by changing family structures.

HISTORICAL THINKING

1. **READING CHECK** How did Title IX benefit college-bound women?
2. **ANALYZE LANGUAGE USE** What did feminists mean by the phrase "the personal is political"?
3. **MAKE GENERALIZATIONS** In what ways did the legal cases won by feminists help change the roles of women in society?

11.10.7 Analyze the women's rights movement from the era of Elizabeth Stanton and Susan Anthony and the passage of the Nineteenth Amendment to the movement launched in the 1960s, including differing perspectives on the roles of women; 11.11.3 Describe the changing roles of women in society as reflected in the entry of more women into the labor force and the changing family structure.

3.3 **MAIN IDEA** After years of living in secret due to fear of discrimination, homosexuals demanded acknowledgment and fair treatment in the 1960s.

The Quest for Equality Expands

Have you ever avoided stating an opinion because you might be teased? On a more serious level, homosexual men and women were at risk of being ridiculed and even persecuted if they did not stay quiet about who they were. In the 1960s, however, these men and women began raising their voices for better treatment.

THE LGBT COMMUNITY MOBILIZES

The mid-20th century saw the beginning of a broader struggle for gay and lesbian rights. At that time, the Lesbian, Gay, Bisexual, and Transgender (LGBT) community endured prejudice and discrimination. Not only was homosexuality against the law at that time, it was also classified as a mental illness by the American Psychiatric Association (APA). Yet in 1948, researcher Alfred Kinsey revealed that homosexual **orientation**, or inclination, was far more common than had been believed, and in 1956, a psychologist found that homosexual and heterosexual males did not differ significantly when responding to a series of psychological tests.

For years, gays and lesbians had kept their sexual orientation quiet because they had no rights or protections under the law. The first gay rights organization in the United States, the Society for Human Rights, had formed in Chicago in 1924, but it soon bowed to political pressure and disbanded. As you have read, Harry Hay founded the Mattachine Society in Los Angeles in 1950, the first national homosexual rights group that provided safe places for homosexuals to gather. Membership in the society helped **Frank Kameny**, a professional astronomer. In 1957, he had been fired from his job at the U.S. Army Map Service for his sexual orientation and barred from future U.S. government employment. Kameny became an activist, working to overturn unfair laws

AMERICAN PLACES

The Stonewall Inn, New York

Designated the birthplace of the modern gay rights movement, the Stonewall Inn still maintains its local neighborhood identity. On June 24, 2016, President Obama announced the Stonewall National Monument at the historic site of the Stonewall Uprising. The site is the first national park focused on LGBT history.

11.10.2 Examine and analyze the key events, policies, and court cases in the evolution of civil rights, including *Dred Scott* v. *Sandford*, *Plessy* v. *Ferguson*, *Brown* v. *Board of Education*, *Regents of the University of California* v. *Bakke*, and California Proposition 209; 11.10.4 Examine the roles of civil rights advocates (e.g., A. Philip Randolph, Martin Luther King, Jr., Malcom X, Thurgood Marshall, James Farmer, Rosa Parks), including the significance of Martin Luther King, Jr.'s "Letter from Birmingham Jail" and "I Have a Dream" speech.

and remove the APA classification of homosexuality as a "mental illness," which the APA did in 1973.

Throughout the 1950s and early 1960s, similar discrete organizations created a supportive network for the LGBT community and fought to secure its rights of expression and assembly. They also cultivated relationships with clergy members, doctors, and legislators to challenge teachings and laws that condemned homosexuality as sinful, sick, or criminal. Lesbians **Del Martin** and **Phyllis Lyon** founded the Daughters of Bilitis in 1955 in San Francisco. For 14 years, the organization educated hundreds of women about their rights. Martin and Lyon had started the Daughters of Bilitis because they were wary of gay bars; police raids were not uncommon, and patrons and employees were often subject to arrest. Usually, the victims of these raids did not resist. Yet one night in New York City, things changed.

The Stonewall Inn served alcohol to homosexuals and allowed same-sex partners to dance together, although both activities were illegal in New York City in 1969. On June 28, police raided the Stonewall. About 200 patrons were in the bar, and they refused to cooperate when police told them to line up and show identification. Two transgender women of color, **Sylvia Rivera** and **Marsha P. Johnson**, resisted arrest and sparked several days of rioting in the neighborhood. Stonewall became the first major event in the modern LGBT rights movement.

Emboldened by the civil rights movements, the LGBT community began openly seeking legal and political changes. Organizations such as the Gay Liberation Front and the Gay Activists Alliance called on people in the movement to "come out" as a personal and political act. In 1961, José Sarria became the first openly gay person to run for office, an impressive but unsuccessful bid for a seat on San Francisco's Board of Supervisors. In 1974, Kathy Kozachenko was elected to the City Council of Ann Arbor, Michigan, becoming the first openly gay American elected to public office. Three years later, **Harvey Milk** won the election to San Francisco's Board of Supervisors. He and fellow California activist Cleve Jones brought new attention to the cause of equal rights for homosexual Americans.

THE MOVEMENT GAINS MOMENTUM

By the mid-1970s, LGBT mobilization efforts had led to successes. The American Psychiatric Association stopped diagnosing homosexuality as a mental illness. Laws criminalizing gay sexual behavior were repealed by 17 states, and 36 cities passed laws banning antigay discrimination. Gains and setbacks occurred in the courts. In 1958 in *One, Inc.* v. *Olesen*, the Supreme Court rejected the U.S. Post Office refusal to distribute a gay and lesbian magazine. But in *Boutilier* v. *Immigration and Naturalization Service* in 1967, the court upheld the exclusion and deportation of gay and lesbian immigrants. Then, in 1975, the first federal gay rights bill was introduced to address discrimination based on sexual orientation, but it was never brought up for a vote.

Harvey Milk worked to protect gays and lesbians from losing a job because of their sexual orientation and led the fight to end state legislation that banned gay teachers. Milk was murdered by a former city supervisor a little more than a year after his election, and protests followed the light five-year sentence given his killer.

In 1993, the Department of Defense issued a directive later called "Don't Ask, Don't Tell," stating that applicants for military service could not be asked about their sexual orientation. But it was not until 2010 that gays and lesbians in the military could serve openly. In 2004, Massachusetts became the first state to recognize same-sex marriage, and in 2015, the U.S. Supreme Court ruled in *Obergefell* v. *Hodges*, that the fundamental right to marry is guaranteed to same-sex couples.

HISTORICAL THINKING

1. **READING CHECK** Why did members of the LGBT community hide their sexual orientation?
2. **DRAW CONCLUSIONS** How did political activism further the cause of LGBT rights?
3. **MAKE CONNECTIONS** Why did Frank Kameny's education and experience make him well suited to leading the fight against the classification of homosexuality as a "mental illness"?

11.11.1. Discuss the reasons for the nation's changing immigration policy, with emphasis on how the Immigration Act of 1965 and successor acts have transformed American society; HI 3 Students interpret past events and issues within the context in which an event unfolded rather than solely in terms of present- day norms and values.

4.1 **MAIN IDEA** Throughout the 1960s, the United States and the Soviet Union intensified their space race to reach the moon first.

THE SPACE RACE CONTINUES

As the United States grappled with civil unrest and struggles for equality at home, the Cold War with the Soviet Union continued. Throughout the 1960s, the two nations battled for supremacy in space. During a time of turmoil, Americans found common ground in cheering on the U.S. space program's goal of putting a man on the moon.

THE DREAM OF SPACE TRAVEL

Life in the United States during the 1950s and 1960s came with an undercurrent of fear. The United States was at odds with the world's only other superpower, the Soviet Union. The two nations struggled with an uneasy and fragile peace. As you have read, one night in 1957, Americans got a fright: orbiting over their heads was a piece of Soviet machinery called *Sputnik 1*, the first artificial satellite ever launched into orbit. It was not just the satellite orbiting over their heads that concerned Americans. It was also the fact that *Sputnik* had been launched into orbit by a powerful rocket.

Rockets had been invented by the Chinese in the 13th century, and they have been used for fireworks and in warfare ever since. But modern rocket science really began in Germany during World War II. After the war, some of Germany's leading scientists surrendered to American forces and were brought to the United States, while others were recruited into the Soviet Union's rocket program. Among those who immigrated to the United States was **Wernher von Braun**, who had developed the powerful V-2 rocket for Hitler. Although his role in producing this rocket during the war is controversial, Von Braun's real desire

The 363-foot-tall Saturn V rocket launches the Apollo 11 spacecraft toward the moon in 1969.

was to design a rocket that would travel into space, and working for the United States gave him that opportunity.

When NASA was set up in 1958, it combined a number of different, individual organizations that had been working on space-age rocket research, including von Braun's team at the Army Ballistic Missile Agency in Huntsville, Alabama. The United States was not about to allow the Soviet Union to gain an advantage in rocket research, so the new agency had 8,000 employees and a budget of $100 million. The space race had begun, and, as you have read, in 1961 President Kennedy set a remarkable goal: the United States would land a man on the moon by the end of the decade.

Edward H. White was the first American to take a spacewalk.

With this ambitious challenge, NASA got to work. The location of many NASA facilities was determined by political influence. For example, Houston, Texas, was chosen as the location for the Johnson Space Center largely because Lyndon Johnson, then vice president, was from Texas. NASA's first major launch site, however, was in **Cape Canaveral**, Florida, and it offered two chief advantages, neither of them political. First, all rocket launches would be directed eastward, over the Atlantic Ocean, which was a safety precaution in case of any rocket malfunction. Second, Cape Canaveral was closer to the Equator than other possible launch sites. By launching rockets eastward from a site near the Equator, NASA could take advantage of Earth's eastward rotation in lifting the rocket into orbit.

FROM GEMINI TO APOLLO

The early efforts in the space race focused on sending astronauts deeper and deeper into orbit and safely bringing them back. The first manned space flights were known as Project Mercury. They culminated with American astronaut John Glenn orbiting Earth three times before touching down in the Caribbean Sea. A second astronaut program, Project Gemini, built on what NASA had learned during Mercury's six flights. In a significant step forward, the Gemini space capsules carried two astronauts instead of one. A highlight of the Gemini mission was the first successful American **spacewalk**, in which an astronaut, Edward H. White, ventured outside the spacecraft on June 3, 1965.

From there, NASA initiated its Apollo program, which set its sights on taking the final crucial steps to achieving a moon landing. The earlier Mercury and Gemini programs had solved many of the major challenges involved with launching humans safely into space, from surviving in extreme conditions to returning safely to Earth. NASA now focused its efforts on developing the procedures and equipment that would make a moon orbit and landing possible.

Early on in the Apollo program, however, tragedy struck. On January 27, 1967, during a launch pad test, the Apollo 1 capsule caught fire, trapping three astronauts inside. Virgil "Gus" Grissom, Roger Chaffee, and Edward H. White—the first American to ever walk in space—died in the accident. In the aftermath of this tragedy, NASA conducted an investigation to discover the cause of the fire. The recommendations the investigators made in their report led to engineering and design improvements to the space capsule as well as advances in quality control, manufacturing, and testing procedures. Despite the horrific event, the space program pushed on.

HISTORICAL THINKING

1. **READING CHECK** What were Wernher von Braun's qualifications for working on the American space program?
2. **COMPARE AND CONTRAST** How were the goals of the Mercury and Gemini programs different from those of Apollo?
3. **DESCRIBE** Describe the effects of America's space program on society and the economy. Use evidence from the text to support your response.
4. **ANALYZE CAUSE AND EFFECT** How did NASA respond to the launch pad tragedy that killed three Apollo astronauts?

11.8.7 Describe the effects on society and the economy of technological developments since 1945, including the computer revolution, changes in communication, advances in medicine, and improvements in agricultural technology.

4.2 **MAIN IDEA** The world watched in amazement as a 10-year effort culminated with two Americans setting foot on the moon.

"ONE GIANT LEAP FOR MANKIND"

Have you ever looked up at the moon and imagined what it would be like to walk on its surface, gazing back at Earth? People had been wondering about this for thousands of years, but it wasn't until 1969 that the technology, and the will to attempt such a challenge, allowed it to become reality.

THE U.S. MOON MISSION

In the years after the tragic loss of the Apollo 1 crew, the United States continued making steady progress toward its moon landing goal. NASA developed a rocket, the Saturn V, which officials believed would be powerful enough to set the astronauts on a course that would send them all the way to the moon. It also developed a command **module**, or unit, called *Columbia*, and a lunar module, nicknamed *Eagle*, that astronaut Michael Collins later described as "the weirdest looking contraption I have ever seen in the sky." Collins was one of the three men chosen as the crew of **Apollo 11**, the mission that would shoot for the moon. Collins piloted *Columbia*. **Neil Armstrong** was mission commander, and **Edwin "Buzz" Aldrin** was *Eagle's* pilot.

Dawn on July 16, 1969, was clear and sunny at Cape Kennedy. (Cape Canaveral's name was changed to Cape Kennedy in 1963 after the president's assassination, but it would revert to its original name in 1973.) At 9:32 a.m., Armstrong, Aldrin, and Collins took off in the nose of a massive Saturn V rocket. Spectators cheered as the rocket, wreathed in fire and smoke, rose into the sky. Twelve minutes later, the crew was in orbit and headed toward the moon. The trip took three days. As they approached the moon, Armstrong and Aldrin climbed into *Eagle*, disengaged from *Columbia*, and headed for the moon's surface. Collins stayed behind, piloting *Columbia*. At 4:18 p.m. eastern daylight time on July 20, with just 30 seconds' worth of fuel left, *Eagle* landed on the moon. Armstrong radioed the news back to Earth: "Houston, Tranquility Base here. The *Eagle* has landed."

People at Mission Control in Houston roared in glee and applauded as they watched the landing. For the first time, human beings were on the surface of another celestial body. Kennedy's dream had been realized: Americans were on the moon before any other nation. Armstrong exited *Eagle*, climbed down its ladder, and

APOLLO 11

The Saturn V rocket launched Apollo 11 to the moon in stages. Each stage was discarded as its fuel was spent, until three module spacecraft remained. The escape launch at the top was available to pull the command module *Columbia* to safety in case of a malfunction during the early stages of the launch.

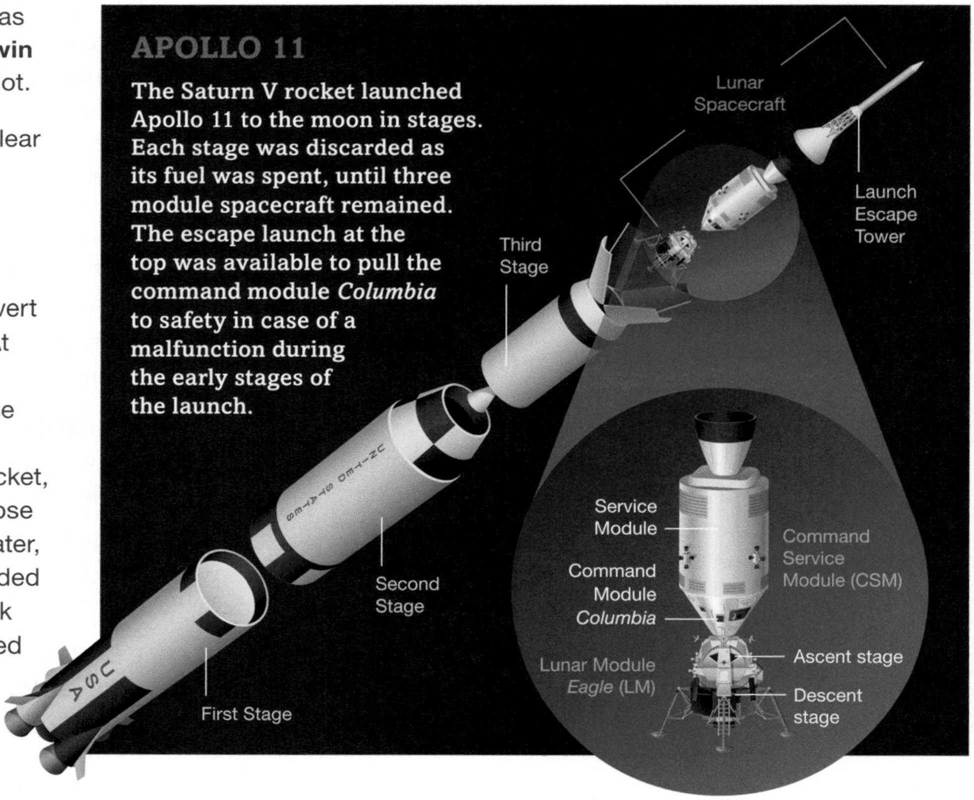

The National Air and Space Museum, Washington, D.C.

The *Columbia*, the Apollo 11 command module, was the living quarters of the three-person crew during the first manned lunar landing mission in July 1969. This command module, no. 107, was one of three parts of the complete Apollo spacecraft and was the only part of the spacecraft to return to Earth, transporting the three astronauts aboard. Its furnishings included a heating unit, water supply, pressure-suit connectors, scientific equipment, and even a vacuum cleaner! The module and its travel ring, or transporting cradle, weighs over 13,600 pounds.

became the first person to walk on the moon. "That's one small step for [a] man, one giant leap for mankind," he radioed back to Earth, where 500 million people—about 14 percent of the world's population—received his words and images broadcast from 238,900 miles away. Together, Aldrin and Armstrong explored and collected samples. "Magnificent desolation" is how Aldrin described the lunar surface.

After two and a half hours, they placed a plaque on the moon memorializing their visit, which described them not as Americans, but as "men of Earth" who came in peace. They also left an American flag, medallions in memory of the Apollo 1 crew and for 2 Russian cosmonauts, and a silicon disk engraved with goodwill wishes from 78 nations. Then they returned to *Eagle,* which was a two-part module: one for descending to the lunar surface, and one for taking off from the surface. Each part of the module had its own fuel supply. The ascent module blasted off, using the descent module as a launching pad, to meet up with Collins and *Columbia*. Upon their return to Earth (after a few days in quarantine), the astronauts were given a huge parade in New York City and were celebrated around the world.

OTHER LUNAR LANDINGS

Five more Apollo missions landed astronauts on the moon between 1969 and 1972. The soil and rock samples the Apollo astronauts brought back from the moon were a treasure trove of information. Scientists confirmed that no life existed on the moon and that its mineral composition was similar to Earth's. The moon is very ancient; its youngest rocks are about the same age as the oldest Earth rocks. These lunar rocks are still being studied.

One of the later Apollo missions, Apollo 13, never reached the moon. Launched on April 11, 1970, it was 200,000 miles from Earth when all water, electrical power, propulsion, and oxygen in the command module were lost. The crew retreated to the lunar module, which kept them alive while the damaged ship did a lunar flyby and headed back to Earth. The men drank only six ounces of water a day as Apollo 13 limped home. All three crewmembers survived. Investigators eventually determined that exposed wires on a fan shorted out, setting the insulation on fire, and causing an oxygen tank to explode.

After the Apollo program ended, NASA's focus shifted away from the moon. Starting in the 1980s, it developed the space shuttle, an orbiter that could be used repeatedly for missions. NASA also began admitting women to the astronaut program. On June 18, 1983, **Sally Ride** became the first American woman to fly in space on a space shuttle mission.

Together, the nations of the world, led by the United States and Russia (the former Soviet Union), began building the International Space Station. Scientists on the space station conduct experiments to learn about how outer space affects living things and study the cosmos without visual interference from Earth's atmosphere. NASA continues to send unmanned probes to explore Mars, Jupiter, Saturn, their moons, and the outer reaches of our solar system.

HISTORICAL THINKING

1. **READING CHECK** What was the major accomplishment of NASA's Apollo program?
2. **ANALYZE CAUSE AND EFFECT** Why do you think NASA has moved away from manned space missions?
3. **ASK AND ANSWER QUESTIONS** What questions do you still have about NASA's technological developments, and where can you find the answers?

11.8.7 Describe the effects on society and the economy of technological developments since 1945, including the computer revolution, changes in communication, advances in medicine, and improvements in agricultural technology.

CHAPTER 19 CHANGES IN SOCIETY

REVIEW

VOCABULARY

Use each of the following vocabulary words in a sentence that shows an understanding of the term's meaning.

1. peer HSS 11.10.5
   His new teammates considered him a peer because his skills were equal to theirs.
2. precedent HSS 11.10.6
3. manifesto HSS 11.10.5
4. militant HSS 11.10.5
5. reparations HSS 11.10.5
6. feminism HSS 11.10.5
7. gender bias HSS 11.10.7
8. spacewalk HSS 11.8.7

READING STRATEGY

ANALYZE CAUSE AND EFFECT

Use a graphic organizer like the one below to describe the civil rights movements, their effect on American society, and how they were influenced by the African-American civil rights movement.

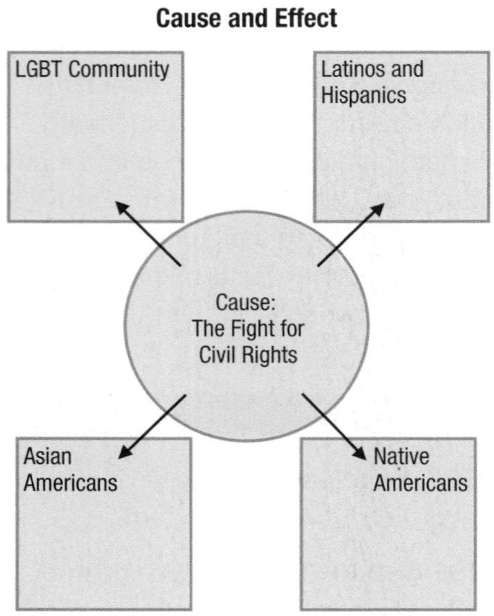

9. How did various groups experiencing discrimination fight for equality and civil rights in the 1960s? HSS 11.10

MAIN IDEAS

Answer the following questions. Support your answers with evidence from the chapter.

10. What factors led to the Latino rights movement? **LESSON 1.1** HSS 11.8.2
11. Why did Larry Itliong ask the Mexican American farmworkers to join the Filipino grape laborers' strike? **LESSON 1.3** HSS 11.6.5
12. What governmental decision made the creation of the Native American Declaration of Purpose necessary? **LESSON 2.1** HSS 11.10.5
13. What was the American Indian Movement (AIM)? **LESSON 2.2** HSS 11.10.5
14. What were the goals of the National Organization for Women (NOW)? **LESSON 3.1** HSS 11.10.7
15. How did Title IX make schools and sports more fair for women? **LESSON 3.2** HSS 11.11.3
16. Why was the declassification of homosexuality as a mental illness an important victory for the LGBT community in 1973? **LESSON 3.3** HSS HI 3
17. How did the technology NASA developed for the Apollo program build on lessons learned from Project Gemini? **LESSON 4.1** HSS 11.8.7
18. What did Neil Armstrong mean when he said, "That's one small step for [a] man, one giant leap for mankind"? **LESSON 4.2** HSS 11.8.7

HISTORICAL THINKING

Answer the following questions. Support your answers with evidence from the chapter.

19. **ANALYZE CAUSE AND EFFECT** Was *The Feminine Mystique* a cause or an effect of the women's movement, or both, and what limitations might prevent you from determining this? HSS HI 2
20. **MAKE GENERALIZATIONS** Why was it important for the LGBT community to become involved in politics? HSS HI 1

21. **DRAW CONCLUSIONS** Which strategies undertaken by Native Americans in pursuit of their civil rights were similar to those strategies undertaken by African Americans, and how effective were they? HSS 11.10.5

22. **FORM AND SUPPORT OPINIONS** Which civil rights movement in this chapter do you think made the greatest strides during this time period? HSS 11.10

INTERPRET VISUALS

Physicist and astronaut Sally Ride monitors the control panel from the pilot's seat on the space shuttle. Ride took her first space flight in 1983 as a mission specialist.

23. **DRAW CONCLUSIONS** What kind of training do you think Ride, or any other astronaut, would need to perform this job in the space shuttle? HSS 11.8.7

24. **MAKE INFERENCES** Why would an astronaut need the large windows shown here, rather than the smaller ones in early capsules? HSS 11.8.7

ANALYZE SOURCES

César Chávez led farmworkers in many protests.

> "The consumer boycott is the only open door in the dark corridor of nothingness down which farm workers have had to walk for many years. It is a gate of hope through which they expect to find the sunlight of a better life for themselves and their families."
>
> —César Chávez, as quoted in *Why We Fight: The Origins, Nature, and Management of Human Conflict*, by David Churchman, 2013

25. Based on the quotation, why do you think Chávez chose boycotts as an effective strategy for achieving equality? HSS 11.10.5

CONNECT TO YOUR LIFE

26. **EXPOSITORY** Talk to family members or other adults you know about one of the civil rights movements described in this chapter. What does the adult remember about it? Ask him or her to explain in what ways civil rights for different groups of Americans have changed or remained unchanged over time. Have these movements made your life today different from what it would have been in the 1960s or 1970s? In a paragraph explain how these movements have affected your life today. HSS CST 1

TIPS

- Use information from the chapter to craft your questions before you conduct any of your interviews.
- Ask the people you interview for concrete details from their memories and experiences.
- Compare your life today with the life described by the adults in your interviews.
- Conclude by drawing from your experiences and feelings to explain why you think these movements had an overall positive or negative impact on American society.
- Use two or three vocabulary terms from the chapter in your response.

NATIONAL GEOGRAPHIC | CONNECTION

Who Was Jim Crow?

BY BECKY LITTLE

Adapted from "Who Was Jim Crow?" by Becky Little, news.nationalgeographic.com, August 2015

In 1944, the Detroit chapter of the National Association for the Advancement of Colored People (NAACP) held a mock funeral for him. In 1963, participants in the March on Washington for Jobs and Freedom symbolically buried him. Racial discrimination existed all over the United States in the 20th century, but it had a special name in the South—Jim Crow.

President Lyndon B. Johnson tried to bury Jim Crow by signing the Voting Rights Act of 1965 into law. The Voting Rights Act and its predecessor, the Civil Rights Act of 1964, fought racial discrimination by banning segregation in public accommodations and outlawing the poll taxes and tests that were used to stop African Americans from voting.

Today, we still use "Jim Crow" to describe that system of segregation and discrimination in the South. But the system's namesake isn't actually Southern. Jim Crow came from the North.

Thomas Dartmouth Rice, a white man, was born in New York City in 1808. He devoted himself to the theater in his 20s. In the early 1830s, he began performing the act that would make him famous: He painted his face black and did a song and dance he claimed were inspired by an African-American slave. The act was called "Jump, Jim Crow" (or "Jumping Jim Crow").

Rice's routine was a hit in New York City, one of many places in the North where working-class whites could see blackface minstrelsy, which was quickly becoming a dominant form of theater and a leading source for popular music in America. Rice took his act on tour. As his popularity grew, his stage name seeped into the culture. Jim Crow became a name that was applied to African Americans in general. "So much so," says Eric Lott, professor at the City University of New York Graduate Center, "that by the time of Harriet Beecher Stowe's *Uncle Tom's Cabin*, which was 20 years later in 1852," one character refers to another as Jim Crow.

Regardless of whether the term Jim Crow existed before Rice took it to the stage, his act helped popularize it as a derogatory term for African Americans. To call someone Jim Crow wasn't just to point out his or her skin color: it was to reduce that person to the kind of caricature that Rice performed on stage.

After the Civil War, southern states passed laws that discriminated against newly freed African Americans. As early as the 1890s, these laws had gained a nickname. In 1899, a North Carolina newspaper published an article subtitled "How 'Capt. Tilley' of the A. & N.C. Road Enforces the Jim Crow Law."

Experts aren't sure how a racist show in the North came to embody racist laws in the South. But they can speculate. Since the term originated in blackface minstrelsy, Lott says that it's almost "perversely accurate . . . that it should come to be the name for official segregation and state-sponsored racism."

"I think probably in the popular white mind, it was just used because that's just how they referred to black people," he says.

"Sometimes in history a movie comes out or a book comes out and it just changes the language . . . and you can point at it," says David Pilgrim, director of the Jim Crow Museum and vice president for Diversity and Inclusion at Ferris State University.

"And in just this case," he says, "I think it just evolved. And I think it was from many sources."

However it happened, the new meaning stuck. Blackface minstrelsy's popularity faded, and Thomas Rice is barely remembered. Most people today don't know his name. But everybody knows the name Jim Crow.

For more from National Geographic, check out "Before Stonewall" online.

UNIT INQUIRY: Design a Museum Exhibit

In this unit, you learned about a turbulent period in American life. The assassinations of three national leaders and a divisive war shattered the hopeful visions of progress proposed in the New Frontier and the Great Society. Protest movements by numerous groups—African Americans, Native Americans, Latinos, women, and antiwar activists—divided the nation and often turned violent. How did the popular culture of the time reflect this great turmoil? Which songs best express the mood of the time? What works of art and literature capture the confusion of those years? How did clothing and hairstyles become protest statements?

ASSIGNMENT

Design a museum exhibit that answers this question: How did popular culture reflect the turbulence of the time period? You might explore popular culture in general or focus on a particular aspect of it, such as music, art, literature, movies, or fashion. Be prepared to present your design to the class.

Plan First choose the subject of your exhibit and identify its main idea or theme. Then research your subject and compile a list of primary sources in diverse formats, such as songs, photographs, works of art, or newspaper articles, that will form your exhibit. You'll use these objects to tell your story. You might use a graphic organizer to outline your theme and arrange your primary sources.

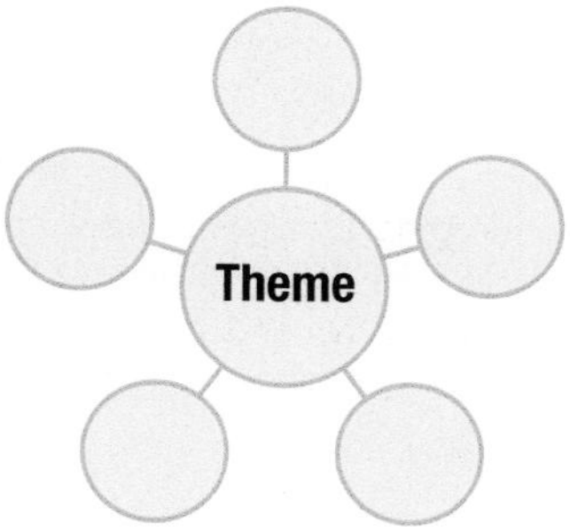

Produce Create a title for your exhibit and write an introduction of one or more paragraphs. Then write a caption for each primary source in your exhibit, providing identifying information and explaining the object's significance.

Present Share your exhibit design with the class. You might consider one of these options:

- Use a computer program to create a virtual museum exhibit and post it on a website that your classmates can access. Invite viewers to share their reactions to the exhibit.
- Create a museum board model for display in the classroom. After viewing one another's displays, hold a class discussion comparing the popular culture of the period with the popular culture of the current time. Discuss how you would characterize the contemporary culture.

NATIONAL GEOGRAPHIC | LEARNING FRAMEWORK ACTIVITIES

Write a Letter

ATTITUDE Responsibility

KNOWLEDGE New Frontiers

Write a letter, addressed to your classmates or to the president of the United States, outlining a "New Frontier" or "Great Society" challenge that you think your generation should tackle. Explain your vision of progress, how you would implement it, and how it will improve people's lives. Compare your ideas with those of either President Kennedy or President Johnson. Share your letter with your classmates, and discuss the ideas and visions presented for the future.

Create a Song

KNOWLEDGE Our Human Story

SKILLS Collaboration, Communication

If you have musical skills, collaborate with one or more partners to compose a song that captures a current conflict in American society, perhaps in the lives of American youth. Consider various styles of music, such as rap, pop, country, folk, and rock. Choose a style and a theme, and play around with lyrics and melody until a song develops. Practice the song and perform it for the class. Discuss how it relates to the conflict. Ask for feedback, inviting suggestions for changes to the lyrics or music.

CST 1 Students compare the present with the past, evaluating the consequences of past events and decisions and determining the lessons that were learned.

UNIT 6

1968–Present

Challenges of a New Century

CRITICAL VIEWING The High Line, an elevated public park built on an old, unused freight rail line, extends between the buildings of Manhattan's West Side. Benches give visitors a peaceful place to rest above the busy New York City streets, and plants, grasses, and trees recall the wild landscape that once ran along the abandoned railway. How might the High Line serve as an example of a solution to a modern urban challenge?

UNIT 6

Challenges of a New Century

The United States

1974
Nixon resigns his presidency in the wake of the Watergate scandal, and Vice President Gerald Ford becomes president. *(official presidential portrait of Ford)*

1986
The space shuttle *Challenger* explodes soon after takeoff, killing all on board. *(The shuttle launches from Cape Canaveral.)*

1970

1980
Ronald Reagan is elected president, ushering in a new conservative movement.

1990

1998
President William Clinton is impeached but is acquitted of all charges.

1980

The World

1975 ASIA
Saigon falls, and Vietnam is reunified under a communist government.

1979 ASIA
Islamic militants hold 52 American hostages in Iran following the overthrow of the ruling monarchy.

1989 EUROPE
The Berlin Wall falls, paving the way to the reunification of Germany a year later. *(Crowds celebrate on top of the wall.)*

1991 EUROPE
The Soviet Union breaks up, and the Cold War comes to an end.

1994 AFRICA
Voters take part in South Africa's first democratic elections and elect Nelson Mandela as president.

HISTORICAL THINKING

DETERMINE CHRONOLOGY Which world event may have occurred in response to the 2001 attacks on the United States?

2008
Barack Obama becomes the first African-American president. *(2012 campaign sticker)*

2001
On September 11, a series of attacks by militants associated with the Islamic terrorist group al Qaeda kill more than 3,000 people. *(security guard badge recovered from the ruins of the World Trade Center)*

2005
Hurricane Katrina hits New Orleans, Louisiana, and devastates the city.

2007
The Great Recession begins, which leads to widespread unemployment and a collapse in housing prices.

2016
Donald Trump is elected president. *(cap featuring Trump's 2016 campaign slogan)*

2000

2010

2020

2003 ASIA
The United States and Britain launch an attack on Iraq. *(Saddam Hussein on a playing card given to coalition forces)*

2008 AMERICAS
Fidel Castro resigns after leading Cuba for 49 years, and his brother Raúl succeeds him.

2015 EUROPE
The Islamic State in Iraq and Syria (ISIS) claims responsibility for a terrorist attack in Paris.

2010 AFRICA
The Arab Spring movement begins in Tunisia. *(Protesters stand on an army tank in Cairo, Egypt, in 2011.)*

CHAPTER 20

PRESIDENTIAL SUCCESSES AND FAILURES

1968–1980

HISTORICAL THINKING What policies and challenges characterized the presidencies of Nixon, Ford, and Carter?

CRITICAL VIEWING During his historic trip to China in 1972, President Nixon toured the Badaling section of China's Great Wall with Chinese Vice Premier Li Xiannian. Known for its striking view, the Badaling section of the Great Wall dates from about 1500. Nixon was the first U.S. president to visit China. What details in the photo convey the mood surrounding Nixon's visit?

"What is most important is that
we have an open world."

—President Richard M. Nixon

1.1 **MAIN IDEA** In 1968, Richard Nixon made a major political comeback to win the presidency.

Nixon's Comeback

Have you ever achieved something important because you refused to give up and simply kept trying? Despite setbacks, Richard Nixon did not give up his quest for the presidency, and in 1968, his perseverance paid off.

NIXON'S RISE, FALL, AND RISE

In the months leading up to the 1968 election, many Americans were anxious about the state of the country. The assassinations of Martin Luther King, Jr., and Robert Kennedy, ongoing demonstrations against the Vietnam War, and changing cultural values left people feeling the country was out of control.

Richard Nixon was a familiar name to most Americans, having served as President Eisenhower's vice president from 1953 to 1961. The son of Quaker parents living in California, Nixon had excelled in academics and debate. After law school, he took a government job, which he left to serve in the U.S. Navy during World War II. After the war, Republican Party leaders suggested he run for a Congressional seat in California, which he won. Nixon appeared to be a rising star in the party.

As a member of Congress, Nixon gained a reputation for being tough on communism. His participation in the trial of Alger Hiss, a suspected Russian spy, in 1949 helped him win a seat in the U.S. Senate in 1950. Just two years later, Dwight Eisenhower chose Nixon as his vice-presidential running mate. However, trouble emerged during the campaign when some critics accused Nixon of accepting an $18,000 campaign contribution and using it for his personal benefit. To silence these critics, Nixon went on national television and admitted to accepting one personal gift from a supporter—a dog, whom his young daughter named Checkers. The speech won over the public.

After serving eight years as Eisenhower's loyal vice president, Nixon seemed destined to win the White House in 1960. As you have read, however, he narrowly lost that election to John F. Kennedy. Two years later, he lost the California governor's race. Many observers thought Nixon's political career was over. In fact, after his defeat, a bitter Nixon told reporters, "You won't have Nixon to kick around anymore."

PRIMARY SOURCE

After being accused of spending campaign money on private expenses, Richard Nixon addressed the nation, claiming that the only gift he had received was a dog named Checkers.

We did get something, a gift, after the election. A man down in Texas heard . . . that our two youngsters would like to have a dog, and, believe it or not . . . we got a message from Union Station in Baltimore, saying they had a package for us. It was a little cocker spaniel dog . . . black and white, spotted, and our little girl Tricia, the six year old, named it Checkers. And you know, the kids, like all kids, loved the dog, and . . . we are going to keep it.

—from Richard Nixon's "Checkers" speech, September 23, 1952

11.11.2 Discuss the significant domestic policy speeches of Truman, Eisenhower, Kennedy, Johnson, Nixon, Carter, Reagan, Bush, and Clinton (e.g., with regard to education, civil rights, economic policy, environmental policy); HI 2 Students recognize the complexity of historical causes and effects, including the limitations on determining cause and effect.

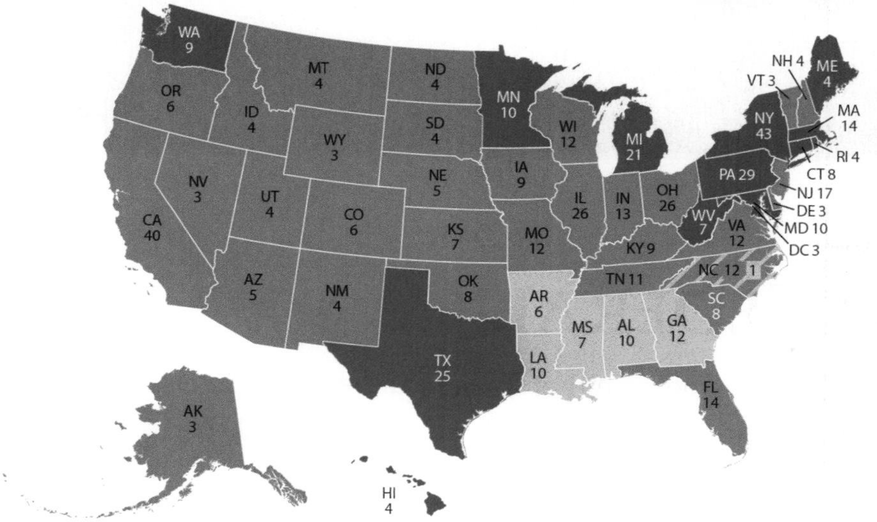

The 1968 Election

Richard Nixon, Republican

Electoral Vote: 301 votes, 55.9%

Popular Vote: 31,785,480 votes, 43.4%

Hubert Humphrey, Democrat

Electoral Vote: 191 votes, 35.5%

Popular Vote: 31,275,166 votes, 42.7%

George Wallace, Independent

Electoral Vote: 46 votes, 8.4%

Popular Vote: 9,906,473 votes, 13.5%

With no political office to keep him in California, Nixon moved to New York City, where he practiced law and successfully rebuilt his reputation by assisting Republican candidates in their campaigns. Despite his election failures, he was regarded as a knowledgeable and experienced politician. After the Republicans lost the 1964 national election, their leaders turned to Nixon, hoping he could regain the White House in 1968. They felt voters were dissatisfied with reform-minded Democrats. Nixon chose Governor **Spiro T. Agnew** of Maryland as his running mate. Agnew was a moderate who supported civil rights but advocated a tough stance on crime. Nixon hoped Agnew would increase the ticket's appeal to both moderate and conservative voters.

THE 1968 ELECTION

The year 1968 marked the beginning of a swing toward conservatism that would last for several decades. Many Americans were upset with the excesses of the 1960s, including the counterculture, illegal drug use, and rising crime rates in cities. In his campaign, Nixon tapped into these feelings of insecurity and appealed to what he called the **silent majority**, those who are not actively involved in politics and do not voice their political opinions publicly. At this time, the silent majority consisted of moderate voters who wanted the United States to take a more stable and conservative course.

At the Republican National Convention, Nixon promised to make law and order his top priority at home and to bring "peace with honor" to Vietnam. The Democrats, on the other hand, were divided over the war in Vietnam, and antiwar protesters were upset with the nomination of Vice President Hubert Humphrey as the Democratic candidate. Demonstrations turned violent outside the Democratic National Convention in Chicago when police officers clashed with protesters. The clashes gave Nixon an advantage with voters who wanted a more peaceful country.

To attract even more voters, Nixon's campaign also targeted people in the southern states who historically voted for Democrats. His southern strategy appealed to white southerners who were disappointed with Democratic support of the civil rights movement. If Nixon could turn these southern states Republican, he stood an excellent chance of winning the election.

However, for the first time since 1948, there was a serious third-party candidate: former Alabama governor George Wallace. Wallace was a segregationist, and now he based his platform on his opposition to civil rights. Wallace proved popular among the white southern voters Nixon had hoped to attract. While these voters rejected Humphrey's support of civil rights, they also did not favor Nixon, who was neither pro-civil rights nor a segregationist. Wallace ended up winning five southern states, but Nixon still won the election.

HISTORICAL THINKING

1. **READING CHECK** Why did some experts believe that Richard Nixon's political career was over by the early 1960s?
2. **ANALYZE CAUSE AND EFFECT** Describe the complex cause-and-effect relationship between the political situation in the country, Nixon's campaign platform, and his victory in the 1968 presidential election.
3. **INTERPRET MAPS** What effect did Wallace's third-party candidacy have on the 1968 election?

1.2 **MAIN IDEA** President Nixon initiated a number of important domestic reforms and built stronger relationships with China and the Soviet Union.

NIXON'S NEW FEDERALISM

Some presidents are easy to categorize as being either conservative, moderate, or liberal. But Richard Nixon is difficult to pigeonhole. His actions covered the entire political spectrum.

NIXON'S DOMESTIC POLICIES

President Nixon advocated a number of reforms in welfare policy, civil rights, and other areas. In 1970, he requested a bill be introduced in Congress called the **Family Assistance Plan (FAP)**. The plan provided direct cash payments to those in need, while requiring participants to work or receive job training. Conservative members of Congress opposed the idea of the government supporting unemployed people. Liberal Congress members thought the minimum household income in order to qualify for Nixon's plan was too low. Because of these and other dissenting views, Congress never passed the FAP.

Also in 1970, Nixon signed amendments that renewed the Voting Rights Act of 1965, which protected African-American voters at the polls by prohibiting literacy tests. Even though African Americans had the right to vote, many still experienced discrimination and intimidation at polling stations, which kept a number of them away from the polls. After Nixon's renewal of the act, the number of African-American voters fully participating in the election process increased. Nixon also issued an executive order supporting affirmative action, which aimed to improve job opportunities for minorities. However, many white citizens opposed the order, believing it was a form of reverse racism, or prejudice against white people.

PRIMARY SOURCE

The Voting Rights Act of 1965 has opened participation in the political process. In the 5 years since its enactment, close to 1 million Negroes have been registered to vote for the first time and more than 400 Negro officials have been elected to local and State offices. These are more than election statistics; they are statistics of hope and dramatic evidence that the American system works. They stand as an answer to those who claim that there is no recourse except to the streets.

—from Richard Nixon's Voting Rights Act Amendments signing speech, 1970

Nixon supported other progressive reforms. For example, he approved legislation that provided automatic cost-of-living adjustments for Social Security recipients. He also signed the bill that established the **Occupational Safety and Health Administration (OSHA)**, which enforces workplace safety standards.

Although he supported some progressive measures, Nixon believed the federal government had assumed too much responsibility for social problems. In 1972, Nixon signed legislation to return some of the authority of the federal government to state and local governments. He created a five-year revenue sharing plan, which required the federal government to collect taxes and then distribute the money directly to state and local governments. The system allowed those governments to allocate, or give out, money to the programs that benefited their constituents most. Nixon called his tax plan the **New Federalism**.

SCHOOL DESEGREGATION

By 1971, Nixon had the rare opportunity to appoint four Supreme Court justices. In 1969, he chose **Warren E. Burger**, a moderate Republican, as chief justice. His other three appointees were conservatives. Some politicians were concerned that Nixon's conservative appointments would shift the Supreme Court radically to the right, but the Burger Court proved more independent than expected.

11.11.2 Discuss the significant domestic policy speeches of Truman, Eisenhower, Kennedy, Johnson, Nixon, Carter, Reagan, Bush, and Clinton (e.g., with regard to education, civil rights, economic policy, environmental policy).

In 1970, two Cincinnati school districts agreed to a busing plan in which African-American children from one district would attend the predominantly white schools of the other. Second graders in one of the newly merged schools say the Pledge of Allegiance together to begin their school day.

Nixon stated that he opposed school segregation, which the Court had found unconstitutional in 1954. However, in one case, his administration won a request in a lower court to allow 33 Mississippi school districts to postpone their school desegregation plans. In a 1969 ruling, the Burger Court overturned the lower court ruling and ordered the immediate desegregration of the Mississippi school districts.

However, the Burger Court went on to issue mixed decisions on the use of forced busing to eliminate *de facto* segregation. *De facto* segregation of schools still existed because children attended neighborhood schools, and neighborhoods were not integrated. In 1964, an African-American couple in Charlotte, North Carolina, Vera and Darius Swann, tried to enroll their son in an integrated public school. The Swanns lived in the attendance area of a school in which all the students were African American, but the integrated school was actually closer to their home. The Swanns' request was denied, and the NAACP brought the case to a federal court on their behalf. In 1969, the court ruled in favor of the Swanns and went further by requiring the Charlotte-Mecklenburg school district to implement a busing program to integrate its schools. As you have read, in the landmark case of *Swann* v. *Charlotte-Mecklenburg Board of Education*, the Supreme Court upheld the lower court's ruling. The ruling also granted the federal courts broad powers in ordering and overseeing school desegregation.

The *Swann* ruling changed, however, in 1974 after the Court's decision on *Milliken* v. *Bradley*. In that case, the NAACP had sued the state of Michigan for failure to desegregate Detroit-area schools. Most African-American families lived in the city, so a desegregation plan would require busing students to suburban areas, which would be similar to the plan in Charlotte. In *Milliken*, however, the Court ruled that the federal government could not force the local government to bus students across school districts' boundaries. The decision shifted most of the responsibility for carrying out integration back to local communities.

11.10.2 Examine and analyze the key events, policies and court cases in the evolution of civil rights, including *Dred Scot* v. *Sandford*, *Plessy* v. *Ferguson*, *Brown* v. *Board of Education*, *Regents of the University of California* v. *Bakke*, and California Proposition 209; 11.10.6 Analyze the passage and effects of civil rights and voting rights legislation (e.g., 1964 Civil Rights Act, Voting Rights Act of 1965) and the Twenty-Fourth Amendment, with an emphasis on equality of access to education and to the political process.

NIXON'S FOREIGN POLICY

Nixon preferred to focus on foreign policy, where presidents sometimes have a more immediate and direct impact than they do on domestic affairs. As you have learned, Henry Kissinger was Nixon's national security advisor and secretary of state, and he aided the president in many diplomatic achievements. Nixon and Kissinger believed in a foreign policy based on realism, as opposed to idealism. They thought national interests, rather than such ideals as freedom and human rights, should dictate foreign policy. In Latin America and the Middle East, for example, they supported dictatorships that furthered U.S. interests.

One of Nixon's first moves as president was to take advantage of the growing divide between communist China and the Soviet Union. Nixon wanted a closer relationship with China for several reasons. He wanted to promote trade with China. He also hoped China, as an ally of North Vietnam, would help the United States achieve a peace settlement in Vietnam. In addition, a close relationship with China would strengthen the United States' bargaining position with the Soviet Union, who feared any alliance between the United States and China.

No American president had visited China or even officially talked with Chinese leaders since China became a communist state in 1949, partly because Nixon and other anti-communist leaders had opposed any contact. Nixon broke this taboo on February 22, 1972, becoming the first American president to visit China. The trip ended with a joint statement that promised closer relations between the two countries in trade, travel, and cultural exchange. Three months later, the president traveled to Moscow for a summit meeting with Soviet leader Leonid Brezhnev (LEHY-uh-nihd BREZH-nehf). Nixon believed that his successful trip to China, coupled with a declining Soviet economy, would make the Soviets more likely to strike serious deals with the United States on arms control and trade. Both countries possessed huge numbers of nuclear weapons that cost billions of dollars and increased the chances of nuclear war. In addition, the Soviets desperately needed grain, heavy equipment, and technical assistance. American farmers and manufacturers were eager to market these goods and services to the Soviet Union.

On May 22, 1972, the United States and the Soviet Union signed an agreement arising out of the **Strategic Arms Limitation Talks**. The agreement

President Nixon (center) already knew how to use chopsticks when he sat down with Premier Chou En-Lai (left) and Communist Party leader Chang Chun-Chiao (right) at a banquet in honor of his visit to China in 1972. Before the trip, Nixon had taken lessons on how to properly use chopsticks, hoping to make a good impression on his hosts.

11.9.6 Describe U.S. Middle East policy and its strategic, political, and economic interests, including those related to the Gulf War.

TOWARD ENERGY INDEPENDENCE

Americans were already aware of the benefits of using less petroleum before the 1973 war between Israel and Egypt and Syria. Although the oil embargo of 1973 was short-lived, it served as a wakeup call that the United States was in a vulnerable position regarding its energy needs.

The Arab countries in OPEC that participated in the embargo provided only a small percentage of all the oil imported, but a decrease in supply of more than a million barrels a day still made a difference. Spurred on by the environmental movement and the development of new technologies, the United States began to work toward energy independence. While petroleum imports increased through the 1980s and 1990s, new sources of energy were being developed. These energy sources included shale oil, natural gas, and such renewables as wind and solar power. Experts think energy independence by 2035 may be an attainable goal for the United States.

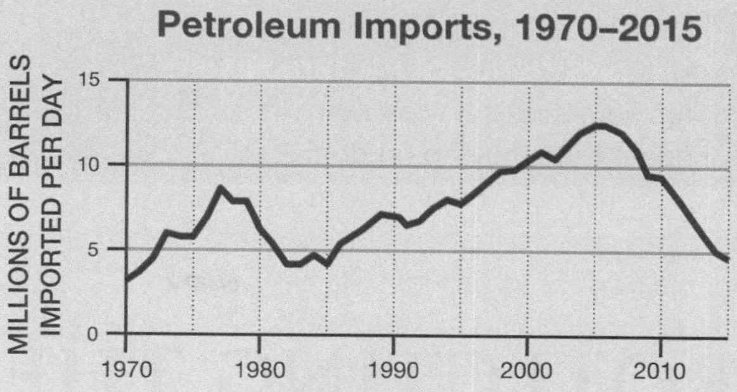

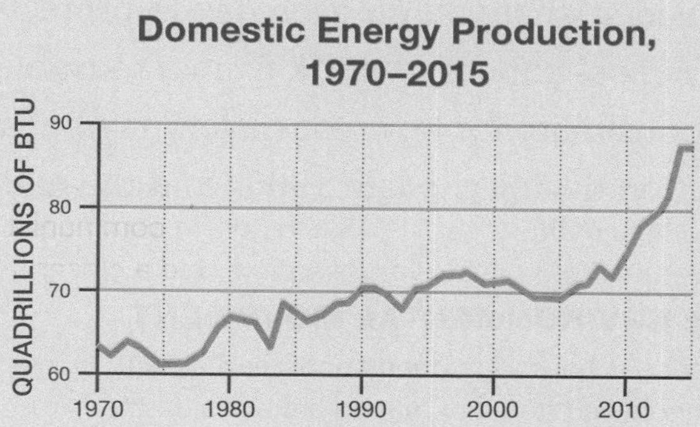

Source: U.S. Energy Information Administration

became known as **SALT I**, and it limited the number of long-range offensive missiles both countries could possess. The two countries also signed an agreement to stop the production of **antiballistic missiles (ABMs)**—missiles designed to destroy other bomb-carrying missiles before they hit the ground—for the next five years. ABMs were a problem because their possession by one side or the other provided an advantage and increased the temptation for those owning them to attack first with their own weapons. Henry Kissinger helped negotiate these treaties, which taken together represented a breakthrough in Soviet-American relations. The Moscow summit provided a solid foundation for **détente** (day-TAHNT), or an easing of tension between countries.

Despite these successes, Nixon continued to face foreign policy challenges in the Middle East. War broke out in the Middle East on the Jewish holiday of Yom Kippur, October 6, 1973. Egypt and Syria attacked the predominantly Jewish country of Israel on two fronts. The United States supported Israel, a longtime ally, by airlifting vital military supplies. These supplies proved essential in helping Israel drive back the attack. The Yom Kippur War lasted less than three weeks and ended when United Nations officials negotiated a cease-fire.

To protest American support of Israel, certain Middle Eastern countries in the **Organization of Petroleum Exporting Countries (OPEC)**, a multinational organization that sets petroleum prices and policies, began an embargo, or official ban, on exports of oil to the United States. While Americans accounted for barely 6 percent of the world's population in 1974, they used more than 30 percent of the world's oil. Between 1968 and 1973, the United States' consumption of imported oil had tripled. The embargo created an immediate panic. It forced Americans to reduce their energy use and wait in long lines to buy high-priced gas for their cars. The oil embargo ended in April 1974, but oil costs continued to rise because OPEC had tripled its prices.

HISTORICAL THINKING

1. **READING CHECK** What was the New Federalism?
2. **SYNTHESIZE** Explain the connections between Nixon's trip to China and larger political and economic developments during his administration.
3. **MAKE INFERENCES** What did Nixon mean when he said that the increase in the number of African-American elected officials and registered voters was evidence that the American system worked?
4. **INTERPRET GRAPHS** How does the overall trend in petroleum imports from 1970 to 2015 compare with that of domestic energy production, and what significant change in the relationship between the two occurred in 2005?

HI 1 Students show the connections, causal and otherwise, between particular historical events and larger social, economic, and political trends and developments; HI 2 Students recognize the complexity of historical causes and effects, including the limitations on determining cause and effect.

1.3 **MAIN IDEA** The modern environmental movement took shape during the presidency of Richard Nixon.

PROTECTING THE ENVIRONMENT

Consider what you do each day to protect the environment. Perhaps you recycle old school papers or drink from a reusable water bottle. The idea of taking responsibility for how your everyday behavior affects the environment gained traction during the late 1960s and the early 1970s.

THE ENVIRONMENTAL MOVEMENT

Americans have long been concerned about the negative effects of human activities on the environment. Near the beginning of the 20th century, conservationists such as John Muir and Theodore Roosevelt took action to protect natural places from human destruction. In the 1950s, activists protested the negative environmental effects of nuclear weapons development and testing and of nuclear energy production.

In the 1960s, American scientists published environmental articles and books that raised public awareness and gave rise to the modern environmental movement. American marine biologist **Rachel Carson** published *Silent Spring* in 1962, bringing concerns about pollution into the spotlight. After years of research, Carson showed how a common pesticide called **DDT** entered the food chain. Farmers sprayed DDT on their crops to kill insects, but the contaminated food ended up killing animals, especially birds, and harming people. If the contamination of the food supply continued, Carson warned, it could lead to a world in which all life would be endangered.

Stanford University biologist **Paul Ehrlich** warned about the global consequences of human population growth in *The Population Bomb* (1968). Ehrlich argued that the global food supply would not be able to support the increasing number of people on Earth. He predicted that the world would experience wide-scale hunger by the 1970s. Ehrlich's predictions did not come true, partly because of a dramatic increase in agricultural production, but he continued to promote the need to curb global population growth.

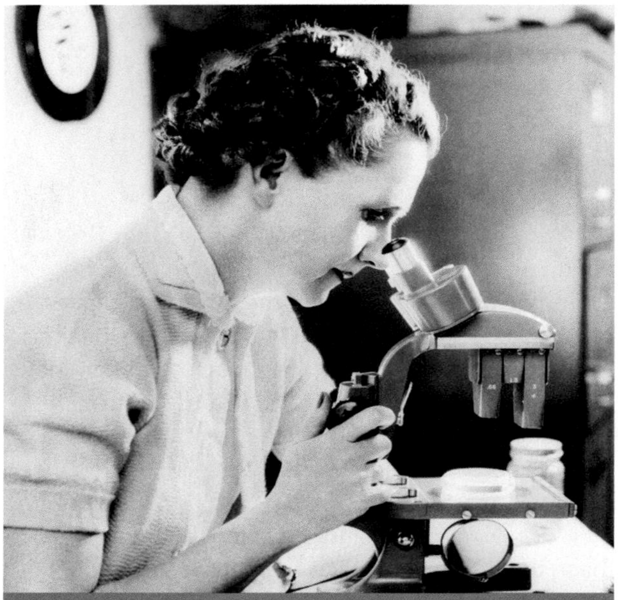

PRIMARY SOURCE

Rachel Carson (above) was a biologist whose gift for writing enabled her to explain environmental science to the public. She sounded an alarm about environmental pollution in her book *Silent Spring*.

The most alarming of all man's assaults upon the environment is the contamination of air, earth, rivers, and sea with dangerous and even lethal materials. This pollution is for the most part irrecoverable; the chain of evil it initiates not only in the world that must support life but in living tissues is for the most part irreversible. In this now universal contamination of the environment, chemicals are the sinister and little-recognized partners of radiation in changing the very nature of the world—the very nature of its life.

—from *Silent Spring*, by Rachel Carson, 1962

CRITICAL VIEWING In the 1940s, cities began to spray DDT in residential neighborhoods to kill mosquitoes. This photo shows a fogger for spraying DDT being tested in Long Island, New York. What details in the photo indicate a lack of public awareness about the dangers of DDT?

During Nixon's presidency, environmental problems often covered the front pages of newspapers. In June 1969, the Cuyahoga River in Cleveland, Ohio, caught fire due to the dumping of industrial waste. Lake Erie was declared "dead," or lacking in any aquatic life, due to pollution. Smog blanketed major cities, such as New York City and Los Angeles. Biologists warned that the national symbol of the United States, the bald eagle, faced extinction due to habitat destruction, illegal hunting, and DDT contamination. The environmental problems were so severe that people around the country began to push for more effective conservation measures.

On April 22, 1970, U.S. Senator Gaylord Nelson and Harvard graduate student Denis Hayes organized the first Earth Day, a celebration to raise awareness about the environmental movement and to educate people on the importance of conservation. Around the country, nearly 20 million people participated. The largest gatherings were in Washington, D.C., and New York City, where conservationists took to the streets to show their support of the movement.

LEGISLATION AND ORGANIZATIONS

Responding to these growing concerns, President Nixon worked with Congress to pass laws to preserve and protect the environment. The **National Environmental Policy Act (NEPA)** was the first law of its kind when it was enacted on January 1, 1970. It required the federal government to consider the environmental impact of any new federally funded construction project. The following year, Nixon created the **Environmental Protection Agency (EPA)** to ensure enforcement of environmental laws. The **Clean Air Act** of 1970 set strict national guidelines to reduce emissions from vehicles and factories and help curb smog. In 1972, Congress passed amendments to the 1948 Federal Water Pollution Control Act, which then became known as the **Clean Water Act**. The amendments allotted $25 billion for the cleanup of polluted lakes and rivers. This costly effort proved effective in bringing polluted waters, such as the Cuyahoga River, back to life. In 1973, Congress passed the **Endangered Species Act** to keep rare plant and animal species from dying out.

The courts also played a role as environmental groups brought lawsuits against various businesses to stop them from polluting. In a 1966 case brought on behalf of all the citizens of Suffolk County in Long Island, New York, the Suffolk County Supreme Court awarded relief in the form of a ban on DDT use in the county. The case was supported by scientists who documented for the court the nearly irreparable environmental damage resulting from use of the pesticide. Interest in the group's success arose across the nation, and in 1967, Charles Wurster and nine other scientists involved in the suit formed the **Environmental Defense Fund (EDF)** to work on a variety of environmental issues. The EDF's efforts led to a New York statewide ban on DDT in 1971 and a nationwide ban by the EPA in 1972. In 1970, a group of law students and attorneys founded the **National Resources Defense Council (NRDC)**.

11.8.6 Discuss the diverse environmental regions of North America, their relationship to local economies, and the origins and prospects of environmental problems in those regions.

AMERICAN PLACES

Yellowstone National Park, Wyoming

Minerva Terrace, part of Mammoth Hot Springs in Yellowstone National Park, consists of a series of multi-colored terraces composed of calcium carbonate deposited by hot springs. Microorganisms tint the terrace rock various colors. Minerva Terrace is one of the many spectacular natural features of Yellowstone, the world's first national park.

This stunning photograph of Minerva Terrace was taken by National Geographic photographer Frans Lanting. By capturing the magnificence of the natural world, National Geographic photographers help people understand the importance of protecting Earth and its diversity.

The EDF and the NRDC were the first nonprofit environmental groups focused initially on bringing about environmental change by filing research-based lawsuits against polluting companies and agencies.

Some conservation organizations that had existed for many years experienced a newfound popularity and purpose as a result of the environmental movement of the late 1960s and the 1970s. The **Sierra Club**, founded in 1892 by naturalist John Muir, was largely responsible for the preservation of lands in the West, including Yosemite National Park in California. By the 1970s, the Sierra Club had become a leading lobbyist group and environmental protection advocate, fighting to protect natural areas from industrial and agricultural development. The club helped protect California's redwood forests as well as wilderness areas in Alaska.

The Sierra Club often joined with other environmental groups to achieve common goals. One of these groups was the **Wilderness Society**, which was founded in 1935 to fight for the protection of America's wild natural areas. Since its founding, the Wilderness Society has succeeded in preserving some 110 million acres of land across 44 states. In 1969, David Brower, a former leader of the Sierra Club, formed the **League of Conservation Voters** to organize support for pro-environmental political candidates and policies.

CONTROVERSY ON REGULATION

The new environmental laws passed in the 1970s restricted business operations and land use. Some corporations and conservative politicians began to criticize what they viewed as **overregulation**, or excessive control and oversight, by the EPA and other federal agencies. They claimed that the regulations limited profits, job creation, and economic progress.

In the early 1970s, for example, officials with the Tennessee Valley Authority (TVA) were attempting to expand construction of a dam along the Little Tennessee River. The dam promised to extend hydroelectric power over a large region. In 1973, researchers discovered a previously unknown species of fish, called the snail darter, in the Little Tennessee River area. Scientists warned that the dam could destroy the snail darter's natural habitat, and thus potentially destroy the entire population of this rare creature. In 1975, government officials listed the snail darter as protected under the Endangered Species Act. After several years of back and forth decisions in the courts, the U.S. Supreme Court ruled in 1978 that the dam would violate the law protecting the snail darter. The Court ordered a halt to construction of the dam. Eventually, Tennessee officials persuaded Congress to pass a law specifically allowing completion of the dam. As a result, the snail darter became extinct in the Little Tennessee River region. However, thanks to relocation efforts, the snail darter was able to survive in other areas.

Meanwhile, the amount of federally protected land was growing. In 1978, Congress passed a law expanding the size of California's Redwood National and State Parks, much to the disappointment of some leaders in the logging industry. Federal officials also expanded the protection of lands in Alaska, where many oil companies wanted to drill in such wilderness areas as the Arctic National Wildlife Range. The range was renamed the **Arctic National Wildlife Refuge** to highlight its protected status. By the end of the 1970s, new legislation more than doubled the size of the national park system, protecting millions of acres of land and thousands of plant and animal species, but at the same time upsetting some business leaders.

The mid-1970s saw the rise of a movement called the **Sagebrush Rebellion**, led by a group of landowners, miners, loggers, and ranchers in certain western states who resented federal laws limiting the extraction of natural resources on federally protected lands. As supporters of **property rights**, or the right to use property as the owner sees fit, they wanted more local control and even ownership of federal lands so they could use the lands for their benefit. The rebellion continued into the early 1980s and inspired similar movements in later years to reclaim western lands from federal control.

HISTORICAL THINKING

1. **READING CHECK** What environmental problems resulted from human modifications of landscapes in the 1960s and 1970s?
2. **COMPARE AND CONTRAST** How was the environmental movement similar to and different from other activist movements of the 1960s and 1970s?
3. **FORM AND SUPPORT OPINIONS** Do you think the U.S. government should own land and control how it is used? Give reasons for your opinion.
4. **ANALYZE ENVIRONMENTAL CONCEPTS** How might the quality of life in the United States be different today if the modern environmental movement had not developed?

11.11.5 Trace the impact of, need for, and controversies associated with environmental conservation, expansion of the national park system, and the development of environmental protection laws, with particular attention to the interaction between environmental protection advocates and property rights advocates; HI 4 Students understand the meaning, implication, and impact of historical events and recognize that events could have taken other directions; HI 5 Students analyze human modifications of landscapes and examine the resulting environmental policy issues.

CRITICAL VIEWING Alaska's Denali National Park and Preserve is home to North America's highest mountain as well as these Dall sheep. The park's strict rules protect wildlife habitats and ecosystems, keeping its 6 million acres of land as they have been for thousands of years. Paul Nicklen believes sea ice and polar ecosystems like those found in the park play an important role in our current climate era. What types of controversies currently exist between environmental protection advocates like Nicklen and property rights activists? Whose views do you support?

11.11.5 Trace the impact of, need for, and controversies associated with environmental conservation, expansion of the national park system, and the development of environmental protection laws, with particular attention to the interaction between environmental protection advocates and property rights advocates.

1.4

THROUGH THE LENS

PAUL NICKLEN

Canadian-born National Geographic photographer and marine biologist Paul Nicklen documents both the beauty and the plight of the world's oceans and Arctic regions for a global audience. His personal mission is to use his emotional, evocative, and inspiring photographs to ignite conversations about the future of our planet's natural wonders and to promote conservation.

CST 4 Students relate current events to the physical and human characteristics of places [illegible] regions.

1.5 **MAIN IDEA** As a result of illegal activities, Richard Nixon became the first president to resign from office.

THE WATERGATE SCANDAL

Have you ever wanted something so badly you were willing to do almost anything to get it? Unfortunately, Richard Nixon wanted to remain president so badly that he was willing to break the law and compromise his entire administration.

NIXON'S BID FOR RE-ELECTION

By the end of his first term, President Nixon had built a strong record, especially in foreign affairs. He had successfully negotiated foreign policy agreements with China and the Soviet Union. He also had made progress in the Vietnam War peace talks.

The Republican Party nominated Nixon and his vice president, Spiro Agnew, for re-election, and they did so enthusiastically. Statisticians and journalists favored Nixon to win handily against any of the 11 Democratic primary candidates who were vying for their party's nomination.

Despite all his accomplishments, Nixon worried about the election. Not only did he want to maintain the presidency, he wanted his party to take control of Congress. To this end, some of his supporters founded a political action group called the **Committee to Re-Elect the President (CRP)** in the

Washington Post reporters Carl Bernstein (left) and Bob Woodward received anonymous tips linking the Watergate break-in to the White House. In 2005, it was revealed that the source had been a deputy director of the FBI.

spring of 1971. Nixon's opponents mocked him by referring to the CRP as "CREEP." Attorney General **John Mitchell** resigned his cabinet position to lead the committee.

Mitchell and other CRP members resorted to what came to be known as "dirty tricks" to ruin the chances of the strongest contenders for the Democratic presidential nomination. For example, one CRP member sent a forged letter to a newspaper in New Hampshire that accused the Democratic primary favorite, Senator Edmund Muskie of Maine, of using an ethnic slur to refer to French Canadians.

CRP's dirty tricks may have worked. In July 1972, the Democratic Party chose an underdog as its nominee, South Dakota Senator **George McGovern**. McGovern was a staunch opponent of the Vietnam War, but otherwise his platform was vague. His relative inexperience in politics, compared to Nixon's broad experience, made him a weak candidate.

CRITICAL VIEWING **Radio microphones hidden in lip balm containers were found in the White House office safe of one of the leaders of the Watergate break-in team. They were displayed, along with many other listening devices, at the trial of the Watergate burglars. What does evidence like this suggest about the nature of the trial?**

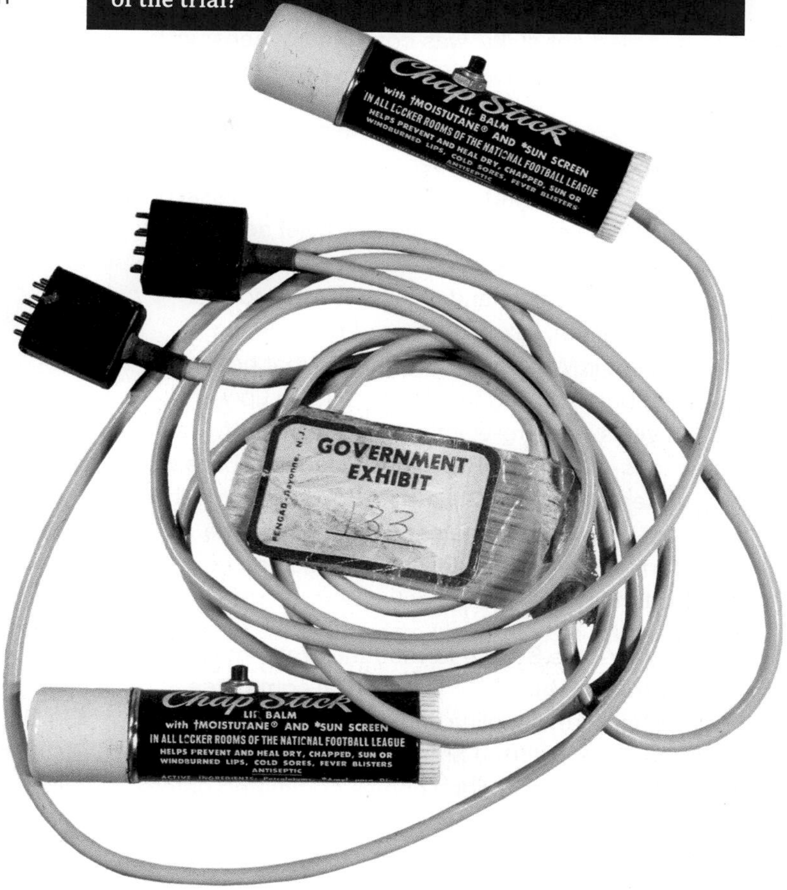

THE WATERGATE BREAK-IN

On June 17, 1972, just weeks before McGovern won the Democratic nomination, a security guard on his rounds of the Watergate building complex in Washington, D.C., noticed a piece of tape that prevented a door from locking. That door was the entrance to the Democratic National Headquarters. The security guard called the police, who surprised and arrested five men in possession of burglary tools, cameras, film, tear gas guns, and surveillance equipment. Among the burglars was **James W. McCord, Jr.**, the security director for CRP. The next day a second CRP member and a former presidential aide were named as accomplices in the burglary. Journalists called the incident the **Watergate break-in**.

In response to news of the break-in, President Nixon assured the public that no one "presently employed" in his administration was involved "in this very bizarre incident." At first, few people paid much attention to the crime. But over the next several months, *Washington Post* reporters **Bob Woodward** and **Carl Bernstein** slowly began to uncover the connection between the break-in and top government officials closely connected to the White House.

Months passed, and the election campaigns continued. The Watergate break-in had little effect on the outcome of the November 1972 election because the journalists were still investigating the incident. Nixon won the presidency by a landslide, but the Democratic Party, much to Nixon's disappointment, kept control of Congress.

THE WATERGATE TRIALS

Woodward and Bernstein continued to publish reports through the end of 1972 describing the dirty tricks that CRP members had played to sabotage Nixon's opponents. In January 1973, the same month as Nixon's inauguration, the trial of the Watergate burglars began with Judge **John Sirica** presiding.

At the time, Nixon's public approval rating was very high, at 68 percent, but it fell sharply as the journalists continued to uncover information about the break-in. The *Post's* reports led Judge Sirica

11.11.4 Explain the constitutional crisis originating from the Watergate scandal.

to suspect a **cover-up**, or an attempt to hide the truth. He did not believe that the burglars had acted without the knowledge of either the CRP or the president. In January, four of the Watergate burglars pled guilty to minor charges of theft and **wiretapping**, or placing a device on a telephone in order to secretly listen to conversations. McCord, who had pled not guilty, was convicted of conspiracy along with the other two offenses.

In March 1973, McCord wrote a letter to Judge Sirica implicating Nixon in the cover-up of the Watergate burglary. McCord's letter resulted in the dismissal or the resignation of several of Nixon's chief advisors, including White House counsel John Dean, chief of staff H. R. Haldeman, and chief domestic advisor John Ehrlichman. Nixon continued to deny any involvement in Watergate. He claimed that he had been too busy running the nation to keep up with the activities of his re-election campaign staff. Many Americans—and most Republican leaders—believed Nixon. Representative **Gerald R. Ford** of Michigan declared, "I have the greatest confidence in the president and am absolutely positive he had nothing to do with this mess."

Nonetheless, the Senate formed the **Watergate Committee** in May 1973. The special committee, chaired by North Carolina senator **Sam Ervin**, heard sworn testimonies from present and former Nixon aides. The aides described crimes committed before the 1972 election that were intended to undermine the president's opponents. Additionally, a former aide to the president revealed that Nixon had been secretly tape-recording his conversations in the White House's Oval Office since 1971.

In May 1973, Attorney General **Elliot Richardson** appointed Harvard Law School professor **Archibald Cox** as a special prosecutor in the Watergate case. Cox, Judge Sirica, and committee chairman Ervin demanded to hear the relevant Oval Office tapes. However, Nixon withheld them, claiming **executive privilege**, the principle that the president may withhold certain information from Congress in the nation's interest. Cox presented the White House with a subpoena demanding the tapes, which Nixon's lawyers asked Sirica to block. Sirica ordered the tapes to be turned over. Now the White House was in a battle with the courts as well as with the Watergate Committee, provoking a constitutional crisis.

At the same time, Vice President Spiro Agnew was enmeshed in his own separate scandal. Beginning in April 1973, the U.S. Justice Department had been investigating allegations that Agnew had accepted illegal payoffs from building contractors while he was governor of Maryland from 1967 to 1969. Initially, Agnew denied the charges. Then, on October 10, 1973, he pleaded no contest in court to income tax evasion, and he resigned as vice president.

PRIMARY SOURCE

As a member of the committee given the task of deciding Nixon's fate, Representative Barbara Jordan asserted that a failure to impeach Nixon went directly against the Constitution.

The President has engaged in a series of public statements and actions designed to thwart the lawful investigation by government prosecutors. Moreover, the President has made public announcements and assertions . . . which the evidence will show he knew to be false. If the impeachment provision in the Constitution of the United States will not reach the offenses charged here, then perhaps that 18th-century Constitution should be abandoned to a 20th-century paper shredder.

—from a speech delivered by Representative Barbara Jordan, House Judiciary Committee, during Watergate hearings, July 25, 1974

On October 20, Nixon ordered Attorney General Richardson to fire Cox, but Richardson refused. Nixon retaliated by firing Richardson. With Richardson gone, the attorney general's second-in-command, Solicitor General Robert Bork, fired Cox and replaced him with a lawyer named Leon Jaworski. These dramatic developments, known as the "Saturday Night Massacre," prompted the House Judiciary Committee to consider hearings for **impeachment**, or formal charges brought against a public official for misconduct while in office. At this point, the White House turned over some, but not all, of the tapes. In December 1973, Congress confirmed Nixon's choice of Gerald Ford to replace Agnew as vice president.

THE TAPES AND THE RESIGNATION

In March 1974, Nixon's chief advisors, who had resigned or were dismissed as a result of McCord's letter to Judge Sirica, were indicted for crimes. In July, prosecutor Jaworski ordered Nixon to release 64 additional tapes of his conversations in the Oval Office. Rather than release the tapes, Nixon handed over more than 1,000 pages of edited transcripts. Jaworski appealed to the Supreme Court. In *United States* v. *Nixon*, the Supreme Court ruled unanimously that the tapes did not fall under the

11.11.4 Explain the constitutional crisis originating from the Watergate scandal.

CRITICAL VIEWING On August 9, 1974, the day after announcing his resignation, Nixon boarded the Marine One helicopter that took him from the White House lawn to Andrews Air Force Base for his flight to his home in southern California. What attitude does Nixon convey in his body language?

protection of executive privilege and that Nixon must surrender them. By this point, Nixon had lost the trust of most American citizens. A Gallup poll taken just months earlier showed Nixon's public approval rating had dropped from 68 to 27 percent.

Also in July 1974, the House Judiciary Committee began debating charges of presidential impeachment before a national television audience. One member of the committee was Representative **Barbara Jordan** of Texas, who became famous for her powerful speeches. Three days after the Supreme Court ordered Nixon to hand over the Oval Office tapes, the committee approved three charges: obstruction of justice, abuse of power, and contempt of Congress. On August 5, the president released the tapes, one of which had an 18-minute gap of silence. The gap led many people to believe that something may have been erased. Although investigators could not prove Nixon knew of the burglary before it occurred, the tapes confirmed that he played an active role in the attempt to cover up the burglary. He offered money to the burglars to keep quiet about their role in the crime. He developed a plan for the CIA to block the FBI's investigation. Ultimately, Nixon was charged with obstruction of justice and abuse of power.

Nixon's impeachment seemed certain. Rather than risk further disgrace, on August 8, 1974, Nixon resigned, becoming the first president to do so. In a tearful farewell to his staff the next morning, he offered advice he himself had ignored. "Always remember," he said, "those who hate you don't win unless you hate them. And then you destroy yourself." Vice President Gerald Ford was sworn in as president shortly after noon on the same day.

Nixon's involvement in Watergate deepened a public distrust of government that had grown during the Vietnam War years. The scandal also demonstrated the dangers of an imperial, or overly powerful, presidency and sent the Congress into constitutional crisis mode. Fortunately, the Constitution's system of checks and balances allowed the judicial and legislative branches to rein in the executive branch. For his part, however, Nixon, who died in 1994 at the age of 81, never directly admitted his guilt in the matter.

HISTORICAL THINKING

1. **READING CHECK** What was Nixon's involvement in the Watergate scandal?
2. **DRAW CONCLUSIONS** Do Representative Jordan's comments indicate bias on her part, or does she present valid arguments? Explain your answer.
3. **SYNTHESIZE** What role did the characteristics of power in Washington, D.C., play in the actions and resignation of Nixon?
4. **EVALUATE** Within the context of the Watergate scandal, identify what you believe to be a valid argument that was used as well as a fallacious argument used to analyze events. Explain your choices.

HREP 1 Students distinguish valid arguments from fallacious arguments in historical interpretations;
HREP 2 Students identify bias and prejudice in historical interpretations.

2.1 **MAIN IDEA** President Ford inherited many challenges that proved difficult to resolve during his brief presidency, including a slow economy and the ongoing conflict in Vietnam.

FORD SUCCEEDS NIXON

Americans felt betrayed by the Watergate scandal. Their president left office barely apologizing for the chaos he had caused and without admitting his guilt. They hoped the man who took his place would prove more trustworthy.

THE WATERGATE LEGACY

When Vice President Agnew resigned in 1973, Gerald Ford rose from Congressional representative to vice president—the first selected under the **25th Amendment**. Ratified under President Johnson in 1967, the amendment calls for the president to nominate and Congress to approve a replacement for the vice president when necessary. On August 9, 1974, the day after President Nixon resigned and less than a year after being confirmed as vice president, Ford became the 38th president of the United States. The American people had a president they had never voted for—another first.

In his 25 years in Congress, Ford had developed a reputation for honesty and openness, traits Americans were looking for in their president. During his vice-presidential confirmation hearing in 1973, Ford had stated he would not give Nixon a presidential pardon. A president has the constitutional right to grant a pardon to anyone. A pardon excuses a person from punishment for a crime. In September 1974, Ford reversed his position and pardoned Nixon for all crimes he "may have committed" during his term in office. Ford's pardon ended any further criminal investigation into Nixon's actions as president.

Ford hoped the pardon would finally allow Americans to move forward and put the Watergate scandal behind them. However, many Americans wanted justice and felt that Ford had betrayed them. As a result, Ford's public approval rating plummeted from 72 percent to 49 percent.

ECONOMIC TROUBLES

Ford inherited an ailing economy that worsened over the course of his presidency. The economy slowed almost to a standstill, a situation called **economic stagnation**. The stagnation was due to years of slow economic growth and high unemployment rates. At the same time, energy costs kept rising, pushing up the inflation rate, or the annual percent increase in the prices of goods and services. Economists called this unusual combination of stagnation and inflation "**stagflation**."

Ford was at odds with the Democratic Congress over economic policies. He did not want to increase the federal deficit, and so he defied Congress's plan to lower taxes and increase government spending. Instead, in October 1974, Ford proposed a plan that involved a tax hike and a reduction in government spending. To get Americans on board with his plan, he initiated a campaign called Whip Inflation Now (WIN), in which he asked citizens to voluntarily limit their spending and consumption through thriftiness.

Stagflation, 1970–1979

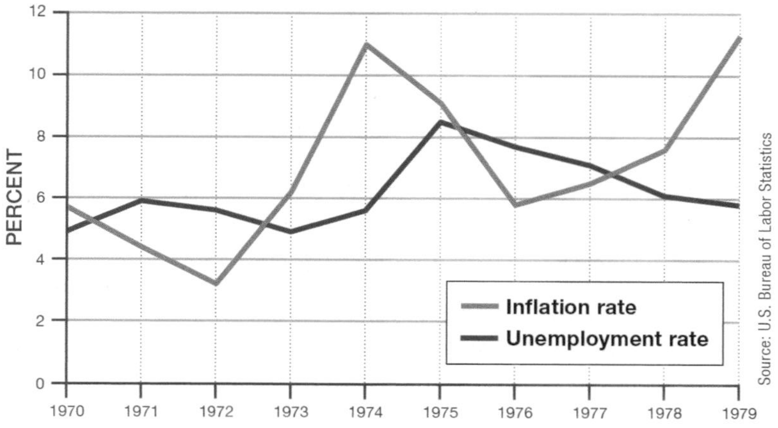

HI 6 Students conduct cost-benefit analyses and apply basic economic indicators to analyze the aggregate economic behavior of the U.S. economy.

In January 1975, he offered a new plan that called for a modest tax cut and a reduction in government spending. Congress approved this plan, but only after adding more tax cuts and raising government spending. In his battle with Congress, Ford vetoed more than 60 bills. Congress overrode the president's veto on several bills, increasing Social Security benefits, funding public works projects, and raising the minimum wage. Ford also battled Congress over energy policy, which had arisen as an issue under Nixon.

President Ford inherited from his predecessor the issue of U.S. dependence on foreign oil. In 1975, to promote conservation and energy independence, Ford imposed an import fee on oil. He hoped the fee would spur consumers to use less energy and so decrease demand for OPEC oil. Here Ford discusses his plan with the press outside the White House.

FOREIGN POLICY

In addition to an ailing economy, Ford also inherited the ongoing conflict in Vietnam and its many geopolitical consequences. As you have read, the United States withdrew combat troops from Vietnam in 1973 but kept an embassy in South Vietnam. However, fighting between the North and South Vietnamese had continued. The South Vietnamese army was no match for the combined North Vietnamese and Viet Cong forces. In October 1974, the leaders of communist North Vietnam prepared their final plans for the conquest of South Vietnam.

In March 1975, the North Vietnamese launched a massive assault, overwhelming South Vietnamese forces near the demilitarized zone (DMZ). As North Vietnamese troops rapidly advanced toward Saigon, the capital of South Vietnam, chaos and panic gripped the city. Thousands of soldiers left their units, and masses of civilians crowded the highways, trying to flee. Ignoring a plea from President Ford, the U.S. Congress refused to extend emergency aid to South Vietnam. A few U.S. forces remained in the city, and they worked to evacuate as many Americans and South Vietnamese as they could. On April 30, 1975, the North Vietnamese took control of Saigon and reunited North and South Vietnam into one communist-led nation. With the fall of Saigon, American efforts to stop the spread of communism in Southeast Asia failed, raising concerns about the limits of U.S. military power.

Communism also spread to neighboring Cambodia with the rise of a rebel guerilla force called the **Khmer Rouge** (kuh-MEHR ROOZH). After a civil war, a brutal communist regime took over Cambodia in 1975. The Khmer Rouge carried out a massive genocide against the Cambodian people. Not wanting to become involved in another war in Southeast Asia, the United States took no military action. By the time the regime was overthrown four years later, the Khmer Rouge had killed almost 2 million people—one-fourth of the nation's population.

Ford continued Nixon's policy of détente with the Soviet Union and signed the Helsinki Accords, or the Helsinki Final Act, in 1975. In this agreement, the 35 signing nations, including the United States and the Soviet Union, agreed to resolve conflicts peacefully, cooperate economically and scientifically, and respect human rights.

HISTORICAL THINKING

1. **READING CHECK** What challenges did President Ford inherit from President Nixon?
2. **ASK AND ANSWER QUESTIONS** What questions do you have about the fall of Saigon, and how can you find the answers to your questions?
3. **INTERPRET GRAPHS** In terms of the economic behavior of the United States, what was the trend in inflation while unemployment was falling from 1975 to 1979?

11.9.3 Trace the origins and geopolitical consequences (foreign and domestic) of the Cold War and containment policy, including the following: • The era of McCarthyism, instances of domestic Communism (e.g., Alger Hiss) and blacklisting • The Truman Doctrine • The Berlin Blockade • The Korean War • The Bay of Pigs invasion and the Cuban Missile Crisis • Atomic testing in the American West, the "mutual assured destruction" doctrine, and disarmament policies • The Vietnam War • Latin American policy.

2.2 **MAIN IDEA** President Carter focused on battling the nation's energy crisis and promoting human rights throughout the world.

CARTER AND THE ENERGY CRISIS

If you're like most people, you probably wouldn't want to be considered an "outsider." But for a presidential candidate, it's sometimes an advantage, particularly if voters don't trust the "insiders."

THE OUTSIDER PRESIDENT

Gerald Ford dreamed of winning the White House in his own right, but he faced a serious challenge in 1976—conservative California governor **Ronald Reagan**. In his primary campaign, Reagan portrayed Ford as a weak president who was unable to control a Democratic Congress or to confront the Soviet Union. Reagan campaigned effectively, but Ford managed a narrow primary victory and became the Republican presidential nominee.

Because Ford appeared vulnerable in 1976, the Democratic race for president attracted a number of candidates. Among them was a little-known politician named **James Earl (Jimmy) Carter, Jr.** Although he was not taken seriously at first, Carter presented the right image for the post-Watergate era. He was a deeply religious man who promised voters, "I will never lie to you." And he was not part of the Washington political establishment, which many Americans had come to distrust.

Born in Plains, Georgia, in 1924, Carter graduated from the U.S. Naval Academy and spent seven years as a naval officer. He returned to Plains to run the family's farm supply and peanut business. As his company prospered, he turned to politics, becoming the governor of Georgia in 1970. Known as a "new South" politician, Carter supported progressive causes and civil rights, which appealed to African-American voters. At the Democratic National Convention, delegates chose Carter as their presidential nominee, and he went on to win the 1976 presidential race against Ford.

Carter won praise for some of his early actions in office, including the appointment of popular civil rights leader **Andrew Young, Jr.**, as U.S. ambassador to the United Nations. Young had been a close associate of Dr. Martin Luther King, Jr., and was elected to Congress in 1972. Carter also supported the creation of the **Department of Education** to coordinate federal education policy. Previously, numerous federal offices had handled education-related issues. Through Carter's efforts, Congress approved the consolidation of these efforts into one cabinet-level department in 1979. Carter was also a strong supporter of affirmative action in federal government hiring. As you have read, affirmative action was challenged and upheld by the Supreme Court in the 1978 case of *Regents of the University of California* v. *Bakke.*

Carter often found himself at odds with Congress, however. Many Congressional representatives considered Carter difficult to work with. A relationship of dislike and distrust developed as Congress voted down bill after bill that Carter proposed. In return, Carter vetoed many of the bills that Congress had approved.

THE ENERGY CRISIS

Like Presidents Nixon and Ford, Carter had to battle an ongoing energy crisis. Since the 1973 oil embargo, the United States had faced rising prices for oil, declining domestic supplies, and growing energy needs. To address the crisis, Carter presented Congress with his plan for the National Energy Program in April 1977. This environmental policy emphasized reducing the demand for energy through conservation. It also called for decreased dependence on foreign oil and increased use of domestic coal as well as the development of alternative energy sources, such as solar, wind, and nuclear power. In promoting his program, Carter appealed to Americans to reduce their consumption of oil and gas.

11.10.2 Examine and analyze the key events, policies, and court cases in the evolution of civil rights, including *Dred Scott* v. *Sandford*, *Plessy* v. *Ferguson*, *Brown* v. *Board of Education*, *Regents of the University of California* v. *Bakke*, and California Proposition 209.

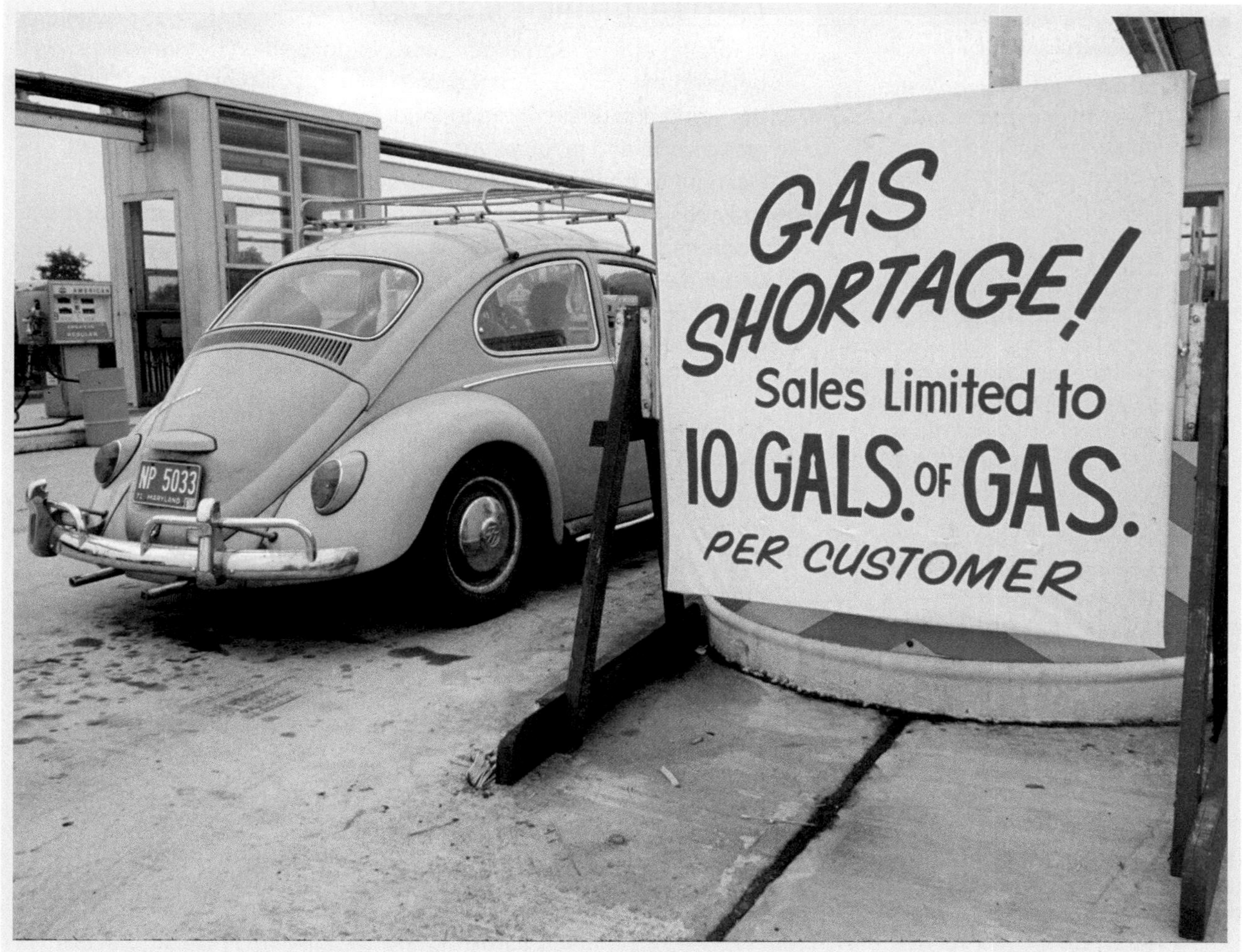

Rising prices and declining supplies of oil in the 1970s resulted in long lines and rationing at gas stations such as this one in Connecticut. States, cities, and individual gas stations themselves imposed limits on gas purchases.

Carter's plan ran into immediate opposition from oil companies, the auto industry, and others who supported the increased production of oil and the removal of restrictions on oil pricing. Nonetheless, in October 1977, President Carter established the **Department of Energy** to oversee federal energy policy and programs. In November 1978, he signed five energy bills into law.

Carter's push for alternative energy sources experienced a setback in 1979. A mechanical failure at the Three Mile Island nuclear power plant in Pennsylvania threatened the East Coast with a possible radiation leak. Even though power plant workers avoided a crisis, the incident raised awareness of the great risks associated with nuclear power.

In early 1979, a public uprising in Iran, as well as a strike by oilfield workers, disrupted the oil supply from that country. In late 1979, two OPEC nations decided to raise oil prices. The oil shortage and price increases led to a high rate of inflation in the United States. The events underscored the need for new sources of energy to build energy independence. But in the meantime, angry and frustrated Americans blamed Carter.

In a nationally televised speech, Carter prefaced his proposals for solving the energy crisis by describing a "crisis of confidence" gripping the nation. He claimed that many Americans no longer believed in a great future for the nation. In what came to be called the "malaise" (muh-LAYZ) speech, Carter portrayed Americans as suffering from low morale. The word ***malaise*** means "a general feeling of illness or unease." In the days following his speech, Carter's approval rating increased, but then negative reviews came out in the press. Carter's speech ultimately undermined confidence in his leadership. Many Americans felt that Carter blamed them, instead of his own lack of leadership, for the state of the country.

11.11.5 Trace the impact of, need for, and controversies associated with environmental conservation, expansion of the national park system, and the development of environmental protection laws, with particular attention to the interaction between environmental protection advocates and property rights advocates.

PRIMARY SOURCE

It's clear that the true problems of our nation are much deeper—deeper than gasoline lines or energy shortages, deeper even than inflation or recession.

The threat is nearly invisible in ordinary ways. It is a crisis of confidence. It is a crisis that strikes at the very heart and soul and spirit of our national will. We can see this crisis in the growing doubt about the meaning of our own lives and in the loss of a unity of purpose for our nation.

The erosion of our confidence in the future is threatening to destroy the social and the political fabric of America.

—from the "malaise" speech by President Carter, July 15, 1979

CARTER'S FOREIGN POLICY

In foreign affairs, Carter centered his policies on human rights. He believed the United States should promote human rights throughout the world, including rights to food, housing, and education as well as civil and political rights. He also believed all people had the right to bodily integrity, or ownership of one's self, which provides freedom from slavery, torture, and unlawful imprisonment. Addressing human rights violations in Latin America, Carter withdrew American support for a military dictatorship in Chile, cut off aid to a repressive regime in Nicaragua, and encouraged the governments of Brazil and Argentina to take steps toward establishing democracy.

Despite having little previous experience in foreign affairs, President Carter proved to be a successful diplomat. Shortly after taking office, he prioritized resolving a long-standing issue with the country of Panama. As you've read, Theodore Roosevelt negotiated for the United States to have control of the Panama Canal Zone in 1904. Over the years, tension grew between the United States and Panama over the issue of canal ownership. In 1977, President Carter and Omar Torrijos (OH-mahr toh-REE-hohs), the dictator of Panama, negotiated two treaties. The first treaty allowed the U.S. military to use the canal for defense. The second treaty outlined the

CRITICAL VIEWING **President Carter (center), Egyptian president Anwar Sadat (left), and Israeli prime minister Mehanchem Begin shake hands together to celebrate the signing of the 1979 treaty that ended 31 years of war between Egypt and Israel. What does the photo convey about the mood of this moment?**

11.9.6 Describe the U.S. Middle East policy and its strategic, political, and economic interests, including those related to the Gulf War; 11.11.2 Discuss the significant domestic policy speeches of Truman, Eisenhower, Kennedy, Johnson, Nixon, Carter, Reagan, Bush, and Clinton (e.g., with regard to education, civil rights, economic policy, environmental policy).

process of transferring ownership of the Panama Canal Zone from the United States back to Panama. Both treaties provoked fierce national debate in the Senate for more than six months, but they were eventually ratified. The treaties greatly improved relations between the United States and Latin America.

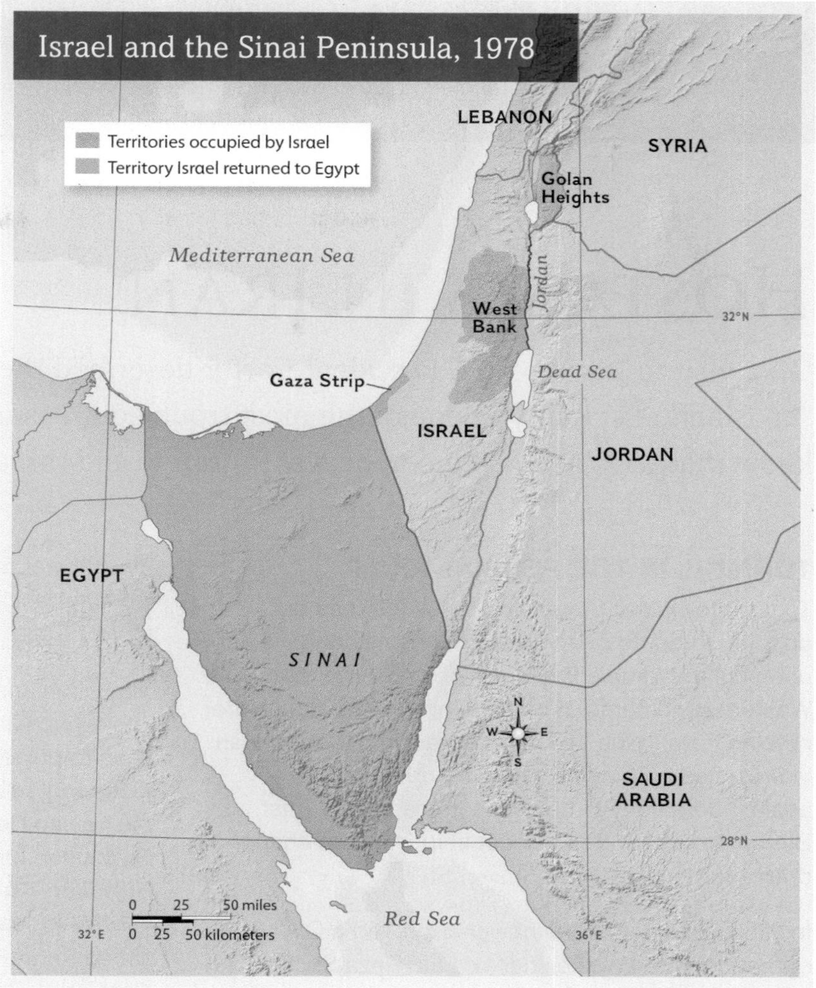

Carter's greatest foreign policy achievement involved the Middle East, however. In 1977, Egyptian President **Anwar Sadat** (AHN-wahr suh-DAHT) stunned the Arab world by visiting Israel to explore the possibility of peace talks with Prime Minister **Menachem Begin** (muh-NAH-khuhm BAY-gihn). Egypt and Israel had been enemies for many years and seemed at an impasse. Their discussions were friendly but unproductive, as neither man seemed willing to take the political risks that peace demanded.

Carter invited Sadat and Begin to join him at the presidential retreat at Camp David in Maryland in September 1978 to negotiate a peace agreement. The **Camp David Accords** led to a historic treaty the following year. Egypt agreed to recognize the state of Israel, previously unthinkable for an Arab nation. Israel agreed to return the Sinai Peninsula, which it had acquired in the 1967 Six-Day War, to Egypt.

Carter also worked to improve foreign relations with the Soviet Union by building upon the SALT I treaty you have read about. A new round of talks, **SALT II**, had begun in 1972, when Nixon was president. For seven years, negotiators refined the language of the treaty. In 1979, President Carter and General Secretary Leonid Brezhnev of the Soviet Union signed the SALT II Treaty, which limited the number of weapons each nation could have and restricted their deployment. When the U.S. Senate received the treaty for ratification, Republicans and conservative Democrats opposed the deal and wrote a letter to Carter in December 1979 explaining, "Ratification of a SALT II Treaty will not reverse trends in the military balance adverse to the United States." Days later, the Soviets invaded neighboring Afghanistan, which resulted in Carter withdrawing the SALT II treaty from consideration and organizing an international boycott of the 1980 Summer Olympics to be held in Moscow. The Soviet invasion was intended to stop a revolt by Islamic fundamentalists against the pro-Soviet regime that ruled the country. The United States then supported and equipped the Afghan fighters, contributing to massive casualties for the Soviet troops. The invasion worsened the tensions between the United States and the Soviet Union.

HISTORICAL THINKING

1. **READING CHECK** How did President Carter plan to address the energy crisis?
2. **IDENTIFY MAIN IDEAS AND DETAILS** Describe the main features of U.S. Middle East policy and outline its strategic, political, and economic objectives.
3. **MAKE INFERENCES** Why were the Camp David Accords historically important?
4. **INTERPRET MAPS** After returning the Sinai Peninsula to Egypt, what territories did Israel still occupy?

HI 4 Students understand the meaning, implication, and impact of historical events and recognize that events could have taken other directions.

2.3 **MAIN IDEA** President Carter lost public support after failing to resolve a hostage crisis in Iran.

HOSTAGES IN IRAN

On a visit to Iran in 1977, President Carter described the Middle Eastern nation as "an island of stability in one of the most troubled areas in the world." He did not know that within two years upheaval in Iran would threaten his own presidency.

TURMOIL IN THE PERSIAN GULF

Today, the United States and the world face an ongoing threat to peace due to uprisings and violent unrest in the Middle East, but the anti-American, anti-Western sentiments of many people in the region are nothing new. In the 1970s, Iran was vital to American interests as both an oil supplier and a political ally against communist influences in the Middle East. But the United States' relationship with Iran changed dramatically in 1979.

In 1953, President Eisenhower approved a CIA operation to return the shah of Iran, Reza Shah Pahlavi, to power by overthrowing the democratically elected prime minister Mohammed Mossadegh. Eisenhower feared that Mossadegh's rise to power would affect American access to oil supplies in the Middle East.

Many Iranians resented the United States for directly interfering with their government by returning the shah to power. They also opposed the shah's dictatorial rule. In January 1979, protesters launched the Iranian Revolution, also referred to as the Islamic Revolution, under the leadership of **Ayatollah Ruhollah Khomeini** (ah-yuh-TOH-luh roo-HOH-luh koh-MAY-nee). An exiled religious leader. Khomeini aimed to turn Iran into an **Islamic republic**, or a state governed by Islamic law. The shah fled Iran, initially for Egypt, as Khomeini returned to the

On November 4, 1979, Iranian militants captured American embassy workers, blindfolded them, and paraded the hostages before television cameras for the world to see.

11.9.6 Describe U.S. Middle East policy and its strategic, political, and economic interests, including those related to the Gulf War;
HI 4 Students understand the meaning, implication, and impact of historical events and recognize that events could have taken other directions.

country and took power. As a result of perceived corruption in the shah's relationship with the United States, the new leadership opposed Western influence. One of Khomeini's first moves was to end oil shipments to the United States, which he called "the Great Satan." Then other OPEC countries raised their oil prices. In the United States, long lines reappeared at gas stations, and the price of gas reached a dollar per gallon—the most expensive it had ever been.

The wreckage of an American helicopter and the plane it crashed into lie in the Iranian desert. The collision occurred during a failed mission in April 1980 to rescue American hostages held in Iran.

THE HOSTAGE CRISIS

In October 1979, President Carter allowed the deposed shah to enter the United States to receive cancer treatments. This decision, which Carter viewed as a simple humanitarian gesture, angered many Iranians. On November 4, militant students in **Tehran**, the capital of Iran, stormed the American embassy and took 66 Americans as hostages, or prisoners held to force another party to do what the holder of the prisoners wants. The world watched as the blindfolded hostages were paraded before television cameras. The militants demanded the United States return the shah to Iran for trial in exchange for the release of the American hostages. Otherwise, the prisoners would be tried and possibly executed as spies.

Carter refused to return the shah to Iran. Diplomats from the United States and other countries tried to negotiate the release of the hostages but failed. The militants ignored Carter's attempts to settle the crisis through the United Nations. A painful standoff ensued.

Many Americans believed the Iran hostage crisis demonstrated that the United States' prestige and power were declining in the world. Television networks flashed nightly pictures of the hostages on humiliating public display in Tehran while crowds shouted "Death to Carter" and "Down with the United States." Americans appeared helpless and discouraged as they faced daunting challenges abroad.

DEATH IN THE DESERT

As the hostage crisis continued, President Carter consulted with the families of the hostages and mobilized his administration to find a diplomatic solution. Finally, desperate to save the Americans, Carter ordered a secret military mission to free them by force. The result was disastrous. In April 1980, two American helicopters involved in the secret rescue mission were disabled by mechanical problems in the Iranian desert. Another helicopter hit a U.S. cargo plane, killing eight members of the mission. Not only did the soldiers fail to free the hostages, they never even made it to Tehran. The Iranians proudly displayed the burned corpses of the helicopter crash victims before the television cameras.

Carter's credibility as a leader plummeted because most Americans blamed him for the failed mission. The 1980 presidential election was approaching, and Carter's chances for re-election did not look good.

HISTORICAL THINKING

1. **READING CHECK** What was the purpose of the Iranian Revolution of 1979?
2. **SYNTHESIZE** Describe the strategies President Carter used to address the hostage crisis in the Middle East, and explain how they related to political and economic interests.
3. **MAKE PREDICTIONS** If President Carter had made different choices during the hostage crisis, how might they have led to an alternative outcome to this historical event?
4. **ANALYZE VISUALS** What message about American power do the two photos on these pages convey?

CHAPTER 20 PRESIDENTIAL SUCCESSES AND FAILURES

REVIEW

VOCABULARY

Use each of the following vocabulary words in a sentence that shows an understanding of the term's meaning.

1. **silent majority** HSS 11.11.2
   Nixon hoped to appeal to the silent majority, rather than to those Americans protesting on the streets.
2. détente HSS 11.9.3
3. DDT HSS 11.11.5
4. overregulation HSS 11.11.5
5. wiretapping HSS 11.11.4
6. stagflation HSS 11.11
7. malaise HSS 11.11.2
8. Islamic republic HSS 11.9.6

READING STRATEGY

IDENTIFY MAIN IDEAS AND DETAILS

Use a graphic organizer like the one below to identify the supporting details about the impact of the Watergate scandal. Then answer the question.

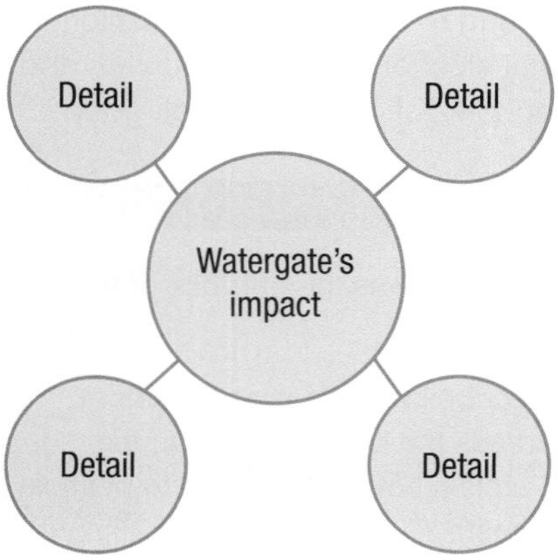

9. What impact did the Watergate scandal have on Nixon's presidency? HSS 11.11.4

MAIN IDEAS

Answer the following questions. Support your answers with evidence from the chapter.

10. What group of Americans made up Nixon's silent majority? **LESSON 1.1** HSS 11.11
11. What were some of the Burger Court's rulings on forced busing to achieve integration? **LESSON 1.2** HSS 11.10.2
12. Why did Nixon create the Environmental Protection Agency? **LESSON 1.3** HSS 11.11.5
13. What conflict arose between environmentalists and property rights advocates in the 1970s? **LESSON 1.3** HSS 11.11.5
14. How did the Watergate scandal provoke a constitutional crisis? **LESSON 1.5** HSS 11.11.4
15. How did the Vietnam War come to an end, and what were the results? **LESSON 2.1** HSS 11.9.3
16. What were the results of the Camp David Accords? **LESSON 2.2** HSS 11.9.6
17. What event initiated the Iran hostage crisis? **LESSON 2.3** HSS 11.9.6

HISTORICAL THINKING

Answer the following questions. Support your answers with evidence from the chapter.

18. **DRAW CONCLUSIONS** What did George Wallace's presidential campaign reveal about changing voting patterns in the United States? HSS 11.11.2
19. **MAKE CONNECTIONS** What aspects of Carter's energy policy are still emphasized today? HSS 11.11
20. **EVALUATE** What were some of Nixon's notable achievements as president? HSS 11.9.4
21. **FORM AND SUPPORT OPINIONS** What is your opinion of President Ford's pardon of Richard Nixon? Give reasons for your answer. HSS 11.11.4

22. **SYNTHESIZE** How did events in the 1970s reflect a more global and interconnected economy? HSS HI 1

23. **COMPARE AND CONTRAST** How did national policies on integration in public schools change during the 1970s? HSS 11.11

INTERPRET GRAPHS

This graph shows the percent change in world oil prices, U.S. gas prices, sales of Japanese-made cars in the United States, and all car sales in the United States from 1978 to 1982. The base year is 1978. A positive percent change represents an increase from the base, while a negative percent change represents a decrease. Study the graph and answer the questions that follow.

Gas Prices and Car Sales in the United States, 1978–1982

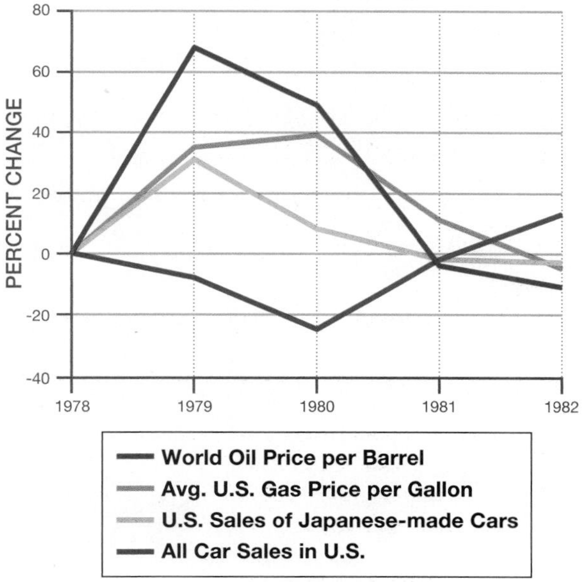

Sources: Inflationdata.com, CQPress, U.S. International Trade Commission

24. Based on the graph and what you know about Japanese-made cars, what is a possible cause of the increase in the sales of these cars in 1979? HSS HI 1

25. What limitations exist in assigning exact cause-and-effect relationships to the factors shown on the graph? In other words, why is it difficult to say for sure that one factor causes another? HSS HI 2

ANALYZE SOURCES

American nature writer Edward Abbey based his book *Desert Solitaire* (1968) on his experiences working as a park ranger in Utah. Abbey's writing, though sometimes controversial, expressed his deep-seated love of the American West. Read this excerpt from *Desert Solitaire* and answer the question that follows.

> No, wilderness is not a luxury but a necessity of the human spirit, and as vital to our lives as water and good bread. A civilization which destroys what little remains of the wild, the spare, the original, is cutting itself off from its origins and betraying the principle of civilization itself.

26. What is your opinion of the reasons Abbey gives for the need to practice environmental conservation? HSS 11.11.5

CONNECT TO YOUR LIFE

27. **EXPLANATORY** President Nixon enacted various measures to address environmental problems in the United States. Choose a region of the United States and identify an environmental issue there. Write an essay in which you describe the policies that address that issue, and explain how these policies affect your life. HSS CST 4

TIPS

- Research the physical and human characteristics of the region you've chosen as well as policies that address the environmental issue you've identified.
- Create a topic sentence that introduces the region and issue you've chosen.
- Develop your topic by describing relevant policies on this issue and explaining their effects on your life.
- Use two or three vocabulary words from the chapter in your essay.
- End your essay with a general statement about the impact of environmental protections.

CHAPTER 21

THE CONSERVATIVE REVOLUTION 1980–1992

HISTORICAL THINKING What major changes occurred in the United States during Ronald Reagan's presidency?

CRITICAL VIEWING *Portrait of President Ronald Reagan in the Oval Office* was taken by American photographer Arnold Newman in 1981, the year Reagan took office. What does the photo convey about the former actor and California governor's attitude toward his new job?

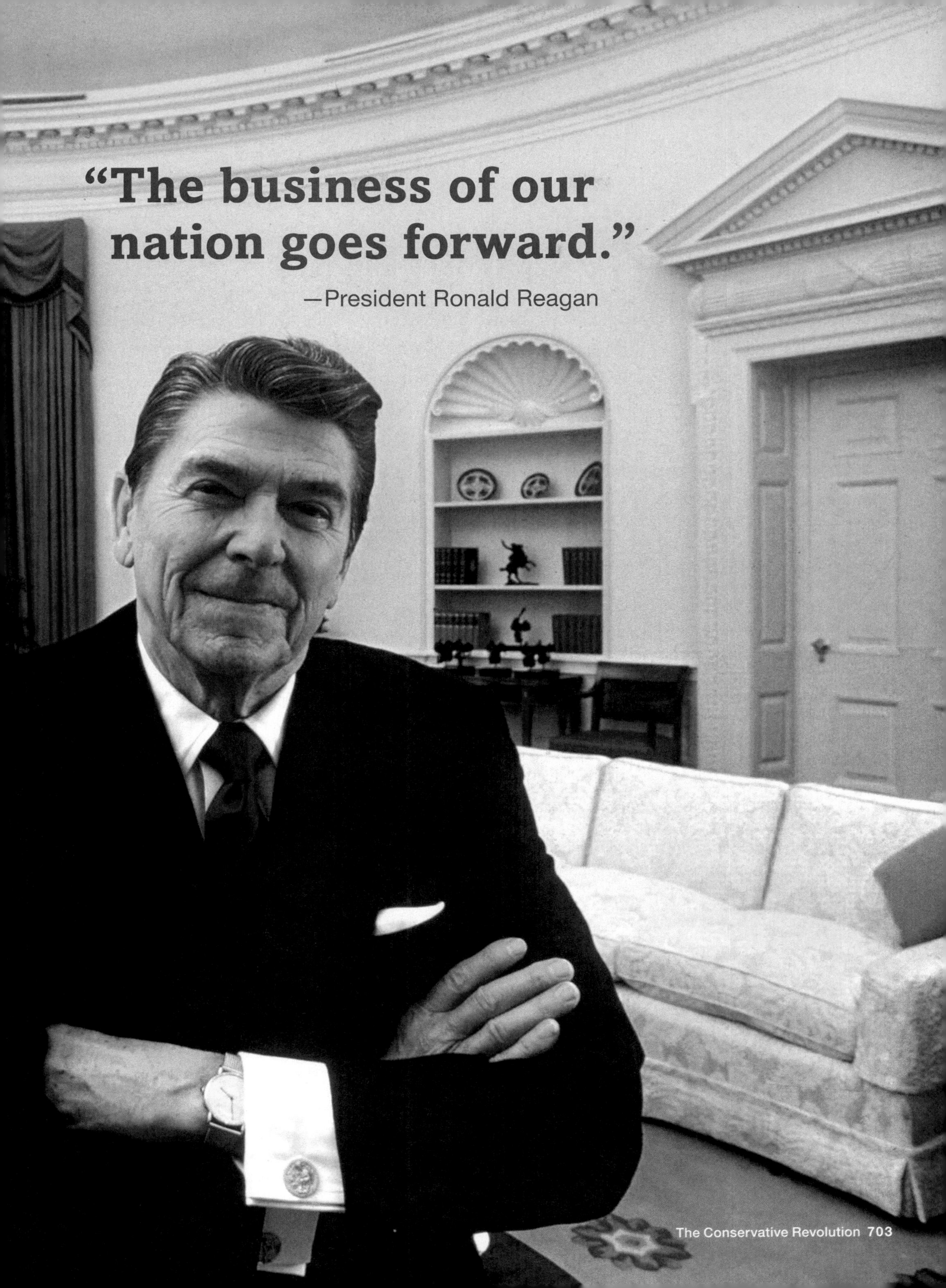

"The business of our nation goes forward."

—President Ronald Reagan

1.1 **MAIN IDEA** The emergence of a conservative movement in the 1970s and 1980s directly affected many aspects of American life.

ROOTS OF THE CONSERVATIVE MOVEMENT

The Republican Party had suffered two major blows in the 1960s and 1970s: the failed 1964 candidacy of Barry Goldwater and Richard Nixon's Watergate scandal. For the 1980 election, the party was looking for an upbeat nominee with the charisma to charm both Republicans and Democrats dissatisfied with Carter's presidency.

A CONSERVATIVE MOVEMENT ARISES

With the nation enduring economic and foreign policy difficulties, Jimmy Carter faced a difficult bid for re-election in 1980. Carter and his fellow Democrats faced another challenge as well—the steady rise of a conservative movement in the country. Several Republican presidential candidates competed for the nomination in 1980. Two notable politicians in the running were former CIA director **George H.W. Bush** and moderate Republican congressman **John B. Anderson** from Illinois. But the favorite to win the nomination was Ronald Reagan, the popular California governor and former movie star. Since delivering a well-received speech endorsing Barry Goldwater for president in 1964, Reagan had emerged as a conservative leader.

The conservative movement began in the late 1960s when numerous grassroots organizations, such as the American Conservative Union (ACU) and Young Americans for Freedom, began working together to promote their ideals. **Conservatives** support traditional policies in economic and social legislation and are more likely to favor established systems of government over progressive ideas

Three teleprompters broadcast Pastor Joel Osteen's Sunday service to about 25,000 people at the Lakewood Church in Houston, Texas. The rise in religious fundamentalism during the 1980s led to the creation of today's megachurches, or very large non-Catholic Christian churches.

11.3.2 Analyze the great religious revivals and the leaders involved in them, including the First Great Awakening, the Second Great Awakening, the Civil War revivals, the Social Gospel Movement, the rise of Christian liberal theology in the nineteenth century, the impact of the Second Vatican Council, and the rise of Christian fundamentalism in current times; 11.3.5 Describe the principles of religious liberty found in the Establishment and Free Exercise clauses of the First Amendment, including the debate on the issue of separation of church and state.

or radical changes. During this time, a number of conservative **think tanks** emerged: groups of experts who conduct research and discuss issues in order to craft potential solutions to social and economic problems. Conservative politicians used the data that think tanks generated to inform their decisions about legislation. Prominent conservative think tanks still active today include the **American Enterprise Institute** and the **Heritage Foundation**. Conservative think tanks, lobbyists, and politicians shared the goal of shaping a compelling message to attract voter support. They hoped to gain more influence throughout the nation and in Washington.

CONSERVATIVE BELIEFS

In general, conservatives favored making the government smaller, decreasing taxes, and deregulating industries. They opposed greater federal regulation of the economy. They argued that if people and businesses had more freedom to make their own economic choices, their purchasing power would stimulate greater growth and a better standard of living for all. Conservatives favored less taxation, arguing that allowing consumers and businesses to keep more of their wages and profits would spur greater investment and growth. In addition, because of their belief that individualism is superior to government action, conservatives opposed government social programs, including many of President Johnson's Great Society welfare reforms, claiming they required high taxation and massive spending by the federal government. As American patriots, however, they did believe in government spending to support a robust, well-funded military.

Many conservatives, but not all, drove a large social agenda that was deeply rooted in religion. This agenda was hotly debated by those who felt that allowing religious views to shape political policies violated the separation of church and state. Still, the 1970s and 1980s were a time of renewed interest in Christian values, much like the First and Second Great Awakenings of the 18th and 19th centuries. Instead of giving powerful sermons in tents, however, the conservative movement built part of its base and conveyed its message through evangelical churches, televangelism, and other media outlets. The Reverend **Jerry Falwell**, a Baptist minister from Virginia, started a grassroots organization called the **Moral Majority**. The organization was made up of Christian fundamentalists, or people who believe in the literal interpretation of the Bible, and **evangelists**, or people who believe it is their duty to spread their religious faith and win converts. According to Falwell, the purpose of the Moral Majority was to press the government into supporting social programs that promoted what they termed "traditional family values." Falwell and his followers spoke out against what they saw as the evils of society: abortion, out-of-wedlock births, homosexuality, the teaching of evolution in schools, and increased drug use among Americans. They also condemned what they perceived as the resulting breakdown of the American family.

PRIMARY SOURCE

Our nation's internal problems are direct results of her spiritual condition. It is now time that moral Americans awakened to the fact that our future depends upon how we stand on moral issues.

—from *Listen, America!*, by Jerry Falwell, 1980

Television programs, magazines, and newspapers featured Falwell regularly. The organization's message became so popular that Pat Robertson, one of Falwell's supporters and a fundamentalist Christian preacher, created a television network to feature the views of prominent members of the Moral Majority. The ideas of the Moral Majority spread throughout American politics as well. Conservative politicians spoke out against abortion and the *Roe* v. *Wade* decision (1973), which made abortion legal under certain circumstances. They demanded that Congress restrict access to abortion, publicly protesting outside abortion clinics and organizing large "Right to Life" demonstrations.

Many religious conservatives also spoke out against Darwin's theory of evolution, an idea they deemed blasphemous, or ungodly, because it contradicted the creation account in the Bible. The growing gay rights and feminist movements as well as the rise in out-of-wedlock births received criticism because the Moral Majority believed these things threatened the traditional definition of family—a married man and woman, and their children. Throughout the late 1970s, and especially in the South and the West, conservatives were becoming a growing and powerful political force.

HISTORICAL THINKING

1. **READING CHECK** What were the conservatives' views on the federal government?
2. **DESCRIBE** What was the main goal of the conservative movement?
3. **MAKE GENERALIZATIONS** The Moral Majority was concerned about the effects of which social changes and movements on the American family, and why?

11.11.7 Explain how the federal, state, and local governments have responded to demographic and social changes such as population shifts to the suburbs, racial concentrations in the cities, Frostbelt-to-Sunbelt migration, international migration, decline of family farms, increases in out-of-wedlock births, and drug abuse.

1.2 **MAIN IDEA** The conservative movement gained momentum in the country's fast-growing southern and western regions.

GROWTH OF THE SUNBELT

Have you ever moved from one part of the country to another, or do you know friends or family members who have? In the decades following World War II, many Americans migrated from the northern part of the country to the South and West—a demographic shift that changed the nation's political landscape.

DEMOGRAPHIC SHIFTS

As you have read, after World War II, the United States experienced a widespread demographic shift as families moved from cities and farms to suburbs. In addition, a large number of Americans began moving from the nation's Frostbelt—the Northeast, the Great Lakes region, and the Midwest—to the nation's southern and western states, a region that became known as the Sunbelt. Population booms occurred in states such as Texas, Florida, and California. In fact, migration to the Sunbelt helped California become the most populous state in the country by 1962. And the migration continued for the next few decades.

Low taxes were one of the primary draws to the Sunbelt for both people and businesses. Taxes had steadily increased in the large cities of the North to help support aging infrastructure and social programs, such as the War on Poverty. In contrast, there were smaller populations and less infrastructure to support across the Sunbelt. Furthermore, land in the Sunbelt states cost a fraction of what it did in the crowded Northeast. Businesses could build

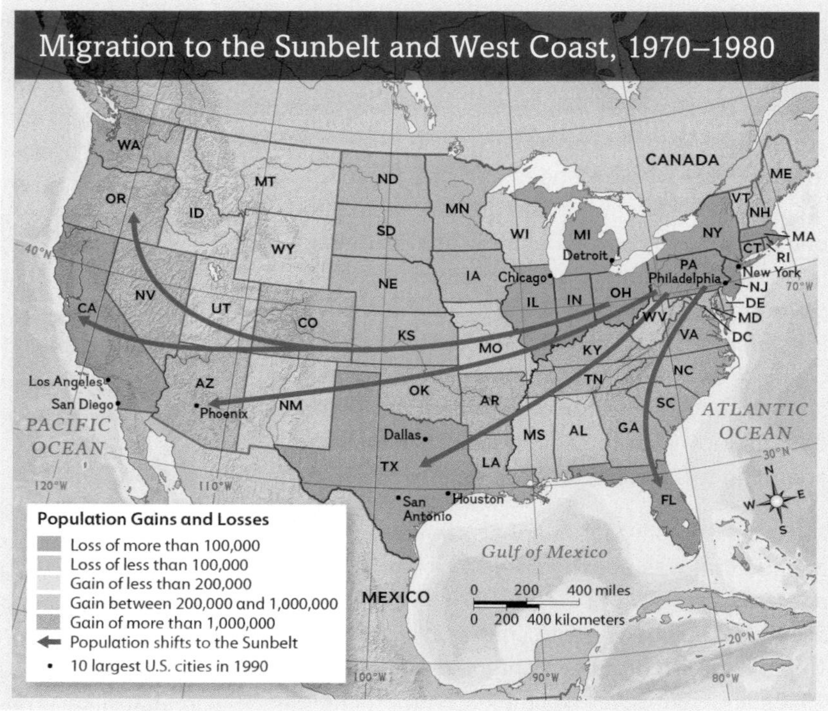

AIR-CONDITIONING AND THE SUNBELT

People first started using mechanical air conditioners in the early 20th century, but air-conditioning units did not become a practical appliance in most homes until after World War II. Innovations during the war made them more portable and less expensive. Air conditioners made it possible for people living in the American South and West to escape the dangerous summer heat. As a result, more people moved to the Sunbelt. With the increased population came increased political representation for Sunbelt states, including Florida, Georgia, Texas, California, Arizona, and New Mexico.

11.11.7 Explain how the federal, state, and local governments have responded to demographic and social changes such as population shifts to the suburbs, racial concentrations in the cities, Frostbelt-to-Sunbelt migration, international migration, decline of family farms, increases in out-of-wedlock births, and drug abuse.

new factories for much less than it cost to update their old facilities in the North. And the warmer weather meant less wear-and-tear on buildings and equipment—another cost saver for businesses. As a result, a number of companies closed their Frostbelt factories and moved south or west. Soon some northern industrial cities became known collectively as the **Rustbelt**, a reference to the way that abandoned tools and machines corrode and rust.

In addition to attracting businesses, the Sunbelt drew many senior citizens. Due to improvements in medicine, life spans in the United States were steadily increasing. Payouts from pensions and Social Security also gave people greater financial security later in life. Healthier and more secure, many elderly Americans chose to enjoy their retirement years in warmer climates.

In 1970, active retirees enjoyed the mild winter weather as they pedaled their bikes around Sun City, Arizona, the first planned retirement community built in the Sunbelt.

POLITICAL IMPACT OF THE SUNBELT

Traditionally, the southern and western regions of the United States have been more politically conservative than the Northeast and upper Midwest. As you have read, the South became even more conservative following the Civil Rights Act of 1964. Many southern Democrats were opposed to civil rights legislation. In the wake of the historic act, a number of southern Democrats switched to the Republican Party as a protest against their more progressive northern counterparts. The influx of new residents strengthened the region's conservatism. Business owners and workers, especially those who flocked to the defense and energy industries in the Sunbelt, tended to be politically conservative. So did many senior citizens. As a result, cities and towns across the Sunbelt grew increasingly conservative during the 1960s and 1970s.

Places such as Orange County, California, located just south of Los Angeles, became centers of conservative thought. In the years leading up to the 1980 election, residents of Orange County sponsored anticommunism events for school students and eagerly backed conservative presidential candidate Barry Goldwater in his 1964 bid. They also spearheaded legislation known as Proposition 6, that, if it had passed in 1978, would have banned members of the LGBT community from teaching in California's public schools. Much like the people involved in the Sagebrush Rebellion, Orange County residents and other Sunbelt conservatives distrusted big government.

With every new resident who migrated to the region, the Sunbelt's political power expanded. As you have learned, a state's population determines the number of representatives it sends to the House of Representatives. The migration to the South and West helped the Sunbelt states gain seats in Congress even as the Rustbelt states were losing them. The shift in population also affected each state's designated number of electoral votes, or votes cast by the representatives who elect the president and the vice president. The combination of conservative northerners' migration to the Sunbelt and southern politicians moving away from the Democratic Party eventually made the South and West strongholds for the Republican Party. The phenomenon became a significant factor in the 1980 presidential election.

HISTORICAL THINKING

1. **READING CHECK** What is the connection between the Sunbelt migration and the rise of the conservative movement?
2. **DESCRIBE** What government and economic factors drew businesses to the Sunbelt?
3. **ANALYZE CAUSE AND EFFECT** How did the Sunbelt migration affect northeastern and upper midwestern states both politically and economically?
4. **INTERPRET MAPS** Which areas of the country experienced the least significant population shift?

HI 1 Students show the connections, causal and otherwise, between particular historical events and larger social, economic, and political trends and developments.

1.3 **MAIN IDEA** Ronald Reagan won the presidency in 1980 by championing conservatism and its principles of limited government, individual accomplishment, and a faith-based culture.

Election of Ronald Reagan

Can a movie actor or entertainer be a good president? What traits and experiences would work in his or her favor, and which ones would work against such a candidate? During the late 1970s, former actor Ronald Reagan leveraged his strong communication skills and his conservative beliefs to reach the highest office in the land.

CRITICAL VIEWING In the 1953 Western movie *Law and Order,* Ronald Reagan played a sheriff who rids a small town of outlaws. How might this photo and the movie itself connect to the conservative trends discussed in previous lessons?

11.11.2 Discuss the significant domestic policy speeches of Truman, Eisenhower, Kennedy, Johnson, Nixon, Carter, Reagan, Bush, and Clinton (e.g., with regard to education, civil rights, economic policy, environmental policy).

THE RISE OF REAGAN

As the 1980 election loomed, the conservative movement found a strong messenger for their cause in California politician Ronald Reagan. Reagan grew up in Illinois and moved to Iowa shortly after graduating from college to work as a sports broadcaster. While on a business trip to California, he auditioned for Hollywood producers, who liked his presence on camera and hired him to act in films. Reagan was cast in 53 roles and, in 1947, became president of the Screen Actors Guild, the union for film actors. During his leadership of the union, his political views shifted. Reagan had been a New Deal Democrat, but the FBI investigations of communist activity in the movie industry led him to adopt more conservative beliefs. During this time, he met Nancy Davis, a film actor whom he would marry in 1952.

From 1954 to 1962, Reagan was a spokesman for the General Electric (GE) company. He was charismatic, and his years in front of the camera had made him a seasoned communicator. Reagan hosted GE's television program, *General Electric Theater*, and toured the country for the company, giving speeches about the dangers of communism, big government, and high taxes. The job prepared him for a televised speech he gave in support of Republican leader Barry Goldwater in 1964. As you've read, that speech caught the attention of California politicians, who later asked Reagan if he was interested in being governor. He ran for governor in 1966 and won. After serving two terms, Reagan moved on to the national scene. In 1976, he challenged incumbent president Gerald Ford in the Republican presidential primary. Reagan narrowly lost, but his strong national showing positioned him well for the future.

THE ELECTION OF 1980

That future came four years later, when Reagan became the Republican candidate in the 1980 presidential election. His opponent, President Jimmy Carter, was seeking a second term. With the ongoing hostage crisis in Iran, a gas shortage, and a struggling economy, many voters in both parties saw President Carter as an ineffective leader. Carter won the Democratic nomination, but only after a strong challenge from U.S. Senator Ted Kennedy of Massachusetts. The race also featured a third-party candidate, Congressman John B. Anderson, a Republican from Illinois, who had run in the Republican primaries in the hope of securing the party's nomination. Arguing that Reagan was too conservative, Anderson ran as an independent candidate and promoted himself as an alternative to the two traditional parties.

PRIMARY SOURCE

We must increase productivity . . . making it possible for industry to modernize . . . bringing government spending back within government revenues. I've already placed a freeze on [government] hiring. I've put a freeze on pending regulations . . . [and] decontrolled oil. We cannot delay in implementing an economic program aimed at both reducing tax rates to stimulate productivity and reducing the growth in government spending to reduce unemployment and inflation.

—from Ronald Reagan's address to the nation on the economy, February 5, 1981

The campaign, however, ultimately pitted Reagan against Carter. As the two candidates prepared for their single televised debate, popularity polls had them tied. During the debate in late October 1980, Carter described Reagan as a dangerous and unreliable political extremist, citing Reagan's plans to repeal the minimum wage, gut social **safety-net programs** that were helping people in poverty, and promote a nuclear arms buildup in the Middle East. Reagan focused on the nation's faltering economy, asking viewers: "Are you better off now than you were four years ago?" referring to when Carter took office. Reagan bet that when Americans thought about gas shortages and rising unemployment, most would answer, "No."

He was right. In November 1980, Reagan won the election in a landslide. Voters cast nearly 44 million ballots for Reagan and 35 million for Carter. John Anderson received 5.7 million votes, a strong showing for a third-party candidate. The Republicans also regained control of the Senate, picking up 12 seats from the Democrats. Reagan won by uniting the growing population of fiscal and social conservatives and by winning over a number of working-class Democrats worried about the economy and jobs. With Ronald Reagan's victory, a new era of conservatism was about to begin.

HISTORICAL THINKING

1. **READING CHECK** What made Ronald Reagan a good choice to lead the conservative movement of the 1980s?
2. **FORM AND SUPPORT OPINIONS** Was President Carter's warning about Ronald Reagan a good argument in support of his re-election? Support your opinion with evidence from the text.
3. **IDENTIFY** In his address to the nation on the economy, how did President Reagan propose to reduce unemployment and inflation?

2.1 **MAIN IDEA** President Reagan worked to put his conservative principles into practice, with varying results.

REDUCING GOVERNMENT

Change is hard—especially when you're in the habit of doing things a certain way. The United States had spent four years under Democratic leadership and was now facing the challenge of shifting to a conservative Republican administration.

THE REAGAN ERA BEGINS

The Reagan administration led a resurgence of the Republican Party with a focus on three key areas that restructured the scope of the federal government. The first was to establish a smaller government by decreasing taxes on individuals and businesses and deregulating industries. The second was to advocate conservative social values, including supporting legislation to outlaw abortion, promoting heterosexual marriage, opposing ratification of the Equal Rights Amendment, and championing individual accomplishment as opposed to funding social safety-net programs.

Also troubled by a rise in out-of-wedlock births and drug abuse, conservatives hoped to affect these and their other social concerns by supporting faith-based **cultural advocacy**, or exerting influence on politicians and social institutions to advance a particular religious belief system—in this case, conservative Christianity. The third area of the administration's focus was to expand the military while managing the Cold War. In all of these areas, the Reagan administration achieved both successes and setbacks.

The first months of Reagan's term were eventful and established the new president as a strong leader. After 444 days in captivity, the U.S. hostages in Iran were released as Reagan took office, a significant victory for the president. In February, his proposed economic program of tax and spending cuts was well received. Then, on March 30, 1981, a would-be assassin named John W. Hinckley, Jr., shot Reagan and his press secretary, James Brady, as the president and his advisors were leaving the Washington Hilton Hotel in Washington, D.C. The president recovered completely, and his courage and good humor during the crisis increased his popularity.

That summer, Reagan took decisive action during a strike by some 13,000 members of the Professional Air Traffic Controllers Organization (PATCO). As government employees, the controllers could not legally strike, and Reagan gave them 48 hours to return to work or lose their jobs. Most of them refused, and they were fired. While some citizens considered Reagan's actions to be extreme, much of the public backed the president. A Gallup poll taken shortly afterward showed that 59 percent of the American people supported firing the striking air traffic controllers.

The risk Reagan took in breaking the PATCO strike paid off for his administration immediately: he achieved a reputation for being a tough negotiator, both domestically and internationally, and particularly with the Soviet Union. The long-term consequences were less positive, though. To restore the air traffic control system to its pre-strike condition cost billions of dollars (an amount much higher than that requested from the strikers for pay increases and revised safety procedures) and took several years. In addition, air travel decreased during that time, thus affecting the earnings of airlines and related travel industries as well.

REAGANOMICS

An urgent focus for the Reagan administration was reviving the stalled U.S. economy and addressing the persistence of poverty. Reagan called for decreasing taxes on individuals and corporations, a strategy his administration termed **supply-side economics**.

11.11.5 Trace the impact of, need for, and controversies associated with environmental conservation, expansion of the national park system, and the development of environmental protection laws, with particular attention to the interaction between environmental protection advocates and property rights advocates; 11.11.6 Analyze the persistence of poverty and how different analyses of this issue influence welfare reform, health insurance reform, and other social policies.

RECOVERING WITH HUMOR
During President Reagan's recovery from the attempt on his life, he and his wife Nancy enthusiastically greeted well-wishers gathered below his hospital room window. Reagan was known for his sense of humor, which was often revealed in short, witty remarks, and for his love of his wife, two traits that endeared him to many of his supporters. Although seriously injured, Reagan still managed to joke with Nancy as he was taken to surgery, saying, "Honey, I forgot to duck."

Reagan administration officials believed that lower taxes would encourage consumers and businesses to spend and invest the money they kept, thus stimulating the economy and leading to job growth. Critics referred to the plan as "trickle-down economics," arguing that it aided the wealthiest Americans most, while only a small amount of job growth and wealth would "trickle down" to the neediest groups. In addition to tax cuts, Reagan called for an increase in military spending. To offset the loss of tax revenue and cover those increases in spending, Reagan proposed significant cuts to social programs, including public education, low-income housing, and Medicaid.

As Reagan worked to implement his policies, the economy worsened. During the early 1980s, unemployment rose to nine million, while thousands of businesses failed and many people lost their homes. The president's popularity plummeted, and Republicans lost seats in the House in the 1982 midterm elections. By the end of 1983, however, the economy began to turn around. Unemployment dropped and so did inflation. The economic growth continued, and Reagan's supporters would eventually cheer what they called "the longest peacetime expansion in American history."

Critics, however, argued that tax cuts continued to benefit mainly the rich and that under Reagan, **income inequality**, or a large gap between what the poorest and the richest citizens earn, had grown wider. Opponents also criticized the administration's continued military spending. While many of Reagan's supporters credited his increased defense spending as part of the reason for the eventual collapse of the Soviet Union, military spending played a big role in tripling the national debt by the end of Reagan's second term.

DEREGULATION

Another campaign promise Reagan sought to fulfill was his pledge to reduce government regulations on American industry. The Carter administration had already begun to eliminate government regulations on the airlines, as well as on the railroad and trucking industries. Reagan, however, felt that these moves didn't go far enough. He initiated a program of **deregulation**, or removing rules and limitations, on a large scale. Among his first targets were environmental regulations.

His choice for secretary of the interior, **James Watt**, was a fierce opponent of environmental protection. Watt proposed a number of changes that outraged environmentalists, including leasing federal lands for oil and gas exploration and reducing funding to national parks. Watt was one of Reagan's most controversial cabinet appointees, and his brief tenure as secretary of the interior was marked not only by his environmentally damaging proposals but also by his frequent insulting remarks, which did not endear him either to Congress or the American people. Watt resigned in October 1983, just as the Senate was drafting a resolution to have him removed from office.

Anne Gorsuch, tapped to direct the Environmental Protection Agency (EPA), was another of Reagan's controversial cabinet picks. During her two years as EPA director, she cut the EPA budget by 22 percent and made moves that critics claimed weakened the Clean Air and Clean Water Acts. In 1982, Congress

11.11.7 Explain how the federal, state, and local governments have responded to demographic and social changes such as population shifts to the suburbs, racial concentrations in the cities, Frostbelt-to-Sunbelt migration, international migration, decline of family farms, increases in out-of-wedlock births, and drug abuse.

demanded that the EPA turn over records for the Superfund program, which was responsible for the cleanup of toxic waste sites. Few of the sites designated for cleanup were actually being cleaned up, and Gorsuch and her agency were accused of mismanagement. When she refused to turn over the records, she was forced to resign.

Of President Reagan's efforts at deregulation, the one that may have had the most long-lasting impact was the lifting of regulations on the savings and loan (S&L) industry. The original S&Ls were small banks designed to help people buy homes at a time when most banks did not issue relatively small loans and mortgages. By the early 1980s, inflation and interest rates were high enough that S&Ls were hurting, and the mortgages they held began to lose value. The government's reaction was to deregulate the S&L industry, which then expanded rapidly.

At the same time, the Reagan administration reduced the number of bank examiners, which contributed to less oversight and fewer inspections of the S&L industry. In addition, the S&Ls carried federal deposit insurance that guaranteed they would be bailed out if they lost money. Those two conditions gave S&L operators a false sense of security and led many of them to plunge into risky and often illegal ventures. In 1983 and 1984, banks and S&L businesses made bad loans, created poorly financed companies, and hired corrupt employees who looted their firms. The reckoning for these actions would not come until 1989, after Reagan had left office, when the S&L industry suffered a catastrophic collapse, leaving taxpayers with the $500 billion bill for reimbursing depositors at the failed institutions. In all, over 1,000 people involved in the banking scandal were prosecuted, and many went to jail.

RESHAPING THE SUPREME COURT

President Reagan also moved the Supreme Court in a more conservative direction. Upon the retirement of Justice Potter Stewart in 1981, Reagan nominated **Sandra Day O'Connor** as his replacement.
A moderate conservative, her nomination had

TROUBLE AT THE EPA

The federal Superfund program was established within the EPA to protect the public and the country's natural resources by cleaning up large contaminated toxic waste sites. In 1982, however, the agency's regulatory actions dropped by about 60 percent, and few highly polluted sites were added to the Superfund list. Of the $700 million in fines owed by corporate polluters of water, land, and air, only $40 million was collected, which left the Superfund budget more reliant on taxpayer funds than on fines collected from polluters during the 1980s.

The site of a Superfund slag heap, or a hill made from industrial or mining waste material, has become a bird haven at the Ormond Beach Wetlands near Oxnard, California. The EPA is working with the local community and the site owners to remove toxic materials, but the entire process will take many years to complete.

11.11.3 Describe the changing roles of women in society as reflected in the entry of more women into the labor force and the changing family structure; HI 5 Students analyze human modifications of landscapes and examine the resulting environmental policy issues.

widespread support from both conservatives and liberals. She made history as the first woman justice to serve on the Supreme Court, a symbol of the changing roles of women in society.

The president would not have another opportunity to appoint a justice until Chief Justice Warren Burger resigned in 1986. Reagan elevated Justice William Rehnquist, a conservative, to replace Burger as Chief Justice and named a conservative federal appeals court judge, Antonin Scalia, to fill the seat Rehnquist had vacated. Scalia was a strong proponent of **originalism**, the belief that when interpreting the Constitution, the courts should refer to what it meant when it was originally adopted, not to what it might mean from a present-day perspective. If people wanted to change the law, he thought, they should use the democratic process and do so through legislation. Scholars and justices who disagreed with Scalia categorized originalism as a **static**, or unchanging, doctrine that does not allow the law to change with the times. While Justice Scalia helped to make the idea of originalism more widespread within academic and popular culture, he was often unable to get other justices to agree in applying it to court cases.

PRIMARY SOURCE

An oil painting of Associate Justice of the Supreme Court Sandra Day O'Connor dressed in her judicial robes hangs in the National Portrait Gallery, Washington, D.C. The painting is by Jean Marcellino.

Yes, I will bring the understanding of a woman to the Court, but I doubt that alone will affect my decisions. I think the important thing about my appointment is not that I will decide cases as a woman, but that I am a woman who will get to decide cases.

—Sandra Day O'Connor, quoted in "Sandra Day O'Connor, Warm, Witty, and Wise," by Pam Hait, *Ladies' Home Journal*, 1982

In 1987, after the Democrats had regained control of the Senate, Justice Lewis Powell resigned, and President Reagan nominated Robert Bork, another conservative appeals court judge, to replace him. Bork had written extensively on many divisive legal issues before becoming a judge, and Senate Democrats and many women and civil rights organizations opposed him. They said he was outside the mainstream of American judicial thinking. The Senate rejected Bork's nomination, but the contentious process had a lasting impact on future Supreme Court nominations. Anthony Kennedy was nominated for the seat and confirmed to the Court early in 1988. Perceived as being balanced and fair in his judicial rulings and writings, he received bipartisan support.

HISTORICAL THINKING

1. **READING CHECK** How was supply-side economics supposed to revive the economy and decrease poverty?
2. **ANALYZE ENVIRONMENTAL CONCEPTS** What human practices of the past led to the designation of Superfund sites for cleanup processes?
3. **MAKE GENERALIZATIONS** What were some of the consequences of President Reagan's deregulation of the savings and loan industry?
4. **ANALYZE LANGUAGE USE** Why did Sandra Day O'Connor make the distinction that it was important that she was "a woman who will get to decide cases"?

2.2 **MAIN IDEA** The primary focus of President Reagan's foreign policy was confronting the Soviet Union and other communist powers.

REAGAN'S FOREIGN POLICY

Think of something you strongly believe in. President Reagan was a strong anticommunist who believed in standing up to the Soviets around the world. This belief would serve as the foundation of U.S. foreign policy during the 1980s.

ANTICOMMUNIST POLICIES

Ronald Reagan's tough stance against communism had long been a part of his image. As president, he vowed to fight the spread of communism around the world. He increased military spending, advocating a policy of "peace through strength."

The Reagan administration put its anticommunist stance into action around the world with results of success as well as failure. When the Soviet Union invaded Afghanistan in 1979 to support a Soviet-backed government, the Carter administration had sent military aid to the anti-Soviet guerillas. Reagan increased the aid, hoping the guerillas could use it to force a Soviet withdrawal.

Reagan also moved against communism in Latin America. The United States invaded the small Caribbean island of Grenada in 1983 after a communist government seized power. Within two days, the Marines had subdued the communist forces and helped establish a new anticommunist government. The United States also took action in Nicaragua after a pro-Soviet group known as the **Sandinistas** seized power and attempted to shape Nicaragua's government along communist lines. In response, the Reagan administration began secretly arming an anti-Sandinista guerilla force known as the **Contras**. The Contras waged a civil war with the Sandinistas throughout the 1980s from the headquarters they established in Honduras, directly north of Nicaragua.

Two days before the invasion of Grenada, tragedy struck the American military half a world away. On October 23, 1983, a suicide bomber drove a truck bomb into a **barracks**, or sleeping quarters, for marines in Beirut, Lebanon. The tremendous explosion had the force of 12,000 pounds of TNT. It destroyed the barracks and killed 241 marines. They had been deployed as peacekeepers during a cease-fire in the hostilities between Lebanese Christians and Muslims, a move that was controversial among Reagan's military advisors, who believed the situation was too unstable to be contained.

Back home, some people accused the president of using the invasion of a tiny, nonthreatening Caribbean country as a distraction from the reckless political blunders that had put those 241 marines in Lebanon in harm's way. The planning done before the October 23 bombing proved that the invasion wasn't merely a reaction to the event. When Reagan ran for re-election in 1984, however, it was clear that the invasion of Grenada had offered the president a public relations boost that helped to distract voters from the Beirut bombing.

IRAN AND SOUTH AFRICA

Congress eventually learned of the secret funding of the Contras and banned further aid to the group in 1984. Two years later, a news story reported that the United States had sold military equipment to Iran—a country that supported international terrorism—as part of an effort to gain the release of the American hostages taken prisoner there in the late 1970s. This contradicted Reagan's claim that the United States would never negotiate with terrorists, but the Reagan administration was afraid of political fallout from another hostage situation. Less than a month later, a follow-up news story revealed that $48 million from the weapons sale to Iran had been turned over to the Contras, which became known as the **Iran-Contra scandal**. Reagan fired the two men most responsible for the scandal: head of the National Security Council

11.9.3 Trace the origins and geopolitical consequences (foreign and domestic) of the Cold War and containment policy, including the following: • The era of McCarthyism, instances of domestic Communism (e.g., Alger Hiss) and blacklisting • The Truman Doctrine • The Berlin Blockade • The Korean War • The Bay of Pigs Invasion and the Cuban Missile Crisis • Atomic testing in the American West, the "mutual assured destruction" doctrine, and disarmament policies • The Vietnam War • Latin American policy.

Lieutenant Colonel Oliver North took an oath to tell the truth during the congressional hearings convened to investigate the Iran-Contra scandal.

But Reagan's policy led South Africa to continue its segregation, and violence erupted. Ironically, Reagan's policy also tarnished American ideals and, ironically, hampered U.S. efforts abroad as the "good guy" in its competition with the Soviet Union. Finally, in 1986, the Senate overrode Reagan's veto of sanctions against South Africa.

THE STRATEGIC DEFENSE INITIATIVE

Meanwhile, tension between the Soviet Union and the United States continued to escalate. In 1983, several false alarms about imminent missile strikes by both sides cast doubt on the effectiveness of the doctrine of mutual assured destruction. And, while neither side overreacted, the arms race between the Soviet Union and the United States had reached its highest point, with the accumulation of more than 69,000 global nuclear weapons.

John Poindexter and one of his aides, Lieutenant Colonel Oliver North of the U.S. Marine Corps. The president appointed John Tower, a former Texas senator, to head a commission to investigate the scandal. Poindexter and North were tried and convicted of lying to Congress and obstruction of justice, among other charges.

President Reagan took full responsibility for the arms-for-hostages deal, but he claimed he knew nothing about the diversion of funds to the Contras. Still, a number of people, including some members of Congress, doubted him. Reagan's popularity declined, but only temporarily. A federal appeals court eventually overturned the convictions of Poindexter and North.

Reagan's strong anticommunist policy also became controversial when he allied the United States with the government of South African prime minister P. W. Botha. The repressive South African regime supported a system of **apartheid**, or extreme official racial segregation. Seeing Botha as a leader who would join him in preventing the spread of communism, Reagan proposed that moderates in the South African government would eventually end apartheid. He vetoed sanctions the U.S. Congress wanted to place on South Africa for its apartheid.

In this atmosphere, Reagan proposed his most ambitious plan for addressing Soviet power: to put a missile defense system in orbit around Earth. Dubbed the **Strategic Defense Initiative (SDI)**, it would use lasers and other technologies to destroy Soviet missiles before they reached their targets. Popularly referred to as "Star Wars," after the movie series, this idea met with many critics who argued that the "other technologies" used to blow the missiles out of the sky didn't even exist yet. They feared that the technical challenges of such a project might swallow the entire defense budget. Ultimately, the proposed SDI technology became too complex and expensive, and the program was never realized.

HISTORICAL THINKING

1. **READING CHECK** How did President Reagan try to achieve his policy of "peace through strength"?
2. **DRAW CONCLUSIONS** Why did some people believe that the invasion of Grenada was a distraction from the bombing in Lebanon?
3. **COMPARE AND CONTRAST** How was U.S. involvement in Nicaragua different from U.S. involvement in Grenada?
4. **MAKE INFERENCES** Why did no president after Reagan continue the Strategic Defense Initiative?

11.9.5 Analyze the role of the Reagan administration and other factors in the victory of the West in the Cold War.

2.3 **MAIN IDEA** New technologies, a health epidemic, and shifting demographics shaped the social structure of the United States during the 1980s.

Social Changes and Tensions

Consider how much computers, smartphones, and tablets are part of your daily life. The 1980s saw a wave of advances in technology—including computer technology—that began to change many aspects of how people lived.

NEW TECHNOLOGIES

Away from the political arena, the 1980s was a time of significant technological progress. In 1981, a communications company called International Business Machines (IBM) announced its plan to sell **personal computers**, small computers for home use. The announcement caused two computer software writers, Bill Gates and Paul Allen, to develop their own graphical user interface system, or GUI, that would appeal to a wide audience by helping people understand how to use the computer. They built their system using a simpler version of a computer language called BASIC. From there, Gates and Allen developed other software programs for their Microsoft company, such as spreadsheets and Microsoft Windows, an operating system that manages computer memory and function.

Apple, a competing company founded in 1976 by Steve Jobs and Steve Wozniak in a garage in Cupertino, California, also developed a GUI and, eventually, a version of a personal computer, named the Apple Macintosh, now known as the Mac. These innovations quickly transformed the personal computer from a novelty item to a common household device. Soon, people would be able to use their computers to publish books, track finances, make travel reservations, and play games.

CRITICAL VIEWING Desktop computers like the one below were among the earliest computers sold in the 1970s in America. This one came with a cassette drive and a tape player attached. It was popular in schools that had just begun teaching computer technology. Although the screen looks like a movable monitor, it was actually an attached built-in display. The computer sold new for about $700. Which of its elements can you identify, and how is the computer similar to or different from the computers you use?

11.8.7 Describe the effects on society and the economy of technological developments since 1945, including the computer revolution, changes in communication, advances in medicine, and improvements in agricultural technology.

After January 1983, sales of personal computers rose to more than half a million per year. New software companies sprang up all over the country, especially in California and Massachusetts. The California tech corridor would become known as "Silicon Valley" for the local resource, silica, used to make silicon computer chips.

Massachusetts companies were able to recruit computer talent from the pool of expertise at MIT, the Massachusetts Institute of Technology. Eventually computers needed to be connected so that people in different cities could collaborate on the same projects. The Pentagon offered its network of computers to computer users and researchers to exchange messages. Other networks in the United States and around the world connected throughout the late 1970s and early 1980s, and this supernetwork became known as the **Internet**, the global system of interconnected computer networks.

At the same time, television technology was expanding. Cable television, a system in which televisions receive transmissions through wires instead of air waves like radios do, had been around since the late 1940s. Its original purpose was to provide television reception to people who lived in geographically isolated communities. By the early 1980s, cable television could provide improved picture and sound quality and offer viewers throughout the whole nation a wide variety of channels. Suddenly every American with cable access could tune in to the same television networks, which contributed to shared cultural experiences. Teenagers watched their favorite bands play in music videos broadcast by MTV. Cable News Network (CNN) reported national news all day, every day.

TEACHER AND ASTRONAUT
Christa McAuliffe was the first candidate accepted for the NASA Teacher in Space Project in 1985. She received her astronaut training and became a payload specialist on board the orbiter *Challenger* when it launched on January 28, 1986. McAuliffe had prepared a science lesson plan for students who would have tuned in to the *Challenger* for the live and taped lessons. After McAuliffe died in the *Challenger* explosion, many of her students told how she had challenged them and inspired them to enter the field of education.

Meanwhile, NASA continued to make strides with its shuttle program in the 1980s. Unfortunately, a catastrophe temporarily set back its efforts. On January 28, 1986, NASA launched the spacecraft *Challenger* from its facility at Cape Canaveral, Florida. Seconds later, however, it disintegrated in midair in a fiery explosion, killing the seven astronauts onboard. One of the astronauts was Christa McAuliffe, a high school teacher from Concord, New Hampshire, who had been selected from thousands of applicants to be the first private citizen in space. An investigation later determined that a damaged rocket booster was to blame for the tragedy. After the investigation, NASA scientists made changes to space shuttles to improve safety conditions, but the shock of the tragedy temporarily stopped work on the space program.

CHANGES IN THE AMERICAN FAMILY

Technology wasn't the only thing changing in the 1980s. The decade saw dramatic shifts in the dynamics of American families. For instance, the number of women giving birth out of wedlock had risen steadily since the 1970s, a social trend that contributed to the 6.7 million increase of single-parent households in the country from 1970 to 1992.

CRITICAL VIEWING In 1996, the AIDS Memorial Quilt (left) made its fifth appearance on the National Mall in Washington, D.C. The quilt held 37,440 panels, or blocks, covering the entire grassy stretch of lawn on the Mall. What do the individual panels (above) tell you about the people they memorialize and the people who made them?

AMERICAN PLACES

The National Mall, Washington, D.C.

The most familiar part of the National Mall is a broad grassy area stretching for almost two miles between the U.S. Capitol Building and the Lincoln Memorial. Americans have historically held rallies and protests here, watched presidential inaugurations, and displayed challenging exhibits, such as the AIDS Memorial Quilt. The Mall is also the gateway to presidential and American memorials and a growing number of museums that house art, cultural artifacts, and unique architecture. An estimated 25 million people visit the Mall each year, free of charge.

Nearly 2,300 American elm trees line the Mall, and more than 26 miles of sidewalks and 8 miles of bike trails extend throughout the surrounding area, officially called the National Mall and Memorial Parks. This larger area encompasses the White House, museums, lush gardens, and the Tidal Basin, where the Cherry Blossom Festival is held each spring. The more than 9,000 trees that cover the larger Mall area not only provide shade and landscaped scenery but also remove about 492 tons of air pollution from Washington, D.C.

The National Mall was originally designed in 1791 by Pierre L'Enfant to be the city's grandest avenue. But it wasn't until 1902 that a commissioned report to Congress advised a restoration, development, and extension of L'Enfant's proposal. The result, with continued modern, sustainable alterations, is the National Mall of today.

Divorce rates reached their highest levels ever in the early 1980s. And women were entering the workforce in record numbers: 67 percent of married women were working in 1986 compared with 26 percent in 1950.

American families were also facing challenges in education. In 1983, a government committee released a document called *A Nation at Risk* on the status of public schools in the United States. The committee's findings were grim. American schools were experiencing low state test scores and high turnover rates among teachers. As many as 23 million American adults could not read or write. The report stated, "If an unfriendly foreign power had attempted to impose on America the mediocre educational performance that exists today, we might well have viewed it as an act of war." *A Nation at Risk* called for massive reform to retain the best teachers and to raise students' academic performances.

One of the most famous educational reforms of the 1980s began in a school in Oakland, California. First Lady Nancy Reagan was addressing an elementary school about the perils of drug use and abuse. A student stood up and asked Mrs. Reagan what students should say if someone asks them to try drugs or alcohol. Mrs. Reagan responded, "Just say no." That advice became a national catchphrase, and schools around the country formed clubs that aimed to teach students how to resist peer pressure. Ultimately, data showed that the programs were not successful.

THE CHALLENGE OF HIV/AIDS

Beginning in the early 1980s, a new disease caused by the **human immunodeficiency virus (HIV)** was attacking its victims' immune systems. In the United States, most of the first victims of HIV were members of the gay community, where the incidence of infection was particularly high. In some patients, the virus destroyed so much of the immune system, the infected person's body could no longer fight off the most common ailments. The last stage of HIV was known as **acquired immunodeficiency syndrome (AIDS)**. Not all HIV patients advanced to this often-deadly stage.

As the 1980s progressed, more HIV/AIDS patients were identified, mostly in large American cities such as New York City and San Francisco. Little was known about the disease then, so panic and confusion rose in the nation and around the world. In 1985, after the New York City school system reported a child with AIDS attending one of its 622 elementary schools, a large number of parents kept their children home out of fear of the virus. This made the gay community and especially those who contracted the virus an even greater target for discrimination.

Eventually, scientists determined that the virus spread through the exchange of certain body fluids, including fluids exchanged during sexual contact. Infected pregnant mothers could pass the disease to their children in the womb. Drug users contracted the virus if they shared contaminated needles, and some hospital patients were stricken after receiving infected blood during transfusions.

In an effort to stop the epidemic, many HIV/AIDS activists promoted safer sex practices, provided clean needles to intravenous drug users, and generated greater awareness about the disease. The Reagan administration as well as leading conservatives resisted such actions. They argued that poor "lifestyle" choices put people at risk for the disease, and they urged a greater adherence to "traditional family values." By 1989, at least 100,000 Americans had contracted HIV/AIDS and thousands of people had died from the disease. The number of deaths rose until the mid-1990s when new drugs were introduced to manage the virus's symptoms.

In 1985, activist Cleve Jones launched the Names Project, enlisting families and friends of people with AIDS to create quilted panels in an effort to keep alive the memory of the thousands who had died. When first displayed in 1987, the quilt covered an area larger than a football field. Since the disease first appeared, 600,000 to 700,000 Americans have died from AIDS.

HISTORICAL THINKING

1. **READING CHECK** What social tensions were caused by changing demographics in the United States during the 1980s?
2. **IDENTIFY** How have personal computers changed the lives of Americans?
3. **MAKE PREDICTIONS** What might have happened if the Reagan administration had chosen to support the educational programs HIV/AIDS activists had suggested?
4. **DESCRIBE** In what ways did women's roles change in society during the 1980s?

11.11.3 Describe the changing roles of women in society as reflected in the entry of more women into the labor force and the changing family structure; 11.11.7 Explain how the federal, state, and local governments have responded to demographic and social changes such as population shifts to the suburbs, racial concentrations in the cities, Frostbelt-to-Sunbelt migration, international migration, decline of family farms, increases in out-of-wedlock births, and drug abuse; CST 2 Students analyze how change happens at different rates at different times; understand that some aspects can change while others remain the same; and understand that change is complicated and affects not only technology and politics but also values and beliefs.

3.1 **MAIN IDEA** In the 1980s, economic dissatisfaction and increasing demands for freedom led to the collapse of the Soviet Union and the fall of communism throughout Eastern Europe.

COLLAPSE OF THE SOVIET UNION

The fall of the Soviet Union and the end of communism in Eastern Europe was surely something people believed they would never witness in their lifetimes. And then it happened.

A WEAKENED SOVIET EMPIRE

Since the aftermath of World War II, the opposing doctrines of the capitalist United States and the communist Soviet Union had generated conflicts that had an impact on the entire world. In 1980, Ronald Reagan took office as president, hoping to promote free-market relations and anticommunist policies throughout the world.

By 1984, the U.S. economy had revived and was growing. This helped Ronald Reagan win a convincing re-election. What also helped was Reagan's strong anticommunist stance, which a majority of Americans favored. As Reagan pursued his anticommunist foreign policy into his second term, the Soviet Union was experiencing a period of inner turmoil. By the mid-1980s, the Soviet Union was struggling with a deteriorating economy and an unpopular war against anticommunist rebels in Afghanistan.

In 1985, the Soviet **Politburo**, the ruling committee of the Communist Party and thus the nation, agreed on a new leader, **Mikhail Gorbachev** (mih-KYL GOR-buh-chof). Younger than most of the aging Communist Party leaders, Gorbachev brought energy and new ideas to the nation. Hoping that increasing freedom of ideas and speech would lead to a stronger nation, he instituted the policy of ***glasnost***, or "openness." For the first time in decades, churches were allowed to open, some political prisoners were released, and journalists were given some freedom to criticize officials.

Central planning, which directed all aspects of Soviet business, farming, and manufacturing, continued to be an inefficient way to govern such a massive country, and people had no economic incentive to pursue innovation. The Soviet Union's economy had stagnated. In addition, in 1979, the Soviet Union had invaded Afghanistan, hoping to intervene on behalf of the country's communist government against anticommunist Muslim rebels. This decision led to a decade-long hostile occupation of Afghanistan, in which thousands of Soviet soldiers died. The conflict drained an enormous amount of money from the Soviet treasury.

Gorbachev reformed the economy more directly through his policy of ***perestroika*** (peh-ruh-STROY-kuh), or economic restructuring. Loosening the nation's strict control over the economy, he gave more freedom to local officials to make decisions. Some people were even allowed to open small businesses. Gorbachev was not trying to overturn communism with his reforms. Rather, he hoped that these changes would lead to a more efficient, more innovative, and wealthier nation. The country's economy remained stalled, however. And the people used their increased freedom to speak up about their dissatisfactions.

Meanwhile, President Reagan had been building a massive military program, the largest in U.S. peacetime history. He also took an aggressive position against the Soviets' hold on Eastern Bloc countries. On June 12, 1987, he delivered a speech in West Berlin about the evils of communism. He stood not far from the Berlin Wall, a symbol of communist rule. He declared, "Mr. Gorbachev, tear down this wall!" That admonition became an iconic moment, marking the peak of the conflict between the two nations. The Soviet Union's economy was too weak to compete with a U.S. military buildup, so Gorbachev began working on a diplomatic program aimed at controlling nuclear arms.

11.9.5 Analyze the role of the Reagan administration and other factors in the victory of the West in the Cold War.

On December 9, 1987, he met with Reagan to sign the Intermediate-Range Nuclear Forces (INF) Treaty, which banned both nations from owning certain kinds of nuclear missiles.

As Soviet power dwindled, Reagan reached the end of his second presidential term. His vice president, George H.W. Bush, ran against Michael Dukakis, the former Democratic governor of Massachusetts. Bush was elected president in 1988 by a large margin of electoral and popular votes. Formerly ambassador to the United Nations and director of the Central Intelligence Agency, Bush had extensive foreign policy experience and was poised to continue the nation's strong stance against the Soviet Union.

Soviet General Secretary Mikhail Gorbachev and President Ronald Reagan strolled on the South Lawn of the White House during the Washington Summit on December 10, 1987. Two days before, they had signed the Intermediate-Range Nuclear Forces Treaty.

END OF THE SOVIET UNION

Gorbachev's economic policies had not energized the Soviet Union as much as he had hoped. He withdrew troops from Afghanistan in 1989, but the Soviet intervention there had been costly and damaging for national morale. *Glasnost*, which had been meant to spur innovation, had encouraged rebellious voices. While Russia was the largest republic in the Soviet Union, non-Russians held the ethnic majority in many of the other Soviet republics, and they wanted freedom from Soviet rule. In 1990, the Baltic republic of Lithuania declared its independence from the union. Worried that other republics would follow its lead, Gorbachev ordered a military assault in 1991 on unarmed citizens in Lithuania's capital.

This assault further damaged Gorbachev's reputation in the Soviet Union. **Boris Yeltsin**, a member of parliament and the newly elected president of the Russian Republic, emerged as a rival to Gorbachev's overarching power. Though he assisted Gorbachev in leading the country, he was a vocal critic of Gorbachev's policies.

On August 18, 1991, conservative members of the Communist Party attempted a coup to overthrow Gorbachev, fearing that their power was diminishing. Tanks and other military vehicles rolled into Moscow, but the party **hardliners**, or staunch Soviet communists, were shocked to find that the people no longer feared such shows of government force.

Despite his disagreements with Gorbachev, Yeltsin jumped onto a tank and rejected the coup, to cheers from the crowd and support from President Bush and other world leaders. Shortly after, the hardliners ordered the military to attack the Soviet parliament, but military leaders refused. The Communist Party and the Politburo had lost. The Russian parliament voted to dissolve them completely. As communist rule collapsed, many of the Soviet republics, such as Estonia and Latvia, declared their independence. Though Gorbachev pushed for unity, the momentum for independence was too great. On December 25, 1991, the Soviet Union ceased to exist, and the former republics of the Union of Soviet Socialist Republics (U.S.S.R.) became independent countries.

As in the Soviet Union, democratic movements arose across the globe during the late 1980s and early 1990s. In China, a solitary demonstrator stands in the way of Chinese army tanks as they roll along the Avenue of Eternal Peace in Beijing. For weeks during the spring of 1989, people had demonstrated in the nearby Tiananmen Square (below) for freedom of speech and the press.

FREEDOM IN CENTRAL AND EASTERN EUROPE

Even before the Soviet Union collapsed, communist rule had fallen throughout Eastern Europe. The reforms instituted by Gorbachev had included granting greater freedom to the Soviet-controlled Eastern Bloc countries. This inspired those countries, starting with Poland, to push for even greater control of their economic and political futures. In 1988, Polish workers, angry at a faltering economy, went on a countrywide strike. Poland's military leaders agreed to legalize a workers' union and cooperate with them, which eventually led to other national reforms and the country's first free elections in 1989 and 1990. The Polish people voted union leader Lech Walesa (LEHK vuh-WEHN-suh) the country's new president in 1990.

In Hungary, reformers were inspired by Poland's drastic transformation. Hungarian leaders adopted policies that moved the country toward a free-market economy and free elections. In 1989, radical reformers took over the Communist Party congress and voted to dissolve the party itself. Czechoslovakia also enjoyed a peaceful transition to democracy. Watching the developments elsewhere, the Czech public marched peacefully against the nation's Communist Party. Massive protests forced the dissolution of the party in 1989. A newly formed parliament elected playwright and activist Václav Havel (VAHT-slav HAH-vehl) president. Romania also saw the fall of communism in 1989, though not without bloodshed. After dictator Nicolae Ceausescu (NIHK-oh-ly chow-CHEHS-kew) ordered the killing of hundreds of peaceful protestors, the Romanian army sided with the uprising against him. Ceausescu and his wife were arrested and executed, and Romania started to hold free elections in 1990.

Meanwhile, people in East Germany organized massive protests for greater freedom. Then, on November 9, 1989, the Berlin Wall was opened. An East German official had mistakenly issued an order to let people cross to West Germany. A series of contradictory instructions followed. Meanwhile, East German crowds at the wall grew by thousands. In an attempt to restore stability, the government first let a few people cross the border and then more. Soon, thousands of people from East and West Germany descended on the scene in joyous celebration. East Germans made it clear that they rejected the Communist Party and wanted reunification with West Germany. About a year later, Germany became one country again, and the Berlin Wall was torn down.

FREEDOM SPREADS

In addition to the spectacular fall of the Soviet Union, the world witnessed other successful freedom movements during this time. In 1989, the newly elected president of South Africa, F. W. de Klerk, began to dismantle apartheid. He lifted restrictions on the media and civil rights groups and ended the plan to force black people to live in separate homelands. In 1990, he freed civil rights leader Nelson Mandela, who had spent 27 years in prison for anti-apartheid activities. The following few years were filled with negotiations led by Mandela and de Klerk to finally end the practice of apartheid and establish the country's first multi-ethnic government. In 1994, Mandela was elected president of South Africa.

Free elections were held in Chile in 1989, ending the military dictatorship that had ruled since 1973. In Nicaragua, the long conflict between the ruling Sandinistas and the rebel Contras, which had sparked the Iran-Contra scandal in the United States, ended when a coalition of anti-Sandinista political parties finally won the national election.

As a wave of activism for democracy rose in China, the nation's communist government stood firm. In 1987, Chinese Communist Party general secretary Hu Yaobang was forced to resign largely for encouraging democratic reforms. When Hu died in 1989, he became a symbol of political democracy. That spring, students demonstrated against the government in **Tiananmen Square**, a large public space in Beijing. Thousands of students protested peacefully and started a hunger strike, gaining support from around the world. On June 4, the military rolled tanks into the square, opening fire and killing hundreds. Despite the democratic movements across the globe, repressive regimes still prevailed in a number of countries, and international tensions still ran high.

HISTORICAL THINKING

1. READING CHECK What were Mikhail Gorbachev's policies of *glasnost* and *perestroika*?
2. **MAKE CONNECTIONS** What larger political trends in Eastern Europe were reflected in the opening of the Berlin Wall?
3. **ANALYZE CAUSE AND EFFECT** How did changes in the Soviet Union lead to the fall of communism in other Eastern Bloc countries?
4. **MAKE INFERENCES** How did Mikhail Gorbachev's policies hurt his own reputation after the Soviet invasion of Lithuania in 1989?

HI 1 Students show the connections, causal and otherwise, between particular historical events and larger social, economic, and political trends and developments.

3.2 CURATING HISTORY

The Newseum Washington, D.C.

Located between the White House and the U.S. Capitol, the interactive Newseum promotes, explains, and defends free expression and the five freedoms of the First Amendment: religion, speech, press, assembly, and petition. The museum's goal is to serve as a neutral forum for fostering open discussions. It engages visitors in the central debates of our time, including the future of investigative journalism, the tensions between national security and privacy, and the role of religious freedom.

The Newseum's 7 levels of interactive exhibits include 15 galleries and 15 theaters. Among the most memorable exhibits are the 9/11 Gallery, which features the broadcast antenna from the top of the World Trade Center and the Pulitzer Prize Photographs Gallery, displaying photographs from every Pulitzer Prize-winning entry since 1942. The Newseum also traces the evolution of electronic communication from the birth of radio to the technologies of the present and the future.

The Berlin Wall Gallery

At the center of the Newseum's Berlin Wall Gallery stand eight 12-foot-high concrete sections of the Berlin Wall—the largest display of unaltered portions of the wall outside of Germany. A three-story East German guard tower that stood near Checkpoint Charlie, Berlin's best-known East-West crossing point, stands nearby. The gallery tells the story of how news and information helped topple a closed and oppressive society, signaling the end of the Cold War.

Documenting the Kennedy Assassination

Before President John F. Kennedy even reached the Dallas hospital after being shot on November 22, 1963, 58-year-old Russian immigrant Abraham Zapruder knew the president was dead. He had watched the assassination unfold through the viewfinder of his 8-millimeter Bell and Howell home movie camera and had unknowingly created one of history's most famous films.

Abraham Zapruder's camera as well as an ID belonging to White House correspondent Sid Davis are part of the Newseum's traveling exhibit devoted to the assassination of President Kennedy.

How does a museum like the Newseum show the connections between historical events and larger social and political trends and developments?

"I am dedicated to keeping the Newseum at the cutting edge of national and international conversations about **the meaning of—and threats to—freedom.**"

—Jeffrey Herbst, Newseum President and CEO

The 9/11 Gallery

Exploring an event like 9/11 through artifacts, such as the newspaper headlines shown here, documentary films, and first-person accounts from journalists who covered the story, has a profound impact on Newseum visitors in this gallery.

Along with police and firefighters, journalists ran toward danger on September 11, 2001. Among the 2,749 people who lost their lives in New York City that day were photojournalist Bill Biggart, who was killed in the collapse of one of the World Trade Center towers, and 6 broadcast engineers who died at their posts at the top of the 110-story complex.

News organizations faced extraordinary challenges that day. From the Pentagon to New York City to Shanksville, Pennsylvania, shocking news broke minute by minute, and journalists scrambled to cover the stories.

11.5.6 Trace the growth and effects of radio and movies and their role in the worldwide diffusion of popular culture; HI 1 Students show the connections, causal and otherwise, between particular historical events and larger social, economic, and political trends and developments.

THE END OF THE COLD WAR

As the general secretary of the Communist Party of the U.S.S.R., Mikhail Gorbachev took office in 1985 with ideas for reform. U.S. President Ronald Reagan had had a few years to develop his foreign policy plan by then, and he had made a commitment to fighting communist forces around the world. Though the two leaders had competing ideologies, they were willing to work with each other to decrease tensions between their countries.

On November 9, 1989, East German officials opened the border between East and West Berlin. That weekend, more than 2 million Berliners flowed across the border, breaking down the concrete and barbed wire barrier that had divided them for 28 years. This photo was taken from the West Berlin side of the wall.

CRITICAL VIEWING Examine the scene in the photo and compare the activity in the foreground on the west side of the Berlin Wall to that in the background on the east side of the wall. How would you describe the scene on both sides of the wall?

DOCUMENT ONE

Primary Source: Article
from *Pravda,* April 24, 1985, by Mikhail Gorbachev

Soon after being appointed general secretary of the Communist Party, Mikhail Gorbachev wrote a newspaper article addressing the country's economic problems. Here, he explains his new ideas of *glasnost* and *perestroika* and how he thinks that restructuring the economy can help the Soviet Union become stronger.

CONSTRUCTED RESPONSE How did Gorbachev's ideas for reform signal a move toward free-market economics?

The main question now is: How, and at what cost, will the country be able to achieve accelerated economic development? Examining this question in the Politburo [a committee made up of the Soviet Union's main policy makers], we have unanimously reached the conclusion that there are real possibilities for this. The task of accelerating growth rates, substantially accelerating them, is completely feasible. We must more boldly advance along the path of expanding the rights of enterprises and their independence, introduce economic accountability and, on this basis, increase the responsibility and stake of labor collectives in the final results of work.

DOCUMENT TWO

Primary Source: Speech
from President Ronald Reagan's speech in West Berlin, June 12, 1987

President Reagan's speech at the Berlin Wall was amplified so that people in East Berlin could hear it as well. He addressed the recent changes in the Soviet Union and wondered where they would lead.

CONSTRUCTED RESPONSE Why did Reagan use the Berlin Wall as a symbol as he addressed changes in the Soviet Union?

Now the Soviets themselves may, in a limited way, be coming to understand the importance of freedom. Are these the beginnings of profound changes in the Soviet state? Or are they token gestures, intended to raise false hopes in the West, or to strengthen the Soviet system without changing it? There is one sign the Soviets can make that would be unmistakable, that would advance dramatically the cause of freedom and peace. General Secretary Gorbachev, if you seek peace, if you seek prosperity for the Soviet Union and Eastern Europe, if you seek liberalization: Come here to this gate! Mr. Gorbachev, open this gate! Mr. Gorbachev, tear down this wall!

DOCUMENT THREE

Primary Source: Speech
from President George H.W. Bush's address to the nation, December 25, 1991

President George H.W. Bush addressed the citizens of the United States on Christmas, announcing the resignation of Mikhail Gorbachev and, essentially, the end of the Cold War.

CONSTRUCTED RESPONSE How did President Bush view Gorbachev's role in the dissolution of the Cold War?

New, independent nations have emerged out of the wreckage of the Soviet empire. Last weekend, these former republics formed a Commonwealth of Independent States. This act marks the end of the old Soviet Union, signified today by Mikhail Gorbachev's decision to resign. Mikhail Gorbachev's revolutionary policies transformed the Soviet Union. His policies permitted the peoples of Russia and the other republics to cast aside decades of oppression and establish the foundations of freedom. The United States applauds and supports the historic choice for freedom by the new states of the Commonwealth. We congratulate them on the peaceful and democratic path they have chosen, and for their careful attention to nuclear control and safety during this transition.

SYNTHESIZE & WRITE

1. **REVIEW** Review what you have learned about the events that led to the end of the Cold War.
2. **RECALL** On your own paper, write details about American and Soviet leaders' actions during the 1980s.
3. **CONSTRUCT** Construct a topic sentence that explains President Reagan's and Mikhail Gorbachev's roles in ending the Cold War.
4. **WRITE** Using evidence from the chapter and these documents, write an informative paragraph that supports your topic sentence in Step 3.

11.9.5 Analyze the role of the Reagan administration and other factors in the victory of the West in the Cold War.

3.4 **MAIN IDEA** During George H.W. Bush's presidency, tensions shifted from the dwindling Cold War to conflicts in the Middle East and a sluggish domestic economy.

George H.W. Bush and the Persian Gulf War

Have you ever had to challenge assumptions that you have held for a long time? What was difficult about it? After decades of sparring with the Soviet Union during the Cold War, the United States faced threats from a new location, which required very different strategies.

An F-14A Tomcat flies over Kuwait where oil well fires set by the Iraqis burned for months after Operation Desert Storm ended.

11.9.6 Describe U.S. Middle East policy and its strategic, political, and economic interests, including those related to the Gulf War.

CONFLICT IN THE MIDDLE EAST

After the Soviet Union collapsed, President Bush was in the position to use his years of experience handling international conflict to assist the former Warsaw Pact countries as they adjusted to democracy. While hope grew in Europe, tensions were about to boil over in Southwest Asia, more commonly known as the Middle East.

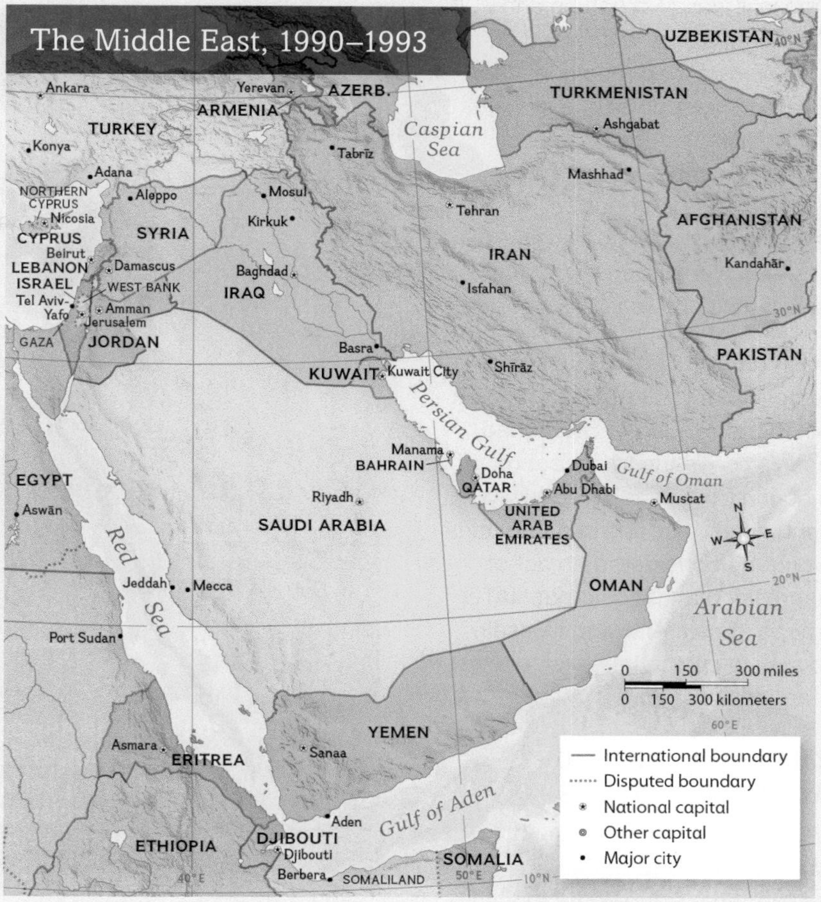

The Middle East, 1990–1993

In the 1980s, the Southwest Asian countries of Iran and Iraq both had authoritarian governments. Since the Iranian Revolution of 1979, Iran had operated as a **theocracy**, or a nation governed by the principles of a single religion. Its leaders were fundamentalist Muslim clerics, or religious leaders. Meanwhile, in Iraq, a member of the Ba'th political party, **Saddam Hussein**, helped his party orchestrate a coup against the country's prime minister. By 1979, Hussein had forced out Iraq's sick and aging president, Ahmad Hasan al-Bakr, and he began a long, tyrannical reign. A brutal dictator, Hussein extinguished any voices of dissent, operating a secret police force that arrested and tortured his enemies.

In 1980, Iran and Iraq went to war. Hussein's goal was to conquer the other countries around the Persian Gulf and preside as the leader over a single, oil-rich Arab nation. In 1980, he attempted an invasion of neighboring Iran's oil fields, leading to the Iran-Iraq War. Religious tensions also played a role in the conflict. Dominated by different branches of Islam, the two countries were often at odds with each other over their beliefs and traditions, especially as they intersected with political and government practices and goals. Hussein was a member of the **Sunni** (SOO-nee) denomination, while Iran was controlled by the **Shi'ite** (SHE-ite) sect. The war between the two countries raged until 1988, when both sides, depleted of funds and resources, agreed to a hostile ceasefire, or an agreement in which the problems being fought over remain unchanged or unresolved, but the parties to the conflict agree to stop fighting while peace plans are made.

OPERATION DESERT STORM

In August 1990, Hussein ordered Iraqi troops to invade another neighboring country, **Kuwait**, in order to take over the small nation's vast oil resources. The conflict, which later became known as the **Persian Gulf War**, expanded to include a buildup of international troops in nearby countries. The presence of Iraq in Kuwait was a major concern for the rest of the world, especially since world leaders suspected that Hussein planned next to attack Saudi Arabia, the world's largest oil producer.

In response, President Bush increased the number of American troops stationed in Saudi Arabia to 400,000, hoping to deter Iraq with a show of force. In addition, the United Nations called for an international ban on trade with Iraq, but neither action deterred Hussein. President Bush then worked with other NATO countries to form a military coalition against Hussein. On January 16, 1991, the coalition moved into Kuwait to force Iraqi troops out.

The coalition effort, called **Operation Desert Storm**, ended quickly. In six weeks it drove Iraq out of Kuwait. The coalition's success was partly owed to modern technology that was used for the first

CST 3 Students use a variety of maps and documents to interpret human movement, including major patterns of domestic and international migration, changing environmental preferences and settlement patterns, the frictions that develop between population groups, and the diffusion of ideas, technological innovations, and goods.

time in a war. Microchips and digital advances were used in precision-guided munitions that relied on laser guidance systems to increase the effectiveness of aerial bombings. On the ground, microcomputers, laser rangefinders, and guided-missile systems were incorporated in new tanks, helicopters, and weapons.

Bush did not pursue Hussein to remove him from power. The goal of Operation Desert Storm had been to drive the Iraqis out of a country they had invaded. To send military troops into Iraq itself would be considered an act of aggression and would put NATO troops at risk. Allowing Hussein to stay in power, however, set the stage for later conflict.

Two hours after U.S. and Allied jets attacked Iraqi military defenses, President George H.W. Bush announced the beginning of Operation Desert Storm on January 16, 1991. During his televised speech, Bush explained that a coalition of 28 nations had "exhausted all reasonable efforts to reach a peaceful resolution."

THE CHALLENGE OF ACHIEVING PEACE

Much like Saddam Hussein, **Manuel Noriega** of Panama had developed a troubled relationship with the United States as he turned from a CIA informer to a criminal liability. Noriega had brutally gained control of Panama and engaged in drug trafficking and racketeering throughout the 1980s. In 1988, the Senate subcommittee on terrorism, narcotics, and international operations declared that Noriega "represents one of the most serious foreign policy failures for the United States."

Americans intervened in Panama in 1989, when President Bush ordered an invasion to depose and capture the dictator. Though the United States was successful, many people around the world criticized its involvement in foreign governments. President Bush was aware of this growing criticism, and during the conflict with Iraq, he presented to Congress and the nation his ideas for achieving peace through cooperation, in what he called a **New World Order**. His emphasis was on ensuring that nations relied on the rule of law, multinational cooperation, and collective security through the United Nations as the Cold War ended.

BUSH'S DOMESTIC POLICIES

President Bush's four years in office were heavily associated with the intervention of the United States in the Persian Gulf. Many items on his domestic agenda still managed to stand out, however. When the liberal-leaning Supreme Court justice William J. Brennan announced his retirement in 1990, President Bush appointed the little-known New Hampshire judge David H. Souter to replace him.

During Souter's first year on the Court, he joined Justice William Rehnquist in several conservative rulings. Then, in 1991, the retirement of Supreme Court justice Thurgood Marshall allowed President Bush to appoint a new justice to the high Court. He nominated **Clarence Thomas**, a federal judge who had held several offices under the Reagan administration. Senate hearings for his appointment to the Court erupted in controversy, however, when law professor Anita Hill testified that Thomas had sexually harassed her when she had worked for him. Despite the contentious hearings, which the nation watched live on television, the Senate eventually approved Thomas's appointment with a vote of 52 to 48.

Republican appointees to the Court held eight seats and seemed ready to move the Court to the right, rolling back rulings on civil rights, abortion, and religion. But Justice Souter surprised conservatives by often voting with the Democrats' appointees and liberal justices. Souter's record on the Court

11.9.4 List the effects of foreign policy on domestic policies and vice versa (e.g., protestsduring the war in Vietnam, the "nuclear freeze" movement); 11.11.2 Discuss the significant domestic policy speeches of Truman, Eisenhower, Kennedy, Johnson, Nixon, Carter, Reagan, Bush, and Clinton (e.g., with regard to education, civil rights, economic policy, environmental policy).

PRIMARY SOURCE

In the following remarks, President Bush introduced the Americans with Disabilities Act that guaranteed civil rights to people with disabilities.

This act is powerful in its simplicity. It will ensure that people with disabilities are given the basic guarantees for which they have worked so long and so hard . . . specifically, first the ADA ensures that employers covered by the act cannot discriminate against qualified individuals with disabilities. Second, the ADA ensures access to public accommodations such as restaurants, hotels, shopping centers, and offices. And third, the ADA ensures expanded access to transportation services. And fourth, the ADA ensures equivalent telephone services for people with speech or hearing impediments.

—from George H.W. Bush's remarks on the signing of the Americans with Disabilities Act, July 26, 1990

disappointed many conservatives and contributed to their growing dissatisfaction with President Bush.

However, President Bush kept a campaign promise and signed significant civil rights legislation for people with disabilities. For years, the disability rights movement had been working to show that the exclusion and segregation of people with disabilities was discrimination. Following the example of the civil rights movement, activists conducted sit-ins at federal buildings, obstructed public transportation, marched in the streets, and took their case to the courts and Congress. Legal changes began in the 1970s, but the most comprehensive civil rights legislation wasn't passed until 1990 when President Bush signed the **Americans with Disabilities Act**, which had passed Congress with bipartisan support.

Another major piece of legislation signed by President Bush was also the result of activism that began in the mid-20th century. In the 1980s, Americans became aware that rainfall made acidic by industrial pollution could travel from the pollution source to other areas, often damaging forests and lakes. In 1989, Bush proposed revisions to the Clean Air Act, specifically targeting acid rain, urban air pollution, and toxic air emissions. The revisions also improved pollution enforcement authority. The bill passed by large votes in both the House of Representatives and the Senate in 1990.

The United States had stopped developing and testing nuclear weapons by the early 1990s. Growing efforts made throughout the 1980s by activists as part of the "nuclear freeze" movement had brought attention and pressure to both the Reagan and Bush administrations to change U.S. nuclear policies. Though complete nuclear disarmament was not achieved, the United States significantly reduced its nuclear weapons. President Bush also signed the Radiation Exposure Compensation Act, which gave partial restitution to people, mostly in western states, who contracted cancer and other diseases as a result of their exposure to atmospheric nuclear testing undertaken during the Cold War or from their employment in the uranium industry.

Bush ran for re-election in 1992, but he was haunted by a campaign promise he had made four years earlier. In 1988, during his speech at the Republican National Convention, he had declared, "Read my lips: no new taxes." His words proved memorable to the American people. But when he took office in 1989, the federal budget debt was about $2.8 trillion, almost three times what it had been in 1980. Unemployment rose, and gas prices spiked during the Gulf War conflicts. Ultimately, the United States faced a recession. The budget deficit was quickly growing, and it limited the president's ability to increase domestic spending. In 1990, President Bush found that he needed to compromise with Congress on a plan of **deficit reduction** that included budget cuts and tax increases to rein in spending and improve the economy.

As Bush explained to the nation why he felt this plan was necessary, people were reminded of his famous pledge to avoid new taxes. Even other Republicans were quick to bring up the broken promise. Despite bipartisan attempts at deficit reduction, people were dissatisfied with the economy by the end of Bush's term. A moderate Democrat, **William Jefferson "Bill" Clinton**, was readying himself to take on the challenge of running for the presidency.

HISTORICAL THINKING

1. **READING CHECK** What were the main criticisms of George H.W. Bush's economic policies?
2. **IDENTIFY MAIN IDEAS AND DETAILS** How did the United States government have to shift its foreign policy during Bush's presidency?
3. **ANALYZE CAUSE AND EFFECT** What was the main cause of the Persian Gulf War?
4. **SUMMARIZE** What impact did President Bush's revisions to the Clean Air Act have on protecting the environment?

11.11.5 Trace the impact of, need for, and controversies associated with environmental conservation, expansion of the national park system, and the development of environmental protection laws, with particular attention to the interaction between environmental protection advocates and property rights advocates.

CHAPTER 21 THE CONSERVATIVE REVOLUTION REVIEW

VOCABULARY

Use each of the following vocabulary words in a sentence that shows an understanding of the term's meaning.

1. conservative HSS 11.11.7
   A person who supports traditional social or economic policies is a conservative.
2. think tank HSS 11.11.7
3. safety net HSS 11.11.7
4. supply-side economics HSS 11.11.2
5. deregulation HSS 11.11.2
6. evangelist HSS 11.11.7
7. income inequality HSS 11.11.7
8. apartheid HSS 11.9.5
9. deficit reduction HSS 11.11.2

READING STRATEGY

ANALYZE CAUSE AND EFFECT

When you identify causes and effects, you determine how events affect later events. Complete the following chart to identify causes and effects related to Ronald Reagan's presidency. Then answer the question.

Causes	→	Effect
the economy		Election of Ronald Reagan
conservatism		
gas shortages		

Causes	→	Effect
		Reducing Government

Causes	→	Effect
		Deregulation

10. What were some of the most influential policies enacted during Reagan's presidency, and how did they affect the nation? HSS 11.11

MAIN IDEAS

Answer the following questions. Support your answers with evidence from the chapter.

11. How did the conservative movement respond to Johnson's Great Society programs? **LESSON 1.1** HSS 11.11.7
12. What aspects of post–World War II life in the United States contributed to Sunbelt migration? **LESSON 1.2** HSS 11.11.7
13. What was the significance of Reagan asking the American people if they were better off under Carter's presidency? **LESSON 1.3** HSS 11.11.2
14. Why did the government deregulate the savings and loan industry? **LESSON 2.1** HSS 11.11
15. What was the Iran-Contra scandal? **LESSON 2.2** HSS 11.9.3
16. How did the Reagan administration address the increased use of drugs in the United States? **LESSON 2.3** HSS 11.11.7
17. How did the collapse of communism after the fall of the Soviet Union affect countries in Central and Eastern Europe? **LESSON 3.1** HSS 11.9.5
18. What international challenges did President George H.W. Bush face during his term? **LESSON 3.4** HSS 11.9.6

HISTORICAL THINKING

Answer the following questions. Support your answers with evidence from the chapter.

19. **COMPARE AND CONTRAST** In what ways did President Reagan's position on the size of government differ from President Carter's? HSS 11.11.2
20. **MAKE CONNECTIONS** The early years of the HIV/AIDS epidemic were confusing and people were fearful. What other events in American history caused similar anxiety? HSS 11.11

21. **DETERMINE CHRONOLOGY** What evidence reveals that the invasion of Grenada was not planned as a distraction from the bombing in Beirut, Lebanon, that killed 241 U.S. marines? HSS 11.9.3

22. **ANALYZE CAUSE AND EFFECT** Why did the Soviet Politburo select Mikhail Gorbachev to become general secretary in 1985? HSS 11.9.5

23. **FORM AND SUPPORT OPINIONS** Do you think President Reagan was right to fire air traffic controllers during the PATCO strike? Support your opinion with evidence from the text. HSS 11.11

24. **IDENTIFY PROBLEMS AND SOLUTIONS** What regional environmental problems did President George H.W. Bush address in legislation? HSS 11.8.6

INTERPRET VISUALS

Look closely at this photo of American medical students who were studying at a university in Grenada when the U.S. military invaded to oust the communist government. Then answer the questions that follow.

25. Why do you think the expressions of the students and that of the soldier appear to convey different emotional states? HSS 11.9.3

26. What details in the photograph help you understand how U.S. intervention in Grenada increased Reagan's popularity among American voters? HSS 11.9.3

ANALYZE SOURCES

Read the excerpt from Ronald Reagan's Farewell Address, January 11, 1989, at the end of his presidency. Then answer the question that follows.

> And in all of that time I won a nickname, "The Great Communicator." I wasn't a great communicator, but I communicated great things, and they didn't spring full bloom from my brow, they came from the heart of a great nation—from our experience, our wisdom, and our belief in the principles that have guided us for two centuries. They called it the Reagan revolution. Well, I'll accept that, but for me it always seemed more like the great rediscovery, a rediscovery of our values and our common sense.

27. How does the excerpt above help demonstrate why President Reagan was considered "The Great Communicator"? HSS 11.11.2

CONNECT TO YOUR LIFE

28. **EXPLANATORY** Think about the challenges, achievements, and shortcomings faced by President Ronald Reagan. Then consider the challenges, achievements, and shortcomings of the current U.S. president. In a short essay, explain how the role of president has changed and stayed the same from Ronald Reagan's two terms to the present day. HSS CST 2

TIPS

- Research legitimate biographical and news sources about the current president. List the challenges, accomplishments, and missteps, if any, faced by the president while in office.
- Read through the chapter for text evidence of Reagan's accomplishments, challenges, and missteps, and list them.
- Chart similarities and differences in a Venn diagram or another graphic organizer.
- Use your findings to craft a solid thesis statement. Write a paragraph containing at least three sentences and three vocabulary words from the chapter in your response.

CHAPTER 22

AMERICA IN A GLOBAL SOCIETY

1992–Present

HISTORICAL THINKING What does it mean to be an American in the 21st century?

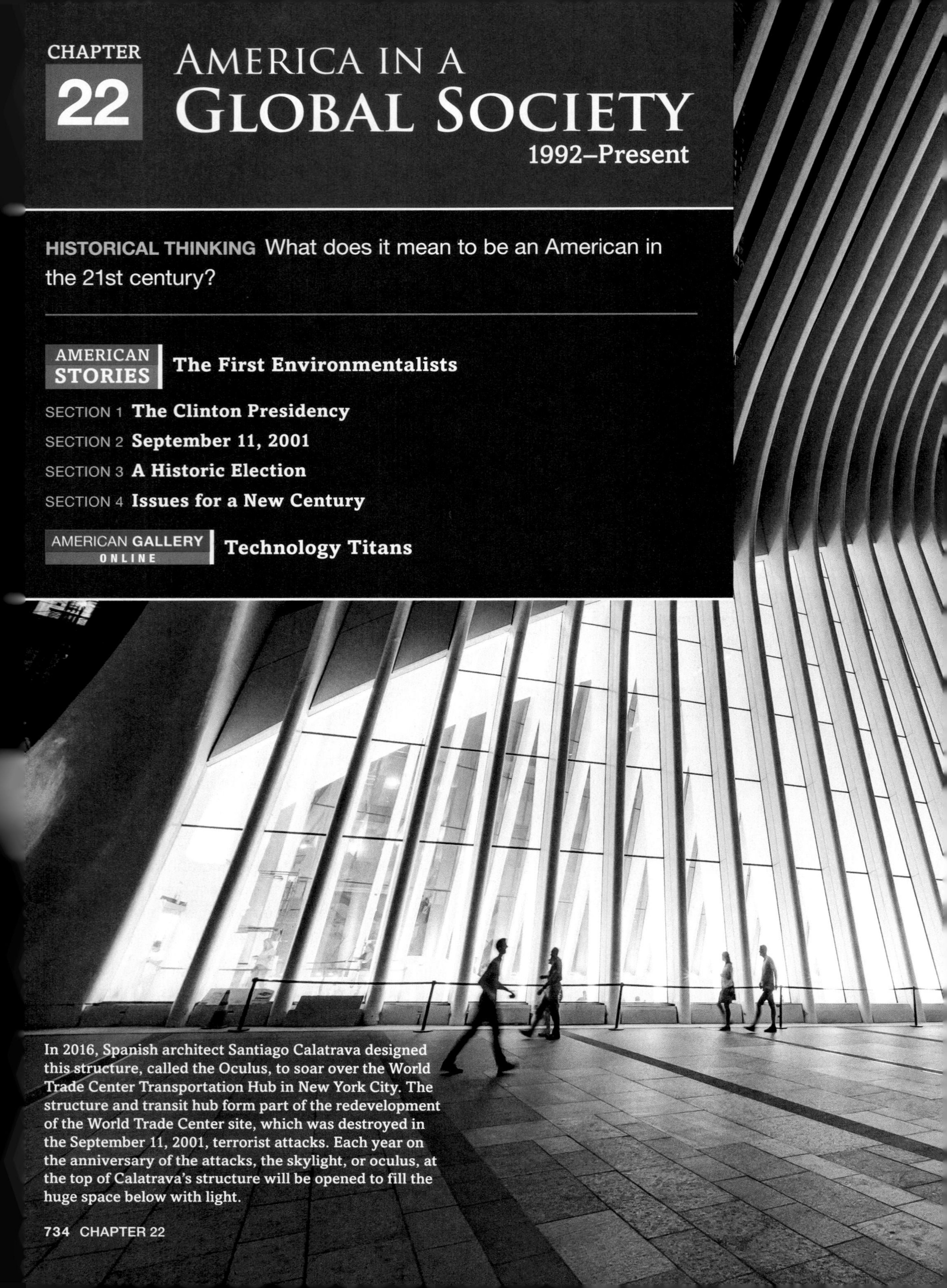

In 2016, Spanish architect Santiago Calatrava designed this structure, called the Oculus, to soar over the World Trade Center Transportation Hub in New York City. The structure and transit hub form part of the redevelopment of the World Trade Center site, which was destroyed in the September 11, 2001, terrorist attacks. Each year on the anniversary of the attacks, the skylight, or oculus, at the top of Calatrava's structure will be opened to fill the huge space below with light.

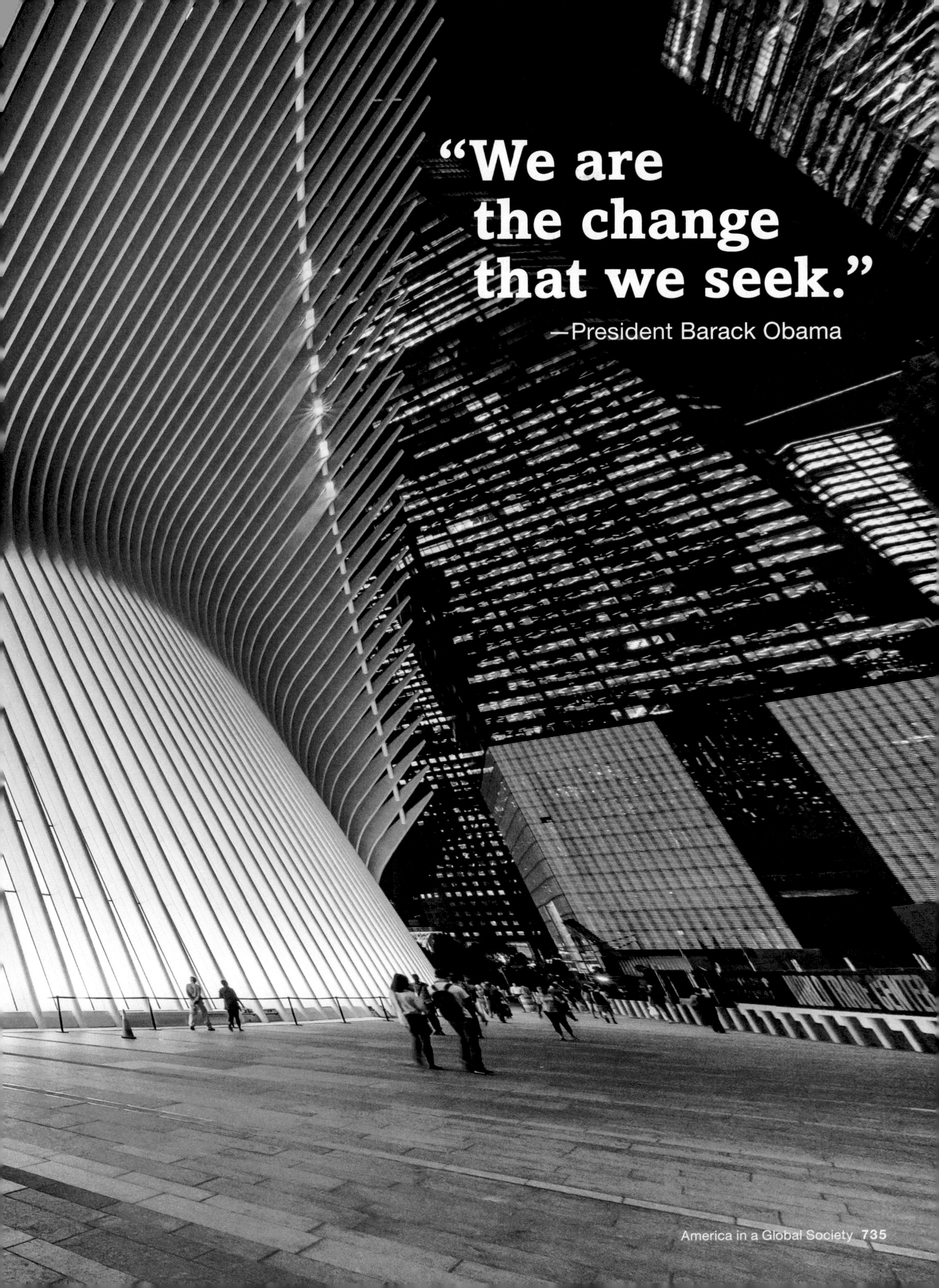

"We are the change that we seek."

—President Barack Obama

AMERICAN STORIES

NATIONAL GEOGRAPHIC

THE FIRST ENVIRONMENTALISTS

Protesters march on the Standing Rock Indian Reservation in North Dakota in 2016, attempting to halt the construction of a pipeline along the northern edge of the reservation.

11.8.6 Discuss the diverse environmental regions of North America, their relationship to local economies, and the origins and prospects of environmental problems in those regions.

In 1971, an organization called Keep America Beautiful launched an anti-pollution advertising campaign that quickly went viral. Billboards, magazine ads, and television commercials featured a solemn-faced Native American man in traditional clothing. As he regarded a landscape littered with garbage, a single tear trickled down his weathered cheek. The image (right), accompanied by slogans such as "Pollution hurts all of us," became instantly recognizable. The "Crying Indian" campaign was hugely successful in enlisting Americans to join the crusade against pollution.

This signature image also effectively illustrates a long-held stereotype of Native Americans as simple hunters or farmers living in harmony with nature, leaving no trace—the first American environmentalists. While some may consider this portrayal as flattering, it may also be an oversimplification. Native Americans have been using natural resources in a variety of sophisticated, evolving ways since long before the first Europeans arrived. Native American groups are as diverse as the nationalities found on any continent, and their complex relationships with nature reflect that diversity.

PRE-CONTACT

The term "pre-contact" is sometimes used to refer to Native Americans during the time before their first encounters with European explorers and settlers. Scholars believe that most pre-contact groups shared a broadly similar worldview incorporating the ideas that animals, plants, and the earth itself harbored sacred spirits, and that humans could ask the spirits to influence the weather, harvests, or the results of an upcoming battle. However, the cultures and survival practices of the tribes varied widely to suit the diverse North American geography. Some groups did indeed leave little trace on the land, while others took an active role in molding the ecosystems that surrounded them. Historian Louis S. Warren wrote, "To claim that Indians lived without affecting nature is akin to saying that they lived without touching anything, that they were a people without a history."

Different groups manipulated their environments in different ways to suit their needs. The Choctaw, Iroquois, and Pawnee, for example, cleared forests to create fields for farming. When those fields were no longer fertile, the tribes would abandon them and clear new land. When land was abundant, this practice could continue for a long time but led to deforestation

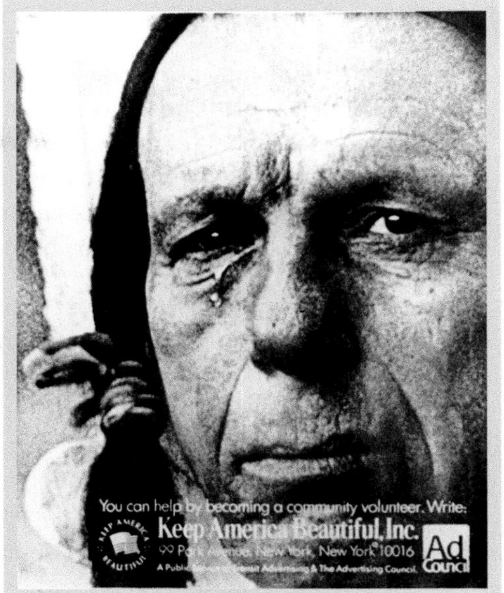

IRON EYES CODY

The story of the "Crying Indian" from the Keep America Beautiful ad campaign contains some curious twists relating to perceptions of Native American identity. The craggy-faced man featured in the ads was an actor named Iron Eyes Cody who had played Native Americans in movies since the 1920s. Sometime after the famous ad campaign, however, it was revealed that Iron Eyes Cody was not of Cherokee and Cree ancestry, as he claimed. In fact, he was a Sicilian American, born in Louisiana with the name Espera Oscar de Corti.

It would be easy to dismiss Cody as a mockery or cheap fake, but he took his pseudo-Native American identity very seriously. He married a Native American woman, adopted two Native American sons, and followed Native American practices and beliefs during his entire adult life. He also vigorously supported numerous Native American causes. In 1995, the Hollywood Native American community honored him for his work, although some were angered by Cody's very public appropriation of Native American identity through actions and beliefs rather than birth.

and stress on local species. There is evidence that certain tribes may have even caused their own downfall by overusing local resources. Some researchers believe the Ancestral Puebloans who once lived in southeastern Utah disappeared from their villages in the 13th century because they had depleted the wood in the region by burning it for fuel.

Fire was a powerful tool groups used to shape an ecosystem to their advantage. For example, some groups used fire to help create open prairies where large game animals such as bison, deer, elk, and antelope could graze. Fires were sometimes used in hunts to force animals into small open areas where they could be easily hunted. Burning was also used to clear ground for crops or drive out pests.

But many pre-contact groups actively practiced conservation techniques to protect the species they relied upon. The Algonquian lived along the Atlantic Coast and divided hunting territories among families. Each family would hunt its land according to systems the group had developed to maintain the game supply. In the Pacific Northwest, some Native American tribes trapped salmon swimming up rivers to spawn, but were also careful to let enough fish escape and lay their eggs so that the supply would be maintained from year to year.

THE PRESENT DAY

For years after European settlers arrived, Native Americans continued to use many of their pre-contact techniques for living within and managing ecosystems. As the groups were relocated and pushed onto reservations in the 19th century, however, most of these systems were disrupted. In the centuries since the first European contact, Native Americans have faced the challenge of adapting to new environments and maintaining their cultures in a changing, sometimes hostile world. Climate change may pose one of the most severe threats to some groups, particularly in Alaska, where melting ice and permafrost are profoundly affecting species including polar bears and caribou.

Native American groups remain at the forefront of conservation efforts, and many tribes are uniquely positioned to protect wild lands. According to one study, "many tribal lands still represent some of the largest intact habitats . . . in North America," and more than 81,236 square miles of land in the lower 48 states and 62,500 square miles of land in Alaska are controlled by Native American tribes. "Much of this land is relatively undisturbed, providing a significant amount of rare and important fish and wildlife habitat," the authors of the study claim.

CRITICAL VIEWING A grizzly bear fishes for salmon in Alaska's Katmai National Park. To what extent do national parks like this one help reduce the effects of human activities on natural systems and habitats?

Examples abound of Native American tribes working to restore habitats and species. One of the most publicly recognized Native American conservation efforts is the fight to restore the American bison. Historically, the bison had provided a living for numerous tribes on the Great Plains and was important to the tribes' cultural and religious lives. By 1884, as a result of overhunting, only 325 wild bison remained in the United States. Today, organizations such as the Intertribal Buffalo Council (ITBC) work to reintroduce American bison to tribal lands in South Dakota, Montana, Oklahoma, and New Mexico. Currently, the ITBC has 58 member tribes, including the Lakota, Crow, Blackfeet, Ho Chunk, and Choctaw. In 2016, ITBC controlled a herd of more than 15,000 bison spread across 19 states. Emphasizing the cultural and environmental importance of bison, the ITBC asserts, "To re-establish healthy buffalo populations on tribal lands is to re-establish hope for Indian people."

Still, it would be shortsighted to view Native Americans' relationship with the environment as one-dimensional. Like all Americans, Native Americans need to make a living, coping with the demands of modern life while maintaining cultural traditions. In some cases, that means balancing conservation with the use of natural resources to earn money. Members of the Hoopa Valley Tribe in California, for example, have a strong belief in conservation and powerful cultural and religious ties to the species that populate their wooded land. At the same time, cutting and selling trees for timber is necessary for the tribe's economy. Thus, the Hoopa have developed ways to maintain a sustainable logging industry while protecting the forest habitat. Similarly, on the Great Plains, some groups harvest and sell bison meat as a healthier alternative to beef and also work to preserve the wild herds.

Occasionally, tribes' traditional practices bring them into conflict with environmental organizations. The Makah Indians in Washington State had been whaling for more than 1,000 years when they stopped in 1929, in the face of a declining whale population. In 1999, they resumed hunting, having been authorized by the government to take five whales a year. The Makah argue that whaling is central to their culture and traditions. They also point to the Treaty of Neah Bay, signed in 1855, which granted whaling rights to the Makah in exchange for tribal lands.

THE GREAT LAW OF PEACE

The Iroquois Confederacy was bound by a constitution that had existed for centuries before the first Europeans arrived. In the present day, it is known by different names, including the Great Law of Peace. In pre-contact times, the constitution was transmitted by oral tradition.

One passage in the constitution has, in recent years, been used to form the basis of an idea called seven-generation sustainability, or the seventh-generation principle. The concept, supported by many environmentalists and other scientists, is that humans should make decisions about natural resources with the fate of our seventh-generation descendants in mind. Today's decisions, in other words, should lead to healthy, sustainable ecosystems for many generations to come.

PRIMARY SOURCE

In all of your deliberations in the Confederate Council, in your efforts at lawmaking, in all your official acts, self-interest shall be cast into oblivion. Cast not over your shoulder behind you the warnings of the nephews and nieces should they chide you for any error or wrong you may do, but return to the way of the Great Law which is just and right. Look and listen for the welfare of the whole people and have always in view not only the present but also the coming generations, even those whose faces are yet beneath the surface of the ground—the unborn of the future Nation.

—from the Constitution of the Iroquois Nations

Environmentalists argue that certain gray whale groups are nearly depleted, and whaling by the Makah could threaten their dwindling numbers. Some also criticize the Makah for using modern technology, in addition to traditional tools, to kill whales.

In 2000, former Tribal Council Chairman Ben Johnson summed up the frustration many Native Americans feel about stereotypes that would simplify Native American culture and freeze it in time. "Times change and we have to change with the times," he said. "[People] want us to be back in the primitive times. We just want to practice our culture."

11.11.5 Trace the impact of, need for, and controversies associated with environmental conservation, expansion of the national park system, and the development of environmental protection laws, with particular attention to the interaction between environmental protection advocates and property rights advocates; CST 4 Students relate current events to the physical and human characteristics of places and regions.

AMERICAN STORIES

THE DAKOTA ACCESS PIPELINE

In 2016, an environmental protest placed the Standing Rock Sioux tribe in headlines across the country. The Sioux were fighting the construction of the Dakota Access Pipeline (DAPL) beneath the Missouri River on land that is adjacent to the Standing Rock Reservation in North Dakota. The DAPL is a 1,170-mile-long underground pipeline intended to transport oil from fields in North Dakota to southern Illinois, where it can be shipped to refineries. The $3.7 billion project is financed by a private company.

The Standing Rock Sioux object to the pipeline on both cultural and environmental grounds. They claim construction will disrupt sacred tribal burial sites and believe that if the DAPL suffers an oil spill, it will permanently contaminate the Missouri River, the reservation's principal source of water. Protesters claim the land through which the pipeline runs is in fact Sioux land, deeded to them in the Treaty of Fort Laramie in 1851. Since 1851, the government has taken much of the land, but the treaty was never nullified.

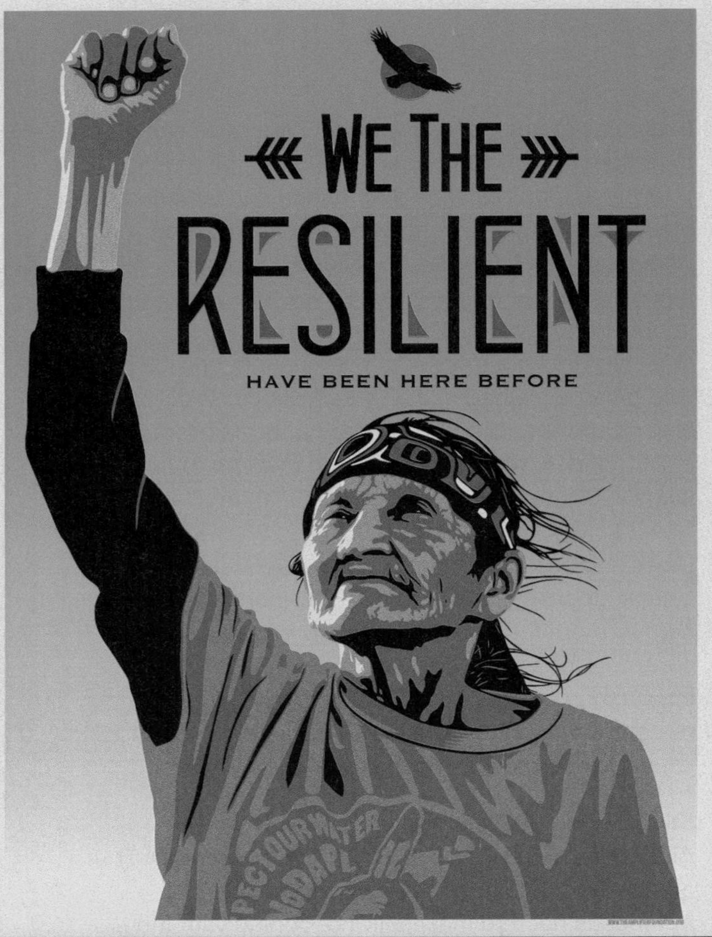

In 2016, artist-activists collaborated with photographers to create a series of images, including this one by Ernesto Yerena, that capture the shared humanity of our diverse America.

In spring of 2016, tribe members set up a camp on the reservation in North Dakota and publicized their mission statement, stating: "Our goal is to peacefully and prayerfully defend our rights, and rise up as one to sustain Mother Earth and her inhabitants." Protests staged from the camp were largely peaceful, although some clashes with police did occur. Environmentalists, celebrities, and others joined the Standing Rock Sioux in their protests. Many others used donations or social media to express their support. For example, in November 2016, when the rumor circulated that police officers were using Facebook check-ins to track the locations of protesters, more than 1 million people across the United States "checked in" at the Standing Rock Reservation.

On the other side of the issue, many Americans favor the construction of the DAPL, which some claim has created thousands of jobs—the reason the pipeline is supported by several labor unions. Others believe transporting oil through a pipeline is much safer than using trucks, tankers, and trains. Experts debate the relative safety of moving oil through pipelines, and a major leak discovered in 2016 in an older North Dakota pipeline added to safety concerns about the new one.

At the end of 2016, the matter of the Dakota Access Pipeline was still unsettled. In November 2016, the Army Corps of Engineers, which must approve the project, determined "additional discussion and analysis are warranted in light of the history of the Great Sioux Nation's dispossessions of lands, the importance of Lake Oahe to the Tribe, our government-to-government relationship, and the statute governing easements through government property." In December, the Army denied a permit to complete the project and said it would continue its environmental impact study.

ANALYZE ENVIRONMENTAL CONCEPTS

What decisions have Native American groups faced in terms of resources and natural systems, and how did those factors influence the groups' actions?

11.8.6 Discuss the diverse environmental regions of North America, their relationship to local economies, and the origins and prospects of environmental problems in those regions.

NATIONAL GEOGRAPHIC

RESTORING THE RIO GRANDE

In September 2016, National Geographic Freshwater Fellow Sandra Postel reported on an innovative collaboration between Native American tribes and Audubon New Mexico, a conservation society, to restore flow to the Rio Grande. Even though the Rio Grande is the second largest river in the Southwest, parts of it dry up in the summer as water is diverted for irrigation and other purposes. This is alarming to water conservationists like Postel because the Rio Grande supports numerous native fish and birds, including some listed as threatened or endangered.

National Geographic Freshwater Fellow (2009–2015) Sandra Postel

Seeking to restore some of the river's flow, Audubon New Mexico asked Native American groups in the Middle Rio Grande Valley to contribute a portion of the water they receive from the river through allocations. In exchange, Audubon committed to use the water for the river's benefit and to seek funding to restore river habitats on tribal lands. The Sandia, Isleta, Santa Ana, and Cochiti Pueblos agreed, transferring over 130 million gallons of water to Audubon New Mexico. With contributions from another user, the total water donation came to more than 260 million gallons.

The water was stored in a reservoir and released at strategic locations during the summer of 2016. At the same time, the Pueblos and Audubon New Mexico worked to plant trees and restore habitats along the river's banks. Postel praised the partnership between Native American groups and an environmental organization to save the threatened Rio Grande. "River by river," she wrote, "the movement of water stewardship and restoration we are working to build is growing."

CRITICAL VIEWING Why is cooperation among tribes and outside agencies important in achieving environmental goals such as the restoration of the Rio Grande, shown below?

11.11.5 Trace the impact of, need for, and controversies associated with environmental conservation, expansion of the national park system, and the development of environmental protection laws, with particular attention to the interaction between environmental protection advocates and property rights advocates; HI 5 Students analyze human modifications of landscapes and examine the resulting environmental policy issues.

1.1 **MAIN IDEA** During his first term as president, Bill Clinton pursued domestic and social reforms and faced growing opposition from Republicans.

Moderate Reform Under Bill Clinton

In 1963, a 16-year-old boy named Bill Clinton visited the White House and shook hands with President John F. Kennedy. Afterward, the boy told his friends that he would have Kennedy's job someday. Three decades later, Clinton became the country's 42nd president.

THE 1992 ELECTION

In February of 1992, President George H.W. Bush announced plans to run for a second term on the Republican Party ticket. A year earlier, he might have seemed unbeatable. However, as you have read, his approval rating had dropped sharply as the result of an economic recession.

Arkansas governor Bill Clinton emerged on the Democratic side as Bush's challenger in the presidential election. For his vice-presidential running mate, Clinton went against political wisdom by selecting another southerner: Senator Al Gore of Tennessee, who had championed many environmental issues in Congress. Clinton campaigned as a "New Democrat," or a moderate member of the party who supported more conservative economic policies than many other Democrats.

As governor, Clinton boasted a strong record in education, civil rights, and economic growth in Arkansas. His critics attacked his character, however, claiming that Clinton, a married man, had had extramarital affairs and

Clinton addresses a rally in front of the courthouse in Carthage, Tennessee, during the 1992 campaign. Gore, along with his wife and children, stand behind Clinton. Growing up, Gore spent his summers working on his family's farm in Carthage.

evaded the draft during the Vietnam War. The legality of some of his business dealings was also questioned.

Disappointed by the Bush-Clinton matchup, many voters—especially Republicans—wanted an alternative. They got one when a Texas computer billionaire named **H. Ross Perot** threw his hat into the ring. Plainspoken and tough-talking, Perot argued that professional politicians lacked the will to tackle the country's most difficult problems. His popularity soared, and he briefly moved ahead of Bush and Clinton in the polls. However, with the Republican base split between Bush and Perot, Clinton won on election day.

Among Clinton's domestic reforms was the Brady Handgun Violence Prevention Act, passed by Congress in 1993. James Brady (left), President Ronald Reagan's press secretary, was shot in the head and left partially paralyzed in the assassination attempt against the president in 1981. After the shooting, Brady and his wife worked tirelessly to promote handgun legislation. The act helped block the sale of an estimated one million guns to dangerous criminals.

DOMESTIC REFORMS

Upon taking office, President Clinton focused on domestic policy. To slash the massive federal budget deficit he had inherited from his predecessor, Clinton proposed an economic package that combined tax increases and spending cuts. He lobbied hard to win support for the plan, and in August 1993, it squeaked through Congress. Other initiatives of the early Clinton administration included the expansion of federal support for housing and nutritional programs aimed at assisting low-income families and addressing the persistence of poverty.

Clinton's most ambitious domestic goal was to overhaul the country's health care system to ensure that all Americans had access to quality, affordable care. Nearly 40 million Americans at that time lacked health insurance, and the costs of medical care were rising at an alarming rate. Just days into his presidency, Clinton created a **task force**, or group organized for a special mission, to reform the health care system. He appointed his wife, Hillary Clinton, to lead it. Mrs. Clinton, an accomplished lawyer, had advocated for children and education as first lady of Arkansas. During the 1992 campaign, Clinton had told the public that, with his election, they would get "two for the price of one," meaning that his wife would play an active role in his administration.

By September 1993, Mrs. Clinton and the task force had developed a proposal called the Health Security Act, which called for universal health coverage, managed care, and a restructured health insurance industry. The proposal met with fierce opposition from insurance companies, small-business organizations, the American Medical Association, and Congress. The "Clinton Health Plan," as it was known, failed to be adopted.

SOCIAL CHANGES

President Clinton also dealt with important social issues. In fact, the first bill he signed into law was the Family and Medical Leave Act, which Bush had vetoed twice. Designed to help employees balance work and family life, the act allowed workers to take up to 12 weeks of unpaid, job-protected leave each year to care for newborn or newly adopted children or seriously ill family members.

The growing activism and prominence of lesbian, gay, bisexual, and transgender (LGBT) groups resulted in further social change. In 1974, a politician and LGBT activist named **Elaine Noble** had won election to the Massachusetts House of Representatives, becoming the first openly lesbian or gay person ever elected to a state legislature. As you may remember, three years later, voters in San Francisco elected a community leader and openly gay activist named Harvey Milk to the city's Board of Supervisors.

In 1992, the year Clinton was elected, the AIDS epidemic remained one of the most critical issues affecting the LGBT community. That year, AIDS became the number one cause of death for

11.11.7 Explain how the federal, state, and local governments have responded to demographic and social changes such as population shifts to the suburbs, racial concentrations in the cities, Frostbelt-to-Sunbelt migration, international migration, decline of family farms, increases in out-of-wedlock births, and drug abuse.

The worst act of domestic terrorism in American history occurred during Clinton's presidency. On the morning of April 19, 1995, a truck bomb exploded at the Alfred P. Murrah Federal Building in Oklahoma City, Oklahoma, killing 168 people, including 19 children, and injuring more than 500. The bombing was carried out by Timothy McVeigh, an antigovernment activist and Persian Gulf War veteran. He was convicted and executed for the crime in 2001.

The Outdoor Symbolic Memorial, part of the Oklahoma City National Memorial, is located where the Murrah Federal Building once stood. Symbolic elements in the memorial include the Field of Empty Chairs, shown here, which contains 168 chairs, one for each victim. Two gates at the entrance to the memorial are carved with the times 9:01 and 9:03, indicating the minute before and after the attack.

American men between the ages of 25 and 44. A disproportionate number of the disease's victims were gay men. The Clinton administration responded to the crisis by establishing the Presidential Advisory Council on HIV/AIDS and by dramatically increasing government funding for AIDS research, prevention, and treatment.

Clinton was the first major presidential candidate to court the gay vote. Shortly after taking office, he reaffirmed a controversial campaign vow to overturn the U.S. military's longstanding ban on homosexuals. Top military leaders wanted to keep the ban, as did many members of Congress, including Senator Sam Nunn of Georgia, the powerful chairman of the Senate Armed Services Committee.

In July 1993, Clinton announced a compromise policy that came to be known as "Don't Ask, Don't Tell." Under the new policy, homosexuals would be allowed to serve in the military as long as they kept their sexual orientation to themselves. But Clinton's support for gay rights had limits. In 1996, he took a stand against same-sex marriage by signing the **Defense of Marriage Act (DOMA)**. This law defined marriage as "a legal union between one man and one woman," and it denied same-sex couples the federal benefits, privileges, and recognition that opposite-sex couples received. Clinton's stand left many of his gay supporters feeling betrayed.

THE REPUBLICAN REVOLUTION

Meanwhile, Republican opponents began to investigate the Clintons' purchase in the late 1970s of a real estate development in Arkansas known as **Whitewater** and charged the couple with financial wrongdoing. In early 1994, the U.S. attorney general appointed a special prosecutor to look into their role in what came to be known as the Whitewater scandal. The resulting inquiry spanned about 6 years and cost more than $50 million, but investigators failed to find sufficient evidence to charge the Clintons with any crime.

The president's rivals had greater success when they challenged him politically. In the 1992 election, Democrats had retained their majorities in both houses of Congress. This political landscape shifted dramatically in 1994, however, after the midterm congressional elections. The Republicans won a sweeping victory, gaining control of both the Senate and the House of Representatives for the first time in four decades. **Newton "Newt" Gingrich**, a congressman from Georgia, became Speaker of the House. Before the elections, Gingrich had co-authored a document called a **Contract with America**, which promised tax cuts for the middle class, strong anticrime legislation, and constitutional amendments requiring a balanced budget and term limits for members of Congress.

When Congress reconvened in January 1995, the House Republicans immediately began to push the legislation detailed in the contract through Congress. Some of the measures eventually passed into law, including a major welfare reform law called the Personal Responsibility and Work Opportunity Reconciliation Act of 1996. This legislation required welfare recipients to work after receiving benefits for two years, limited the time they could stay on welfare, and shifted much of the responsibility for social welfare administration from the federal government to the states. Critics argued that the act destroyed the safety net that protected the country's neediest and most vulnerable citizens. Still, many of the measures proposed by the House were rejected by the Senate or vetoed by Clinton.

The 1994 midterm elections seemed to make Clinton's re-election in 1996 unlikely, but missteps on the part of Republicans in 1995 helped the president regain popularity. One of these errors occurred toward the end of the year when the White House and Congress became deadlocked over the federal budget. Rather than negotiate, Gingrich and other members of the GOP majority in the House shut down the government. They hoped this action would pressure the White House into agreeing with their position. The strategy backfired when the public blamed the Republicans for the budget impasse. By early January 1996, the government had resumed normal operations.

HISTORICAL THINKING

1. **READING CHECK** How did H. Ross Perot's candidacy affect the 1992 presidential election?
2. **ANALYZE CAUSE AND EFFECT** Describe the causes that may have led to the Republicans gaining control of both the Senate and House of Representatives in 1994.
3. **EXPLAIN** How did the government respond to social changes during the Clinton administration? Provide examples from the text.
4. **DRAW CONCLUSIONS** How did the persistence of poverty influence the social policies of President Clinton?

11.11.6 Analyze the persistence of poverty and how different analyses of this issue influence welfare reform, health insurance reform, and other social policies; HI 2 Students recognize the complexity of historical causes and effects, including the limitations on determining cause and effect.

1.2 **MAIN IDEA** Globalization and immigration were key issues during the presidency of Bill Clinton.

GLOBALIZATION AND IMMIGRATION

"Nothing is permanent except change." In the 1990s, this saying might have rung truer than ever. The world was shrinking, and everything seemed to be in a state of flux. What would all this change mean for Americans?

GLOBALIZED BUSINESS

During the Clinton presidency, **globalization**, or the faster and freer flow of people, resources, goods, and ideas across national borders, had a powerful effect on the United States. Through trade, investments, migration, and the rapid sharing of information, countries and people around the world became increasingly interconnected.

Globalization had a profound impact on U.S. manufacturing. Many American companies began moving their operations to Mexico, where lower labor costs meant they could produce goods for less money. In time, some companies moved their operations from Mexico to China and then to smaller nations such as Bangladesh, to take advantage of even lower labor costs. These shifts resulted in falling prices for many goods that Americans consumed. However, producing these goods outside of the United States also led to **job dislocations**, or the movement of jobs to other places. These dislocations caused many Americans to lose their jobs.

Some American businesses, including computer software, retail, and automobile companies, have fared well in the globalized world. These industries established research centers and factories abroad and expanded their businesses in European, Asian, and African markets. American industrial leaders also recruited the best and the brightest from around the world to work in their companies.

THE UNITED STATES AND MEXICO

The growth of world trade in the second half of the 20th century came largely as a result of international trade agreements. In 1947, as you may recall, 23 countries signed the General Agreement on Tariffs and Trade (GATT), whose purpose was to reduce tariffs and other trade barriers so that countries could trade more freely with one another. In 1994, the World Trade Organization (WTO) replaced GATT. The WTO strives to set and enforce rules for trade, resolve trade disputes, ensure that developing countries benefit from the growth in international trade, and continue to support free trade.

The success of the European Economic Community—which, as you know, formed in 1958—prompted leaders in North America to consider creating a similar union. In 1988, the United States and Canada signed a free-trade pact that called for the elimination of most trade barriers. Then, in 1992, the United States, Canada, and Mexico ceremonially signed the **North American Free Trade Agreement (NAFTA)**. In the United States, George H.W. Bush had proposed and led the fight for the agreement during his presidency. NAFTA played a central role in fostering close relationships among the three countries and created the world's largest trading bloc.

The economic ties between the United States and Mexico had begun to deepen after the Cold War ended. These ties were strengthened by manufacturing plants called *maquiladoras* (mah-kee-luh-DOOR-uhz), which were established along the border between the United States and Mexico in the 1960s. A **maquiladora** is a plant located in an export-processing zone. A plant in this zone imports materials and then uses them to manufacture products for export. The plants allow

Many American workers and labor unions united in their opposition to NAFTA. When a bill was proposed in 1997 that would require Congress to vote yes or no on a trade agreement submitted by a president within 90 days, these Maryland steelworkers protested. The legislation was defeated.

U.S. companies to take advantage of low labor costs in Mexico. In addition, maquiladoras operate as **free-enterprise zones**, which allow the suspension of both Mexican and U.S. tax and custom laws. As a result, goods flowed between the two countries at freer and faster rates from the 1980s through the 2000s.

In the early 1990s, Mexico prepared for **integration**, or the process of joining economic forces, with the United States and Canada under NAFTA by instituting a series of economic reforms. One of these called for communally owned farms in the southern Mexico state of Chiapas to be privatized, or transferred from public to private ownership. In response, an armed uprising called the **Chiapas Rebellion** took place in 1994. The rebellion was launched by a revolutionary force made up of local, rural people called Zapatistas (zah-puh-TEES-tuhz). They called for "a world in which many worlds fit," not a mono, or single, world with no space for them. Their response was an example of **disintegration**, or the endurance of nationalist, tribalist, and separatist alternatives to globalization.

Implementation of NAFTA was and continues to be controversial on both sides of the border. In the United States, critics feared the agreement would cause the country to lose even more manufacturing jobs to Mexico. And although it is true that the United States did lose some jobs, the loss was not as large as

PRIMARY SOURCE

Before Clinton signed NAFTA into law in 1993, the president addressed those assembled to witness the signing. In this excerpt from his speech, Clinton explains how he thinks NAFTA will benefit the United States and the world.

I believe we have made a decision now that will permit us to create an economic order in the world that will promote more growth, more equality, better preservation of the environment, and a greater possibility of world peace. We are on the verge of a global economic expansion that is sparked by the fact that the United States at this critical moment decided that we would compete, not retreat.

—from President William Clinton's remarks on the signing of NAFTA, December 8, 1993

11.9.7 Examine relations between the United States and Mexico in the twentieth century, including key economic, political, immigration, and environmental issues; 11.11.2 Discuss the significant domestic policy speeches of Truman, Eisenhower, Kennedy, Johnson, Nixon, Carter, Reagan, Bush, and Clinton (e.g., with regard to education, civil rights, economic policy, environmental policy).

some critics had predicted. Still, tensions remain on issues related to economic regulation, labor conditions, increased immigration from Mexico, and damage to the environment. However, on the plus side, trade between the United States and Mexico has grown dramatically since NAFTA. A huge increase in exports bolstered Mexico's economy, and a similar increase in imports gave Mexican consumers access to lower-priced, better-quality goods. The borderland between the United States and Mexico is the scene of dynamic interactions in work, commerce, and culture.

NEW IMMIGRATION PATTERNS

As you've read, many critics of NAFTA were concerned that the agreement would result in a rise in the number of Mexican immigrants. The Immigration Act of 1965 had already liberalized country-of-origin policies by opening the United States to people of all nationalities. The act emphasized family reunification by giving special preference to relatives of immigrants who were already citizens of the United States. The new policy soon brought about major demographic and social changes. The U.S. population became increasingly diverse as immigration increased and newcomers arrived from all parts of the world. Immigration from Mexico jumped dramatically, from approximately 575,000 Mexicans in 1960 to more than 4 million in 1990.

As legal immigration to the United States increased, so did illegal immigration. Many of the people who crossed the border illegally—without proper documentation—came from Mexico or Central America in search of work and a better future. Illegal immigration emerged as a major issue in the 1990s, especially in states along the U.S.-Mexico border. Many people felt that these undocumented immigrants took jobs away from Americans, caused crime rates to rise, and took advantage of the country's social services without paying taxes. In 1996, Congress addressed the flood of illegal immigrants by allocating funds for increased border security.

People in some states bordering Mexico also took steps against illegal immigration. For example, in 1994, California voters approved **Proposition 187**, a controversial ballot measure that denied illegal immigrants state services such as public education

During the 1994 Chiapas Rebellion against NAFTA, a man known as "Subcomandante Marcos" (shown below wearing a black mask) led the Zapatistas. His army, consisting mostly of poor Maya farmers, briefly occupied several towns before agreeing to a truce with the Mexican government.

11.10.2 Examine and analyze the key events, policies, and court cases in the evolution of civil rights, including *Dred Scott* v. *Sandford*, *Plessy* v. *Ferguson*, *Brown* v. *Board of Education*, *Regents of the University of California* v. *Bakke*, and California Proposition 209; 11.11.1 Discuss the reasons for the nation's changing immigration policy, with emphasis on how the Immigration Act of 1965 and successor acts have transformed American society.

Vendors at the Little Saigon Night Market in Westminster, California, grill fresh fish and other street food in this 2015 photo. These open-air stalls are common in Vietnam, and immigrants brought the tradition to the United States. Night markets have sprung up across the country.

and health care. All but one provision of Proposition 187 was blocked by federal courts throughout the 1990s, but other anti-immigrant measures soon followed. **Proposition 209**, which won approval in 1996, prohibited state-supported affirmative action that was intended to help minority groups suffering from discrimination. Two years later came **Proposition 227**, which banned bilingual education in California's public schools.

Major world events also affected immigration patterns in the last decades of the 20th century. As you've learned, the end of the Vietnam War in 1975 brought hundreds of thousands of refugees from Vietnam and neighboring Southeast Asian countries to the United States. Immigration from Vietnam continued to grow as relatives sought to join family members who had arrived earlier. Similarly, the 1979 Islamic Revolution in Iran drove a large influx of Iranians to U.S. shores.

The United States has always been made up of people from many different cultures. However, the growing diversity of the U.S. population led to debate over the concept of multiculturalism. In the early 1990s, conservatives accused liberals of using multiculturalism to divide society into conflicting groups, limit free speech on campuses by suppressing conservative views, and reject traditional Western culture. Liberals countered that multiculturalism was necessary to tackle problems that arise as our society becomes more diverse.

As Clinton dealt with globalization and immigration, he also concentrated on seeking a second term as president. He would be aided in achieving this goal by the country's strong economy. Clinton's second four years, however, would not be smooth sailing.

HISTORICAL THINKING

1. **READING CHECK** Why did some American companies move to Mexico, China, and Bangladesh?
2. **COMPARE AND CONTRAST** What have been some of the advantages and disadvantages of NAFTA?
3. **FORM AND SUPPORT OPINIONS** Based on what you have read in this lesson, do you think globalization is a good thing? Support your opinion with evidence from the text.
4. **SUMMARIZE** How did the federal government and California voters respond to international migration in the 1990s?

11.11.7 Explain how the federal, state, and local governments have responded to demographic and social changes such as population shifts to the suburbs, racial concentrations in the cities, Frostbelt-to-Sunbelt migration, international migration, decline of family farms, increases in out-of-wedlock births, and drug abuse.

1.3 **MAIN IDEA** The economy remained robust during Clinton's second term, but scandals and an impeachment trial plagued his presidency.

ECONOMIC BOOM AND SCANDALS

Websites, blogs, Wi-Fi, and social media are part of everyday life today, but before the technology boom of the 1990s, they were all but unknown. They all have to do with the Internet, which fueled major cultural changes and big economic growth.

SECOND-TERM ACCOMPLISHMENTS

After Clinton defeated Republican candidate Robert Dole and Reform Party candidate H. Ross Perot in the 1996 election, the nation's economy continued to improve. Unemployment fell from 5.4 to 4.9 percent in 1997, and by 2000, it had dropped to 4 percent—the lowest level in three decades. The stock market soared to record levels, and inflation fell. In 1998, the president presented the first balanced budget since 1969. The federal government took in more money than it spent in 1998 and in each of the next three years, allowing for a rare budget surplus. With Americans enjoying plentiful jobs and stable prices, a sense of optimism swept the nation and kept Clinton's job approval ratings around 60 percent.

One of the main forces driving this strong economic growth was the rise of the Internet and the rapid development of companies that took advantage of this revolutionary new mode of information-sharing. The result was a "dot-com" boom in the stock market, named for the suffix of most corporate web pages. Investors poured money into the stocks of Internet-related companies, and entrepreneurs who started popular social media and commercial websites became millionaires almost overnight. The center of this rapid growth in technology was California's Silicon Valley where, as you know, the personal computer was developed.

In his second term, as in his first, Clinton pursued an agenda of moderate domestic reforms. Addressing Americans' concerns about the soaring costs of higher education, for example, he proposed and signed a bill calling for tax breaks, tuition grants, and scholarships to help working- and middle-class families pay for college. In foreign policy matters, Clinton led efforts to expand the North Atlantic Treaty Organization (NATO) by bringing in former communist countries in Eastern Europe. In 1995, during his first term, Clinton had worked to bring about a cease-fire among warring Serbs, Croats, and Bosnians in the Balkans, a mountainous region in Eastern Europe that was once part of Yugoslavia. In 1999, Clinton authorized NATO to carry out air strikes against Serbia to end its mass killing of ethnic Albanians in the Serbian province of Kosovo. Clinton's administration also played an important role in implementing the **Oslo Accords**, which were aimed at ending the decades-long conflict between the Israelis and Palestinians.

The Dot-Com Boom, 1995–2004

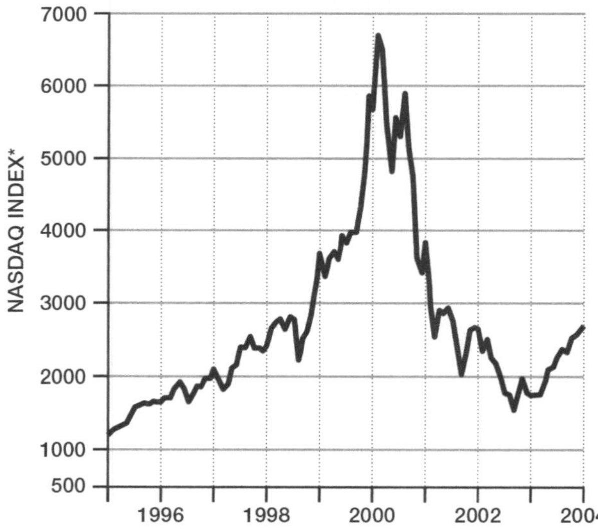

Source: Federal Reserve Bank of St. Louis

* The NASDAQ is a stock market of stocks that are traded electronically. The index expresses stocks' values with respect to a 1971 base index of 100.

11.8.7 Describe the effects on society and the economy of technological developments since 1945, including the computer revolution, changes in communication, advances in medicine, and improvements in agricultural technology.

CLINTON'S IMPEACHMENT

While Clinton achieved many political successes during his second term, a serious scandal arose that threatened to end his presidency. In 1994, a former Arkansas state employee named Paula Jones had filed a sexual harassment suit against Clinton, accusing him of unwanted sexual advances. Kenneth Starr, the special prosecutor in charge of the Whitewater inquiry, expanded his investigation to include the Paula Jones case, even though there was no connection between the two. In late 1997, stories began to surface about another sexual relationship, this one between Clinton and a young female White House intern named Monica Lewinsky. Lawyers for Jones subpoenaed Lewinsky as a witness, but in a sworn statement, she denied any relationship with the president. When Clinton testified under oath in the case, he, too, denied the relationship.

However, Starr eventually uncovered strong evidence of sexual encounters between Clinton and Lewinsky. Faced with this evidence, the president testified before a grand jury in August 1998 and admitted to having had "inappropriate intimate contact" with her. The following month, Starr submitted a report to Congress that identified 11 possible grounds on which the president could be impeached, or formally charged with "treason, bribery, or other high crimes and misdemeanors." Impeachment is limited to the president, vice president, and other civil officers of the United States. An official convicted of the charge is removed from office.

According to the Constitution, the House of Representatives votes to impeach an official, while the Senate tries the case. In December 1998, the Republican-controlled House voted largely along party lines to bring two charges against Clinton. The first alleged the president had committed **perjury**, or had lied under oath. The second claimed he had obstructed justice by attempting to hide his relationship with the intern and encouraging her to lie in her sworn statement. The only other president ever to be impeached was Andrew Johnson in 1868.

In January 1999, Clinton's impeachment trial began. After just four weeks of testimony, the Senate voted to acquit Clinton of both charges, having failed to obtain the two-thirds majority needed for conviction. He remained in office, but the scandals and trial damaged his reputation with the American people. As a result, concern over candidates' moral character would have a big impact on the election of 2000.

SPORTS ★ ★ ★ ★ FINAL

DAILY NEWS

$1.00

NEW YORK'S HOMETOWN NEWSPAPER

Sunday, December 20, 1998

IMPEACHED

After being impeached, the President vows to serve until 'the last hour of the last day of my term.

16-PAGE SPECIAL REPORT ON AMERICA'S HISTORIC DAY

The *New York Daily News* ran this special edition of its newspaper on December 20 1998, the day after the House voted to impeach Clinton. Before his acquittal, the president told the American people that he was "profoundly sorry for all I have done wrong in words and deeds."

HISTORICAL THINKING

1. **READING CHECK** What were some of the indicators of the strong economy during Clinton's second term, and how did the Internet play a role?
2. **MAKE INFERENCES** What might the Republicans in Congress have hoped to gain by impeaching President Clinton?
3. **FORM AND SUPPORT OPINIONS** Do you think Clinton's presidency was a success or a failure? Explain your opinion.
4. **INTERPRET GRAPHS** What stock market trend began just after 2000, and what impact did this probably have on Internet-related companies?

MAIN IDEA Although Al Gore won the popular vote, George W. Bush emerged as the winner of the controversial 2000 presidential election.

THE CONTESTED ELECTION OF 2000

Most elections are decided easily: the candidate receiving the most votes is the winner. But as Americans learned in 2000, sometimes U.S. presidential elections are not so straightforward.

THE 2000 CAMPAIGN

During Clinton's impeachment trial, many leading political figures were already looking ahead to the 2000 presidential election—particularly among Republicans. They knew Clinton's scandals had weakened the Democratic Party. By early July 1999, nine Republicans had announced their candidacy. After a long primary battle, the Republican Party nominated Texas governor **George W. Bush**, the eldest son of former president George H.W. Bush.

HANGING CHADS
Many Florida voters used punch-card ballots in the 2000 presidential election. However, a number of voters failed to punch a hole in their card, leaving a fragment of paper, called a "hanging chad," attached. Election officials, like the one shown here, studied the ballots, trying to determine the voter's intent in each instance.

Bush embraced what he called **compassionate conservatism**, a political philosophy that blended traditional conservative ideas about economic policies with a concern for disadvantaged people. He echoed Ronald Reagan's populist stand in the 1980s. Like Reagan, Bush criticized establishment elites and supported a smaller, contracted government and advocated for social programs that promoted traditional family values. He also vowed to restore executive power, which he felt Congress had weakened.

As his vice president, Bush chose Richard Cheney, who had served as secretary of defense under George H.W. Bush. Politically, Cheney was a neoconservative. A **neoconservative**, or "neocon," is someone who strongly supports a free-market economy with few regulations and believes the United States should use its influence and military power to actively promote its ideals and national interests around the world. For example, neocons shared the view that Saddam Hussein, the autocratic president of Iraq, was a destabilizing influence in Southwest Asia (often referred to as the Middle East), one of the world's most troubled regions. Neocons regretted that George H.W. Bush had not removed Hussein from power during the 1990–91 Persian Gulf War. They also believed strongly in what they called **American exceptionalism**—the idea that the United States is superior to other nations due to its history and ideology. As such, neocons claimed the country had a mission to spread democracy and change the world.

On the Democratic side, Vice President Al Gore easily won his party's nomination. In the minds of many Americans, however, Gore had been tarnished by the scandals of the Clinton presidency, and many

CST 1 Students compare the present with the past, evaluating the consequences of past events and decisions and determining the lessons that were learned.

The 2000 Election

Al Gore, Democrat

Electoral Vote: 266 votes, 49.4%

Popular Vote: 50,992,335 votes, 48.4%

George W. Bush, Republican

Electoral Vote: 271 votes, 50.4%

Popular Vote: 50,455,156 votes, 47.9%

Ralph Nader, Green

Popular Vote: 2,882,738 votes, 2.7%

The 2000 election was one of the closest in modern U.S. history. In this photo, candidate Bush shakes hands with supporters at a campaign rally.

voters thought he was arrogant. In televised debates with Bush, Gore sighed, rolled his eyes, and seemed to talk down to his opponent. Ralph Nader ran as the candidate of the Green Party, which supported nonviolence, environmentalism, and social justice. During his candidacy, Nader promoted universal health care and spoke out against the power of big business. Because he drew much of his support from young, liberal, politically independent voters, some people would later claim that Nader took votes away from Gore and cost the vice president the election.

BUSH v. *GORE*

On election day, the voting was very close in many states. By the end of the night, with final and projected counts still being reported, Gore led in the popular vote. Still, neither candidate had yet gained the 270 electoral votes needed to win the election. It became clear that Florida, with 25 electoral votes, would determine the next president.

Shortly after 2 a.m., news outlets began declaring that Bush had won Florida and, therefore, the election. Gore called Bush to concede, or accept, defeat but soon took back his concession when he learned the count in Florida was much closer than had been previously reported. Bush led by fewer than 600 votes, and the gap continued to narrow as the counting continued. Furthermore, Gore's aides had noted irregularities and compromised ballots at polling places in several Democratic counties.

The slimness of the margin called for the application of a Florida law, which required a statewide recount by machine. The recount reduced Bush's lead to 327. Some counties then initiated manual recounts, although the legality of these recounts was challenged in court. The Gore and Bush camps exchanged charges of fraud, manipulation, and the exercise of excessive political pressure throughout November.

In early December, the Florida Supreme Court ordered a manual statewide recount of the roughly 45,000 undervotes—ballots that had not been counted by the voting machines because the voter's intent was unclear. Days later, lawyers for both sides argued the ***Bush* v. *Gore*** case before the U.S. Supreme Court. In a decision that many commentators considered both hasty and biased toward Republicans, the Court declared the Florida Supreme Court's recount order unconstitutional. As a result, Bush became the president-elect. Although Gore had won the nationwide popular vote by more than 500,000 votes, he accepted the outcome as final and conceded the election.

HISTORICAL THINKING

1. **READING CHECK** How could the election of 2000 have taken other directions?
2. **ANALYZE CAUSE AND EFFECT** What impact did the closeness of the election and its controversial results have on the American people and on Bush's authority as president?
3. **FORM AND SUPPORT OPINIONS** Based on past elections, including the 2000 election, do you think American voters should directly elect the president, or do you think the current system is fine as it is? Explain your answer.

HI 4 Students understand the meaning, implication, and impact of historical events and recognize that events could have taken other directions.

2.2 **MAIN IDEA** On September 11, 2001, the United States suffered a series of deadly attacks by terrorists associated with an Islamic extremist group.

SEPTEMBER 11, 2001

A list of the darkest dates in U.S. history would certainly include April 12, 1861, the day the Civil War broke out, and December 7, 1941, when Japanese warplanes attacked Pearl Harbor. It would also include September 11, 2001, the day of the deadliest terrorist attacks ever on American soil.

UNDER ATTACK

As Americans went about their normal routines on the morning of Tuesday, September 11, 2001, news outlets reported an odd event in New York City. At 8:46 a.m., an airplane crashed into one of the twin 110-story towers of the World Trade Center in the city's downtown financial district. Smoke and flames billowed out of a gaping hole near the top of the north tower, and firefighters and police officers rushed to the scene. At first, many people assumed the crash had been an accident. Seventeen minutes later, however, people around the country looked on in disbelief as news cameras filmed another large jetliner slamming into the south tower. There could no longer be any question: the United States was under attack by terrorists.

The Federal Aviation Administration (FAA) immediately ordered all takeoffs to be halted at U.S. airports. Airplanes in the air were directed to land at the nearest airport. Minutes after the FAA issued this order, another plane crashed into the Pentagon, the headquarters of the U.S. Department of Defense, near Washington, D.C. Soon news came that a fourth airplane had crashed. This one was not flown into a building, however. It plunged into a field in a rural area of southwestern Pennsylvania. Passengers onboard the plane had struggled with the terrorists and prevented the aircraft from hitting its intended target, believed to have been the White House or the U.S. Capitol Building.

The attacks ended with the fourth crash, but there were more horrors to come. Around 10 a.m., as emergency responders worked desperately to evacuate the World Trade Center and battle the fires that engulfed it, the south tower collapsed. The collapse created a thick cloud of dust in the air that spread outward in every direction. Less than a half hour later, the north tower collapsed. The site of the collapsed towers became known as Ground Zero. In the hours after the attack, people with missing loved ones began gathering at the site, hoping desperately for good news. "Missing" posters soon covered walls, lampposts, and store windows in the area.

Over the next few days, authorities pieced together the story of the attacks. Nineteen terrorists, divided into groups of four or five, had boarded four

National September 11 Memorial Museum, New York City

The New York firefighter who wore this helmet on 9/11 was last seen carrying a woman from the north tower lobby when the building collapsed on top of them. His helmet, partially melted by the heat in the tower after it was hit, is one of thousands of artifacts on display in the museum.

The day after the attack on the World Trade Center, firefighters, city workers, members of the National Guard, and others began searching the wreckage for the bodies of victims, as well as any possible survivors.

commercial airplanes—two in Boston, one in Newark, New Jersey, and one in Washington, D.C. All four planes were originally scheduled to fly to the West Coast, so they were carrying full fuel tanks. After takeoff, the terrorists seized control of each airplane, perhaps using box cutters as weapons. They then piloted the planes toward targets selected for their symbolic significance. On the fourth airplane, however, the passengers and crew had learned about the other plane crashes and, as you've read, fought back.

Authorities believed the terrorists were linked to **al Qaeda** (al KY-duh), an Islamic extremist organization founded in the late 1980s. A Saudi Arabian militant named **Osama bin Laden** led this group from his base in Afghanistan. There, al Qaeda was protected and supported by the **Taliban**, an ultraconservative Islamic group that had gained control of much of the country. Determined to bring an end to U.S. influence in Southwest Asia, bin Laden employed **terrorism**, or the use of violent acts and threats to achieve a political goal, as his principal tactic. He had masterminded other attacks against the United States, including the 1998 bombing of U.S. embassies in Kenya and Tanzania, which left 224 people dead, and the 2000 bombing in Yemen of a U.S. warship called the U.S.S. *Cole*, which killed 17 sailors. The September 11, 2001, attacks were far deadlier. About 2,750 people were killed in New York City alone. The death toll at the Pentagon was 184, and the plane crash in Pennsylvania claimed 40 lives.

THE NATION UNITES

The September 11 attacks left Americans feeling profoundly sad, angry, and vulnerable. But the attacks also drew Americans together. In his first months in office, George W. Bush had governed a deeply divided populace. Increasingly, Americans saw their country as split between Democrats and Republicans. The public was also divided over the tax cuts passed by the president and the Republican-controlled Congress. Democrats claimed the tax cuts mainly benefited the wealthy.

However, 9/11, as the day of the terrorist attacks came to be called, inspired strong feelings of patriotism that united all Americans. The night of the attacks, Bush addressed the country saying, "These [terrorist] acts shattered steel, but they cannot dent the steel of American resolve." Many Americans displayed the flag or wore flag pins. People in countries around the world also condemned the attacks and expressed their solidarity with the United States. On September 12, a French newspaper declared, "We are all Americans."

AMERICAN PLACES

The Freedom Tower New York City

The Freedom Tower, also known as One World Trade Center, is the main building of the rebuilt World Trade Center complex and opened in 2014. At a symbolic 1,776 feet tall, the office building is the tallest in the Western Hemisphere. The tower stands before the 9/11 Memorial, shown in the foreground of this photo. Bronze panels inscribed with the names of the terrorists' victims edge two reflecting pools that sit within the footprints of the original twin towers.

11.9.4 List the effects of foreign policy on domestic policies and vice versa (e.g., protests during the war in Vietnam, the "nuclear freeze" movement); HI 1 Students show the connections, causal and otherwise, between particular historical events and larger social, economic, and political trends and developments.

Stories of heroism, sacrifice, and resilience during and after the attacks also drew people together. Many of the stories involved firefighters, police, and other first responders who had rushed bravely into the burning towers of the World Trade Center and led countless people to safety. But when the towers collapsed, more than 400 of the responders lost their own lives. Thousands more later developed severe health problems related to the smoke and toxic dust they inhaled. The collapse of the twin towers released dust containing high levels of lead, mercury, asbestos, and other harmful substances.

The mayor of New York City, Rudy Giuliani, also emerged as a hero. The calm, courage, and humanity he showed after the attacks helped comfort distressed New Yorkers. He spoke with many rescue workers and grieving families and, as victims were buried, attended as many as five funerals a day.

THE AFTERMATH

In the wake of the attacks, U.S. foreign policy, especially on the Middle East, underwent great change. The Bush administration shifted its focus from rival superpowers Russia and China to the connections between terrorist groups such as al Qaeda and **rogue states**. These states included countries, such as Iraq, Iran, and North Korea, that were perceived to violate international law and threaten world peace. Government officials suspected some rogue states of possessing **weapons of mass destruction (WMD)**, or weapons that use nuclear, chemical, or biological substances to harm large numbers of people.

Domestically, the attacks led to a dramatic increase in governmental vigilance. New laws passed during the Bush administration strengthened border and airport security and tightened screening of international travelers. The **USA Patriot Act** greatly expanded the government's powers to conduct surveillance on its own citizens. The act allowed federal agencies to tap the phones of those suspected of terrorist activity. Critics argued that the new policies focusing on national security and defense impinged upon Americans' civil liberties, especially freedom of speech and protection from unreasonable search and seizure.

The attacks also resulted in a rise in hate crimes against Muslims. Although the attacks had been carried out by an Islamic extremist group, some Americans blamed all Muslims for 9/11. Hate crimes were also carried out against those believed to be Muslims—notably Sikhs. Within days of the attacks, a Sikh gas station owner in Arizona, who had just donated $75 to help 9/11 victims, was shot by a man who had announced his intention to kill Muslims.

Following September 11, the Bush administration embraced the idea of taking pre-emptive, or preventive, military action against countries that harbored or actively supported terrorist groups. In a nationally broadcast speech before Congress 10 days after the attacks, Bush promised a "war on terror." Addressing the leaders of the Taliban, he made a non-negotiable demand: "Deliver to United States authorities all the leaders of al Qaeda who hide in your land." Bush went on to say that if the Taliban refused to hand over the terrorists, the Islamic group would "share in their fate." The president soon took steps to make good on this threat.

PRIMARY SOURCE

In a speech to Congress after the 9/11 attacks, Bush addressed Muslims everywhere. Note that the term *Allah* used in the speech is an Arabic word Muslims use to refer to God.

I also want to speak tonight directly to Muslims throughout the world. We respect your faith. It's practiced freely by many millions of Americans and by millions more in countries that America counts as friends. Its teachings are good and peaceful, and those who commit evil in the name of Allah blaspheme [insult] the name of Allah. The terrorists are traitors to their own faith, trying, in effect, to hijack Islam itself. The enemy of America is not our many Muslim friends. It is not our many Arab friends. Our enemy is a radical network of terrorists and every government that supports them.

—from George W. Bush's presidential address to Congress, September 20, 2001

HISTORICAL THINKING

1. **READING CHECK** How did foreign and domestic policies change after the 9/11 attacks?
2. **MAKE INFERENCES** Al Qaeda chose its targets for their symbolic value. What do you think the World Trade Center symbolized?
3. **FORM AND SUPPORT OPINIONS** Does the Patriot Act protect U.S. citizens or violate their civil liberties? Research both arguments to formulate a response.
4. **MAKE CONNECTIONS** How do the events leading up to and following 9/11 relate to the U.S. Middle East policy at the time? Use information from this chapter and other sources to explain.

11.9.6 Describe U.S. Middle East policy and its strategic, political, and economic interests, including those related to the Gulf War.

2.3 **MAIN IDEA** Bush's war on terror led the United States and its allies to launch prolonged military attacks on Afghanistan and Iraq.

THE WAR ON TERROR

It was a high-stakes game of hide-and-seek. Osama bin Laden, leader of al Qaeda, was believed to be hiding out somewhere in the mountains of Afghanistan. The U.S. government was determined to find him.

WAR AGAINST THE TALIBAN

Less than a month after September 11, President Bush put his war on terror in motion. The first phase of the war focused on the Southwest Asian country of Afghanistan, which, as you know, was largely controlled by the Taliban. Since the mid-1990s, the group had instituted policies based on a strict interpretation of *shari'a*, or Islamic law, over the Afghani people. These laws enforced the unequal treatment of women and harsh punishments for crimes such as theft. When the Taliban refused to hand over suspected terrorists—and, in particular, Osama bin Laden—the United States initiated Operation Enduring Freedom on October 7, 2001.

The war began with U.S. and British air strikes launched against Taliban and al Qaeda targets in Afghanistan. Within weeks, both the United States and Britain also began sending ground troops to Afghanistan. Soon, other countries, including France and Germany, joined the coalition, while other allies provided intelligence and the use of their military bases. These nations believed the United States had the right to strike those who had supported and sheltered the 9/11 terrorists. By December, the multinational coalition had driven the Taliban out of power. U.S. intelligence services then began an exhaustive but unsuccessful search for bin Laden.

Afghanistan held democratic elections and passed a new constitution, but fighting in the country continued. Taliban insurgents, or rebels, reorganized and took up arms against the coalition forces. More troops went to fight in Afghanistan as the war dragged on and crossed into neighboring Pakistan. Finally, in May 2011, the U.S. military located bin Laden in a compound in Pakistan and killed the al Qaeda leader. Major U.S. combat operations in Afghanistan officially ended in December 2014. It became the longest war the United States had ever fought.

WAR IN IRAQ

While U.S. troops were engaged in Afghanistan, the Bush administration also focused its efforts on Iraq and ousting its brutal president, Saddam Hussein. The Bush administration claimed that Hussein's regime was linked to al Qaeda. Officials also believed Iraq possessed weapons of mass destruction (WMD)

Following the invasion of Iraq and capture of Saddam Hussein, U.S. forces remained in the country to keep order. The U.S. troops shown here are accompanying Iraqi school children in 2009 after attending the reopening of a Baghdad elementary school that had been damaged during the war.

that could be used against the United States. In November 2002, the United Nations demanded that Iraq allow weapons inspectors to search for WMD. The inspectors failed to find any such weapons, but the Bush administration remained skeptical. Vice President Cheney and other neocons didn't trust the Iraqi government. They had called for Hussein's elimination since the Persian Gulf War in 1990.

On March 19, 2003, coalition forces, again led by the United States and Britain, launched strikes against government and military targets in Iraq. This time, though, few other countries joined the coalition. Days later, ground troops invaded the country. Within a few weeks, they had defeated the Iraqi army and brought an end to Saddam Hussein's rule. Hussein himself went into hiding, but he was eventually captured, tried in an Iraqi court, and executed.

After Iraq's defeat, inspectors continued to search for WMD, but none were ever found. Further, no links were uncovered between Hussein's regime and al Qaeda. Many Americans became angry after learning the Bush administration had led the United States into war based on faulty intelligence.

Meanwhile, the United States and Britain occupied Iraq and began rebuilding the country and preparing its people for a democratic form of government. But democracy never really took hold in Iraq. Government corruption and a civil war between the country's two main religious groups, the Sunni Muslims and the Shi'ite Muslims, prevented Iraq from becoming the stable state the United States had envisioned.

The war in Iraq was a major issue in the 2004 presidential election. Bush faced a strong challenge from the Democratic Party's nominee, Senator John Kerry of Massachusetts. Bush won a narrow victory, but his second term got off to a rocky start. As the violence continued in Iraq and more American soldiers died, Bush's approval rating fell. It dropped even further following his mismanagement of the Hurricane Katrina relief effort in August 2005, when the storm flooded low-lying areas of New Orleans where the city's poor and minority populations lived. Tens of thousands of people were left stranded on the tops of buildings, and more than 1,500 died. These factors helped the Democrats gain control of both houses of Congress in the 2006 elections and allowed Democrat Nancy Pelosi of California to become the first female Speaker of the House.

In January 2007, President Bush announced plans for a **surge**, or quick increase, in the number of U.S. troops in Iraq to halt the ongoing fighting and restore security. The United States sent roughly 30,000 additional troops to Iraq, bringing total troop strength to about 170,000, but still the war continued. Soon, however, Bush was forced to shift his focus from Iraq to a crisis at home that threatened the United States with economic collapse.

HISTORICAL THINKING

1. **READING CHECK** What U.S. interests led to the war in Afghanistan?
2. **SYNTHESIZE** How did U.S. involvement in the wars in Afghanistan and Iraq demonstrate neoconservative views?
3. **INTERPRET MAPS** Why were some of the U.S. military bases for operations in Afghanistan located outside of that country?

11.9.6 Describe U.S. Middle East policy and its strategic, political, and economic interests, including those related to the Gulf War.

THROUGH THE LENS **AMERICAN PLACES**

NEW ORLEANS, LOUISIANA

Built in a bowl-shaped geographic depression, much of New Orleans lies below sea level. When Hurricane Katrina, the most destructive storm in U.S. history, struck the Gulf Coast on August 29, 2005, it sent a storm surge barreling toward the low-lying city. The floodwaters demolished New Orleans' ineffective levee system, flooding the streets and leaving most of the city underwater. Nearly 2,000 people died in the city and along the Gulf Coast, and more than 1 million lost their homes.

Stranded and desperate for aid that was slow to come, the people of New Orleans felt abandoned by President George W. Bush and the government agencies tasked with providing support during disasters. According to the *New York Times*, "New Orleans became a global symbol of American dysfunction and government negligence. At every level and in every duty, from engineering to social policy to basic logistics, there were revelations of malfunction and failure before, during and after Katrina."

CRITICAL VIEWING What does this 2015 photo of New Orleans' Lower Ninth Ward reveal about its recovery from Katrina and the neighborhood's relationship with the Mississippi River?

Fortunately, New Orleans has slowly rebounded. Neighborhoods destroyed by flooding, like the Lower Ninth Ward (opposite page), are being rebuilt, and billions of dollars in federal aid have funded new schools and hospitals, replacing some that were in dire need of an overhaul before Katrina even hit. Many residents have also returned—although local demographics have changed dramatically. In 2013, nearly 100,000 fewer African Americans lived in New Orleans than in 2000. Population shifts are common in port towns, but for a city challenged by racial and class inequalities throughout history, the fallout from Katrina has been especially hard to overcome.

While the economic and social impact of the hurricane may affect New Orleans long after the restoration of the city is complete, its music, culture, and character remain strong and dynamic. The bustling, vibrant French Quarter (shown below), filled with music and colorful historic buildings, celebrates the city's distinctive Creole culture and is as unique, diverse, and rich in history as ever. Hundreds of thousands of people flock to New Orleans' legendary Mardi Gras festivities, boosting the city's continued rebuilding efforts with tourism dollars and establishing New Orleans as an example of the strength and resilience of great American cities.

CRITICAL VIEWING On Bourbon Street in New Orleans' French Quarter, you might suddenly find yourself marching in a second line parade, made up of people who follow the band just to enjoy the music. What do you observe about the physical and human characteristics of the city from the photos in this lesson, and how might those characteristics have been impacted by Hurricane Katrina?

11.11.7 Explain how the federal, state, and local governments have responded to demographic and social changes such as population shifts to the suburbs, racial concentrations in the cities, Frostbelt-to-Sunbelt migration, international migration, decline of family farms, increases in out-of-wedlock births, and drug abuse; CST 4 Students relate current events to the physical and human characteristics of places and regions.

3.1 **MAIN IDEA** The collapse of the housing market in 2007 triggered the worst economic downturn in the United States since the Great Depression.

THE GREAT RECESSION

We all know that bubbles burst pretty quickly. In the first years of the 21st century, a housing bubble developed, fueled by the high demand for new homes. When the bubble burst, it had terrible consequences for the country's economy.

HOUSING MARKET RISE AND FALL

The housing market crash was many years in the making. Banks and other lenders had begun to adopt unwise economic policies and lending strategies—mostly related to home-buying—in the 1980s and 1990s. These practices continued into the first decade of the 2000s, setting the stage for the economic problems that developed in 2007, toward the end of George W. Bush's second term.

Owning a home is a big part of the American dream, but rates of homeownership are usually significantly lower among minorities and people with low incomes. Spurred by their own business interests and by affordable-housing goals established by the federal government, lenders took steps to increase the pool of potential home buyers. They relaxed down-payment and employment-history requirements and began to offer more **subprime mortgages**, or home loans to buyers with poor credit history. To entice people to buy, banks also offered loans with low initial interest rates, called adjustable-rate mortgages. After a certain period of time, though, the interest rates on these loans would be raised, increasing the borrowers' payments—often to amounts few could afford.

Although subprime mortgages were risky, banks felt comfortable offering them because they could sell many of the mortgages to two government-sponsored enterprises: Fannie Mae (the Federal National Mortgage Association) and Freddie Mac (the Federal Home Loan Mortgage Corporation). Wall Street investment banks bundled groups of mortgages into what they called "managed packages" and sold them on the international financial market as profitable but highly unstable investments. An **investment bank** is a financial institution that purchases and sells stocks and bonds and helps other companies raise capital and manage their assets.

As demand for housing increased, prices rose dramatically. The widespread belief was that rising prices would cause the real estate to increase significantly in value. But then the bubble burst in 2007, and housing prices fell. Increasing numbers of subprime mortgage holders found they could not afford their loan payments. To make matters worse, they could not sell their homes. There were too many homes up for sale at the same time, and demand was low. Housing prices tumbled. Many of these homes went into **foreclosure**—that is, the banks took possession of them because the buyers could no longer make their house payments. Millions of families lost their homes to foreclosure. The housing market crash triggered a severe recession that, because of globalization, spread quickly around the world. Japan and many countries in Europe were hit especially hard due to their strong financial and

Stock Market Index, 2000–2010

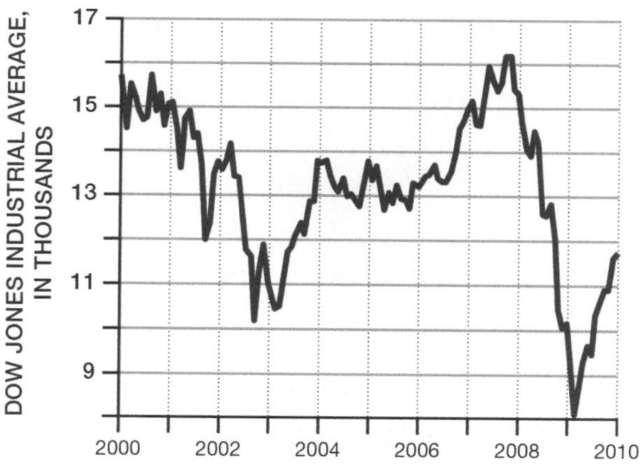

Source: Federal Reserve Bank of St. Louis

In 2009, a woman in San Antonio, Texas, wrote these words on her house to announce she was facing foreclosure. She had recently lost her job and could no longer make her mortgage payments.

trade ties to the United States. Echoing the Great Depression of the 1930s, the downturn became known as the **Great Recession**.

LOOMING ECONOMIC COLLAPSE

The Great Recession grew steadily worse in 2008. Many small banks went bankrupt, and other banks severely limited their lending. Wall Street financial institutions that had invested heavily in managed packages tied to subprime mortgages suffered huge losses. Plunging real estate prices meant that Americans could no longer finance major purchases such as cars by borrowing against the value of their homes. As a result, the recession also devastated the American automobile industry. A reduction in spending by wary consumers hurt many other industries, including those related to travel, construction, and home furnishings. Many companies were forced to make cuts, and millions of people lost their jobs. As government revenues shrank, cities and states also cut their budgets and laid off workers. As a result, the unemployment rate climbed to around 10 percent.

The terrible state of the economy raised the concern that some investment banks were "too big to fail." And if they did, many economists believed the country's entire financial system would collapse. But after some powerful firms did go bankrupt, Congress passed the Emergency Economic Stabilization Act (EESA) of 2008. This act, which Bush signed into law in October, provided the Treasury Department with up to $700 billion to buy mortgages and other "troubled assets," or unstable investments, from banks. The legislation also established the Troubled Asset Relief Program (TARP), designed to help individuals and businesses secure bank loans. But much of this money was used to save large investment banks. The costly **bailout** spurred widespread resentment. Some critics blamed the recession on the greed of the banks and argued that the government should have let them fail.

While the bailout was being debated, the stock market plunged on September 29. The crash erased much of the savings ordinary Americans had been counting on. The recession affected almost everyone. And with so many people unemployed and in debt, the recession and the persistence of poverty became the main issues of the 2008 presidential election.

HISTORICAL THINKING

1. **READING CHECK** Why were lenders eager to offer subprime mortgages to potential buyers?
2. **FORM AND SUPPORT OPINIONS** Who do you think played the biggest role in the housing market crash: home buyers, mortgage companies, or investment banks? Explain.
3. **INTERPRET GRAPHS** How many points did the stock market plunge between 2008 and 2009?

11.11.6 Analyze the persistence of poverty and how different analyses of this issue influence welfare reform, health insurance reform, and other social policies; HI 6 Students conduct cost-benefit analyses and apply basic economic indicators to analyze the aggregate economic behavior of the U.S. economy.

3.2 **MAIN IDEA** Barack Obama won the 2008 presidential election, becoming the first African-American president in U.S. history.

The Election of 2008

At the beginning of 2008, an atmosphere of gloom hung over the United States. The Great Recession was worsening, and the war in Iraq was dragging into its sixth year. As the 2008 election approached, many Americans were ready for a change.

HISTORY IS MADE

With George W. Bush's approval rating around 30 percent, Democrats felt they had the advantage over Republicans in 2008. The early Democratic favorite was New York senator Hillary Clinton, wife of former president William Clinton. She faced a strong challenge, however, from Senator **Barack Obama** of Illinois. A historic outcome was guaranteed. If Clinton won, she would become the first female nominated for president by a major party. If Obama won, he would become the first African American nominated by a major party.

On election night, November 4, 2008, President-elect Barack Obama delivered his victory speech before 240,000 people gathered in Chicago's Grant Park. With his family beside him, Obama said, "If there is anyone out there who still doubts that America is a place where all things are possible; who still wonders if the dream of our founders is alive in our time; who still questions the power of our democracy, tonight is your answer."

Ceding many of the most populated states to Clinton, Obama focused his efforts on winning as many convention delegates as he could in less populous states. The strategy worked. Even though Clinton won the popular vote in the primaries, Obama secured more convention delegates and thus became the Democratic nominee. For his vice-presidential running mate, he chose Senator Joe Biden of Delaware.

On the Republican side, the leading candidates in the primary elections included former Massachusetts governor Mitt Romney, former Arkansas governor Mike Huckabee, and Senator John McCain of Arizona. McCain eventually secured the Republican nomination, winning all but one of the final 21 primaries. For his running mate, he chose Alaska governor Sarah Palin, who was not well known outside her home state. Her controversial remarks, however, quickly brought her a great deal of public attention. The outspoken Palin drew large crowds to her campaign speeches.

Both presidential candidates addressed the financial crisis facing the nation. But while McCain seemed uncertain about what measures he would take, Obama's focused, confident response to the crisis won over many voters. With his message of hope and change, Obama won the election in November with relative ease and became the first African-American president in the country's 232-year history.

OBAMA'S PRIORITIES

One of Obama's top priorities as president was to lead the country out of the Great Recession. Soon after taking office, he signed into law the American Recovery and Reinvestment Act, which authorized $787 billion in government spending as an **economic stimulus**, or a measure aimed at promoting and enabling financial recovery and growth. The act was designed to save existing jobs and to create new ones. Obama and the federal government also bailed out the auto industry, providing $80 billion to the three major U.S. automakers to prevent them from failing. By the end of Obama's two terms as president, the unemployment rate had dropped to 5 percent, and the auto industry had recovered—and repaid the bailout money.

Initiating comprehensive health care reform was another of Obama's goals. Like Bill Clinton, the new president sought to extend the scope of the government and provide health care insurance for all U.S. citizens. In a speech to Congress in September 2009, he pointed out that more than 30 million Americans lacked health insurance. He also spoke of rising health care costs, unethical insurance practices and claims, and the heavy burden government programs such as Medicare and Medicaid put on taxpayers. The House passed a health care bill in early November, and on Christmas Eve, the Senate passed its own version of the bill.

A development in Massachusetts, however, threatened to doom the legislation. Scott Brown, a conservative Republican, won a special election to fill the vacancy created by the death of Democratic Senator Edward Kennedy, the brother of John and Robert Kennedy. By picking up a seat in the Senate, Republicans gained the ability to block legislation through the use of filibusters. Congressional Democrats, meanwhile, retreated from their commitment to health care reform.

Prospects for passage of the president's initiative seemed bleak. However, the determination of Speaker of the House Nancy Pelosi and Obama's persistence helped secure the passage of a health care package in March 2010. The bill that Obama signed into law was called the **Patient Protection and Affordable Care Act (PPACA)**, but it became popularly known as Obamacare. Although Republicans tried to block it through legislation and in the federal courts, the act had provided health insurance coverage to nearly 20 million Americans by 2016.

Passage of the Affordable Care Act and other progressive bills inspired the rise of a conservative populist movement known as the **Tea Party**. It was not a formal organization but rather a loose confederation of individuals and groups united by their antigovernment, antitax, and anti-immigration views. Most of those in the grassroots movement were Republicans who hoped to influence the direction of the party. Energized by the fast-growing Tea Party, Republicans gained 6 seats in the Senate and took control of the House by picking up 63 seats there in the 2010 midterm elections. As a result, Obama would face strong opposition to many of his initiatives during the rest of his time in office.

HISTORICAL THINKING

1. **READING CHECK** What factors helped Obama win the 2008 presidential election?
2. **EVALUATE** How did President Obama seek to address U.S. poverty and economic problems?
3. **MAKE INFERENCES** How do you think most members of the Tea Party felt about the economic stimulus legislation and Obamacare?

11.11.6 Analyze the persistence of poverty and how different analyses of this issue influence welfare reform, health insurance reform, and other social policies.

BARACK HUSSEIN OBAMA II 1961–

MICHELLE LAVAUGHN ROBINSON OBAMA 1964–

"If you were going to list the 100 most popular things that I have done as president, being married to Michelle Obama is number one."—Barack Obama

The president probably wasn't exaggerating. When Barack Obama's approval numbers were at their lowest in 2013—due to controversies over both his domestic and foreign policies—his wife, Michelle, still drew adoring crowds wherever she appeared in public. Initially reluctant to embrace Washington and relinquish her own career, Michelle threw her full support behind her husband when he first ran for the presidency. Barack and Michelle entered the White House as a team, but their path to its door could hardly have been more different.

The Obamas stroll along the Colonnade of the White House in 2010. In his final speech, the president told his wife, "You have made me proud, and you have made the country proud."

EARLY LIVES

Barack Obama had an unsettled childhood. His parents met as students at the University of Hawaii. His mother, Ann Dunham, was a white American from Kansas. His father, Barack Obama, Sr., was a black African from Kenya. The couple divorced when their child was two years old, and Barack had very little contact with his father after that. His mother later married an Indonesian, and the family lived in Indonesia for a time. Then, when Barack was 10, his mother sent him to live with his grandparents in Hawaii. She eventually returned to Hawaii and her parents' home after divorcing her second husband. Barack's parents died when he was a young man: his father in 1982, his mother in 1995.

By contrast, Michelle Obama grew up in a stable, close-knit family. Her parents, Marian and Fraser Robinson, raised their children in a small house in Chicago. Michelle and her brother, Craig, slept in the living room and strung up a sheet to divide the space and provide some privacy. Education was a priority in the Robinson home, and both children did well in school. Michelle would later say, "I liked being smart. I thought being smart was cooler than anything in the world."

Barack Obama pursued education as well. After graduating from Columbia University in New York City and working as a community organizer in Chicago, he enrolled in Harvard Law School in 1988. After his first year at Harvard, he interned at a law firm in Chicago. His supervisor was Michelle Robinson, and he was immediately attracted to her. At first, Michelle resisted his advances, but eventually the pair fell in love. They married in 1992. Meanwhile, Barack completed his law degree at Harvard. Soon he decided to enter politics.

Michelle often accompanied her husband on state visits, including this trip in March 2011 to the Central American country of El Salvador. Here, shortly after their arrival in the country's capital of San Salvador, the POTUS and FLOTUS greet school children waving American flags.

POTUS and FLOTUS

Running as a Democrat, Obama won an Illinois state senate seat in 1996. Then, in 2004, he was elected to the U.S. Senate representing Illinois. That same year he gave the keynote speech at the Democratic National Convention to endorse presidential candidate John Kerry. However, the speech is best remembered for launching Obama onto the national stage and paving the way for his successful presidential run in 2008. In his speech, he delivered a message of unity that resonated with many Americans: "There's not a liberal America and a conservative America—there's the United States of America. There's not a black America and white America and Latino America and Asian America; there's the United States of America." Because of speeches like this, Obama is considered one of the most powerful orators of his generation.

As you know, Obama faced a host of political issues when he became president of the United States (POTUS), but he also endured challenges to the legitimacy of his presidency. Members of the so-called "birther movement" claimed the president had not been born in the United States and so was ineligible to hold the office. Some birthers also asserted that Obama was Muslim, a charge designed to suggest the president was somehow "un-American." Despite concrete evidence disproving birther allegations—his Hawaiian birth certificate, for example—the contentions dogged Obama throughout his presidency.

While lies swirled during his presidency, Obama depended on Michelle—his "rock," as he called her—to help keep him grounded. Levelheaded and funny, Michelle was not part of what Obama called the "silliness of Washington." As first lady of the United States (FLOTUS), Michelle undertook an initiative called "Let's Move" to get kids to exercise and eat healthy foods. She and the POTUS also protected the privacy of their daughters, Malia and Sasha, as they grew up in the White House.

At the end of his second term, Obama delivered a farewell address in Chicago. After encouraging Americans not to take their democracy for granted, he said: "I do have one final ask of you as your president—the same thing I asked when you took a chance on me eight years ago. I am asking you to believe. Not in my ability to bring about change—but in yours." And in her final speech, Michelle Obama had a special message, based on her own experience, for young Americans: "Empower yourself with a good education. Then get out there and use that education to build a country worthy of your boundless promise. Lead by example with hope: never fear."

HISTORICAL THINKING

1. **READING CHECK** How did Barack and Michelle Obama's early lives differ?
2. **MAKE INFERENCES** What does Barack Obama's speech at the Democratic National Convention suggest about politics in the country at that time?
3. **EVALUATE** What false charges were leveled against President Obama, and what did those who alleged them hope to accomplish?

HREP 1 Students distinguish valid arguments from fallacious arguments in historical interpretations; HI 1 Students show the connections, causal and otherwise, between particular historical events and larger social, economic, and political trends and developments.

4.1 **MAIN IDEA** In the 21st century, progress has been made in civil rights for women, minorities, and the LGBTQ community, but these groups continue to fight for full equality.

CIVIL RIGHTS IN THE 21ST CENTURY

To oppressed people around the world, the United States symbolizes freedom and opportunity. Some Americans, however, are still denied their full rights as citizens. The fight for these rights goes on.

ADVANCES AND SETBACKS FOR WOMEN

Women have made great strides in gaining their civil rights in recent decades. In business, some have broken through the "glass ceiling"—an invisible barrier of attitudes and prejudices that prevents women and minorities from advancing to high-level positions. In 1998, for instance, Meg Whitman was named president and chief executive officer of a major online auction company. The following year, Carly Fiorina was appointed head of a giant software and computer services company. Women continue to increase their representation in politics as well. Since 1990, about half of the 50 states have elected female governors. In 2007, as you've learned, Congresswoman Nancy Pelosi became the first female Speaker of the House. And in 2016, women held about 20 percent of the seats in Congress.

Nevertheless, little progress has been made in other areas. For decades, women have been demanding equal pay for equal work. They make up about half of the American workforce and are the main wage-earners in roughly 4 of every 10 families. Yet white women are paid about 20 percent less than men, African-American women earn around 35 percent less, and Latinas make about 40 percent less.

As more women have moved into the workforce, access to affordable, quality childcare has also posed a significant problem, especially for low-income women. Although traditional ideas about the family structure and gender roles in society are changing, the primary responsibility for taking care of children is still more often assumed by women than by men. This means that women face a greater challenge in balancing work and family commitments. In a 2015 survey, the majority of women said that being a working parent made it harder for them to advance in their career.

Legal access to abortion was one of the most divisive issues in the United States in the second half of the 20th century, and it remains so in the 21st. Despite being challenged many times, the landmark 1973 Supreme Court ruling in *Roe* v. *Wade*, which legalized abortion nationwide, has never been overturned. The Department of Health and Human Services, at both the federal and state levels, has provided family planning and pregnancy prevention and care programs. However, some lawmakers have tried to cut off the funding for such programs. In addition, many states have passed laws restricting women's access to abortion.

THE AMERICANS WITH DISABILITIES ACT

In 1990, President George H.W. Bush signed the Americans with Disabilities Act (ADA), which granted civil rights for Americans with a disability, defined as "a physical or mental impairment that substantially limits one or more major life activities." Amendments were added to the ADA in 2008 that broadened the definition of "disability" and protected more people. Considered one of America's most comprehensive pieces of civil rights legislation, the ADA prevents discrimination in employment and guarantees access to public services, accommodations, and transportation.

JUSTICE FOR ALL

As you know, the civil rights movement of the 1950s and 1960s achieved major breakthroughs in the struggle to end segregation and discrimination against African Americans. Activists have continued to fight for further progress, but full racial equality

11.10.6 Analyze the passage and effects of civil rights and voting rights legislation (e.g., 1964 Civil Rights Act, Voting Rights Act of 1965) and the Twenty-Fourth Amendment, with an emphasis on equality of access to education and to the political process.

has remained elusive. Many African Americans continue to live in segregated city neighborhoods where schools, housing, and public services are inferior. Public housing funded by federal and state governments has contributed to keeping these neighborhoods segregated. In addition, federal, state, and local laws that had ended in the late 20th century still impact racial segregation today. These laws include those that designated white neighborhoods as residential areas and black neighborhoods as commercial areas, and those that prohibited the sale of property to African Americans.

Crime rates in segregated neighborhoods are higher, and drug abuse and out-of-wedlock births are more prevalent. Prison sentences for many of the crimes are also longer. For example, blacks convicted of drug offenses serve substantially more time in prison than do whites convicted of similar offenses. Local law enforcement often focuses on urban areas and, in particular, low-income communities. Blacks are also less likely than whites to graduate from high school and attend college. They suffer higher rates of unemployment and poverty. And although their incomes have risen, their pay is still, on average, far below those of whites.

In the 21st century, increasing charges of local police brutality against African Americans have been leveled. In some instances, police officers have used excessive force and sometimes shot and killed unarmed African Americans. One of the most widely publicized of these shootings occurred in Ferguson, Missouri, a predominantly African-American suburb of St. Louis. As you read in the American Story on civil rights, in 2014, a white Ferguson police officer shot and killed an unarmed black teenager named Michael Brown, touching off angry protests that continued for weeks. Remember that in the wake of this event and others like it, **Black Lives Matter** rose to national prominence. Activists in the movement organized protests to draw attention to unwarranted police violence toward African Americans and to demand justice for victims of this violence.

The movement polarized Americans. Some people believed it increased the violence. At a Black Lives Matter protest in Dallas, Texas, in July 2016, a sniper opened fire on police officers, killing five of them. A week and a half later, another gunman ambushed and killed three police officers in Baton Rouge, Louisiana. The African-American men who carried out the shootings were killed by the police.

In December 2014, Black Lives Matter supporters marched in New York City to take part in a "Justice for All" demonstration. A similar march took place in Washington, D.C. Protesters called for an end to racial profiling and police violence and demanded change in the justice system.

11.11.3 Describe the changing roles of women in society as reflected in the entry of more women into the labor force and the changing family structure;
11.11.7 Explain how the federal, state, and local governments have responded to demographic and social changes such as population shifts to the suburbs, racial concentrations in the cities, Frostbelt-to-Sunbelt migration, international migration, decline of family farms, increases in out-of-wedlock births, and drug abuse.

The incidents increased racial tensions and led some to accuse Black Lives Matter of encouraging violence against police. However, white citizens also directed racially charged violence against African Americans. In June 2015, Dylann Roof, a self-proclaimed white supremacist, massacred nine African-American worshipers attending a prayer meeting at the Emanuel African Methodist Episcopal Church in Charleston, South Carolina. When arrested, Roof claimed he wanted to start a race war.

ISSUES IN THE LGBT COMMUNITY

In the American Story on civil rights, you also read about the LGBT community's struggle to achieve marriage equality. **Marriage equality** is the legal right of gays and lesbians to marry their partners and have the same privileges that married heterosexual couples enjoy. However, even after same-sex marriage became legal in 2015, other issues arose that challenged the LGBT community's civil rights. One of these involved the right of transgender individuals to use the public restroom that corresponds to their gender identity rather than their gender at birth. In 2013, California became the first state to pass a law guaranteeing this right for transgender students in public schools. The law allowed them to use whichever restroom they wanted. Over the next few years, other states passed similar laws. Then, in 2016, President Obama issued guidelines to all school districts in the country, detailing the steps they should take to make sure their students were not discriminated against. The guidelines included allowing students to use the restroom of their choice.

Supporters of transgender laws suffered a number of setbacks in 2017. The federal government withdrew its position on bathroom protections for transgender students and declared the issue was one of states' rights. Soon after this declaration, North Carolina, which had passed a bathroom bill in 2016, repealed the measure after just a year. In Virginia, a transgender high school student named Gavin Grimm sought to ban discrimination based on gender identity at his school, where separate facilities had

John Lewis, left, and his husband, Stuart Gaffney, who were key activists in the struggle for marriage equality, celebrate the U.S. Supreme Court's decision to legalize same-sex marriage in 2015.

11.9.7 Examine relations between the United States and Mexico in the twentieth century, including key economic, political, immigration, and environmental issues; 11.11.1 Discuss the reasons for the nation's changing immigration policy, with emphasis on how the Immigration Act of 1965 and successor acts have transformed American society.

been set aside for him alone. Grimm took his case to the Supreme Court, but it would not hear the case. In spite of the legal defeat, Grimm and others pledged to continue fighting against transgender discrimination.

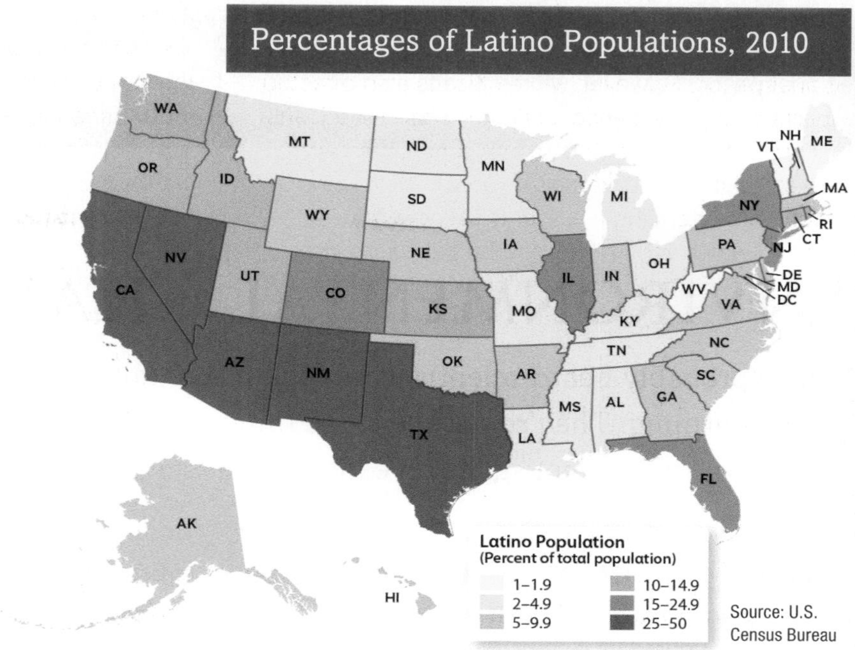

Source: U.S. Census Bureau

MEXICAN IMMIGRATION

American civil rights leaders in the 21st century consider immigration a civil rights issue because they claim that many immigrants are not given a chance to succeed economically—especially those from Mexico. By the 2000s, the status of Mexican Americans and Mexican immigrants became a national political discussion. The wave of immigration from Mexico—in particular, the estimated 6 million who entered the United States illegally, or without documentation—worried and angered many Americans. Some claimed these immigrants hurt the economy by taking jobs from American citizens, driving down wages, avoiding paying taxes, and putting pressure on social service agencies. Many economists dismissed such claims, stating that immigrants actually benefit the economy by taking jobs Americans don't want, paying their share of taxes, and buying products and services.

After the September 11, 2001, terrorist attacks, fear for national security led Congress to provide for increased border enforcement. And so, in 2006, President George W. Bush signed into law the Secure Fence Act, authorizing the construction of 700 miles of fencing along the U.S.-Mexico border. Still, the influx of immigrants continued, and many of them settled in California. As a result, in 2010, Latino men and women comprised the largest ethnic group in California, and Latino boys and girls made up more than 51 percent of the children in public schools. It was within this context that those in the Latino community became increasingly active in politics. In 2013, Mexican American Eric Garcetti became mayor of Los Angeles, and a number of Latino organizations, often run by school board members and elected local officials, have arisen throughout the state. These organizations work to improve education, health care, and jobs and economic development for Latinos.

Meanwhile, Democrats and Republicans both pushed for the passage of comprehensive immigration legislation, but time and again the legislation died in Congress due to a lack of consensus, or agreement. Frustrated by the inaction of Congress, President Obama issued an executive order in 2014 aimed at strengthening border security. After issuing the order, he addressed the nation about the actions he was taking on immigration. In his address, Obama emphasized that the efforts of immigration authorities would be focused on "Felons, not families. Criminals, not children. Gang members, not a mom who's working hard to provide for her kids." Republican leaders and many American citizens were angered by the order, claiming that the president's actions would lead to more illegal immigration, not less. During his presidency, Obama wrestled with many other issues that divided Americans, including one that scientists said affected the entire planet: climate change.

HISTORICAL THINKING

1. **READING CHECK** How have beliefs about women's roles changed, and how have they stayed the same?
2. **FORM AND SUPPORT OPINIONS** Since the civil rights movement, do you think African Americans have continued to make significant gains in achieving equality? Explain your answer.
3. **MAKE INFERENCES** Why do you think making same-sex marriage legal was an important goal of the LGBT community?
4. **INTERPRET MAPS** Which states had the largest percentages of Latino populations in the country in 2010, and why do you think that was so?

CST 2 Students analyze how change happens at different rates at different times; understand that some aspects can change while others remain the same; and understand that change is complicated and affects not only technology and politics but also values and beliefs.

4.2 **MAIN IDEA** Climate change is affecting the environment, but people disagree about what is causing it.

ENVIRONMENTAL CHALLENGES

You've probably heard scientists and politicians talk about climate change and global warming. They're not the same thing, but the two terms are related. The vast majority of scientists believe global warming is driving climate change.

CLIMATE CHANGE OR GLOBAL WARMING?

Climate change is a gradual shift in Earth's overall climate. Throughout its history, Earth has undergone many climate changes. Global warming, on the other hand, is a term used by many scientists to describe the rapid warming of Earth's surface observed over the last century. These scientists believe this warming is causing climate change and is largely due to human activities. Experts say that the heavy use of nonrenewable fossil fuels, including coal, oil, and natural gas, contributes to rising temperatures. Burning these energy sources releases **greenhouse gases**, such as carbon dioxide and methane. The greenhouse gas emissions trap the sun's heat and warm Earth's surface, causing its temperature to rise. This warming is called the **greenhouse effect**.

Scientists believe the greenhouse effect began to significantly increase around 1750 with the Industrial Revolution, when people began burning more fossil fuels to run factories. Consumption of these fuels has intensified during the last 250 years or so, with the introduction of trains, automobiles, and airplanes. As a result, since the beginning of the 20th century, the average temperature of the globe has risen 1.4° F. That number may seem small, but a change of even one degree is cause for concern.

Researchers believe they have already detected evidence of the impact of this seemingly small rise in global temperature. The vast ice sheets that cover Antarctica and Greenland, for example, have begun to melt and shrink. And oceans are warming, causing sea ice to melt and sea levels to rise. Scientists say these changes are already destroying habitats and changing ecosystems. Earth's warming may also result in more intense hurricanes and typhoons, which in turn could lead to high casualty tolls and damage to coastlines and other geographic features.

AN INCONVENIENT TRUTH

In this 2006 documentary film, former vice president Al Gore seeks to educate the public about global warming. Throughout the film, Gore uses photos, graphs, and flow charts to make his case that global warming is real and caused by human activities. Stressing that global warming is a moral issue rather than a political one, Gore encourages his audience to take steps to combat it. He says, "We have everything that we need to reduce carbon emissions, everything but political will. But in America, the will to act is a renewable resource."

COMBATING GLOBAL WARMING

The majority of scientists believe that global warming will continue unless greenhouse gas emissions are dramatically reduced. Such a reduction will not be easy to achieve, however. In 1988, as concern about global warming was growing, the United Nations and the World Meteorological Organization took a step toward addressing the problem by creating the **Intergovernmental Panel on Climate Change (IPCC)**. The panel is made up of top climate experts from around the world. Its mission is to assess "the scientific, technical, and socioeconomic information relevant to understanding the scientific basis of risk of human-induced climate change." The panel's reports help world leaders set climate policies.

International action on climate change was undertaken in 1997 with a treaty called the **Kyoto Protocol**, which committed countries to reducing greenhouse gas emissions to below 1990 levels. Eventually, nearly 200 countries implemented the treaty, but the United States—which at the time was

CRITICAL VIEWING National Geographic photographer Peter McBride took this picture of a Cocopah tribesman standing at the end of the Colorado river in Mexico. The river used to flow at this point into the Gulf of California, but drought and irrigation demands have reduced it to a trickle. How have human activities influenced the extent, biological diversity, and viability of the Colorado River?

the world's largest emitter of these gases—was not among them. President George W. Bush, who was skeptical about what caused climate change, opposed the treaty, arguing that it would "harm our economy and hurt our workers." He also objected to the fact that developing countries were exempt from complying with the treaty.

Since then, however, the United States has made efforts to reduce emissions by moving toward the use of more renewable energy sources, such as solar, wind, and geothermal power. In 2009, President Obama allocated billions of dollars to promote renewable and clean energy programs. In 2016, the country's first offshore wind farm was completed in the Atlantic Ocean near Rhode Island's Block Island, and federal agencies announced a plan to accelerate the development of additional offshore wind energy.

Obama and the U.S. Environmental Protection Agency unveiled the Clean Power Plan in 2015. The president called the plan "the single most important step America has ever taken in the fight against global climate change." It established nationwide standards aimed at greatly reducing carbon dioxide emissions from power plants.

In 2016, the United States made its most ambitious commitment to date toward dealing with global warming by ratifying the Kyoto Protocol's successor, a climate treaty known as the **Paris Agreement**. The goal of the agreement was to prevent Earth from warming more than 2° C, or approximately 3.6° F. Scientists believe that allowing Earth to warm beyond that limit would result in destructive and dangerous climate change. It remains to be seen whether the countries that signed the agreement will meet the pledge—and even if they do, whether their efforts will help protect the environment.

HISTORICAL THINKING

1. **READING CHECK** What controversies are associated with the concept of climate change and with environmental conservation?
2. **ANALYZE ENVIRONMENTAL CONCEPTS** How might our consumption of natural resources, such as coal, oil, and natural gas, influence the geographic extent, composition, biological diversity, and viability of natural systems?
3. **DESCRIBE** How has the human modification of landscapes contributed to global warming, and what types of environmental policies have resulted from it?

11.11.5 Trace the impact of, need for, and controversies associated with environmental conservation, expansion of the national park system, and the development of environmental protection laws, with particular attention to the interaction between environmental protection advocates and property rights advocates; HI 5 Students analyze human modifications of landscapes and examine the resulting environmental policy issues.

4.3 **MAIN IDEA** Globalization has had profound impacts on the U.S. economy, environment, and culture.

GLOBALIZING AMERICAN SOCIETY

Not so long ago, Americans found satisfying, well-paid work in automobile plants and steel factories. In our global economy, those days seem to be over.

ECONOMY AND ENVIRONMENT

Beginning in the 1970s and continuing through recent times, U.S. economic production has shifted away from heavy industry and toward the service sector. The **service sector** provides services rather than goods and includes jobs in banking, education, retail, and health care. This de-industrialization has altered the daily lives of many working- and middle-class American families.

Over the past 30 years, the gaps in income between top earners and middle- and working-class earners have become wider and more pronounced. Working-class wages have stagnated as higher-paying unionized blue collar factory jobs have been outsourced and replaced with minimum-wage paying service sector jobs. The stagnant or decreasing wealth of working- and middle-class Americans has been compounded by changes in tax structures and safety-net programs. It has also been amplified by higher costs for education, child care, and housing. In the early 2010s, a populist movement called Occupy Wall Street sought to bring attention to the income gap through protests and demonstrations. Some members of the movement tried to provide solutions through education or organization.

Part of the reason for the decreasing income of many Americans is globalization and the rise of **multinational corporations**, or companies that have offices and factories in multiple countries. In the first 15 years of the 21st century, the United States lost an estimated 5 million manufacturing jobs. Many of these jobs were outsourced to Mexico or China, where wages are much lower than in the United States.

In many ways, the globalized economy has had a broad, negative impact on the environment. The rapid industrialization of countries with lax environmental standards, such as China, Mexico, and India, has resulted in severe air, water, and soil pollution. Globalization has also led to a tremendous increase in deforestation. Around the world, people have cleared vast tracts of forest so that the land can be developed for homes or factories or used as farmland or pasture for grazing cattle. Because trees absorb carbon dioxide through the process of photosynthesis, the loss of immense numbers of them is a major factor in global warming. Even the use of large, standardized containers to ship goods all over the world has played a role in increasing the levels of carbon dioxide released into the air.

SOCIAL IMPACT

The way we work has become globalized, and so has the way we communicate, thanks to new media. **New media** refers to digital products and services that provide content through the Internet, and it has fundamentally changed the way people work, learn, interact socially, and spend their leisure time. Today, texting, instant messaging, and social networking allow fast and easy communication among people around the world. Much of this is done with smartphones, which combine communication and software applications into one handheld device. The technology enables people all over the world to connect with one another and share ideas and information instantaneously. As a result, culture sometimes forms around shared ideas or interests, rather than in a physical location.

Globalization has even affected what the world eats. Multinational fast food chains have popped up all over the planet. In just about any country, you can find some of your favorite restaurants. Some fear this will create a universal food culture, one in which people in all parts of the world eat the same things rather than the traditional foods of their culture. A universal food culture could result in the loss of regional cuisines and a wide range of crop varieties.

11.8.1 Trace the growth of service sector, white collar, and professional sector jobs in business and government; 11.11.5 Trace the impact of, need for, and controversies associated with environmental conservation, expansion of the national park system, and the development of environmental protection laws, with particular attention to the interaction between environmental protection advocates and property rights advocates.

In January 2013, Beijing, China's capital, registered a near record level of air pollution. The dense smog is visible over the city as these tourists, wearing masks to protect them from the polluted air, visit the Temple of Heaven, a complex of religious buildings.

Foods from other countries are also imported to the United States. But because food production in some of these countries lacks safety standards, some Americans worry about possible contamination and public health issues. Many are also concerned about the explosion of genetically modified (GM) foods. **Genetically modified foods** are grown from plants that have been changed in a way that does not occur naturally, often through the introduction of a gene from a different organism. Plants are sometimes modified in this way to make them disease-resistant and to increase crop yields. While the practice is controversial, GM foods may provide a sustainable way to feed the world's population.

HISTORICAL THINKING

1. **READING CHECK** Why did the wealth gap between top earners and the majority of Americans grow between the 1970s and 2010s?
2. **ANALYZE ENVIRONMENTAL CONCEPTS** How have global industrialization and the modification of landscapes affected natural systems around the world?
3. **ANALYZE CAUSE AND EFFECT** How do you think the aspects of globalization discussed in the lesson might define U.S. environmental policy issues?
4. **EVALUATE** What are some of the advantages and disadvantages of new media?

HI 5 Students analyze human modifications of landscapes and examine the resulting environmental policy issues.

4.4 NATIONAL GEOGRAPHIC EXPLORER TRISTRAM STUART

USING FOOD WASTE TO FEED THE WORLD

"We want to catalyze a food-waste revolution one person, one town, one country at a time."—Tristram Stuart

Tristram Stuart has an ambitious goal in mind: to create a healthy planet with zero hunger. He knows it can be done. After all, one-third of all food produced on Earth ends up in landfills and garbage heaps, and the impact extends far beyond the dinner plate. Growing food and raising animals takes its toll on the land. Water and other precious resources are wasted, trees are cut down. Pollution is greatly increased. Stuart is starting a food-waste revolution, and he urges you to join him: to eat less, buy less, waste less.

^ National Geographic Explorer, author, and campaigner Tristram Stuart is also a renowned activist fighting against worldwide food waste at a farmer's market near you.

MAIN IDEA Tristram Stuart is creating a food-waste revolution to stop hunger and save our planet.

WASTED FOOD

For thousands of years, pigs have been fed what their human owners didn't need. In fact, National Geographic Explorer Tristram Stuart says that's the exact reason pigs were domesticated—to recycle human food scraps. So when Stuart raised pigs as a teen, he fed them leftovers from his school cafeteria and local stores—good-quality leftovers that would otherwise have been discarded. But most pigs are now fed soy, wheat, and corn—foods that could nourish hungry people.

Food waste is a big problem, and it goes well beyond the pigs. As Stuart attests, "About a third of all food globally is wasted in the same world in which 1 billion people don't have enough to eat." From the moment he became aware of this global epidemic, Stuart hasn't looked back. He has written two best-selling books and has spoken to people around the world about curbing food waste. "I'd seen bins full of food being trucked off to landfill sites. And I thought, surely there is something more sensible to do with food than waste it."

What's unfortunate is that the food being thrown away is not rotten at all—it's good, fresh food that may not meet strict grocery store regulations of size, shape, or appearance. Before Stuart intervened, as much as 40 percent of these "ugly" fruits and vegetables were left in fields to rot around the world—even in countries where millions suffer from malnutrition.

This immense waste extends beyond produce. Bakeries throw away the ends of bread, edible parts of animals are discarded, fish that are too small are dumped back in the sea. In addition, harvesting food that ends up getting thrown away creates pollution, wastes water, and greatly impacts the land.

ADDRESSING A GLOBAL ISSUE

To demonstrate just how much actually gets wasted, Stuart and his organization, Feedback, set up an initiative called Feeding the 5,000. Food that would have been discarded is cooked up by local chefs and served to the community—for free. This public event first took place in London in 2009 and has since expanded to many locations around the world, including New York City in 2016. The goal is to create awareness while calling on individuals and companies to strategize more responsible ways to waste less—whether by buying less or by planning better—so that everything purchased is consumed.

CRITICAL VIEWING Imperfect yet edible produce like this typically gets rejected by stores and consumers. Why might shoppers pass up food like this, contributing to potential food waste?

Food waste is a global issue, and its solution is one that we must all take part in. Stuart recognizes that it is nearly impossible to have a world with zero waste. However, he draws attention to the burdens that our wastefulness is putting on Earth. "We are reaching the ecological limits that our planet can bear. And when we chop down forests—as we are every day to grow more and more food—when we extract water from depleting water reserves, when we emit fossil fuel emissions in the quest to grow more and more food and then we throw away so much of it—we have to start thinking about what we can start saving."

Through his books and public campaigns—including Gleaning Network, which coordinates the collection of produce that would normally have been left to rot—Tristram Stuart is on a mission to end food waste and save the world, 5,000 meals at a time.

HISTORICAL THINKING

1. **READING CHECK** What do Tristram Stuart's Feeding the 5,000 events aim to accomplish and inspire among their participants?
2. **ANALYZE CAUSE AND EFFECT** How does a global issue like hunger relate to the physical and human characteristics of places and regions?
3. **DRAW CONCLUSIONS** How can you and your family contribute to Stuart's mission to end food waste and improve the world?

11.11 Students analyze the major social problems and domestic policy issues in contemporary American society; CST 4 Students relate current events to the physical and human characteristics of places and regions.

4.5 **MAIN IDEA** In the 2010s, the United States tried to reach out to other nations and kept a watchful eye on terrorists.

AN INTERCONNECTED WORLD

During the 20th century, the United States became so powerful and dominant that historians began speaking of "the American century." How will the country's role change in the interconnected world of the 21st century?

PURSUING A MORE HOPEFUL WORLD

During his terms in office, President Obama favored a diplomatic approach in shaping U.S. relations with other countries. In 2009, the president began working to improve relations with Cuba. The two countries had been at odds since Fidel Castro seized power in Cuba in 1959 and established a communist dictatorship there. Then in 2008, with his health declining, Castro handed over power to his brother Raúl, who soon began to institute reforms. The following year, Obama lifted restrictions on travel to Cuba from the United States, and in 2015, the two countries restored diplomatic ties. In March 2016, Obama became the first sitting U.S. president to visit Cuba in nearly 90 years. Fidel Castro died at the age of 90 in November 2016.

Obama also attempted to improve relations between the United States and Iran. The two countries had been adversaries since the 1979 Iranian Revolution, which brought an anti-American Muslim cleric, or religious leader, to power. Tensions between the two countries increased early in the 21st century when the United States accused Iran of secretly developing a nuclear weapons program. As a result, the United States imposed harsh economic sanctions on Iran. In 2012, diplomats representing the two nations began discussing the nuclear issue and struck a deal in 2015. Iran promised to use its nuclear research for peaceful purposes and to provide inspectors greater access to the program, and the United States agreed to lift its sanctions. Obama said the agreement marked "one more chapter in our

National Geographic photographer David Guttenfelder took this photo of a passenger waving the American and Cuban flags as his ship arrived in Havana, Cuba's capital, in May 2016. The vessel was one of the first cruise ships to travel from the United States to Cuba in decades.

pursuit of a safer, more helpful and more hopeful world." However, the deal drew criticism from many Americans who did not believe Iran would keep its promise.

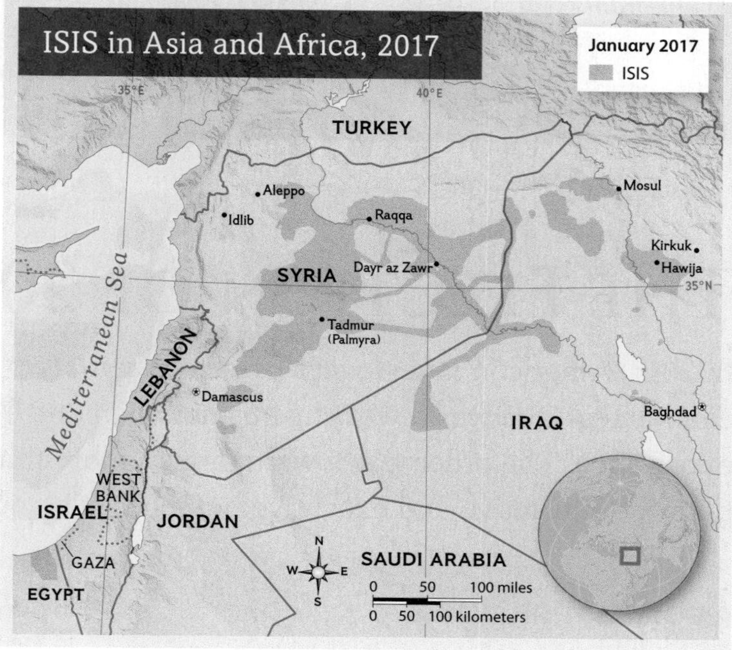

GLOBAL TERRORISM

No deals can be made with terrorists, however. Terrorist groups have emerged as major threats to world security. Foremost among these groups is al Qaeda, which you have read about. During the ongoing war on terror, President Obama ordered American soldiers to hunt down and kill al Qaeda leaders, including Osama bin Laden, the mastermind of the September 11, 2001, terror attacks. Nevertheless, the group has survived and continues to commit acts of terrorism.

Another terrorist organization called the **Islamic State in Iraq and Syria (ISIS)** may be more dangerous than al Qaeda. ISIS is a militant extremist group that has taken control of large areas of Syria and Iraq. The group first gained widespread attention in early 2014 when its forces seized control of cities and territories in Iraq and Syria, which was being torn apart by a bloody civil war. In the summer of 2015, ISIS destroyed ancient buildings and artifacts in and around the Syrian city of Palmyra. Leaders of the group claimed the ancient Greek and Roman ruins had no value because they weren't made by Muslims. The rest of the world condemned this misguided attack on our common heritage. In the end, however, terrorism can't destroy the enduring record of human life on Earth.

Europe also came under attack. In November 2015, ISIS members carried out terrorist attacks in Paris, killing roughly 130 people. Five months later, the militant Muslim group claimed credit for killing more than 30 people in Brussels, Belgium. Some of the men who carried out the attacks were born and raised in Europe. ISIS and other terrorist groups have been able to recruit new members through the Internet. Their message of inclusion appeals to many economically disadvantaged and alienated people—particularly young men—around the world.

The fighting in Syria and Iraq displaced millions of people and contributed to a worldwide refugee crisis. By 2015, about 4 million refugees had fled from Syria. In the United States, the question of whether or not to accept Syrian refugees sparked intense debate. Opponents expressed fear that some of the refugees might carry out terrorist attacks on U.S. soil.

Yet as the leader of the world's democratic societies, the United States has long been a magnet for people all over the world who yearn for a life of freedom and opportunity—and political stability. Under our democratic political system, the United States has achieved a level of freedom and economic prosperity that has made it a model for other nations.

As you know, Americans' rights and freedoms are the result of a carefully defined set of political principles embodied in the Constitution. But these freedoms are imperfect. For example, even though Americans elected an African-American president in 2008, poverty, incarceration, and lower life-expectancy rates continue to afflict communities of color at rates that are far higher than those of white communities. Still, the enduring significance of the United States lies in its free political system, its pluralistic nature, and its promise of opportunity. The country has demonstrated the strength and dynamism of a racially, religiously, and culturally diverse people. Our democratic political system depends on them—as educated citizens—to survive and prosper.

HISTORICAL THINKING

1. **READING CHECK** What steps did President Obama take to improve relations with Cuba?
2. **SYNTHESIZE** How has globalization helped encourage the rise of terrorist groups?
3. **FORM AND SUPPORT OPINIONS** Do you think the United States should pursue diplomatic solutions to problems with other countries, or use force? Explain your answer.

11.9.6 Describe U.S. Middle East policy and its strategic, political, and economic interests, including those related to the Gulf War; HI 1 Students show the connections, causal and otherwise, between particular historical events and larger social, economic, and political trends and developments.

4.6 **MAIN IDEA** Donald Trump's populist message that he would "Make America Great Again" attracted enough voters to secure him the electoral votes needed to win the 2016 presidential election.

THE ELECTION OF 2016

In 2016, American voters were presented with two historic major party candidates. One was a wealthy businessman and TV personality with no political experience. The other was a woman with more than a decade of experience in both the legislative and executive branches. The outcome surprised many.

A POPULIST PREVAILS

As you have read, populists such as William Jennings Bryan and H. Ross Perot launched presidential bids in the past. In 2016, after emerging from a crowded field of candidates to become the Republican nominee, **Donald J. Trump** ran a populist campaign in which he claimed that only he, with his business expertise, could solve the nation's problems.

Trump's opponent, Democratic nominee Hillary Rodham Clinton, had served as U.S. Senator from New York and as President Obama's secretary of state. She was the wife of former president Bill Clinton. Trump, on the other hand, had never run for or served in public office prior to 2016. A real-estate developer and reality TV celebrity, Trump was known for speaking his mind. He chose **Mike Pence**, the governor of Indiana, as his running mate. Clinton's running mate was Tim Kaine, a senator from Virginia.

While Clinton ran a traditional campaign based on issues and proposed solutions, Trump's populist campaign was fueled by his message: The interests of the United States should be placed above those of all other nations. His lively rallies attracted the support of traditional Republicans and a number of independent voters. His promises to build a wall along the entire length of the border with Mexico, deport undocumented immigrants, and ban foreign Muslims from entering the United States appealed to nativists. He pledged to repeal the Affordable Care Act, put an end to NAFTA, and bring a quick end to international terrorism.

During the campaign, U.S. intelligence agencies and the Department of Justice gathered evidence that Russia had engaged in a complex, high-tech effort to disrupt the nation's electoral process. According to the Department of Homeland Security, Russian hackers attempted to access voter databases in 21 states and succeeded in breaching the systems of three states. There was no evidence these efforts affected the actual vote. Russian operatives also spread misinformation and negative "news" about Clinton on social media and hacked into both parties' email systems, leaking information that tended to be primarily unfavorable to Clinton and the Democrats.

On Election Day, Trump won a narrow majority of voters in a number of **swing states**, or states where the election might go to either party. Even though almost 3 million more Americans cast their votes for Clinton, Trump won the electoral vote 306 to 232.

Trump and Clinton take the stage for their second presidential debate, held in St. Louis, Missouri, on October 9.

11.2.8 Examine the effect of political programs and activities of Populists; 11.11.1 Discuss the reasons for the nation's changing immigration policy, with emphasis on how the Immigration Act of 1965 and successor acts have transformed American society;

The 2016 Election

Donald J. Trump, Republican

Electoral Vote: 306 votes, 56.9%

Popular Vote: 62,979,636 votes, 46.1%

Hillary Rodham Clinton, Democrat

Electoral Vote: 232 votes, 43.1%

Popular Vote: 65,844,610 votes, 48.2%

Write-Ins & Others

7,804,213 votes, 5.7%

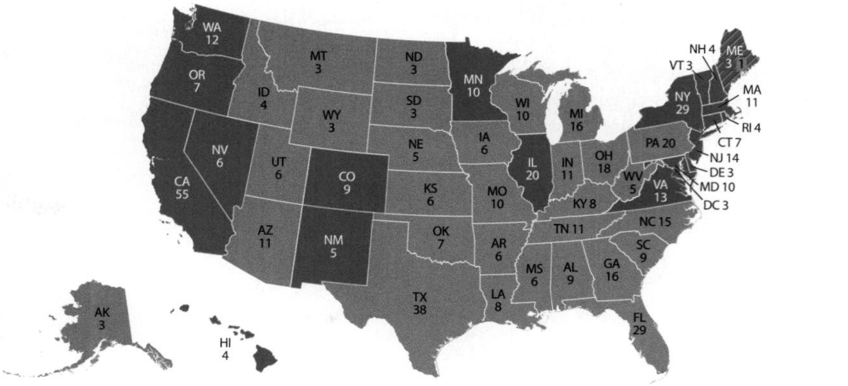

In 2017, Congress voted to add new sanctions to those already in place to address Russia's cyberattacks during the election. The unusual election also raised suspicion that Trump's campaign had **colluded**, or conspired, with the Russians. Even though Trump denied the allegations, the Department of Justice appointed a special prosecutor, **Robert Mueller**, to investigate. As of early 2018, the investigation was still ongoing, while Trump declined to impose the additional sanctions on Russia. He claimed existing sanctions were effective enough.

TRUMP'S FIRST YEAR

Trump began his presidency by issuing a number of executive orders, including a directive banning people from seven specific, primarily Muslim, nations from entering the United States. Enforcement of the order began as many travelers were already on their way to the United States, causing widespread confusion at airports. Federal courts initially blocked this order, stating it was unconstitutional. Parts of the ban were reinstated and the government issued new versions of the ban in 2017. These were also contested in federal courts.

Trump attempted to secure funding for the construction of a border wall early in his term, but Congress approved only a small portion of the money required. He also ordered a sharp increase in the number of **Immigration and Customs Enforcement (ICE)** agents, raising the deportation rate of undocumented immigrants. In September 2017, Trump chose to end the **Deferred Action for Childhood Arrivals (DACA)** program, which had been created by President Barack Obama in 2012. The program allowed the children of illegal immigrants who came to the United States before 2007 to defer deportation and apply for work permits in the country for a two-year renewable period. Applicants had to undergo a thorough background check every two years. In 2012, about 800,000 young people—who came to be known as "Dreamers"—enrolled in DACA. Trump handed Congress the responsibility of passing an act to protect the Dreamers. Otherwise, these immigrants would face deportation to the place of their birth. Trump also insisted that Congress should pass tougher immigration laws.

Congress failed to repeal the Affordable Care Act, but a clause in its Tax Cuts and Jobs Act, which passed in December 2017, ended the individual mandate, a funding measure requiring Americans not covered by an insurance plan to pay a tax. This threatened the affordability and the future of the ACA. The tax bill lowered tax rates for individuals temporarily and corporations permanently but took no steps to make up the lost revenue caused by these cuts. Some economists believed this new tax plan would result in a sharp rise to the national debt.

On the international front, Trump ended U.S. involvement in the **Trans-Pacific Partnership (TPP)**, a trade agreement with Asia. He threatened to leave NAFTA, but ultimately decided to try to renegotiate it. Trump also withdrew the United States from the Paris Agreement on climate change, asserting that the agreement was not fair to the American people or to U.S. businesses.

HISTORICAL THINKING

1. **READING CHECK** How did the swing states affect the 2016 election?
2. **DETERMINE WORD MEANINGS** How did Trump fit the definition of a populist?
3. **EVALUATE** How effective was Trump in meeting his campaign promises during his first year as president?

11.11.5 Trace the impact of, need for, and controversies associated with environmental conservation, expansion of the national park system, and the development of environmental protection laws, with particular attention to the interaction between environmental protection advocates and property rights advocates; HI 4 Students understand the meaning, implication, and impact of historical events and recognize that events could have taken other directions.

African migrants wait to be rescued from their rubber boat in the Mediterranean Sea in 2014. Many countries patrol international waters to rescue refugees and transfer them safely to shore in Europe, where more than 1.3 million applied for asylum in 2015 alone.

CRITICAL VIEWING Addario captured this photo of refugees from Egypt, Syria, and other countries being examined and treated by medical personnel from Doctors Without Borders. What role do relief organizations play in the refugee crisis? Do online research to support your answer.

CST 4 Students relate current events to the physical and human characteristics

Hanaa, age 12, (center) rides to her job before dawn with other Syrian refugees from their temporary tent settlement in Lebanon. Hanaa and her family fled Syria in 2011 to escape the civil war.

4.7

THROUGH THE LENS

Lynsey Addario

After studying international relations in college, Lynsey Addario had a thought: photojournalism could be a marriage between international relations and art, telling stories with pictures. Fast-forward a few years, and Addario is one of National Geographic's most accomplished conflict photographers. Refugees are a primary focus of her work. "My philosophy has always been that I'm there for the people I'm covering," says Addario. "I'm just a messenger documenting whatever is going on and bringing their message to people in power who may be able to do something about it."

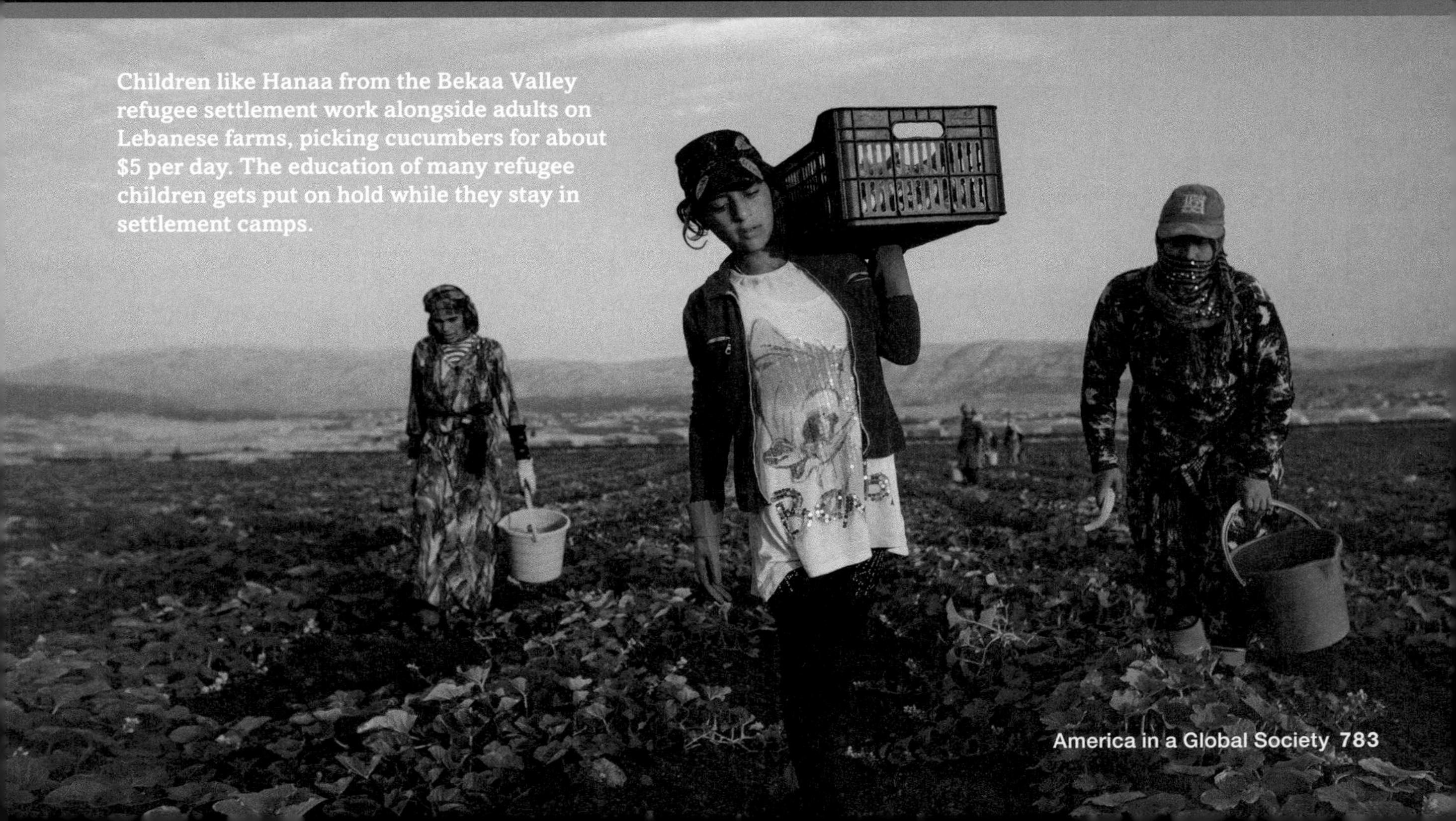

Children like Hanaa from the Bekaa Valley refugee settlement work alongside adults on Lebanese farms, picking cucumbers for about $5 per day. The education of many refugee children gets put on hold while they stay in settlement camps.

CHAPTER 22 AMERICA IN A GLOBAL SOCIETY

REVIEW

VOCABULARY

For each of the following vocabulary terms, write a sentence in which you use the term correctly.

1. globalization HSS 11.11.1
   Globalization, which has allowed for the faster and freer flow of people and goods across national borders, has powerfully affected the United States.
2. free-enterprise zone HSS 11.9.7
3. compassionate conservatism HSS 11.11.2
4. neoconservative HSS 11.9.6
5. rogue state HSS 11.9.6
6. bailout HSS 11.11.6
7. foreclosure HSS 11.11.6
8. marriage equality HSS 11.10.6
9. greenhouse gas HSS 11.11.5
10. new media HSS 11.8.7

READING STRATEGY

FORM AND SUPPORT OPINIONS

When you form an opinion, you determine and assess the importance and significance of an issue. Your opinion is your personal judgment, not a fact, so you should support your opinion with examples and facts. Use a chart like this one to form and support an opinion about issues in the 21st century. Then answer the question.

Example/Fact	Example/Fact	Example/Fact

Opinion

11. What do you think is the most critical issue facing the United States in the 21st century? HSS 11.11

MAIN IDEAS

Answer the following questions. Support your answers with evidence from the chapter.

12. What was the Contract with America? **LESSON 1.1** HSS 11.11
13. How did globalization affect U.S. manufacturing jobs during the 1990s? **LESSON 1.2** HSS 11.9.7
14. Explain why many commentators believed bias played into the outcome of the 2000 presidential election. **LESSON 2.1** HSS HREP 2
15. Why did President George W. Bush order the invasion of Iraq? **LESSON 2.3** HSS 11.9.6
16. What impact did the Great Recession have on American industries and the employment rate? **LESSON 3.1** HSS 11.11
17. What were Obama's priorities when he became president? **LESSON 3.2** HSS 11.11.6
18. What evidence of global warming have scientists detected? **LESSON 4.2** HSS 11.11.5
19. What are genetically modified foods? **LESSON 4.3** HSS 11.11.5
20. Why were many voters surprised by the outcome of the 2016 election? **LESSON 4.6** HSS HI 4

HISTORICAL THINKING

Answer the following questions. Support your answers with evidence from the chapter.

21. **COMPARE AND CONTRAST** Why is the United States more diverse now than it was in the middle of the 20th century? HSS 11.11.1
22. **DRAW CONCLUSIONS** How have shifts in foreign policy and immigration affected America's national identity from the 1980s through recent times? HSS 11.11.1
23. **MAKE INFERENCES** How do you think Muslims in the United States may have been regarded by some other Americans after September 11, 2001? HSS HI 3

24. **EVALUATE** How has the role of the federal government—and especially the presidency—changed from the 1970s through more recent times? HSS 11.11.7

25. **SYNTHESIZE** What does globalization mean, and how has it affected Americans? HSS 11.11

26. **FORM AND SUPPORT OPINIONS** Do you think groups such as Black Lives Matter and Occupy Wall Street are ultimately effective? Why or why not? HSS HI 1

27. **ANALYZE ENVIRONMENTAL CONCEPTS** How has deforestation affected the natural system of photosynthesis and increased global warming? HSS HI 5

INTERPRET GRAPHS

Study the graphs below, which show the relative populations of ethnic groups in the United States between 1950 and 2010. Then answer the questions that follow.

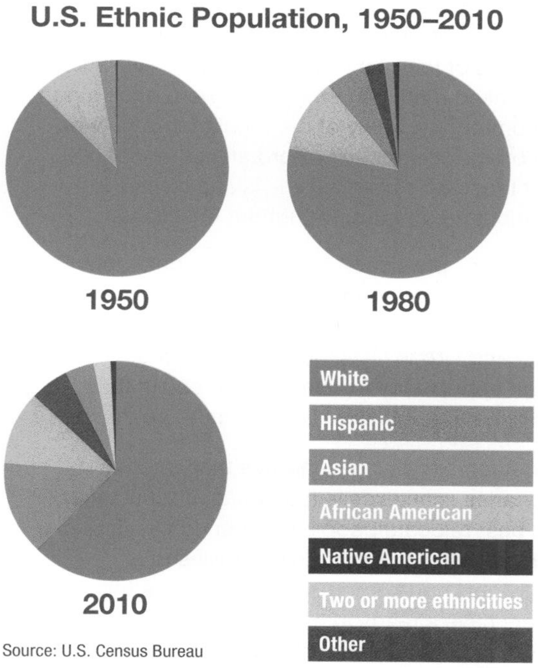

Source: U.S. Census Bureau

28. How did the composition of the United States shift between 1950 and 1980? HSS 11.11.7

29. What additional shifts occurred between 1980 and 2010? HSS 11.11.7

ANALYZE SOURCES

In this excerpt from an address to the nation on immigration that President Obama delivered on November 20, 2014, he explains why he welcomes immigrants to the United States.

> My fellow Americans, we are and always will be a nation of immigrants. We were strangers once, too. And whether our forebears were strangers who crossed the Atlantic, or the Pacific, or the Rio Grande, we are here only because this country welcomed them in, and taught them that to be an American is about something more than what we look like, or what our last names are, or how we worship. What makes us Americans is our shared commitment to an ideal—that all of us are created equal, and all of us have the chance to make of our lives what we will.

30. What vision of the United States does Obama describe in his address? HSS 11.11.1

CONNECT TO YOUR LIFE

31. **EXPLANATORY** Grassroots movements such as the Tea Party, Occupy Wall Street, and Black Lives Matter formed in the early 21st century. Why do you think such movements form, and why are people drawn to them? Write a paragraph in which you explain the connection between such groups and larger issues. HSS HI 1

TIPS

- State the purpose of grassroots movements in a main idea statement.
- Describe the social, economic, and political factors that may be involved in the movements' formation.
- Explain what people who join the movements hope to get out of them.
- Use information from the chapter to help support your ideas.
- Conclude your paragraph with a sentence summarizing your ideas.

NATIONAL GEOGRAPHIC | CONNECTION

U.S. Climate Refugees Race Against Time

BY CAROLYN VAN HOUTEN

Adapted from "The First Official Climate Refugees in the U.S. Race Against Time," by Carolyn van Houten, news.nationalgeographic.com, May 2016

A shot rings out across what remains of Isle de Jean Charles as the sun drops behind the gnarled skeletons of what once were massive oak trees. Rifle in hand, Howard Brunet, 14, looks down at the rabbit he shot. His sister Juliette, 13, leaps down the stairs to retrieve the body. Next comes rabbit stew. It's a normal evening at the Brunet household. The kids are tough. The water forces them to be.

Since 1955, the Isle de Jean Charles band of the Biloxi-Chitimacha-Choctaw tribe has lost 98 percent of its land to the encroaching Gulf waters. Of the 22,400-acre island that stood at that time, only several hundred acres remain. The island is located deep in the southern bayous of Louisiana, about 15 miles (24 kilometers) from the Gulf of Mexico. As the land has eroded, the tribe's identity, food, and culture have slowly eroded with it.

In response, in 2016, the Department of Housing and Urban Development awarded the tribe $48 million to relocate. But moving isn't a simple solution. The tribe is receiving funding, but the fight to save their culture is not over. The federal grant will help save the tribe from the eroding landscape, but addressing the effects of cultural erosion is far more difficult. "Once our island goes, the core of our tribe is lost," says Chantel Comardelle, the deputy tribal chief's daughter. "We've lost our whole culture—that is what is on the line."

For generations, the Biloxi-Chitimacha-Choctaw have sustained themselves off of the island's natural resources. But today, residents say the land loss has made that untenable. The land is disappearing into the Gulf of Mexico because of a combination of coastal erosion, rising sea levels, lack of soil renewal, and shifting soil due to dredging for oil and gas pipeline placement. The soil that remains is nutrient depleted due to saltwater intrusion enabled by eroding marshes.

As the effects of climate change transform coastal communities around the world, the people of Isle de Jean Charles will be only 60 of the estimated 200 million people globally who could be displaced by 2050 because of climate change.

The only way into or out of Isle de Jean Charles is on Island Road. In 1953, the year the road was built, land and thick marsh surrounded the road. But erosion is eating away at it. Every time a strong storm heads toward the island, residents have to decide whether they will evacuate. Once the storm arrives, the road out of the island will be flooded. The water has overtaken many structures that were once a part of the community. Many of the tribal members who remain on the island can't afford any other option. Most of those who have left the island remain in the tribe but are spread throughout Louisiana.

"The tribe has physically and culturally been torn apart with the scattering of members," states the resettlement proposal submitted to the Department of Housing and Urban Development. "A new settlement offers an opportunity for the tribe to rebuild their homes and secure their culture on safe ground."

The resettlement proposal argues that Isle de Jean Charles is an excellent test case for deciding how to best relocate people threatened by climate change. The plan aims to move families to a culturally appropriate community. Because tribe members have already lost so much of their land and their tribal heritage to the water, relocation is crucial not just for their personal safety but also for the longevity of their culture and traditions.

"At one time, water was our life, and now it's almost our enemy because it is driving us out, but it still gives us life," Comardelle says. "It's a double-edged sword. It's our life and our death."

For more from National Geographic, check out "Shell Shock" online.

UNIT INQUIRY: Conduct Oral History Interviews

In this unit, you learned about recent American history, which includes events that your parents and many adults alive today have witnessed. You'll have no difficulty finding adults who watched TV news reports of the Watergate investigation and of President Nixon leaving the White House after resigning. These adults have vivid, emotional memories of the 9/11 terrorist attacks on the World Trade Center in New York City and on the Pentagon in Washington, D.C. What can you learn from these adults about the way average Americans reacted to such events? How has life in the United States changed over the course of their lives? What is better about life today? What is worse?

ASSIGNMENT

Conduct oral history interviews with people who were adults in the years after 1970. Find out how they and other Americans reacted to major events that occurred between 1970 and 2010. Be prepared to present your findings to the class.

Plan Review the major events covered in this unit and choose a couple to focus on. Compose a list of questions about those events and about changes in the United States between 1970 and 2010. You might use a graphic organizer to help you formulate your questions or to take notes. Then identify three adults and ask if they would be willing to be interviewed.

Who? ______________________

What? ______________________

Where? ______________________

When? ______________________

Why? ______________________

____

____

Produce Decide if you want to take notes during your interviews or make an audio or video recording. Then schedule and conduct the interviews. In your notes or at the beginning of a recording, be sure to identify each interviewee by name and birthdate.

Present Share your interviews with the class. You might consider one of these options:

- If you made audio or video recordings, write and record an introduction to them. Then edit your recordings and produce a final version to play for the class. (You have created your own primary source.)
- Either transcribe your interviews or write a summary of what you learned from them and distribute your written account to the class.
- Prepare and deliver an oral report of the highlights of your interviews.

Check out the History Notebook for another oral history project.

NATIONAL GEOGRAPHIC | LEARNING FRAMEWORK ACTIVITIES

Create a History Game

ATTITUDE Curiosity

SKILLS Communication, Collaboration

Perhaps you've played board games that require you to answer questions about literature, science, popular culture, and other subjects. Work with a partner to create a history game modeled on such board games. Using the information in this unit, write 50 questions that can be answered in a word or phrase. Use the questions as the basis of a board game, and play the game with a group of classmates. As an alternative, create a crossword puzzle using key words and names from the unit. Give the puzzle to a classmate to solve.

Form a Political Party

ATTITUDES Responsibility, Empowerment

KNOWLEDGE Our Human Story

You've read about the beliefs, policies, and agendas of a number of American political parties during this course. Now form a political party that represents your beliefs. Decide on a name for your party, and write a platform and a description of the programs you'd like to institute. Tell how your party differs from the Democratic and Republican parties in the United States. Identify groups of Americans who would be likely to support your party. Give an oral presentation in which you describe your political party to the class.

CST 2 Students analyze how change happens at different rates at different times; understand that some aspects can change while others remain the same; and understand that change is complicated and affects not only technology and politics but also values and beliefs; HREP 4 Students construct and test hypotheses; collect, evaluate, and employ information from multiple primary and secondary sources; and apply it in oral and written presentations.

THROUGH THE LENS

AMERICA THROUGH THE DECADES

A picture is worth a thousand words. You've probably heard that before—now see if you agree. Each image in this photo essay represents one of the decades you have learned about, starting with the 1900s and going through the 2010s. Test your knowledge of American history by identifying each photograph according to its decade while you consider the historical events, important people, and social and cultural movements you have studied.

1775

RUN
DMC
KING OF ROCK

STUDENT REFERENCES

BIG SUR, CALIFORNIA

CITIZENSHIP HANDBOOK

This Citizenship Handbook will help you take an in-depth look at our nation's two most important documents: the Declaration of Independence and the U.S. Constitution, which contains the Bill of Rights. The handbook includes notes to help you understand the formal language and difficult concepts contained in the more than 225-year-old documents. The handbook also provides background information and historical context to better help you understand the thinking and motivations of the Framers. At the end of the handbook, you will read about citizenship and the rights and responsibilities that come along with it. You will also find out how you can build and practice citizenship skills in the classroom and beyond.

The Charters of Freedom, as the Declaration of Independence, U.S. Constitution, and Bill of Rights are collectively known, are housed in the National Archives Museum in Washington, D.C.

11.1.1 Describe the Enlightenment and the rise of democratic ideas as the context in which the nation was founded; 11.1.2 Analyze the ideological origins of the American Revolution, the Founding Fathers' philosophy of divinely bestowed unalienable natural rights, the debates on the drafting and ratification of the Constitution, and the addition of the Bill of Rights.

DECLARATION OF INDEPENDENCE

Introduction

The American colonists wrote the Declaration of Independence in 1776 to formally call for their separation and independence from Britain. Up until then, colonists who were legally British citizens had lived in relative isolation from the king's authority and largely governed themselves. They modeled their colonial governments on Parliament, Britain's legislative body, by forming elected assemblies similar to the House of Commons. Unlike the British legislature, however, elected officials in colonial assemblies lived in the areas they represented. The colonists believed representatives who lived among those who elected them would better understand local interests and needs. At the same time, the colonists had no representatives in Parliament and sometimes resented what they felt to be unfair treatment by Britain.

ROAD TO REVOLUTION

The colonists' resentment grew after they fought alongside the British in the French and Indian War. The Americans had joined the fight so they could expand their settlements westward into Native American territory. But after Britain won the war against the French in 1763, British king George III wanted to keep the peace. To do so, he believed he needed to limit contact between the Native Americans and the colonists. As a result, the British government issued the Proclamation of 1763, which stated that colonists could not settle west of the Appalachian Mountains.

Furthermore, victory in the war had left Britain with overwhelming debt. To help pay it down, King George introduced a series of taxes against the colonists, including customs duties, the Sugar Act of 1764, and the Stamp Act of 1765, which taxed printed materials in the colonies. The Stamp Act was the first direct tax Britain had imposed on the colonists.

The American colonists protested the British legislation with shouts of "No taxation without representation." Angry colonists formed secret groups, such as the Sons of Liberty, and organized demonstrations and boycotts of British goods. As tensions continued to rise, violence erupted. In 1770, the Boston Massacre resulted in the deaths of five colonists at the hands of British soldiers. Three years later, colonists demonstrated their anger over a law on the sale of tea by staging the Boston Tea Party in Boston Harbor.

Finally, in 1775, feelings on both sides reached the boiling point. After British troops learned the colonists had stored weapons in Concord, Massachusetts, the troops marched to the town. Colonial militiamen rushed to face down the British soldiers in nearby Lexington. During the clash, shots rang out at what would later be called the first battle of the American Revolution.

BREAK WITH BRITAIN

American leaders had convened a conference of colonial delegates to respond to British taxation in 1774. At this conference in Philadelphia, known as the First Continental Congress, some delegates had called for the colonies to separate completely from Britain. By 1775, the Second Continental Congress was prepared to take action. The Congress raised an army and formed a committee to write an official document to declare independence from Britain. This "Committee of Five" included Thomas Jefferson, John Adams, Benjamin Franklin, Roger Sherman, and Robert Livingston. Jefferson, the youngest member of the Congress at 33, was chosen to be the principal author of the Declaration of Independence.

Enlightenment thinkers such as John Locke influenced the ideological origins of the American Revolution and the Declaration. Locke argued that humans were born free and equal and that a leader could rule only with the consent of the people. Jefferson was also inspired by the Enlightenment philosophy of unalienable, or natural, rights. The Founding Fathers considered that these rights were "divinely bestowed," or God-given. Unalienable rights, Jefferson insisted, could not be taken away.

On July 4, 1776, the delegates to the Continental Congress adopted the Declaration of Independence. In 1782, seven years after the first shots were fired, the American Revolution officially ended. The American colonists had fought for and won their freedom and independence from Britain.

THE DECLARATION OF INDEPENDENCE

IN CONGRESS, JULY 4, 1776

The Declaration of Independence begins by explaining why the colonists at the Continental Congress want to break away from Britain and become independent. Jefferson and the other Founding Fathers believed it was necessary to explain their motivations.

The unanimous Declaration of the thirteen united States of America, When in the Course of human events, it becomes necessary for one people to dissolve the political bands which have connected them with another, and to assume among the powers of the earth, the separate and equal station to which the Laws of Nature and of Nature's God entitle them, a decent respect to the opinions of mankind requires that they should declare the causes which impel them to the separation.

Here, Jefferson states that people are born equal and have rights, including life, liberty, and the pursuit of happiness, that should be safeguarded by the government. John Locke's idea that government is based on the consent of the people is also established. Jefferson claims that when a government takes away the people's rights, they must overthrow the government. But this step should not be taken lightly.

We hold these truths to be self-evident, that all men are created equal, that they are endowed by their Creator with certain unalienable Rights, that among these are Life, Liberty and the pursuit of Happiness.—That to secure these rights, Governments are instituted among Men, deriving their just powers from the consent of the governed, —That whenever any Form of Government becomes destructive of these ends, it is the Right of the People to alter or to abolish it, and to institute new Government, laying its foundation on such principles and organizing its powers in such form, as to them shall seem most likely to effect their Safety and Happiness. Prudence, indeed, will dictate that Governments long established should not be changed for light and transient causes; and accordingly all experience hath shown, that mankind are more disposed to suffer, while evils are sufferable, than to right themselves by abolishing the forms to which they are accustomed. But when a long train of abuses and usurpations, pursuing invariably the same Object evinces a design to reduce them under absolute Despotism, it is their right, it is their duty, to throw off such Government, and to provide new Guards for their future security.—Such has been the patient sufferance of these Colonies; and such is now the necessity which constrains them to alter their former Systems of Government. The history of the present King of Great Britain is a history of repeated injuries and usurpations, all having in direct object the establishment of an absolute Tyranny over these States. To prove this, let Facts be submitted to a candid world.

The Declaration goes on to explain exactly what King George has done by listing the colonists' grievances against him.

HISTORICAL THINKING Why do you think Jefferson lists the colonists' grievances against the king?

The king has failed to approve or disapprove laws needed by the people. At the time, colonial laws had to be approved by the king. Britain could also veto colonial legislation.

He has refused his Assent to Laws, the most wholesome and necessary for the public good.

11.1 Students analyze the significant events in the founding of the nation and its attempts to realize the philosophy of government described in the Declaration of Independence.

He has forbidden his Governors to pass Laws of immediate and pressing importance, unless suspended in their operation till his Assent should be obtained; and when so suspended, he has utterly neglected to attend to them. He has refused to pass other Laws for the accommodation of large districts of people, unless those people would relinquish the right of Representation in the Legislature, a right inestimable to them and formidable to tyrants only.

The king has ordered his royal governors to block colonial legislation. He has claimed that unless people in the colonies give up the right to have representatives in their own government in America, he will not pass laws those people need.

He has called together legislative bodies at places unusual, uncomfortable, and distant from the depository of their public Records, for the sole purpose of fatiguing them into compliance with his measures.

He has dissolved Representative Houses repeatedly, for opposing with manly firmness his invasions on the rights of the people.

The king has dissolved many colonial lawmaking bodies because they stood up against laws that threatened the rights of Americans. By 1776, many colonial assemblies had been dissolved.

He has refused for a long time, after such dissolutions, to cause others to be elected; whereby the Legislative powers, incapable of Annihilation, have returned to the People at large for their exercise; the State remaining in the mean time exposed to all the dangers of invasion from without, and convulsions within.

After the legislatures were dissolved, some colonies had no laws to protect them. Citizens often created special assemblies to maintain some form of government.

He has endeavored to prevent the population of these States; for that purpose obstructing the Laws for Naturalization of Foreigners; refusing to pass others to encourage their migrations hither, and raising the conditions of new Appropriations of Lands.

He has obstructed the Administration of Justice, by refusing his Assent to Laws for establishing Judiciary powers.

He has made Judges dependent on his Will alone, for the tenure of their offices, and the amount and payment of their salaries.

Some colonial legislatures tried to establish courts, but the king dismissed them. Judges have also been appointed who favored the king's interests.

He has erected a multitude of New Offices, and sent hither swarms of Officers to harass our people, and eat out their substance.

He has kept among us, in times of peace, Standing Armies without the Consent of our legislatures.

He has affected to render the Military independent of and superior to the Civil power.

The king has sent soldiers to America without the consent of colonial legislatures. He has made his soldiers more powerful than the colonists.

The king has allowed others to pass and enforce new laws in the colonies that the colonists consider to be invalid ("pretended").

He has combined with others to subject us to a jurisdiction foreign to our constitution, and unacknowledged by our laws; giving his Assent to their Acts of pretended Legislation:

Jefferson introduces acts of Parliament the colonists considered to be unconstitutional. For example:

- making sure that soldiers who kill colonists are given a fake trial and not held accountable for murder;
- stopping American trade with other countries;
- taxing without permission;
- often refusing the right of trial by jury;
- sending colonists far away to be tried in courts for things they have not done;
- abolishing laws made by the colonies;
- stopping lawmaking groups in America and declaring that only the British government can make laws for people in America.

For Quartering large bodies of armed troops among us:

For protecting them, by a mock Trial, from punishment for any Murders which they should commit on the Inhabitants of these States:

For cutting off our Trade with all parts of the world:

For imposing Taxes on us without our Consent:

For depriving us in many cases, of the benefits of Trial by Jury:

For transporting us beyond Seas to be tried for pretended offences

For abolishing the free System of English Laws in a neighboring Province, establishing therein an Arbitrary government, and enlarging its Boundaries so as to render it at once an example and fit instrument for introducing the same absolute rule into these Colonies:

For taking away our Charters, abolishing our most valuable Laws, and altering fundamentally the Forms of our Governments:

For suspending our own Legislatures, and declaring themselves invested with power to legislate for us in all cases whatsoever.

The colonists claim that the king has essentially given up, or abdicated, his power to govern them. Now the king refuses to protect the colonists and has started a war against them.

He has abdicated Government here, by declaring us out of his Protection and waging War against us.

He has plundered our seas, ravaged our Coasts, burnt our towns, and destroyed the lives of our people.

The king is sending foreign soldiers to fight and suppress the colonists—an act of barbarism unworthy of a civilized nation.

He is at this time transporting large Armies of foreign Mercenaries to complete the works of death, desolation and tyranny, already begun with circumstances of Cruelty & perfidy scarcely paralleled in the most barbarous ages, and totally unworthy the Head of a civilized nation.

He has constrained our fellow Citizens taken Captive on the high Seas to bear Arms against their Country, to become the executioners of their friends and Brethren, or to fall themselves by their Hands.

He has excited domestic insurrections amongst us, and has endeavored to bring on the inhabitants of our frontiers, the merciless Indian Savages, whose known rule of warfare, is an undistinguished destruction of all ages, sexes and conditions.

He has encouraged Native Americans to attack the colonists.

In every stage of these Oppressions We have Petitioned for Redress in the most humble terms: Our repeated Petitions have been answered only by repeated injury. A Prince whose character is thus marked by every act which may define a Tyrant, is unfit to be the ruler of a free people.

The colonists have repeatedly and unsuccessfully made formal requests for this behavior to stop. However, the king has become a tyrant.

Nor have We been wanting in attentions to our British brethren. We have warned them from time to time of attempts by their legislature to extend an unwarrantable jurisdiction over us. We have reminded them of the circumstances of our emigration and settlement here. We have appealed to their native justice and magnanimity, and we have conjured them by the ties of our common kindred to disavow these usurpations, which, would inevitably interrupt our connections and correspondence. They too have been deaf to the voice of justice and of consanguinity. We must, therefore, acquiesce in the necessity, which denounces our Separation, and hold them, as we hold the rest of mankind, Enemies in War, in Peace Friends.

We have appealed to the British people, pointing out the injustice of our treatment and our close ties to them ("consanguinity"), but they have ignored us. We have no choice but to consider them our enemies.

We, therefore, the Representatives of the united States of America, in General Congress, Assembled, appealing to the Supreme Judge of the world for the rectitude of our intentions, do, in the Name, and by Authority of the good People of these Colonies, solemnly publish and declare, That these United Colonies are, and of Right ought to be Free and Independent States; that they are Absolved from all Allegiance to the British Crown, and that all political connection between them and the State of Great Britain, is and ought to be totally dissolved; and that as Free and Independent States, they have full Power to levy War, conclude Peace, contract Alliances, establish Commerce, and to do all other Acts and Things which Independent States may of right do. And for the support of this Declaration, with a firm reliance on the protection of divine Providence, we mutually pledge to each other our Lives, our Fortunes and our sacred Honor.

For all these reasons, Jefferson declares that the United Colonies are free and independent states with no further allegiance to Britain. As free and independent states, they can declare war, negotiate peace, make agreements to work with other countries, establish commerce, and participate in all other activities allowed by independent states.

CONSTITUTION OF THE UNITED STATES

Introduction

In 1787, delegates at the Constitutional Convention in Philadelphia engaged in debates for four months as they drafted the Constitution. Among other issues, they debated how the legislative branch should work, how to elect the president, and whether enslaved people should be included in a state's population. After agreeing to a series of compromises, the Framers signed the U.S. Constitution, which, once ratified by the states, became the supreme law of the land in the United States. Considering the size and complexity of the United States today and its position as a world power, the U.S. Constitution is relatively simple. It consists of a Preamble, 7 articles, and currently 27 amendments, based on the 7 key principles below.

1. Popular Sovereignty The phrase means "the authority of the people." The opening words of the Constitution, "We the people" emphasize the idea that people together create a social contract in which they agree to be governed. Government authority is derived from the citizens, who determine how much power the government should have and what rules it must follow.

2. Republicanism This is a form of representational democracy. In a republic, citizens have the power and authority to make decisions as to how they are governed. Citizens elect representatives, who then have the power to write and enforce laws. Most Americans today use the terms *representational democracy* and *republicanism* interchangeably.

3. Federalism Federalism is a form of government in which power is distributed among several levels of government. A federalist system features a strong central government, but states do not lose all rights and power. States pursue and protect their interests as they see fit, while working together as a nation. In American federalism, the federal government's powers are enumerated, or listed. The states have powers that are reserved, or unwritten. Concurrent powers are powers shared by the federal and state governments.

4. Separation of Powers To reduce the potential for abuse of power and to prevent one branch from becoming too powerful, government was divided into three branches: the legislative branch (Congress, consisting of the Senate and the House of Representatives), which writes laws; the executive branch (led by the president), which enforces the laws written by Congress; and the judicial branch (made up of the U.S. Supreme Court and additional lower federal courts), which interprets and applies the laws.

5. Checks and Balances Each branch of government can limit the power of the other two, and so exert a check on the others. As with separation of powers, a system of checks and balances helps prevent one branch from becoming too powerful. For example, the judicial branch can declare a law passed by Congress to be unconstitutional. The president can veto a law written by Congress, but Congress can override the presidential veto. Congress can confirm or reject the president's nominees to his cabinet and the courts.

6. Limited Government The Articles of Confederation had failed because the central government was too weak and lacked the authority to tax or regulate trade. A stronger, stable central government was needed, but the Framers did not want to give it too much power or allow it to abuse what power it had. This principle of limited government seeks to protect rights by restricting the power of the central government. The Framers explicitly outlined the powers of the federal government and set additional limits in the Bill of Rights and other amendments.

7. Individual Rights Amendments, or changes and additions to the Constitution, have become part of the U.S. Constitution over the years. The first 10 amendments, known as the Bill of Rights, were added in 1791. These amendments address many individual rights, such as freedom of religion, freedom of speech, and the right to trial by jury. The Bill of Rights also places strict limits on what the federal government can do. The Bill of Rights was added to the Constitution to ensure that all states would accept and ratify this new plan for government.

11.1.2 Analyze the ideological origins of the American Revolution, the Founding Fathers' philosophy of divinely bestowed unalienable natural rights, the debates on the drafting and ratification of the Constitution, and the addition of the Bill of Rights.

THE CONSTITUTION

Preamble We the People of the United States, in Order to form a more perfect Union, establish Justice, insure domestic Tranquility, provide for the common defense, promote the general Welfare, and secure the Blessings of Liberty to ourselves and our Posterity, do ordain and establish this Constitution for the United States of America.

Article I Legislative Branch

SECTION 1: CONGRESS

All legislative Powers herein granted shall be vested in a Congress of the United States, which shall consist of a Senate and House of Representatives.

SECTION 2: THE HOUSE OF REPRESENTATIVES

1 The House of Representatives shall be composed of Members chosen every second Year by the People of the several States, and the Electors in each State shall have the Qualifications requisite for Electors of the most numerous Branch of the State Legislature.

2 No Person shall be a Representative who shall not have attained to the Age of twenty five Years, and been seven Years a Citizen of the United States, and who shall not, when elected, be an Inhabitant of that State in which he shall be chosen.

3 *Representatives and direct Taxes shall be apportioned among the several States which may be included within this Union, according to their respective Numbers, which shall be determined by adding to the whole Number of free Persons, including those bound to Service for a Term of Years, and excluding Indians not taxed, three fifths of all other Persons.* The actual Enumeration shall be made within three Years after the first Meeting of the Congress of the United States, and within every subsequent Term of ten Years, in such Manner as they shall by Law direct. The Number of Representatives shall not exceed one for every thirty Thousand, but each State shall have at Least one Representative; and until such enumeration shall be made, the State of New Hampshire shall be entitled to choose three, Massachusetts eight, Rhode-Island and Providence Plantations one, Connecticut five, New-York six, New Jersey four, Pennsylvania eight, Delaware one, Maryland six, Virginia ten, North Carolina five, South Carolina five, and Georgia three.

4 When vacancies happen in the Representation from any State, the Executive Authority thereof shall issue Writs of Election to fill such Vacancies.

5 The House of Representatives shall choose their Speaker and other Officers; and shall have the sole Power of Impeachment.

NOTE Boldfaced headings, section numbers, margin notes, and questions have been inserted to help you understand and interpret this rich and evolving document. Passages that are no longer part of the Constitution have been printed in italic type.

PREAMBLE
UNDERSTANDING THE CONSTITUTION The Preamble to the Constitution outlines the goals of the U.S. government. With the words, "We the People," the Framers establish that the Constitution's authority comes from the people of the United States.

ARTICLE I
UNDERSTANDING THE CONSTITUTION Sections 1 and 2 The Constitution establishes a bicameral, or two-house, Congress. Representatives in the House serve the members of their districts and are elected every two years. The House provides one of the most direct and effective ways in which citizens can participate in the political process. Constituents can contact their representatives by mail, email, and phone, and by visiting their lawmakers' offices. Representatives must be responsive to the needs and interests of their constituents or face losing their seats.

UNDERSTANDING THE CONSTITUTION 2.3 The number of seats in the House is based on each state's population. Populous states have more representatives than less-populated states.

HISTORICAL THINKING How might changes in a state's population affect its political power?

UNDERSTANDING THE CONSTITUTION 2.5 The Speaker of the House presides over sessions of Congress, but the Constitution says nothing about further responsibilities of the Speaker or those of other officers.

UNDERSTANDING THE CONSTITUTION 3.1 Section 3 describes the Senate. Originally, state legislatures chose the senators. With the passage of the 17th Amendment in 1913, senators were elected by voters, which made the process of selecting these federal officials more democratic.

UNDERSTANDING THE CONSTITUTION 3.2 The terms of senators are staggered. One class of senators begins its term in an even-numbered year, the next class begins two years later, and the third class begins two years after that.

As president of the Senate, Vice President Richard Cheney is shown here presiding over the daily proceedings of the legislative body in 2009. House Speaker Nancy Pelosi stands beside him.

UNDERSTANDING THE CONSTITUTION 3.6 The House of Representatives has the power to bring impeachment charges, but the Senate conducts the trial and determines if the individual is to be removed from office. The president, vice president, all civil officers, and federal judges can be impeached.

HISTORICAL THINKING Do you think the power to impeach is essential to the system of checks and balances? Explain why or why not.

SECTION 3: THE SENATE

1 The Senate of the United States shall be composed of two Senators from each State, chosen by the Legislature thereof, for six Years; and each Senator shall have one Vote.

2 Immediately after they shall be assembled in Consequence of the first Election, they shall be divided as equally as may be into three Classes. The Seats of the Senators of the first Class shall be vacated at the Expiration of the second Year, of the second Class at the Expiration of the fourth Year, and of the third Class at the Expiration of the sixth Year, so that one third may be chosen every second Year; and if Vacancies happen by Resignation, or otherwise, during the Recess of the Legislature of any State, the Executive thereof may make temporary Appointments until the next Meeting of the Legislature, which shall then fill such Vacancies.

3 No Person shall be a Senator who shall not have attained to the Age of thirty Years, and been nine Years a Citizen of the United States, and who shall not, when elected, be an Inhabitant of that State for which he shall be chosen.

4 The Vice President of the United States shall be President of the Senate, but shall have no Vote, unless they be equally divided.

5 The Senate shall choose their other Officers, and also a President pro tempore, in the Absence of the Vice President, or when he shall exercise the Office of President of the United States.

6 The Senate shall have the sole Power to try all Impeachments. When sitting for that Purpose, they shall be on Oath or Affirmation. When the President of the United States is tried, the Chief Justice shall preside: And no Person shall be convicted without the Concurrence of two thirds of the Members present.

7 Judgment in Cases of Impeachment shall not extend further than to removal from Office, and disqualification to hold and enjoy any Office of honor, Trust or Profit under the United States: but the Party convicted shall nevertheless be liable and subject to Indictment, Trial, Judgment and Punishment, according to Law.

SECTION 4: CONGRESSIONAL ELECTIONS

1 The Times, Places and Manner of holding Elections for Senators and Representatives, shall be prescribed in each State by the Legislature thereof; but the Congress may at any time by Law make or alter such Regulations, except as to the Places of choosing Senators.

2 *The Congress shall assemble at least once in every Year, and such Meeting shall be on the first Monday in December, unless they shall by Law appoint a different Day.*

11.1.3 Understand the history of the Constitution after 1787 with emphasis on federal versus state authority and growing democratization.

SECTION 5: RULES

1 Each House shall be the Judge of the Elections, Returns and Qualifications of its own Members, and a Majority of each shall constitute a Quorum to do Business; but a smaller Number may adjourn from day to day, and may be authorized to compel the Attendance of absent Members, in such Manner, and under such Penalties as each House may provide.

2 Each House may determine the Rules of its Proceedings, punish its Members for disorderly Behavior, and, with the Concurrence of two thirds, expel a Member.

3 Each House shall keep a Journal of its Proceedings, and from time to time publish the same, excepting such Parts as may in their Judgment require Secrecy; and the Yeas and Nays of the Members of either House on any question shall, at the Desire of one fifth of those Present, be entered on the Journal.

4 Neither House, during the Session of Congress, shall, without the Consent of the other, adjourn for more than three days, nor to any other Place than that in which the two Houses shall be sitting.

SECTION 6: PAY AND EXPENSES

1 The Senators and Representatives shall receive a Compensation for their Services, to be ascertained by Law, and paid out of the Treasury of the United States. They shall in all Cases, except Treason, Felony and Breach of the Peace, be privileged from Arrest during their Attendance at the Session of their respective Houses, and in going to and returning from the same; and for any Speech or Debate in either House, they shall not be questioned in any other Place.

2 No Senator or Representative shall, during the Time for which he was elected, be appointed to any civil Office under the Authority of the United States, which shall have been created, or the Emoluments whereof shall have been increased during such time; and no Person holding any Office under the United States, shall be a Member of either House during his Continuance in Office.

SECTION 7: PASSING LAWS

1 All Bills for raising Revenue shall originate in the House of Representatives; but the Senate may propose or concur with Amendments as on other Bills.

2 Every Bill which shall have passed the House of Representatives and the Senate, shall, before it become a Law, be presented to the President of the United States; If he approve he shall sign it, but if not he shall return it, with his Objections to that House in which it shall have originated, who shall enter the Objections at large on their Journal, and proceed to reconsider it. If after such Reconsideration two thirds of that House shall agree to pass the Bill, it shall be sent, together with

UNDERSTANDING THE CONSTITUTION Section 5 This section empowers each house of Congress to make its own rules. The House and Senate have developed different rules over the years that affect how they operate. For example, only members of the Senate can engage in a filibuster, which allows a senator to speak in the chamber as long as it may take to block a piece of legislation. The filibuster gives the minority party in the Senate some power to block or slow the passage of legislation.

UNDERSTANDING THE CONSTITUTION 7.2

How a Bill Becomes a Law in Congress

A The first step in the legislative process is the introduction of a bill to Congress. Although anyone can write a bill or request certain legislation, only a member of Congress can introduce a bill.

B The bill is debated and usually revised. Congressional committees and their subcommittees are the key groups that move bills through the process. Once out of committee, the full House or Senate votes on the bill.

C Each house reviews, debates, and amends the bill, often resulting in different versions. A committee made up of members from both houses then works to resolve differences and create one final version of the bill.

D If both houses accept the compromises, Congress sends the bill to the president.

E The president can either sign the bill—and it becomes law—or veto the bill, which prevents the bill from becoming law. Congress can, however, override the veto with a vote of two-thirds of the members present in each house, in which case the bill becomes law.

the Objections, to the other House, by which it shall likewise be reconsidered, and if approved by two thirds of that House, it shall become a Law. But in all such Cases the Votes of both Houses shall be determined by yeas and Nays, and the Names of the Persons voting for and against the Bill shall be entered on the Journal of each House respectively. If any Bill shall not be returned by the President within ten Days (Sundays excepted) after it shall have been presented to him, the Same shall be a Law, in like Manner as if he had signed it, unless the Congress by their Adjournment prevent its Return, in which Case it shall not be a Law.

3 Every Order, Resolution, or Vote to which the Concurrence of the Senate and House of Representatives may be necessary (except on a question of Adjournment) shall be presented to the President of the United States; and before the Same shall take Effect, shall be approved by him, or being disapproved by him, shall be re-passed by two thirds of the Senate and House of Representatives, according to the Rules and Limitations prescribed in the Case of a Bill.

UNDERSTANDING THE CONSTITUTION Section 8 Section 8 begins with a list of 17 enumerated powers given to Congress, which cannot be modified by the states. The Constitution includes little detail as to how some of these powers should be carried out. The authority to collect taxes—perhaps the most important power granted to Congress—is often referred to as the "power of the purse."

HISTORICAL THINKING Why do you think the authority to collect taxes is an important power?

SECTION 8: POWERS OF CONGRESS

1 The Congress shall have Power To lay and collect Taxes, Duties, Imposts and Excises, to pay the Debts and provide for the common Defense and general Welfare of the United States; but all Duties, Imposts and Excises shall be uniform throughout the United States;

2 To borrow Money on the credit of the United States;

3 To regulate Commerce with foreign Nations, and among the several States, and with the Indian Tribes;

UNDERSTANDING THE CONSTITUTION 8.3 This clause is generally referred to as the commerce clause. Regulating commerce with foreign nations means controlling imports and exports to provide maximum benefit for U.S. businesses and consumers. Regulating commerce between states means maintaining a common market among the states, with no restrictions.

HISTORICAL THINKING Without the commerce clause, what kinds of disputes might arise between states engaged in interstate commerce?

4 To establish an uniform Rule of Naturalization, and uniform Laws on the subject of Bankruptcies throughout the United States;

5 To coin Money, regulate the Value thereof, and of foreign Coin, and fix the Standard of Weights and Measures;

6 To provide for the Punishment of counterfeiting the Securities and current Coin of the United States;

7 To establish Post Offices and post Roads;

8 To promote the Progress of Science and useful Arts, by securing for limited Times to Authors and Inventors the exclusive Right to their respective Writings and Discoveries;

9 To constitute Tribunals inferior to the supreme Court;

10 To define and punish Piracies and Felonies committed on the high Seas, and Offences against the Law of Nations;

11 To declare War, grant Letters of Marque and Reprisal, and make Rules concerning Captures on Land and Water;

12 To raise and support Armies, but no Appropriation of Money to that Use shall be for a longer Term than two Years;

13 To provide and maintain a Navy; To make Rules for the Government and Regulation of the land and naval Forces;

14 To provide for calling forth the Militia to execute the Laws of the Union, suppress Insurrections and repel Invasions;

15 To provide for organizing, arming, and disciplining, the Militia, and for governing such Part of them as may be employed in the Service of the United States, reserving to the States respectively, the Appointment of the Officers, and the Authority of training the Militia according to the discipline prescribed by Congress;

16 To exercise exclusive Legislation in all Cases whatsoever, over such District (not exceeding ten Miles square) as may, by Cession of particular States, and the Acceptance of Congress, become the Seat of the Government of the United States, and to exercise like Authority over all Places purchased by the Consent of the Legislature of the State in which the Same shall be, for the Erection of Forts, Magazines, Arsenals, dock-Yards, and other needful Buildings;—And

17 To make all Laws which shall be necessary and proper for carrying into Execution the foregoing Powers, and all other Powers vested by this Constitution in the Government of the United States, or in any Department or Officer thereof.

UNDERSTANDING THE CONSTITUTION Section 8 The last of the enumerated powers has been referred to as the "elastic clause" or the "necessary and proper clause." This clause allows Congress "to make all laws which shall be necessary and proper" to support its duties and responsibilities. It is called the "elastic clause" because it allows Congress to expand its authority and handle issues that might not have been anticipated. The vagueness of the phrase "necessary and proper" has created controversy. The Supreme Court provided some guidance in the 1819 case of ***McCulloch*** v. ***Maryland*** when it gave Congress wide authority to determine what is "necessary and proper."

SECTION 9: RESTRICTIONS ON CONGRESS

1 *The Migration or Importation of such Persons as any of the States now existing shall think proper to admit, shall not be prohibited by the Congress prior to the Year one thousand eight hundred and eight, but a Tax or duty may be imposed on such Importation, not exceeding ten dollars for each Person.*

2 The Privilege of the Writ of Habeas Corpus shall not be suspended, unless when in Cases of Rebellion or Invasion the public Safety may require it.

3 No Bill of Attainder or ex post facto Law shall be passed.

4 *No Capitation, or other direct, Tax shall be laid, unless in Proportion to the Census or Enumeration herein before directed to be taken.*

5 No Tax or Duty shall be laid on Articles exported from any State.

6 No Preference shall be given by any Regulation of Commerce or Revenue to the Ports of one State over those of another: nor shall Vessels bound to, or from, one State, be obliged to enter, clear, or pay Duties in another.

UNDERSTANDING THE CONSTITUTION Section 9 Section 9 lists specific areas in which Congress may not legislate.

UNDERSTANDING THE CONSTITUTION 9.4 A "capitation tax" is a tax charged on an individual.

UNDERSTANDING THE CONSTITUTION 9.6 Congress cannot pass laws that favor commerce in one state over that in another. For example, Congress cannot pass a law requiring shipping to go through a particular state's port.

UNDERSTANDING THE CONSTITUTION 9.8 This provision, known as the "emoluments clause," is a commitment to transparency and to the prevention of corruption. The clause prohibits federal government officials from benefiting financially from the office they hold by receiving payments from foreign governments.

HISTORICAL THINKING Why might a violation of the emoluments clause by a federal government official have significant consequences?

UNDERSTANDING THE CONSTITUTION Section 10 Section 10 limits the power of the states by preventing them from entering into a treaty, coining money, or passing laws that interfere with contracts.

7 No Money shall be drawn from the Treasury, but in Consequence of Appropriations made by Law; and a regular Statement and Account of the Receipts and Expenditures of all public Money shall be published from time to time.

8 No Title of Nobility shall be granted by the United States: And no Person holding any Office of Profit or Trust under them, shall, without the Consent of the Congress, accept of any present, Emolument, Office, or Title, of any kind whatever, from any King, Prince, or foreign State.

SECTION 10: LIMITING THE AUTHORITY OF STATES

1 No State shall enter into any Treaty, Alliance, or Confederation; grant Letters of Marque and Reprisal; coin Money; emit Bills of Credit; make any Thing but gold and silver Coin a Tender in Payment of Debts; pass any Bill of Attainder, ex post facto Law, or Law impairing the Obligation of Contracts, or grant any Title of Nobility.

2 No State shall, without the Consent of the Congress, lay any Imposts or Duties on Imports or Exports, except what may be absolutely necessary for executing its inspection Laws: and the net Produce of all Duties and Imposts, laid by any State on Imports or Exports, shall be for the Use of the Treasury of the United States; and all such Laws shall be subject to the Revision and Control of the Congress.

3 No State shall, without the Consent of Congress, lay any Duty of Tonnage, keep Troops, or Ships of War in time of Peace, enter into any Agreement or Compact with another State, or with a foreign Power, or engage in War, unless actually invaded, or in such imminent Danger as will not admit of delay.

ARTICLE II
UNDERSTANDING THE CONSTITUTION Section 1 Article II establishes an executive branch of government to carry out the laws passed by Congress. Section 1 describes a detailed process for choosing the president, although this process was replaced in 1804 by the 12th Amendment.

HISTORICAL THINKING Why might some Americans object to the electoral college?

Article II The Executive Branch

SECTION 1: ELECTING THE PRESIDENT

1 The executive Power shall be vested in a President of the United States of America. He shall hold his Office during the Term of four Years, and, together with the Vice President, chosen for the same Term, be elected, as follows

2 Each State shall appoint, in such Manner as the Legislature thereof may direct, a Number of Electors, equal to the whole Number of Senators and Representatives to which the State may be entitled in the Congress: but no Senator or Representative, or Person holding an Office of Trust or Profit under the United States, shall be appointed an Elector.

3 *The Electors shall meet in their respective States, and vote by Ballot for two Persons, of whom one at least shall not be an Inhabitant of the same State with themselves. And they shall make a List of all the Persons voted for, and of the Number of Votes for each; which List they shall sign and certify, and transmit sealed to the Seat of the Government of the United States, directed to the President of the Senate. The President of the Senate shall, in the Presence of the Senate and House of Representatives, open all the Certificates, and the Votes shall then be counted. The Person having the greatest Number of Votes shall be the President, if such Number be a Majority of the whole Number of Electors appointed; and if there be more than one who have such Majority, and have an equal Number of Votes, then the House of Representatives shall immediately choose by Ballot one of them for President; and if no Person have a Majority, then from the five highest on the List the said House shall in like Manner choose the President. But in choosing the President, the Votes shall be taken by States, the Representation from each State having one Vote; A quorum for this Purpose shall consist of a Member or Members from two thirds of the States, and a Majority of all the States shall be necessary to a Choice. In every Case, after the Choice of the President, the Person having the greatest Number of Votes of the Electors shall be the Vice President. But if there should remain two or more who have equal Votes, the Senate shall choose from them by Ballot the Vice President.*

4 The Congress may determine the Time of choosing the Electors, and the Day on which they shall give their Votes; which Day shall be the same throughout the United States.

5 No Person except a natural born Citizen, or a Citizen of the United States, at the time of the Adoption of this Constitution, shall be eligible to the Office of President; neither shall any Person be eligible to that Office who shall not have attained to the Age of thirty five Years, and been fourteen Years a Resident within the United States.

6 *In Case of the Removal of the President from Office, or of his Death, Resignation, or Inability to discharge the Powers and Duties of the said Office, the Same shall devolve on the Vice President, and the Congress may by Law provide for the Case of Removal, Death, Resignation or Inability, both of the President and Vice President, declaring what Officer shall then act as President, and such Officer shall act accordingly, until the Disability be removed, or a President shall be elected.*

7 The President shall, at stated Times, receive for his Services, a Compensation, which shall neither be increased nor diminished during the Period for which he shall have been elected, and he shall not receive within that Period any other Emolument from the United States, or any of them.

UNDERSTANDING THE CONSTITUTION 1.3 The italicized text refers to how vice presidents were originally elected. In the presidential election of 1800, the top two vote winners (Thomas Jefferson and Aaron Burr) received the same number of electoral votes. The selection of the president then fell to the House of Representatives, which chose Jefferson. Today, presidential candidates select a running mate, and voters cast a single vote for the entire ticket.

UNDERSTANDING THE CONSTITUTION 1.4 The Constitution does not stipulate when federal elections are to be held. Congress determined in 1792 that federal elections should be held in November. In 1845, it established election day as the Tuesday following the first Monday in November in years divisible by four.

UNDERSTANDING THE CONSTITUTION 1.8 Beginning with George Washington, every president has taken the oath of office as it appears in the Constitution.

UNDERSTANDING THE CONSTITUTION Section 2 Section 2 outlines the president's authority. Among other duties, the president serves as commander in chief of the armed forces, has the power to make treaties, and can appoint ambassadors and Supreme Court justices. However, the powers of the presidency increased during the Great Depression, World War II, and the Cold War. For example, although the Constitution states that only Congress can declare war, President Harry Truman began an undeclared war against North Korea in the Cold War.

HISTORICAL THINKING Do you think a president is justified to exceed constitutional powers in some situations? Why or why not?

8 Before he enter on the Execution of his Office, he shall take the following Oath or Affirmation:—"I do solemnly swear (or affirm) that I will faithfully execute the Office of President of the United States, and will to the best of my Ability, preserve, protect and defend the Constitution of the United States."

SECTION 2: EXECUTIVE POWERS

1 The President shall be Commander in Chief of the Army and Navy of the United States, and of the Militia of the several States, when called into the actual Service of the United States; he may require the Opinion, in writing, of the principal Officer in each of the executive Departments, upon any Subject relating to the Duties of their respective Offices, and he shall have Power to grant Reprieves and Pardons for Offences against the United States, except in Cases of Impeachment.

2 He shall have Power, by and with the Advice and Consent of the Senate, to make Treaties, provided two thirds of the Senators present concur; and he shall nominate, and by and with the Advice and Consent of the Senate, shall appoint Ambassadors, other public Ministers and Consuls, Judges of the supreme Court, and all other Officers of the United States, whose Appointments are not herein otherwise provided for, and which shall be established by Law: but the Congress may by Law vest the Appointment of such inferior Officers, as they think proper, in the President alone, in the Courts of Law, or in the Heads of Departments.

3 The President shall have Power to fill up all Vacancies that may happen during the Recess of the Senate, by granting Commissions which shall expire at the End of their next Session.

In this photo, President Barack Obama delivers his annual State of the Union address to Congress in 2016. To fulfill the rule in Section 3 on keeping Congress informed "from time to time," presidents present this address every year except in the first year of a new president's term.

SECTION 3: THE PRESIDENT AND CONGRESS

He shall from time to time give to the Congress Information of the State of the Union, and recommend to their Consideration such Measures as he shall judge necessary and expedient; he may, on extraordinary Occasions, convene both Houses, or either of them, and in Case of Disagreement between them, with Respect to the Time of Adjournment, he may adjourn them to such Time as he shall think proper; he shall receive Ambassadors and other public Ministers; he shall take Care that the Laws be faithfully executed, and shall Commission all the Officers of the United States.

UNDERSTANDING THE CONSTITUTION Section 4 In the phrase "high crimes and misdemeanors," the word *high* does not mean "more serious" but rather refers to highly placed public officials.

SECTION 4: IMPEACHMENT

The President, Vice President and all civil Officers of the United States, shall be removed from Office on Impeachment for, and Conviction of, Treason, Bribery, or other high Crimes and Misdemeanors.

11.8.5 Describe the increased powers of the presidency in response to the Great Depression, World War II, and the Cold War.

Article III The Judiciary Branch

SECTION 1: SUPREME COURT AND LOWER COURTS

The judicial Power of the United States, shall be vested in one supreme Court, and in such inferior Courts as the Congress may from time to time ordain and establish. The Judges, both of the supreme and inferior Courts, shall hold their Offices during good Behavior, and shall, at stated Times, receive for their Services, a Compensation, which shall not be diminished during their Continuance in Office.

The Supreme Court justices posed for this photo in 2017. In the top row, from left to right, are Elena Kagan, Samuel Alito, Jr., Sonia Sotomayor, and Neil Gorsuch. In the bottom row, from left to right, are Ruth Bader Ginsburg, Anthony Kennedy, John Roberts, Jr. (chief justice), Clarence Thomas, and Stephen Breyer.

SECTION 2: AUTHORITY OF THE SUPREME COURT

1 The judicial Power shall extend to all Cases, in Law and Equity, arising under this Constitution, the Laws of the United States, and Treaties made, or which shall be made, under their Authority;—to all Cases affecting Ambassadors, other public Ministers and Consuls;—to all Cases of admiralty and maritime Jurisdiction;—to Controversies to which the United States shall be a Party;—*to Controversies between two or more States;—between a State and Citizens of another State;—between Citizens of different States;—between Citizens of the same State claiming Lands under Grants of different States, and between a State, or the Citizens thereof, and foreign States, Citizens or Subjects.*

2 In all Cases affecting Ambassadors, other public Ministers and Consuls, and those in which a State shall be Party, the supreme Court shall have original Jurisdiction. In all the other Cases before mentioned, the supreme Court shall have appellate Jurisdiction, both as to Law and Fact, with such Exceptions, and under such Regulations as the Congress shall make.

3 The Trial of all Crimes, except in Cases of Impeachment, shall be by Jury; and such Trial shall be held in the State where the said Crimes shall have been committed; but when not committed within any State, the Trial shall be at such Place or Places as the Congress may by Law have directed.

SECTION 3: TREASON

1 Treason against the United States, shall consist only in levying War against them, or in adhering to their Enemies, giving them Aid and Comfort. No Person shall be convicted of Treason unless on the Testimony of two Witnesses to the same overt Act, or on Confession in open Court.

2 The Congress shall have Power to declare the Punishment of Treason, but no Attainder of Treason shall work Corruption of Blood, or Forfeiture except during the Life of the Person attainted.

ARTICLE III

UNDERSTANDING THE CONSTITUTION Section 1 Article III Section 1 establishes the federal court system. The Supreme Court of the United States is the highest court in the land and the only part of the federal judiciary specifically required by the Constitution. Lower courts were established by Congress by the Judiciary Act of 1789.

UNDERSTANDING THE CONSTITUTION Section 2 The italicized portion in 2.1 was changed in 1795 by the 11th Amendment. The last part of 2.2 describes the Supreme Court as the final appeals court. As a result of the landmark 1803 case *Marbury* v. *Madison*, the Court is often asked to rule on the constitutionality of a law.

UNDERSTANDING THE CONSTITUTION Section 3 Treason is the only crime specifically defined in the Constitution. Between 1954 and 2016, one person was charged with treason for collaborating in the production of propaganda videos for the terrorist group al Qaeda. Protesting or opposing U.S. government actions or policies, however, is protected by the free speech clause in Amendment 1.

Article IV States and Citizens

ARTICLE IV
UNDERSTANDING THE CONSTITUTION Section 1 "Full faith and credit" means that states agree to respect and honor each other's laws, court decisions, and documents. For example, a driver's license issued by one state must be honored by all other states. Section 1 was included as a way to create cohesiveness among individual states.

SECTION 1: MUTUAL RESPECT AMONG STATES

Full Faith and Credit shall be given in each State to the public Acts, Records, and judicial Proceedings of every other State. And the Congress may by general Laws prescribe the Manner in which such Acts, Records and Proceedings shall be proved, and the Effect thereof.

SECTION 2: CITIZENS OF STATES AND OF THE UNITED STATES

1 The Citizens of each State shall be entitled to all Privileges and Immunities of Citizens in the several States.

2 A Person charged in any State with Treason, Felony, or other Crime, who shall flee from Justice, and be found in another State, shall on Demand of the executive Authority of the State from which he fled, be delivered up, to be removed to the State having Jurisdiction of the Crime.

UNDERSTANDING THE CONSTITUTION 2.3 The text in italics is known as the fugitive slave clause, which barred people who had escaped slavery in the South from living as free people in northern states. It became obsolete with the abolition of slavery. It is interesting to note that the words *slave* and *slavery* do not appear in the Constitution.

HISTORICAL THINKING Why might the Framers have chosen not to mention slavery in the Constitution?

3 *No Person held to Service or Labor in one State, under the Laws thereof, escaping into another, shall, in Consequence of any Law or Regulation therein, be discharged from such Service or Labor, but shall be delivered up on Claim of the Party to whom such Service or Labor may be due.*

SECTION 3: NEW STATES

1 New States may be admitted by the Congress into this Union; but no new State shall be formed or erected within the Jurisdiction of any other State; nor any State be formed by the Junction of two or more States, or Parts of States, without the Consent of the Legislatures of the States concerned as well as of the Congress.

2 The Congress shall have Power to dispose of and make all needful Rules and Regulations respecting the Territory or other Property belonging to the United States; and nothing in this Constitution shall be so construed as to Prejudice any Claims of the United States, or of any particular State.

UNDERSTANDING THE CONSTITUTION Section 4 In the "guarantee clause," the Constitution commits the U.S. government to protecting the people of a state from attack by a foreign government as well as from domestic violence or terrorism.

SECTION 4: PROTECTION OF STATES BY THE UNITED STATES

The United States shall guarantee to every State in this Union a Republican Form of Government, and shall protect each of them against Invasion; and on Application of the Legislature, or of the Executive (when the Legislature cannot be convened), against domestic Violence.

Article V Amending the Constitution

1 The Congress, whenever two thirds of both Houses shall deem it necessary, shall propose Amendments to this Constitution, or, on the Application of the Legislatures of two thirds of the several States, shall call a Convention for proposing Amendments, which, in either Case, shall be valid to all Intents and Purposes, as Part of this Constitution, when ratified by the Legislatures of three fourths of the several States, or by Conventions in three fourths thereof, as the one or the other Mode of Ratification may be proposed by the Congress.

2 Provided that no Amendment which may be made prior to the Year One thousand eight hundred and eight shall in any Manner affect the first and fourth Clauses in the Ninth Section of the first Article; and that no State, without its Consent, shall be deprived of its equal Suffrage in the Senate.

Article VI The Supreme Law of the Land

1 All Debts contracted and Engagements entered into, before the Adoption of this Constitution, shall be as valid against the United States under this Constitution, as under the Confederation.

2 This Constitution, and the Laws of the United States which shall be made in Pursuance thereof; and all Treaties made, or which shall be made, under the Authority of the United States, shall be the supreme Law of the Land; and the Judges in every State shall be bound thereby, any Thing in the Constitution or Laws of any State to the Contrary notwithstanding.

3 The Senators and Representatives before mentioned, and the Members of the several State Legislatures, and all executive and judicial Officers, both of the United States and of the several States, shall be bound by Oath or Affirmation, to support this Constitution; but no religious Test shall ever be required as a Qualification to any Office or public Trust under the United States.

ARTICLE V
UNDERSTANDING THE CONSTITUTION Article V This article describes the process for amending the Constitution but states that the first and fourth clauses in Article 1's ninth section cannot be amended before 1808. These clauses refer to the importation of slaves and to a tax charged on an individual. The Framers realized that the Constitution would need to be amended at some point, but they made the amendment process extremely difficult. According to U.S. Senate records, approximately 11,699 bills have been proposed as amendments to the Constitution. However, as of 2017, only 27 amendments had been added to the Constitution.

HISTORICAL THINKING Do you think the amendment process should be made easier? Explain why or why not.

ARTICLE VI
UNDERSTANDING THE CONSTITUTION Article VI Paragraph 2 is known as the "supremacy clause." The clause establishes the Constitution and all federal laws and treaties as the supreme law of the land. When state law is in conflict with federal law, federal law prevails. The Supreme Court has used the supremacy clause to ensure that federal law pre-empts, or takes priority over, state law. This is known as the doctrine of pre-emption.

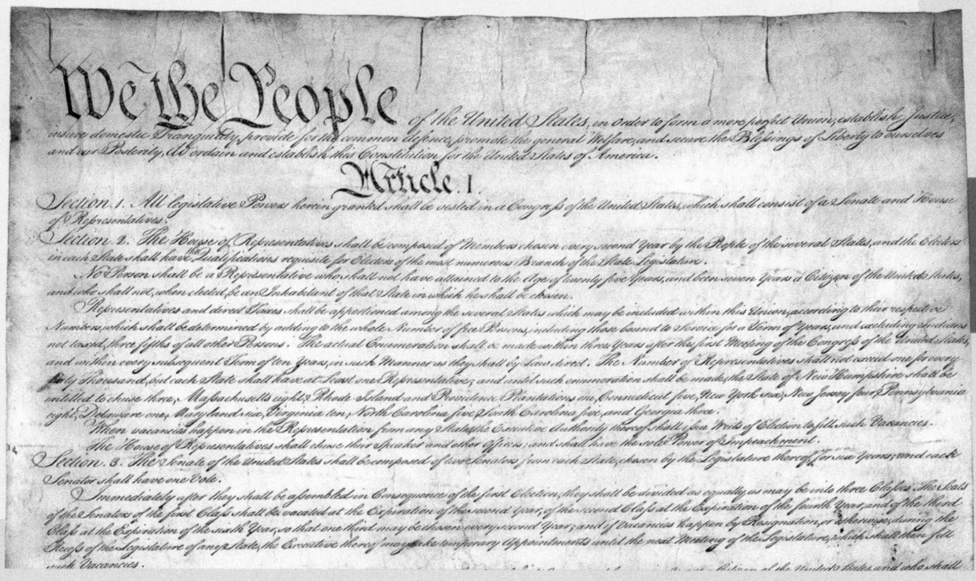
We the People of the United States, in Order to form a more perfect Union, establish Justice, insure domestic Tranquility, provide for the common defence, promote the general Welfare, and secure the Blessings of Liberty to ourselves and our Posterity, do ordain and establish this Constitution for the United States of America.

Article. I.

Section. 1. All legislative Powers herein granted shall be vested in a Congress of the United States, which shall consist of a Senate and House of Representatives.

Section. 2. The House of Representatives shall be composed of Members chosen every second Year by the People of the several States, and the Electors in each State shall have the Qualifications requisite for Electors of the most numerous Branch of the State Legislature.

Today, "the people" referred to in the Constitution includes all adult U.S. citizens.

ARTICLE VII

UNDERSTANDING THE CONSTITUTION Article 7 The Framers clearly stated in Article 7 that the Constitution required the approval of only 9 states, not the entire 13. This contrasted with the Articles of Confederation, which required the consent of all 13 states. In addition, the Framers decided to hold a special ratification convention in each state. Delegates to these conventions were chosen by the state's citizens.

On June 21, 1788, New Hampshire became the 9th state to ratify the Constitution and make it the law of the United States. However, the Framers knew that the new nation's survival depended on the populous and wealthy states of Virginia and New York, which were slow to ratify. After lengthy debates, first Virginia and then New York approved the measure, becoming the 11th and 12th states to ratify the Constitution. Rhode Island was the only obstacle to unanimous approval. It officially joined the United States only after being warned that it would be treated like a foreign government if it did not.

HISTORICAL THINKING Why did the Framers call for ratification conventions in the 13 states?

Article VII Ratification

The Ratification of the Conventions of nine States, shall be sufficient for the Establishment of this Constitution between the States so ratifying the Same.

[Here appears some text noting corrections that were made on the original copy of the document.]

Done in Convention by the Unanimous Consent of the States present the Seventeenth Day of September in the Year of our Lord one thousand seven hundred and Eighty seven and of the Independence of the United States of America the Twelfth In witness whereof We have hereunto subscribed our Names,

G°. Washington
President and deputy from Virginia

Massachusetts
Nathaniel Gorham
Rufus King

New York
Alexander Hamilton

Delaware
George Read
Gunning Bedford, Jr.
John Dickinson
Richard Bassett
Jacob Broom

Virginia
John Blair
James Madison, Jr.

Pennsylvania
Benjamin Franklin
Thomas Mifflin
Robert Morris
George Clymer
Thomas Fitzsimons
Jared Ingersoll
James Wilson
Gouverneur Morris

New Hampshire
John Langdon
Nicholas Gilman

New Jersey
William Livingston
David Brearley
William Paterson
Jonathan Dayton

Connecticut
William Samuel Johnson
Roger Sherman

North Carolina
William Blount
Richard Dobbs Spaight
Hugh Williamson

South Carolina
John Rutledge
Charles Cotesworth Pinckney
Charles Pinckney
Pierce Butler

Maryland
James McHenry
Daniel of St. Thomas Jenifer
Daniel Carroll

Georgia
William Few
Abraham Baldwin

11.1.3 Understand the history of the Constitution after 1787 with emphasis on federal versus state authority and growing democratization.

Introduction

Individual rights are fundamental to liberty. The Magna Carta, the charter of English liberties granted in 1215, helped inspire the Bill of Rights. Those who sailed to North America from Britain had enjoyed the freedoms granted to them under both the Magna Carta and the English Bill of Rights. They believed they were entitled to these same rights when they settled their colonies.

No one argued whether Americans should have these rights, but there was debate as to whether it was necessary and advisable to include them in the Constitution. At first, James Madison didn't believe the rights needed to be included. He argued that state constitutions already offered the explicit protection of individual liberties. Stating the rights in the Constitution might actually have the effect of limiting them. However, in 1787, Thomas Jefferson wrote to Madison, "[A] bill of rights is what the people are entitled to against every government on earth, general or particular, and what no just government should refuse." After long discussion among the Framers, Madison changed his mind. He drafted 19 amendments. On December 15, 1791, 10 of them were ratified, and the Bill of Rights was added to the Constitution.

The following is a transcription of the Bill of Rights. Over time, as you'll see, more amendments were added to the Constitution to address issues that arose as the nation grew and changed.

The Preamble to the Bill of Rights

Congress of the United States begun and held at the City of New York, on Wednesday the fourth of March, one thousand seven hundred and eighty nine.

THE Conventions of a number of the States, having at the time of their adopting the Constitution, expressed a desire, in order to prevent misconstruction or abuse of its powers, that further declaratory and restrictive clauses should be added: And as extending the ground of public confidence in the Government, will best ensure the beneficient ends of its institution.

RESOLVED by the Senate and House of Representatives of the United States of America, in Congress assembled, two thirds of both Houses concurring, that the following Articles be proposed to the Legislatures of the several States, as amendments to the Constitution of the United States, all, or any of which Articles, when ratified by three fourths of the said Legislatures, to be valid to all intents and purposes, as part of the said Constitution; viz.

UNDERSTANDING THE PREAMBLE *Viz* is Latin for "that is to say" or "namely."

11.1.2 Analyze the ideological origins of the American Revolution, the Founding Fathers' philosophy of divinely bestowed unalienable natural rights, the debates on the drafting and ratification of the Constitution, and the addition of the Bill of Rights.

UNDERSTANDING AMENDMENT 1
Amendment 1 protects the free exercise of religious liberty by prohibiting the government from establishing a church, endorsing a particular religion, or favoring one set of religious beliefs over another. Thomas Jefferson's 1786 Statute for Religious Freedom, which he wrote for the Virginia legislature, influenced the protection of religious freedom. In his statute, Jefferson also called for the separation of church and state. This idea is contained—although not explicitly—in the "establishment" clause. The Framers debated the wording of the clause and finally adopted that shown here.

UNDERSTANDING AMENDMENT 2
This amendment has been debated for decades. Many Americans believe the amendment ensures the right to possess guns. Others think gun ownership should be controlled. In 2008, the Supreme Court ruled in *District of Columbia* v. *Heller* that Amendment 2 guarantees the right to possess a firearm for self-defense and hunting. There has been debate as to whether the amendment protects ownership of any type of weapon, however.

HISTORICAL THINKING Do you think gun ownership should be controlled? Why or why not?

ARTICLES in addition to, and Amendment of the Constitution of the United States of America, proposed by Congress, and ratified by the Legislatures of the several States, pursuant to the fifth Article of the original Constitution.

Amendment 1 (1791)

Congress shall make no law respecting an establishment of religion, or prohibiting the free exercise thereof; or abridging the freedom of speech, or of the press; or the right of the people peaceably to assemble, and to petition the Government for a redress of grievances.

Amendment 2 (1791)

A well regulated Militia, being necessary to the security of a free State, the right of the people to keep and bear Arms, shall not be infringed.

Amendment 3 (1791)

No Soldier shall, in time of peace be quartered in any house, without the consent of the Owner, nor in time of war, but in a manner to be prescribed by law.

Amendment 4 (1791)

The right of the people to be secure in their persons, houses, papers, and effects, against unreasonable searches and seizures, shall not be violated, and no Warrants shall issue, but upon probable cause, supported by Oath or affirmation, and particularly describing the place to be searched, and the persons or things to be seized.

11.3.5 Describe the principles of religious liberty found in the Establishment and Free Exercise clauses of the First Amendment, including the debate on the issue of separation of church and state.

Amendment 5 (1791)

No person shall be held to answer for a capital, or otherwise infamous crime, unless on a presentment or indictment of a Grand Jury, except in cases arising in the land or naval forces, or in the Militia, when in actual service in time of War or public danger; nor shall any person be subject for the same offence to be twice put in jeopardy of life or limb; nor shall be compelled in any criminal case to be a witness against himself, nor be deprived of life, liberty, or property, without due process of law; nor shall private property be taken for public use, without just compensation.

Amendment 6 (1791)

In all criminal prosecutions, the accused shall enjoy the right to a speedy and public trial, by an impartial jury of the State and district wherein the crime shall have been committed, which district shall have been previously ascertained by law, and to be informed of the nature and cause of the accusation; to be confronted with the witnesses against him; to have compulsory process for obtaining witnesses in his favor, and to have the Assistance of Counsel for his defence.

Amendment 7 (1791)

In Suits at common law, where the value in controversy shall exceed twenty dollars, the right of trial by jury shall be preserved, and no fact tried by a jury, shall be otherwise re-examined in any Court of the United States, than according to the rules of the common law.

Amendment 8 (1791)

Excessive bail shall not be required, nor excessive fines imposed, nor cruel and unusual punishments inflicted.

Amendment 9 (1791)

The enumeration in the Constitution, of certain rights, shall not be construed to deny or disparage others retained by the people.

Amendment 10 (1791)

The powers not delegated to the United States by the Constitution, nor prohibited by it to the States, are reserved to the States respectively, or to the people.

UNDERSTANDING AMENDMENTS 4–6 These three amendments protect people who are suspected of a crime or are being tried for one.

Amendment 4 says that police must have "probable cause" (a good reason) before they can seize someone's possessions. It also protects people from unreasonable searches by government officials.

Amendment 5 protects those accused of crimes. The Due Process Clause was the basis for the defense of Fred Korematsu, an American citizen and and the son of Japanese parents, who refused to obey President Franklin Roosevelt's executive order and report to an internment camp during World War II. Under Roosevelt's order, Korematsu's lawyers argued, Japanese Americans were "deprived of life, liberty, or property, without due process of law." The case, *Fred Korematsu* v. *United States of America*, finally went to the Supreme Court, which upheld Korematsu's removal to an internment camp.

Amendment 6 guarantees a speedy public trial to those accused of a crime.

HISTORICAL THINKING Why do you suppose the Supreme Court upheld Roosevelt's executive order?

UNDERSTANDING AMENDMENTS 9 and 10 Amendment 9 prevents the government from denying rights that are not listed in the Bill of Rights. These are called "unenumerated" rights and include the right to travel and to vote.

The Framers added Amendment 10 to better define the balance of power between the states and the federal government. Each state is given the power to make laws that are not covered by the Constitution.

11.7.5 Discuss the constitutional issues and impact of events on the U.S. home front, including the internment of Japanese Americans (e.g., *Fred Korematsu* v. *United States of America*) and the restrictions on German and Italian resident aliens; the response of the administration to Hitler's atrocities against Jews and other groups; the roles of women in military production; and the roles and growing political demands of African Americans.

Amendment 11 (1798)

[**Note:** Article 3, Section 2, of the Constitution was modified by the 11th Amendment.]

The Judicial power of the United States shall not be construed to extend to any suit in law or equity, commenced or prosecuted against one of the United States by Citizens of another State, or by Citizens or Subjects of any Foreign State.

Amendment 12 (1804)

[**Note:** Part of Article 2, Section 1, of the Constitution was replaced by the 12th Amendment.]

The Electors shall meet in their respective states and vote by ballot for President and Vice-President, one of whom, at least, shall not be an inhabitant of the same state with themselves; they shall name in their ballots the person voted for as President, and in distinct ballots the person voted for as Vice-President, and they shall make distinct lists of all persons voted for as President, and of all persons voted for as Vice-President, and of the number of votes for each, which lists they shall sign and certify, and transmit sealed to the seat of the government of the United States, directed to the President of the Senate; —the President of the Senate shall, in the presence of the Senate and House of Representatives, open all the certificates and the votes shall then be counted; —The person having the greatest number of votes for President, shall be the President, if such number be a majority of the whole number of Electors appointed; and if no person have such majority, then from the persons having the highest numbers not exceeding three on the list of those voted for as President, the House of Representatives shall choose immediately, by ballot, the President. But in choosing the President, the votes shall be taken by states, the representation from each state having one vote; a quorum for this purpose shall consist of a member or members from two-thirds of the states, and a majority of all the states shall be necessary to a choice. *And if the House of Representatives shall not choose a President whenever the right of choice shall devolve upon them, before the fourth day of March next following, then the Vice-President shall act as President, as in case of the death or other constitutional disability of the President.* The person having the greatest number of votes as Vice-President, shall be the Vice-President, if such number be a majority of the whole number of Electors appointed, and if no person have a majority, then from the two highest numbers on the list, the Senate shall choose the Vice-President; a quorum for the purpose shall consist of two-thirds of the whole number of Senators, and a majority of the whole number shall be necessary to a choice. But no person constitutionally ineligible to the office of President shall be eligible to that of Vice-President of the United States.

UNDERSTANDING AMENDMENT 12
Amendment 12 established the electoral college. As you know, prior to its passage, the presidential candidate who received the most electoral votes won the presidency. The candidate with the second most votes became the vice president. The amendment changed this system by allowing the delegates of each party to choose its nominees for both president and vice president.

The electoral college was challenged in 2000 and 2016, when the candidates who won the popular vote (Al Gore in 2000 and Hillary Clinton in 2016) lost the elections to George W. Bush and Donald Trump, respectively.

HISTORICAL THINKING Do you think the electoral college should be abolished? Why or why not?

Amendment 13 (1865)

[**Note:** A portion of Article 4, Section 2, of the Constitution was superseded by the 13th Amendment.]

SECTION 1: Neither slavery nor involuntary servitude, except as a punishment for crime whereof the party shall have been duly convicted, shall exist within the United States, or any place subject to their jurisdiction.

SECTION 2: Congress shall have power to enforce this article by appropriate legislation.

Amendment 14 (1868)

[**Note:** Article 1, Section 2, of the Constitution was modified by Section 2 of the 14th Amendment.]

SECTION 1: All persons born or naturalized in the United States, and subject to the jurisdiction thereof, are citizens of the United States and of the State wherein they reside. No State shall make or enforce any law which shall abridge the privileges or immunities of citizens of the United States; nor shall any State deprive any person of life, liberty, or property, without due process of law; nor deny to any person within its jurisdiction the equal protection of the laws.

SECTION 2: Representatives shall be apportioned among the several States according to their respective numbers, counting the whole number of persons in each State, excluding Indians not taxed. But when the right to vote at any election for the choice of electors for President and Vice-President of the United States, Representatives in Congress, the Executive and Judicial officers of a State, or the members of the *Legislature thereof, is denied to any of the male inhabitants of such State, being twenty-one years of age, and citizens of the United States,* or in any way abridged, except for participation in rebellion, or other crime, the basis of representation therein shall be reduced in the proportion which the number of such male citizens shall bear to the whole number of male citizens twenty-one years of age in such State.

SECTION 3: No person shall be a Senator or Representative in Congress, or elector of President and Vice-President, or hold any office, civil or military, under the United States, or under any State, who, having previously taken an oath, as a member of Congress, or as an officer of the United States, or as a member of any State legislature, or as an executive or judicial officer of any State, to support the Constitution of the United States, shall have engaged in insurrection or rebellion against the same, or given aid or comfort to the enemies thereof. But Congress may by a vote of two-thirds of each House, remove such disability.

UNDERSTANDING AMENDMENTS 13–15 Amendments 13–15 are often referred to as the "civil war" or "reconstruction" amendments because they were created in the aftermath of the war. These post-Civil War amendments laid the foundation for the legal phase of the 20th-century civil rights movement.

UNDERSTANDING AMENDMENT 13 This amendment outlawed slavery.

UNDERSTANDING AMENDMENT 14 Section 1 This section defines citizenship and ensures that all citizens enjoy the same rights and the same protections by the law. The amendment has been continually reinterpreted and applied to different contexts by the courts. For example, sometimes it has been employed as a protection for workers and other times as a protection for corporations. In the 1877 case, *Munn* v. *Illinois*, the Supreme Court upheld the idea that a corporation and its business activities were protected by the 14th Amendment.

UNDERSTANDING AMENDMENT 14 Section 2 This section overrides the three-fifths clause in Article I. As a result of this amendment, each citizen is counted as a whole person. Section 2 also calls for reducing the number of representatives of a state if it denies some citizens the right to vote.

SECTION 4: The validity of the public debt of the United States, authorized by law, including debts incurred for payment of pensions and bounties for services in suppressing insurrection or rebellion, shall not be questioned. But neither the United States nor any State shall assume or pay any debt or obligation incurred in aid of insurrection or rebellion against the United States, or any claim for the loss or emancipation of any slave; but all such debts, obligations and claims shall be held illegal and void.

SECTION 5: The Congress shall have the power to enforce, by appropriate legislation, the provisions of this article.

UNDERSTANDING AMENDMENT 15
The 15th Amendment prohibits federal and state governments from limiting or denying an individual's ability to vote because of "race, color, or previous conditions of servitude." Section 2 of the amendment gives Congress the authority to enforce the amendment by passing federal laws that guarantee voting rights. Note that the amendment granted African-American men voting rights but not women of any race. In addition, some states imposed literacy tests, white primaries, poll taxes, and other barriers to keep African Americans from voting. Almost 100 years would pass before African Americans secured stronger protections through federal legislation and the 24th Amendment.

HISTORICAL THINKING Why might some states have made it difficult for African-American men to vote?

Amendment 15 (1870)

SECTION 1: The right of citizens of the United States to vote shall not be denied or abridged by the United States or by any State on account of race, color, or previous condition of servitude—

SECTION 2: The Congress shall have the power to enforce this article by appropriate legislation.

The 15th Amendment, a print from 1870, illustrates a parade celebrating the amendment's passage.

UNDERSTANDING AMENDMENT 16
The 16th Amendment was the first of four "Progressive" amendments. During the Progressive Era (1890–1920), many Americans worked to reform government. Seeking to reduce tariffs and still provide revenue for the federal government, progressives pushed for this amendment, which established an income tax.

Amendment 16 (1913)

[**Note:** Article 1, Section 9, of the Constitution was modified by the 16th Amendment.]

The Congress shall have power to lay and collect taxes on incomes, from whatever source derived, without apportionment among the several States, and without regard to any census or enumeration.

11.2.9 Understand the effect of political programs and activities of the Progressives (e.g., federal regulation of railroad transport, Children's Bureau, the Sixteenth Amendment, Theodore Roosevelt, Hiram Johnson).

Amendment 17 (1913)

[**Note:** Article 1, Section 3, of the Constitution was modified by the 17th Amendment.]

The Senate of the United States shall be composed of two Senators from each State, elected by the people thereof, for six years; and each Senator shall have one vote. The electors in each State shall have the qualifications requisite for electors of the most numerous branch of the State legislatures.

When vacancies happen in the representation of any State in the Senate, the executive authority of such State shall issue writs of election to fill such vacancies: Provided, That the legislature of any State may empower the executive thereof to make temporary appointments until the people fill the vacancies by election as the legislature may direct.

This amendment shall not be so construed as to affect the election or term of any Senator chosen before it becomes valid as part of the Constitution.

UNDERSTANDING AMENDMENT 17
The 17th Amendment changed the process by which Senators are elected. Through the popular election of senators, the amendment made the process more democratic.

Amendment 18 (1919)

Repealed by the 21st Amendment.

SECTION 1: *After one year from the ratification of this article the manufacture, sale, or transportation of intoxicating liquors within, the importation thereof into, or the exportation thereof from the United States and all territory subject to the jurisdiction thereof for beverage purposes is hereby prohibited.*

SECTION 2: *The Congress and the several States shall have concurrent power to enforce this article by appropriate legislation.*

SECTION 3: *This article shall be inoperative unless it shall have been ratified as an amendment to the Constitution by the legislatures of the several States, as provided in the Constitution, within seven years from the date of the submission hereof to the States by the Congress.*

Philadelphia's Director of Public Safety, Smedley Butler, smashes casks of beer in 1924 to enforce Prohibition.

UNDERSTANDING AMENDMENT 18
Known as the Prohibition Amendment, the 18th Amendment prohibited the production, sale, or transportation of alcoholic beverages in the United States. Many of those who supported the amendment also supported the temperance movement, which advocated for the control of alcohol consumption. Many progressives viewed alcohol abuse as a significant social problem. Congress passed the Volstead Act in 1919, which gave the U.S. Treasury Department the power to enforce Prohibition.

HISTORICAL THINKING In what way was Amendment 18 different from the preceding amendments?

11.1.3 Understand the history of the Constitution after 1787 with emphasis on federal versus state authority and growing democratization; 11.5.3 Examine the passage of the Eighteenth Amendment to the Constitution and the Volstead Act (Prohibition).

Following the passage of the 19th Amendment, the women shown here voted for the first time in a 1920 election in New York City.

UNDERSTANDING AMENDMENT 19
Although many states had granted some voting privileges to women before 1920, the 19th Amendment extended equal voting rights to all women in the country. In the 1800s, women's rights leaders such as Elizabeth Cady Stanton and Susan B. Anthony dedicated their lives to securing political and social equality for women. Their actions helped inspire and launch another movement in the 1960s, which called for further rights for women and offered differing perspectives on the roles of women.

HISTORICAL THINKING Why does the amendment specify that women's right to vote "shall not be denied or abridged by the United States or by any state"?

UNDERSTANDING AMENDMENT 20
This amendment is often called the "Lame Duck Amendment." In government, a lame duck is an elected official whose term in office is about to end. So, for instance, a president who has already served two terms is a lame duck. Officials who have not won re-election are also considered lame ducks. Congress has little incentive to work with a lame duck president.

Amendment 19 (1920)

The right of citizens of the United States to vote shall not be denied or abridged by the United States or by any State on account of sex.

Congress shall have power to enforce this article by appropriate legislation.

Amendment 20 (1933)

[**Note:** Article 1, Section 4, of the Constitution was modified by Section 2 of the 20th Amendment. In addition, a portion of the 12th Amendment was superseded by Section 3.]

SECTION 1: The terms of the President and the Vice President shall end at noon on the 20th day of January, and the terms of Senators and Representatives at noon on the 3d day of January, of the years in which such terms would have ended if this article had not been ratified; and the terms of their successors shall then begin.

SECTION 2: The Congress shall assemble at least once in every year, and such meeting shall begin at noon on the 3d day of January, unless they shall by law appoint a different day.

SECTION 3: If, at the time fixed for the beginning of the term of the President, the President elect shall have died, the Vice President elect shall become President. If a President shall not have been chosen before the time fixed for the beginning of his term, or if the President elect shall have failed to qualify, then the Vice President elect shall act as President until a President shall have qualified; and the Congress may by law provide for the case wherein neither a President elect nor a Vice President elect

11.5.4 Analyze the passage of the Nineteenth Amendment and the changing role of women in society.; 11.10.7 Analyze the women's rights movement from the era of Elizabeth Cady Stanton and Susan B. Anthony and the passage of the Nineteenth Amendment to the movement launched in the 1960s, including differing perspectives on the roles of women.

shall have qualified, declaring who shall then act as President, or the manner in which one who is to act shall be selected, and such person shall act accordingly until a President or Vice President shall have qualified.

SECTION 4: The Congress may by law provide for the case of the death of any of the persons from whom the House of Representatives may choose a President whenever the right of choice shall have devolved upon them, and for the case of the death of any of the persons from whom the Senate may choose a Vice President whenever the right of choice shall have devolved upon them.

SECTION 5: Sections 1 and 2 shall take effect on the 15th day of October following the ratification of this article.

SECTION 6: This article shall be inoperative unless it shall have been ratified as an amendment to the Constitution by the legislatures of three-fourths of the several States within seven years from the date of its submission.

Amendment 21 (1933)

SECTION 1: The eighteenth article of amendment to the Constitution of the United States is hereby repealed.

SECTION 2: The transportation or importation into any State, Territory, or possession of the United States for delivery or use therein of intoxicating liquors, in violation of the laws thereof, is hereby prohibited.

SECTION 3: This article shall be inoperative unless it shall have been ratified as an amendment to the Constitution by conventions in the several States, as provided in the Constitution, within seven years from the date of the submission hereof to the States by the Congress.

Amendment 22 (1951)

SECTION 1: No person shall be elected to the office of the President more than twice, and no person who has held the office of President, or acted as President, for more than two years of a term to which some other person was elected President shall be elected to the office of the President more than once. But this Article shall not apply to any person holding the office of President when this Article was proposed by the Congress, and shall not prevent any person who may be holding the office of President, or acting as President, during the term within which this Article becomes operative from holding the office of President or acting as President during the remainder of such term.

SECTION 2: This article shall be inoperative unless it shall have been ratified as an amendment to the Constitution by the legislatures of three-fourths of the several States within seven years from the date of its submission to the States by the Congress.

UNDERSTANDING AMENDMENT 21
Amendment 21 repealed Amendment 18 and ended Prohibition. Amendment 21 is the only amendment that was ratified by state conventions rather than state legislatures. Section 2 of the amendment returned the regulation of alcohol to the states, giving them significant control of alcohol within and across their borders. Consequently, alcohol laws vary throughout the states. States also have the power to establish the legal drinking age within their borders. In an effort to prohibit the sale of alcohol to minors, the federal government provides federal funds only to states who set the legal drinking age at 21. All 50 states have done so.

HISTORICAL THINKING What potential problems or issues might arise when states have different laws regulating people of the same age?

UNDERSTANDING AMENDMENT 22
Democrat Franklin D. Roosevelt served three terms as president of the United States and was elected to a fourth term shortly before he died in 1945. George Washington had declined to run for a third term. All presidents before Roosevelt followed this unwritten custom and served no more than two terms. Within months of Roosevelt's death, Republicans in Congress presented the 22nd Amendment for consideration.

HISTORICAL THINKING Do you think a president should be able to serve for more than two terms? Explain your answer.

UNDERSTANDING AMENDMENT 23
The District of Columbia is the official seat of the U.S. government, but it is a federal territory, not a state, and has only a nonvoting representative in Congress. Washington, D.C., began as a small community, but by 1960, more than 760,000 people who paid federal taxes and could be drafted into the military lived there. The states ratified Amendment 23 in 1961 to allow residents of the District to vote in presidential elections. The District of Columbia has three electoral votes.

Amendment 23 (1961)

SECTION 1: The District constituting the seat of Government of the United States shall appoint in such manner as the Congress may direct:

A number of electors of President and Vice President equal to the whole number of Senators and Representatives in Congress to which the District would be entitled if it were a State, but in no event more than the least populous State; they shall be in addition to those appointed by the States, but they shall be considered, for the purposes of the election of President and Vice President, to be electors appointed by a State; and they shall meet in the District and perform such duties as provided by the twelfth article of amendment.

SECTION 2: The Congress shall have power to enforce this article by appropriate legislation.

UNDERSTANDING AMENDMENT 24
This amendment abolished poll taxes and election fees charged by states to keep low-income and mostly African-American citizens from voting. The successful push to get the amendment passed was in part based on the support and demands of the civil rights movement. The amendment gave African Americans greater access to the political process. As written, Amendment 24 prohibits poll taxes only in federal elections. The Voting Rights Act of 1965 and a 1966 Supreme Court decision banned poll taxes in state elections as well.

HISTORICAL THINKING Why do you think the amendment refers to the "right of citizens of the United States to vote," rather than name specific minority groups?

Amendment 24 (1964)

SECTION 1: The right of citizens of the United States to vote in any primary or other election for President or Vice President, for electors for President or Vice President, or for Senator or Representative in Congress, shall not be denied or abridged by the United States or any State by reason of failure to pay any poll tax or other tax.

SECTION 2: The Congress shall have power to enforce this article by appropriate legislation.

11.10.6 Analyze the passage and effects of civil rights and voting rights legislation (e.g., 1964 Civil Rights Act, Voting Rights Act of 1965) and the Twenty-Fourth Amendment, with an emphasis on equality of access to education and to the political process.

Amendment 25 (1967)

[**Note:** Article 2, Section 1, of the Constitution was affected by the 25th Amendment.]

SECTION 1: In case of the removal of the President from office or of his death or resignation, the Vice President shall become President.

SECTION 2: Whenever there is a vacancy in the office of the Vice President, the President shall nominate a Vice President who shall take office upon confirmation by a majority vote of both Houses of Congress.

SECTION 3: Whenever the President transmits to the President pro tempore of the Senate and the Speaker of the House of Representatives his written declaration that he is unable to discharge the powers and duties of his office, and until he transmits to them a written declaration to the contrary, such powers and duties shall be discharged by the Vice President as Acting President.

SECTION 4: Whenever the Vice President and a majority of either the principal officers of the executive departments or of such other body as Congress may by law provide, transmit to the President pro tempore of the Senate and the Speaker of the House of Representatives their written declaration that the President is unable to discharge the powers and duties of his office, the Vice President shall immediately assume the powers and duties of the office as Acting President.

Thereafter, when the President transmits to the President pro tempore of the Senate and the Speaker of the House of Representatives his written declaration that no inability exists, he shall resume the powers and duties of his office unless the Vice President and a majority of either the principal officers of the executive department or of such other body as Congress may by law provide, transmit within four days to the President pro tempore of the Senate and the Speaker of the House of Representatives their written declaration that the President is unable to discharge the powers and duties of his office. Thereupon Congress shall decide the issue, assembling within forty-eight hours for that purpose if not in session. If the Congress, within twenty-one days after receipt of the latter written declaration, or, if Congress is not in session, within twenty-one days after Congress is required to assemble, determines by two-thirds vote of both Houses that the President is unable to discharge the powers and duties of his office, the Vice President shall continue to discharge the same as Acting President; otherwise, the President shall resume the powers and duties of his office.

UNDERSTANDING AMENDMENT 25
The 25th Amendment was ratified in 1967 to establish procedures to follow if a president becomes disabled while in office. The amendment was proposed after the assassination of President John F. Kennedy in 1963. Following his death, many questioned what would have happened if he had survived the shooting but been unable to govern. Eight presidents have died and one resigned while in office. In addition, seven vice presidents have died while in office and two have resigned. This amendment provides for an orderly transfer of power.

HISTORICAL THINKING Why is there a plan of succession for the presidency?

Pat Keefer, a leader in advocating for the youth vote in the early 1970s, holds signs urging 18-year olds to vote.

UNDERSTANDING AMENDMENT 26
Amendment 26 continued the Constitution's expansion of voting rights. In 1954, President Dwight Eisenhower proposed lowering the voting age to 18 years. The movement acquired new momentum in the late 1960s during the Vietnam War. People began to question why 18-year-old men could be drafted to serve in the military but could not vote.

HISTORICAL THINKING Do you think the voting age should be reduced even more? Explain your answer.

UNDERSTANDING AMENDMENT 27
Amendment 27 defers any congressional pay raise to the next election cycle. The amendment was first proposed in 1789 by James Madison. However, it was ratified more than 200 years later, thanks to a college student's research project. In his research, the student found that a proposed amendment remains pending, no matter how much time passes before action is taken on it. The student decided to see if he could get the amendment passed and found that he was able to gather enough support to do so.

Amendment 26 (1971)

[**Note:** Amendment 14, Section 2, of the Constitution was modified by Section 1 of the 26th Amendment.]

SECTION 1: The right of citizens of the United States, who are eighteen years of age or older, to vote shall not be denied or abridged by the United States or by any State on account of age.

SECTION 2: The Congress shall have power to enforce this article by appropriate legislation.

Amendment 27 (1992)

No law, varying the compensation for the services of the Senators and Representatives, shall take effect, until an election of Representatives shall have intervened.

11.10.6 Analyze the passage and effects of civil rights and voting rights legislation (e.g., 1964 Civil Rights Act, Voting Rights Act of 1965) and the Twenty-Fourth Amendment, with an emphasis on equality of access to education and to the political process.

Citizenship and You

For many high school students, getting to a job, meeting with friends, and participating in activities require some source of transportation. Many young adults borrow a car from their parents to get around. To continue to enjoy this privilege, you have to handle responsibilities and prove you are dependable. You have to obey the rules of the road and be a careful, alert driver. Similarly, our responsibilities to our communities, states, and nation balance the rights we receive as citizens. Let's examine some aspects of American citizenship—of being a full member of a country in exchange for certain responsibilities.

STRUGGLE FOR EQUAL RIGHTS

As you have learned by studying the U.S. Constitution and Bill of Rights, privileges and rights such as citizenship and voting have been contested, reshaped, and amended during our country's history. Beginning with freedoms and rights cherished and protected in the Constitution by the Framers, Americans from all walks of life have struggled to expand their own rights and those of others. People gained rights they had been denied through the efforts of the civil rights movement, including the right to participate in government, the right to free expression—in all its forms—and the right to equal treatment under the law. Federal, state, and local governments have responded to these social changes with more equitable laws. For example, in response to demands by the LGBT community, the Supreme Court legalized same-sex marriage in 2015. The efforts and sacrifices of rights activists have helped move all Americans forward in our continuing struggle to become a more perfect union—a struggle that continues today.

Individuals act as participatory citizens by exercising their right to vote in local, state, and federal elections.

WE THE PEOPLE

What role do rules play in your life? Have you ever considered what your life would be like if there were no rules? Imagine arriving at school on the first day of your senior year of high school. You discover that there are no schedules. No one knows where to go, what classes to attend, which locker to use. No one understands the processes and procedures that allow a school to operate efficiently.

This is similar to what would happen in a government without clear rules—or laws—that define the rights and responsibilities of citizens. Order, organization, equality, and safety would all be threatened without laws and established procedures and processes. The most concrete example of our society's rules are our laws, and the most fundamental duty of an American citizen is to obey them.

Is it fair that a government makes laws that people must follow? As you learned while studying the Constitution, the United States is a representative democracy, as demonstrated by the phrase "We the people." Your exploration of the Constitution has revealed that the American people hold the power to shape the government and determine its practices. When our government and representatives act in ways that oppose our rules and ideals, we have the means to point the country in the right direction. Americans work to be *good citizens* by obeying laws, *participatory citizens* by voting and serving on juries, and *socially-just citizens* by standing up for the rights of others.

THINK ABOUT IT

SUMMARIZE Why are rules and laws important, and what would happen without them?

11.11.7 Explain how the federal, state, and local governments have responded to demographic and social changes such as population shifts to the suburbs, racial concentrations in the cities, Frostbelt-to-Sunbelt migration, international migration, decline of family farms, increases in out-of-wedlock births, and drug abuse.

The Rights and Responsibilities of Citizens

Our Constitution defines many of the rights we enjoy as Americans. These rights apply to all citizens, regardless of whether they were born here or immigrated from another country. Knowing your rights can help you better understand the responsibilities that come with being a citizen, and help you determine what you must do to support and protect those rights. Responsibilities include doing what is right, showing good character, and acting in an ethical manner. As you read, think about specific actions you already perform and other steps you might take to be a good, participatory, and socially just citizen.

AMERICAN CITIZENSHIP

Some residents of the United States are citizens because they were born in the country. They are native-born citizens. Others came legally from foreign countries to live in the United States. Our democratic principles have fostered high levels of freedom, political stability, and economic prosperity. These features have attracted people to our nation for hundreds of years. In addition, our political and economic systems have become models for other nations throughout the world. People looking for opportunity and freedom are drawn to our country.

A person who has immigrated to the United States and desires to become a legal citizen goes through a process called **naturalization**. Individuals may qualify for naturalization if they are at least 18 years old and have been a permanent resident in the United States for at least 5 years (or 3 years if they are married to a U.S. citizen). They must learn the laws, rights, and responsibilities of American citizenship.

Following a successful interview with government officials, a prospective citizen must pass a citizenship test. After completing all the steps in this process, a new citizen is sworn in during a naturalization ceremony. As you know, the United States is a country of immigrants. Throughout our country's history, immigrants have helped build our nation, strengthen our economy, and enhance our society. It is a proud day when they become U.S. citizens.

For both native and naturalized citizens, being an American means much more than just living in the United States. After all, Americans living in foreign countries are still citizens of the United States. They are always connected to the United States and other Americans because of their citizenship. Citizenship also encompasses elements of the American tradition, which includes a shared history, customs, and political and cultural beliefs and values. These values include freedom, liberty, and equality—those principles Thomas Jefferson described in the Declaration of Independence.

Rights of Citizens
Right to freedom of religion
Right to freedom of speech (with some limits)
Right to freedom of the press
Right to assemble
Right to trial by jury (in specific types of cases)
Right to vote
Right to buy and sell property
Right to freely travel across the country and to leave and return to the country

RESTRICTIONS ON RIGHTS

By now, you're probably familiar with the basic rights of citizens as guaranteed in the Constitution. These rights also carry responsibilities and are subject to interpretation by the courts. For example, Amendment 1 guarantees the right to free speech—to state one's views or ideas without fear of punishment. Nonetheless, an employer or teacher, for example, can limit speech to what is appropriate in the circumstances. Speech intended to cause harm to others is not protected. For example, crying "Fire!" in a crowded theater when there is no fire is not protected by the right to free speech. The person's "speech" could cause harm to others. The Supreme Court has also placed limits on speech intended to motivate an individual to break the law. Threats of violence are also restricted.

New citizens are sworn in at a naturalization ceremony on July 4, 2016, in Seattle, Washington.

TWO TYPES OF RESPONSIBILITIES

American citizens have two different types of responsibilities: civic and personal. **Civic responsibilities** include voting, paying taxes, and serving on juries. Some of these responsibilities are duties: actions required by law. For example, all citizens must obey laws, pay taxes, and perform jury duty when notified. Neglecting these duties may result in legal penalties. Males over the age of 18 must register with the government in case they are needed for military service.

Personal responsibilities are not required, but they contribute to a more civil society. These include respecting others and their rights, helping in the community, standing up for others, and staying informed about important issues. Personal responsibilities are not as clearly defined as civic duties. They are, however, vital to maintaining an effective government and just society.

All American citizens over the age of 18 have the right to vote. Many people take that right for granted but don't bother to exercise it. Perhaps they don't consider the fact that the right to vote is a privilege that is not granted to people in some countries. These people have no say in how they are governed. Voters also have a responsibility to become informed about issues. They have an obligation to use reliable sources to learn about candidates and their positions on issues. Informed voters can then analyze the credibility of a candidate's claims.

BEING A RESPONSIBLE CITIZEN

When you think of your personal responsibilities as a citizen, consider the choices you make in terms of your actions. Being a responsible citizen means behaving in ways that are right, moral, and just, and acting in a way that benefits you and those around you. Considering the rights of all people, not just the rights of a select few, will help you be a personally responsible citizen.

Citizens have many personal responsibilities, such as being open-minded, respecting the opinions of others, and showing respect for the beliefs and individuality of people with different backgrounds. People of any age can take on personal responsibilities by doing community service projects, standing up for the rights of others, and respecting all people regardless of ethnicity, nationality, gender identity, sexual orientation, or beliefs. Tolerance for others is an important part of being an American citizen.

Tolerance of differences is essential in a democracy, especially one that is as diverse as the United States. Responsible citizens are also willing to give time, effort, and money to improve their communities. Living up to these personal responsibilities helps citizens contribute to an environment of respect and caring and one that protects and promotes the health and welfare of everyone. Responsible citizens work to contribute to the common good.

THINK ABOUT IT

EXPLAIN How does taking on personal responsibilities as a citizen contribute to the common good?

Building and Practicing Citizenship Skills

Building citizenship skills is like learning to play an instrument. It takes hard work and repetition, but the rewards make the effort worth it. Some citizenship skills, such as helping raise voter participation, will require you to seek out specific opportunities. Others, such as refusing to tolerate unjust behavior, can be exercised whenever appropriate situations arise. Citizenship affords many rights and requires many responsibilities. Enjoying these rights and responsibilities is the reward of being a good citizen.

The following chart includes ways you can build and apply citizenship skills in the classroom and in your community to become an active participant in our democracy. Study the chart and check out the Active Citizenship for the Environment Activities in this program's online resources. Then brainstorm more ways you can be a good, participatory, and socially just citizen and put them to practice.

After a gunman terrorized her Parkland, Florida high school on February 14, 2018, killing 17 people and injuring many others, Emma González transformed from a high school student into an activist and gun control advocate. As an engaged citizen, González lobbies for changes to gun legislation, and participates in peaceful protests such as the March For Our Lives, which was held on March 24, 2018, in hundreds of U.S. cities.

THINK ABOUT IT

DESCRIBE What opportunities for active citizenship appeal to you? Explain what you could do to be involved and engaged in your community and country.

ACTIVE CITIZENSHIP

Responsibilities	Citizenship Projects: Ways to Promote Civic Engagement
Become engaged.	• Get information from reliable, unbiased sources. • Ask questions of others who are well informed. • Attend or organize peaceful public demonstrations about issues important to you. • Register to vote, encourage others to vote, and consider becoming an election judge or poll watcher. • Serve your country and your fellow citizens through the military or by participating in organizations such as AmeriCorps, AmeriCorps VISTA, and the Peace Corps. • Participate in citizen journalism by reporting information accurately through blogs, news sites, and social media.

Responsibilities	Citizenship Projects: Ways to Promote Civic Engagement
Do historical research.	• Conduct oral histories with family or community members to better understand historical trends. • Interview citizens who served in the military, took part in social justice movements, or were involved in bringing about social change in schools or the workplace. • Research how you and your classmates can participate in National History Day at a state or national level.
Participate in the democratic process.	• Ask a teacher to organize a trip to a local courtroom to see the legal system in action. • Contact a local political candidate whose ideas you support to see how you might help with his or her campaign. • With the help of a parent or teacher, seek opportunities to witness a naturalization ceremony.
Lobby for change.	• Form a lobbying committee with other students to influence legislation or public policy. • Establish a goal for your lobbying campaign. • Identify whom to lobby. (Who are the people who can help you accomplish your goal?) • Find information and statistics to support your goal. • Get public support for your cause. You might consider gathering signatures on a petition or creating flyers to publicize your campaign. • Present your case to the appropriate individuals.
Volunteer in your community.	• Determine how your skills and interests could help someone else. • Talk with your parents, teachers, and friends to learn what types of volunteer services your community needs. • Make volunteering a regular part of your life. You could consider serving food to the homeless, collecting clothing or canned goods to help a local shelter, cleaning or restoring a local park or playground, or tutoring students who are struggling with their school work.
Pay taxes.	• Read more about your local and state taxes, and what the revenue is used for. • Recognize that you are already paying sales taxes when you purchase many items.
Express political opinions.	• Write a letter or an email to a newspaper editor about an issue that concerns you.
Obey the law.	• Become familiar with the laws in your state, city, and town that apply to people your age.
Stand up for the rights of others.	• Work to stop the discrimination of all people. • Write articles and blog posts about the importance of protecting and supporting the rights of people of different races, religions, and sexual orientations.
Listen to the opinions of others. Discuss differences of opinion in a kind and civil manner.	• When friends or acquaintances express opinions that differ from yours, politely explain why you disagree, if you do.
Respect the value of individuals. Respect differences among people.	• Enjoy and appreciate the differences among people from various backgrounds. • Make friends with people who are different from you. • Volunteer in your community to interact with and help others.
Accept responsibility for your actions.	• If someone asks about a mistake you have made, tell the truth. • Ask what you might do to make up for the mistake.

PRIMARY AND SECONDARY SOURCE

HANDBOOK

THINKING ABOUT TIME AND PLACE

Historians ask questions that are rooted in time and place. The most basic information historians must establish is when and where a person lived or an event occurred. Because time and place are so basic to the study of history, time lines and maps are crucial tools for historians.

Time lines indicate how major events, people, and periods are related to one another in time. Maps show the physical and cultural features of neighborhoods, cities, states, and countries. They help explain such events as the historical migration of a group of people, or the growth of an empire or economic system. This book contains many time lines and maps with this kind of information.

Yet the study of history is not limited to when or where. Historians also ask how events relate to each other. They wonder about the lessons we can learn from analyzing the multiple causes, developments, and effects of the past. To answer these questions, historians first accept that change over time affects not only technology, politics, and economics, but also our very ideas and values. The people, places, and events that make up history are constantly driving how we both frame and interpret the present.

PRIMARY AND SECONDARY SOURCES

As you've learned, historians begin their research by asking questions about a particular time and place. They then conduct research by examining evidence from primary and secondary sources.

Primary sources are writings or recordings created by someone who witnessed or lived through a historical event. These sources include letters, diaries, autobiographies, photographs, and oral histories. An **oral history** is a recorded interview with a person whose experiences and memories have historical significance. **Secondary sources** are writings or recordings created after an event by someone who did not see it or live during the time when it occurred. Secondary sources include history books and biographies and are often based on primary sources. Historians apply reasoning skills to evaluate information in primary and secondary sources. For example, to evaluate a piece of writing, a historian asks such questions as:

- Is the author biased?
- Does the author make sound generalizations or misleading oversimplifications?
- Which explanation of events best accords with the textual evidence available?
- Can the author's premise or claim be corroborated with other information?
- Does the author present sufficient evidence or clear reasons to support his or her argument?

From *Rediscovering Jacob Riis*, by Bonnie Yochelson and Daniel Czitrom, 2014

The 2014 book from which the following excerpt was taken is considered a secondary source because it was written about a historical person, photographer Jacob Riis, by someone who did not live during his lifetime. Secondary sources are sometimes based on other secondary sources, which are themselves based on primary sources. That is the case with this book, which cites a key secondary source translation of Riis's original pocket diaries in its bibliography.

SECONDARY SOURCE

[Jacob Riis's] nationwide lecture tours and steady stream of magazine stories had kept his message in public view. The twin themes of his writing—urban poverty and the Americanization of the immigrant—are as relevant today as in his time. Riis's original photographs . . . constitute a unique pictorial record of New York's late-nineteenth-century slums—[and] added another dimension to his fame. His most enduring legacy remains the written descriptions, photographs, and analysis of the conditions in which the majority of New Yorkers lived in the late nineteenth century.

INTERPRETING EVIDENCE

After historians examine and evaluate evidence, they try to put together a whole picture or story. They explain the central issues, placing people and events in a particular setting. They identify causes, effects, and sequence of events. But they also look for connections between events and larger social, economic, and political developments. Realizing there are limitations in making such connections, historians must be both perceptive and discerning as they examine primary and secondary sources for evidence of such connections, and as they identify patterns that continue over time and place.

Historians also use sources as evidence to identify the emergence of new patterns. One example of a new pattern might be global terrorism, a relatively recent form of warfare against private citizens across the world. Historians can draw upon evidence in primary and secondary sources to determine and establish new historical patterns as they develop.

Historians also must learn to interpret evidence in the context in which an event occurred, rather than applying present-day values when making judgments about a historical event. For example, in the period leading up to the Civil War, it was common for people to speak about enslaved people as if they were property. Therefore, a historian analyzing primary sources from this era must consider how the values and views of that time period shaped the purpose, style, and content of the sources.

Additionally, the lens through which a historian examines a source depends partly on the time and place being studied. A historian examining immigration in the early 1900s in California might focus on basic indicators of economic performance—statistics that might connect to the influx of new immigrants seeking jobs. He or she might then analyze the costs and benefits of economic and political decisions. A historian studying human migration into the Americas would not choose such a focus because such statistics are not available. As you continue to study history, be prepared to apply the intellectual reasoning, reflection, and research skills of a historian, especially as you examine primary and secondary sources.

PRIMARY SOURCE

As part of his focus on photographing immigrants and the disadvantaged in New York City in the late 1800s, Jacob Riis captured this group of men in an alley behind Mulberry Street known as "Bandit's Roost." After working as a police photographer, Riis developed an emotional connection to his subjects that led him to document all aspects of life in the city.

HISTORICAL THINKING

1. **READING CHECK** What is the difference between a primary source and a secondary source?
2. **CONSTRUCT A HYPOTHESIS** Using information from both sources, why do you think Riis became famous for his work involving urban poverty and immigrants?
3. **EVALUATE INFORMATION** Examine the primary and secondary sources on these pages. Write a paragraph in which you evaluate whether the evidence presented in the sources is sufficient to support the generalization that the majority of urban immigrants to the United States at the turn of the 20th century worked and lived in poverty.

HI 1 Students show the connections, causal and otherwise, between particular historical events and larger social, economic, and political trends and developments.

"Binder on Top of the World," advertisement, 1800s

Ironically, as American farmers became more efficient and productive, agriculture made up a smaller portion of the national economy. This was largely due to a reduction in crop prices and less demand for farm labor, as farmers began to use machines like the grain binder (right) to do the work of human workers. This advertisement from the late 1800s provides insight into the impact of industrialization on farmers' productivity and efficiency.

DOCUMENT-BASED QUESTIONS:

1. How does the ad suggest the development of the McCormick grain binder made farming more efficient?
2. How has the illustrator represented the phrase "on top of the world," and what does the phrase mean in this context?
3. Explain why you think this ad would or would not have influenced you to buy a grain binder if you were a farmer during the 1800s.

11.2.1 Know the effects of industrialization on living and working conditions, including the portrayal of working conditions and food safety in Upton Sinclair's *The Jungle*.

CHAPTER 6

From *The Octopus: A Story of California*, by Frank Norris, 1901

During the early 1900s, capitalism was fueled by industrialization and large monopolistic corporations were beginning to dominate the American economy. Journalist Frank Norris challenged the simplistic idea that progress was good by highlighting the ways in which large corporations negatively affected workers. This excerpt from Norris's novel, *The Octopus*, provides an image of how the railroad, representing big business, terrorizes the countryside.

> Then, faint and prolonged . . . he heard the engine whistling. Again and again, at rapid intervals in its flying course, it whistled for road crossings, for sharp curves, for trestles; ominous notes, hoarse, bellowing, ringing with the accents of menace and defiance; and abruptly Presley saw again, in his imagination, the galloping monster, the terror of steel and steam, with its single eye, cyclopean, red . . . but saw it now as the symbol of a vast power, huge, terrible, flinging the echo of its thunder over all the reaches of the valley, leaving blood and destruction in its path; the leviathan, with tentacles of steel clutching into the soil, the soulless Force, the iron-hearted Power, the monster, the Colossus, the Octopus.

DOCUMENT-BASED QUESTIONS:

1. What details in the excerpt suggest that the railroad exerted great power over those living along its route?
2. What does the excerpt reveal about Norris's bias or prejudices toward big business?
3. What does the excerpt reveal about the controversies surrounding the rise of large corporations during the early industrial era in America?

11.2.6 Trace the economic development of the United States and its emergence as a major industrial power, including its gains from trade and the advantages of its physical geography; HREP 2 Students identify bias and prejudice in historical interpretations.

From *What Social Classes Owe Each Other*, by William Graham Sumner, 1884

At the turn of the 20th century, the process of industrialization had allowed a few individuals to accumulate great wealth, while the majority worked for wages at levels that made it difficult for them to afford the necessities of life. This stark contrast sparked intense social debate over why such inequalities existed in the first place. In this primary source, William Sumner, a leading Social Darwinist of the late 1800s, explains what he believes are the root causes of those inequalities.

DOCUMENT-BASED QUESTIONS:

1. What is the main idea of Sumner's argument?
2. How does Sumner believe the practice of "self-denial" differentiates individuals within society?
3. Compare the differences between Sumner's beliefs and Washington Gladden's beliefs (below) in terms of how society should respond to social inequalities. Based on the evidence, who makes a better argument and why?

Capital is only formed by self-denial, and if the possession of it did not secure advantages and superiorities of a high order men would never submit to what is necessary to get it. The possession of capital is, therefore, an indispensable prerequisite of educational, scientific, and moral goods. Hence it appears that the man who has his self-denial before him, however good may be his intention, cannot be as the man who has his self-denial behind him. Some seem to think that this is very unjust, but they get their notions of justice from some occult source of inspiration, not from observing the facts of this world as it has been made and exists. That it requires energy, courage, perseverance, and prudence is not to be denied.

11.2.7 Analyze the similarities and differences between the ideologies of Social Darwinism and Social Gospel (e.g., using biographies of William Graham Sumner, Billy Sunday, Dwight L. Moody); HREP 1 Students distinguish valid arguments from fallacious arguments in historical interpretations.

CHAPTER 6

From *Social Salvation*, by Washington Gladden, 1902

Proponents of the Social Gospel movement, such as the pastor Washington Gladden, viewed social inequality largely as the result of greed and called for broader private and public support for reforms. This excerpt is from a lecture entitled "The State and the Unemployed," one of a series of lectures Gladden presented at the Yale Divinity School in 1902. The lectures were collected in the book *Social Salvation*. The title reflects Gladden's view that one's salvation comes from working to remedy social ills.

DOCUMENT-BASED QUESTIONS:

1. Based on the excerpt, what is the meaning of the title of the lecture, "The State and the Unemployed"?
2. What can you infer about the assistance poor and unskilled workers received from private agencies?
3. How does Gladden believe social inequalities should be relieved?
4. Is Gladden making a valid argument? Why or why not?

It is the salvation of these people [and] the recognition of this high responsibility on the part of the state for which I am pleading . . . which cannot be done by private agencies. It involves a measure of compulsion which only the state can exercise. And the state can never do it as it ought to be done until it gets a new conception of its function as the representative of the divine power and the divine goodness. The skilless workman in this age of highly developed industry is, especially in cities, at a terrible disadvantage. We must do one of two things. We must feed him as a pauper . . . or we must try to teach him some kind of industry. Our systems of education ought to make large provision for instruction of this kind.

11.3.2 Analyze the great religious revivals and the leaders involved in them, including the First Great Awakening, the Second Great Awakening, the Civil War revivals, the Social Gospel Movement, the rise of Christian liberal theology in the nineteenth century, the impact of the Second Vatican Council, and the rise of Christian fundamentalism in current times; HREP 1 Students distinguish valid arguments from fallacious arguments in historical interpretations.

From "Anarchism: What It Really Stands For," by Emma Goldman, 1910

Emma Goldman, a Russian Jewish immigrant, was a committed antiwar and anticapitalist activist and writer. She was eventually jailed and deported from the United States for promoting her views at public engagements. In this primary source, Goldman shares her views on the core tenets of anarchism and why she believes religious, economic, and political systems serve to repress, not enhance.

Anarchism, then, really stands for the liberation of the human mind from the dominion of religion; the liberation of the human body from the dominion of property; liberation from the shackles and restraint of government. Anarchism stands for a social order based on the free grouping of individuals for the purpose of producing real social wealth; an order that will guarantee to every human being free access to the earth and full enjoyment of the necessities of life, according to individual desires, tastes, and inclinations.

DOCUMENT-BASED QUESTIONS:

1. What is the main idea of this passage, and which details support it?
2. What is Goldman's point of view on the relevance and purpose of government?
3. What do you think Goldman means by "social wealth"? How does her idea of social wealth demonstrate her personal biases?
4. How does Goldman define the "necessities of life"?

HREP 2 Students identify bias and prejudice in historical interpretations.

From *Modern Industry in Relation to the Family, Health, Education, Morality*, by Florence Kelley, 1914

As a result of progressive efforts in the early 1900s, many women gained new educational and employment opportunities that were previously reserved for men. Factory inspector, writer, and social reformer Florence Kelley came to Hull House in the late 1800s to escape an abusive husband. She stayed for a decade, working to address unfair and unsafe labor practices with Julie Lathrop, an advocate for women, children, immigrants, and the mentally ill. In this excerpt, Kelley writes of the negative impact working at night can have on young women.

The absence from home at night of thousands of young girls in the telephone service has become a matter of course. Seventy-five percent of these young workers at night are at the age of 18 years, according to the latest official report of this state. Sleep lost at night cannot be made up by day by people who live in the industrial districts of any city. What nation ever before took it for granted that thousands of young girls 18 years old should, in the way of earning their bread, be away from home at night? This employment of young girls may well be taken as an index of cynicism of public opinion which accepts, under the corrupting influence of industry, such disintegration of the family as inevitable.

DOCUMENT-BASED QUESTIONS:

1. How is Kelley's argument related to the views of the progressives?
2. What does Kelley suggest about the causal relationship between the girls' jobs and the family?
3. According to Kelley, how did the arrival of the telephone service change the lives and roles of women?

CST 2 Students analyze how change happens at different rates at different times; understand that some aspects can change while others remain the same; and understand that change is complicated and affects not only technology and politics but also values and beliefs.

From *A Farewell to Arms*, by Ernest Hemingway, 1929

American author and poet Gertrude Stein called Ernest Hemingway and other writers who actively participated in World War I a "lost generation." With diminished moral and religious values and the feeling that life lacked meaning, these authors created characters who sought to make sense of life and find purpose in it. Hemingway served as an ambulance driver in World War I and captured his experiences in his 1929 novel, *A Farewell to Arms*. The novel tells the story of a young American, Henry, in Italy during the war. In this excerpt, Henry considers the impact of war on people.

I had seen nothing sacred, and the things that were glorious had no glory and the sacrifices were like the stockyards at Chicago if nothing was done with the meat except to bury it. There were many words that you could not stand to hear and finally only the names of places had dignity. Certain numbers were the same way and certain dates and these with the names of the places were all you could say and have them mean anything. Abstract words such as glory, honor, courage, or hallow [to hold in utter respect] were obscene beside the concrete names of villages, the numbers of roads, the names of rivers, the numbers of regiments and the dates.

DOCUMENT-BASED QUESTIONS:

1. How does this excerpt suggest that Hemingway was indeed part of the lost generation?
2. What textual evidence demonstrates that Henry chooses to focus on real things that have meaning rather than on abstract concepts? Why might he do so?
3. How is Henry's perspective that of someone whose initial views toward war might have changed?

11.4.5 Analyze the political, economic, and social ramifications of World War I on the home front.

From *The Making of Americans*, by Gertrude Stein, 1925

After World War I ended, young people, including many war veterans, felt lost or aimless. Some focused on gaining material wealth to re-establish their sense of purpose. Additionally, the standard of living rose in the 1920s for middle-class white Americans, so the overall desire for new types of consumer goods such as automobiles and household appliances increased. In her novel *The Making of Americans*, Gertrude Stein explores the changes that occur from generation to generation in two fictional families, as well as the impact of increasing social pressures.

The father had always been convinced and proud even when he had disapproved the opinions of his daughter. He now took a solid satisfaction in the completeness of accomplishment she now had in her. To her father, to know well what one wanted, and to win it, by patient steady fighting for it, was the best act a man or woman could accomplish, and well had his daughter done it. She had won it, she knew very well what she wanted and she had it. He still shook his head at her new fangled notions, her literary effects, the artistic kind of new improvement, as he called it, that she put into her new house to make it perfect. He did not understand it and he always said it, but he was very proud to see her do it, and he bragged to everybody.

DOCUMENT-BASED QUESTIONS:

1. What does the father like and dislike in regard to his daughter's house, and why?
2. What biases are evident in how the father views his daughter?
3. What does the excerpt indicate about the social effects resulting from the rise of consumer goods?

11.5 Students analyze the major political, social, economic, technological, and cultural developments of the 1920s; HREP 2 Students identify bias and prejudice in historical interpretations.

From *The Interpretation of Dreams*, by Sigmund Freud, 1900

In the early 20th century, new scientific theories challenged traditional beliefs. Psychologist Sigmund Freud described the workings of the unconscious mind and explained how it influenced behavior. The ideas of scientists like Freud opposed more superstitious ideas about the causes of mental illness that were prevalent at the time. This new understanding of the unconscious mind formed part of the foundation for the rise of the different schools of psychotherapy practiced today.

At any rate, the interpretation of dreams is the [royal highway] to a knowledge of the unconscious element in our psychic life. By the analysis of dreams we obtain some insight into the composition of this most marvelous and most mysterious of instruments [the mind]; it is true that this only takes us a little way, but it gives us a start which enables us, setting out from the angle of other (properly pathological [unhealthy]) formations, to penetrate further in our disjoining of the instrument [separating out the parts of the mind].

DOCUMENT-BASED QUESTIONS:

1. What does Freud suggest about the relationship between dreams and the mind?
2. Why might a scientist studying the mind want to identify and separate out its parts?
3. What lasting effect did Freud have on the mental health community? Use this source material and do additional research to find out.

HI 2 Students recognize the complexity of historical causes and effects, including the limitations on determining cause and effect.

Ad from the *Chicago Defender*, 1917

During the Progressive Era, attitudes about race were challenged, especially in the South, in part due to new information reaching the public through print media. The *Chicago Defender*, a newspaper founded in 1905 by Robert S. Abbott, quickly became a prominent weekly. Filled with news and commentary, the paper had a large readership outside the city of Chicago. Abbott's periodical helped publicize issues of racial injustice. In this ad from 1917, the *Defender* issues a call to African Americans living with Jim Crow laws in the South to migrate to cities like Chicago in the North during World War I.

The *Defender* invites all to come north. Plenty of room for the good, sober, industrious men. Plenty of work. For those who will not work, the jails will take care of you. When you have served your 90 days at hard labor, you will then learn how to work. Anywhere in God's country is far better than the southland. Cast the yoke from around your neck. See the light, when you have crossed the Ohio River, breathe fresh air and say, "Why didn't I come before?"

DOCUMENT-BASED QUESTIONS:

1. How does this advertisement describe the lives of African Americans in the South?
2. What kind of influence do you think this ad might have had in both the North and South over ideas about race and equality?
3. What larger historical development does the ad represent?

11.5.7 Discuss the rise of mass production techniques, the growth of cities, the impact of new technologies (e.g., the automobile, electricity), and the resulting prosperity and effect on the American landscape; CST 3 Students use a variety of maps and documents to interpret human movement, including major patterns of domestic and international migration, changing environmental preferences and settlement patterns, the frictions that develop between population groups, and the diffusion of ideas, technological innovations, and goods.

Sun on Prospect Street (Gloucester, Massachusetts), by Edward Hopper, 1934

Edward Hopper was a painter known for his realism—emphasis upon contemporary reality and the lives of everyday people. The realist movement originally began with the literature of such early 20th century authors as John Dos Passos. It then spread to the visual arts. Of particular interest to Hopper were architecture and landscapes, as can be seen in his painting, *Sun on Prospect Street*. At the time he painted it, Gloucester, Massachusetts, on the Atlantic Coast, was a thriving New England fishing town.

DOCUMENT-BASED QUESTIONS:

1. How does Hopper's painting reflect the realist movement?
2. How does the painting represent the modernization of American life?
3. How do you think Hopper feels about this prosperous middle-class fishing town? Use details from the painting to support your answer.

11.5.7 Discuss the rise of mass production techniques, the growth of cities, the impact of new technologies (e.g., the automobile, electricity), and the resulting prosperity and effect on the American landscape; 11.8.8 Discuss forms of popular culture, with emphasis on their origins and geographic diffusion (e.g., jazz and other forms of popular music, professional sports, architectural and artistic styles).

From the author's prologue to *U.S.A.,* by John Dos Passos, 1938

In 1938, John Dos Passos's three previous novels—*42nd Parallel, 1919*, and *The Big Money*—were combined and published as a trilogy entitled *U.S.A.* In the novels of *U.S.A.,* Dos Passos set out to represent the diversity of people that made up the United States in terms of their accents and dialects, the work they did, and their aspirations and struggles. In the prologue he wrote for the trilogy edition, Dos Passos provides a look at the setting in which his characters moved and spoke.

U.S.A. is the slice of a continent. U.S.A. is a group of holding companies, some aggregations of trade unions, a set of laws bound in calf, a radio network, a chain of moving picture theaters, a column of stock quotations rubbed out and written in by a Western Union boy on a blackboard, a public-library full of old newspapers and dogeared history books with protests scrawled on the margins in pencil. U.S.A. is the world's greatest river valley fringed with mountains and hills, U.S.A. is a set of big mouthed officials with too many bank accounts. U.S.A. is a lot of men buried in their uniforms in Arlington Cemetery. U.S.A. is the letters at the end of an address when you are away from home. But mostly U.S.A. is the speech of the people.

DOCUMENT-BASED QUESTIONS:

1. What is Dos Passos's perception of the United States?
2. What is the meaning of the phrase "with protests scrawled on the margins in pencil"?
3. How is the image of the United States conveyed in the last sentence different from the images conveyed in the rest of the excerpt?

Tenement Flats, by Millard Sheets, 1933–1934

Artist Millard Sheets was supported by and served the Public Works of Art Project, a New Deal program to fund art documenting the Depression. The scene Sheets depicts in *Tenement Flats* is in a California neighborhood called Bunker Hill. The area first consisted of mansions that were then abandoned during the Depression and converted to or replaced with tenements like those in the painting. By 1934, when this painting was completed, the neighborhood had become one of the most impoverished in the Los Angeles area. However, mansions remained at the top of the hill, and in the painting we see a person, possibly a servant, trudging up toward one of those houses.

DOCUMENT-BASED QUESTIONS:

1. How does this scene compare with that in Edward Hopper's painting *Sun on Prospect Street*?
2. What image of the urban poor during the Depression and the New Deal does this painting convey?
3. What controversy might arise from the fact that Sheets was employed by a New Deal program while the people he depicted lived in poverty?

11.6.4 Analyze the effects of and the controversies arising from New Deal economic policies and the expanded role of the federal government in society and the economy since the 1930s (e.g., Works Progress Administration, Social Security, National Labor Relations Board, farm programs, regional development policies, and energy development projects such as the Tennessee Valley Authority, California Central Valley Project, and Bonneville Dam).

From *What We Knew: Terror, Mass Murder, and Everyday Life in Nazi Germany*, by Eric A. Johnson, 2005

Historian Eric A. Johnson studies the history of violence, especially the Holocaust. Johnson and Karl-Heinz Reuband, a German sociologist, compiled an oral history providing insight into everyday life for Jews during the Holocaust. In this excerpt from an interview, Armin Hertz describes his experience of Kristallnacht as a 12-year-old Jewish boy in Berlin.

During the Kristallnacht, our store was destroyed, glass was broken, the synagogues were set on fire. There was a synagogue in the same street where we lived. It was on the first floor of a commercial building; downstairs were stores, and upstairs was a synagogue. In the back of that building, there was a factory so they could not set that synagogue on fire because people were living and working there. But they threw everything out of the window—the Torah scrolls, the prayer books, the benches, everything was lying in the street.

DOCUMENT-BASED QUESTIONS:

1. What was the impact of Kristallnacht on Jews in Germany and on the world?
2. What does the passage suggest about how Nazi policies toward Jews were evolving?
3. During World War II, some Americans believed the reports of the persecution of Jews in Europe were exaggerated or simply propaganda created so the U.S. government would give Jews special treatment. Today, a small number of people even deny the Holocaust occurred. How could this historian's excerpt be used to debate such alternative interpretations of the Holocaust and the mistreatment of Jews and other groups by the Nazis?

11.3.3 Cite incidences of religious intolerance in the United States (e.g., persecution of Mormons, anti-Catholic sentiment, anti-Semitism); HREP 3 Students evaluate major debates among historians concerning alternative interpretations of the past, including an analysis of authors' use of evidence and the distinctions between sound generalizations and misleading oversimplifications.

From *An American Dilemma*, by Gunnar Myrdal, 1944

Gunnar Myrdal was a Swedish economist and sociologist who studied the problems of African Americans in the late 1930s and early 1940s. During this period, African Americans experienced the sharp contrast between American principles of freedom and equality and the practice of racial segregation. In his writing, Myrdal details the systematic oppression of African Americans.

In spite of all race prejudice, few Americans seem to doubt that it is the ultimate fate of this nation to incorporate without distinction not only all the Northern European stocks, but also the people from Eastern and Southern Europe, the Near East and Mexico. The Negroes, on the other hand, are commonly assumed to be unassimilable. Considerable efforts are directed toward "Americanizing" all groups of alien origin. But in regard to the colored peoples, the American policy is the reverse. They are excluded from assimilation. They are usually advised to keep to themselves and develop a race pride of their own.

DOCUMENT-BASED QUESTIONS:

1. How does the excerpt point to a dilemma, as reflected in the title of the work from which it comes?
2. Given the date of this excerpt—the fourth year of direct U.S. participation in World War II—how does the attitude toward African Americans described in the excerpt exemplify hypocrisy on the part of Americans?
3. In what ways does Myrdal oversimplify in his account of assimilation by the minority groups he identifies in addition to African Americans?

From a speech by General George C. Marshall, 1947

George C. Marshall was the chief of staff of the U.S. armed forces during World War II. After the war, he served as President Truman's secretary of state. In this speech, Marshall outlines the need for an economic aid plan to help Europe recover from the destruction of World War II. His speech became the basis for the Marshall Plan, which many credit as saving Western Europe from economic collapse. For his plan, General Marshall was awarded the Nobel Peace Prize in 1953.

Our policy is directed not against any country or doctrine but against hunger, poverty, desperation and chaos. Its purpose should be the revival of a working economy in the world so as to permit the emergence of political and social conditions in which free institutions can exist. Any government that is willing to assist in the task of recovery will find full cooperation, I am sure, on the part of the United States Government. Any government which maneuvers to block the recovery of other countries cannot expect help from us. Furthermore, governments, political parties or groups which seek to perpetuate human misery in order to profit therefrom politically or otherwise will encounter the opposition of the United States.

DOCUMENT-BASED QUESTIONS:

1. Using clues from the text, what is the meaning of "free institutions"?
2. What threat does Marshall believe European nations face in the aftermath of the war?
3. What evidence from the excerpt supports the idea that the Marshall plan was not a policy for controlling Europe?

11.7.8 Analyze the effect of massive aid given to Western Europe under the Marshall Plan to rebuild itself after the war and the importance of a rebuilt Europe to the U.S. economy.

From President Truman's veto of the Taft-Hartley Labor Bill, 1947

Following World War II, the number of labor strikes in the United States increased. Workers generally had agreed to limit such strikes during the war, but when the war ended, millions of soldiers went back to work, and the frequency and duration of labor strikes increased. To limit unions' abilities to organize and strike, the Taft-Hartley Act of 1947 was passed despite the veto of President Harry Truman. In this excerpt, Truman explains to Congress his reasons for vetoing the bill.

I heartily condemn abuses on the part of unions and employers, and I have no patience with stubborn insistence on private advantage to the detriment of the public interest. But this bill is far from a solution of those problems. The bill taken as a whole would reverse the basic direction of our national labor policy, inject the Government into private economic affairs on an unprecedented scale, and conflict with important principles of our democratic society. Its provisions would cause more strikes, not fewer. It would contribute neither to industrial peace nor to economic stability and progress. It contains seeds of discord which would plague this Nation for years to come.

DOCUMENT-BASED QUESTIONS:

1. What does the excerpt suggest about Truman's beliefs about the efficacy, or success, of previous labor laws?
2. Based on this excerpt, what can you infer about Truman's labor policy?
3. What evidence does Truman offer to support the idea that the revised labor act would have the opposite effect of what was intended?

11.8.3 Examine Truman's labor policy and congressional reaction to it.

CHAPTER 14

From a speech by Senator Robert A. Taft, 1947

Senator Robert A. Taft, a Republican who served as chair of the Senate Labor Committee in 1947, co-sponsored the Taft-Hartley Act of 1947, in large part due to his belief that the Wagner Act had given too much power to labor unions. Here, Taft explains why he supports banning what he believes to be unfair union practices. Despite President Truman's veto of the bill, Taft was able to work with members of both the House and Senate to gather enough votes to override the veto.

The Taft-Hartley Act was written for only one purpose: to restore justice and equality in labor-management relations. It was not a new law, but a revision of elaborate existing laws such as the Wagner Act . . . that were so one-sided they conferred on labor-union leaders arbitrary power over all but the largest employers, and even more important, over their own members. These former laws are written on sound principles, to correct excessive power formerly exercised by employers. But they were so sweeping, and so broadly construed, that they gave no one—employer, public or workmen, any remedy whatever against the acts of union-labor leaders, no matter how arbitrary and unjust those acts might be.

DOCUMENT-BASED QUESTIONS:

1. What does the excerpt suggest about how most lawmakers in 1947 felt about the effectiveness of previous labor laws?
2. How did Taft and Truman differ in regard to how they expected the revised act to affect labor-management relations?
3. Which author, Taft or Truman, gives the best support for his ideas? Explain your answer.

11.8.3 Examine Truman's labor policy and congressional reaction to it.

From Article 5 of the NATO Treaty, 1949

World War II left Europe economically devastated and politically divided. The communist bloc and the western democracies, which had conflicting aims, each assumed the other would seek political, economic, and military advantages. The western democracies formed the North Atlantic Treaty Organization (NATO) to protect members against a military invasion by the Soviet bloc, with the hope that it would discourage such an invasion from occurring in the first place.

The parties agree that an armed attack against one or more of them in Europe or North America shall be considered an attack against them all, and consequently they agree that, if such an armed attack occurs, each of them, in exercise of the right of individual or collective self defense recognized by Article 51 of the Charter of the United Nations, will assist the Party or Parties so attacked by taking forthwith, individually, and in concert with the other Parties, such action as it deems necessary, including the use of armed force, to restore and maintain the security of the North Atlantic area.

DOCUMENT-BASED QUESTIONS:

1. What is the meaning of "collective self defense"?
2. Based on the excerpt, what was the original purpose of NATO?
3. In what way are members who signed the NATO treaty required to support the alliance?
4. What do you hypothesize Article 51 of the Charter of the United Nations states, based on the context in which it appears in the excerpt?

11.9.2 Understand the role of military alliances, including NATO and SEATO, in deterring communist aggression and maintaining security during the Cold War.

From Dalton Trumbo's Laurel Award acceptance speech, 1970

Dalton Trumbo was an Oscar-winning screenwriter who was blacklisted as one of the Hollywood Ten. When he refused to identify fellow actors and screenwriters as communist sympathizers, he was held in contempt and jailed for 10 months. Looking back on that time more than 20 years later, he had this advice to offer.

When you who are in your 40s or younger look back with curiosity on that dark time . . . it will do no good to search for villains or heroes or saints or devils because there were none; there were only victims. Some suffered less than others, some grew and some diminished, but in the final tally we were all victims because almost without exception each of us felt compelled to say things he did not want to say, to do things that he did not want to do, to deliver and receive wounds he truly did not want to exchange. That is why none of us—right, left, or center [conservative, liberal, or moderate]—emerged from that long nightmare without sin.

DOCUMENT-BASED QUESTIONS:

1. Based on the excerpt, what can you infer about how the Cold War affected ordinary Americans?
2. How does Trumbo's claim that "we were all victims" reflect the historical context of the events being described?
3. What is Trumbo suggesting by stating "none of us . . . emerged from that long nightmare without sin"?
4. Based on this excerpt, do you think blacklisting was an effective strategy to rid the film industry of communist sympathizers?

11.9.3 Trace the origins and geopolitical consequences (foreign and domestic) of the Cold War and containment policy, including the following:
• The era of McCarthyism, instances of domestic Communism (e.g., Alger Hiss) and blacklisting • The Truman Doctrine • The Berlin Blockade • The Korean War • The Bay of Pigs invasion and the Cuban Missile Crisis • Atomic testing in the American West, the "mutual assured destruction" doctrine, and disarmament policies • The Vietnam War • Latin American policy; HI 3 Students interpret past events and issues within the context in which an event unfolded rather than solely in terms of present-day norms and values.

Salk Institute, San Diego, California, 1965

American architect Louis Kahn was born in Estonia and immigrated to the United States at a young age. After studying in the United States, he toured Europe for sources of architectural ideas and was strongly influenced by classical buildings such as the Pantheon in Rome. Part of the post–World War II modernist movement, Kahn's architectural style is described as brutalist, referring to his use of unfinished concrete arranged in bold, geometric formations. In 1959, Kahn was commissioned to design the Salk Institute for Biological Studies, near San Diego, California. The institute's brutalist design revolves around its construction materials: concrete, wood, and travertine.

DOCUMENT-BASED QUESTIONS:

1. Which architectural details in this photo of the Salk Institute exemplify Kahn's brutalist style?
2. Based on what you know of Kahn's architectural work, would you think the phrase "form follows function" best exemplifies it, or "function follows form"? Explain.
3. Why might an architectural style such as brutalism have originated after World War II?

11.8.8 Discuss forms of popular culture, with emphasis on their origins and geographic diffusion (e.g., jazz and other forms of popular music, professional sports, architectural and artistic styles); HI 1 Students show the connections, causal and otherwise, between particular historical events and larger social, economic, and political trends and developments.

From President Dwight D. Eisenhower's State of the Union Address, 1954

Citizens 18 years and older received the right to vote in 1971, when the 26th Amendment was ratified, but it may surprise you to know that President Eisenhower proposed the idea in his first State of the Union address in 1954. Suffrage was the last topic of Eisenhower's address, and the president also recommended that the vote be extended to citizens of the District of Columbia, to armed forces serving overseas, and to the people of Hawaii, by awarding statehood to the then-territory.

> For years our citizens between the ages of 18 and 21 have, in time of peril, been summoned to fight for America. They should participate in the political process that produces this fateful summons. I urge Congress to propose to the States a constitutional amendment permitting citizens to vote when they reach the age of 18.

DOCUMENT-BASED QUESTIONS:

1. Would Eisenhower's proposal have increased African-American voting? Explain why or why not.
2. What is Eisenhower's reasoning in asking to extend the vote to citizens 18 years and older?
3. Does Eisenhower make a valid argument as to why citizens 18 years of age should be able to vote? Why or why not? Use evidence from the text to support your answer.

11.11.2 Discuss the significant domestic policy speeches of Truman, Eisenhower, Kennedy, Johnson, Nixon, Carter, Reagan, Bush, and Clinton (e.g., with regard to education, civil rights, economic policy, environmental policy); HREP 1 Students distinguish valid arguments from fallacious arguments in historical interpretations.

From *A Raisin in the Sun*, by Lorraine Hansberry, 1959

Lorraine Hansberry was the first African-American woman to write a play that was performed on Broadway. In *A Raisin in the Sun*, Hansberry portrays challenges African Americans faced in trying to overcome racial prejudice and discrimination in the post–World War II era. In this scene, Mama has contracted to buy a house in an all-white neighborhood, but her son Walter has accepted a buyout offer from a white man who wants to prevent them from actually moving in. Mama and her daughter, Beneatha, reflect on Walter's decision.

MAMA: Son—I come from five generations of people who was slaves and sharecroppers—but ain't nobody in my family never let nobody pay 'em no money that was a way of telling us we wasn't fit to walk the earth. We ain't never been that poor. We ain't never been that—dead inside.

BENEATHA: Well—we are dead now. All the talk about dreams and sunlight that goes on in this house. It's all dead now.

DOCUMENT-BASED QUESTIONS:

1. How does Mama's last sentence in this excerpt reflect her opinion about her son accepting a buyout?
2. Based on the excerpt, how did racial attitudes toward African Americans in the 1950s represent a continuation of past attitudes?
3. How does the difference in the way Mama and Beneatha speak reflect generational differences?

CST 2 Students analyze how change happens at different rates at different times; understand that some aspects can change while others remain the same; and understand that change is complicated and affects not only technology and politics but also values and beliefs.

CORE-SUNY Downstate Medical Center, July 1963, by Bob Adelman

Beginning in 1963, Bob Adelman worked as a volunteer photographer for the Congress for Racial Equality (CORE) and the Student Nonviolent Coordinating Committee (SNCC), producing some of the most powerful images of the civil rights movement. On July 10, 1963, he photographed a protest in which CORE members blocked access to a construction site at the SUNY Downstate Medical Center in Brooklyn, New York. The demonstrators were protesting hiring discrimination in the construction industry. In this photo, a woman using nonviolent resistance to prevent a cement truck from entering the site is arrested by police.

DOCUMENT-BASED QUESTIONS:

1. Based on details in this photo, how would you describe the methods of nonviolent resistance being used by the protesters?
2. What emotion do you think the woman in the photo was experiencing at this moment?
3. How is this photo and the event it captured related to *A Raisin in the Sun*?

From *The Autobiography of Malcolm X*, by Malcolm X with Alex Haley, 1965

At the time of his murder, Malcolm X had done extensive interviews with a writer named Alex Haley. From these interviews, Haley wrote The Autobiography of Malcolm X. The book became a best seller and helped make Malcolm X a spiritual and ideological hero to people of many different backgrounds.

Yesterday I . . . was studying a document about how the United Nations proposes to ensure the human rights of the oppressed minorities of the world. The American black man is the world's most shameful case of minority oppression. What makes the black man think of himself as only an internal United States issue is just a catch-phrase, two words, "civil rights." How is the black man going to get "civil rights" before first he wins his *human rights*? If the American black man will start thinking about his *human* rights, and then start thinking of himself as part of one of the world's great peoples, he will see he has a case for the United Nations.

DOCUMENT-BASED QUESTIONS:

1. What distinction does Malcolm X make between civil rights and human rights?
2. Explain why you do or do not think Malcolm X makes a valid argument.
3. Why would it have been unusual for African Americans to take their case to the United Nations during the 1960s? Do you think it would have been effective?
4. Why do you think Malcolm X identifies the status of African Americans as the "most shameful case of minority oppression" in the world?

11.10.4 Examine the roles of civil rights advocates (e.g., A. Philip Randolph, Martin Luther King, Jr., Malcolm X, Thurgood Marshall, James Farmer, Rosa Parks), including the significance of Martin Luther King, Jr.'s "Letter from Birmingham Jail" and "I Have a Dream" speech; HREP 1 Students distinguish valid arguments from fallacious arguments in historical interpretations.

CHAPTER 17

From President John F. Kennedy's televised speech on Civil Rights, June 11, 1963

When John F. Kennedy became President of the United States in 1961, civil rights were one of the most important and visible issues facing the nation. African Americans encountered discrimination in all aspects of life. Civil rights leaders and activists had effectively managed to draw attention to this racial discrimination, and yet, segregation and discrimination continued. In his televised speech to the nation, Kennedy called not only on lawmakers but on all Americans to join together to acknowledge and honor the rights of African Americans.

This is one country. It has become one country because all of us and all the people who came here had an equal chance to develop their talents.

We cannot say to 10 percent of the population that you can't have that right; that your children cannot have the chance to develop whatever talents they have; that the only way that they are going to get their rights is to go into the streets and demonstrate. I think we owe them and we owe ourselves a better country than that.

DOCUMENT-BASED QUESTIONS:

1. To what larger American principle does Kennedy connect specific aspects of the civil rights movement?
2. What is Kennedy's view of civil rights demonstrations?
3. What does Kennedy convey through the phrase "we owe ourselves"?

11.11.2 Discuss the significant domestic policy speeches of Truman, Eisenhower, Kennedy, Johnson, Nixon, Carter, Reagan, Bush, and Clinton (e.g., with regard to education, civil rights, economic policy, environmental policy).

From "Vue Vang's Life Story" in *Hmong Means Free*, edited by Sucheng Chan, 1994

Laos lies to the east of Vietnam, and, until its independence in 1953, it was part of French Indochina, along with Vietnam and Cambodia. The Hmong are an ethnic group from the mountains of Laos, and in the early 1960s, the CIA recruited Hmong people to fight against the Pathet Lao, the communists in Laos. Like Vietnam, Laos fell to the communists in 1975, and many Hmong refugees came to live in the United States. In this excerpt, a Hmong woman named Vue Vang, who resettled with her husband in California, describes a particular challenge in her new country.

Some other Hmong women and I were eager to learn English so that we could understand and communicate with our American friends. We wanted to be able to go to the grocery store, read prices, and understand the cashier. When I first got here, I always brought extra money with me to make sure I would have enough to pay for the groceries I bought. I bought only those products I recognized—that is, meat and vegetables. I simply handed [the cashier] all my money, with the hope that he or she was honest and would take the correct amount.

DOCUMENT-BASED QUESTIONS:

1. What geopolitical consequence of the Vietnam War is evidenced by this excerpt?
2. Identify a larger social development related to the Vietnam War that is indicated in the excerpt.
3. Why did Vue Vang hand all of her money to the cashier?

11.9.3 Trace the origins and geopolitical consequences (foreign and domestic) of the Cold War and containment policy, including the following: • The era of McCarthyism, instances of domestic Communism (e.g., Alger Hiss) and blacklisting • The Truman Doctrine • The Berlin Blockade • The Korean War • The Bay of Pigs invasion and the Cuban Missile Crisis • Atomic testing in the American West, the "mutual assured destruction" doctrine, and disarmament policies • The Vietnam War • Latin American policy; HI 1 Students show the connections, causal and otherwise, between particular historical events and larger social, economic, and political trends and developments.

From a speech by César Chávez, 1974

César Chávez was the son of a farm labor activist and the grandson of immigrants from Mexico. Born in 1927 in the border town of Yuma, Arizona, Chávez moved with his family to California, where they worked as migrant farmworkers. By the early 1960s, Chávez had organized workers to form the National Farm Workers Association, which pushed for labor reform and civil rights for immigrant farmworkers, using nonviolent methods such as strikes. In this speech, Chávez speaks to other union organizers about one government response to the strikes he organized: injunctions, which are court orders to stop a particular action, such as a strike.

We have some of the most ridiculous injunctions against us. We are now striking in 10 different places in California. Not only in grapes and lettuce; there are some strawberry strikes, cantaloupe strikes[. I]n every single place . . . they have a standard injunction. Every time we have a strike, they just [invoke the same injunction] and they come up with a restraining order. Last year we had almost 5,000 people arrested for breaking the injunction, which means [the growers] are free to go to Mexico and import numbers of illegals to come and break the strike. And because of that, the boycott must continue.

DOCUMENT-BASED QUESTIONS:

1. What explanation does Chávez provide for the presence of undocumented Mexican immigrants in the United States?
2. What was the importance of the boycott in bringing about the farmworkers' success?
3. What does this excerpt suggest as a causal relationship between immigration and the farm labor movement?

11.6.5 Trace the advances and retreats of organized labor, from the creation of the American Federation of Labor and the Congress of Industrial Organizations to current issues of a postindustrial, multinational economy, including the United Farm Workers in California; 11.8.2 Describe the significance of Mexican immigration and its relationship to the agricultural economy, especially in California.

From "Grapes Of Wrath: The Forgotten Filipinos Who Led A Farmworker Revolution," by Lisa Morehouse, 2015

Larry Dulay Itliong was a Filipino American labor organizer. He organized California agricultural workers starting in the 1930s and rose to national prominence in 1965. Itliong's methods and overall impact on the farm labor movement are described in this secondary source.

For decades the migrant, bachelor, Filipino farmworkers—called *manongs*, or elders—had fought for better working conditions. So in the summer of 1965, with pay cuts threatened around the state, these workers were prepared to act, says historian Dawn Mabalon. [Larry Itliong] urged local families in Delano [California] to join manongs in asking farmers for a raise. The growers balked. César Chávez and others had been organizing Mexican workers around Delano for a few years, but a strike wasn't in their immediate plans. But Larry Itliong appealed to Chávez, and two weeks later, Mexican workers joined the strike. Soon, the two unions came together to form what would become United Farm Workers.

DOCUMENT-BASED QUESTIONS:

1. What do you think is the purpose of this secondary source excerpt?
2. What inferences can you make about the methods Larry Itliong used to help Filipino farmworkers fight for better working conditions?
3. What do this excerpt and the excerpt you read from Chávez's speech suggest about the significance of immigrants to California's agricultural economy?
4. How does the excerpt from Chávez's speech help explain why he was not planning a strike?

11.8.2 Describe the significance of Mexican immigration and its relationship to the agricultural economy, especially in California.

From "Aria," by Richard Rodriguez, 1982

The *Latino Reader* is a collection of writings from the Hispanic Americas from the mid-16th century to the late 1900s. The collection includes this excerpt by writer and journalist Richard Rodriguez. The son of Mexican immigrants, Rodriguez grew up in a home where only Spanish was spoken, and immersed in Mexican culture. In this excerpt, Rodriguez describes some of the sights and sounds associated with that experience.

I'd rarely leave home all alone or without reluctance. Walking down the sidewalk . . . I'd warily notice the—suddenly—silent neighborhood kids who stood warily watching me. Nervously, I'd arrive at the grocery store to hear there the sounds of the gringo—foreign to me—reminding me. I was a foreigner. Walking back toward our house, climbing the steps . . . I'd hear voices beyond the screen door talking in Spanish. For a second or two I'd stay, linger there, listening. Smiling, I'd hear my mother call out, saying in Spanish: "Is that you, Richard?" All the while her sounds would assure me: You are home now; come closer; inside. With us. "*Sí*," I'd reply.

DOCUMENT-BASED QUESTIONS:

1. What is the main idea of this passage?
2. How does the last sentence support the main idea?
3. Based on the excerpt, what is the meaning of "gringo"?
4. How does Rodriguez's state of mind change as he moves from silence to hearing English and then to hearing Spanish?

From the U.S. Immigration Act of 1965

The Immigration and Naturalization Act of 1952 regulated immigration by a quota system, which placed strict limits on the number of immigrants who could enter the United States from certain nations of origin. The 1952 act favored immigrants from northern and western Europe and made it more difficult for immigrants from Asia, Africa, and Latin America to enter the country. In 1965, changes were made to the 1952 act, resulting in new legislation that became known as the Immigration Act of 1965. This excerpt references some of the significant changes to the 1952 act.

The Immigration and Nationality Act [is to] be amended to read as follows: No person shall receive any preference or priority or be discriminated against in the issuance of an immigrant visa because of his race, sex, nationality, place of birth, or place of residence . . . provided . . . the total number of immigrant visas and the number of conditional entries made available to natives of any single foreign state . . . shall not exceed 20,000 in any fiscal year.

DOCUMENT-BASED QUESTIONS:

1. How might the quota system have been an attack on immigrant civil liberties?
2. What significant change in the 1952 act's immigration policy is described in this excerpt?
3. Based on the excerpt, what can you infer about the reason for the proposed changes to immigration policy?

11.5.2 Analyze the international and domestic events, interests, and philosophies that prompted attacks on civil liberties, including the Palmer Raids, Marcus Garvey's "back-to-Africa" movement, the Ku Klux Klan, and immigration quotas and the responses of organizations such as the American Civil Liberties Union, the National Association for the Advancement of Colored People, and the Anti-Defamation League to those attacks; 11.11.1 Discuss the reasons for the nation's changing immigration policy, with emphasis on how the Immigration Act of 1965 and successor acts have transformed American society.

From the Refugee Act of 1980

The end of the Vietnam War in 1975 generated the first of several waves of refugees from war and oppression to the United States. As people fled from Vietnam, Laos, Cambodia, and Cuba to escape political oppression, and from El Salvador in Central America to escape war, the U.S. government amended the Immigration Act of 1965 to accommodate an increase in refugee immigrants. The resulting Refugee Act of 1980 gave the president flexibility in determining the number of refugees to admit based on circumstances. The part of the act in the excerpt provides background for the immigration policy changes put in effect.

[I]t is the historic policy of the United States to respond to the urgent needs of persons subject to persecution in their homelands, including, where appropriate, humanitarian assistance for their care and maintenance in asylum areas, efforts to promote opportunities for resettlement or voluntary repatriation, aid for necessary transportation and processing, admission to this country of refugees of special humanitarian concern to the United States, and transitional assistance to refugees in the United States. [F]urther, it is the policy of the United States to encourage all nations to provide assistance and resettlement opportunities to refugees to the fullest extent possible.

DOCUMENT-BASED QUESTIONS:

1. How did this act alter U.S. immigration policy?
2. What does the last sentence of the excerpt indicate about the goals of the act?
3. How might lessons learned from the passage of the Immigration Act of 1965 relate to the changes to immigration policy reflected in this act?

11.11.1 Discuss the reasons for the nation's changing immigration policy, with emphasis on how the Immigration Act of 1965 and successor acts have transformed American society.

From *Native American Testimony*, by Peter Nabokov, 1991

In 1969, a group of Native Americans organized an occupation of Alcatraz Island in San Francisco Bay. The occupiers had previously petitioned the government to establish a Native American university on the island, on which, from 1934 to 1963, a federal prison was located. In this excerpt, Adam Fortunate Eagle, a Chippewa, describes the group's effort to land protesters on the island after an initial attempt had been unsuccessful. The "skipper" was the captain of a private fishing boat the protesters had hired to take them to the island.

"Hurry up, you guys," the skipper yelled, "we've got to get going!" [A]t the Alcatraz dock . . . we gently nudged the barge. Indians spilled over the bow [the front of a ship], one securing a line while the rest clambered overboard. Sleeping bags and blankets were passed after them. "What's going on?" the skipper asked. In an offhand way, I said, "We're taking over the island." His sudden realization that he might be charged with a crime, plus his worry about the rushing tides, made him throw the gears into reverse.

As we accelerated for San Francisco . . . we spotted fourteen Indians on the island's shore. The occupation of Alcatraz was now a fact.

DOCUMENT-BASED QUESTIONS:

1. Summarize in your own words the events that are being described in the excerpt.
2. Which details support the conclusion that the occupation was politically motivated?
3. Why do you think the protesters chose this strategy in their quest to establish a Native American university on the island?

11.10.5 Discuss the diffusion of the civil rights movement of African Americans from the churches of the rural South and the urban North, including the resistance to racial desegregation in Little Rock and Birmingham, and how the advances influenced the agendas, strategies, and effectiveness of the quests of American Indians, Asian Americans, and Hispanic Americans for civil rights and equal opportunities.

From a speech by Harvey Milk, 1978

This excerpt from a speech by Harvey Milk, who became the first openly gay elected official in the United States in 1977, is part of a 1982 book called *The Mayor of Castro Street: The Life and Times of Harvey Milk*, by Randy Shilts. Milk and other California activists such as Cleve Jones were part of a broader LGBT activism movement that emerged following the 1969 police raid on the Stonewall Inn in New York, which you have read about.

Gay brothers and sisters, what are you going to do about it? You must come out. Come out . . . to your parents . . . I know that it is hard and will hurt them but think about how they will hurt you in the voting booth! Come out . . . to your relatives. Come out to your friends . . . if they indeed are your friends. Come out to your neighbors . . . to your fellow workers . . . to the people who work, where you eat and shop. Come out only to the people you know, and who know you, not to anyone else. But once and for all, break down the myths. Destroy the lies and distortions. For your sake. For their sake.

DOCUMENT-BASED QUESTIONS:

1. How does the phrase "come out" relate to the movement for equal rights for the LGBT community?
2. What does Milk mean when he says, "think about how they will hurt you in the voting booth"?
3. Why might a lack of openness and honesty about their sexual identity hinder members of the LGBT community in their quest for equal rights?

From *When We Rise*, by Cleve Jones, 2016

In the 1970s, activists began to draw significant attention to the cause of equal rights for LGBT Americans by holding public demonstrations. Cleve Jones was one such activist. This excerpt from his memoir *When We Rise* captures a conversation Jones had with his friend, Doug, as they prepared to march in San Francisco in 1976. Jones asks Doug, "So how many of us [members of the LGBT community] do you think there are, anyway?" This excerpt begins with Doug's response to Jones.

"Well, how do you define 'us'? I think the definition of 'us' is people who say 'us.' It's those of us who know what we are and identify ourselves as gay and feel some connection to other gay people even if we're still closeted to our families and at work."

I laughed.

"What's funny?" Doug asked.

"Just a few years ago I thought I was the only one in the whole wide world."

"Me too."

I imagined all the others getting ready for Friday night—not 10 million, of course, but those who had gotten away and come to this city; those who had fled and found each other, we few thousand who were now ready to declare ourselves, to march, to organize, to dance, and to rise.

DOCUMENT-BASED QUESTIONS:

1. What does Doug mean by "people who say 'us'"?
2. Which details support the conclusion that the LGBT community felt discriminated against in the 1970s?
3. How does this excerpt corroborate Harvey Milk's premise that by not coming out, members of the LGBT community limit their own ability to vote for supportive policies and candidates in elections?
4. What is the meaning of the title of Jones's book, considering the last line of this excerpt?

From "Bug Suspect Got Campaign Funds," by Carl Bernstein and Bob Woodward, in the *Washington Post*, August 1, 1972

On Sunday, June 18, 1972, the *Washington Post* newspaper printed a front-page story breaking the Watergate scandal. The *Post* would continue to run a series of articles over the next two years, covering details of the scandal that eventually led to President Nixon's resignation. The excerpt below is from a story by journalists Bernstein and Woodward that ran in the *Post* about six weeks after the break-in at the Watergate Hotel.

A $25,000 cashier's check, apparently earmarked for President Nixon's re-election campaign, was deposited in April in a bank account of [Bernard L. Barker] one of the five men arrested in the break-in at Democratic National Headquarters here [in Washington, D.C.] June 17.

Barker's bank account in which the $25,000 was deposited was the same account from which Barker later withdrew a large number of hundred-dollar bills. About 53 of these $100 bills were found on the five men after they were arrested at the Watergate.

In a related development . . . another $89,000 . . . was deposited during May. This makes a total of $114,000 deposited in Barker's account.

DOCUMENT-BASED QUESTIONS:

1. What details in the excerpt likely inspired curiosity in readers as to whether President Nixon could have been connected to the break-in?
2. How does the excerpt suggest a "follow the money" hypothesis in investigating the Watergate break-in?
3. How could the fact that the burglars received cash from the $25,000 payment tie the burglary to a constitutional crisis?

11.11.4 Explain the constitutional crisis originating from the Watergate scandal.

Ignorance = Fear, by Keith Haring, 1989

As the AIDS epidemic of the 1980s spread, Americans struggled to understand its causes and find solutions. Prominent artists such as Keith Haring sought to counter the trend of misinformation and fear by creating art that would inspire public awareness and dialogue about the disease. Haring himself had been diagnosed with AIDS in 1988, and shortly thereafter began designing posters such as this one to promote AIDS awareness. Haring died in 1990 from AIDS-related complications.

DOCUMENT-BASED QUESTIONS:

1. What do the hand motions of each person in the poster represent?
2. What message do you believe Haring sought to communicate through this work of art? What details support your theory?
3. What connection does this work of art suggest exists between the AIDS epidemic and broader government efforts to investigate the crisis?

11.11.7 Explain how the federal, state, and local governments have responded to demographic and social changes such as population shifts to the suburbs, racial concentrations in the cities, Frostbelt-to-Sunbelt migration, international migration, decline of family farms, increases in out-of-wedlock births, and drug abuse.

From "Surgeon General's Report on Acquired Immune Deficiency Syndrome," by C. Everett Koop, M.D., 1987

Everett Koop served as U.S. surgeon general from 1982–1989 under presidents Reagan and Bush. A fundamentalist Christian, he faced resistance from liberals who predicted he would impose religious beliefs on the nation's health issues. For his first four years, Koop was nearly silent about the AIDS outbreak, but in 1987 he issued his report, surprising nearly everyone with its frankness and objectivity.

Many people—especially our youth—are not receiving information that is vital to their future health and well-being because of our reticence in dealing with the subjects of sex, sexual practices, and homosexuality. This silence must end. We can no longer afford to sidestep frank, open discussions about sexual practices—homosexual and heterosexual. Education about AIDS should start at an early age so that children can grow up knowing the behaviors to avoid to protect themselves from exposure to the AIDS virus.

AIDS education must start at the lowest grade possible. There is now no doubt that we need sex education in schools and that it [must] include information on sexual practices that may put our children at risk for AIDS.

DOCUMENT-BASED QUESTIONS:

1. Considering the outspoken nature of LGBT activists such as Harvey Milk, Cleve Jones, and Keith Haring during the 1970s and 1980s, where do you think "the silence" Koop refers to in this excerpt comes from?
2. Why does Koop feel it necessary to educate children about AIDS and its causes?
3. How do Koop's comments verbalize the ideas presented visually in Keith Haring's poster above?

11.11.7 Explain how the federal, state, and local governments have responded to demographic and social changes such as population shifts to the suburbs, racial concentrations in the cities, Frostbelt-to-Sunbelt migration, international migration, decline of family farms, increases in out-of-wedlock births, and drug abuse.

President George H.W. Bush's statement on signing the Americans with Disabilities Act (ADA), 1990

In 1986, while George H.W. Bush was serving as vice president under President Reagan, a report was issued by the National Council on Disability, formed by President Reagan, which recommended legislation to ban discrimination against people with disabilities. As president, Bush signed the ADA in 1990. In this excerpt from his statement, Bush explains why he signed the act.

This legislation is comprehensive because the barriers faced by individuals with disabilities are wide-ranging. Existing laws and regulations under the Rehabilitation Act of 1973 have been effective. However, they have left broad areas of American life untouched or inadequately addressed. Many of our young people, who have benefited from the equal educational opportunity guaranteed under [previous acts], have found themselves on graduation day still shut out of the mainstream of American life. They have faced persistent discrimination in the workplace and barriers posed by inaccessible public transportation, public accommodations, and telecommunications.

DOCUMENT-BASED QUESTIONS:

1. What does Bush suggest about the impact of previous legislation on discrimination against people with disabilities?
2. What evidence does Bush provide to support his claim that the new act is "comprehensive"?
3. Do you believe Bush's justification of the signing of the Americans with Disabilities Act to be valid? Why or why not?

11.11 Students analyze the major social problems and domestic policy issues in contemporary American society; HREP 1 Students distinguish valid arguments from fallacious arguments in historical interpretations.

From "Why I Wrote the Americans with Disabilities Act," by Robert Burgdorf, Jr., in the *Washington Post*, July 24, 2015

Robert Burgdorf, Jr., is a rights scholar who advocates for people with disabilities. He played a key role in developing the content of what would eventually become the Americans with Disabilities Act of 1990. In this excerpt, he reflects on factors that motivated him to work on legislation to protect disabled persons.

The ADA was a response to an appalling problem: widespread, systemic, inhumane discrimination against people with disabilities. Large numbers of [people] with disabilities were systematically excluded from American public schools . . . routinely denied rights . . . to vote . . . to obtain a driver's license . . . to hold public office. Early groundbreaking successes in the courts focused on access to public school education and confinement in residential treatment facilities, but subsequent court decisions and protest actions . . . addressed unequal treatment in other contexts, including transportation, guardianship, housing, medical services, involuntary sterilization, contracts and voting.

DOCUMENT-BASED QUESTIONS:

1. How does this excerpt confirm the reasons George H.W. Bush provided in the previous excerpt for why the Americans with Disabilities Act needed to be passed?
2. What provisions of the new act does Burgdorf discuss in addition to those mentioned in the excerpt from President Bush's statement above?
3. Based on both excerpts, what role did past policy reforms play in the federal government's recognition of the need for the Americans with Disabilities Act?

11.11 Students analyze the major social problems and domestic policy issues in contemporary American society.

From President William J. Clinton's remarks on Earth Day, April 21, 1993

In the 1970s, legislation was passed that served to protect different aspects of the environment, including water, air, and wildlife. But decades later, as ongoing scientific research continued to point to additional links between human activity and environmental degradation and climate change, many people, including President Bill Clinton, felt that more needed to be done.

For all that has been done to protect the air and the water, we haven't halted the destruction of wetlands at home and the rain forest abroad. For all that has been learned, we still struggle to comprehend such dangers to our planet's delicate environment as the shroud of greenhouse gases and the dangerous thinning of the ozone layer.

[W]e yearn to move beyond the false choices that the last few years have imposed upon us. For too long we have been told that we have to choose between the economy and the environment, between our jobs, between our obligations to our own people and our responsibilities to the future and to the rest of the world, between public action and private economy.

DOCUMENT-BASED QUESTIONS:

1. Do additional research to determine what environmental issues had and had not yet been addressed when President Clinton gave this speech.
2. What does this excerpt reveal about people's perceived choices and trade-offs regarding the environment and the economy?
3. Compare the issues presented in President Clinton's speech with the attitude the U.S. government has toward environmental issues today.

11.11.2 Discuss the significant domestic policy speeches of Truman, Eisenhower, Kennedy, Johnson, Nixon, Carter, Reagan, Bush, and Clinton (e.g., with regard to education, civil rights, economic policy, environmental policy); CST 1 Students compare the present with the past, evaluating the consequences of past events and decisions and determining the lessons that were learned.

President George W. Bush's remarks on signing the No Child Left Behind Act (NCLB), 2002

President George W. Bush signed the No Child Left Behind Act (NCLB) into law in January 2002. The act was based on the belief that it was necessary, and also possible, to close the achievement gap—a gap in educational skills that had arisen between different socioeconomic and racial groups. In the process, NCLB sought to increase local school and teacher accountability for student achievement. This excerpt details President Bush's discussion of one aspect of the accountability principle of the act.

No longer is it acceptable to hide poor performance. No longer is it acceptable to keep results away from parents. [T]his bill says that we're never going to give up on a school that's performing poorly; that when we find poor performance, a school will be given time and incentives and resources to correct their problems. A school will be given time to try other methodologies, perhaps other leadership, to make sure that people can succeed. If, however, schools don't perform, if, however, given the new resources, focused resources, they are unable to solve the problem of not educating their children, there must be real consequences. Parents must be given real options in the face of failure in order to make sure reform is meaningful.

DOCUMENT-BASED QUESTIONS:

1. Based on the excerpt, what can you conclude about the reasons why the NCLB Act was passed?
2. What inferences can you make about the criteria used to label a school with "poor performance"?
3. Based on the excerpt, how did the NCLB Act affect the educational opportunities of students?

11.11.2 Discuss the significant domestic policy speeches of Truman, Eisenhower, Kennedy, Johnson, Nixon, Carter, Reagan, Bush, and Clinton (e.g., with regard to education, civil rights, economic policy, environmental policy); HREP 2 Students identify bias and prejudice in historical interpretations.

From *Greenhouse Effect and Global Climate Change: Hearings before the Committee on Energy and Natural Resources*, 1988

Dr. James E. Hansen, Director of the NASA Goddard Institute for Space Studies, played a pivotal role in calling attention to scientific research about the reality, as well as the causes and effects, of climate change. In 1988, Hansen testified before a Senate committee, outlining research pointing to the "greenhouse mechanism"—the trapping of heat in the atmosphere under a carbon dioxide layer—as a factor contributing to climate change.

[L]et me turn to . . . causal association of the greenhouse effect and the global warming. Causal association requires first that the warming be larger than natural climate variability and, second, that the magnitude and nature of the warming be consistent with the greenhouse mechanism. The observed warming during the past 30 years . . . the period when we have accurate measurements of atmospheric composition . . . is almost 0.4° C by 1987 relative to . . . the 30 year mean . . . and . . . the warming is more than 0.4° C in 1988. The probability of a chance warming of that magnitude is about 1 percent. So, with 99 percent confidence we can state that the warming during this time period is a real warming trend.

DOCUMENT-BASED QUESTIONS:

1. Is Hansen's connection of the greenhouse effect to global warming a sound generalization? Why or why not?
2. Based on the excerpt, how is the greenhouse effect linked to the probability of extreme climate-related events?
3. How does the evidence presented in the excerpt indicate a likely human role in climate change?
4. Why might a rise of 0.4° C in 30 years be a concern?

11.11.5 Trace the impact of, need for, and controversies associated with environmental conservation, expansion of the national park system, and the development of environmental protection laws, with particular attention to the interaction between environmental protection advocates and property rights advocates; HREP 3 Students evaluate major debates among historians concerning alternative interpretations of the past, including an analysis of authors' use of evidence and the distinctions between sound generalizations and misleading oversimplifications.

From "ALEC Energy Principles," by the American Legislative Exchange Council, 2013

The climate change debate brought to light opposing environmental and economic concerns. Many who opposed government regulation of industries and practices that impacted the climate did recognize climate change as a fact, but did not acknowledge a human role in bringing it about. They believed government regulation hindered necessary economic growth. The American Legislative Exchange Council (ALEC) was one such opponent of regulation to limit the greenhouse gases that contribute to climate change. This excerpt presents ALEC's reasons for its position.

Global climate change is inevitable. Climate change is a historical phenomenon and the debate will continue on the significance of natural and [human] contributions. ALEC will continue to monitor the issue and support the use of sound science to guide policy, but ALEC will also incorporate economic and political realism. Unilateral efforts by the United States or regions within the United States will not significantly decrease carbon emissions globally. Policy makers in most cases are not willing to inflict economic harm on their citizens with no real benefit. ALEC discourages impractical visionary goals that ignore economic reality, and that will not be met without serious consequences for worldwide standard of living.

DOCUMENT-BASED QUESTIONS:

1. How might describing climate change as "inevitable" and using the word "sound" with "science" bias people toward supporting ALEC's stance on government regulation?
2. Do you agree that there is "no real benefit" in measures taken to limit climate change? Why or why not?
3. What are the main differences between this excerpt and Dr. James Hansen's argument in the excerpt above?

11.11.5 Trace the impact of, need for, and controversies associated with environmental conservation, expansion of the national park system, and the development of environmental protection laws, with particular attention to the interaction between environmental protection advocates and property rights advocates; HREP 1 Students distinguish valid arguments from fallacious arguments in historical interpretations.

GEOGRAPHY AND THE ENVIRONMENT

HANDBOOK

MAPS

READING MAPS

If you've ever needed to figure out how to get to a friend's house, you probably used the GPS on your phone to navigate. But imagine if the only resource you had was a globe, which would have to be enormous in order to show enough detail for you to locate your friend's house. Since a globe is way too big to carry around in your pocket, maps—which are more portable than globes—come in handy.

REPRESENTING EARTH

Geography includes studying features of Earth's surface. Geographers use maps, which are two-dimensional, flat models of Earth, as well as globes, which are three-dimensional, spherical models of Earth, to study the planet. A globe is useful when you need to see Earth as a whole, but it is not helpful if you need to see a small section of the planet. If you took a small part of a globe and flattened it out, you'd have a map that would showcase a smaller section of our planet. Maps and globes represent Earth differently, but they have similar features that help us navigate our world.

MAP AND GLOBE FEATURES

Most maps and globes share a common set of features. The letters below identify the location of important features on the maps at the right.

A A **title** tells the subject of the map or globe.

B **Symbols** represent information such as natural resources and economic activities.

C **Labels** are the names of places, such as cities, countries, rivers, and mountains.

D **Colors** represent different kinds of information. For example, the color green usually represents a park.

E A **legend**, or key, explains what the symbols or colors on the map represent.

F A **compass rose** shows the directions north, south, east, and west.

LATITUDE AND LONGITUDE

G **Lines of latitude** are imaginary lines that run east to west, parallel to the equator, which is the center line of latitude. Distances north and south of the equator are measured in degrees (°). There are 90 degrees north of the equator and 90 degrees south.

H **Lines of longitude** are imaginary lines that run north to south from the North Pole to the South Pole. They measure distance east or west of the prime meridian, Earth's zero line of longitude, which runs through Greenwich, England. There are 180 degrees east of the prime meridian and 180 degrees west. The equator and the prime meridian are both 0°.

These two lines divide Earth into hemispheres, or halves. The equator divides Earth into the Northern Hemisphere, where North America is located, and the Southern Hemisphere, where most of South America and all of Antarctica is located. Similarly, the prime meridian divides Earth into the Western Hemisphere, where North America is located, and the Eastern Hemisphere, where most of Europe is located.

SCALE

I A map's **scale** shows how much distance on Earth is shown on the map and is usually shown in both inches and centimeters. One inch or centimeter on the map represents a much larger distance on Earth, such as a number of miles or kilometers. A large-scale map covers a small area but shows many details, a small-scale map covers a large area but includes few details, and a medium-scale map falls somewhere in between.

THINK LIKE A GEOGRAPHER

SUMMARIZE What are the purposes of a small-scale map and a large-scale map?

Large-Scale Map

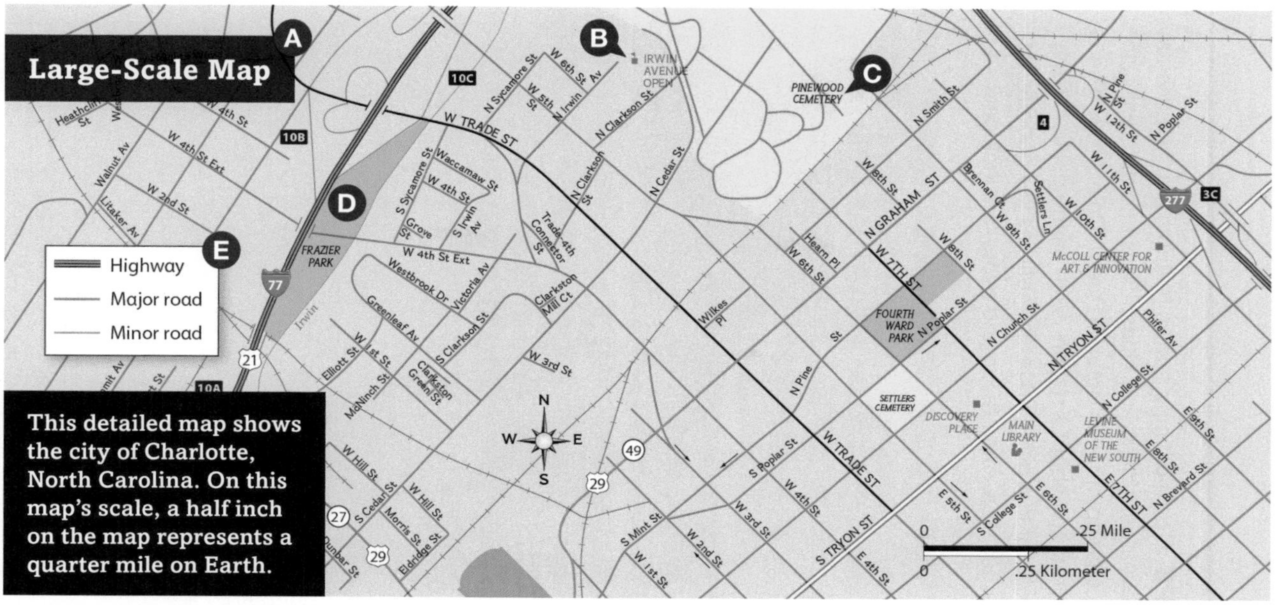

This detailed map shows the city of Charlotte, North Carolina. On this map's scale, a half inch on the map represents a quarter mile on Earth.

Medium-Scale Map

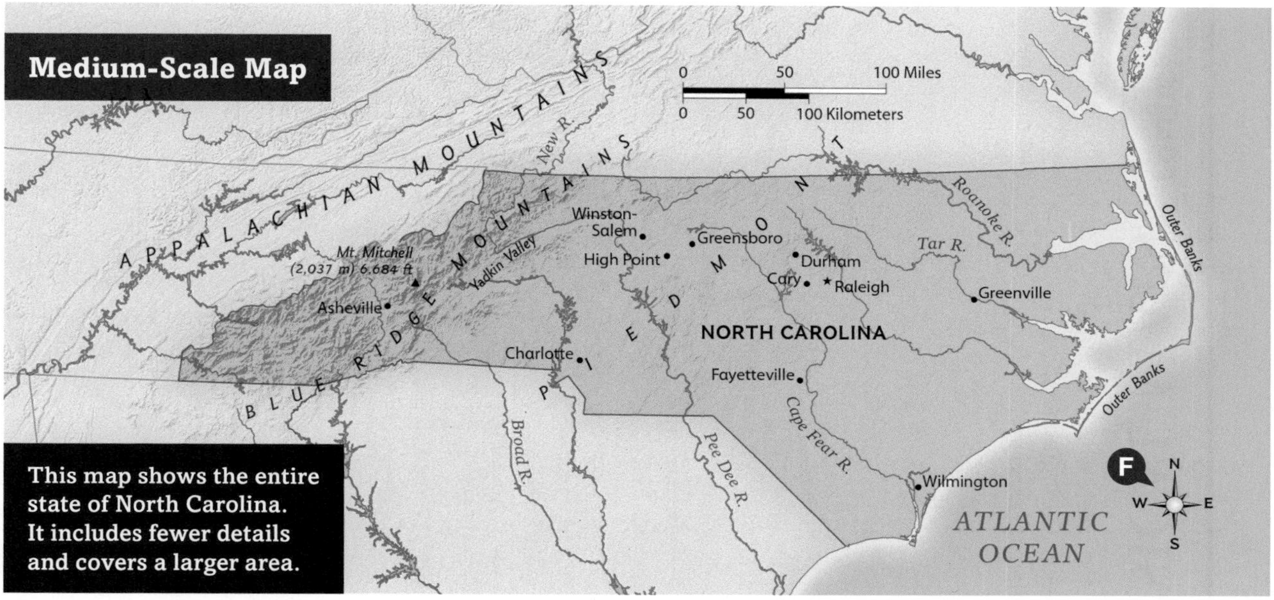

This map shows the entire state of North Carolina. It includes fewer details and covers a larger area.

Small-Scale Map

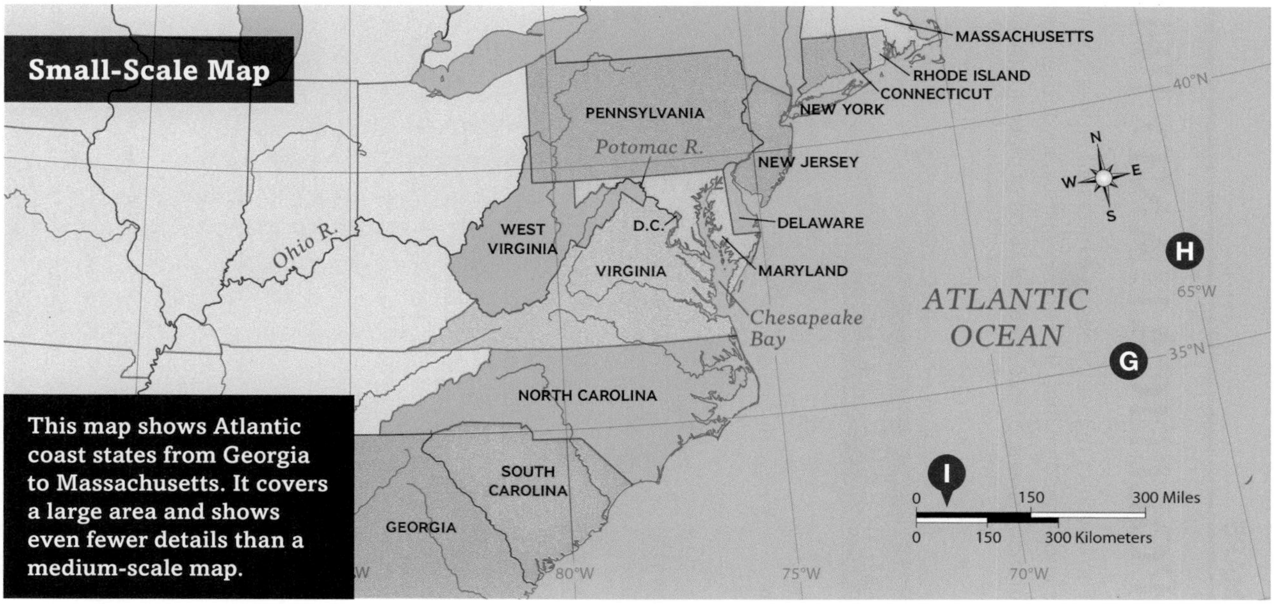

This map shows Atlantic coast states from Georgia to Massachusetts. It covers a large area and shows even fewer details than a medium-scale map.

POLITICAL AND PHYSICAL MAPS

The governor of a state needs a map that shows counties and cities, while a mountain climber needs a map that shows cliffs, canyons, and ice fields. Cartographers, or mapmakers, create different kinds of maps for these different purposes.

POLITICAL MAPS A political map shows features that humans have created, such as countries, states, and cities. Lines and different colors may be used to indicate boundaries between them. Colors may also be used to provide information about a region, such as the political party that most people vote for in a given state. Sometimes key geographic features, such as large lakes, mountains, and rivers, are included.

United States Political

PHYSICAL MAPS A physical map shows landforms and other natural features of physical geography, such as mountain ranges, plains, valleys, deserts, oceans, lakes, rivers, and other bodies of water.

A physical map can also show elevation, or the height of a physical feature above sea level, and many use colors to represent different ranges of elevation. Many physical maps also use textures or patterns to show relief, or the change in elevation from one place to another.

THINK LIKE A GEOGRAPHER

COMPARE AND CONTRAST How is a political map different from a physical map?

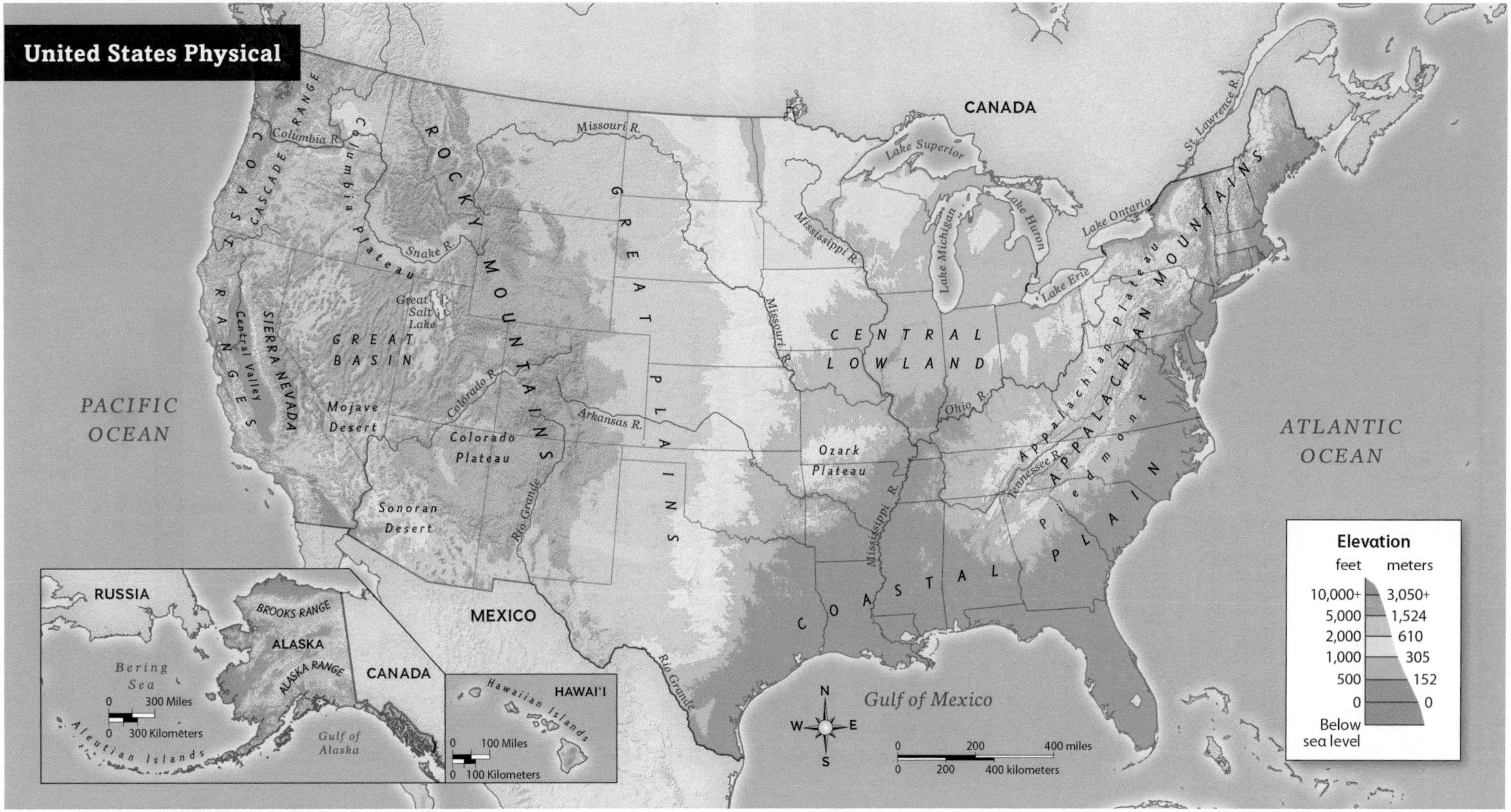

THEMATIC MAPS

If you wanted to create a map showing the location of sports fields in your community, you would create a thematic map, which focuses on a specific theme, or topic.

TYPES OF THEMATIC MAPS

Thematic maps are useful for showing a variety of geographic information, including economic activity, natural resources, and population density. Common types of thematic maps are the point symbol map, the dot density map, and the proportional symbol map.

Point symbol maps use symbols to indicate where certain features or activities are located. Some point symbol maps focus on one type of feature or activity and use a simple shape to show where it occurs on the map, while others use different shapes or symbols to differentiate between a variety of different features or activities. For example, a point symbol map showing the location of natural resources might use an oil well to indicate petroleum and a tree to indicate lumber.

Dot density maps use dots to represent data. For example, a dot density map showing the location of groundwater resources will have more dots in areas where there are numerous reservoirs of groundwater, while areas with fewer groundwater resources will be indicated by a lower density of dots.

Proportional symbol maps use symbols of varying sizes to show how much of something occurs in a given location. They are similar to dot density maps except that instead of using multiple dots to indicate a higher quantity, proportional symbol maps use a larger dot or other shape.

THINK LIKE A GEOGRAPHER

ANALYZE VISUALS Look through your U.S. history program and identify an example of a thematic map. What geographic information does the map show?

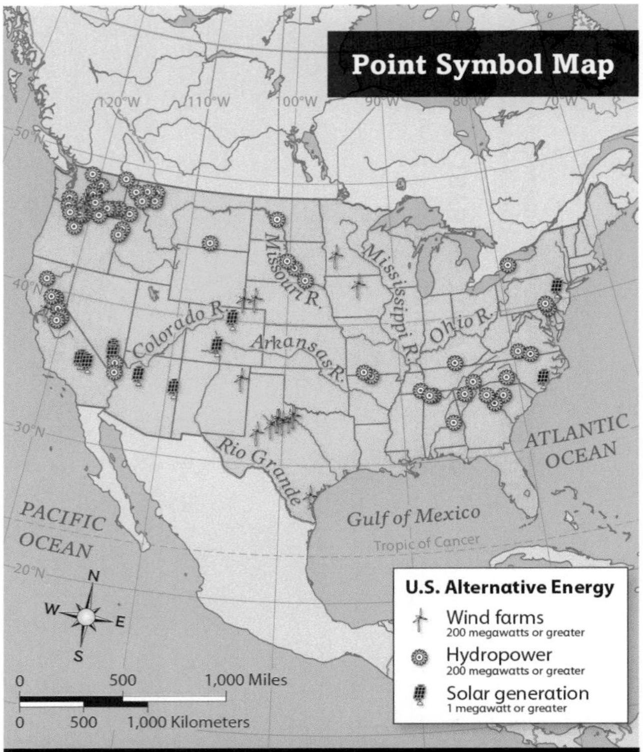

A point symbol map shows the location of activities at different points. For example, this map has symbols that show some sources of wind, water, and solar energy in the United States.

The 48 turbines at the Golden Hills Wind Energy Center in Alameda County, California, generate enough electricity to power 25,000 homes.

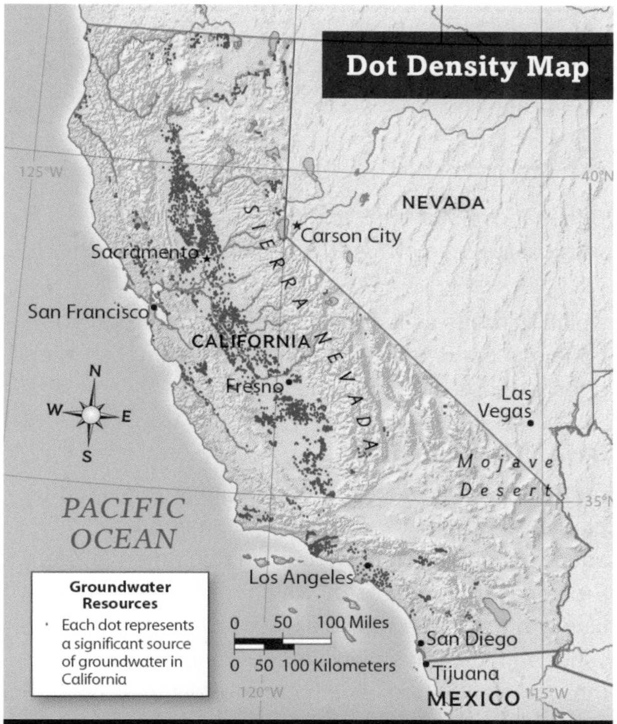

Dot density maps use dots to show how something is distributed in a country or region. Each dot indicates the presence of something in a given area. For example, each dot on this map represents a significant source of groundwater in California.

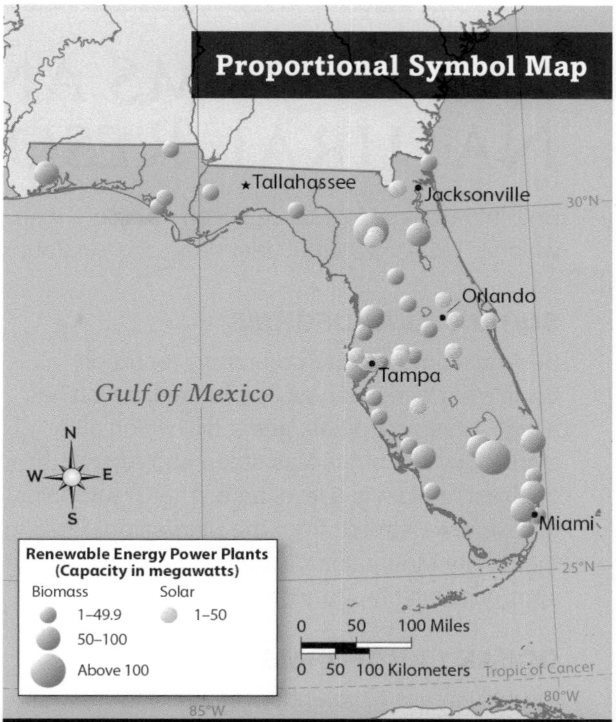

Proportional symbol maps use symbols of different sizes to show the amount of something in an area. For example, the sizes of the circles on this map show the renewable energy capacity of various regions in Florida.

Landforms and Natural Resources

Both the Rocky Mountains, which rise more than 14,000 feet above sea level, and the Grand Canyon, which is more than 5,000 feet deep, are landforms, or physical features on Earth's surface.

SURFACE LANDFORMS

Several landforms are commonly found on Earth's surface, such as a mountain, which has a high, steep elevation, and a hill, which also slopes upward but is less steep and rugged. In contrast, a plain is a level area. The Great Plains, for example, stretch from the Mississippi River to the Rocky Mountains. A valley is a low-lying area surrounded by mountains or hills.

OCEAN LANDFORMS

Earth's oceans have underwater landforms, such as mountains and valleys that rise and fall along the ocean floor. Volcanoes erupt with hot magma, which hardens as it cools to form a new crust. The edge of a continent is called the continental shelf and often extends out under the water.

CHANGING EARTH

Earth is always changing, and the changes affect plant and animal life. For example, a flood can cause severe erosion, which can ruin an ecosystem. Erosion is the process by which rocks and soil slowly break apart and are swept away. Air, water, wind, and ice can slowly wear away rock and soil through weathering, which contributes to erosion. For example, the rock formations of Arches National Park in Utah were created by weathering and erosion over a span of millions of years.

Surface landforms take a variety of shapes. This natural stone arch is one of 2,000 arches found in Arches National Park in Utah.

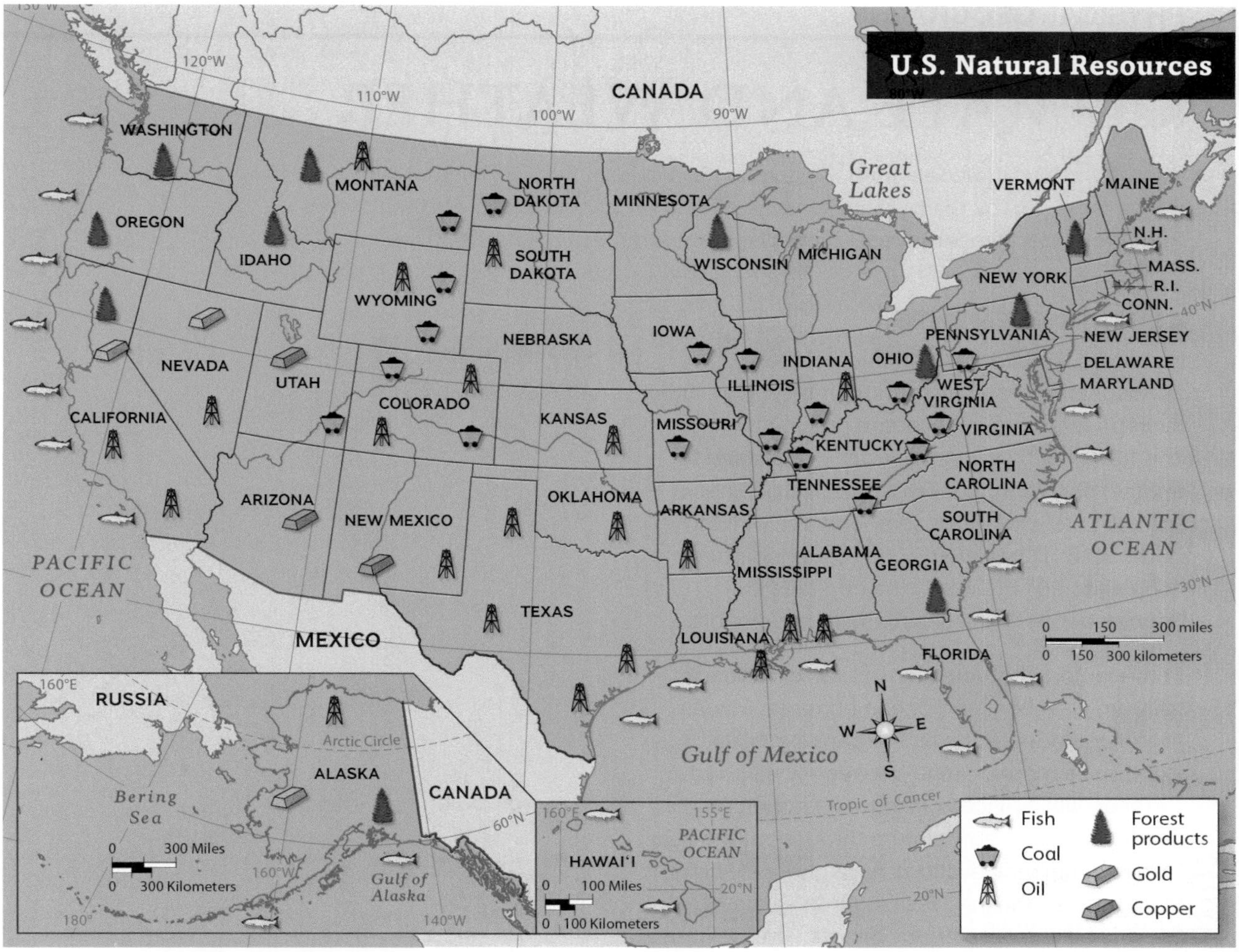

EARTH'S RESOURCES

What materials make up a pencil? Wood comes from trees, and the material you write with is a mineral called graphite. The pencil is made from natural resources, which are materials on Earth that people use to live and to meet their needs.

There are two kinds of resources. The first, biological resources, are living things, such as livestock, plants, and trees that provide humans with important things like food, shelter, and clothing.

The second, mineral resources, are nonliving resources buried within Earth, such as oil and coal. Some mineral resources are raw materials, or materials used to make products. Iron ore, for example, is a raw material used in making steel. The steel, in turn, is used to make skyscrapers and automobiles.

The methods people use to extract, harvest, transport, and process biological and mineral resources affect the geologic makeup, diversity, and health of natural systems.

RESOURCE CATEGORIES

Geographers classify resources in two categories: nonrenewable and renewable. Nonrenewable resources, such as oil, coal, and natural gas, are limited and cannot be replaced. For example, oil comes from wells that are drilled into Earth's crust, and once a well runs dry, the oil is gone.

Renewable resources, such as wind, water, and solar power, never run out, or a new supply develops over time. Trees are also considered to be a renewable resource because a new supply can grow to replace those that have been cut down.

The diverse resources of the United States helped it become an industrial powerhouse. However, overuse is a concern, and the federal and state governments have put an emphasis on resource conservation.

THINK LIKE A GEOGRAPHER

ANALYZE ENVIRONMENTAL CONCEPTS
How do physical processes reshape Earth's landforms, and how do human processes affect Earth's natural systems?

HI 5 Students analyze human modifications of landscapes and examine the resulting environmental policy issues.

CLIMATE AND WEATHER

People who live in Sacramento, California, have mild winters. When they go skiing in the nearby Sierra Nevada range, they wear parkas to protect themselves from the colder temperatures—they adapt temporarily to a different climate.

CLIMATE ELEMENTS

Climate is the average condition of the atmosphere over a long period of time. It includes average temperature, average precipitation, and the amount of change from one season to another. For example, Fairbanks, Alaska, has a cold climate with winter temperatures dipping down to -8° F; however, summer temperatures can rise to 90° F. Clearly, the changes that happen between the seasons are observable.

Three factors that affect a region's climate are latitude, elevation, and ocean currents. Places at high latitudes, such as Fairbanks, Alaska, experience more change between winter and summer, while places close to the equator have nearly the same temperature throughout the year. Places at higher elevations have generally colder temperatures than places closer to sea level. Ocean currents also affect climate. The California Current carries cool waters from northern latitudes down the western coast of the United States. Warm air flowing over the cold water creates California's characteristic fog.

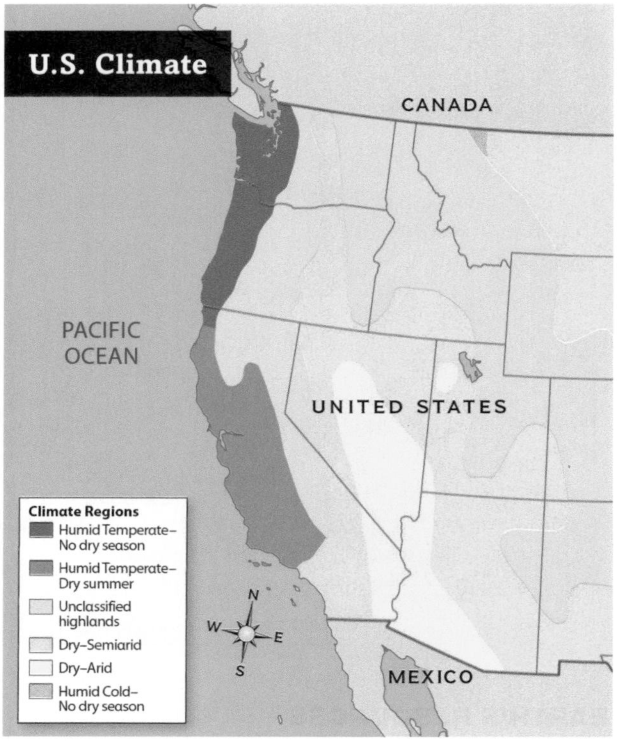

WEATHER CONDITIONS

Weather is the condition of the atmosphere at a particular time, and it includes the temperature, precipitation, and humidity, or the amount of water vapor in the air, for a particular day or week.

Weather changes because of air masses. An air mass is a large area of air that has uniform temperature, humidity, and pressure throughout. The boundary between two air masses is called a front. If a forecaster talks about a warm, humid front, he or she usually means that thunderstorms are headed toward the area.

Extreme weather is weather that is powerful enough to affect people's lives. The most common types of extreme weather in the United States are tornadoes, hurricanes, blizzards, and drought. Because of improvements in technology, however, it is possible to broadcast warnings before extreme weather strikes.

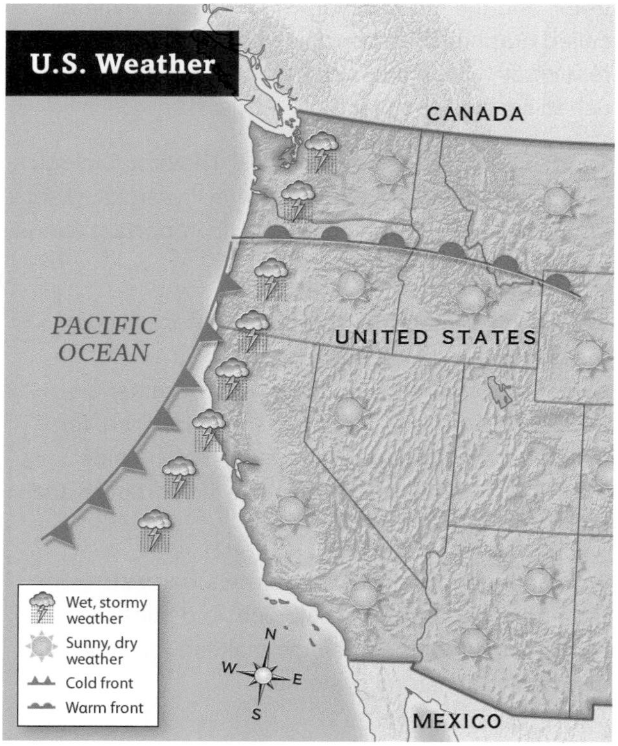

CLIMATE REGIONS AND VEGETATION

A climate region is a group of places that have similar temperatures, precipitation levels, and changes in weather. Geographers have identified five climate regions, each of which has subcategories. Places located in the same subcategory often have similar vegetation, as well as transition areas, such as a montane, where vegetation changes depending on the elevation.

Dry climates have little to no rain or snow and both hot and cold temperatures. Plant life includes shrubs and cacti as a source of vegetation. Dry climates are divided into arid and semiarid.

Humid temperate climates have cool winters, warm summers, and ample rainfall. Plant life includes mixed forests with evergreens and leafy trees. Humid temperate climates are divided into those with no dry season and those with dry winters or dry summers.

Humid equatorial climates are located near the equator and have high temperatures and rainfall all or most of the year. Plant life includes tropical plants and rain forests or grasslands with trees. Humid equatorial climates are divided into those with no dry season and those with short or long dry seasons.

Tundra or ice climates are north of the Arctic Circle and south of the Antarctic Circle, and they have long, cold winters and short summers. Plant life includes mosses or no vegetation.

Humid cold climates have cold winters, warm summers, rain, and snow. Plant life includes evergreen or deciduous (leafy) forests. Humid cold climates are divided into those with dry winters and those with no dry season.

The predominant climate regions of the United States are dry, humid temperate, and humid cold.

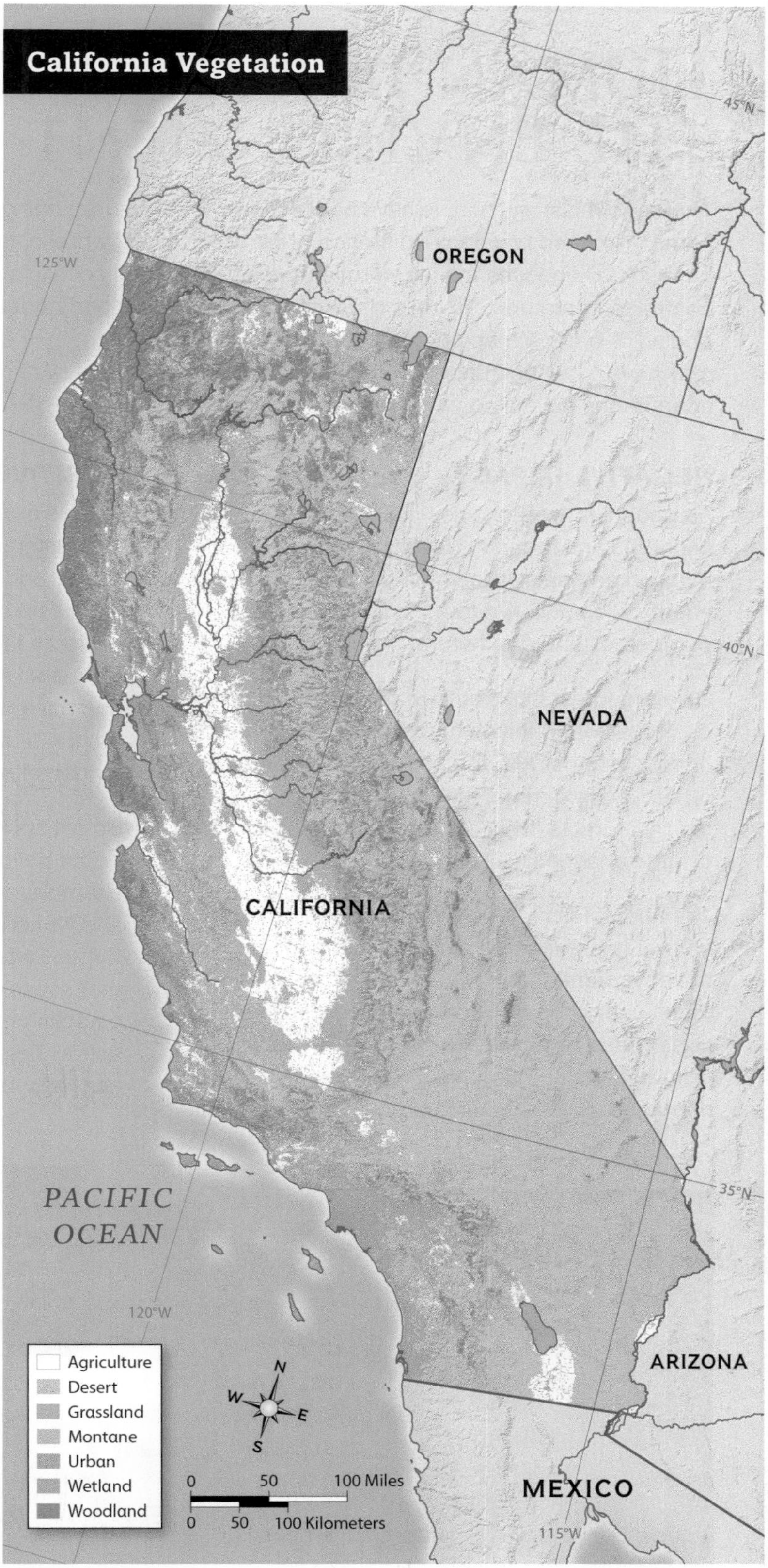

THINK LIKE A GEOGRAPHER

COMPARE AND CONTRAST What are the similarities and differences between climate and weather?

HUMAN IMPACT ON THE ENVIRONMENT

Throughout history, people have had to adapt to their surroundings. Early humans learned how to build fires to warm themselves, while in modern times, we also build houses to stay warm and use heating and cooling systems to control temperature. We build dams to hold water back and bridges to span bodies of water. When people adapt to their surroundings, their actions may have a lasting impact on the environment and natural systems. Some adaptations have a positive impact, while others can be harmful.

NEGATIVE IMPACT

As people moved to cities over the last few centuries and industry developed, the need for housing and energy increased. To provide this energy, we cut down forests, dug mines, and pumped oil and and natural gas out of the earth.

Clearing forests and other natural systems destroys communities of plants and animals, or ecosystems. Altering one ecosystem affects others. For example, the destruction of the rain forests likely contributes to global climate change.

The use of fossil fuels—including coal, oil, and natural gas—has had a negative impact on the environment and natural systems. Burning these energy sources has polluted the air and contributed to global warming, while oil spills from tankers and underwater oil rigs have damaged Earth's waters, shorelines, and wildlife.

POSITIVE IMPACT

People around the world have taken steps to save ecosystems, preserve natural systems, and protect our air and water. In 1973, for example, the United States passed the Endangered Species Act, which protects the habitats of endangered species. People have also restored forest habitats by planting trees and have passed laws and regulations to limit the amounts of pollutants released by vehicles and industrial plants.

Scientists have worked to educate the public about pollution's effect on the environment. For example, some scientists, including oceanographer and National Geographic Explorer-in-Residence Sylvia Earle, have formed Mission Blue, a program that seeks to heal and protect Earth's oceans and establish marine-protected areas in endangered hot spots. These "hope spots" are ocean habitats that can recover and grow if human impact is limited.

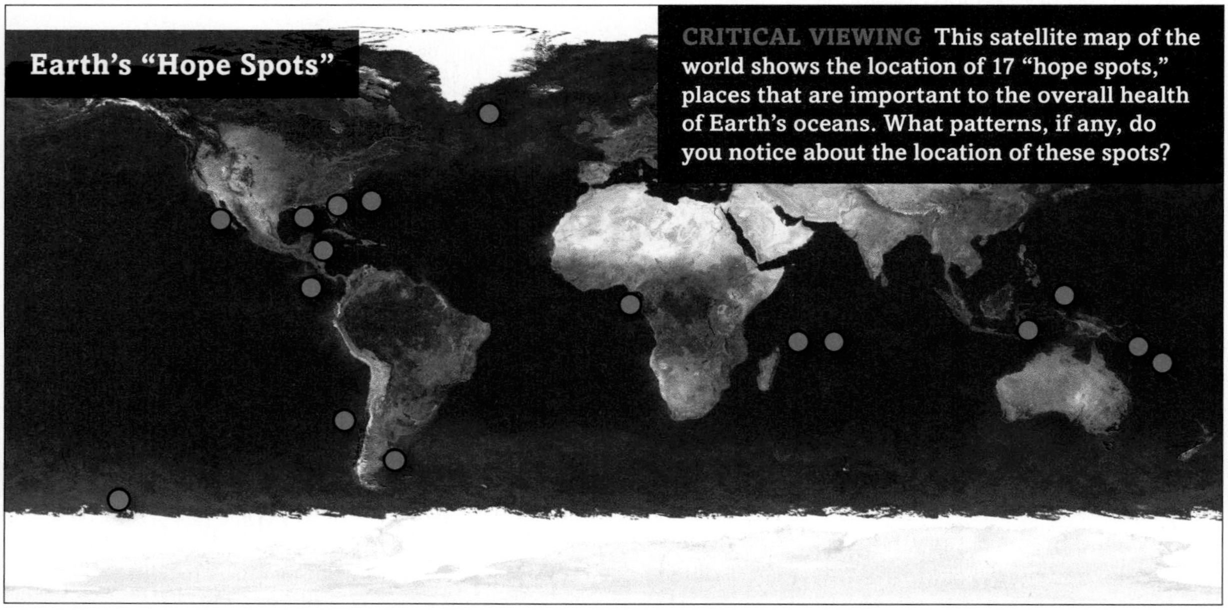

Earth's "Hope Spots"

CRITICAL VIEWING This satellite map of the world shows the location of 17 "hope spots," places that are important to the overall health of Earth's oceans. What patterns, if any, do you notice about the location of these spots?

11.11.5 Trace the impact of, need for, and controversies associated with environmental conservation, expansion of the national park system, and the development of environmental protection laws, with particular attention to the interaction between environmental protection advocates and property rights advocates; HI 5 Students analyze human modifications of landscapes and examine the resulting environmental policy issues.

THINK LIKE A GEOGRAPHER

ANALYZE ENVIRONMENTAL CONCEPTS In what way can the byproducts of human activity negatively impact a natural system, such as a body of water?

In 2010, the Deepwater Horizon oil rig exploded in the Gulf of Mexico. The explosion killed 11 people and released more than 200 million gallons of oil in the Gulf. Thousands of birds, fish, and marine mammals were harmed by the disaster.

The seven-mile-long Elkhorn Slough, an estuary of Monterey Bay in California, serves as a protective home to many species. This harbor seal mother and her pup loaf along the shore, soaking in the warm sunshine.

VOCABULARY WORDS BY CHAPTER

Chapter 5
Expansion and Conflict in the West

allotment (page 122)
aquifer (page 110)
cooperative (page 114)
debt peonage (page 112)
dime novel (page 127)
dry farming (page 107)
egalitarian (page 126)
Exoduster (page 106)
forage (page 118)
free silver movement (page 115)
genocide (page 121)
Ghost Dance (page 122)
gold standard (page 115)
Homestead Act (page 106)
hydraulic mining (page 108)
lien (page 112)
lode (page 108)
manifest destiny (page 106)
placer mining (page 108)
populism (page 115)
posse (page 126)
reservation (page 118)
reservoir (page 110)
shaft mining (page 108)
sharecropper (page 112)
sluice (page 108)
subtreasury system (page 114)
tenant farming (page 112)

Chapter 6
Industrial America

Americanization (page 154)
anarchism (page 151)
anti-Semitism (page 160)
assimilate (page 160)
Bessemer process (page 139)
corporation (page 139)
deflation (page 149)
department store (page 167)
depression (page 139)
Haymarket Riot (page 151)
horizontal integration (page 139)
Interstate Commerce Act (page 139)
Jim Crow laws (page 171)
labor union (page 150)
laissez-faire economics (page 149)
monoculture (page 145)
monopoly (page 139)
muckrakers (page 141)
nativist (page 162)
parent company (page 145)
patent (page 144)
phonograph (page 145)
political machine (page 168)
poll tax (page 171)
progressivism (page 169)
propaganda (page 162)
push-pull factor (page 154)
recession (page 139)
referendum (page 169)
robber barons (page 139)
sanitation (page 168)
scabs (page 151)
segregation (page 171)
separate but equal (page 172)
Social Darwinism (page 139)
socialism (page 153)
streetcar (page 167)
subsidiary (page 145)
suburb (page 167)
telegraph (page 144)
tenement (page 160)
trust (page 141)
vaudeville (page 166)
vertical integration (page 139)
workers' compensation (page149)

Chapter 7
The Progressive Era and Expansionism

American Anti-Imperialist League (page 217)
annex (page 209)
archipelago (page 208)
Boxer Rebellion (page 210)
Children's Bureau (page 190)
commission government (page 196)
conscription (page 189)
conservation (page 198)
direct primary (page 197)
enfranchisement (page 191)
expansionism (page 208)
exposé (page 189)
franchise (page 191)
guerrilla war (page 217)
imperialism (page 208)
income tax (page 207)
initiative (page 197)
insurrection (page 219)
isolationism (page 208)
isthmus (page 219)
merger (page 199)
Open Door Policy (page 210)
Progressive Era (page 188)
prohibition (page 193)
protectorate (page 208)
recall (page 197)
reparations (page 211)
scientific management (page 206)
social security (page 206)
sphere of influence (page 210)
suffragist (page 191)
syndicate (page 204)
temperance movement (page 193)
trustbuster (page 200)
women's suffrage (page 190)
yellow journalism (page 213)

Chapter 8
The Great War

alliance (page 236)
American Expeditionary Forces (AEF) (page 244)
antiaircraft gun (page 248)
armistice (page 261)
assassinate (page 236)
civil liberties (page 246)
Committee on Public Information (CPI) (page 246)
communism (page 261)
conscientious objector (page 246)
declaration of war (page 243)
dissent (page 246)
espionage (page 241)
Fourteen Points (page 259)
front (page 239)
Great Migration (page 255)
influenza (page 257)
League of Nations (page 262)
Liberty Bond (page 244)
machine gun (page 248)
militarism (page 236)
moral diplomacy (page 240)
nationalism (page 236)
neutrality (page 240)
pandemic (page 257)
Prohibition (page 255)
Schlieffen Plan, The (page 238)
sedition (page 246)
sovereignty (page 262)
tank (page 248)
Treaty of Versailles (page 262)
trench warfare (page 239)
U-boat (page 242)
War Industries Board (WIB) (page 244)
Zimmermann Telegram (page 243)

Chapter 9
The Jazz Age and Mass Culture

American Civil Liberties Union (ACLU) (page 279)
Anti-Defamation League (ADL) (page 279)
assembly line (page 287)
back-to-Africa movement (page 301)
bootlegger (page 282)
capitalism (page 278)
constituency (page 299)
eugenics (page 280)
flapper (page 296)
fundamentalism (page 283)
Harlem Renaissance (page 302)
jazz (page 290)
mass market (page 287)
modernism (page 294)
nativism (page 280)
Pan-Africanism (page 301)
radical (page 279)
Red Scare (page 278)
speakeasy (page 282)
stalactite (page 284)
stalagmite (page 284)
welfare capitalism (page 289)

Chapter 10
The Great Depression

Bonus Army (page 337)
deport (page 327)
disposable income (page 321)
Dow Jones Industrial Average (page 322)
drought (page 330)
Dust Bowl (page 331)
fascism (page 335)
Great Depression (page 323)
gross national product (GNP) (page 323)
Hooverville (page 334)
injunction (page 336)
Kellogg-Briand Pact (page 321)
margin (page 322)
mass media (page 332)
repatriation (page 327)
speculation (page 322)
stock market (page 321)
trading pool (page 324)
underwrite (page 334)

Chapter 11
The New Deal

bank holiday (page 352)
brain trust (page 352)
breadwinner (page 370)
coalition (page 361)
collective bargaining (page 364)
court-packing plan (page 366)
deficit (page 352)
deficit spending (page 378)
economic planning (page 355)
fireside chat (page 352)
First Hundred Days (page 352)
lame duck (page 351)
mandate (page 365)
mobilization (page 377)
National Socialism (page 360)
Nazi Party (page 360)
New Deal (page 353)
pension fund (page 358)
picket line (page 365)
planned scarcity (page 354)
polio (page 351)
populist (page 360)
Second New Deal (page 358)
sit-down strike (page 367)
totalitarian (page 360)
voting bloc (page 372)
welfare state (page 378)

Chapter 12
A Threatening World

active defense (page 407)
Allied Powers (page 391)
appeasement (page 397)
arsenal (page 404)
Atlantic Charter (page 406)
Axis Powers (page 391)
belligerent (page 404)
embargo (page 403)
Gestapo (page 390)
Long March (page 401)
Munich Agreement (page 397)
nonaggression pact (page 397)
pacifism (page 394)
purge (page 400)
rearmament (page 390)
refugee (page 395)
Rome-Berlin Axis (page 391)
Third Reich (page 390)

Chapter 13
America in World War II

amphibious assault (page 437)
amphibious landing craft (page 440)

GLOSSARY

A

acquired immunodeficiency syndrome (AIDS) *n.* (uh-KWYRD ih-MYOO-noh-dih-FIH-shun-see SIHN-drohm) the final stage of a virus that attacks the system in the human body that fights off illnesses (page 719)

active defense *n.* (ACK-tihv DEE-fehns) a policy allowing U.S. warships to defend against attacks by German submarines on ships in shipping traffic lanes in the Atlantic Ocean (page 407)

aerospace industry *n.* (AIR-oh-spayss IHN-duhs-tree) the business of building airplanes, spacecrafts, and other vehicles that travel in the air (page 470)

affirmative action *n.* (uh-FUR-muh-tihv AK-shuhn) a government policy that institutes racial quotas to favor groups that suffer from discrimination (page 597)

Agent Orange *n.* (AY-juhnt OR-ihnj) a potent herbicide used to kill vegetation (page 613)

agribusiness *n.* (A-gruh-bihz-nuhs) the commercial business of agriculture (page 495)

Agricultural Revolution *n.* (AHG-rih-kuhl-chuhr-uhl REV-oh-luh-shuhn) the transition in human history from hunting and gathering food to planting crops and raising animals (page xxxiv)

alliance *n.* (uh-LY-uhnss) an agreement of mutual support between countries (page 236)

Allied Powers *n.* (AHL-ayhd POHW-uhrs) Several countries, including France and Great Britain, working together to oppose the Axis Powers of Germany, Italy, and Japan during World War II. (page 391)

allotment *n.* (uh-LOT-muhnt) a piece of land given to a Native American for farming (page 122)

American Anti-Imperialist League *n.* (uh-MAIR-uh-kuhn AN-ty ihm-PIHR-ee-uhl-ist LEEG) an organization that formed in 1898 to oppose the United States' annexation of the Philippines (page 217)

American Civil Liberties Union (ACLU) *n.* (uh-MAIR-uh-kuhn SIH-vuhl LIH-bur-teez YOON-yuhn) an organization, formed in 1920, dedicated to defending the individual rights and freedoms of all Americans (page 279)

American exceptionalism *n.* (uh-MAIR-uh-kuhn ek-SEHP-shuhn-uh-lih-zuhm) the idea that the United States is superior to other countries due to its history and ideology (page 752)

American Expeditionary Forces (AEF) *n.* (uh-MAIR-uh-kuhn ehk-spuh-DIH-shuhn-air-ee FORS-uhz) the corps of American soldiers sent to fight in Europe during World War I (page 244)

Americanization *n.* (uh-mair-uh-kan-ih-ZAY-shuhn) an effort to immerse immigrants in what some people defined as American culture and transform them into "true" Americans (page 154)

amphibious assault *n.* (am-FIH-bee-uhs uh-SAWLT) an attack that uses naval support to protect military forces invading by land and air (page 437)

amphibious landing craft *n.* (am-FIH-bee-uhs LAN-ding KRAFT) boats used to convey soldiers and equipment from the sea to the shore during military attacks (page 440)

anarchism *n.* (AN-ahr-kih-zuhm) the idea that governments are not necessary and that all social and political cooperation should be voluntary (page 151)

annex *v.* (A-neks) to take possession of a territory or country (page 209)

Anti-Defamation League (ADL) *n.* (AN-ty deh-fuh-MAY-shun LEEG) an international Jewish service organization founded to combat anti-Semitism, religious and racial intolerance, and all forms of organized discrimination based on stereotypical beliefs (page 279)

anti-Semitism *n.* (AN-ty SEHM-ih-tih-zuhm) discrimination, prejudice, and hostility against the Jewish people (page 160)

antiaircraft gun *n.* (AN-ty-AIR-kraft GUHN) a piece of heavy artillery modified so that it can be pointed skyward at enemy planes (page 248)

antiballistic missile (ABM) *n.* (AN-ty-buh-LIHS-tihk MIH-suhl) a missile designed to destroy a bomb-carrying missile before it hits its target (page 681)

apartheid *n.* (uh-PAHR-tayt) the legal separation of the races in South Africa (page 715)

appeasement *n.* (uh-PEEZ-muhnt) a policy of making political compromises in order to avoid conflict (page 397)

aquifer *n.* (AH-kwuh-fur) a geologic formation below Earth's surface that can hold a large groundwater reservoir (page 110)

archipelago *n.* (ahr-kuh-PEH-luh-go) a chain of islands (page 208)

armistice *n.* (AHR-muh-stuhss) an agreement between opposing sides in a conflict to stop fighting (page 261)

arms race *n.* (AHRMZ RAYSS) a political situation in which rival countries try to gather or produce the most military weapons (page 470)

arsenal *n.* (AHRS-uh-nuhl) a place where weapons and other miltary equipment are stored (page 404)

artifact *n.* (AHR-tif-ackt) an item made by a human that has historical or cultural meaning (page 90)

assassinate *v.* (uh-SA-suh-nayt) to murder for political reasons (page 236)

assembly line *n.* (uh-SEHM-blee LYN) a method of manufacturing in which the work passes from one worker to another, each of whom has a specific, specialized task (page 287)

assimilate *v.* (uh-SIHM-uhl-ate) to take on the qualities and similarities of another culture and take on a culture's way of life (page 160)

Atlantic Charter *n.* (aht-LAHN-tick CHAHR-tuhr) a charter that lists eight principles for a better world, composed during a meeting between President Franklin Roosevelt and British Prime Minister Winston Churchill (page 406)

atomic bomb *n.* (uh-TAH-mihk BAHM) a type of nuclear bomb whose violent explosion is triggered by splitting atoms, which releases intense heat and radioactivity (page 446)

atrocity *n.* (uh-TRAH-suh-tee) an extremely cruel and shocking act of violence (page 455)

autocrat *n.* (AW-tuh-krat) a tyrant with absolute power (page 606)

Axis Powers *n.* (ACK-sihs POHW-uhrs) Germany, Italy, and Japan, which formed an alliance together at the start of World War II (page 391)

B

baby boom *n.* (BAY-bee BOOM) a significant increase in the birthrate (page 498)

back-to-Africa movement *n.* (BAK TOO A-frih-kuh MOOV-muhnt) a movement headed by Marcus Garvey that encouraged African Americans to leave the United States and return to Africa (page 301)

bailout *n.* (BAY-lowt) during the Great Recession, the act of buying mortgages and unstable investments from banks (page 763)

ballistic missile *n.* (buh-LIHS-tihk MIH-suhl) a nuclear weapon that is propelled by a rocket and guided using a GPS system (page 572)

bank holiday *n.* (BANGK HAH-luh-day) a day or period when banks are closed by government order (page 352)

barrack *n.* (BAIR-uhk) a military building used for sleeping quarters (page 714)

belligerent *n.* (buh-LIH-juh-ruhnt) a country fighting in a war (page 404)

Bering Land Bridge *n.* (BARE-ingh LAND BRIJ) a piece of land between Alaska and Siberia that was above sea level 13,000 years ago and allowed early humans to cross into North America (page xxxii)

Bessemer process *n.* (BEH-seh-mur PRAH-sehs) a process in which workers use forced air to remove impurities such as carbon from iron, which transforms the iron into steel (page 139)

bipartisan *adj.* (by-PAHR-tuh-zuhn) relating to both parties in a two-party system (page 585)

black separatist *n.* (BLAK SEH-puh-ruh-tihst) radical African-American activist who believed that the only way to achieve equality and justice in the United States was to separate themselves culturally and economically from whites (page 594)

Bonus Army *n.* (BOH-nuhs AHR-mee) the thousands of veterans, determined to collect promised cash bonuses early, who came to Washington during the summer of 1932 to listen to Congress debate the bonus proposal (page 337)

bootlegger *n.* (BOOT-leh-gur) an individual who made, transported, or supplied alcohol illegally to saloons or "speakeasies" where city dwellers congregated in the evenings (page 282)

Boxer Rebellion *n.* (BAHK-sur rih-BEL-yuhn) a 1900 political uprising in northern China against foreigners in the country (page 210)

Bracero Program *n.* (brah-SEH-roh PROH-gram) a program designed to import Mexican laborers to replace native-born agricultural and transportation industry workers who were mobilizing for World War II (page 424)

brain trust *n.* (BRAYN TRUHST) a group of experts who advised President Franklin Roosevelt during the Great Depression (page 352)

breadwinner *n.* (BREHD-wih-nur) a member of a household who contributes to the family's income (page 370)

brinkmanship *n.* (BRIHNGK-muhn-ship) the practice of pushing a conflict to the edge of violence without getting into a war, usually as a tactic to gain a favorable outcome (page 496)

bulwark *n.* (BUHL-wurk) something that provides protection or defense (page 497)

busing *n.* (BUH-sing) transporting students of all races to schools outside their neighborhoods or school districts to assure integration and provide equal opportunities in education (page 597)

C

capitalism *n.* (KAP-ih-tuh-lih-zuhm) an economic system in which private individuals or groups own the resources and produce goods for a profit (page 278)

charter *n.* (CHAHR-tur) a document that establishes the main goal of an endeavor (page 651)

chiefdom *n.* (CHEEF-duhm) a large community of people ruled by a chief (page xxxiv)

Children's Bureau *n.* (CHIHL-druhnz BYUR-oh) a U.S. government agency that was created in 1912 and is focused on improving the lives of children and families (page 190)

civic responsibility *n.* (SIH-vihk rih-SPAWN-suh-BIHL-uh-tee) responsibility that is either required or essential that people perform, such as voting, paying taxes, and serving on juries (page R35)

civil disobedience *n.* (SIH-vuhl dihs-uh-BEE-dee-uhnts) the nonviolent disobeying of laws as a form of protest (page 547)

civil liberties *n.* (SIH-vuhl LIH-bur-teez) individual rights protected by law from government interference (page 246)

coalition *n.* (koh-uh-LIH-shuhn) an alliance of people, parties, or states focused on a common goal (page 361)

collective bargaining *n.* (kuh-LEHK-tihv BAHR-guhn-ihng) negotiation between an employer and union leaders on behalf of all union members (page 364)

collude *v.* (kuh-LOOD) to conspire; to construct a plot with others (page 781)

commission government *n.* (kuh-MIH-shuhn GUH-vur-muhnt) a form of city government in which voters elect a small number of officials called commissioners, each of whom heads a city department (page 196)

Committee on Public Information (CPI) *n.* (kuh-MIH-tee ON PUH-blihk ihn-fur-MAY-shuhn) a committee established during World War I to counter possible dissent and raise the country's enthusiasm for the war (page 246)

communism *n.* (KAHM-yuh-nih-zuhm) a form of government in which all the means of production and transportation are owned by the state (page 261)

compassionate conservatism *n.* (kuhm-PAH-shuh-nuht kuhn-SUR-vuh-tih-zuhm) a political philosophy that blended traditional conservative ideas about economic policies with a concern for disadvantaged people (page 752)

concentration camp *n.* (kahnt-suhn-TRAY-shuhn KAMP) a place where prisoners of war or members of persecuted minorities are confined; in World War II, the camps where Jews and others were held and murdered by the Nazis (page 450)

conscientious objector *n.* (KAHN-shee-ehnt-shuhs ahb-JEHK-tur) a person who refuses to fight in a war for religious reasons (page 246)

conscription *n.* (kuhn-SKRIHP-shuhn) the requirement to enlist for service in a country's armed forces (page 189)

conservation *n.* (kahn-sur-VAY-shuhn) the management and protection of natural resources (page 198)

conservative *n.* (kuhn-SUR-vuh-tihv) a member of a political party who believes in traditional values, social structure, and gradual change in policies (page 704)

constituency *n.* (kuhn-STIH-chu-uhn-see) a group of citizens that has elected, or is entitled to elect, a representative to the government (page 299)

consumer society *n.* (kuhn-SOO-mur suh-SY-uh-tee) a society in which shopping and buying goods has become an important part of people's lifestyles (page 500)

consumerism *n.* (kuhn-SOO-muh-rih-zuhm) a theory stating that the economy flourishes when people buy, or consume, a lot of goods and services (page 495)

containment *n.* (kuhn-TAYN-muhnt) a U.S. security policy during the Cold War in which military action was used to stop the Soviet Union from spreading communism (page 463)

context *n.* (KAHN-text) the circumstances and setting in which an object is located that give an understanding of how an object is used (page 90)

contraceptive *n.* (kahn-truh-SEHP-tihv) a means of preventing pregnancy (page 658)

cooperative *n.* (koh-AH-pruh-tihv) an organization run and funded by its members (page 114)

corporation *n.* (kor-puh-RAY-shuhn) companies or groups of people that invest in a business and then share its profits (page 139)

counterculture *n.* (kown-tur-KUHL-chur) a movement in the 1960s that promoted a way of life that was in opposition to American society's established rules and behavior (page 622)

coup *n.* (KOO) an illegal overthrow of the government (page 607)

court-packing plan *n.* (KORT PA-king PLAN) President Franklin Roosevelt's controversial plan to increase the number of justices on the Supreme Court from nine to fifteen by adding six justices who shared his progressive views (page 366)

cover-up *n.* (KUH-vur UHP) an attempt to hide the truth from the public (page 690)

covert action *n.* (KOH-vurt AK-shuhn) an activity performed secretly to influence the political, economic, or military situation in another country (page 496)

credibility gap *n.* (kreh-dih-BIHL-uh-tee GAP) an increasing skepticism among Americans about government reports on the Vietnam War (page 615)

crematorium *n.* (kree-muh-TOR-ee-uhm) a furnace or oven used to burn human or animal remains; in World War II, the ovens used by Nazis to burn their victims' bodies (page 453)

Cuban Missile Crisis *n.* (KYOO-buhn MIH-suhl CRY-suhs) a political showdown in 1962 between the United States and the Soviet Union caused by the presence of nuclear weapons in Cuba (page 572)

cultural advocacy *n.* (KUHLCH-ruhl AD-vuh-kuh-see) a political strategy in which members of a religion influence politicians and social institutions in an effort to promote their beliefs (page 710)

D

D-Day *n.* (DEE DAY) the day, June 6, 1944, in World War II when Allied forces invaded northern France by landing on beaches at Normandy (page 440)

DDT *n.* (DEE-DEE-TEE) a pesticide, now banned in the United States and many other countries, that was found to be harmful to animals and to cause long-term contamination of the environment (page 682)

de facto segregation *n.* (dih FAK-toh seh-grih-GAY-shuhn) segregation that is present in society despite no laws enforcing it (page 594)

de jure segregation *n.* (dee JUR-ee seh-grih-GAY-shuhn) segregation enforced by law (page 594)

debt peonage *n.* (DEHT PEE-uh-nihj) a form of labor in which a person works just to pay off a debt (page 112)

declaration of war *n.* (deh-kluh-RAY-shun UHV WOR) a formal announcement made by a country's leader of the intention to wage war (page 243)

deferment *n.* (dih-FUR-muhnt) an official permission to delay conscription (page 616)

deficit *n.* (DEH-fuh-suht) a negative monetary balance that occurs when expenditures exceed income (page 352)

deficit reduction *n.* (DEH-fuh-suht rih-DUHK-shun) the steps taken by a government to pay off debt (page 731)

deficit spending *n.* (DEH-fuh-suht SPEHND-ihng) spending more money than the government receives from taxes (page 378)

deflation *n.* (dee-FLAY-shuhn) a decrease in the prices of goods and services (page 149)

dehumanize *v.* (dee-HYOO-mahn-ize) to treat people as if they are not human beings (page 541)

delegate *n.* (DEH-lih-guht) a person representing his or her state in a nominating convention (page 621)

GLOSSARY

demilitarized zone *n.* (dee-MIH-luh-tuh-ryzd ZOHN) an area in which military personel and weapons are not allowed (page 476)

demobilization *n.* (dih-moh-buh-ly-ZAY-shuhn) the release of soldiers from military duty (page 427)

demographic composition *n.* (dem-uh-GRA-fihk kahm-puh-ZIH-shuhn) the make-up of the population of a specific area based on ethnicity (page 591)

department store *n.* (dee-PAHRT-mehnt STOHR) large store that provides a wide variety of merchandise, organized into different departments but all under one roof (page 167)

deport *v.* (dih-PORT) to forcibly remove from the country, or to pressure to leave (page 327)

depression *n.* (dee-PREH-shuhn) a severe and longterm economic decline characterized by a number of business failures, reduced industrial output, and high unemployment (page 139)

depth charge *n.* (DEHPTH CHAHRJ) an underwater bomb that is programmed to explode at a certain depth (page 435)

deregulation *n.* (dee-reh-gyuh-LAY-shun) the act of repealing laws on a large scale and usually related to a particular industry (page 711)

desegregation *n.* (dee-seh-grih-GAY-shuhn) the process of ending a policy that forces the separation of groups of people in public spaces (page 543)

détente *n.* (day-TAHNT) an easing of tensions and an improvement in relations between countries (page 681)

dime novel *n.* (DYM NAH-vuhl) popular fiction that sold for 10 cents a book in the late 18th and early 19th centuries (page 127)

direct primary *n.* (duh-REKT PRY-mair-ee) a preliminary election in which voters choose the party candidates to run in a later election for public office (page 197)

disenfranchise *v.* (dihs-ihn-FRAN-chyz) to deprive someone of a legal right or privilege (page 587)

disintegration *n.* (dihs-ihn-tuh-GRAY-shuhn) the endurance of nationalist, tribalist, and separatist alternatives to globalization (page 747)

disposable income *n.* (dih-SPOH-zuh-buhl IHN-kuhm) spending money (page 321)

dissent *n.* (dih-SEHNT) disagreement with the government's official opinion (page 246)

domestication *n.* (doh-mehs-TIH-kay-shuhn) the practice of raising animals and growing plants for human benefit (page xxxiv)

domesticity *n.* (doh-mehs-TIH-suh-tee) life inside the home (page 498)

domino theory *n.* (DAH-muh-noh THEER-ee) an idea during the Cold War that countries that neighbor communist countries are more likely to fall to communism (page 473)

dove *n.* (DUHV) a person who opposes war (page 616)

Dow Jones Industrial Average *n.* (DAU JOHNZ ihn-DUH-stree-uhl A-vuh-rihj) an index of the stock of leading companies, tracked daily and used as a measure of general stock market trends (page 322)

drought *n.* (DROWT) a prolonged period with little or no rainfall (page 330)

dry farming *n.* (DRY FAHR-mihng) agricultural techniques used in areas with little rainfall (page 107)

Dust Bowl *n.* (DUHST BOHL) areas of Kansas, Colorado, Oklahoma, Texas, and New Mexico that, during the 1930s, suffered ecological devastation and turned into a barren desert (page 331)

E

economic planning *n.* (eh-kuh-NAH-mihk PLAN-ihng) management of the economy by the federal government (page 355)

economic stagnation *n.* (eh-kuh-NAH-mihk stahg-NAY-shuhn) a period of little or no economic growth (page 692)

economic stimulus *n.* (eh-kuh-NAH-mihk STIHM-yuh-luhs) a measure aimed at promoting and enabling financial recovery and growth (page 765)

egalitarian *adj.* (ih-gal-uh-TAIR-ee-uhn) the belief that all people are equal (page 126)

embargo *n.* (ihm-BAHR-goh) a ban against engaging in commerce with specified countries (page 403)

enemy alien *n.* (EH-nuh-mee AY-lyuhn) someone whose loyalty to the nation in which the person lives is suspect (page 430)

enfranchisement *n.* (ihn-FRAN-chyz-muhnt) the granting of the rights of citizenship, especially the right to vote (page 191)

escalation *n.* (ehs-kuh-LAY-shuhn) an increase of intensity, as during war (page 608)

espionage *n.* (EH-spee-uh-nahj) spying (page 241)

eugenics *n.* (yoo-JEH-nihks) the belief that some races were superior to others and that breeding should be controlled so that populations of superior races increase (page 280)

evangelist *n.* (ih-VAN-juh-lihst) a person whose religion requires them to recruit more believers (page 705)

executive order *n.* (ihg-ZEH-kyuh-tihv OR-dur) a directive issued by a president that has the force of law (page 431)

executive privilege *n.* (ihg-ZEH-kyuh-tihv PRIHV-lij) the principle that in the nation's interest, the president may withhold certain information from Congress (page 690)

Exoduster *n.* (EKS-oh-duhs-tur) an African American who migrated from the South to the Great Plains after Reconstruction had failed (page 106)

expansionism *n.* (ihk-SPAN-shuh-nih-zuhm) a policy or practice of increasing a country's territory (page 208)

exposé *n.* (ehk-spoh-ZAY) a work of writing that publicizes a scandal or injustice (page 189)

F

fascism *n.* (FA-shih-zuhm) a political movement based on extreme nationalism, militarism, and racism promoting the superiority of a particular people over all others (page 335)

feminism *n.* (FEH-muh-nih-zuhm) the idea that women are equal to men socially and politically (page 657)

filibuster *n.* (FIH-luh-buhs-tur) a political strategy in which a small group of legislators take turns speaking and refuse to stop the debate or allow a bill to come to a vote (page 585)

fireside chat *n.* (FY-ur-syd CHAT) one of a series of radio broadcasts that President Franklin Roosevelt made to the nation throughout his presidency (page 352)

First Hundred Days *n.* (FURST HUHN-druhd DAYZ) President Franklin Roosevelt's first 100 days in office, during which he produced 15 laws that formed the basis of the New Deal (page 352)

flapper *n.* (FLA-pur) young women in the 1920s who embraced a freer style of dress and the use of cosmetics (page 296)

forage *v.* (FOR-ihj) to search for plants (page 118)

foreclosure *n.* (for-KLOH-zhur) the action of a bank taking possession of a property because the buyer can no longer make payments (page 762)

Fourteen Points *n.* (FOR-teen PAWIHNTS) President Woodrow Wilson's proposed program for peace at the end of World War I (page 259)

franchise *n.* (FRAN-chyz) a constitutional right, especially the right to vote (page 191)

free silver movement *n.* (FREE SIHL-vur MOOV-mehnt) a monetary system that would allow private citizens to mint their silver into U.S. coins (page 115)

free-enterprise zone *n.* (FREE EHN-tur-pryz ZOHN) an area that allows the suspension of both tax and custom laws (page 747)

Freedom Riders *n.* (FREE-duhm RY-durz) interracial groups who rode buses in the South and ignored "white" and "colored" signs when they stopped at restrooms and lunch counters so that a series of federal court decisions declaring segregation illegal in facilities serving travelers would not be ignored by white officials (page 553)

front *n.* (FRUHNT) a battle line between armies (page 239)

Frostbelt *n.* (FRAHST-behlt) the north-central and northeastern regions of the United States, which have cold winters (page 495)

fundamentalism *n.* (FUHN-duh-mehn-tah-lih-zuhm) a movement that promoted the idea that every word of the Bible was the literal truth (page 283)

G

gender bias *n.* (JEHN-dur BY-uhs) the preference for one gender over another (page 658)

genetically modified food *n.* (juh-NEH-tik-lee MAH-duh-fyd FOOD) food grown from plants that have been changed in a way that does not occur naturally (page 775)

genocide *n.* (JEH-nuh-syd) the deliberate murder of a large number of people belonging to a specific racial, cultural, or political group (page 121)

Gestapo *n.* (guh-SHTAH-poh) Nazi secret police force (page 390)

Ghost Dance *n.* (GOHST DANSS) a ceremonial dance performed by some Native Americans who believed the dance would summon a deliverer who would restore their world (page 122)

GI Bill *n.* (JEE I BIHL) a government program started in 1944 that helped veterans returning from WWII buy homes and attend college (page 469)

glacial period *n.* (GLAY-shuhl PEER-ee-uhd) a period of time in history during which huge sheets of ice covered much of Earth (page xxxi)

glasnost *n.* (GLAZ-nohst) a government policy of open communication in the former Soviet Union (page 720)

globalization *n.* (gloh-buh-luh-ZAY-shuhn) the faster and freer flow of people, resources, goods, and ideas across national borders (page 746)

gold standard *n.* (GOHLD STAN-durd) a monetary system in which a nation's currency is backed by gold (page 115)

government-in-exile *n.* (GUH-vur-muhnt IHN EHG-zyl) a government that has been deposed and attempts to rule from another land (page 472)

grassroots activism *n.* (GRAS-roots AK-tih-vih-zuhm) political movements driven by people who individually do not have much power, but who, working together, can be very effective (page 538)

Great Depression *n.* (GRAYT dee-PREH-shuhn) worldwide economic downturn in the 1930s, marked by poverty and high unemployment (page 323)

Great Migration *n.* (GRAYT my-GRAY-shuhn) a massive movement of African Americans who left the South for cities in the North, beginning in 1910 (page 255)

greenhouse effect *n.* (GREEN-hows uh-FEHKT) the warming of Earth's surface caused when greenhouse gas emissions trap the sun's heat (page 772)

greenhouse gas *n.* (GREEN-hows GAS) a gas such as carbon dioxide or methane (page 772)

gross national product (GNP) *n.* (GROHS NA-shuh-nuhl PRAH-duhkt) the total goods and services produced by the nation plus the income earned by its citizens (page 323)

guerrilla war *n.* (guh-RIH-luh WOR) war in which small, mobile groups of irregular forces use hit-and-run tactics to battle conventional military forces (page 217)

H

hardliner *n.* (HAHRD-ly-nur) a person, usually within a political or special-interest group, who strictly supports a set of ideas or policies (page 721)

Harlem Renaissance *n.* (HAHR-luhm reh-nuh-SAHNTS) a cultural movement that originated in Harlem in the 1920s and promoted African-American writers, artists, and musicians (page 302)

hawk *n.* (HAWK) a person who supports war (page 616)

Haymarket Riot *n.* (HAY-mahr-kuht RY-uht) a violent confrontation between workers and police on May 4, 1886, which began as a protest against police conduct during a strike at a factory of the McCormick Company in Chicago, Illinois (page 151)

Holocaust *n.* (HOH-luh-cawst) the mass slaughter by the Nazis of six million Jews and others during World War II (page 453)

Homestead Act *n.* (HOHM-stehd AKT) a law introduced in 1862 that encouraged American citizens to settle in the Great Plains by offering plots of land in the region (page 106)

homogeneity *n.* (hoh-muh-juh-NAY-uh-tee) the state of being the same or similar (page 503)

Hooverville *n.* (HOO-vur-vil) makeshift villages for homeless Americans, usually at the edge of a city with shelters made of cardboard, scrap metal, or whatever was cheap and available (page 334)

horizontal integration *n.* (hor-uh-ZAHN-tuhl ihn-tuh-GRAY-shuhn) purchasing other companies that offer the same goods and services in order to reduce the number of competitors and achieve control within an industry (page 139)

human immunodeficiency virus (HIV) *n.* (HYOO-muhn ih-MYOO-noh-dih-FIH-shun-see VY-ruhs) a virus that attacks the system in the human body that fights off illnesses (page 719)

hunter-gatherer *n.* (HUHN-tuhr GAHTH-uhr-uhr) a human who hunts animals and gathers wild plants to eat (page xxxiii)

hydraulic mining *n.* (hy-DRAW-lik MY-nihng) a process of uncovering precious minerals by using pressurized water to remove soil (page 108)

hydrogen bomb *n.* (HY-druh-juhn BAHM) a nuclear weapon that explodes due to compacted gases inside (page 471)

I

ice age *n.* (AISS AJ) a period of time in history during which huge sheets of ice covered much of Earth (page xxxi)

impasse *n.* (IHM-pass) a situation in which no progress is possible (page 621)

impeachment *n.* (ihm-PEECH-muhnt) formal charges brought against a public official for misconduct in office (page 690)

imperialism *n.* (ihm-PIHR-ee-uh-lih-zuhm) a policy or practice of exerting control over weaker nations or territories (page 208)

income inequality *n.* (IHN-kuhm ih-nih-KWAH-luh-tee) an economic phenomenon in which a large gap exists between what the poorest and the richest citizens in a nation earn (page 711)

income tax *n.* (IHN-kuhm TAKS) a tax that is based on the amount a person earns (page 207)

induction *n.* (ihn-DUHK-shun) the act of being drafted into the military (page 625)

infamy *n.* (IHN-fuh-me) refers to an extremely shameful or evil act (page 420)

influenza *n.* (ihn-floo-EHN-zuh) an acute and highly contagious illness commonly called "the flu" (page 257)

infrastructure *n.* (IHN-fruh-struhk-chur) the basic systems of a society including roads, bridges, sewers, and electricity (page 470)

initiative *n.* (ih-NIH-shuh-tihv) a procedure by which citizens can propose new laws to be voted on by the public or by the legislature (page 197)

injunction *n.* (ihn-JUHNGK-shuhn) court orders that demand or forbid certain actions (page 336)

insurgent *n.* (ihn-SUR-juhnt) a rebel or revolutionary (page 606)

insurrection *n.* (ihn-suh-REK-shun) a violent rebellion against a government or political authority (page 219)

integrated *adj.* (IHN-tuh-gray-tuhd) allowing the free association of people of different races or ethnicities (page 543)

integration *n.* (ihn-tuh-GRAY-shuhn) the process of joining economic forces (page 747)

interned *v.* (ihn-TURND) confined in prisons or camps for military or political reasons during wartime (page 430)

Internet *n.* (IHN-tur-neht) the worldwide network of computers (page 717)

internment camp *n.* (ihn-TURN-muhnt KAMP) a prison camp to hold enemy aliens and other prisoners of war during wartime (page 431)

Interstate Commerce Act *n.* (IHN-tur-stayt KAH-murs AKT) a law that established a commission that supervised and regulated the nation's railroads, investigated complaints about business practices, and sued companies that violated its regulations (page 139)

Interstate Highway System *n.* (IHN-tur-stayt HY-way SIHS-tuhm) the network of highways launched by President Eisenhower in 1956 to span the United States and connect states and major cities (page 502)

investment bank *n.* (ihn-VEHST-muhnt BANK) a financial institution that purchases and sells stocks and bonds and helps companies raise capital and manage their assets (page 762)

iron curtain *n.* (I-urn KUR-tuhn) the military and political divide in Europe between Western capitalist and Eastern communist countries (page 463)

Islamic republic *n.* (IZ-lahm-ik RE-puhb-lik) a state either incorporating, or based entirely on Islamic law (page 698)

island hopping *n.* (I-luhnd HAH-pihng) a strategy that involves capturing and setting up military bases on island groups one island at a time (page 439)

isolationism *n.* (I-soh-LAY-shuh-nih-zuhm) a policy in which a nation stays out of the affairs of other nations (page 208)

isthmus *n.* (IHS-muhs) a narrow strip of land connecting two larger land areas (page 219)

J

jazz *n.* (JAZ) a style of music originating among African-American musicians that contains lively rhythms, sounds from a variety of instruments, and improvisation (page 290)

GLOSSARY

Jim Crow laws *n.* (JIHM KROH LAWZ) laws established after the Reconstruction Period that enforced racial segregation across the southern states (page 171)

job dislocation *n.* (JAHB dihs-loh-KAY-shuhn) the movement of jobs to other places (page 746)

K

kamikaze *n.* (kah-mih-KAH-zee) one of a group of Japanese suicide bomber pilots who crashed their planes, loaded with explosives, into American ships (page 444)

Kellogg-Briand Pact *n.* (KEH-lawg bree-AHN PAKT) a multinational agreement from 1928 in which the signing countries agreed to reject war (page 321)

L

labor union *n.* (LAY-bur YOON-yuhn) groups of workers who band together to achieve better pay, safer working conditions, and other benefits (page 150)

laissez-faire economics *n.* (LEH-say FAIR eh-kuh-NAH-mihks) a policy that calls for less government involvement in economic affairs, so that businesses choose how they will operate, with little or no oversight (page 149)

lame duck *n.* (LAYM DUHK) an outgoing elected official soon to be replaced by a successor (page 351)

landmark legislation *n.* (lahnd-MARK lehj-iss-LAY-shun) important and historic law (page 593)

League of Nations *n.* (LEEG UHV NAY-shuhnz) President Woodrow Wilson's plan proposed after World War I for a general assembly of countries that would stabilize relations among countries and help preserve peace (page 262)

libel *n.* (LY-buhl) the crime of making verbal or written negative claims about someone without evidence (page 479)

liberal consensus *n.* (LIH-buh-ruhl kuhn-SEHN-suhs) the agreement between the Democrats and Republicans in Congress made after World War II to continue welfare, develop a national security system, and strengthen the executive branch of government (page 468)

Liberty Bond *n.* (LIH-bur-tee BAHND) a government bond sold to individuals to help support U.S. involvement in World War I (page 244)

lien *n.* (LEEN) a legal claim to a person's property and income if debts aren't paid (page 112)

lode *n.* (LOHD) vein of ore (page 108)

Long March *n.* (LOHNGH MAHRCH) a 6,000 mile journey by Chinese communists to relocate the communist revolutionary base from southeast China to central China (page 401)

loyalty oath *n.* (LOY-uhl-tee OHTH) a sworn statement confirming a person does not belong and has never belonged to various organizations including those identified as communist (page 479)

M

machine gun *n.* (muh-SHEEN GUHN) a gun designed to fire hundreds of bullets per minute (page 248)

malaise *n.* (muh-LAYZ) a general feeling of illness or unease (page 695)

mandate *n.* (MAN-dayt) the authority to carry out a course of action, given to a representative by voters (page 365)

manifest destiny *n.* (MAN-uh-fehst DEHS-tuh-nee) the belief that Americans were intended to settle all the land between the Atlantic and Pacific coasts (page 106)

manifesto *n.* (man-uh-FEHS-toh) a written declaration of intent (page 648)

maquiladora *n.* (mah-kee-luh-DOR-uh) a manufacturing plant located in an export-processing zone (page 746)

margin *n.* (MAHR-juhn) money borrowed from a bank in order to pay for an investment, such as stocks (page 322)

marriage equality *n.* (MEHR-ihj ih-KWAH-luh-tee) the legal right of gays and lesbians to marry their partners and have the same privileges that married heterosexual couples enjoy (page 770)

Marshall Plan *n.* (MAHR-shuhl PLAN) a U.S. economic aid program to restore economic stability to Western Europe after World War II (page 461)

mass market *n.* (MAS MAHR-kuht) a large number of consumers to whom manufacturers can sell goods that are manufactured in mass quantities (page 287)

mass media *n.* (MAS MEE-dee-uh) forms of communication such as radio, film, and musical recordings with the potential to reach large audiences (page 332)

material record *n.* (muh-TEEHR-ee-uhl REK-uhrd) the buildings and objects that survive from a previous era (page 90)

McCarthyism *n.* (muh-KAHR-thee-ih-zuhm) the practice of accusing people of being traitors to their country without offering proof (page 481)

Medicaid *n.* (MEH-dih-kayd) a U.S. government program started in 1965 that gives medical insurance to impoverished people (page 590)

Medicare *n.* (MEH-dih-kair) a U.S. government program started in 1965 that gives medical insurance to elderly people (page 590)

merger *n.* (MUR-jur) the act of incorporating two or more businesses into one (page 199)

militant *adj.* (MIH-luh-tuhnt) overly aggressive in achieving a goal (page 652)

militarism *n.* (MIH-luh-tuh-rih-zuhm) the belief that a government must create a strong military and be prepared to use it to achieve the country's goals (page 236)

military-industrial complex *n.* (mih-luh-tair-EE ihn-DUS-tree-uhl CAHM-plehks) a country's military establishment and industries producing arms or other military materials (page 471)

miscegenation *n.* (MIH-sehj-ehn-a-shuhn) marriage between people of different races (page 597)

misogyny *n.* (MISS-ah-jihn-ee) a dislike or contempt for or hatred of women; prejudice against women (page 659)

mobilization *n.* (moh-buh-luh-ZAY-shuhn) the act of assembling and organizing military forces (page 377)

modernism *n.* (MAH-dur-nih-zuhm) a modern artistic and literary style, featuring a hard, realistic tone and a tendency to reject or avoid artistic and literary practices of the past (page 294)

module *n.* (MAH-jool) a segment of a spacecraft that can function on its own (page 664)

monoculture *n.* (mahn-oh-KUHL-chuhr) growing a single crop (page 145)

monopoly *n.* (muh-NAH-puh-lee) the complete control of an industry or the market for a service or product (page 139)

Montgomery Bus Boycott *n.* (mahnt-GUH-muh-ree BUHS BOY-kaht) a mass protest, sparked by the arrest of Rosa Parks, against the racial segregation practices of the public bus system in Montgomery, Alabama (page 547)

moral diplomacy *n.* (MOR-uhl duh-PLOH-muh-see) the concept that the United States should drastically reduce its intervention in the affairs of other countries (page 240)

mortar *n.* (MOR-tur) a short-range, muzzle-loaded cannon (page 611)

muckrakers *n.* (MUHK-ray-kurs) investigative journalists of the early 1900s who exposed misconduct by powerful organizations or people (page 141)

multinational corporation *n.* (muhl-tee-NA-shuh-nuhl kor-puh-RAY-shuhn) a company that has offices and factories in multiple countries (page 774)

Munich Agreement *n.* (MYOO-nihk uh-GREE-muhnt) an agreement Hitler made with the rulers of Great Britain, France, and Italy, declaring that Germany had the right to seize the Sudetenland, a portion of Czechoslovakia (page 397)

N

napalm *n.* (NAY-pahlm) a thick flammable, jellylike substance used in bombs to cause and spread fires (page 422)

National Socialism *n.* (NA-shuh-nuhl SOH-shuh-lih-zuhm) the political doctrine of the Nazi Party in Germany, which promoted the superiority of Germany and the German people, rejected communism, and carried anti-Semitism—hatred of Jewish people—to extreme levels (page 360)

nationalism *n.* (NA-shuh-nuh-lih-zuhm) a strong sense of loyalty to one's country and belief in its superiority to others (page 236)

nativism *n.* (NAY-tih-vih-zuhm) an ideology favoring people born in the United States over more recent immigrants (page 280)

nativist *n.* (NAY-tih-vihst) someone who opposes immigration and wants to protect the interests of the native-born population (page 162)

naturalization *n.* (NACH-uh-ruh-lih-ZAY-shuhn) the process of becoming a U.S. citizen for people who are not native-born citizens (page R34)

naval quarantine *n.* (NAY-vuhl KWAWR-uhn-teen) a blockade imposed on the ports of another country (page 572)

Nazi Party *n.* (NAHT-see PAHR-tee) a political party that was led by Adolf Hitler and used force to exert complete control over Germany from 1933 to 1945 (page 360)

neoconservative *n.* (nee-oh-kuhn-SUR-vuh-tihv) a person who strongly supports a free-market economy and believes the United States should actively promote its ideals around the world (page 752)

neutrality *n.* (noo-TRA-luh-tee) the refusal to take sides or become involved in a conflict (page 240)

New Deal *n.* (NOO DEEL) the laws, agencies, and programs initiated by President Franklin Roosevelt and his administration in response to the Great Depression of the 1930s (page 353)

New Federalism *n.* (NOO FEH-duh-ruh-lih-zuhm) a plan by President Richard Nixon to turn the control of some federal programs over to the states (page 678)

New Frontier *n.* (NOO fruhn-TEER) a U.S. political strategy in 1960 in which President Kennedy stressed creative problem solving, foreign diplomacy, and technological advancements to overcome the country's problems (page 568)

new media *n.* (NOO MEE-dee-uh) digital products and services that provide content through the Internet (page 774)

nonaggression pact *n.* (nahn-uh-GREH-shuhn PAKT) an agreement made in 1939 between Nazi Germany and the Soviet Union, declaring that they would not take military action against each other for the next 10 years (page 397)

nuclear deterrence *n.* (NOO-klee-ur dih-TUR-unts) a strategy of using nuclear weapons as a threat to ward off an enemy attack (page 496)

nuclear power *n.* (NOO-klee-ur POW-ur) energy that is created by either splitting or fusing the nuclei of atoms (page 501)

O

occupation zone *n.* (AH-kyoo-pay-shuhn ZOHN) an area of a country in which a foreign military takes control (page 463)

Open Door Policy *n.* (OH-puhn DOHR PAH-luh-see) an American proposal that aimed to establish equal access to ports among countries trading with China in 1900 (page 210)

oral history *n.* (OR-uhl HISS-tuh-ree) recorded interview with a person whose experiences and memories have historical significance (page R38)

orientation *n.* (or-ee-uhn-TAY-shun) a person's identification of sexual attraction (page 660)

originalism *n.* (OH-rihj-ihn-uh-lih-zuhm) a belief system used to interpret the U.S. Constitution from the point of view of the intent of the document when it was originally written (page 713)

overregulation *n.* (oh-vur-reh-gyuh-LAY-shuhn) excessive rules and regulations (page 685)

P

pacifism *n.* (PA-suh-fih-zuhm) the belief that war is morally wrong (page 394)

Pan-Africanism *n.* (PAN A-frih-kuh-nih-zuhm) a movement in the early 1900s that sought to unify people of African descent (page 301)

pandemic *n.* (pan-DEH-mihk) sudden outbreak of a disease that spreads over a wide geographic area (page 257)

panzer *n.* (PAHN-zur) a thickly armored German tank with impressive firepower used during World War II (page 435)

parent company *n.* (PAIR-uhnt KUHM-puh-nee) a company that controls all or part of other, smaller companies (page 145)

patent *n.* (PA-tuhnt) a license that gives an inventor exclusive rights to use, sell, or make an invention for a specific number of years (page 144)

peer *n.* (PEER) a person of the same age, rank, or social status as another (page 642)

penicillin *n.* (peh-nuh-SIH-luhn) an antibiotic, or bacteria killer, made from mold and used to treat infections and disease (page 422)

pension fund *n.* (PEHN-shuhn FUHND) a pool of money used to pay people a small, established income after they retire (page 358)

perestroika *n.* (peh-ruh-STROY-kuh) a government policy of reform in the former Soviet Union (page 720)

perjury *n.* (PUR-juh-ree) the act of lying under oath (page 751)

personal computer *n.* (PURS-uh-nuhl kuhm-PYOO-tur) an electronic device that processes data and is specifically designed for home use (page 716)

personal responsibility *n.* (PURS-uh-nuhl rih-SPAWN-suh-BIHL-uh-tee) responsibility that is not required but that contributes to a more civil society, such as respecting and standing up for others' rights, helping in the community, and staying informed (page R35)

phonograph *n.* (FOH-nuh-graf) a machine that reproduces sounds from a record (page 145)

picket line *n.* (PIH-kuht LYN) a group of strikers who form a barrier to keep scabs, or strikebreakers, from entering a building to work in their place (page 365)

placer mining *n.* (PLAH-sur MY-nihng) mining techniques involving the use of lightweight tools to pan for gold in rivers and streams (page 108)

planned scarcity *n.* (PLAND SKEHR-suh-tee) the economic theory that lowering the supply of a product will increase demand for it and raise its price (page 354)

Pleistocene epoch *n.* (PLEIS-tuh-seen EH-puhk) a period in the history of Earth in which large animals and plants existed and glaciers covered Earth (page xxxi)

polio *n.* (POH-lee-oh) an infectious disease that sometimes causes muscle weakness or paralysis (page 351)

Politburo *n.* (PAW-luht-byoor-oh) the main ruling government committee that made policy decisions in the Communist Party; often refers to those of China or the former Soviet Union (page 720)

political machine *n.* (poh-LIH-tih-kuhl muh-SHEEN) a political organization in which one person or a small group is able to maintain control over a city or a state (page 168)

poll tax *n.* (POHL TAKS) a tax on every individual, regardless of income, often connected to the right to vote (page 171)

populism *n.* (PAH-pyuh-lih-zuhm) the belief that ordinary people should control government (page 115)

populist *n.* (PAH-pyuh-lihst) a politician who claims to represent the concerns of ordinary people (page 360)

posse *n.* (PAH-see) group of armed men formed to capture an outlaw (page 126)

post-traumatic stress disorder (PTSD) *n.* (POHST truh-MAH-tihk STREHS dihs-AWR-dur) a condition brought on by injury or psychological trauma (page 629)

poverty rate *n.* (PAH-vur-tee RAYT) the percentage of the population living in poverty (page 514)

precedent *n.* (PREH-suh-duhnt) a previous determination in a court case to set a standard for comparison with similar, new cases (page 642)

primary sources *n.* (PRY-mehr-ee SOR-ses) writings or recordings that were created by someone who witnessed or lived through a historical event (page R38)

Progressive Era *n.* (pruh-GREH-sihv EHR-uh) a period from about 1890 to 1920 in which reformers sought to correct many social, economic, and political inequalities and injustices in the United States (page 188)

progressivism *n.* (pruh-GREH-sih-vih-zuhm) reform movement from 1890 to 1920 that sought to make state and national politics more democratic and government more efficient (page 169)

prohibition *n.* (proh-uh-BIH-shuhn) the act of outlawing the production, distribution, and sale of alcohol (page 193)

Prohibition *n.* (proh-uh-BIH-shuhn) constitutional ban on the sale of alcoholic beverages that was in effect between 1920 and 1933 (page 255)

propaganda *n.* (prah-puh-GAN-duh) misleading ideas and information that are spread in order to influence people's opinions or advance an organization's or party's ideas (page 162)

property rights *n.* (PRAH-puhr-tee RITES) the legal ownership of property and the authority to determine how it is used (page 685)

protectorate *n.* (pruh-TEK-tuh-ruht) a country that is partly governed by a more powerful country (page 208)

proxy war *n.* (PRAHK-see WOR) a series of battles that are provoked by a nation that does not participate in the fighting (page 474)

purge *n.* (PUHRJ) removing or eliminating something (page 400)

push-pull factor *n.* (PUSH PUL FAK-tur) reason why people migrate; "push" factors cause them to leave; "pull" factors make them come to a place (page 154)

GLOSSARY

R

radical *n.* (RA-dih-kuhl) a person who wants an extreme change or holds an extreme political position (page 279)

ration *v.* (RA-shuhn) to control the supply of goods made available to the public, especially in wartime (page 424)

rearmament *n.* (ree-AHR-muh-muhnt) for a nation to rebuild a stockpile of weapons to replace those that are out-of-date or have been taken away (page 390)

recall *n.* (REE-kawl) a procedure by which citizens can vote to remove an elected public official from office (page 197)

recession *n.* (rih-SEH-shuhn) a relatively short-lasting slowdown in economic growth, often part of a normal business cycle (page 139)

Red Scare *n.* (REHD SKAIR) a period in 1919 and 1920 when the federal government targeted suspected communists, anarchists, and radicals (page 278)

referendum *n.* (reh-fuh-REN-duhm) when the people vote directly on specific measures (page 169)

refugee *n.* (REH-fyoo-jee) a person seeking shelter and protection from political persecution (page 395)

reparations *n.* (reh-puh-RAY-shunz) money paid to the victors by the losing side in a war (page 211)

reparations *n.* (reh-puh-RAY-shunz) the money paid to compensate for damages (page 655)

repatriation *n.* (ree-PAY-tree-ay-shuhn) returning or being returned to the country of one's origin or citizenship (page 327)

reservation *n.* (reh-zur-VAY-shuhn) an area of land designated for and managed by a particular Native American tribe (page 118)

reservoir *n.* (REH-zuh-vwahr) a large, contained body of water that can be tapped (page 110)

robber barons *n.* (RAHB-ur BA-ruhns) railroad industry leaders such as Cornelius Vanderbilt and Jay Gould who became renowned for their ruthless methods against competitors (page 139)

rock and roll *n.* (RAHK AND ROHL) a form of music, derived from rhythm and blues, that became popular in the 1950s (page 509)

rogue state *n.* (ROHG STAYT) a country perceived to violate international law and threaten world peace (page 757)

Rome-Berlin Axis *n.* (ROHM-burh-LIHN ACK-sihs) an agreement formed between Germany and Italy in 1936 (page 391)

rural electrification *n.* (RUR-uhl ih-LEHK-truh-fuh-kay-shuhn) a government program that ran power lines through rural communities (page 469)

Rustbelt *n.* (RUHST-behlt) the area in the northeastern and midwestern United States in which manufacturing has diminished significantly (page 707)

S

safety-net programs *n.* (SAFE-tee neht PRO-grams) a collection of programs provided by the state or federal government designed to prevent people from falling deeper into poverty (page 709)

sanitation *n.* (sa-nuh-TAY-shuhn) measures such as sewers to protect public health (page 168)

scabs *n.* (SKABS) nonunion workers willing to cross strike lines in order to work (page 151)

Schlieffen Plan *n.* (SHLEE-fuhn PLAN) a German plan to make a rapid conquest of France, followed by a march on Russia (page 238)

scientific management *n.* (sy-uhn-TIH-fihk MA-nihj-muhnt) a management method that relies on experimental studies to identify the most efficient way to execute tasks in a factory or other workplace (page 206)

Second New Deal *n.* (SEHK-und NOO DEEL) a second set of New Deal programs, which President Franklin Roosevelt presented to Congress after the 1934 midterm elections (page 358)

secondary sources *n.* (SEK-uhn-dehr-ee SOR-ses) writings, recordings, or objects created after an event by someone who did not see it or live during the time when it occurred (page R38)

sedition *n.* (sih-DIH-shuhn) the criminal act of trying to persuade individuals to undermine the government (page 246)

segregation *n.* (seh-grih-GAY-shuhn) the separation of different groups of people, usually based on race (page 171)

separate but equal *n.* (SEHP-uh-reht BUHT EE-kwuhl) a policy that allowed businesses and institutions to segregate African Americans from whites as long as the facilities or services provided were about equal (page 172)

service sector *n.* (SUR-vuhss SEHK-tur) the part of the economy that provides services rather than goods (page 774)

shaft mining *n.* (SHAFT MY-nihng) mining technique in which a vertical channel is blasted into a mountain and people are lowered down the shaft to mine (page 108)

sharecropper *n.* (SHAIR-krah-pur) a farmer who works a landowner's land and, in exchange for supplies and shelter, turns over most of the crops to the landowner (page 112)

silent majority *n.* (SY-luhnt muh-JOR-uh-tee) a term used by Richard Nixon in the late 1960s to describe a large group of moderate voters who did not publicly express their political opinions (page 677)

sit-down strike *n.* (SIHT DAUN STRYK) a strike in which the workers do not walk out, but rather stay at their place of employment and refuse to do any work (page 367)

sit-in *n.* (SIHT IN) an organized protest where people sit down and refuse to leave (page 551)

situation comedy *n.* (sih-chuh-WAY-shuhn KAH-muh-dee) a weekly series that features a familiar setting and a group of characters who face amusing problems (page 508)

sluice *n.* (SLOOSS) an inclined wooden trough used in mining to strain water from gold (page 108)

smog *n.* (SMAHG) a noxious combination of fog and smoke from factories (page 495)

Social Darwinism *n.* (SOH-shuhl DAHR-wuh-nih-zuhm) nineteenth-century philosophy that argued that human social history could be understood as a struggle between the wealthy and poor, with the strongest and the fittest invariably triumphing (page 139)

social security *n.* (SOH-shuhl sih-KYOOR-ih-tee) a government program that provides income to the elderly, disabled, and unemployed (page 206)

socialism *n.* (SOH-shuh-lih-zuhm) a system of government in which the community or government controls economic resources (page 153)

solitary confinement *n.* (SAHL-it-tar-ee cuhn-FINE-ment) a form of punishment, isolating a prisoner from contact with other people (page 554)

sovereignty *n.* (SAH-vuh-ruhn-tee) freedom from external control (page 262)

space race *n.* (SPAYSS RAYSS) the competition between the United States and the Soviet Union to be the first to travel outside Earth's atmosphere (page 570)

spacewalk *n.* (SPAYSS-wawk) any period of time when an astronaut ventures outside the spacecraft (page 663)

speakeasy *n.* (SPEEK-ee-zee) an illegal drinking club where people secretly gathered in the evenings during Prohibition (page 282)

speculation *n.* (speh-kyuh-LAY-shuhn) taking on a business risk, such as buying stocks on margin even though there is no guarantee that they will increase in value (page 322)

sphere of influence *n.* (SFEER UHV IHN-floo-ents) the claim by a country to exclusive control over a foreign area or territory (page 210)

stagflation *n.* (stag-FLAY-shuhn) an economic condition in which stagnation, or slow economic growth, is accompanied by inflation, or rising prices (page 692)

stalactite *n.* (stuh-LAK-tyt) a column of minerals that hangs from the roof of a cave (page 284)

stalagmite *n.* (stuh-LAG-myt) a column of minerals that form upward from the floor of a cave (page 284)

stalemate *n.* (STAYL-mayt) a situation in which neither side in a conflict can claim victory (page 619)

static *adj.* (stat-IK) something that does not move or change (page 713)

stock market *n.* (STAHK MAHR-kuht) the buying and selling of shares in companies (page 321)

streetcar *n.* (STREET-kahr) a vehicle that runs on rails through city streets and carries passengers (page 167)

subdivision *n.* (SUHB-duh-vih-zhuhn) a tract of land that has been divided into smaller lots on which houses are built (page 503)

subprime mortgage *n.* (SUHB-prym MOR-gihj) home loan issued to buyers with poor credit history (page 762)

subsidiary *n.* (suhb-SIH-dee-ehr-ee) a secondary business (page 145)

subtreasury system *n.* (suhb-TREH-zhuh-ree SIHS-tuhm) a system proposed by which farmers would store their crops in silos until prices rose and the government would lend the farmer money to buy new seeds for the next year's crops (page 114)

suburb *n.* (SUH-burb) a community near or on the outskirts of a city (page 167)

suburban sprawl *n.* (suh-BUR-buhn SPRAWL) the spread of housing developments over more and more suburban and rural land (page 505)

suburbanization *n.* (suh-bur-buh-nuh-ZAY-shuhn) a population shift from cities to outlying communities (page 502)

subversion *n.* (suhb-VUR-zhuhn) an act of destabilizing a major social or political system in an attempt to destroy it (page 480)

suffragist *n.* (SUH-frih-jihst) a person who supports women's right to vote (page 191)

Sunbelt *n.* (SUHN-behlt) the southern and southwestern region of the United States, which have mild winters (page 495)

supply-side economics *n.* (suh-PLY SYD eh-kuh-NAH-mihks) a financial theory in which tax rates are lowered for businesses and investors in the hope of boosting production and trade in the country (page 710)

surge *n.* (SURJ) a sudden increase (page 759)

swing state *n.* (SWING STAYT) a U.S. state in which both a Democratic and a Republican presidential candidate have a strong chance of being elected to office; especially when the state plays an important part in the outcome of the election (page 780)

syndicate *n.* (SIHN-dih-kuht) a group of criminals who control organized criminal activities (page 204)

T

tank *n.* (TANGK) an armored, heavily armed vehicle that uses treads instead of wheels (page 248)

task force *n.* (TASK FORSS) group of people organized for a special mission (page 743)

telegraph *n.* (TEHL-uh-graf) a device that transmits messages along connected wires, to communicate over long distances (page 144)

temperance movement *n.* (TEHM-pur-uhns MOOV-mehnt) a social and political movement in the 1800s and early 1900s that encouraged people to limit their consumption of alcohol or to abstain from alcohol altogether (page 193)

tenant farming *n.* (TEH-nuhnt FAHR-mihng) a system in which farmland is rented from a property owner (page 112)

tenement *n.* (TEH-nuh-muhnt) a large building that rents rooms and apartments, and which is usually overcrowded and badly maintained (page 160)

termination policy *n.* (tur-muh-NAY-shuhn PAH-luh-see) a policy enacted under President Eisenhower that removed Native Americans from reservations, while the government ended the limited sovereignty of individual tribes and nations (page 518)

terrorism *n.* (TEHR-ur-ih-zuhm) the use of violent acts and threats to achieve a political goal (page 756)

theocracy *n.* (thee-AH-kruh-see) a government ruled by a religious leader or religious leaders (page 729)

think tank *n.* (THIHNK TAYNK) a group of experts who conduct research and discuss issues in order to craft potential solutions to social and economic problems (page 705)

Third Reich *n.* (THURD RYK) name used by the Nazi party to describe the time when Adolph Hitler believed he was creating a third German empire (page 390)

third world *adj.* (THURD WURLD) during the Cold War, a country that was not aligned with either the United States or the Soviet Union (page 605)

totalitarian *adj.* (toh-ta-luh-TAIR-ee-uhn) relating to a government that is headed by a dictator and requires complete obedience to the state (page 360)

trading pool *n.* (TRAYD-ihng POOL) groups formed to buy and sell large amounts of stocks (page 324)

transistor *n.* (tran-ZIHS-tur) an electronic device used to control the flow of electricity in electronic equipment (page 501)

Treaty of Versailles *n.* (TREE-tee UHV vur-SY) the treaty that officially brought World War I to a close (page 262)

trench warfare *n.* (TREHNCH WOR-fair) a type of warfare in which long ditches dug deep in the ground provided protection for soldiers (page 239)

tribunal *n.* (try-BYOO-nuhl) a court of justice with authority over a specific matter (page 455)

trust *n.* (TRUHST) a company managed by members of a board rather than by owners or stockholders (page 141)

trustbuster *n.* (TRUHST-buhst-ur) a person who seeks to break up business trusts, or monopolies, especially a federal official who enforces antitrust laws (page 200)

U

U-boat *n.* (YOO BOHT) a German submarine (page 242)

underwrite *v.* (UHN-dur-ryt) to take on the financial responsibilities—including the risks—of a set of assets (page 334)

urban renewal *n.* (UR-buhn rih-NOO-uhl) a program that involves clearing slums and replacing them with large, publicly funded housing projects (page 514)

V

vaudeville *n.* (VOD-vihl) theatrical show that involved singing and dancing acts (page 166)

vertical integration *n.* (VUR-tih-kuhl ihn-tuh-GRAY-shuhn) a procedure in which a company takes control of all phases of production from start to finish (page 139)

Vietnamization *n.* (vee-eht-nuh-muh-ZAY-shun) a military strategy that allowed for the gradual replacement of U.S. troops with South Vietnamese troops during the Vietnam War (page 624)

voter fraud *n.* (VOH-tur FRAWD) illegal manipulation of ballots to help win an election (page 565)

voter registration drive *n.* (VOH-tur reh-juh-STRAY-shuhn DRYV) an effort by groups or government to sign up as many eligible voters in a targeted area as possible (page 558)

voting bloc *n.* (VOHT-ihng BLOK) a large group of citizens who share a common concern and tend to vote the same in elections (page 372)

W

wage discrimination *n.* (WAYJ dihs-krih-muh-NAY-shuhn) receiving lower pay for the same job based on gender, race, or ethnicity (page 426)

war bond *n.* (WOR BAHND) a debt security issued by the government to help finance military expenses during wartime (page 422)

War Industries Board (WIB) *n.* (WOR IHN-duh-streez BAWRD) a board that oversaw manufacturing in the United States during World War I (page 244)

war of attrition *n.* (WOR UHV uh-TRIH-shun) a military strategy in which an army wears another down by conducting many small battles over a long period of time (page 611)

Watergate break-in *n.* (WAH-tur-gayt BRAYK IHN) a break-in at the Democratic National Headquarters in the Watergate complex in Washington, D.C., in 1972 by burglars associated with President Richard Nixon's re-election committee (page 689)

weapons of mass destruction (WMD) *n.* (WEH-puhnz UHV MAS dih-STRUHK-shuhn) weapons that use nuclear, chemical, or biological substances to harm large numbers of people (page 757)

welfare capitalism *n.* (WEHL-fair KA-puh-tuh-lih-zuhm) a business practice in which companies offer workers extra benefits, including recreational facilities, benefit plans, and profit-sharing opportunities (page 289)

welfare state *n.* (WEHL-fair STAYT) a system in which the government provides for the health and well-being of its citizens (page 378)

white-collar *adj.* (HWYT-KAH-lur) relating to the class of people whose jobs typically take place in an office or professional environment and don't involve manual labor (page 469)

wiretapping *v.* (WY-urh-tap-ihng) placing a device on a telephone in order to secretly listen to conversations (page 690)

women's suffrage *n.* (WIH-muhnz SUH-frihj) the right of women to vote (page 190)

workers' compensation *n.* (WUR-kurz kahm-puhn-SAY-shuhn) insurance for employees injured while on the job, providing assistance for medical care and loss of income (page 149)

Y

yellow journalism *n.* (YEH-loh JUR-nuh-lih-zuhm) a type of journalism that stresses sensationalism over facts (page 213)

Z

Zimmermann Telegram *n.* (ZIH-mur-muhn TEH-luh-gram) secret German telegram sent to the German ambassador in Mexico laying out a plan to ally with Mexico (page 243)

ACADEMIC VOCABULARY

acquiesce *v.* (a-kwee-EHS) to agree, especially after an argument (page 655)
affluence *n.* (A-floo-ehns) wealth, prosperity (page 498)
agitator *n.* (A-juh-TAY-tuhr) someone who stirs up anger and rebellion (page 122)
allocate *v.* (A-luh-kayt) to give out, to distribute (page 678)
amenity *n.* (uh-MEH-nih-tee) a benefit that promotes comfort and ease of use or lifestyle (page 152)

blacklist *v.* (BLAK-lihst) to put one or more people on a list indicating they are to be shunned or punished (page 479)
blasphemous *adj.* (BLAS-fuh-muhs) ungodly, sacrilegious (page 705)

depository *n.* (dih-PAH-suh-tor-ee) a warehouse; a place where items are stored (page 575)
disproportionate *adj.* (dihs-pruh-POR-shuh-nuht) unequal, unbalanced, usually weighed to the larger part (page 745)
diversify *v.* (dih-VUR-sih-fy) to expand one's options (page 113)

effigy *n.* (EH-fuh-jee) a dummy representing a person, particularly a famous person (often a politician) who is hated or reviled (page 476)
eke *v.* (eek) to obtain with great effort (page 108)
eradicate *v.* (ih-RA-duh-kayt) to wipe out, to destroy utterly (page 198)
erratic *adj.* (ih-RA-tihk) unpredictable, inconsistent (page 480)
exorbitant *adj.* (ihg-ZOR-buh-tuhnt) excessive, overpriced (page 108)
expedient *adj.* (ehk-SPEE-dee-uhnt) convenient, practical (page 651)
extortion *n.* (ecks-TOR-shuhn) the act of obtaining something—usually money or information—through forceful coercion; blackmail (page 595)

frugality *n* (froo-GA-luh-tee) thriftiness (page 289)

ghetto *n.* (GEH-toh) a section of a city in which certain groups, usually Jews, were required to live; more recently, a section of a city where certain minority groups live, usually due to poverty (page 450)

herbicide *n.* (UR-buh-syd) a chemical substance used to kill plants (page 613)
homogenous *adj.* (hoh-MAH-juh-nuhs) uniform, equal, consistent, standardized (page 511)
hostage *n.* (HAH-stihj) someone who is held prisoner to force another party to follow the demands of those who hold him or her (page 699)

illicit *adj.* (ih-LIH-suht) illegal, unlawful (page 291)
immolate *v.* (IH-muh-layt) to destroy by setting on fire (page 607)
inception *n* (ihn-SEHP-shuhn) the act of beginning (page 301)
incorporate *v.* (ihn-COR-puh-rayt) to blend, to unite (page 541)
influx *n.* (IHN-fluhks) an arrival, an entry (as of immigrants) (page 154)
insubordination *n.* (ihn-suh-bor-dih-NAY-shuhn) disobedience, rebelliousness (page 204)
interventionist *n.* (ihn-tur-VEHN-shuh-nishst) someone who supports getting involved, as in a war (page 398)
invincible *adj.* (ihn-VIHN-suh-buhl) impossible to conquer, indestructible (page 193)

laudable *adj.* (LAW-duh-buhl) praiseworthy (page 294)
lease *v.* (lees) to either sign or provide a contract that gives rights to land or facilities for a certain amount of time at an agreed upon rent (page 215)
lucrative *adj.* (LOO-kruh-tihv) profitable, well-paid (page 495)

mystique *n.* (mih-STEEK) an air of mystery, or the unknown, that surrounds a person, thing, or idea (page 657)

normalcy *n.* (NOR-muhl-see) a condition or situation that is typical, usual, or expected, such as the general social, political, and economic conditions of a nation (page 265)
notorious *adj.* (noh-TOR-ee-uhs) famous for having a bad reputation, dishonorable (page 282)
noxious *adj.* (NAHK-zhuhs) foul, offensive, digusting (page 168)

obstruction *n.* (uhb-STRUHK-shuhn) something that blocks a path or an action (page 691)
oratorical *adj.* (or-uh-TOR-ih-kuhl) having to do with speechmaking (page 544)

philanthropic *adj.* (fih-lahn-THRAW-pihk) charitable (page 141)
pluralism *n.* (PLUR-uh-lih-zuhm) the coexistence of different cultural groups within a single larger civilization (page 154)
pragmatism *n.* (PRAG-muh-tihzm) practicality, rationality (page 352)
pre-emptive *adj.* (pree-EHMP-tihv) preventive, defensive (page 757)
privatize *v.* (PRY-vuh-tyz) to transfer from public to private control (page 747)
proponent *n.* (pruh-POH-nuhnt) supporter, advocate (page 115)
protagonist *n.* (proh-TA-guh-nihst) the main character of a work of fiction (page 127)

quota *n.* (KWOH-tuh) a proportional amount, percentage, or share, often in reference to proportion of members of minority or gender groups allotted for a particular benefit (page 327)

redress *n.* (rih-DREHS) compensation for wrongdoing (page 431)
relinquish *v.* (ree-LIHNG-kwihsh) to give up, to surrender (page 546)
renounce *v.* (rih-NOWNTS) to reject, to give up (page 321)
repressive *adj.* (rih-PREH-sihv) oppressive, brutally authoritarian (page 715)

scurrilous *adj.* (SKUR-uh-luhs) insulting, slanderous, scandalous (page 246)
solidarity *n.* (saw-luh-DAIR-uh-tee) unity of purpose (page 153)
subjugation *n.* (suhb-jih-GAY-shuhn) the act of bringing a group of people under control by force (page 467)
subpoena *n.* (suh-PEE-nuh) a legal demand to appear before a court, judge, or government committee (page 479)

unanimous *adj.* (yoo-NA-nuh-muhs) undisputed, with all votes the same (page 543)

warlord *n.* (WOR-lord) a local military leader who holds great power in his limited region (page 400)

GLOSARIO

A

activismo comunitario *s.* movimiento políticos impulsados por personas que individualmente no tienen mucho poder, pero que trabajando juntos logran obtener resultados (página 538)

Acuerdos de Múnich *s.* acuerdos que realizó Hitler con los gobernantes de Gran Bretaña, Francia e Italia, declarando que Alemania tenía el derecho de apoderarse de los Sudetes, que formaba parte de Checoslovaquia (página 397)

acuífero *s.* formación geológica debajo de la superficie de la tierra que puede albergar un gran depósito de agua subterránea (página 110)

adjudicación *s.* lote de tierra entregado a un indígena para su cultivo (página 122)

Agente Naranja *s.* herbicida potente usado para matar la vegetación (página 613)

agroindustria *s.* el negocio comercial de la agricultura (página 495)

aislacionismo *s.* política en la cual una nación permanece fuera de los asuntos de otras naciones (página 208)

Aliados *s.* varios países, entre ellos Francia y gran Bretaña, que lucharon juntos para oponerse a las Potencias del Eje de Alemania, Italia y Japón (página 391)

alianza *s.* acuerdo de apoyo mutuo entre dos o más países (página 236)

alimentos genéticamente modificados *s.* alimentos producidos a partir de plantas que han sido modificadas de una manera que no ocurre naturalmente (página 775)

allanamiento de Watergate *s.* allanamiento en la sede nacional del Partido Demócrata dentro del complejo de Watergate en Washington, D.C., en 1972 por ladrones asociados con el comité para la reelección del presidente Richard Nixon (página 689)

amarillismo *s.* tipo de periodismo que hace hincapié en el sensacionalismo en lugar de los hechos (página 213)

Amenaza Roja *s.* período en 1919 y 1920 en el que el gobierno federal acosó a presuntos comunistas, anarquistas y radicales (página 278)

americanización *s.* proceso de inmersión dirigido hacia los inmigrantes para que aprendieran lo que algunos definen como la cultura estadounidense y así transformarlos en "verdaderos" estadounidenses (página 154)

ametralladora *s.* pistola diseñada para disparar cientos de balas por minuto (página 248)

anarquía *s.* concepto que postula que los gobiernos no son necesarios y que toda la cooperación social y política debe ser voluntaria (página 151)

anexar *v.* tomar posesión de un territorio o país (página 209)

anticonceptivo *s.* medio o manera de prevenir el embarazo (página 658)

antisemitismo *s.* discriminación, prejuicio y hostilidad contra el pueblo judío (página 160)

apaciguamiento *s.* política de hacer compromisos para evitar conflictos (página 397)

aparcero *s.* agricultor que trabaja la tierra de un terrateniente y, a cambio de provisiones y refugio, entrega la mayor parte de sus cultivos al terrateniente (página 112)

aparecería *s.* sistema en el que las tierras de cultivo se alquilan a un propietario (página 112)

apartheid *s.* separación legal entre las razas en Sudáfrica (página 715)

aplazamiento *s.* permiso oficial para demorar el reclutamiento (página 616)

archipiélago *s.* conjunto de islas (página 208)

armas de destrucción masiva (ADM) *s.* armas que usan material nuclear, químico o biológico para causar un inmenso daño a un gran número de personas (página 757)

arsenal *s.* lugar donde se almacenan armas y otros equipos militares (página 404)

artefacto *s.* artículo hecho por un ser humano que tiene un significado histórico o cultural (página 90)

artículo investigativo *s.* escrito que revela un escándalo o una injusticia (página 189)

artillería antiaérea *s.* arma pesada modificada para poder ser dirigida hacia el cielo y disparar contra aviones enemigos (página 248)

asegurar *v.* asumir las responsabilidades financieras, incluidos los riesgos, de un conjunto de activos (página 334)

asimilar *v.* asumir las cualidades de otra cultura, así como su modo de vida (página 160)

B

baluarte *s.* algo que proporciona protección o defensa (página 497)

banco de inversión *s.* institución financiera que compra y vende acciones y bonos y ayuda a las empresas a recaudar capital y administrar sus activos (página 762)

bar clandestino *s.* club ilegal de bebedores en el que la gente se reunía secretamente por las tardes durante la Prohibición (página 282)

beligerante *s.* país que está en guerra (página 404)

bimetalismo *s.* sistema monetario que permitiría a los ciudadanos acuñar monedas estadounidenses a partir de la plata que poseían (página 115)

bipartidista *adj.* relativo a ambas partes en un sistema de dos partidos políticos (página 585)

bloque electoral *s.* grupo grande de ciudadanos que comparten ideologías y tienden a votar por igual en las elecciones (página 372)

bloqueo naval *s.* bloqueo impuesto a los puertos de otro país (página 572)

boicot de autobuses de Montgomery *s.* protesta masiva, provocada por el arresto de Rosa Parks, en contra de las prácticas de segregación racial del sistema de autobuses públicos en Montgomery, Alabama (página 547)

bomba atómica *s.* tipo de bomba nuclear cuya explosión violenta es desencadenada por la fisión de átomos, lo cual libera calor intenso y radiactividad (página 446)

bomba de hidrógeno *s.* una arma nuclear que explota debido a los gases compactados dentro (página 471)

bono de guerra *s.* título de deuda emitido por el gobierno para ayudar a financiar los gastos militares durante una guerra (página 422)

Bono *Liberty* *s.* bono del gobierno vendido a ciudadanos para ayudar a apoyar la participación de los Estados Unidos en la Primera Guerra Mundial (página 244)

Brain Trust *s.* grupo de expertos que asesoró al presidente Franklin Roosevelt durante la Gran Depresión (página 352)

brecha de credibilidad *s.* creciente escepticismo de los estadounidenses acerca de los informes gubernamentales sobre la guerra de Vietnam (página 615)

C

cacicazgo *s.* comunidad grande de personas gobernadas por un cacique o jefe indígena (página xxxiv)

callejón sin salida *s.* situación en la que no es posible progresar (página 621)

caminata espacial *s.* cualquier período de tiempo en el que un astronauta sale de la nave espacial (página 663)

campaña de registro electoral *s.* esfuerzo realizado por grupos independientes o por el gobierno para inscribir la mayor cantidad posible de votantes en un área determinada (página 558)

campo de concentración *s.* lugar donde se encuentran confinados prisioneros de guerra o miembros de minorías perseguidas; en la Segunda Guerra Mundial , los campos donde judíos y otros fueron detenidos y asesinados por los nazis (página 450)

campo de internamiento *s.* campo de prisioneros para detener a extranjeros enemigos y otros prisioneros de guerra durante la guerra (página 431)

capitalismo *s.* sistema económico en el que los individuos o grupos privados son dueños de los recursos y producen bienes con fines de lucro (página 278)

capitalismo benefactor *s.* práctica empresarial en la que las empresas ofrecen a los trabajadores beneficios adicionales, incluyendo instalaciones recreativas, cobertura médica y oportunidades de participación en las ganancias (página 289)

carga de profundidad *s.* bomba submarina que está programada para explotar a cierta profundidad (página 435)

carrera de armamentos *s.* situación política en la que países rivales tratan de acumular o producir la mayor cantidad de armas militares (página 470)

GLOSARIO

carrera espacial *s.* competencia entre los Estados Unidos y la Unión Soviética para ser el primero en realizar un viaje fuera de la atmósfera terrestre (página 570)

Carta del Atlántico *s.* carta que enumera ocho principios para lograr un mundo mejor, compuesta durante una reunión entre el presidente Franklin Roosevelt y el primer ministro británico Winston Churchill (página 406)

casa de vecindad *s.* edificio grande que alquila habitaciones y apartamentos, y que suele estar abarrotado y mal mantenido (página 160)

Catorce Puntos *s.* programa propuesto por el presidente Woodrow Wilson para establecer la paz al final de la Primera Guerra Mundial (página 259)

cazador y recolector *s.* ser humano que caza animales y recolecta plantas silvestres para alimentarse (página xxxiii)

cédula real *s.* documento que establece el objetivo principal de un proyecto (página 651)

coalición *s.* alianza de personas, partidos o estados centrada en un objetivo común (página 361)

colega *s.* persona de la misma edad, rango o estatus social que otra (página 642)

coludir *v.* conspirar o armar un complot para hacer daño a otros (página 781)

combativo *adj.* extremadamente agresivo en la búsqueda de un objetivo (página 652)

cometer magnicidio *v.* asesinar por razones políticas (página 236)

Comité de Información Pública (CPI) *s.* comité establecido durante la Primera Guerra Mundial para contrarrestar la posible disensión y estimular el entusiasmo del país por la guerra (página 246)

comité de vigilancia *s.* grupo de hombres armados reunidos para capturar a un proscrito (página 126)

complejo industrial-militar *s.* dirigencia militar de un país y las industrias que producen armas u otros materiales bélicos (página 471)

composición demográfica *s.* composición de la población de un área específica basada en la etnicidad (página 591)

computadora personal *s.* dispositivo electrónico que procesa datos y está específicamente diseñado para el uso doméstico (página 716)

comunismo *s.* forma de gobierno en la que todos los medios de producción y transporte son propiedad del estado (página 261)

confinamiento solitario *s.* forma de castigo en la que se aísla a un prisionero del contacto con otras personas (página 554)

consenso liberal *s.* acuerdo entre demócratas y republicanos en el Congreso, pactado después de la Segunda Guerra Mundial, para continuar las prestaciones sociales, desarrollar un sistema de seguridad nacional y fortalecer el poder ejecutivo (página 468)

conservador *s.* miembro de un partido político que cree en los valores tradicionales, la estructura social y el cambio gradual en las políticas (página 704)

conservadurismo compasivo *s.* filosofía política que combinaba las ideas conservadoras tradicionales sobre las políticas económicas con una preocupación por las personas desfavorecidas (página 752)

consumismo *s.* teoría que sostiene que la economía florece cuando la gente compra o consume muchos bienes y servicios (página 495)

contención *s.* política de seguridad estadounidense durante la Guerra Fría en la que se utilizó la acción militar para impedir que la unión soviética propagara el comunismo (página 463)

contención nuclear *s.* estrategia de usar las armas nucleares como amenaza para evitar un ataque enemigo (página 496)

contexto *s.* las circunstancias y el entorno en el que se encuentra un objeto que ayudan a comprender cómo se utiliza un objeto (página 90)

contrabandista *s.* individuo que fabricaba, transportaba o suministraba alcohol ilegalmente a tabernas o "bares clandestinos" donde los habitantes se congregaban por las tardes (página 282)

contracultura *s.* movimiento de los años sesenta que promovió un modo de vida que estaba en oposición a las reglas y el comportamiento establecidos por la sociedad estadounidense (página 622)

contrato colectivo *s.* negociación entre un empleador y un sindicato

conversación junto a la chimenea *s.* serie de emisiones de radio que el presidente Franklin Roosevelt hizo a la nación durante su presidencia (página 352)

cooperativa *s.* organización dirigida y financiada por sus miembros (página 114)

corporación *s.* empresas o grupos de personas que invierten en un negocio y luego comparten sus beneficios (página 139)

cortina de hierro *s.* división militar y política en Europa entre los países capitalistas occidentales y los países comunistas orientales (página 463)

crematorio horno utilizado para quemar restos humanos o animales; en la Segunda Guerra Mundial , los hornos utilizados por los nazis para quemar los cuerpos de sus víctimas (página 453)

Crisis de los Misiles en Cuba *s.* enfrentamiento político de 1962 entre los Estados Unidos y la Unión Soviética causado por la presencia de armas nucleares en Cuba (página 572)

cuartel *s.* edificio militar utilizado para alojar a los soldados (página 714)

cuerpo especial *s.* grupo de personas organizadas para una misión especial (página 743)

cultivo en secano *s.* conjunto de técnicas agrícolas utilizadas en zonas con escasa precipitación (página 107)

D

Danza de los Espíritus *s.* danza ceremonial realizada por algunos indígenas con la esperanza de que esta convocaría a un libertador que restauraría su mundo (página 122)

darwinismo social *s.* filosofía del siglo XIX que sostenía que la historia social humana podía entenderse como una lucha entre los ricos y los pobres, con los más fuertes y los más aptos invariablemente triunfando (página 139)

DDT *s.* insecticida, actualmente prohibido en los Estados Unidos y muchos otros países, que resultó ser perjudicial para los animales y causar contaminación a largo plazo del medio ambiente (página 682)

de cuello blanco *adj.* relacionado con la clase de personas cuyos trabajos suelen tener lugar en una oficina o entorno profesional y no implican trabajo manual (página 469)

declaración de guerra *s.* anuncio formal hecho por el líder de un país sobre la intención de este de librar una guerra (página 243)

defensa activa *s.* política que permite a los buques de guerra de los Estados Unidos defenderse contra los ataques de submarinos alemanes sobre buques en tránsito dentro del océano Atlántico (página 407)

déficit *s.* saldo monetario negativo que ocurre cuando los gastos exceden los ingresos (página 352)

deflación *s.* disminución en los precios de bienes y servicios (página 149)

delegado *s.* persona que representa a su estado en una convención política (página 621)

deportar *v.* expulsar por la fuerza del país, o presionar para que esto se haga (página 327)

depresión *s.* deterioro económico severo y a largo plazo, caracterizado por una serie de fracasos empresariales, reducción de la producción industrial y elevado desempleo (página 139)

derechos civiles *s.* derechos individuales protegidos por la ley contra el abuso gubernamental (página 246)

derechos de propiedad *s.* posesión legal de una propiedad y la autoridad para determinar cómo se usa (página 685)

desagravio *s.* dinero pagado para compensar por daños hechos (página 655)

desapoderar *v.* privar a una persona de un derecho legal (página 587)

desegregación *s.* proceso mediante el cual se pone fin a una política que obliga a la separación de grupos de personas en espacios públicos (página 543)

deshumanizar *v.* tratar a las personas como si no fueran seres humanos (página 541)

desigualdad económica *s.* fenómeno económico en el que existe una gran brecha entre lo que ganan los ciudadanos más pobres y los más ricos de una nación (página 711)

desintegración *s.* resistencia por parte de alternativas nacionalistas, tribales y separatistas a la globalización (página 747)

desmovilización *s.* liberación de soldados del servicio militar (página 427)

desobediencia civil *s.* desobediencia no violenta de las leyes como forma de protesta (página 547)

desplazamiento urbano *s.* desplazamiento de la población de las ciudades a las comunidades periféricas (página 502)

desregulación *s.* acto de derogar a gran escala algunas leyes, generalmente relacionadas con una industria en particular (página 711)

destino manifiesto *s.* creencia de que era el destino de los estadounidenses colonizar toda la tierra entre las costas atlántica y pacífica (página 106)

Día-D *s.* 6 de junio de 1944, día en el que los Aliados invadieron el norte de Francia durante la Segunda Guerra Mundial, desembarcando en las playas de Normandía (página 440)

diplomacia moral *s.* concepto de que los Estados Unidos debería reducir drásticamente su intervención en los asuntos de otros países (página 240)

discriminación positiva *s.* política gubernamental que instituye cuotas raciales para favorecer a los grupos que sufren discriminación (página 597)

discriminación salarial *s.* ganar un sueldo más bajo por el mismo trabajo debido al género, la raza o el origen étnico (página 426)

discriminación sexual *s.* preferencia por un género sobre otro (página 658)

disidencia *s.* desacuerdo con la opinión oficial del gobierno (página 246)

dislocación de empleo *s.* movimiento de los trabajos a otros lugares (página 746)

distensión alivio de tensiones y mejoría en las relaciones entre países (página 681)

domesticación *s.* práctica de criar animales y cultivar plantas para el beneficio humano (página xxxiv)

domesticidad *s.* vida hogareña (página 498)

Dust Bowl *s.* áreas de Kansas, Colorado, Oklahoma, Texas y Nuevo México que, durante la década de 1930, sufrieron devastación ecológica y se convirtieron en un desierto árido (página 331)

E

ecologismo *s.* gestión y protección de los recursos naturales (página 198)

economía de la oferta *s.* teoría financiera en la que las tasas de impuestos se reducen para las empresas y los inversionistas con la esperanza de impulsar la producción y el comercio en el país (página 710)

economía *laissez-faire* *s.* política que exige menos participación del gobierno en los asuntos económicos, para que las empresas escojan cómo operar, con poca o ninguna supervisión (página 149)

efecto invernadero *s.* calentamiento de la superficie de la Tierra que ocurre cuando las emisiones de gases de efecto invernadero atrapan el calor del Sol (página 772)

Eje Roma-Berlín *s.* acuerdo entre Alemania e Italia firmado en 1936 (página 391)

ejecución hipotecaria *s.* acción que realiza un banco para tomar posesión de una propiedad porque el comprador ya no puede hacer los pagos de la hipoteca (página 762)

Ejército del Bono *s.* grupo de miles de veteranos de guerra, decididos a cobrar los bonos en efectivo que les habían sido prometidos, que acudieron a Washington, D.C., durante el verano de 1932 para escuchar el debate del Congreso sobre la propuesta de bonificación (página 337)

elección primaria directa *s.* elección preliminar en la cual los votantes eligen a los candidatos de su partido que luego se postularán a elecciones para cargos públicos (página 197)

electorado *s.* grupo de ciudadanos que ha elegido o tiene derecho a elegir un representante para el gobierno (página 299)

electrificación rural *s.* programa gubernamental que trajo electricidad a las comunidades rurales (página 469)

embalse *s.* gran cuerpo de agua que puede ser aprovechada (página 110)

embargo *s.* prohibición de comerciar con determinados países (página 403)

empoderamiento *s.* concesión de derechos de ciudadanía, especialmente del derecho al voto (página 191)

empresa matriz *s.* empresa que controla la totalidad o parte de otras empresas más pequeñas (página 145)

encubrimiento *s.* intento de esconder la verdad del público (página 690)

energía nuclear *s.* energía que se crea dividiendo o fusionando los núcleos de átomos (página 501)

era glacial *s.* período de tiempo en la historia durante el cual enormes capas de hielo cubrieron gran parte de la Tierra (página xxxi)

Era Progresista *s.* período de 1890 a 1920 en el que los reformadores trataron de corregir muchas desigualdades e injusticias sociales, económicas y políticas en los Estados Unidos (página 188)

escasez planificada *s.* teoría económica de que bajar la oferta de un producto aumentará su demanda y por lo tanto su precio (página 354)

esfera de influencia *s.* afirmación de un país al control exclusivo de una zona o territorio extranjero (página 210)

esmog *s.* combinación nociva de niebla y humo de fábricas (página 495)

especulación *s.* asumir un riesgo empresarial, como comprar acciones con reserva, sin garantía de que aumenten en valor (página 322)

espionaje *s.* la actividad de espiar (página 241)

estado benefactor *s.* sistema en el que el gobierno proporciona los servicios de salud y beneficios a sus ciudadanos (página 378)

estado clave *s.* un estado de los Estados Unidos en el cual tanto un candidato demócrata como un candidato republicano tienen altas posibilidades de ganar la elección, especialmente cuando el estado juega un rol importante en el resultado de las elecciones (página 780)

estado paria *s.* país percibido como violador del derecho internacional y que amenaza la paz mundial (página 757)

estalactita *s.* columna de minerales que cuelga del techo de una cueva (página 284)

estalagmita *s.* columna de minerales que se forma hacia arriba desde el suelo de una cueva (página 284)

estancamiento económico *s.* período de poco o ningún crecimiento económico (página 692)

estanflación *s.* condición económica con estancamiento, o crecimiento económico lento, acompañado de inflación, o aumento de los precios (página 692)

estático *adj.* que no se mueve ni cambia (página 713)

estímulo económico *s.* medida destinada a promover y permitir la recuperación y el crecimiento financieros (página 765)

eugenesia *s.* creencia de que algunas razas son superiores a otras y que la reproducción humana debe ser controlada para que aumenten las poblaciones de razas superiores (página 280)

evangelizador *s.* persona cuya religión requiere que reclute a más creyentes (página 705)

exceso de regulación *s.* conjunto de reglas excesivas (página 685)

exoduster *s.* afroamericano que emigró del Sur a las Grandes Llanuras después de que la Reconstrucción había fracasado (página 106)

expansión suburbana *s.* expansión de las urbanizaciones sobre un número cada vez mayor de terrenos rurales y suburbanos (página 505)

expansionismo *s.* política o práctica de ampliar el territorio de un país (página 208)

explosión de natalidad *s.* aumento significativo en la tasa de natalidad (página 498)

extranjero enemigo *adj.* persona cuya lealtad a la nación en la que vive es poco fiable (página 430)

F

factor de expulsión o atracción *s.* razón por la cual las personas emigran; los factores de "expulsión" hacen que se vayan; los factores de "atracción" hacen que vayan hacia un lugar (página 154)

fascismo *s.* movimiento político basado en el nacionalismo extremo, el militarismo y el racismo, que promueve la superioridad de un pueblo en particular sobre todos los demás (página 335)

feminismo *s.* principio de que las mujeres son iguales a los hombres social y políticamente (página 657)

feriado bancario *s.* día o período de tiempo en el que los bancos están cerrados por orden del gobierno (página 352)

flapper *s.* mujer joven en la década de 1920 que adoptó un estilo más libre de vestir y el uso de cosméticos (página 296)

GLOSARIO

fondo de pensiones *s.* reserva de dinero usada para pagar a una persona un pequeño ingreso establecido después de jubilarse (página 358)

fonógrafo *s.* máquina que reproduce sonidos de un disco (página 145)

forrajear *v.* buscar plantas para comer (página 118)

fraude electoral *s.* manipulación ilegal de boletas para ganar una elección (página 565)

Freedom Riders *s.* grupos interraciales que viajaban en autobuses por el Sur, haciendo caso omiso a las leyes de segregación cuando usaban los baños públicos y los cafés, para así asegurar que las decisiones judiciales federales que habían establecido como ilegal la segregación en lugares de atención públicos para viajeros fuesen cumplidas por los funcionarios blancos (página 553)

frente *s.* línea de batalla entre dos ejércitos (página 239)

Frostbelt *s.* región del centro-norte y noreste de los Estados Unidos, que tiene inviernos fríos (página 495)

fuentes primarias *s.* grabaciones o escritos creados por alguien que fue testigo de o vivió un evento histórico (página r38)

fuentes secundarias escritos, grabaciones u objetos creados después de un evento por alguien que no lo vio o vivió en el momento en que ocurrió (página r38)

Fuerzas Expedicionarias Estadounidenses (AEF) *s.* cuerpo de soldados estadounidenses enviados a luchar en Europa durante la Primera Guerra Mundial (página 244)

fundamentalismo *s.* movimiento que promulgó la idea de que cada palabra de la Biblia debía ser tomada literalmente (página 283)

fusión *s.* acto de incorporar dos o más negocios en uno (página 199)

G

G.I. Bill *s.* programa del gobierno iniciado en 1944 que ayudó a los veteranos que regresaban de la Segunda Guerra Mundial a comprar casas y asistir a la universidad (página 469)

gas de efecto invernadero *s.* gas como el dióxido de carbono o metano (página 772)

gastar públicamente déficit *v.* gastar más dinero del que el gobierno recibe por impuestos (página 378)

genocidio *s.* asesinato intencional de un gran número de personas pertenecientes a determinado grupo racial, cultural o político (página 121)

Gestapo *s.* policía secreta nazi (página 390)

glasnost *s.* política gubernamental de comunicación abierta en la ex Unión Soviética (página 720)

globalización *s.* flujo más rápido y libre de personas, recursos, bienes e ideas a lo largo de las fronteras entre países (página 746)

gobierno en exilio *s.* gobierno que ha sido depuesto e intenta gobernar desde otro país (página 472)

gobierno por comisión *s.* forma de gobierno citadino en la que los votantes eligen un pequeño número de funcionarios llamados comisionados, cada uno de los cuales dirige un departamento de la ciudad (página 196)

golpe *s.* derrocamiento ilegal del gobierno (página 607)

Gran Depresión *s.* recesión económica mundial en la década de 1930, marcada por la pobreza y el alto desempleo (página 323)

Gran Migración *s.* movimiento masivo de afroamericanos que se fueron del Sur para las ciudades del norte, comenzando en 1910 (página 255)

gravamen *s.* reclamación legal sobre los bienes e ingresos de una persona si no se pagan deudas (página 112)

grupo de comercio *s.* grupo formado para comprar y vender grandes cantidades de acciones (página 324)

guerra de desgaste *s.* una estrategia militar en la que un ejército lleva a otro abajo conduciendo muchas pequeñas batallas durante un largo período de tiempo (página 611)

guerra de guerrillas *s.* guerra en la que pequeños grupos móviles de fuerzas anómalas usan tácticas de ataque y huida para luchar contra fuerzas militares convencionales (página 217)

guerra de trincheras *s.* tipo de guerra en la que se excavan largas y profundas zanjas en el suelo para proteger a los soldados (página 239)

guerra subsidiaria *s.* conjunto de batallas provocadas por una nación que luego no participa en la lucha (página 474)

H

halcón *s.* persona que apoya la guerra (página 616)

hipotecas de alto riesgo *s.* préstamos hipotecarios otorgados a compradores que tenían un historial de crédito pobre (página 762)

historia oral *s.* entrevista grabada con una persona cuyas experiencias y recuerdos tienen significado histórico (página r38)

hito legislativo *s.* legislación importante e histórica (página 593)

Holocausto *s.* matanza en masa de seis millones de judíos y otros pueblos por parte de los nazis durante la Segunda Guerra Mundial (página 453)

hombre de paja *s.* funcionario electo que está por finalizar su mandado y será reemplazado por un sucesor (página 351)

homogeneidad *s.* estado de similitud o igualdad (página 503)

Hooverville *s.* aldeas improvisadas, construidas para los estadounidenses sin techo, por lo general en la afueras de las ciudades, que albergaban refugios hechos de cartón, chatarra y otros materiales baratos (página 334)

huelga de brazos caídos *s.* huelga en la que los trabajadores no se van del lugar trabajo, sino que permanecen ahí sin realizar labor alguna (página 367)

I

igualdad matrimonial *s.* derecho legal de las personas homosexuales a casarse con sus parejas y tener los mismos privilegios que disfrutan las parejas heterosexuales casadas (página 770)

igualitario *adj.* creencia de que todas las personas son iguales (página 126)

imperialismo *s.* política o práctica de ejercer control sobre naciones o territorios más débiles (página 208)

impuesto electoral *s.* impuesto sobre cada individuo, independientemente de sus ingresos, a menudo relacionado con el derecho al voto (página 171)

impuesto sobre la renta *s.* impuesto que se basa en la cantidad de dinero que gana una persona (página 207)

indemnización *s.* dinero pagado a los vencedores por el lado perdedor en una guerra (página 211)

indemnización laboral *s.* seguro que cubre a los empleados lesionados en el trabajo y que ofrece asistencia médica y compensación por la falta de ingresos (página 149)

índice bursátil Dow Jones *s.* índice de las acciones de empresas líderes, que tiene seguimiento diario y es utilizado como medida de las tendencias generales del mercado bursátil (página 322)

índice de pobreza *s.* porcentaje de la población que vive en la pobreza (página 514)

industria aeroespacial *s.* negocio comercial relacionado a la construcción de aviones, naves espaciales y otros vehículos que vuelan (página 470)

infamia *s.* maldad o vileza extrema (página 420)

influenza *s.* enfermedad aguda y altamente contagiosa comúnmente llamada "gripe" (página 257)

infraestructura *s.* sistemas físicos básicos de una sociedad, incluyendo carreteras, puentes, alcantarillas y electricidad (página 470)

iniciativa *s.* procedimiento mediante el cual los ciudadanos pueden proponer nuevas leyes para ser votadas por el público o por los legisladores (página 197)

injuria *s.* delito de hacer declaraciones negativas verbales o escritas sobre alguien sin evidencia (página 479)

insurgente *s.* rebelde o revolucionario (página 606)

insurrección *s.* rebelión violenta contra un gobierno o una autoridad política (página 219)

integración *s.* proceso mediante el cual se juntan recursos económicos (página 747)

integración horizontal *s.* compra por parte de una compañía de otras que ofrecen los mismos bienes y servicios para reducir el número de competidores y lograr el dominio de una industria (página 139)

integración vertical *s.* procedimiento en el que una empresa toma el control de todas las etapas de producción (página 139)

integrado *adj.* que permite la libre asociación de personas de diferentes razas o grupos étnicos (página 543)

intensificación *s.* aumento de intensidad en algo, por ejemplo, durante la guerra (página 608)

interdicto *s.* orden judicial que exige o prohíbe ciertas acciones (página 336)

internar *v.* confinar a una prisión o campo por razones militares o políticas durante la guerra (página 430)

internet *s.* red mundial de ordenadores (página 717)

intervención telefónica *s.* la colocación de un dispositivo en un teléfono para poder escuchar en secreto las conversaciones ajenas (página 690)

intransigente *s.* persona que generalmente pertenece a un grupo político o de intereses especiales y que apoya de manera estricta y dura un conjunto de ideas o políticas (página 721)

istmo *s.* estrecha franja de tierra que conecta dos áreas de tierra más grandes (página 219)

J

jazz *s.* estilo de música que se originó entre los músicos afroamericanos y que contiene ritmos vivos, sonidos de una variedad de instrumentos y mucha improvisación (página 290)

juicio político *s.* cargos formales presentados contra un funcionario público por mala conducta en el cargo (página 690)

Junta Militar de Industrias (WIB) *s.* consejo que supervisó la industria de manufactura dentro de los Estados Unidos durante la Primera Guerra Mundial (página 244)

juramento de lealtad *s.* declaración jurada que confirma que una persona no pertenece y nunca ha pertenecido a determinadas organizaciones, por ejemplo, aquellas identificadas como comunistas (página 479)

K

kamikaze *s.* miembro de un grupo de pilotos japoneses que estrellaban su avión, cargado con explosivos, en los barcos estadounidenses (página 444)

L

laboratorio de ideas *s.* grupo de expertos que realizan investigaciones y discuten temas para elaborar soluciones potenciales a problemas sociales y económicos (página 705)

Larga Marcha *s.* viaje de 6.000 millas realizado por los comunistas chinos para trasladar la base revolucionaria comunista del sureste al centro de China (página 401)

Ley de Asentamientos Rurales *s.* ley promulgada en 1862 que alentaba a los ciudadanos estadounidenses a establecerse en las Grandes Llanuras al ofrecerles terrenos en esa región (página 106)

Ley del Comercio Interestatal *s.* ley que establecía una comisión para supervisar y regular los ferrocarriles del país, investigar quejas sobre las prácticas comerciales y presentar demandas legales en contra de las empresas que violaban sus reglamentos (página 139)

Leyes de Jim Crow *s.* leyes establecidas después de la Reconstrucción que imponían la segregación racial a lo largo de los estados sureños (página 171)

Liga antidifamación (ADL) *s.* organización judía internacional de servicio fundada para combatir el antisemitismo, la intolerancia religiosa y racial y todas las formas de discriminación organizada basadas en estereotipos (página 279)

Liga estadounidense antiimperialista *s.* organización formada en 1898 para oponerse a la anexión de las Filipinas por los Estados Unidos (página 217)

línea de ensamblaje *s.* método de fabricación en el que el objeto a ser fabricado pasa de un trabajador a otro, cada uno de los cuales tiene una tarea específica y especializada (página 287)

M

macartismo *s.* la práctica de acusar a la gente de ser traidores a su país sin ofrecer pruebas (página 481)

mafia *s.* grupo de delincuentes que controlan actividades criminales organizadas (página 204)

magnates ladrones *s.* líderes de la industria ferroviaria, como Cornelius Vanderbilt y Jay Gould, que se hicieron famosos por sus métodos despiadados en contra de sus competidores (página 139)

malestar *s.* sensación general de enfermedad (página 695)

mandato *s.* autoridad para llevar a cabo alguna acción, otorgado a un representante por los votantes (página 365)

manejo científico *s.* gestión basada en estudios experimentales para identificar la forma más eficiente de ejecutar tareas en una fábrica u otro lugar de trabajo (página 206)

manifiesto *s.* declaración de intenciones por escrito (página 648)

maquiladora *s.* planta de manufactura ubicada en una zona de exportación (página 746)

maquinaria política *s.* organización política en la que una persona o un grupo pequeño es capaz de mantener el control sobre una ciudad o un estado (página 168)

mayoría silenciosa *s.* término usado por Richard Nixon a finales de los años sesenta para describir a un gran grupo de votantes moderados que no expresaban públicamente sus opiniones políticas (página 677)

Medicaid *s.* programa del gobierno de los Estados unidos iniciado en 1965 para ofrecer cobertura médica a la gente pobre (página 590)

Medicare *s.* programa del gobierno de los Estados Unidos iniciado en 1965 para ofrecer cobertura médica a personas de edad avanzada (página 590)

medios de comunicación de masas *s.* formas de comunicación como la radio, el cine y las grabaciones musicales que tienen el potencial de alcanzar grandes audiencias (página 332)

medios de comunicación modernos *s.* productos y servicios digitales que proporcionan contenido a través de internet (página 774)

mercado de valores *s.* sistema de compra y venta de acciones empresariales (página 321)

mercado general *s.* gran número de consumidores a los que los fabricantes pueden vender bienes fabricados en grandes cantidades (página 287)

mestizaje *s.* matrimonio entre personas de diferentes razas (página 597)

militarismo *s.* creencia de que un gobierno debe desarrollar un ejército fuerte y estar preparado para usarlo para alcanzar sus objetivos (página 236)

minería aluvial *s.* técnicas mineras que incluyen el uso de herramientas ligeras para encontrar oro en ríos y arroyos (página 108)

minería hidráulica *s.* proceso de descubrimiento de minerales preciosos mediante el uso de agua a presión para eliminar el suelo (página 108)

minería subterránea *s.* técnica minera en la que se abre un túnel vertical en una montaña para que los mineros bajen hacia la mina (página 108)

misil antibalístico (ABM) *s.* misil diseñado para destruir un misil portador de bomba antes de que este alcance su objetivo (página 681)

misil balístico *s.* arma nuclear propulsada por un cohete y guiada por un sistema GPS (página 572)

misoginia *s.* aversión, desprecio u odio hacia las mujeres; prejuicio contra las mujeres (página 659)

modernismo *s.* estilo artístico y literario moderno, con tono duro y realista y una tendencia a rechazar o evitar las prácticas artísticas y literarias del pasado (página 294)

módulo *s.* segmento de una nave espacial que puede funcionar de manera independiente (página 664)

monocultivo *s.* cultivo único de una especie vegetal (página 145)

monopolio *s.* control total de una industria o el mercado de un servicio o producto (página 139)

mortero *s.* cañón de corto alcance cuya carga se inserta por la boca (página 611)

movilización militar *s.* acto de reunir y organizar fuerzas militares (página 377)

movimiento de retorno a África *s.* movimiento encabezado por Marcus Garvey, quien alentó a los afroamericanos a abandonar los Estados Unidos y regresar a África (página 301)

movimiento por la moderación *s.* movimiento social y político del siglo XIX y principios del siglo XX que animaba a las personas a limitar su consumo de alcohol o abstenerse del alcohol por completo (página 193)

muckrakers *s.* periodistas de investigación de principios del siglo XX que revelaron las conductas indebidas de organizaciones o personas poderosas (página 141)

multinacional *s.* empresa que tiene oficinas y fábricas en varios países (página 774)

GLOSARIO

N

nacionalismo *s.* fuerte sentido de lealtad al país al que uno pertenece y la creencia en la superioridad del mismo los demás países (página 236)

nacionalsocialismo *s.* doctrina política del partido nazi en Alemania, que promovió la superioridad de Alemania y del pueblo alemán, rechazó el comunismo y llevó el antisemitismo (el odio al del pueblo judío) a niveles extremos (página 360)

napalm *s.* substancia espesa, inflamable y gelatinosa usada en bombas para causar y propagar incendios (página 422)

nativismo *s.* ideología que favorece a las personas nacidas en los Estados Unidos sobre los inmigrantes más recientes (página 280)

nativista *s.* persona que se opone a la inmigración y quiere proteger los intereses de la población nativa (página 162)

naturalización *s.* proceso mediante el cual una persona que no nació en los Estados Unidos se convierte en ciudadana (página r34)

neoconservador *s.* persona que apoya firmemente una economía de libre mercado y cree que los Estados Unidos debe promover activamente sus ideales en todo el mundo (página 752)

neutralidad *s.* negativa a tomar partido o involucrarse en un conflicto (página 240)

New Deal *s.* leyes, organismos y programas iniciados por el presidente Franklin Roosevelt y su administración en respuesta a la Gran Depresión de la década de 1930 (página 353)

novela de diez centavos *s.* publicación de literatura popular que se vendía por 10 centavos a finales del siglo XVIII y principios del XIX (página 127)

Nueva Frontera *s.* estrategia política de los Estados Unidos en 1960, en la que el presidente Kennedy enfatizó la resolución creativa de problemas, la diplomacia extranjera y los avances tecnológicos para superar los problemas del país (página 568)

Nuevo Federalismo *s.* plan del presidente Richard Nixon para transferir el control de algunos programas federales a los estados (página 678)

O

objetor de conciencia *s.* persona que se niega a luchar en una guerra por razones religiosas (página 246)

obstrucción *s.* estrategia política en la que un pequeño grupo de legisladores se turnan para hablar y evitar así que finalice un debate o que un proyecto de ley sea sometido a votación (página 585)

Oficina de Protección al Menor *s.* agencia gubernamental estadounidense creada en 1912 para mejorar la vida de los niños y sus familias (página 190)

oleada *s.* aumento repentino (página 759)

operación anfibia *s.* ataque que utiliza el apoyo naval para proteger a las fuerzas militares que invaden por tierra y por aire (página 437)

operación encubierta *s.* actividad realizada secretamente para influir en la situación política, económica o militar en otro país (página 496)

orden ejecutiva *s.* directiva emitida por un presidente que tiene fuerza de ley (página 431)

orientación *s.* identificación que hace una persona de su atracción sexual (página 660)

originalismo *s.* sistema de creencias utilizado para interpretar la constitución de los Estados Unidos desde el punto de vista de la intención del documento cuando fue escrito originalmente (página 713)

P

pacifismo *s.* creencia de que la guerra es moralmente incorrecta (página 394)

Pacto de Briand-Kellogg *s.* acuerdo multinacional de 1928 en el que los países firmantes aceptaron rechazar la guerra (página 321)

país de tercer mundo *s.* durante la Guerra Fría, cualquier país que no estaba alineado ni con los Estados Unidos ni con la Unión Soviética (página 605)

paloma *s.* persona que se opone a la guerra (página 616)

pan-africanismo *s.* movimiento de principios del siglo XX que procuró unificar a la gente de ascendencia africana (página 301)

pandemia *s.* brote repentino de una enfermedad que se extiende sobre una amplia área geográfica (página 257)

panzer *s.* tanque alemán fuertemente blindado y que poseía gran potencia de fuego, utilizado durante la Segunda Guerra Mundial (página 435)

Partido Nazi *s.* partido político dirigido por Adolf Hitler y que mediante la fuerza ejerció control total sobre Alemania de 1933 a 1945 (página 360)

patente *s.* licencia que otorga a un inventor derechos exclusivos para usar, vender o hacer una invención durante un número específico de años (página 144)

patrón oro *s.* sistema monetario en el que la moneda de una nación está respaldada por oro (página 115)

penicilina *s.* antibiótico hecho de moho y utilizado para tratar infecciones y enfermedades (página 422)

perestroika *s.* política gubernamental de reforma en la antigua Unión Soviética (página 720)

período glacial *s.* período de tiempo en la historia durante el cual enormes capas de hielo cubrieron gran parte de la Tierra (página xxxi)

perjurio *s.* acto de mentir bajo juramento (página 751)

piquete *s.* grupo de huelguistas que forman una barrera para evitar que los rompehuelgas entren en un edificio para trabajar en su lugar (página 365)

plan de desbordamiento de la corte *s.* controvertido plan del presidente Franklin Roosevelt para aumentar el número de jueces de la Corte Suprema de nueve a quince, sumando seis jueces que compartían sus valores progresistas (página 366)

Plan Marshall *s.* programa de ayuda económica de los Estados Unidos para restablecer la estabilidad económica en Europa occidental después de la Segunda Guerra Mundial (página 461)

Plan Schlieffen, *s.* plan alemán para conquistar rápidamente a Francia, seguido por un ataque a Rusia (página 238)

planificación económica *s.* administración de la economía por el gobierno federal (página 355)

Pleistoceno *s.* era de la historia de la Tierra en la que vivieron grandes animales y plantas y los glaciares cubrieron la tierra (página xxxi)

polio *s.* enfermedad infecciosa que a veces causa debilidad muscular o parálisis (página 351)

politburó *s.* principal comité gubernamental que tomó decisiones políticas en el partido comunista; a menudo se refiere al comité de China o la antigua Unión Soviética (página 720)

Política De Puertas Abiertas *s.* propuesta estadounidense que pretendía establecer la igualdad de acceso a los puertos de los países que comerciaban con china en 1900 (página 210)

política de terminación *s.* política promulgada bajo el presidente Eisenhower que sacó a los indígenas de sus reservas a la vez que el gobierno ponía fin a la limitada soberanía de las tribus y pueblos (página 518)

política arriesgada *s.* práctica de llevar a un conflicto al borde de la violencia sin entrar en una guerra, usualmente como táctica para obtener un resultado favorable (página 496)

populismo *s.* creencia de que la gente común debe controlar el gobierno (página 115)

populista *s.* político que dice representar las preocupaciones de la gente común (página 360)

Potencias del Eje *s.* Alemania, Italia y Japón, que formaron una alianza a comienzos de la Segunda Guerra mundial (página 391)

precedente *s.* determinación previa en un caso judicial para establecer una comparación con casos nuevos similares (página 642)

presión cultural *s.* estrategia política en la que los miembros de una religión influyen en los políticos y las instituciones sociales en un esfuerzo por promover sus creencias (página 710)

Primeros Cien Días *s.* los primeros 100 días del presidente Franklin Roosevelt en el gobierno, durante los cuales promulgó 15 leyes que formaron la base del *New Deal* (página 352)

privilegio ejecutivo *s.* principio que sostiene que, para proteger los intereses de la nación, el Presidente puede no divulgar cierta información al Congreso (página 690)

privilegio estadounidense *s.* la idea de que los Estados Unidos es superior a otros países debido a su historia e ideología (página 752)

Procedimiento Bessemer *s.* proceso en el que se utiliza aire forzado para eliminar impurezas del hierro, como el carbono, transformando así el hierro en acero (página 139)

producto nacional bruto (PNB) *s.* total de bienes y servicios producidos por un país, más los ingresos obtenidos por sus ciudadanos (página 323)

Programa Bracero *s.* programa diseñado para importar obreros mexicanos para reemplazar a los trabajadores agrícolas y de transporte estadounidenses que eran reclutados para la Segunda Guerra Mundial (página 424)

progresismo *s.* reforma entre 1890 y 1920 que buscaba hacer más democráticas las políticas estatales y nacionales y hacer más eficiente el gobierno (página 169)

prohibición *s.* acto de prohibir la producción, distribución y venta de alcohol (página 193)

Prohibición *s.* prohibición constitucional de la venta de bebidas alcohólicas, vigente entre 1920 y 1933 (página 255)

propaganda *s.* ideas e información engañosas que se difunden para influir en las opiniones de las personas o promover las ideas de una organización o un partido (página 162)

protectorado *s.* país que es gobernado en parte por un país más poderoso (página 208)

puente de Beringia *s.* pedazo de tierra entre Alaska y Siberia que estaba por encima del nivel del mar hace 13.000 años y que permitió a los primeros humanos cruzar hacia Norteamérica (página xxxii)

punto muerto *s.* situación en la que ninguna de las partes en un conflicto puede afirmar la victoria (página 619)

purga *s.* eliminación de algo (página 400)

R

racionar *v.* controlar el suministro de bienes puestos a disposición del público, especialmente en tiempos de guerra (página 424)

radical *s.* persona que quiere un cambio extremo o tiene una posición política extrema (página 279)

rearmamento *s.* actividades que realiza una nación para reaprovisionar su arsenal y reemplazar aquellas que están desfasadas o han sido eliminadas (página 390)

rebelión de los bóxer *s.* levantamiento político de 1900 en el norte de China contra los extranjeros en el país (página 210)

recesión *s.* desaceleración relativamente breve del crecimiento económico, a menudo parte de un ciclo económico normal (página 139)

reclutamiento *s.* acto de ser ingresado en el ejército (página 625)

redes de seguridad *s.* conjunto de programas proporcionados por el gobierno estatal o federal diseñados para evitar que la gente permanezca en la pobreza (página 709)

reducción del déficit *s.* medidas adoptadas por un gobierno para pagar una deuda (página 731)

referendo *s.* voto directo del pueblo sobre medidas específicas (página 169)

refugiado *s.* persona que busca refugio y protección contra la persecución política (página 395)

registro material *s.* edificios y objetos que sobreviven de una época anterior (página 90)

Renacimiento de Harlem *s.* movimiento cultural que se originó en Harlem en la década de 1920 y dio a conocer a muchos escritores, artistas y músicos afroamericanos (página 302)

renovación urbana *s.* programa que consiste en rehabilitar los barrios pobres y construir grandes proyectos de vivienda financiados con fondos públicos (página 514)

renta disponible *s.* dinero del que se dispone para gastos (página 321)

repatriación *s.* el acto de devolver a un ciudadano a su país de origen (página 327)

república islámica *s.* estado o país que incorpora o se basa enteramente en la ley islámica (página 698)

rescate financiero *s.* durante la Gran Recesión, el acto de comprar hipotecas e inversiones inestables de los bancos (página 763)

reserva *s.* área de tierra designada y administrada por una tribu indígena (página 118)

reserva *s.* dinero tomado en préstamo de un banco para pagar una inversión, como acciones (página 322)

responsabilidad cívica *s.* obligación requerida o necesaria por parte de la población, como votar, pagar impuestos y formar parte de los jurados (página r35)

responsabilidad personal *s.* responsabilidad que no es regulada pero que contribuye a una sociedad más civil, como respetar y defender los derechos de los demás, ayudar en la comunidad y mantenerse informado (página r35)

revocatoria *s.* proceso mediante el cual los ciudadanos pueden votar para sacar del poder a un funcionario público (página 197)

Revolución agrícola *s.* transición en la historia humana de la caza y la recolección de alimentos a la siembra de cultivos y la cría de animales (página xxxiv)

Revuelta de Haymarket *s.* enfrentamiento violento entre los trabajadores y la policía el 4 de mayo de 1886, que comenzó como una protesta contra la conducta policial durante una huelga en una fábrica de la compañía McCormick, en Chicago, Illinois (página 151)

rock and roll *s.* estilo musical derivado del *rhythm and blues*, que se popularizó en la década de 1950 (página 509)

rompehuelgas *s.* trabajadores no sindicalizados dispuestos a desafiar los piquetes para trabajar (página 151)

rustbelt *s.* el área en el Noreste y Medio Oeste de los Estados Unidos en la que la industria manufacturera ha disminuido significativamente (página 707)

S

saetín *s.* canal de madera inclinado utilizado en la minería para separar el agua del oro (página 108)

salto de rana *s.* estrategia en la que se capturan grupos de islas una por una para establecer en ellas bases militares (página 439)

saneamiento *s.* medidas como las alcantarillas para proteger la salud pública (página 168)

sector de servicios *s.* parte de la economía que proporciona servicios en lugar de bienes (página 774)

sedición *s.* acto criminal de tratar de persuadir a las personas para rebelarse o menoscabar el gobierno (página 246)

segregación *s.* separación de diferentes grupos de personas, generalmente basada en la raza (página 171)

segregación *de facto* *s.* segregación presente en la sociedad a pesar de que no hay leyes que la impongan (página 594)

segregación *de iure* *s.* segregación impuesta por la ley (página 594)

Segundo *New Deal* *s.* segundo conjunto de programas del New Deal, que el presidente Franklin Roosevelt presentó al Congreso después de las elecciones del Congreso de 1934 (página 358)

seguridad social *s.* programa gubernamental que proporciona ingresos a los ancianos, discapacitados y desempleados (página 206)

sentada *s.* protesta organizada donde la gente se sienta y se niega a irse (página 551)

separados pero iguales *s.* política que permitió a las empresas e instituciones segregar a los afroamericanos de los blancos, siempre y cuando las instalaciones o servicios proporcionados fueran casi iguales (página 172)

separatista negro *s.* activista afroamericano radical que creía que la única manera de lograr la igualdad y la justicia en los Estados Unidos era separarse cultural y económicamente de los blancos (página 594)

sequía *s.* período prolongado con poca o ninguna lluvia (página 330)

servicio militar *s.* obligación de alistarse para el servicio en las fuerzas armadas de un país (página 189)

servidumbre por mora *s.* tipo de servidumbre en la cual una persona trabaja únicamente para pagar una deuda (página 112)

sindicato de trabajadores *s.* grupos de trabajadores que se unen para lograr mejores salarios, condiciones de trabajo más seguras y otros beneficios (página 150)

síndrome de inmunodeficiencia adquirida (SIDA) *s.* etapa final de un virus que ataca al sistema del cuerpo humano que combate las enfermedades (página 719)

sistema de carreteras interestatales *s.* red de autopistas inaugurada por el presidente Eisenhower en 1956 para poder atravesar los Estados Unidos y conectar entre sí estados y grandes ciudades (página 502)

GLOSARIO

sistema de sub-tesorería *s.* propuesta mediante la cual los agricultores almacenarían sus cultivos en silos hasta que los precios subieran, mientras que el gobierno les prestaría dinero para comprar semillas para los cultivos del siguiente año (página 114)

soberanía *s.* libertad de control por parte de potencias externas (página 262)

socialismo *s.* sistema de gobierno en el que la comunidad o el gobierno controla los recursos económicos (página 153)

sociedad de consumo *s.* sociedad en la que la comprar de bienes y productos se ha convertido en una parte muy importante del estilo de vida de las personas (página 500)

Sociedad de las Naciones *s.* plan que propuso el presidente Woodrow Wilson después de la Primera Guerra Mundial, en el que habría una asamblea general de países para estabilizar las relaciones entre sí y ayudar a preservar la paz (página 262)

sociedad fiduciaria *s.* empresa administrada por miembros de una junta directiva en lugar de por propietarios o accionistas (página 141)

sostén de familia *s.* miembro del hogar que contribuye a los ingresos de la familia (página 370)

subdivisión *s.* parcela de terreno que ha sido dividida en lotes más pequeños en los que se construyen casas (página 503)

suburbio *s.* comunidad cerca o en las afueras de una ciudad (página 167)

subversión *s.* acto de desestabilización de un sistema social o político importante en un intento por destruirlo (página 480)

sucursal *s.* negocio secundario (página 145)

sufragio *s.* derecho constitucional, especialmente el derecho al voto (página 191)

sufragio femenino *s.* derecho de las mujeres al voto (página 190)

sufragista *s.* persona que apoya el derecho de las mujeres a votar (página 191)

sunbelt *s.* la región del sur y suroeste de los Estados Unidos, que tienen inviernos templados (página 495)

T

tanque *s.* vehículo blindado y fuertemente armado que usaba bandas de rodadura en lugar de ruedas (página 248)

telecomedia *s.* serie televisiva semanal que cuenta con un entorno familiar y un grupo de personajes que se enfrentan a problemas divertidos (página 508)

telégrafo *s.* dispositivo que transmite mensajes a lo largo de cables conectados, para comunicarse a largas distancias (página 144)

telegrama Zimmermann *s.* telegrama secreto alemán enviado al embajador alemán en México, exponiendo un plan para la alianza con México (página 243)

teocracia *s.* gobierno por uno o más líderes religiosos (página 729)

teoría del dominó *s.* idea concebida durante la Guerra Fría y que sostiene que los países vecinos de los países comunistas tienen más probabilidades de caer en el comunismo (página 473)

Tercer Reich *s.* nombre utilizado por el Partido Nazi para describir la época en que Adolf Hitler creía que estaba creando un tercer imperio alemán (página 390)

terrorismo *s.* el uso de actos violentos y amenazas para lograr un objetivo político (página 756)

tienda por departamentos *s.* tienda grande que ofrece una amplia variedad de mercancías, organizadas en diferentes departamentos, pero todos bajo un mismo techo (página 167)

totalitario *adj.* relativo a un gobierno que está encabezado por un dictador y que requiere completa obediencia al estado (página 360)

transistor *s.* dispositivo electrónico utilizado para controlar el flujo de electricidad en equipos electrónicos (página 501)

transporte escolar de minorías *s.* transporte de estudiantes de diferentes razas a escuelas fuera de sus vecindarios o distritos escolares para asegurar la integración y proporcionar igualdad de oportunidades en la educación (página 597)

tranvía *s.* vehículo que corre sobre rieles por las calles de la ciudad y transporta pasajeros (página 167)

trastorno por estrés postraumático (TEPT) *s.* condición causada por lesión o trauma psicológico (página 629)

Tratado de no Agresión *s.* acuerdo hecho en 1939 entre la Alemania nazi y la Unión Soviética, declarando que no tomarían acción militar el uno contra el otro durante los siguientes 10 años (página 397)

Tratado de Versalles *s.* tratado que oficialmente puso fin a la Primera Guerra Mundial (página 262)

tribunal *s.* corte de justicia con autoridad sobre un asunto específico (página 455)

trustbuster *s.* persona que busca deshacer las sociedades fiduciarias o los monopolios, especialmente un funcionario federal que hace cumplir las leyes antimonopolio (página 200)

U

U-boot *s.* submarino alemán (página 242)

Unión Estadounidense por las Libertades Civiles (ACLU) *s.* organización formada en 1920, dedicada a defender los derechos y las libertades individuales de todos los estadounidenses (pág. 279)

V

vehículo de desembarco militar *s.* barco utilizado para transportar soldados y equipos desde el mar hasta la costa durante los ataques militares (página 440)

veta *s.* filón mineral (página 108)

vietnamización *s.* estrategia militar que permitió la sustitución gradual de tropas estadounidenses por tropas survietnamitas durante la guerra de Vietnam (página 624)

virus de la inmunodeficiencia humana (VIH) *s.* virus que ataca al sistema del cuerpo humano que combate las enfermedades (página 719)

vodevil *s.* espectáculo teatral que incluía canto y danza (página 166)

Z

zona de libre empresa *s.* área que permite la suspensión de leyes fiscales y de aduanas (página 747)

zona de ocupación *s.* área de un país en la que el ejército de otro país toma el control (página 463)

zona desmilitarizada *s.* área en la que se prohíbe la presencia de personal y armas militares (página 476)

VOCABULARIO ACADÉMICO

adjudicar *v.* asignar, distribuir (página 678)

agitador *s.* persona que provoca ira y rebelión (página 122)

arrendar *v.* firmar o proporcionar un contrato que otorgue derechos a tierras o a propiedades por un tiempo en base a un alquiler acordado (página 215)

asentir *v.* aceptar, especialmente después de un argumento (página 655)

caudillo militar *s.* líder militar local con gran poder en su región limitada (página 400)

citatorio *s.* exigencia legal para comparecer ante un tribunal, un juez o un comité gubernamental (página 479)

comodidad *s.* beneficio que facilita el uso de algo o el estilo de vida de alguien (página 152)

conveniente, *adj.* oportuno (página 651)

cuota *s.* proporción, porcentaje o participación, a menudo en referencia a la proporción de grupos minoritarios o de género que obtienen algún beneficio en particular (página 327)

depósito *s.* almacén, lugar donde se almacenan artículos (página 575)

desagravio *s.* compensación por daños recibidos (página 431)

desproporcionado *adj.* desigual, desequilibrado, generalmente en comparación a la mayoría (página 745)

dimitir *v.* ceder, renunciar (página 546)

diversificar *v.* ampliar las opciones (página 113)

efigie *s.* muñeco que representa a una persona, particularmente a una persona famosa (a menudo un político) que es odiada (página 476)

erradicar *v.* destruir o eliminar por completo (página 198)

errático *adj* impredecible, incoherente (página 480)

exorbitante *adj.* excesivo, caro (página 108)

extorsión *s.* acto de obtener algo, generalmente dinero o información, mediante el uso de coacción; chantaje (página 595)

filantrópico *adj.* caritativo, bondadoso (página 141)

frugalidad *s.* economía en gastos o uso (página 289)

gueto *s.* sección de una ciudad en la cual ciertos grupos, generalmente judíos, estaban obligados a vivir; en uso moderno se refiere a la sección de una ciudad donde viven ciertos grupos minoritarios, generalmente debido a la pobreza (página 450)

herbicida *s.* sustancia química usada para matar plantas (página 613)

homogéneo *adj.* uniforme, igual, coherente, estandarizado (página 511)

ilícito *adj.* ilegal (página 291)

incorporar *v.* unir (página 541)

influjo *s.* llegada, entrada (por ejemplo, de inmigrantes) (página 154)

inicio *s.* comienzo (página 301)

injurioso *adj.* insultante, calumnioso, escandaloso (página 246)

inmolar *v.* destruir mediante el fuego (página 607)

insubordinación *s.* desobediencia, rebeldía (página 204)

intervencionista *s.* persona cuya tendencia es involucrarse en algo, como en una guerra (página 398)

invencible *adj.* imposible de vencer, indestructible (página 193)

laudable *adj.* alabable, digno de felicitación (página 294)

lucrativo *adj.* rentable, que genera dinero (página 495)

mística *s.* aire de misterio que rodea a una persona, cosa o idea (página 657)

nocivo *adj.* ofensivo, desagradable (página 168)

normalidad *s.* condición o situación típica, usual o esperada, como las condiciones sociales, políticas y económicas generales de una nación (página 265)

notorio *adj.* famoso por tener mala reputación (página 282)

obstrucción *s.* algo que bloquea una ruta de acceso o una acción (página 691)

opulencia *s.* riqueza, gran prosperidad (página 498)

oratorio *adj.* relacionado a los discursos (página 544)

partidario *s.* que apoya o aboga por algo (página 115)

pluralismo *s.* coexistencia de diferentes grupos culturales dentro de una misma sociedad más grande (página 154)

poner en la lista negra *v.* poner a una o más personas en una lista indicando que deben ser rechazadas o castigadas (página 479)

pragmatismo *s.* utilidad, sentido práctico (página 352)

preventivo *adj.* que prevé, defensivo (página 757)

privatizar *v.* transferir del control público al privado (página 747)

protagonista *s.* personaje principal de una obra de ficción (página 127)

rehén *s.* persona detenida para obligar a alguien a cumplir las demandas de quienes han detenido a esa persona (página 699)

renegar *v.* rechazar, renunciar (página 321)

represivo *adj.* opresivo, brutalmente autoritario (página 715)

sacrílego *adj.* profano, infame (página 705)

solidaridad *s.* unidad en el propósito o los objetivos (página 153)

subsistir *v.* lograr sobrevivir (página 108)

subyugación *s.* acto de controlar a un grupo de personas mediante el uso de la fuerza (página 467)

unánime *adj.* indiscutible, que ha obtenido todos los votos (página 543)

INDEX

A

INDEX

C

INDEX

D

E

F

INDEX

G

INDEX

INDEX

M

N

INDEX

INDEX

Q

R

INDEX

T

INDEX

SKILLS INDEX

ACKNOWLEDGMENTS

NATIONAL GEOGRAPHIC LEARNING | CENGAGE

National Geographic Learning gratefully acknowledges the contributions of the following National Geographic Explorers and affiliates to our program:

Lynsey Addario, National Geographic Photographer
Robert Ballard, National Geographic Explorer-in-Residence
Ari Beser, Fulbright-National Geographic Fellow
Jimmy Chin, National Geographic Photographer
Leslie Dewan, National Geographic Explorer
Jeffrey Gusky, National Geographic Photographer
David Guttenfelder, National Geographic Photographer
Kevin Hand, National Geographic Explorer
Fredrik Hiebert, National Geographic Archaeologist-in-Residence
Kathryn Keane, Vice President, National Geographic Exhibitions
Paul Nicklen, National Geographic Photographer
William Parkinson, National Geographic Explorer
Robert Reid, National Geographic Digital Nomad
Andrés Ruzo, National Geographic Explorer
Sandra Postel, National Geographic Freshwater Fellow (2009–2015)
Tristram Stuart, National Geographic Explorer

Photographic Credits

Front Cover (tr) ©Eduardo Frederiksen/500px. (tl) Underwood Photo Archives/Underwood Photo Archives/Superstock. (cr) David Becker/Getty Images. (cl) nsf/Alamy Stock Photo. (clb) ©Design Pics Inc/National Geographic Creative. (c) Library of Congress, Prints & Photographs Division, Reproduction number LC-DIG-ppmsca-36413. (br) ©Design Pics Inc/National Geographic Creative. (bc) The Art Archive/Superstock. (bl) ©Yreina Cervantez/SPARC. **Back Cover** ©Evgeny Tchebotarev/500px.

i (tl) Courtesy of the Burke Museum of Natural History and Culture, catalog number 1991-58/6. **i** (c) IRA BLOCK/National Geographic Creative. **ii** (c) IRA BLOCK/National Geographic Creative. **ii** (tr) Collection 9/11 Memorial Museum, Gift of the Weinberg family in memory of our beloved Michael, Photograph by Michael Hnatov. **iii** (l) Mark Thiessen/National Geographic. **iii** (c) ©Mary Lynne Ashley Photography/National Geographic Learning. **iii** (l) National Geographic Learning. **iv** (tl) ©KMK/National Geogrpahic Creative. **iv** (tr) ©Robert Reid/National Geographic Creative. **iv** (cl) ©Brian Nelson/National Geographic Learning. **iv** (cr) Courtesy of Andres Ruzo. **v** (tl) MARK THIESSEN/National Geographic Creative. **v** (tl) ©Ari Beser. **v** (tr) ©Lynn Johnson/National Geographic Creative. **v** (tr) MARK THIESSEN/National Geographic. **v** (cl) ©Mark Thiessen/National Geographic Creative. **v** (cl) HOGUE KAT KEENE/National Geographic Creative. **v** (bl) Roberto Ricciuti/Getty Images. **v** (bl) MIKEY SCHAEFER/National Geographic Creative. **v** (bc) ©Jeff Gusky. **v** (br) DAVID GUTTENFELDER/National Geographic Creative. **v** (br) ©Christina Mitermeier/National Geographic Creative. **vi** ©Metropolitan Museum of Art, New York, USA/Bridgeman Images. **vii** ©Metropolitan Museum of Art. New York. USA/Bridgeman Images. **viii** Library of Congress, Prints & Photographs Division, Reproduction number LC-DIG-det-4a09036. **ix** Library of Congress, Prints & Photographs Division, LC-DIG-det-4a09036. **x** Allentown Art Museum; Purchase: Leigh Schadt and Edwin Schadt Art Museum Trust. 2012. (2012.09). **xi** Allentown Art Museum; Purchase: Leigh Schadt and Edwin Schadt Art Museum Trust. 2012. (2012.09). **xii** ©Robert Capa/ International Center of Photography/Magnum Photos. **xiii** ©Robert Capa/International Center of Photography/Magnum Photos. **xiv** Bettmann/Getty Images. **xv** Bettmann/Getty Images. **xvi** DIANE COOK. LEN JENSHEL/National Geographic Creative. **xvii** DIANE COOK. LEN JENSHEL/National Geographic Creative. **xviii** ©Mapping Specialist/National Geographic Learning. **xix** MARK THIESSEN/National Geographic Creative. **xx** (t) AP Images/Pablo Martinez Monsivais. **xx** (b) Division of Political History, National Museum of American History,Smithsonian Institution. **xxi** (bl) ©Official White House Photo by Pete Souza. (tr) Car Culture/Getty Images. (cr) ©Bruno Barbey/Magnum Photos. **xxx** (bkgd) Daniel Gomes Lacerda / EyeEm/Getty Images. **xxxii** ©Levi Stroud/Michigan News. **xxxiii** ©David Coventry/National Geographic Creative. **xxxiv** IRA BLOCK/National Geographic Creative. **xxxv** (tl) Philippe Psaila/Science Source. (t) Nicolle Rager Fuller, National Science Foundation. **xxxvi** (tr) Werner Forman/Getty Images. (cr) IRA BLOCK/National Geographic Creative. (cr) Paul Chesley/National Geographic Creative. (br) ©Werner Forman Archive/Heritage Image Partnership Ltd/Alamy Stock Photo. **xxxvii** (tr) ©National Museum of the American Indian, Smithsonian Institution 5/4385. (cr) Werner Forman/Getty Images. (bc) ©musée du quai Branly - Jacques Chirac, Dist. RMN-Grand Palais/Art Resource, NY. (br) Human effigy vessel, Late Mississippian period, 1300-1500 (ceramic)/Mississippian culture (c.800-1500)/DIRK BAKKER PHOTOGRAPHY/Private Collection/Bridgeman Images. (bl) IRA BLOCK/National Geographic Creative. **1** (bl) nsf/Alamy Stock Photo. **1** (tl) ©Design Pics Inc/National Geographic Creative. **1** (tr) ©Design Pics Inc/National Geographic Creative. **1** (br) David Becker/ Getty Images. **1** ©Metropolitan Museum of Art. New York. USA/Bridgeman Images. **2** (tl) The Art Archive/Superstock. **2** (tr) Library of Congress. Prints & Photographs Division. LC-DIG-ppmsca-. **2** (cl) Simon Dannhauer/Shutterstock.com. **2** (br) Fine Art Images/Fine Art Images/Superstock. **3** (tl) Joseph Sohm; Visions of America/Getty Images. **3** (cl) George Washington. 1796-1803 (oil on canvas)/Stuart. Gilbert (1755-1828)/CLARK ART INSTITUTE/Sterling and Francine Clark Art Institute. Williamstown, Massachusetts, USA/Bridgeman Images. **3** (bl) Science & Society Picture Library/Getty Images. **4** Joe Raedle/Getty Images News/Getty Images. **5** Joe Raedle/Getty Images News/Getty Images. **7** Damon Winter/The New York Times/Redux. **8** Tony Linck/Tony Linck/ Superstock. **9** ©National Museum of the American Indian. Smithsonian Institution 14/9624. **10** National Geographic Stock. **11** IRA BLOCK/National Geographic Creative. **12** ROBERT SISSON/National Geographic Creative. **13** Head of Squanto (wood)/American School, (17th century)/Private Collection/Bridgeman Images). **14** ©US Capitol. **15** ©JC Shamrock/500px. **16** Bill Grant/Alamy Stock Photo. **17** Cameron Davidson/Getty Images. **19** Ralph Earl Gentleman with Attendant. 1785 - 88 Oil on canvas 30 ¾ x 25 ¾ in. Courtesy of the New Britain Museum of American Art Harriet Russell Stanley Fund 1948.6. **22** ©Crossroads of the American Revolution NHA. **23** ©Crossroads of the American Revolution NHA. 24 SuperStock/ SuperStock. **25** SuperStock/SuperStock. **26** SuperStock/Getty Images. **27** ©Museum of the American Revolution. **28** IllustratedHistory/Alamy Stock Photo. **29** Prisma/Prisma/Superstock. **30** ©National Archives. **31** RGB Ventures/SuperStock/Alamy Stock Photo. **32** Mark Summerfield/ Alamy Stock Photo. **33** L. Toshio Kishiyama/Getty Images. **34** George Washington. 1796-1803 (oil on canvas)/Stuart. Gilbert (1755-1828)/CLARK ART INSTITUTE/Sterling and Francine Clark Art Institute. Williamstown, Massachusetts. USA/Bridgeman Images. **35** ©Photographs in the Carol M. Highsmith Archive, Library of Congress. Prints and Photographs Division. **36** ©2004 White House Historical Association. **37** ©Armed Forces History Division. National Museum of American History. Smithsonian Institution. **40** ©iStock/Getty Images Plus/Getty Images. **41** ©iStock/Getty Images Plus/Getty Images. **43** ©Missouri History Museum. St. Louis. **45** ©From the Collections of The Henry Ford/Henry Ford Museum. **47** Erik Sampers/Getty Images. **48** Wim Wiskerke/Alamy Stock Photo. **49** ©National Museum of the American Indian. **50** Fotosearch/Getty Images. **51** Chicago History Museum. ICHi-052442. **52** ©Old Dartmouth Historical Society-New Bedford Whaling Museum. **53** Tomas Abad/Alamy Stock Photo. **54** Library of Congress/Getty Images. **55** Jim West/Alamy Stock Photo. **57** American Progress. 1872 (oil on canvas)/Gast. John (1842-1896)/CHRISTIES IMAGES/Private Collection/Bridgeman Images. **58** ©HerronStock.com. **61** Inge Johnsson/Alamy Stock Photo. **62** Gold Rush prospector, 1849 (b/w photo)/American Photographer. (19th century)/PETER NEWARK'S PICTURES/Private Collection/Bridgeman Images. **63** Garden Photo World/David C Phillips/Getty Images. **66** ©Damir Frkovic/Masterfile. **67** ©Damir Frkovic/Masterfile. **68** ©National Geographic Learning/Cengage Learning. **70** Abraham Lincoln and Stephen A. Douglas debating at Charleston. Illinois on 18th September 1858. 1918 (oil on canvas)/Root. Robert Marshall (1863-1937)/Private Collection/Bridgeman Images. **71** ©Kenneth Garrett. **72** ©ARS. NY. Photo: The Jacob and Gwendolyn Lawrence Foundation/Art Resource. NY. **73** Library of Congress Prints and Photographs Division [LC-USZ62-7816]. **74** Abraham Lincoln (1809-65) 1860 (b/w photo)/Hesler. Alexander (1823-95)/PETER NEWARK'S PICTURES/Private Collection/Bridgeman Images. **75** Jason Demek/500px. **77** ©Confederate Memorial Hall Museum. New Orleans. **78** Science & Society Picture Library/Getty Images. **80** The Library of Congress. **81** Frederick Douglass. 1847-52 (daguerreotype)/Miller, Samuel J. (1822-88)/ART INSTITUTE OF CHICAGO/The Art Institute of Chicago. IL. USA/Bridgeman Images. **83** ©Confederate Memorial Hall Museum. **84** TOM LOVELL/National Geographic Creative. **85** Chicago History Museum. USA/Bridgeman Images. **86** ©Library of Congress Prints and Photographs Division Washington. D.C. **87** Angus Osborn/Getty Images. **90** (tl) Wynne Brewer/National Geographic Learning. (b) John Elk III/Getty Images. **91** (t) TED S. WARREN/Getty Images. (b) IRA BLOCK/National Geographic Creative. **92** (cl) Courtesy of the Burke Museum of Natural History and Culture, catalog number 1991-58/6. (cr) IRA BLOCK/National Geographic Creative. **93** (cr) Collection 9/11 Memorial Museum, Gift of the Weinberg family in memory of our beloved Michael, Photograph by Michael Hnatov. (bc) IRA BLOCK/National Geographic Creative. **94** ©National Geographic Learning. **95** ©National Geographic Learning. **96** (tr) Collection of the Smithsonian National Museum of African American History and Culture; Gift of the Descendants of Garfield Logan. In Honor of Philip Henry Logan. **96** (cl) DEA PICTURE LIBRARY/Getty Images. **96** (br) ©Nick Norman/National Geographic Creative. **97** (tl) Gift of Mr. James Harvey Young. Division of Medicine & Sceince. National Museum of American History. Smithsonian Institution. **97** (c) David Frent/Getty Images. **97** (b) Steve Speller/Alamy Stock Photo. **98–99** Jim Brandenburg / Minden Pictures / Superstock. **100** Columbia Pictures/Courtesy Everett Co/Everett Collection. **101** Columbia Pictures/Courtesy Everett Co/Everett Collection. **102** Transcendental Graphics/Getty Images. **103** The Library of Congress. **104** Silver Screen Collection/Getty Images. **105** (background) AF archive/Alamy Stock Photo. **105** (br) ©National Museum of American History/Smithsonian Institution. A Mexican Vaquero. 1890 (oil on canvas)/Remington, Frederic (1861-1909)/ART INSTITUTE OF CHICAGO/The Art Institute of Chicago. IL. USA/Bridgeman Images. **110** Library of Congress. Prints & Photographs Division. LC-DIG-fsa-8b27566. **111** (b) ©Randy Olson/National Geographic Creative. **112** Howard Cheek Photography. **113** Lightfoot/Getty Images. **114** Jake Lyell/Alamy Stock Photo. **116** Rick Herrmann/500px. **117** Rick Herrmann/500px. **120** ANAND VARMA/National Geographic Creative. **121** Library of Congress. Prints & Photographs Division, LC-USZ62-49148. **123** (t) ©National Museum of the American Indian/Smithsonian Institution. **123** (b) ©National Museum of the American Indian/Smithsonian Institution. **124** ©The Field Museum Chicago. **125** (tr) ©The Field Museum Chicago. **126** (bl) ©The Field Museum Chicago. **127** Library of Congress, Prints and Photographs Division, LC-DIG-ppmsca-24362. **130** Bettmann/Getty Images. **131** Bettmann/Getty Images. **132** Bill Pugliano/Getty Images. **133** Bill Pugliano/Getty Images. **134** The Library of Congress. **135** Everett Collection Inc/Alamy Stock Photo. **136** STEVE RAYMER/National Geographic Creative. **137** Marcie Goodale/National Geographic Learning. **142** (tr) California State Railroad Museum Library. **142** (bl) California State Railroad Museum Library. **143** (Background) LeighSmithImages/Alamy Stock Photo. **143** (br) California State Railroad Museum Library. **143** (cl) California State Railroad Museum Library. **144** ullstein bild/Getty Images. **147** (t) Anthony Barboza/Getty Images. **147** (bl) Graphic Arts Collection. National Museum of American History. Smithsonian Institution. **148** National Archives and Records Administration. **151** Front cover of booklet entitled' The Chicago Riot: A record of the terrible scenes of May 4'. 1886 by Paul C. Hull. 1886 (colour litho)/Williams. True (19th Century)/CHICAGO HISTORY MUSEUM/©Chicago History Museum. USA/Bridgeman Images. **153** Lorenzo Dow Turner papers. Anacostia Community Museum Archives. Smithsonian Institution, gift of Lois Turner Williams. **155** (tl) Jordan J. Lloyd/Dynamichrome. **157** Courtesy of California State Parks. Image 231-18-9. **161** Lewis W. Hine/George Eastman House/Getty Images. **162** ©The Ohio State University Billy Ireland Cartoon Library & Museum. **163** Riverside Metropolitan Museum. Harada Family Archival Collection. **164** Bettmann/Getty Images. **165** Wallace Kirkland/Getty Images. **166** Library of Congress. Prints & Photographs Division. Reproduction number LC-USZC4-6075. **167** ©Museum of the City of New York/The Art Archive at Art Resource. NY. **168** Chicago History Museum/Archive Photos/Getty Images. **170** MPI/Getty Images. **172** Library of Congress. Prints and Photographs Division [LCUSZC2-1058]. **174** ©Smithsonian American Art Museum. Washington. DC/Art Resource. NY. **178** Gary Crabbe/Enlightened Images/Alamy Stock Photo. **179** Gary Crabbe/Enlightened Images/Alamy Stock Photo. **181** National Archives. **183** (bl) ©The New York Public Library Digital Collections. **183** (br) ©From the Collections of The Henry Ford. **184** (t) National Archives. **184** (b) National Geographic Learning. **185** INTERFOTO/Alamy Stock Photo. **186** The Library of Congress. **187** AFP/Getty Images. **188** George Rinhart/Getty Images. **191** AP Images. **192** Library of Congress. Prints & Photographs Division. Reproduction number LC-USZ62-683 (b&w film copy neg.). **194** (Background) "Votes for Men". cover of 'Life' magazine. 15 September 1910 (litho)/O'Malley. Power (b.1909)/TOPHAM PICTURE SOURCE/Private Collection/Bridgeman Images. **194** (b) NEW YORK HISTORICAL SOCIETY/Collection of the New-York Historical Society. USA/Bridgeman Images. **195** From the Collections of The Henry Ford. **196** Niday Picture Library/Alamy Stock Photo. **198** ©Division of Political History/National Museum of American History. **199** Bettmann/Getty Images. **200** Library of Congress. Prints & Photographs Division, LC-DIG-ppmsca-36413. **202** PETE MCBRIDE/National Geographic Creative. **203** PETE MCBRIDE/National Geographic Creative. **205** Everett Collection Inc/Alamy Stock Photo. **206** ullstein bild/Getty Images. **209** DESIGN PICS INC/National Geographic Creative. **211** China: Official portrait of Empress Dowager Cixi (1835-1908) by court photographer Yu Xunling. c. 1895/Yu Xunling (c.1880–1943)/PICTURES FROM HISTORY/Bridgeman Images. **212** Destruction of the U.S. Battleship Maine in Havana Harbor. February 15th. 1898 (colour litho)/Kurz and Allison (fl.1880-98)/NEW YORK HISTORICAL SOCIETY/Collection of the New-York Historical Society. USA/Bridgeman Images. **214** Buyenlarge/Getty Images. **216** Damir Sagol/Reuters. **218** Bettmann/Getty Images. **224** Allentown Art Museum; Purchase: Leigh Schadt and Edwin Schadt Art Museum Trust. 2012. (2012.09). **225** Allentown Art Museum; Purchase: Leigh Schadt and Edwin Schadt Art Museum Trust. 2012. (2012.09). **226** (tr) Car Culture/Getty Images. **226** (cl) Library of Congress. Prints & Photographs Division. LC-DIG-ppmsc-03521. **226** (b) Akademie/Alamy Stock Photo. **227** (tl) Fotosearch/Getty Images. **227** (tr) Fotosearch/Getty Images. **227** (b) Eddie Gerald/Alamy Stock Photo. **228** Buyenlarge\UIG/AGE Fotostock. **229** Buyenlarge\UIG/AGE Fotostock. **230** Bettmann/Getty Images. **231** National Geographic Learning. **232** ©MPI / Stringer/Getty. **233** DeAgostini/Superstock. **235** (Background) ©Ken Marschall. **235** (tr) MARK THIESSEN/National Geographic Creative. **239** Popperfoto/Getty Images. **240** Bettmann/Getty Images. **241** National Geographic Learning. **242** Bygone Collection/Alamy Stock Photo. **245** (tl) FPG/Getty Images. **245** (tr) Bettmann/Getty Images. **247** (c) ©The National World War I Museum. **247** (br) Library of Congress. Prints & Photographs Division, LC-USZC4-4455. **247** (bl) swim ink 2 llc/Getty Images. **248** (c) ©Photodisc. **249** (t) Lachina/National Geographic Learning. (b) Artville. **250** ©National Portrait Gallery, Smithsonian Institution. **251** Buyenlarge/Getty Images. **252** ©Jeffrey Gusky. **253** ©Jeffrey Gusky. **254** The Migration Series. Panel No.1: During World War I there was a great migration north by southern African Americans. 1940-41 (casein tempera on hardboard)/Lawrence, Jacob (1917-2000)/PHILLIPS COLLECTION/The Phillips Collection. Washington, D.C. USA/Bridgeman Images. **255** David Frent/Getty Images. **256** Bettmann/Getty Images. **257** National Geographic Learning. **260** (t) Rick Herrmann/500px. **260** (b) Neil Hall/Reuters. **262** Hulton Archive/Getty Images. **264** Bettmann/Getty Images. **265** (tr) ©University of Washington Libraries. Special Collections Division. **267** PARIS PIERCE/Alamy Stock Photo. **268** AF archive/Alamy Stock Photo. **269** AF archive/Alamy Stock Photo. **270** Robert Holmes/Alamy Stock Photo. **271** Robert Holmes/Alamy Stock Photo. **272** Nightlife. 1943 (oil on canvas)/Motley Jr. Archibald J. (1891-1981)/ART INSTITUTE OF CHICAGO/The Art Institute of Chicago. IL. USA/Bridgeman Images. **273** (t) The Estate of David Gahr/Premium Archive/Getty Images. **273** (b) INTERFOTO/Alamy Stock Photo. **274** (bl) ©National Museum of African American History and Culture. (br) National Geographic Learning. **275** ClassicStock/Alamy Stock Images. **276** Dosfotos/Getty Images. **277** (tr) Everett Collection Historical/Alamy Stock Photo. **277** (cr) ©Everett Collection. **277** (br) Michael Ochs Archives/Getty Images. **278** Library of Congress Prints and Photographs Division Washington. D.C. **281** ©COURTESY OF THE SYRACUSE UNIVERSITY ART COLLECTION. **282** Image Asset Management/AGE Fotostock. **283** GL Archive/Alamy Stock

Photo. 286 (l) Mary Evans/Jazz Age Club Collection/AGE Fotostock. 286 (r) Mary Evans Picture Li/ AGE Fotostock. 290 Pictorial Press Ltd/Alamy Stock Photo. 291 Blank Archives/Getty Images. 292 (bl) Glasshouse Images/Alamy Stock Photo. 292 (br) Herbert Dorfman/Getty Images. 293 ©Richard T. Nowitz/Getty Images. 294 ©National Baseball Hall of Fame. 295 National Air and Space Museum. Smithsonian Institution. 296 Kirn Vintage Stock/Getty Images. 297 Hulton Deutsch/Corbis Premium Historical/Getty Images. 298 Governor Nellie Ross. c.1925 (b/w photo)/ Bain. George Grantham (1865-1944)/Private Collection/Bridgeman Images. 301 Bettmann/Getty Images. 302 State Archives of Florida/Florida Memory/Alamy Stock Photo. 303 The Jacob and Gwendolyn Lawrence Foundation/Art Resource. NY. 304 Photo Researchers. Inc/Alamy Stock Photo. 306 Robert W. Kelley/Getty Images. 307 (t, c, b) National Geographic Learning. 309 Universal History. Archive/Getty Images. 310 Library of Congress. Prints & Photographs Division. LC-DIG-ppmsca-. 311 Library of Congress. Prints & Photographs Division. LC-DIGppmsca-15611. 312 The Library of Congress. 313 The Library of Congress. 314 The Library of Congress. 315 Library of Congress Prints and Photographs Division Washington. D.C. 316 Artepics/Alamy Stock Photo. 318 The Library of Congress. 319 (tl) The Library of Congress. 319 (tr) The Library of Congress. 319 (b) The Library of Congress. 320 Everett Collection Inc/Alamy Stock Photo. 322 Everett Collection Inc/Alamy Stock Photo. 326 New York Times Co./Getty Images. 328–329 (l) ©Jimmy Chin Photography. 329 (tr) MIKEY SCHAEFER/National Geographic Creative. 330 Everett Collection Inc/Alamy Stock Photo. 332 National Air and Space Museum. 333 Eric Schaal/Getty Images. 335 Bettmann/Getty Images. 336 Everett Collection Inc/Alamy Stock Photo. 339 (tr) ©Brigham Young University Museum of Art. gift of Herald R. Clark. 339 (bl) Photo Researchers/Getty Images. 340 Francois Galland/Getty Images. 341 Francois Galland/Getty Images. 342 Universal History Archive/Getty Images. 343 National Baseball Hall of Fame Library. 344 (c) PhotoQuest/Getty Images. 344 (b) ©National Baseball Hall of Fame. 345 Ronald Gabriel Baseball Memorabilia Collection. 1912-2009. Archives Center. National Museum of American History. 346 Transcendental Graphics/Getty Images. 347 (cr) Transcendental Graphics/Getty Images. 347 (t) ©National Baseball Hall of Fame Library/MLB Photos/Getty Images. 348 TASOS KATOPODIS/Getty Images. 349 Ron Vesely/Getty Images. 350 (b) Bettmann/Getty Images. 350 (br) Blank Archives/Getty Images. 352 ©National Museum of American History. Kenneth E. Behring Center. 353 Stock Montage/Getty Images. 354 AP Images. 355 David Frent/Getty Images. 356 Historical/Getty Images. 359 (tl) Library of Congress, Prints & Photographs Division, LC-USZC2-854. 359 (tr) Library of Congress, Prints & Photographs Division, LC-USZC2-987. 359 (bl) Library of Congress. Prints & Photographs Division. LC-USZC2-1174. 359 (br) Library of Congress. Prints & Photographs Division. Reproduction number LCUSZC2-5653. 360 Bettmann/ Getty Images. 362–363 ©Images Courtesy of Milwaukee Public Museum. 364 MARK RALSTON/ Getty Images. 366 Bettmann/Getty Images. 367 Bloomberg/Getty Images. 368 ©Tom Till/ SuperStock. 369 ©Tom Till/SuperStock. 370 Bettmann/Getty Images. 372 Bettmann/Getty Images. 373 David Frent/Getty Images. 375 Library of Congress. Prints & Photographs Division. LC-USZC2-936. 377 Bettmann/Getty Images. 379 Kerrick James/Getty Images. 381 ©Courtesy of The Buffalo News. 382 ©Jeffrey Gusky. 388 Hulton Deutsch/Getty Images. 389 Hulton Deutsch/ Getty Images. 391 Print Collector/Getty Images. 392 Guernica. 1937 (oil on canvas)/Picasso. Pablo (1881-1973)/Museo Nacional Centro de Arte Reina Sofia. Madrid. Spain/Bridgeman Images. 393 UniversalImagesGroup/Getty Images. 397 SZ Photo/Scherl/The Image Works. 399 Paul Popper/Popperfoto/Getty Images. 400 Fototeca Storica Nazionale./Getty Images. 402 VCG/Getty Images. 403 VCG/Getty Images. 405 Fox Photos/Getty Images. 407 Franklin D. Roosevelt Presidential Library & Museum/National Archives. 409 Bettmann/Getty Images. 410 Everett Collection Inc/Alamy Stock Photo. 411 Everett Collection Inc/Alamy Stock Photo. 412 Everett Collection Inc/Alamy Stock Photo. 415 (l) AP Images/Dean Hanson. 415 (r) Lyn Alweis/Getty Images. 416 Science & Society Picture Library/Getty Images. 417 ©Weinstein Company/Courtesy Everett Collection/Everett Collection. 419 Pictorial Press Ltd/Alamy Stock Photo. 420 Library of Congress. Prints & Photographs Division, LC-USW33-038539-ZC. 421 Library of Congress. Prints & Photographs Division, LC-USW33-038539-ZC. 423 Library of Congress. Prints & Photographs Division. LC-DIG-ppmsca-13259. 424 Bettmann/Getty Images. 425 Bettmann/Getty Images. 427 Peter Stackpole/Getty Images. 428 Printed by permission of the Norman Rockwell Family Agency Copyright ©1942 the Norman Rockwell Family Entities. Library of Congress. Prints & Photographs Division. Reproduction number LC-DIG-ppprs-00368. 429 Library of Congress. 430 Library of Congress. Prints & Photographs Division. Reproduction number LC-DIG-ppprs-00368. 431 ©Manzanar National Historic Site/NPS. 432 Japanese American National Museum. Gift of Ibuki Hibi Lee (96.601.8). 433 (tr) Japanese American National Museum. Gift of June Hoshida Honma. Sandra Hoshida and Carole Hoshida Kanada (97.106.1EN). 433 (tl) Japanese American National Museum. Gift of June Hoshida Honma. Sandra Hoshida and Carole Hoshida Kanada (97.106.2CA). 433 (b) Japanese American National Museum. Gift of Jack and Peggy Iwata (93.102.127). 436 Thomas D. McAvoy/Getty Images. 437 Historical/Getty Images. 438 ANDREW CABALLERO-REYNOLDS/Getty Images. 439 ©Aviation History Collection/Alamy Stock Photo. 441 (b) Hulton Archive/Getty Images. 442 LAPI/Getty Images. 443 Library of Congress. Prints & Photographs Division. Reproduction number LC-USZ62-7449. 446 Photo Researchers. Inc/Alamy Stock Photo. 447 Alfred Eisenstaedt/Pix Inc./Time & Life Pictures/Masters/Getty Images. 448 ©Ari Beser. 449 KIMIMASA MAYAMA/Newscom/European Pressphoto Agency/ HIROSHIMA/HIROSHIMA/JAPAN. 450 ©United States Holocaust Memorial Museum. 451 National Archives/Getty Images. 452 Historical/Getty Images. 453 Anne Frank Fonds Basel/ Premium Archive/Getty Images. 454 ©United States Holocaust Memorial Museum. 457 Galerie Bilderwelt/Hulton Archive/Getty Images. 458–459 Cameron Davidson/Getty Images. 460 ©WHO/E. Soteras Jalil. 462 Heritage Images/Getty Images. 464–465 Walter Sanders/Getty Images. 466 ©Leslie Illingworth Associated Newspaper/Solo Syndication, London. 468 National Archives. 471 BRUCE DALE/National Geographic Creative. 472 Keren Su/Getty Images. 476 AFP/ Getty Images. 477 AFP/Getty Images. 478 ©REUTERS/Bobby Yip. 481 Everett Collection Inc/ Alamy Stock Photo. 483 Universal History Archive/Getty Images. 484 Margaret Bourke-White/ Getty Images. 485 Margaret Bourke-White/Getty Images. 486 ©Tony Frank/Sygma/Sygma/Getty Images. 487 ©Tony Frank/Sygma/Sygma/Getty Images. 488 INTERFOTO/Alamy Stock Photo. 489 New York Daily News Archive/Getty Images. 490 Hulton Archive/Getty Images. 491 (t) The Advertising Archives/Alamy Stock Photo. 491 (tc) Apic/Getty Images. 491 (c) ©C12/Corbis. 491 (bc) CBW/Alamy Stock Photo. 491 (b) Marc Tielemans/Alamy Stock Photo. 492 Michael Ochs Archives/Getty Images. 493 (t) RB/Getty Images. 493 (b) ZUMA Press. Inc./Alamy Stock Photo. 494 Everett Collection/AGE Fotostock. 496 (tl) ©Collection of the New-York Historical Society. 496 (tr) Bettmann/Getty Images. 497 (tl) Frederic Neema/Getty Images. 497 (c) Hulton Deutsch/ Getty Images. 497 (tr) ©UN Photo. 499 Yale Joel/Getty Images. 500 PhotoQuest/Getty Images. 501 ClassicStock/Alamy Stock Photo. 503 Everett Collection Inc/Alamy Stock Photo. 504 Bettmann/Getty Images. 506 (tl) ©Wayne Miller/Magnum Photos. 506 (tr) Three Lions/Getty Images. 506 (cl) Thomas D. McAvoy/Getty Images. 506 (cr) Car Culture/Getty Images. 506 (bl) ©Carol M. Highsmith/The Library of Congress. 506 (br) ©Dennis Stock/Magnum Photos. 507 (t) Corbis Premium Historical/Getty Images. 507 (bl) ZUMA Press. Inc./Alamy Stock Photo. 507 (br) Bryan Mitchell/Getty Images. 509 (tl) Bettmann/Getty Images. 509 (tr) Blank Archives/ Getty Images. 510 Charles Trainor/Getty Images. 511 Charles Trainor/Getty Images. 512 ©National Baseball Hall of Fame. 513 ©National Baseball Hall of Fame. 515 ©Wayne Miller/Magnum Photos. 519 ©Leonard Nadel/National Museum of American History/Kenneth E. Behring Center. 521 ©Buyenlarge/Getty Images. 522 Bettmann/Getty Images. 524 Bettmann/Getty Images. 525 Bettmann/Getty Images. 526 (tr) Independent Picture Service/Alamy Stock. 526 (c) Ian Dagnall/Alamy Stock Photo. 526 (br) Library of Congress. Prints & Photographs Division, LC-DIG-ppmsc-07978. 526 (bl) Ulrich Doering/Alamy Stock Photo. 527 (tl) Gary Ombler/Getty Images. 527 (c) New York Daily News Archive/Getty Images. 527 (br) Bettmann/Getty Images. 527 (bl) Pacific Press/Getty Images. 528 ©Danny Lyon/Magnum Photos. 529 ©Danny Lyon/ Magnum Photos. 530 AP Images/Pablo Martinez Monsivais. 531 ©Leonard Freed/Magnum Photos. 532 AP Images/Jacquelyn Martin. 533 (tl) AP Images/Jacquelyn Martin. 533 (br) Carl Iwasaki/ Getty Images. 534 AP Images/Molly Riley. 535 ©REUTERS/Jim Young. 536 ©Eli Reed/Magnum Photos. 537 ©National Museum of African American History and Culture. 539 Arthur Brower/ Getty Images. 540 The Library of Congress- Prints & Photographs Online Catalog, LC-GLB23- 0425. 541 'Invisible Man' by Ralph Ellison (1914-94) published by Random House. New York. 1952/ American School. (20th century)/CHRISTIES IMAGES/Private Collection/Bridgeman Images. 542 Bettmann/Getty Images. 544 Cornell Capa/Getty Images. 545 Bettmann/Getty Images. 546 UniversalImagesGroup/Getty Images. 547 Don Cravens/Getty Images. 548 (tr) AP Images. 548 (b) AP Images/Anonymous. 549 Bettmann/Getty Images. 550 Smithsonian National Museum of African American History and Culture. 551 Bettmann/Getty Images. 552 Underwood Archives/ Getty Images. 553 ©Collection of the Smithsonian National Museum of African American History and Culture. 555 AP Images/BILL HUDSON. 556 ©Wyatt Tee Walker/Everett Collection/CSU Archives. 559 Uncredited/AP Images. 561 ©Copyright 1960. St. Louis Post-Dispatch/Library of Congress [LC-DIG-ppmsca-05522]. 562 Bettmann/Getty Images. 563 Bettmann/Getty Images. 564 (bl) Bettmann/Getty Images. 564 (br) Bettmann/Getty Images. 567 (t) Corbis Historical/Getty Images. 567 (b) Ulrich Baumgarten/Getty Images. 569 Photo Courtesy of Peace Corps. 570 NASA. 571 NASA. 573 (bl) Underwood Archives/Getty Images. 573 (br) Bettmann/Getty Images. 574 Art Rickerby/Getty Images. 575 Bettmann/Getty Images. 576 Bettmann/Getty Images. 577 Bachrach/ Getty Images. 578 (tl) Historical/Getty Images. 578 (tr) Bettmann/Getty Images. 579 (t) Bettmann/ Getty Images. 579 (b) Everett Collection Historical/Alamy Stock Photo. 580 ©Lynn Johnson/ National Geographic Creative. 581 Phil Degginger/Alamy Stock Photo. 582 DAVIDGUTTENFELDER/National Geographic Creative. 583 (l) DAVID GUTTENFELDER/National Geographic Creative. 583(tr) DAVID GUTTENFELDER/National Geographic Creative. 584 Keystone-France/Getty Images. 586 UniversalImagesGroup/Getty Images. 587 ©Danny Lyon/ Magnum Photos. 589 AP Images/Charles Kelly. 590 ©Bob Stefko. 592 ©Copyright held by Spider Martin/The Spider Martin Civil Rights Collection. NASA. 598 (bkgd) Brooks Kraft/Getty Images. (br) ©National Geographic Learning. 599 (tr) Ian Dagnall / Alamy Stock Photo. (tl) Paul Briden/ Alamy Stock Photo. (br) Raymond Boyd/Getty Images. 602 ©Bruno Barbey/Magnum Photos. 603 ©Bruno Barbey/Magnum Photos. 604 AP Images. 605 Vietnam: Communist propaganda poster: 'Victorious Ham Rong'/PICTURES FROM HISTORY/Bridgeman Images. 606 AP Images/HORST FAAS. 609 AP Images. 610 AP Images/HENRI HUET. 611 ©National Air and Space Museum. 613 ©Ian Berry/Magnum Photos. 614 Tim Page/Getty Images. 615 AP Images/Anonymous. 617 ©Marc Riboud/Magnum Photos. 619 CBS Photo Archive/Getty Images. 620 Julian Wasser/Getty Images. 623 John Dominis/Getty Images. 625 ©Burt Glinn/Magnum Photos. 626 John Filo/Getty Images. 628 Photograph courtesy of the National Mall and Memorial Parks. National Park Service. 629 Juan Valdez/National Geographic Learning. 630 Historical/Getty Images. 630–631 MICHAEL S. LEWIS/National Geographic Creative. 634–635 Aaron Huey. 635 Courtesy of NASA. 636 Courtesy of NASA. 638 EVERETT COLLECTION. INC. 639 ©Smithsonian National Air and Space Museum. 640 NASA. 641 (t) MARK THIESSEN/National Geographic Creative. 641 (b) NASA/Getty Images. 643 ZUMA Press. Inc./Alamy Stock Photo. 644 (c) ©Kattia Zanetta. 644–645 (portraits) ©Angélica Dass. 647 (cr) Library of Congress Prints and Photographs Division Washington, LC-DIG-ds-03091. 647 (tl) Cathy Murphy/Getty Images. 647 (cl) Tim Graham/Getty Images. 647 (bl) ©National Geographic Learning. 649 ©Los Angeles Public Library. 650 Bettmann/Getty Images. 652 ©Minnesota Historical Society. 653 ©Bob Kreisel/Alamy Stock Photo. 654 Bettmann/Getty Images. 656 (bl) ©Library of Congress Prints and Photographs Division Washington. D.C. 656 (c) Blank Archives/Getty Images. 656 NCAA Photos/Getty Images. 660 jcarillet/Getty Images. 661 Bettmann/Getty Images. 662 ©Ralph Morse/The LIFE Picture Collection/Getty Images. 663 Science & Society Picture Library/Getty Images. 664 Kenneth Batelman/National Geographic Learning. 665 ©Transferred from the National Aeronautics and Space Administration/ Smithsonian Institution. National Air and Space Museum. 667 ©NASA. 670–671 (spread) DIANE COOK, LEN JENSHEL/National Geographic Creative. 672 (tr) Bettmann/Getty Images. 672 (tl) Universal History Archive/Getty Images. 672 (b) Tom Stoddart Archive/Contributor. 673 (tl) Dennis Tarnay. Jr./Alamy Stock Photo. 673 (cr) JEFF KOWALSKY/Newscom/European Pressphoto Agency/WARREN/MI/UNITED STATES. 673 (cl) MICKE Sebastien/Getty Images. 673 (bl) ©Mark Stewart/Camera Press/Redux. 673 (cr) Peter Macdiarmid/Getty Images. 674–675 Bettmann/Getty Images. 676 George Silk/Getty Images. 679 Bettmann/Getty Images. 680 Bettmann/Getty Images. 682 George Rinhart/Getty Images. 683 Bettmann/Getty Images. 686 PAUL NICKLEN/National Geographic Creative. 687 PAUL NICKLEN/National Geographic Creative. 687 (tr) ©Christina Mitermeier/National Geographic Creative. 688 AP Images. 689 ©National Archives. 691 Bettmann/Getty Images. 693 ©Library of Congress Prints and Photographs Division Washington. D.C. 695 Owen Franken/Getty Images. 696 ©Government Press Office. 698 Bettmann/Getty Images. 699 Bettmann/Getty Images. 702 Arnold Newman/Getty Images. 703 Arnold Newman/ Getty Images. 704 Timothy Fadek/Getty Images. 708 ©National Geographic Learning. 708 Ralph Crane/Getty Images. 708 Entertainment Pictures/Alamy Stock Photo. 711 Diana Walker/Getty Images. 712 Al Seib/Getty Images. 713 ©National Portrait Gallery. Smithsonian Institution/Art Resource. NY. 715 Terry Ashe/Getty Images. 716 Retro Ark/Alamy Stock Photo. 717 Encyclopaedia Britannica/Getty Images. 718 (tl) ZUMA Press. Inc./Alamy Stock Photo. 718 (tr) Richard Ellis/ Alamy Stock Photo. 721 AP Images/Boris Yurchenko. 722 (t) Bettmann/Getty Images. 722 (b) David Turnley/Getty Images. 724 Rolf Adlercreutz/Alamy Stock Photo. 725 (tl, tr) BRENDAN SMIALOWSKI/Getty Images. 725 (b) Alex Wong/Getty Images. 726 AP Images/LIONEL CIRONNEAU. 728 Historical/Getty Images. 729 ©National Geographic Learning. 730 jean-Louis Atlan/Contributor. 733 DOD Photo/Alamy Stock Photo. 734 Michael Lee/Getty Images. 735 Michael Lee/Getty Images. 736 ©Alyssa Schukar/The New York Times/Redux. 737 Everett Collection Inc/Alamy Stock Photo. 738 ©Matthias Breiter/Minden Pictures. 740 ©Amplifier Foundation. 741 (t) ©Mark Thiessen/National Geographic Creative. 741 (b) Robert Alexander/ Getty Images. 742 AP Images/Cliff Schiappa. 743 Mark Reinstein/Getty Images. 744 (t) AP Images/ Anonymous. 744 (b) Joe Raedle/Getty Images. 747 Richard Ellis/Alamy Stock Photo. 750 ©National Geographic Learning. 751 New York Daily News. 752 Robert King/Getty Images. 753 Brooks Kraft/Getty Images. 754 ©Michael Hnatov/Gift in Memory of Firefighter Jimmy Riches FDNY. 755 Everett Collection Historical/Alamy Stock Photo. 758 Wathiq Khuzaie/Getty Images. 759 ©National Geographic Learning. 760 The Washington Post/Getty Images. 761 (background) The Washington Post/Getty Images. 761 Photoservice/Getty Images. 762 ©National Geographic Learning. 763 AP Images/Eric Gay. 764 The Washington Post/Getty Images. 766 ©Official White House Photo by Pete Souza. 767 ©Official White House Photo by Pete Souza. 769 AP Images/John Minchillo. 770 Bloomberg/Getty Images. 773 PETE MCBRIDE/National Geographic Creative. 775 Lou Linwei/Alamy Stock Photo. 776 ©Kat Keene Hogue/National Geographic Creative. 777 BRIAN FINKE/National Geographic Creative. 778 DAVID GUTTENFELDER/National Geographic creative. 779 ©National Geographic Learning. 780 MANDEL NGAN/Getty Images. 782 (t) ©Lynsey Addario/Reportage/Getty Images. 782 (b) ©Lynsey Addario/Reportage/Getty Images. 783 (t) ©Lynsey Addario/Reportage/Getty Images. 783 (c) Roberto Ricciuti/Getty Images. 783 (b) ©Lynsey Addario/Reportage/Getty Images. 785 ©National Geographic Learning. Archive/Getty Images. 786 CAROLYN VAN HOUTEN/National Geographic Creative. 788 (tl) AP Images. 788 (tr) Pictorial Press Ltd / Alamy Stock Photo. 788 (bl 1) J. R. EYERMAN/Getty Images. 788 (bl 2) Galerie Bilderwelt/Getty Images. 788 (br) The Library of Congress. 789 (tl) Bruno Barbey/Magnum Photos. 789 (tr) Historical/Getty Images. 789 (cl) Bettmann/Getty Images. 789 (cr) ©Spencer Platt/Getty Images. 789 (bl) tekinturkdogan/Getty Images. 789 (br 1) The Library of Congress. 789 (br 2) Jonathan Bachman/Reuters. 789 (bl) Ebet Roberts/Redferns/Getty Images. R00–R1 ©Tim Fitzharris/Minden Pictures. R2 ©Kumar Sriskandan/Alamy Stock Photo. R10 ©Chip Somodevilla/Getty Images. R16 ©Mark Wilson/Getty Images. R17 ©Jonathan Ernst/Reuters. R19 ©National Archives. R26 ©Courtesy Everett Collection/Alamy. R27 ©Underwood Archives/Getty Images. R28 ©Photo by Underwood Archives/Getty Images. R32 ©Bettmann/Contributor/Getty Images. R33 Blend Images-Hill Street Studios/Getty Images. R35 ©REUTERS/David Ryder. R36 RHONA WISE/AFP/Getty Images. R39 Jacob A. Riis/Getty Images. R40 PARIS PIERCE/Alamy Stock Photo. R45 Prospect Street, Gloucester, 1928 (w/c on paper laid down on board)/Hopper, Edward (1882-1967)/CHRISTIES IMAGES/Private Collection/Bridgeman Images. R46 Smithsonian American Art Museum, Washington, DC/Art Resource, NY. R50 Andriy Blokhin/Alamy Stock Photo. R51 ©Bob Adelman. R58 ©Keith Haring Foundation. R66–R67 (b) Steve Proehl/Getty Images. R68 ©NPS/Jacob W. Frank. R72 NASA Goddard Space Flight Center Image by Reto Stockli (land surface, shallow water, clouds). Enhancements by Robert Simmon (ocean color, Compositing, 3D globes, animation). Data and technical support: MODIS Land Group; MODIS Science Data Support Team; MODIS Atmosphere Group; MODIS Ocean Group Additional data: USGS EROS Data Center (topography); USGS Terrestrial Remote Sensing Flagstaff Field Center (Antarctica); Defense Meteorological Satellite Program (city lights)/NASA. R73 (t) U.S. Coast Guard photo. R73 (b) ©Suzi Eszterhas/Minden Pictures.

Text Credits

Pg. 557 "Letter from Birmingham City Jail," by Dr. Martin Luther King Jr. April 16, 1963. Reprinted by arrangement with The Heirs to the Estate of Martin Luther King Jr., c/o Writers House as agent for the proprietor New Nork, NY. ©1963 Dr. Martin Luther King Jr. ©Renewed 1991 Loretta Scott King.

Pg. 558 "I Have a Dream," by Dr. Martin Luther King Jr. Reprinted by arrangement with The Heirs to the Estate of Martin Luther King Jr., c/o Writers House as agent for the proprietor New Nork, NY. ©1963 Martin Luther King Jr. ©Renewed 1991 Coretta Scott King.

Map Credits

Unless otherwise indicated, all maps were created by Mapping Specialists.

Illustrator Credits

Unless otherwise indicated, all illustrations were created by Lachina.